CENSUS OF INDIA 1931

CENSUS OF INDIA, 1931

BOOK - 3: VOLUME - I

INDIA

PART III: ETHNOGRAPHICAL
AND
PART V: ADMINISTRATION REPORT

A. Racial Affinities of the Peoples of India

B.S. GUHA

B. Ethnographic Notes by Various Authors

Edited By

J. H. HUTTON

GYAN

Published by

Gyan Publishing House
5, Ansari Road
Daryaganj, New Delhi-110002
Phone: 011-47034999, 9811692060
E-mail: books@gyanbooks.com

Distribution Network
gyanbooks.com
India, USA, Canada, UK, Australia

ISBN: 978-81-212-7123-3 (Set) 28 Vols. In 52 Bindings

ISBN: 978-81-212-7611-5 (PB) Vol. III, Pt. V

First Published, 1935

2nd Impression 2024

Printed at: Gyan Press, Delhi.

CENSUS OF INDIA 1931

Census of India, 1931

VOL. I—INDIA

Part III—Ethnographical

A. Racial Affinities of the Peoples of India

by

B. S. GUHA, Ph. D.,

Anthropologist, Zoological Survey of India.

B. Ethnographic Notes by various Authors

edited by

J. H. HUTTON.

SIMLA
GOVERNMENT OF INDIA PRESS
1935.

List of Agents from whom Government of India Publications are available.

ENGLAND.

THE HIGH COMMISSIONER FOR INDIA, INDIA HOUSE, ALDWYCH, LONDON, W. C. 2.

PALESTINE.

Steimatzky, Jerusalem.

INDIA.

(*a*) Provincial Government Book Depots.

MADRAS :—Superintendent, Government Press, Mount Road, Madras.

BOMBAY :—Superintendent, Government Printing and Stationery, Queen's Road, Bombay.

SIND :—Library attached to the Office of the Commissioner in Sind, Karachi.

UNITED PROVINCES OF AGRA AND OUDH :—Superintendent of Government Press, United Provinces of Agra and Oudh, Allahabad.

PUNJAB :—Superintendent, Government Printing, Punjab, Lahore.

BURMA :—Superintendent, Government Printing, Burma, Rangoon.

CENTRAL PROVINCES AND BERAR :—Superintendent, Government Printing, Central Provinces, Nagpur.

ASSAM :—Superintendent, Assam Secretariat Press, Shillong.

BIHAR AND ORISSA :—Superintendent, Government Printing, Bihar and Orissa, P. O. Gulzarbagh, Patna.

NORTH-WEST FRONTIER PROVINCE :—Manager, Government Printing and Stationery, Peshawar.

(*b*) Private Book-sellers.

Advani Bros., Cawnpore.
Aero Stores, Karachi City.*
Albert Library, Dacca.
Banerjee & Bros., Ranchi, Messrs. G.
Banthiya & Co., Ltd., Kucheri Road, Ajmer.
Bengal Flying Club, Dum Dum Cantt.*
Bhawnani & Sons, New Delhi.
Book Company, Calcutta.
Booklover's Resort, Taikad, Trivandrum, South India.
Burma Book Club, Ltd., Rangoon.
Butterworth & Co. (India), Ltd., Calcutta.
Calcutta Book Agency, 16-1, Shama Charan Dey Street, Calcutta.
Chatterjee & Co., 3, Bacharam Chatterjee Lane, Calcutta.
Chukervertty, Chatterjee & Co., Ltd., 13, College Square, Calcutta.
City Book Co., Madras.
City Book House, Meston Road, Cawnpore.
Commercial Book Co., Lahore.
Das Gupta & Co., 54|3, College Street, Calcutta.
Deccan Book Stall, Poona 4.
Delhi and U. P. Flying Club, Ltd., Delhi.*
English Book Depot, Ferozepore.
English Book Depot, Taj Road, Agra, and Saddar Bazar, Jhansi.
English Book Depot, Bank Road, Ambala Cantt., Kasauli.
English Bookstall, Karachi.
Fakir Chand Marwah, Peshawar Cantt.
Gaya Prasad & Sons, Agra.
Grantha Mandir, Cuttack.
Higginbothams, Madras.
Hindu Library, 137|F., Balaram De Street, Calcutta.
Hyderabad Book Depot, Chaderghat, Hyderabad (Deccan).
Imperial Book Depot and Press, near Jama Masjid (Machhliwalan), Delhi.
Indian Army Book Depot, Dayalbagh, Agra.
Indian Army Book Depot, Jullundur City and Daryaganj, Delhi.
Indian Book Shop, Benares City.
Indian School Supply Depot, 309, Bow Bazar St., Calcutta.
Insurance Publicity Co., Ltd., Lahore.
International Book Service, Poona 4.
Jaina & Bros., Mori Gate, Delhi, Messrs. J. M.
James Murray & Co., 12, Govt. Place, Calcutta (for Meteorological publications only).
Kali Charan & Co., Municipal Market, Calcutta.
Kamala Book Depot, 15, College Square, Calcutta.
Kamala Book Stores, Bankipore, Patna.
Karnataka Publishing House, Bangalore City.
Keale & Co., Karachi.
Krishnaswami & Co., Teppakulam P. O., Trichinopoly Fort, Messrs. S.
Lahiri & Co., Calcutta, Messrs. S. K.
Law Printing House, 11, Mount Road, Madras.
Law Publishing Co., Mylapore, Madras.
Lawrence and Mayo, Ltd., Bombay (for Meteorological publications only).
Local Self Govt. Institute, Bombay.
London Book Co. (India), Arbab Road, Peshawar Murree, Nowshera, Rawalpindi.
London Book Depot, B. I. Bazar, Bareilly, U. P.
Malhotra & Co., Quetta, Messrs. U. P.
Mohanlal Dossabhai Shah, Rajkot.
Nandkishore & Bros., Chowk, Benares City.
Nateson & Co., Publishers, George Town, Madras, Messrs. G. A.
New Book Co., "Kitab Mahal", 192, Hornby Road, Bombay.
Newman & Co., Ltd., Calcutta, Messrs. W.
North India Christian Tract and Book Society, 18, Clive Road, Allahabad.
Oriental Book Supplying Agency, 15, Shukrawar, Poona City.
Oxford Book and Stationery Company, Delhi, Lahore, Simla, Meerut and Calcutta.
Parikh & Co., Baroda, Messrs. B.
Pioneer Book Supply Co., 20, Shib Narayan Das Lane, Calcutta and 219, Cloth Market, Delhi.
Popular Book Depot, Grant Road, Bombay.
Punjab Religious Book Society, Lahore.
Punjab Sanskrit Book Depot, Saidmitha Street, Lahore.
Raghunath Prasad & Sons, Patna City.
Rama Krishna & Sons, Booksellers, Anarkali, Lahore.
Ram Krishna Bros., Opposite Bishrambag, Poona City.
Ram Narain Lal, Katra, Allahabad.
Ramesh Book Depot, Stationery Mart, Kashmere Gate, Delhi.
Ray & Sons, 43, K. & L. Edwardes Road, Rawalpindi, Murree and Peshawar, Messrs. J.
Ray Chowdhury & Co., 68|5, Ashutosh Mukherjee Road, Calcutta.
Rochouse & Sons, Madras.
Roy Chowdhury & Co., 11, College Square, Calcutta, Messrs. N. M.
Sampson William & Co., 127-B., The Mall, Cawnpore.
Sarcar & Sons, 15, College Square, Calcutta, Messrs. M. C.
Sarkar & Co., 2, Shama Charan De Street, Calcutta, Messrs. P. C.
Scientific Publishing Co., 9, Taltola Lane, Calcutta.
Seshachalam & Co., Masulipatam, Messrs. M.
Shivji & Co., P. O. Chauliaganj, Cuttack.
Shri Shankar Karnataka Pustaka Bhandara, Malamuddi, Dharwar.
S. P. Bookstall, 21, Budhwar, Poona.
Standard Bookstall, Karachi.
Standard Book Depot, Lahore, Dalhousie and Delhi.
Standard Law Book Society, 5, Hastings Street, Calcutta.
Standard Literature Company, Ltd., Calcutta.
Students' Popular Depot, Kacheri Road, Lahore.
Surat and District Trading Society, Surat.
Taraporevala Sons & Co., Bombay, Messrs. D. B.
Thacker & Co., Ltd., Bombay.
Thacker, Spink & Co., Ltd., Calcutta.
Tripathi & Co., Booksellers, Princes Street, Kalbadevi Road, Bombay, Messrs. N. M.
Union Stores, Indore City.
University Book Agency, Kachari Road, Lahore.
Upper India Publishing House, Ltd., Literature Palace, Ammuddaula Park, Lucknow.
Varadachary & Co., Madras, Messrs. P.
Wheeler & Co., Allahabad, Calcutta and Bombay, Messrs. A. H.
Young Man & Co., Ajmer and Egerton Road, Delhi.

*Agent for publications on Aviation only.

PREFACE.

The last time that the Census of India published a volume of ethnographic Appendices was in 1901 when Sir Herbert Risley supplemented his famous report with a volume of papers on the physical and cultural anthropology of various castes and tribes. The present volume consists of two parts A and B with separate pagination. Part A is the work of Dr. B. S. Guha alone; part B is a collection of papers, many of which have already appeared in provincial census volumes, by various hands. Part A deals primarily with physical and part B with cultural anthropology.

It has unfortunately been impossible for Dr. Guha to finish his report on the somatic affinities of the castes and tribes measured by him in time for me to see it before closing my office and leaving India on furlough, and I therefore write under this disadvantage, but I have seen his diagrams and the admirable photographs obtained by him with the help of the Zoological Survey's photographers, and likewise his tables of the co-efficients of racial likeness, and it is not too much to say that his is easily the most important contribution to the physical anthropology of India since Sir Herbert Risley's. Anyone who is familiar with the labour involved in the lengthy calculations required to produce such co-efficients as he has given us will express no surpise at the time taken to complete the report on his survey. The survey itself involved visits to many parts of India, some of them not too easy of access, and the taking of exhaustive measurements on many individuals. The taking of these measurements and the extraction of the reduced co-efficients of racial likeness has been a laborious task.

It has long been apparent to students of Indian anthropology that some of Risley's conclusions were unsatisfactory and open in some respects to grave doubt. His conception of India as isolated from the rest of Asia and inhabited entirely by barbarous tribes until the Aryan invasion of c. 1500 B. C., already impugned, has been proved to be erroneous by the discovery of Mohenjo-daro. His explanation of brachycephaly in the west of India as due to Scythian invasion in historic times has been justifiably attacked on the score that the population so introduced was never numerous enough to make a complete and permanent change in the somatic characteristics of the population. His explanation of brachycephaly in Bengal as Mongolian has been impeached, largely on sentimental grounds, but the impeachment is almost entirely justified by facts. From the date on which I was appointed Census Commissioner I was in touch with Colonel Seymour Sewell, then Director of the Zoological Survey of India, and with Dr. Guha, who is the anthropologist attached to that department, both of whom were as anxious as I was that the opportunity of the 1931 Census should be made use of to obtain fresh light on the racial constitution of India. It was easy therefore to obtain the co-operation both of Dr. Guha in particular and of the Zoological Survey in general, but that increases rather than reduces my indebtedness to them for their help, and the plan of campaign was Dr. Guha's not mine.

Dr. Guha will have seen his own manuscript through the press and it was only considerations of economy which prevented part A's appearing as a separate volume. The first proofs of part B were received in time for me to look through them in haste and to add an occasional note, but I am indebted to the Government of India Press at Simla for their final reading. I owe some apology to a number of authors whose contributions have been freely cut down in order to reduce the volume of material presented. This has unfortunately been inevitable, and I have endeavoured to restrict my regrettable excisions to points of theory rather than of fact. In many cases the articles here incorporated will be found in full in provincial volumes, and generally speaking those which have so appeared can be distinguished from those not published elsewhere in the census series by their being printed in smaller type.

I should also here make it clear that a large proportion of the contributions in part B were received in reply to a questionnaire, which is printed as an appendix at the end which has frequently determined the form taken by the papers constituting that part. I take this opportunity of expressing my indebtedness and my thanks to all those, whether or not their contributions appear here, who have so kindly endeavoured to comply with the importunate questions of my Census Superintendents and of myself.

SIMLA; J. H. HUTTON.

June, 1st 1933.

M53CO

PART III A.

The Racial Affinities of the Peoples of India

by

B. S. GUHA, Ph. D.,
Anthropologist, Zoological Survey of India.

LIST OF CONTENTS.

(Plates I—X.)

THE RACIAL AFFINITIES OF THE PEOPLES OF INDIA.

INTRODUCTION.

The classification of the races of India based on anthropometric measurements was first attempted by Sir Herbert Risley in the Census of 1901 which was revised and published as a separate volume in 1908 under the title of *The People of India*. This work was really an extension of his earlier work on *The Castes and Tribes of Bengal* undertaken at the instructions of Sir Rivers Thompson, then Lieutenant-Governor of Bengal and published in four volumes in 1891. Risley was not however the first to apply the methods of anthropometry to an Indian race. Between the years 1879-84, Baron Mezö-Kövesd von Ujfalvy, the distinguished Hungarian anthropologist, carried out an extensive series of investigations in Kashmir and the West Himalayan regions under the auspices of the Societè d'Anthropologie de Paris, the results of which were published in his well-known works "*Aus dem Westlichen Himalaja*" and "*Les Aryens .. l'Hindou-Kouch*" in 1884 and 1896 respectively. For nearly thirty years Ujfalvy's writings were the only works on the people of this region, and though in recent years greatly supplemented by the researches of Stein Dainelli and the present writer,[1] they still remain among the most authoritative sources of our information on the population of both sides of the Hindukush and the Upper Indus Valley. Nevertheless, being restricted in their scope and confined mainly[2] to the races of this region they cannot take the place of Risley's more comprehensive work as the first scientific study of the racial characteristics of the entire population of India

Although some excellent descriptions of the somatic traits of Indian tribes were available before Risley's Survey, in such works as *Dalton's Descriptive Ethnology of Bengal* (1872), no systematic attempt was made to isolate the physical types concealed in the linguistic groups, *e.g.*, Aryan, Dravidian, etc., into which the people of India were broadly divided. One effect of such a classification has been the unrestricted use of philological terms in the ethnical sense—a practice which unfortunately lingers even to-day in many pseudo-anthropological writings, in spite of Frederick Müller's protest forty years ago. Risley's endeavour to introduce exact methods in the differentiation of Indian races must therefore be regarded as a landmark in the study of Man in India. It gave the orientation necessary for such studies by drawing attention to the necessity of keeping clear the respective fields of Race and Culture in scientific investigations.

Having had no training in the subject himself, Risley wisely sought the help of Sir William Flower, before venturing to give a practical shape to his ideas. Sir William referred him to Topinard's standard work on Anthropology and Risley prepared a scheme based on the latter's system.[3] This was tried as an experimental measure by Risley in the Rangpur district and was sent to both Topinard and Flower for approval before being finally put into operation.

Risley's Survey was at first confined to Bengal, but later on extended to the North-Western Province (United Provinces), the Punjab, Baluchistan, Rajputana, Bombay, Behar, Orissa, Ceylon and Burma. Assam and Madras were excluded from the scope of its operations. Lieutenant-Colonel Waddell however published the measurements of a large number of tribes in Assam in 1901.[4] and Thurston performed a similar task in the Madras Presidency in 1909.[5]

The actual work of taking the measurements was in the hands of Messrs. Kumud Behari Samanta, Ala-ud-din, Chandi Singh and B. A. Gupte. The first was responsible for measurements in Bengal, Behar, Orissa, Ceylon and Rajputana, the second and the third respectively for the Punjab and the North-Western Provinces (United Provinces) and the last for Bombay, Baluchistan and Burma. Mr. Samanta's work in Ceylon in 1892 was under the direct supervision of Risley[6] but we have the testimony of Lieutenant-Colonel Waddell, that his measurements in Bengal and other parts of the country were taken under "no body's immediate supervision."[7] Mr. Ala-ud-din's work in the Punjab was under the supervision of the Deputy Surgeon-General Stephen and lastly Mr. Chandi Singh's measurements in the North-Western Provinces (United Provinces) were supervised by Mr. J. C. Nesfield.[8] So far as can be judged, Mr. Gupte carried

---

[1] To be published soon.

[2] Ujfalvy's works include also some measurements of the Parsis of Bombay.

[3] Risley, H. H.—The Tribes and Castes of Bengal, Official Edition, Volume I, pages XXIII—XXV, Calcutta, 1891.

[4] Waddell, L. A.—The Tribes of the Brahmaputra Valley. J. A. S. B., Volume LXIX, Part III, Calcutta, 1901.

[5] Thurston, E.—The Castes and Tribes of Southern India, Volume I, Madras, 1909.

[6] Risley, H. H.—Measurements of Cingalese Moormen and Tamils taken at Ceylon in November 1892. J. A. S. B., Volume LXII, Part III, page 33, Calcutta, 1893.

[7] Waddell, L. A.—Op. cit., page 73.

[8] Risley, H. H.—Op. cit., 1891, page XXV.

out the work himself though acting under Risley's general advice[1]. Risley's own share[2] lay in teaching the measurers the use of the instruments, in exercising a general control over the whole work and in supplying them with detailed printed instructions regarding the technique of the measurements described in his "Anthropometric Instructions."[3] These instructions relate to the selection of the subjects, the manner in which they should be seated and the position of the operator in relation to the subject, etc. In selecting subjects for measurements, Risley's instructions are unexceptionable except in so far as the rejection of men of "very black complexion with broad depressed noses" and "of very fair complexion with high-caste type of features," is advised from samples respectively of the upper and lower castes.[4] An amount of caution is undoubtedly necessary in guarding against spurious cases from being included among those measured, but there is no justification for excluding persons on grounds of physical appearance alone and of attempting to set up a preconceived "standard type for each caste."[4]

The number of measurements taken on each individual in Risley's Survey was not uniform throughout. In the majority of the castes and tribes of Bengal, Behar, United Provinces and the Punjab, 14 measurements were taken.[5] The Bi-malar and the Naso-malar breadths however, were not taken in the case of 8 castes of Bengal, 6 castes of Behar and 22 castes of the United Provinces.[5] The measurements taken by Gupte in Bombay,[6] the North-West Frontier Provinces[7] and Burma,[8] comprise 8 additional measurements, namely, Cephalic Volume, Nasio-mental length, Bigonial breadth, Height (sitting and kneeling), Height to Sternal Notch, Height to Chin and Bi-Iliac Crest breadth. But Gupte did not measure the Minimum Frontal breadth and Weight, and instead of taking the measurement of the Height from Vertex to Inter-Superciliary point, as was advised by Risley, he measured the distance from the Vertex to the root of the Nose.

The technique of the measurements described by Risley, in so far as the Cephalic length, Cephalic breadth, Maximum Bizygomatic breadth, Bigoniac diameter and Nasal width are concerned, are in general conformity with that adopted subsequently at the International Agreement of Monaco, as it was based largely on the system propounded by the French School of Broca and Topinard.

There are no instructions regarding Stature and the Minimum Frontal diameter. In the absence of any directions it may be presumed that Topinard's technique was followed, as in the case of the measurement of the Height of the Head, where "the centre of the tragus"[9] was taken as the lower terminus, instead of "the upper border of the auditory meatus" of the subsequent Monaco Agreement. With regard to the Bi-malar breadth and the Naso-malar breadth, Risley followed the technique of Oldfield Thomas, for the living.[10] In measuring the Nasal height, Risley advised that the deepest point of the depression at the nasal root should be taken as the upper terminus, but in all cases where this depression was not marked, the instrument should be placed either on the transverse fold, or between the two folds when both were present. These grooves usually occur near the root of the nose and according to Risley at about 2mm. *above* the transverse axis of the eyes.[11] In another place, however, of the same paper, *viz.*, Fig. 1, opp. page 1, the nasal root itself is stated to be from 1mm. to 3mm. *below* the transverse axis of the eyes!

In taking the transverse folds as land-marks Risley no doubt was guided by the advice of Topinard, though to be correct the latter regarded the lower groove and not the spot between the two as corresponding to the nasion,[12] but I have not come across any reference in Topinard's works as to his considering the deepest point of the nasal depression as equivalent to the nasal root. On the other hand there is definite evidence that the nasal root in the living was regarded by him to correspond to the median point in the fronto-nasal suture.[13] It is interesting to note in this connection that in the second edition of the *Notes and Queries on Anthropology*, published by the Royal Anthropological Institute in 1892, the foregoing definitions appear almost verbatim, but as Risley's paper was published six years earlier, it is not improbable that they were taken from his account.

1 Risley, H. H.—The People of India, page 22, Calcutta, 1915.

2 Op. cit., 1891, page XXV.

3 Risley, H. H.—Anthropometric Instructions, Calcutta, 1886.

4 *Ibid.*, page 1.

5 Risley, H. H.—Anthropometric Data, Volumes 1 and 2, Calcutta, 1891.

6 Anthropometric Data from Bombay, Calcutta, 1906.

7 Anthropometric Data from N. W. Borderland, Calcutta, 1909.

8 Anthropometric Data from Burma, Calcutta, 1906.

9 Risley.—Op. cit., page 6.

10 Oldfield Thomas.—Account of a Collection of human crania from Torres Straits, J. R. A. I., Volume XIV, pages 332—334, London, 1885.

11 Op. cit., page 3.

12 See footnote on page 367 in Duckworth's Morphology and Anthropology, Cambridge, 1904.

13 Topinard, Paul—Anthropology, pages 367, 256 and 247 (Fig. 29), London, 1894.

The most serious objection, however, with regard to the measurement of this character is his instruction that "the pointed end of the lower limb (of the nasometer) should be placed at the junction of the nasal cartilage with the upper lip and pressed inwards and upwards until it meets with steady resistance from the nasal spine."[1] It is clear from this that a great amount of pressure will be required before a steady resistance from the nasal spines can be felt; and pressed in this way the nose is bound to be considerably distorted and the nasal height measured, will thus fall much below the true height of the nose measured without the application of pressure.

The methods and results of Risley's work received wide recognition, though at the same time critics were not wanting who questioned the reliability of the data published by him, but actually taken by people whose competence for the work was not beyond question. In addition, Prof. Karl Pearson[2] showed that there were errors in the calculations of means and indices.[3]

As will have appeared from the accounts given in the preceding pages, that besides these objections, there are other drawbacks in Risley's work which considerably impair its value. They relate to his failure to take necessary steps to ensure uniformity in the measurements of the different workers to render them comparable; for, as is well known, in anthropometrical training the main desideratum is not so much the theoretical acquaintance with the technique, as is the capacity to carry it out in practice correctly. Risley employed four distinct workers, who measured independently under the supervisions of three different men. There is no evidence to show that the measurers received the necessary practical training under a competent person or that the results of the different workers attained a reasonable amount of uniformity, particularly as the control exercised was very superficial and in one case at least, *e.g.*, J. C. Nesfield, the supervisor himself could not lay claim to an adequate knowledge of the subject.

In view of these defects, opinion has long been prevalent among many anthropologists regarding the necessity of collecting fresh data by trained men to check Risley's measurements, and revise, if necessary, the views based on them. Investigations, such as have taken place since, also strengthened the suspicion about the validity of Risley's findings, with regard specially to the classification of the Dravidian speaking races[4] and the possible presence of a Negrito strain among the aboriginal population of India.[5] In October 1929, soon after his assumption of the Office of the Census Commissioner for India, Dr. J. H. Hutton, sought my advice about the desirability of taking fresh measurements and the publication of the results in connection with the Census Operations of 1931. A detailed scheme was prepared for taking anthropometric measurements on selected tribes and castes and was sent to Dr. Hutton for approval. The scheme was sanctioned by the Government in 1930 and with the active support of Lieutenant-Colonel R. B. Seymour Sewell, F.R.S., then Director of the Zoological Survey of India, my services were placed at the disposal of the Census Commissioner to carry out the work. As the funds available were limited and the time none too long, a comprehensive scheme, embracing the majority of the castes and tribes of India, was not practicable. It was necessary to restrict the scope of the work, but to make sure at the same time that the results of the survey were capable of yielding positive results.

The Nature and Scope of the Work.

In deciding the most effective way of carrying out the work, consideration had to be given primarily to those regions on which our materials were scantiest, and in the selection of castes and tribes for measurements, preference had likewise to be given to those which appeared to throw greater light on the racial structure of the population. I have pointed out elsewhere[6] the paucity of reliable data from Southern India. The Vedic literature contains many references to the 'Aryan' invasion of N. W. India, but of the racial movements that probably entered through a more southern gate and passed into the Deccan and beyond, we have no authentic information. It is true the discovery of the ancient civilisation of Mohenjo-daro has indicated the early advent of races from Western Asia, but we are still in the dark as to how far their penetration east and southwards had actually taken place. In the present enquiries therefore, I have attempted a more detailed survey of the country below the Vindhyas and paid special attention to all the strategic approaches through which such racial drifts could conceivably have entered. In the second place, for reasons already stated the investigations had to be restricted to the groups among whom chances of miscegenation would appear to be the smallest, and those with whom,

---

[1] Op. cit., page 3.

[2] Biometrika, Volume II, page 348, London, 1902.

[3] Risley's figures have since been checked and a revised list has been published by Prof. P. C. Mahalanobis. *Sankhya*—pages 76–100, Volume I, Part I, Calcutta, 1933.

[4] Richards, F. G.—Some Dravidian Affinities and their Sequel. Quarterly Journal of the Mythic Society, pages 243—284, Volume VII, Bangalore, 1917.

[5] Guha, B. S.—*Nature*—May 19, 1928 and June 22, 1929, London.

[6] Presidential Address before the Anthropological Section of the Indian Science Congress, Calcutta, 1928.

if at all, such mixing of blood could have taken place. Translated into the actual social conditions of the country, the project really meant the comparative study of the somatic characters of the Brahmins with the castes next in order of precedence. The old four-fold divisions of Hindu Society are no longer in existence. The Brahmins doubtless occupy the highest position everywhere in India, but there appears to be no uniformity regarding the caste next in position. For instance, in Upper India the Rajputs or Chattris come just below the Brahmins but in Bombay and Bengal the Prabhus and Kayasthas occupy that position. In Southern India, on the other hand, the gap between the Brahmins and all other castes is wide and there is no clear social canon about the position of any one caste corresponding to those named in Northern India.

The scheme proposed to include in addition, the so-called lowest castes, and the major aboriginal groups in the survey, but the numerous intermediate castes were omitted as they did not appear to have the same strategic importance. Pursued in this manner, the survey, it was felt, would disclose *(i)* the racial types present among the upper and the lower classes, of the Indian population and *(ii)* the extent to which intermixture may have occurred between *(a)* the Brahmins and the upper stratum of the rest of the population and *(b)* between the latter and the aboriginal tribes. Further, the enquiry was expected to throw light on the question as to whether the Brahmins all over the country could still be regarded as carrying the blood of the "Vedic Aryans" in their veins or there are racial differences between their different divisions, and in some parts at least, particularly in the southern provinces, they are in reality the upper classes of the indigenous population who were Aryanised earlier and acted subsequently as the disseminators of the Vedic culture.

The investigations commenced in 1930 and lasted till the summer of 1933 during which the greater portions of the Central, Western and Southern India were toured. Visits were also paid to selected areas in the North and the East and the total distance thus covered amounted to over ten thousand miles.

The main body of the work was divided into two parts, namely (1) an intensive study of the Peninsular India and (2) in the rest of the country, with a view to filling up the gaps in our existing knowledge, only chosen areas were examined. In the former were included *(a)* a survey of the western littoral from Kathiawar to Cochin, lying approximately between lats. 24° and 9°N. and longs. 71° and 77° E. *(b)* a survey of Central India along the Malwan plateau from Birwani to Rewa, between lats. 25° and 22°N. and longs. 74° and 82°E. and *(c)* a survey of the Eastern parts from Orissa to Madura, between lats. 20° and 10°N. and longs. 78° and 86°E. and including the states of Hyderabad and Mysore.

In the north, besides the examination of selected Bengal castes, visits were paid to the United Provinces and the Khasi Hills of Assam. In addition, measurements were taken for the first time on a large number of Nicobarese by Dr. Naidu, a medical officer of the Andamans Government who was deputed for training in our laboratory in the Indian Museum, and was supplied with one set of our instruments. He visited the islands of Great Nicobar, Little Nicobar, Camorta, Terressa, Chaura and Bompoka during the enumeration of the Census and measured 121 men and 50 women.

The total number of racial groups examined during this Survey was 34 of which 14 were Brahmins, 16 belonging to various Hindu castes, and 4 tribal; the member of individuals measured being, 1,004 Brahmins, 884 caste Hindus, and 275 Aborigines, besides 5 female groups consisting of 348 women, making a grand total of 2,511 persons. With the exception of the Nicobarese (121 ♂ and 50 ♀) all the others were measured by me.

The average size of the samples of the 39 groups is 64·4, of which 7 were from 100 to 143 26 between 50 to 99 and only 6 were below 50. It will be evident from these figures that barring the Chenchus, where out of a total adult male population of about 445,[1] 23 were measured, the size of the samples was fair, though not large, in the majority of the cases.

An important consideration that has to be borne in mind in this connection is the need for care and precaution in getting the subjects for measurement. In India, due to the social prestige and privileges enjoyed by upper castes, there is always a tendency for individuals to surreptitiously pass off as members of castes higher than the ones to which they rightly belong. Usually by adopting generic surnames like Roy, Dutt, Singh, Chowdhuri, etc., attempts are made to mask the caste origins, and in those parts, *e.g.*, S. India, where the use of surnames is not customary, it is still more difficult to detect these cases. It is not realised that this complication often takes away the value of the works of foreign and not infrequently of Indian investigators who do not happen to be familiar with the conditions prevalent in different localities. In order to guard against this possibility, measurements of each caste were taken in the particular centre of its concentration and the help and guidance of the Caste Organisations and prominent members of the castes were sought, so that unauthorised persons were not included in my samples. In a few cases, like some Rajput States of Central India, actual Registers are kept containing the

[1] Census of India, Volume XXIII, Part II, pages 100-101, 1931.

lists of the genuine Rajput families and my subjects were procured from the members of these families through the kind offices of influential state officials. It should however be distinctly understood that no selection was made in the subjects for measurement and they are to be regarded as random samples in the strict sense of the word.

These measurements, taken expressly for the Census of 1931, do not form the entire materials of this Report. Soon after my joining the Zoological Survey of India in 1927, I took a large series of measurements on two aboriginal tribes in the interior of the Cochin Hills, and in the summer of 1929, I participated in a scientific expedition to Chitral and Kaffiristan, in collaboration with Dr. Morgenstierne, who was sent by the "Norwegian Instituttet for Sammenlignende Kulturforskning" to study the languages spoken in that area. During this expedition, a large number of people living in the mountain valleys south of the Hindu Kush, including the Kaffir tribes of Rambur and Bamboret, were studied. Altogether about 700 individuals belonging to 10 different races were measured. If these measurements are now added, the total number of individuals measured by the present writer will increase to 3,227 belonging to 51 racial groups from all parts of India and directly comparable to one another. Over and above this, the results of other investigators, totalling measurements on 3,774 persons have also been included for comparison and discussion, along with most of the cranial materials so far discovered and worked out. The account, given in the following pages, may therefore be considered to be based on most of the available metric data, and purports to give a comprehensive view of the racial characteristics of the Indian population.

In carrying out the work I have been greatly indebted to the Governments of Bhavnagar, Birwani, Dhar and Rewa in Kathiawar and Central India, and Hyderabad and Cochin in Southern India for giving all the facilities for my investigations during my visits to their States. Among the many individuals who have given me their help and advice, my special thanks are due to Messrs. Natvarlal Surati and Ramanlal Trivedi, Superintendent and Assistant Superintendent of the Census operations in Bhavnagar; Messrs. Sankara Menon and Venkateswar Iyangar, Census Superintendents of Cochin and Mysore; Principal Findlay Shirras, Professor Dhruva. Messrs. D. P. Derasarai, S. C. Bose and Mr. and Mrs. Ambalal Sarabai of Ahmedabad; Professor S. Belvalkar, Mr. Kodanda Rao, Principal Mahajani and Mr. and Mrs. K. C. Naik of Poona; Lieutenant-Colonel A. C. G. de Silva Correia of Nova Goa; Messrs. Achutya Menon, Gobinda Menon, Romani Menon and Narayan Menon of Trichur; Mr. J. Foulkes of Madura; Sir S. Radhakrishanan of Vizagapatam; Mr G. C. Banerji and Professor A. C. Banerji of Allahabad; Rai Bahadurs Ramaprasad Chanda, Nagendra Nath Bose and Mr. Upendra Nath Mukherjee of Calcutta; the Lindoh of Mawflong and Barik Singh Mantri of Mylliem, Khasi Hills; and finally, Mr. C. S. Venkatachar, I.C.S., Census Superintendent of Central India, who not only arranged my programme but accompanied me throughout my tours in Central India and helped me with advice and suggestions regarding the racial distribution of the people of that region.

To Dr. J. H. Hutton, D.Sc., I.C.S., Census Commissioner for India, who initiated the enquiry and provided the necessary funds for carrying it out, my obligations are very great for his constant help and advice throughout the investigations and preparation of this report. I am indebted also to Lieutenant-Colonel R. B. Seymour Sewell, F.R.S., late Director of the Zoological Survey of India, for active support and help during my work and to Dr. Baini Prashad, the present Director, for valuable suggestions and help, specially during my temporary absence in Europe.

To Prof. Roland B. Dixon of Harvard, I am also indebted for allowing me to use his unpublished data on the Hunzas.

My acknowledgments are due to Mr. D. N. Bagchi who is responsible for the photographs taken in Northern, Central, Eastern and Western India; Messrs. P. C. Basu of the Bose Research Institute, A. K. Mitra, Mr. C. C. Roy and my wife Mrs. Uma Guha for allowing me to use their unpublished materials and finally to Messrs. H. K. Basu, B. K. Chatterjee, R. K. Paul, A. K. Mitra, S. S. Sarkar, J. N. Sen Gupta, Bhupendra S. Guha, Surendra S. Guha and Panchcowrie Chakravarty for the statistical reduction of the data. But for the labour and untiring devotion of these workers, the huge task of computation involved in this Report could hardly have been completed within this time.

The Technique of the Measurements.

Measurements were taken on each individual on 18 different characters with a set of Herman and Rickenboch's anthropometric instruments. Besides these a large number of observations were recorded including tints of skin, eye and hair colours. For this purpose von Luschan's Hautfarbentafel, Martin's Augenfarbentafel and Fischer's Haarfarbentafel were used. The following measurements were taken :—

(1) Stature, (2) Auricular height, (3) Maximum Head length, (4) Maximum Head breadth, (5) Minimum Frontal breadth, (6) Maximum Bizygomatic breadth, (7) Bigonial breadth, (8) Inter-Orbital breadth, (9) Orbito-Nasal breadth, (10) Orbito-Nasal arc, (11) Nasal length, (12) Nasal breadth, (13) Nasal height or depth, (14) Upper Facial length, (15) Total Facial length, (16) Hor. Circumference of the Head, (17) Sagittal arc, and (18) Transverse arc. They correspond to No. 1,[1] and Nos. 15, 1,[2] 3, 4, 6,

[1] Martin, Rudolf.—Lehrbuch der Anthropologie, Volume I, page 150, 1928.
[2] Op. cit., page 180.

8, 9, 10 (1), 10 (2), 21, 13, 22, 20, 18, 45, 48 and 49 described by Martin[1] and are in agreement with the technique adopted by the International Agreement of Monaco except in the case of Nos. 9 and 10. The latter two are after the measurements described by Oldfield Thomas; but by gently passing the steel tape over the nasion from the ectoconchions, instead of measuring the distance from the edges of either of the orbits, to a spot in the centre of the bridge of the nose and then doubling the result[2]—a slightly modified technique was adopted.[3] The Auricular height was measured in projection by subtracting the height up to the tragions from the height up to the vertex and I have followed Hrdlicka[4] in preferring to retain the term "Nasal length" for "Nasal height" of the Monaco Agreement and used the latter for the height of the Septum or Nasal elevation or depth. Slight amount of pressure was used in all measurements except Nos. 1, 2, 8, 9, 10, 11, 12 13, 14 and 15 of my list which were all contact measurements.

The measurements were supplemented by visual observations on some of the characteristic features of the head and the face, which though incapable of quantitative expression, are nevertheless of some importance in the discrimination of races. There is no fixed procedure, however, regarding the number and particulars of these observations and it is usually left to the discretion of the observer himself to record what he considers to be the most salient. In the present Survey, altogether 20 observations were made on each individual including among others, the character of the Hair, form of the Eye, shape of the Nose, Chin, Face, Forehead, Prognathism and the presence or absence of the Epicanthic Fold.

In recording the shades of colours of the Skin, Eye and the Hair, one is handicapped for want of an International Agreement, and recourse was necessarily had to the artificial standards that have come into general use. Of these von Luschan's Scale for skin colours, which has replaced Broca's in recent years, is more suitable for the white and black races, but is rather inadequate for the intermediate shades of the brown and the light brown which are found in the Indian races. As providing a well-known comparative standard, its use however is essential, though it was noticed that shades intermediate between 9—10 and 18—22 are lacking and the existing ones do not correctly represent the tints found. Similarly, Fischer's Haarfarbentafel needs a larger representation of tints varying between dark brown and black (Nos. 4—27) and between dark and reddish brown (Nos. 4—6). But Martin's Augenfarbentafel is more suitable, as with the exception of a small percentage, the eye colours of the Indians vary within the shades of brown, which are adequately represented in Martin's scale.

I have tried however to record the nearest approaches to the shades given in the scales, where they do not quite match, with as much accuracy as possible and the observations were made in good day light by holding the scales against the persons of the individuals. As being the first records taken on European standards, they give definite information on the integumentary colours of the Indian races in a form comparable with those available for peoples of other parts of the world.

The Method of Investigations.

Races are usually differentiated by anthropologists either on qualitative grounds or on the basis of a single or combination of physical characters. The value of the first depends on the insight of the observer and his special knowledge of the tribes, but as there is no means of evaluating that judgment, it remains at best the expression of an individual opinion only. Comparison of single characters is equally unsatisfactory as it is not always clear how far significant differences or similarities can be deduced from them. Racial discrimination, in order to be reliable, must be based on the entire somatic constitution of peoples, specially when the data are limited to a few characters obtained from small samples, and a single numerical measure of all the differences is therefore required to show the degree of resemblance or divergence of the two races or tribes compared. An attempt in this direction was first made by T. A. Joyce[5] in his analysis of the anthropometric data obtained by Sir Aurel Stein from the Pamirs and Chinese Turkistan. Joyce used the following expression at the suggestion of Mr. H. E. Soper of the Biometric Laboratory of the University College, London :—

$$\Sigma \frac{M_1 - M_2}{\sqrt{\sigma_1^2 + \sigma_2^2}}$$

and called it the "Differential Index" where M_1 and σ_1 are the mean and the standard deviation of one character in the first race and M_2 and σ_2 the corresponding quantities of the same character in the second race ; Σ standing for the total sum of all the characters considered.

---

1 Op. cit. pages 182—195.

2 Oldfield Thomas.—Op. cit., pages 332—334.

3 Op. cit., No. 102 (2), page 184.

4 Hrdlicka, Ales.—Anthropometry, page 74 ; Philadelphia, 1920.

5 Joyce, T. A.—Notes on the Physical Anthropology of Chinese Turkistan and the Pamirs. J. R. A. I., Volume XLII, pages 451—452 ; London, 1912.

The drawback of this expression is that it does not consider either the number of individuals measured or the number of characters considered. The value of this kind of statistical test depends on the number of characters used and it has also been shown that the size of the samples has an appreciable influence on the Co efficient.[1] Consequently no quantitative test, which aims at getting the true measure of racial divergence can afford to neglect these factors.

For a satisfactory study of the resemblance or difference of the physical characters of two races, Professor Pearson[2] has suggested another Co-efficient known as the Co-efficient of Racial Likeness, which takes into account not only the mean characters and their standard deviations but also the number of the individuals and characters measured. The following expression has been given for this Co-efficient, after it has received extensive trial in the Biometric Laboratory of the University College, London. If m_s is the mean, σ_s the standard deviation and n the number of individual measurements of the sth. character in the first race and m'_s, σ'_s and n'_s are the corresponding quantities in the second race then the Co-efficient of Racial Likeness is given by :—

$$S\left\{\frac{1}{M}\left(\frac{(m_s-m'_s)^2}{\dfrac{\sigma_s^2}{n_s}+\dfrac{\sigma'^2_s}{n'_s}}\right)\right\}-1+\frac{1}{M}$$

where M is the number of characters measured. If the races are then samples of the same population, then the expression will be sensibly zero, with a probable error of :—

$$\pm\cdot 67449\sqrt{\frac{2}{M}\left(1-\frac{1}{M}\right)}$$

As however the size of the samples measured is usually very small and the standard deviations can hardly be determined with sufficient accuracy from such samples, it has become the common practice to regard σ_s as equal to those of the longest series available which belong to the same family of races, on the assumption that the variability of the different races of men is not greatly divergent.[3] If $\sigma_s=\sigma'_s$ then the Co-efficient becomes :—

$$C.\ R.\ L.=S\left\{\frac{1}{M}\cdot\frac{n_s n'_s}{n_s+n'_s}\times\frac{(m_s-m'_s)^2}{\sigma_s^2}\right\}-1+\frac{1}{M}\pm\cdot 67449\sqrt{\frac{2}{M}\left(1-\frac{1}{M}\right)}\ \ldots\ldots\ldots(1)$$

Values calculated from this expression are called " Crude " Co-efficients.

The values of the Crude Co-efficients have however been shown to be affected by the size of the samples compared[4] and it was found necessary to devise some means for eliminating this factor. Professor Pearson[5] introduced the correction by reducing the Crude Co-efficient to the value it would have when each of the samples was of a standard size of 100 individuals.

If $\bar{n}_s$ is the mean number of individuals available for the characters used in the first series and $\bar{n}'_s$ is the same for the second series then the " Reduced " Co-efficient is defined to be :—

$$50\times\frac{\bar{n}_s+\bar{n}'_s}{\bar{n}_s\times\bar{n}'_s}\times S\left\{\frac{1}{M}\cdot\frac{n_s n'_s}{n_s+n'_s}\times\frac{(m_s-m'_s)^2}{\sigma_s^2}\right\}-1+\frac{1}{M}$$

$$\pm\ 50\times\frac{\bar{n}_s+\bar{n}'_s}{\bar{n}_s\times\bar{n}'_s}\times\cdot 67449\sqrt{\frac{2}{M}\left(1-\frac{1}{M}\right)}\ \ldots\ldots\ldots(2)$$

The values of this Reduced Co-efficient are directly comparable to one another and this is the form which has been used in this paper.

In calculating the C. R. L.'s, it has been customary to use the idea of a general human variability obtained from large samples for σ_s, modified a little from one race to another. In this instance, unfortunately standard deviations based on large number of the living subjects of an allied race are not available, and recourse must therefore be had to those of the group in the present series which most nearly fulfil these conditions. After careful considerations the standard deviations of the Nagar Brahmins were selected as having smaller probable errors than those of any other sample of over 100 individuals, and though the size of the same is not large the σ_s approach very closely the values of one of the largest samples of living subjects for

---

[1] Morant, G. M.—A Preliminary Classification of European Races, Biometrika, Volume XX-B, pages 307—309.

[2] Pearson, Karl—On the Co-efficient of Racial Likeness, Biometrika, Volume—XVIII, pages 105—117,

[3] Op. cit., page 108.

[4] Morant. G. M.—Op. cit., pages 307—309.

[5] Pearson, Karl—Biometrika, Volume XX-B, pages 376—378.

which figures are available, namely, the Swedish group of 46,983 measured by Lundborg and Linders[1] and from which it may be inferred that they represent a fair approximation of the true value of the σ_s of Indian races.

It is true that there will be slight variations in the values of the C. R. L.'s if the latter could have been substituted for the σ_s of the Nagar Brahmins—which is unavoidable whenever a constant set of σ_s is used[2]—but that they are small and do not affect the general conclusions, may be shown from the following table in which are given the C. R. L.'s calculated from the mean standard deviations of the 30 samples given in Tables XXII and XXIIa, in the Appendix[3] for 10 pairs showing very low, moderate and high Co-efficients.

Names of Castes and Tribes compared.	Crude Co-efficients of Racial Likeness.			Reduced Co-efficients of Racial Likeness.		
	With σ_s of Nagar Brahmins.	With mean of σ_s.	Difference.	With σ_s of Nagar Brahmins.	With mean of σ_s.	Difference.
Bengali Brahmins and Kayasthas	0·99 ±0·17	1·48 ±0·17	0·49	1·49 ±0·26	2·22 ±0·26	0·73
Baghel Rajputs and Miscellaneous Rajputs.	0·28 ±0·17	0·45 ±0·17	0·17	0·55 ±0·34	0·90 ±0·34	0·35
Telegu Brahmins and Non-Brahmins.	—0·10 ±0·17	0·12 ±0·17	0·22	—0·20 ±0·34	0·24 ±0·34	0·44
Upper Chitralis and Lower Chatralis	—0·01 ±0·17	0·21 ±0·17	0·22	0·01 ±0·15	0·19 ±0·15	0·20
Red Kaffirs and Nagar Brahmins	24·96 ±0·17	29·58 ±0·17	4·62	24·46 ±0·17	28·99 ±0·17	4·53
Audich Brahmins and Kanarese Brahmins.	2·21 ±0·17	2·62 ±0·17	0·41	3·40 ±0·26	4·03 ±0·26	0·63
U. P. Brahmins and Nambudiris	3·30 ±0·17	4·10 ±0·17	0·80	6·30 ±0·32	7·85 ±0·32	1·53
Bengali Pods and Mahrattas ..	3·53 ±0·17	3·13 ±0·17	0·40	6·53 ±0·31	5·79 ±0·31	0·74
Nagar Brahmins and Bania-Jains	1·12 ±0·17	1·52 ±0·17	0·40	1·10 ±0·17	1·49 ±0·17	0·39
Bengali Pods and Swaraswat Gour Brahmins.	2·23 ±0·17	2·91 ±0·17	0·68	4·46 ±0·34	5·82 ±0·34	1·36

The point that has to be considered next is the relative significance of the different values of the C. R. L.'s as measures of racial divergence. This was discussed by Professor Pearson and a provisional classification attempted by him on the basis of 760 C. R. L.'s worked out in the Biometric Laboratory up to the time of his writing.[4] Professor Pearson's classification relates to cranial materials only and its application to living subjects has not yet been considered. He appears inclined however to ascribe higher values in the case of living subjects on theoretical grounds,[5] but for want of adequate materials the matter has not been decided. In his paper on the "Preliminary Classification of European Races" Morant[6] has compared 820 C. R. L.'s belonging to 41 distinct racial groups and Woo[7] has done the same for Asiatic Races in which 337 C. R. L.'s of 27 races were compared. The mean values of the 820 Reduced C. R. L.'s of European races and 337 Reduced C. R. L.'s of Asiatic races based entirely on cranial materials are 35·96 and 80·25 respectively. Against this, the mean value of the 627 Reduced C. R. L.'s discussed in this paper is 24·96 and of the 136 Reduced C. R. L.'s of the Swedish people[8] it is as low as 1·38

[1] Lundborg, H. and Linders, F. J.—The Racial Characters of the Swedish Nation, pages 64—100; Uppsala, 1926.

[2] Morant, G. M.—Op. cit., pages 306-307.

[3] Pages 35-36.

[4] Pearson Karl—Op. cit., page 112.

[5] *See* footnote on page 74, Biometrika, Volume XX-A

[6] Morant, G. M.—Op. cit., page 309.

[7] Biometrika, Volume XXIV, pages 117—128.

[8] Mahalanobis, P. C.—*A Statistical Study of certain Anthropometric measurements from Sweden*—Biometrika, Volume XXII, page 100.

only. The mean value of the Crude Co-efficients of the latter is however 24·85 and the extremely low values of the Reduced Co-efficients, to which Professor Mahalanobis[1] has drawn attention, as compared to those obtained from skulls, is undoubtedly due to the reduction of these values computed from large samples of several thousands to those of the standard size of 100. It is to be remembered in this connection that of the 627 Co-efficients of the Indian races 520 were based on the measurements taken by me and the remaining 107 only, on the data collected by 8 other workers. In the case of the Swedish materials Drs. Dahlburg and Wahlund were responsible for the greater part of the materials and the remaining portions only were the works of 10 assistants.[2] Consequently the influence of personal equation of the values on the living subjects, has been very much smaller than on those based on the cranial materials of a large number of investigators. Nevertheless in the face of these values, it was thought advisable to adhere to the provisional classification given by Professor Pearson with slight modification until a different set of values can definitely be ascribed to the C. R. L.'s computed from the measurements on the living.

In the computation of the C. R. L.'s 29 characters, including linear, arcal, indical and denoting both size and shape were taken into account. The condition that the characters should all be theoretically uncorrelated, has not been tested. In view of our ignorance on this point and also of the comparative small size of many of the samples, a large number of characters was included to overcome this deficiency and which appeared in the circumstances to be the safest procedure adoptable.[3] In one respect the materials dealt with in this paper, have an advantage over similar ones, namely the almost negligible effect of personal equation. For, out of 627 C. R. L.'s calculated, 520 are based on my measurements, and of the remaining 107, 56 are concerned with the data taken by three of my assistants who followed the same theoretical principles. The C. R. L.'s given here do not only form the largest number yet calculated on living subjects but also comprise the greatest number of racial groups studied ; 83 p. c. of which at least are *directly* comparable with one another, being based on the measurements taken by one person. It should not however be forgotten that though the method of the Co-efficient of Racial Likeness is without doubt the best available criterion of racial divergence, it is nevertheless not an absolute test, but only a rough measure of "how far *on the given data* significant resemblance or divergence can be asserted".[4] In assigning an equal value to every-one of the characters, it furthermore neglects the differences in the relative biological significance of the various characters as measures of racial difference. Other factors such as the systematic observations of non-measurable characters, should therefore be duly considered. The problem of unravelling racial kinships is a very complicated one and involves many elements, and though the help given by the statistical method is a substantial one it is still only a rough measure and the results obtained by its aid, should be taken with a little caution unless corroborative evidence is forthcoming.

---

[1]Mahalanobis, P. C.—Op. cit., page 100.

[2]Lundborg, H. and Linders, F.—Op. cit., page 3.

[3]Morant, G. M.—Op. cit., page 303.

[4]Pearson, Karl—Loc. cit., page 105.

CONSIDERATIONS OF THE RESULTS.

The mean measurements with the Indices and Statistical Constants are given in Tables I—V, and the Co-efficients of Racial Likeness in Tables VI—XXIV (a)[1]. In the former, only the Castes and Tribes examined for the Census of 1931 are included, but in the latter the values of all the groups compared are given.

The best way of discussing the results of the statistical analysis would seem to be to divide them first into several groups, constituted on the basis of the topography and known history of the country and then to consider the inter relationships between these groups. India has, very well defined natural boundaries, with lofty mountains guarding its northern, western and eastern limits and the sea protecting its southern shores. From its western extremity the Kirthar range stretches northwards into the Sulaiman mountains in almost unbroken chains until the Hindukush is reached. The mountain wall then continues eastwards through the Pamirs to the Karakoram ranges and finally into the Himalayas which stretches in a long curve through the entire northern boundaries of the country for upwards of 1,500 miles. From the eastern end again, there is an extension of mountain chains southwards through the Patkoi, Naga, Lushai and the Arakan Yoma Hills until the shores of the Bay of Bengal are touched near the Cape Negrais. There can be no doubt that this great mountain wall protected India from the main impact of racial movements which had their sources in Central Asia, and were deflected westwards into Asia Minor and Europe. Similarly the main drive of the mongolian races from China went southwards into the Malay Peninsula and the Indonesian Islands; though it is true that the Passes on its northwestern frontiers and gaps in the eastern ranges furnished pathways through which for many centuries hordes of invaders have poured into the country and greatly influenced the history and the racial composition of her people. The regions surrounding these routes are strategic centres and form the nuclei of several distinct zones into which the racial map of India naturally divides itself. The first of these is the mountainous country between longitudes 70° to 80°E and latitudes 33° to 37°N and protected by the barriers of the Hindukush and Karakoram ranges on the west and the north. It consists of the narrow defiles of the Chitral, Kunar, Panjkora and Swat on the west, the valleys of the Upper Indus including Ladakh, Baltistan, Hunza Nagar and Gilgit on the north, and the vales of Kashmir and Jammu on the south. This zone forms the most important of all ethnic divisions, as containing India's famous gateways on the west and the north, and the only means of its communication with Central and Western Asia.

I.—THE NORTH WESTERN HIMALAYAN REGION.

The materials regarding the somatic traits of the inhabitants of this tract are fairly extensive and include the main racial groups of the Upper Indus Valley and Hindukush. On Kashmir proper and Jammu however, our data are very scanty. The first scientific survey of the tribes of this region was due to the labours of Ujfalvy, who supplemented his earlier work in Russian Turkistan and the Pamirs [2] by his investigations in Kashmir and Little Tibet between 1881-82. The measurements taken by him during this period include 82 Baltis, 44 Dardis, 36 Ladakhis, 40 Kashmiris, besides 20 Paharis and 27 Lahulis from Kulu[3]. After Ujfalvy, the next important work was that of Sir Aurel Stein. In the course of his second *Archæological Expedition* to Chinese Turkistan, he found time to measure a large number of tribes around the Taklamakan desert and the mountainous country lying south of it within the borders of India[4]. His measurements taken on 600 individuals belonging to 29 tribes, were analysed by T. A. Joyce[5]. and published in 1912.

In the same year, Prof. Roland B. Dixon of Harvard, measured 92 Burushaskis in Hunza during his short visit to that region, and I am indebted to him for allowing me to use his unpublished data here. The Italian expedition under De Filippi to the Upper Himalaya and the Karakoram ranges in 1913-14 is responsible for an excellent series of measurements comprising 380 individuals belonging to 6 racial groups which were taken by Prof. G. Dainelli but analysed by Prof. Renato Biasutti in his paper entitled " I tipi somatici nelle popolazioni dell 'Alto Indo" and published in 1925[6]. Finally in 1929, as a member of a Scientific Expedition sent by the Government of India, the present writer visited the Chitral Valley and Kaffiristan and carried out an extensive survey of the races living in these parts. Altogether over 700 men were measured belonging to the Kaffir tribes of Rambur and Bamboret, the Khos of Upper and Lower Chitral, the Pathans of Bijaur and the Ashretis and Damelis of the Ashret Valley. Measurements were also taken on the Tadjiks, Uzbegs and other peasant traders from Badakshan who came to Chitral at this time through the Dorah Pass, as well as the pilgrims from Khasgar in Chinese Turkistan who used the high Baroghil Pass to cross the frontiers.

---

[1] *Vide* Appendix, pages 1—22 and 24—38.

[2] Expèdition Sciéntifique francaise en Russie, en Sibérie et dans le Turkestan, 3 Volumes, Paris, 1880.

[3] Ujfalvy, Karl Eugen von — Aus dem Westlichen Himalaja. Leipzing 1884—See tables at the end of the volume. And Les Aryens de l'Hindou-Kouch—By the same author. Paris, 1896. Pages 387—434.

[4] Stein, Sir Aurel—Serindia, page 1351, Appendix C. Volume III; Oxford, 1921.

[5] Joyce, T. A.—Notes on the Physical Anthropology of Chinese Turkistan and the Pamirs—J. R. A. I., Volume XLII, pages 450—484.

[6] Spedizione Italiana de Filippi, Serie II, Volume IX, pages 181—269; Bologna, 1925.

All these materials taken together cover the major racial groups living south of the Hindukush and Karakoram mountains, but with the exception of the Pathans of Bijaur and a few Kashmiris we have no information regarding the somatic types of the inhabitants of the lower valleys.

In Tables VI and VIa[1] are given the values of both Crude and Reduced Co-efficients of Racial Likeness of the people of the Western parts including three samples from Badakshan and Russian Turkistan. As the influence of personal equation on C. R. L. appears to be very great,[2] I have thought it advisable to restrict the computation of their values to the measurements taken by a single worker wherever possible, so that they can be directly compared. In Text–fig. 1

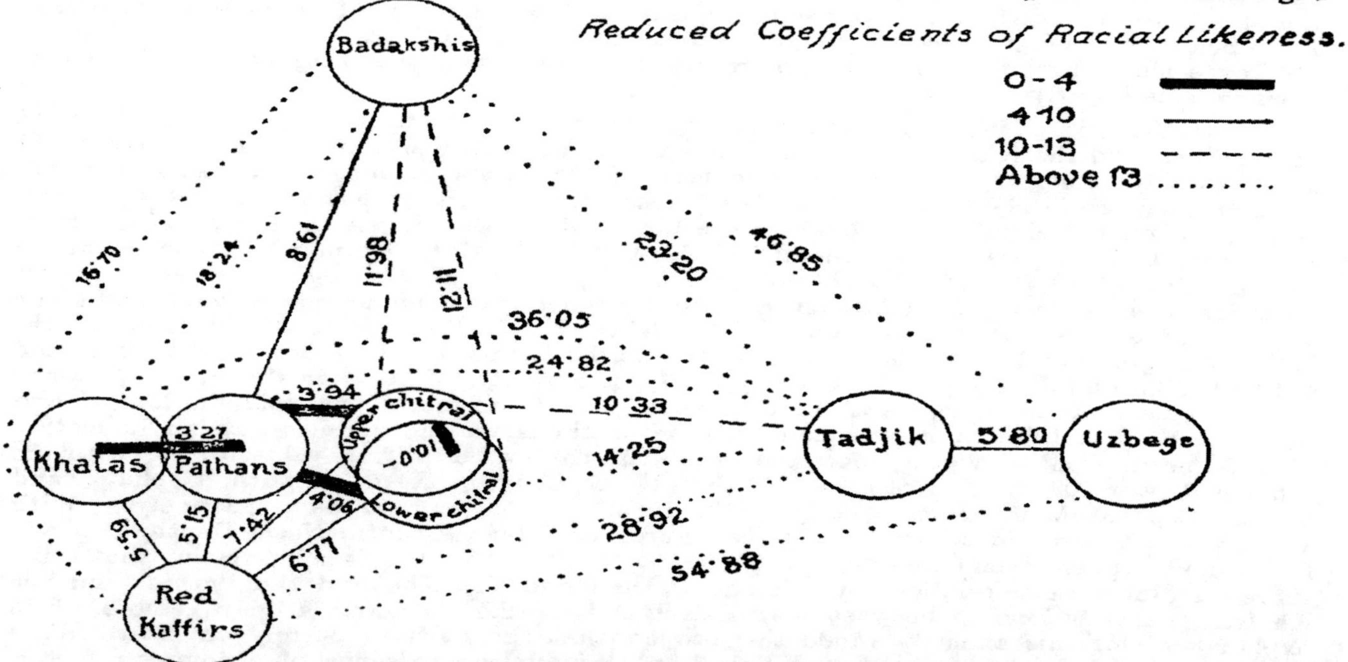

Text—fig. 1. Inter-relationship of North Western Indian Races.

the affinities between the various groups as disclosed by the C. R. L.'s are diagramatically shown. It will be seen from this Fig. that there is an intimate association between the Khos of the Upper and Lower Chitral with the surprisingly small value of — 0·01±0·15, or 0·19±0·15, if the mean standard deviations of the groups are substituted for those of the Nagar Brahmins. Further when the values of the function 'α '[3] are compared, in 19 characters they are found to be below 1, in three only, they exceed 3, but in none the value is over 6 to indicate any suggestion of racial difference[4]. Against this, Joyce [5] obtained the value of 4·84 for his Differential Index between the Chitrali and Mastuji and 4·18 between the latter and the Kaffir, and came to the conclusion that there is a closer relationship between the Mastuji, Sarikoli and Pakho than between the Mastuji and Chitrali, as a result probably of the presence of "some foreign element" in the latter[6]. It should be mentioned here that the tribal name of the people of Chitral and Mastuj is *Kho*, who speak an Indo-Aryan language known as *Khowar*. It has been identified with 'Kin-wei', the old Chinese name for Mastuj or Upper Chitral which they originally occupied and later spread to Chitral in the south. Inspite of the independence of the two principalities of Chitral and Mastuj for a long time, there is no evidence that the unity of the people was not maintained as is indicated by the absence of any dialectical differences in the Khowar spoken in the two areas[7]. I have considered it proper therefore to name my two samples of the Chitrali people as Khos of Lower and Upper Chitral instead of calling them by the separate names of Chitrali and Mastuji, as Stein has done. Among the latter are included all inhabitants up to Reshun, which is the natural boundary of the two valleys, and among the former all those whose homes were in Turikho, Mulikho, and Mastuj. Stein's subjects came from the same general localities, though among his Chitrali he included some men who came from Kusht (Kosht), Mulkho (Mulikho), Yasin, and one from Ashreth (No. 3 in his list)[8] who probably was not a Kho at all, as this village is inhabited by a small colony of Palula speaking people who are said to have immigrated from the Shina country.[9]

---

[1] Appendix, page 25.
[2] Pearson, Karl, 1928—Op. cit., page 376.
[3] $\alpha = \frac{n_s \times n_s'}{n_s + n_s'} \left(\frac{m_s - m_s'}{\sigma^s} \right)^2$. These values are not shown in the Tables but will be published in the detailed report on these tribes.
[4] Biometrika, Volume XVIII, page 26.
[5] Joyce. T. A. —Op. cit., page 476.
[6] *Ibid.*, page 462.
[7] Morgenstierne, Georg,—Report on a Linguistic Mission to Northwestern India, pages 46 50; Oslo, 1932.
[8] Stein, Sir Aurel,—Op. cit., page 1362.
[9] Morgenstierne, Georg,—Op. cit., page 54.

The results of my statistical analysis corroborate this unity and demonstrate clearly the complete racial homogeneity of the two Kho groups. The conflicting nature of Joyce's conclusions is due in the first instance to the unsoundness of his method and secondly to the extremely small size of the samples (*e.g.*, 22 Chitralis and 28 Mastuji against my 90 and 150 respectively for the two groups), to which this method was applied. If instead of the Differential Index, the method of C. R. L. is followed, the following values of the Reduced C. R. L. are obtained from his data, namely, for the Chitrali and Mastuji, $14 \cdot 58 \pm 1 \cdot 06$ and for the Chitrali and Kaffir, $21 \cdot 87 \pm 1 \cdot 31$, showing a comparatively closer degree of association between the two Kho groups than between the Chitrali and Kaffir. The high values in this case are no doubt due to the small size of the samples and the lesser number of characters considered. Prof. Pearson[1] has deprecated the use of his method for small samples and the values obtained by Joyce show how misleading are the results when the quantitative tests are applied to extremely small groups.

From Text-fig. I, it will be further observed that there is an intimate association between the Pathan and the Khalash, popularly known as the Black Kaffir on the one hand, and the Pathan and the Khos on the other. The values of the Crude and Reduced C. R. L.'s in the case of the former are $1 \cdot 90 \pm 0 \cdot 17$ and $3 \cdot 27 \pm 0 \cdot 29$ respectively. But when the individual characters are compared significant differences are observed in Stature, Auricular Height, Transverse Arc, Trans. Cephalo-Facial Index and the Orbito-Nasal Index in which the values of 'α' are 7·38, 7·99, 8·70, 7·03 and 6·45 respectively, showing that though both the groups are somatically closely related, the Pathans are slightly taller with a higher cranial vault and a less flat but more pronounced facial cast than the Khalash. In the case of the Pathans and the Khos of Upper and Lower Chitral, the Crude and the Reduced C. R. L.'s are $2 \cdot 96 \pm 0 \cdot 17$ and $3 \cdot 94 \pm 0 \cdot 23$; and $2 \cdot 60 \pm 0 \cdot 17$ and $4 \cdot 06 \pm 0 \cdot 27$ respectively. The main differences between the Pathans and the Khos as a whole, consists in the former's possessing a longer and narrower head and face in comparison with that of the latter and there is also an indication that the nasal profile is slightly more pronounced in the former. The values of 'α' with the Khos of Upper Chitral in respect of the Head Length, Head Breadth, Cephalic and Trans. Cephalo-Facial Indices being 9·17, 10·22, 24·55 and 12·85 respectively. With the Khos of Lower Chitral the respective figures for Head Length, Nasal Depth, Cephalic Index and Upper Facial Index are 9·00, 7·93, 17·62 and 7·35. It is interesting that while there is an intimate association between the Pathan and the Kho and the Pathan and the Khalash, the relationship between the Khalash and the Kho is comparatively remote. The explanation for this anomaly would seem to be that the Pathans occupy an intermediate position with whom the two others are linked up through the presence of a common factor, though the dominant elements in the two are different.

The Red Kaffirs considered here belong to the Kati tribe which forms their easternmost section and occupy the Bashgul valley in Afghan Kaffiristan and the Rambur and Bamboret valleys of Chitral. They are undoubtedly the most important of the Kaffir groups and include the famous Kam tribe[2]. The subjects measured by me came from Bargromatal in Afghan Kaffiristan and the villages of Kunist and Brumotul in the Rambur and Bamboret valleys to which some of them took refuge after Abdur Rahman's conquest of Kaffristan.

The C. R. L.'s given in Tables VI and VI (*a*) do not disclose intimate relationship of the Kaffir with any group, though associations with both the Pathan and the Khalash are close. With the Kho, the kinship is more distant though not quite so much as that existing between the Khalash and the latter. When the individual characters are scrutinised it is found that the Red Kaffir differ from the Pathans in being somewhat taller but possessing a larger head with a slightly shorter facial profile. Compared to the Khalash, they are again much taller, with larger and broader head and slightly shorter face but showing more pointed features. The values of 'α' in respect of Stature, Head Breadth, Horizontal Circumference of head, Cephalic Index, Orbito-Nasal Index and Trans. Cephalo-Facial Index being 31·34, 12·52, 9·37, 7·08, 36·49 and 9·92 respectively.

From the Kho groups the Red Kaffirs differ in having a higher stature and a larger and more elongated head. The nose is also pitched higher and the cast of the face sharper. The values of 'α' in Stature, Head Length, Horizontal Circumference, Cephalic Index, Nasal Depth and the Orbito-Nasal Index with the Khos of Upper and Lower Chitral are respectively 11·93, 43·87, 7·51, 41·80, 4·57, 17·74 and 17·36, 37·50, 11·72, 27·79, 7·19, and 19·52.

The races living across the frontier whom I measured in Chitral are the Badakshi, the Tadjik and Uzbeg. The first two belong to the provinces of Munjan, Zabak, Sanglech, Rostock and Warduz and the latter to Russian Turkistan. Among the Badakshis were included the upper stratum of the population of Badakshan, whereas the Tadjiks comprised the cultivating communities only.

---

[1] **Pearson, Karl,** 1928—*Op. cit., foot-note on page* 377.

Morgenstierne, 1932—*Op. cit.,* page 63.

From Text-fig. I, it will be observed that while there is a close relationship of the Tadjiks with the Uzbegs and to a lesser degree with the Khos of Upper Chitral, the former do not show any kinship with the upper classes of their own country, who, on the other hand disclose some association with the Pathans, and also with the Khos, albeit distant.

These results appear rather startling in view of Ujfalvy's definite conclusions regarding the affinities of the Tadjiks with the Galchas and other members of the Pamir group.[1] In his Expedition to Russian Turkistan, Ujfalvy measured 60 Tadjiks and 73 Uzbegs.[2]

In the following Table are given the measurements of the Tadjik and the Uzbegs taken by Ujfalvy and myself :—

Tribes.	Head length.	Head breadth.	Cephalic Index.	Inter-orbital breadth.	Horizontal Circumference.	Transverse arc.	Stature.
Tadjik (Ujfalvy) ..	184	156	84·78	30·37	557·5	350	1705
Uzbeg (Ujfalvy) ..	188	159	84·57	32·50	557·0	348	1687
Tadjik (Guha) ..	182·7	151·6	83·12	31·26	542·4	342	1660
Uzbeg (Guha).. ..	183·5	156·6	85·42	32·82	550·1	348	1648

It will be seen from these figures that the Tadjiks of Russian Turkistan are evidently taller, more brachycephalic and possess larger heads and probably a more prominent nasal bridge than their kinsmen south of the Oxus. The two Uzbeg groups appear however to be closer though the one measured by me has shorter stature.

It has been suggested by several writers that the Tadjiks were the aboriginal population of Persia[4] from where they spread to western Afganistan, Badakshan and Russian Turkistan.[5] It appears from the figures given above that the "Pamiri" or "Iranian" element considered by Ujfalvy to be the dominant factor among the Tadjiks is stronger among those of Russian Turkistan than in their kinsmen in Badakshan who are related to the Uzbegs. Haddon's[6] view however that they "preserved themselves more or less free from the last Uzbeg invasion" of Russian Turkistan appears untenable in the face of the C. R. L.'s obtained between the two, and the only explanation that fits in with the facts, seems to be that in their expansion westwards the Tadjiks absorbed other elements, and the section that settled in Badakshan was Tartarised in blood, though not in speech and remained racially separate from the Badakshis whose basic strain is the same as that which has entered into the ethnic composition of the northern Pathans and other tribes on the north-western frontiers of India.

North and East of the Khos along the southern boundaries of the Pamirs, are the settlements of the Wakhis who have moved from their barren home in the North and occupied the highlands of the Upper Mastuj and Hunza valleys[7]. They are regarded by Joyce[8] as the purest of the Iranian races in these parts and closely akin to the Galchas. I was able to measure only a few, but Stein[9] took measurements on 9 Wakhis.

The mean Head Length and Head Breadth calculated from his measurements are 184·74 $\pm$ 0·95 and 156·68 $\pm$0·91 respectively and the Cephalic Index 84·81 $\pm$0·60. Besides the Galchas, they appear to be racially allied to the people living around the Taklamakan desert such as the Turfan, Khotan, Hami, Charlick and the Sarikoli, if the values obtained for the Differential Index of Joyce are to be entirely relied upon. Whatever may, however, be the exact degrees of kinship between these groups, there appears to be no doubt, from the measurements taken by Stein, that the basic element among these people is the same and is spread across the highlands of Central Asia from Persia to the Taklamakan desert.

[1] Ujfalvy, Charles de, 1896—Op. cit., pages 149—155.

[2] Ujfalvy is not consistent about the number of Uzbegs he measured; on page 388 he mentions 73 but on page 392, he gives the figure as 74.

[3] The figures given by Ujfalvy (Op. cit., page 388) were found inaccurate and correct values as given in the above Table were calculated from his measurements.

[4] Ruggeri, G. V.—The first outlines of a systematic Anthropolgy of Asia, page 33; Calcutta, 1921; and Haddon, A. C.—The Races of Man, page 102; Cambridge, 1924.

[5] Deniker, J.—The Races of Man, page 419; London, 1900.

[6] Haddon, A. C.—Op. cit., page 104.

[7] Morgenstierne, G.—Op. cit., page 68.

[8] Joyce, T. A.—Op. cit., page 467.

[9] Stein, Sir Aurel Op. cit., Appendix C.

East of Chitral and south of the Karakoram ranges, the country is divided into several high narrow valleys of the Upper Indus, and the vale of Kashmir on the southwest of the same river. The northern parts of this territory contains the home of the Burish and several Dardic speaking tribes separated by lofty mountain ranges from one another with Tibetan encroachment on the east. The valleys south of the western Himalayan ranges are inhabited by the Kashmiri people. Of these, the Burish or the Yeshkun occupy the northern side valleys of Yasin, Hunza, and Nagar and speak the archaic Burushaski which is unrelated to any of the Indian languages. The data available for these interesting tribes consist of the measurements of one Nagar by Ujfalvy, a Hunza and Yasin by the present writer and the series of 92 Hunzas by Prof. Roland B. Dixon. The latter took his measurements during his visit to north-western Kashmir and I am very grateful to him for permitting me to use his unpublished materials for this paper.

The solitary Hunza measured by me (see Figs. 1 and 1 a, in Plate VII) was of medium height, with a long head, squarish face and long and moderately prominent nose. The Yasinese was considerably shorter but the shape of his head, face and nose was similar Ujfalvy considers the somatic characters of the Burish to be similar to those of the Dardi but found certain differences between the types represented by the Hunza and the Nagar, the latter being somewhat shorter[1].

In Tables VII and VII(*a*) are given the Crude and Reduced C. R. L.'s of the Hunzas with different groups, based on the measurements taken by Dixon. The figures published in these tables show that the Hunzas have the lowest Co-efficient with the Khalash, and next to them with the Khos of Upper Chitral. The values of the Reduced C. R. L.'s with the Red Kaffir and the Pathan[2] are however smaller, being $28 \cdot 07 \pm 0 \cdot 29$ and $30 \cdot 88 \pm 0 \cdot 43$ respectively. Ordinarily such high values are regarded as indicating racial divergence rather than association, but as these are based on the measurements of two different workers, the influence of personal equation on the Co efficient has to be taken into account. That the values would have been much lower, had this disturbing factor been absent, admits of hardly any doubt, but whether any relationship between these groups would have ensured thereby is a matter impossible to determine.

On examining the individual characters it is found that the high Co-efficients of the Hunzas with the Khalash and the Khos are mainly due to differences in Stature, Nasal Length, Nasal Breadth and Nasal Index ; the values of 'α' in these characters being 50·42, 48·10, 19·33, 79·25 and 27·92, 64·00, 46·33 and 137·65 respectively in the two series. In the case of the Red Kaffirs and the Pathans, the values of α for Nasal Length, Nasal Breadth and Nasal Index are similarly very high, the figures being 87.16, 24.68, 118.59 and 57.74, 14.69, 78.04 respectively in the two series. Judging from these figures the effect of personal equation does not alone seem to have influenced the C. R. L.'s. The presence of a strong broad-nosed element among the Burish appears unmistakable, which probably differentiates them from their western neighbours as well as the Dardi speaking Balti on the east, with whom their Reduced C. R. L.'s is as high as $117 \cdot 00 \pm 0 \cdot 26$; and is also perhaps the explanation of their comparatively closer approach to the mongoloid Ladakhi with whom the Reduced C. R. L. is only $33 \cdot 50 \pm 0 \cdot 47$. On scrutinising the individual characters however it is found that the differences in the values of 'α' in Facial width with the last two, are as much as 846·81 and 78·43 respectively. As, such high figures appeared unlikely to be the results of racial differences, Dainelli's measurements were examined again. He is stated to have taken his measurements according to the Convention of Monaco [3] and his "*Larghezza facciale*" was regarded therefore as corresponding to the 'Bizygomatic diameter' of the Monaco Agreement, and the C. R. L.'s were calculated from the tables of measurements given on pages 272-299. On looking through Biasutti's text[4] however it was found that Dainelli's "*Larghezza facciale*" was really "Larghezza bimalare" and his "Indice Facciale" was calculated from this measurement. Consequently the Facial Width and the Faccial Index were omitted and fresh values of the C. R. L.'s were calculated. The Co-efficients thus obtained became only $13 \cdot 25 \pm 0 \cdot 28$ with the Baltis and $8 \cdot 71 \pm 0 \cdot 52$ with the Ladakhis. These latter figures, appear likely to be more indicative of the true relationship between these races and if the personal equation could have been eliminated, these would probably have shown further eductions.

The existence of a broad nosed strain among the Burish, deduced from an analysis of Dixon's measurements, seems also to receive support from the few Burish crania that have so far been studied. In 1899, Garson[5] published an account of 3 skulls from Garkush belonging to three middle aged Yasinese slain by a local Khan by the name of Ger Bhenau. The mean Cubic Capacity of these skulls is 1376 c.c., the mean Head Length and Head Breadth are 178·66 and 132·66 respectively and the mean Cranial Index is 74·40. The mean Nasal Index

---

[1] Ujfalvy, Charles de, 1896—Op. cit., page 276.

[2] These values are not shown in the Tables.

[3] Biasutti, R. 1925—Op. cit., page 181.

[4] *Ibid.*, page 222.

[5] Garson, J. G.—On Skulls from the Hindukush District. J. A. I., Volume XVIII, pages 20-26, 1899.

of the three skulls is 48·70 and the Facial Index 87·60. Duckworth[1] also described 2 Nagar skulls brought by Mr. Conway from an exploration of the Karakoram regions in 1894, one of which was male and the other female. The Cranial Index of the male skull was 70·45 and the Nasal 52·72. In the female skull the corresponding figures are 69·94 and 50·00. These measurements on the skulls are therefore in agreement with the values obtained by Dixon on the living and do not lead to the conclusion of the leptorrhinic character of the Burish.

Taking all these facts together the Hunzas seem to exhibit closer affinities with their eastern neighbours the Baltis and more specially with the Ladakhis than with the tribes living on their southwest. At first sight the close association with the Ladakhis seems contrary to the views expressed by many observers but if the broad-nosed strain among the Burish is admitted the kinship suggested by the C. R. L.'s is at once understood. The Dardic strain observed by Ujfalvy clearly points out the association of the Hunzas with the Baltis, but this factor does not appear to be predominating when the visual impressions are reduced to a quantitative basis. The broad-nosed strain which is present among the Burish appears also to be strong among the Ladakhi, though in their case, an additional mongoloid factor must have intruded, but which had not penetrated so far west and north as the Burish country.

South and east of the Burish country is the Gilgit Valley or Dardistan, the home of the Dardi. The Brokpa, as the eastern section of the Dardis are called, extend further east into Baltistan and occupy the valley south of the Indus. North of the Brokpa between the Balti and the Ladakhi there lives in the narrow defiles of the upper stream of the same river, another section of the Dardis, known as the Machnopa. The language of this tribe is Dardi or Shina from which the entire branch of the Indo-Aryan languages of the North Western Himalayan regions has derived its name.

In the Baltis who inhabit the northern valleys of Baltistan and the Purigi, who live immediately south of the Machnopa and east of the Brokpa we have races who have adopted Tibetan languages without apparently undergoing racial metamorphism. Finally the easternmost part of the territory or the little Tibet is occupied by the Ladakhi and the barren uplands further north east, by the Chiangpa, the last of whom are a Mongoloid race who crossed the Tibetan frontiers at an early date.

The data regarding these tribes consists of the measurements taken by Ujfalvy[2] in 1881 on 45 Dardis, 41 Baltis and 36 Ladakhis and by Dainelli[3] on 146 Balti, 49 Brokpa, 44 Machnopa, 47 Purigi, 47 Ladakhi and 47 Chiangpa.

The Dardis proper, who form the western section of the Dardi or Shina speaking peoples occupy the Gilgit valleys. Ujfalvy describes them as possessing tall slim figures, with aquiline nose, deep set eyes and well marked supra-orbital ridges. The C. R. L.'s of the Dardis based on Ujfalvy's measurements, with the tribes living on their west and east are given in the following Table :—

CO-EFFICIENTS OF RACIAL LIKENESS.

The Dardi (Ujfalvy) *and others.*

—	Khos (Guha) (Upper Chitral).	Burish (Hunza) (Dixon).	Balti (Ujfalvy).	Brokpa (Dainelli).
Reduced	33·80±0·38	43·04±0·46	20·30±0·69	13·20±0·74
Crude	22·69±0·26	25·32±0·29	7·90±0·25	6·06±0·34

It appears from this Table that the Dardis have the lowest value with the Brokpa. As the C. R. L.'s were based on the measurements of two workers, it is possible that the values would have been smaller, if the factor of personal equation could have been eliminated. With the Balti the Co-efficient is considerably higher, and as no disturbing factor is involved in this case (the C. R. L.'s being calculated from Ujfalvy's and not Dainelli's measurements of the Baltis), the values signify actual conditions existing between these tribes. On examining the individual characters it is found that the main difference between the Dardi and the Brokpa lies in

[1] Duckworth, W. L. H.—Studies from the Anthropological Laboratory of Cambridge, pages 212-224; ambridge, 1904.

[2] Ujfalvy, Charles de,—Aus dem Westlichen Himalaja—Tables. Leipzig, 1884.

[3] Dainelli, G.—Op. cit., pages 272-299.

the greater Nasal breadth of the latter, the value of 'α' in this character being 20·52. The differences of the Dardis from Baltis consist in the smaller head and the longer and narrower nose of the former. The values of 'α' in the Horizontal circumference of the head, the Sagittal and Transverse arcs, the Nasal length and the Nasal Index are 49·58, 6·86, 13·66, 6·39 and 10·68 respectively. The above figures tend to demonstrate the basic affinity of the two western and eastern sections of the Dardi speaking groups but the Tibetan speaking Baltis living north of the Brokpa appear to be somewhat different. It is probable that this divergence has been caused by the presence of some alien strain among the Baltis.

With their western neighbours the Dardis do not seem to show any association. The C. R. L.'s with the Burish of Hunza, the Khos and the Red Kaffirs are high. It is difficult of course to determine how far they are affected by personal equation. The values of 'α' of the Dardi with the Burish in Stature, Nasal length, Nasal breadth, Bizygomatic breadth and Nasal Index are 11·47, 8·25, 49·95, 67·15, 68·27 respectively, showing that the differences in these characters are real and not fortuitous. Between the Dardis and the Khos the values of 'α' in respect of Head breadth, Min. Frontal breadth, Bizygomatic breadth, Nasal length, Horizontal circumference of the head are 9·81, 21·11, 52·81, 9·02 and 57·27 respectively. With the Red Kaffirs similarly the values for Head length, Bizygomatic breadth, Nasal length, Nasal breadth, Horizontal circumference of head, Sagittal arc and Length Breadth Index are 10·53, 65·08, 19 58, 10·48, 83·33, 53·30 and 10·35 respectively, signifying true racial differences between these two tribes in these characters.

In Tables VIII and VIII(*a*) are given the C. R. L.'s, Crude and Reduced, of the 6 eastern tribes measured by Dainelli, of which the Brokpa and the Machnopa, as stated already, are Dardic speaking and the rest speak languages belonging to the Tibetan family.

The lowest value of the C. R. L. shown in the Tables is that between the Balti and the Brokpa where it is only — 0·56 ± 0·38, proving unmistakably that they are the samples of the same race, though speaking different languages. The Reduced C. R. L. between the Brokpa and the other Dardic tribe Machnopa living slightly further east and north is also very low, namely 1·09 ± 0·60 ; between the Balti and the Machnopa it is a little higher namely 3·76 ± 0·41. Examination of the individual characters show that in the first two pairs, the values of 'α' in every case is much below 6. With regard to the latter pair, in the Facial Index only it is 8·80, *i.e.*, over 6. Dainelli's Facial Index was obtained from the ratio of the Bimalar breadth to the Naso-mental height[1] and shows that the Machnopa in comparison with the Brokpa have wider malars and shorter face. This is not probably the result of a Mongoloid admixture because the two Tibetan groups Ladakhi and Chiangpa show not only greater facial width but have also larger facial height. The Bimalar breadth and the Naso-mental height in the three being 119, 128, 130 and 117, 123 and 122 respectively. Among the Balti on the other hand, the values for both the characters are ow, namely 117 and 117. Consequently the rise in the value of the C. R. L. between the Balti and the Machnopa cannot be attributed to a Mongoloid strain. All these three tribes, are however, closely allied and belong to the same racial stock inspite of Tibetan acculturation of the Balti, which does not seem to have affected the southern valleys occupied by the Brokpa and from which the Machnopa appear also to have escaped though living in continuous territories with the Ladakhis, as a result probably of the high mountain ranges which prevented ingress from outside.

The Purigi also show certain affinities to the Machnopa, their northern neighbours, and to a lesser extent with the Brokpa and the Balti, but do not seem to be connected with either the Ladakhi or the Chiangpa with both of whom the Co-efficients are high. Comparisons of the individual characters indicate that the values of 'α' between the Purigi and the Balti are 40·04, 9·37, 17·34, 17·22 and 6·91 in respect of the Bimalar breadth, Nasal length, Nasal Index, Facial Index and Stature respectively. With the Brokpa their main differences are in Stature, Bimalar breadth, Nasal Index and Facial Index in which the values of 'α' are 10·53, 16·80, 8·85 and 10·76 respectively. In relation to the Balti and Brokpa, therefore, the Purigi have shorter stature, broader face and nose. It is probable that these differences are due to the presence of a slight Mongoloid strain, traces of which have been noticed[2], though their basic type does not seem to have been much affected by it.

The two Mongoloid tribes, the Ladakhi and the *Chiangpa* have a Reduced C. R. L. of 17·23 ± 0·60, slightly less than that between the former and the Purigi. Their Co-efficient with the Machnopa is 22·84 ± 0·62 but with the rest the values are very high. The Chiangpa do not show any association with any of these groups excepting perhaps the Ladakhi. Ujfalvy has drawn attention to the Mongoloid character of the Ladakhi among whom prominent cheek bones and oblique slit eyes were seen by him[3]. The observations recorded by Dainelli show that 38 per cent. among the Ladakhi do not have facial hair and 98 per cent. body hair. Among the Chiangpa the corresponding figures are 58 and 100 respectively[4]. It appears probable from these

---

[1] Biasutti, R.—Op. cit., page 224.
[2] Biasutti, R.—Op. cit., page 256.
[3] Ujfalvy, Charles de, 1884—page 184.
[4] Biasutti, R.—Op. cit., page 194.

figures that the Chiangpa represent a pure Mongoloid type unrelated to any of the other groups except the Ladakhi with whom there is the indication of relationship. Their truer affinities would however seem to be with the inhabitants across the border. The Ladakhis, though Mongoloid likewise in basis, have apparently absorbed another element which has entered into the composition of the Purigi and the Machnopa, and with whom there have been closer contacts due to the contiguity of their territories.

The country south of the Western Himalayan ranges, is the vale of Jammu and Kashmir, famous for its beauty and climate. Unfortunately, information about the somatic traits of the people of this part is very scanty. We have some excellent descriptions no doubt, but the only metric data that we possess are the measurements on 20 Pandits and 20 Kashmiris taken by Ujfalvy[1] in 1881 and by Chanda[2] on 14 Kashmiri Pandits in 1922. Sir George Campbell[3] describes the Brahmins of Kashmir " as high Aryan, very fair and handsome, with high chiselled features, and no trace of intermixture of the blood of any lower race. The high nose is slightly aquiline, but is by no means ' Jewish ' or ' nut-cracker ' type. Raise a little the brow of a Greek statue and give the nose a small turn at the bony point in front of the bridge (though straight noses are quite common) and you have then the model type of this part of India." Ujfalvy[4] also found them above medium height with well built powerful body, long straight nose, and sharp oval face. The measurements taken by Ujfalvy show that the head is long ; the mean Cephalic Index of the 20 Pandits and Kashmiris being 71·90 and 72·52 respectively, and the mean Horizontal circumference of head of the two groups 540 mm. each and the Transverse arc 325 and 335 respectively. Chanda likewise found them dolichocephalic, the Index varying from 66·8 to 78·9. None of these two workers has published any other measurement and it is not possible to calculate the C. R. L.'s and obtain a quantitative assessment of their relationship with the neighbouring races.

The hilly region south west of Kashmir, but outside its political boundary, lying between the lower ranges of the Western Himalayas up to Nepal, includes Chamba, Kangra, Garhwal and the Kumaon districts. The data available on the people living in this region consist of the measurements taken by Holland[5] on the Kanets of Kulu and Lahoul, by von Eickstedt[6] on 13 Garhwalis, 27 Gurung from Western Nepal and 69 Gurkhas measured during the war.

The Tracts of Lahoul and Kulu are really the south eastern extension of Ladakh and are separated from each other by a mountain barrier over which all communication is carried on through the Rotang Pass (13326 ft.) which passes on again from Lahoul to Ladakh and thence to Central Asia. The Kanets are an agricultural community living in this hilly country but their kinsmen across the mountains in Lahoul speak a language which is almost a modified form of Tibetan[7]. In his very able paper on this tribe, Holland considers that as a result of this contact-metamorphism, there has also been a distinct infusion of Tibetan blood among the Kanets of Lahoul, though the basic type remains Indian[8].

The C. R. L.'s calculated from his measurements are given in the following Table :—

The C. R. L.'s of the Kanets of Kulu and others.

—	Kanets of Lahoul. (Holland).	Purigi. (Dainelli).	Machnopa. (Dainelli).
Reduced C. R. L.	9·10±0·70	9·47±0·62	14·17±0·65
Crude C. R. L.	3·64±0·28	5·01±0·33	7·23±0·33

The values of the C. R. L.'s as shown in the above Table between the two sections of the Kanets point definitely to their racial kinship. On examining the individual characters it is found that the main differences between them lie in Stature, Cephalic Index, Nasal Index and Naso-Malar Index in which the values of 'α' are 12·96, 10·24, 59·29 and 6·76 respectively. Holland[9] has observed that due to the infusion of Tibetan blood, the Kanets of Lahoul show modifications on the Kulu average by 2·9 per cent. in Stature, 4·1 per cent. in Cephalic Index, 10·4 per cent. in Nasal Index and 2·3 per cent. in Naso-Malar Index. His conclusions are therefore in accord with the statistical results, illustrating the gradual absorption of Tibetan blood among the Lahoulis though as yet their essential Indian character remains unaltered.

1 Ujfalvy, Charles de, 1896—Op. cit., pages 387-434.
2 Chanda, Ramaprasad—Races of India. The Journal of the Department of Letters, Calcutta University, Volume VIII, pages 10-11. 1922.
3 Campbell, G.—The Ethnology of India, J. A. S. B., Volume XXXV, Part II, Suppl. No. 1867, Calcutta.
4 Ujfalvy, Charles de, 1884—Op. cit., page 153.
5 Holland, T. A.—The Kanets of Kulu and Lahoul. J. A. I., Volume XXXII, page 101, 1902.
6 Eickstedt, E.—The Races and Types of the Western and Central Himalaya, *Man in India*, Volume VI, pages 237—276, 1926.
7 Holland—Op. cit., page 102.
8 *Ibid.*, page 104.
9 *Ibid.*, page 120.

With the tribes further north and west, the Kanets appear also to be racially allied. The values of the C. R. L.'s with the Purigi are only slightly less than those found with the Lahoulis, but as the Co-efficients have been computed form the measurements of two persons, their true values are most likely to be much smaller. For similar reasons the C. R. L.'s with the Machnopa would probably have given lower values than are shown at present. In individual characters, the main differences with the Purigi lie in Stature and Head breadth. With the Machnopa on the other hand, they consist in Head length and Cephalic Index ; the values of 'α' with the former in the two characters being 26·97 and 12·51 respectively and with the latter 34·61 and 10·77. In the case of the Lahoulis, the increase in the value of the Cephalic Index has been shown by Holland[1], to have been due to the influence of Tibetan blood. It is probably the same with the Machnopa who appear likewise to have absorbed some Tibetan blood. With the Purigi, the increase in the Head breadth may also be due to the same factor but the shortness of Stature in the Purigi had probably to be accounted for by the presence of some other element.

Further east, along the entire Sub-Himalayan tract to the borders of Nepal, the same racial type as seen among the Kanets, probably prevails. The measurements taken by Eickstedt[2] on 1? Garhwalis of British Garhwal show that the mean Stature of these people is 1598 mm., Cephalic Index 76·8 and Nasal Index 73·8. Measurements by the same writer on 27 Gurungs[3] of Western Nepal give 1623 mm., 79·6 and 75·3 as their mean Stature, Cephalic and Nasal Indices respectively. Eickstedt has measured also 69 Gurkhas whose mean Stature is 1617 mm., Cephalic Index 82·7 and Nasal Index 73·4[3].

It is not possible on such meagre data to assess quantitatively the amount of kinship between these groups, but it appears probable as Eickstedt[4] also thinks, that there is a common racial substratum in all these people with a gradual increase of Mongoloid blood extending up to the western parts of Nepal.

Integumentary Colours.

Considerations have so far been confined to the statistical analysis of the metric data, of the North-Western Himalayan tribes. While no systematic observations on the integumentary colours are given in the early accounts on these tribes, many observers mention the presence of light eyed and light haired persons in these regions. Ujfalvy[5] speaks of 37 per cent. and 15 per cent. respectively of blonds among the Tadjiks and Galchas of Russian Turkistan and the sporadic occurrence of the same element in the people of the Hindukush mountains. Robertson[6] also mentions the existence of people with light eyes and hair among the Kaffirs. It was Stein[7] however who for the first time carefully recorded the various shades of skin, eye and hair colours of the people measured by him around the Pamir region, and Dainelli[8] performed a similar task for the tribes of the Upper Indus Valley according to the recognised standards of Broca and von Luschan.

Stein's observations on the skin, hair and eye colours of the three tribes living within the frontiers of India are summarised in the following Table :—

Tribes.	Skin Colour.			Eye Colour.			Hair Colour.		
	Brown.	Rosy Brown.	Rosy.	Dark.	Medium.	Light.	Black.	Dark Brown.	Fair and Medium.
Kaffir	22	..	78	11	61	28	17	56	28
Chitrali	..	..	100	..	91	9	5	91	4
Mastuji	4	..	93	14	79	7	14	82	4

It will be seen from these records that the Kaffirs have the largest element of blond people (28 per cent.) with rosy white skin colour, light eye and fair to medium hair. The percentages of this strain among the two Khos groups are much smaller, only 9 and 7 per cent. of

[1] *Ibid.*, page 121.

[2] Eickstedt, E., Zur Anthropologie der Garhwali im Himalaja. Mitt. Anthr. Ges. Volume LVI, pages 173—183 ; Wien, 1926.

[3] Eickstedt, E.-*Man in India*, 1926— Op. cit., page 275.

[4] *Ibid.*, page 265.

[5] Ujfalvy, 1896—Op. cit., pages 428—429.

[6] Robertson, Sir George Scott,—The Kaffirs of the Hindukush, page 170 ; London, 1896.

[7] Stein, Sir Aurel, 1931—Op. cit., pages 1387—1388.

[8] Biasutti, R. 1925—Op. cit., pages 184—194.

whom have light eyes and 4 per cent. fair and medium hair, though the average skin colour of the latter is lighter than that of the Kaffirs who contain a distinct brown element. Stein's observations, valuable as they undoubtedly are, were not taken according to any of the recognised colour scales and as the number of subjects observed was also very small, *e.g.*, 18 Kaffirs, 22 Chitralis, and 28 Mastujis—it is doubtful how far percentages calculated from such small samples are truly indicative of the real conditions of these people.

During the course of my enquiries among the races of the Hindukush mountains, systematic observations were made on their integumentary colours according to the standard sca es of von Luschan and Martin. In recording the skin colour, both the exposed and the unexposed parts of the body were observed and the colour tints on the forehead the ventral side of the upper arm and chest were noted. In the following Table, a summary of the observations on the skin colour is given :—

Skin Colour (after von Luschan).

—	Forehead (approx. %).				Upper Arm (Ventral side) (approx. %).				Chest (approx. %).			
	9 R	10-11	12-13	14-18	9	10-11	12-14	15-18	9	10-11	12-14	15-18
Pathan	4	45	26	25	60	18	14	8	38	31	20	11
Red Kaffir	33	31	20	16	44	26	17	13	42	25	18	15
Khalash	30	36	27	7	27	35	27	11	25	35	28	14
Khos (Lower)	20	45	25	10	50	30	14	6	25	45	23	7
Khos (Upper)	30	40	21	9	56	28	12	4	38	35	19	8
Tadjik	35	35	20	10	82	9	9	..	64	21	13	2
Badakshi	64	4	12	20	58	21	11	10	36	36	15	14
Uzbeg	25	35	27	13	69	15	16	..	60	25	15	..

It will be noticed from the figures given in the above Table that the lightest skin colour recorded is No. 9 of von Luschan's scale, though on the forehead the shade is mixed with a reddish tint. Martin[1] regards all the shades between Nos. 9—11 as 'reddish white'. The highest percentage of this colour is found among the two tribes living north and west of India's political boundaries namely the Tadjik and Badakshi of Badakshan. The Khos, specially of Upper Chitral appears to be almost equally light but the two Kaffir tribes are slightly behind. When the skin colour of the exposed portion alone is considered, the Pathan seems to contain a smaller percentage of the 'reddish white' people, but in the unexposed parts the difference in skin colour is not marked. Taking the tints of both the exposed and unexposed parts together, all the tribes living in these regions appear in the main to be of rosy white complexion but there is also a distinctly dark element present in varying degrees. The percentage of this latter is greater among the Pathan, the Kaffir and the Badakshi, but considerably less in the others.

In the colour of the eyes shown in the Table below, the highest percentages

Eye Colour (after Martin).

	Between 1-4 (%).	Between 5-6 (%).	Between 7-8 (%).	Between 9-12 (%).	Between 13-16 (%).
Pathan	80·0	8·0	6·0	2·0	4·0
Red Kaffir	66·0	22·0	7·0	2·0	3·0
Khalash	60·0	24·3	8·6	5·7	1·4
Khos (Lower)	68·9	20·0	6·7	2·2	2·2
Khos (Upper)	57·3	28·7	9·3	4·7	..
Tadjik	67·7	24·2	6·5	1·6	..
Badakshi	64·7	35·3	..	..	..
Uzbeg	72·7	15·2	6·1	3·0	3·0

[1] Martin, Rudolf—*Lehrbuch der Anthropologie*, Volume 1, page 206; Jena, 1928.

of blue and grey-blue eyes (Nos. 9—16)[1] are found among the Pathan and the Kaffir tribes—the much despised Khalash being on the top of the list. Among the Khos it is slightly lower but among the Tadjik and the Badakshi it is almost entirely absent. Among all these tribes however there is an appreciable percentage of hazel eyes (Nos. 7—8)[1] but the shades of the brown (Nos. 1—6)[1] are undoubtedly preponderant. It may therefore be concluded that against 88 per cent. of people with brown eyes, the Pathan has 12 per cent. of light eyed people, the Red Kaffir the same, the Khalash 85 per cent. against 15 per cent., the Khos of lower Chitral 89 per cent. against 11 per cent., the Khos of Upper Chitral 86 per cent. against 14 per cent., the Tadjik 92 per cent. against 8 per cent. and the Uzbeg 88 per cent. against 12 per cent. The Badakshi appear however to be entirely brown eyed.

It will be seen from the figures given above that the observations made by me are not in strict accord with those published by Stein with regard specially to the percentages of men having dark and light eyes. It is difficult of course to institute strict comparisons, as his records were based on personal impressions as against mine taken in conformity with recognised objective standards. It is difficult to know for instance whether No. 4 of Martin's scale will be regarded by him as 'Medium' or whether Nos. 5—6 of the same scale will be included among his 'Light' eyes. I have regarded all of the three shades within 'Brown' after Martin, but a great difference in the final results would have revealed if they were included among the 'Light' eyes. Stein's observations might also have differed owing to the small sizes of his samples. It is desirable to have all observations on skin, eyes and hair colours, taken after some standard scale, otherwise their value for comparative purposes becomes uncertain.

Systematic observations on the integumentary colours of the tribes living further east in the Karakoram regions were recorded by Dainelli[2] and quite recently Mr. A. Paskevicius, a Lithuanian student, who travelled widely in the Burushaski country and measured a large number of men with a set of instruments lent by Sir Aurel Stein. I am indebted to him for permitting me to use his observations here. Mr. Paskevicius did not have with him any standard scale and had to be content with recording his visual impressions only. The subjects observed by him were mostly Burish or Yashkin of Hispar-Hupar and Hunza Nagar, and the Dardi or Shin of Ishkoman and Yasin. The former were found by him to be somewhat lighter than the latter; the exposed portions of the body being of a rich brown tint but the unexposed parts approached the shade of ivory. The eye colour of most of the men was of a brown shade but many people in Nagar were seen to possess hazel eyes (Nos. 7—8 of Martin). In the Hispar-Hupar country, men with grey blue eyes and chestnut hair were observed, and in Hunza several individuals with red hair and white complexion were noticed. The prevailing hair colour however, among both the Burish and the Shin varied from dark brown to light brown, though individuals with black hair were not wanting.

Dainelli's observations were taken according to the scales of Broca and von Luschan. The tints of the skin colour however were confined to the exposed part of the body *viz.*, forehead only. Nevertheless, as some of these were based on von Luschan's scale they are directly comparable to those of the western tribes mentioned in the foregoing Tables.

According to Dainelli's records none of the tribes observed seem to have a rosy white tint on the forehead. Of light brown colour (Nos. 13—14) the Baltis have only 17·2 per cent., the Brokpa 12 per cent. and the Purigi only 2 per cent., the rest being all dark brown[3]. In the colour of the eyes 35·5 per cent. of the Baltis are dark brown, 47·8 per cent. brown, 11·5 per cent. light brown and 5·2 per cent. hazel. Among the Brokpa, the corresponding figures for dark brown, brown and light brown are 47·9 per cent., 40·6 per cent. and 12 per cent. The Machnopa have 36 per cent. of dark brown, 46·6 per cent. of brown, 14 per cent. of light brown and 2 per cent. hazel. Among the Ladakhi the respective figures are 55·1 per cent., 32·6 per cent., 10·3 per cent. and 2 per cent. The Chiangpa show only brown tint in their eyes. In the Purigi, besides 50 per cent. of dark, 40 per cent. of brown, 8 per cent. of light brown and 2 per cent. of hazel, there are 2 per cent. of blue eyes[4]. Dainelli's tables also show that 88·7 per cent. of the Baltis possess black hair, 7·1 per cent. dark chestnut and 4·2 per cent. chestnut. The Brokpa have 97·9 per cent. of black hair and 2·1 dark chestnut; the Machnopa 97·9 per cent. black and 2·1 per cent. chestnut. The Ladakhi and the Chiangpa possess only balck hair[5].

From these figures it is clear that among the Eastern tribes of the Himalaya, the prevailing skin colour of the forehead is dark brown, the eye colour also dark brown and the colour of the hair black. But there is a small element with hazel and even blue eyes (Purigi) and chestnut hair. It is unfortunate that Dainelli's observations on the skin colour were confined to the exposed parts. If the tint of the unexposed parts of the body, such as the ventral side of the upper arm were taken, it is not impossible that a much lighter shade would have been noticed.

---

[1] *Ibid.*, page 218.

[2] Biasutti, R.—Op. cit., pages 185—191.

[3] *Ibid.*, page 185.

[4] *Ibid.*, page 191.

[5] *Ibid.*, page 190.

for, as is well known the extreme dirt on the face of the N. W. Himalayan tribes—a fact mentioned by Robertson and also noticed by Paskevicius among the Burish and Shin—and by the present writer among the Kaffirs, is liable to give a wrong impression of the true skin colour of these people. But even after making allowance for this factor, the Western tribes appear undoubtedly to be of lighter complexion with a definite blond element among them. This latter strain is very slight in the Eastern tribes, (only 2 per cent. of the Purigi, showing blue eyes) who are predominantly of a darker type.

Conclusions.

From the comparisons of measurements and integumentary colours given in the preceding pages, it appears that several racial strains have gone into the composition of the tribes, living in the North Western Himalayan regions. There is first of all the underlying substratum of a tall dolichocephalic leptorrhine element with light skin, eye and hair colours in the Pathans of the north, the Red Kaffirs and rather unexpectedly and in a greater degree in the Khalash of Rambur and Bamboret. The latter were once the occupants of the Chitral valley up to Reshun but must have been pushed into the mountain defiles on the south and west by the Khos expansion from the north, and probably their lowly conditions and comparative isolation have helped them to preserve in a purer form the original characteristics of this race. The conclusion reached by Joyce[1] that the basic constituent of the Kaffirs is 'brown', is not possible to maintain in view of the high percentage of the blond element among these tribes. Want of personal knowledge of these tribes no doubt, made him argue from the skin colour of the exposed part of the body only to the exclusion of the eye and hair colours[2] and led him to regard the dark factor absorbed from other autochthonous tribes, as the fundamental racial element among the Kaffirs.

This light dolichocephalic strain forms also an important element in the racial composition of the Khos of Chitral and Mastuj. From the meagre data available, it appears that the Pandits if not the other people of Kashmir, apparently possess the same strain in their blood. How far it has entered into the Burish and Dardi tribes on the east, it is difficult to determine properly from the present data, but as shown from the observations of Paskevicius on the Burish of Hispar-Hupar and Hunza, and of Dainelli on the Purigi, its presence among them cannot altogether be denied.

From comparative evidence, the advent of this race in the N. W. Himalayan regions appears to be contemporaneous with the 'Aryan' invasion of India—probably a part of the same wave which swept over the Punjab.

The second racial strain which is also foreign to these parts is the brachycephalic race with long and frequently aquiline nose, light complexion but medium hair and eyes and allied to the Dinaric race of Eastern Europe or what Fischer calls the "Near Eastern Race", which entered from across the Hindukush and Pamir mountains. Its intrusion must have taken place later, but seems to have affected the racial type of the northern tribes as shown by the increase of Cephalic Index and the frequent occurrence of aquiline noses among them. It has been partially observed amongst the Red Kaffirs and the northern Pathans but the Khalash are free from its influence. The Khos of Chitral, the Burish, and the Dardi of the Gilgit valley appear to have been more affected. This Asiatic Dinaric race was probably dislodged from Russian Turkistan by the Mongol invasion and its penetration in the Indian territories has since been steadily continuing, as the occupation of Sarikol and the Upper Mastuj and Hunza valleys by the Wakhis in recent years shows.

The other two Racial strains which have intruded from outside are the *Oriental Race* of Fischer[3] represented by the Badakshis of Badakshan. It is characterised by a long head, aquiline nose, rosy white complexion but brown eyes and hair. How far it has actually entered in the composition of the N. W. Himalayan tribes is difficult to determine, but from the values of the C. R. L.'s its presence among the Pathans seems clear. It is possible that this type also underlies the rank and file of the Kashmiri population judged by descriptions. And the *Mongoloid Element* which has crossed over from Tibet and is found all along the Ladakh plateau and the southern hilly districts. The Chiangpa are its purest representatives but the Ladakhis, Lahoulis, the Gurung and other tribes of western Nepal show preponderance of this element. The Purigi and the Machnopa of the N. W. parts of Ladakh seem also to have absorbed a small amount of this strain.

Finally over and above these foreign elements there is one which appears to be indigenous to the N. W. Himalayan regions and underlies the population of the entire territory from Gilgit to western Nepal. This Race possesses a short stature, dolichocephalic head, medium nose, broad face but brown complexion. It is found in comparatively pure form among the Machnopa, Purigi and the Kanets of Kulu, but also forms the basis of the racial structure of the Dardis, Baltis and the Brokpa. The Burish of Nagar and Hunza seem also to be mainly formed by this

[1] Op. cit., pages 467—468.

[2] See Tables 11 and 12, Stein's Serindia, Appendix C., Volume II, 1921.

[3] Fischer, Eugen.—Human Heredity, page 201; London, 1931.

strain. Though overlaid by other more predominant elements it appears also as one of the constituents of the racial type of the Khos. From the values of the Reduced C. R. L.'s given in the following Table, it will be seen that the racial substratum of all these tribes has a

	Dardi and Balti.	Dardi and Brokpa.	Khos and Balti.	Khos and Machnopa.	Khos and Brokpa.	Purigi and Kanet.	Machnopa and Kanet.
Reduced C. R.L.	20·30 ±0·67	13·21 ±0·74	17·14 ±0·22	19·77 ±0·47	16·17 ±0·44	9·47 ±0·62	14·17 ±0 65

common element though infused in varying proportions with other strains in different parts of the country. In the Kaffirs of the Western valleys however it does not seem to have entered as the Reduced C. R. L. of 36·37±0·43 between the Dardis and the Red Kaffirs shows.

The existence of an autochthonous race in the N. W. Himalayan tracts is indicated by the Khalash traditions of the Bakaliks who were supposed to have occupied Chitral in early times, and the Kati accounts also speak of the Jasis in the lower Bashgul valley[1]. Kalhana[2] similarly mentions the existence of several tribes in Kashmir such as the Khasas, Dombas and Vitals, and Hiuen Tsang[3] speaks of the Kilotas who were opposed to the Bauddhas. To Biasutti[4] belongs the credit of first isolating this short statured Himalayan Race and Eickstedt[5] has named it ' Garhwali ' on the basis of the measurements of 13 Garhwali soldiers during the war. The expression is hardly appropriate as the major distribution of this type is in the North Himalayan regions, and Eickstedt's claim that it is found in its purest form among the Garhwalis can only be justified when an adequate sample of the latter is subjected to anthropometric tests. The name proposed here for this Race therefore is ' Himalayan ', which had been its home from ancient times.

2.—THE INDO-GANGETIC PLAINS.

(a) *The Punjab and Sindh.*

Immediately south of the mountain valley of the North-Western Himalayas there is a swift descent into the historic plains watered by the Indus and the Ganges which do not rise over 500 ft. above the sea level. The Aravalli Hills running in a north easterly direction separate the southern portions of the valleys of these two rivers and are connected through the Malwan plateau with the Vindhyan ranges. From the earliest times these hills have formed the boundaries between Upper India and the table lands of the Deccan and have proved formidable barriers against ' Aryan ' expansion in the south. Of the Indus Valley proper, apart from the measurements of 7 castes taken by Alauddin for Risley's Ethnographical Survey, the available data are (*i*) those published by Eickstedt[6] on 144 Punjabi soldiers captured by Germany during the war, of which 76 were Sikhs from eastern and 68 Moslems from western Punjab ; and (*ii*) the measurements taken by Lieutenant-Colonel R. B. Seymour Sewell and Mr. C. C. Roy on 100 Sindhi and 100 Brahui coolies at Mohenjo daro during the excavation season of 1927-28. The latter are being worked out now, and I am grateful to Colonel Sewell for permitting me to use these unpublished materials here. Both Eickstedt[7], Sewell and Roy took their measurements according to the International Agreement of Monaco as described by Martin, and the technique adopted by these workers is thus in agreement with that followed in the present enquiries.

By careful comparisons of the measurements, Eickstedt was able to distinguish two types in the Punjab, namely (1) a robust coarse type with broader nose, smaller head, but having overhanging occiput and prominent superciliary arches and (2) a more refined type with larger head, narrow and high pitched nose, but possessing a slightly darker skin colour than the first. The two types appear to be well mixed in the population of both the Eastern and Western Punjab and Eickstedt considers the entire population of the province to be composed of one great race consisting of these two elements.[8] In his opinion there is no somatic difference between the Sikhs of the east and the Moslems of the west, and the illusion of racial difference between the two is due to the peculiar modes in which clothing and hair are worn by these people.[9] He further considers that Pandit Harikissen Kaul's surmise of 15% of foreign blood among the Moslems[10] of the Punjab appears to be a higher estimate than is warranted by anthropometry.

[1]Morgenstierne, Georg.—Op. cit., pages 47 and 52.

[2]Stein's Rajatarangini, VIII, page 1082.

[3]Beal, S.—Hiuen Tsang, pages 64—77 ; London, 1911.

[4]Biasutti, R.—1925, Op. cit.

[5]Eickstedt.—1926, Op. cit., page 268.

[6]Eickstedt, Egon.—Rassenelemente der Sikh. Zeitschrift für Ethnologie, pages 317—394 ; Berlin, 1921. And A Comparative Anthropometry of 144 Punjabis by the same author—*Man in India*, Vol. III, pages 161—189 ; Ranchi, 1923.

[7]Eickstedt, 1923., Op. cit., page 162. [8]Op. cit., page 170. [9]Op. cit., page 162. [10]Kaul, Harikissen—Census Report, page 128, Vol. XIV, 1911.

In Tables IX and IX (*a*) are given the C. R. L.'s of the Punjabi Sikhs and Moslems based on Eickstedt's measurements in relation to other racial groups. Unfortunately Eickstedt is not very careful about his figures and the mean values of the measurements of the Sikhs and the Moslems given by him[1] contain numerous errors. They had therefore to be recalculated from the tables of individual measurements, for computation of the C. R. L.'s. In the following Tables I have given the correct values against those published by Eickstedt.

Eickstedt's Values.

Tribes.	Head Length.	Head Breadth.	Min. Frontal Diam.	Bizygomatic Breadth.	Bigonial Breadth.	Morph. Facial Length.	Nasal Height.	Nasal Breadth.	Length-Breadth Index.	Nasal Index.	Morph. Facial Index.	Trans. Fronto-P. Index.	Stature.
Sikhs	195	144·86	103·37	136·66	102·96	123·20	55·55	35·51	73·79	64·83	89·98	71·87	172·18
Moslems.. ..	193·3	145·7	103·3	137·9	103·8	123·1	55·4	35·8	75·2	64·6	89·2	70·0	172·0

Corrected Values.

Tribes.	Head Length.	Head Breadth.	Min. Frontal Diam.	Bizygomatic Breadth.	Bigonial Breadth.	Morph. Facial Length.	Nasal Height.	Nasal Breadth.	Length-Breadth Index.	Nasal Index.	Morph. Facial Index.	Trans. Fronto-P. Index.	Stature.
Sikhs	194·95	143·97	102·37	136·16	103·96	122·62	55·16	35·67	73·74	64·71	90·11	71·25	1718
Moslems ..	193·4	146·3	103·0	137·7	103·8	122·9	55·4	35·7	75·6	64·7	89·2	70·0	1720

As will appear from Tables IX and IX (*a*) the values of the Crude and Reduced C. R. L.'s between the Sikhs and the Moslems of the Punjab are 0·91 ± 0·25 and 1·27 ± 0·35 respectively, showing the close somatic unity of the two. There is no individual character in which the value of "α" is over 6, and the results of the statistical test therefore fully corroborate the conclusions already reached by Eickstedt regarding the racial homogeneity of the people of the Punjab irrespective of caste or creed.

In 1892 Dr. Havelock Charles[2] published the measurements of 50 crania belonging mainly to the Chuhra and Chamar castes. These skulls were taken from bodies brought to the dissecting room of the Medical College at Lahore and their caste, age and sex are said to be authentic. The mean Cranial Capacity of the 36 male adult crania measured by Dr. Charles was 1375 c. c. The mean length and breadth of these Crania are 183 and 129·5 mm. respectively, with 70 as the mean of the proportions between the two. The mean Altitudinal Index is 72 and the Orbital Index 88·8. The mean Gnathic Index is 92 and the Nasal Index is 49·6. These figures show that compared to the main population of the Punjab, the two "outcaste" groups have, smaller heads and broader nose, but like the former they are dolichocephalic and orthognathous.

These differences are probably due to the presence of another blood from indigenous inhabitants which does not appear to have been absorbed in any appreciable degree in the rest of the people of the Punjab.

The values of the C. R. L.'s given in Tables IX and IX (*a*) between the Sikhs and the Northern Pathans are 5·78 ± 0·25 for the Crude and 9·59±0·42 for the Reduced Coefficient. The chief differences lie in Stature, Head length and Cephalic Index in which the values of 'α' are 51·61, 9·86 and 6·05 respectively. In all other characters the values are below 6. This, together with the allowance that has to be made for personal equation would undoubtedly indicate a much closer association between the Sikhs and the Pathans than the actual values of the C. R. L.'s would seem to suggest.

The measurements taken by Sewell and Roy on the Sindhi Mussalmans and Brahuis comprise 100 adult men of each group. The Co-efficients of Racial Likeness between the two is 7·57±0·18. In individual characters, the chief differences lie in Stature, the Auricular height.

[1] Eickstedt, 1921, Op. cit., pages 334-335 and 1923, Op. cit., pages 188-189.

[2] Charles, R. Havelock,—Notes on the Craniometry of some of the Outcaste Tribes of the Punjab—Journal of Anatomy and Physiology, Volume XXVI, pages 1—25; London, 1892.

Inter-orbital breadth, Orbito-nasal breadth, Nasal length, Length-breadth Index and breadth-height Index with 6·77, 36·54, 29·08, 15·31, 11·98, 10·03 and 37·34 as the values of 'α' respectively, showing that the Sindhis in comparison with the Brahuis are slightly taller, rounder headed and possess a longer nose. The vault of the head, however, is higher and the Inter-orbital breadth greater among the Brahuis. These figures, while indicating a racial association between the two, also suggest the substratum of a long and high skulled race with broader nose among the Brahuis. It has been suggested by close observers[1] that the Brahuis have absorbed the blood of the intruding Baluch so much, that at the present they are hardly distinguishable from the latter. While this may be true in general, the statistical analysis reveals the persistence of the primitive dolichocephalic strain among them in a greater degree than in their Sindhi neighbours.

The values of the Crude and Reduced C. R. L.'s between the Sindhis and the Sikhs are 49·81$\pm$0·25 and 57·78$\pm$0·29 respectively. Comparison of individual characters shows that the values of 'α' are highest in Head length, Length-Breadth Index, Stature, Facial length, Nasal Index, Bizygomatic breadth, Bigonial diameter with 284·89, 141·57, 59·52, 38·96, 29·30, 41·91 and 21·71 respectively. As shown by these figures, the Sindhis as compared to the Sikhs are broader headed, shorter in stature, have a more rounded face and broader nose and are certainly racially divergent. It would seem therefore, that the racial alignment of the Sikhs and Punjabis is with the people living north and west rather than with those of the lower Indus Valley who disclose a different racial strain.

(b) *The United Provinces.*

Of the people living in the Upper Ganges valley the only caste that was measured was the Brahmin belonging to the Sarbaria, Sarjupari and Kanyakubja sections of Allahabad and the adjoining districts. The values of the Crude and Reduced C. R. L.'s as shown in Tables IX and IX (*a*), between the U. P. Brahmins and Sikhs are 8·91 $\pm$ 0·25 and 14·79$\pm$ 0·42, respectively. The main differences between the two lie in Stature, Head breadth, Bizygomatic breadth, Bigonial diameter, Nasal breadth and Nasal Index with 38·84, 12·96, 12·54, 8·17, 7·91 and 15·72, as the respective values of 'α' for these characters, showing that the Sikhs are taller than the U. P. Brahmins and possess a slightly larger head and longer nose but broader face.

With the Mussalmans of Western Punjab, the U. P. Brahmins have 21·10 $\pm$ 0·44, as the value of the Reduced and 12·13 $\pm$ 0·25, as that of the Crude C. R. L. The differences being with regard to Bizygomatic breadth, Facial length, Head breadth, Cephalic Index and Stature. The values of 'α' for these characters are 28·81, 10·50, 23·81, 13·80 and 39·29, respectively. As in the case of the Sikhs, the Mussalmans of Western Punjab are taller, broader headed and wider faced than the Brahmins of U. P. and possess also a longer nose.

In assessing the true relationship between these groups, the disturbing influence of 'personal equation' must be taken into account. Attention has already been drawn to Pearson's remark that the influence of personal equation is much higher than ordinarily rated[2], and in the case of living subjects, where the location of the anatomical landmarks is much more difficult, giving a greater scope for individual variations—the amount of this influence certainly becomes considerable even when the same theoretical technique is followed. The values of the C. R. L.'s obtained between the U. P. Brahmins and particularly the Sikhs though falling outside the sphere indicating relationship, would most probably have shown very close association if the factor of personal equation could have been eliminated. It should also be remembered that Eickstedt's "Sikhs" were from a selected group, namely, soldiers captured by Germany during the War, which may account for certain marked differences, *e.g.*, in Stature. This view is strengthened by a comparison of the values of the Reduced C. R. L. between the U. P. Brahmins and the Pathans and the Red Kaffirs measured by me for which the figures obtained are 10·62 $\pm$ 0·34 and 11·64 $\pm$ 0·27 respectively. If the values of the C. R. L. can be so low with the two Frontier tribes, it stands to reason that they would have been far smaller with the neighbouring Sikhs who show a Co-efficient of 9·59 $\pm$ 0·42 with the Pathans (Table IX).

Integumentary colours.

Besides the measurements discussed above, the skin, eye and hair colours were recorded by both Eickstedt and myself. Eickstedt has not published the details, but has given very brief summaries of his observations. But as the same standards were used by both of us, our results can certainly be compared. Of the people of the Punjab, Eickstedt[3] finds the men coming from the Siwalik Hills to be fairer—the mean skin colour observed being No. 11 of von Luschan's scale. The people of the plains are, however, darker with No. 15 as the mean colour of the skin. The colour of the hair in both is black (No. 27 of Fischer's scale) and the eye colour varies between Nos. 2—4 of Martin's scale. In one Sikh[4] from Hoshiarpur, however, he noticed a light brown hair (between Nos. 4-5) and an eye shade matching No. 8 of Martin's scale. Eickstedt does not mention what portion of the body was observed for the skin colour possibly it was the exposed part of the forehead. In the records kept by me the tints of

[1] Denys Bray.—The Census of Baluchistan, 1911.
[2] Pearson, Karl, 1928,—Op. cit., page 376.
[3] Eickstedt, E. 1923.—pages 179-182.
[4] Eickstedt, E. 1926.—page 258.

the skin of the forehead, the ventral part of the upper arm and the breast were observed and noted separately. In the case of the U. P. Brahmins,[1] the lightest skin colour was found to be No. 12 and the darkest No. 23 of von Luschan's scale. The percentage of people having a skin colour of the forehead equivalent to Nos. 12-13 was 10·2, between Nos. 14-15, 55·1 and between Nos. 17-23, 34·69. On the ventral part of the upper arm the respective figures are 10·2, 61·23 and 28·57 and on the breast they are 12·34, 46·94 and 40·82. These figures, show that among the Brahmins of U. P. between 10-12 per cent. of the people have very light brown, 50–60 per cent. brown and the rest have tawny brown complexion. Six per cent. of the people have black eyes (No. 1), 68 per cent. dark brown, 22 per cent. light brown (Nos. 4–6) and 4 per cent. hazel eyes (No. 7)[2]. Lastly about 13 per cent. of the people have brown hair (No. 4) and 74 per cent. black (No. 27)[3]. As far as can be judged from the brief summary given by Eickstedt, the integumentary colours of the Punjabi are not much different from those of the people of U. P. who seem also to show the same average tints and among whom a lighter element is also present.

As will appear from Table LV (*b* and *c*), the supra-orbital ridges among the U. P. Brahmins are marked but not specially developed. The face is longish and 4 p. c. showing alveolar prognathism. The nose is usually prominent, the lips are from thin to medium. The epicanthic fold is present in 2 p. c. of people among whom the eye is also slanting. Eickstedt does not appear to have recorded these traits among his Sikhs, so comparison cannot unfortunately be made with them.

To sum up, the people of the Punjab appear to be homogeneous and closely allied to the Pathans and the dolichocephalic races of the North Western Himalayan regions. There is a lighter element present but its percentage is very much smaller than that found among the latter. Among the lowest classes, however, a shorter, broad-nosed strain is observed. The U. P. Brahmins are closely associated with the people of the Punjab and the N.-W. Frontier regions and there can be no doubt that the fundamental racial strain in the valleys of the Indus and Ganges is one. In Sind an intruding brachycephalic race seems to have superimposed on the original longheaded population, from southern Baluchistan.

3.—CENTRAL INDIA AND GUZRAT.

(*a*) *Central India.*

The country south east of the Punjab and below the valleys of the Jumna and the Ganges extends up to Sind on the west, and Behar on the east, and is separated by the Vindhyas from the Deccan plateau. Its northern and western portions are semi-desert, but the southern tableland of Malwa and Guzrat are fertile. In language and culture this part of the country is allied to Upper India and really forms its lower extremity.

The groups measured in this area consist (1) of the Brahmins, Rajputs and Bhils of the Malwan plateau and (2) the six major sections of the Guzrati population namely the Kathis, the Nagar and Audich Brahmins, the Brahma Kshatris, the Bania-Jains and the Kunbi-Patidars who have migrated to the southern parts of Malwa.

The Malwa Brahmins measured by me belonged to the Sree Gaur and Dasodha divisions. The Rajputs came from the Rathor, Gahiot, Paramar, Salonki, Bundela, Kalchuri and Baghel clans. These are as a rule endogamous divisions but the three Agnikulas, the Chauhan, Paramar, and Salonki, intermarry with one another[4]. All of these are famous Rajput clans who migrated to Central India during the medieval times due to the pressure of Islamic forces from Delhi. Of these, the Chauhans were once the rulers of the whole country from Mount Abu to Hissar, and from the Aravalli hills to Bundelkhand, and the Salonkis, of Guzrat and Kathiawar with their capital at Anilvad Patan. The Kalchuris now found in a few villages in Rewa, were known as the Chedi or Haihaiya and occupied the eastern portions of the Narbada valley. The Baghels are a branch of the Salonkis, and migrated from Guzrat, and founded the state of Rewa in the 13th. century A. D. The Rathors were formerly known as Gaharwar and migrated to Rajputana after the fall of Kanauj[5].

In Tables XII and XII(*a*) are given the values of the Crude and Reduced C. R. L.'s of the three Central Indian groups—the Bhils being reserved for consideration later on with the other Aboriginal tribes.

The figures given in these Tables show that there is an intimate relationship between the two sections of the Rajputs. The relation between the Miscellaneous Rajputs and Malve Brahmins is also very close, the value of the Reduced C. R. L. being $3{\cdot}08 \pm 0{\cdot}34$. The Baghels however have a somewhat higher Co-efficient with the Malve Brahmins, namely $5{\cdot}31 \pm 0{\cdot}34$. This apparent anomaly is explained when the individual characters are examined. The values of 'α' for Stature, Head breadth, Length-Breadth Index, Trans. Fronto-Parietal Index and Trans-Cephalo-Facial Index are 18·7, 8·52, 6·35, 14·55 and 8·93 respectively, showing that in comparison with the Malve Brahmins, the Baghels are taller, broader headed and possess a shorter

[1] See Table LV— Appendix, page 100.

[2] See Table LV (*b*).

[3] See Table LV (*a*).

[4] Venktachar, C. S.—Census of India, Volume XX, Part I., pages 234-235 ; Delhi, 1933.

[5] Op. cit., pages 274-275.

face. In these respects the Miscellaneous Rajput group occupies a somewhat intermediate position, having intimate affinities with the Baghels and at the same time showing close association with the Malve Brahmins. There appears therefore a common racial substratum in the three sections representing the population of Central India, but the Baghels contain, a small brachycephalic strain, which is very slight in the other Rajput (see Figs. 2—3a, Plate No. III) group but not noticeable among the Malve Brahmins.

The value of the Crude and Reduced C. R. L.'s of the Malve and the U. P. Brahmins are $5\cdot73\pm0\cdot17$ and $11\cdot46\pm0\cdot34$, and of the combined Rajput groups and the U. P. Brahmins are $5\cdot47\pm0\cdot17$ and $8\cdot21\pm0\cdot26$ respectively. The relationship of the U. P. Brahmins is therefore closer to the Rajputs than the Malves. With the Sikhs, the Malves have much higher values namely $19\cdot95\pm0\cdot25$ and $33\cdot12\pm0\cdot42$ respectively for the Crude and the Reduced C. R. L.'s. The values of the function "α" of the Malve with the U. P. Brahmins in respect of the Head length, Inter-orbital breadth, Nasal length, Nasal depth, Sagittal arc and Nasal Elevation Index are 20·29, 23·02, 7·02, 16·84, 70·62 and 14·80 respectively, showing that the latter possess a longer head and a longer and a more highly pitched nose in comparision with the former. Between the Sikhs and the Malves, the values of "α" for Stature, Head length, Head breadth, Max. bizygomatic breadth, Nasal length, Nasal breadth, Facial length, Trans. Fronto-Parietal Index and Nasal Index are 53·81, 47·79, 17·33, 12·86, 26·54, 12·14, 20·45, 26·92, 45·05 respectively. In other words the Sikhs are taller and have a longer face and longer and finer nose.

Integumentary colours.

In the case of the Malve Brahmins[1] two per cent. of people show reddish-white skin colour (No. 11) on the forehead, 22·44% between Nos. 12-13 and 75% between 14—23. In the ventral part of the upper arm 4·08% have rosy white skin colour (Nos. 9-11), 36·73% light brown (Nos. 12-13), 44·89% brown (No. 14) and 15·30% tawny brown (Nos. 15-28).

In the colour of the eyes, the commonest shade is dark brown (Nos. 2-3) with 87·75%, 10·2% have light brown (No. 4) and 2·04% hazel (No. 7). Lastly 40·81% of the people examined have brown hair (No. 4), 36·73% black (No. 27) and 2·04% light brown (No. 5).

The Baghel Rajputs[2] have 2% of rosy white skin colour (No. 11) on the forehead, 34% brown (Nos. 13-14), 60% dark brown (Nos. 15-23) and 4% tawny brown (No. 27). On the ventral part of the upper arm, the figures are approximately the same. Seventy per cent. of the Baghels have dark brown eyes (Nos. 2-3), 28% light brown (Nos. 4-6) and 2% hazel (No. 7). Forty four per cent. of the people have brown hair (No. 4), six per cent. light brown (No. 5) and forty six per cent. black (No. 27). Among the Miscellaneous Rajputs[3] the percentage of light brown skin colour on the forehead is only 6 (Nos. 12-13), 22 brown (No. 14), 64 dark brown (Nos. 15-23) and 4 tawny brown. In the ventral part of the upper arm the percentage of light brown is 22, 48 brown, 28 dark brown and 2 tawny brown. Eighty eight per cent. of people have dark eyes (Nos. 2-3) and 12 light brown eyes (No. 4). Lastly 55·19% show brown hair (No. 4), and 40·81% black hair (No. 27).

These records of the integumentary colours show that among the people of Malwa, the average skin colour is brown (Nos. 14-15), the eye colour dark brown (Nos. 2-3) and the hair colour black (No. 27). The proportion of men with light brown skin colour, light brown eyes and brownish hair is smaller. There is however a distinct percentage of people having a rosy white skin colour, brown hair and hazel eyes. This element is smallest among the Miscellaneous Rajputs, who have a correspondingly higher percentage of darker people, and slightly less than that seen among the U. P. Brahmins. As will appear from Table LV (*b and c*) the supra orbital ridges are moderatly prominent in all the three groups, specially the Rajputs. The eyes are usually horizontal and open, but in a small percentage (4%) traces of epicanthic fold were noticed. The nose is usually prominent and among a small number (10 to 14%) it is distinctly convex. Among the Malves there is an appreciable percentage showing slight depression of the nasal root. Similarly among the latter, about 10% of the men measured, had slight alveolar prognathism as against 6% of the Miscellaneous Rajputs, indicating probably the presence of some amount of aboriginal blood.

(*b*) *Guzrat.*

In Kathiawar and Guzrat, measurements were taken on all the principal ethnic groups. Of these the Kathis, from whom the name Kathiawar was derived, are a military caste who came from the Cutch about the 14th. century A. D. according to their tradition.[4] I measured them in Shelna, one of their important centres in southern Bhavnagar.

The two Brahmin groups are the Audich or the Northerners, who were said to have been invited to Guzrat from Upper India by Mularaja in the 10th. century A. D.[5], and the Nagars, who are the most aristocratic and influential community in Guzrat. According to Bhandarkar[6]

[1] See Tables LV—LV(*b*).
[2] *Ibid.*
[3] *Ibid.*
[4] Enthoven, R. E.—The Tribes and Castes of Bombay, Volume II, 1922, page 165.
[5] *Ibid.*, Volume 1, page 228.
[6] *Ibid.*, page 235.

they were found for the first time in Kathiawar and Guzrat during the sixth century A. D. Measurements were taken on their four principal endogamous subdivisions, namely, Vadnagra, Sathodra, Visnagra and Prashnora, in Ahmedabad and Bhavnagar. The Brahma-Kshatris are a small community almost entirely confined to these parts and are supposed to have been originally Kshatris of Upper India who migrated to Guzrat in the 15th. century as a result of Moslem oppression. The name is considered to signify those Kshatris who gave up their original pursuits for those of the Brahmins. The subjects included under the Bania-Jains are the members of the great mercantile caste of North Guzrat and are really members of the same Bania caste, though some of them profess Jain and the others Hindu religion.

In addition, the Guzrati speaking Kunbis who have settled in the state of Birwani, were measured at Anjar, and have been included among the Guzrati rather than the Central Indian groups.

In Tables XIII and XIII(*a*) are given the Crude and Reduced C. R. L.'s of the Guzrati castes. When the figures are scrutinised it will be found that intimate relationship exists between the Nagar Brahmins and the Bania-Jains with 1·10±0·17 as the value of the Reduced C. R. L. With the exception of one, namely the Trans. Cephalo-Facial Index the value of "α" does not exceed 6 in any character. Between the Audich Brahmins and the Bania-Jains, the Nagar Brahmins and the Kathis, and the Kathis and Brahma-Kshatris, the relationships are very close; the values of the Reduced C. R. L.'s being 3·75±0·18, 4·10±0·29, 4·52±0·49 respectively. There are also definite associations between the Nagar and the Audich Brahmins, the Nagar Brahmins and the Brahma-Kshatri, and the Kathis and the Bania-Jains; the respective Coefficients of the three pairs being 5·58±0·17, 6·13±0·36 and 6·32±0·30. Finally associations are also found between the Audich Brahmins and the Brahma-Kshatri, and between the Audich Brahmins, and the Kunbi-Patidars and the Kathis. The Kunbi-Patidars however do not show any association with any other caste. In Text—fig. 2, these results are diagrammatically illustrated.

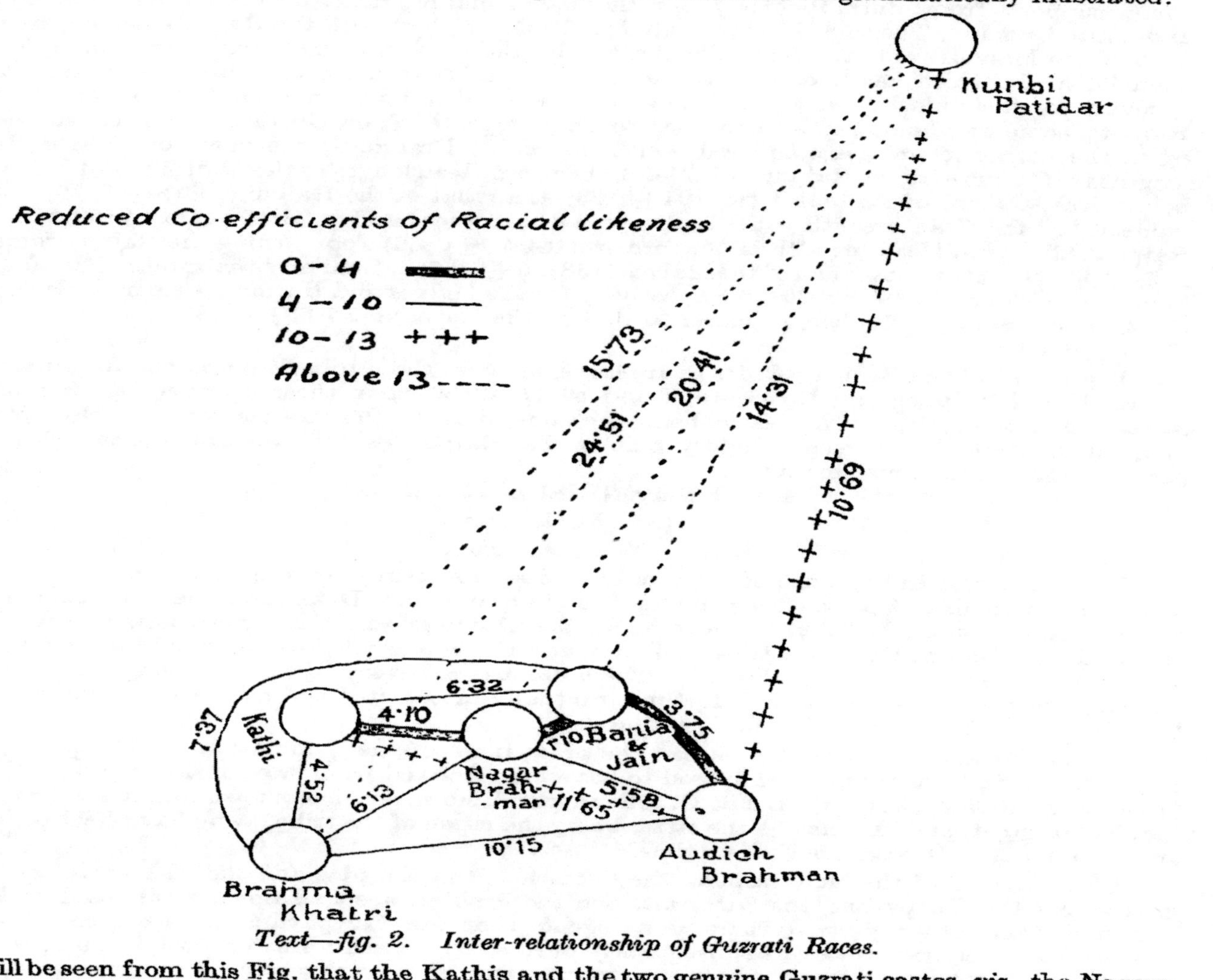

Text—fig. 2. Inter-relationship of Guzrati Races.

It will be seen from this Fig. that the Kathis and the two genuine Guzrati castes, *viz.*, the Nagars and the Bania-Jains are intimately related, but the relationship with the Brahma-Kshatri and the Audich Brahmint hough definite, is not so close. The Kunbi-Patidars do not show any association with any other group except the Audich. According to their chronicles the Kunbis migrated in a body from Guzrat in the 11th. century[1]. They migrated to Southern Malwa as a result of the pressure from the Rajput tribes, and it is possible that this agricultural community had originally a different racial substratum from the other people of Guzrat.

Though morphologically the main Guzrati castes are so closely allied, there is a marked difference in integumentary colours[2] between the Nagar Brahmins and the others. The former, who are one of the lightest communities living in the plains of India, have 13·3% of people showing rosy white skin colour on the forehead, and 28·55% on the ventral side of the upper arm. The percentages of light brown on the two parts of the body are 33·34 and 36·19, of brown 22·86 each and of dark brown 30·47 and 12·38 only. The Bania Jains have only 2·02% of people with rosy white skin colour on the forehead, and 7·07% on the ventral part of the upper arm, 11·11% and 28·28 , light brown, 23·33% and 26·26% brown and the rest are dark brown. The Kathis appear to be darker than the others, with only 17·5% and 35% light brown, 45% and 35% brown, and 35% and 27·5% tawny brown. There is no person with rosy white skin colour, but there is a distinct element of 2·5% of, dark tawny brown (No. 28) people. The Brahma-Kshatri approach the Nagar Brahmins in skin colour and show approximately the same percentage of a lighter element. It will be noticed from Table LVI (*b*) that all the five Guzrati castes show well marked supra orbital ridges and usually have open horizontal eyes but a small percentage specially among the Baina Jains show traces of epicanthic fold and have slanting eyes. Similarly the latter has 12% of people with alveolar prognathism, and over 15% with slight depression of the nasal root. These traits together with darker skin colour, would appear to suggest that among the Baina Jains, some amount of aboriginal blood has probably entered.

When the Guzrati castes are compared with those of Central India, the only group that shows definite association are the Audich Brahmins, who have a reduced C. R. L. of 7·81±0·18 with the combined samples of the Rajputs, and 10·46±0·26 with the Malve Brahmins. There is thus some support from anthropometry for the traditional migration of the former from Upper India into Guzrat. The slightly lower value of the Co-efficient with the Rajputs as compared to that of the Malve Brahmins, may be explained by the fact that the absorption of the brachycephalic strain which has taken place among the Audich to a considerable extent and which accounts for their kinship with the Guzrati castes—is also found in a small degree among the Rajputs, some of whom are also supposed to have migrated from Guzrat. This becomes clear when the values of 'α' are compared—with the Malve Brahmins, the value of 'α' for Head length is 6·97, but with the Rajputs it is 21·28, the mean Head length of the Audich (184·00±0·45) being closer to that of the Malve (186·94±0·63) than that of the Rajput (188·22±0·75). The value of 'α' for Head breadth with the Malves on the other hand is 24·59 against 7·00 with the Rajputs, the mean Head breadth of the former (144·73±0·32) approaching the Rajput value of 142·13±0·55 rather than that of the Malves (138·80±0·56). Similarly the values of 'α' for the Cephalic Index are 42·07 and 30·76 respectively for the Malves and Rajputs—the mean Index of the Audich (78·77±0·24) being nearer to that of the Rajputs (75·63±0·38) than the Malve's (74·30±0·30).

The values of the Reduced C. R. L. are lower between the Bania-Jain and the Rajputs, and the Kathi and Rajputs, *viz.*, 15·39±0·17 and 16·77±0·30, than those of other Central Indian castes with the Guzratis. The reason being the same, namely, the absence of the brachycephalic strain in Central India, except slightly among the Rajputs which associates them with the people of Guzrat to a small extent.

4.—THE PENINSULAR INDIA.

(*a*) *The Deccan.*

(*i*). *The Maharashtra.*

The Peninsular India, south of the Vindhyas, does not form a single geographical unit. It is made up of two distant parts—the plateau of the Deccan (from 'Dakkhan', the vernacular form of the sanskrit word 'Dakshina' meaning southern) comprising the region between the Western and the Eastern Ghats up to the Nilgiris, and the country below latitude 14 degree North, known in ancient times as Tamilakan[3]. The latter has a history of its own independent of the Deccan, excepting in so far as their fortunes mutually intersected and has been the home of the Dravidian civilisation from the earliest times.

In the Western parts of the Deccan the great mass of the population are Marathi. The term 'Mahratta' was formerly supposed to have been derived from two sanskrit words, 'Maha' (great) and 'Rathi' (warrior). Sir R. G. Bhandarkar[4], however, has shown that it really means 'Maha' or great, and 'Rathas'—the latter being the name of the tribe, who have held political supremacy in the Deccan from a long time.

Of the castes of the Maharashtra, the Desasthas, the Karadas and the Mahrattas are local groups, but the Chitpavans, the Saraswats and the Prabhus are traditionally supposed to have migrated from other parts. There is a legend that the Chitpavans were descended from shipwrecked foreigners, who were subsequently purified by Parashurama into the Brahmin caste,

---

1 Venkatachar, C. S.—Op. cit., page 278.
2 See Tables LVI, LVI(*a*) and LVI(*b*).
3 Bhandarkar, R. G.—Early History of the Deccan. Bombay Gazetteer, Volumes I and II, pages 133-275; Bombay, 1896.
4 Op. cit.

as their name " Chitpavan " implies[1]. On the basis of this legend, and the alleged similarity of Chitpavan names with place-names in Palestine, Prof. D. R. Bhandarkar has ascribed their *origin to Asia Minor*[2].

The Prabhus measured, belong to the Chandraseniya Kayastha section. According to their chornicles, the Prabhu Ratnamala, their original home was Oudh, from where they migrated to the Bombay Presidency during the times of Mahapadmanand and his successors[3]. The Chandraseniyas do not intermarry with any other sections of the Prabhus excepting the Davne *who are considered to* be their sub section.

The Saraswat Brahmins measured by me at Nova Goa, claim their descent from the Gour Saraswats of Northern India, and were supposed to have been brought by Parashurama and settled in Gomanchal, the ancient name for Goa. Their surnames, *e.g.*, Debasharma, Lomasharma, Shivasharma and titular deities such as Shantadurga are adduced as proofs of their affinities, with the Brahmins of Eastern India (Bengal)[4]. Unlike the rest of the people in Maharashtra, neither the Chitpavans nor the Saraswats marry their maternal uncles' daughters[5]. This custom has been considered as one of the distinguishing features of Dravidian speaking peoples of Southern India[6], and lends some support to their traditional migration from Northern India.

Outside the present data, the only other measurements available are those taken by B. A. Gupte for Risley's Survey, and a careful study of 100 Saraswat Brahmins of Goa by Prof. Germano de Silva Correia's pupil Voicunta Camotin[7].

After comparing the values obtained by him[8] with the figures published by Risley, Camotin came to the conclusion that the Gour Saraswats of Goa were racially akin to the Brahmins of Bengal, and considered that they were not a section of the Punjab Saraswats as supposed, but belonged rather to the Brahmins of the Gaurdeshã or old Bengal[9]. To this extent the traditions about their origins appeared to receive support from anthropometry.

In Tables XIV (*a*) and XIV are given the Crude and Reduced C. R. L.'s of the 5 Mahrathi and 1 Konkani castes. The lowest value of the Reduced C. R. L., $0 \cdot 15 \pm 0 \cdot 24$ is found between the Chitpavan Brahmins and the Prabhu Kayasthas. Between the Desastha Brahmins and the Mahratta, the Desastha and the Chitpavan, Desastha and the Prabhu, the Chitpavan and the *Prabhu, the Chitpavan and the Karada, the* Karada and the Prabhu, the relationships are very intimate. Between the Chitpavan and the Mahratta, the Desastha and Karada, the Karada and the Mahratta, the Mahratta and the Prabhu there are also intimate associations. The Konkani speaking Saraswat Gour Brahmins of Goa are intimately related to the Prabhus, and show close relationship with the Karada, but exhibit only a moderate degree of association with the rest of the castes. In Text—fig. 3, the mutual relationships of the Mahrathi Races

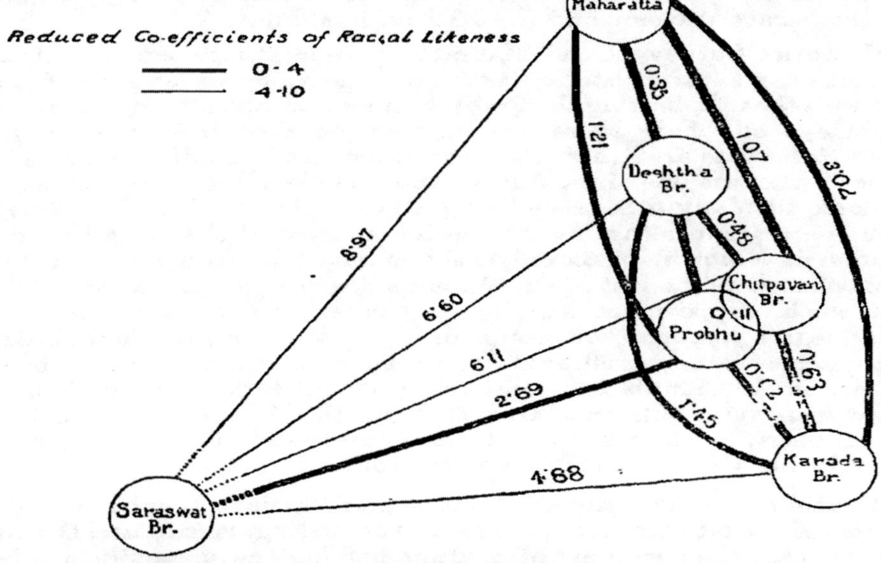

Text—fig. 3. Inter relationship of the Mahrathi Races.

---

[1] Enthoven, Op. cit., Volume I, page 242.

[2] *Ibid.*, foot note on page 242.

[3] Enthoven, Op. cit., Volume III, pages 237-240.

[4] Op. cit., Volume I, pages 249-250.

[5] Op. cit.

[6] Ghuriye, G. S.—Dual Organisation in India, J. R. A. I., Volume LIII, pages 79 91, 1923.

[7] Camotin, Voicunta— Os Bramanes Sarasvatas de Goa. Nova Goa. 1929.

[8] Op. cit., pages 14-49.

[9] Op. cit., pages 63-64.

are diagrammatically shown from which it will be seen that all the castes of the Maharashtra proper are so intimately related that they must strictly be considered as samples of the same race.

Integumentary colours.

Comparisons of skin colours show that the Chitpavans have the lightest tints, with 4·85 per cent. rosy white (Nos. 10-11), 52·43 per cent. light brown, 26·21 per cent. brown and only 16·50 per cent. dark brown complexion on the forehead. On the ventral part of the upper arm the proportion of the rosy white tint (Nos. 9-11) rises to 30·09, the highest figure observed among the people of the plains of India. The rest of the castes are darker and do not possess any person with rosy skin colour, with the exception of the Prabhus who show 1·82 per cent. of this element on the forehead. Among the Deshastha, Mahratta and the Saraswats there is a small proportion showing a distinct tawny shade (Nos. 23-27) which is absent among the first two, and the Karada Brahmins.

In the colour of the eyes the Chitpavans have 4 per cent. of grey (Nos. 8-9), 4 per cent. of hazel and 20 per cent. of clear light brown eyes. The Deshastha show 0·94 per cent. of hazel (No. 7), and the Prabhus 9 per cent. of clear light brown eyes. The Saraswats have however 2 per cent.ot grey and 2 per cent. of hazel eyes. In no other caste were light eyes found[1].

Similarly in hair colour, 3 per cent. of the Chitpavans have reddish brown hair (No. 6) and 5 per cent. brown. The Prabhus have 2 per cent. of reddish brown, and one Desastha Brahmin had red hair (No. 3). The Saraswats show 12 per cent. of brown hair. The rest of the people have drak brown to black hair[2].

Dr. Mrs. Irawati Karve[3], a Chitpavan lady, has published her observations on the eye colours of 3,097 Chitpavans consisting o 1,591 men and 1,506 women between the ages of 1–54. She finds 5 per cent. grey blue, 8 per cent. hazel 8 per cent. clear light brown, 27 per cent. brown, 33 per cent. dark brown and 19 per cent. black brown eyes among the Chitpavans. The figures published by her therefore correspond to those given in Table LVII (*b*), except the percentages for the hazel and clear light brown eyes. As her observations, however, were not taken with the help of Martin's "Augenfarbentafel" but from visual impressions only, these differences can very well be understood.

It will be noticed from Tables LVII (*b*) and (*c*) that the Mahrathi castes have only very slightly marked supra orbital ridges. The eye is usually horizontal and open, but among the Deasatha Brahmins there is a small percentage showing traces of the epicanthic fold. Alveolar prognathism is however present in all except the Prabhus, being specially noticeable in the Mahrattas, the Saraswat Gours and the Karada Brahmins.

To conclude this brief Survey of the Mahrathi people, there can hardly be any doubt, that they belong to the same racial stock, with the possible exception of the Saraswats, whose relationship with the rest, barring the Prabhus, does not appear to be so close. In the colours of the skin, eye and hair there are however marked differences. The Chitpavans, the Prabhus and the Saraswats are lighter than the others, and contain a definite blond element, specially the former, who are one of the fairest, and include a higher percentage of light eyed and light haired people than any other race living in the plains of India. This probably has occasioned so much speculations regarding the possible sources of their origin, and their descent from foreigners from Asia Minor, shipwrecked on the coasts of the Konkan. The intimate associations of the Chitpavans with the rest of the Maharashtra people, as disclosed by quantitative tests are against such suppositions. The lighter element, so well marked among them, but noticed in a smaller degree among other groups of Western India, is undoubtedly due to an alien strain, but there seems no justification to suppose that it originated from Asia Minor where excepting the Mountain Kurds the people are in general dark eyed, and belong to a certain well known racial types very different from that of the Chitpavans. As has happened in many other parts of India, but possibly in a lesser extent—this lighter element probably had its source in some early racial drift from N. Western India.

Besides the Marathi castes, I measured 36 adult male Parsis in Bombay in 1926 through the kind help and interest of the late Sir Jivanji J. Modi, the distinguished Parsi Orientalist. These measurements showed that the Parsis are of medium height, the mean Stature being 1667·44. The maximum Head length and the Head breadth are 181·78 ± 0·62 and 151·08 ± 0·66 respectively, and the mean proportions between the two is 83·15±0·38, showing the Parsis to be highly brachycephalic. The nose is very long and prominent and not infrequently aquiline, the mean Nasal and Orbito-Nasal Indices being 62·83 ± 0·71 and 118·13± 0·68 respectively. The face is wide but rather short, the Total Facial Index being 87·04±0·59.

---

[1] See Table LVII (*b*).

[2] See Table LVII(*a*).

[3] Karve, Irawati,—Beobachtungen über die Augenfarben an Chitpavan Brahmanen. Zeits für Morph. und Anthro. Band XXIX, pages 498—501.

The values of the C.R.L.'s of the Parsis and the two main Guzrati groups given in Table XIII (*b*) indicate their racial divergence from the people among whom they took shelter in the 12th. century.

While the Parsis appear to be somatically different from the Indian races, it is interesting to compare them with the remnants of the old Persian population still professing Zoroastrianism and known as the Guebres. Baer measured 5 Guebre crania from Yezd and Kirman, belonging to adult males, now in the St. Petersburg Academy. The mean Cranial Index of these five crania is 69·9 showing them to be markedly longheaded. Danilov[1] has published the measurements of 5 other Guebre crania from a cemetery called "Kala Gebri" in the mountains south east of Tehran. The mean values of the measurements taken by Danilov on the 3 adult male skulls are given in the following Table :—

The mean values of three adult male Guebre crania from Kala Gebri (*Tehran*)[2]

Name.	Hor. Circumference.	Cranial length.	Cranial breadth.	Cranial height.	Cranial Index.	Length height Index.	Min. Front. Diam.	Facial width.	Upper facial length.	Upper facial Index.	Nose length.	Nose breadth.	Nasal Index.	Facial angle.
Guebre Crania	502·3	184	133·6	134·3	72·2	73·2	92·6	127·3	67	52·4	50	22·3	44·8	63

From these figures it will be observed that the Guebres of 'Kala Gebri' near Tehran are also dolichocranial with a high cranial vault—the height of the skull exceeding the greatest Transverse diameter, and the Length-height Index being 73·2 against 72·2, the mean value of the Cranial Index for the skulls. The face is narrow and orthognathous and the nose leptorhine.

The Guebres of Yezd, Kirman and Kala Gebri are longheaded, and are therefore racially very different from the Parsis of Bombay, but appear to be allied to the other Aryan speaking people of N. W. Asia. It seems likely, as suggested by Dixon[3], that the Parsi emigrants to Bombay represent a brachycephalic group of Persian population who were converted to Zoroastrianism, while their brethren in faith, the Guebres who remained at home represented the older racial stock.

The values of the C. R. L. of the Mahrathi castes when compared with those of Guzrat, are given in Tables XV-XV (*a*). It is seen from these figures that intimate relationship exists between the Audich and the Deshastha Brahmins—the Reduced Co efficient being only $2 \cdot 56 \pm 0 \cdot 17$. In the case of the Audich and the Prabhu, Audich and Mahratta, Audich and Chitpavan there are also close associations. In a lesser degree, relationship is also shown by the other Guzrati and Mahrathi castes, excepting the Kathi and the Brahma-Kshatri. The latter however appears to have a slight association with the Karada and the Saraswat Gour, who are unrelated to the Kunbi-Patidars. When the values of 'α' are scrutinized, it is noticed that the differences between the Guzrati and the Mahrathi castes are caused by the greater preponderance of the brachycephalic strain in the former, who appear also to have a longer and finer nose. This explains the closer relationship of the Mahrathi with those castes of Guzrat who migrated there from Upper India barring the Brahma-Kshatris, and would appear to suggest the existence of a common racial substratum from Central India to Maharashtra. This substratum seems to have been overlaid by a brachycephalic element in Western India, particularly in Guzrat, which accounts for the difference of the Guzrati from both the Central Indian and Mahrathi population.

Besides the Mahrathi, the people of Deccan consist mainly of the Kannada, who occupy the western portions of the table-land including Mysore and south western Hyderabad, and the Telegu, who predominate in the northern and eastern parts up to the Ceded Districts. Between the Maharashtra and Mysore however there is a small section of Tulu speaking people in South Kanara, which is closely connected with, if not a dialect of Kanarese.

Thurston[4] took the measurements of 120 Tulu speaking castes including 40 Bants, 50 Billavas and 30 Shivali Brahmins. The mean Cephalic Indices of the Bant, the Billava and the Shivalli are 78·0, 80·1 and 80·4 respectively. The corresponding figures for the Nasal Index are 72·2, 72·6 and 71·4. The total mean Cephalic Index for the entire Tulu castes is 79·5 and the total mean Nasal Index for the same is 72·0. Of these, the Billavas, who are toddy drawers, are the most numerous, and form about one fifth of the total population

[1] Danilov, N. P.—"K charakteristikye antropologicheskich i fiziologicheskich chert sovremennago nasaleniya Persii "in *Izvjestiya imperatorskago obschestva lyubitelei estestvoznaniya anthropologii i etnografii*, Volume LXXXVIII. Moscow, 1984. Columns 137—146.

[2] I am indebted to Prof. Roland B. Dixon of Harvard for sending me the measurements published by Baer and Danilov from the original Russian.

[3] Dixon, Roland B.—*The Racial History of Man*, page 310.

[4] Thurston, E.—*The Castes and Tribes of South India*. Volume I. pages LXI—LXXIII, 1909.

of the region. The Bants, who are the chief land-owning class (given to military pursuits), and occupy the same position as the Nairs in Malabar, come next to them in number [1]. The Shivalli, one of the chief groups of the Tulu Brahmins, are most numerous at Udipi in South Canara. Physically there is not much to choose between these groups, excepting that the Shivalli Brahmins are much lighter [1] and slightly more brachy and leptorhine, and the Bants more dolichocephalic. Regarding the last, Mr. Logan writes as follows :[2] " Both men and women of the Bant community are among the comeliest of Asiatic races, having high foreheads and well-turned, aquiline noses." All of the three observe the typical Southern Indian " Marumakkattayam " form of inheritance (*i.e.*, inheritance through the female line), and the dead are usually cremated ; though among the Billavas occasional recourse to burial still takes place ; when a small, conical mound is raised over the burial, and on the thirteenth day after the burial, four poles are planted around the mound. It is probable that like the Lingayats [1], the Kurubas [1], and other sects and tribes of the western parts of the Deccan, burial was the common custom at one time, and was abandoned later on, due to the influence of Hinduism. Nothing definitely is known about the origin of either the Billavas or the Bants, though traditions suggest that both of them are immigrants into this region. As regards the Shivalli Brahmins, there is a distinct tradition, that they were brought to the west coast by Mayur Varma, founder of the Kadamba Dynasty, about 750 A. D., from Ahikshetra in Northern India, identified by Mr. Bhandarkar as Rohilkhand (Oudh), and were settled in thirty-two villages near Udipi, forming the most important (if not the first) centre of Brahmanism in this region. There is little doubt that the Hinduization of the other two was due to the influence of the last, for whom they still act as priests [1].

(*ii*). *Kanara.*

Of the Kannada proper, Thurston [3] has published the measurements of 410 men from Mysore belonging to 8 distinct groups and 290 men belonging to the districts of Bellary and Karnul. The mean Cephalic Index of the Mysore groups is 79·3 and the Nasal Index 73·5. The corresponding figures for the latter are 78·8 and 75·3 respectively. The Kanarese of the Bellary and Karnul districts appear to possess a slightly longer head and broader nose, to judge from Thurston's measurements.

The mean values of the measurements taken by me are given in Table IV . It will be observed from these figures that the stature of the Kanarese Brahmins is short, the mean value being only 1618·70±5·16. The head is nearly round, though not falling strictly within the brachycephalic class—the mean Cephalic Index being 79·34±0·50. The vault of the head is not high, though it seems so in relation to the length—the mean Length-Auricular height Index being 65·97±0·38. The forehead is broad and arched but decidedly receeding in a few cases. The cheek bones are well spread out, but the width between the gonia is comparatively narrow, giving a pear shaped appearance to the face. The nose is long (N. I. 71·20±0·70) but the nostrils are broad with a moderately high bridge. In several cases aquiline noses were also found.

The Non-Brahmins are somewhat taller with a mean Stature of 1654·92±4.83. The head is distinctly broad with a mean Cephalic Index of 83·06±0·44. The vault is high in relation to the length but not absolutely—the mean Length Auricular-height Index being 68·34±0·38. The forehead is broad and generally well arched. The face is broad but short and of a pear-shape. The nose is moderately long (N. I. 72·46±0·67) and well pronounced with frequent occurrence of aquiline noses [4]. The measurements taken by me on the Brahmins appear therefore to agree on the whole with those published by Thurston but the mean Cephalic Index of my non-Brahmin group is considerably higher. This is probably due to the fact that in my non-Brahmin sample only the upper stratum of the population, *viz.*, the Vakkaliga, Banajiga and Devanga were included, on the advice of Mr. Venkateswar Iyanger, the Census Superintendent of Mysore, as the Kannada do not have one single caste ranking immediately below the Brahmin. The Vakkaliga measured by Thurston also gave a high value for the Cephalic Index (81·7).

In Tables XVI and XVI (*a*) are given the Reduced and Crude C. R. L.'s, of the Kannada groups. The value of the former between the Brahmins and the Non-Brahmins is 4·70±0·34 and that of the latter is 2·35±0·17, showing that the two groups are closely related. When the individual characters are compared the values of the function " α " for Stature, Head length, Cephalic, Length-height and the Trans. fronto-parietal Indices are 10·51, 13·81, 22·41, 7·25 and 9·51 respectively. In the rest they are below 6. It will be seen from these figures that the chief difference between the Brahmins and the non-Brahmins consist in the higher stature and broader head of the latter.

In the colour of the skin (Table LVIII), the Non-Brahmins appear to be darker with higher percentages of dark brown and tawny brown elements. In eye colour [Table LVIII(*b*)], both are predominantly dark brown, and black, with a small percentage of men showing a light brown shade (No. 5). Similarly the colour of the hair is mainly black with a small percentage of

---

[1] Thurston, Op. cit., 1909.
[2] Logan, 1906.
[3] Op. cit., Volume I.
[4] Guha, B. S.—A Note on the Somatic Characters of the Kanarese People, Census of India, Volume, XXV, page 358 ; Bangalore, 1932.

dark brown (No. 4). As in skin colours, the Brahmins show a slightly higher proportion of people having a lighter shade of the eye and hair colours.

As will appear from Tables LVIII (*b*) and (*c*), the supra orbital ridges are on the whole well developed among both the Brahmins and the Non-Brahmins ; only 2 per cent. of the latter not showing any ridges. The epicanthic fold is present in 6 per cent. of the Brahmins and 4 per cent. of the Non-Brahmins, and 6 per cent. of the former and 10 per cent. of the latter, also show slanting eyes. The nasal root is depressed among 14 per cent. Brahmins and 22 per cent. Non-Brahmins, but on the average the nose is fairly prominent in both. In 22 per cent. of the Brahmins and 10 per cent. of the Non-Brahmins it is however convex. The face is either round or squarish, with 10 per cent. of the Brahmins and 8 per cent. Non Brahmins showing traces of prognathism. In the latter group, 2 per cent. of the people show marked alveolar prognathism.

South west of Mysore and bounded by South Kanara on the west, and Malabar on the south, there is the small State of Coorg perched on the slopes of the Western Ghats, inhabited by the Coorgi, whose language Kodagu is a dialect of Kanarese and forms a link between it and Tulu. Sir Thomas Holland [1] is responsible for an excellent series of measurements on 32 Coorgis and 25 Yeruvas, an aboriginal tribe who live also in these hills. Sir Thomas [2] describes the Coorgi "as the finest race without exception in Southern India," and considers them to be superior to the Brahmins of this area, in respect of skin colour, stature and the prominence of the nose. The mean Cephalic Index of the 32 Coorgi is 79·9 and the Nasal Index 72·2.

In Tables XVII and XVII (*a*) are given the values of the Crude and Reduced C. R. L.'s calculated from the measurements published by Holland. It is interesting that the smallest Co-efficient obtained, is with the Tamil Brahmins (12·24±0·74), and slightly higher with the Kanarese Non Brahmin (14·39±0·74), with the Kanarese Brahmin however, the value of the Reduced C. R. L. is 18·33±0·74. The three groups, the Coorgi, the Tamil Brahmin and the Kanarese Non-Brahmin, would therefore appear to be related, and if allowance can be made for personal equation, this relationship will probably be very close. With the brachycephalic groups from Bengal and Guzrat however, the values of the C. R. L.'s are very high.

(*iii*). *Andhra.*

The North Eastern parts of the Deccan and the coastal strips from Ganjam to the Ceded Districts are occupied by the Andhras. Thurston [3] has published the measurements of 9 Andhra castes from the Karnul and Bellary districts. The mean Cephalic and Nasal Indices of these groups are given in the following Table :—

The Andhras (Thurston).

Name.	C. I.	N. I.	Number.
Madiga (Adoni)	75·0	80·8	30
Madiga (Hospet)	76·5	77·5	40
Mala	77·1	76·2	30
Galla	77·5	74·1	60
Boya	77·9	75·0	50
Tota Balija	78·0	74·4	39
Kapu	78·0	72·8	49
Padma Sala	78·7	73·2	30
Togata	80·0	77·5	30
Grand Average.	77·6	75·4	358

The mean values of the Cephalic and Nasal Indices of the 358 men measured by Thurston are 77·6 and 75·4 respectively. Of these castes however, the Boyas are the Telegu speaking sub-division of the Kanarese Bedars, who were brought by Hyder Ali and Tipu Sultan from Mysore during the Carnatic Wars. The Galla (from Sanskrit Gopala) are a pastoral people with distinct traditions of having migrated from Northern India. At the present time they are tending towards the Lingayat sect, and have extensively intermixed with the Kapus and Balijas. The Kapus are traditionally said to be a branch of the "Rattas" (from which the Mahrattas derive their origin), and from which their main title "Reddi" is said to have been derived. The Tota Balijas or Bnnjaras (from Sanskrit, Banijya, *i.e.*, trade) are the main trading caste

[1] Holland, T. H.—The Coorgs and Yeruvas. J.A.S.B., Part III, pages 59—98. 1901.

[2] Loc. cit., page 59.

[3] Thurston, E.—Op. cit., 1909.

north of Mysore. At present the Gallas, Kapus and Balijas have largely intermixed, due to the influence of Lingyatism, to which the largest portion of the trading communities of the Central Deccan belong, and from the anthropological standpoint may therefore be considered as one unit. The Padma Salas, like the castes mentioned, are also Lingyats, and have also intermixed. It will be seen from these accounts that the people belonging to all these castes are greatly intermixed due to the Lingyat influence which took converts from all classes. Consequently how far these western castes can be regarded as true representatives of the Telegu people seems very doubtful.

In taking the measurements of the Telegu speaking people, therefore, attention was directed to the Central and Eastern regions, and two groups of the Andhras, the Brahmins and Vaisya Kumtis [1], *i.e.*, the caste next to the Brahmins, were measured by me in the " Telangana " of the Hyderabad State, and Vizagapatam, which have been the chief centres of the Telegus from the earliest times.

In Table IV are given the measurements of the Telegu groups. Both of the castes are of medium stature, having long face and moderate but fairly prominent nose.

The values of the Crude and Reduced C. R. L. [Tables XVI and XVI (*a*)] between the two are as low as—0·10±0·17 and—0·20±0·34 or 0·12±0·17 and 0·24±0·34 respectively, when the mean standard deviations are substituted for those of the Nagar Brahmins. When the individual characters are compared, the value of 'α' in no case is found to exceed 6. There can therefore be no doubt that the Brahmins and Komtis are samples of the same Telegu population. In skin colour the Brahmins are however lighter, with 8 per cent. of light brown element (Table LVIII) on the forehead and 10 per cent. on the ventral side of the upper arm, against nil of the Kumtis, who have on the other hand 42 per cent. and 40 per cent. of people with tawny brown skin colour. The eye colour in both—Table LVIII (*b*)—varies from black to dark-brown, with 2 per cent. of the Brahmins having light brown eyes. The colour of the hair—Table LVIII (*a*) —similarly in the majority is black in both, with 38 per cent. of the dark brown.

A reference to Tables LVIII (*b*) and (*c*) will indicate that the supra-orbital ridges are on the whole well developed, in 2 per cent. of each of the castes the ridges are distinctly stout and in only 8 per cent. Brahmins and 12 per cent. Non-Brahmins they are absent. The eyes are usually round, but 4 per cent. of both the groups show epicanthic fold. Ten per cent. of the Brahmins and 8 per cent. of the Non-Brahmins have convex noses, but 20 per cent. of the former and 48 per cent. of the latter show depressed nasal roots. On the average however the nasal dorsum is moderately prominent. The face varies from a long to a pear shape, and 16 per cent. of the Brahmins have traces of prognathism.

Recently 68 male and 12 female skulls belonging to the peasant classes of Vizagapatam, Ganjam and Godavari districts have been measured by Dr. R. K. Rau, Professor of Anatomy of the Vizagapatam Medical College.[2] These skulls belonged to the Cadavars brought to the Department of Anatomy from King George's Hospital, Vizagapatam, and particulars regarding their caste, etc., are known. The mean Cranial Index of the 68 male skulls is 73·74 and of the 12 female skulls 75·78. The mean of the Breadth-Height Index for the two groups are 94·76 and 92·59 respectively The values of the Superior Facial Index are 50·53 and 51·90, and those of the Nasal Index 50·28 and 54·32, showing that the face is medium and the nose is broad. The orbits are high, the mean Orbital Index being 85·63 in the male and 84·53 in the female. The palate is broad in the male and medium in the female—the values of the Palatal Index being 90·00 and 88·13 respectively. These measurements confirm the dolichocephalic character of the Telegu head, but in the lower communities (the peasant classes) the nose appear to be much broader, specially in the females.

(*b*) *Tamilakan.*

The people living in the area below the Ghats may be divided into two classes, *viz.*, (*a*) The Malayali living in Malabar or Western and (*b*) The Tamils living in the eastern ends of the Peninsula.

(*i*). *The Malayali.*

Thurston [3] has published the measurements of 175 Malayali belonging to 5 groups as shown in the following Table :—

The Malayali (Thurston).

Name	Number.	C. I.	N. I.
Tiyan	40	73·0	74·2
Cheruman	25	73·9	78·1
Nayar	40	74·4	71·1
Syrian Christian	30	75·5	71·9
Mukkuvan	40	75·1	81·0
Total	175	74·36	75·21

[1] Guha, B. S.—Anthropometric Notes on Telegu Brahmins and Kumtis, Census of India, Volume XXIII (Hyderabad), page 280, 1933.

[2] Rau, R. K. and Guha, B. S.—A comparative study of the skulls of the Telegu speaking people of the Northern Circars (under publication).

[3] Thurston, E.—Op. cit., 1909.

The mean Cephalic Index of the five groups is 74·36 and the mean Nasal Index 75·21. Fawcett,[1] in addition published measurements on 25 Nambudiri Brahmins and 186 Nairs. The mean Cephalic Index obtained by him for the former is 76·3 and for the latter 73·1; the respective values of the Nasal Index for the two being 75.5 and 76·8. In the year 1931, I measured 55 Nambudiris, 60 Nairs and 50 Illuvas in Cochin, representing the upper, middle and lower strata of the Malayali population. The Nambudiris were measured in different Taluks of the Cochin State and I am grateful to Messrs. Achutya Menon and Sankara Menon for the help rendered by them when taking these measurements. The three groups measured, consisted of genuine members of the three castes. In Table IV, the measurements of the Malayali castes are given, from which it will be seen that the Nairs are of tall, the Nambudiris medium and the Illuva short stature. All the three are dolichocephalic, the Cephalic Index being 74·18±0·30, 72·51±0·28 and 73·38±0·28 respectively. The absolute length and size of the Nambudiri head is however greater, the face longer and the nose more highly pitched.

In Tables XVI and XVI (a) are given the values of the C. R. L.'s. The Reduced Coefficient between the Nambudiri and the Nair is 2·31±0·29 showing the two castes are intimately associated. But the Illuva, do not show any relationship with either of the two—the values of the Reduced C. R. L. for the two being 14·52±0·32 and 14·31±0·31 respectively. When the individual characters between the Nambudiri and the Nair are scrutinised, the only one in which the value of 'α' exceeds 6 is found to be in Stature (23·68). Between the Illuva and the Nambudiri the values of 'α' for Stature, Head length, Auricular height, Bizygomatic breadth, Orbito-nasal arc, Nasal length, Nasal height, Upper and Total Facial length, Breadth-height Index, Orbito-nasal Index and Nasal Elevation Index are 13·88, 15·40, 20·41, 13·78, 19·51, 12·93, 30·90, 14·51, 10·30, 8·79, 13·76 and 21·60 showing the all round differences between the two groups. With the Nairs similarly, the values of 'α' for Stature, Auricular height, Max. Bizygomatic breadth, Orbito-nasal arc, Nasal length, Nasal depth, Upper and Total Facial length, Length-height Index and Nasal Elevation Index are 72·78, 15·43, 19·18, 7·29, 17·22, 18·37, 15·28, 15·12, 6·82 and 8·81 respectively.

In the colour of the skin, the proportion of the light brown is greatest (29 per cent.) among the Nambudiris, who show also a very much smaller percentage of darker people. Among the Nairs the average skin colour varies between brown and tawny brown. The Illuva on the other hand, have a much greater proportion of darker colours as compared to the Nambudiri and the Nair. The colour of the eye in all the three are in the main from black to dark brown, but the Nambudiri have a small percentage of clear light brown (No. 6), and the Illuva of light brown (No. 5) eyes. The hair colour in all the three is generally black with a small proportion of dark brown.

The supra-orbital ridges are well marked. The eyes are usually round. Among the Nambudiris no one showed any trace of epicanthic fold, but among the Nair and the Illuva it was 1·67 per cent. and 10 per cent. respectively; the latter also have 12 per cent. of slanting eyes amongst them. The Nambudiri has a high prominent nose, 16 per cent. of which are convex. Among the Nairs the nasal prominence, as well as convexity is less marked, who in this respect are slightly nearer to the Illuva than to the Nambudiri. The face is longish among the Nambudiri on the average, and only 1·82 per cent. show any traces of prognathism. Among the Nairs the face is less elongated, and 15 per cent. have prognathism. Among the Illuva the face is more squarish and fully 30 per cent. show the presence of prognathism.

The Nambudiris are not indigeneous to Malabar but were supposed to have settled in Southern India during the time of the Western Chalukyas in the early centuries of the Christian era.[2] Due however to the system of "Sambandham" prevalent among them, the younger sons of the Nambudiri, contract informal alliances with Nair women, with the result that the Nairs contain a large amount of Nambudiri blood. The value of the C. R. L. between these two confirm this intermixture, and show that the absorption of Nambudiri blood among the Nairs has been going on at such a pace, that at the present day the two have become intimately allied in somatic characters, the difference being mostly in integumentary colours and finer cut features noticeable among the former.

---

[1] Fawcett, F.W.—Madras Government Museum Bulletin, No. 3, Volume III, pages 36 and 191; Madras 1901.

[2] Fawcett, F. W.—Op. cit.

(*ii*). *The Tamils.*

Of the Tamils proper, who may roughly be said to occupy the southern parts of the Peninsula below the Ghats and the rich eastern coastal lands up to approximately latitude 14 degree North, Thurston[1] has published the measurements on 541 men, belonging to 11 groups as shown in the following Table :—

The Tamils (Thurston).

Name.	C. I.	N. I.	Number.
Agamudaiyan	74·0	74·2	40
Ambattan	73·4	72·4	29
Chakkilyan	74·9	78·9	50
Idaiyan	76·0	73·6	42
Kammalan	75·0	77·3	40
Malaiyali	74·3	77·8	50
Palli	73·0	77·3	40
Paraiyan	73·6	80·0	40
Tamil Brahmin	76·5	76·7	40
Shanan	76·6	79·5	130
Vellala	74·1	73·21	40
Grand Average	74·6	76·4	541

The total mean values of the Cephalic and Nasal Indices of the 541 Tamils are 74·6 and 76·4 respectively. Of the groups mentioned in the Table, only three have mean Cephalic Index of 76 and over, namely the Idaiyans, the Tamil Brahmins and the Shanans. The measurements taken by Mr. Samanta[2] in 1892 on 56 Tamils settled in Northern Ceylon, gave 77·7 and 83·8 as the mean of these two Indices. Hornell[3] also published measurements on three Tamil castes from the Tinnevelly district, namely, the Parawar, the Shanan and the Parayan. The mean Cephalic and Nasal Indices of the 50 male Parawars, were 79·39 and 77·72 respectively. Of the 100 male Shanans, and 31 male Parayans, the respective values were 80·72 and 74·43, and 80·34 and 77·89 respectively. In 1931, I measured three Tamil castes in the Madura district, namely, the Brahmin, the Vaisya Chetti and the Kalla. In Table IV, are given the measurements of these castes, from which it will be seen that the mean values of the Cephalic Index are 77·36±0·34, 79·49±0·28 and 75·26±0·30 respectively. The respective figures for the Nasal Index of the three castes are 71·92±0·58, 71·19±0·72 and 76·26±0·77. The Reduced C. R. L. (Table XVI) between the Tamil Brahmin and Tamil Chetti is 4·28±0·34, showing the existence of a close relationship between the two. With the Kalla however, both the upper castes have only a very slight association ; the Co-efficients being 12·85±0·38 and 13·01±0·38 respectively. When the individual characters are compared, the main differences between the Brahmin and the Chetti are noticed in the Bizygomatic breadth, Inter-orbital breadth, Orbito-nasal arc, Length-breadth Index and Orbito-nasal Index, the values of 'α' for these characters being 11·48, 13·53, 6·15, 7·34 and 8·94 respectively, showing that the Chettis have a broader head and face than the Brahmins. The differences of the Brahmins from the Kallas consist in the Auricular height, Inter-orbital breadth, Orbito-nasal breadth, Orbito-nasal arc, Nasal length, Nasal depth, Cephalic Index, Length-height Index, Orbito-nasal Index, Nasal Index and Trans. Cephalo-facial Index, the values of 'α' in these characters being 6·08, 12·17,13·97, 28·56, 6·82, 7·02, 6·35, 6·23, 9·28, 9·32, 23·31 respectively. From the Chettis, the Kallas differ in Stature, Head breadth, Orbito-nasal breadth, Orbito-nasal arc, Nasal length, Total facial length, Cephalic Index, Trans. Fronto-parietal Index, Nasal Index and Trans. Cephalo-facial Index with 10·78, 20·37, 11·07, 9·04, 13·93, 9·66, 25·75, 11·44, 12·72 and 18·34 as the respective values of 'α' for these characters It is evident from these figures, that the differences of the Kallas from the Brahmins and the Chettis, relate to the shape and proportions of the head and the face taken as a whole, and not confined to one or two traits only.

In skin colour, the Tamil Brahmins (Table LVIII) have 8 per cent. of light brown (No. 13) 4 per cent. of tawny brown (Nos. 23—27) but the majority are of dark brown (Nos. 15—17D). The Chettis have only 2 per cent. of light brown, 46 per cent. of tawny brown, but 40 per cent. of dark brown. The Kallas have 5 per cent. of dark chocolate brown (No. 29) and 90 per cent. of dark tawny brown. The eye colour in all the three groups, varies from black to dark brown, excepting 6% of Brahmins with light clear brown eyes. The majority have either black or dark brown hair, but 6 per cent. of the Brahmins possess brown hair. These figures show that the Tamil groups are in general dark, barring a small percentage of people with light brown skin and eye colours.

From Tables LVIII (*b*) and (*c*) it will appear that the supra-orbital ridges are moderately prominent among the Tamil group, and 2 per cent. among the Brahmins, 5 per cent. among the Kallas and 12 per cent. among the Chettis have well developed supra-orbital ridges. Twenty

[1] Thurston, E.—Op. cit., 1909.

[2] Risley, H.H.—Measurements of the Cingalese Moormen and Tamils, taken at Ceylon in November 1892. J.A.S.B., *Volume LXII, Part III, pages* 33—45, 1893.

[3] Hornell, James.—The Origins and Ethnological significance of Indian Boat Designs, Mem. A.S.B., Volume VII, pages 139-246.

four per cent. of the Brahmins, 20 per cent. of the Kallas and 30 per cent. of the Chettis do not show the ridge at all. The eye is usually round but 4 per cent. of the Brahmins, 10 per cent. of the Kallas and 8 per cent. of the Chettis have slightly slanting eyes. In the Brahmins the epicanthic fold is altogether absent, but it is present among 2 per cent. of the Chettis and 7·5 per cent. of the Kallas. The nose is prominent among both the Brahmins and the Chettis, who show also 16 per cent. and 4 per cent. respectively of convex noses. In the Kallas the nose is however medium to flat, with 27·5 per cent. of the people having depressed nasal root. On the average, the face varies from a pear to a roundish shape and among 12 per cent. of the Brahmins, 12·5 per cent. of the Kallas and 16 per cent. of the Chettis there is distinct prognathism.

Measurements of several series of crania have been published but with the exception of 35 male and 4 female skulls belonging to Tamil coolies who died in the Singapore Hospital [1], the locality and race of these crania are uncertain. Of the 14 skulls measured by Montegazza [2] the only information available is that they belonged to 'Hindus' of Southern India. Nothing is said as to what race or caste the skulls belonged or the locality from where they were procured. Similarly, of the 37 male Maravar crania in the collections of the Royal College of Surgeons, London, there is no information as to how and where the skulls were obtained from. Dr. Shortt, who made the presentation, seemed even doubtful if all the skulls really belonged to the Maravar caste [3]. In any consideration of the racial characteristics of the different Dravidian speaking peoples of South India therefore, the data derived from a study of these skulls, should not properly find any place.

The mean Cubic Capacity of the 35 male Tamil crania measured by Harrower is 1350·25, the Cranial length 179·6, the Cranial breadth 131·5, and the mean of the proportions between the two is 73·45. The Max. Bizygomatic breadth is 127·8 and the mean Nasal Index is 51·64. As the Tamil coolies come from the lower classes, it is only to be expected that the values of their measurements should approach those of the Kallas rather than either those of the Brahmins or the Chettis.

A comparison of all the measurements published on the Tamil groups discussed above, makes it clear, that the physical type of the Tamils is made up of two racial strains—a brachycephalic and a dolichocephalic element predominating in the higher and lower castes respectively.

In Tables XVI and XVI (*a*), are given the Reduced and the Crude C. R. L.'s of the South-Indian castes. From Text-fig. 4, which sums up the relationships disclosed by the C. R. L.'s

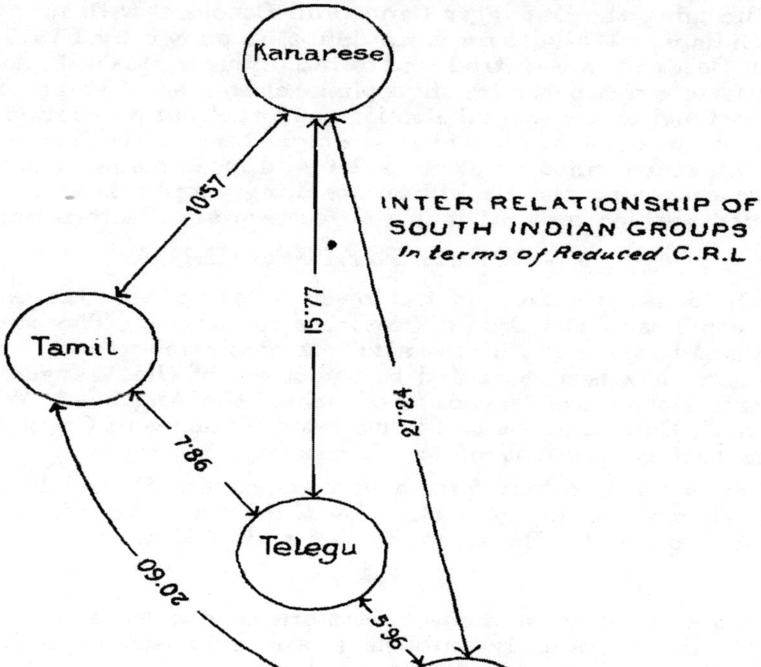

Text.-fig. 4.—Inter relationship of South Indian Groups.

[1] Harrower, Gordon.—A study of the Hokien and Tamil skulls, Trans. Roy. Soc. of Edinburgh, Volume LIV, pages 573—599.

[2] Archivio L'Antropologia e la Etnologia, Volume XIII, pages 177—241. Firenze, 1883.

[3] Biometrika, Volume XXB, Parts III and IV, page 298.

it appears that the Telegu and Malayali are closely related with a mean value of 5·96 only—the association between the Telegu and the Tamil is also close (7·86). The Telegu thus forms a link between the Malayali and the Tamil, who have a mean C. R. L. of 20·6. The relationship of the Tamil with the Kanarese is also apparent, but there is no association between the Kanarese and the Malayali. The Kanarese and the Malayali are therefore at the two ends, the former representing the broadheaded and the latter the longheaded type. The Tamil seems to have absorbed the brachycephalic strain considerably, but retains a strong substratum of the dolichocephalic element, and stands midway between the Kanarese and the Telegu; the last being closer to the Malayali type than any other of the Dravidian speaking higher groups.

We have little information regarding the ancient races of Southern India. The earliest reference occurs in the Aitareya Brahmana [1] about the Andhras, who are mentioned as occupying the country near the mouth of the Godavari river (lat. 16 degree N.). Katyana,[2] who wrote a commentary on the Sutras of Panini, and is supposed to have flourished about the 4th century B. C., mentions three separate kingdoms in Southern India, namely Pandya in the extreme southeast, Kerala on the southwest and Chola north of Pandya. In the Ramayana[3] similar references occur regarding the Andhra, and the three states of Kerala, Pandya and Chola in the extreme south of the Peninsula. The Mahabharata[4] also mentions these kingdoms. According to the Tamil traditions[5] however there was at first only one kingdom, namely, 'Tamilkan' which extended from Mahe, on the Malabar coast to Calicut, a little north of Madras, and was essentially the land of the Tamil race and speech. Gradually, Tamilkan was split up into different states. We have no information either from the archæological or traditional sources as to the periods when the Dravidian speaking peoples of the South separated from one another. It seems certain however, that the Telegu and the Kanarese, developed into distinct divisions much earlier, but the Tamil and the Malayali remained together till very much later. The closer relationship of the Telegu and the Malayali, and the divergence of the Malayali from the Tamil, must therefore be explained as due to the intrusion of a later racial strain, which moving along the western littoral, passed through the Kanarese country into the south eastern parts occupied by the Tamils, but did not penetrate Malabar, nor appeared to have moved northwards into the Telegu regions. The Kanarese seem to have been most affected by this movement, the Tamils partially, the Telegue only very slightly, but the Malayalis remained altogether unaffected. In his very suggestive paper, on the "Origins and Ethnological Significance of the Indian Boat Designs", Hornell [6] has attempted to explain the brachycephalic character of the Parawar, Shanan and Parayan of the Tinnevelly district, as due to a Polynesian immigration into Southern India, bringing the Outrigger Canoe and Cocoanut with it, prior to or soon after the arrival of the Dravidians. While there is no doubt, as shown by Hornell, that both the Outrigger Canoe and the Cocoanut were introduced from Polynesia, it is not necessary to postulate a Polynesian racial drift to explain the brachycephalic character of some of the Tamil castes. Brachycephaly is not confined to the coastal Tamils, as Hornell supposed, but is dominant among all the upper castes, and runs north-westwards through the entire Kanarese country into Maharashtra and Guzrat, and cannot be explained by supposing the presence of Polynesian blood only. Its presence among the Dravidian speaking peoples is apparently the result of the same racial movements which brought it in the Western and Eastern parts of Upper India.

5.—NORTH EASTERN INDIA.

North-Eastern India consists mainly of the lower valleys of the Ganges and Brahmaputra and extends from the confines of the United Provinces to Assam. The coastal plains formed by the deltas of the Mahanadi on the south have also been associated with it; and from the earliest historical times this region has been regarded as the home of the Vratyas. The Vaidehis of Eastern U. P. and North Behar, the Magadhas of Behar, the Angas of Western Bengal, the Paundras of North Bengal, Bangas of Central Bengal and Kalingas of Orissa, were mentioned as the inhabitants of the various portions of this territory.

Topographically however it does not form a homogeneous unit, and its racial history also does not appear to be the same in every part. The three distinct zones into which the region is divided at the present time are (a) Behar, (b) Bengal and (c) Orissa.

(a) *Behar*.

Of Behar proper—one of my students, Chatterjee, now working under Prof. Rivet in the University of Paris, recently published an exhaustive study of two of the

---

1 Aitareya Brahmana VII, 18.

2 Bhandarkar, R. G.—Early History of the Deccan. Bombay Gazetteer, Volumes I and II, pages 133-275; Bombay, 1896.

3 The Ramayana, III, 13.

4 The Mahabharata, III, 96-97.

5 Aiyangar, S. K.—Ancien India, pages 1—14; London, 1911.

6 Op. cit., page 234.

most important sections of its population, namely the Maithil and Kanaujiya Brahmins.[1] Chatterjee took the measurements of 190 Maithilis and 160 Kanaujiyas, and obtained the value of $2 \cdot 25 \pm 0 \cdot 10$ for the Reduced C. R. L. between them, and came to the conclusion that the two groups belong undoubtedly to the same racial stock.[2] In Tables X and X (*a*) are given the Reduced and Crude C. R. L.'s of the Behari Brahmins measured by Chatterjee, with the main racial groups of Northern and Southern India, from which it will be seen that their closest relations are with the Uriya and the Telegu Brahmins, and slightly less with the Nambudiris of Malabar. If the disturbing factor of personal equation was absent, it is not improbable that the values of the C. R. L.'s would have been much less. With the Bengali castes, the U. P. Brahmins and the Sikhs, the Behari Brahmins do not appear to be related. in spite of the historical associations of Behar and Bengal.

(*b*) *Bengal.*

Geographically, the province of Bengal extends from the foot of the Himalayas to the Bay of Bengal, and from Chotanagpur to the frontiers of Assam and Burma. The northern parts of Jalpaiguri, Rangpur and Cooch Behar however, until the middle of the 16th century formed part of the Koch Kingdom of Kamrupa.[3] Similarly, the territories bordering on the Chittagong Hill tracts, came under the influence of the Magh tribes settled in the adjoining hills. Ethnologically therefore these two tracts should be considered separately from the Central Deltaic plains of the Ganges and Brahmaputra, the Centre of the Bengali speaking people.

Risley was the first to have anthropometric measurements taken on the people of Bengal on 20 groups, of which 5 were from the Chittagong Hills.[4] The mean value of the Cephalic Index of the 15 Bengali groups obtained by Risley was 76·9, and of the 5 hill tribes of Chittagong 79·9. The corresponding values of the Nasal Indices were given as 78·7 and 82·7 respectively[5] but the corrected figures for the mean Cephalic and Nasal Indices of the 15 Bengali castes should be 77·1 and 79·2.[6] In the higher castes however, an increase in the value of the Cephalic and a decrease in that of the Nasal Index were observed ; the mean Cephalic and Nasal Indices of the Brahmins being 78·8 and 70·8 and of the Kayastha 78·3 and 70·7 respectively.[7]

Risley's views[8] regarding the ethnic origins of the Bengali are well known and were based on the assumption that brachycephaly and platyrhiny are the respective characters of the Mongolian and Dravidian Races. Consequently, brachycephaly noticed among the Chittagong tribes and platyrhiny found among the semi-aboriginal tribes living on the borders of Western Bengal were grouped together, and the racial alloy thus derived, was termed the Mongolo-Dravidian or the Bangali! Unfortunately, the groups selected by Risley as representatives of the Mongolo-Dravidian type, namely, the Brahmins, the Kayasthas, the Rajbansi Magh of Chittagong, the Mals of Bankura and Midnapur and the Koch of Jalpaiguri and Rangpur, cannot all be regarded as forming parts of the Bengali people, though living within the political boundaries of Bengal. Thus, for example the Rajbansi Magh, who live in the hill tracts of Chittagong and are one of the three main endogamous divisions of the Magh tribe, originally came from Arakan and are considered to be Indo-Chinese in race.[9] Their social and clan organisation, and such names as Ahong, Sepotang, Pangdung, Thafasu, Thianga [10], *etc.*, of the men measured for Risley at Rangamati (the head-quarters of the Chittagong Hill Tracts), show conclusively that though settled in the Chittagong hill districts for a considerable time, their tribal characters and names are still intact. Similarly, the Mals, now settled in Bankura, Birbhoom, etc., as Risley himself admits, migrated from the Rajmahal hills and are racially identical with the Mal Paharias, Mals, etc., of the Santhal Parganas.[11] Lastly. the Rajbansi Kóch of Jalpaiguri and Rangpur are really the descendants of the Koch tribe who conquered North Bengal. Most of the men measured for Risley have such names as Paia, Lethru, Lobu, Alinga, Enna, Tandu, Lobai [12], etc., which are certainly not Bengali names. Col. Waddell who also measured these Koch in Jalpaiguri, considered them to be "distinctly mongoloid" [13]. Conclusions based on these tribes, therefore, which are admittedly of foreign origin, though now settled for sometime in the outlying

[1] Chatterjee, B. K.—A Comparative Study of the Somatic Affinities of the Maithil and Kanaujiya Brahmins of Behar. Anthr. Bull. of the Z.S.I., No. II ; Calcutta, 1934.

[2] *Ibid., pages 108-109.*

[3] Gait, E. A.—The History of Assam, 1894.

[4] Risley, H. H.—The Tribes and Castes of Bengal, Anthropometric Data, Volume I, pages 1—229, Calcutta, 1891.

[5] Op. cit., pages I—VII.

[6] Mahalanobis, P. C.—A revision of Risley's Anthropometric Data—*Sankhya*, pages 93—105: Volume I, Part I ; Calcutta, 1933.

[7] Mahalanobis, P. C.—Op. cit., 1933.

[8] Risley, H. H.—The People of India, Calcutta, 1915.

[9] Risley, H. H.—The Tribes and Castes of Bengal, Volume II, pages 28-30 : Calcutta, 1891.

[10] Anthropometric Data, pages 206—212.

[11] Tribes and Castes of Bengal, Volume II, page 46.

[12] Anthropometric Data, Volume I, pages 166—171.

[13] J. A. S. B.—Volume LXIX. Part III, page 48.

districts of Bengal, cannot be regarded as applicable to the true Bengali people. If Risley had tried to determine the racial affinities of the Bengali, from the measurements of the castes living in the lower central valleys of the Ganges and Bramahputra, it would have been clear to him, that groups such as the Brahmins and the Kayasthas, differ materially from the foregoing tribes, both in the shape of the head and the nose. They have neither the flatness of the face, the paucity of the facial and body hair, nor the epicanthic fold characteristic of the mongoloid tribe like the Magh and Koch. As early as 1916 Mr. Ramaprasad Chanda, [1] called attention to these defects in Risley's account of the origin of the Bengali people, but with the notable exception of the late Giuffrida Ruggeri, [2] who gave his whole hearted support to his criticisms, Mr. Chanda's views, until very recently did not receive the attention they deserved. The origin of the brachycephalic characters of the Bengali head has therefore to be sought elsewhere.

In the course of the present enquiry I took measurements of three Bengali castes, *e.g.*, the Rarhi Brahmins, the Dakshin Rarhiya Kayasthas, and the Pods of the 24 Parganas, as representing the three sections of the Bengali people of the Central Deltaic region removed from the zone of Mongoloid influence. Measurements of these castes are given in Table I. It will be seen from the figures given in Table I, that the Bengali Brahmins are of moderate Stature with $1680 \cdot 30 \pm 5 \cdot 14$ as their mean Stature. The head is nearly round (C. I. $78 \cdot 93 \pm 0 \cdot 33$) though not falling strictly within the brachycephalic class. The vault of the head is high, the mean Auricular height being $123 \cdot 38 \pm 0 \cdot 84$. The forehead is broad and well arched. The cheek bones are well spread out. The nose is long, and high the mean Nasal Index and the mean Nasal elevation or depth being $67 \cdot 71 \pm 0 \cdot 62$ and $26 \cdot 78 \pm 0 \cdot 22$ respectively.

The Kayasthas have about the same Stature ($1670 \cdot 71 \pm 3 \cdot 87$) but compared to the Brahmins, they are more broad headed (C. I. $80 \cdot 84 \pm 0 \cdot 26$), and of slightly higher vault, the mean Auricular height being $124 \cdot 66 \pm 0 \cdot 46$. The forehead and the cheek bones are also slightly broader and the general shape of the face is a little more rounded. The nose is long and high pitched, the mean Nasal Index and the Nasal elevation or depth being respectively $68 \cdot 11 \pm 0 \cdot 38$ and $26 \cdot 42 \pm 0 \cdot 17$. In contrast to the Brahmins and the Kayasthas, the Pods are shorter (mean Stature $1628 \cdot 26 \pm 4 \cdot 63$). The head is less round (C. I. $77 \cdot 13 \pm 0 \cdot 37$) and the vault of the head somewhat lower (Aur. height $120 \cdot 62 \pm 0 \cdot 62$). The face is also narrower and shorter, and the nose somewhat shorter and less prominent; the mean Nasal Index and the Nasal elevation or depth being $71 \cdot 81 \pm 0 \cdot 52$ and $24 \cdot 06 \pm 0 \cdot 17$ respectively.

Tables XI and XI (*a*) contain the values of the Reduced and Crude C. R. L.'s. It will be seen from the figures given in these Tables that the Brahmins and the Kayasthas are intimately related, the value of the Reduced Co-efficient being only $1 \cdot 49 \pm 0 \cdot 26$. When the individual characters are compared, the values of 'α' are below 6 in all, excepting three, *viz.*, the Sagittal Arc, Cephalic Index and Total Facial Index where they are $11 \cdot 99$, $7 \cdot 88$ and $6 \cdot 53$ respectively. With the Pods however, neither of the two appears to show any relation, as indicated by the high values of the Co-efficients—the Reduced C. R. L. between the Brahmins and the Pods being $15 \cdot 70 \pm 0 \cdot 34$, and that between the Kayasthas and the Pods $18 \cdot 89 \pm 0 \cdot 25$.

In skin colour (Table LV), (considering both the exposed and the unexposed parts of the body), both the Brahmins and the Kayasthas show a small percentage of men having a rosy white tint (5-6 per cent.), 14-22 per cent. of light brown, 62 per cent. of brown and 24 and 31 per cent. of dark brown respectively. Among the Pods the light brown element is absent, 6% are brown, but, 64 per cent. of them are dark brown, and 28 per cent. tawny brown. In the colour of the eyes there is a small percentage of light clear brown (Nos. 6-7) among both the Brahmins and the Kayasthas, but the majority have dark brown eyes (Nos. 2-3). The Pods have either black or dark brown eyes. In hair colour, though the majority have a black tint (No. 27), among both the Brahmins and the Kayasthas there is a small brown element and among the latter one individual was observed with reddish hair (No. 3) and two with light brown hair (Nos. 5-6).

From Table LV (*a*) it will appear that large percentages of all the three castes have well developed pilious system—in the Pods it is slightly less than among the other two. The supra-orbital ridges are prominent [Table LV (*b*)], and the form of the eye is round among both the Brahmins and the Kayasthas. Among the Pods however 10 per cent. of the people have slightly oblique eyes. Among the Brahmins no case of epicanthic fold was noticed. Among the Kayasthas 2 per cent. of the people, and among the Pods 4 per cent. showed the presence of epicanthic fold. Among the Brahmins 74 per cent. of the people had high pitched noses, of which 6 per cent. were convex. Among the Kayasthas 61 per cent. had high pitched noses, 10 per cent. of which were convex. As against this, the Pods had 54 per cent. well developed noses, none of which were convex. Against 2 and 3 per cent. of the Brahmins and Kayasthas respectively, the Pods showed 18 per cent. of the people with flat noses. Traces of prognathism were found in 6 per cent. of the Brahmins and Kayasthas and 24 per cent. of the Pods. Both in the form and size of their physical structure and integumentary colours therefore, the Pods appear to be different from the Brahmins and Kayasthas of Bengal.

---

[1] Chanda, Ramaprasad.—The Indo-Aryan Races, pages 65—70; Rajshahi, 1916.

[2] The First Outlines of a Systemtic Anthropology of Asia by V. Giuffrida Ruggeri,—pages 44-46. (English translation by Prof. H. C. Chakladar, University of Calcutta, Anthropological Papers No. 6.) Calcutta, 1921.

In addition to these data, one of my students, Mr. A. K. Mitra, now working under Prof. Mollison in the University of Munich, Germany, has recently taken a large number of measurements on 875 Bengalis belonging to 5 different castes, and I am grateful to him for allowing me to use his unpublished data here.

In the Tables below are given the Crude and the Reduced C. R. L.'s of the 5 castes measured by Mitra :—

Crude C. R. L.'s (24 characters only).

Names of castes.	R. Vaidya.	B. Vaidya.	Subarnabanik.	Mahisya.	Namasudra.
Rarhiya Vaidya.	..	1·09	5·37	6·67	15·55
Bangaja Vaidya.	1·09	..	3·23	5·59	14·70
Subarnabanik.	5·37	3·23	..	12·28	32·93
Mahisya..	6·67	5·59	12·28	..	4·79
Namasudra.	15·55	14·70	32·93	4·79	..

The probable error is ±0·19 in all cases.

Reduced C. R. L.'s (*24 characters only*).

Names of castes.	Rarhia Vaidya.	Bangaja Vaidya.	Subarnabanik.	Mahisya.	Namasudra.
Rahriya Vaidya. (125)	..	0·87 ±0·15	3·22 ±0·11	5·34 ±0·15	9·33 ±0·11
Bangaja Vaidya. (125)	0·87 ±0·15	..	1·94 ±0·11	4·47 ±0·15	8·82 ±0·11
Subarnabanik. (250)	3·22 ±0·11	1·94 ± 0·11	..	7·37 ±0·11	13·17 ±0·08
Mahisya. (125)	5·34 ±0·15	4·47 ±0·15	7·37 ±0·11	..	2·87 ±0·11
Namasudra. (250)	9·33 ± 0·11	8·82 ±0·11	13·17 ±0·08	2·87 ±0·11	..

It will appear from the figures given in these Tables that the lowest value of 0·87±0·15 is found between the two sections of the Vaidya caste. Between the Subarnabaniks and the Vaidyas the relationship is also intimate—the Bangaja Vaidya showing a somewhat lower value. With the Mahisyas there is also distinct relationship, but with the Namasudras the associations of the Vaidyas and Subarnabaniks are more distant.

The C. R. L.'s of the five castes measured by Mitra, with the three taken by me, are given in the following Tables :—

Crude C. R. L.'s (*22 characters only*).

Names of castes.	Rahriya Vaidya.	Bangaja Vaidya.	Subarnabanik.	Mahisya.	Namasudra.
Brahmin	16·40	12·26	20·89	20·45	19·19
Kayastha	18·12	14·86	29·93	28·67	34·16
Pod	11·50	10·71	18·21	9·02	4·70

Reduced C. R. L.'s (*22 characters only*).

Names of casts.	Rahriya Vaidya.	Bangaja Vaidya.	Subarnabanik.	Mahisya.	Namasudra.
Brahmin	22·96 ±0·28	17·16 ±0·28	25·07 ±0·24	28·63 ±0·28	23·02 ±0·24
Kayastha	16·31 ±0·18	13·37 ±0·18	20·95 ±0·14	25·80 ±0·18	23·91 ±0·14
Pod	16·10 ±0·28	14·99 ±0·28	21·85 ±0·24	12·63 ±0·28	5·56 ±0·24

The lowest value of the Reduced C. R. L. is between the Pod and the Namasudra, namely 5·53±0·24 and next to it are the values between the Pod and the Mahisya, the Kayastha and the Vaidya, the Pod and the Vaidya and the Brahmin and the Vaidya. Between the rest the values are somewhat higher. As however the factor of personal equation has to be taken into account, it is probable the degrees of true relationships between all these groups are much smaller, than the figures given seem to indicate. It may consequently be concluded that the racial basis of the Pod, the Mahisya and the Namasudra is fundamentally the same. The upper section formed the Brahmins and the Kayasthas, however appear to be somewhat different. The relationship of these two, with the Vaidyas and the Subarnabaniks appears to be close, but exactly how much, cannot be actually determined owing to our ignorance of the part played by personal equation in these comparisons.

Dainelli[1] has published the measurements of 65 crania (42 male and 23 female) purported to have belonged to the Chandalas or Pariah caste of Bengal. The mean Cranial Capacity of the male crania was found to be 1368 c.c. and that of the females 1277 c.c. Of the 42 male skulls, 26 had a Cranial Index below 75 and 5 between 80·1—83·34. Of the 23 female skulls only 2 showed Brachycranial Index. Twenty one, among the male skulls were orthocranial, and 20 hypsicranial; the corresponding figures for the female skulls being 11 and 11. The mean Min. Frontal Diameter of the male skulls was 91·67, and that of the females 91·38. The mean Horizontal Circumference for the males was 488·33mm. and for the females 476·08mm. The mean Naso-alveolar length of the male skulls was 67·26 and the Max. Bizygomatic breadth 124·26. In the female skulls the corresponding values are 63·53 and 116·25. The mean Nasal Index of the male skulls is 50·56 and that of the female skulls 51·47. These figures show the skulls to be of small size, dolichocranial in the main, of moderate to high cranial vault, of narrow long face and of short broad nose. It will be noticed however, that they are not in agreement with any of the genuine Bengali castes mentioned before, and it is doubtful whether they belonged at all to the Bengali. These skulls, it may be mentioned, were presented by Dr. Hacks to the Société d'Anthropologie de Paris, and are mentioned in its catalogue as belonging to Bengalis of the lower castes living on the lower banks of the Ganges.[2] But Dainelli, who searched for detailed information regarding these skulls, was unable to find precise information either of the locality from which they were taken, or of the race or caste to which they belonged. For, the maps which accompanied the gift were lost, or probably burnt, as happened with so many other documents belonging to the great Broca. In the minutes of the Committee of the Société d' Anthropologie de Paris however, to which these crania were presented, they were referred to as that of the Pariahs. On one of the crania the word "Hugli" was written.[3] This scanty available information, Dainelli very justly considered, only gave the right to classify these crania as roughly belonging to the Pariahs or more correctly to the Chandalas inhabiting the banks of the Hugli.[4] In the writings of the Biometric School however, these crania have figured prominently as those of the Bengalis, and its classification of the latter race is based on these skulls. Those who are acquainted with the Hindu Funerary customs are aware that it is the invariable practice with the Hindus to burn their dead, and in only exceptional cases such as that of the Jugis or Vaisnavas that the dead are interred. Among the Bengali, there is strictly speaking no such caste as the Pariahs; and the Chandalas, Doms, Scavangers, etc., who occupy a somewhat analogous position are not generally indigenous to the province but are formed by the semi-hinduised aboriginals from Chota Nagpur and Santal Parganas, who come to Bengal for these works. The Mills, on the banks of the Hugli, also employ large numbers of labourers belonging to the lower castes of Bihar and Orissa, some of whom observe burial as a method of disposal of their dead.

In view of these facts it would be unsafe to regard these skulls as those of the 'Bengali' but more probably of some of the semi-hinduised aboriginals from neighbouring hills, with whom they agree also in the shape and proportions of the head and the face.

(c) *Orissa.*

The valley of the Mahanadi, southwest of Bengal is the ancient kingdom of Kalinga inhabited by one of the eastern Vratyas. Measurements of 586 Uriyas belonging to 14 groups were taken under Risley's directions and he considered them to be the southernmost section of the Mongolo-Dravidians.[5] One hundred and forty three Sasana Brahmins of Orissa were measured by me in the interior of the Puri district (Table 1). The mean Stature of the Sasanas obtained by me was 1642·92±3·32, the mean Cephalic Index 77·31±0·26, and the mean Nasal Index was 70·46±0·35.

---

[1] Dainelli, Jacopo—Studio sui crani Bengalesi—Archivio L'Antropologia e la Etnologia, Volume XXII, Fasc. 2, pages 291-341 and Fasc. 3, pages 371—448; Firenze, 1892.

[2] *Ibid.*, page 339.

[3] Dainelli, Jacopo—Studio sui crani Bengalesi—Archivio L'Antropologia e la Etnologia, Volume XXII, pages 338-340.

[4] *Ibid.*, page 340.

[5] Risley, H. H., 1915, Op. cit., page 40.

In skin colour the Uriyas are darker than the Brahmins of Bengal and U. P. with a much higher percentage of the darker and a smaller percentage of the lighter shades (Table LV). The colour of the eye is mostly dark brown but there is a small percentage of clear light brown eyes (Nos 6-7). Similarly the hair colour is mostly black but there is small percentage of dark brown hair.

As will appear from Tables LV (*b* and *c*), the supra-orbital ridges are moderately prominent. In 14 per cent. the eyes were found to be slanting, and 7 per cent. had epicanthic folds. The nose is on the average prominent, but 17 per cent. of those measured had depressed nasal roots. The face varied from a pear to a square shape, and in 17 per cent. of the people alveolar prognathism was noticed.

The values of the C.R.L.'s given in Tables XI and XI (*a*) show that their closest relationship is with the Pods of Bengal with a value of 8·19±0·23 for the Reduced C. R. L. With the Brahmins and Kayasthas of Bengal no association seems to exist, but with the Brahmins of Behar (see *ante*), of whom they were traditionally supposed to have once formed a part, there appears to be a definite kinship.

There is a series of 25 male Uriya skulls in the collections of the Indian Museum which have been measured by Sir William Turner.[1] From the examination of these skulls, Turner found several types, which led him to think that " no proper history of the dead had been obtained and in consequence the skulls had not been properly identified". For this he was taken to task by Prof. Karl Pearson who considered that his act " has succeeded in casting discredit on the series as a homogeneous group".[2] If however Pearson had taken the trouble to read an easily available book like Risley's People of India,[3] a little carefully he would have found that Turner's doubts were thoroughly justified. Risley [4] remarks that "as a matter of fact most of these skulls were acquired during the Orissa famine of 1866, and the only description they bear is "Uriya" or "Orissa", the word 'Hindu' being occasionally added. To any one who is acquainted with the conditions which prevailed in Orissa at that time it was obvious that a given skull may have belonged to a broad-nosed Dravidian from the hill tracts, to a high caste Hindu of the coast strip, or to a Mongoloid pilgrim from Nepal, who died of starvation or cholera while seeking salvation at Jagannath." It is evident from these statements that these skulls cannot be taken as genuine Uriya as Prof. Pearson appears to consider, and are consequently of little value in throwing light on the Uriya racial type. It is a matter of great regret that Prof. Pearson and his followers while rightly laying stress on precise mathematical reduction of Anthropometric data, have taken for granted the authenticity of many of their cranial series without adequate enquiries. Of the 7 different series of Indian skulls given prominence to by the Biometric School, it has been shown that at least four, *viz*., the Maravar, the South Indian skulls measured by Montegazza, the so-called Bengali and Uriya skulls measured by Dainelli and Turner respectively, we have no precise information regarding their locality and race, and however persistent efforts may be made to re-establish their authenticity on purely theoretical grounds, as was done recently by Prof. Pearson, [5] all careful workers acquainted with Indian conditions will agree with Harrower,[6] in regarding them as having little bearing on the racial affinities of the people studied, in view of the 'much too obscurity of the origin and source of these skulls'.

6.—ASSAM.

The easternmost part of Northern India separated from Bhutan by the Himalayan range and from Upper Burma by the Patkoi mountains, and connected with the plains of Bengal on the north-west, is known as Assam (from Ahom, the Burmese conquerors of the land). It is a land consisting mostly of mountains, with two fertile plains separated by the Khasi-Jaintia hills. From the purely anthropological standpoint there is no part of India which is more interesting than Assam. Situated as it is, between the Eastern Himalayas, Southern Tibet, China, Burma and Bengal, its population has been derived from all these sources. From the former three it has received the bulk of its population, while Burma supplied it with its Ruling Dynasty from 1228 A. D. till the advent of the British in 1887. Besides these, the rich fertile valleys of the land have invited Hindu immigrants from North-Eastern India who carried the Hindu civilisation and social organisation into Assam at a very early date. The latter have formed the upper classes, with various degrees of intermixture, while the bulk of the population has remained since the days of Hiuen Tsang (7th century) "Indo-Chinese" in the main.[7] The nature of the topography of the country has kept the larger portion of the hill tribes in extreme isolation, with all their primitive habits and institutions almost intact.

---

1 Turner, Sir William.—Trans. of the Royal Society of Edinburgh, Volume XL, Part I, pages 59—129.

2 Pearson, Karl,—The Co-efficient of Racial Likeness as a test of samples, Biometrika, Volume XXB, pages 296-297.

3 Pages 19-20.

4 Loc. cit.; page 20.

5 Biometrika, Volume XXB, Parts III and IV, pages 294-300.

6 *Ibid*., page 248.

7 Si-yu-ki, Beal's translation, II, page 196.

The metric data available on the people of Assam consist of (1) the measurements of Waddell [1] on the different hill tribes, (2) on the Naga tribes by Hutton, and (3) the Khasis by the present writer, besides accounts of several series of skulls.

Col. Waddell measured 580 individuals belonging to 21 Assamese and 3 Foreign tribes, but as most of these series consist of a small number of individuals, the Co-efficients of Racial Likeness were calculated on 3 Assamese and one Sikkimese tribes only, as shown in the following Table [2]:—

Assam & Sikkim Tribes.

Tribes.	Crude C. R. L.	Reduced C. R. L.
Mande (Garo) and Lepcha	18·06	51·47
Lepcha (Rong) and Khasia	10·40	20·90
Khasia and Bodo (Kachari)	3·21	6·74
Bodo and Lepcha	8·13	23·57
Mande and Khasia	10·89	22·76
Mande and Bodo	3·69	10·89

It will be noticed from these figures that the lowest Co-efficient is found between the Khasia and the Kachari. The value of the C. R. L. between the Mande and the Bodo is also close, showing that these three tribes have a common racial substratum. With the Lepcha however none of the Assam tribes seems to bear any relationship.

Of the Assamese proper, of the Brahmaputra Valley, we have no metric data excepting 6 Kolitas measured by Waddell. In the absence of reliable measurements, it is impossible to determine how far they are racially allied to the neighbouring people of Bengal and Behar, though the inhabitants of the Eastern Surma Valley being composed of later immigrants from Eastern Bengal, are probably still closely related to them.

The tribes living along the hills on the Eastern frontiers as disclosed by Hutton's measurements of the Angami Naga,[3] and Turner's [4] 'Studies of Chin Lushai skulls', are in the main dolichocephalic in the shape and proportions of the head, but containing a small element of brachycephalic type allied to the Burmese. An examination of the large series of the Naga crania recovered by the Dewar Expedition from the Triangular Area in Upper Burma,[5] also confirmed this conclusion of the dolichocephalic character of the Naga head, but showed at the same time the presence of a definite Negrito strain. This is in agreement with Hutton's [6] discovery of frizzly haired men among the Angami Nagas.

7.—BURMA.

Though politically Burma still forms a part of India, and has been profoundly influenced by Hindu and later on Buddhistic religions and culture, ethnologically, like the outskirts of Assam, it forms an altogether separate kingdom, through which successive waves of mongolian tribes from Southern China have passed into the Malay Peninsula and beyond ; parts of which, having also penetrated Assam. In any successful attempt to unravel the racial affinities of the peoples living on the borders of Eastern India, a consideration of the various tribes living in Burma is almost indispensible. From the anthropo-geographical points of view the country may be divided into three distinct zones : i) a broad belt of wild and rugged hills adjoining the frontiers of Assam and Bengal, ii) the valleys of the Irawadi and its great tributory the Chindwin, and iii) the eastern hills and tablelands, traversed from north to south by the Salween river. Thanks to the labours of the late B. A. Gupte [7], we possess a fairly large number of measurements of the principal tribes of Burma. We have also serveral important Memoirs on 'Burmese' crania, published by Turner [8], Tildesley [9] and Basu[10]. In Tables XXIII and XXIII (a) are given the C. R.L.'s of the 10 principal tribes measured by Gupte. It will be observed from these Tables that the lowest value of the Reduced C. R. L. namely $3 \cdot 52 \pm 0 \cdot 23$ is found between the two groups of the Karens living near the deltaic plains. Between the Pwo-Karens and the Taungthus, the value of the C. R. L. is only slightly higher, namely $3 \cdot 54 \pm 0 \cdot 24$, but that of the latter and the Sgaw-Karens is considerably higher namely $9 \cdot 89 \pm 0 \cdot 23$. Between the Taungthus and the Talaings there is also close relationship, the value of the Reduced C. R. L. being $7 \cdot 26 \pm 0 \cdot 24$. According to the traditions [11] of the former, they were descended from the Talaings, and statistical analysis of their anthropometric measurements seems to bear this out. We must regard therefore all these four tribes, who live in contiguous districts, to be also racially related. How far there is a relationship between the

Waddell, L. A.—The Tribes of the Brahmaputra Valley, J.A.S.B., Volume LXIX, Part III, pages 1—127. Based on Waddell's measurements.

3 Hutton, J. H.—Angami Nagas, London, 1921.

4 Turner, Sir William.—Trans. of Royal Society Edinburgh, Volume XXXIX, Part III, pages 703—747.

5 Guha, B. S. and Basu, P. C.—Anthropological Bulletin of the Zoological Survey of India, No. I., page II. Calcutta, 192[illegible].

6 Hutton, J. H.—*Man in India*, Volume VII, pages 257—262, 1927.

7 Gupte, B.A. Anthronometric Data from Burma. Calcutta. 19[illegible]6.

8 Turner, Sir William- Trans. Roy. Soc. Edinburgh, Volume XXXIX. pages 700-747 ; 1900.

9 Tildesley, M. L.-Biometrika, Volume XIII. pages 176-262. 1920-21.

10 Basu P. C.- Trans. Bose. Inst. Calcutta, Volume VII, pages 271—318, 1933.

11 Census of India, Volume IX, Part 1, 1911.

Talaings and the Burmese it is not clear, for the value of the C. R. L., namely 15·52 ± 0·24 is just outside the figure usually considered to exhibit association between two racial samples, though from historical records we know that there has been close contact between these two races. It is to be presumed therefore that the Mons or the Talaings who built a powerful kingdom in the vicinity of Prome, which was subsequently broken up by the Burmese, did not mix their blood with that of their conquerors as much as one would otherwise have imagined. Ingenious attempts have been made by Phayre and Yule to derive the Burmese name for the Mons, namely Talaing from " Telinga," supposed to be a variant of " Kalinga " the ancient name for Orissa. They might have derived it more appropriately from " Telengana," the country of the Telegus, somewhat further south. Unfortunately a comparison of the somatic traits of these two peoples, does not lend any support to the theory of their common origin, and as has been shown already, the Mons or the Telaings form a common racial unit with the Karens of the Plains and the Taungthus and are wholly unconnected with the " Telegus " of Telengana, the one being a highly brachycephalic and the other a highly dolichocephalic race.

Between the Talaings and the Palaungs there is no racial kinship though both of them, speak Mon-Khmer languages. The latter however are closely related to the southern Chin with a value of 5·18±0·23 for the Reduced C. R. L., and also to the Kachin, the Shan and the Burmese, the values of the C. R. L. with the three last groups being 7·09±0·24 ; 8·05±0·24 and 8·14±0·24 respectively. The value of the Reduced C. R. L. with the Taungthus is also fairly low, namely 14·86±0·24, indicating probably slight relationship.

The Kachin, living in the Kachin hills extending from Bhamo to Hsipaw, are related to the Palaung, Southern Chin and the Chinese Shan or " Shan-ta-loi " with 7·09 ± 0·24 ; 8·27±0·23 and 11·23±0·24 as the values of the C. R. L.'s with these three tribes. Gupte [1] has called the last " Shan-ta-loke " but in the Upper Burma Gazetteer, compiled by Scott [2] and the Census Reports [3] they have been referred to as "Shan-ta-loi." Due to his unfamiliarity with the region and its languages, it is apparent that Gupte has made a mistake in the transliteration of the correct name of the tribe. " The classification of the races of Burma," as Captain Green [4] has rightly observed, " has been complicated, as the names now applied to them are not their own names, but those given to them by their neighbours. Thus the words, Kachin, Chin and Karen appear to be derived from three different pronounciations of the original Burmese word for the wild hill tribes 'Kakhyen.'" However that be, the Chinese Shans or the "Shan-ta-loi" though closely related to the Kachin and the Southern Chin, do not appear to have any affinities with the Shans proper or any of the other tribes of Burma. Mr. Morgan Webb [5] regards the Southern Chin as an advance guard of the Kachin, so called, to distinguish them from the Chin tribes living within the Chinese frontiers. The small value of the Reduced C. R. L. between the two tribes (8·27±0·23) seems to indicate that there is probably a great deal of truth in his contention.

All these northern hill tribes again seem to be closely related to the Burmese proper of the lower Irawady valley and the latter shows more intimate association with them, than with any of the other tribes of the Plains. Their C. R. L.'s with the Kachin and the Shan are the smallest, namely 6·57±0·24 and 7·42±0·24 respectively, but with the Chinese Shan no kinship appears to be indicated (19·02±0·24). Lastly with the Plains-Karen groups, the Taungthu and possibly also with the Talaing as already noted, the Burmese possess some association.

We have therefore two broad racial groups among the tribes living within the territories of Burma, namely, i) the southern group of the Plains-peoples, living along the lower course of the Salween river and consisting of the Sgaw and Pwo Karens, the Taungthu and the Talaing and ii) the northern group of hill tribes composed of the Palaung, the Kachin, the Southern Chin and the Chinese Shan who live n the hills between Bhamo and the Shan States. The Burmese proper belong also to this group and the somewhat distant association that is seen between the Burmese and the tribes belonging to group i) may probably have been due to close historical contact lasting through several centuries rather than to a basic racial unity.

With regard to skin colour the northern hill tribes, are much lighter, specially the Palaung but the mongoloid characteristics of the eye and the face are found equally strongly marked among both, with the exception of the Karens in whom these features are not so prominent [6].

In addition to the anthropometric measurements taken by Gupte and discussed above, some excellent series of measurements on Burmese crania are also available. Chief among them are those published by Turner [7] on 28 male Burmese crania from Prome, Tharawaddy, Hanthawaddy and Ava. The mean Cranial Capacity of these skulls is 1388c.c. The mean Cranial length and breadth are 172·8mm. and 141·7mm. respectively and the proportions between the two 82·1. The mean Basi-Bregmatic height is 135.1mm. and the Length-Height Index 78·2. The mean Nasal length is 52mm., the mean Nasal breadth 25·3mm. and the proportions between the two 48·6. The Maximum Bizygomatic breadth is 134 mm. and the mean Orbital

[1] Gupte, B. A.- *General Indefinite Characteristics of the Tribes of Burma*, Calcutta, 1906.
[2] Scott, Sir J. George- Gazetter of Upper Burma and the Shan States, 1891.
[3] Census of India, Volume IX, 1901 and 1911.
[4] Green, J.H.- Appendix C, pages 245-247 ; Census of India, Volume XI, 1931.
[5] Census of India, Volume IX, 1911.
[6] Gupte, B. A.- Op. cit., 1906.
[7] Turner, Sir William, 1900, Op. cit., pages 700 747.

Index is 85·0. The 27 male skulls of Tildesley's "A" series[1] belonging to authentic Burmese, have a mean Cranial Capacity of 1406·9c.c. The mean Cranial length and breadth of these skulls are 173·5mm. and 143·7mm. respectively and the mean proportions between the two 82·9. The Basi-Bregmatic height obtained by Tildesley is 136·8mm. and the Length-Height Index 78·8. The mean Nasal length and breadth are 53·1mm. and 28·1mm. respectively and the Nasal Index 52·7. The Max. Bizygomatic breadth is 134·0 mm. Recently Basu[2] has measured 36 Burmese crania belonging to the collections of the Anthropological Section of the Indian Museum of which 30 were male and 6 female. These crania were obtained from a known Burmese Cemetery near Prome. The mean Cranial Capacity of the 30 male Cranial calculated by means of Lea-Pearson formula No. 10 is found to be 1450c.c. The Max. Cranial length and breadth are 173·3mm. and 141·1mm. respectively and the proportions between the two 81·4. The mean Basi-Bregmatic height is 134·6 and the Length-Height Index 77·6. The mean Nasal length and breadth are 51·2mm. and 26·7mm. respectively and Nasal Index 52·5. The Max. Bizygomatic breadth is 131·2mm.

Basu[3] has also investigated the forward growth of the facial parts by means of projections drawn from the Trans. auricular Axis at right angles to the Frankfort Plane. His studies showed, that in the Burmese skulls, the retrocession of the lateral nasal walls and the forward growth of the zygomatic bones were present in the same extent as in the Naga Group I,[4] and Chinese skulls.[5] These features, as Sir Arthur Keith[5] has called attention to, give the Mongolian face, its charactristic flattened appearance.

The anthropometric and the cranial measurements therefore agree in showing the Burmese tribes to be brachycephalic with broad nose and flattened mongolian face. The aboriginal tribes living across the Assam frontiers tend however towards dolichocephaly and are medium-nosed though exhibiting the other characteristic mongloid features. In his classification of the Burmese races that Captain Green[6] has recently attempted, he has included the Nagas of the Hukong Valley and the adjoining tracts, with the Palaung-Wa tribes, the Mons and the Lulo-Muhso into one racial group, mainly on cultural and liguistic grounds. The Naga skulls recovered by the Dewar Expedition from the Triangle,[7] as had already been stated belong to a dolichocephalic race and are essentially different from the Palaung, Wa and Mon groups who are all markedly brachycephalic. They therefore form one racial unit with the Naga tribes across the Assam borders and the tribes living within Lats. 25°-28° N. and Longs. 94°-98° E. in the Namphuk Tanai and Torung valleys of the unadministered northernmost parts of Burma and are therefore racially aligned to the Assam tribes rather than to those of Burma. In his other two groups Green, included the Kachin and the Southern Chin in one, and the Plains-Karens (the Sgaw and the Pwo) and the Taungthu (though he seems doubtful about the latter) in the other. He considers the Hkahku (of the Triangle) and the Hukong Valley Kachins to be different from the Bhamo and the Lashio Kachins and the Hill Karens to be allied to the Palaung-Wa rather than to the Plains-Karens. We have no metric data on the Kachins of the Triangle and the Hukong Valley, but all the available measurements, including the Kachins of Hsipaw and Bhamo indicate the fundamental racial unity of the northern hill tribes and the Burmese proper and their difference from the plains-people, inhabiting the southwestern parts. Green's classifications so far as they relate to the Kachin, Southern Chin and the Karen Taungthu groups receive support from anthropometry but his inclusion of the Palaung-Wa and the Mons in the division composed of the Nagas and the Nunai Valley tribes seems unjustified even though they may "lie along to the same line of migration."

8.—THE TRIBAL GROUPS.

In Table V, are given the measurements of three tribal groups of which the Khasis and the Chenchus were measured by me and the Nicobarese by Dr. Naidu. The Khasis measured by me came from Cherapunji, Mylliem and Mawflong. As some amount of miscegenation is supposed to have taken place among tne Khasis of Shillong, no person was taken from that quarter.

The Khasis, as will appear from the measurements are of short stature (1569·10 ± 4·67) of medium but high head (Mean C. I. 77·30 ± 0·20), broad flat squarish face, and low medium nose (Mean N. I. 77·40 ± 0·52). A small percentage of people show reddish-white skin colour (No. 10) and light brown (Nos. 12-14), 67 % dark brown (Nos. 15-18) and the rest tawny brown. The eye colour varies from black to brown (Nos. 1-3) and no instance of light brown or hazel eyes was noticed in a Khasi of unmixed blood. Similarly, the colour of the hair is uniformly black (No. 27), but a small percent (1·23) shows a dark brown tint. The character of the hair is usually staight but a small percent (4) has wavy hair. In about 4 % the beard and the moustache are moderate but among 46 % they are absent. Similarly, on the body the hair is either absent (59%) or slightly noticeable only. The supra-orbital ridges in the average Khasi are moderately strong but a large section, about 44 % do not show any. In 45 %, the eye is found to be round

---

[1] Tildesley, M. L.- 1920-21.. Op. cit.
[2] Basu, P. C. 1933.—Op. cit.
[3] *Ibid.*, pages 309-314.
[4] Guha, B. S. and Basu, P. C., 1931.—Op. cit., pages 15-19.
[5] Keith, Sir Arthur—J. R. A. I., Volume LXI, page 170.
[6] Green, Capt. J. H. 1933.—Op. cit. [7] Guha, B.S. and Basu, P.C. 1932.—Op. cit

and in 55 % it is slanting, while in 32 % traces, and on 31 % a marked degree of the epicanthic fold were noticed. The nasal bridge is usually flat and in the majority the nasal root is considerably depressed. In a few however, about 9 %, the nose is fine and prominent. Alveolar prognathism was noticed in 20 % of the people measured.

The Nicobarese measured by Dr. Naidu belong to Chaura, Great Nicobar, Little Nicobar, Camorto, Terressa and Bompoka. The purest type among the Nicobarese is considered to be found among the people of Chaura[1]. In Kar Nicobar, miscegenetion with the Burmese has taken place and in Teressa and Nankauri also some amount of Chinese and Malay blood undoubtedly exist[2]. For this reason, Dr. Naidu avoided Kar Nicobar and Nankauri altogether and got the larger portion of his subjects from Chaura. A few individuals however, were measured in Teressa but all possible precautions were taken to ensure that no one suspected of having Malay or Chinese blood was included among his subjects. The sample of the Nicobarese discussed here may therefore be regarded as that of pure Nicobarese as far as it was possible to ascertain.

The Shompen or the tribe living in the islands of Great Nicobar who are of much darker skin colour and not infrequently possess wavy and curly hair and are linguistically and culturally very different from the coastal Nicobarese[3] have not been included. Dr. Naidu measured 11 men at a Shompen village on the Alexandria river in the interior of Great Nicobar, but as this number was too small, it was not thought safe to make any comparisons with the Nicobarese.

From the measurements given in Table V, it will appear that the Nicobarese like the Khasis are short (mean St. 1589·25 ± 3·22) of medium but high head —the mean Cephalic Index being 76·76 ± 0·27 and the Auricular height 126·07 ± 0·38. The nose verges on platyrhiny, as the mean Nasal Index (83·87 ± 0·43) indicates, with a sunken bridge (the mean Orbito-nasal Index being 111·81±0·22). The face is low but broad with 82·08±0·26 as the mean Total Facial Index and 138·31 ± 0·26 as the mean Bizygomatic breadth. The Bigonial breadth is also large, namely, 102·26 ± 0·24 giving the face a squarish shape[4]. The skin colour varies from dark to tawny brown (Nos. 17-24) and therefore much darker than that of the average Khasi. The eye colour is uniformly dark brown and the hair black (No. 27). Almost all have straight hair but a very small percentage (1 %) shows curly hair. There is an abundant growth of hair on the head, but the beard and the moustache is either absent or only slightly present. The supra-orbital ridges are slightly marked but in a few cases (1%) they are rather prominent. In the majority, the eye is oblique and in 89% traces, and in 11% a marked degree of the epicanthic fold were noticed. In nearly every case prognathism was found. Lt.-Col. R. B. Seymour Sewell [5], who as Surgeon-Naturalist to the Government of India, spent 20 years in the Bay of Bengal and has very intimate knowledge of both the Nicobarese and the Andamanese, is of the opinion that the alveolar proganathism generally found among the adult Nicobarese is due to their peculiar manner of eating raw cocoanut but is not a true racial character as it is not found among the children.

In Tables XVIII and XVIII (*a*) are given the C. R. L.'s of three Mongoloid tribes of which the Uzbeg are a Turki speaking people from Russian Turkistan, and the Khasis and the Nicobarese are both Monkhmer speaking peoples from Assam and the Nicobar Islands respectively. The value of the Reduced C. R. L. between the Uzbeg and the Khasi is 67·22 ± 0·38 and that of the Uzbeg and the Nicobarese 108·50 ± 0·33. There can therefore be no suggestion of any relation between the Uzbeg and these two tribes. Between the Khasis and the Nicobarese however, the value is 21·59 ± 0·19. Considering that the measurements have been taken by two persons, the Co-efficient in my opinion is sufficiently low to denote some amount of relationship between these two tribes and the fact that both speak Monkhmer languages is not without significance.

It is generally agreed that the Nicobarese have migrated from the Tenassarim district of Burma and have occupied the coastal portions of the Nicobar Islands. They do not exhibit however any somatic affinity with either of the Monkhmer speaking tribes of Burma, namely the Mons (Talaings), and the Palaung-Wa of northern Shan States, who are both brachycephalic races and are markedly different from the Nicobarese. If the view advanced here, namely the existence of a racial kinship between the Nicobarese and the Khasis be correct, it is probable that the racial strain which the Nicobarese brought with them and still retain along with the Khasis, once formed the common racial substratum of the Monkhmer speaking peoples of Assam and Burma ; and the Mons and the Palaung—Wa tribes were of different racial affinities as their kinships respectively with the Karen-Taungthu and the Kachin-Southern Chin groups indicate—who subsequently adopted Monkhmer languages as a result probably of intimate contact with these peoples.

The other aboriginal tribes of which the C. R. L.'s have been calculated are the Chenchu, the Bhil, the Kadar and Nattu Malayan of Southern India. These four tribes were measured by me and I am indebted to Dr. P. C. Basu for allowing me to use his unpublished data on the two Chota Nagpur tribes.

---

1 Bonington, B. C.—Census of India. Volume II, page 69, 1931.
2 *Ibid.*,—pages 68—69.
3 Mans, E. H.—*Ibid.*, pages 68—69.
4 Guha, B.S.—Census of India, 1931, Volume II, Part I, page 69.
5 Sewell, Seymour, R. B.— *Journal of the Bombay Natural History Society*, page 972, 1922.

The Chenchus occupy mainly the Nalaimallais hill ranges in the Karnool and Ganturdistricts of the Madras Presidency, but are also found across the Krishna in the hills of the Mahbubnagar district of the Nizam's dominions. Out of a total populaton of 8,078, nearly half are found in the Karnool and about one fourth in the Gantur districts. Due to close contact with the neighbouring people of the plains, the Chenchus of these districts are being rapidly assimilated among the lower classes of the Hindu population, though intermarriage does not as yet openly take place[1]. In the Nizam's dominions however, due to their complete isolation—for until "a track was cut through the woods, over the hills, 30 years ago by Mr. Yusufuddin, they were not traversed by any men" [2], the Chenchus are still to be found in a state of purity.

In December 1931, at the invitation of his Exalted Highness the Nizam's Government, I spent some time in the interior of the hills at Farhabad and measured some Chenchus with the kind and very helpful co-operation of Mr. Gulam Ahmed Khan, the Census Commissioner of the State. As a very large part of the hills was not even then opened out and as all adult males were out in the jungles during the day in search of food and minor forest produce, we succeeded in getting only 23 adult men, out of a total population of 445 souls [3], even though we visited all the Pentas (Chenchu stettlements) from Manarum to Vettul-Palli.

From the measurements given in Table V, it will be seen that the Chenchus are medium statured (mean Stature $1649 \cdot 52 \pm 9 \cdot 23$) with long head, (the mean Cephalic Index being $72 \cdot 89 \pm 0 \cdot 53$). The vault of the Cranium is moderately high (mean Auricular height $120 \cdot 48 \pm 0 \cdot 85$) and the face short and narrow, the Total Facial length being only $110 \cdot 00 \pm 1 \cdot 01$. The nose is broad at the root, the Inter orbital breadth being $30 \cdot 30 \pm 0 \cdot 27$ and also very wide at the nostrils. It is moderately low, as shown by the depth (mean Nasal depth $21 \cdot 11 \pm 0 \cdot 32$), and gives an almost Chamaerrhine Index, (mean N. I. $81 \cdot 38 \pm 0 \cdot 95$). The skin colour varies from tawny brown to dark chocolate brown (Nos 23—33), and the hair is generally black (No. 27). The character of the hair is usually wavy but 13% had straight hair and 8% curly. No instance, however of a genuinely frizzly or wooly hair was met with. The hair is plentiful on the head but scanty on the face and very little on the body. [4] Supra-orbital ridges are well marked and in a few cases (4%) they were very prominent. The eye is round and no traces of the epicanthic fold were found in any individual. A slight amount of prognathism was found in most individuals and in some (9%) it was quite marked.

The Bhils measured came from the western ranges of the Vindhya hills. The total number of the Bhils enumerated in the Census of 1931[5] is 363,124; of which only 218,288 still adhere to tribal customs and religion. Of the three divisions into which the Bhils are divided, namely, Patlia, Mankar and Tarvi, the first two are considerably mixed and it is only among the last that miscegenation has not taken place.[6] In 1931, at the suggestion and with the active help of Mr. C. S. Venkatachar I.C.S., then Census Superintendent of the Central Indian States, and who has a very wide and intimate knowledge of the Bhils, I visited several Bhil settlements in the western Vindhyas and took measurements on 50 adult men, belonging to the Tarvi division and as far as could be ascertained of pure blood.

The other two tribes from Southern India, namely the Kadars and the Nattu Malayans, with whom comparisons have been made, came from the hills in the Cochin State where I spent several months in the winters of 1928 and 1929. The latter live in the lower parts of the hills and the adjoining forests and I measured 44 adult men with the help of Mr. Romoni Menon, then Divisional Forest Officer of the Cochin State. The Kadars live in the upper ranges of these hills which are continuous with the Annaimallais hills of the Coimbatore district. The Kadars measured by me belonged to Perambicullam and Vellaripallam in the extreme interior of these hills, where I camped for several weeks in 1928 and 1929 and measured over 112 men and 31 women. The semi-nomadic habits of the Kadars, the great difficulty of communications and the highly malarious conditions of these hills, would have made it impossible for me to take these measurements without the help and enthusiastic co-operation of Messrs. K. Govinda Menon and Narayan Menon, then Conservator of Forests and Divisional Forest Officer of the Cochin State; the former has contributed an excellent account of the habits and social institutions of the Kadars in this Volume.

In Tables XIX and XIX (a) are given the Reduced and Crude C. R. L.'s of the six principal aboriginal tribes of Southern and Central India. It will be seen from the figures given in these Tables that the lowest value of the C. R. L. is between the Mundas and the Oraons who must therefore be regarded as racially akin. Between the Chenchu and the Bhil the Co-efficient is also small ($6 \cdot 11 \pm 0 \cdot 59$). When the individual characters are compared it is found that excepting the Auricular height and Bigonial breadth in which the values of "α" are $8 \cdot 57$ and $11 \cdot 26$ respectively, there is no significant difference in the other characters considered. The Chenchus have also a low Co-efficient, namely $10 \cdot 32 \pm 0 \cdot 49$ with the Kadars, the differences being mainly in Stature, Bigonial breadth and Orbito-Nasal breadth in which the values of "α" are

[1] Census of India 1931, Volume XIV, Part I, page 362.
[2] Gulam Ahmed Khan—The Chenchus in Census of India 1931, Volume XXIII, Part I, page 261.
[3] Census of India, Volume XXIII, Part II, pages 100—101, 1931.
[4] Guha, B. S.—Anthropological work in the Hyderabad State in Census of India, Volume XXIII, pages 277—279.
[5] Census of India 1931, Volume XX, Part II, page 306.
[6] Venkatachar, C. S.—Ethnographic account of the Bhils of Central India in Census of India, Volume XX. Part I, Appendix I, pages 238—266. 1933.

52·93, 13·89 and 12·00 respectively. The latter however do not appear to show relationship with any of the other tribes, the lowest values obtained being 18·98±0·27 and 19·76±0·30 with the Bhils and Nattu Malayans respectively. Similarly the Nattu Malayans seem to be unrelated to the others, their lowest Co-efficient of 19·76±0·30 being, as stated, with the Kadars.

The values of the C. R. L.'s given above were computed from 26 characters including the Auricular height. While all other measurements were taken by the same instruments (Herman's), the Auricular height in the Kadars and Nattu Malayans were measured by means of Pearson's 'Head spanner,' but among the rest it was measured in projection with the Anthropometer. It was thought therefore that for a more correct comparison, fresh values of the C. R. L.'s were necessary to be calculated after omitting the Auricular height and the Indices based on it. The additional values, based on 22 characters, are given in Table XX, and it will be noticed that the Co-efficients between the Kadars and the Nattu Malayans, and the Kadars and the Bhils, have considerably diminished bringing the tribes within the limits of relationship. In the rest of the groups (excepting between the Kadars and the Chenchus where the value is slightly raised) though the values of the C. R. L.'s have decreased, they are still very much outside the limits signifying any kinship.

In Tables XXI and XXI (a) are given the C. R. L.'s of the Yeruvas with the four tribes mentioned above. Holland is responsible for the measurements of 25 Yeruvas [1] who live in the southernmost parts of Coorg and those portions of Mysore and Wynaad which adjoin it as only 10 of the measurements appeared to be strictly comparable, the C. R. L.'s had to be computed from these. Too much emphasis therefore should not be laid on the results obtained, but such as they are, they suggest relationship with the Kadar (11·22±0·74) and probably also with the Nattu-Malayan and the Chenchu, if allowance can be made for personal equation. With the Bhil, however no association is indicated.

In Text-fig 5. the Inter-relationship of these aboriginal tribes are diagrammatically illus-

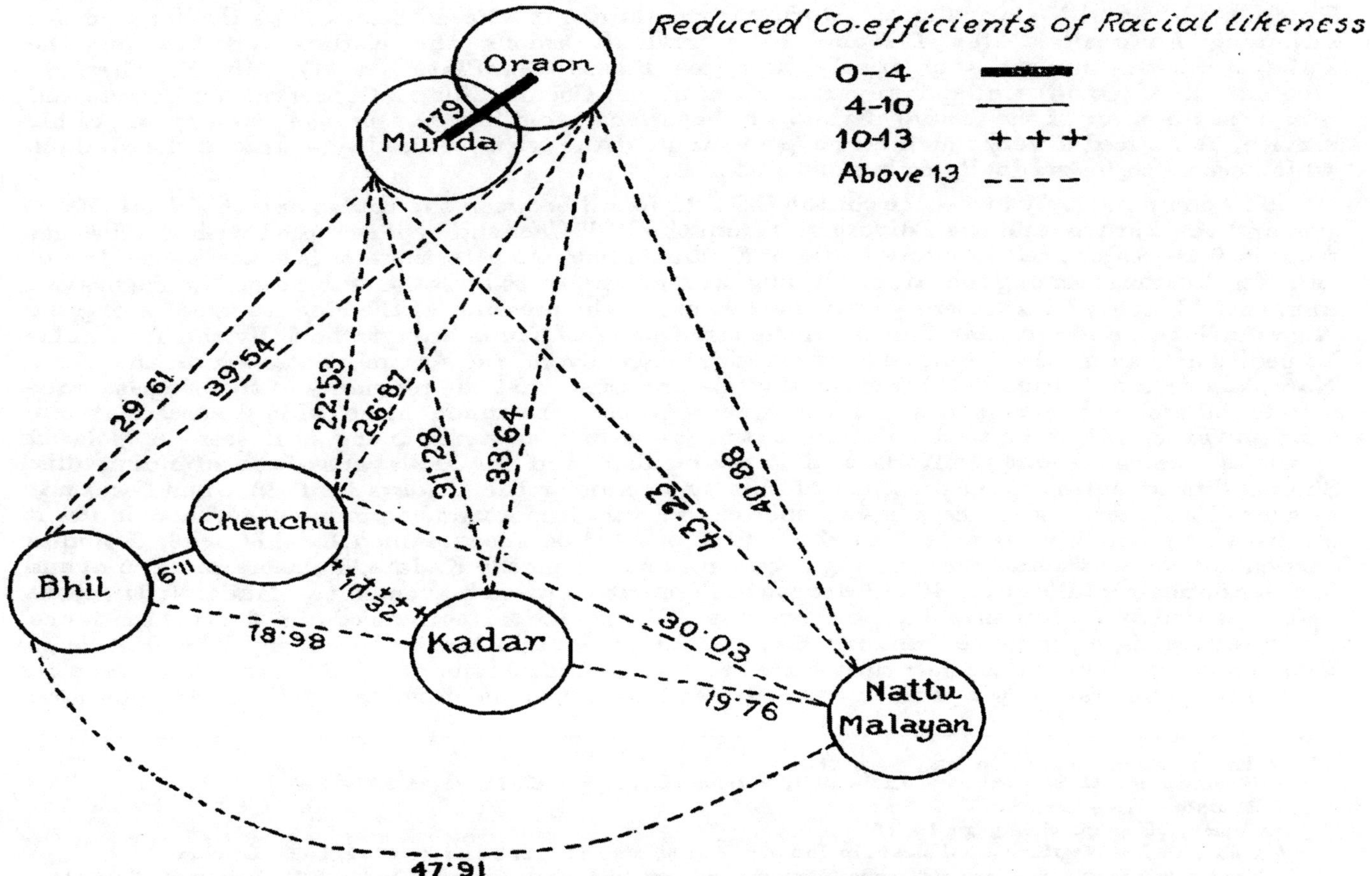

Text-fig 5. Inter-relationship of Aboriginal Tribes.

trated. It will be observed that the relationship between the two Chota Nagpur tribes is very intimate. This is in agreement with the conclusion reached by Sir William Turner[2] and

[1] Holland, T.H.—1901. Op. cit.
[2] Turner, Sir William, 1901—Op. cit., Part I.

adopted subsequently by Risley [1]. From a comparative study of the skulls of these two tribes in the collection of the Indian Museum, it appears that there is some difference in the formation of the forehead, which may not however be important. In an excellent paper, Venkatachar [2] has recently discussed the history of migrations of tribes in Central India, and from traditions present among the Oraons and the Gonds, he considers that both of these tribes migrated from Southern India in comparatively recent historical times. There is a great deal to be said in favour of this view, which explains why the Oraons and the Gonds speak Dravidian languages among tribes who are Austric speaking. The values of the C. R. L.'s given in Tables XIX and XIX (a) would at first sight appear to go against this supposition, for while showing an intimate association with the Mundas, the Oraons do not exhibit any relationship with any of the South Indian tribes. But as the values of the C. R. L.'s between these tribes and the Bhils of Central India are even higher it is probable that they do not represent true values of relationships between these tribes but are rather due to individuals of mixed parentage being included in Basu's samples of the Mundas and Oraons which were obtained from the outskirts of the town of Ranchi. It is only after his investigations in the interior of the hills are completed that we can be certain on this point.

However that be, the racial strain represented by the Bhils is found among the Chenchu of the Nallaimallais hills and seems also to form a constituent of the Kadar who contain in addition a definite Negrito element.

The presence of a Negrito racial strain in the aboriginal population of South India was suspected by some observers, but definite evidence as to its existence was lacking and many distinguished anthropologists, refused to entertain the supposition. Thus Thurston, [3] writing in 1909 remarked that the only individual with wooly hair seen by him was of "mixed Tamil and African parentage." Similarly Risley [4] observed that " although the terms wooly and frizzly had been loosely applied to the wavy hair, not uncommon among the Dravidians, no good observer had as yet found among any of the Indian races, a head of hair that could be correctly described as wooly."

I have drawn attention elsewhere [5] to the presence of frizzly hair among the Kadars of Perambiculam and Vellaripallam. During my enquiries in the interior of the Cochin and the adjoining Anaimallais hills, I found 14 individuals among the Kadars and 1 among the Pullayans with unmistakably frizzly hair (see Figs. 1—3a, Plate No. II). Mr. K. Govinda Menon, B. A. (Oxon) who spent over 25 years in the Cochin hills as Conservator of forests and is a close observer of the Kadar habits and customs,[6] told me that in the early years of his service, he noticed a very much larger percentage of the frizzly haired type among the Kadars, which seems to be gradually dying out since.

The comparatively low values of the C. R. L. found between the Kadar and the Nattu Malayan and the Yeruva, and their divergence from the Bhil-Chenchu type, coupled with the distinct negroid features noticed in many of the individuals belonging to these tribes, seem also due to this Negrito strain among the latter, although it may appear to be rather submerged at the present moment. Hutton [7] has recently drawn attention to the presence of the Negrito type among the Angami Nagas, and our examination of the large series of skulls brought back by the Triangular Expedition[8] has made it quite clear that it extends beyond the Assam frontiers into the trans-Namphuk area of Burma. It may therefore be presumed that the remnants of the Negrito race now found among the Semangs and the Andamanese, were much more widely spread at one time and extended well into the Indian continent—a few survivals being still seen in isolated 'pockets' such as among the Kadars of Perambiculam and the Pullayans of the adjoining hills. Since calling attention to the presence of this type, among the Kadars in 1928, when I was not aware of Lapique's researches, I have come across a very important communication[9] here in Paris published by this investigator. In the winter of 1903 04 accompanied by his wife, Lapique carried out some extremely interesting investigations among the Kadars, Malasers and Poulayans in the Anaimalais hills about 40 miles south of Coimbatore when he visited two Kadar settlements and measured 32 adult men and 24 adult women. His researches convinced him that the existence of " une race nigre primitive " among these people is incontestable[10]. Accepting the definition of Quatrefage, however that the negritos are brachycephalic he remarks, " J' arrivais alors a la conception d'une race negre primitive voisine des Negritos, mais distincte parl'indice Cephalique

---

[1] Risley, H. H.—1915. Op. cit., page 21.

[2] Venkatachar, C. S.—Census of India 1931, Volume XX, Appendix II, pages 267—279.

[3] Thurston, E.— Loc. cit.

[4] Risley, H.—Op. cit., page 16, 1915.

[5] Guha, B. S.—Negrito Racial strain in India. *Nature*, May 19, 1928 and June 22, 1929. London.

[6] For his excellent account of the Kadar customs and institution see Census of India 1931, Volume I, Part III.

[7] Hutton, J. H.—A Negrito Substratum in the population of Assam, *Man in India*. Volume VII, pages 257—262.

[8] Guha, B. S. and Basu, P. C. 1931.—Op. cit., pages 21—26.

[9] Lapique, Louis—Note sommaire sur un mission ethnologique dans le Sud de l'Inde. Bull. du Museum D'Histoire Naturelle, Volume II, pages 283—285 ; Paris, 1905.

[10] Op. cit., page 284.

dolichocephala[1]". In my notes published in *Nature* in 1928—29 referred to before I stated that though the mean Cephalic Index of the Kadars was dolichocephalic among the individuals with frizzly hair there was a marked tendency for a rise in the Index to mesorrhiny as shown by two individuals having 77·34 and 79·29 as the values of their Index [2] which in my opinion indicated that the basis of this negrito type was probably brachycephalic or at least meso. as in the Semangs (mean C. I. 79), but large admixture with a primitive dolichocephalic race had affected the general shape of their head. To the same admixture was probably also due the long spirals now seen among most of the Kadars and Pulayans with frizzly hair, in two individuals, namely the right hand man in Figs. 3—3a[3] and in Figs. 2—2a[4] (Plate II) of this Volume, short spirals similar to 'h' instead of 'g' of Martin's scheme [5] were noticed. At the present day these Negritos are found to be closely similar to the Melanesian type both in hair and head form, but judging from the presence of two men with short spirals and higher Cephalic Index, it would seem that the original type was not probably unlike that of the Semangs and the Andamanese, among the former of whom designs on the bamboo combs identical with those used by Kadar women, are found.[6] Whatever might have been the original type, there can at any rate be no doubt that th's was Negrito, a conclusion reached independently by both Lapique and myself and the photos of the Kadars in this Volume (see Figs. 1—3a, Plate II) it is hoped will remove all further doubts about it.

We are not directly concerned with the Semangs in this Report, but the Andamanese come within our purview. As survivals of a very primitive ancient type they have naturally attracted the attention of well known anthropologists and several excellent reports have been published on their skeletons such as those of Sir William Flower [7], Sir William Turner[8] and L. R. Sullivan. [9] The most exhaustive and authoritative account of their somatic characters, however was published by M. V. Portman and William Molesworth in 15 Vols. in 1893—94,[10] of which Vols. VIII, IX, XII and XIII contained detailed anthropometric measurements and the rest photographs. Mr. Portman was then the Officer in charge of the Andamanese and Captain Molesworth, who took the measurements, was a member of the Indian Medical Service, stationed at Port Blair. The photographs comprise every sphere of the life of the Andamanese and are the best published, two of which are reproduced in Figs. 1—2a, Plate I. The measurements were taken on 200 individuals and are the most complete and exhaustive data that we possess on this dying race. Unfortunately only three copies of this valuable work were published and it was after a great deal of search that I was able to get access to one.

Molesworth measured 50 men and 50 women belonging to the North Andamanese Group comprising the Ti Chari, the Ta Yeri, the Ta Jeru and the Ta Keda tribes, who "inhabit the country from Landfall Island to a line drawn through the Middle Andaman from Flat Island on the west coast, to 'Amit-la-Ted' on the east coast. [11]"

The same numbers were measured from the South Andaman Group comprising the Aka-Bea-Da, the Akar-Bale, the Pichikwar, the Okko-Juwai and the Kol tribes, "inhabiting the remaining portion of the Middle Andaman and most of the South Andaman and adjacent islands, to and including Rutland Island.[12]" The tribes in each of these 'divisions are culturally and linguistically allied and the divisions are regarded as real by the Andamanese themselves. [13]'

The mean Stature of the 50 ♂ North Andamanese is 1486mm. against 1482 mm. of the 50 ♂ South Andamanese. The mean Head length and the Head breadth of the former are 172·90 and 141·80 respectively against 173·10 and 143·70 of the latter, giving a mean Cephalic Index of 82·00 in the former against 83·00 of the latter. The mean Nasal length and breadth are respectively 41·40 and 38·30 and the Nasal Index 92·50 in the former. The corresponding figures for the latter are 43·70 mm., 37·40 mm. and 85·58.

The females of the Northern Group have a mean Stature of 1386 mm. against 1402 mm. of the Southern. The mean Head length, Head breadth and the Cephalic Index of the former are 165·20, 135·30 and 81·90 respectively against 166·00, 137·4 and 82·77 of the latter. The mean

---

1 Op. cit., page 285.
2 Guha, B. S. —Op. cit., 1928, page 793.
3 Op. cit. 1928, page 793.
4 Op. cit., 1929, page 943.
5 Martin, R.—Lehrbuch, 2nd Edition. Volume I, page 213.
6 Preufs, Dr. K. Th.—*Die Zauberbidderschriften der Negrito in Malakka—Globus*, Volume LXXV, pages 345—348 and pages 364—369 ; Brounschweig, 1899.
7 J. A. I., Volumes IX and XIV.
8 Op. cit., Volume XL, Part I.
9 Sullivan, L. R.—Anth. Papers. A. M. N. H., Volume XXIII, Part IV, 1921.
10 Portman, M.V. and Molesworth, W.—*The Andaman Islanders*, 15 Volumes, Calcutta, 1893—94.
11 Loc. cit., Volume VIII, page 1.
12 Loc. cit., page 1.
13 *Ibid.*

Nasal length, Nasal breadth and Nasal Index are respectively 36·90, 34·80 and 94·30 in the former against 38·70, 34·60 and 89·40 of the latter. The value of the C. R. L. based on the measurements published by Molesworth, between the males of the North and the South Andamanese groups, is found to be $0 \cdot 62 \pm 0 \cdot 32$, showing that the Andamanese of both these places are without doubt, samples of the same population. In the case of the female groups the value of the Co-efficient is a little higher, namely $2 \cdot 00 \pm 0 \cdot 32$ but not large enough to indicate any difference of type, though from comparison of the values of "α" it is clear that among both the males and the females of the Northern group the nose is somewhat shorter and gives a more Chaemerrhine Index.

They are both however very short in stature and in this respect not unlike the Semangs of the Malay Peninsula and the Aetas of the Phillipine Islands.

The colour of the skin on parts not exposed is usually that of black lead and reddish or yellowish brown under the axilla, corresponding to Nos. 28—43 in Broca's scale. Comparatively speaking the Onges are the lightest and the South Andamanese the darkest, among whom instances of 'absolute black' are not wanting [1]. In a few cases, specially among the North Andamanese, Dr. Molesworth [2] noticed "a reddish tinge on the skin on the cheek bones and other prominent parts of the face and body." The pigment is however so strong that "a patch of black skin kept free from the light for years, as in the case of the skin of the head covered with a thick mat of hair, does not become lighter in colour [3]".

The eye colour varies slightly from very dark brown to dark brown with 'a ring of black round the iris'. The colour of the hair is usually sooty black which often turns to red and light brown from the bleaching action of the sea water [4]. In form the hair is invariably wooly and often of a pepper corn type and deviation from it was not observed in a single individual. The amount of hair, either on the face or the body in all cases is very scanty but total absence of hair is unknown. There is a little hair under the axilla and the pubic parts and in some men slight beard and moustache, but excessive hairiness does not occur. [5]

The face is usually short and broad with a tendency to prognathism, which is never very marked. The lips are usually thick and in some cases everted. Molesworth did not find any evidence of artificial deformation excepting "the mark across the skull caused by the strap used in carrying loads", which is specially noticeable in women who carry big bundles of fire wood and as this commences at an early age, it not infrequently causes an actual depression in the skull[6]. Baron von Eickstedt, [7] who not long ago published an account of his trip to to the Andaman Islands and spoke of this deformity as the unique characteristic of the Onge women, whose skulls could on that account be easily distinguished, was apparently unaware that the trait was not so restricted as he imagined, but is found among all the Andaman tribes both men and women, and was mentioned by Molesworth as early as 1893. His further claims that the pepper corn type of hair and steotopygia among the Andamanese were first noticed by him are equally unfounded for in addition to Molesworth [8], they are mentioned by Lt. Col. R. B. Seymour Sewell F. R. S.,[9] who during 20 years of his service as Surgeon Naturalist on board the "Investigator" visited almost every part of the Islands, including Titaje [10] which the Baron thinks he was the first 'white Man' to visit and had renamed as "Weule-Bay" and "Weule-Creek" [11].

Again his contention that the scantiness of hair on the body of the Andamanese is due to their inveterate habit of shaving [12], finds no confirmation from Molesworth, who mentions that eye brows no doubt are often shaved as a sign of ornament but in none of the individuals examined by him was there any sign of shaving the hair on the body which by nature was very scanty [13].

---

[1] Op. cit., Volume VIII, page 7.

[2] Loc. cit., Volume XII, page 1.

[3] Loc. cit., Volume VII, page 7.

[4] *Ibid*, pages 6—7.

[5] Op. cit., Volulme VIII, page 6.

[6] Loc. cit., page 7.

[7] Eickstedt, Baron von.—*Die Negritos der Andamanen. Anthr. Anz.*, pages 259—268, 1928.

[8] Op. cit., Voumes VIII, IX and XII.

[9] Sewell, R.B.S.—*Racial Ethnology of India* (VIIth. Congress of the Far Eastern Association of Tropical Medicine. Calcutta. 1927.)

[10] Sewell. R. B. S. —1922. Op. cit.

[11] As a matter of fact Titaje was also visited by Portman and Wright, Chief Commissioners of the Andaman Islands and Tipper and Gee of the Geological Survey of India; the last two published the *results of their investigations in the Memoirs* of that Survey.

[12] Eickstedt—Op. cit.

[13] Op. cit., Volume VIII page 6.

In the paper [1] mentioned, Eickstedt disputes the uniformity of type among the Andamanese and thinks that the "Great" (North ?) Andamanese are more graceful, slimmer and possess a longer face and finer features than the Onges of Rutland (of whom he measured 42 men 38 women and 20 children), and comes to the conclusion that the latter represent a different type and belong to an earlier wave of migration. Molesworth [2] on the other hand regards the North Andamanese to be More 'Platyprosopic' and as his observations were based on a much longer sample and on a very much longer acquaintance with the Andamanese of every part of the Island, the former's theories—derived from a trip of a few weeks duration and on measurements of 35 men and women only obtained from the "Andaman Homes" near Port Blair and Rutland Island where, as is well known, all the inmates are not of pure blood,—need not be taken very seriously. The values of the C. R. L.'s given above prove conclusively the racial homogeneity of the Andamanese though, minor local variations occur, as suggested by Molesworth, between the Northern and the Southern groups, but there seems no justification to assume, as Eickstedt did, that they constitute any fundamental difference of type.

The distinctiveness of the Andamenese as racial type has not hitherto been questioned and from the time of their discovery till now they have been universally recognised as one of the few remnants of the ancient race characterised by a dwarfish stature, black complexion and wooly hair who have survived as a result of isolation in the Islands of Bay of Bengal [3]. As Eickstedt has put it "only very few race groups are known of which one can say with a certain probability that they have remained almost free from outside influence [4]." The task was left however to Drs. T. L. Woo and G. M. Morant of the Biometric School, to discover that they are not Negritos at all, but degenerated Burmese![5] In their opinion the shape of the Andamanese head "is very similar to those of the neighbouring Burmese and Javanese. The close resemblance between the shapes in these cases can not be supposed fortuitous and it seems to point clearly to the fact that the Andamanese came originally from Java or from the neighbouring mainland and that they have degenerated since. This theory can not be reconciled to the Negrito hypothesis however [6]." Again "it is reasonable to suppose that this (the resemblance of head shape) indicates a true relationship and that the stock degenerated after reaching the Islands and then becoming isolated [7]."

The basis of this amazing conclusion was a comparison of the values of the C. R. L.'s obtained from Tildesley's 'A' Series of 44 Burmese male crania, some Javanese and the "pooled" means of several short series of Andamanese skulls, totalling 34 in all.

Drs. Woo and Morant have not told us exactly when this Burmese or Javanese migration to the Andaman Islands took place, for we find no mention of this event in their chronicles and the Burmese occupation of Burma at least, is not so ancient. Nor have they enlightened us as to why the Burmese or for the matter of that the Javanese, felt the necessity of inventing an altogether new and unrelated tongue in place of Burmese or Javanese after reaching their new habitat (the Andamans) unless they happened to be the results of "degeneracy" to which no doubt their present primitive but very different habits are also to be attributed! There must be something very extraordinary in the climate of the Andaman Islands which wrought these wonders and changed the straight hair of the Burmese or Javanese into the woolly hair of the Andamanese, transformed their slanting eyes with epicanthic folds into the horizontal open eyes of the latter, made them dwarfish, gave them a sooty black skin colour in place of their original dark brown and produced steotopygia in their women, though in their immediate south, the Nicobarese retain the somatic, cultural, and linguistic characters of their kinsmen of Assam and Northern Burma after thousands of years of migration!

The danger of the application of the statistical method to racial questions by persons with insufficient knowledge of Anthropology is nowhere better illustrated than in the case of these two authors who never stopped to think that some amount of similarity in the cranial shape is bound to exist between two races who are both brachy—and chaemaerrhine, without the one being a degenerated form of the other. The microcephalic character of the Andamanese skull, disclosed also by statistical analysis [8], is a distinguishing mark of the Negrito race along with pigmy stature and woolly hair and not a product of "degeneracy." Values derived from "pooled" means of various short series measured by different men in which no allowance is made for personal equation, and the additive nature of the method of the C. R. L. which assigns

[1] Op. cit., 1928.

[2] Op. cit., Volume XII, page 1.

[3] Peake, H. and Fleure, H. J.—The Corridors of Time, Volume IV. page 180. 1927.

[4] Eickstedt, E. Fr.—Loc. cit., page 259.

[5] Op. cit., 1932, pages 108—134.

[6] Loc. cit., page 129.

[7] Loc. cit., page 130.

[8] Op. cit., page 129.

an equal value to all the characters, may produce altogether misleading results and the closeness of the Co-efficients thus obtained should not, therefore, be taken to be indicative of racial identity, without considering other relevant factors, for which a knowledge of the racial history of the tribes compared is essential, and the mere ability to use the calculating machine—however important—is not enough.

9.—FEMALE GROUP.

In addition to the different groups of males discussed above, measurements were taken by me on 94 Guzrati, 102 Mahrathi, 71 Malayali and 31 Kadar women. The values of the C. R. L.'s, both Crude and Reduced are given in Tables XXIV and XXIV(a). It will be seen from there values that there is a definite relationship between the Guzrati and Mahrathi women and there is also some association between the Mahrathi and the Malayali but there does not seem to be any between the Gujrati and the Malayali. The Kadar women stand altogether separate from the above three groups. When the individual characters are compared the differences between the Guzrati and the Mahrathi women are found mainly in Head breadth, Min. Frontal diameter, Bizygomatic breadth, Nasal length and depth, Transverse arc, Cephalic Index and Breadth-Height Index; the values of 'α' in these characters being 20·73, 27·72, 17·25, 11·32, 18·95, 20·71, 35·33 and 34·77 respectively; showing that in comparison with the Mahrathi, the Guzrati women have broader head and face, and longer and more prominent nose. The differences between the Mahrathi and Malayali women lie in Head length, Inter-Orbital breadth, Orbito-Nasal breadth, Nasal depth, Total Facial length, Sagittal and Transverse arcs, Cephalic Index, and Upper Facial Index; the values of 'α' being 17·37, 21·82, 9·79, 16·69, 113·96, 17·84, 8·88 and 26·49 respectively. Compared to the Mahrathi, the Malayali women are more longheaded and possess narrower and more elongated face and a slightly broader, but more pronounced nose. The Guzrati and the Malayali therefore represent two distinct types, the brachycephalic and the dolichocephalic, the Mahrathi occupying an intermediate position between the two. The racial types disclosed from the analysis of the data on the males seem to be strictly followed by the female samples.

In addition to the groups compared above my wife has measured 250 Bengali women belonging to the Brahmin, Vaidya and the Kayastha castes and I am indebted to her for permitting me to use her unpublished data here. In the following Tables are given the values of the C. R. L.'s [1] of the Bengali women :—

Crude Co efficints of Racial Likeness.

	Brahmin.	Vaidya.	Kayastha.
Brahmin	..	0·12	1·14
Vaidya	0·12	..	0·11
Kayastha	1·14	0·11	..

Probable Error ±0·17 in all cases.

Reduced Coefficients of Racial Likeness.

	Brahmin.	Vaidya.	Kayastha.
Brahmin	..	0·16±0·23	1·36±0·20
Vaidya	0·16±0·23	..	0·13±0·20
Kayastha	1·36±0·20	0·13±0·20	..

These figures show conclusively that all the three groups are intimately related though the values of the Co-efficients between the Brahimin and Vaidya and the Vaidya and the Kayastha are somewhat smaller than that between the Brahmin and the Kayastha.

When the women of Bengal taken as a whole are compared to those of Guzrat, the value of the Reduced C. R. L. is found to be 29·95±0·15. With the Mahrathi, the Co-efficient is 31·21 ±0·18 and with the Malayali it is 35·24±0·15, showing that the Bengali women are nearer to to the Guzrati and the Mahrathi than to the Malayali though the values as such are much too high to indicate any relationship.

When discussing the comparative values of the male groups however it was noticed how they were affected by the presence of personal equation. The above figures therefore must not be taken strictly on their face values and considered as indicative of racial divergence. Judging from the relationships shown between the women of Guzrat and Maharashtra, and between the Brahmin and Kayastha women of Bengal, there seems no reason to think that the true relationships of the three groups taken in their entireties, are anything different from what were seen between the males of these regions.

[1] Based on 28 characters only.

INTER-RELATIONSHIPS.

In the foregoing pages the somatic traits of the peoples of India were discussed separatively in each of the 8 ethnic groups into which they were divided. In the following paragraphs it is proposed to discuss their inter relationships. In Tables XXII and XXII (a) are given the Reduced and Crude C. R. L.'s of the 30 representative castes and tribes belonging to these groups, of which (*i*) five were selected from the North-Western Himalayan region, namely (*a*) the Uzbeg, (*b*) the Tadjik, (*c*) the Red Kaffir, (*d*) the Pathan and (*e*) the Khos. In the Text fig.

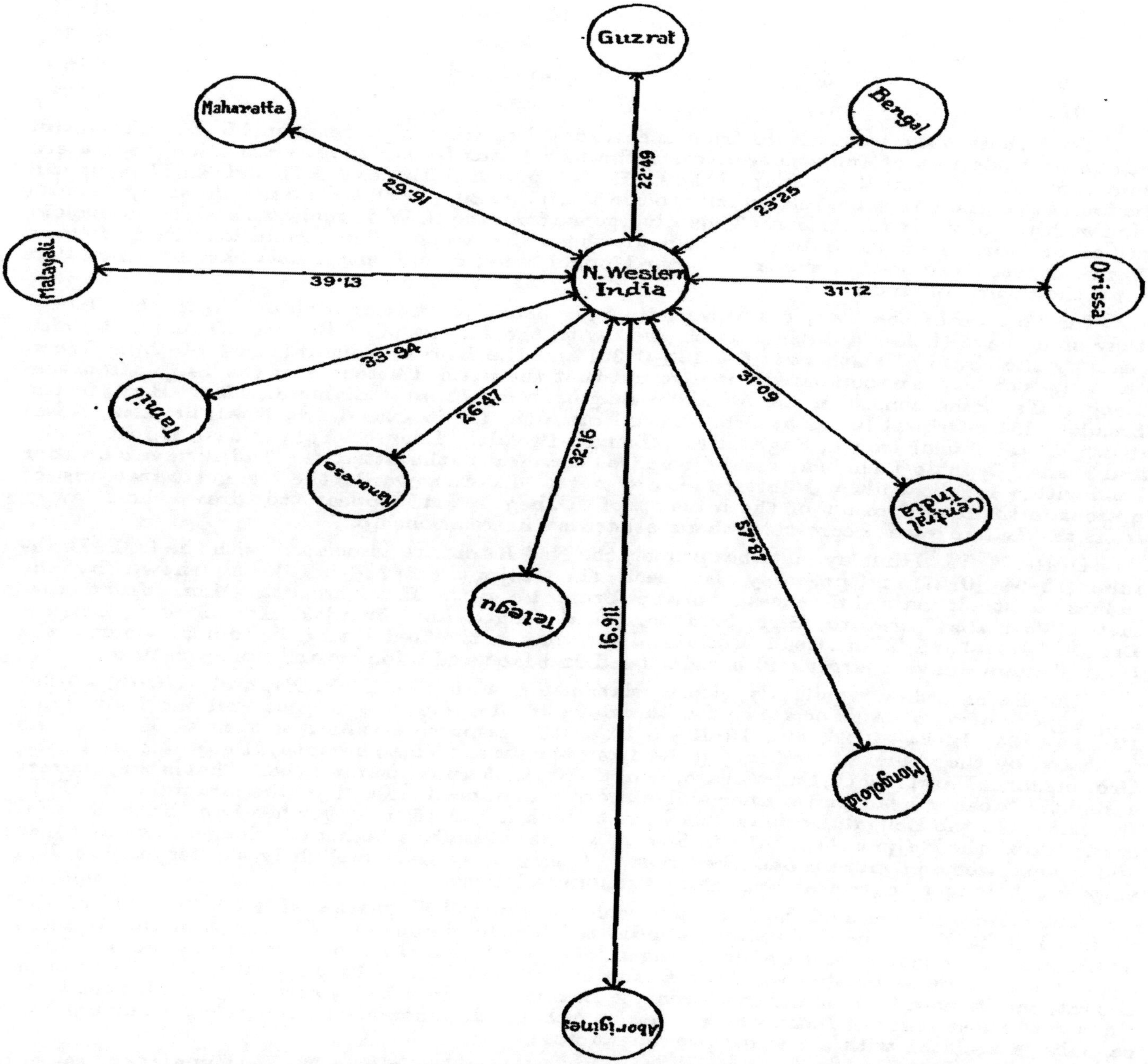

Text fig. 6. Inter-relationship of North Western India with other Groups.

6. are shown the inter-relationships of N. W. Himalayan egion with the rest of India. It will be observed from this that its closest relationship is with Guzrat and Bengal with 22·49 and 23·25 respectively as the total values of the C. R. L.'s. Next to these come Kannada with 26·47, Maharashtra with 29·91, Central India with 31·09. Orissa with 31·12, Telengana with 32·16, Tamil-Nadu with 33·94, U. P. (not shown in the Text-fig.) with 37·85 and Malabar with 39·13. If however the first two groups (the Uzbeg and the Tadjik) who really do not

belong to India but come from the Russian Turkistan and Badakshan, are omitted and fresh values of the C. R. L.'s are calculated, we get the following figures ;—

1. North-West Himalayan Region and	U. P.	13·71
2. ,, ,, ,,	Bengal	15·64
3. ,, ,, ,,	Central India	16·13
4. ,, ,, ,,	Telengana	18·77
5. ,, ,, ,,	Guzrat	18·89
6. ,, ,, ,,	Kannada	19·69
7. ,, ,, ,,	Maharashtra	21·75
8. ,, ,, ,,	Malabar	22·65
9. ,, ,, ,,	Tamil-nadu	23·65
10. ,, ,, ,,	Orissa	24·93

That these values constitute truer measures of relationships between N. W. Himalayan region and the rest of India is seen when the two Trans-Indian groups are taken separately and compared. From the values of the C. R. L.'s given in Tables XXII and XXII (a) it will be found that the Uzbeg are related only to the Tadjik (5·80±0·39) but do not show any association with any of the Indian tribes. Their divergence from the N. W. Himalayan and the Mongoloid tribes of North-Eastern India have already been discussed. The conclusion that follows from this, seems to be that the true Tartar-Mongol blood from Central Asia has not penetrated into the heart of India.

In the case of the Tadjik however, though their closest relationship is with the Uzbeg, they show nevertheless a distinct association with the Kayastha of Bengal (10·82±0·22) also possibly the Kathi of Kathiawar (14·18±0·35) and the Kho of Chitral (14·25±0·23). When the values of 'α' are compared [1] it is found that the main differences of the Tadjik from the Bengali Kayastha consist in the Auricular height, Min. Frontal diameter, Max. Bizygomatic breadth, Inter-Orbital breadth, Orbito-Nasal breadth, Orbito-Nasal arc, Nasal breadth, Nasal depth, Total Facial length, Sagittal arc, Length-Breadth, Length height, Nasal, Upper Facial and Trans. Cephalo-Facial Indices. Compared therefore to the latter, the Tadjik have a broader head with a higher vault and flatter face and nose. In other words, the Mongol characteristics present in them as a result of the infusion of Uzbeg blood, appear to draw them away from the Indian races nearest to them otherwise in relationship.

Of the N. W. Himalayan tribes proper, the Red Kaffir are associated with the U. P. Brahmins (11·64±0·27) and probably also with the Rajput (13·72±0·17). As shown by the values 'α' their main differences from the former lie in the Head breadth, Min. Front. diameter, Max. Bizy. breadth, Bigo. breadth, Nasal length and breadth, Hor. circum., Length-Breadth, Nasal and Trans. Ceph. Facial Indices, that is, the Red Kaffir, in comparison with the U. P. Brahmin have a larger and broader head and face and a longer and norrower nose.

The Pathan show a slightly closer relationship with the U. P. Brahmin (10·62±0·34) and appear also to be associated with the Bengali Brahmin, the Rajput and the Nair with 12·62±0·34, 12·24±0·26, and 12·13±0·31 as the respective values of their C. R. L.'s. As indicated by the values of 'α' they differ from the first in Head breadth, Min. Front. and Int.-Orb. breadth, Nasal length, Sagittal arc, Length-Breadth and Nasal Indices. That is they possess a slightly broader head and a finer and a more pronounced nose than the Brahmins of U. P. In relation to the Bengali Brahmin, they are taller and possess a longer head and sharper facial cast. From the Rajput they differ in having a taller stature, a higher and longer head and face and a narrower and more pronounced nose. Lastly, they have a slightly shorter stature, but very much longer, narrower and more pronounced nose.

The closest affinities of the Khos are with the Bengali Kayastha with 10·76±0·18 as the Reduced C. R. L. The differences as indicated by the values of 'α' consist in the former's having a slightly shorter stature but a longer head and face and a more pronounced nose. They appear also to be associated with the Brahmin and the Pod of Bengal, all the four castes of Guzrat, the Saraswat Gour and the Kanarese Brahmins. In other words, they exhibit relationships with those parts of India where, there is either a dominance or strong element or brachycephaly associated with a narrow prominent nose.

We may therefore conclude that the closest relationship of the N. W. Himalayan region is with U. P. followed closely by Bengal and Central India. With Western and Southern India, its associations are more distant. Considered individually however, we notice on the one hand an alignment of the dolicocephalic Red Kaffir and the Pathan with the long headed groups of Northern India like the Brahmin and the Rajput, and on the other the relationships of the more broad headed Khos with the brachycephalic castes of Bengal, Guzrat and Mysore ; while both the groups evince some associations with castes occupying a more intermediate position.

[1] Table XXVIII, Appendix, pages 46-47.

(*ii*) From the values of the C. R. L.'s given in Tables XXII and XXII (*a*) the nearest relations of the U. P. Brahmins would seem to be the Nambudiris and the Nairs of Malabar with 6·30±0·32 and 7·72±0·31 respectively as the values of the C. R. L.'s. There s also a difinite relationship with the Rajput of Central India (8·21±0·26) and the Telegu Brahmin (9·04±0·34) and some association with the Brahmin of Malwa (11·46±0·34) and the Pod o. Bengal (13·92±0·34).

The relationship of U. P. with North Western and Central India has already been discussed. Its closer affinities with the Nambudiris, who are supposed to have migrated from the United Provinces and the Nair who contain an appreciable amount of the latter's blood, are also evident. The values of the C. R. L.'s, as noted above, would appear further to indicate the existence of some common bond between it and Andhra and Bengal.

(*iii*) In Text-fig. 7, are shown the relationships of Bengal with the rest of India.

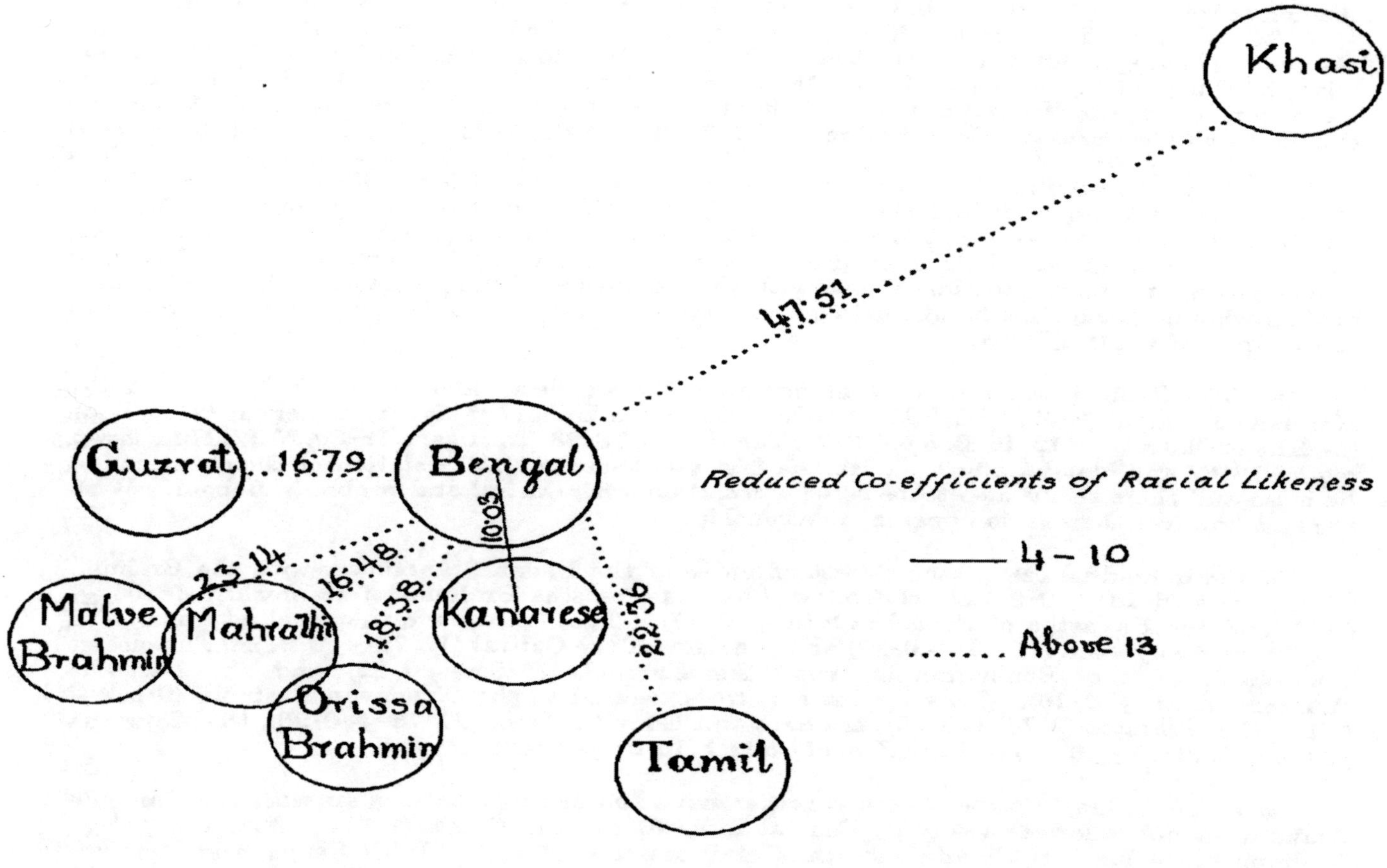

Text-fig. 7. Inter-relationship of Bengal with Others.

It will be seen that the closest relationship of Bengal is with Kanarese (Mysore) with 10·03 as the value of the C. R. L. The Maharashtra comes next with 16·48, Guzrat with 16·79 and Orissa with 18·38. Taken as a whole, there does not appear to be much relationship between Bengal and Tamil-nadu and Central India. If however, the individual castes are compared, both the Brahmin and the Kayastha show their nearest relationships with the Tamil Brahmin, the values of the Reduced C. R. L. being 7·40 ± 0·34 and 8·34 ± 0·26 respectively, followed by the Kanarese and the Saraswat Gour Brahmin and the Khos of Chitral. Besides these, affinities are also shown by the Nair of Malabar and the Pathan of N. W. India with the Bengali Brahmin; and by the Nagar Brahmin, the Tadjik, the Kathi and the Bania-Jain with the Bengali Kayastha. The Pods however show much wider relationships, being connected with the Uriya and the Malve Brahmins, the Rajput, the Audich, Chitpavan and the Desastha Brahmins, the Maharatta, the Illuva, the Kannada and the Telegu Brahmins. On the other hand no relationship is shown with the Khasi of Assam, either collectively or individually, as indicated by the high values of the C. R. L.'s. This should dispose of finally the hypothesis of the Mongolian origin of the Bengali people.

(*iv*) The closest relationships of the Sasan Brahmin of Orissa appear to be with the Saraswat Gour Brahmin (8·11 ± 0·23,) the Bengali Pod (8·19 ± 0·23) and the Maharatta (8·22 ± 0·21) closely followed by the Telegu Brahmin (9·78 ± 0·23). As shown by the values of 'α', their chief differences from these groups consist in their having a higher cranial vault and a broader nasal root. From the Saraswat and the Telegu Brahmin, they differ also in having a shorter head and a more squarish type of face.

(*v*) Taken as a whole Central India shows nearer affinities to Telangana and Maharashtra with 6·20 and 6·47 respectively as the values of the C. R. L.'s closely followed by U. P. with 9·83. With the Tamil-nadu the value is 12·15, with Kannada it is 13·57, Orissa 13·87, Malabar 13·84, Guzrat 15·54, N. W. H. 16·13 and Bengal 19·03. Individually, however the Malve Brahmins are most closely related to the Chitpavan and the Telegu Brahmins with 5·27 ± 0·25 and 6·44 ± 0·34 respectively as the values of the C. R. L.'s. The Tamil Kalla (7·22 ± 0·38) the Bengali Pod (7·40 ± 0·34), the Mahratta (7·54 ± 0·32) and the Desastha Brahmin (7·82 ± 0·25) come next in points of relationship. There appear also to be some associations with the Audich (10·46 ± 0·26), the U. P. (11·46 ± 0·34) and the Saraswat Gour Brahmin of Goa (11·76 ± 0·34). They differ from the Kalla in having a longer and more prominent nose and from the rest in having a much narrower head. Similarly the closest relationships of the Rajput are with the Chitpavan (5·45 ± 0·17) and the Telegu Brahmin (5·96 ± 0·26). They are also related to the Pod, the Mahratta, the Audich, the Kalla, the Desastha and the U. P. Brahmins, the Nair and the Saraswat Gour Brahmin with 7·73 ± 0·26, 7·80 ± 0·23, 7·81 ± 0·18, 7·95 ± 0·30, 8·02 ± 0·16, 8·21 ± 0·26, 8·40 ± 0·22 and 8·78 ± 0·26 respectively as the values of C. R. L.'s. In addition there seems also some associations with the Khos of Chitral (11·55 ± 0·18), the Pathan of Bijaur (12·24 ± 0·26), the Kannada Brahmin (21·48 ± 0·26), the Tamil Brahmin (13·29 ± 0·26), and the Red Kaffir of Kaffiristan (13·72 ± 0·17). As indicated by the values of 'α' their chief differences from the above tribes consist in their having a taller stature and more prominent nose with the exception of the Pathan and the Red Kaffir, both of whom, on the other hand, are taller and possess a narrower and more prominent nose than the Rajput of Central India.

(*vi*) The Guzrati castes taken together have the smallest value of the C. R. L. with the Kannada Brahmin (8·47). With Maharashtra the value is slightly higher, namely 10·74. With the Kho of Chitral it is 12·16, Bengal 16·79, Tamil-nadu 18·28, Telangana 18·80, N. W. Himalayan region 18·89 and Malabar 29·0. With the first two therefore the relation of Guzrat seems to be close and there seems also to be some association with Chitral and probably Bengal. With the rest however there is no apparent relationship.

Of the individual castes, the closest affinities of the Nagar Brahmin are with the Brahmin of Kannada (6·48 ± 0·27) closely followed by the Desastha Brahmin of Mahrashtra (8·54 ± 0·16) and the Kayastha of Bengal (10·46 ± 0·17). The Kathi have the smallest value with the Bengali Kayastha (11·06 ± 0·30) and the Kho of the Chitral (11·75 ± 0·31). The closest relationship of the Bania-Jain are with the Kannada (5·91 ± 0·26) and the Desastha Brahmin (5·94 ± 0·16). They appear also to be related to the Chitpavan Brahmin (9·53 ± 0·17), the Māhratta (9·75 ± 0·23), the Saraswat Gour Brahmin (11·73 ± 0·26), the Kayastha of Bengal (12·65 ± 0·17) and the Kho of Chitral (13·01 ± 0·18).

(*vii*) The Mahrathi castes taken together have the closest relationship with the Kannada Brahmin (4·55) followed closely by Central India (6·47) and Orissa (7·47). With the Telegu Brahmin the value is 8·35, and with the Tamil castes it is 9·38. With Bengal and Malabar, the association is more distant, namely 16·48 and 17·93 respectively. There seems, therefore to be no doubt of the close relationship of Maharashtra, Kannada, Central India, Guzrat, Andhra and Tamil-nadu. With the rest of India, the affinities of the Mahrathi are more distant.

Of the individual castes the Chitpavans have the closest affinities with the Audich Brahmins (3·45 ± 0·17), followed by Malve Brahmin of Central India (5·27 ± 0·25), the Rajputs (5·45 ± 0·17), the Kannada Brahmins (5·53 ± 0·25), and the Tamil Kalla (5·74 ± 0·29). They are related also to the Bengali Pod (7·46 ± 0·25) and the Telegu Brahmin (7·99 ± 0·25). There may also be some association between them and the Nagar Brahmins of Guzrat and the Sasan Brahmins of Orissa. The closest relationship of the Desastha are with the Audich Brahmins of Guzrat (2·56 ± 0·17) and the Brahmins of Kannada (4·87 ± 0·25). They are closely related also to the Bania-Jain (5·94 ± 0·16), the Bengali Pod (6·69 ± 0·25), the Tamil Kalla (6·76 ± 0·29), the Malve Brahmin (7·82 ± 0·25), the Rajput (8·02 ± 0·16), the Nagar Brahmin (8·54 ± 0·16) and the Brahmins of the Telangana (9·07 ± 0·25).

The nearest relationship of the Saraswat Gour Brahmins are with the Kannada and the Tamil Brahmins with 1·20 ± 0·34 and 1·32 ± 0·34 respectively as the values of the C. R. L.'s. They are closely related to the Telegu Brahmins (4·26 ± 0·34), the Bengali Pod (4·46 ± 0·34), the Brahmins of Orissa (8·11 ± 0·23) and the Rajputs of Central India (8·78 ± 0·26).

Curiously enough there seems to be a relationship with the Khasis of Assam (9·40 ± 0·29). With the Kayasthas and Brahmins of Bengal, the Kho of Chitral and the Brahmins of Malwa there appear also to be some associations. The Mahrattas show the smallest values with the Audich Brahmins of Guzrat (3·56 ± 0·24) followed by the Pod of Bengal (6·53 ± 0·31), the Kannada Brahmin (6·60 ± 0·31), the Malve Brahmin (7·54 ± 0·32), the Rajput (7·80 ± 0·23), the Tamil Kalla (8·13 ± 0·36), the Brahmins of Orissa (8·22 ± 0·21), the Saraswat Gour (8·97 ± 0·31) and the Bania-Jains of Guzrat (9·75 ± 0·23). There appear moreover to be some associations between them and the Nagar and the Telegu Brahmins.

(*viii*) The Malayali as a whole is most closely related to the Telegu with a Co-efficient of 5·96 followed by the U. P. Brahmins with 10·19 and the Central Indian castes with 13·94. There does not appear to be much relationship with other parts of India, the values of the Co-efficient being with Maharashtra 17·93, Orissa 19·60, Bengal 20·23, Tamil-nadu 20·60, Kannada 27·24, Guzrat 29·00 and N. W. Himalayan region 39·13.

Individually however, the Nambudiri is closely related to the U. P. Brahmin (6·30 ± 0·32), as noted already, the Telegu Brahmins (6·56 ± 0·32) and the Rajputs of Central India (14·93 ± 0·24). The Nair is most closely related to the Telegu Brahmin (3·66 ± 0·31) followed by the Tamil Brahmin (6·39 ± 0·31) the Saraswat Gour Brahmin (7·32 ± 0·31), the U. P. Brahmin (7·72 ± 0·31), and the Rajput (8·40 ± 0·22). There appear to be some relationship also with the Bengali Brahmin (10·21 ± 0·31), the Tamil Kalla (10·59 ± 0·35), the Pathan (12·13 ± 0·31) and the Bengali Pod (12·48 ± 0·31). The nearest relationships of the Illuva are with the Telegu Brahmin (5·56 + 0·34) and the Tamil Kalla (5·76 ± 0·38) followed closely by the Bengali Pod (7·00 ± 0·34). They seem also to be associated with the Saraswat Gour Brahmin (10·24 ± 0·34), the Malve Brahmin (10·60 ± 0·34), the Chitpavan (12·83 ± 0·25) and the Tamil Brahmins (13·94 ± 0·34).

(*ix*) The relationship of the Tamil castes appears to be closest with Telegu (7·86) followed closely by Maharashtra (9·38) and Kannada (10·57). They are also found to be related to Central India (12·15) and Orissa (12·73). With the rest of India the relationship is not close, namely with U. P. (18·04), Guzrat (18·28), Malabar (20·60), Bengal (22·36) and N. W. H. (33·94).

Individually however the Tamil Brahmin has the smallest Co-efficient with the Saraswat Gour Brahmin (1·32 ± 0·34) closely followed by those of the Kannada Brahmin (4·72 ± 0·34), Telegu Brahmin (5·96 ± 0·34), the Nair (6·39 ± 0·31) and the Bengali Brahmin (7·40 ± 0·34). They are also related to the Pod and Kayastha of Bengal, the Nambudiri and the Tamil Kalla. The latter, as noted already shows the smallest value with the Telegu Brahmins (3·26 ± 0·38) closely followed by the Chitpavan Brahmins (5·74±0·29), the Illuva (5·76±0·38), the Bengali Pod (6·17±0·38), the Desastha Brahmin (6·76 ± 0·29), Malve Brahmin (7·22 ± 0·38), the Rajput (7·95 ± 0·30), the Mahratta (8·13 ± 0·36) and the Saraswat Gour Brahmin (8·89 ± 0·38). They seem also to be associated with the Nair, the Kannada Brahmin, the Audich and the Orissa Brahmins.

(*x*) The closest affinities of the Kannada rather unexpectedly are with the Guzrati (8·47), closely followed by the Bengali (10·03), the Tamil (10·57) and the Mahrathi (10·74). There appears also to be some association with Central India (13·57) and Telangana (15·77). With the rest of India there does not appear to be any relationship ; the values of the Co-efficient being 23·66 with the U. P., 26·47 with N. W. H. region and lastly 27·24, the highest, with their near neighbour the Malayali.

Individually however the closest relationship of the Kannada Brahmins is with the Saraswat Gour Brahmins (1·20 ± 0·34) closely followed by the Audich (3·40 ± 0·26), the Tamil (4·72 ± 0·34) and the Desastha Brahmins (4·87 ± 0·25). They are also related to the Chitpavan, the Telegu Brahmins, the Bania-Jains, the Nagar Brahmin, the Mahratta and the Bengali Pod.

(*xi*) The relationship of the Telegu people is closest with the Malayali (5·96) followed by the people of Central India (6·20), the Tamils (7·86), Mahrathi (8·35), the U. P. (9·04), and the Uriya Brahmins (9·78). With the rest of India the relationship is not close, the value of the Co-efficient being 15·77 with Kannada, 15·88 with Bengal, 18·80 with Guzrat and 32·16 with North Western Himalayan region.

Considered individually the Brahmin of Telangana, are most intimately related to the Tamil Kalla (3·26 ± 0·38) and the Nair (3·66 ± 0·31) closely followed by the Saraswat Gour Brahmin of Goa (4·26 ± 0·34). They are also related to the Illuva (5·56 ± 0·34), the Kannada Brahmins (5·84 ± 0·34), the Rajput (5·96 ± 0·26), the Tamil Brahmin (5·96 ± 0·34), the Malve Brahmin (6· 44 ± 0·34), the Nambudiri (6·56 ± 0·32), the Bengali Pod (6·68 ± 0·34), the Chitpavan (7·99 ± 0·25), the U. P. (9·04 ± 0·34), the Desastha (9·07 + 0·25) and the Audich Brahmin (10·80 ± 0·26).

(*xii*) Of the three tribal groups, (Kadar, Bhil and Khasi), the Kadar do not appear to show relationship with any other, with the possible exception of the Bhil, with whom the corrected value of their C. R. L.'s as given in Table XX (Appendix, page 33) is 12·47±0·29, just sufficient to bring the two within the limits of relationship. The latter however would seem to be more widely associated, having some connection with the Malve Brahmin of Central India (13·24 ± 0·34) and al o possibly the Mahratta (15·43 ± 0·31), the Chitpavan Brahmin (16·15 ± 0·25) and the Tamil Kalla (16·58 ± 0·38). As the Bhil and the Malve Brahmin are close neighbours and the Mahratta and the Chitpavans live not far distant, the closeness of the Co-efficients is suspicious although strictly speaking they are not indicative of any relationship.[1]

The only relationship shown by the Khasis, as judged by the values of the C. R. L. is with the Saraswat Gour Brahmin (9·40 ± 0·29) as mentioned already. It would seem to be quite unexpected but the smallness of the value is difficult to be explained otherwise except on the assumption oı the existence of a racial strain which has entered into the composition of both which probably explains the presence of a small element among the Khasis with fine and prominent nose.

GENERAL CONCLUSIONS.

The results derived from the values of the C. R. L.'s discussed above are summarised in Text-figures 8 and 9. In the former are shown the inter-relationships of all the groups having

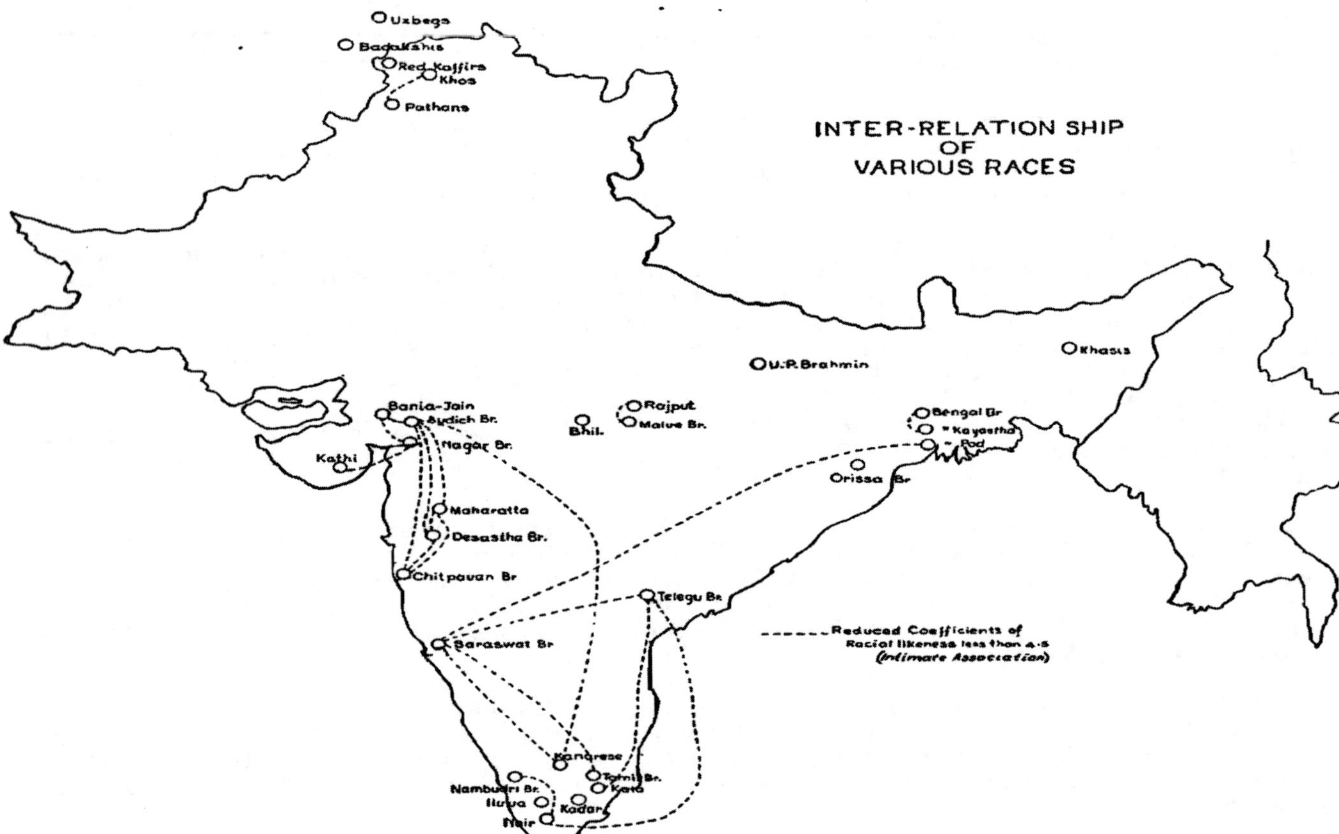

Text.-fig. 8. Inter-relationship of Various Races.

values of the C. R. L.'s below 4·5, *i.e.*, having intimate affinities. On examining this Fig. it will be noticed that besides the intra-regional groupings seen in N. W. Himalaya, Guzrat, Bengal, Maharashtra and Malabar, intimate relationships are exhibited by the Audich Brahmin of Guzrat with all the Mahrathi castes and the Kannada Brahmin ; the Pod of Bengal with the Saraswat Gour Brahmin of Konkan and the latter with the Telegu, Tamil and the Kannada Brahmins. Similarly the Telegu Brahmin are intimtately associated with both the Saraswat Gour and the Kalla Nair group. We find, on the one hand, therefore, a very intimate relationship between (*i*) the long-headed peoples of Andhra, Tamil-nadu and Malabar and on the other, between (*ii*) the peoples having a mo e intermediate head form in Guzrat, Maharashtra, Kannada, Tamil-nadu

[1] Venkatachar, C. S.-Op. cit., pages 267-279, where he suggests the infusion of Bhil blood among the Malves due to the former's repeated encroachments in historical times.

and Bengal. If however the values of the C. R. L.'s are raised from 4·5 to 7 (Text-fig. 9.), some

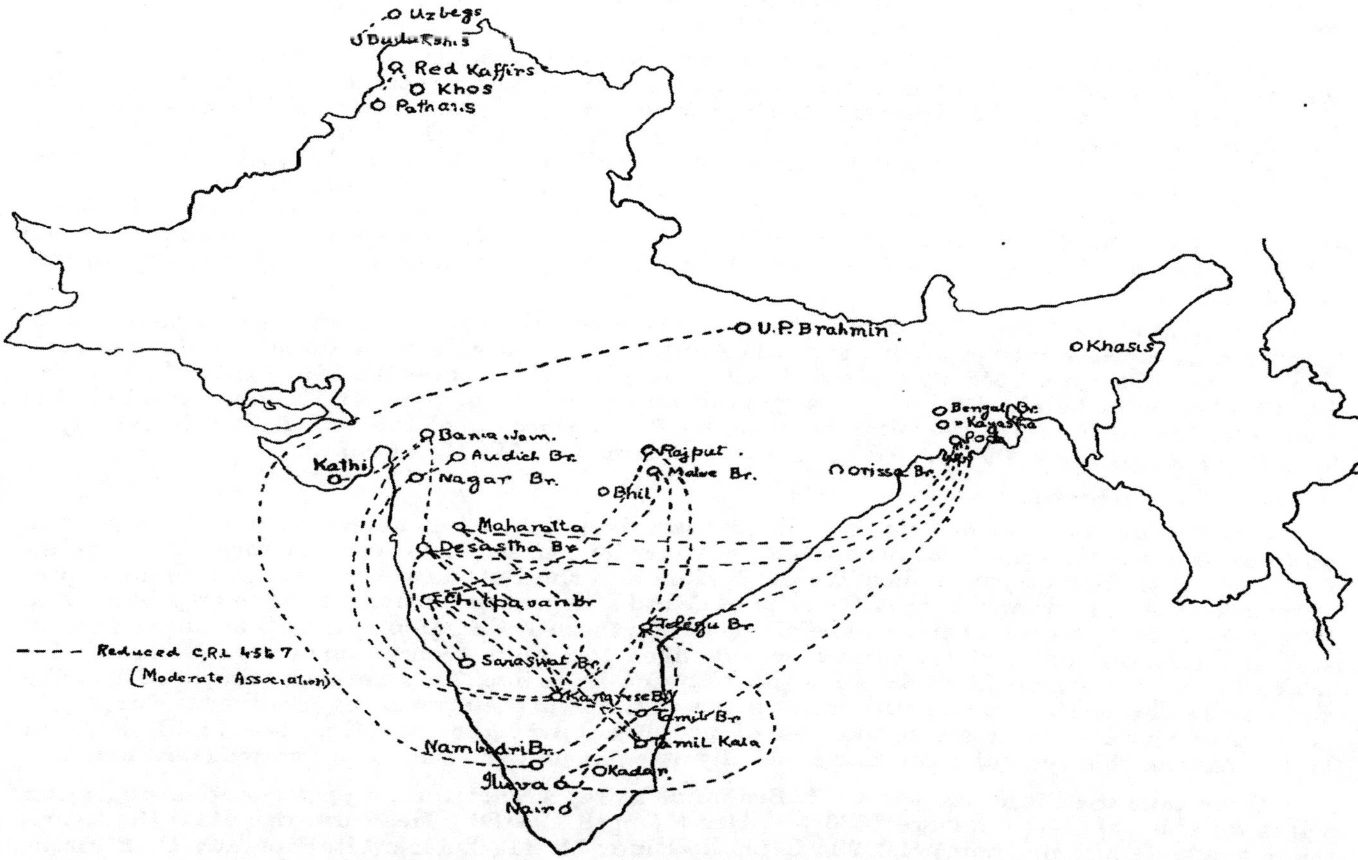

Text-fig 9. Inter-relationship of Various Races.

definite relationships of the former, *i.e.*, (*i*), are established with the long-headed elements of Maharashtra and Central India ; and of the whole of this long-headed group of the Maharashtra, Andhra, Tamil nadu and Malabar with the second, *i.e.*, (*ii*). Last y close affinities are also found between the Brahmin of the United Provinces and the Nambudiri and between the broad-headed peoples of Guzrat and Kannada.

When the C. R. L. values are still further raised (to 13), the the common dolichocephalic strain which underlies the entire population of the Peninsular and Central India and also partially of Guzrat and Bengal becomes still more explicit and appears to show some morphological similarities with the long-headed strain of Northern India. Similarly the brachycephalic strain which enters predominantly into the population of Guzrat, Bengal, Kannada, Maharashtra and Tamil nadu appears not wholly unlike the one seen among the Tadjik of Badakshan and which forms also one of the component element of the Khos of Chitral.

In the racial composition of the peoples of India we can discern therefore :—(A) a short statured long headed element with high cranial vault but faintly marked supra-orbital ridges and broad, short but orthognathous face, with medium lips. The nose is prominent and long but the alae moderately spread out, giving a Mesorrhine Index. The colour of the skin varies from light brown (Nos. 14-15) in the Telegu Brahmin to a dark tawny brown (Nos. 23—27) among the Kalla, the eye colour is dark brown (Nos. 1-3), and colour of the hair is usually black (No. 27). The latter is in general straight, but is inclined to waviness and the amount is moderate both on the face and the body.

It is found in its purest form among the Telegu Brahmin but the Kallas of Southern Tamil country and the Illuvas of Cochin also furnish good examples. Taking these three as representative samples, we get the following mean values for its somatic characters :—

Stature 1634·23 ; Head length 189·68 ; Head breadth 140·92 ; Cephalic Index 74·34 ; Auricular height 121·69 ; Bizygomatic breadth 131·18 ; Total Facial length 115·40 ; Facial Index 88·05 ; Inter-orbital breadth 31·20 ; Orbito-nasal Index 111·20 ; Nasal depth 23·97 and Nasal Index 73·05.

This type forms the predominant element in the greater part of the lower stratum of the population of Northern India, including to some extent the Punjab, where among the Chuhra and

Chamar, Havelock Charles[1] noticed the presence of a small-headed, broad-nosed element which appears to be closely related to the Mediterranean stock of Europe. (Fig. 5-5(*a*) 6-6(*a*) in Plate VII and Figs. 1-1(*a*), 2-2(*a*) and 4-4(*a*) in Plate IX.

On this basic substratum there appears to have superimposed :— *In the western littoral and Bengal* (B) a brachycephalic element of medium stature with flattened occiput but having also h'gh head and not infrequently receding forehead. Like the former the face is short and orthognathous but somewhat broader. The nose is long and highly pitched but quite often arched and convex. The skin colour varies from a pale white (Nos. 10—13) to light brown (Nos. 14—15) among the Nagar Brahmin, to tawny brown (Nos. 23—28) among the Kannada Non-Brahmins. The co'our of the eye is usually dark brown (Nos. 2—4) but a small per cent. shows light eyes (Nos. 5—9). The hair colour similarly is black (No. 27) with a small proportion showing a dark brown t:nt (Nos. 4—6). The hair is generally straight and the pilous system well developed.

If we take the Nagar Brahmin of Guzrat, the Kayastha of Bengal and the Kannada non-Brahmin as representatives of this type , the following mean values are found for their somatic characters :—Stature 1658·08 ; Head length 183·25 ; Head breadth 149·60 ; Cephalic Index 81·76 ; Auricular height 122·76 ; Bizygomatic breadth 134·59 ; Total Facial length 116·34 ; *Facial Index 86·58 ; Inter-orbital breadth 30·88 ; Orbito-nasal Index 112·38 ; Nasal depth* 25·18 and Nasal Index 69·85. (Figs. 1—6*a*, in Plates III, IV, V and X).

And in Northern India :—

(C) Another long-headed strain with comparatively lower but longer head and tall stature and possess:ng a long face and prominent narrow long nose. In its purest form it is found the Northwest Himalayan tr:bes like the Kaffirs and the Pathan where the skin colour is predominantly of a rosy white tint (Nos. 9—11) and an appreciable number have grey blue eyes (Nos. 7—16) and chestnut hair. In the plains of Northern India, among the Sikhs of the Punjab and the Brahmin of U. P. the skin colour changes to a light transparent brown (Nos. 12—15) which in the language of Emil Schmidt quoted by Risley is like, " the milk just tinged with coffee and hardly darker than is met with in members of the swartheir races of Southern Europe "[2]. Here also there is a small proportion of people having light eyes (Nos. 5—7) and brownish hair. Among this type also the hair is usually straight and the pilous system well developed.

If we take the Sikhs and the U. P. Brahmins as representatives, we get the following mean value for this type :— Stature 1686·39 : Head length 193·80 ; Head breadth 141·73 ; Auricular height (U. P. Brahmin) 120·92 ; Cephalic Index 73·11 ; Inter-orbital breadth (U. P. Brahmin) 29·44 ; Bizygomatic breadth 134·58 ; Total Facial length 120·91 ; Facial Index 89·88 Orbito nasal Index (U. P. Brahmin) 114·24 ; Nasal Depth (U. P. Brahmin) 26·78 and Nasal Index 67·13. (Figs. 1—4*a* in Plate VI, Figs. 1—6*a* in Plate VII and Figs. 3—3*a* in Plate IX.)

The two long-headed strains (A) and (C) show some similarity in the shape of the head as revealed in the comparative closeness of the values of the C. R. L.'s between the U. P. and the Telegu Brahmins and the Pathan and the Nair. A somewhat like similarity was also noticed by Harrower[3] in the shape of the cranium of the Tamil coolies and the Scottish people.

Significant differences are however, visible not only in stature, in the absolute length, and height of the cranial vault, but also in the form and proportions of the face and the nose. These together with the d fferences :n the integumentary colours mark out the long headed people of Southern from those of Northern India. If as Peake and Fleure[4] consider, that long- and high-headedness are associated with dark hair and eyes and are the characteristics of a very early type of modern men, the type designated here as (A) must be a south eastward drift of this race, which reached India in very early times. The other long headed type, as history would seem to suggest, belonged to a late drift from the north west though both may have been evolved of a common ancestral stock like the Cro-magnon or some pre-Cro-magnon race but were differentiated very early.

In addition to these three types, the aboriginal population of India discloses :—

(D) A short long- and moderately high-headed strain with often strongly marked brow ridges broad short face, the mouth sightly inclined forwards and small flat nose with the alae extended. The hair varies from wavy to curliness and the skin colour is a shade of dark chocolate brown approaching black. This type is predominant among the aboriginal tribes of Central and Southern India, but seems also to have entered in a considerable degree in the ower stratum of the Indian population *This type is closely allied to the Veddas of Ceylon*, the Toalas of Celebes and the Sakais of the Malay Peninsula. A more primitive form of this type is seen among the aborigines of Australia among whom some of its traits are found in an intensified form.

---

[1] Charles, R. H.—1892. Op. cit.
[2] Risley, H. H. 1901—Op. cit., page 490.
[3] Harrower, Gordon.—Trans. Roy. Soc. of Edinburgh, Volume LIV. Op. cit.
[4] Peake, H. and Fleure, H. J.—Priests and Kings. pages 181—188 ; Oxford, 1927.

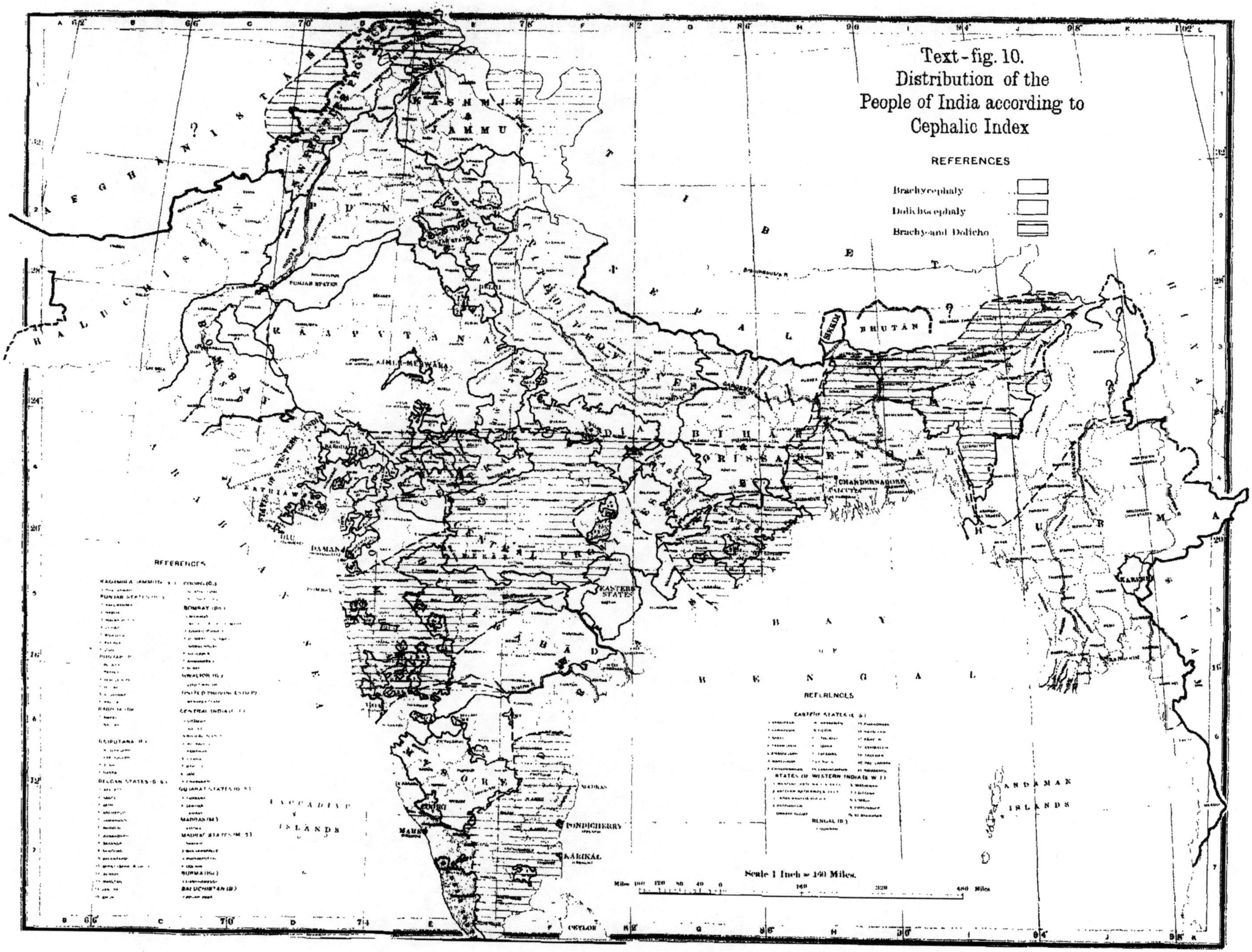

Text-fig. 10. Distribution of the People of India according to Cephalic Index

The Bhils of the Vindhya and the Chenchus of the Farhabad Hills may be regarded as representatives of this type. (Figs. 4—7*a*, in Plate II and Figs. 5—6*a*, in Plate IX.)

It seems probable that at a very early time, this type displaced and partially intermixed with :—

(E) a dark pigmy strain having spirally curved hair, remnants of which are still found among the Kadars and the Pulayans of the Peramabicullan Hills but which is mostly submerged in India at the present time. (Figs. 1—2*a*, in Plate I and Figs. 1—3*a*, in Plate II).

From the evidence supplied by anthropometry the mongoloid racial strain does not appear to have entered in any considerable extent in the population of the mainlands of India. The true Mongol element as seen among the Uzbegs, still remains outside the Indian frontiers but all along the sub-Himalayan region from the Chiang-pa and Ladakhi of N.E. Kashmir to the Lepcha or Rong of Bhuatan :—

(F) a brachycephalic mongolid type, having, not improbably some affinities with the former, seems to have penetrated, and constitutes today, the main component of the population of these parts. The type that forms the dominant element in Burma is also brachycephalic but somewhat shorter in stature and having a short flat nose and a tendency to alveolar prognathism. It appears to exhibit certain affinities with and may not improbably be a sub-type of (F) but having closer relationships with the Siamese, the Malay and the Cochin Chinese, all of whom undoubtedly belong fundamentally to a common racial stock.

In Assam and Northern Burma there seems to have entered :—

(G) a second mongoloid strain, characterised by medium stature, longish head and medium nose, but exhibiting like (F) the typical mongoloid characteristics of the face and the eye. This element constitutes the major strain in the population of the hills and not inconsiderably of that of the Brahmaputra Valley, though mixed with the type (G) in many places. The Angami Nagas may be considered to be the best representative of this type, but the Mikir-Bodo group also furnishes a good example. (Figs. 1—7, in Plate VIII.)

RELATIONSHIP WITH OLDER STRAINS.

In trying to trace the history of these different racial strains we are confronted with a lack of skeletal materials belonging to early periods of India's racial history though relics of early man are scattered extensively all over the country. In Text fig. 11, are given the distribution

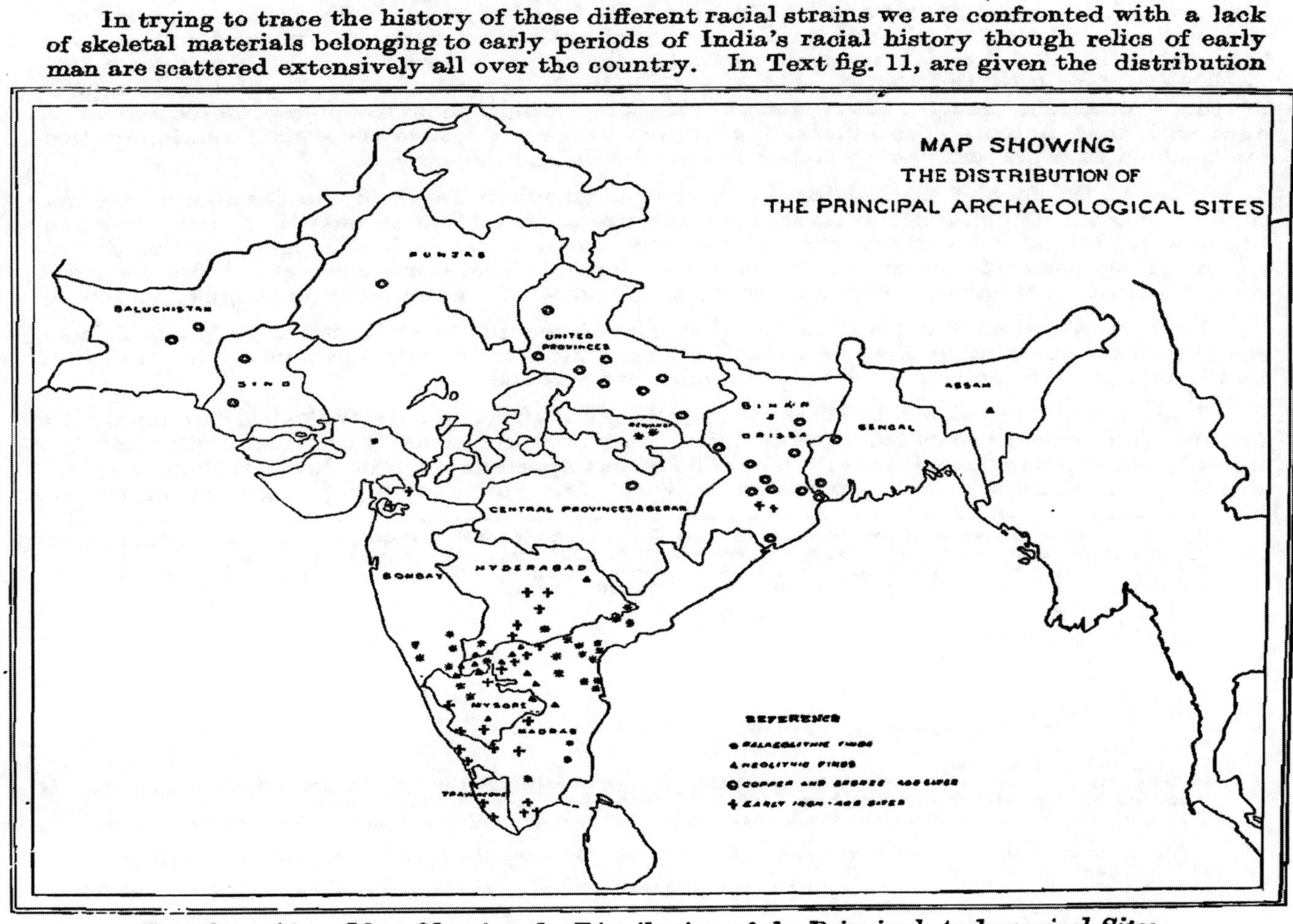

Text-fig.—11. Map Showing the Distribution of the Principal Archæoogical Sites.

of the principal prehistoric sites so far discovered. Of the early stone age, implements have been found in Rewa, Kathiawar, Maharashtra, Pallavaram, Arkonam, Pundi in the southernmost parts of the Peninsula and higher up along the Penner river. There is also evidence in many places of Southern Deccan that the Neolithic man used some of the rock shelters on the granite hills which rise abruptly out of the plains, but as yet no traces of human habitation or inhumation which can be assigned definitely to the Palæolithic or Neolithic age, have been discovered.[1] Innumerable sites belonging to the Chalcolithic times, numbering well over a hundred, have however been found principally in Northwestern India, some of which *e.g.*, Mohenjo-daro and Harappa cover many hundreds of acres. Similarly megalithic remains and burials of the Iron Age, occur in all parts of the Central and Southern India, of which nearly a million were counted in the Hyderabad State alone.[2]

The earliest accounts of the latter were published by Meadows Taylor [3] and Breeks[4] in 1873. Taylor opened hundreds of Cairns and Kistaevans in the Shorapur State, above the junction of the Bheema and Krishna rivers, of which the most important and complete were the cairns of Jewurgi numbering 268, and occupying an area of 336, 216 yards.[5] Throughout these remains red and black earthenware, red cornelian beads, copper, bronze, iron implements and objects of gold and silver were found. From the manner of the disposal of the dead, Taylor came to the conclusion that two different cultures were represented—i) when burial was resorted to, and, ii) when cremation came into general use.[6] He found also evidence of human sacrifice, specially in Cairns A, B, D and E at Jewurgi[7] and in Cairn A at Andola about 5 miles south-east of Jewurgi[8]. Three skeletons were found in Cairn A[9] at Jewurgi, of which the largest measured 5—5½ft., 3 in Cairn B[10] of which two were probably of women judging from the pelvic breadth, 5 skulls in Cairn D and 1 in Cairn E. The last was " very long headed with prominent eyebrows and marked *prognathism*"[11]. Unfortunately none of these skeletal remains could be preserved as they decayed soon after having been exposed to air.

The Megalithic remains of the Nilgiri hills described by Breeks[12], who as a member of the Madras Civil Service was stationed for many years in the Nilgiris,—belong apparently to two periods, the earlier of which was the age of the Cairn builders and the latter of that of the Cromlechs, which were found at lower levels close to the Ghats leading from the Plains. Red and black earthenware and bronze and iron objects were found throughout these remains but from the changes in orientation and nature of the objects differences of time and culture were inferred[13]. It is of special interest to note the representations of human figures on horsebacks found in the Cairns, and the same with swords in the sculptured figures of the Cromlechs, though the portrayal of horse would seem to suggest limited acquaintance with that animal. The human figures are uncovered above the waist, wearing quilted and padded drawers and having elaborate sword-belt and dagger[14].

Close to the foot of the Nilgiris, in the Satyamangalam Taluk of the Coimbatore district (lat. 11° N), Mr. Longhurst[15] excavated a certain number of Cairns and stone cists, red and black ware, beads and various iron objects were found along with four-legged earthen sarcophagi. Fragments of human skulls were also found. The same excavator[16] also opened a rock-cut tomb in Malabar, about 5 miles from Calicut where a similar sarcophagus was found.

In the Hyderabad State, Mr. Yazdani[17] opened a large number of Cairns near Maula Ali in a rocky country covering an area of about 40 acres. Red and black ware and bronze and iron implements and fragments of human remains were found.

Besides Mr. Yazdani, Mr. L. Munn [18] in the Raigir District and Mr. Wakefield[19] at Janampitt (Warangal District) excavated several Cairns and Cromleches, in which also similar pottery, iron objects and sarcophagi were found. The most important work in this part, however, was done by Dr. Hunt[20], who excavated a very large number of cist graves in Raigir,

---

1 Foote, Robert Bruce—*Indian Prehistoric and Proto-Historic Antiquities*—pages 2 and 11, Madras, 1916.
2 Hyderabad Cairn burials and their significance—*J. R. A. I.*, Volume LIV, page 141, London.
3 Taylor, Capt. Meadows,—Trans. Roy. Irish Academy. Volume XXIV, pages 329—362; Dublin, 1865.
4 Breeks, J. W. —Primitive Tribes of the Nilgiris; London, 1873.
5 *Ibid.*, page 337.
6 *Ibid.*, page 358.
7 *Ibid.*, pages 340—342.
8 page 345.
9 page 339.
10 page 340.
11 *Ibid.*, page 334.
12 Breeks, J. W.—*Op. cit.*—pages 72—110.
13 *Ibid.*, page 100.
14 *Ibid.*, pages 102—105.
15 Longhurst, A. H.—A Report *on* the excavation of certain cairns in the Coimbatore District. Ann. Report of the Archæological Survey—Southern Circle, *for* 1913—14, pages 43—45, Madras.
16 Longhurst, A. H.—A Rock-cut tomb near Calicut. Ann. Report of the Archæological Survey for 1911—12, pages 159—160.
17 Yazdani, G.—Ann. Report of the Arch. Dept. of His Highness the Nizam's Dominions for 1915—16.
18 *Ibid.*, page 10.
19 Wakefield, G. E. C.—Note on a *visit* to the prehistoric burial grounds of Janampitt in the Warangal Dist. of Hyderabad; Ann. Rep. Arch. Sur. Hyder. State for 1917—18, *pages* 24 39.
20 Hunt, E. H.—Op. cit.

and other places in the Hyderabad State. Dr. Hunt[1] distinguishes two kinds of pottery (1) red and (2) black with red bases, both hand and wheel made with symbolic marks. Copper objects, lapis lazuli, quartz and cornelian beads associated with female burials, gold and silver ornaments and iron objects of all kinds were found throughout. There was evidence of human sacrifice here, as at Jewurgi[2] and several skeletons were found both in a contracted and extended position, seven of which were discovered in Raigir Cairn XVII, one in Raigir V and another in Raigir XXIV.[3]

In the Tamil country, in the south, Mr. Richards[4] excavated three stone circles at Odygathur in the Palar Valley, about 18 miles from Vellore, not far from the site of Kanchi the ancient capital of the Pallavas. These stone circles occur at about 1,100 ft. above the sea level. Red and black wares, copper and iron objects and three-legged earthen sarcophagi were found along with two terracotta spindle whorls.

In the south of the Chingleput district, at Perambour, Mr. Rea[5] excavated some stone circles on the lower end of the hill slope and found the same kind of red and black-wares, iron implements and earthen sarcophagi, with three rows of legs instead of two. Two human skeletons were found, one of which was in a flexed position. Somewhat further south on the Coromandel Coast, about 20 kilometres from Pondichery, Dr. Numa Laffitte[6] of the French Colonial Health Service, has recently carried out some notable excavations in the villages of Tiruvicar, Perimbe and Montapalam. In these three villages, he found a large number of burial jars and sarcophagi having both two and three rows of legs. Besides the usual red and black wares, he got in these urns, a large number of bronze, copper and iron objects and gold and cornelian trinkets. He recovered also a large number of human crania[7]. The nature and content of the objects and the geometrical symbols (?) on the outer surface of the earthen ware were similar to those found at Chingleput and other parts of the Presidency.

The largest and apparently the most important of these remains however, occur in the southernmost part of the Peninsula, in the district of Tinnevelley, in the delta of the Tamraparni river, which at Aditanallur alone extends over 114 acres[8]. Mr. Rea, of the Archæological Survey of India carried out some excavations during 1901-02 and opened a large number of burial urns, in which besides red and black-ware, gold ornaments and objects of copper, bronze and iron in large quantities were found. Some human skeletons were found in a flexed position.

That the megalithic remains of the Deccan and S. India reveal an uniform culture throughout as judged by the nature and contents of the objects found, admits hardly of any doubt, though several phases of the same can probably be distinguished. But what exactly were the origins and the precise period of time to which this culture may be assigned, are questions that cannot be settled definitely until further excavations take place. Meadows Taylor has shown that the round holes, in the centre of the slabs on the southern sides of the Deccan Kistvaens are identical with those of Circassia, Brittany and England,[9] and Dr. Hunt[10] has called attention to the striking resemblance of the burial arrangements of the Raigir Cairn with those of Tarkham in Egypt, the similarity of interwined snakes and rosettes and of the polished black and red ware with those with "Ka" marks of the Middle Predynastic Egypt pointed out originally by Mr. Henry Balfour of Oxford. But as shown by Sir Flinders Petrie, [11] this connection could not have been direct for the iron found in the Indian remains was not known in Egypt before the time of Rameses the Great *i.e.*, about 13th century B. C. Similarly the bronze found in the South Indian graves contains a much higher percentage of tin than the Egyptian bronzes, which did not come into use, according to Petrie, till the 18th Dynasty. The bronze vases from the Nilgiri Cairns analysed by Mr. Broughton [12] had 19·8% of tin and a similar cup from Maula Ali (Hyderabad) when analysed showed 21% of tin. [13]

From the evidence derived from Sanskritic sources, both Sir John Marshall[14] and Prof. Rapson[15] have attributed the introduction of iron in S. India to the Vedic Aryan colonists about the 5th century B. C. when S. India was still supposed to be in the Neolithic stage. But iron ores of excellent quality are found on the surface in large quantities in S. India and earthen

---

1 Op. cit., page 150.
2 Op. cit., page 148.
3 Op. cit., pages 148—149.
4 Richards, F. J.—Note on some Iron Age graves at Odymegathur. N. Arcot Dist. S. India. J.R.A.I., Volume LIV, pages 157—165.
5 Rea, A.—Prehistoric Remains at Perambur. Ann. Rept. Arch. Survey, 1908—09, pages 92—99.
6 Laffite, Numa—Rapport D'ensemble sur les Fouilles Executees dans le Sud De L'Inde. Paris, 1932.
7 Op. cit., pages 16—39.
8 Annual Report of the Archæological Survey of India for 1902—03, pages 114—119.
9 Meadows Taylor, Op. cit., page 329.
10 Hunt, E. H.—Op. cit., page 155.
11 *Ibid.*, page 156.
12 Brooks, J. W.—Op. cit.
13 Ann. Rept. of the Arch. Sur. of the Hyderabad State for 1915—16, page 8.
14 Marshall, Sir John—Cambridge History of India. Volume I, pages 612—648; Cambridge, 1922.
15 Rapson, E. G.— *Ibid.*, pages 37—62.

crucibles for smelting them, corresponding in size and shape to those now used, have been discovered at Aditanallur[1]. The possibility of acquiring the knowledge of its reduction independently therefore in Southern India, cannot altogether be ignored and one must admit the force of Dr. Hunt's argument that the presence of iron should not be regarded as setting a limiting date to these remains [2].

In Northern India remains of prehistoric settlements belonging to the Chalcolithic times exisit all along the lower beds of the Indus river from Gujo to Harappa. The explorations of Sir Aurel Stein [3] have shown that they exist further westwards "at a great line of Mounds stretching long the barren foot of the South-Western Waziristan hills". Three of these important sites have been excavated so far, namely, Nal, Mohenjo-daro and Harappa and the publication of Sir John Marshall's monumental work [4], a short time ago has shown the high state of civilisation reached in the Indus Valley in the 4th mellenium B. C. and its close association with the contemporary civilisation of the Tigris-Euphrates Valley.

Besides these remains definitely attributable to the Chalcolithic Age, there occur numerous Cairns, harrows and rough other stone structures in the Mol and other valleys of the Kirthar range and on the Rorhi Hills in Sind and across the mountain ranges and plateaus of Central India. A group of earthen mounds, believed to be of the Vedic period has also been found at Lauriya, near Nandangarh in Behar. Four of these mounds were excavated by Dr. T. Bloch [5] in 1906-07. In one of them (Mound I) "human skeletons in leaden coffins" were reported to have been found. In two others (Mounds M and N), Dr. Bloch discovered two gold leaves with the figure of the Mother Goddess inscribed on them, and fragments of charred bones mixed with charcoal.

In the Vedic funerary rituals described in the verses 13 and 18 of Mandala 10 of the R. K. Veda the bones of cremated persons are ordained to be consecrated in a *Smasana* made of earth or brick after the invocation of Prithvi or Mother Goddess [6]. From the presence of the figures of the latter and the conical shape of the mound with an wooden post in the centre, as described in the Vedic Prayogas, Dr. Bloch came to the conclusion that the mounds at Lauriya were some Royal tombs belonging to the Vedic Period[7].

The remains of ancient megalithic sites occur in the hills and plateaus of Central India, and copper object have been found in many places, including the enormous find of 828 lbs. at Gungeria in the Balaghat district of the Central Provinces. Similar objects have been reported from all along the Chota Nagpur plateau from Palamau to Dalbhum near Tatanagar. Any systematic, excavations of these ancient sites has not so far been attempted but we are indebted to the distinguished anthropologist, Mr. Sarat Ch. Roy[8] for an excellent account of the remains in the Ranchi and Singbhum districts. Quite recently Mr. E. A. Murry,[9] an Engineer working in the copper mines has excavated some ruins at Raungarh in the Dalbhum district.

From the vicinity of the Kandri river near Kalamati to the banks of the Phulghar river in the Ranchi district and extending into the neighbouring Singbhum and Manbhum districts, Mr. Roy found the remains of ancient brick structures, silted up tanks and huge slabs and columns of sepulchral stones attributed by the Mundas to "Asuras" who were supposed to have occupied the land before the latter came to occupy it.[10] Over 18 of these ancient sites were examined by Mr. Roy from Belwadag, 4 miles southwest of Khunti, the sub divisional headquarters of the Mundas, to Sangrigaon and Indpirl on the southern extremity of the Ranchi District.

These remains, which are situated everywhere on high lands, near river banks and commanding a good view of the surrounding country,[11] can be divided into two kinds, namely (*a*) ruins of settlements containing large brick structures, silted up tanks and sometimes kilns for smelting iron, and (*b*) graveyards, adjacent to the former with huge monolithic stones under each of which 3 to 4 cinerary urns were buried. At Khuntit'a Kunjla, 2 miles east of Belwadag and believed to be the latter's graveyard, 50 of these monoliths were counted. The manner of erecting these structures was different from that of the Munda graves where the stone slabs are supported on 4 corner-stones and in the "Asura" graves they lie flat on the ground, with the urns placed from 1 to 2 ft. below the surface under the monoliths.[12] Similarly, unlike the

---

[1] Thurston, E.—The Madras Presidency, page 74; Cambridge, 1913.

[2] Hunt, E. H.—Op. cit., pages 153—154.

[3] Stein, Sir Aurel—Prehistory of Indo-Iranian Borderlands. Huxley Lecture for 1934.

[4] Marshall, Sir John—Mohenjo-daro and the Indus Civilisation. 3 Volumes, London, 1931.

[5] Bloch, T.—Excavations at Lauriya, Nandangarh—Ann. Report. Arch. Survey of India for 1906—07, pages 119-126.

[6] Op. cit., pages 123—124.

[7] Op. cit., pages 125—126.

[8] Roy, Sarat Ch.—A Note on some Remains of the Ancient Asuras in the Ranchi District, Journal of the Behar and Orissa Research Society, Volume I, Part. II, pages 229—253.

[9] Mr. Murray's account will shortly be published by the Asiatic Society of Bengal.

[10] Op. cit., page 229.

[11] Op. cit., page 258.

[12] Op. cit., page 238.

Munda who bury only a few selected bones, these urns contain all the bones [1], though found in extremely decayed state at present. A large number of these earthen jars were opened by Mr. Roy, who found their nature and contents to be similar. Polished stone implements of various kinds, cornelian beads, large quantities of copper and bronze objects and ornaments were discovered in the jars. Few pieces of what look like lapis lazuli were found at Bichna, six miles from Khunti[2]. Besides these, phallic symbols in stone were found in several places including Sangrigaon and Indpirl[3], iron arrow heads, ornaments and implements at Kamanta, Anigara, Dargana, Bichna and Toner. At Belwadag[4] and Oskea[5] large quantities of iron slags and kilns for smelting them were seen showing that the art of reducing the raw metal was not unknown to these ancient dwellers. The pottery was found to be wheel-made ornamented with geometric designes and beautifully polished but not glazed[6].

Ruangarh ruins excavated by Mr. E. A. Murray occur on the spur of a hill in the copper belt of the Dalbhum district near Tatanagar. Among the objects found in these ruins by Mr. Murray are a large number of polished stone implements potsherds, cornelian beads, copper and gold ornaments, iron slags and two skulls in a fairly good state of preservation.

From an examination of the nature and contents of the Chota Nagpur ruins, Mr. Roy came to the conclusion that they ranged over a long-period of time, in which two stages could be distinguished, namely (*i*) a Neolithic and (*ii*) a copper—the latter overlapping an Iron Age culture.[7]

It is true that in Europe, the megalithic remains have been assigned to the latter part of the Neolithic Age, and some of the crude stone monuments of Sind, specially those of the Rorhi hills are believed to have belonged to the same time.[8] The ruins of Chota Nagpur on the other hand show everywhere the association of stone implements with copper, bronze and in several places iron objects[9]. While therefore, further excavations may yet disclose here a definitely Neolithic basis we cannot at the present state of our knowledge avow anything beyond a possible Chalcolithic stage before iron came into general use.

The relationship of the megalithic remains of Chota Nagpur with those of Southern India. has not as yet been closely examined, as a result probably of the very important discoveries of Messrs. Roy and Murray being not widely known. It is significant however that the large bronze vessel dicovered by Mr. Roy inside a burial jar at Bahea,[10] appeared on examination to be similar to some of the bronze objects of Southern India[11]. The percentage of tin in the bronze objects of Chota Nagpur is also very high, though not quite as great as that of the Southern Indian specimens referred to before. In the 11 specimens sent by Mr. Roy for examination, Dr. Caldwell of the Geological Survey of India found the amount of tin to be varying from 5·8 to 23·8%[12], on the other hand the highest percentage of tin found at Mohenjo-daro did not exceed 12·13 [13]. I am informed further by Mr. Sana Ullah, the Archæological Chemist, that the chemical composition of the copper objects of Aditanallur analysed by him is similar to that of Chota Nagpur, from which he infers that the former was imported from the latter region.

All these points taken together establish in my opinion a very strong case for linking up the negalithic culture of Central and Southern India. If the distribution of the remains further west be now taken into consideration we can trace an almost continuous line up to Sind, where it apprently existed in the Neolithic times. We are not certain when it moved eastwards but not probably earlier than the Chalcolithic Age and certainly not later than the time when Iron just came into use, for out of a total of 248 objects found by Mr. Roy, only 20 were of iron and all the rest were of copper and bronze [14]. In the Southern Indian remains, on the other hand iron objects far outnumber the objects of copper and bronze. The probability therefore would seem to be that the megalithic culture was introduced into Southern India after the use of iron has already been acquired in Central India.

The introduction of iron in Northern India appears to be synchronous with the invasion of the "Vedic Aryans" who also brought horse with them. It is significant therefore that not

---

[1] Op. cit., page 235.

[2] Op. cit., page 240.

[3] Op. cit., page 248.

[4] Op. cit., pages 230—231.

[5] Op. cit., page 244.

[6] Coggin Brown, J.—Note on Ancient Pottery found in the Munda country—J.B.O.R.S., Volume I, Part II, page 130.

[7] Roy, Sarat Chandra,—Distribution and Nature of "Asura" sites in Chota Nagpur— J. B. O. R. S., Volume VI, Part III, pages 393—423.

[8] Marshall, Sir John—*Op. cit., Volume I, page 93.*

[9] *Roy, Sarat Chandra—Note on some prehistoric stone implements found in the Ranchi District. Ibid.,* Volume II, page 65.

[10] Roy, Sarat Chandra—A find of ancient bronze articles in the Ranchi District. J.B. O. R. S., Volume II, Part IV, pages 485—487.

[11] See, *Ibid.*, page 486 for Mr. Coggin Brown's Report.

[12] Roy, Sarat Chandra—Op. cit., Volume VI, page 410.

[13] Sana Ullah, M.—Mohenjo-daro and the Indus Civilisation, Volume, II, page 481.

[14] Roy, Sarat Chandra—Op. cit., Volume VI, Part III, page 397.

far from the Chota Nagpur ruins at Nandangarh, a Vedic site seemed to have existed, and a gold coin of the Kushan period was discovered by Mr. Roy at Belwadag where the remains of an ancient kiln for smelting iron were also found[1]. Similarly the discovery of sculptured figures of men riding horses in "quilted and padded trousers," with drawn sword inside the Cairns of the Nilgiri hills,[2] along with iron and bronze objects would seem to indicate some association between the northern invaders—to whom alone these figures can refer—and the introduction of the 'black' metal in Southern India. That the people of Southern India had as yet only limited acquaintance with the horse is shown from their poor representations of that noble animal.[3] These considerations would seem to far outweigh in my opinion those advanced in favour of the discovery of the knowledge of the use of iron independently in Southern India and until it is proved otherwise, it will be safer to regard the megalithic remains of South India as post-Vedic and later than similar remains of the Central Indian plateau, from where the culture would seem to have spread southwards.

The human skeletons found in these pre-historic sites fall therefore into two broad groups namely (*a*) the Chalcolithic, and (*b*) the Iron Age remains, excepting two whose precise ages are uncertain. Of these two, one was found by Mr. Wolf at Bayana, near Agra, 35 ft, below the level of the bed of the Gumbhir river while building a railway bridge over it in 1912. This skull, which has been presented by the Bombay Anthropological Society to the Anthropological section of the Indian Museum through the kind offices of the late Sir J. J. Modi, is of considerable antiquity as judged by the complete mineralisation which it has undergone. In character it is dolichocranial, and though the facial part is missing, portions of the nasal bones left, show that the nose was high pitched[4]. The other skull discovered by Capt. Hingston, near Sialkot is of a later date and in "the general nature and consistency of the bones not unlike the bronze age human remains of England[5]." The shape and proportions of this skull are closely allied to that found by Mr. Hargreaves at Nal,[6] though somewhat smaller, due probably to its female sex.[7]

(*a*) The human remains that have been definitely ascribed to the Chalcolithic times all belong to the Indus Valley Civilisation and recovered from Nal, Mohenjo-daro and Harappa. Two human skulls have also been discovered by Sir Aurel Stein in similar Chalcolithic sites in Makran.[8] Col. R. B. Seymour Sewell F. R. S., late Director of the Zoological Survey and the present writer have already published their reports on the Nal.[9] Makran[10] and the first lot of the Mohenjo-daro remains[11]. Studies on the second collection of the Mohenjo-daro skulls by Dr. P. C. Basu of the Bose Research Institute, Calcutta, and the present writer[12], and on the Harappa skeletons by the latter[13] are also under publication. Detailed descriptions of these remains therefore are not necessary here. It is sufficient to note that the majority of these remains belong to the dolichocranial class, of which the greater proportion have a small, but high vaulted head with smooth forehead and narrow prominent nose. The muscular attachments are feeble and judging from the long bones the living stature was moderate. The rest however are much larger, with a mean cubic capacity of 1490c.c., lower cranial vault, prominent supra-orbital ridges and an enormous growth of the post-auricular part, which forms 55 per cent. of the total cranium.[14] This type occurs at Makran (skull B),[15] the lower strata of Mohenjo-daro, and also at Harappa where it is found in the Open Burials, some parts of the G. site and by one skeleton (H. 255) in the Jar burials of a much later date.[16] From the formation of its lower forehead, moderately broad nose and post-auricular development, Col. Sewell and I provisionally classified it as "Proto-Australoid."[17] The discovery of more remains of this type later on, however, with a narrow high pitched nose, both at Mohenjo daro and Harappa, and my examination of the ancient Sumerian skulls found at Al-Ubaid and Kish in the collections of the Royal College of Surgeons, London, and the Anatomy Department of the Oxford University, as well as the Long Barrow English skulls, have convinced me that in spite of the prominence of the supra-orbital ridges the true affinities of

1 Roy, Sarat Chandra. Op. cit., Volume I, Part II, pages, 230—232.

2 Breeks, J. W. —Op. cit., pages 95—102.

3 *Ibid.*

4 Keith, Sir Arthur—Journal of the Anthropological Society of Bombay, Volume XI, No. 6, pages 663—672; Bombay, 1917.

5 *Ibid.*, page 664.

6 Sewell, R. B. S. and Guha, B. S.—Report on the bones excavated at Nal, Mem. Arch. Survey of India; No. 35, pages 56—80.

7 *Ibid.*, page 65.

8 Stein, Sir Aurel—Mem. Arch. Survey of India, No. 43.

9 *Op. cit.*,

10 Sewell, Col. R. B. S. and Guha, B. S.—Report on a collection of bones made by Aurel Stein in Makran, Mem. Arch. Survey of India, No 43, pages 191—200.

11 Sewell, Col. R. B. S. and Guha, B. S.—Op. cit., 1931.

12 Guha, B. S. and Basu, P. C.—Report on the Human Remains excavated at Mohenjo-daro in 1928-29 in Further Excavations at Mohenjo-daro, edited by Ernest Mackay, pages 634—653 (in the press).

13 Guha, B. S.—Report on the Human Remains excavated at Harappa (in the press).

14 Guha, B. S. and Bose, P. C.—Op. cit., pages 647—649.

15 Sewell, R. B. S. and Guha, B. S.—Op. cit., page 199.

16 Guha, B. S.—Report on the Human Remains at Harappa. Op. cit.

17 Op. cit., 1931, pages 638—642.

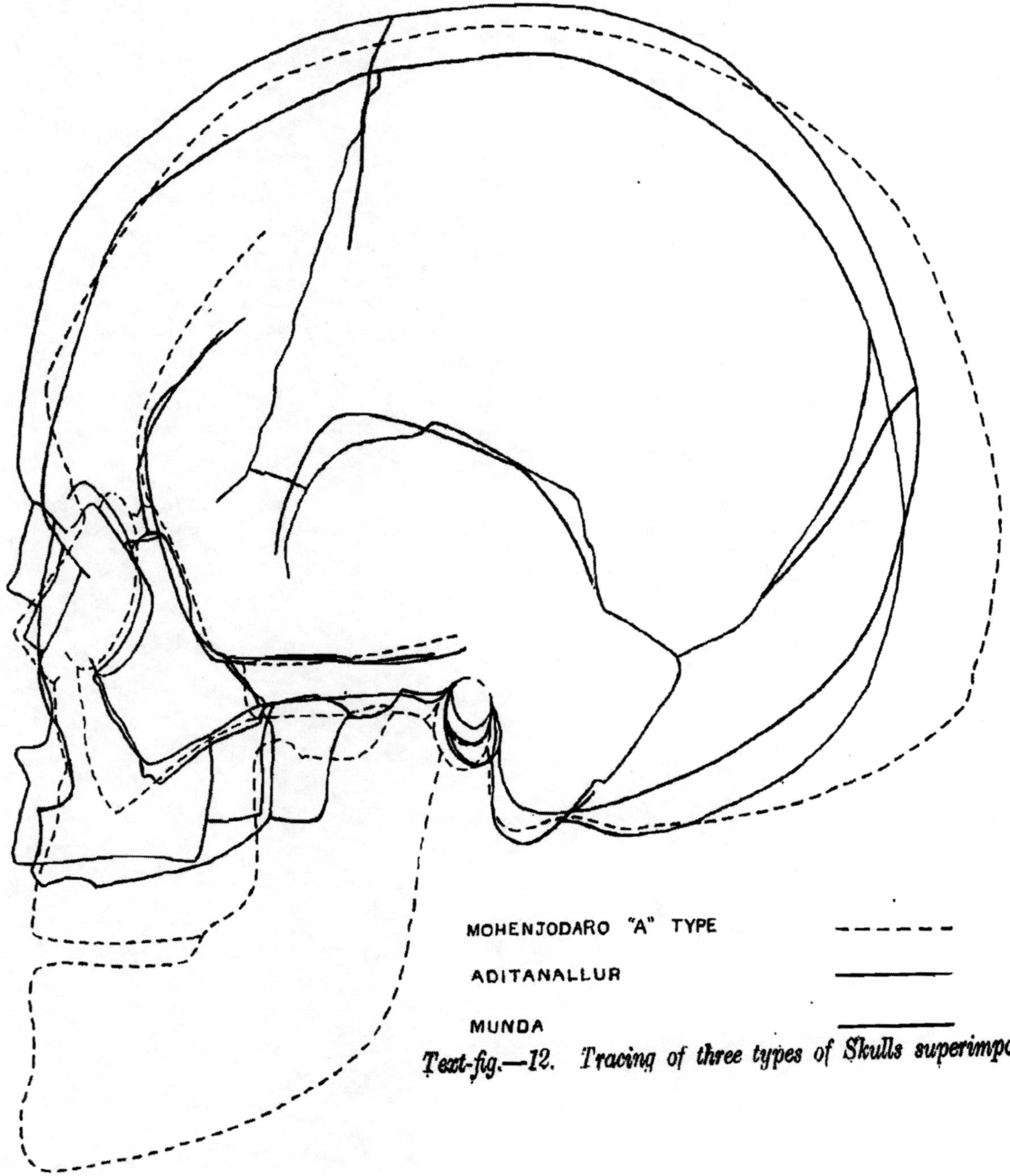

Text-fig.—12. Tracing of three types of Skulls superimposed.

this case are not "Australoid," as we formerly supposed, but "Caucasic", to use Keith's [1] not very happy expression.

Eickstedt's discovery in the present population of the Indus Valley, of "a course type with robust proportions, overhanging occiput and prominent superciliary ridges but lighter complexion" seems further to corroborate this view and its continued existence to-day [2].

Besides these two long-headed types, there is a distinctly broad headed one among the crania found at Mohenjo-daro and specially Harappa with high cranial vault, large head and moderately marked supra-orbital ridges. The nose is narrow and prominent but not so fine and high pitched as in the skulls of the Mediterranean type. There is no evidence of any Mongolian strain either in the forward growth of the cheek-bones or the retrocession of the nasal walls as suspected from skull 13*b* found in the earlier lot of Mohenjo-daro remains. The occipital parts are not usually flattened in these skulls but in one No. 11635 it is markedly so,[3] showing definitely the presence of the Armenoid strain in the Indus Valley during the Chalcolithic times.

(*b*) Of the remains recovered from the Iron Age sites, the most numerous and important are the skeletons from Aditanallur. Two of the skulls were taken by Prof. Elliot Smith from the Madras Museum one of which was found to be Australoid [4] and in the other he recognised Armenoid characteristics. Of the remainder, which are now being studied by the present writer, two at least are definitely Australoid with a low sagittal ridge, prominent supra-orbital ridges and chamaerrhine nose with nasal gutter at the lower margins. The others appear to belong to a branch of the Mediterranean race with a high cranial vault, low broad face and also chamaerrhine nose but with sharp lower margins. In Text-fig. 12, is superposed the composite profile view of the three massive Mohenjo-daro skulls, formerly termed by us "Proto-Australoid" on those of 4 male Aditanallur and 4 male Munda skulls from the collections of the Indian Museum. It will be noticed that the former differ from the other two in the forward position of the Auditory Meatus, and the development of the occipital region giving support to powerful neck muscles. The Aditanallur skulls on the other hand have a much higher vault of the cranium and a greater development of the frontal parts which distinguish these from the aboriginal Munda crania.

Of the other sites belonging to the Iron Age we have very little information about the racial types, as most of the human remains found have either been lost or destroyed. A broken skull was found by Mr. Roy at Khuntitola which appeared to be of the long-headed type[5] and Mr. Murray recovered two skulls from Ruangarh ruins which were measured by Mr. Pycraft of the Natural History Museum of London. The Cranial Index of the two skulls are 73·4 and 72·3 and the Nasal Index 48·0 and 57·4 respectively.[6] All the three skulls from Chota Nagpur fall therefore within the dolichocranial class of which one at least is very chamaerrhine.

In the cairns of Jewurgi, Meadows Taylor [7] found many skeletons, both male and female (judging from the breadth of the pelvis).[8] The height of the male skeletons was about 5—5½ ft. and that of the female 4 ft. 9½ in., remains probably of the victims of human sacrifice.[8] In Cairn E[9] he found a skull which was "long-headed with prominent eyebrows and marked prognathism." From the drawings published by him of this skull[10] there can be no doubt that it was definitely negroid.

The skeletons found in the Raigir Cairns and believed by Dr. Hunt[11] to be those of the cairn builders also average about 5 ft. 6 in. in length but the bodies of the victims of human sacrifice were more powerful and massive. Of the three skulls recovered by him in good condition from cairns XVII, and V and XXIV, one had a Cranial Index of 75·0, another 90·0 and the lady with lapis lazuli for whom the cairn was supposed to have been built, 76·0.

SUMMARY OF THE RESULTS.

The accounts of the human remains from prehistoric sites given above though extremely meagre, with the exception of those of the Indus Valley, enable us nevertheless to visualise the broad outlines of the racial history of India in these early times. From the beginning of the 4th millenium B. C. Northwestern India seemed to have been in the occupation of a long-headed race with high cranial vault, long face and narrow prominent nose. Side by side with them we find the existence of another very powerfully built race also long-headed, but with lower cranial vault, and equally long-faced and narrow nose, though the latter was not so high pitched as that of the former.

---

[1] Keith, Sir Arthur—*Illustrated London News*, December 19, 1931, page 1002.
[2] Eickstedt, E.—Loc. cit., 1923, page 164.
[3] Guha, B. S. —Op. cit.
[4] Smith, G. Elliot—Evolution of Man, page 130.
[5] Roy, Sarat Chandra,—Op. cit., page 379.
[6] I am indebted to Mr. Murray for these figures.
[7] Taylor, Meadows—Op. cit., pages 339—345.
[8] *Ibid.*, page 340.
[9] *Ibid.*, page 334.
[10] *Ibid.*, page 334.
[11] Hunt, E. H.—Op. cit., pages 148—149.

A third type with broader head and apparently Armenoid affinities also existed but whose advent occurred probably somewhat later judged by the age of the site at Harappa from which most of these latter type of skulls came.

The presence at Bayana of a small, long, and moderately high vaulted skull with prominent nose seems to indicate that a drift of this race eastwards had taken place even earlier and the whole of the Indo-Gangetic basin seems to have been in its occupation as early as these times.

We have no evidence that this or any of the other two races had penetrated into Southern India at this early period. But later on in the Iron Age, the Peninsula seems to have been occupied by a long but high skulled race with low broad face and nose, resembling the Combe Capelle type. Fischer [1] has stated that the megalithic population of Europe was racially related to the Cro-magnon or more correctly the Combe Capelle type. If this view is correct it would seem that the same people also had introduced this culture in India in the Neolithic times but were driven subsequently from the hills of Northwestern India into Central and Eastern India from where they migrated southwards. They appeared to have dispossessed the aboriginal occupants of the land whose remains are found in various Cairns as victims of human sacrifice. Over this there has superimposed at a later date a race with Armenoid affinities seen from the remains of two persons at Raigir and Aditanallur.

To sum up, though we have no direct evidence of the Negrito race in the old skeletal remains of India the skull of a victim of human sacrifice found in a Cairn at Jewurgi is unmistakeably negroid. The Australoid type found so largely in the present day Indian aborigines, is however abundantly represented both in the Southern Indian and Chota Nagpur sites, and judging from the description given by the " Vedic Aryans " there seems hardly any doubt that they were the " Nisadas " who formerly as to-day occupied the hills and forests of India. [2] Various names have been given to this race such as " Pre-Dravidian ", " Proto-Australoid " and " Veddoid " but none of them seems to be as appropriate as " Nisadic " the generic name given to them by the " Vedic Aryans ", and resuscitated by Mr. Chanda,[3] and which should henceforth be used to designate the non-Negritoid Indian aborigines.

The Combe Capelle type or a race very closely allied to it, from skeletons found in the megalithic remains of Central and Southern India, entered probably with that culture as early as Neolithic times. Mixed with the long-headed Mediterranean race which constituted the major part of the Indus Valley people in the Chalcolithic times, it forms to-day the bulk of the population of the Peninsular and a considerable portion of Northern India, in the upper classes of which another strain with undoubted northern affinities is clearly distinguishable. Fischer[4] has stated that the upper castes of Northern India, retain the Nordic characters of stature, head and nose forms without the fair tint of the skin. The figures published in the Appendix[5] will show that the lighter element though constituting a very small percentage, is still present among the upper classes of the Indian people not only in N. India but also slightly in the south where among the Tamil Brahmins [6] at least it is noticeable. But the largest percentage of this element is found among the Chitpavan or Konkonstha Brahmins of Maharashtra who constitute one of the lightest racial groups in India. In a pure form, however, it is prevalent only among the Indo-Aryan speaking tribes south of the Hindukush mountains, who are in this respect comparable to the European races. It is probable that the powerfully built large-headed strain found at Mohenjo-daro forms one of the constituents of this race whose advent in India appears to synchronise with the " Aryan " invasion.

The brachycephalic race, who forms the dominant element in the population of the western and southwestern parts of India as well as Bengal, must have come at an earlier period, as judged by the remains at Harappa. But that it penetrated Southern India somewhat later seems certain, as judged by the age of the Aditanallur and Raigir skeletons. When it had moved eastwards into Bengal we have no definite evidence, but probably earlier than in Southern India as racial drifts along the Gangetic Valley would seem to have been easier and more rapid.

Mr. Chanda,[7] who first pointed out the non-Mongolic character the brachycephalic people of Bengal, postulates the invasion of an Alpine race from the Pamir regions, speaking a Tokharian speech to explain its existence in India. The presence of broad-headed skulls in the early strata of Mohenjo-daro and Harappa would seem however to militate against this supposition. Recent discoveries of Bertram Thomas analysed by Sir Arthur Keith have definitely shown the existence of brachycephalic types in South Arabia, of which the " Omani " displayed Armenoid affinities,[8]

---

[1] **Fischer, Eugen, endasl—Op. cit., page 191.**

[2] **Chanda, Ramaprasad—Op. cit., 1916, pages 4—8.**

[3] **Chanda, Ramaprasad.—1916. Op. cit.**

[4] **Fischer, E.—Op. cit., page 199.**

[5] **Pages 100—116.**

[6] ***Ibid.*, page 112.**

[7] **Chanda, R.—Op. cit., pages 37—78.**

[8] **Keith, Sir Arthur—The Racial characters of the Southern Arabs in Arabia Felix by Bertram Thomas, pages 301—333.**

which according to Keith[1] must have come from Persia and Baluchistan. There seems no reason to think that the Indian brachycephals with definite Armenoid affinities resembling the "Omani"[2] had a different origin. That it was not mongoloid would seem to be quite clear from both the character of the Indus Valley skulls and the values of the C. R. L.'s discussed before. From the frequency of the epicanthic fold given in Tables LV-LIX(a),[3] it will be seen that except in the Sub-Himalayan region and along the eastern frontiers, the mongoloid element does not constitute an important factor in the racial composition of the Indian population. In Upper India, Bengal, Guzrat and Maharashtra, its presence is slight but from Orissa to Malabar it occurs as a small element. In the Tamil country and Malabar this mongoloid strain is due no doubt to an oceanic migration whose northern limit may not improbably have reached Orissa, or there may exist still in the latter place, remnants of an earlier wave allied to that found in the Brahmaputra Valley but which has been submerged in Bengal.

Recently Eickstedt[4] has published the results of his Indian Expedition in which he has sought to find in the potency of geographical control and explanation of the racial types seen in India, but has offered no evidence to show that this control was ever exercised in the manner described by him. Similarly with the exception of a few figures regarding his "type groups"[5] he has given no anthropometric data to indicate that the classification advanced by him had really a somatic basis. He classifies the races of India into an aboriginal or old group, called "Vedide", an intermediate or dark, called "Melanide" and a recent, called "Indide". The "Vedide" again is subdivided into a "Gondide" and "Malide" type; the "Melanide" into a "Melinide" and "Kolide"; and the "Indide" into a "Graceful" and a "Coarser" type. Eickstedt, who seems to have a fancy for new names is apparently not satisfied with these, but will also have a "Kiralide" type in Malabar and a "Gharwali" in southeastern Kashmir.[6] His "Gondide" race corresponds however to what we have called the 'Nisadic' element in the aboriginal *population of India and though he speaks of* a very primitive 'Malide' group, he does not seem to recognise the existence of the Negritos. There do not appear also sufficient grounds to distinguish the Central Indian "Kolide" type from the non-negritoid Southern Indian aborigines.

Lastly the 'Graceful' type of his new or 'Indide' race appears to correspond to what we have called the Mediterranean and the "Coarser" to our Proto-Nordic North Indian type I o oes not sufficiently seem to realise the differences between the two, which do not consist merely in the gracefulness of the former. As stated before, the North Indian type is not only taller but has a much larger head, with a lower cranial vault, longer face and a narrower and more porminent nasal profile, in addition to having a light blondish element which is best preserved among the N. Western mountain tribes. The greatest weakness of his racial scheme, however, lies in the absence of any place given to the brachycephalic Armenoid race whom he dismisses as a late "Turanian" (whatever that may mean) thrust in the Maharatta country[7] and the whole of Guzrat, Bengal, Maharashtra and Kannada is shown in his map[8] as the homeland of the 'Indide' race. The skeletal remains from the late Indus Valley Period in Sind and lower Punjab, to the Iron Age remains of Hyderabad and Tinnevelley, testify to the early intrusion of this race in India and the anthropometic values given in this Volume[9] as well as those published by Risley, Chanda, Thurston and Hoernle prove, that in the whole of Bengal and the western littoral as far as Kannada and Southwestern Tamil land, it forms the dominant element in the present population. Eickstedt's failure to recognise it can only be attributed to his limited acquaintance with the somatic characters of the Indian people.

---

1 *Ibid.*, page 322.

2 *Ibid.*, page 310.

3 Appendix. pages 100—116.

4 Eickstedt, Egon Freiherr von—*Die Rassengeschichte von Indien mit besonderer Berücksichtigung von Mysore.* —Zeits. Morph. Anthropol. Bd XXXII, pages 77—124, 1933.

5 Eickstedt, E. F.—Op. cit., page 122.

6 Eickstedt, E. F.—Op. cit., page 98.

7 Eickstedt, E. F. —Op. cit., page 121.

8 *Ibid.*, page 84.

9 Appendix, pages 1—19.

PART III-A.
Tables I to XXIV.

M 5300

TABLE I.

United Provinces, Central India, Bengal and Orissa.

M53CC

TABLE

United Provinces, Central

Measurements and Indices.	Bengali Brahmin.				Bengali Kayastha.			
	Total No.	Mean with P. E.	S. D. with P. E.	Co-eff. of variation with P. E.	Total No.	Mean with P. E.	S. D. with P. E.	Co-eff. of variation with P. E.
Stature	50	1,680·30±5·14	53·91±3·63	3·21±0·22	100	1,670·71±3·87	57·34±2·73	3·43±0·16
Auricular Height	50	123·38±0·84	8·77±0·59	7·11±0·48	100	124·66±0·46	6·87±0·33	5·51±0·26
Max. Head Length	50	186·36±0·58	6·04±0·41	3·24±0·22	100	185·25±0·43	6·32±0·30	3·41±0·16
Max. Head Breadth	50	146·96±0·49	5·16±0·35	3·51±0·24	100	149·59±0·37	5·43±0·26	3·63±0·17
Min. Frontal Breadth	50	104·46±0·45	4·67±0·31	4·47±0·30	100	105·23±0 26	3·84±0·18	3·65±0·17
Max. Bizygomatic Breadth	50	132·84±0·48	5·03±0·34	3·79±0·26	100	134·7[illegible]±0·37	5·52±0·26	4·10±0·2[illegible]
Bigonial Breadth	50	101·16±0·56	5·91±0·40	5·84±0·39	100	101·63±0·40	5·89±0·28	5·80±0·28
Inter-orbital Breadth	50	29·38±0·21	2·15±0·15	7·32±0·50	100	29·66±0·14	2·12±0·10	7·15±0·34
Orbitonasal Breadth	50	101·10±0·43	4·53±0·31	4·48±0·30	100	101·30±0·30	4·49±0·21	4·43±0·21
Orbitonasal Arc	50	114·30±0·58	6·04±0·41	5·28±0·36	100	114·21±0·40	5·97±0·28	5·22±0·25
Nasal Length	50	54·20±0·34	3·52±0·24	6·49±0·44	100	54·61±0·21	3·05±0·15	5·59±0·27
Nasal Breadth	50	36·58±0·29	3·05±0·21	8·34±0·57	100	37·09±0·17	2·46±0·12	6·63±0·32
Nasal Height or Depth	50	26·78±0·22	2·27±0·15	8·48±0·58	100	26·42±0·17	2·44±0·12	9·24±0·44
Upper Facial Length	50	70·16±0·45	4·70±0·32	6·70±0·45	100	69·93±0·27	3·99±0·19	5·71±0·27
Total Facial Length	50	121·66±0·57	6·00±0·40	4·93±0·33	100	120·12±0·37	5·48±0·26	4·56±0·22
Horizontal Cirm. of the Head ..	50	540·96±1·31	13·71±0·92	2·53±0·17	100	541·51±0·94	13·87±0·66	2·56±0·12
Sagittal Arc	50	361·62±1·20	12·62±0·85	3·49±0·24	100	352·64±0·90	13·34±0·64	3·78±0·18
Transverse Arc	50	340·54±1·34	14·08±0·95	4·13±0·28	100	341·27±0·80	11·91±0·57	3·49±0·17
Length Breadth Index	50	78·93±0·33	3·42±0·23	4·33±0·29	100	80·84±0·26	3·89±0·19	4·81±0·22
Length Height Index	50	66·26±0·47	4·95±0·33	7·47±0·51	100	67·33±0·25	3·74±0·18	5·55±0·27
Breadth Height Index	50	83·93±0·45	4·74±0·32	5·65±0·38	100	83·44±0·33	4·93±0·24	5·91±0·28
Trans. Fronto-Parietal Index	50	71·11±0·27	2·82±0·19	3·97±0·27	100	70·39±0·15	2·26±0·11	3·21±0·15
Orbitonasal Index	50	113·07±0·34	3·60±0·24	3·18±0·21	100	112·76±0·24	3·51±0·17	3·11±0·15
Nasal Index	50	67·71±0·62	6·48±0·44	9·57±0·65	100	68·11±0·38	5·70±0·27	8·37±0·40
Nasal Elevation Index	50	73·65±0·78	8·17±0·55	11·09±0·76	100	71·51±0·56	8·25±0·39	11·54±0·58
Upper Facial Index	50	52·87±0·36	3·78±0·25	7·15±0·48	100	51·98±0·24	3·54±0·17	6·81±0·33
Total Facial Index	50	91·68±0·48	5·02±0·34	5·48±0·37	100	89·32±0·36	5·39±0·26	6·03±0·29
Trans. Cephalo-Facial Index	50	90·44±0·30	3·12±0·21	3·45±0·23	100	90·08±0·19	2·88±0·14	3·20±0·15
Vertical Cephalo-Facial Index ..	50	98·96±0·64	6·67±0·45	6·74±0·45	100	96·56±0·37	5·48±0·26	5·68±0·27

ndia, Bengal and Orissa.

Bengali Pod.				Orissa Brahmin.				
otal No.	Mean with P. E.	S. D. with P. E.	Co-eff. of variation with P. E.	Total No.	Mean with P. E.	S. D. with P. E.	Co-eff. of variation with P. E.	Measurements and Indices.
50	1,628·26±4·63	48·57±3·28	2·98±0·20	143	1,642·92±3·32	58·88±2·34	3·58±0·14	Stature.
50	120·62±0·62	6·46±0·44	5·36±0·36	100	128·43±0·41	6·02±0·29	4·69±0·22	Auricular Height.
50	184·08±0·64	6·68±0·45	3·63±0·24	143	183·13±0·38	6·74±0·26	3·68±0·15	Max. Head Length.
50	141·80±0·47	4·95±0·33	3·49±0·24	143	141·34±0·31	5·49±0·21	3·88±0·15	Max. Head Breadth.
50	102·60±0·40	4·24±0·29	4·13±0·28	140	102·83±0·23	4·16±0·16	4·05±0·16	Min. Frontal Breadth.
50	130·75±0·36	3·80±0·26	2·91±0·20	143	131·70±0·26	4·72±0·18	3·58±0·14	Max. Bizygomatic Breadth.
50	100·46±0·54	5·61±0·38	5·58±0·38	142	100·55±0·33	5·94±0·23	5·91±0·24	Bigonial Breadth.
50	30·96±0·23	2·37±0·16	7·66±0·52	143	32·13±0·15	2·65±0·10	8·25±0·33	Inter-orbital Breadth.
50	96·80±0·40	4·20±0·28	4·34±0·29	143	97·76±0·22	3·93±0·15	4·02±0·16	Orbitonasal Breadth.
50	109·30±0·40	4·18±0·28	3·82±0·26	142	109·87±0·30	5·38±0·21	4·89±0·20	Orbitonasal Arc.
50	51·18±0·29	3·00±0·20	5·86±0·40	143	51·76±0·21	3·72±0·14	7·19±0·29	Nasal Length.
50	36·66±0·22	2·32±0·16	6·33±0·43	143	36·36±0·14	2·47±0·10	6·79±0·27	Nasal Breadth.
50	24·06±0·17	1·83±0·12	7·61±0·52	143	24·05±0·14	2·48±0·10	10·31±0·42	Nasal Height or Depth.
50	66·96±0·35	3·69±0·25	5·51±0·37	143	66·46±0·26	4·61±0·18	6·94±0·28	Upper Facial Length.
50	117·38±0·45	4·69±0·32	4·00±0·27	143	117·29±0·37	6·57±0·26	5·60±0·22	Total Facial Length.
50	528·78±1·30	13·68±0·92	2·59±0·17	142	527·44±0·74	13·06±0·52	2·48±0·10	Horizontal Cirm. of the Head.
50	354·82±1·15	12·07±0·81	3·40±0·23	143	346·38±0·74	13·19±0·53	3·81±0·15	Sagittal Arc.
50	329·28±0·94	9·84±0·66	2·99±0·20	143	330·85±0·62	11·04±0·44	3·34±0·13	Transverse Arc.
50	77·13±0·37	3·89±0·26	5·04±0·34	143	77·31±0·26	4·66±0·18	6·03±0·24	Length Breadth Index.
50	65·60±0·38	3·90±0·26	5·95±0·40	100	70·48±0·28	4·12±0·20	5·85±0·28	Length Height Index.
50	85·14±0·51	4·96±0·33	5·83±0·39	100	91·00±0·38	5·66±0·27	6·22±0·30	Breadth Height Index.
50	72·24±0·30	3·12±0·21	4·32±0·29	140	72·85±0·17	2·99±0·12	4·10±0·16	Trans. Fronto-Parietal Index.
50	113·01±0·38	3·99±0·27	3·53±0·24	142	112·22±0·22	3·98±0·15	3·55±0·14	Orbitonasal Index.
50	71·81±0·52	5·42±0·37	7·55±0·51	143	70·46±0·35	6·25±0·24	8·87±0·36	Nasal Index.
50	65·93±0·67	7·02±0·47	10·65±0·73	143	66·37±0·43	7·55±0·30	11·38±0·46	Nasal Elevation Index.
50	51·24±0·29	3·06±0·21	5·97±0·40	143	50·41±0·22	3·92±0·16	7·78±0·31	Upper Facial Index.
50	89·83±0·43	4·46±0·30	4·96±0·33	143	89·21±0·33	5·90±0·23	6·61±0·26	Total Facial Index.
50	92·14±0·28	2·94±0·20	3·19±0·22	143	92·61±0·28	4·99±0·19	5·39±0·21	Trans. Cephalo-Facial Index.
50	97·53±0·52	5·47±0·37	5·61±0·38	100	90·89±0·42	6·24±0·30	6·87±0·33	Vertical Cephalo-Facial Index.

TABLE

United Provinces, Central

Measurements and Indices.	U. P. Brahmin.				Malve Brahmin.			
	Total No.	Mean with P. E.	S. D. with P. E.	Co-eff. of variation with P. E.	Total No.	Mean with P. E.	S. D. with P. E.	Co-eff. of variation with P. E.
Stature	50	1,654·78±5·24	54·91±3·70	3·32±0·22	50	1,643·56±5·70	59·77±4·03	3·64±0·24
Auricular Height	50	120·92±0·70	7·36±0·50	6·09±0·41	50	119·16±0·68	7·08±0·48	5·94±0·40
Max. Head Length	50	192·66±0·65	6·85±0·46	3·56±0·24	50	186·94±0·63	6·27±0·42	3·35±0·23
Max. Head Breadth	50	139·50±0·45	4·72±0·32	3·38±0·23	50	138·80±0·56	5·90±0·40	4·25±0·29
Min. Frontal Breadth ..	50	101·82±0·34	3·57±0·24	3·51±0·24	50	102·88±0·38	3·94±0·27	3·83±0·26
Max. Bizygomatic Breadth ..	50	133·00±0·33	3·45±0·23	2·59±0·17	50	132·96±0·45	4·72±0·32	3·55±0·24
Bigonial Breadth	50	100·52±0·59	6·18±0·42	6·15±0·41	50	101·66±0·66	6·89±0·46	6·78±0·46
Inter-orbital Breadth	50	29·44±0·19	2·03±0·14	6·90±0·47	50	31·58±0·23	2·44±0·16	7·73±0·52
Orbitonasal Breadth . ..	50	98·18±0·33	3·50±0·24	3·56±0·24	49	97·90±0·39	4·07±0·28	4·16±0·29
Orbitonasal Arc	50	112·16±0·50	5·22±0·35	4·65±0·31	50	111·74±0·48	5·02±0·34	4·49±0·30
Nasal Length	50	53·64±0·34	3·52±0·24	6·56±0·44	50	51·68±0·29	3·07±0·21	5·94±0·40
Nasal Breadth	50	37·18±0·25	2·61±0·18	7·02±0·48	50	37·54±0·28	2·89±0·19	7·70±0·52
Nasal Height or Depth ..	50	26·78±0·21	2·18±0·15	8·14±0·55	50	24·40±0·20	2·06±0·14	8·44±0·57
Upper Facial Length	50	68·80±0·43	4·48±0·30	6·51±0·44	50	66·58±0·32	3·31±0·22	4·97±0·34
Total Facial Length	50	119·20±0·58	6·07±0·41	5·09±0·34	50	117·30±0·62	6·53±0·44	5·57±0·38
Horizontal Cirm. of the Head ..	50	539·20±1·52	15·98±1·08	2·96±0·20	50	533·36±1·60	16·73±1·13	3·14±0·21
Sagittal Arc	50	362·66±1·55	16·27±1·10	4·49±0·30	50	337·50±1·27	13·28±0·90	3·93±0·27
Transverse Arc	50	326·46±1·10	11·49±0·78	3·52±0·24	50	325·98±1·12	11·72±0·79	3·60±0·24
Length Breadth Index ..	50	72·48±0·31	3·23±0·22	4·46±0·30	50	74·30±0·30	3·19±0·22	4·29±0·29
Length Height Index	50	62·77±0·32	3·37±0·23	5·37±0·36	50	63·66±0·35	3·70±0·25	5·81±0·39
Breadth Height Index ..	50	86·74±0·52	5·45±0·36	6·28±0·42	50	86·04±0·50	5·29±0·36	6·15±0·42
Trans. Fronto-Parietal Index ..	50	73·05±0·29	3·00±0·20	4·11±0·28	50	74·16±0·24	2·55±0·17	3·44±0·23
Orbitonasal Index	50	114·24±0·35	3·65±0·25	3·20±0·22	49	114·19±0·33	3·43±0·23	3·00±0·20
Nasal Index	50	69·56±0·58	6·12±0·41	8·80±0·60	50	72·92±0·70	7·37±0·50	10·11±0·69
Nasal Elevation Index ..	50	72·32±0·68	7·10±0·48	9·81±0·67	50	65·28±0·61	[illegible]·41±0·43	9·83±0·67
Upper Facial Index	50	51·75±0·33	3·46±0·23	6·69±0·45	50	50·06±0·28	2·97±0·20	5·93±0·40
Total Facial Index	50	89·66±0·47	4·95±0·33	5·52±0·37	50	88·30±0·51	5·32±0·36	6·02±0·41
Trans. Cephalo-Facial Index ..	50	95·41±0·28	2·95±0·20	3·09±0·21	50	95·86±0·26	2·74±0·18	2·86±0·19
Vertical Cephalo-Facial Index ..	50	98·25±0·61	6·43±0·43	6·54±0·44	50	98·63±0·60	6·34±0·43	6·43±0·44

I.

India, Bengal and Orissa.

Baghel Rajput.				Miscellaneous Rajput.				
Total No.	Mean with P. E.	S. D. with P. E.	Co-eff. of variation with P. E.	Total No.	Mean with P. E.	S. D. with P. E.	Co-eff. of variation with P. E.	Measurements and Indices.
50	1,691·86±5·84	61·25±4·13	3·62±0·24	50	1,684·42±5·83	61·09±4·12	3·63±0·24	Stature.
50	121·16±0·62	6·47±0·44	5·34±0·36	50	120·38±0·63	6·59±0·44	5·47±0·37	Auricular Height.
50	187·40±0·56	5·84±0·39	3·12±0·21	50	189·04±0·85	8·95±0·60	4·73±0·32	Max. Head Length.
50	142·78±0·48	5·00±0·34	3·50±0·24	50	141·48±0·62	6·52±0·44	4·61±0·31	Max. Head Breadth.
50	102·48±0·35	3·62±0·24	3·53±0·24	50	101·54±0·40	4·24±0·29	4·18±0·28	Min. Frontal Breadth.
50	134·02±0·42	4·39±0·30	3·28±0·22	50	134·56±0·42	4·44±0·30	3·30±0·23	Max. Bizygomatic Breadth.
50	100·32±0·55	5·75±0·39	5·73±0·39	50	99·32±0·62	6·49±0·44	6·53±0·44	Bigonial Breadth.
50	29·76±0·25	2·57±0·17	8·64±0·59	50	30·94±0·20	2·07±0·14	6·69±0·45	Inter-orbital Breadth.
50	95·86±0·46	4·78±0·32	4·99±0·34	50	97·86±0·44	4·61±0·31	4·71±0·32	Orbitonasal Breadth.
50	109·94±0·50	5·26±0·35	4·78±0·32	49	112·86±0·50	5·23±0·36	4·63±0·32	Orbitonasal Arc.
50	52·74±0·36	3·62±0·24	6·86±0·46	50	52·38±0·33	3·46±0·25	6·61±0·45	Nasal Length.
50	36·90±0·24	2·52±0·17	6·83±0·46	50	36·56±0·25	2·59±0·17	7·10±0·48	Nasal Breadth.
50	25·14±0·22	2·30±0·16	9·15±0·62	50	25·00±0·25	2·65±0·18	10·60±0·72	Nasal Height or Depth.
50	67·32±0·40	4·14±0·28	6·15±0·42	50	66·74±0·41	4·35±0·29	6·52±0·44	Upper Facial Length.
50	117·12±0·59	6·16±0·42	5·26±0·36	50	116·96±0·58	6·06±0·41	5·18±0·35	Total Facial Length.
50	538·46±1·31	13·73±0·93	2·55±0·17	50	540·00±1·85	19·41±1·31	3·59±0·24	Horizontal Cirm. of the Head.
50	343·84±1·07	11·22±0·76	3·26±0·22	50	341·62±1·66	17·38±1·17	5·09±0·35	Sagittal Arc.
50	329·24±1·04	10·88±0·73	3·30±0·22	50	328·58±1·19	12·47±0·84	3·80±0·26	Transverse Arc.
50	76·28±0·33	3·45±0·23	4·52±0·31	50	74·98±0·44	4·56±0·31	6·08±0·41	Length Breadth Index.
50	64·71±0·36	3·82±0·26	5·90±0·40	50	63·62±0·40	4·25±0·29	6·68±0·45	Length Height Index.
50	84·93±0·47	4·88±0·33	5·75±0·39	50	85·21±0·46	4·90±0·33	5·75±0·39	Breadth Height Index.
50	71·81±0·23	2·38±0·16	3·31±0·22	50	71·88±0·36	3·79±0·26	5·27±0·36	Trans. Fronto-Parietal Index.
50	114·75±0·32	3·39±0·23	2·95±0·20	49	115·48±0·41	4·23±0·29	3·66±0·25	Orbitonasal Index.
50	70·42±0·68	7·11±0·48	10·09±0·69	50	70·03±0·70	7·33±0·49	10·47±0·71	Nasal Index.
50	68·40±0·70	7·32±0·49	10·70±0·73	50	68·82±0·76	7·95±0·54	11·55±0·80	Nasal Elevation Index.
50	50·24±0·27	2·82±0·19	5·61±0·38	50	49·64±0·33	3·41±0·23	6·87±0·47	Upper Facial Index.
50	87·40±0·37	3·90±0·26	4·46±0·31	50	86·97±0·44	4·61±0·31	5·30±0·36	Total Facial Index.
50	93·90±0·24	2·51±0·17	2·67±0·18	50	95·33±0·33	3·42±0·23	3·59±0·24	Trans. Cephalo-Facial Index.
50	96·87±0·60	6·34±0·43	6·54±0·44	50	97·42±0·65	6·84±0·46	7·02±0·48	Vertical Cephalo-Facial Index.

TABLE II.

Guzrat and Kathiawar.

TABL

Guzrat an

Measurements and Indices.	Nagar Brahmin.				Bania-Jain.			
	Total No.	Mean with P. E.	S. D. with P. E.	Co-eff. of variation with P. E.	Total No.	Mean with P. E.	S. D. with P. E.	Co-eff. of variation with P. E.
Stature	105	1,648·60±3·67	55·85±2·60	3·38±0·16	99	1,642·69±3·95	58·33±2·79	3·55±0·17
Auricular Height	105	121·24±0·49	7·51±0·35	6·19±0·29	99	120·48±0·58	8·55±0·14	7·10±0·37
Max. Head Length	105	185·12±0·42	6·35±0·30	3·43±0·16	99	185·30±0·54	7·91±0·38	4·27±0·21
Max. Head Breadth	105	150·59±0·45	6·82±0·32	4·52±0·21	99	149·16±0·45	6·67±0·32	4·47±0·22
Min. Frontal Breadth ..	105	106·35±0·24	3·72±0·17	3·50±0·16	99	105·38±0·28	4·20±0·20	3·99±0·21
Max. Bizygomatic Breadth ..	105	135·41±0·32	4·90±0·23	3·62±0·17	99	136·61±0·33	4·84±0·23	3·54±0·16
Bigonial Breadth	105	99·94±0·44	6·61±0·31	6·61±0·31	99	101·13±0·44	6·56±0·31	6·49±0·31
Inter-orbital Breadth	105	31·44±0·15	2·23±0·10	7·09±0·33	99	31·80±0·18	2·63±0·13	8·33±0·40
Orbitonasal Breadth	104	99·22±0·30	4·59±0·21	4·62±0·22	99	100·73±0·28	4·13±0·20	4·10±0·20
Orbitonasal Arc	105	112·40±0·41	6·21±0·29	5·07±0·24	99	112·82±0·39	5·73±0·27	5·08±0·24
Nasal Length	105	52·95±0·24	3·70±0·17	5·98±0·28	99	53·36±0·28	4·07±0·19	7·63±0·37
Nasal Breadth	105	36·41±0·19	2·94±0·14	8·07±0·38	99	37·40±0·19	2·81±0·13	7·51±0·36
Nasal Height or Depth ..	105	25·07±0·19	2·90±0·14	11·56±0·55	99	24·95±0·23	3·34±0·16	13·38±0·65
Upper Facial Length	105	66·09±0·29	4·42±0·21	6·68±0·31	99	65·78±0·31	4·50±0·22	6·84±0·33
Total Facial Length	105	113·48±0·43	6·46±0·30	5·69±0·27	99	113·56±0·45	6·64±0·32	5·85±0·28
Horizontal Cirm. of the Head ..	105	545·14±1·04	15·80±0·74	2·90±0·14	99	540·24±1·02	15·00±0·72	2·78±0·13
Sagittal Arc	105	344·98±0·99	14·97±0·70	4·34±0·20	99	345·68±1·18	17·39±0·83	5·03±0·24
Transverse Arc	105	338·65±0·89	13·51±0·63	3·98±0·19	99	336·28±1·33	19·55±0·94	5·81±0·28
Length Breadth Index ..	105	81·38±0·26	3·93±0·18	4·82±0·22	99	80·58±0·29	4·22±0·20	5·24±0·25
Length Height Index ..	105	65·55±0·29	4·40±0·20	6·71±0·31	99	65·08±0·29	4·24±0·20	6·52±0·31
Breadth Height Index ..	105	80·67±0·40	6·11±0·28	7·57±0·35	99	80·88±0·37	5·53±0·26	6·84±0·33
Trans. Fronto-Parietal Index ..	105	70·78±0·20	3·08±0·14	4·35±0·20	99	70·74±0·22	3·31±0·16	4·68±0·23
Orbitonasal Index	104	113·38±0·30	4·58±0·21	4·03±0·19	99	111·99±0·27	3·96±0·19	3·54±0·17
Nasal Index	105	69·05±0·44	6·70±0·31	9·70±0·46	99	70·26±0·44	6·56±0·31	9·34±0·45
Nasal Elevation Index ..	105	69·19±0·60	9·15±0·43	13·22±0·63	99	66·85±0·52	7·65±0·37	11·44±0·56
Upper Facial Index	105	48·87±0·24	3·70±0·17	7·57±0·35	99	48·22±0·23	3·33±0·16	6·91±0·33
Total Facial Index	105	83·66±0·35	5·33±0·25	6·37±0·30	99	83·21±0·37	5·50±0·26	6·61±0·32
Trans. Cephalo-Facial Index ..	105	89·95±0·22	3·28±0·15	3·64±0·17	99	91·66±0·21	3·08±0·15	3·30±0·16
Vertical Cephalo-Facial Index ..	105	93·82±0·52	7·85±0·37	8·36±0·39	99	94·52±0·47	6·96±0·33	7·36±0·35

Kathiawar.

Audich Brahmin.				Kathi.				Measurements and Indices.
Total No.	Mean with P. E.	S. D. with P. E.	Co-eff. of variation with P. E.	Total. No.	Mean with P. E.	S. D. with P. E.	Co-eff. of variation with P. E.	
93	1,647·82±3·74	53·37±2·67	3·24±0·16	40	1,670·05±5·05	47·23±3·54	2·83±0·21	Stature.
92	118·66±0·53	7·52±0·38	6·34±0·32	40	121·45±0·63	5·87±0·44	4·83±0·37	Auricular Height.
93	184·00±0·45	6·38±0·32	3·47±0·16	40	187·58±0·65	6·07±0·46	3·24±0·23	Max. Head Length.
93	144·73±0·32	4·52±0·23	2·12±0·11	40	151·25±0·75	7·01±0·53	4·63±0·35	Max. Head Breadth.
92	105·27±0·30	4·26±0·21	4·05±0·20	40	104·73±0·51	4·80±0·36	4·58±0·35	Min. Frontal Breadth.
93	134·48±0·28	3·95±0·20	2·94±0·15	40	139·48±0·63	5·91±0·44	4·24±0·32	Max. Bizygomatic Breadth.
93	99·37±0·42	6·04±0·30	6·08±0·31	40	100·58±0·71	6·59±0·49	6·55±0·50	Bigonial Breadth.
93	31·60±0·17	2·46±0·12	7·78±0·39	40	31·53±0·22	2·10±0·16	6·66±0·51	Inter-orbital Breadth.
93	98·90±0·29	4·08±0·20	4·13±0·20	40	100·25±0·40	3·73±0·28	3·72±0·28	Orbitonasal Breadth.
92	111·89±0·38	5·43±0·27	4·85±0·24	40	114·08±0·58	5·41±0·41	4·74±0·36	Orbitonasal Arc.
93	51·92±0·23	3·29±0·16	6·34±0·32	40	54·90±0·33	3·07±0·23	5·59±0·42	Nasal Length.
93	36·08±0·16	2·38±0·12	6·60±0·33	40	36·48±0·31	2·92±0·22	8·00±0·61	Nasal Breadth.
93	25·13±0·21	2·93±0·15	11·66±0·59	40	25·80±0·32	2·99±0·22	11·59±0·89	Nasal Height or Depth.
93	64·76±0·29	4·19±0·21	6·47±0·32	40	68·48±0·43	4·03±0·30	5·88±0·46	Upper Facial Length.
93	113·77±0·40	5·69±0·28	5·00±0·25	40	116·38±0·46	4·29±0·32	3·69±0·28	Total Facial Length.
92	535·54±1·02	14·42±0·70	2·69±0·13	40	548·80±1·62	15·18±1·14	2·77±0·21	Horizontal Cirm. of the Head.
93	342·91±1·08	15·39±0·77	4·49±0·22	40	335·15±1·30	12·19±0·91	3·64±0·28	Sagittal Arc.
93	332·99±0·78	11·19±0·56	3·36±0·17	40	337·95±1·31	12·21±0·92	3·61±0·27	Transverse Arc.
93	78·77±0·24	3·40±0·17	4·32±0·22	40	80 71±0·47	4·43±0·33	5·49±0·43	Length Breadth Index.
92	64·51±0·29	4·17±0·21	6·46±0·32	40	64·78±0·33	3·05±0·23	4·71±0·36	Length Height Index.
92	82·07±0·35	4·93±0·25	6·01±0·30	40	80·39±0·45	4·17±0·31	5·19±0·39	Breadth Height Index.
92	72·81±0·22	3·11±0·16	4·27±0·21	40	69·30±0·32	2·97±0·22	4·30±0·32	Trans. Fronto-Parietal Index.
92	113·15±0·26	3·67±0·18	3·24±0·16	40	113·99±0·45	4·25±0·32	3·72±0·28	Orbitonasal Index.
92	69·70±0·40	5·71±0·29	8·19±0·41	40	66·38±0·71	6·66±0·50	10·03±0·76	Nasal Index.
93	69·90±0·62	8·82±0·44	12·62±0·64	40	71·11±1·19	11·12±0·83	15·64±1·20	Nasal Elevation Index.
93	48·21±0·22	3·08±0·15	6·39±0·32	40	49·16±0·35	3·26±0·24	6·63±0·50	Upper Facial Index.
93	84·66±0·30	4·22±0·21	4·98±0·25	40	83·52±0·40	3·72±0·28	4·45±0·34	Total Facial Index.
93	92·96±0·19	2·69±0·13	2·89±0·14	40	92·34±0·39	3·68±0·28	3·99±0·30	Trans. Cephalo-Facial Index.
92	96·37±0·49	6·93±0·35	7·19±0·35	40	96·01±0·71	6·65±0·50	6·93±0·53	Vertical Cephalo-Facial Index.

TABLE II.

Guzrat and Kathiawar.

Measurements and Indices.	Brahma Kshatri. Total No.	Mean with P. E.	S. D. with P. E.	Co-eff. of variation with P. E.
Stature	31	1,639·52±7·48	61·74±5·29	3·77±0·32
Auricular Height	31	124·19±1·28	10·55±0·90	8·50±0·73
Max. Head Length	31	186·26±0·63	5·24±0·45	2·81±0·24
Max. Head Breadth	31	149·06±0·72	5·98±0·51	4·01±0·34
Min. Frontal Breadth	31	108·29±0·45	3·70±0·32	2·42±0·20
Max. Bizygomatic Breadth	31	137·10±0·52	4·29±0·37	3·13±0·27
Bigonial Breadth	31	100·65±0·71	5·83±0·50	5·79±0·50
Inter-oribital Breadth	31	31·45±0·22	1·81±0·16	5·76±0·50
Orbitonasal Breadth	31	100·90±0·41	3·41±0·29	3·38±0·29
Orbitonasal Arc	31	115·29±0·71	5·85±0·50	5·18±0·45
Nasal Length	31	55·13±0·35	2·85±0·24	5·17±0·45
Nasal Breadth	31	36·23±0·32	2·67±0·29	7·37±0·63
Nasal Height or Depth	31	25·74±0·27	2·27±0·19	8·82±0·76
Upper Facial Length	31	69·48±0·52	4·26±0·37	6·13±0 53
Total Facial Length	31	118·10±0·83	6·86±0·59	5·81±0·50
Horizontal Cirm. of the Head	31	545·48±1·76	14·52±1·24	2·66±0·23
Sagittal Arc	31	343·84±1·67	13·83±1·19	4·02±0·34
Transverse Arc	31	341·65±1·49	12·27±1·05	3·59±0·31
Length Breadth Index	31	79·70±0·44	3·60±0·31	4·52±0·39
Length Height Index	31	66·67±0·50	4·15±0·36	6·22±0·54
Breadth Height Index	31	83·34±0·76	6·31±0·54	7·57±0·65
Trans. Fronto-Parietal Index	31	72·95±0·36	2·96±0·25	5·06±0·43
Orbitonasal Index	31	114·28±0·48	3·94±0·34	3·45±0·30
Nasal Index	31	65·84±0·66	5·45±0·47	8·28±0·71
Nasal Elevation Index	31	71·49±1·08	8·89±0·76	12·44±1·08
Upper Facial Index	31	50·49±0·42	3·48±0·30	6·89±0·59
Total Facial Index	31	86·18±0·59	4·89±0·42	5·67±0·49
Trans. Cephalo-Facial Index	31	92·03±0·30	2·48±0·21	2·69±0·23
Vertical Cephalo-Facial Index	31	95·53±0·88	7·28±0·62	7·62±0·66

TABLE III.

Maharashtra.

TABL...

Mahar...

Measurements and Indices.	Chitpavan Brahmin. Total No.	Mean with P. E.	S. D. with P. E.	Co-efficient of variation with P. E.	Deshastha Brahmin. Total No.	Mean with P. E.	S. D. with P. E.	Co-efficient of variation with P. E.
Stature	103	1,646·61±3·67	52·47±2·62	3·19±0·15	107	1,636·94±3·86	55·09±2·75	3·37±0·16
Auricular Height	103	120·38±0·52	7·43±0·37	6·17±0·29	107	120·16±0·63	8·98±0·45	7·47±0·35
Max. Head Length	103	*185·83±0·51*	*7·30±0·37*	3·93±0·19	107	184·57±0·51	7·27±0·36	3·93±0·18
Max. Head Breadth	103	143·78±0·39	5·50±0·28	3·83±0·18	107	144·55±0·43	6·20±0·31	4·22±0·19
Min. Frontal Breadth	103	104·38±0·31	4·48±0·22	*4·30±0·20*	107	104·53±0·29	4·17±0·21	*3·99±0·18*
Max. Bizygomatic Breadth	103	133·94±0·32	4·60±0·23	*3·43±0·16*	107	133·80±0·37	5·35±0·27	4·00±0·18
Bigonial Breadth	103	98·48±0·42	5·94±0·30	*6·04±0·29*	107	100·64±0·43	6·19±0·31	6·15±0·29
Inter-orbital Breadth	103	30·97±0·18	2·52±0·13	8·14±0·38	107	31·60±0·16	2·29±0·11	7·23±0·33
Orbitonasal Breadth	103	98·14±0·28	4·01±0·20	4·09±0·19	107	97·77±0·33	4·68±0·23	4·79±0·22
Orbitonasal Arc	103	113·06±0·41	5·90±0·30	5·22±0·25	107	111·77±0·36	5·54±0·26	4·96±0·28
Nasal Length	103	50·97±0·24	3·43±0·17	6·73±0·32	107	51·25±0·27	3·92±0·20	7·63±0·35
Nasal Breadth	103	37·02±0·19	2·65±0·13	7·16±0·34	107	37·40±0·20	2·90±0·15	7·75±0·36
Nasal Height or Depth	103	23·30±0·14	2·05±0·10	8·80±0·42	107	23·35±0·17	2·49±0·12	10·66±0·50
Upper Facial Length	103	64·75±0·27	3·89±0·19	6·01±0·28	107	64·97±0·28	3·95±0·20	6·08±0·28
Total Facial Length	103	115·79±0·40	5·66±0·28	4·89±0·23	107	114·44±0·39	6·01±0·28	5·25±0·24
Horizontal Cirm. of the Head	103	536·53±1·00	14·23±0·71	2·65±0·13	107	536·93±1·06	15·17±0·76	3·01±0·14
Sagittal Arc	103	337·81±1·03	14·72±0·74	4·36±0·21	107	340·51±0·99	14·08±0·70	4·13±0·19
Transverse Arc	103	327·70±0·75	10·73±0·54	3·30±0·16	107	333·32±0·82	11·69±0·58	3·51±0·16
Length Breadth Index	103	77·49±0·30	4·24±0·21	5·48±0·26	107	78·36±0·33	4·66±0·23	5·95±0·27
Length Height Index	103	64·73±0·28	3·93±0·20	6·07±0·29	107	65·13±0·35	5·06±0·25	7·77±0·36
Breadth Height Index	103	83·80±0·38	5·47±0·27	6·53±0·31	107	83·22±0·44	6·34±0·32	7·62±0·35
Trans. Fronto-Parietal Index	103	72·66±0·23	3·22±0·16	4·43±0·14	107	72·45±0·22	3·10±0·16	4·28±0·20
Orbitonasal Index	103	115·24±0·30	4·24±0·21	3·68±0·17	107	114·41±0·25	3·52±0·18	3·08±0·14
Nasal Index	103	73·27±0·51	7·25±0·36	9·89±0·46	107	73·41±0·49	6·97±0·35	9·49±0·44
Nasal Elevation Index	103	63·78±0·57	8·19±0·41	12·86±0·61	107	62·75±0·55	7·87±0·39	12·53±0·58
Upper Facial Index	103	48·28±0·22	3·13±0·16	6·48±0·31	107	48·51±0·23	3·26±0·16	6·72±0·31
Total Facial Index	103	86·55±0·31	4·46±0·22	5·17±0·43	107	85·70±0·35	5·00±0·25	5·83±0·27
Trans. Cephalo-Facial Index	103	93·23±0·21	3·06±0·15	3·28±0·15	107	92·57±0·29	4·08±0·20	4·42±0·20
Vertical Cephalo-Facial Index	103	96·45±0·47	7·10±0·33	7·36±0·35	107	95·64±0·62	8·92±0·45	9·33±0·43

htra.

Prabhu.				Karada Brahmin.				
Total No.	Mean with P. E.	S. D. with P. E.	Co-efficient of variation with P. E.	Total No.	Mean with P. E.	S. D. with P. E.	Co-efficient of variation with P. E.	Measurements and Indices.
55	1,639·71±4·76	52·30±3·35	3·19±0·20	48	1,639·31±4·59	47·37±3·32	2·89±0·20	Stature.
55	120·15±0·70	7·70±0·49	6·41±0·41	48	121·63±0·62	6·43±0·45	5·29±0·37	Auricular Height.
55	185·69±0·67	7·33±0·41	3·95±0·25	48	187·38±0·69	7·07±0·49	3·77±0·26	Max. Head Length.
55	143·25±0·42	4·64±0·30	3·24±0·21	48	142·90±0·55	5·71±0·40	4·00±0·28	Max. Head Breadth.
55	104·16±0·34	3·78±0·24	3·63±0·23	48	105·33±0·43	4·46±0·31	4·24±0·30	Min. Frontal Breadth.
55	131·93±0·38	4·20±0·27	3·18±0·20	48	133·73±0·39	3·97±0·28	2·97±0·21	Max. Bizygomatic Breadth.
55	98·86±0·48	5·27±0·34	5·33±0·34	48	100·23±0·53	5·49±0·38	5·48±0·38	Bigonial Breadth.
55	31·00±0·24	2·59±0·17	8·35±0·53	48	31·29±0·20	2·08±0·15	6·65±0·47	Inter-orbital Breadth.
55	98·76±0·49	5·35±0·34	5·42±0·35	48	98·50±0·37	3·83±0·27	3·89±0·27	Orbitonasal Breadth.
55	112·67±0·61	6·74±0·43	5·98±0·38	48	113·00±0·49	5·03±0·35	4·46±0·31	Orbitonasal Arc.
55	51·82±0·33	3·67±0·23	7·08±0·46	48	51·60±0·34	3·48±0·24	6·72±0·47	Nasal Length.
55	36·91±0·23	2·55±0·16	6·91±0·44	48	37·13±0·25	2·56±0·18	6·89±0·48	Nasal Breadth.
55	23·42±0·20	2·17±0·14	9·27±0·60	48	23·42±0·19	1·91±0·13	8·16±0·57	Nasal Height or Depth.
55	66·09±0·37	4·05±0·26	6·13±0·39	48	65·17±0·42	4·33±0·30	6·64±0·47	Upper Facial Length.
55	115·33±0·50	5·44±0·35	4·72±0·30	48	115·54±0·53	5·51±0·39	4·77±0·33	Total Facial Length.
55	537·04±1·47	16·11±0·13	3·00±0·19	48	540·77±1·36	14·02±0·98	2·59±0·18	Horizontal Cirm. of the Head.
55	336·67±1·42	15·66±1·00	4·65±0·30	48	343·54±1·48	15·26±1·07	4·47±0·31	Sagittal Arc.
55	330·60±1·04	11·47±0·73	3·47±0·22	48	335·50±1·03	10·61±0·74	3·16±0·22	Transverse Arc.
55	77·23±0·30	3·25±0·21	4·21±0·27	48	76·38±0·43	4·44±0·31	5·81±0·41	Length Breadth Index.
55	64·77±0·40	4·42±0·28	6·82±0·41	48	64·98±0·37	3·77±0·26	5·80±0·41	Length Height Index.
55	83·68±0·49	5·33±0·34	6·37±0·41	48	85·23±0·51	5·27±0·37	6·18±0·43	Breadth Height Index.
55	72·77±0·29	3·17±0·20	4·36±0·28	48	73·75±0·30	3·12±0·22	4·23±0·30	Trans. Fronto-Parietal Index.
55	114·22±0·37	4·11±0·26	3·60±0·23	48	114·79±0·41	4·22±0·30	3·68±0·26	Orbitonasal Index.
55	71·54±0·58	6·32±0·40	8·83±0·57	48	72·27±0·67	6·95±0·49	9·62±0·68	Nasal Index.
55	63·42±0·54	5·98±0·38	9·43±0·61	48	63·44±0·73	7·51±0·53	11·84±0·84	Nasal Elevation Index.
55	49·87±0·34	3·73±0·24	7·48±0·48	48	48·76±0·32	3·34±0·23	6·85±0·46	Upper Facial Index.
55	87·48±0·41	4·48±0·29	5·12±0·33	48	86·47±0·45	4·68±0·33	5·41±0·38	Total Facial Index.
55	92·16±0·28	3·05±0·20	3·31±0·21	48	93·67±0·31	3·16±0·22	3·37±0·24	Trans. Cephalo-Facial Index.
55	96·39±0·71	7·77±0·50	8·06±0·52	48	95·44±0·61	6·27±0·44	6·58±0·46	Vertical Cephalo-Facial Index.

TABLE III

Maharashtra

Measurements and Indices.	Mahratta.				Saraswat-Gour Brahmin.			
	Total No.	Mean with P. E.	S. D. with P. E.	Co-efficient of variation with P. E.	Total No.	Mean with P. E.	S. D. with P. E.	Co-efficient of variation with P. E.
Stature	59	1,638·14±4·53	51·43±3·19	3·14±0·20	50	1,629·76±4·66	48·86±3·30	3·00±0·20
Auricular Height	57	120·37±0·65	7·29±0·46	6·06±0·38	50	124·06±0·59	6·14±0·41	4·95±0·34
Max. Head Length ..	59	182·51±0·68	7·75±0·48	4·25±0·26	50	186·86±0·59	6·18±0·42	3·31±0·23
Max. Head Breadth ..	59	143·42±0·48	5·45±0·34	3·80±0·24	50	144·52±0·45	4·70±0·32	3·25±0·22
Min. Frontal Breadth ..	59	104·07±0·36	4·13±0·26	3·97±0·25	50	103·78±0·32	3·26±0·22	3·14±0·21
Max. Bizygomatic Breadth ..	59	133·93±0·45	5·13±0·32	3·83±0·24	50	131·74±0·46	4·80±0·32	3·64±0·24
Bigonial Breadth	59	100·69±0·44	5·01±0·31	4·98±0·31	50	95·08±0·47	4·93±0·33	5·19±0·35
Inter-orbital Breadth ..	59	31·10±0·23	2·58±0·16	8·30±0·52	50	30·62±0·23	2·40±0·16	7·84±0·53
Orbitonasal Breadth ..	59	96·34±0·43	4·32±0·27	4·48±0·28	50	100·26±0·32	3·37±0·23	3·36±0·23
Orbitonasal Arc	59	110·20±0·46	5·06±0·31	4·59±0·29	50	113·02±0·45	4·72±0·31	4·48±0·30
Nasal Length	59	51·36±0·31	3·56±0·22	6·93±0·43	50	51·94±0·32	3·25±0·22	6·26±0·42
Nasal Breadth	59	37·14±0·24	2·73±0·17	7·35±0·46	50	36·82±0·28	2·98±0·21	8·09±0·55
Nasal Height or Depth ..	59	23·24±0·16	1·85±0·11	7·96±0·50	50	24·24±0·23	2·31±0·16	9·53±0·65
Upper Facial Length ..	59	64·73±0·27	3·06±0·19	4·73±0·30	50	66·70±0·37	3·94±0·26	5·91±0·40
Total Facial Length ..	59	114·49±0·50	5·63±0·35	4·92±0·31	50	118·30±0·56	5·90±0·40	4·99±0·34
Horizontal Cirm. of the Head	59	531·64±1·27	14·48±0·90	2·72±0·17	50	537·12±1·34	14·04±0·94	2·61±0·18
Sagittal Arc	59	334·64±1·33	15·17±0·94	4·53±0·29	50	345·08±1·60	16·70±1·13	4·84±0·33
Transverse Arc	59	329·49±1·05	11·88±0·74	3·61±0·23	50	337·34±1·07	11·22±0·76	3·33±0 23
Length Breadth Index ..	59	78·71±0·37	4·25±0·26	5·40±0·34	50	77·42±0·35	3·65±0·24	4·71±0 32
Length Height Index ..	57	66·45±0·36	4·00±0·25	6·02±0·38	50	66·42±0·29	3·11±0·21	4·68±0 31
Breadth Height Index ..	57	84·27±0·45	5·09±0·32	6·04±0·38	50	85·92±0·46	4·66±0·32	5·42±0·37
Trans. Fronto-Parietal Index	59	72·61±0·25	2·79±0·17	3·84±0·24	50	71·87±0·26	2·73±0·18	3·80±0·26
Orbitonasal Index	59	114·46±0·32	3·68±0·23	3·22±0·20	50	112·78±0·32	3·36±0·23	2·98±0·20
Nasal Index	59	72·42±0·60	6·78±0·42	9·36±0·59	50	71·18±0·75	7·84±0·53	11·01±0·76
Nasal Elevation Index ..	59	62·99±0·54	6·08±0·38	9·65±0·61	50	66·29±0·73	7·66±0·52	11·56±0·80
Upper Facial Index ..	59	48·55±0·24	2·70±0·17	5·56±0·35	50	50·67±0·29	3·11±0·21	6·14±0·41
Total Facial Index	59	85·57±0·38	4·27±0·26	4·99±0·32	50	89·87±0·45	4·76±0·31	5·30±0·36
Trans. Cephalo-Facial Index ..	59	93·32±0·28	3·22±0·20	3·45±0·21	50	91·21±0·33	3·43±0·24	3·76±0·25
Vertical Cephalo-Facial Index.	57	95·45±0·54	6·11±0·38	6·40±0·41	50	95·55±0·57	5·96±0·41	6·24±0·42

TABLE IV.

Southern India.

TABI

Souther

Measurements and Indices.	Nambudiri. Total No.	Mean with P. E.	S. D. with P. E.	Co-eff. of variation with P. E.	Nair. Total No.	Mean with P. E.	S. D. with P. E.	Co-eff. of variation with P. E.
Stature	55	1,635·55±4·37	48·10±3·09	2·94±0·10	60	1,689·97±5·34	61·34±3·80	3·63±0·2
Auricular Height	55	126·25±0·55	6·06±0·39	4·80±0·31	60	125·27±0·58	6·63±0·41	5·29±0·3
Max. Head Length	55	194·89±0·49	5·43±0·35	2·79±0·18	60	192·28±0·47	5·43±0·34	2·82±0·1
Max. Head Breadth	55	141·24±0·51	5·65±0·36	4·00±0·26	60	142·52±0·45	5·21±0·32	3·66±0·2
Min. Frontal Breadth	55	102·33±0·39	4·33±0·28	4·23±0·27	60	102·88±0·34	3·87±0·24	3·76±0·2
Max. Bizygomatic Breadth ..	54	132·33±0·46	4·96±0·32	3·75±0·24	60	132·87±0·34	3·95±0·24	2·97±0·1
Bigonial Breadth	55	97·49±0·55	6·05±0·39	6·21±0·40	60	98·83±0·45	5·19±0·32	5·26±0·3
Inter-orbital Breadth	55	30·96±0·19	2·10±0·14	6·78±0·44	60	31·00±0·20	2·32±0·14	7·48±0·4
Orbitonasal Breadth	55	100·84±0·30	3·27±0·21	3·24±0·21	60	100·75±0·33	3·78±0·23	3·75±0·2
Orbitonasal Arc	55	116·58±0·43	4·73±0·30	4·06±0·26	60	114·43±0·47	5·43±0·34	4·75±0·2
Nasal Length	55	51·98±0·37	4·07±0·26	7·83±0·51	60	52·32±0·31	3·61±0·22	6·90±0·4
Nasal Breadth	55	37·22±0·24	2·68±0·17	7·20±0·47	60	37·70±0·20	2·35±0·15	6·23±0·3
Nasal Height or Depth ..	55	26·47±0·20	2·18±0·14	8·24±0·53	60	25·70±0·22	2·53±0·16	9·84±0·61
Upper Facial Length	55	67·55±0·40	4·45±0·29	6·59±0·43	60	67·57±0·37	4·27±0·26	6·32±0·3
Total Facial Length	55	119·49±0·53	5·88±0·38	4·92±0·32	60	120·25±0·47	5·36±0·33	4·46±0·28
Horizontal Cirm. of the Head ..	55	546·40±1·33	14·60±0·94	2·67±0·17	60	542·53±0·96	10·99±0·68	2·03±0·13
Sagittal Arc	55	364·00±1·07	11·79±0·76	3·24±0·21	60	357·05±0·90	10·32±0·64	2·92±0·18
Transverse Arc	55	337·47±1·19	13·09±0·84	3·88±0·25	60	340·68±0·93	10·72±0·66	3·15±0·2
Length Breadth Index	55	72·51±0·28	3·10±0·20	4·28±0·28	60	74·18±0·30	3·42±0·21	4·62±0·28
Length Height Index	55	64·80±0·28	3·05±0·20	4·71±0·30	60	65·20±0·34	3·90±0·24	5·98±0·37
Breadth Height Index	55	89·50±0·46	5·01±0·32	5·60±0·36	60	87·98±0·45	5·16±0·32	5·86±0·3
Trans. Fronto-Parietal Index ..	55	72·52±0·31	3·39±0·22	4·67±0·30	60	72·26±0·28	3·22±0·20	4·46±0·28
Orbitonasal Index	55	115·63±0·32	3·55±0·23	3·07±0·20	60	113·62±0·37	4·25±0·26	3·74±0·23
Nasal Index	55	72·28±0·72	7·87±0·51	10·89±0·71	60	72·37±0·55	6·30±0·37	8·71±0·54
Nasal Elevation Index	55	71·51±0·48	5·30±0·34	7·41±0·48	60	68·40±0·67	7·73±0·48	11·30±0·71
Upper Facial Index	54	51·09±0·32	3·50±0·23	6·85±0·45	60	50·89±0·30	3·45±0·21	6·78±0·42
Total Facial Index	54	90·39±0·43	4·70±0·31	5·20±0·34	60	90·56±0·39	4·45±0·28	4·91±0·30
Trans. Cephalo-Facial Index ..	54	93·83±0·27	2·91±0·19	3·10±0·20	60	93·31±0·29	3·36±0·21	3·61±0·22
Vertical Cephalo-Facial Index ..	55	94·78±0·47	5·20±0·33	5·49±0·35	60	96·24±0·55	6·27±0·39	6·51±0·40

India.

Iluva.				Tamil Brahmin.				
Total No.	Mean with P. E.	S. D. with P. E.	Co-eff. of variation with P. E.	Total No.	Mean with P. E.	S. D. with P. E.	Co-eff. of variation with P. E.	Measurements and Indices.
50	1,594·00±4·33	45·61±3·06	2·86±0·19	50	1,640·68±5·95	62·40±4·21	3·80±0·26	Stature.
50	119·62±0·64	6·74±0·45	5·63±0·38	50	125·46±0·58	6·03±0·41	4·81±0·32	Auricular Height.
50	190·02±0·48	5·04±0·34	2·65±0·18	50	188·32±0·69	7·26±0·49	3·86±0·26	Max. Head Length.
50	139·34±0·50	5·28±0·35	3·79±0·25	50	145·50±0·46	4·81±0·32	3·31±0·22	Max. Head Breadth.
50	101·22±0·36	3·76±0·25	3·71±0·25	50	102·94±0·32	3·36±0·23	3·26±0·22	Min. Frontal Breadth.
50	128·76±0·43	4·51±0·30	3·51±0·23	50	131·02±0·45	4·69±0·32	3·58±0·24	Max. Bizygomatic Breadth.
50	96·64±0·55	5·74±0·38	5·94±0·40	50	97·92±0·53	5·57±0·38	5·69±0·38	Bigonial Breadth.
50	31·22±0·26	2·72±0·18	8·71±0·58	50	29·68±0·19	1·99±0·13	6·70±0·45	Inter-orbital Breadth.
50	99·24±0·38	3·98±0·27	4·12±0·28	50	102·42±0·37	3·83±0·26	3·74±0·25	Orbitonasal Breadth.
50	111·22±0·50	5·26±0·35	4·73±0·32	50	115·42±0·51	5·35±0·36	4·64±0·31	Orbitonasal Arc.
50	49·38±0·31	3·25±0·22	6·58±0·34	50	51·38±0·35	3·69±0·25	7·18±0·49	Nasal Length.
50	36·98±0·22	2·32±0·16	6·28±0·42	50	36·82±0·24	2·50±0·17	6·79±0·46	Nasal Breadth.
50	23·32±0·21	2·21±0·15	9·48±0·65	50	25·08±0·18	1·84±0·12	7·34±0·50	Nasal Height or Depth.
50	64·26±0·38	4·02±0·27	6·27±0·42	50	66·68±0·41	4·29±0·29	6·43±0·44	Upper Facial Length.
50	115·44±0·60	6·36±0·43	5·51±0·37	50	117·74±0·54	5·70±0·38	4·84±0·33	Total Facial Length.
50	534·44±1·48	15·60±1·05	2·92±0·20	50	540·20±1·54	16·12±1·09	2·98±0·20	Horizontal Cirm. of the Head.
50	357·12±1·13	11·93±0·80	3·34±0·22	50	354·72±1·31	13·69±0·92	3·86±0·26	Sagittal Arc.
50	331·46±0·91	9·55±0·64	2·88±0·19	50	337·68±1·17	12·31±0·83	3·65±0·25	Transverse Arc.
50	73·38±0·28	2·95±0·20	4·02±0·27	50	77·36±0·34	3·53±0·24	4·56±0·31	Length Breadth Index.
50	63·00±0·37	3·86±0·26	6·13±0·41	50	66·70±0·36	3·79±0·26	5·68±0·38	Length Height Index.
50	85·96±0·53	5·55±0·37	6·46±0·43	50	86·25±0·34	3·53±0·24	4·09±0·28	Breadth Height Index.
50	72·70±0·27	2·80±0·19	3·85±0·26	50	70·81±0·27	2·81±0·19	3·97±0·27	Trans. Fronto-Parietal Index.
50	112·31±0·38	3·97±0·27	3·53±0·24	50	112·74±0·41	4·35±0·29	3·86±0·26	Orbitonasal Index.
50	75·20±0·63	6·68±0·45	8·88±0·59	50	71·92±0·58	6·03±0·41	8·38±0·57	Nasal Index.
50	63·20±0·64	6·74±0·45	10·66±0·72	50	68·45±0·69	7·20±0·49	10·52±0·72	Nasal Elevation Index.
50	49·97±0·34	3·54±0·24	7·08±0·47	50	50·93±0·35	3·72±0·26	7·30±0·49	Upper Facial Index.
50	89·74±0·52	5·49±0·37	6·23±0·42	50	89·94±0·44	4·63±0·31	5·15±0·35	Total Facial Index.
50	92·49±0·34	3·59±0·24	3·88±0·26	50	90·07±0·25	2·64±0·18	2·93±0·20	Trans. Cephalo-Facial Index.
50	96·82±0·73	7·72±0·52	7·97±0·53	50	94·00±0·52	5·47±0·37	5·82±0·39	Vertical Cephalo-Facial Index.

TABLE

Southern

Measurements and Indices.	Tamil Kala. Total No.	Mean with P. E.	S. D. with P. E.	Co-eff. of variation with P. E.	Tamil Chetti. Total No.	Mean with P. E.	S. D. with P. E.	Co-eff. of variation with P.E.
Stature	40	1,661·80±6·74	63·22±4·77	3·80±0·29	50	1,623·00±5·20	54·53±3·68	3·36±0·23
Auricular Height	40	121·53±0·70	6·55±0·49	5·39±0·41	50	124·14±0·68	7·11±0·48	5·73±0·39
Max. Head Length	40	188·83±0·49	4·61±0·35	2·44±0·18	50	187·04±0·59	6·21±0·42	3·32±0·22
Max. Head Breadth	40	142·05±0·52	4·87±0·37	3·43±0·26	50	148·58±0·47	4·92±0·33	3·31±0·21
Min. Frontal Breadth	40	101·30±0·34	3·16±0·24	3·12±0·24	50	102·68±0·36	3·77±0·25	3·67±0·25
Max. Bizygomatic Breadth	40	132·63±0·43	4·05±0·31	3·05±0·23	50	134·34±0·51	5·39±0·36	4·01±0·27
Bigonial Breadth	40	100·00±0·66	6·16±0·46	6·16±0·47	50	101·36±0·56	5·88±0·40	5·80±0·39
Inter-orbital Breadth	40	31·33±0·20	1·85±0·14	5·90±0·45	50	31·32±0·24	2·53±0·17	8·08±0·55
Orbitonasal Breadth	40	98·78±0·37	3·48±0·26	3·52±0·27	50	102·12±0·37	3·83±0·26	3·75±0·25
Orbitonasal Arc	40	108·38±0·40	3·79±0·29	3·50±0·26	50	112·34±0·52	5·48±0·37	4·88±0·33
Nasal Length	40	49·33±0·41	3·83±0·29	7·76±0·59	50	52·26±0·32	3·39±0·23	6·49±0·44
Nasal Breadth	40	37·40±0·26	2·44±0·18	6·52±0·49	50	37·02±0·27	2·84±0·19	7·68±0·52
Nasal Height or Depth	40	23·45±0·19	1·79±0·13	7·63±0·58	50	24·22±0·18	1·84±0·12	7·60±0·52
Upper Facial Length	40	64·78±0·32	3·01±0·23	4·65±0·35	50	66·86±0·41	4·32±0·29	6·46±0·44
Total Facial Length	40	115·48±0·52	4·88±0·37	4·23±0·32	50	119·74±0·66	6·90±0·47	5·76±0·39
Horizontal Cirm. of the Head	40	532·73±1·01	9·49±0·72	1·78±0·13	50	540·98±1·40	14·65±0·99	2·71±0·18
Sagittal Arc	40	346·98±1·00	9·35±0·71	2·69±0·20	50	355·26±1·15	12·02±0·81	3·38±0·23
Transverse Arc	40	331·20±0·90	8·45±0·64	2·55±0·19	50	339·18±0·89	9·33±0·63	2·75±0·19
Length Breadth Index	40	75·26±0·30	2·82±0·21	3·75±0·28	50	79·49±0·28	2·97±0·20	3·74±0·25
Length Height Index	40	64·37±0·35	3·26±0·25	5·06±0·38	50	66·42±0·38	4·00±0·27	6·02±0·41
Breadth Height Index	40	85·63±0·53	4·95±0·37	5·78±0·44	50	83·64±0·52	5·45±0·37	6·52±0·44
Trans. Fronto-Parietal Index	40	71·38±0·30	2·82±0·21	3·95±0·30	50	69·17±0·24	2·55±0·17	3·69±0·25
Orbitonasal Index	40	109·78±0·37	3·51±0·26	3·20±0·24	50	110·00±0·30	3·15±0·21	2·86±0·19
Nasal Index	40	76·26±0·77	7·26±0·55	9·52±0·72	50	71·19±0·72	7·52±0·51	10·56±0·72
Nasal Elevation Index	40	62·92±0·62	5·84±0·44	9·28±0·71	50	65·89±0·76	7·97±0·54	12·10±0·83
Upper Facial Index	40	48·90±0·28	2·59±0·20	5·30±0·40	50	49·83±0·34	3·61±0·24	7·24±0·49
Total Facial Index	40	87·12±0·41	3·89±0·29	4·47±0·34	50	89·26±0·57	5·97±0·40	6·69±0·45
Trans. Cephalo-Facial Index	40	93·43±0·37	3·49±0·26	3·74±0·28	50	90·45·±0·30	3·14±0·21	3·47±0·23
Vertical Cephalo-Facial Index	40	95·22±0·57	5·34±0·40	5·61±0·42	50	96·72±0·68	7·18±0·48	7·42±0·50

IV.

India.

Telegu Brahmin.				Telegu Non-Brahmin.				
Total No.	Mean with P. E.	S. D. with P. E.	Co-eff. of variation with P. E.	Total No.	Mean with P. E.	S. D. with P. E.	Co-eff. of variation with P. E.	Measurements and Indices.
50	1,645·90±4·67	49·19±3·30	2·99±0·20	50	1,650·86±5·78	60·86±4·08	3·69±0·25	Stature.
50	123·88±0·73	7·69±0·52	6·21±0·42	50	121·64±0·89	9·35±0·63	7·67±0·52	Auricular Height.
50	190·20±0·50	5·22±0·35	2·74±0·18	50	189·88±0·61	6·41±0·43	3·38±0·23	Max. Head Length.
50	141·36±0·47	4·96±0·33	3·49±0·23	50	140·90±0·54	5·66±0·38	4·02±0·27	Max. Head Breadth.
50	102·52±0·34	3·60±0·24	3·51±0·24	50	103·24±0·44	4·59±0·31	4·45±0·30	Min. Frontal Breadth.
50	132·16±0·43	4·54±0·30	3·44±0·23	50	132·76±0·53	5·60±0·38	4·22±0·28	Max. Bizygomatic Breadth.
50	97·48±0·57	6·01±0·40	6·17±0·41	50	97·32±0·55	5·74±0·38	5·90±0·40	Bigonial Breadth.
50	31·08±0·27	2·81±0·19	9·04±0·61	50	31·38±0·24	2·48±0·17	7·90±0·54	Inter-orbital Breadth.
50	100·40±0·43	4·57±0·31	4·55±0·30	50	99·80±0·46	4·81±0·32	4·82±0·32	Orbitonasal Breadth.
50	111·94±0·56	5·89±0·39	5·26±0·35	50	111·90±0·57	5·95±0·40	5·32±0·36	Orbitonasal Arc.
50	51·52±0·30	3·18±0·21	6·17±0·41	50	51·40±0·32	3·32±0·22	6·46±0·43	Nasal Length.
50	37·82±0·26	2·77±0·19	7·35±0·49	50	38·38±0·26	2·78±0·19	7·24±0·49	Nasal Breadth.
50	25·16±0·19	2·01±0·13	7·99±0·54	50	24·62±0·18	1·86±0·12	7·55±0·51	Nasal Height or Depth.
50	66·42±0·39	4·07±0·27	6·14±0·41	50	65·94±0·33	3·45±0·23	5·23±0·35	Upper Facial Length.
50	115·30±0·46	4·88±0·33	4·23±0·28	50	117·16±0·54	5·65±0·38	4·82±0·32	Total Facial Length.
50	539·76±1·05	11·06±0·74	2·05±0·14	50	538·18±1·56	16·46±1·10	3·06±0·21	Horizontal Cirm. of the Head.
50	351·04±1·38	14·48±0·97	4·12±0·28	50	346·60±1·51	15·87±1·06	4·58±0·31	Sagittal Arc.
50	332·70±1·10	11·57±0·78	3·48±0·23	50	331·38±1·02	10·72±0·72	3·23±0·22	Transverse Arc.
50	74·39±0·34	3·58±0·24	4·81±0·32	50	74·27±0·34	3·54±0·24	4·77±0·32	Length Breadth Index.
50	65·18±0·42	4·42±0·30	6·78±0·45	50	64·12±0·49	5·16±0·35	8·05±0·54	Length Height Index.
50	87·80±0·54	5·69±0·38	6·48±0·43	50	86·41±0·63	6·64±0·44	7·68±0·52	Breadth Height Index.
50	72·59±0·29	3·03±0·20	4·17±0·28	50	73·32±0·28	2·92±0·20	3·98±0·27	Trans. Fronto-Parietal Index.
50	111·53±0·37	3·91±0·26	3·51±0·24	50	112·18±0·36	3·81±0·26	3·40±0·23	Orbitonasal Index.
50	73·70±0·68	7·18±0·48	9·74±0·66	50	74·93±0·64	6·71±0·45	8·96±0·61	Nasal Index.
50	66·90±0·70	7·35±0·49	10·99±0·75	50	64·54±0·71	7·44±0·50	11·53±0·79	Nasal Elevation Index.
50	50·32±0·31	3·29±0·22	6·54±0·44	50	49·73±0·27	2·87±0·19	5·77±0·39	Upper Facial Index.
50	87·30±0·37	3·94±0·26	4·51±0·30	50	88·14±0·45	4·69±0·31	5·32±0·36	Total Facial Index.
50	93·51±0·31	3·27±0·22	3·50±0·23	50	94·26±0·28	2·93±0·20	3·11±0·21	Trans. Cephalo-Facial Index.
50	93·29±0·67	7·02±0·47	7·52±0·50	50	96·43±0·74	7·82±0·52	8·11±0·55	Vertical Cephalo-Facial Index.

TABLE IV.

Southern India.

Measurements and Indices.	Kanarese Brahmin. Total No.	Mean with P. E.	S. D. with P. E.	Co-eff. of variation with P. E.	Kanarese Non-Brahmin. Total No.	Mean with P. E.	S. D. with P. E.	Co-eff. of variation with P. E.
Stature	50	1,618·70±5·16	54·10±3·64	3·34±0·23	50	1,654·92±4·83	50·88±3·43	3·07±0·2[illegible]
Auricular Height	50	121·24±0·59	6·16±0·42	5·08±0·34	50	122·38±0·63	6·64±0·45	5·42±0·3[illegible]
Max. Head Length	50	184·02±0·67	7·05±0·48	3·88±0·26	50	179·30±0·71	7·44±0·50	4·15±0·28
Max. Head Breadth	50	145·74±0·65	6·85±0·46	4·70±0·32	50	148·74±0·61	6·40±0·43	4·30±0·29
Min. Frontal Breadth	50	104·72±0·37	3·92±0·26	3·74±0·25	50	104·10±0·40	4·26±0·29	4·09±0·28
Max. Bizygomatic Breadth ..	50	132·60±0·36	3·82±0·26	2·88±0·19	50	133·76±0·49	5·20±0·35	3·89±0·27
Bigonial Breadth	50	96·22±0·45	4·71±0·32	4·90±0·33	50	98·18±0·50	5·30±0·36	5·40±0·36
Inter-orbital Breadth	50	30·14±0·25	2·61±0·18	8·66±0·59	50	30·56±0·25	2·61±0·18	8·54±0·58
Orbitonasal Breadth	50	100·86±0·31	3·27±0·22	3·24±0·22	50	100·54±0·32	3·37±0·23	3·35±0·23
Orbitonasal Arc	50	112·78±0·41	4·33±0·29	3·84±0·26	50	111·68±0·46	4·86±0·33	4·35±0·30
Nasal Length	50	51·58±0·36	3·84±0·26	7·44±0·51	50	50·52±0·35	3·66±0·25	7·24±0·49
Nasal Breadth	50	36·46±0·21	2·25±0·15	6·17±0·42	50	36·48±0·27	2·80±0·19	7·66±0·51
Nasal Height or Depth	50	24·94±0·22	2·35±0·16	9·42±0·64	50	24·06±0·19	1·99±0·13	8·27±0·56
Upper Facial Length	50	65·94±0·31	3·26±0·22	4·94±0·33	50	65·08±0·36	3·77±0·25	5·79±0·39
Total Facial Length	50	115·64±0·43	4·48±0·30	3·87±0·26	50	115·96±0·62	6·55±0·44	5·65±0·38
Horizontal Cirm. of the Head ..	50	533·16±1·38	14·48±0·98	2·72±0·18	50	530·48±1·39	14·60±0·98	2·75±0·18
Sagittal Arc	50	345·00±1·36	14·28±0·96	4·14±0·28	50	339·48±1·26	13·29±0·89	3·91±0·26
Transverse Arc	50	334·92±1·10	11·51±0·78	3·44±0·23	50	339·28±1·00	10·53±0·71	3·10±0·21
Length Breadth Index	50	79·34±0·50	5·23±0·35	6·59±0·45	50	83·06±0·44	4·66±0·31	5·61±0·38
Length Height Index	50	65·97±0·38	4·00±0·27	6·06±0·41	50	68·34±0·38	4·03±0·27	5·90±0·40
Breadth Height Index	50	83·33±0·48	5·04±0·34	6·05±0·41	50	82·38±0·47	4·94±0·33	6·00±0·41
Trans. Fronto-Parietal Index ..	50	71·97±0·33	3·45±0·23	4·79±0·32	50	70·07±0·31	3·31±0·22	4·72±0·32
Orbitonasal Index	50	111·85±0·33	3·51±0·24	3·14±0·21	50	111·11±0·34	3·55±0·24	3·20±0·21
Nasal Index	50	71·20±0·70	7·36±0·50	10·34±0·70	50	72·46±0·67	7·14±0·48	9·85±0·67
Nasal Elevation Index	50	68·65±0·73	7·61±0·51	11·09±0·76	50	66·26±0·63	6·59±0·44	9·95±0·68
Upper Facial Index	50	49·76±0·26	2·74±0·18	5·51±0·37	50	48·69±0·28	2·99±0·20	6·14±0·42
Total Facial Index	50	87·30±0·44	4·59±0·31	5·26±0·36	50	86·77±0·49	5·13±0·35	5·91±0·40
Trans. Cephalo-Facial Index ..	50	91·11±0·33	3·42±0·23	3·75±0·25	50	90·00±0·30	3·20±0·22	3·56±0·24
Vertical Cephalo-Facial Index ..	50	95·64±0·60	6·30±0·42	6·59±0·45	50	94·96±0·61	6·47±0·44	6·81±0·46

TABLE V.

Tribal Group.

TABLE V.

Tribal Group.

Measurements and Indices.	Khasi.				Chenchu.			
	Total No.	Mean with P. E.	S. D. with P. E.	Co-efficient of variation with P. E.	Total No.	Mean with P. E.	S. D. with P. E.	Co-efficient of variation with P. E.
Stature	81	1,569·10±4·67	62·34±3·30	3·97±0·21	23	1,649·52±9·23	65·67±6·53	3·98±0·40
Auricular Height ..	76	125·60±0·46	6·02±0·33	4·78±0·26	23	120·48±0·85	6·03±0·60	5·00±0·50
Max. Head Length ..	81	186·90±0·42	5·57±0·30	3·00±0·16	23	185·17±0·79	5·61±0·56	3·03±0·30
Max. Head Breadth ..	81	144·50±0·40	5·26±0·28	3·67±0·19	23	134·83±0·74	5·26±0·52	3·90±0·39
Min. Frontal Breadth ..	81	101·40±0·39	5·22±0·28	5·13±0·27	23	100·83±0·55	3·89±0·39	3·86±0·38
Max. Bizygomatic Breadth..	81	133·80±0·41	5·53±0·29	4·11±0·22	23	129·00±0·66	4·67±0·46	3·62±0·36
Bigonial Breadth ..	81	106·10±0·64	8·62±0·46	8·11±0·43	23	93·39±1·29	9·15±0·91	9·80±0·98
Inter-orbital Breadth ..	16	31·10±0·50	2·45±0·35	7·88±1·13	23	30·30±0·27	1·90±0·19	6·27±0·62
Orbitonasal Breadth ..	81	96·30±0·42	5·64±0·30	5·82±0·31	23	97·15±0·51	3·65±0·36	3·76±0·37
Orbitonasal Arc	81	104·60±0·39	5·22±0·28	4·97±0·26	23	108·74±0·70	4·99±0·50	4·59±0·46
Nasal Length	81	49·10±0·29	3·89±0·21	7·94±0·42	23	48·22±0·63	4·47±0·44	9·27±0·93
Nasal Breadth	81	37·90±0·20	2·74±0·14	7·12±0·38	23	38·98±0·32	2·27±0·23	5·82±0·58
Nasal Height or Depth ..	81	19·20±0·22	3·03±0·16	1·56±0·08	23	21·11±0·32	2·26±0·23	10·71±1·08
Upper Facial Length ..	81	67·00±0·29	3·89±0·21	5·82±0·31	23	61·35±0·76	5·39±0·54	8·79±0·88
Total Facial Length ..	81	113·10±0·44	5·81±0·31	5·13±0·27	23	110·00±1·01	7·17±0·71	6·52±0·65
Horizontal Cirm. of the Head	16	538·75±3·30	16·25±2·34	3·02±0·43	23	525·35±1·86	13·21±1·31	2·51±0·25
Sagittal Arc	16	351·56±2·69	13·23±1·90	3·76±0·54	23	344·52±2·18	15·51±1·54	4·50±0·45
Transverse Arc	16	334·44±2·86	14·04±2·02	4·20±0·60	23	326·82±1·74	12·40±1·23	3·79±0·38
Length Breadth Index ..	81	77·30±0·20	2·70±0·14	3·49±0·18	23	72·89±0·53	3·76±0·37	5·16±0·51
Length Height Index ..	76	67·10±0·27	3·50±0·19	5·22±0·28	23	65·11±0·49	3·51±0·35	5·39±0·54
Breadth Height Index ..	76	87·20±0·37	4·77±0·26	5·50±0·30	23	89·46±0·73	5·18±0·52	5·79±0·58
Trans Fronto-Parietal Index	81	70·30±0·31	4·09±0·22	5·83±0·31	23	74·85±0·43	3·06±0·30	4·09±0·41
Orbitonasal Index ..	81	108·60±0·25	3·43±0·18	3·13±0·17	23	111·98±0·73	5·17±0·52	4·62±0·46
Nasal Index	81	77·40±0·52	6·94±0·37	8·91±0·48	23	81·38±0·95	6·72±0·67	8·26±0·83
Nasal Elevation Index ..	81	50·70±0·61	8·10±0·43	15·98±0·87	23	54·19±0·72	5·09±0·51	9·39±0·94
Upper Facial Index ..	81	50·00±0·25	3·33±0·17	6·60±0·35	23	47·56±0·54	3·82±0·38	8·03±0·80
Total Facial Index ..	81	84·50±0·34	4·49±0·24	5·33±0·28	23	85·26±0·61	4·36±0·43	5·11±0·51
Trans Cephalo-Facial Index	81	92·70±0·29	3·90±0·21	4·21±0·22	23	95·75±0·49	3·47±0·35	3·62±0·36
Vertical Cephalo-Facial Index	76	90·10±0·51	6·59±0·36	7·33±0·40	23	91·48±0·96	6·85±0·68	7·49±0·75

TABLE V.

Tribal Group.

Nicobarese.				Measurements and Indices.
Total No.	Mean with P. E.	S. D. with P. E.	Co-efficient of variation with P. E.	
121	1,589·25±3·22	52·49±2·28	3·30±0·14	Stature.
112	126·07±0·38	5·94±0·27	4·71±0·21	Auricular Height.
121	187·04±0·39	6·30±0·27	3·37±0·15	Max. Head Length.
121	143·36±0·31	5·02±0·22	3·50±0·15	Max. Head Breadth.
121	103·99±0·22	3·68±0·16	3·54±0·15	Min. Frontal Breadth.
121	138·31±0·26	4·31±0·19	3·12±0·13	Max. Bizygomatic Breadth.
121	102·26±0·24	3·90±0·17	3·81±0·16	Bigonial Breadth.
121	33·55±0·14	2·31±0·10	6·89±0·30	Inter-orbital Breadth.
121	94·77±0·23	3·69±0·16	3·89±0·17	Orbitonasal Breadth.
121	105·93±0·30	4·87±0·21	4·60±0·20	Orbitonasal Arc.
121	47·79±0·20	3·25±0·14	6·80±0·29	Nasal Length.
121	39·86±0·12	2·01±0·09	5·04±0·22	Nasal Breadth.
121	14·30±0·09	1·51±0·06	1·06±0·05	Nasal Height or Depth.
121	66·44±0·27	4·44±0·19	6·68±0·29	Upper Facial Length.
121	113·49±0·37	6·05±0·26	5·33±0·23	Total Facial Length.
121	542·40±0·71	11·62±0·50	2·14±0·09	Horizontal Cirm. of the Head.
121	352·30±0·75	12·25±0·53	3·48±0·15	Sagittal Arc.
121	340·83±0·61	9·95±0·43	2·92±0·13	Transverse Arc.
121	76·76±0·27	4·35±0·19	5·67±0·26	Length Breadth Index.
112	67·61±0·25	3·87±0·17	5·72±0·26	Length Height Index.
112	88·14±0·30	4·66±0·21	5·29±0·24	Breadth Height Index.
121	72·60±0·19	3·05±0·13	4·20±0·18	Trans Fronto-Parietal Index.
121	111·81±0·22	3·62±0·16	3·24±0·14	Orbitonasal Index.
121	83·87±0·43	6·98±0·30	8·32±0·36	Nasal Index.
121	35·93±0·24	3·90±0·17	3·81±0·16	Nasal Elevation Index.
121	48·05±0·18	2·92±0·13	6·08±0·26	Upper Facial Index.
121	82·08±0·26	4·24±0·18	5·17±0·23	Total Facial Index.
121	96·56±0·22	3·60±0·16	3·73±0·16	Trans Cephalo-Facial Index.
112	90·01±0·37	5·76±0·26	5·40±0·24	Vertical Cephalo-Facial Index.

REDUCED AND CRUDE

Co-efficients of Racial Likeness.

EXPLANATION

of

Reduced Co-efficients of Racial Likeness.

From 0—4	..	**Intimate association.**
From 4·1—13	..	**Association.**
Above 13	..	*Divergence.*

TABLE VI.

Reduced Co-efficients of Racial Likeness.

North Western India.

	Red-Kaffir.	Pathan.	Uzbeg.	Badakshi.	Tadjik.	Khos [Lower Chitral].	Khalash.	Khos [Upper Chitral].
Red-Kaffir	..	5·15 ±0·26	54·88 ±0·34	16·70 ±0·59	28·92 ±0·22	6·77 ±0·18	5·59 ±0·21	7·42 ±0·14
Pathan	5·15 ±0·26	..	44·50 ±0·43	8·61 ±0·67	24·82 ±0·31	4·06 ±0·27	3·27 ±0·29	8·94 ±0·23
Uzbeg	54·88 ±0·34	44·50 ±0·43	..	46·85 ±0·76	5·80 ±0·39	32·62 ±0·35	64·25 ±0·38	30·91 ±0·31
Badakshi	16·70 ±0·59	8·61 ±0·67	46·85 ±0·76	..	23·20 ±0·64	12·11 ±0·60	18·24 ±0·62	11·98 ±0·56
Tadjik	28·92 ±0·22	24·82 ±0·31	5·80 ±0·39	23·20 ±0·64	..	14·25 ±0·23	36·05 ±0·26	10·33 ±0·19
Khos [Lower Chitral] ..	6·77 ±0·18	4·06 ±0·27	32·62 ±0·35	12·11 ±0·60	14·25 ±0·23	..	8·94 ±0·22	—0·01 ±0·15
Khalash	5·59 ±0·21	3·27 ±0·29	64·25 ±0·38	18·24 ±0·62	36·05 ±0·26	8·94 ±0·22	..	10·68 ±0·18
Khos [Upper Chitral]	7·42 ±0·14	8·94 ±0·23	30·91 ±0·31	11·98 ±0·56	10·33 ±0·19	—0·01 ±0·15	10·68 ±0·18	..

TABLE VI (a).

Crude Co-efficients of Racial Likeness.

North Western India.

	Red-Kaffir.	Pathan.	Uzbeg.	Badakshi.	Tadjik.	Khos [Lower Chitral].	Khalash.	Khos [Upper Chitral].
Red-Kaffir	..	3·43	27·17	4·84	22·08	6·45	4·58	8·94
Pathan	3·43	..	17·66	2·18	13·71	2·60	1·90	2·96
Uzbeg	27·17	17·66	..	10·48	2·50	15·76	28·81	16·71
Badakshi	4·84	2·18	10·48	..	6·17	3·45	4·97	3·64
Tadjik	22·08	13·71	2·50	6·17	..	10·48	23·72	9·06
Khos [Lower Chitral] ..	6·45	2·60	15·76	3·45	10·48	..	7·04	—0·01
Khalash	4·58	1·90	28·81	4·97	23·72	7·04	—	10·17
Khos [Upper Chitral] ..	8·94	2·96	16·71	3·64	9·06	—0·01	10·17	..

Probable Error is ± 0·17 in all cases.

TABLE VII.

Reduced Co-efficients of Racial Likeness.

Hunza (Dixon) and others.

(10 characters only.)

	Hunza (Dixon).	Khos [Upper Chitral] (Guha).	Khalash (Guha).	Balti (Dainelli).	Ladaki (Dainelli).
Hunza (Dixon)	..	39·67 ±0·38	35·28 ±0·37	117·00 ±0·26	33·50 ±0·47
Khos [Upper Chitral] (Guha)	39·67 ±0·38	..	×	104·64 ±0·20	×
Khalash (Guha)	35·28 ±0·37	×	..	×	×
Balti (Dainelli)	117·00 ±0·26	104·64 ±0·20	×	..	×
Ladaki (Dainelli)	33·50 ±0·47	×	×	×	..

TABLE VII (a).

Crude Co-efficients of Racial Likeness.

Hunza (Dixon) and others.

(10 characters only.)

	Hunza (Dixon).	Khos [Upper Chitral] (Guha).	Khalash (Guha).	Balti (Dainelli).	Ladaki (Dainelli).
Hunza (Dixon).	..	30·28	28·00	132·95	20·81
Khos [Upper Chitral] (Guha).	30·28	..	×	*153·88*	×
Khalash (Guha).	28·00	×	..	×	×
Balti (Dainelli).	132·95	153·88	×	..	×
Ladaki (Dainelli). — ..	20·81	×	×	×	..

Probable Error is ±0·29 in all cases.

TABLE VIII.

Reduced Co-efficients of Racial Likeness.

Balti (Dainelli) and others.

(10 characters only.)

	Balti.	Brokpa.	Machnopa.	Purigi.	Ladaki.	Changpa.
Balti	..	—0·56 ±0·38	3·76 ±0·41	12·96 ±0·39	*41·88 ±0·39*	*74·83 ±0·39*
Brokpa	—0·56 ±0·38	..	1·09 ±0·60	10·07 ±0·59	*33·96 ±0·59*	*65·71 ±0·59*
Machnopa	3·76 ±0·41	1·09 ±0·60	..	7·26 ±0·62	*22·84 ±0·62*	*49·15 ±0·62*
Purigi	12·96 ±0·39	10·07 ±0·59	7·26 ±0·62	..	*17·44 ±0·60*	*47·24 ±0·60*
Ladaki	*41·88 ±0·39*	*33·96 ±0·59*	*22·84 ±0·62*	*17·44 ±0·60*	..	*17·23 ±0·60*
Changpa	*74·83 ±0·39*	*65·71 ±0·59*	*49·15 ±0·62*	*47·24 ±0·60*	*17·23 ±0·60*	..

TABLE VIII (a).

Crude Co-efficients of Racial Likeness.

Balti (Dainelli) and others.

(10 characters only.)

	Balti.	Brokpa.	Machnopa.	Purigi.	Ladaki.	Changpa.
Balti	..	—0·41	2·54	9·19	29·71	53·07
Brokpa	—0·41	..	0·50	4·82	16·25	31·44
Machnopa	2·54	0·50	..	3·30	10·38	22·34
Purigi	9·19	4·82	3·30	..	8·19	22·18
Ladaki	29·71	16·25	10·38	8·19	..	8·09
Changpa	53·07	31·44	22·34	22·18	8·09	..

Probable Error is ± 0·28 in all cases.

TABLE IX.

Reduced Co-efficients of Racial Likeness.

Sikh (Eickstedt) and others.

(13 characters only.)

	Sindhi.	Pathan.	U. P. Brahmin.	West Punjabi (Eickstedt).	Telegu Brahmin.	Nambudiri Brahmin.	Malve Brahmin.
Sikh (Eickstedt)	*57·78* ±*0·29*	9·59 ±0·42	*14·79* ±*0·42*	1·27 ±0·35	*32·37* ±*0·42*	*24·35* ±*0·39*	*33·12* ±*0·42*

TABLE IX(a).

Crude Co-efficients of Racial Likeness.

Sikh (Eickstedt) and others.

(13 characters only.)

	Sindhi.	Pathan.	U. P. Brahmin.	West Punjabi (Eickstedt).	Telegu Brahmin.	Nambudiri Brahmin.	Malve Brahmin.
Sikh (Eickstedt)	49·81	5·78	8·91	0·91	19·50	15·51	19·95

Probable Error is × 0·25 in all cases.

TABLE X.

Reduced Co-efficients of Racial Likeness.

Maithil and Kanaujia Brahmins (Chatterjee) of Bihar and others.

(25 characters only.)

	Telegu Brahmin.	U. P. Brahmin.	Bengali Brahmin.	Bengali Kayastha.	Bengali Pod.	Nambudiri Brahmin.	Malve Brahmin.	Oriya Brahmin.	Sikh* (Eickstedt).
Maithil Brahmin (Chatterjee).	*18·48* ±*0·24*	*30·68* ±*0·24*	*32·85* ±*0·24*	*33·12* ±*0·14*	*25·14* ±*0·24*	*19·68* ±*0·22*	*27·08* ±*0·24*	*16·90* ±*0·12*	*31·49* ±*0·23*
Kanaujia Brahmin (Chatterjee).	*16·30* ±*0·25*	*25·58* ±*0·25*	*29·59* ±*0·24*	*30·46* ±*0·15*	*17·58* ±*0·25*	*20·18* ±*0·23*	*21·24* ±*0·25*	*14·63* ±*0·13*	*36·64* ±*0·24*

* Based on 13 characters only.

TABLE X (a).

Crude Co-efficients of Racial Likeness.

Maithil and Kanaujia Brahmins (Chatterjee) of Bihar and others.

(25 characters only.)

	Telegu Brahmin.	U. P. Brahmin.	Bengali Brahmin.	Bengali Kayastha.	Bengali Pod.	Nambudiri Brahmin.	Malve Brahmin.	Oriya Brahmin.	Sikh.* (Eickstedt).
Maithil Brahmin (Chatterjee).	14·67 ±0·19	24·35 ±0·19	26·07 ±0·19	43·58 ±0·19	19·95 ±0·19	16·82 ±0·19	21·49 ±0·19	26·83 ±0·19	34·23 ±0·25
Kanaujia Brahmin (Chatterjee).	12·44 ±0·19	19·30 ±0·19	22·59 ±0·19	37·61 ±0·19	13·42 ±0·19	16·54 ±0·19	16·21 ±0·19	21·52 ±0·19	37·78 ±0·25

* Based on 13 characters only.

TABLE XI.

Reduced Co-efficients of Racial Likeness.

Bengal and Orissa.

	Bengali Brahmin.	Bengali Kayastha.	Bengali Pod.	Orissa Brahmin.
Bengali Brahmin	..	1·49 ±0·26	*15·70 ±0·34*	*23·59 ±0·23*
Bengali Kayastha	1·49 ±0·26	..	*18·89 ±0·25*	*23·35 ±0·15*
Bengali Pod	*15·70 ±0·34*	*18·89 ±0·25*	..	8·19 ±0·23
Orissa Brahmin	*23·59 ±0·23*	*23·35 ±0·15*	8·19 ±0·23	..

TABLE XI (a).

Crude Co-efficients of Racial Likeness.

Bengal and Orissa.

	Bengali Brahmin.	Bengali Kayastha.	Bengali Pod.	Orissa Brahmin.
Bengali Brahmin	..	0·99	7·85	17·22
Bengali Kayastha	0·99	..	12·59	26·84
Bengali Pod	7·85	12·59	..	5·98
Orissa Brahmin	17·22	26·84	5·98	..

Probable Error is ±0·17 in all cases.

TABLE XII.

Reduced Co-efficients of Racial Likeness.

Central India.

	Baghel Rajput.	Miscellaneous Rajput.	Malve Brahmin.
Baghel Rajput	..	0·55 ±0·34	5·31 ±0·34
Miscellaneous Rajput	0·55 ±0·34	..	3·08 ±0·34
Malve Brahmin	5·31 ±0·34	3·08 ±0·34	..

TABLE XII (a).

Crude Co-efficients of Racial Likeness.

Central India.

	Baghel Rajput.	Miscellaneous Rajput.	Malve Brahmin.
Baghel Rajput	..	0·28	2·66
Miscellaneous Rajput	0·28	..	1·54
Malve Brahmin	2·66	1·54	–

Probable Error is ±0·17 in all cases.

TABLE XIII.

Reduced Co-efficients of Racial Likeness.

Guzrati group.

	Nagar Brahmin.	Bania-Jain.	Brahma-Kshatri.	Kathi.	Audich Brahmin.	Kunbi-Patidar.
Nagar Brahmin	..	*1·10* ±0·17	*6·13* ±0·36	4·10 ±0·29	5·58 ±0·17	*20·41* ±0·4
Bania-Jain	1·10 ±0·17	..	7·37 ±0·36	6·32 ±0·30	3·75 ±0·18	*14·31* ±*0·43*
Brahma-Kshatri	6·13 ±0·36	7·37 ±0·36	..	4·52 ±0·49	10·15 ±0·37	*24·51* ±*0·6*
Kathi	4·10 ±0·29	6·32 ±0·30	4·52 ±0·49	..	11·65 ±0·30	*15·73* ±*0·55*
Audich Brahmin	5·58 ±0·17	3·75 ±0·18	10·15 ±0·37	11·65 ±0·30	..	10·69 ±0·43
Kunbi-Patidar	*20·41* ±*0·42*	*14·31* ±*0·43*	*24·51* ±*0·61*	*15·73* ±*0·55*	10·69 ±0·43	--

TABLE XIII (a).

Crude Co-efficients of Racial Likeness.

Guzrati group.

	Nagar Brahmin.	Bania-Jain.	Brahma-Kshatri.	Kathi.	Audich Brahmin.	Kunbi-Patidar.
Nagar Brahmin	..	1·12	2·92	2·38	5·49	8·23
Bania-Jain	1·12	..	3·51	3·61	3·61	5·70
Brahma-Kshatri	2·92	3·51	..	1·58	4·72	6·79
Kathi	2·38	3·61	1·58	..	6·51	4·84
Audich Brahmin	5·49	3·61	4·72	6·51	..	4·21
Kunbi-Patidar	8·23	5·70	6·79	4·84	4·21	..

Probable Error is ± 0·17 in all cases.

TABLE XIII (b).

Reduced and Crude Co-efficients of Racial Likeness.

Parsi and Others.

(25 characters only.)

		Nagar Brahmin.	Bania-Jain.
Parsi	Reduced	*33·08* *0·36*	*43·81* ±*0·36*
	Crude	17·69 ±0·19	3·18 ±0·19

TABLE XIV.

Reduced Co-efficients of Racial Likeness.

Mahrati group.

	Chitpavan Brahmin.	Desastha Brahmin.	Karada Brahmin.	Mahratta.	Prabhu.	Saraswat-Gour Brahmin.
Chitpavan Brahmin	..	0·48 ·' *0·16*	0·68 ±*0·26*	1·07 ±*0·23*	0·15 ±0·24	6·11 ±0·25
Desastha Brahmin	0·48 ±0·16	..	1·45 ±0·26	0·35 ±0·22	0·92 ±0·23	6·60 ±0·25
Karada Brahmin	0·68 ±0·26	1·45 ±0·26	..	3·02 +0·32	0·62 ±0·33	4·88 ±0·35
Mahratta	1·07 ±0·23	0·35 ±0·22	3·02 ±0·32	..	1·21 ±0·30	8·97 ±0·31
Prabhu	0·15 ±0·24	0·92 ±0·23	0·62 ±0·33	1·21 +0·30	..	2·69 ±0·32
Saraswat-Gour Brahmin ..	6·11 ±0·25	6·60 ±0·25	4·88 +0·35	8·97 ±0·31	2·69 ±0·32	..

TABLE XIV (a).

Crude Co-efficients of Racial Likeness.

Mahrati group.

	Chitpavan Brahmin.	Desastha Brahmin.	Karada Brahmin.	Mahratta.	Prabhu.	Saraswat-Gour Brahmin
Chitpavan Brahmin	..	0·50	0·41	0·80	0·11	4·10
Desastha Brahmin	0·50	..	0·96	0·27	0·67	4·49
Karada Brahmin	0·41	0·96	..	1·60	0·32	2·39
Mahratta	0·80	0·27	1·60	..	0·69	4·85
Prabhu	0·11	0·67	0·32	0·69	..	1·41
Saraswat-Gour Brahmin ..	4·10	4·49	2·39	4·85	1·41	..

Probable Error is ±0·17 in all cases.

TABLE XV.

Reduced Co-efficients of Racial Likeness.

Guzrati and Mahrati Groups.

——	Nagar Brahmin.	Bania-Jain.	Brahma-Kshatri.	Kathi.	Audich Brahmin.	Kunbi-Patidar.	Chitpavan Brahmin.	Desastha Brahmin.	Karada Brahmin.	Mahratta.	Prabhu.	Saraswat Gour Brahmin.
gar Brahmin ..	..	1·10 ±0·17	6·13 ±0·36	4·10 ±0·29	5·58 ±0·17	*20·41 ±0·42*	12·24 ±0·16	8·54 ±0·16	12·19 ±0·26	11·57 ±0·23	10·97 ±0·24	12·14 ±0·25
nia-Jain	1·10 ±0·17	..	7·37 ±0·36	6·32 ±0·30	3·75 ±0·18	*14·31 ±0·43*	9·53 ±0·17	5·94 ±0·16	9·35 ±0·26	9·75 ±0·23	9·05 ±0·24	11·73 ±0·26
rahma-Kshatri ..	6·13 ±0·36	7·37 ±0·36	..	4·52 ±0·49	10·15 ±0·37	*24·51 ±0·61*	*16·91 ±0·36*	*15·00 ±0·35*	12·48 ±0·45	*18·92 ±0·42*	*13·96 ±0·43*	11·67 ±0·44
athi	4·10 ±0·29	6·32 ±0·30	4·52 ±0·49	..	11·65 ±0·30	*15·73 ±0·55*	*18·51 ±0·30*	*16·37 ±0·29*	*18·50 ±0·39*	*19·91 ±0·36*	*17·37 ±0·37*	*18·75 ±0·38*
udich Brahmin ..	5·58 ±0·17	3·75 ±0·18	10·15 ±0·37	11·65 ±0·30	..	10·69 ±0·43	3·45 ±0·17	2·56 ±0·17	3·75 ±0·27	3·56 ±0·24	3·47 ±0·25	8·38 ±0·26
unbi-Patidar ..	*20·41 ±0·42*	*14·31 ±0·43*	*24·51 ±0·61*	*15·73 ±0·55*	10·69 ±0·43	..	6·63 ±0·43	8·92 ±0·59	11·92 ±0·52	9·63 ±0·48	7·97 ±0·49	*18·03 ±0·51*
hitpavan Brahmin ..	12·24 ±0·16	9·53 ±0·17	*16·91 ±0·36*	*18·51 ±0·30*	3·45 ±0·17	6·63 ±0·43	..	0·48 ±0·16	0·63 ±0·26	1·07 ±0·23	0·15 ±0·24	6·11 ±0·25
esastha Brahmin ..	8·54 ±0·16	5·94 ±0·16	*15·00 ±0·35*	*16·37 ±0·29*	2·56 ±0·17	8·92 ±0·59	0·48 ±0·16	..	1·45 ±0·26	0·35 ±0·22	0·92 ±0·23	6·60 ±0·25
arada Brahmin ..	12·19 ±0·26	9·35 ±0·26	12·48 ±0·45	*18·50 ±0·39*	3·75 ±0·27	11·92 ±0·52	0·63 ±0·26	1·45 ±0·26	..	3·02 ±0·32	0·62 ±0·33	4·88 ±0·35
ahratta	11·57 ±0·23	9·75 ±0·23	*18·92 ±0·42*	*19·91 ±0·36*	3·56 ±0·24	9·63 ±0·48	1·07 ±0·23	0·35 ±0·22	3·02 ±0·32	..	1·21 ±0·30	8·97 ±0·31
Prabhu	10·97 ±0·24	9·05 ±0·24	*13·96 ±0·43*	*17·37 ±0·37*	3·47 ±0·25	7·97 ±0·49	0·15 ±0·24	0·92 ±0·23	0·62 ±0·33	1·21 ±0·30	..	2·69 ±0·32
Saraswat-Gour Brahmin	12·14 ±0·25	11·73 ±0·26	11·67 ±0·44	*18·75 ±0·38*	8·38 ±0·26	*18·03 ±0·51*	6·11 ±0·25	6·60 ±0·25	4·88 ±0·35	8·97 ±0·31	2·69 ±0·32	—

TABLE XV(a).

Crude Co-efficients of Racial Likeness.

Guzrati and Mahrati Groups.

——	Nagar Brahmin.	Bania-Jain.	Brahma Kshatri.	Kathi.	Audich Brahmin.	Kunbi-Patidar.	Chitpavan Brahmin.	Desastha Brahmin.	Karada Brahmin.	Mahratta.	Prabhu.	Saraswat-Gour Brahmin.
Nagar Brahmin ..	..	1·12	2·92	2·38	5·49	8·23	12·75	9·08	8·02	8·70	7·89	8·20
Bania-Jain	1·12	..	3·51	3·61	3·61	5·70	9·63	6·12	6·03	7·17	6·42	7·77
Brahma Kshatri ..	2·92	3·51	..	1·58	4·72	6·79	8·05	7·21	4·71	7·69	5·54	4·47
Kathi	2·38	3·61	1·58	..	6·51	4·84	10·64	9·52	8·08	9·48	8·04	8·37
Audich Brahmin ..	5·49	3·61	4·72	6·51	..	4·21	3·38	2·53	2·36	2·56	2·30	5·44
Kunbi-Patidar ..	8·23	5·70	6·79	4·84	4·21	..	2·61	3·61	3·92	3·38	2·74	6·01
Chitpavan Brahmin ..	12·75	9·63	8·05	10·64	3·38	2·61	..	0·50	0·41	0·80	0·11	4·10
Desastha Brahmin ..	9·08	6·12	7·21	9·52	2·53	3·61	0·50	..	0·96	0·27	0·67	4·49
Karada Brahmin ..	8·02	6·03	4·71	8·08	2·36	3·92	0·41	0·96	..	1·60	0·32	2·39
Mahratta	8·70	7·17	7·69	9 48	2·56	3·38	0·80	0·27	1·60	..	0·69	4·85
Prabhu	7·89	6·42	5·54	8·04	2·39	2·74	0·11	0·67	0·32	0·69	..	1·41
Saraswat-Gour Brahmin ..	8·20	7·77	4·47	8·37	5·44	6·01	4·10	4·49	2·39	4·85	1·41	--

Probable Error is ±0·17 in all cases.

TABLE XVI.

Reduced Co-efficients of Racial Likeness.

Southern India.

—	Kanarese Brahmin.	Kanarese Non-Brahmin.	Tamil Brahmin.	Tamil Chetti.	Tamil Kalla.	Telegu Brahmin.	Telegu Non-Brahmin.	Nambudiri.	Nair.	Iluva.
Kanarese Brahmin	..	4·70 ±0·34	4·72 ±0·34	6·04 ±0·34	11·00 ±0·38	5·84 ±0·34	9·62 ±0·34	*22·48 ±0·32*	*15·46 ±0·31*	*18·68 ±0·34*
Kanarese Non-Brahmin	4·70 ±0·34	..	*13·56 ±0·34*	9·18 ±0·34	*18·92 ±0·38*	*23·12 ±0·34*	*24·50 ±0·34*	*45·13 ±0·32*	*30·30 ±0·31*	*31·36 ±0·34*
Tamil Brahmin	4·72 ±0·34	*13·56 ±0·34*	..	4·28 ±0·34	12·85 ±0·38	5·96 ±0·34	10·18 ±0·34	10·43 ±0·32	6·39 ±0·31	*13·94 ±0·34*
Tamil Chetti	6·04 ±0·34	9·18 ±0·34	4·28 ±0·34	..	13·01 ±0·38	10·28 ±0·34	*14·96 ±0·34*	*21·62 ±0·32*	11·46 ±0·31	*23·04 ±0·34*
Tamil Kalla	11·00 ±0·38	*18·92 ±0·38*	12·85 ±0·38	13·01 ±0·38	..	3·26 ±0·38	2·54 ±0·38	*20·37 ±0·37*	10·59 ±0·35	5·76 ±0·38
Telegu Brahmin	5·84 ±0·34	*23·12 ±0·34*	5·96 ±0·34	10·28 ±0·34	3·26 ±0·38	..	—0·20 ±0·34	6·56 ±0·32	3·66 ±0·31	5·56 ±0·34
Telegu Non-Brahmin	9·62 ±0·34	*24·50 ±0·34*	10·18 ±0·34	*14·96 ±0·34*	2·54 ±0·38	—0·20 ±0·34	..	9·70 ±0·32	5·00 ±0·31	5·30 ±0·34
Nambudiri	*22·48 ±0·32*	*45·13 ±0·32*	10·43 ±0·32	*21·62 ±0·32*	*20·37 ±0·37*	6·56 ±0·32	9·70 ±0·32	..	2·31 ±0·29	*14·52 ±0·32*
Nair	*15·46 ±0·31*	*30·30 ±0·31*	6·39 ±0·31	11·46 ±0·31	10·59 ±0·35	3·66 ±0·31	5·00 ±0·31	2·31 ±0·29	..	*14·31 ±0·31*
Iluva	*18·68 ±0·34*	*31·36 ±0·34*	*13·94 ±0·34*	*23·04 ±0·34*	5·76 ±0·38	5·56 ±0·34	5·30 ±0·34	*14·52 ±0·32*	*14·31 ±0·31*	..

TABLE XVI (a).

Crude Co-efficients of Racial Likeness.

Southern India.

—	Kanarese Brahmin.	Kanarese Non-Brahmin.	Tamil Brahmin.	Tamil Chetti.	Tamil Kalla.	Telegu Brahmin.	Telegu Non-Brahmin.	Nambudiri	Nair.	Iluva.
Kanarese Brahmin	..	2·35	2·36	3·02	4·89	2·92	4·81	11·83	8·45	9·34
Kanarese Non-Brahmin	2·35	..	6·78	4·59	8·41	11·56	12·25	23·63	16·55	15·68
Tamil Brahmin	2·36	6·78	..	2·14	5·71	2·98	5·09	5·49	3·49	6·97
Tamil Chetti	3·02	4·59	2·14	..	5·78	5·14	7·48	11·32	6·26	11·52
Tamil Kalla	4·89	8·41	5·71	5·78	..	1·45	1·13	9·43	5·09	2·56
Telegu Brahmin	2·92	11·56	2·98	5·14	1·45	..	—0·10	3·45	2·00	2·78
Telegu Non-Brahmin	4·81	12·25	5·09	7·48	1·13	—0·10	..	5·08	2·73	2·65
Nambudiri	11·83	23·63	5·49	11·32	9·43	3·45	5·08	..	1·33	7·64
Nair	8·45	16·55	3·49	6·26	5·09	2·00	2·73	1·33	..	7·82
Iluva	9·34	15·68	6·97	11·52	2·56	2·78	2·65	7·64	7·82	..

Probable Error is ±0·17 in all cases.

TABLE XVII.

Reduced Co-efficients of Racial Likeness.

Coorgi (Holland) and others.

(10 characters only.)

	Tamil Brahmin.	Kanarese Brahmin.	Kanarese Non-Brahmin.	Bengali Kayastha.	Bengali Brahmin.	Nagar Brahmin.
Coorgi (Holland).	12·24 ±0·74	*18·33 ±0·74*	*14·39 ±0·74*	*114·52 ±0·60*	*109·72 ±0·74*	*170·81 ±0·59*

TABLE XVII (a).

Crude Co-efficients of Racial Likeness.

Coorgi (Holland) and others.

(10 characters only.)

	Tamil Brahmin.	Kanarese Brahmin.	Kanarese Non-Brahmin.	Bengali Kayastha.	Bengali Brahmin.	Nagar Brahmin.
Coorgi (Holland).	4·78	7·16	5·62	55·59	42·86	83·73

Probable Error is ±0·29 in all cases.

TABLE XVIII.

Reduced Co-efficients of Racial Likeness.

The Mongoloid group.

	Khasi.	Nicobarese.	Uzbeg.
Khas	..	*21·59 ±0·19*	*67·22 ±0·38*
Nicobarese	*21·59 ±0·19*	..	*108·50 ±0·33*
Uzbeg	*67·22 ±0·38*	*108·50 ±0·33*	..

TABLE XVIII (*a*).

Crude Co-efficients of Racial Likeness.

The Mongoloid group.

	Khasi.	Nicobarese.	Uzbeg.
Khasi	..	19·28	30·28
Nicobarese	19·28	..	56·22
Uzbeg	30·28	56·22	..

Probable Error is ±0·17 in all cases.

TABLE XIX.

Reduced Co-efficients of Racial Likeness.

The Aboriginal group.

(26 characters only.)

	Kadar.	Bhil.	Chenchu.	Nattu Malayan.	Munda* (Basu).	Oraon* (Basu).
Kadar	..	*18·98 ±0·27*	10·32 ±0·49	*19·76 ±0·30*	*31·28 ±0·19*	*33·64 ±0·19*
Bhil	*18·98 ±0·27*	..	6·11 ±0·59	*47·91 ±0·40*	*29·61 ±0·29*	*39·54 ±0·29*
Chenchu	10·32 ±0·49	6·11 ±0·59	..	*30·03 ±0·62*	*22·53 ±0·52*	*26·87 ±0·52*
Nattu Malayan	*19·76 ±0·30*	*47·91 ±0·40*	*30·03 ±0·62*	..	*43·23 ±0·31*	*40·88 ±0·31*
Munda (Basu)	*31·28 ±0·19*	*29·61 ±0·29*	*22·53 ±0·52*	*43·23 ±0·31*	..	1·79 ±0·20
Oraon (Basu)	*33·64 ±0·19*	*39·54 ±0·29*	*26·87 ±0·52*	*40·88 ±0·31*	1·79 ±0·20	..

*Based on 24 characters.

TABLE XIX (a).

Crude Co-efficients of Racial Likeness.

The Aboriginal Group.

(26 characters only.)

	Kadar.	Bhil.	Chenchu.	Nattu Malayan.	Munda* (Basu).	Oraon* (Basu).
Kadar	..	13·09 ±0·19	3·97 ±0·19	12·47 ±0·19	32·93 ±0·20	35·42 ±0·20
Bhil	13·09 ±0·19	..	1·94 ±0·19	22·44 ±0·19	19·74 ±0·20	26·36 ±0·20
Chenchu	3·97 ±0·19	1·94 ±0·19	..	9·10 ±0·19	8·50 ±0·20	10·14 ±0·20
Nattu Malayan	12·47 ±0·19	22·44 ±0·19	9·10 ±0·19	..	27·02 ±0·20	25·55 ±0·20
Munda (Basu)	32·93 ±0·20	19·74 ±0·20	8·50 ±0·20	27·02 ±0·20	..	1·79 ±0·20
Oraon (Basu)	35·42 ±0·20	26·36 ±0·20	10·14 ±0·20	25·55 ±0·20	1·79 ±0·20	..

*Based on 24 characters.

TABLE XX.

Reduced Co-efficients of Racial Likeness.

The Aboriginal group.

Omitting Auricular Height and the Indices containing it (*i.e.*, Length-Height Index, Breadth-Height Index and the Vertical Cephalo-Facial Index) in the case of the Kadar and Nattu Malayan.

	Kadar.	Bhil.	Chenchu.	Nattu Malayan.
Kadar	..	12·47 ±0·29	11·63 ±0·53	10·92 ±0·32
Bhil	12·47 ±0·29	..	6·11 ±0·59	*26·57 ±0·43*
Chenchu	11·63 ±0·53	6·11 ±0·59	..	*24·60 ±0·66*
Nattu Malayan	10·92 ±0·32	*26·57 ±0·43*	*24·60 ±0·66*	..

TABLE XXI.

Reduced Co-efficients of Racial Likeness.

Yeruvas (Holland) and others.

(10 characters only.)

	Bhil.	Kadar.	Chenchu.	Nattu Malayan.
Yeruvas (Holland)	*25·29 ±0·87*	11·22 ±0·74 *	*16·64 ±1·21*	*15·32 ±0·94* *

TABLE XXI(a).

Crude Co-efficients of Racial Likeness.

Yeruvas (Holland) and others.

(10 characters only.)

	Bhil.	Kadar.	Chenchu.	Nattu Malayan.
Yeruvas (Holland)	8·43 ±0·29	4·58 ±0·30 *	3·99 ±0·29	4·88 ±30 *

* In the cases of Kadar and Nattu Malayan, 9 characters only, have been taken into consideration.

ALL INDIA.

TABLE XXII.

Reduced Co-efficients of Racial Likeness.

All India.

	Red-Kaffir.	Pathan.	Uzbeg.	Tadjik.	Khos (Lower Chitral).	U. P. Brahmin.	Bengali Brahmin.	Bengali Kayastha.	Bengali Pod.	Orissa Brahmin.	Malve Brahmin.	Rajput.	Nagar Brahmin.	Audich Brahmin.	Kathi.
Red-Kaffir ..	..	5·15 ±0·26	54·88 ±0·34	28·92 ±0·22	6·77 ±0·18	11·64 ±0·27	15·56 ±0·26	19·44 ±0·17	23·76 ±0·26	35·13 ±0·15	22·73 ±0·26	13·72 ±0·17	24·46 ±0·17	20·77 ±0·18	18·87 ±0·30
Pathan ..	5·15 ±0·26	..	44·50 ±43	24·82 ±0·31	4·06 ±0·27	10·62 ±0·34	12·62 ±0·34	16·32 ±0·26	18·34 ±0·34	20·34 ±0·23	18·93 ±0·34	12·24 ±0·26	25·64 ±0·25	20·47 ±0·26	21·24 ±0·36
Uzbeg ..	54·88 ±0·34	44·50 ±0·43	..	5·80 ±0·39	32·62 ±0·35	88·25 ±0·43	42·06 ±0·43	24·98 ±0·34	63·75 ±0·43	53·99 ±0·32	74·79 ±0·43	62·58 ±0·34	34·88 ±0·33	32·77 ±0·35	35·19 ±0·47
Tadjik ..	28·92 ±0·22	24·82 ±0·31	5·80 ±0·39	..	14·25 ±0·23	49·79 ±0·31	16·32 ±0·67	10·82 ±0·22	32·27 ±0·31	26·77 ±0·20	44·54 ±0·31	32·03 ±0·22	16·67 ±0·22	21·60 ±0·23	14·18 ±0·36
Khos (Lower Chitral).	6·77 ±0·18	4·06 ±0·27	32·62 ±0·35	14·25 ±0·23	..	18·94 ±0·27	11·96 ±0·27	10·76 ±0·18	12·09 ±0·27	19·36 ±0·16	17·75 ±0·27	11·55 ±0·18	12·65 ±0·18	11·24 ±0·19	11·75 ±0·31
U. P. Brahmin	11·64 ±0·27	10·62 ±0·34	88·25 ±0·43	49·79 ±0·31	18·94 ±0·27	..	13·04 ±0·34	27·50 ±0·26	13·92 ±0·34	25·65 ±0·23	11·46 ±0·34	8·21 ±0·26	37·39 ±0·25	23·70 ±0·26	37·53 ±0·38
Bengali Brahmin.	15·56 ±0·26	12·62 ±0·34	42·06 ±0·43	16·32 ±0·67	11·95 ±0·27	13·04 ±0·34	..	1·40 ±0·26	15·70 ±0·34	23·59 ±0·23	29·80 ±0·34	17·76 ±0·26	18·50 ±0·25	21·18 ±0·26	14·29 ±0·38
Bengali Kayastha.	19·44 ±0·17	16·32 ±0·26	24·98 ±0·34	10·82 ±0·22	10·76 ±0·18	27·50 ±0·26	1·40 ±0·26	..	18·89 ±0·25	23·35 ±0·15	22·21 ±0·26	19·32 ±0·17	10·46 ±0·17	17·63 ±0·18	11·06 ±0·30
Bengali Pod ..	23·76 ±0·26	18·34 ±0·34	63·75 ±0·43	32·27 ±0·31	12·09 ±0·27	13·92 ±0·34	15·70 ±0·34	18·89 ±0·25	..	8·10 ±0·23	7·40 ±0·34	7·73 ±0·26	19·80 ±0·25	9·16 ±0·26	28·60 ±0·38
Orissa Brahmin	35·13 ±0·15	20·34 ±0·23	53·99 ±0·32	26·77 ±0·20	19·36 ±0·16	25·65 ±0·23	23·59 ±0·23	23·35 ±0·15	8·19 ±0·33	..	13·69 ±0·23	14·06 ±0·15	25·28 ±0·14	15·07 ±0·15	33·82 ±0·27
Malve Brahmin	22·73 ±0·26	18·93 ±0·34	74·79 ±0·43	44·54 ±0·31	17·75 ±0·27	11·46 ±0·34	29·80 ±0·34	32·21 ±0·26	7·40 ±0·34	13·69 ±0·23	..	4·26 ±0·26	27·81 ±0·25	10·46 ±0·26	30·22 ±0·38
Rajput ..	13·72 ±0·17	12·24 ±0·26	62·58 ±0·34	32·03 ±0·22	11·55 ±0·18	8·21 ±0·26	17·76 ±0·26	19·32 ±0·17	7·73 ±0·26	14·06 ±0·15	4·26 ±0·26	..	19·74 ±0·17	7·81 ±0·18	16·77 ±0·30
Nagar Brahmin	24·46 ±0·17	25·64 ±0·25	34·88 ±0·33	16·67 ±0·22	12·65 ±0·18	37·99 ±0·25	18·50 ±0·25	10·46 ±0·17	19·80 ±0·25	25·28 ±0·14	27·81 ±0·25	19·74 ±0·17	..	5·58 ±0·17	4·10 ±0·29
Audich Brahmin	20·77 ±0·18	20·47 ±0·26	32·77 ±0·35	21·60 ±0·23	11·24 ±0·19	23·70 ±0·26	21·18 ±0·26	17·63 ±0·18	9·16 ±0·26	15·07 ±0·15	10·46 ±0·26	7·81 ±0·18	5·58 ±0·17	..	11·65 ±0·30
Kathi ..	18·87 ±0·30	21·24 ±0·38	35·19 ±0·47	14·18 ±0·36	11·75 ±0·31	37·53 ±0·38	14·29 ±0·38	11·06 ±0·30	28·60 ±0·38	33·82 ±0·27	30·22 ±0·38	16·77 ±0·30	4·10 ±0·29	11·65 ±0·30	..
Bania-Jain ..	22·30 ±0·17	24·31 ±0·26	38·66 ±0·34	19·13 ±0·22	13·01 ±0·18	33·64 ±0·26	20·57 ±0·26	12·65 ±0·17	17·60 ±0·26	21·55 ±0·15	22·13 ±0·26	15·39 ±0·17	1·10 ±0·17	3·76 ±0·18	6·32 ±0·30
Chitpavan Brahmin.	23·05 ±0·17	24·50 ±0·25	61·14 ±0·34	33·28 ±0·22	16·04 ±0·18	22·02 ±0·25	26·02 ±0·25	23·05 ±0·17	7·46 ±0·25	12·84 ±0·14	5·27 ±0·25	5·45 ±0·17	12·24 ±0·16	3·45 ±0·17	18·51 ±0·30
Desastha-Brahmin.	27·07 ±0·16	22·40 ±0·25	45·95 ±0·29	26·53 ±0·22	15·15 ±0·17	26·11 ±0·25	25·58 ±0·25	21·03 ±0·16	6·69 ±0·25	11·79 ±0·14	7·82 ±0·25	8·02 ±0·16	8·54 ±0·16	2·58 ±0·17	16·37 ±0·29
Saraswat-Gour Brahmin.	23·57 ±0·26	14·14 ±0·34	51·36 ±0·43	24·34 ±0·31	11·70 ±0·27	17·78 ±0·34	11·16 ±0·34	10·73 ±0·26	4·46 ±0·34	8·11 ±0·23	11·76 ±0·34	8·78 ±0·26	12·14 ±0·25	8·38 ±0·26	18·75 ±0·38
Mahratta ..	31·13 ±0·23	27·21 ±0·31	76·52 ±0·30	29·85 ±0·28	16·96 ±0·24	27·05 ±0·31	30·14 ±0·31	24·85 ±0·23	6·53 ±0·31	8·22 ±0·21	7·54 ±0·32	7·80 ±0·23	11·67 ±0·23	3·56 ±0·24	19·91 ±0·36
Nambudiri ..	21·16 ±0·24	15·74 ±0·32	71·23 ±0·41	49·35 ±0·29	26·93 ±0·25	6·30 ±0·32	18·76 ±0·32	26·31 ±0·24	18·62 ±0·32	26·20 ±0·22	18·28 ±0·32	14·93 ±0·24	36·38 ±0·24	27·01 ±0·25	37·15 ±0·37
Iluva ..	36·90 ±0·26	30·10 ±0·34	97·40 ±0·44	62·70 ±0·31	29·02 ±0·27	16·56 ±0·34	33·34 ±0·34	40·68 ±0·26	7·00 ±0·34	13·56 ±0·23	10·60 ±0·34	15·91 ±0·26	27·39 ±0·27	19·17 ±0·26	46·53 ±0·38
Tamil Brahmin	25·76 ±0·26	19·38 ±0·34	56·19 ±0·44	29·27 ±0·31	17·57 ±0·27	17·26 ±0·34	7·40 ±0·34	8·34 ±0·26	8·28 ±0·34	13·28 ±0·23	20·06 ±0·34	13·29 ±0·26	14·59 ±0·27	14·35 ±0·26	21·89 ±0·38
Tamil Kalla ..	32·38 ±0·30	25·81 ±0·38	69·17 ±0·47	43·86 ±0·35	21·03 ±0·31	18·83 ±0·38	29·48 ±0·38	29·75 ±0·30	6·17 ±0·38	12·18 ±0·27	7·22 ±0·38	7·95 ±0·30	22·68 ±0·29	11·24 ±0·30	30·05 ±0·43
Kanarese Brahmin.	25·94 ±0·26	21·18 ±0·34	49·06 ±0·43	24·24 ±0·31	11·95 ±0·27	23·66 ±0·34	11·92 ±0·34	10·38 ±0·26	7·80 ±0·34	11·86 ±0·23	14·66 ±0·34	12·48 ±0·26	6·48 ±0·27	3·40 ±0·26	15·12 ±0·38
Telegu Brahmin	22·65 ±0·26	15·66 ±0·34	65·70 ±0·43	38·77 ±0·31	18·02 ±0·27	9·04 ±0·34	19·36 ±0·34	21·60 ±0·26	6·68 ±0·34	9·78 ±0·23	6·44 ±0·34	5·96 ±0·26	19·12 ±0·27	10·80 ±0·26	26·51 ±0·33
Nair ..	17·25 ±0·23	12·13 ±0·31	68·81 ±0·42	32·14 ±0·28	17·15 ±0·24	7·72 ±0·31	10·21 ±0·31	15·67 ±0·23	12·48 ±0·31	14·05 ±0·20	12·97 ±0·31	8·40 ±0·22	25·44 ±0·22	18·59 ±0·23	26·17 ±0·35
Kadar ..	142·24 ±0·16	134·60 ±0·25	213·90 ±0·32	161·83 ±0·21	131·64 ±0·17	109·71 ±0·25	157·96 ±0·25	155·79 ±0·16	74·58 ±0·23	81·04 ±0·14	68·31 ±0·25	90·94 ±0·16	103·43 ±0·16	100·65 ±0·17	154·50 ±0·29
Bhil ..	66·06 ±0·26	63·30 ±0·34	115·61 ±0·44	85·88 ±0·31	54·13 ±0·27	43·04 ±0·34	72·46 ±0·34	71·76 ±0·26	23·58 ±0·34	30·00 ±0·23	13·24 ±0·34	26·70 ±0·26	52·91 ±0·27	27·13 ±0·26	64·73 ±0·38
Khasi ..	67·40 ±0·20	57·21 ±0·29	67·22 ±0·38	52·06 ±0·26	45·47 ±0·21	54·81 ±0·29	61·32 ±0·29	56·16 ±0·20	25·04 ±0·29	28·79 ±0·18	34·29 ±0·29	32·59 ±0·20	42·92 ±0·20	39·12 ±0·21	54·87 ±0·33

	Bania-Jain.	Chitpavan Brahmin.	Desastha Brahmin.	Saraswat-Gour Brahmin.	Mahratta.	Nambu-diri.	Iluva.	Tamil Brahmin.	Tamil Kalla.	Kanarese Brahmin.	Telegu Brahmin.	Nair.	Kadar.	Bhil.	Khasi.
Red-Kaffir.	22·30 ±0·17	23·05 ±0·17	27·07 ±0·16	23·57 ±0·26	31·13 ±0·29	21·16 ±0·24	36·90 ±0·26	25·76 ±0·26	32·32 ±0·30	25·94 ±0·26	22·65 ±0·26	17·25 ±0·23	142·24 ±0·16	66·06 ±0·26	67·40 ±0·20
Pathan.	24·31 ±0·26	24·50 ±0·25	22·40 ±0·25	14·14 ±0·34	27·21 ±0·31	15·74 ±0·32	30·10 ±0·34	19·38 ±0·34	25·81 ±0·33	21·18 ±0·34	15·66 ±0·34	12·13 ±0·31	134·60 ±0·25	63·30 ±0·34	57·21 ±0·29
Uzbeg.	38·66 ±0·34	61·14 ±0·34	45·95 ±0·39	51·36 ±0·43	76·52 ±0·30	71·23 ±0·41	97·40 ±0·44	56·19 ±0·44	69·17 ±0·47	49·06 ±0·43	65·70 ±0·43	68·81 ±0·42	213·90 ±0·32	115·61 ±0·44	67·22 ±0·38
Tadjik.	19·12 ±0·22	33·28 ±0·22	26·53 ±0·22	24·34 ±0·31	29·85 ±0·28	49·35 ±0·29	62·76 ±0·31	29·27 ±0·31	43·86 ±0·35	24·24 ±0·31	38·77 ±0·31	32·14 ±0·28	161·83 ±0·21	85·88 ±0·31	52·06 ±0·26
Khos (Lower Chitral).	13·61 ±0·18	16·04 ±0·18	15·15 ±0·17	11·70 ±0·27	16·96 ±0·24	25·93 ±0·25	29·02 ±0·27	17·57 ±0·27	21·03 ±0·31	11·95 ±0·27	18·02 ±0·27	17·15 ±0·24	131·64 ±0·17	54·13 ±0·27	45·47 ±0·21
U. P. Brahmin.	32·64 ±0·26	22·02 ±0·25	26·11 ±0·25	17·78 ±0·34	27·05 ±0·31	6·30 ±0·32	16·56 ±0·34	17·26 ±0·34	18·83 ±0·38	23·66 ±0·34	9·04 ±0·34	7·72 ±0·31	109·71 ±0·25	43·04 ±0·34	54·81 ±0·29
Bengali Brahmin.	20·57 ±0·26	26·02 ±0·25	25·58 ±0·25	11·16 ±0·34	30·14 ±0·31	18·76 ±0·32	33·34 ±0·34	7·40 ±0·34	29·48 ±0·38	11·92 ±0·34	19·36 ±0·34	10·21 ±0·31	157·96 ±0·25	72·46 ±0·34	61·32 ±0·29
Bengali Kayastha.	12·05 ±0·17	23·05 ±0·17	21·03 ±0·16	10·73 ±0·26	24·85 ±0·23	26·31 ±0·24	40·68 ±0·26	8·34 ±0·26	29·75 ±0·30	10·38 ±0·26	21·60 ±0·26	15·67 ±0·23	155·79 ±0·16	71·78 ±0·26	56·16 ±0·20
Bengali Pod.	17·50 ±0·26	7·46 ±0·25	6·69 ±0·26	4·46 ±0·34	6·53 ±0·31	16·62 ±0·32	7·00 ±0·34	8·28 ±0·34	6·17 ±0·38	7·80 ±0·34	6·68 ±0·34	12·48 ±0·31	74·58 ±0·23	23·58 ±0·34	25·04 ±0·23
Orissa Brahmin.	21·55 ±0·15	12·84 ±0·14	11·70 ±0·14	8·11 ±0·23	8·22 ±0·21	26·20 ±0·21	13·56 ±0·23	13·28 ±0·23	12·18 ±0·27	11·86 ±0·23	9·78 ±0·23	14·05 ±0·20	81·04 ±0·14	30·00 ±0·23	28·79 ±0·18
Malve Brahmin.	22·13 ±0·26	5·27 ±0·25	7·82 ±0·25	11·76 ±0·34	7·54 ±0·32	18·23 ±0·31	10·60 ±0·34	20·06 ±0·34	7·22 ±0·38	14·66 ±0·34	6·44 ±0·34	12·97 ±0·31	68·31 ±0·25	13·24 ±0·34	34·29 ±0·29
Rajput.	15·39 ±0·17	5·45 ±0·17	8·02 ±0·16	8·78 ±0·26	7·80 ±0·23	14·93 ±0·24	15·91 ±0·26	13·29 ±0·26	7·95 ±0·30	12·48 ±0·26	5·96 ±0·26	8·40 ±0·22	90·94 ±0·16	26·70 ±0·26	32·59 ±0·20
Nagar Brahmin.	1·10 ±0·17	12·24 ±0·16	8·54 ±0·16	12·14 ±0·25	11·67 ±0·23	36·38 ±0·24	27·39 ±0·27	14·59 ±0·27	22·68 ±0·29	6·48 ±0·27	19·12 ±0·27	25·44 ±0·22	103·43 ±0·16	52·91 ±0·27	42·92 ±0·20
Audich Brahmin.	3·75 ±0·18	3·45 ±0·17	2·58 ±0·17	8·38 ±0·26	3·56 ±0·24	27·01 ±0·25	19·17 ±0·26	14·35 ±0·26	11·24 ±0·30	3·40 ±0·26	10·80 ±0·26	18·59 ±0·23	100·65 ±0·17	27·13 ±0·26	39·12 ±0·21
Kathi.	6·32 ±0·30	18·51 ±0·30	16·37 ±0·29	18·75 ±0·38	19·91 ±0·36	37·15 ±0·37	46·53 ±0·38	21·39 ±0·38	30·05 ±0·43	15·12 ±0·38	26·51 ±0·38	26·17 ±0·35	154·50 ±0·29	64·73 ±0·33	54·87 ±0·33
Bania-Jain.	..	9·53 ±0·17	5·94 ±0·16	11·73 ±0·26	9·75 ±0·23	33·06 ±0·24	28·19 ±0·26	14·70 ±0·26	16·75 ±0·30	5·91 ±0·26	15·90 ±0·26	22·86 ±0·23	118·00 ±0·16	42·98 ±0·26	33·32 ±0·21
Chitpavan Brahmin.	9·53 ±0·17	..	0·48 ±0·16	6·11 ±0·25	1·07 ±0·23	23·03 ±0·24	12·63 ±0·25	13·04 ±0·25	5·74 ±0·29	6·53 ±0·25	7·99 ±0·25	15·71 ±0·22	76·88 ±0·16	16·15 ±0·25	30·96 ±0·20
Desastha Brahmin.	5·94 ±0·16	0·48 ±0·16	..	6·60 ±0·25	0·35 ±0·22	26·55 ±0·23	14·04 ±0·25	13·33 ±0·25	6·76 ±0·29	4·87 ±0·25	9·07 ±0·25	17·64 ±0·22	83·51 ±0·16	18·99 ±0·25	23·73 ±0·20
Saraswat-Gour Brahmin.	11·73 ±0·26	6·11 ±0·25	6·60 ±0·25	..	8·97 ±0·31	13·25 ±0·33	10·24 ±0·34	1·32 ±0·34	8·89 ±0·38	1·20 ±0·34	4·26 ±0·34	7·32 ±0·31	93·53 ±0·23	34·68 ±0·34	9·40 ±0·29
Mahratta.	9·75 ±0·23	1·07 ±0·23	0·35 ±0·22	8·97 ±0·31	..	34·11 ±0·30	17·67 ±0·31	17·83 ±0·31	8·13 ±0·36	6·60 ±0·31	12·08 ±0·31	22·81 ±0·29	67·57 ±0·22	15·43 ±0·31	22·92 ±0·26
Nambudiri.	33·06 ±0·24	23·03 ±0·24	26·55 ±0·23	13·25 ±0·33	34·11 ±0·30	..	14·52 ±0·32	10·43 ±0·32	20·37 ±0·37	22·48 ±0·32	6·56 ±0·32	2·81 ±0·29	123·58 ±0·23	52·79 ±0·32	52·29 ±0·27
Iluva.	28·19 ±0·26	12·83 ±0·25	14·04 ±0·25	10·24 ±0·34	17·67 ±0·31	14·52 ±0·32	..	13·94 ±0·34	5·76 ±0·38	18·58 ±0·34	5·56 ±0·34	14·31 ±0·31	88·71 ±0·25	19·74 ±0·34	27·10 ±0·29
Tamil Brahmin.	14·70 ±0·26	13·04 ±0·25	13·33 ±0·26	1·32 ±0·34	17·83 ±0·31	10·43 ±0·32	13·94 ±0·34	..	12·86 ±0·38	4·72 ±0·34	5·96 ±0·34	6·39 ±0·31	125·02 ±0·25	46·86 ±0·34	36·81 ±0·29
Tamil Kalla.	16·75 ±0·30	5·74 ±0·29	6·76 ±0·29	8·89 ±0·38	8·13 ±0·36	20·37 ±0·37	5·76 ±0·38	12·85 ±0·38	..	11·00 ±0·38	3·26 ±0·38	10·59 ±0·35	83·15 ±0·29	16·53 ±0·38	18·04 ±0·33
Kanarese Brahmin.	5·91 ±0·26	6·53 ±0·25	4·87 ±0·25	1·20 ±0·34	6·60 ±0·31	22·48 ±0·32	18·68 ±0·34	4·72 ±0·34	11·00 ±0·38	..	5·84 ±0·34	15·46 ±0·31	94·07 ±0·23	32·64 ±0·34	33·56 ±0·29
Telegu Brahmin.	15·90 ±0·26	7·99 ±0·25	9·07 ±0·25	4·26 ±0·34	12·08 ±0·31	6·56 ±0·32	5·56 ±0·34	5·96 ±0·34	3·26 ±0·38	5·84 ±0·34	..	8·66 ±0·31	81·99 ±0·23	27·94 ±0·34	29·12 ±0·29
Nair.	22·86 ±0·23	16·71 ±0·22	17·64 ±0·22	7·32 ±0·31	22·81 ±0·29	2·81 ±0·29	14·31 ±0·31	6·30 ±0·31	10·59 ±0·35	15·46 ±0·31	3·66 ±0·31	..	121·74 ±0·22	46·56 ±0·31	46·24 ±0·26
Kadar.	118·00 ±0·16	76·88 ±0·16	83·51 ±0·16	93·53 ±0·23	67·57 ±0·22	123·58 ±0·23	88·71 ±0·25	125·02 ±0·25	83·15 ±0·29	94·07 ±0·23	81·99 ±0·23	121·74 ±0·22	..	18·98 ±0·27	51·44 ±0·20
Bhil.	42·98 ±0·26	16·15 ±0·25	18·99 ±0·25	34·68 ±0·34	15·43 ±0·31	52·79 ±0·32	19·74 ±0·34	46·86 ±0·34	16·58 ±0·38	32·64 ±0·34	27·94 ±0·34	46·56 ±0·31	18·98 ±0·27	..	35·58 ±0·29
Khasi.	33·32 ±0·21	30·96 ±0·20	23·73 ±0·20	9·40 ±0·29	22·92 ±0·26	52·29 ±0·27	27·10 ±0·29	36·81 ±0·29	18·04 ±0·33	33·56 ±0·29	29·12 ±0·29	46·24 ±0·26	51·44 ±0·20	35·58 ±0·29	..

TABLE XXII (a).

Crude Co-efficients of Racial Likeness.

All India.

	Red-Kaffir.	Pathan.	Uzbeg.	Tadjik.	Khos (Lower Chitral).	U. P. Brahmin.	Bengali Brahmin.	Bengali Kayastha.	Bengali Pod.	Orissa Brahmin.	Malve Brahmin.	Rajput.	Nagar Brahmin.	Audich Brahmin.	Kathi.	Bania-Jain.	Chitpavan Brahmin.	Desastha Brahmin.	Saraswat Gour Brahmin.	Mahratta.	Nambudiri.	Iluva.	Tamil Brahmin.	Tamil Kalla.	Kanarese Brahmin.	Telegu Brahmin.	Nair.	Kadar.	Bhil.	Khasi.	
Red-Kaffir ..	..	3·43	27·17	22·08	6·45	7·76	10·37	19·44	15·84	40·38	15·15	13·72	24·96	19·97	10·78	22·08	23·28	27·91	15·71	23·06	16·01	24·60	17·17	18·50	17·29	15·10	12·97	149·73	44·04	56·17	Red-Kaffir.
Pathan ..	3·43	..	17·66	13·71	2·60	5·31	6·31	10·88	9·17	14·85	9·46	8·16	17·18	13·29	9·44	16·10	16·42	15·24	7·70	14·71	8·24	15·05	9·69	11·47	10·59	7·83	6·63	92·83	31·65	33·65	Pathan.
Uzbeg ..	27·17	17·66	..	2·50	15·76	35·02	16·69	12·37	25·30	28·72	29·68	30·98	17·53	25·74	9·16	19·14	30·57	27·03	20·38	42·75	29·31	37·75	21·39	24·97	19·47	26·07	29·28	108·68	44·81	30·28	Uzbeg.
Tadjik ..	22·08	13·71	2·50	..	10·48	27·51	4·12	8·26	17·83	22·86	24·61	24·45	13·02	16·05	6·88	14·60	25·80	20·89	13·45	17·98	28·69	34·64	16·17	21·29	13·39	21·42	19·60	128·85	47·45	34·48	Tadjik.
Khos (Lower Chitral).	6·45	2·60	15·76	10·48	..	12·14	7·66	10·15	7·75	21·04	11·38	10·90	12·28	10·31	6·49	12·27	15·42	14·85	7·50	12·03	17·64	18·60	11·26	11·62	7·66	11·55	12·34	130·24	34·70	36·09	Khos. (Lower Chitral).
U. P. Brahmin	7·76	5·31	35·02	27·51	12·14	..	9·02	18·33	6·96	18·72	5·73	5·47	25·67	15·39	16·68	22·28	14·78	17·76	8·89	14·62	3·30	8·28	8·63	8·37	11·83	4·52	4·22	75·66	21·52	32·24	U. P. Brahmin.
Bengali Brahmin.	10·37	6·31	16·69	4·12	7·66	9·02	..	0·99	7·85	17·22	14·90	11·84	12·50	13·75	6·35	13·67	17·46	17·40	5·58	16·29	9·82	16·67	3·70	13·10	5·96	9·68	5·58	108·94	36·23	36·07	Bengali Brahmin.
Bengali Kayastha.	19·44	10·88	12·37	8·26	10·15	18·33	0·99	..	12·59	26·84	21·47	19·32	10·67	16·95	6·32	12·52	23·28	21·68	7·15	18·44	18·66	27·12	5·56	17·00	6·92	14·40	11·78	163·09	47·84	46·80	Bengali Kayastha.
Bengali Pod ..	15·84	9·17	25·30	17·83	7·75	6·96	7·85	12·59	..	5·98	3·70	5·15	13·38	5·95	12·71	11·59	5·01	4·55	2·23	3·53	9·75	3·50	4·14	2·74	3·90	3·34	6·62	54·84	11·79	14·73	Bengali Pod.
Orissa Brahmin	40·38	14·85	28·72	22·86	21·04	18·72	17·22	26·84	5·98	..	9·99	16·23	30·02	16·65	20·93	24·77	15·10	14·21	5·92	6·74	20·47	13·55	9·69	7·54	8·66	7·14	11·71	98·83	21·90	26·91	Orissa Brahmin.
Malve Brahmin	15·15	9·46	29·68	24·61	11·38	5·73	14·90	21·47	3·70	9·99	..	2·84	19·18	6·79	13·43	14·65	3·54	5·32	5·88	3·97	9·57	5·30	10·03	3·21	7·33	3·22	7·09	47·11	6·62	20·17	Malve Brahmin.
Rajput ..	13·72	8·16	30·98	24·45	10·90	5·47	11·84	19·32	5·15	16·23	2·84	..	20·14	7·51	9·58	15·24	5·50	8·27	5·85	5·78	10·59	10·61	8·86	4·54	8·32	3·97	6·41	95·73	17·80	27·16	Rajput.
Nagar Brahmin	24·96	17·18	17·53	13·02	12·28	25·67	12·50	10·67	13·38	30·02	19·18	20·14	..	5·49	2·38	0·95	12·75	9·08	8·20	8·70	25·73	18·51	9·86	13·11	4·38	12·92	19·42	111·21	35·75	36·37	Nagar Brahmin.
Audich Brahmin	19·97	13·29	25·74	16·05	10·31	15·39	13·75	16·95	5·95	16·65	6·79	7·51	5·49	..	6·51	3·61	3·38	2·53	5·44	2·56	18·63	12·45	9·32	6·28	2·21	7·01	13·57	101·67	17·62	31·55	Audich Brahmin.
Kathi ..	10·78	9·44	9·16	6·88	6·49	16·68	6·35	6·32	12·71	20·93	13·43	9·58	2·38	6·51	..	3·61	10·64	9·52	8·37	9·48	17·20	20·68	9·73	12·02	6·72	11·78	12·58	90·88	28·77	28·14	Kathi.
Bania-Jain ..	22·08	16·10	19·14	14·60	12·27	22·28	13·67	12·52	11·59	24·77	14·65	15·24	0·95	3·61	3·61	..	9·63	6·12	7·77	7·17	23·28	18·73	9·77	9·57	3·93	10·63	17·06	124·21	28·56	27·63	Bania-Jain.
Chitpavan Brahmin.	23·28	16·42	30·57	25·80	15·42	14·78	17·46	23·28	5·01	15·10	3·54	5·50	12·75	3·38	10·64	9·63	..	0·50	4·10	0·80	16·45	8·61	8·75	3·31	3·71	5·36	11·90	82·67	10·84	26·02	Chitpavan Brahmin.
Desastha Brahmin.	27·91	15·24	27·03	20·89	14·85	17·76	17·40	21·68	4·55	14·21	5·32	8·27	9·08	2·53	9·52	6·12	0·50	..	4·49	0·27	19·24	9·55	9·07	3·93	3·31	6·17	13·57	90·77	12·92	20·28	Desastha Brahmin.
Saraswat-Gour Brahmin.	15·71	7·70	20·38	13·45	7·50	8·89	5·58	7·15	2·23	5·92	5·88	5·85	8·20	5·44	8·37	7·77	4·10	4·49	..	4·85	6·90	5·12	0·66	3·95	0·60	2·13	4·00	68·77	17·34	5·53	Saraswat-Gour Brahmin.
Mahratta ..	23·06	14·71	42·75	17·98	12·03	14·62	16·29	18·44	3·53	6·74	3·97	5·78	8·70	2·56	9·48	7·17	0·80	0·27	4·85	..	19·38	9·55	9·64	3·87	3·57	6·53	13·58	51·98	8·34	14·79	Mahratta.
Nambudiri ..	16·01	8·24	29·31	28·69	17·64	3·30	9·82	18·66	9·75	20·47	9·57	10·59	25·73	18·63	17·20	23·28	16·45	10·24	6·90	19·38	..	7·64	5·49	9·43	11·83	3·45	1·33	90·87	27·64	32·48	Nambudiri.
Iluva ..	24·60	15·05	37·75	34·64	18·60	8·28	16·67	27·12	3·50	13·55	5·30	10·61	18·51	12·45	20·68	18·73	8·61	9·55	5·12	9·55	7·64	..	6·97	2·56	9·34	2·78	7·82	61·18	9·87	15·94	Iluva.
Tamil Brahmin	17·17	9·69	21·39	16·17	11·26	8·63	3·70	5·56	4·14	9·69	10·03	8·86	9·86	9·32	9·73	9·77	8·75	9·07	0·66	9·64	5·49	6·97	..	5·71	2·36	2·98	3·49	86·22	23·43	21·65	Tamil Brahmin.
Tamil Kalla ..	18·50	11·47	24·97	21·29	11·62	8·37	13·10	17·00	2·74	7·54	3·21	4·54	13·11	6·28	12·02	9·57	3·31	3·93	3·95	3·87	9·43	2·56	5·71	..	4·89	1·45	5·09	48·91	7·37	9·25	Tamil Kalla.
Kanarese Brahmin.	17·29	10·59	19·47	13·39	7·66	11·83	5·96	6·92	3·90	8·66	7·33	8·32	4·38	2·21	6·72	3·93	3·71	3·31	0·60	3·57	11·83	9·34	2·36	4·89	..	2·92	8·45	69·17	16·32	19·74	Kanarese Brahmin.
Telegu Brahmin	15·10	7·83	26·07	21·42	11·55	4·52	9·68	14·40	3·34	7·14	3·22	3·97	12·92	7·01	11·78	10·63	5·36	6·17	2·13	6·53	3·45	2·78	2·98	1·45	2·92	..	2·00	60·29	13·97	17·18	Telegu Brahmin.
Nair ..	12·97	6·63	29·28	19·60	12·34	4·22	5·58	11·78	6·62	11·71	7·09	6·41	19·42	13·57	12·58	17·06	11·90	13·57	4·00	13·58	1·33	7·82	3·49	5·09	8·45	2·00	..	95·11	25·44	30·22	Nair.
Kadar ..	149·73	92·83	108·68	128·85	130·24	75·66	108·94	163·09	54·84	98·83	47·11	95·73	111·21	101·67	90·88	124·21	82·67	90·77	68·77	51·98	90·87	61·18	86·22	48·91	69·17	60·29	95·11	..	13·09	44·73	Kadar.
Bhil ..	44·04	31·65	44·81	47·45	34·70	21·52	36·23	47·84	11·79	21·90	6·62	17·80	35·75	17·62	28·77	28·56	10·84	12·92	17·34	8·34	27·64	9·87	23·43	7·37	16·32	13·07	25·44	13·09	--	20·93	Bhil.
Khasi ..	56·17	33·65	30·28	34·48	36·09	32·24	36·07	46·80	14·73	26·91	20·17	27·16	36·37	31·55	28·14	27·63	26·02	20·28	5·53	14·79	32·48	15·94	21·65	9·25	19·74	17·13	30·22	44·73	20·93	--	Khasi.
MSSCC																															

Probable Error is ± 0·17 in all cases.

TABLE XXIII.

Reduced Co-efficients of Racial Likeness.

Burma (Gupte).

(15 characters only.)

	Chinese Shan.	Kachin.	Southern Chin.	Palaung.	Lower Burman.	Shan.	Sgaw Karen.	Taung-thu.	Talaing.	Pwo Karen.
Chinese Shan ..	..	11·23 ±0·24	9·67 ±0·23	19·89 ±0·24	19·02 ±0·24	36·77 ±0·24	49·31 ±0·23	27·00 ±0·24	40·66 ±0·24	37·90 ±0·24
Kachin	11·23 ±0·24	..	8·27 ±0·23	7·09 ±0·24	6·57 ±0·24	15·93 ±0·24	26·93 ±0·23	14·42 ±0·24	27·81 ±0·24	18·51 ±0·24
Southern Chin ..	9·67 ±0·23	8·27 ±0·23	..	5·18 ±0·23	9·80 ±0·23	20·34 ±0·23	27·45 ±0·22	14·14 ±0·23	30·89 ±0·23	17·07 ±0·23
Palaung	19·89 ±0·24	7·09 ±0·24	5·18 ±0·23	..	8·14 ±0·24	8·05 ±0·24	29·36 ±0·23	14·86 ±0·24	25·86 ±0·24	15·92 ±0·24
Lower Burman ..	19·02 ±0·24	6·57 ±0·24	9·80 ±0·23	8·14 ±0·24	..	7·42 ±0·24	21·63 ±0·24	13·28 ±0·24	15·52 ±0·24	13·66 ±0·24
Shan	36·77 ±0·24	15·93 ±0·24	20·34 ±0·23	8·05 ±0·24	7·42 ±0·24	..	38·31 ±0·23	25·02 ±0·24	24·11 ±0·24	25·48 ±0·24
Sgaw Karen ..	49·31 ±0·23	26·93 ±0·23	27·45 ±0·22	29·36 ±0·23	21·63 ±0·23	38·31 ±0·23	..	9·89 ±0·23	26·14 ±0·23	3·52 ±0·23
Taungthu ..	27·00 ±0·24	14·42 ±0·24	14·14 ±0·23	14·86 ±0·24	13·28 ±0·24	25·02 ±0·24	9·89 ±0·23	..	7·26 ±0·24	3·54 ±0·24
Talaing	40·66 ±0·24	27·81 ±0·24	30·89 ±0·23	25·86 ±0·24	15·52 ±0·24	24·11 ±0·24	26·14 ±0·23	7·26 ±0·24	..	14·93 ±0·24
Pwo Karen ..	37·90 ±0·24	18·51 ±0·24	17·07 ±0·23	15·92 ±0·24	13·66 ±0·24	25·48 ±0·24	3·52 ±0·23	3·54 ±0·24	14·93 ±0·24	..

TABLE XXIII (a).

Crude Co-efficients of Racial Likeness.

Burma (Gupte).

(15 characters only.)

	Chinese Shan.	Kachin.	Southern Chin.	Palaung.	Lower Burman.	Shan.	Sgaw Karen.	Taung-thu.	Talaing.	Pwo Karen.
Chinese Shan ..	..	11·12	10·07	19·89	19·02	36·41	51·90	27·00	40·66	37·90
Kachin	11·12	..	8·53	7·02	6·47	15·77	28·05	14·28	27·53	18·33
Southern Chin ..	10·07	8·53	..	5·40	10·21	20·97	29·84	14·73	32·18	17·78
Palaung	19·89	7·02	5·40	..	8·14	7·97	30·90	14·86	25·86	15·92
Lower Burman ..	19·02	6·47	10·21	8·14	..	7·35	22·77	13·28	15·52	13·66
Shan	36·41	15·77	20·97	7·97	7·35	..	39·91	24·77	23·87	25·23
Sgaw Karen ..	51·90	28·05	29·84	30·90	22·77	39·91	..	10·41	27·52	3·71
Taungthu ..	27·00	14·28	14·73	14·86	13·28	24·77	10·41	..	7·26	3·54
Talaing	40·66	27·53	32·18	25·86	15·52	23·87	27·52	7·26	..	14·98
Pwo Karen ..	37·90	18·33	17·78	15·92	13·66	25·23	3·71	3·54	14·93	..

Probable Error is ±0·24 in all cases.

TABLE XXIV.

Reduced Co-efficients of Racial Likeness.

Guzrati and others.

(Female group.)

	Guzrati.	Mahrati.	Malayali.	Kadar.
Guzrati	..	8·50 ±0·18	*16·11 ±0·21*	*115·41 ±0·37*
Mahrati	8·50 ±0·18	..	11·95 ±0·20	*77·20 ±0·36*
Malayali	*16·11 ±0·21*	11·95 ±0·20	..	*115·54 ±0·39*
Kadar	*115·41 ±0·37*	*77·20 ±0·36*	*115·54 ±0·39*	..

TABLE XXIV (a).

Crude Co-efficients of Racial Likeness.

Guzrati and others.

(Female group.)

	Guzrati.	Mahrati.	Malayali.	Kadar.
Guzrati	..	8·25	12·99	53·68
Mahrati	8·25	..	9·96	36·59
Malayali	12·99	9·96	..	49·80
Kadar	53·68	36·59	49·80	..

Probable Error is ± 0·17 in all cases.

Tables XXV to LIV.

TABLE—XXV.

Values of $\frac{N_s N_s'}{N_s+N_s'} \left(\frac{M_s-M_s'}{\sigma_s}\right)^2$ for Red

Characters.	Pathan.	Uzbeg.	Tadjik.	Khos (Lower Chitral).	U. P. Brahmin.	Bengali Brahmin.	Bengali Kayastha.	Bengali Pod.	Orissa Brahmin.	Malve Brahmin.	Rajput.	Nagar Brahmin.	Audich Brahmin.	Kathi.	Bania Jain.
Stature	4·54	2·47	0·38	17·36	1·28	2·27	0·40	15·00	9·81	5·25	8·11	4·81	4·95	0·17	8·46
Auricular Height ..	10·43	49·43	44·19	1·15	0·01	3·93	13·21	0·02	51·61	1·59	0·00	0·17	3·89	0·21	0·09
Max. Head Length ..	4·34	62·64	112·35	37·50	0·75	43·45	86·67	75·07	160·30	36·77	36·03	91·56	110·37	25·76	7·47
Max. Head Breadth	1·95	60·05	26·45	1·57	30·18	0·67	13·93	12·58	27·36	37·04	16·02	23·30	1·64	17·06	10·75
Min. Frontal Breadth	12·74	1·52	1·32	6·15	52·75	10·02	5·83	36·63	56·77	32·97	72·84	0·08	5·24	6·47	4·51
Max. Bizygomatic Breadth.	3·29	44·21	15·12	0·76	16·05	17·59	6·02	44·16	54·14	16·43	9·37	2·09	7·40	11·29	9·14
Bigonial Breadth ..	8·36	2·43	0·44	3·63	11·78	8·26	9·10	12·14	20·43	5·94	24·63	23·84	28·46	9·79	12·55
Inter-Orbital Breadth	17·16	29·22	17·08	4·94	6·18	6·97	5·51	2·10	35·42	9·33	0·03	11·14	13·96	7·34	19·61
Orbitonasal Breadth	0·06	9·90	5·13	0·00	3·15	29·66	48·70	0·00	2·74	1·99	0·03	14·52	10·38	16·42	37·03
Orbitonasal Arc ..	4·45	0·06	0·97	9·49	2·13	11·90	16·99	1·44	0·79	1·14	0·83	4·35	2·10	9·02	6·42
Nasal Length ..	0·01	0·01	0·47	5·67	12·55	7·12	6·17	54·47	74·03	43·56	40·99	32·78	56·04	2·15	23·63
Nasal Breadth ..	0·07	1·57	0·05	0·60	9·03	3·34	12·00	3·93	3·43	13·78	6·14	3·42	1·03	2·28	17·63
Nasal Height or Depth	0·38	22·31	9·44	7·19	0·54	0·54	0·00	21·89	38·98	16·01	10·68	10·94	9·39	1·26	12·61
Upper Facial Length	0·81	14·42	3·41	1·09	0·21	1·74	1·56	8·18	21·80	11·27	11·51	24·55	47·54	0 66	28·92
Total Facial Length	1·70	15·16	6·88	0·53	1·89	0·68	0·46	9·02	16·78	9·45	16·40	64·69	56·10	7·73	61·46
Horizontal Cirm. of the Head.	5·27	0·33	13·15	11·72	21·87	16·41	22·04	71·99	141·79	46·39	32·66	9.65	52·01	1·17	27·61
Sagittal Arc ..	1·95	23·99	21·42	13·73	8·46	6·28	1·37	0·01	20·06	46·18	34·25	23·50	32·06	50·84	19·78
Transverse Arc ..	1·47	58·58	41·45	3·63	0·40	28·99	48·68	0·33	2·73	0·70	0·26	32·19	6·73	14·87	18·96
Length Breadth Index	0·02	161·28	147·68	27·79	18·40	26·89	95·81	6·46	13·90	2·61	0·17	118·59	35·43	52·33	86·43
Length Height Index	15·09	108·47	131·62	15·29	0·19	25·12	61·76	17·19	166·95	2·56	7·73	25·59	10·60	8·08	17·91
Breadth Height Index	13·10	0·97	5·19	0·01	13·79	1·12	0·53	4·85	89·84	9·32	6·84	6·28	0·70	4·48	4·97
Trans. Fronto-Parietal Index.	1·98	48·38	19·88	11·24	0·02	12·16	35·09	1·87	0.00	4·98	6·61	25·90	0·13	40·87	26·09
Orbitonasal Index ..	7·48	48·60	16·64	19·52	0·03	2·69	6·18	2·94	12·93	0·05	1·30	2·38	3·23	0·20	13·43
Nasal Index ..	0·01	0·73	0·27	0·66	21·81	9·46	17·56	43·68	52·36	57·24	41·31	27·51	33·19	3·10	41·61
Nasal Elevation Index	0·15	25·46	9·01	4·15	2·00	0·33	5·56	29·65	47·15	34·28	21·15	17·64	12·50	4·06	35·32
Upper Facial Index..	2·79	0·00	0·91	1·70	2·43	10·94	5·52	0·58	0·49	1·16	2·40	13·23	22·71	5·28	23·26
Total Facial Index ..	5·08	0·26	0·03	1·41	1·32	11·13	0·91	1·78	0·77	0·11	3·50	44·00	26·33	25·95	50·87
Trans. Cephalo-Facial Index.	0·00	10·07	7·17	6·45	11·78	28·25	53·10	5·40	3·95	17·84	6·26	53·66	1·12	3·33	14·98
Vertical Cephalo-Facial Index.	2·59	7·24	10·14	0·11	2·16	0·90	11·05	4·00	71·09	1.42	7·80	34·36	11·71	8·38	26·51

TABLE—XXV.

...ffir with other races.

...hit-van ...ah-min.	Desastha Brah-min.	Saras-wat Gour Brahmin.	Mah-ratta.	Nam-budiri Brah-min.	Iluva.	Tamil Brah-min.	Tamil Kala.	Kana-rese Brah-min.	Telegu Brah-min.	Nair.	Kadar.	Bhil.	Khasi.	Characters.
5·94	13·72	13·82	9·05	10·35	53·59	6·70	0·13	23·62	4·20	7·07	1·44	19·98	133·93	Stature.
0·16	0·39	6·28	0·12	18·68	0·83	12·87	0·27	0·11	5·61	13·20	2·34	20·29	17·64	Auricular Height.
6·17	104·76	37·66	113·39	1·44	10·65	23·13	16·19	76·02	9·61	1·65	170·27	110·27	49·97	Max. Head Length.
5·33	2·31	1·55	5·27	17·21	31·69	0·17	9·54	0·05	15·36	9·71	195·51	67·84	2·13	Max. Head Breadth.
16·48	14·49	17·82	15·83	44·58	67·15	30·52	55·83	7·63	38·15	35·51	96·87	57·83	84·11	Min. Frontal Breadth.
2·79	14·55	30·14	9·43	24·19	81·03	40·18	16·91	20·05	24·96	19·46	172·34	33·33	12·60	Max. Bizygomatic Breadth.
1·39	17·17	66·97	12·01	39·34	46·53	32·53	12·95	51·67	37·02	27·11	35·52	22·82	2·79	Bigonial Breadth.
3·31	16·50	0·32	3·66	2·24	4·51	3·48	4·97	0·45	3·17	2·72	1·30	1·13	1·36	Inter-Orbital Breadth.
4·52	2·46	19·27	0·33	27·90	9·65	50·50	5·48	26·46	20·86	28·20	26·65	0·19	0·47	Orbitonasal Breadth.
3·03	1·87	5·10	0·14	33·01	0·12	20·50	3·62	4·15	1·64	14·35	13·48	0·57	41·64	Orbitonasal Arc.
0·45	81·99	38·37	56·12	40·03	103·81	49·96	90·36	45·65	46·86	35·30	239·02	138·78	151·59	Nasal Length.
1·02	18·31	5·28	9·53	10·12	6·82	5·28	10·12	2·53	18·18	18·23	107·82	35·17	26·21	Nasal Breadth.
8·36	57·55	18·66	44·34	0·01	37·84	7·01	29·76	8·56	6·25	2·25	234·51	66·95	276·61	Nasal Height or depth.
0·28	46·23	10·24	37·11	4·65	40·80	10·41	27·93	17·58	12·75	4·79	78·56	89·67	10·59	Upper Facial Length.
9·79	49·16	4·76	34·73	1·33	22·43	7·19	18·94	20·77	23·64	0·22	177·76	49·72	62·59	Total Facial Length.
·64	47·02	29·56	61·62	4·46	41·17	18·59	42·50	47·39	20·02	13·47	599·17	110.28	9·70	Horizontal Cirm. of the Head.
·64	49·23	14·99	69·46	12·49	0·59	0·02	8·45	15·23	2·54	0·62	286·65	62·75	0·78	Sagittal Arc.
·02	8·20	16·14	0·40	17·65	2·26	17·32	1·66	8·90	4·20	33·35	737·58	21·77	3·19	Transverse Arc.
·35	29·32	8·81	26·33	19·19	8·81	8·31	0·04	33·43	2·27	3·61	19·70	0·42	10·46	Length Breadth Index.
·75	19·32	27·27	30·16	10·21	0·54	31·24	5·50	21·41	12·96	14·76	61·63	0·97	48·44	Length Height Index.
·33	0·23	8·64	2·07	42·51	8·86	10·57	6·09	0·24	22·24	26·85	122·92	2·34	22·29	Breadth Height Index.
·51	1·47	4·25	0·50	0·76	0·26	16·39	7·61	3·51	0·58	1·99	57·19	9·34	33·63	Trans. Fronto-Parietal Index.
·83	0·01	4·02	0·01	2·69	6·74	4·22	28·70	10·09	12·85	1·01	0·21	0·34	71·03	Orbitonasal Index.
·22	98·95	36·80	56·68	52·37	90·82	44·94	93·49	37·01	67·73	56·58	432·49	196·30	175·28	Nasal Index.
·43	86·11	27·23	59·34	3·94	51·37	14·86	46·23	13·91	23·36	17·00	344·93	111·43	304·29	Nasal Elevation Index.
·61	18·94	0·02	13·12	0·29	1·48	0·08	7·14	2·39	0·52	0·05	1·94	33·15	1·84	Upper Facial Index.
50	15·30	1·80	11·99	3·95	1·52	2·11	2·20	1·98	2·05	5·07	17·87	8·62	26·47	Total Facial Index.
25	3·80	15·69	0·07	0·45	2·91	35·60	0·00	17·11	0·08	0·08	32·18	29·39	2·40	Trans. Cephalo-Facial Index.
89	17·83	11·95	13·58	17·23	6·36	21·13	11·73	11·50	26·20	9·78	99·63	2·99	72·19	Vertical Cephalo-Facial Index.

TABLE—XXVI.

Values of $\frac{N_s \; N_s'}{N_s+N_s'}\left(\frac{M_s-M_s'}{\sigma_s}\right)^2$ for

Characters.	Red Kaffir.	Uzbeg.	Tadjik.	Khos (Lower Chitral).	U. P. Brahmin.	Bengali Brahmin.	Bengali Kayastha.	Bengali Pod.	Orissa Brahmin.	Malve Brahmin.	Rajput.	Nagar Brahmin.	Audich Brahmin.	Kathi.	Bania-Jain.
Stature	4·54	0·06	2·06	1·79	0·75	9·93	7·01	2·27	0·06	0·02	19·79	0·13	0·08	4·44	0·06
Auricular Height	10·43	14·44	7·48	5·23	7·38	1·16	0·07	8·50	6·95	15·12	10·57	8·49	23·08	4·96	12·03
Max. Head Length ..	4·34	29·99	51·57	9·00	1·11	15·25	30·46	32·50	61·63	11·84	7·94	32·18	43·21	7·71	29·86
Max. Head Breadth	1·95	64·24	32·46	5·77	12·59	3·69	19·75	34·68	7·17	16·50	3·50	28·44	0·11	22·81	16·59
Min. Frontal Breadth	12·74	14·89	18·20	2·14	10·23	0·12	2·56	4·63	5·00	3·15	11·55	11·31	2·68	0·45	3·34
Max. Bizygomatic Breadth.	3·29	54·06	25·05	1·13	3·60	4·25	0·04	17·50	15·41	3·76	0·45	0·43	0·20	19·75	4·24
Bigonial Breadth ..	8·36	13·17	4·36	1·61	0·22	0·00	0·18	0·27	0·30	0·16	1·33	1·12	2·33	0·16	0·00
Inter-Orbital Breadth	17·16	2·69	0·07	5·00	32·95	34·51	36·70	5·44	0·13	0·89	18·25	2·14	1·05	0·99	0·27
Orbitonasal Breadth	0·06	9·01	4·68	0·04	3·04	24·24	35·24	0·06	2·45	2·05	0·12	11·17	8·31	14·21	27·16
Orbitonasal Arc ..	4·45	0·33	1·20	0·22	9·56	23·18	29·98	0·62	2·30	7·58	8·04	14·62	10·70	19·12	17·44
Nasal Length ..	0·01	0·03	0·27	3·55	9·00	5·03	3·80	40·00	45·49	31·91	26·61	20·95	36·87	1·50	15·16
Nasal Breadth ..	0·07	0·85	0·00	0·79	5·67	1·85	6·62	2·24	1·44	8·96	3·12	1·55	0·34	1·26	10·09
Nasal Height or Depth	0·38	22·13	10·26	7·93	0·01	0·01	0·36	21·03	31·41	16·00	10·79	10·96	9·78	2·24	12·37
Upper Facial Length	0·81	7·31	0·57	3·04	1·39	0·13	0·01	10·62	21·67	13·60	13·47	24·38	42·96	2·10	28·03
Total Facial Length	1·70	6·14	1·11	0·47	5·39	0·18	3·46	13·92	21·40	14·38	21·26	61·71	55·38	18·03	59·42
Horizontal Cirm. of the Head.	5·27	1·58	1·00	0·32	4·26	2·27	2·37	28·74	49·50	15·30	5·62	0·04	13·45	0·84	4·00
Sagittal Arc ..	1·95	10·73	7·23	2·83	13·90	11·43	0·19	1·23	4·33	21·87	11·44	6·43	10·38	26·51	5·02
Transverse Arc ..	1·47	34·98	19·44	0·14	2·56	13·05	20·09	0·31	0·00	3·16	0·64	11·49	0·87	6·26	5·50
Length Breadth Index	0·02	126·66	105·94	17·62	14·76	19·04	61·54	4·30	7·86	2·33	0·04	75·82	22·51	39·05	55·50
Length Height Index	15·09	39·98	39·36	0·35	8·93	0·96	6·40	0·05	44·43	3·91	2·60	0·04	1·32	0·44	0·18
Breadth Height Index	13·10	3·66	1·89	12·24	0·01	4·92	9·14	1·51	16·97	0·24	2·20	32·34	18·12	23·25	29·52
Trans. Fronto-Parietal Index.	1·98	26·41	6·42	1·91	1·82	3·25	11·76	0·00	1·54	9·92	0·48	7·40	1·19	19·97	7·67
Orbitonasal Index ..	7·48	17·04	0·97	0·91	4·96	0·90	0·50	0·78	0·00	4·67	13·28	2·24	1·48	3·39	0·07
Nasal Index ..	0·01	0·45	0·11	0·30	15·53	6·55	10·89	31·58	31·52	41·57	26·29	17·17	21·28	2·18	26·46
Nasal Elevation Index	0·15	23·23	8·62	4·26	2·44	0·70	5·36	25·55	34·35	29·27	17·18	14·52	10·83	4·40	27·53
Upper Facial Index ..	2·79	1·60	5·54	7·35	0·01	2·01	0·06	0·62	5·38	5·66	8·61	21·53	30·94	11·48	31·45
Total Facial Index ..	5·08	4·80	4·89	1·52	0·92	0·88	2·17	0·64	2·82	4·09	14·89	58·75	41·49	40·10	48·95
Trans. Cephalo-Facial Index.	0·00	8·07	5·28	4·37	8·84	21·19	35·39	4·05	2·49	13·39	4·17	38·70	0·75	2·59	10·01
Vertical Cephalo-Facial Index.	2·59	1·36	1·56	1·71	0·02	0·33	1·22	0·12	31·47	0·13	0·45	9·88	1·50	1·52	6·76

TABLE—XXVI.

Pathan with other races.

Chitpavan Brahmin.	Desastha Brahmin.	Saregwat Gour Brahmin.	Mahratta.	Nambudiri Brahmin.	Ilnva.	Tamil Brahmin.	Tamil Kala.	Kanarese Brahmin.	Telegu Brahmin.	Nair.	Kadar.	Bhil.	Khasi.	Characters.
0·02	0·65	1·89	0·42	0·76	20·20	0·16	2·01	5·59	0·01	17·60	87·00	4·10	57·25	Stature.
12·75	12·71	0·39	10·12	0·73	12·83	0·10	4·74	6·27	0·56	0·04	4·21	44·86	0·19	Auricular Height.
25·19	34·44	12·33	52·09	8·28	1·05	5·58	3·42	33·04	0·78	0·62	71·15	53·16	14·98	Max. Head Length.
0·23	0·03	0·02	0·49	5·41	13·44	0·72	2·50	1·05	4·77	1·94	97·78	35·09	0·02	Max. Head Breadth.
0·08	0·24	0·32	0·03	6·62	16·04	2·87	13·50	0·49	5·10	3·43	19·62	12·21	17·52	Min. Frontal Breadth.
1·19	1·47	10·14	0·97	6·92	38·75	15·35	4·60	5·32	7·59	4·50	76·94	11·76	14·33	Max. Bizygomatic Breadth.
5·46	0·17	21·01	0·12	7·99	11·59	5·93	0·66	93·85	7·67	3·33	3·52	2·67	17·41	Bigonial Breadth.
7·19	0·71	9·58	4·41	5·70	3·06	27·06	2·01	17·39	4·26	5·48	10·86	7·12	1·97	Inter-Orbital Breadth.
3·89	2·05	16·07	0·07	22·56	8·40	40·47	5·10	21·74	17·32	22·51	15·47	0·03	0·11	Orbitonasal Breadth.
19·63	9·41	14·32	2·48	46·34	5·45	32·68	0·00	12·90	3·50	26·40	0·69	1·38	11·09	Orbitonasal Arc.
58·86	47·32	28·06	40·03	28·80	76·68	36·65	69·21	33·45	34·40	24·96	154·82	102·72	103·21	Nasal Length.
6·00	9·25	3·13	5·79	6·28	4·17	3·13	6·75	1·34	12·04	11·63	66·23	24·16	16·08	Nasal Breadth.
46·87	51·16	18·28	38·97	0·19	34·36	8·00	28·25	9·42	7·24	3·37	169·42	58·08	207·91	Nasal Height or Depth.
44·69	37·00	12·62	36·17	7·03	30·85	12·78	29·12	19·46	14·97	7·19	65·41	80·68	12·76	Upper Facial Length.
33·18	43·98	9·11	38·54	4·61	27·38	11·92	24·04	25·78	28·52	2·48	146·75	42·37	61·35	Total Facial Length.
11·40	9·43	7·41	21·49	0·05	12·74	3·05	15·02	15·80	3·56	1·11	304·99	50·52	2·36	Horizontal Cirm. of the Head.
[illegible]·18	16·43	4·60	34·32	18·26	3·52	1·16	2·03	4·71	0·02	3·75	150·65	31·94	0·00	Sagittal Arc.
1·75	1·08	5·90	0·25	6·42	0·06	6·52	0·02	2·35	0·51	14·64	538·48	25·94	0·89	Transverse Arc.
8·64	16·14	5·97	18·05	15·16	7·28	5·60	0·08	23·87	2·00	3·08	13·99	0·47	6 49	Length Breadth Index.
0·78	0·12	1·34	1·52	0·49	7·44	2·18	1·22	0·42	0·06	0·06	5·79	6·31	4·50	Length Height Index.
7·28	9·55	0·35	4·01	5·74	0·31	0·10	0·61	7·34	0·90	1·31	27·91	3·27	0·25	Breadth Height Index.
0·69	0·17	0·32	0·43	0·25	0·61	5·24	1·65	0·17	0·36	0·01	57·34	14·93	12·02	Trans. Fronto-Parietal Index.
14·84	7·10	0·40	6·59	14·69	0·02	0·35	6·20	0·15	0·54	2·62	9·92	3·49	19·10	Orbitonasal Index.
60·67	56·60	26·56	39·94	37·34	66·41	32·51	71·04	26·67	49·42	39·76	278·89	144·72	118·57	Nasal Index.
52·31	56·25	23·60	48·03	4·21	42·86	13·53	39·89	12·73	20·47	14·97	237·84	89·89	221·32	Nasal Elevation Index.
30·85	24·39	2·42	21·14	1·01	6·25	1·45	13·84	7·75	4·11	1·72	8·00	41·38	7·48	Upper Facial Index.
30·23	26·61	0·58	24·87	0·08	0·78	0·48	9·91	10·05	10·05	0·01	32·65	20·19	41·57	Total Facial Index.
0·17	2·24	11·77	0·05	0·33	2·19	26·71	0·00	12·83	0·01	0·06	21·06	22·05	1·66	Trans. Cephalo-Facial Index.
1·42	2·90	2·56	2·94	4·57	0·62	6·69	2·91	2·38	9·23	1·47	41·39	0·01	31·01	Vertical Cephalo-Facial Index.

TABLE—XXVII.

Values of $\frac{N_s\ N_s'}{N_s+N_s'}\left(\frac{M_s-M_s'}{\sigma_s}\right)^2$ for

Characters.	Red Kaffir.	Pathan.	Tadjik.	Khos (Lower Chitral).	U. P. Brahmin.	Bengali Brahmin.	Bengali Kayastha.	Bengali Pod.	Orissa Brahmin.	Malve Brahmin.	Rajput.	Nagar Brahmin.	Audich Brahmin.	Kathi.	Bania Jain.
Stature.	2·47	0·06	1·01	2·03	0·28	6·61	4·07	2·42	0·23	0·13	12·76	0·00	0·00	2·76	0·23
Auricular Height	49·43	14·44	2·44	38·08	46·45	22·67	19·98	41·09	3·88	51·56	49·71	45·96	69·90	31·32	52·33
Max. Head Length	62·64	29·99	0·33	11·81	41·19	3·98	1·84	0·15	0·10	5·63	13·59	1·59	0·14	7·29	19·45
Max. Head Breadth	60·05	64·24	11·30	45·59	124·98	39·72	26·20	91·41	134·23	132·22	111·68	19·50	74·00	10·98	29·45
Min. Frontal Breadth	1·52	14·89	0·08	8·91	45·05	12·59	8·60	119·93	40·66	28·91	52·47	2·08	8·11	9·33	7·44
Max. Bizygomatic Breadth.	44·21	54·06	10·74	51·57	81·81	84·46	70·16	16·31	141·07	80·52	77·32	59·30	72·82	8·90	41·30
Bigonial Breadth	2·43	13·17	3·81	8·41	16·38	13·07	13·58	13·50	21·84	10·49	25·49	24·88	22·59	14·40	16·46
Inter-Orbital Breadth	29·22	2·69	3·75	14·03	45·67	47·31	4·98	7·59	2·57	6·00	30·44	9·62	7·31	5·97	5·18
Orbitonasal Breadth	9·90	9·01	1·32	9·84	2·10	1·93	3·13	1·60	4·64	2·93	9·30	0·24	0·69	0·29	1·32
Orbitonasal Arc	6·06	0·33	2·42	0·05	11·10	23·70	28·79	32·94	3·83	8·96	9·61	15·51	12·03	19·91	18·03
Nasal Length.	0·01	0·03	0·39	3·31	8·09	4·71	3·50	0·16	22·21	26·46	21·45	17·06	29·71	1·58	12·60
Nasal Breadth.	1·57	0·85	0·99	3·20	1·44	0·08	1·41	0·37	0·00	2·97	0·24	0·00	0·27	0·02	2·92
Nasal Height or Depth	22·31	22·13	4·40	7·54	23·01	23·01	22·45	30·71	0·49	1·26	5·87	5·94	6·28	9·71	4·90
Upper Facial Length	14·42	7·31	4·63	20·17	14·08	5·67	8·52	32·90	50·40	35·05	38·28	53·14	75·30	14·90	57·55
Total Facial Length	15·16	6·14	2·75	11·05	20·69	8·12	19·11	35·61	46·42	33·52	45·32	91·18	84·58	37·85	88·71
Horizontal Cirm. of the Head.	0·33	1·58	4·78	3·53	9·60	6·77	7·47	18·01	55·47	22·06	11·92	2·56	20·86	0·13	9·80
Sagittal Arc	23·99	10·73	1·19	4·78	43·96	39·94	16·59	40·11	4·28	0·73	0·60	2·35	0·69	2·19	3·08
Transverse Arc	58·58	34·98	5·30	38·33	54·36	7·25	7·51	32·59	46·80	54·90	53·24	13·90	33·03	11·29	20·92
Length Breadth Index	161·28	126·66	7·38	76·84	215·53	54·21	33·69	86·37	114·17	155·40	153·96	26·34	69 95	25·62	37·54
Length Height Index	108·47	39·98	1·20	55·99	80·79	29·72	23·81	36·58	17·24	63·85	71·51	48·10	63·78	43·37	68·96
Breadth Height Index	0·97	3·66	0·62	0·85	3·94	0·00	2·24	0·65	32·38	2·12	0·73	7·55	2·48	6·30	6·54
Trans. Fronto-Parietal Index.	48·38	26·41	9·82	19·96	60·66	12·48	7·74	26·08	49·19	61·67	26·45	11·78	43·91	0·75	11·18
Orbitonasal Index	48·60	17·04	11·80	13·86	37·38	24·75	27·25	23·60	23·17	36·49	60·32	35·08	31·55	3·09	19·16
Nasal Index.	0·73	0·45	0·17	0·07	8·08	2·59	4·40	18·38	15·96	25·17	13·49	7·91	10·58	0·47	13·62
Nasal Elevation Index	25·46	23·23	6·00	12·41	11·74	16·60	11·46	0·10	0·37	0·00	3·27	4·56	6·20	7·22	0·72
Upper Facial Index	0·00	1·60	0·55	13·33	1·40	6·40	2·65	3·13	0·25	0·71	1·25	6·62	11·69	3·38	11·76
Total Facial Index	0·26	4·80	0·12	1·81	1·79	9·17	1·38	2·14	1·24	0·04	0·66	17·06	9·92	12·91	20·44
Trans. Cephalo-Facial Index.	10·07	8·07	0·90	1·74	30·16	1·60	3·84	1·07	3·83	36·37	24·36	4·71	5·74	1·56	0·19
Vertical Cephalo-Facial Index.	7·24	1·36	0·01	5·84	1·62	2·81	0·12	0·73	10·55	2·16	0·52	1·95	0·05	0·00	0·89

TABLE XXVII.

…ng with other races.

	Desastha Brahmin.	Saraswat Gour Brahmin.	Mahratta.	Nambudiri Brahmin.	Iluva.	Tamil Brahmin.	Tamil Kalla.	Kanarese Brahmin.	Telegu Brahmin	Nair.	Kadar.	Bhil.	Khasi.	Characters.
·02	1·01	21·41	0·67	0·01	11·89	0·35	1·10	5·37	0·03	11·97	63·55	4·18	46·91	Stature.
·81	56·59	18·99	45·08	9·70	48·91	12·44	31·23	35·52	19·46	14·19	36·77	95·50	13·73	Auricular Height.
·31	0·69	5·50	0·54	66·14	20·83	11·36	12·64	0·12	21·48	40·52	10·85	1·05	6·64	Max. Head Length.
·20	78·73	63·37	79·03	104·64	127·33	52·66	82·29	49·22	96·92	90·74	308·60	176·83	73·82	Max. Head Breadth.
·69	15·22	19·04	17·16	38·62	55·22	28·83	48·94	10·23	33·68	31·71	64·37	48·66	61·41	Min. Frontal Breadth.
·31	87·75	103·86	71·54	9·58	166·49	117·65	80·04	86·43	93·94	90·80	251·45	108·36	81·59	Max. Bizygomatic Breadth.
·97	19·96	59·55	16·46	4·26	44·41	33·65	17·59	47·13	36·30	28·82	32·73	25·87	0·09	Bigonial Breadth.
·20	6·82	19·35	12·59	14·35	10·23	39·42	8·07	28·03	11·82	14·18	21·96	16·15	6·41	Inter-Orbital Breadth.
·78	4·32	3·28	11·14	1·34	0·17	7·14	0·68	1·30	0·49	1·18	45·90	9·97	12·64	Orbitonasal Breadth.
·80	11·81	15·59	3·94	43·91	7·06	32·17	0·35	13·92	9·83	26·38	0·00	2·63	5·18	Orbitonasal Arc.
·18	41·57	23·94	33·28	24·35	63·63	30·99	58·75	27·70	28·46	21·06	118·27	84·76	81·55	Nasal Length.
·15	2·98	0·43	1·38	1·64	0·80	0·43	2·13	0·01	4·59	4·23	35·30	11·96	6·19	Nasal Breadth.
·38	0·29	0·80	0·44	19·37	0·27	4·77	0·09	3·78	5·19	10·53	34·22	4·37	55·46	Nasal Height or Depth.
·23	73·59	34·47	65·73	26·08	69·43	34·70	55·44	43·02	36·97	26·70	100·12	114·77	36·47	Upper Facial Length.
·88	77·85	26·72	64·75	19·62	51·03	30·87	46·05	47·92	51·18	15·66	174·45	79·76	9[illegible]·49	Total Facial Length.
65	17·74	13·58	29·14	1·18	19·73	7·93	22·05	22·52	8·44	4·99	269·66	57·71	5·64	Horizontal Circm. of the Head.
75	0·00	1·94	3·13	51·27	24·83	18·19	3·49	1·83	9·81	26·34	46·18	3·00	5·99	Sagittal Arc.
38	32·69	14·06	42·78	14·26	32·37	13·23	30·34	20·19	27·22	7·50	708·75	109·31	12·01	Transverse Arc.
75	81·39	82·38	616·84	222·62	186·59	83·62	120·84	46·46	152·39	174·30	254·58	14·08	100·11	Length Breadth Index.
·63	55·21	27·98	29·08	49·85	76·66	25·06	49·36	32·23	41·84	45·61	25·96	73·32	24·50	Length Height Index.
·03	0·43	1·92	0·04	16·59	2·00	2·65	1·25	0·25	7·43	89·43	44·91	0·09	7·33	Breadth Height Index.
·04	37·99	21·46	34·63	32·23	34·03	9·60	14·00	22·28	31·44	28·92	146·55	73·69	6·57	Trans. Fronto-Parietal Index.
14	50·02	22·02	42·62	57·86	17·93	21·65	2·85	14·00	11·79	32·52	54·31	31·66	0·46	Orbitonasal Index.
35	37·04	15·36	23·96	22·45	43·49	19·47	48·47	15·10	30·58	23·77	184·39	101·11	76·61	Nasal Index.
	1·04	0·24	1·34	9·53	1·04	2·37	1·21	2·62	0·60	2·46	60·61	13·21	59·62	Nasal Elevation Index.
	9·41	0·01	7·62	0·15	0·93	0·04	4·62	14·46	0·29	0·02	0·99	10·99	1·02	Upper Facial Index.
	4·03	2·29	4·61	3·93	1·97	2·47	0·56	0·39	0·39	4·67	5·87	3·28	10·39	Total Facial Index.
	3·37	0·05	7·48	11·60	2·32	3·12	7·13	0·12	8·26	7·45	51·23	49·39	3·86	Trans. Cephalo-Facial Index.
	0·06	0·07	0·10	0·51	0·21	1·30	0·18	0·04	[illegible]·33	0·02	17·69	1·15	13·04	Vertical Cephalo-Facial Index.

TABLE XXVIII.

Values of $\frac{N_s N_s'}{N_s+N_s'}\left(\frac{M_s-M_s'}{\sigma_s}\right)^2$ for

Characters.	Red Kaffir.	Pathan.	Uzbeg.	Khos (Lower Chitral).	U. P. Brah-min.	Bengali Brah-min.	Bengali Kayas-tha.	Bengali Pod.	Orissa Brah-min.	Malve Brah-min.	Rajput.	Nagar Brah-min.	Audich Brah-min.	Kathi.	Bania —Jain.
Stature ..	0·38	2·06	1·01	9·42	0·26	2·31	1·35	9·05	4·14	2·46	9·58	1·68	1·83	0·76	3·75
Auricular Height	44·19	7·48	2·44	30·99	31·02	0·00	12·03	33·40	0·13	46·27	44·52	40·24	68·76	23·73	47·58
Max. Head Length	112·35	51·57	0·33	24·90	67·69	0·14	6·03	1·25	0·17	12·17	28·61	5·52	1·49	14·18	6·24
Max. Head Breadth	26·45	32·46	11·30	15·49	87·99	2·90	3·52	57·86	99·04	98·42	74·73	0·96	9·87	0·09	5·12
Min. Frontal Breadth	1·32	18·20	0·08	10·93	57·68	0·19	10·62	42·14	59·02	37·15	74·48	1·54	9·91	10·63	9·02
Max. Bizygomatic Breadth.	15·12	25·05	10·74	20·93	41·50	2·61	36·42	87·66	109·03	49·01	42·94	26·89	38·73	0·00	13·08
Bigonial Breadth ..	0·44	4·36	3·81	1·05	6·57	0·27	3·90	6·81	10·05	2·74	13·46	12·88	16·26	5 56	5·94
Inter-Orbital Breadth	17·08	0·07	3·75	4·38	33·40	8·45	38·29	4·82	0·50	0·52	18·26	1·59	0·63	0·63	0·06
Orbitonasal Breadth	5·13	4·68	1·52	5·10	0·10	15·67	14·75	3·58	0·98	0·39	4·59	1·09	0·36	3·74	9·40
Orbitonasal Arc ..	0·97	1·20	2·42	3·05	4·70	2·42	21·09	0·06	0·08	3·29	3·17	7·94	5·06	12·65	10·25
Nasal Length ..	0·47	0·27	0·39	2·03	6·99	5·34	2·22	37·73	44·19	29·50	24·16	18·52	34·83	0·64	12·75
Nasal Breadth ..	0·05	0·00	0·99	0·82	6·46	12·60	7·83	2·60	1·80	10·15	3·75	1·91	0·44	1·46	11·87
Nasal Height or Depth	9·44	10·26	4·40	0·42	10·78	0·92	9·57	2·73	4·35	1·07	0·05	0·05	0·11	1·99	0·00
Upper Facial Length	3·41	0·57	4·63	7·44	3·95	3·56	0·57	17·45	35·59	21·44	23·18	38·27	62·07	4·93	42·91
Total Facial Length	6·88	1·11	2·75	3·73	12·15	3·00	10·35	24·68	39·71	25·33	38·04	93·41	84·05	29·37	89·89
Horizontal Cirm. of the Head.	13·15	1·00	4·78	0·29	1·39	1·43	0·23	21·61	40·47	9·75	1·89	0·90	7·69	3·58	0·34
Sagittal Arc ..	21·42	7·23	1·19	1·62	43·38	10·86	12·99	14·68	1·17	5·09	0·24	0·19	0·17	7·34	0·53
Transverse Arc	41·45	19·44	5·30	21·42	36·62	13·88	0·11	24·54	29·46	38·92	35·93	2·40	16·55	2·19	6·83
Length Breadth Index	147·68	105·94	7·38	52·73	202·89	1·78	12·89	64·32	94·56	139·46	139·05	7·64	45·59	9·15	15·93
Length Height Index	131·62	39·36	1·20	60·74	87·66	0·05	21·14	35·74	0·03	68·86	81·73	51·35	7·10	42·53	60·00
Breadth Height Index	5·19	1·89	0·62	4·72	2·09	1·29	2·69	0·01	36·17	0·71	0 00	20·13	8·87	14·20	17·84
Trans. Fronto-Parietal Index. .	19·88	6·42	9·82	2·00	15·43	12·28	0·52	6·47	19·97	33·92	4·88	0·00	16·56	5·38	0·00
Orbitonasal Index	16·64	0·97	11·80	0·01	11·02	6·35	3·63	3·63	1·56	10·52	25·69	7·63	5·91	8·08	0·74
Nasal Index ..	0·27	0·11	0·17	0·04	14·57	18·73	9·91	31·17	31·97	41·66	26·07	16·43	20·72	1·53	26·25
Nasal Elevation Index	9·01	8·62	6·00	1·31	1·60	2·44	0·88	5·80	7·27	7·74	1·04	0·40	0·02	0·28	4·87
Upper Facial Index	0·91	5·54	0·55	0·04	4·99	0·67	9·06	2·27	0·17	0·03	0·16	4·89	10·55	1·85	10·70
Total Facial Index	0·03	4·89	0·12	1·45	1·40	0·31	1·00	1·83	0·86	0·02	2·17	31·61	18·91	20·88	36·98
Trans. Cephalo-Facial Index.	7·17	5·28	0·90	0·15	29·22	15·29	13·66	0·02	1·31	37·40	23·67	15·83	2·93	0·20	0·51
Vertical Cephalo-Facial Index.	10·14	1·56	0·01	7·98	1·87	1·76	0·08	0·78	17·58	2·62	0·55	3·61	0·01	0·01	1·77

TABLE XXVIII.

with other races.

Desastha Brahmin.	Saraswat Gour Brahmin.	Mahratta.	Namburi Brahmin.	Iluva.	Tamil Brahmin.	Tamil Kata.	Kanarese Brahmin.	Telegu Brahmin.	Nair.	Kadar.	Bhil.	Khasi.	Characters.
6·81	8·22	4·72	5·68	37·84	3·38	0·02	15·28	1·82	8·66	137·60	12·62	93·44	Stature.
52·92	11·35	38·05	3·55	41·39	5·71	23·22	28·57	12·22	7·01	29·80	95·23	6·47	Auricular Height.
3·30	11·71	0·04	106·90	36·49	21·43	22·44	1·14	38·31	38·48	0·27	0·31	15·15	Max. Head Length.
42·66	30·34	44·13	68·05	90·33	22·58	48·27	20·83	63·18	54·77	302·93	141·14	38·71	Max. Head Breadth.
20·06	23·26	21·26	49·75	71·28	36·13	60·94	12·22	43·62	40·92	95·04	62·50	85·07	Min. Frontal Breadth.
52·74	69·06	38·78	61·35	132·48	82·51	47·51	54·57	61·77	53·48	233·57	73·41	47·19	Max. Bizygomatic Breadth.
8·64	47·51	6·44	26·06	31·94	21·43	7·78	35·83	21·83	16·82	20·27	14·36	4·48	Bigonial Breadth.
0·42	8·98	3·80	5·07	2·59	27·29	1·53	17·03	3·63	4·83	10·41	6·50	1·60	Inter-Orbital Breadth.
0·86	4·30	6·39	7·90	0·82	20·70	0·13	7·63	5·00	7·63	46·22	5·41	7·71	Orbitonasal Breadth.
4·79	8·40	0·28	36·83	1·80	21·31	0·94	7·26	3·93	18·45	4·80	0·02	22·77	Orbitonasal Arc.
51·79	25·63	37·85	26·38	75·73	34·32	67·60	31·07	32·03	22·62	16·27	103·08	105·08	Nasal Length.
12·22	3·60	6·66	7·19	4·77	3·60	7·57	1·57	13·60	13·28	77·27	27·13	18·61	Nasal Breadth.
12·25	1·75	10·76	7·80	8·93	0·04	6·63	0·00	0·12	10·85	103·40	23·46	130·03	Nasal Height or Depth.
0·70	20·13	50·97	12·72	51·63	20·35	40·28	30·50	23·23	13·12	91·93	104·04	21·61	Upper Facial Length.
76·86	17·30	58·54	11·12	42·88	21·85	37·28	40·77	41·38	7·62	203·58	74·95	90·63	Total Facial Length.
5·31	3·50	11·92	1·57	7·64	0·71	9·76	10·18	0·90	0·01	308·81	42·08	0·81	Horizontal Cirm. of the Head.
2·04	0·17	11·62	61·88	21·52	14·41	1·02	0·14	6·26	1·33	99·73	10·78	3·31	Sagittal Arc.
16·20	0·33	25·02	3·28	16·85	2·83	15·54	7·60	13·12	0·20	910·81	94·60	3·98	Transverse Arc.
57·60	58·24	38·08	212·53	170·07	50·48	97·27	25·61	133·63	157·83	261·73	119·37	77·05	Length Breadth Index.
60·66	24·98	26·42	50·65	82·58	21·75	48·74	30·65	42·00	45·92	23·83	58·75	21·60	Length Height Index.
3·55	0·55	0·50	15·30	0·60	1·05	0·21	2·22	5·37	6·97	53·44	0·29	4·19	Breadth Height Index.
1·95	3·66	11·03	9·62	11·09	0·01	1·02	4·34	8·83	7·33	122·91	43·23	0·75	Trans. Fronto-Parietal Index.
7·52	2·70	13·94	25·15	1·22	2·55	2·83	0·33	0·04	7·49	20·71	8·65	12·63	Orbitonasal Index.
6·33	25·80	40·14	37·31	67·98	22·14	72·37	23·05	40·65	39·96	309·60	151·99	5·70	Nasal Index.
5·47	4·85	18·36	0·67	15·83	0·92	15·05	0·71	3·43	1·08	171·01	49·94	138·21	Nasal Elevation Index.
3·00	0·48	5·87	1·75	0·00	1·14	2·91	0·36	0·04	1·12	0·03	10·63	0·08	Upper Facial Index.
0·52	0·10	8·69	3 78	1·30	2·13	1·54	1·31	1·31	1·73	12·31	6·44	19·30	Total Facial Index.
1·02	0·18	4·60	8·59	0·52	9·93	4·37	2·23	5·36	4·37	58·76	52·09	1·42	Trans. Cephalo-Facial Index.
)·17	0·20	0·28	6·97	0·17	2·20	0·39	0·15	3·50	0·00	29·42	1·28	20·68	Vertical Cephalo-Facial Index.

TABLE XXIX.

Values of $\frac{N_s N_s'}{N_s+N_s'}\left(\frac{M_s-M_s'}{\sigma_s}\right)^2$ for

Characters.	Red Kafir.	Pathan.	Uzbeg.	Tadjik.	U. P. Brahmin.	Bengali Brahmin.	Bengali Kayastha.	Bengali Pod.	Orissa Brahmin.	Malve Brahmin.	Rajput.	Nagar Brahmin.	Andich Brahmin.	Kathi.	Bania-Jain.
Stature	17·36	1·79	2·03	2·77	5·39	24·13	22·86	0·14	2·15	1·50	48·02	4·33	3·71	12·91	1·76
Auricular Height ..	1·15	5·23	38·08	0·53	0·63	1·13	6·08	1·04	35·05	4·00	1·21	0·46	8·84	0·13	1·86
Max. Head Length ..	37·50	9·00	11·81	1·81	17·61	2·04	8·03	12·00	31·96	0·93	0·08	9·09	17·79	0·10	8·27
Max. Head Breadth	1·57	5·77	45·59	3·83	41·29	0·05	5·67	20·37	41·20	49·21	26·49	11·76	6·15	9·62	3·78
Min. Frontal Breadth	6·15	2·14	8·91	1·32	25·91	1·14	0·02	15·22	21·49	12·17	33·96	4·96	0·04	0·37	0·16
Max. Bizygomatic Breadth.	0·76	1·13	61·57	0·31	10·35	11·57	2·30	33·73	38·30	10·74	4·38	0·28	3·22	15·78	1·35
Bigonial Breadth ..	3·63	1·61	8·41	1·92	3·24	1·57	1·06	3·43	5·40	0·78	8·50	7·97	11·06	2·64	2·39
Inter-Orbital Breadth	4·94	5·00	14·03	0·02	18·24	19·57	20·30	0·16	11·33	1·47	5·65	1·00	2·12	0·94	4·38
Orbitonasal Breadth	0·00	0·04	9·84	0·37	3·16	29·00	46·75	0·01	2·73	2·03	0·03	14·08	10·13	16·19	35·62
Orbitonasal Arc ..	9·49	0·22	0·05	5·30	15·77	35·10	50·31	1·85	6·06	12·97	15·67	26·47	19·64	28·22	30·68
Nasal Length ..	5·67	3·55	3·31	4·05	2·30	0·43	0·00	27·94	33·24	20·53	14·83	9·99	24·54	0·15	5·55
Nasal Breadth ..	0·60	0·79	3·20	4·61	12·86	5·90	17·17	6·68	6·91	18·05	10·14	6·66	3·06	4·31	23·59
Nasal Height or Depth	7·19	7·93	7·54	0·88	8·60	8·60	7·32	5·69	9·94	2·96	0·25	0·25	0·12	0·89	0·61
Upper Facial Length	1·09	3·04	20·17	11·83	0·17	4·64	5·10	3·80	11·54	6·04	5·10	14·17	32·40	0·00	17·59
Total Facial Length	0·53	0·47	11·05	3·92	3·80	0·04	1·92	12·57	22·58	13·17	21·78	73·21	64·15	16·85	69·79
Horizontal Cirm. of the Head.	11·72	0·32	3·53	4·13	3·14	1·30	1·31	30·38	61·55	15·06	4·56	0·19	13·48	2·41	2·87
Sagittal Arc ..	13·73	2·83	4·78	0·03	34·90	30·40	6·58	8·64	0·12	13·11	3·96	0·94	3·52	17·52	0·40
Transverse Arc ..	3·63	0·14	38·33	2·18	4·80	13·82	23·87	1·02	0·21	5·72	1·99	12·90	0·43	5·96	5·46
Length Breadth Index.	27·79	17·62	76·84	0·84	73·18	0·56	18·11	3·41	4·33	35·25	23·70	27·68	0·38	9·48	14·37
Length Height Index	15·29	0·35	55·99	1·87	7·82	2·89	13·97	0·72	75·10	2·82	1·45	0·93	0·44	0·04	0·05
Breadth Height Index	0·01	12·24	0·85	3·47	12·89	0·97	0·41	4·44	83·87	8·75	6·14	6·28	0·78	4·56	5·00
Trans. Fronto-Parietal Index	11·24	1·91	19·96	17·14	8·46	0·44	5·83	2·01	11·00	24·62	0·72	2·43	8·61	13·74	2·65
Orbitonasal Index ..	19·52	0·91	13·86	16·23	12·10	4·12	3·99	3·82	1·64	11·52	30·43	8·75	6·64	8·65	0·71
Nasal Index ..	0·66	0·30	0·07	9·15	15·35	5·53	10·67	33·89	37·63	45·81	29·64	18·32	23·19	1·30	29·83
Nasal Elevation Index	4·15	4·26	12·41	5·77	0·08	1·24	0·07	13·45	19·81	16·67	5·94	4·09	2·08	0·18	14·08
Upper Facial Index	1·70	7·35	13·33	14·07	6·78	18·67	12·89	3·32	0·08	0·00	0·04	4·93	11·31	1·60	11·53
Total Facial Index ..	1·41	1·52	1·81	4·53	0·02	5·28	0·07	0·11	0·19	1·78	9·05	58·58	38·03	35·08	66·07
Trans. Cephalo-Facial Index.	6·45	4·37	1·74	4·26	29·83	9·79	20·73	0·04	0·66	39·03	24·73	23·83	2·15	0·02	1·53
Vertical Cephalo-Facial Index.	0·11	1·71	5·84	0·94	1·37	10·07	8·42	2·86	61·99	0·80	5·69	28·79	9·09	6·69	21·90

TABLE XXIX.

hos (Lower Chitral) with other races.

hitpa-van Brah-min.	Desastha Brah-min.	Saraswat Gour Brah-min.	Mah-ratta.	Nam-budiri Brah-min.	Iluva.	Tamil Brah-min.	Tamil Kala.	Kana-rese Brah-min.	Telegu Brah-min.	Nair.	Kadar.	Bhil.	Khasi.	Characters.
3·33	0·40	0·05	0·44	0·14	14·11	0·79	7·98	1·80	2·02	38·91	90·97	0·92	53·92	Stature.
2·15	2·87	2·49	1·58	11·09	3·15	6·94	0·09	0·30	2·08	6·95	0·15	28·16	9·62	Auricular Height.
5·40	13·00	0·96	26·25	40·66	3·38	0·10	0·52	12·37	4·00	16·66	40·92	27·75	1·19	Max. Head Length.
12·29	7·55	5·07	11·12	26·34	43·02	2·07	15·97	1·53	23·81	17·17	221·23	83·16	6·83	Max. Head Breadth.
2·11	1·40	4·42	3·06	19·76	36·05	11·21	29·80	0·45	16·19	13·53	50·12	29·43	43·55	Min. Frontal Breadth.
6·77	7·98	21·85	5·08	16·73	65·97	39·33	11·44	13·54	17·54	12·70	140·77	24·52	6·96	Max. Bizygomatic Breadth.
18·84	4·38	41·82	3·04	20·56	26·31	16·25	4·35	30·13	19·44	11·84	14·72	9·74	11·82	Bigonial Breadth.
0·22	2·86	1·62	0·00	0·17	0·06	13·40	0·25	6·21	0·01	0·10	1·37	0·62	0·00	Inter-Orbital Breadth.
4·47	2·46	18·90	0·68	27·24	9·54	49·22	5·47	25·90	20·43	27·48	24·71	0·16	0·39	Orbitonasal Breadth.
34·33	19·87	22·62	5·28	68·09	9·69	48·26	0·23	20·59	14·22	40·91	0·17	3·24	11·39	Orbitonasal Arc.
17·00	40·79	16·99	27·84	17·51	64·71	24·80	56·80	21·84	22·71	14·03	158·78	92·30	95·23	Nasal Length.
6·06	24·46	8·37	13·66	14·26	10·46	8·37	13·85	4·83	23·24	7·93	118·47	41·73	32·83	Nasal Breadth.
2·39	21·65	4·13	17·63	5·75	14·68	15·29	11·02	0·44	0·04	0·76	147·15	33·94	187·38	Nasal Height or Depth.
4·21	30·82	5·21	25·65	0·64	29·30	5·33	19·40	10·61	6·98	1·53	56·91	71·23	4·78	Upper Facial Length.
6·48	57·07	7·50	41·01	3·05	27·54	10·44	18·63	25·73	28·85	1·18	187·73	58·56	70·71	Total Facial Length.
1·14	10·18	6·34	22·31	0·70	12·11	2·00	14·44	15·52	2·47	0·37	411·10	56·13	1·58	Horizontal Circm. of the Head.
3·34	9·36	0·56	24·53	43·72	14·51	8·41	0·00	0·61	2·27	16·03	160·05	22·34	1·23	Sagittal Arc.
1·17	0·72	5·64	0·94	6·27	0·01	6·34	0·04	1·85	0·18	15·98	803·73	37·84	0·57	Transverse Arc.
·63	0·01	2·04	2·08	76·94	52·65	2·29	17·78	1·80	33·63	41·71	94·56	24·77	3·40	Length Breadth Index.
·11	0·09	3·64	4·11	0·03	6·25	5·14	0·47	1·76	0·10	0·13	13·16	5·08	9·93	Length Height Index.
·11	0·16	8·01	1·84	40·20	8·22	9·83	5·65	0·18	20·92	25·18	114·62	2·10	20·69	Breadth Height Index.
·17	4·95	0·54	4·88	3·97	5·13	1·48	0·02	0·85	4·25	2·37	115·20	33·19	6·15	Trans. Fronto-Parietal Index.
·24	20·70	2·79	15·60	28·71	1·19	2·63	3·59	0·27	0·02	8·23	24·62	9·42	16·28	Orbitonasal Index.
·42	78·30	27·97	44·54	41·08	75·52	34·98	79·15	28·15	55·07	44·39	375·53	171·35	147·67	Nasal Index.
·36	48·35	11·87	33·42	0·05	28·72	4·44	26·37	3·93	9·41	5·12	254·65	75·46	227·77	Nasal Elevation Index.
·99	8·47	0·90	5·86	2·67	0·02	1·82	2·67	0·20	0·17	1·85	0·00	20·99	0·01	Upper Facial Index.
·91	25·11	0·14	19·57	0·90	0·05	0·20	5·60	5·58	5·58	1·37	28·38	14·91	37·82	Total Facial Index.
·29	0·46	3·23	3·70	7·83	0·17	14·20	3·58	3·88	4·74	3·76	65·92	54·98	0·80	Trans. Cephalo-Facial Index.
·12	14·19	9·74	11·04	14·35	4·85	17·97	9·71	9·33	22·58	7·70	87·58	2·02	63·82	Vertical Cephalo-Facial Index.

TABLE XXX.

Values of $\frac{N_s N_s'}{N_s+N_s'}\left(\frac{M_s-M_s'}{\sigma}\right)^2$ for U. P.

Characters.	Red Kaffir.	Pathan.	Uzbeg.	Tadjik.	Khos (Lower Chitral).	Bengali Brahmin.	Bengali Kayastha.	Bengali Pod.	Orissa Brahmin.	Malve Brahmin.	Rajput.	Nagar Brahmin.	Audich Brahmin.	Kathi.	Bania-Jain.
Stature ..	1·28	0·75	0·28	0·26	5·39	5·22	2·71	5·64	1·67	1·01	11·89	0·41	0·30	16·61	1·59
Auricular Height	0·01	7·38	46·45	31·02	0·63	2·68	8·27	0·04	33·33	1·37	0·01	0·06	2·93	0·11	0·11
Max. Head Length ..	0·75	1·11	41·19	67·69	17·61	24·61	45·39	45·64	83·45	20·29	16·30	47·75	60·48	14·22	44·63
Max. Head Breadth	30·18	12·59	124·98	87·99	41·29	29·91	72·95	2·84	2·70	0·26	4·96	89·56	19·13	65·95	66·65
Min. Frontal Breadth	52·75	10·23	45·05	57·68	25·91	12·59	28·01	1·10	2·72	2·03	0·09	50·23	27·86	13·60	30·42
Max. Bizygomatic Breadth.	16·05	3·60	81·81	41·50	10·35	0·03	4·01	5·23	2·61	0·00	2·31	8·19	2·97	38·86	18·03
Bigonial Breadth ..	11·78	0·22	16·38	6·57	3·24	0·24	0·94	0·00	0·00	0·75	0·37	0·26	0·99	0·00	0·25
Inder-Orbital Breadth	6·18	32·95	45·67	33·40	18·24	0·02	0·32	11·62	53·91	23·02	5·55	27·25	30·51	19·52	37·21
Orbitonasal Breadth	3·15	3·04	2·10	0·10	3·16	10·12	15·40	2·26	0·31	0·09	2·76	1·73	0·80	4·52	10·25
Orbitonasal Arc ..	2·13	9·56	11·10	4·70	15·77	2·97	3·63	5·30	5·03	0·12	0·51	0·05	0·06	2·12	0·38
Nasal Length ..	12·55	9·00	8·09	6·99	2·30	0·57	2·29	11·05	9·57	7·02	2·84	1·17	7·03	2·58	0·19
Nasal Breadth ..	9·03	5·67	1·44	6·46	12·86	1·04	0·03	0·78	2·88	0·38	0·96	2·32	4·55	1·26	0·19
Nasal Height or Depth	0·54	0·01	23·01	10·78	8·60	0·00	0·51	21·99	32·83	16·84	11·59	11·78	10·53	2·54	13·23
Upper Facial Length	0·21	1·39	14·08	3·95	0·17	2·37	2·18	4·33	10·39	6·31	5·35	12·73	27·17	0·12	15·51
Total Facial Length	1·89	5·39	20·69	12·15	3·80	3·63	0·68	1·99	3·24	2·16	3·73	26·55	22·98	4·24	25·32
Horizontal Circm. of the Head.	21·87	4·26	9·60	1·39	3·14	0·31	0·71	10·87	20·49	3·42	0·00	4·79	1·74	8·20	0·14
Sagittal Arc ..	8·46	13·90	43·96	43·38	34·90	0·12	14·93	6·86	43·82	70·62	59·07	47·24	56·60	75·04	42·74
Transverse Arc ..	0·40	2·56	54·36	36·62	4·80	27·16	40·05	1·09	3·91	0·03	1·10	27·57	7·60	16·07	17·53
Length Breadth Index	18·40	14·76	215·53	202·89	73·18	67·34	150·82	35·00	55·96	5·36	21·41	173·71	83·30	97·45	141·12
Length Height Index	0·19	8·93	80·79	87·66	7·82	15·73	35·80	10·34	102·34	1·02	3·37	13·52	5·07	4·64	9·16
Breadth Height Index	13·70	0·01	3·94	2·09	12·89	5·29	9·72	1·72	16·20	0·33	2·49	33·43	18·92	24·00	30·56
Trans. Fronto-Parietal Index.	0·02	1·82	60·66	15·43	8·46	9·92	24·86	1·73	0·15	3·25	5·06	18·40	0·20	32·94	18·69
Orbitonasal Index ..	0·03	4·96	37·38	11·02	12·10	1·63	3·48	1·80	7·19	0·00	1·19	1·19	1·74	0·07	8·02
Nasal Index ..	21·81	15·53	8·08	14·57	15·35	1·91	1·36	2·82	0·67	6·29	0·33	0·20	0·01	5·01	0·36
Nasal Elevation Index	2·00	2·44	11·74	1·60	0·08	0·53	0·26	12·19	13·99	14·80	5·48	3·96	2·28	0·39	11·87
Upper Facial Index ..	2·43	0·01	1·40	4·99	6·78	2·29	0·13	0·48	4·86	5·22	7·98	20·52	29·77	10·89	30·24
Total Facial Index ..	1·32	0·92	1·79	1·40	0·02	3·59	0·14	0·03	0·26	1·63	7·16	42·92	28·62	29·49	48·65
Trans. Cephalo-Facial Index.	11·78	8·84	30·16	29·22	29·83	57·40	88·01	24·85	27·00	0·47	1·93	93·85	18·14	19·47	43·42
Vertical Cephalo-Facial Index.	2·16	0·02	1·62	1·87	1·37	0·21	1·54	0·21	29·30	0·06	0·65	10·79	1·86	1·81	7·50

TABLE XXX.

Brahmin with other races.

Chitpavan Brahmin.	Desastha Brahmin.	Saraswat Gour Brahmin.	Mahratta.	Nambudiri Brahmin.	Iluva.	Tamil Brahmin.	Tamil Kala.	Kanarese Brahmin.	Telegu Brahmin.	Nair.	Kadar.	Bhil.	Khasi.	Characters.
0·72	3·48	5·02	2·40	3·11	28·74	1·59	0·36	10·43	0·63	10·83	107·05	8·36	72·77	Stature.
0·18	0·36	4·37	0·14	13·19	0·75	9·14	0·15	0·05	3·88	9·15	1·31	15·85	11·71	Auricular Height.
38·94	55·32	20·86	69·14	3·23	4·32	11·68	8·08	46·28	3·75	0·10	93·62	69·66	25·44	Max. Head Length.
13·26	18·69	13·55	8·94	1·70	0·02	19·35	3·11	20·93	1·86	5·35	32·67	5·64	16·62	Max. Head Breadth.
15·94	18·09	6·94	9·90	0·49	0·65	2·27	0·43	15·19	0·89	2·21	0·51	0·00	0·39	Min. Frontal Breadth.
1·24	0·91	1·65	0·97	0·49	18·72	4·08	0·13	0·17	0·74	0·02	42·77	2·34	0·83	Max. Bizygomatic Breadth.
3·20	0·01	16·93	0·02	5·50	8·62	3·87	0·14	10·58	5·29	1·78	1·76	1·36	22·03	Bigonial Breadth.
15·84	33·78	7·00	14·99	12·17	15·93	0·29	15·96	2·46	13·52	13·36	11·93	9·44	6·72	Inter-Orbital Breadth.
0·00	0·27	5·14	4·35	8·79	1·33.	12·46	0·38	8·52	5·85	8·55	35·79	3·68	5·19	Orbitonasal Breadth.
0·71	0·14	0·48	2·70	13·27	0·57	6·89	8·23	0·25	0·03	3·64	19·86	3·67	45·82	Orbitonasal Arc.
17·53	14·22	5·28	10·27	5·27	33·14	9·33	30·15	7·75	8·21	3·47	79·47	50·86	46·55	Nasal Length.
0·10	0·19	0·38	0·01	0·01	0·12	0·38	0·12	1·50	1·19	0·85	28·51	6·42	1·86	Nasal Breadth.
48·47	47·67	19·18	40·32	0·30	35·59	8·59	29·30	10·07	7·80	3·78	172·60	59·66	211·24	Nasal Height or Depth.
28·26	25·59	5·64	22·94	2·10	26·38	5·75	18·38	10·47	7·25	2·11	44·95	60·93	5·13	Upper Facial Length.
9·38	18·50	0·49	14·39	0·05	8·47	1·28	7·37	7·59	9·11	0·72	88·05	24·16	27·57	Total Facial Length.
0·96	0·70	0·43	6·19	5·44	2·27	0·10	3·73	3·65	0·03	1·21	226·13	25·45	0·01	Horizontal Circm. of the Head.
12·73	74·61	34·48	67·74	0·21	3·43	7·03	24·38	34·79	15·05	3·83	277·46	87·98	6·66	Sagittal Arc.
0·29	8·79	16·22	1·36	17·39	3·43	17·24	2·74	9·80	5·33	30·21	454·76	12·21	4·23	Transverse Arc.
4·70	76·29	39·50	68·00	0·00	1·31	38·55	11·12	76·17	5·91	5·10	0·60	9·96	46·51	Length Breadth Index.
6·68	9·80	17·20	18·63	5·58	0·07	19·95	2·94	13·22	7·50	8·32	35·04	0·23	29·21	Length Height Index.
7·79	11·31	0·45	4·35	5·34	6·41	0·16	0·73	7·79	0·75	1·12	26·90	3·57	0·17	Breadth Height Index.
0·54	1·29	3·67	0·55	0·78	0·32	13·22	6·53	8·08	6·56	9·21	38·11	6·33	24·65	Trans. Fronto-Parietal Index.
1·61	0·05	2·54	0·06	2·41	4·44	2·68	21·07	6·81	8·75	0·50	0·29	0·13	46·89	Orbitonasal Index.
0·32	11·25	1·46	4·93	4·32	17·72	3·10	22·22	1·50	9·55	4·80	145·60	65·44	42·34	Nasal Index.
9·32	57·28	10·86	28·13	0·20	24·84	4·47	23·45	4·02	8·77	5·00	184·53	62·70	172·63	Nasal Elevation Index.
9·60	26·13	2·13	20·24	0·63	5·79	1·23	13·18	7·23	3·74	1·47	7·38	40·17	6·92	Upper Facial Index.
1·46	18·81	0·04	15·93	0·49	0·01	0·07	5·05	4·90	4·90	0·7	21·06	12·51	28·98	Total Facial Index.
4·87	25·55	40·99	10·99	6·02	19·81	66·26	8·10	42·97	8·39	11·18	1·20	2·97	21·11	Trans. Cephalo-Facial Index.
1·77	3·77	2·96	8·39	5·12	6·83	7·33	3·31	2·76	9·98	1·79	43·25	0·05	32·51	Vertical Cephalo-Facial Index.

TABLE XXXI.

Values of $\frac{N_s \; N_s'}{N_s+N_s'}\left(\frac{M_s-M_s'}{\sigma_s}\right)^2$ for Bengali

Characters.	Red Kaffir.	Pathan.	Uzbeg.	Tadjik.	Khos (Lower Chitral.)	U. P. Brahmin.	Bengali Kayastha.	Bengali Pod.	Orissa Brahmin.	Malve Brahmin.	Rajput.	Nagar Brahmin.	Audich Brahmin.	Kathi.	Bania-Jain.
Stature	2·27	9·93	6·61	2·31	24·13	5·22	0·98	21·71	16·60	10·82	0·66	10·91	11·00	0·75	15·07
Auricular Height	3·93	1·16	22·67	0·00	1·13	2·68	0·97	3·38	15·07	7·90	4·03	2·75	12·79	1·47	4·95
Max. Head Length ..	43·45	15·25	3·98	0·14	2·04	24·61	1·02	3·22	9·58	0·21	2·86	1·29	4·49	0·82	0·93
Max. Head Breadth	0·67	3·69	39·72	2·90	0·05	29·91	4·96	14·31	25·16	35·79	16·72	9·60	3·48	8·79	3·46
Min. Frontal Breadth	10·02	0·12	12·59	0·19	1·14	12·59	1·43	6·25	7·07	4·51	14·46	8·74	1·54	0·12	2·03
Max. Bizygomatic Breadth	17·59	4·25	84·46	2·61	11·57	0·03	4·80	4·51	2·00	0·02	2·93	9·32	3·64	36·03	19·67
Bigonial Breadth ..	8·26	0·00	13·07	0·27	1·57	0·24	0·17	0·28	0·31	0·14	1·37	1·15	2·38	0·17	0·00
Inter-Orbital Breadth	6·97	34·51	47·31	8·45	19·57	0·02	0·53	12·56	36·34	24·33	6·31	28·92	32·25	20·67	39·15
Orbitonasal Breadth	29·66	24·24	1·93	15·67	29·00	10·12	0·06	21·94	19·64	12·15	28·44	5·66	7·47	0·76	0·22
Orbitonasal Arc ..	11·90	23·18	23·70	2·42	35·10	2·97	0·01	16·21	18·82	4·25	7·30	3·17	4·88	0·03	1·89
Nasal Length ..	7·12	5·03	4·71	5·34	0·43	0·57	0·41	16·66	16·11	11·60	6·55	3·86	12·35	0·80	1·71
Nasal Breadth ..	3·34	1·85	0·08	12·60	5·90	1·04	1·00	0·02	0·21	2·67	0·04	0·11	0·94	0·03	2·58
Nasal Height or Depth	0·54	0·01	23·01	0·92	8·60	0·00	0·51	20·41	32·83	16·84	11·59	11·78	10·53	2·54	13·23
Upper Facial Length	1·74	0·13	5·67	3·56	4·64	2·37	0·09	13·10	25·96	16·40	16·71	28·71	48·53	3·21	32·63
Total Facial Length	0·68	0·18	8·12	3·00	0·04	3·63	1·89	10·98	16·95	11·39	17·05	54·31	48·51	14·85	52·23
Horizontal Cirm. of the Head.	16·41	2·27	6·77	1·43	1·30	0·31	0·04	14·86	27·08	5·79	0·40	2·37	3·81	5·47	0·07
Sagittal Arc ..	6·28	11·43	39·94	10·86	30·40	0·12	11·99	5·16	38·40	64·90	53·07	41·85	50·80	4·15	37·66
Transverse Arc ..	28·99	13·05	7·25	13·88	13·82	27·16	0·10	17·37	19·06	29·04	24·70	0·66	10·16	0·82	3·39
Length Breadth Index	26·89	19·04	54·21	1·78	0·56	67·34	7·88	5·25	6·29	34·70	23·50	13·17	0·06	4·56	5·86
Length Height Index	25·12	0·96	29·72	0·05	2·89	15·73	1·97	0·56	30·66	8·73	7·52	0·88	5·12	2·51	2·39
Breadth Height Index	1·12	4·92	0·00	1·29	0·97	5·29	0·21	0·98	44·63	2·98	1·16	9·04	3·00	7·46	8·28
Trans. Fronto-Parietal Index.	12·16	3·25	12·48	12·28	0·44	9·92	1·82	3·37	11·76	24·52	1·92	0·39	9·86	7·67	0·48
Orbitonasal Index ..	2·69	0·90	24·75	6·35	4·12	1·63	0·15	0·01	1·27	1·50	6·59	0·16	0·02	0·90	1·86
Nasal Index ..	9·46	6·55	2·59	18·73	5·53	1·91	0·12	9·36	6·24	15·12	4·72	1·35	2·87	0·86	4·81
Nasal Elevation Index	0·33	0·70	16·60	2·44	1·24	0·53	1·82	17·80	23·45	20·92	10·11	8·05	5·46	1·71	18·85
Upper Facial Index ..	10·94	2·01	6·40	0·67	18·67	2·29	1·93	4·85	16·38	14·42	20·90	39·58	51·58	22·34	52
Total Facial Index ..	11·13	0·88	9·17	0·31	5·28	3·59	6·53	3·01	7·96	10·05	23·65	76·68	56·41	52·08	83
Trans. Cephalo-Facial Index.	28·25	21·19	1·60	15·29	9·79	57·40	0·40	6·72	16·22	68·27	54·13	0·76	19·19	7·45	4
Vertical Cephalo-Facial Index..	0·90	0·33	2·81	1·76	10·07	0·21	3·12	0·83	35·22	0·05	1·77	14·52	3·53	3·14	10

TABLE XXXI.

...amin with other races.

...h-...	Desastha Brahmin.	Saraswat Gour Brahmin.	Mahratta.	Nambudiri Brahmin.	Iluva.	Tamil Brahmin.	Tamil Kala.	Kanarese Brahmin.	Telegu Brahmin.	Nair.	Kadar.	Bhils.	Khasi.	Characters.
25	20·64	20·47	15·42	16·81	58·45	12·58	2·41	30·41	9·49	0·82	169·86	26·80	122·58	Stature.
37	6·30	0·21	4·28	3·82	6·27	1·92	1·35	2·03	0·11	1·73	0·61	31·58	2·64	Auricular Height.
24	2·71	0·16	9·95	47·26	8·31	2·38	3·36	3·40	9·14	23·70	14·76	11·47	0·22	Max. Head Length.
32	4·26	3·20	7·29	18·42	31·21	1·15	11·52	0·80	16·86	11·56	147·56	61·54	4·02	Max. Head Breadth.
02	0·01	0·84	0·30	8·59	18·97	4·18	10·03	0·12	6·80	4·92	23·37	14·78	20·92	Min. Frontal Breadth.
70	1·31	1·26	1·34	0·28	17·33	3·45	0·04	0·06	0·48	0·00	40·29	1·87	1·19	Max. Bizygomatic Breadth.
53	0·21	21·15	0·14	8·07	11·69	6·01	0·68	13·96	7·75	3·39	3·59	2·72	17·27	Bigonial Breadth.
12	35·62	7·73	16·10	13·15	17·02	0·45	16·99	2·90	14·53	2·11	13·05	10·28	7·21	Inter-Orbital Breadth.
00	17·94	0·84	29·10	0·08	4·11	2·07	5·68	0·07	0·58	0·16	94·53	25·99	33·81	Orbitonasal Breadth.
34	5·66	1·06	11·80	3·53	6·15	0·81	20·19	1·50	3·61	0·01	41·95	13·25	75·44	Orbitonasal Arc.
65	21·66	9·33	15·94	9·43	42·43	14·52	38·49	12·54	13·12	7·04	96·13	62·28	58·74	Nasal Length.
75	2·65	0·17	0·98	1·24	0·46	0·17	1·73	0·04	4·45	3·96	42·77	12·64	6·23	Nasal Breadth.
47	47·67	19·18	40·32	0·30	35·59	8·69	29·30	10·07	7·80	3·78	172·61	59·66	211·24	Nasal Height or depth.
43	46·99	15·32	40·84	9·13	44·55	15·50	32·92	22·79	17·90	9·36	72·48	87·31	15·80	Upper Facial Length.
79	42·57	6·76	33·34	2·95	23·18	9·21	20·34	0·22	24·23	1·30	135·09	46·50	54·29	Total Facial Length.
65	2·22	1·48	9·42	3·10	4·26	0·06	6·03	6·09	0·15	0·27	246·26	31·38	0·24	Horizontal Cirm. of the Head.
15	67·77	30·52	87·90	0·66	2·26	5·31	21·25	30·82	12·49	2·54	264·01	81·57	5·47	Sagittal Arc.
41	9·73	1·40	18·10	1·35	11·29	1·12	10·62	4·33	8·42	0·00	753·65	75·77	2·47	Transverse Arc.
52	0·72	3·69	0·08	69·89	49·86	3·99	19·38	0·27	33·36	39·84	78·71	25·51	5·32	Length Breadth Index.
07	2·25	0·03	0·05	2·88	13·72	0·25	4·10	0·11	1·51	1·58	1·56	12·17	1·10	Length Height Index.
02	0·46	2·65	0·08	21·77	2·76	3·61	1·72	0·24	10·03	11·98	02·26	0·17	8·64	Breadth Height Index.
53	6·45	1·52	6·42	5·49	6·66	0·24	0·17	1·95	5·77	3·80	93·38	32·10	2·14	Trans. Fronto-Parietal Index.
56	2·92	0·10	2·49	8·18	0·69	0·13	11·47	1·78	2·83	0·39	4·14	8·40	29·45	Orbitonasal Index.
18	24·67	6·71	13·37	12·18	31·24	9·87	36·19	6·78	19·98	13·19	187·41	89·68	64·08	Nasal Index.
17	48·36	16·18	36·73	1·43	32·61	8·08	30·56	7·47	13·61	8·98	208·48	74·73	194·52	Nasal Elevation Index.
80	47·32	8·84	36·89	6·01	15·36	6·87	25·58	17·66	11·88	7·81	20·22	61·64	18·60	Upper Facial Index.
18	42·90	2·88	35·56	1·52	3·31	2·67	16·26	16·88	16·88	1·21	46·48	29·50	56·11	Total Facial Index.
36	14·37	1·38	20·86	27·73	9·77	0·32	18·46	1·04	21·90	20·88	100·05	86·47	14·68	Trans. Cephalo-Facial Index.
44	6·10	4·72	5·33	7·42	1·86	9·98	5·04	4·47	13·04	3·28	50·52	0·46	38·42	Vertical Cephalo-Facial Index.

TABLE XXXII.

Values of $\frac{N_s N_s'}{N_s+N_s'}\left(\frac{M_s-M_s'}{\sigma_s}\right)^2$ for Benga

Characters.	Red Kaffir.	Pathan.	Uzbeg.	Tadjik.	Khos (Lower Chitral).	U. P. Brahmin.	Bengali Brahmin.	Bengali. Pod.	Orissa Brahmin.	Malve Brahmin.	Rajput.	Nagar Brahmin.	Audich Brahmin.	Kathi.	Bania Jain
Stature	0·40	7·01	4·07	1·35	22·86	2·71	0·98	19·25	14·57	7·88	4·87	8·03	8·10	0·00	12·5
Auricular Height	13·21	0·07	19·98	12·03	6·08	8·27	0·97	9·65	12·60	18·87	13·41	10·62	30·59	5·22	15·4
Max. Head Length ..	86·67	30·46	1·84	6·03	8·63	45·39	1·02	1·13	6·56	2·36	10·94	0·02	1·87	3·85	0·0
Max. Head Breadth	13·93	19·75	26·20	3·52	5·67	72·95	4·96	43·49	86·12	83·43	59·83	1·10	24·47	1·69	0·2
Min. Frontal Breadth	5·83	2·56	8·60	10·62	0·02	28·01	1·43	16·66	24·28	13·30	37·46	4·64	0·00	0·52	0·0
Max. Bizygomatic Breadth.	6·02	0·04	70·16	36·42	2·30	4·01	4·80	21·54	22·07	4·20	0·35	1·08	0·10	27·19	7·5
Bigonial Breadth ..	9·10	0·18	13·58	3·90	1·06	0·94	0·17	1·04	1·57	0·00	3·75	3·35	5·63	0·72	0·2
Inter-Orbital Breadth	5·51	36·70	4·98	38·29	20·30	0·32	0·53	11·33	72·20	24·71	4·79	32·63	36·47	20·09	45·8
Orbitonasal Breadth	48·70	35·24	3·13	14·75	46·75	15·40	0·06	32·03	35·00	18·05	46·79	10·47	13·18	1·49	0·7
Orbitonasal Arc ..	16·99	29·98	28·79	21·09	50·31	3·63	0·01	20·83	28·66	5·27	10·26	4·35	6·69	0·01	2·4
Nasal Length ..	6·17	3·80	3·50	2·22	0·00	2·29	0·41	28·63	34·92	20·90	15·35	10·31	25·47	0·17	5·(
Nasal Breadth ..	12·00	6·62	1·41	7·83	17·17	0·03	1·00	0·71	3·63	0·78	0·97	2·74	5·69	1·23	0·[illegible]
Nasal Height or Depth	0·00	0·36	22·45	9·57	7·32	0·51	0·51	22·07	39·31	16·17	10·84	11·10	9·54	1·31	12·7
Upper Facial Length	1·56	0·01	8·52	0·57	5·10	2·18	0·09	15·05	36·27	19·14	21·53	38·66	65·93	3·07	43·
Total Facial Length	0·46	3·46	19·11	10·35	1·92	0·68	1·89	6·00	11·29	6·35	11·37	54·11	46·56	9·58	51·
Horizontal Cirm. of the Head.	22·04	2·37	7·47	0·23	1·31	0·71	0·04	21·63	46·53	8·87	1·04	2·70	6·84	6·08	0
Sagittal Arc ..	1·37	0·19	16·59	12·99	6·58	14·93	11·99	0·71	10·29	34·09	21·91	13·41	20·36	39·00	10
Transverse Arc ..	48·68	20·09	7·51	0·11	23·87	40·05	0·10	26·25	35·01	42·69	41·85	1·93	18·10	1·73	6·
Length Breadth Index	95·81	61·54	33·69	12·89	18·11	150·82	7·88	29·70	47·48	92·30	87·88	0·97	13·37	0·03	0·
Length Height Index	61·76	6·40	23·81	21·14	13·97	35·80	1·97	5·15	25·63	23·19	25·79	8·38	19·69	9·60	13·
Breadth Height Index	0·53	9·14	2·24	2·69	0·41	9·72	0·21	2·58	78·55	6·04	3·56	10·53	2·41	7·12	8·
Trans. Fronto-Parietal Index.	35·09	11·76	7·74	0·52	5·83	24·86	1·82	19·40	37·21	49·94	11·24	0·82	29·58	3·58	0·
Orbitonasal Index ..	6·18	0·60	27·25	3·63	3·99	3·48	0·15	0·10	0·82	3·21	13·10	0·93	0·40	2·06	
Nasal Index ..	17·56	10·89	4·40	9·91	10·67	1·56	0·12	10·17	7·24	17·18	5·01	1·01	2·71	1·91	5·
Nasal Elevation Index	5·56	5·38	11·46	0·88	0·07	0·26	1·82	12·40	18·57	15·45	5·03	3·29	1·49	0·05	12·
Upper Facial Index ..	5·52	0·06	2·65	9·06	12·89	0·13	1·93	1·33	10·60	8·98	15·20	36·19	50·03	16·60	51·
Total Facial Index ..	0·91	2·17	1·38	1·00	0·07	0·14	6·53	0·31	0·02	1·22	7·99	57·76	36·84	33·83	65·
Trans. Cephalo-Facial Index.	53·10	35·39	3·84	13·66	20·73	88·01	0·40	13·15	35·02	103·50	95·80	0·08	37·15	13·57	11·
Vertical Cephalo-Facial Index.	11·05	1·22	0·12	0·08	8·42	1·54	3·12	0·51	26·09	2·32	0·28	6·24	0·03	0·14	3

TABLE XXXII.

…stha with other races.

…	Desastha Brahmin.	Saraswat Gour Brahmin.	Mahratta.	Nambudiri Brahmin.	Iluva.	Tamil Brahmin.	Tamil Kala.	Kanarese Brahmin.	Telegu Brahmin.	Nair.	Kadar.	Bhil.	Khasi.	Characters.
15	18·90	17·92	12·62	14·06	61·41	9·64	0·71	28·90	6·58	4·46	220·92	24·85	148·12	Stature.
18	18·64	0·21	11·85	1·59	15·01	0·38	4·96	6·91	0·36	0·25	4·87	55·83	0·68	Auricular Height.
12	0·59	2·14	6·91	81·77	18·81	7·79	9·08	1·25	20·25	45·96	12·11	8·41	3·02	Max. Head Length.
32	28·23	18·42	30·37	53·18	75·29	11·99	34·92	10·62	48·54	40·30	317·53	127·33	24·93	Max. Head Breadth.
55	1·83	5·06	3·61	21·56	38·73	12·63	31·89	0·63	17·69	14·97	54·92	31·74	47·44	Min. Frontal Breadth.
12	1·74	12·16	0·92	8·20	48·98	18·80	5·10	6·12	8·96	5·23	112·49	14·22	1·51	Max. Bizygomatic Breadth.
52	1·16	32·73	0·75	13·92	18·99	10·50	1·74	22·33	13·14	6·73	8·17	5·36	20·46	Bigonial Breadth.
51	41·58	6·16	15·47	12·06	16·31	0·00	16·02	1·54	13·52	13·54	12·62	8·86	5·75	Inter-Orbital Breadth.
05	30·57	1·71	43·33	0·35	6·71	1·98	8·61	0·31	1·28	0·54	152·17	37·68	53·10	Orbitonasal Breadth.
74	7·98	1·22	15·47	5·17	7·73	1·27	25·18	1·77	4·45	0·05	62·25	16·96	107·17	Orbitonasal Arc.
11	42·63	17·35	28·63	17·93	66·59	25·40	58·18	22·35	23·25	4·56	167·08	95·10	99·24	Nasal Length.
03	0·57	0·28	0·01	0·07	0·05	0·28	0·32	1·53	2·06	1·61	46·56	9·63	3·40	Nasal Breadth.
13	57·93	18·83	44·62	0·01	38·09	7·12	29·97	8·68	6·29	2·31	235·28	67·27	277·38	Nasal Height or Depth
19	65·09	17·80	51·36	10·29	54·85	18·02	38·79	27·16	21·02	10·69	102·94	110·01	19·66	Upper Facial Length.
10	39·96	2·65	28·19	0·34	17·49	4·52	14·74	16·03	18·55	0·02	159·65	42·21	54·36	Total Facial Length.
4	4·34	2·57	14·48	3·40	6·67	0·23	8·82	9·31	0·41	1·56	386·21	44·47	0·42	Horizontal Circm. of the Head.
0	33·94	8·50	53·65	20·43	2·99	0·64	4·09	8·68	0·38	3·26	247·32	48·51	0·07	Sagittal Arc.
9	17·90	2·82	28·21	2·81	17·57	2·35	15·87	7·36	13·41	0·07	1178·56	107·39	3·52	Transverse Arc.
7	20·58	25·24	10·90	159·40	120·09	26·13	57·60	4·86	89·78	107·70	210·25	74·61	36·31	Length Breadth Index.
2	12·92	1·43	1·45	11·73	32·28	0·68	12·93	3·18	7·96	8·79	0·05	29·51	0·12	Length Height Index.
8	0·07	5·49	0·67	34·90	5·67	7·05	3·67	0·01	16·97	20·70	106·86	0·88	16·35	Breadth Height Index.
3	23·12	7·70	19·28	16·97	18·75	0·62	2·95	8·77	17·00	13·82	183·04	62·27	0·04	Trans. Fronto-Parietal Index.
8	6·71	0·00	5·11	13·93	32·33	0·00	12·10	1·32	2·40	1·32	9·01	2·10	36·92	Orbitonasal Index.
9	32·35	7·00	15·36	13·74	37·32	10·78	42·28	7·09	23·20	15·16	271·91	112·15	86·04	Nasal Index.
l	47·38	10·85	32·17	0·00	27·49	3·73	25·18	3·26	8·46	4·33	260·81	74·50	231·47	Nasal Elevation Index.
	45·46	4·18	31·89	2·03	9·84	2·68	19·80	11·76	6·71	3·26	14·52	58·93	12·82	Upper Facial Index.
	23·85	0·35	18·37	1·41	0·21	0·45	4·87	4·79	4·79	2·03	27·14	13·80	36·60	Total Facial Index.
	29·79	3·96	36·21	45·83	17·99	0·00	29·80	1·70	36·45	36·36	173·26	129·29	28·55	Trans. Cephalo-Facial Index.
	0·71	0·55	0·73	1·82	0·04	3·55	0·83	0·46	11·78	0·06	43·09	0·97	29·24	Vertical Cephalo-Facial Index.

TABLE XXXIII.

Values of $\frac{N_s\ N_s'}{N_s+N_s'}\left(\frac{M_s-M_s'}{\sigma_s}\right)^2$ for Beng

Characters.	Red Kaffir.	Pathan.	Uzbeg.	Tadjik.	Khos. (Lower Chitral).	U. P. Brahmins.	Bengali Brahmin.	Bengali Kayastha.	Orissa Brahmin.	Malve Brahmin.	Rajput.	Nagar Brahmin.	Audich Brahmin.	Kathi.	Ba Ja
Stature	15·00	2·27	2·42	9·05	0·14	5·64	21·71	19·25	2·55	1·88	38·31	4·49	3·99	12·44	
Auricular Height ..	0·02	8·50	41·09	33·40	1·04	0·04	3·38	9·65	36·05	0·95	0·01	0·23	2·21	0·27	
Max. Head Length ..	75·07	32·50	0·15	1·25	12·00	45·64	3·22	1·13	0·83	5·07	14·17	0·91	0·00	6·75	
Max. Head Breadth	12·58	34·68	91·41	57·86	20·37	2·84	14·31	43·49	0·17	4·84	0·08	56·26	6·03	42·66	
Min. Frontal Breadth	36·63	4·63	119·93	42·14	15·22	1·10	6·25	16·66	0·14	0·14	0·84	34·42	16·69	7·29	
Max. Bizygomatic Breadth.	44·16	17·50	16·31	87·66	33·73	5·23	4·51	21·54	1·36	5·04	17·30	30·50	18·74	70·37	
Bigonial Breadth ..	12·14	0·27	13·50	6·81	3·43	0·00	0·28	1·04	0·00	0·83	3·12	2·10	0·89	0·01	
Inter-Orbital Breadth	2·10	5·44	7·59	4·82	0·16	11·62	12·56	11·33	10·20	1·93	2·49	1·57	3·78	1·45	
Orbitonasal Breadth	0·00	0·06	1·60	3·58	0·01	2·26	21·94	32·03	1·62	1·42	0·01	9·39	6·81	12·55	
Orbitonasal Arc ..	1·44	0·62	32·94	0·06	1·85	5·30	16·21	20·83	0·31	3·86	3·76	8·44	5·63	13·17	
Nasal Length ..	54·47	40·00	0·16	37·73	27·94	11·05	16·66	28·63	0·95	0·46	4·64	7·75	1·30	22·46	
Nasal Breadth ..	3·93	2·24	0·37	2·60	6·68	0·78	0·02	0·71	3·86	2·24	0·00	0·24	1·27	0·18	
Nasal Height or Depth	21·89	21·03	30·71	2·73	5·69	21·99	20·41	22·07	0·00	0·34	4·04	4·11	4·43	8·00	
Upper Facial Length	8·18	10·62	32·90	17·45	3·80	4·33	13·10	15·05	0·47	0·19	0·01	0·56	8·06	2·63	
Total Facial Length	9·02	13·92	35·61	24·68	12·57	1·99	10·98	6·00	0·01	0·01	0·09	12·35	10·16	0·53	
Horizontal Cirm. of the Head.	71·99	28·74	18·01	21·61	30·38	10·87	14·86	21·63	0·27	2·10	14·58	36·31	5·93	35·67	
Sagittal Arc ..	0·01	1·23	40·11	14·68	8·64	6·86	5·16	0·71	11·78	33·47	21·74	14·64	20·59	38·36	
Transverse Arc ..	0·33	0·31	32·59	24·54	1·02	1·09	17·37	26·25	0·07	1·49	0·03	23·99	2·45	9·15	
Length Breadth Index	6·46	4·30	86·37	64·32	3·41	35·00	5·25	29·70	0·08	12·96	4·86	39·61	5·66	18·44	
Length Height Index	17·19	0·05	36·58	35·74	0·72	10·34	0·56	5·15	41·00	4·86	3·52	0·00	1·99	0·77	
Breadth Height Index	4·85	1·51	0·65	0·01	4·44	1·72	0·98	2·58	30·66	0·54	0·00	18·13	8·18	13·43	
Trans. Fronto-Parietal Index.	1·87	0·00	26·08	6·47	2·01	1·73	3·37	19·40	1·44	9·72	0·54	7·61	1·11	20·25	
Orbitonasal Index ..	2·94	0·78	23·60	3·63	3·82	1·80	0·01	0·10	1·10	1·64	7·01	0·22	0·05	1·02	
Nasal Index ..	43·68	31·58	18·38	31·17	33·89	2·82	9·36	10·17	1·50	0·69	1·85	5·75	3·23	14·59	
Nasal Elevation Index.	29·65	25·55	0·10	5·80	13·45	12·19	17·80	12·40	0·09	1·26	2·86	4·30	6·12	7·12	
Upper Facial Index ..	0·58	0·62	3·13	2·27	3·32	0·48	4·85	1·33	1·86	2·54	4·14	13·90	21·81	7·02	
Total Facial Index ..	1·78	0·64	2·14	1·83	0·11	6·03	3·01	0·31	0·49	2·06	8·16	45·28	30·52	28·84	
Trans. Cephalo-Facial Index.	5·40	4·05	1·07	0·02	0·04	24·85	6·72	13·15	0·76	32·16	19·05	15·10	2·03	0·08	
Vertical Cephalo-Facial Index.	4·00	0·12	0·73	0·78	2·86	0·21	0·83	0·51	23·85	0·49	0·08	7·57	0·71	0·83	

TABLE XXXIII.

'ith other races.

Desastha Brahmin.	Saraswat Gour Brahmin.	Mahratta.	Nambudiri Brahmin.	Iluva.	Tamil Brahmin.	Tamil Kala.	Kanarese Brahmin.	Telegu Brahmin.	Nair.	Kadar.	Bhil.	Khasi.	Characters.
0·83	0·02	0·85	0·33	8·92	1·24	8·10	0·73	2·50	33·29	57·07	0·03	34·60	Stature.
1·34	5·25	0·03	14·72	0·44	10·38	0·33	0·17	4·71	10·46	1·90	14·30	13·26	Auricular Height.
0·20	4·79	1·65	75·90	21·83	11·15	12·43	0·00	23·22	45·48	3·00	2·53	6·10	Max. Head Length.
5·54	4·23	1·53	0·18	3·25	7·36	0·03	8·35	0·11	0·30	59·27	16·50	4·85	Max. Head Breadth.
9·17	2·52	4·23	0·14	3·44	0·21	2·71	8·12	0·01	0·16	3·74	1·81	3·22	Min. Frontal Breadth.
13·12	1·00	11·32	2·66	4·17	0·70	3·24	3·53	2·04	6·06	14·84	0·57	11·90	Max. Bizygomatic Breadth.
0·02	16·56	0·03	5·29	8·35	3·69	0·11	10·29	5·08	1·00	1·62	1·25	22·51	Bigonial Breadth.
3·36	0·58	0·11	0·00	0·34	0·40	0·61	3·28	0·07	0·01	0·31	0·11	0·05	Inter-Orbital Breadth.
1·52	14·21	0·27	20·29	7·07	37·48	4·14	19·56	15·38	20·20	17·76	0·17	0·37	Orbitonasal Breadth.
5·39	8·97	0·57	35·99	2·39	24·28	0·49	7·85	4·52	18·61	3·08	0·15	17·71	Orbitonasal Arc.
0·01	1·06	0·06	1·22	5·92	0·07	5·56	0·29	0·21	2·59	25·06	14·52	9·77	Nasal Length.
2·16	0·08	0·72	0·95	0·30	0·08	1·41	0·12	3·89	3·41	40·70	11·69	5·50	Nasal Breadth.
2·04	0·10	2·16	18·09	1·63	3·09	0·98	2·30	3·60	8·72	58·11	9·21	86·84	Nasal Height or Depth.
6·91	0·09	6·89	0·47	9·33	0·10	5·41	1·33	0·37	0·53	1·81	32·77	0·00	Upper Facial Length.
7·06	0·51	5·41	2·79	2·26	0·08	1·92	1·81	2·59	5·38	59·71	12·29	13·57	Total Facial Length.
9·07	6·97	0·89	32·57	3·21	13·06	1·39	1·92	12·07	20·65	124·55	3·05	4·83	Horizontal Circm. of the Head.
31·14	10·58	12·51	9·85	0·59	0·00	6·09	10·76	1·60	0·61	184·35	45·70	0·57	Sagittal Arc.
3·05	8·90	0·01	9·62	0·65	9·67	0·45	4·36	1·60	19·42	508·61	20·59	1·77	Transverse Arc.
3·34	0·14	4·37	36·19	22·76	0·09	5·03	7·91	12·15	15·37	38·18	7·62	0·06	Length Breadth Index.
0·39	0·87	1·01	0·87	8·73	1·56	1·74	0·18	0·28	0·23	4·57	7·50	3·50	Length Height Index.
3·37	0·41	0·55	13·34	0·45	0·83	0·14	2·20	4·74	5·89	45·25	0·34	3·43	Breadth Height Index.
0·16	0·36	0·39	0·22	0·56	5·39	1·73	0·19	0·32	0·01	56·77	14·68	12·27	Trans. Fronto-Parietal Index.
3·18	0·06	2·71	8·57	0·59	0·09	11·05	1·60	2·61	0·48	4·46	0·97	28·67	Orbitonasal Index.
1·94	0·22	0·22	0·13	6·40	0·01	0·80	0·21	1·99	0·19	101·85	41·10	21·52	Nasal Index.
4·12	0·04	2·79	9·74	2·23	1·90	2·40	2·21	0·28	1·99	89·83	19·59	85·66	Nasal Elevation Index.
18·55	0·59	14·30	0·04	2·95	0·18	8·89	4·00	1·55	0·24	3·64	31·91	3·47	Upper Facial Index.
20·41	0·00	17·24	0·29	0·01	0·01	5·73	5·62	5·62	0·51	22·76	13·63	30·92	Total Facial Index.
0·59	2·01	3·50	6·95	0·29	9·96	3·44	2·47	4·36	3·47	48·37	44·99	0·87	Trans. Cephalo-Facial Index.
1·98	1·59	1·90	3·21	0·21	5·06	1·92	1·45	7·29	0·74	36·44	0·06	27·02	Vertical Cephalo-Facial Index.

TABLE XXXIV.

Values of $\frac{N_s\, N_s'}{N_s+N_s'}\left(\frac{M_s-M_s'}{\sigma_s}\right)^2$ for Orissa

Characters.	Red Kaffir.	Pathan.	Uzbeg.	Tadjik.	Khos (Lower Chitral).	U. P. Brahmin.	Bengali Brahmin.	Bengali Kayastha.	Bengali Pod.	Malvo Brahmin.	Rajput.	Nagar Brahmin.	Audich Brahmin.	Kathi.	Bania-Jain.
Stature	9·81	0·03	0·23	4·14	2·15	1·67	16·60	14·57	2·55	0·00	38·58	0·62	0·43	7·38	0·00
Auricular Height ..	51·61	6·95	3·83	0·13	35·05	33·33	15·07	12·60	33·05	53·78	52·02	47·04	81·10	24·68	55·75
Max. Head Length ..	160·30	61·63	0·10	0·17	31·96	83·45	9·58	6·50	0·83	13·34	37·82	50·46	1·06	15·35	6·83
Max. Head Breadth	27·36	7·17	134·23	69·04	41·20	2·70	25·16	86·12	0·17	5·14	0·79	111·38	13·02	66·01	75·02
Min. Frontal Breadth	56·77	5·00	40·66	59·02	21·49	2·72	7·07	24·28	0·14	0·01	2·83	53·72	23·88	8·11	27·24
Max. Bizygomatic Breadth.	54·14	15·41	141·07	109·03	38·30	2·61	2·00	22·07	1·36	2·45	16·44	34·71	18·14	78·81	58·74
Bigonial Breadth ..	20·43	0·30	21·84	10·05	5·40	0·00	0·31	1·57	0·00	1·04	0·72	0·51	1·79	0·00	0·45
Inter-Orbital Breadth	35·42	0·13	2·57	0·50	11·33	53·91	36·34	72·20	10·20	2·20	37·52	5·80	3·18	2·26	1·29
Orbitonasal Breadth	2·74	2·45	4·64	0·98	2·73	0·31	19·64	35·00	1·62	0·03	2·26	6·09	3·48	0·20	24·49
Orbitonasal Arc ..	0·79	2·30	3·83	0·08	6·06	5·03	18·82	28·66	0·31	3·35	3·48	10·02	5·91	14·34	13·20
Nasal Length ..	74·03	45·49	32·21	44·19	33·24	9·57	16·11	34·92	0·95	0·02	2·75	6·26	0·11	22·51	10·94
Nasal Breadth ..	3·43	1·44	0·00	1·80	6·91	2·88	0·21	3·63	3·86	5·97	0·70	0·02	0·51	0·05	7·39
Nasal Height or Depth	38·98	31·41	0·49	4·35	9·94	32·83	32·83	39·31	0·00	0·54	7·28	7·40	7·82	11·38	5·63
Upper Facial Length	21·80	21·67	50·40	35·59	11·54	10·39	25·96	36·27	0·47	0·03	0·98	0·44	8·33	6·53	1·39
Total Facial Length	16·78	21·40	46·42	39·71	22·58	3·24	16·95	11·29	0·01	0·00	0·09	21·06	16·73	0·62	19·50
Horizontal Cirm. of the Head.	141·79	49·50	55·47	40·47	61·55	20·49	27·08	46·53	0·27	5·19	32·67	75·75	14·67	57·04	38·28
Sagittal Arc ..	20·03	4·33	4·23	1·17	0·12	43·82	38·40	10·29	11·78	13·04	3·50	0·53	3·03	17·59	0·13
Transverse Arc ..	2·73	0·00	46·80	29·46	0·21	3·91	19·06	35·01	0·07	4·81	1·21	20·18	1·41	8·63	9·45
Length Breadth Index.	13·90	7·83	114·17	94·56	4·33	55·96	6·29	47·48	0·08	21·74	10·76	64·95	22·08	23·40	40·51
Length Height Index	166·95	44·43	17·24	0·03	75·10	102·34	30·66	25·63	41·00	89·08	102·83	64·30	88·22	47·95	74·93
Breadth Height Index	89·84	16·97	32·38	36·17	83·87	16·20	44·63	76·55	30·66	21·96	47·10	146·41	102·37	86·16	136·49
Trans. Fronto-Parietal Index.	0·09	1·34	49·19	19·97	11·00	0·15	11·76	37·21	1·44	6·66	6·15	27·09	0·01	41·31	27·20
Orbitonasal Index ..	12·93	0·00	23·17	1·33	1·64	7·19	1·27	0·82	1·10	6·74	23·22	3·85	2·51	4·66	0·13
Nasal Index ..	52·36	31·52	15·93	31·97	37·63	0·67	6·24	7·24	1·50	1·76	0·07	2·68	0·73	11·59	0·05
Nasal Elevation Index	47·15	34·35	0·37	7·27	19·81	13·99	23·45	13·57	0·00	0·53	3·53	5·75	4·31	12·30	0·10
Upper Facial Index ..	0·49	5·38	0·25	0·17	0·08	4·80	16·38	10·60	1·86	0·33	0·95	10·49	19·02	3·57	20·49
Total Facial Index ..	0·77	2·82	1·24	0·86	0·19	0·26	7·96	0·02	0·40	1·08	8·45	65·64	41·06	35·02	74·15
Trans. Cephalo-Facial Index.	3·95	2·49	3·83	1·31	0·66	27·00	16·22	35·02	0·76	36·37	22·10	38·81	0·64	0·21	4·01
Vertical Cephalo-Facial Index.	71·09	34·47	10·55	17·58	61·99	29·30	35·22	26·09	23·85	32·40	31·80	7·13	23·35	17·60	10·64

TABLE XXXIV.

Brahmin with other races.

Chitpavan Brahmin.	Desastha Brahmin.	Saraswat Gour Brahmin.	Mahratta.	Nambudiri Brahmin.	Iluva.	Tamil Brahmin.	Tamil Kala.	Kanarese Brahmin.	Telegu Brahmin.	Nair.	Kadar.	Bhil.	Khasi.	Characters.
0·26	0·70	2·06	0·31	0·69	27·39	0·06	3·61	6·97	0·10	30·00	150·38	1·86	90·34	Stature.
58·30	62·83	11·29	41·81	2·90	45·87	5·21	24·12	30·55	12·24	6·64	34·09	7·20	6·13	Auricular Height.
10·82	3·15	12·79	0·40	136·24	43·62	24·75	25·19	0·73	45·93	87·77	1·32	1·05	18·23	Max. Head Length.
7·66	13·56	8·05	3·88	0·01	3·19	13·79	0·34	15·42	0·00	1·26	96·88	20·03	11·10	Max. Head Breadth.
10·30	12·66	2·40	4·61	0·71	6·90	0·03	5·26	9·51	0·25	0·01	9·26	4·08	7·58	Min. Frontal Breadth.
12·51	11·24	0·00	8·65	0·65	13·34	0·72	1·13	1·25	0·33	2·41	45·05	0·06	9·50	Max. Bizygomatic Breadth.
5·86	0·01	25·32	0·02	8·49	12·94	5·83	0·22	15·87	7·98	2·86	3·31	2·09	36·36	Bigonial Breadth.
16·21	2·72	17·00	8·92	10·94	6·17	44·75	4·03	29·52	8·22	10·86	24·07	12·99	3·07	Inter-Orbital Breadth.
0·41	0·00	10·99	4·00	17·88	3·85	38·18	1·54	16·90	12·26	17·94	53·85	3·16	5·23	Orbitonasal Breadth.
15·75	5·71	9·51	0·12	46·28	1·75	29·54	1·80	8·12	4·11	22·75	9·49	0·01	37·15	Orbitonasal Arc.
2·73	1·16	0·09	0·49	0·14	15·33	0·39	13·48	0·09	0·16	0·97	63·83	31·29	26·72	Nasal Length.
3·02	7·66	0·91	2·94	3·40	0·44	0·91	3·91	0·04	9·14	8·78	88·54	22·88	14·19	Nasal Breadth.
4·01	3·57	0·16	3·26	27·66	2·35	4·67	1·34	3·49	5·43	13·68	105·02	33·32	144·63	Nasal Height or Depth.
8·96	6·95	0·11	6·40	2·41	9·18	0·09	4·51	0·51	0·00	2·67	22·43	39·43	0·77	Upper Facial Length.
5·39	11·91	0·90	7·85	4·61	3·04	0·18	2·45	2·42	3·52	8·83	106·21	17·50	21·75	Total Facial Length.
19·76	22·02	13·83	2·95	57·08	7·26	24·12	3·50	4·85	22·48	38·47	205·86	2·59	7·37	Horizontal Circm. of the Head.
19·62	9·41	0·28	25·69	55·03	19·07	11·50	0·05	0·31	3·59	21·47	191·37	23·02	6·19	Sagittal Arc.
3·26	2·04	8·55	0·42	9·54	0·07	9·47	0·02	3·36	0·70	22·38	980·93	38·83	3·65	Transverse Arc.
0·13	4·37	0·03	5·30	59·27	37·06	0·01	8·51	9·80	20·47	26·82	75·57	13·25	0·00	Length Breadth Index.
86·65	76·42	28·38	30·46	59·12	96·32	24·60	55·09	35·02	48·36	5·40	29·10	91·49	25·48	Length Height Index.
70·46	83·81	23·04	1·21	2·14	22·68	20·14	22·07	52·52	9·14	0·16	1·80	38·54	16·70	Breadth Height Index.
0·23	1·02	3·73	0·25	0·45	0·09	16·15	7·08	3·01	0·26	1·54	71·86	11·89	35·16	Trans. Fronto-Parietal Index.
25·95	13·95	0·55	9·97	21·97	0·01	0·48	8·86	0·24	0·84	0·70	17·59	5·03	32·22	Orbitonasal Index.
10·53	11·87	0·43	3·58	2·93	18·54	1·76	23·43	0·45	8·67	1·85	231·04	81·55	55·48	Nasal Index.
4·80	9·58	0·00	5·70	12·54	4·45	1·92	4·45	2·30	0·13	1·84	173·10	32·27	151·67	Nasal Elevation Index.
19·84	16·14	0·18	10·56	1·32	0·52	0·73	5·21	1·14	0·02	12·72	0·63	30·37	0·64	Upper Facial Index.
14·91	26·54	0·57	19·48	1·92	0·37	0·70	4·81	4·76	4·76	0·34	30·43	14·38	40·33	Total Facial Index.
2·14	0·01	6·75	1·96	5·42	0·05	22·22	1·95	7·75	2·79	7·16	67·88	53·18	0·04	Trans. Cephalo-Facial Index.
25·46	18·93	11·75	12·24	8·71	19·02	5·23	8·69	12·26	3·12	0·30	1·72	26·58	0·44	Vertical Cephalo-Facial Index.

TABLE XXXV.

Values of $\frac{N_s N_s'}{N_s+N_s'}\left(\frac{M_s-M_s'}{\sigma_s}\right)^2$ for Rajput

Characters.	Red Kaffir.	Pa-than.	Uzbeg.	Tad-jik.	Khos (Lower Chitral).	U. P. Brah-min.	Bengali Brah-min.	Bengali Kayas-tha.	Bengali Pod.	Orissa Brah-min.	Malve Brah-min.	Nagar Brah-min.	Audich Brah-min.	Kathi.	Bania —Jain
Stature	8·11	19·79	12·70	9·58	48·02	11·89	0·66	4·87	38·31	38·58	21·23	25·67	25·12	3·00	32·9
Auricular Height ..	0·00	10·57	49·71	44·52	1·21	0·01	4·03	13·41	0·01	52·02	1·53	0·20	3·78	0·23	0·0
Max. Head Length ..	36·03	7·94	13·59	28·61	0·08	16·30	2·86	10·94	14·17	37·82	1·35	12·21	21·28	0·29	10·5
Max. Head Breadth	16·02	3·50	111·68	74·73	26·49	4·96	16·72	59·83	0·08	0·79	7·95	78·82	7·00	51·09	52·8
Min. Frontal Breadth	72·84	11·55	52·47	74·48	33·96	0·09	14·46	37·46	0·84	2·83	1·82	69·72	36·80	15·27	40·8
Max. Bizygomatic Breadth.	9·37	0·45	77·32	42·94	4·38	2·31	2·93	0·35	17·30	16·44	2·46	2·67	0·07	32·05	11·1
Bigonial Breadth ..	24·63	1·33	25·49	13·46	8·50	0·37	1·37	3·75	3·12	0·72	2·58	0·02	0·22	0·38	1·9
Inter-Orbital Breadth	0·03	18·25	30·44	18·26	5·65	5·55	6·31	4·79	2·40	37·52	10·14	12·24	15·14	8·00	21·0
Orbitonasal Breadth	0·03	0·12	9·30	4·59	0·03	2·76	28·44	46·79	0·01	2·23	1·69	13·48	9·52	15·58	35·3
Orbitonasal Arc ..	0·83	8·04	9·61	3·17	15·67	0·51	7·30	10·26	3·76	3·48	0·11	1·36	0·31	5·34	2·6
Nasal Length ..	40·99	26·51	21·45	24·16	14·83	2·84	6·55	15·35	4·64	2·75	1·89	0·57	1·44	11·43	2·3
Nasal Breadth ..	6·14	3·12	0·24	3·75	10·14	0·96	0·04	0·97	0·00	0·70	2·85	0·43	2·09	0·13	2·4
Nasal Height or Depth	10·68	10·79	5·87	0·05	0·25	11·59	11·59	10·84	4·04	7·28	1·78	0·00	0·02	1·81	0·0
Upper Facial Length	11·51	13·47	38·28	23·18	5·10	5·35	16·71	21·53	0·01	0·98	0·35	2·32	12·71	3·07	3·9
Total Facial Length	16·40	21·26	45·52	38·04	21·78	3·73	17·05	11·37	0·09	0·09	0·05	15·56	12·35	0·30	14·4
Horizontal Cirm. of the Head.	32·66	5·62	11·92	1·89	4·56	0·00	0·40	1·04	14·58	32·67	4·60	7·17	2·61	10·48	0·2
Sagittal Arc ..	34·25	11·44	0·60	0·24	3·96	59·07	53·07	21·91	21·74	3·50	4·07	1·16	0·00	7·33	1·9
Transverse Arc ..	0·26	0·64	53·24	35·93	1·99	1·10	24·70	41·85	0·03	1·21	1·57	26·62	4·39	12·79	14·8
Length Breadth Index.	0·17	0·04	153·96	139·05	23·70	21·41	23·50	87·88	4·86	10·76	3·82	109·65	30·76	47·74	78·9
Length Height Index	7·73	2·60	71·51	81·73	1·45	3·37	7·52	25·79	3·52	102·83	0·45	50·39	0·29	0·55	2·1
Breadth Height Index	6·84	2·20	0·73	0·00	6·14	2·49	1·16	3·56	0·00	47·10	0·84	26·56	11·55	16·76	23·4
Trans. Fronto-Parietal Index.	6·61	0·48	26·45	4·88	0·72	5·06	1·92	11·24	0·54	6·15	18·75	6·18	4·65	19·58	6·4
Orbitonasal Index ..	1·30	13·28	60·32	25·69	30·43	1·19	6·59	13·10	7·01	23·22	1·32	7·24	8·47	1·70	22·9
Nasal Index ..	41·31	26·29	13·49	26·07	29·64	0·33	4·72	5·01	1·85	0·07	5·37	1·59	0·30	9·43	0·0
Nasal Elevation Index.	21·15	17·18	3·27	1·04	5·94	5·48	10·11	5·03	2·86	3·53	4·41	0·22	0·96	2·13	1·8
Upper Facial Index..	2·40	8·61	1·25	0·16	0·04	7·98	20·90	15·20	4·14	0·95	0·04	4·28	10·53	1·27	10·7
Total Facial Index ..	3·50	14·89	0·66	2·17	9·05	7·16	23·65	7·99	8·16	8·45	1·45	22·41	10·83	13·51	27·6
Trans. Cephalo-Facial Index.	6·26	4·17	24·36	23·67	24·73	1·93	54·13	95·80	19·05	22·10	4·76	103·83	12·34	13·81	40·5
Vertical Cephalo-Facial Index.	7·80	0·45	0·52	0·55	5·69	0·65	1·77	0·28	0·08	31·80	1·18	9·21	0·47	0·60	5·5

TABLE XXXV.

with other races.

Chitpavan Brahmin.	Desastha Brahmin.	Saraswat Gour Brahmin.	Mahratta.	Nambudiri Brahmin.	Iluva.	Tamil Brahmin.	Tamil Kala.	Kanarese Brahmin.	Telegu Brahmin.	Nair.	Kadar.	Bhil.	Khasi.	Characters.
28·07	43·44	36·42	29·74	31·46	92·79	24·07	6·31	51·52	19·06	0·04	203·45	46·07	20·33	Stature.
0·14	0·35	6·40	0·10	18·89	0·78	13·00	0·29	0·13	5·72	13·46	2·43	20·08	17·86	Auricular Height.
7·19	17·08	1·53	30·01	39·15	2·68	0·01	0·26	14·58	3·24	15·33	47·32	31·37	1·93	Max. Head Length.
2·97	6·51	4·09	1·33	0·60	5·58	8·14	0·00	9·34	0·42	0·12	97·37	24·69	5·41	Max. Head Breadth.
20·60	23·72	7·55	11·38	0·26	1·50	2·08	1·04	17·69	0·63	2·05	1·55	0·40	1·20	Min. Frontal Breadth.
0·26	0·52	9·03	0·20	5·61	42·45	14·85	3·28	3·97	6·30	3·15	99·94	10·81	0·45	Max. Bizygomatic Breadth.
2·09	0·80	17·14	0·64	4·41	7·71	2·75	0·02	9·89	4·18	0·84	0·76	0·54	40·39	Bigonial Breadth.
3·92	17·84	0·49	4·20	2·65	5·07	3·01	5·52	0·30	3·57	3·19	1·70	1·42	1·56	Inter-Orbital Breadth.
8·95	2·03	18·29	0·48	26·68	8·96	48·91	5·00	25·31	19·82	26·93	28·14	0·31	0·67	Orbitonasal Breadth.
3·65	0·19	2·29	1·36	24·20	0·02	13·99	6·67	1·66	0·26	8·95	21·08	2·23	53·26	Orbitonasal Arc.
9·37	6·48	0·94	3·90	0·87	24·62	3·39	21·77	2·34	2·63	0·16	79·18	42·95	39·13	Nasal Length.
0·68	3·10	0·08	0·91	1·20	0·35	0·08	1·71	0·20	5·01	4·52	61·41	15·27	7·71	Nasal Breadth.
18·90	18·18	2·73	14·78	8·27	12·14	0·00	8·92	0·07	0·03	1·77	142·90	30·41	183·35	Nasal Height or Depth.
13·50	11·23	0·19	10·06	0·49	13·09	0·21	7·40	2·03	0·63	0·56	28·91	44·90	0·00	Upper Facial Length.
1·90	8·37	1·27	5·78	5·10	2·04	0·39	1·67	1·57	2·42	9·26	84·07	14·02	16·65	Total Facial Length.
1·48	1·10	0·59	8·56	7·31	3·06	0·13	4·83	4·92	0·04	1·64	346·02	34·05	0·01	Horizontal Cirm. of the Head.
5·48	1·14	0·82	10·84	71·63	30·80	21·38	2·30	0·77	10·27	34·31	119·11	9·88	4·80	Sagittal Arc.
0·41	5·51	12·98	0·07	14·25	1·19	14·05	0·82	6·59	2·62	28·46	766·05	25·82	2·31	Transverse Arc
11·37	24·94	6·92	13·77	22·36	10·93	6·46	0·25	29·70	3·32	5·10	23·65	0·97	8·08	Length Breadth Index.
0·82	2·46	8·72	9·75	0·73	2·36	11·02	0·06	5·58	1·76	20·55	25·05	1·65	19·15	Length Height Index.
2·19	4·74	0·65	0·62	18·65	0·71	1·24	0·24	2·70	6·65	8·51	70·52	0·37	5·25	Breadth Height Index.
3·51	0·20	0·00	2·26	1·68	2·54	3·80	0·67	0·05	1·92	0·66	3·08	26·57	11·34	Trans. Fronto-Parietal Index.
0·04	1·20	8·60	0·75	0·45	12·42	8·90	38·68	16·83	20·30	3·95	0·51	2·28	90·01	Orbitonasal Index.
10·45	11·65	0·67	3·96	3·32	18·34	2·12	23·14	0·70	8·94	3·83	201·31	76·80	51·25	Nasal Index.
14·24	21·20	2·14	14·00	3·57	11·65	0·01	11·05	0·00	1·16	0·02	191·67	46·26	171·45	Nasal Elevation Index.
10·21	7·72	1·30	5·24	3·39	0·00	2·39	2·26	0·08	0·35	2·47	0·04	20·19	0·01	Upper Facial Index.
0·73	4·03	8·43	3·43	12·63	7·63	8·87	0·01	0·01	0·01	7·41	5·31	1·98	11·40	Total Facial Index.
9·11	20·19	36·02	5·83	2·03	14·06	64·14	3·76	38·17	3·82	5·98	9·62	11·42	15·34	Trans. Cephalo-Facial Index.
0·41	1·91	1·38	1·70	3·24	0·06	5·37	1·73	12·33	8·06	0·50	50·56	0·30	34·83	Vertical Cephalo-Facial Index.

TABLE XXXVI.

Values of $\frac{N_s N_s'}{N_s+N_s'}\left(\frac{M_s-M_s'}{\sigma_s}\right)^2$ for Ma

Characters.	Red Kaffir.	Pathan.	Uzbeg.	Tadjik.	Khos (Lower Chitral).	U. P. Brahmin.	Bengali Brahmin.	Bengali Kayastha.	Bengali Pod.	Orissa Brahmin.	Rajput.	Nagar Brahmin.	Audich Brahmin.	Kathi.	Ba Ja
Stature	5·25	0·02	0·13	2·46	1·50	1·01	10·82	7·88	1·88	0·00	21·23	0·27	0·19	5·00	
Auricular Height ..	1·59	15·12	51·56	46·27	4·60	1·37	7·90	18·87	0·95	50·78	1·53	2·60	0·14	2·07	
Max. Head Length ..	36·77	11·84	5·63	12·17	0·93	20·29	0·21	2·36	5·07	13·34	1·35	2·78	6·97	0·23	
Max. Head Breadth	37·04	16·50	132·22	98·42	49·21	0·26	35·79	83·43	4·84	5·14	7·95	101·22	24·59	74·05	
Min. Frontal Breadth	32·97	3·15	28·91	37·15	12·17	2·03	4·51	13·30	0·14	0·01	1·82	29·47	13·37	5·50	
Max. Bizygomatic Breadth.	16·43	3·76	80·52	49·01	10·74	0·00	0·02	4·20	5·04	2·45	2·46	8·47	3·13	39·34	
Bigonial Breadth ..	5·94	0·16	10·49	2·74	0·78	0·75	0·14	0·00	0·83	1·04	2·58	2·29	4·00	0·59	
Inter-Orbital Breadth	9·33	0·89	6·00	0·52	1·47	23·02	24·33	24·71	1·93	2·26	10·14	0·13	0·00	0·01	
Orbitonasal Breadth	1·99	2·05	2·93	0·39	2·03	0·09	12·15	18·05	1·42	0·03	1·69	2·75	1·52	6·19	
Orbitonasal Arc ..	1·14	7·58	8·96	3·29	12·97	0·12	4·25	5·27	3·86	3·35	0·11	0·38	0·02	3·16	
Nasal Length ..	43·56	31·91	26·46	29·50	20·53	7·02	11·60	20·90	0·46	0·02	1·89	3·99	0·14	16·83	
Nasal Breadth ..	13·78	8·96	2·97	10·15	18·05	0·38	2·67	0·78	2·24	5·97	2·85	5·00	8·02	2·89	
Nasal Height or Depth	16·01	16·00	1·26	1·07	2·96	16·84	16·84	16·17	0·34	0·54	1·78	1·81	2·06	5·18	
Upper Facial Length	11·27	13·60	35·05	21·44	6·04	6·31	16·40	19·14	0·19	0·03	0·35	0·42	5·52	4·11	
Total Facial Length	9·45	14·38	33·52	25·33	13·17	2·16	11·39	6·35	0·01	0·00	0·05	11·84	9·71	0·45	
Horizontal Circm. of the Head.	46·39	15·30	22·00	9·75	15·06	3·42	5·79	8·87	2·10	5·19	4·60	18·83	0·62	21·22	
Sagittal Arc ..	46·18	21·87	0·73	5·09	13·11	70·62	64·90	34·09	33·47	13·04	4·07	8·46	4·25	0·55	
Transverse Arc ..	0·70	3·16	54·90	38·92	5·72	0·03	29·04	42·69	1·49	4·81	1·57	29·79	8·75	17·44	
Length Breadth Index	2·61	2·33	155·40	139·46	35·25	5·36	34·70	92·30	12·96	21·74	3·82	109·93	42·07	59·11	
Length Height Index	2·56	3·91	63·85	68·86	2·82	1·02	8·73	23·19	4·86	80·08	0·45	6·25	1·21	1·44	
Breadth Height Index	9·32	0·24	2·12	0·71	8·75	0·33	2·98	6·04	0·54	21·96	0·84	26·16	13·68	19·00	
Trans. Fronto-Parietal Index.	4·98	9·92	61·67	33·92	24·62	3·25	24·52	49·94	9·72	6·66	18·75	40·79	6·22	55·32	
Orbitonasal Index ..	0·05	4·67	36·49	10·52	11·52	0·00	1·50	3·21	1·64	6·74	1·32	1·04	1·55	0·04	
Nasal Index ..	57·24	41·57	25·17	41·66	45·81	6·29	15·12	17·18	0·69	1·76	5·37	11·30	7·51	21·17	
Nasal Elevation Index.	34·28	29·27	0·00	7·74	16·67	14·80	20·92	15·45	1·26	0·53	4·41	6·18	8·29	0·02	
Upper Facial Index..	1·16	5·66	0·71	0·03	0·00	5·22	14·42	8·98	2·54	0·33	0·04	3·50	8·13	1·32	
Total Facial Index ..	0·11	4·99	0·04	0·02	1·78	1·63	10·05	1·22	2·06	1·08	1·45	25·67	15·17	17·87	
Trans. Cephalo-Facial Index.	17·84	13·39	36·37	37·40	39·03	0·47	68·27	103·50	32·16	36·37	4·76	109·96	25·42	25·59	
Vertical Cephalo-Facial Index.	1·42	0·13	2·16	2·62	0·80	0·06	0·05	2·32	0·49	32·40	1·18	12·71	2·69	2·48	

TABLE XXXVI.

...min with other races.

Desastha Brahmin.	Saraswat Gour Brahmin.	Mahratta.	Nambudiri Brahmin.	Iluva.	Tamil Brahmin.	Tamil Kala.	Kanarese Brahmin.	Telegu Brahmin.	Nair.	Kadar.	Bhil.	Khasi.	Characters.
0·48	1·53	0·25	0·54	18·98	0·07	2·40	4·95	0·05	18·82	84·00	3·56	54·96	Stature.
0·59	10·64	0·69	23·34	0·10	17·59	2·21	1·92	9·88	18·05	6·35	7·90	22·18	Auricular Height.
4·75	0·01	13·17	41·05	5·88	1·18	1·97	5·29	6·59	19·29	19·18	14·77	0·00	Max. Head Length.
24·22	17·59	12·42	3·35	0·16	24·13	5·05	25·89	3·52	8·11	26·13	3·47	21·60	Max. Head Breadth.
6·70	1·46	2·77	0·57	4·98	0·01	4·01	6·12	0·24	0·00	5·62	2·96	4·89	Min. Frontal Breadth.
1·00	1·55	1·06	0·43	18·37	3·92	0·10	0·14	0·67	0·01	42·14	2·22	0·91	Max. Bizygomatic Breadth.
0·81	24·77	0·58	10·42	14·42	8·00	1·40	16·93	10·00	5·00	5·47	4·11	13·95	Bigonial Breadth.
0·04	4·63	1·25	2·02	0·65	18·15	0·28	10·43	1·26	1·84	4·79	2·98	0·56	Inter-Orbital Breadth.
0·03	6·54	3·09	10·63	2·11	24·00	0·81	10·29	7·34	10·40	31·19	2·57	3·71	Orbitonasal Breadth.
0·00	1·06	1·66	15·91	0·18	8·78	6·50	0·70	0·03	5·12	16·49	2·49	40·87	Orbitonasal Arc
0·46	0·12	0·20	0·17	9·66	0·17	8·96	0·02	0·05	0·82	33·64	20·13	15·03	Nasal Length.
0·08	1·50	0·50	0·31	0·91	1·50	0·05	3·37	0·23	0·08	21·34	3·69	0·46	Nasal Breadth.
4·47	0·08	4·33	13·34	3·47	1·38	2·38	0·87	1·72	5·48	69·10	13·11	99·41	Nasal Height Depth.
4·52	0·02	4·74	1·26	6·89	0·01	3·68	0·53	0·03	1·37	14·07	28·03	0·28	Upper Facial Length.
6·68	0·60	5·12	3·01	2·07	0·12	1·76	1·65	2·40	5·69	58·59	11·86	13·07	Total Facial Length.
1·74	1·42	0·32	17·84	0·12	4·69	0·04	0·01	4·10	9·18	165·49	10·22	1·41	Horizontal Cirm. of the Head.
1·38	6·41	0·99	82·07	42·94	33·08	8·91	6·28	20·45	46·51	45·90	0·95	10·69	Sagittal Arc.
10·06	17·68	1·83	18·94	4·11	18·75	3·32	10·95	6·19	32·28	445·89	11·00	4·75	Transverse Arc.
36·37	15·76	34·07	5·43	1·37	15·16	1·33	41·12	0·01	0·02	3·78	0·71	18·02	Length Breadth Index.
3·80	9·84	10·71	1·76	0·56	11·94	0·58	6·89	2·98	3·34	22·38	0·29	18·43	Length Height Index.
7·26	0·01	2·24	8·40	0·01	0·03	0·10	4·92	2·08	2·75	34·35	1·74	1·09	Breadth Height Index.
10·50	13·82	6·85	7·42	5·62	29·58	18·10	12·64	6·50	10·38	15·35	0·51	48·56	Trans. Fronto-Parietal Index.
0·08	2·35	0·09	2·56	4·18	2·48	20·41	6·46	8·35	0·42	0·36	0·09	45·48	Orbitonasal Index.
0·18	1·69	0·15	0·24	2·90	0·56	5·52	1·65	0·34	0·18	83·13	31·16	13·82	Nasal Index.
2·61	0·31	1·69	12·14	1·29	3·00	1·48	3·39	0·78	3·17	82·09	16·57	78·51	Nasal Elevation Index.
5·98	0·68	4·51	2·01	0·02	1·38	2·18	0·17	0·12	1·37	0·00	16·44	0·01	Upper Facial Index.
8·11	2·17	7·10	3·99	1·83	2·37	1·09	0·88	0·88	4·90	9·54	5·11	15·72	Total Facial Index.
34·29	50·25	16·23	9·94	26·39	77·90	12·20	52·43	12·83	16·48	0·08	1·08	28·70	Trans. Cephalo-Facial Index.
4·95	3·85	4·37	6·30	1·33	8·70	4·19	3·63	11·57	2·53	47·07	0·22	35·61	Vertical Cephalo-Facial Index.

TABLE XXXVII.

Values of $\frac{N_s\ N_s'}{N_s+N_s'}\left(\frac{M_s-M_s'}{\sigma_s}\right)^2$ for

Characters.	Red Kaffir.	Pathan.	Uzbeg.	Tadjik.	Khos (Lower Chitral).	U. P. Brahmin.	Bengali Brahmin.	Bengali Kayastha.	Bengali Pod.	Orissa Brahmin.	Malvo Brahmin.	Rajput.	Audich Brahmin.	Kathi.	Bania Jain.
Stature	4·81	0·13	0·00	1·68	4·33	0·41	10·91	8·03	4·49	0·62	0·27	25·67	0·01	4·27	0·57
Auricular Height ..	0·17	8·49	45·96	40·24	0·46	0·06	2·75	10·62	0·23	47·04	2·60	0·20	5·72	0·02	0·52
Max. Head Length ..	91·56	32·18	1·59	5·52	9·69	47·75	1·29	0·02	0·91	59·46	2·78	12·21	1·53	4·35	0·04
Max. Head Breadth	23·30	28·44	19·50	0·96	11·76	89·56	9·60	1·10	56·26	111·38	101·22	78·82	36·41	0·27	2·24
Min. Frontal Breadth	0·08	11·31	2·08	1·54	4·96	50·23	8·74	4·64	34·42	53·72	29·47	69·72	4·16	5·49	3·46
Max. Bizygomatic Breadth.	2·09	0·43	59·30	26·89	0·28	8·19	9·32	1·08	30·50	34·71	8·47	2·67	1·76	19·98	3·06
Bigonial Breadth ..	23·84	1·12	24·88	12·88	7·97	0·26	1·15	3·35	2·10	0·51	2·29	0·02	0·36	0·27	1·65
Inter-Orbital Breadth	11·14	2·14	9·62	1·59	1·00	27·25	28·92	32·63	1·57	5·80	0·13	12·24	0·26	0·05	1·33
Orbitonasal Breadth	14·52	11·17	0·24	1·09	14·08	1·73	5·66	10·47	9·39	6·09	2·75	13·48	0·24	1·46	5·51
Orbitonasal Arc ..	4·35	14·62	15·51	7·94	26·47	0·05	3·17	4·35	8·44	10·02	0·38	1·36	0·33	2·12	0·23
Nasal Length ..	32·78	20·95	17·06	18·52	9·99	1·17	3·86	10·31	7·75	6·26	3·99	0·57	3·82	8·05	0·63
Nasal Breadth ..	3·42	1·55	0·00	1·91	6·66	2·32	0·11	2·74	0·24	0·02	5·00	0·43	0·62	0·02	5·7
Nasal Height or Depth	10·94	10·96	5·94	0·05	0·25	11·78	11·78	11·10	4·11	7·49	1·81	0·00	0·02	1·84	0·0
Upper Facial Length	24·55	24·38	53·14	38·27	14·17	12·73	28·71	38·66	0·56	0·44	0·42	2·32	4·46	8·47	0·2
Total Facial Length	64·69	61·71	91·18	93·41	73·21	26·55	54·31	54·11	12·35	21·06	11·84	15·56	0·10	5·84	0·0
Horizontal Circm. of the Head.	9·65	0·04	2·56	0·90	0·19	4·79	2·37	2·70	36·31	75·75	18·83	7·17	18·21	1·56	4·9
Sagittal Arc ..	23·50	6·43	2·35	0·19	0·94	47·24	41·86	13·41	14·64	0·53	8·46	1·16	0·94	0·00	0·1
Transverse Arc ..	32·19	11·49	13·90	2·40	12·90	27·57	0·66	1·93	23·99	20·18	29·79	26·62	8·66	0·08	1·5
Length Breadth Index	118·59	75·82	26·54	7·64	27·68	173·71	13·17	0·97	39·61	64·95	109·93	109·65	21·76	0·84	2·1
Length Height Index	25·59	0·04	48·10	51·35	0·93	13·52	0·88	8·38	0·00	64·30	6·25	50·39	2·76	0·89	0·5
Breadth Height Index	6·28	32·34	7·55	20·13	6·28	33·43	9·64	10·53	18·13	146·41	26·16	26·56	2·63	0·06	0·0
Trans. Fronto-Parietal Index.	25·90	7·40	11·78	0·00	2·43	18·40	0·39	0·82	7·61	27·09	40·79	6·18	21·41	6·69	0·0
Orbitonasal Index ..	2·38	2·24	35·08	7·63	8·75	1·19	0·16	0·93	0·22	3·85	1·04	7·24	0·10	0·51	4·
Nasal Index ..	27·51	17·17	7·91	16·43	18·32	0·20	1·35	1·01	5·75	2·68	11·30	1·59	0·46	4·60	1·
Nasal Elevation Index	17·64	14·52	4·56	0·40	4·09	8·96	8·05	3·29	4·30	5·76	6·18	0·22	0·30	1·27	3·
Upper Facial Index..	13·23	21·53	6·62	4·89	4·93	20·52	39·58	36·19	13·90	10·49	3·50	4·28	1·57	0·18	1·
Total Facial Index ..	44·00	58·75	17·06	31·61	58·58	42·92	76·68	57·76	45·28	65·64	25·67	22·41	1·74	0·02	0·
Trans. Cephalo-Facial Index.	58·66	38·79	4·71	15·83	23·83	93·85	0·76	0·08	15·10	38·81	109·96	103·83	41·53	15·38	13·
Vertical Cephalo-Facial Index.	34·36	9·88	1·95	3·61	28·79	10·79	14·52	6·24	7·57	7·13	12·71	9·21	5·20	2·25	0·

TABLE XXXVII.

Nagar Brahmin with other races.

Chit-pavan Brahmin.	Desastha Brahmin.	Saraswat-Gour Brahmin.	Mahratta.	Nambudiri Brahmin.	Iluva.	Tamil Brahmin.	Kalo.	Kanarese Brahmin.	Telegu Brahmin.	Nair.	Kadar.	Bhil.	Khasi.	Characters.
0·07	2·31	3·86	1·33	1·97	31·31	0·68	1·64	9·71	0·08	20·95	147·36	7·41	92·66	Stature.
0·68	1·12	4·78	0·50	16·06	1·57	10·70	0·04	0·00	4·19	11·00	1·25	23·83	14·86	Auricular Height.
0·65	0·40	2·54	6·38	85·43	20·17	8·57	9·89	1·02	21·68	48·54	11·38	7·86	3·59	Max. Head Length.
51·85	41·57	26·83	41·75	67·83	92·16	18·87	45·42	17·13	62·03	53·46	365·83	149·53	36·47	Max. Head Breadth.
14·58	12·69	16·17	14·19	42·15	64·41	28·46	53·39	6·50	35·91	33·22	93·56	55·22	80·97	Min. Frontal Breadth.
4·68	5·72	19·00	3·44	14·09	62·38	27·19	9·33	11·14	14·90	10·26	139·44	21·57	4·93	Max. Bizygomatic Breadth.
2·54	0·59	18·31	0·49	4·96	8·44	3·20	0·00	10·73	4·69	1·08	1·03	0·71	39·72	Bigonial Breadth.
2·31	0·61	4·58	0·88	1·67	0·31	21·10	0·07	11·51	0·88	0·15	5·19	2·70	0·32	Inter-Orbital Breadth.
2·87	5·26	1·73	14·82	4·48	0·00	16·41	0·27	4·31	2·23	4·23	85·81	12·57	18·43	Orbitonasal Breadth.
0·59	0·55	0·34	4·74	16·35	1·22	8·01	12·14	0·13	0·19	4·08	34·27	6·03	72·14	Orbitonasal Arc.
14·89	11·19	2·52	6·98	2·48	31·53	6·10	27·73	4·64	5·06	1·11	95·82	52·12	49·51	Nasal Length.
2·24	6·01	0·66	2·33	2·74	1·27	0·66	3·29	0·01	7·79	7·35	74·19	20·01	11·74	Nasal Breadth.
19·37	18·65	2·77	15·04	8·41	12·33	0·00	9·04	0·07	0·03	1·80	146·61	30·90	187·36	Nasal Height or Depth.
4·78	3·40	0·64	3·58	3·94	5·81	0·60	2·54	0·04	0·19	4·28	15·06	30·44	1·94	Upper Facial Length.
6·65	1·17	18·86	0·92	31·24	3·12	14·73	2·78	3·79	2·69	41·93	27·36	0·32	0·16	Total Facial Length.
15·44	14·31	8·73	27·58	0·23	15·53	3·31	17·87	19·47	3·93	1·04	466·34	64·95	2·27	Horizontal Cirm. of the Head.
11·93	4·73	0·00	18·02	58·26	22·27	14·34	0·52	0·00	5·55	24·82	147·88	16·35	2·68	Sagittal Arc.
14·16	8·25	0·32	17·36	0·27	9·59	0·18	8·81	2·58	6·57	0·86	111·17	86·82	1·35	Transverse Arc.
10·94	31·30	34·39	17·43	183·84	14·04	35·44	70·25	9·12	107·15	128·15	246·39	90·39	49·29	Length Breadth Index.
1·80	0·48	1·32	1·54	1·05	11·38	2·31	2·08	0·31	0·24	0·24	7·62	9·74	5·47	Length Height Index.
3·64	9·23	26·01	0·13	75·37	25·39	28·25	19·09	6·42	34·09	54·65	190·64	12·83	50·36	Breadth Height Index.
9·38	15·58	4·24	5·37	11·52	13·16	0·00	1·10	5·06	11·70	8·82	163·42	52·10	1·11	Trans. Fronto-Parietal Index.
8·53	2·67	0·58	2·09	8·68	1·84	0·66	17·85	3·77	5·51	0·10	4·18	0·45	49·60	Orbitonasal Index.
0·63	22·45	3·42	9·56	8·39	28·54	6·22	33·55	3·49	16·32	9·37	245·48	97·20	71·02	Nasal Index.
1·18	2[illegible]·26	3·40	17·34	2·32	14·51	0·22	13·60	0·12	2·12	0·29	209·94	52·21	186·74	Nasal Elevation Index.
1·32	0·50	8·02	0·28	12·84	2·99	10·50	0·00	1·96	5·20	11·38	5·42	8·11	4·27	Upper Facial Index.
5·29	7·76	45·98	4·85	56·85	44·07	47·02	12·21	15·80	1·58	63·99	6·46	5·93	1·13	Total Facial Index.
1·00	33·82	5·00	39·87	49·90	20·31	0·04	32·61	4·24	39·90	40·07	185·59	136·72	32·14	Trans. Cephalo-Facial Index.
6·83	2·85	1·65	1·52	0·54	4·95	0·02	0·92	1·82	0·16	3·63	16·64	9·15	9·90	Vertical Cephalo-Facial Index.

TABLE XXXVIII.

Values of $\frac{N_s\ N_s'}{N_s+N_s'}\left(\frac{M_s-\bar{M}_s'}{\sigma_s}\right)^2$ for

Characters.	Red Kaffir.	Pathan.	Uzbeg.	Tadjik.	Khos. (Lower Chitral).	U. P. Brahmin.	Bengali Brahmin.	Bengali Kayastha.	Bengali Pod.	Orissa Brahmin.	Malve Brahmin.	Rajput.	Nagar Brahmin.	Audich Brahmin.	Kathi.
Stature	8·46	0·06	0·23	3·75	1·76	1·59	15·07	12·53	2·22	0·00	0·01	32·94	0·57	0·40	
Auricular Height	0·09	12·03	52·33	47·58	1·86	0·11	4·95	15·41	0·01	55·75	1·36	0·07	0·52	2·81	
Max. Head Length ..	7·47	29·86	19·45	6·24	8·27	44·63	0·93	0·00	1·23	6·83	2·22	10·52	0·04	2·01	
Max. Head Breadth	10·75	16·59	29·45	5·12	3·78	66·65	3·46	0·20	38·69	75·92	76·66	52·86	2·24	20·23	
Min. Frontal Breadth	4·51	3·34	7·44	9·02	0·16	30·42	2·03	0·08	18·55	27·24	15·00	40·83	3·46	0·04	
Max. Bizygomatic Breadth.	9·14	4·24	41·30	13·08	1·35	18·03	19·67	7·56	47·35	53·74	18·43	11·15	3·06	9·06	
Bigonial Breadth ..	12·55	0·00	16·46	5·94	2·39	0·25	0·00	0·28	0·34	0·45	0·21	1·96	1·65	3·40	
Inter-Orbital Breadth	19·61	0·27	5·18	0·06	4·38	37·21	39·15	45·81	4·71	1·28	0·32	21·03	1·33	0·38	
Orbitonasal Breadth	37·03	27·16	1·32	9·40	35·62	10·25	0·22	0·77	24·35	24·42	12·46	25·37	5·51	7·62	
Orbitonasal Arc ..	6·42	17·44	18·03	10·25	30·68	0·38	1·89	2·49	10·67	13·20	1·10	2·62	0·23	1·07	
Nasal Length ..	23·63	15·16	12·60	12·75	5·55	0·19	1·71	5·68	11·53	10·94	6·95	2·32	0·63	7·26	
Nasal Breadth ..	17·63	10·09	2·92	11·87	23·59	0·19	2·58	0·55	2·11	7·32	0·08	2·49	5·78	9·67	
Nasal Height or Depth	12·61	12·37	4·90	0·00	0·61	13·23	13·23	12·78	3·13	5·63	1·20	0·08	0·09	0·19	
Upper Facial Length	28·92	28·03	57·56	42·91	17·59	15·51	32·62	43·86	2·37	1·39	1·09	3·98	0·25	2·55	
Total Facial Length	61·46	59·42	88·71	89·89	69·79	25·32	52·23	51·30	11·62	19·50	11·14	14·44	0·01	0·06	
Horizontal Cirm. of the Head.	27·61	4·00	9·80	0·34	2·87	0·14	0·07	0·32	17·48	38·28	6·30	0·20	4·90	4·24	
Sagittal Arc ..	19·78	5·02	3·08	0·53	0·40	42·74	37·66	10·76	12·38	0·13	10·02	1·93	0·11	1·64	
Transverse Arc ..	18·96	5·50	20·92	6·83	5·46	17·55	3·30	6·79	8·92	9·45	19·31	14·81	1·57	2·84	
Length Breadth Index	86·43	55·50	37·54	15·93	14·37	141·12	5·86	0·22	25·60	40·51	84·82	78·92	2·11	10·17	
Length Height Index	17·91	0·18	68·96	60·00	0·05	0·16	2·39	13·01	0·47	74·93	3·46	2·13	0·58	0·81	
Breadth Height Index	4·97	29·52	6·54	17·84	5·00	30·56	8·28	8·73	16·15	136·49	23·69	23·40	0·06	1·82	
Trans. Fronto-Parietal Index.	26·08	7·67	11·18	0·00	2·65	18·69	0·48	0·64	7·88	27·20	40·96	6·46	0·01	21·65	
Orbitonasal Index ..	13·43	0·07	19·16	0·74	0·71	8·02	1·85	1·41	16·48	0·15	7·56	22·97	4·69	3·24	
Nasal Index ..	41·51	26·46	13·62	26·25	29·83	0·36	4·81	5·12	1·78	0·05	5·24	0·00	1·64	0·32	
Nasal Elevation Index	35·32	27·53	0·72	4·87	14·08	11·87	18·35	12·91	0·37	0·16	0·98	1·84	3·33	5·33	
Upper Facial Index ..	23·26	31·45	11·76	10·70	11·53	30·24	52·47	51·38	22·13	20·49	8·22	10·75	1·57	0·00	
Total Facial Index ..	50·87	48·95	20·44	38·98	66·07	48·65	83·89	65·38	49·95	74·13	30·40	27·67	0·36	3·55	
Trans. Cephalo-Facial Index.	14·98	10·01	0·19	0·61	1·53	43·42	4·59	11·54	0·71	4·91	54·47	40·52	13·85	7·53	
Vertical Cephalo-Facial Index.	26·51	6·76	0·89	1·77	21·90	7·50	10·63	3·36	4·88	10·64	9·11	5·58	0·41	2·66	

TABLE XXXVIII.

Bania —Jain with other races.

Chitpavan Brahmin.	Desastha Brahmin.	Saraswat-Gour Brahmin.	Mahratta.	Nambudiri Brahmin.	Iluva.	Tamil Brahmin.	Kala.	Kanarese Brahmin.	Telegu Brahmin.	Nair.	Kadar.	Bhil.	Khasi.	Characters.
0·25	0·55	1·78	0·24	0·58	24·32	0·04	3·37	6·13	0·11	26·78	125·15	4·35	0·18	Stature.
0·01	0·10	7·55	0·01	20·87	0·44	14·61	0·56	0·34	6·81	15·20	3·37	18·08	19·98	Auricular Height.
0·35	0·68	2·01	7·14	80·66	18·35	7·51	8·81	1·35	19·78	45·14	12·44	8·65	2·63	Max. Head Length.
31·41	23·49	15·38	26·19	47·69	68·88	9·57	30·97	8·35	43·46	35·42	299·82	118·86	20·80	Max. Head Breadth.
3·65	2·68	6·15	4·58	23·77	41·54	14·29	34·27	1·05	19·63	18·25	53·95	34·30	50·99	Min. Frontal Breadth.
14·99	16·91	32·81	11·06	26·66	85·40	43·24	18·79	22·25	27·40	21·77	179·65	36·13	14·65	Max. Bizygomatic Breadth.
8·11	0·28	27·83	0·16	10·72	15·33	7·83	0·83	18·33	10·13	4·52	5·30	3·51	25·19	Bigonial Breadth.
6·99	0·20	9·30	3·64	5·02	2·25	80·04	1·26	18·42	8·46	4·81	11·66	6·82	1·36	Inter-Orbital Breadth.
16·07	21·39	0·35	33·82	0·02	3·50	4·50	5·14	0·03	0·17	0·00	130·01	29·29	41·49	Orbitonasal Breadth.
0·08	1·47	0·03	6·58	12·96	2·21	5·82	14·56	0·00	0·67	2·51	39·11	7·96	78·06	Orbitonasal Arc.
21·06	16·72	4·89	10·80	4·92	21·55	9·51	33·80	7·69	8·22	2·95	109·05	60·67	59·06	Nasal Length.
6·84	0·00	1·29	0·29	0·13	0·68	1·29	0·00	3·40	0·68	0·39	36·51	6·20	1·29	Nasal Breadth.
16·34	15·65	1·99	12·85	9·71	10·49	0·07	7·62	0·00	0·17	2·50	13·61	27·74	175·14	Nasal Height or Depth.
2·74	1·73	1·44	2·09	5·67	3·93	1·38	1·46	0·04	0·70	6·13	10·97	25·59	3·39	Upper Facial Length.
6·02	0·96	17·89	0·77	29·80	2·81	13·91	2·52	3·44	2·41	40·07	27·46	0·40	0·23	Total Facial Length.
2·78	2·26	1·30	10·95	5·37	4·49	0·00	6·44	6·67	0·03	0·78	361·66	38·37	0·12	Horizontal Cirm. of the Head.
13·95	6·13	0·05	20·11	52·96	19·40	12·12	0·21	0·07	4·26	21·55	151·64	18·26	2·12	Sagittal Arc.
20·36	2·47	0·21	9·34	0·28	4·23	0·36	4·03	0·34	2·33	3·96	996·12	67·52	0·25	Transverse Arc.
31·21	16·41	21·48	8·37	148·14	111·54	22·31	52·23	3·31	82·44	99·11	195·55	67·95	31·04	Length Breadth Index.
3·20	0·01	3·08	3·50	0·14	7·42	4·50	0·74	1·36	0·02	0·03	12·20	6·13	9·06	Length Height Index.
11·53	7·54	22·60	11·13	70·38	22·96	25·57	17·22	5·34	42·61	60·45	178·17	11·22	46·00	Breadth Height Index.
19·62	15·85	4·47	13·63	11·81	13·45	0·02	1·23	5·30	11·98	9·10	160·91	52·51	0·91	Trans. Fronto-Parietal Index.
25·42	14·36	0·99	10·75	22·33	0·16	0·89	6·63	0·03	0·34	4·73	17·71	5·84	24·40	Orbitonasal Index.
10·19	10·85	0·63	3·84	3·21	18·06	2·04	22·85	0·65	8·76	3·71	199·36	76·09	50·60	Nasal Index.
5·08	10·33	0·12	6·58	9·17	5·29	1·02	5·26	1·29	0·00	1·07	154·13	32·28	138·79	Nasal Elevation Index.
0·02	0·51	14·57	0·30	21·02	7·44	17·82	0·96	5·75	8·76	19·45	12·72	3·27	10·30	Upper Facial Index.
19·82	11·22	51·87	7·25	63·40	40·86	52·96	15·33	19·56	19·56	71·04	10·57	8·40	2·61	Total Facial Index.
11·56	3·96	0·62	9·47	15·38	2·13	7·81	8·30	0·93	10·57	9·45	92·84	73·52	4·48	Trans. Cephalo-Facial Index.
3·10	1·04	0·57	0·51	0·04	2·85	0·15	0·23	0·68	0·82	1·79	21·75	6·16	13·63	Vertical Cephalo-Facial Index.

TABLE XXXIX.

Values of $\frac{N_s\ N_s'}{N_s+N_s'}\left(\frac{M_s-M_s'}{\sigma_s}\right)^2$

Characters.	Red Kaffir.	Pathan.	Uzbeg.	Tadjik.	Khos. (Lower Chitral).	U. P. Brahmin.	Bengali Brahmin.	Bengali Kayastha.	Bengali Pod.	Orissa Brahmin.	Malve Brahmin.	Rajput.	Nagar Brahmin.	Audich Brahmin.	Bania Jain
Stature	0·17	4·44	2·76	0·76	12·91	16·61	0·75	0·00	12·44	7·38	5·00	3·00	4·27	4·43	
Auricular Height ..	0·21	4·96	31·32	23·73	0·13	0·11	1·47	5·22	0·27	24·68	2·07	0·23	0·02	3·86	
Max. Head Length ..	25·76	7·71	7·29	14·18	0·10	14·22	0·82	3·85	6·75	15·35	0·23	0·29	4·35	8·89	
Max. Head Breadth	17·06	22·81	10·98	0·09	9·62	65·95	8·79	1·69	42·66	66·01	74·05	51·09	0·27	25·56	
Min. Frontal Breadth	6·47	0·45	9·33	10·63	0·37	13·60	0·12	0·52	7·29	8·11	5·50	15·27	5·49	4·79	
Max. Bizygomatic Breadth.	11·29	19·75	8·90	0·00	15·78	38·86	36·03	27·19	70·37	78·81	39·34	32·05	19·98	29·12	
Bigonial Breadth ..	9·79	0·16	14·40	5·56	2·64	0·00	0·17	0·72	0·01	0·00	0·59	0·38	0·27	0·94	
Inter-orbital Breadth	7·34	0·99	5·97	0·63	0·94	19·52	20·67	20·09	1·45	2·26	0·01	8·00	0·05	0·03	
Orbitonasal Breadth	16·42	14·21	0·29	3·74	16·19	4·52	0·76	1·49	12·55	9·20	6·19	15·58	1·46	2·42	
Orbitonasal Arc ..	9·02	19·12	19·91	12·65	28·22	2·12	0·03	0·01	13·17	14·34	3·16	5·34	2·12	3·48	
Nasal Length ..	2·15	1·50	1·58	0·64	0·15	2·58	0·80	0·17	22·46	22·51	16·83	11·43	8·05	18·14	
Nasal Breadth ..	2·28	1·26	0·02	1·46	4·31	1·26	0·03	1·23	0·18	0·05	2·89	0·13	0·02	0·52	
Nasal Height or depth	1·26	2·24	9·71	1·99	0·89	2·54	2·54	1·31	8·00	11·38	5·18	1·81	1·84	1·49	
Upper Facial Length	0·66	2·10	14·90	4·93	0·00	0·12	3·21	3·07	2·63	6·53	4·11	3·07	8·47	19·81	
Total Facial Length	7·73	18·03	37·85	29·37	16·85	4·24	14·85	9·58	0·53	0·62	0·45	0·30	5·84	4·56	
Horizontal Cirm. of the Head.	1·17	0·84	0·13	3·58	2·41	8·20	5·47	6·08	35·67	57·04	21·22	10·48	1·56	19·67	
Sagittal Arc ..	50·84	26·51	2·19	7·34	17·52	75·04	4·15	39·00	38·36	17·59	0·55	7·33	0·00	7·52	
Transverse Arc ..	14·87	6·26	11·29	2·19	5·96	16·07	0·82	1·73	9·15	8·63	17·44	12·79	0·08	3·77	
Length Breadth Index	52·33	39·05	25·62	9·15	9·48	97·45	4·56	0·03	18·44	23·40	59·11	47·74	0·84	6·82	
Length Height Index	8·08	0·44	43·37	42·53	0·04	4·64	2·51	9·60	0·77	47·95	1·44	0·55	0·89	0·11	
Breadth Height Index	4·48	23·25	6·30	14·20	4·56	24·00	7·46	7·12	13·43	86·16	19·00	16·76	0·06	2·11	
Trans. Fronto-Parietal Index.	40·87	19·97	0·75	5·38	13·74	32·94	7·67	3·58	20·25	41·31	55·32	19·58	6·69	36·31	
Orbitonasal Index ..	0·20	3·39	3·09	8·08	8·65	0·07	0·90	2·06	1·02	4·66	0·04	1·70	0·51	0·86	
Nasal Index ..	3·19	2·18	0·47	1·53	1·30	5·01	0·86	1·91	14·59	11·59	21·17	9·43	4·60	6·87	
Nasal Elevation Index	4·06	4·40	7·22	0·28	0·18	0·39	1·71	0·05	7·12	12·30	9·02	2·13	1·27	0·49	
Upper Facial Index..	5·28	11·48	3·38	1·85	1·60	10·89	22·34	16·60	7·02	3·57	1·32	1·27	0·18	1·84	
Total Facial Index ..	25·95	40·10	12·91	20·88	35·08	29·49	52·08	33·83	28·84	35·62	17·87	13·51	0·02	1·28	
Trans. Cephalo Facial Index.	3·33	2·59	1·56	0·20	0·02	19·47	7·45	13·57	0·08	0·21	25·59	13·81	15·38	1·00	
Vertical Cephalo-Facial Index.	8·33	1·52	0·00	0·01	6·69	1·81	3·14	0·14	0·83	17·60	2·48	0·60	2·25	0·06	

TABLE XXXIX.

Kathi with other races.

Chitpavan Brahmin.	Desastha Brahmin.	Saraswat-Gour Brahmin.	Mahratta.	Nambudiri Brahmin.	Iluva.	Tamil Brahmin.	Kala.	Kanarese Brahmin.	Telegu Brahmin.	Nair.	Kadar.	Bhil.	Khasi.	Characters.
3·20	10·24	11·56	7·78	8·84	40·23	6·14	0·43	18·78	4·16	3·05	121·82	16·12	87·49	Stature.
0·60	0·87	2·68	0·48	9·46	1·32	6·33	0·00	0·02	2·33	6·21	0·45	16·70	8·00	Auricular Height.
2·24	6·57	0·29	15·19	30·69	3·28	0·30	0·78	6·98	3·78	13·15	21·08	16·79	0·31	Max. Head Length.
35·40	28·10	21·64	31·41	49·89	67·76	15·79	36·39	14·50	46·73	39·33	214·04	107·34	26·23	Max. Head Breadth.
0·26	0·08	1·45	0·75	9·64	19·78	5·14	17·00	0·00	7·84	5·94	23·64	15·73	21·46	Min. Frontal Breadth.
37·72	39·13	55·44	30·57	48·93	106·35	66·24	39·09	43·80	49·59	43·67	174·69	58·93	35·98	Max. Bizygomatic Breadth.
2·98	0·00	15·38	0·01	5·06	7·89	3·60	0·15	9·67	4·89	1·68	1·62	1·30	18·68	Bigonial Breadth.
1·86	0·10	3·70	0·89	1·51	0·43	15·29	0·16	8·63	0·90	1·36	3·60	2·32	0·43	Inter-Orbital Breadth.
6·24	8·50	0·00	17·29	0·38	1·08	4·97	2·05	0·39	0·02	0·29	63·54	15·47	19·83	Orbitonasal Breadth.
0·80	4·03	0·65	9·30	3·75	4·71	1·04	16·85	0·97	2·64	0·08	33·53	10·65	62·41	Orbitonasal Arc.
3·29	28·34	14·22	21·81	14·42	49·46	20·11	45·32	17·88	18·54	11·67	101·60	69·42	65·81	Nasal Length.
0·99	2·85	0·30	1·20	1·47	0·64	0·30	1·96	0·00	4·62	4·13	38·72	12·33	6·25	Nasal Breadth.
21·93	20·78	6·43	18·57	1·24	16·25	1·37	13·13	1·95	1·08	0·03	106·00	32·37	138·71	Nasal Height or Depth.
21·02	18·36	3·60	17·15	1·03	20·25	3·68	14·01	7·34	4·83	1·02	33·61	48·99	3·00	Upper Facial Length.
0·24	2·63	1·96	2·04	5·37	0·47	0·98	0·39	0·29	0·62	8·61	39·62	6·63	6·90	Total Facial Length.
17·80	16·44	12·14	28·11	0·53	18·35	6·58	20·69	21·77	16·17	3·78	295·24	58·06	4·62	Horizontal Cirm. of the Head.
0·93	3·73	9·76	0·03	86·02	47·86	37·97	12·49	9·62	25·04	51·36	29·20	0·03	13·73	Sagittal Arc.
16·99	3·42	0·04	9·34	0·03	5·13	0·01	4·99	1·12	3·36	0·98	590·79	53·33	0·77	Transverse Arc.
19·81	10·41	15·57	6·17	100·83	77·30	16·15	38·46	2·70	57·46	66·26	113·42	47·57	20·16	Length Breadth Index.
0·00	0·18	3·09	3·32	0·00	3·64	4·23	0·17	1·62	0·18	0·22	8·91	2·90	7·29	Length Height Index.
9·19	6·25	18·20	9·29	51·49	18·47	20·44	14·71	5·14	32·68	37·03	108·80	9·71	32·56	Breadth Height Index.
35·12	30·46	15·47	27·52	25·31	27·08	5·34	9·12	16·70	25·35	22·17	146·27	65·79	2·82	Trans. Fronto-Parietal Index.
2·20	0·24	1·55	0·25	2·97	2·99	1·66	16·90	4·85	6·41	0·16	0·63	0·01	37·09	Orbitonasal Index.
31·21	32·06	11·40	19·37	17·98	38·51	15·19	43·49	11·50	26·52	19·18	188·17	97·29	72·45	Nasal Index.
18·94	24 31	6·17	18·77	0·04	16·61	1·88	16·02	1·61	4·70	2·10	139·81	46·81	133·25	Nasal Elevation Index.
1·67	0·90	3·70	0·65	6·25	1·06	5·08	0·10	0·58	2·18	5·35	1·67	7·16	1·38	Upper Facial Index.
9·54	4·87	31·54	3·52	38·18	30·26	32·24	9·12	11·18	11·18	41·87	4·07	4·39	0·91	Total Facial Index.
2·17	0·14	2·64	2·13	4·74	0·05	10·64	2·21	3·12	2·83	2·10	37·10	36·43	0·32	Trans. Cephalo-Facial Index.
0·01	0·06	0·08	0·12	0·57	0·24	1·46	0·20	0·05	2·67	0·02	20·46	1·29	14·86	Vertical Cephalo-Facial Index.

TABLE XL.

Values of $\frac{N_s N_s'}{N_s+N_s'}\left(\frac{M_s-M_s'}{\sigma_s}\right)^2$ for

Characters.	Red Kaffir.	Pathan.	Uzbeg.	Tadjik.	Khos. (Lower Chitral).	U. P. Brahmin.	Bengali Brahmin.	Bengali Kayastha.	Bengali Pod.	Orissa Brahmin.	Malve Brahmin.	Rajput.	Nagar Brahmin.	Kathi.	Bania-Jain.
Stature	4·95	0·08	0·00	1·83	3·71	0·50	11·00	8·10	3·99	0·43	0·19	25·12	0·01	4·43	
Auricular Height ..	3·69	23·08	69·90	68·76	8·84	2·93	12·79	30·59	2·21	81·10	0·14	3·78	5·72	3·86	
Max. Head Length	110·37	43·21	0·14	1·49	17·79	60·48	4·49	1·87	0·00	1·06	6·97	21·28	1·53	8·89	
Max. Head Breadth	1·64	0·11	74·00	9·87	6·15	19·13	3·48	24·47	6·03	13·92	24·59	7·00	36·41	25·56	
Min. Frontal Breadth	5·24	2·68	8·11	9·91	0·04	27·86	1·54	0·00	16·69	23·88	13·37	36·80	4·16	4·79	
Max. Bizygomatic Breadth.	7·40	0·20	72·82	38·73	3·22	2·97	3·64	0·10	18·74	18·14	3·13	0·07	1·76	29·12	
Bigonial Breadth ..	28·46	2·33	22·59	16·26	11·06	0·99	2·38	5·63	0·89	1·79	4·00	0·22	0·36	0·94	
Inder-Orbital Breadth	13·96	1·05	7·31	0·63	2·12	30·51	32·25	36·47	3·78	3·18	0·00	15·14	0·26	0·03	
Orbitonosal Breadth	10·38	8·81	0·69	0·36	10·13	0·80	7·47	13·18	6·81	3·48	1·52	9·52	0·24	2·42	
Orbitonasal Arc ..	2·10	10·70	12·03	5·06	19·64	0·06	4·88	6·69	5·63	5·91	0·02	0·31	0·33	3·48	
Nasal Length ..	56·04	36·87	29·71	34·83	24·54	7·03	12·35	25·47	1·30	0·11	0·14	1·44	3·82	18·14	
Nasal Breadth ..	1·03	0·34	0·27	0·44	3·06	4·55	0·94	5·69	1·27	0·51	8·02	2·00	0·62	0·52	
Nasal Height or Depth	9·39	9·78	6·28	0·11	0·12	10·53	10·53	9·54	4·43	7·82	2·06	0·02	0·02	1·49	
Upper Facial Length	47·54	42·96	75·30	62·07	32·40	27·17	48·53	65·93	8·06	8·33	5·52	12·71	4·46	19·81	
Total Facial Length	56·10	55·38	84·58	84·05	64·15	22·98	48·51	46·56	10·16	16·73	9·71	12·35	0·10	4·56	
Horizontal Cirm. of the Head.	52·01	13·45	20·86	7·69	13·48	1·74	3·81	6·84	5·93	14·67	0·62	2·61	18·21	19·07	
Sagittal Arc ..	32·06	10·38	0·69	0·17	3·52	56·60	50·80	20·36	20·59	3·03	4·25	0·00	0·94	7·52	
Transverse Arc ..	6·73	0·87	33·03	16·55	0·43	7·00	10·16	18·10	2·45	1·41	8·75	4·39	8·66	3·77	
Length Breadth Index	35·43	22·51	69·95	45·59	0·38	83·30	0·06	13·37	5·66	22·08	42·07	30·76	21·76	6·82	
Length Height Index	10·60	1·32	63·78	7·10	0·44	5·07	5·12	19·69	1·99	88·22	1·21	0·29	2·76	0·11	
Breadth Height Index	0·70	18·12	2·48	8·87	0·78	18·92	3·00	2·41	8·18	102·37	13·68	11·55	2·63	2·11	
Trans. Fronto-Parietal Index.	0·13	1·19	43·91	16·56	8·61	0·20	9·86	29·58	1·11	0·01	6·22	4·65	21·41	36·31	
Orbitonasal Index ..	3·23	1·48	31·55	5·91	6·64	1·74	0·02	0·40	0·05	2·51	1·55	8·47	0·10	0·86	
Nasal Index ..	33·19	21·28	10·58	20·72	23·19	0·01	2·87	2·71	3·23	0·73	7·51	0·30	0·46	6·87	
Nasal Elevation Index	12·50	10·83	6·20	0·02	2·08	2·28	5·46	1·49	6·12	4·31	8·29	0·96	0·30	0·49	
Upper Facial Index..	22·71	30·94	11·69	10·55	11·31	29·77	51·58	50·03	21·81	19·92	8·13	10·53	1·57	1·84	
Total Facial Index ..	26·33	41·49	9·92	18·91	38·03	28·62	56·41	36·84	30·52	41·06	15·17	10·83	1·74	1·28	
Trans. Cephalo-Facial Index.	1·12	0·75	5·74	2·93	2·15	18·14	19·19	37·15	2·03	0·64	25·42	12·34	41·53	1·00	
Vertical Cephalo-Facial Index.	11·71	1·05	0·05	0·01	9·09	1·86	3·53	0·03	0·71	23·35	2·69	0·47	5·20	0·06	

TABLE XL.

Audich Brahmin with other races.

Chitpavan Brahmin.	Desastha Brahmin.	Saraswat-Gour Brahmin.	Mahratta	Nambudiri Brahmin.	Iluva.	Tamil Brahmin.	Kala.	Kanarese Brahmin.	Telegu Brahmin.	Nair.	Kadar.	Bhil.	Khasi.	Characters.
0·02	1·89	3·41	1·08	1·67	29·20	0·53	1·78	8·84	0·04	20·77	135·84	6·70	86·00	Stature.
2·55	1·95	16·80	1·82	35·16	0·53	26·56	4·07	3·82	15·65	28·14	12·40	7·95	35·54	Auricular Height.
4·06	0·40	6·60	2·00	101·64	29·23	15·05	16·18	0·00	31·00	62·01	4·04	3·03	9·03	Max. Head Length.
0·95	0·03	0·03	1·34	9·05	20·31	0·41	4·32	0·71	7·94	3·83	153·65	50·16	0·05	Max. Head Breadth.
2·78	1·96	5·20	3·77	21·50	38·39	12·71	31·75	0·71	17·70	14·99	53·68	31·53	46·63	Min. Frontal Breadth.
0·59	0·96	10·17	0·45	6·58	44·32	16·21	3·98	4·79	7·29	3·94	101·63	12·03	0·84	Max. Bizygomatic Breadth.
0·88	1·84	13·70	1·44	2·80	5·55	1·56	0·25	7·39	2·66	0·24	0·13	0·11	44·87	Bigonial Breadth.
9·90	0·03	6·28	1·83	2·85	0·94	24·11	0·41	13·84	1·77	2·64	7·38	4·08	0·69	Inter-Orbital Breadth.
1·34	3·02	2·86	11·26	6·17	0·18	19·13	0·02	5·93	3·47	5·92	70·07	9·49	13·89	Orbitonasal Breadth.
1·72	0·02	1·08	2·66	19·63	0·38	10·47	8·90	0·66	0·00	6·08	25·73	3·74	59·37	Orbitonasal Arc.
3·22	1·63	0·00	0·80	0·01	15·33	0·69	13·70	0·27	0·38	0·43	56·16	30·11	25·15	Nasal Length.
4·99	10·03	2·07	0·01	5·20	3·05	2·06	5·64	0·55	11·39	11·07	83·55	25·24	16·59	Nasal Breadth.
18·46	18·74	3·06	14·41	7·38	12·67	0·01	9·38	0·14	0·00	1·41	140·94	30·94	181·01	Nasal Height or Depth.
0·00	0·11	6·28	0·00	13·77	0·42	6·14	0·00	2·32	4·59	14·74	2·60	13·62	11·12	Upper Facial Length.
4·78	0·54	10·00	0·45	27·10	2·18	12·28	1·96	2·73	1·82	36·70	29·00	0·66	0·47	Total Facial Length.
0·19	0·38	0·32	2·19	16·26	0·16	2·82	0·88	0·74	2·31	7·11	273·26	19·57	0·56	Horizontal Cirm. of the Head.
5·67	1·28	0·68	11·02	68·59	29·30	20·24	2·07	0·63	9·59	32·53	116·42	10·07	4·56	Sagittal Arc.
7·49	0·03	3·37	2·42	3·80	0·42	3·92	0·49	0·66	0·02	11·82	858·41	45·44	0·02	Transverse Arc.
5·19	0·54	3·84	0·01	87·69	61·17	4·19	22·30	0·68	40·39	49·75	109·53	30·57	6·06	Length Breadth Index.
0·12	0·98	6·12	6·84	0·15	3·82	8·02	0·03	3·57	0·75	0·89	18·88	2·92	14·42	Length Height Index
3·90	1·75	12·86	4·56	50·90	13·13	15·16	9·47	1·38	28·49	33·98	136·93	4·83	29·34	Breadth Height Index
0·12	0·68	3·02	0·15	0·31	0·04	13·66	6·01	2·41	0·17	1·16	60·26	10·94	28·61	Trans. Fronto-Parieta Index.
9·83	3·57	0·25	2·89	9·85	1·17	0·30	15·36	2·73	4·20	0·33	5·23	0·83	43·08	Orbitonasal Index.
13·87	15·26	1·59	5·96	5·13	21·92	3·57	26·80	1·63	11·59	5·79	209·66	82·94	57·18	Nasal Index.
21·86	30·38	5·06	20·59	1·07	17·44	0·82	16·27	0·61	3·50	0·98	212·68	56·59	190·61	Nasal Elevation Index.
0·02	0·33	14·40	0·31	20·70	7·36	17·57	0·97	5·71	10·58	19·13	12·43	3·14	10·13	Upper Facial Index.
6·14	1·90	31·08	1·05	39·48	29·54	31·91	5·96	7·98	7·98	44·69	1·26	1·73	0·04	Total Facial Index.
0·33	0·70	9·26	0·44	2·40	0·67	25·25	0·57	10·34	0·91	0·42	44·23	38·74	0·27	Trans. Cephalo-Facial Index.
0·00	0·43	0·35	0·48	1·41	0·11	2·95	0·60	0·28	4·98	0·01	39·02	1·23	26·55	Vertical Cephalo-Facial Index.

TABLE XLI.

Values of $\frac{N_s \; N_s'}{N_s+N_s'}\left(\frac{M_s-M_s'}{\sigma_s}\right)^2$ for

Characters.	Red Kaf-fir.	Pathan.	Uzbeg.	Tad-jik.	Khos. (Lower Chitral).	U. P. Brah-min.	Ben-gali Brah-min.	Ben-gali Kayas-tha.	Bengali Pod.	Orissa Brah-min.	Malve Brah-min.	Rajput.	Nagar Brah-min.	Audich Brah-min.	Kathi.
Stature	5·94	0·02	0·02	2·29	3·33	0·72	12·25	9·45	3·64	0·26	0·10	28·07	0·07	0·02	5·20
Auricular Height ..	0·16	12·75	53·81	49·46	2·15	0·18	5·37	16·48	0·05	58·30	0·89	0·14	0·68	2·55	0·60
Max. Head Length ..	76·17	25·19	3·31	9·22	5·40	38·94	0·24	0·42	2·56	10·82	1·03	7·19	0·65	4·06	2·24
Max. Head Breadth	5·33	0·23	88·30	51·67	12·29	13·26	7·32	36·82	2·84	7·66	17·95	2·97	51·85	0·95	35·40
Min. Frontal Breadth	16·48	0·06	16·69	22·08	2·11	15·94	0·02	2·65	7·71	10·0	5·47	0·60	14·58	2·78	0·26
Max. Bizygomatic Breadth.	12·79	1·19	84·31	49·47	6·77	1·24	1·70	1·22	14·18	12·51	1·35	0·26	4·68	0·59	37·72
Bigonial Breadth ..	41·39	5·46	36·97	24·51	18·84	3·20	5·53	11·52	3·02	5·86	7·79	2·09	2·54	0·88	2·98
Inter-Orbital Breadth	3·31	7·19	17·20	6·59	0·22	15·84	17·12	17·51	0·00	16·21	2·52	3·92	2·31	3·90	1·86
Orbitonasal Breadth	4·52	3·89	2·78	0·18	4·47	0·00	14·00	24·05	2·87	0·41	0·09	3·95	2·87	1·34	6·24
Orbitonasal Arc ..	8·03	19·63	19·89	12·02	34·33	0·71	1·34	1·74	12·34	15·75	1·52	3·65	0·59	1·72	0·80
Nasal Length ..	90·45	58·86	46·18	58·01	47·00	17·53	25·65	49·11	0·11	2·73	1·24	9·37	14·89	3·22	33·29
Nasal Breadth ..	11·02	6·00	1·15	7·11	16·06	0·10	0·75	0·03	0·50	3·02	1·05	0·68	2·24	4·99	0·99
Nasal Height or Depth	58·36	46·87	0·38	12·83	22·39	48·47	48·47	58·73	2·31	4·01	4·84	18·90	19·37	19·46	21·93
Upper Facial Length	50·28	44·69	77·23	64·80	34·21	28·26	50·43	69·69	8·42	8·96	5·77	13·50	4·78	0·00	21·02
Total Facial Length	29·79	33·18	59·88	54·84	36·48	9·38	27·79	22·80	2·04	5·39	1·84	1·90	6·65	4·78	0·24
Horizontal Cirm. of the Head.	48·64	11·40	18·65	5·98	11·14	0·96	2·65	5·04	8·10	19·76	1·36	1·48	15·44	0·19	17·80
Sagittal Arc ..	1·64	28·18	0·75	6·45	18·34	92·75	85·15	49·80	43·46	19·62	0·01	5·48	11·93	5·67	0·93
Transverse Arc ..	0·02	1·75	60·38	43·36	4·17	0·29	30·41	51·19	0·46	3·26	0·55	0·41	34·16	7·49	16·99
Length Breadth Index	14·35	8·64	101·75	79·45	2·63	54·70	4·52	36·87	0·28	0·13	22·18	11·37	50·94	5·19	19·81
Length Height Index	13·75	0·78	61·63	68·88	0·11	6·68	4·07	17·72	1·32	86·65	1·99	0·82	1·80	0·12	00·0
Breadth Height Index	1·33	7·28	0·03	1·64	1·11	7·79	0·02	0·18	1·62	70·46	4·52	2·19	13·64	3·90	9·19
Trans. Fronto-Parietal Index.	0·51	0·69	41·94	14·88	7·17	0·54	8·53	27·56	0·63	0·23	7·98	3·51	19·38	0·12	35·12
Orbitonasal Index ..	1·83	14·84	63·14	27·91	33·24	1·61	7·56	14·88	7·98	25·95	1·75	0·04	8·53	9·83	2·20
Nasal Index ..	94·22	60·67	35·45	63·32	74·42	10·32	23·18	30·09	1·60	10·53	0·09	10·45	20·63	13·87	31·21
Nasal Elevation Index	70·43	52·31	0·68	18·58	37·36	29·32	39·17	36·21	1·86	4·80	0·91	14·14	18·18	21·86	18·94
UpperFacial Index ..	22·61	30·85	11·32	10·21	10·99	29·60	51·80	50·74	21·54	19·84	7·79	10·21	1·32	0·02	1·67
Total Facial Index ..	7·50	20·23	2·00	4·97	14·91	11·46	31·18	13·70	12·71	14·91	3·63	0·73	15·29	6·14	9·5[illegible]
Trans. Cephalo Facial Index.	0·25	0·17	8·04	5·09	4·29	14·87	24·36	46·80	3·72	2·14	21·64	9·11	2·00	0·33	2·1[illegible]
Vertical Cephalo Facial Index.	11·89	1·42	0·08	0·03	9·12	1·77	3·44	0·01	0·64	25·46	2·60	0·41	5·83	0·00	0·0[illegible]

TABLE XLI.

[Chit]pavan Brahmin with other races.

Desastha Brahmin.	Sarasvat Gour Brahmin.	Mahratta.	Numbudiri Brahmin.	Iluva.	Tamil Brahmin.	Kala.	Kanarese Brahmin.	Telegu Brahmin.	Nair.	Kadar.	Bhil.	Khasi.	Characters.
1·57	3·06	0·86	1·41	28·85	0·38	2·16	8·40	0·01	23·6[illegible]	139·69	0·28	132·67	Stature.
0·05	·8·08	0·00	21·90	0·34	15·40	0·67	0·44	7·31	16·07	3·80	17·66	21·13	Auricular Height.
2·07	0·89	10·26	72·98	14·66	5·18	6·43	2·74	15·94	39·12	17·44	11·87	1·29	Max. Head Length
0·70	0·40	0·11	4·97	14·27	2·40	1·85	2·78	4·24	1·29	137·33	40·93	0·50	Max. Head Breadth.
0·08	0·88	0·26	10·88	24·29	5·04	19·75	0·28	8·42	6·16	33·94	18·80	29·09	Min. Frontal Breadth.
0·04	6·79	0·00	3·83	37·62	11·95	2·06	2·52	4·44	1·81	91·25	8·35	0·04	Max. Bizygomatic Breadth.
5·60	8·91	4·19	0·80	2·61	0·24	1·52	3·93	0·77	0·11	0·37	0·19	60·26	Bigonial Breadth.
5·03	0·83	0·13	0·00	0·42	11·27	0·75	4·67	0·08	0·01	0·52	0·18	0·05	Inter-Orbital Breadth.
0·34	7·18	5·77	12·40	1·93	29·26	0·56	11·81	8·16	12·26	54·59	4·73	7·29	Orbitonasal Breadth.
2·27	0·00	7·96	11·52	2·96	4·86	1·64	0·07	1·09	1·85	43·57	9·39	84·16	Orbitonasal Arc.
0·30	2·31	0·42	2·67	6·22	0·41	5·66	0·92	0·74	5·05	33·88	16·75	11·58	Nasal Length.
0·88	0·15	0·06	0·16	0·01	0·15	0·48	1·22	2·49	2·03	49·74	10·61	4·06	Nasal Breadth
0·02	3·54	0·02	42·84	0·00	12·68	0·08	10·76	13·85	25·96	57·43	4·00	90·63	Nasal Height or Depth.
0·13	6·55	0·00	14·38	0·41	6·42	0·00	2·44	4·80	15·43	2·69	13·99	11·75	Upper Facial Length
2·29	5·08	1·52	11·76	0·10	3·07	0·07	0·02	0·20	18·07	61·22	6·97	7·86	Total Facial Length.
0·03	0·05	3·59	13·99	0·59	1·82	1·67	1·53	1·41	5·47	306·15	23·74	0·27	Horizontal Cirm. of the Head.
1·71	7·94	1·68	109·73	56·01	42·95	10·81	7·77	26·29	62·62	73·84	1·57	11·69	Sagittal Arc.
9·08	17·14	0·66	18·75	2·61	18·37	1·93	9·61	4·61	34·99	742·06	21·03	3·45	Transverse Arc.
2·57	0·01	3·62	50·41	36·82	0·04	9·28	7·46	20·95	26·90	70·06	12·61	0·10	Length Breadth Index.
0·44	4·96	5·73	0·01	5·20	6·75	0·19	2·67	0·35	0·43	16·91	4·12	12·69	Length Height Index.
0·47	4·05	0·22	31·20	4·21	5·41	2·58	0·20	14·43	17·75	99·74	0·36	13·54	Breadth Height Index.
0·24	2·21	0·01	0·08	0·01	12·14	4·97	1·69	0·02	0·64	69·55	13·35	26·61	Trans. Frontol-Parietal Index.
1·72	9·71	1·09	0·26	13·77	10·03	40·94	18·44	22·08	4·74	0·85	2·84	95·28	Orbitonasal Index.
0·02	3·28	0·60	0·78	2·79	1·37	5·74	3·21	0·14	0·68	120·49	38·12	17·23	Nasal Index.
0·67	2·53	0·28	25·59	0·13	8·77	0·25	9·54	3·91	9·66	101·76	14·23	92·66	Nasal Elevation Index.
0·20	14·04	0·20	20·44	7·02	17·27	0·81	5·39	10·23	18·86	12·14	3·66	9·80	Upper Facial Index.
1·33	13·06	1·27	18·39	12·06	13·62	0·33	0·67	0·67	21·46	2·08	0·51	6·71	Total Facial Index.
2·13	12·76	0·03	1·19	1·71	31·24	0·11	14·06	0·25	0·02	38·82	34·27	1·18	Trans. Cephalo-Facial Index.
0·56	0·44	0·61	1·62	0·07	3·28	0·71	0·36	5·46	0·03	42·43	1·15	28·62	Vertical Cephalo-Facial Index.

TABLE XLII.

Values of $\frac{N_s\,N_s'}{N_s+N_s'}\left(\frac{M_s-M_s'}{\sigma_s}\right)^2$ for

Characters.	Red Kaf-fir.	Pathan	Uzbeg.	Tad-jik.	Khos. (Lower Chitral).	U. P. Brah-min.	Ben-gali Brah-min.	Ben-gali Kayas-tha.	Bengali Pod.	Orissa Brah-min.	Malve Brah-min.	Rajput	Nagar Brah-min.	Audich Brah-min.	Kathi.
Stature	13·72	0·65	1·01	6·81	0·40	3·48	20·54	18·90	0·83	0·70	0·48	43·44	2·31	1·89	10·24
Auricular Height	0·39	12·71	56·59	52·92	2·87	0·36	6·30	18·64	1·34	62·83	0·59	0·35	1·12	1·95	0·87
Max. Head Length ..	104·76	34·44	0·69	3·30	13·00	55·32	2·71	0·59	0·20	3·15	4·75	17·08	0·40	0·40	6·57
Max. Head Breadth	2·31	0·03	78·73	42·66	7·55	18·69	4·26	28·23	5·54	13·56	24·22	6·51	41·57	0·03	28·10
Min. Frontal Breadth	14·49	0·24	15·22	20·06	1·40	18·09	0·01	1·83	9·17	12·66	6·70	23·72	12·69	1·96	0·08
Max. Bizygomatic Breadth.	14·55	1·47	87·75	52·74	7·98	0·91	1·31	1·74	13·12	11·24	1·00	0·52	5·72	0·96	39·13
Bigonial Breadth ..	17·17	0·17	19·96	8·64	4·38	0·01	0·21	1·16	0·02	0·01	0·81	0·80	0·59	1·84	0·00
Inter-Orbital Breadth	16·50	0·71	6·82	0·42	2·86	33·78	35·62	41·58	3·36	2·72	0·04	17·84	0·51	0·03	0·10
Orbitonasal Breadth	2·46	2·05	4·32	0·86	2·46	0·27	17·94	30·57	1·52	0·00	0·03	2·03	5·26	3·02	8·50
Orbitonasal Arc ..	1·87	9·41	11·81	4·79	19·87	0·14	5·66	7·98	5·39	5·71	0·00	0·19	0·55	0·02	4·03
Nasal Length ..	81·99	47·32	41·57	51·79	40·79	14·22	21·66	42·63	0·01	1·16	0·46	6·48	11·19	1·63	28·34
Nasal Breadth ..	18·31	9·25	2·98	12·22	24·46	0·19	2·65	0·57	2·16	7·66	0·08	3·10	6·01	10·03	2·85
Nasal Height or Depth.	57·55	41·16	0·29	12·25	21·65	47·67	47·67	57·93	2·04	3·57	4·47	18·18	18·65	18·74	20·78
Upper Facial Length	46·23	37·00	73·59	0·76	30·82	25·59	46·99	65·09	6·91	6·95	4·52	11·23	3·40	0·11	18·36
Total Facial Length	49·16	43·98	77·85	76·86	57·07	18·50	42·57	39·96	7·06	11·91	6·68	8·37	1·17	0·54	2·65
Horizontal Cirm. of the Head.	47·02	9·43	17·74	5·31	10·18	0·70	2·22	4·34	9·07	22·02	1·74	1·10	14·31	0·38	16·44
Sagittal Arc ..	49·23	16·43	0·00	2·04	9·36	74·61	67·77	33·94	31·14	9·41	1·38	1·14	4·73	1·28	3·73
Transverse Arc ..	8·20	1·08	32·69	16·20	0·72	8·79	9·73	17·90	3·05	2·04	10·06	5·51	8·25	0·03	3·42
Length Breadth Index.	29·32	16·14	81·39	57·60	0·01	76·29	0·72	20·58	3·34	4·37	36·37	24·94	31·30	0·54	10·41
Length Height Index	19·32	0·12	55·21	60·66	0·09	9·80	2·25	12·92	0·39	76·42	3·80	2·46	0·48	0·38	0·1[illegible]
Breadth Height Index	0·23	9·55	0·43	3·56	0·16	11·31	0·46	0·07	3·37	83·81	7·26	4·74	9·23	1·75	6·25
Trans. Fronto-Parietal Index.	1·47	0·17	37·99	11·95	4·95	1·29	6·45	23·12	0·16	1·02	10·50	0·20	15·58	0·68	30·46
Orbitonasal Index ..	0·01	7·10	50·02	17·52	20·70	0·05	2·92	6·71	3·18	13·95	0·08	1·20	2·67	3·57	0·24
Nasal Index ..	98·95	56·60	37·04	66·33	78·30	11·25	24·67	32·35	1·94	11·87	0·18	11·65	22·45	15·26	32·06
Nasal Elevation Index.	86·11	56·25	1·94	25·47	48·35	37·28	48·36	47·38	4·12	9·58	2·61	21·20	26·26	30·38	24·31
Upper Facial Index ..	18·94	24·39	9·41	8·00	8·47	26·13	47·32	45·46	18·55	16·14	5·98	7·72	0·50	0·33	0·90
Total Facial Index ..	15·30	26·61	4·93	10·52	25·11	18·81	42·90	23·85	20·41	26·54	8·11	4·03	7·76	1·90	4·87
Trans. Cephalo-Facial Index.	3·80	2·24	3·37	1·02	0·46	25·55	14·37	29·79	0·59	0·01	34·29	20·19	33·82	0·70	0·14
Vertical Cephalo-Facial Index.	17·83	2·90	0·06	0·17	14·19	3·77	6·10	0·71	1·98	18·93	4·95	1·91	2·85	0·43	0·06

TABLE XLII.

...astha Brahmin with other races.

...nia ...n.	Chit-pavan. Brah-min.	Saraswat Gour Brah-min.	Mah-ratta.	Num-budiri Brah-min.	Iluva.	Tamil Brah-min.	Kala.	Kana-rese Brah-min.	Telegu Brah-min.	Nair.	Kadar.	Bhil.	Khasi.	Characters.
...0·55	1·57	0·56	0·02	0·02	19·31	0·15	5·82	3·64	0·88	34·66	113·51	2·28	68·02	Stature.
...0·10	0·05	9·24	0·03	23·97	0·17	17·04	0·98	0·72	8·41	17·87	4·83	16·40	23·40	Auricular Height.
...0·68	2·07	4·43	4·00	95·96	25·10	11·89	13·11	0·26	26·80	56·67	7·56	5·32	6·21	Max. Head Length.
...3·49	0·70	0·00	1·05	8·56	19·89	0·06	3·91	1·04	7·46	3·41	160·49	50·35	0·00	Max. Head Breadth.
...2·68	0·08	1·38	0·58	12·71	26·98	6·23	21·95	0·09	9·95	7·56	38·11	21·14	32·64	Min. Frontal Breadth.
...5·91	0·04	6·02	0·03	3·23	36·06	10·97	1·66	2·04	3·82	1·38	89·02	7·51	0·00	Max. Bizygomatic Breadth.
...9·28	5·60	24·11	0·00	8·25	12·48	5·77	0·27	15·24	7·79	2·88	3·24	2·15	31·45	Bigonial Breadth.
...9·20	5·03	7·41	2·40	3·58	1·33	26·87	0·64	15·83	2·30	3·37	9·11	4·95	0·88	Inter-Orbital Breadth.
...1·39	0·34	10·03	3·69	16·46	3·50	34·98	1·41	15·45	11·19	16·20	47·14	2·95	4·73	Orbitonasal Breadth.
...1·47	2·27	1·38	2·43	21·79	0·27	11·77	8·68	0·90	0·02	7·05	26·37	3·50	61·46	Orbitonasal Arc.
...8·72	0·30	1·19	0·03	1·41	8·70	0·04	7·84	0·27	0·18	3·21	41·44	20·79	15·57	Nasal Length.
...0·00	0·88	1·32	0·30	0·13	0·70	1·33	0·00	3·48	0·70	0·40	38·00	6·36	1·33	Nasal Breadth.
...5·65	0·02	3·21	0·05	42·05	0·00	12·13	0·03	10·24	13·27	25·24	60·53	4·47	94·41	Nasal Height or depth.
...1·78	0·13	5·22	0·11	12·38	0·88	5·10	0·05	1·64	3·67	13·30	4·10	16·44	9·72	Upper Facial Length.
...0·96	2·29	12·17	0·00	22·20	0·82	8·89	0·75	1·18	0·60	31·09	40·39	2·07	1·98	Total Facial Length.
...2·26	0·03	0·00	4·26	13·05	0·94	1·46	2·06	1·94	1·09	4·83	318·85	25·51	0·19	Horizontal Cirm. of the Head.
...8·13	1·71	3·18	5·85	89·45	41·96	30·71	5·44	3·07	16·86	46·93	100·23	5·35	7·59	Sagittal Arc.
...2·47	9·08	3·02	3·06	3·43	0·65	3·55	0·72	0·48	0·07	11·41	935·49	49·61	0·10	Transverse Arc.
...3·41	2·57	1·95	0·30	80·50	54·72	2·20	18·12	2·12	34·78	43·49	101·78	25·51	3·35	Length Breadth Index.
...0·01	0·44	2·93	3·42	0·20	7·98	4·34	0·87	1·24	0·00	0·01	12·11	6·63	8·91	Length Height Index.
...7·54	0·47	6·66	1·12	38·38	6·85	8·38	4·53	0·01	19·15	23·33	116·36	1·34	18·86	Breadth Height Index.
...5·85	0·24	1·21	0·10	0·02	0·22	9·66	3·51	0·83	0·07	0·15	79·47	16·61	22·46	Trans. Fronto-Parietal Index.
...4·36	1·72	4·32	0·00	2·58	7·16	4·53	29·76	10·65	13·48	1·15	0·16	0·41	74·18	Orbitonasal Index.
...0·85	0·02	3·78	0·83	1·03	2·43	1·69	5·27	3·71	0·06	0·93	119·47	37·09	16·35	Nasal Index.
...0·33	0·67	5·10	0·03	33·30	0·08	13·23	0·01	14·17	7·01	14·66	87·49	9·85	79·95	Nasal Elevation Index.
...0·31	0·20	11·61	0·00	17·45	5·31	14·58	0·32	3·89	8·16	15·91	9·36	5·23	7·48	Upper Facial Index.
...11·22	1·33	20·86	0·02	27·79	19·58	21·57	0·07	3·07	3·07	31·96	0·08	0·04	2·34	Total Facial Index.
...3·96	2·13	5·86	2·00	5·30	0·02	19·80	2·00	6·75	2·80	1·96	60·54	49·93	0·07	Trans. Cephalo-Facial Index.
...1·04	0·56	0·00	0·02	0·44	0·77	1·49	0·08	0·00	3·05	0·22	33·81	2·83	22·14	Vertical Cephalo-Facial Index.

TABLE XLIII.

Values of $\frac{N_s\ N_s'}{N_s+N_s'}\left(\frac{M_s-M_s'}{\sigma_s}\right)^2$

Characters.	Red Kaf-fir.	Pathan.	Uzbeg.	Tadjik	Khos. (Lower Chitral).	U. P. Brah-min.	Bengali Brah-min.	Bengali Kayas-tha.	Bengali Pod.	Orissa Brah-min.	Malve Brah-min.	Rajput.	Nagar Brah-min.	Audich Brah-min.	Ka
Stature	9·05	0·42	0·67	4·72	0·44	2·40	15·42	12·62	0·85	0·31	0·25	29·74	1·33	1·08	
Auricular Height ..	0·12	10·12	45·08	38·05	1·58	0·14	4·28	11·85	0·03	41·81	0·69	0·10	0·50	1·82	
Max. Head Length ..	113·39	52·09	0·54	0·04	26·25	69·14	9·95	6·91	1·65	0·40	13·17	30·01	6·38	2·00	
Max. Head Breadth	5·27	0·49	79·03	44·13	11·12	8·94	7·29	30·37	1·53	3·88	12·42	1·33	41·75	1·34	
Min. Frontal Breadth	15·83	0·03	17·16	21·26	3·06	9·90	0·30	3·61	4·23	4·61	2·77	11·38	14·19	3·77	
Max. Bizygomatic Breadth.	9·43	0·97	71·54	38·78	5·08	0·97	1·34	0·92	11·32	8·65	1·06	0·20	3·44	0·45	
Bigonial Breadth ..	12·01	0·12	16·46	6·44	3·04	0·02	0·14	0·75	0·03	0·02	0·58	0·64	0·49	1·44	
Inter-Orbital Breadth	3·66	4·41	12·59	3·80	0·00	14·99	16·10	15·47	0·11	8·92	1·25	4·20	0·88	1·83	
Orbitonasal Breadth	0·33	0·07	11·14	6·39	0·68	4·35	29·10	43·33	0·27	4·00	3·09	0·48	14·82	11·26	
Orbitonasal Arc ..	0·14	2·48	3·94	0·28	5·28	2·70	11·80	15·47	0·57	0·12	1·66	1·36	4·74	2·66	
Nasal Length ..	56·12	40·03	33·28	37·85	27·84	10·27	15·94	28·63	0·06	0·49	0·20	3·90	6·98	0·80	
Nasal Breadth ..	9·53	5·79	1·38	6·66	13·66	0·01	0·98	0·01	0·72	2·94	0·50	0·91	2·33	0·01	
Nasal Height or Depth.	44·34	38·97	0·44	10·76	17·63	40·32	40·32	44·62	2·16	3·26	4·33	14·78	15·04	14·41	
Upper Facial Length	37·11	30·17	65·73	50·97	25·65	22·94	40·84	51·36	6·39	6·40	4·74	10·05	3·58	0·00	
Total Facial Length	34·73	38·54	64·75	58·54	41·01	14·39	33·34	28·19	5·41	7·85	5·12	5·78	0·92	0·45	
Horizontal Cirm. of the Head.	61·62	21·49	29·14	14·92	22·31	6·19	9·42	14·48	0·89	2·95	0·32	8·56	27·58	2·19	
Sagittal Arc ..	69·46	34·32	3·13	11·62	24·53	67·74	87·90	53·65	12·51	25·69	0·99	10·84	11·02	11·02	
Transverse Arc ..	0·49	0·25	42·78	25·92	0·94	1·36	18·10	28·21	0·01	0·42	1·83	0·07	17·36	2·42	
Length Breadth Index.	26·33	18·05	616·84	38·08	2·08	68·00	0·08	10·90	4·37	5·30	34·07	13·77	17·43	0·01	
Length Height Index	30·16	1·52	29·08	26·42	4·11	18·63	0·05	1·45	1·01	30·46	10·71	9·75	1·54	6·84	
Breadth Height Index	2·07	4·01	0·04	0·50	1·84	4·35	0·08	0·67	0·55	1·21	2·24	0·62	0·13	4·56	
Trans. Fronto-Parietal Index.	0·50	0·43	34·63	11·02	4·88	0·55	6·42	19·28	0·39	0·25	6·85	2·26	5·37	0·15	
Orbitonasal Index ..	0·01	6·59	42·62	13·94	15·60	0·06	2·49	5·11	2·71	9·97	0·09	0·75	2·09	2·89	
Nasal Index ..	56·68	39·94	23·96	40·14	44·54	4·93	13·37	15·36	0·22	3·58	0·15	3·96	9·56	5·96	
Nasal Elevation Index.	59·34	48·03	1·34	18·36	33·42	28·13	36·73	32·17	2·79	5·70	1·69	14·00	17·34	20·59	
Upper Facial Index..	13·12	21·14	7·62	5·87	5·86	20·24	36·89	31·89	14·30	10·56	4·51	5·24	0·28	0·31	
Total Facial Index ..	11·99	24·87	4·61	8·89	19·57	15·93	35·56	18·37	17·24	19·48	7·10	3·43	4·85	1·05	
Trans. Cephalo-Facial Index.	0·07	0·05	7·48	4·60	3·79	10·99	20·86	36·21	3·50	1·96	16·23	5·83	39·87	0·44	
Vertical Cephalo-Facial Index.	13·59	2·94	0·10	0·28	11·04	3·39	5·33	0·73	1·90	12·94	4·37	1·70	1·52	0·48	

TABLE XLIII.

Mahratta with other races.

Bania-Jain.	Chitpavan Brahmin.	Desastha Brahmin.	Saraswat Gour Brahmin.	Nambudiri Brahmin.	Iluva.	Tamil Brahmin.	Kala.	Kanarese Brahmin.	Telegu Brahmin.	Nair.	Kadar.	Bhil.	Khasi.	Characters.
0·24	0·86	0·02	0·61	0·06	16·22	0·06	4·31	3·28	0·52	25·62	82·57	2·13	52·17	Stature.
0·01	0·00	0·03	6·43	17·16	0·27	12·24	0·56	0·36	5·82	12·44	2·71	13·93	15·80	Auricular Height.
7·14	10·26	4·00	12·70	108·18	37·85	22·65	23·61	1·63	39·69	70·42	0·09	0·14	16·32	Max. Head Length.
26·19	0·11	1·05	0·70	2·91	9·68	2·52	0·96	3·13	2·47	0·52	9·39	29·83	0·86	Max. Head Breadth.
4·58	0·26	0·58	0·17	6·23	15·88	2·50	13·21	0·83	4·70	3·04	19·91	11·93	17·59	Min. Frontal Breadth.
11·06	0·00	0·03	5·41	3·01	30·12	9·54	1·68	1·99	3·53	1·39	65·50	6·65	0·02	Max. Bizygomatic Breadth.
0·16	4·19	0·00	19·49	6·67	10·16	4·75	0·26	12·37	6·38	2·36	2·44	1·81	22·87	Bigonial Breadth.
3·64	0·13	2·40	1·25	0·11	0·08	10·97	0·25	5·01	0·00	0·12	0·95	0·46	0·00	Inter-Orbital Breadth.
33·82	5·77	3·69	19·74	27·36	10·80	47·48	6·73	26·24	21·17	27·46	14·60	0·01	0·00	Orbitonasal Breadth.
6·58	7·96	2·43	5·58	30·04	0·73	19·12	2·05	4·67	2·12	13·80	7·58	0·12	27·76	Orbitonasal Arc.
10·80	0·42	0·03	0·67	0·80	7·75	0·00	7·17	0·09	0·05	1·62	31·30	17·79	12·74	Nasal Length.
0·29	0·06	0·30	0·32	0·02	0·08	0·32	0·19	1·45	1·45	1·08	32·83	7·33	2·28	Nasal Breadth.
12·85	0·02	0·05	3·22	35·30	0·02	10·89	0·12	9·30	11·80	21·41	39·67	2·84	66·26	Nasal Height or Depth.
2·09	0·00	0·11	5·37	11·59	0·31	5·27	0·00	2·03	3·96	12·28	1·86	11·09	9·01	Upper Facial Length.
0·77	1·52	0·00	9·41	17·05	0·58	6·85	0·56	0·86	0·42	23·65	29·04	1·74	1·58	Total Facial Length.
10·95	3·59	4·26	3·26	24·84	0·85	7·94	0·11	0·25	7·15	14·13	167·03	7·61	2·55	Horizontal Cirm. of the Head.
20·11	1·68	5·85	13·16	109·47	61·02	48·69	16·19	12·96	32·48	66·67	35·70	0·00	16·08	Sagittal Arc.
9·34	0·66	3·06	9·14	9·93	0·58	9·94	0·38	4·37	1·53	20·41	573·10	23·06	1·69	Transverse Arc.
8·37	3·62	0·30	2·91	70·83	49·77	3·19	18·36	0·70	32·70	39·53	81·57	24·64	4·39	Length Breadth Index.
3·50	5·73	3·42	0·00	3·94	16·38	0·09	5·25	0·32	2·22	2·86	1·10	14·62	0·71	Length Height Index.
11·13	0·22	1·12	1·94	20·51	2·04	2·80	1·16	0·63	8·89	10·78	62·52	0·02	7·49	Breadth Height Index.
13·63	0·01	0·10	1·56	0·03	0·02	9·24	3·80	1·17	0·00	0·38	52·10	11·30	19·20	Trans. Fronto-Parietal Index.
10·75	1·09	0·00	3·04	1·86	5·96	3·82	24·88	8·79	11·08	1·00	0·07	0·39	55·89	Orbitonasal Index.
3·84	0·60	0·83	0·93	0·01	4·66	0·15	7·83	0·90	0·99	0·00	102·08	38·39	18·36	Nasal Index.
6·53	0·28	0·03	3·52	24·67	0·01	9·64	0·00	10·35	4·94	10·40	64·37	8·61	61·59	Nasal Elevation Index.
0·30	0·20	0·00	8·88	13·29	3·99	11·20	0·21	2·89	6·19	11·90	6·27	4·39	5·24	Upper Facial Index.
7·25	1·27	0·02	17·61	23·05	16·56	18·19	0·27	2·85	2·85	26·08	0·07	0·10	1·38	Total Facial Index.
9·47	0·03	2·00	11·20	0·68	1·73	26·57	0·03	12·29	0·09	0·00	26·18	26·08	1·22	Trans. Cephalo-Facial Index.
0·51	0·61	0·02	0·01	20·39	0·81	0·91	0·02	0·02	2·02	0·30	21·92	2·59	15·13	Vertical Cephalo-Facial Index.

53CO

TABLE XLIV.

Values of $\frac{N_s N_s'}{N_s+N_s'}\left(\frac{M_s-M_s'}{\sigma_s}\right)^2$

Characters.	Red Kaffir.	Pathan.	Uzbeg.	Tadjik.	Khos. (Lower Chitral).	U. P. Brahmin.	Bengali Brahmin	Bengali Kayastha	Bengali Pod.	Orissa Brahmin.	Malve Brahmin.	Rajput.	Nagar Brahmin.	Audich Brahmin.	Kati
Stature	13·82	1·89	21·41	8·22	0·05	5·02	20·47	17·92	0·02	2·06	1·53	36·42	3·85	3·41	
Auricular Height	6·28	0·39	18·99	11·35	2·49	4·37	0·21	0·21	5·25	11·29	10·64	6·40	4·78	16·80	
Max. Head Length ..	37·66	12·33	5·50	11·71	0·96	20·86	0·16	2·14	4·79	12·79	0·01	1·53	2·54	6·60	
Max. Head Breadth	1·55	0·02	62·37	30·34	5·07	13·55	3·20	18·42	4·23	8·05	17·59	4·09	26·83	0·03	
Min. Frontal Breadth	17·82	0·32	19·04	23·26	4·42	6·94	0·84	5·06	2·52	2·40	1·46	7·55	16·17	5·20	
Max. Bizygomatic Breadth.	30·14	10·14	103·86	69·06	21·85	1·65	1·26	12·16	1·00	0·00	1·55	9·03	19·00	10·17	
Bigonial Breadth ..	66·97	21·01	59·55	47·51	41·82	16·93	21·15	32·73	16·56	25·32	24·77	17·14	18·31	13·70	
Inter-Orbital Breadth	0·32	9·58	19·35	8·98	1·62	7·00	7·73	6·18	0·58	17·00	4·63	0·49	4·58	6·28	
Orbitonasal Breadth	19·27	16·07	3·28	4·30	18·90	5·14	0·84	1·71	14·21	10·99	6·54	18·29	1·73	2·86	
Orbitonasal Arc ..	5·10	14·32	15·59	8·40	22·62	0·48	1·06	1·22	8·97	9·51	1·06	2·29	0·34	1·08	
Nasal Length ..	38·37	28·06	23·94	25·63	16·99	5·28	9·33	17·35	1·06	0·09	0·12	0·94	2·52	0·00	
Nasal Breadth ..	5·28	3·13	0·43	3·60	8·37	0·38	0·17	0·28	0·08	0·91	1·50	0·08	0·66	2·07	
Nasal Height or Depth.	18·66	18·28	0·80	1·75	4·13	19·18	19·18	18·83	0·10	0·16	0·08	2·73	2·77	3·06	
Upper Facial Length	10·24	12·62	34·47	20·13	5·21	5·64	15·32	17·80	0·09	0·11	0·02	0·19	0·64	6·28	
Total Facial Length	4·76	9·11	26·72	17·80	7·50	0·49	6·76	2·65	0·51	0·90	0·60	1·27	18·86	16·00	
Horizontal Cirm. of the Head.	29·56	7·41	13·58	3·50	6·34	0·43	1·48	2·57	6·97	13·88	1·42	0·59	8·73	0·32	
Sagittal Arc ..	14·99	4·60	1·94	0·17	0·56	34·48	30·52	8·50	10·58	0·28	6·41	0·82	0·00	0·68	
Transverse Arc ..	16·14	5·90	14·06	0·33	5·64	16·22	1·40	2·82	8·90	8·55	17·68	12·98	0·32	3·37	
Length Breadth Index.	8·81	5·97	82·38	58·24	2·04	39·50	3·69	25·24	0·14	0·03	15·76	6·92	34·39	3·84	
Length Height Index.	27·27	1·34	27·98	24·98	3·64	17·20	0·03	1·43	0·87	28·38	9·84	8·72	1·32	6·12	
Breadth Height Index	8·64	0·35	1·92	0·55	8·01	0·45	2·65	5·49	0·41	23·04	0·01	0·65	25·01	12·86	
Trans. Fronto-Parietal Index.	4·25	0·32	21·46	3·66	0·54	3·67	1·52	7·70	0·36	3·73	13·82	0·00	4·24	3·02	
Orbitonasal Index ..	4·02	0·40	22·02	2·70	2·79	2·54	0·10	0·00	0·06	0·55	2·35	8·60	0·58	0·25	
Nasal Index ..	36·80	26·56	15·36	25·89	27·97	1·46	6·71	7·00	0·22	0·43	1·69	0·67	3·42	1·59	
Nasal Elevation Index.	27·23	23·60	0·24	4·85	11·87	10·86	16·18	10·85	0·04	0·00	0·31	2·14	3·40	5·06	
Upper Facial Index ..	0·02	2·42	0·01	0·48	0·90	2·13	8·84	4·18	0·59	0·18	0·68	1·30	8·02	14·40	
Total Facial Index ..	1·89	0·58	2·29	0·19	0·14	0·04	2·88	0·35	0·00	0·57	2·17	8·43	45·98	31·08	
Trans. Cephalo-Facial Index.	15·69	11·77	0·05	0·18	3·23	40·99	1·38	3·96	2·01	6·75	50·25	36·02	5·00	9·26	
Vertical Cephalo-Facial Index	11·95	2·56	0·07	0·20	9·74	2·96	4·72	0·55	1·59	11·75	3·85	1·38	1·64	0·35	

TABLE XLIV.

swat—Gour Brahmin with other races.

Chitpavan Brahmin.	Desastha Brahmin.	Mahratta.	Nambudiri Brahmin.	Iluva.	Tamil Brahmin.	Kala.	Kanarese Brahmin.	Telegu Brahmin.	Nair.	Kadar.	Bhil.	Khasi.	Characters.
3·06	0·56	0·61	0·28	9·74	0·96	7·36	0·98	2·09	31·69	59·48	0·43	36·48	Stature.
8·08	9·24	6·43	2·23	8·74	0·87	3·00	3·53	0·02	0·71	1·73	36·87	1·27	Auricular Height.
0·89	4·43	12·70	41·88	6·19	1·32	2·14	5·00	6·92	19·87	18·54	14·29	0·00	Max. Head Length.
0·40	0·00	0·70	6·06	14·42	0·52	2·92	0·80	5·37	2·35	100·88	36·67	0·00	Max. Head Breadth.
0·88	1·38	0·17	3·98	11·84	1·28	9·87	1·60	2·87	1·60	14·24	8·59	12·66	Min. Frontal Breadth.
6·79	6·02	5·41	0·38	9·25	0·54	0·73	0·77	1·84	1·45	25·28	0·06	5·46	Max. Bizygomatic Breadth.
8·91	24·11	19·49	3·48	1·39	4·62	12·31	0·74	3·30	8·78	12·34	8·70	85·94	Bigonial Breadth
0·83	7·41	1·25	0·61	1·81	4·44	2·25	1·16	1·07	0·79	0·12	0·18	0·56	Inter-Orbital Breadth
7·18	10·03	19·74	0·42	1·24	5·54	2·31	0·43	9·02	0·31	74·35	17·50	23·01	Orbitonasal Breadth.
0·00	1·38	5·58	8·61	2·10	3·74	12·41	0·04	0·76	1·41	27·91	6·81	56·84	Orbitonasal Arc.
2·31	1·19	0·67	0·00	11·97	0·57	11·06	0·24	0·32	0·29	38·60	23·41	18·22	Nasal Length.
0·15	1·32	0·32	0·48	0·08	0·00	0·86	0·38	2·89	2·44	36·72	9·90	96·93	Nasal Breadth.
3·54	3·21	3·22	15·49	2·52	2·10	1·65	1·46	2·52	6·91	63·81	11·20	93·39	Nasal Height or Depth.
6·55	5·22	5·37	0·97	7·62	0·00	4·19	0·74	0·10	1·06	15·29	29·48	0·14	Upper Facial Length.
5·08	12·17	9·41	0·89	4·90	0·19	4·24	4·24	5·39	2·48	73·35	17·80	20·04	Total Facial Length.
0·05	0·00	3·26	9·04	0·72	0·95	1·72	1·57	0·70	3·20	203·45	19·24	0·13	Horizontal Cirm. of the Head.
7·94	3·18	13·16	41·83	16·17	10·37	0·32	0·00	3·96	17·44	95·11	12·30	2·27	Sagittal Arc.
17·14	3·02	9·14	0·00	4·74	0·02	4·59	0·80	2·95	1·67	679·13	56·56	0·56	Transverse Arc.
0·01	1·95	2·91	40·88	26·42	0·01	6·71	5·97	14·86	18·54	43·73	9·80	0·03	Length Breadth Index.
4·96	2·93	0·00	3·55	15·11	0·10	4·82	0·26	1·99	2·10	1·09	13·47	0·72	Length Height Index.
4·05	6·66	1·94	8·99	0·00	u·07	0·05	4·49	2·37	3·10	35·71	1·49	1·32	Breadth Height Index.
2·21	1·21	1·56	1·17	1·82	2·96	0·56	0·03	1·37	0·44	67·76	19·64	8·03	Trans. Fronto-Parietal Index.
9·71	4·32	3·64	10·14	0·26	0·00	9·53	1·03	1·86	0·92	5·79	1·52	25·76	Orbitonasal Index.
3·28	3·78	0·93	0·71	9·00	0·31	12·77	0·00	3·54	0·86	113·31	47·34	26·65	Nasal Index.
2·53	5·10	3·52	8·52	2·85	1·39	3·01	1·66	0·11	1·45	94·27	21·37	89·76	Nasal Elevation Index.
14·04	11·61	8·88	0·33	0·90	0·12	5·08	1·51	0·22	0·10	1·00	23·80	1·03	Upper Facial Index.
13·06	20·86	17·61	0·25	0·02	0·01	5·91	5·81	5·81	0·46	23·24	13·94	31·39	Total Facial Index.
12·76	5·86	11·20	16·55	3·81	3·02	10·18	0·02	12·29	11·18	74·34	66·02	6·38	Trans. Cephalo-Facial Index.
0·44	0·00	0·01	0·25	0·66	0·98	0·04	0·00	2·07	0·21	20·74	2·24	14·54	Vertical Cephalo-Facial Index.

TABLE XLV.

Values of $\frac{N_s N_s'}{N_s + N_s'}\left(\frac{M_s - M_s'}{\sigma_s}\right)^2$ f

Characters.	Red Kaffir.	Pathan.	Uzbeg.	Tadjik.	Khos. (Lower Chitral).	U. P. Brahmin.	Bengali Brahmin.	Bengali Kayastha.	Bengali Pod.	Orissa Brahmin.	Malve Brahmin.	Rajput.	Nagar Brahmin.	Audich Brahmin.	Kat
Stature	23·62	5·59	5·37	15·28	1·80	10·43	30·41	28·90	0·73	6·97	4·95	51·52	9·71	8·84	
Auricular Height ..	0·11	6·27	35·52	28·57	0·30	0·05	2·03	6·91	0·17	30·55	1·92	0·13	0·00	3·82	
Max. Head Length ..	76·02	33·04	0·12	1·14	12·37	46·28	3·40	1·25	0·00	0·73	5·29	14·58	1·02	0·00	
Max. Head Breadth	0·05	1·05	49·22	20·86	1·53	20·93	0·80	10·62	8·35	15·42	25·89	9·34	17·13	0·71	
Min. Frontal Breadth	7·63	0·49	10·23	12·22	0·45	15·19	0·12	0·63	8·12	9·51	6·12	17·69	6·50	0·71	
Max. Bizygomatic Breadth.	20·05	5·32	86·43	54·57	13·54	0·17	0·06	6·12	3·53	1·25	0·14	3·97	11·14	4·79	
Bigonial Breadth ..	51·67	13·85	47·13	35·83	30·13	10·58	13·96	22·33	10·29	15·87	16·93	9·89	10·73	7·39	
Inter-Orbital Breadth	0·45	17·39	28·03	17·06	6·21	2·46	2·90	1·54	3·38	29·52	10·43	0·30	11·51	13·84	
Orbitonasal Breadth	26·46	21·74	1·30	7·63	25·90	8·52	0·07	0·31	19·56	16·90	10·29	25·31	4·31	5·93	
Orbitonasal Arc ..	4·15	12·90	13·92	7·26	20·59	0·25	1·50	1·77	7·85	8·12	0·70	1·66	0·13	0·66	
Nasal Length ..	45·65	33·45	27·70	31·07	21·84	7·75	12·54	22·35	0·29	0·09	0·02	2·34	4·64	0·27	
Nasal Breadth ..	2·53	1·34	0·01	1·57	4·83	1·50	0·04	1·53	0·12	0·04	3·37	0·20	0·01	0·55	
Nasal Height or Depth	8·56	9·42	3·78	0·00	0·44	10·07	10·07	8·68	2·30	3·49	0·87	0·07	0·07	0·14	
Upper Facial Length	17·58	19·46	43·02	30·59	10·61	10·47	22·79	27·16	1·33	0·51	0·53	2·03	0·04	2·32	
Total Facial Length	20·77	25·78	47·92	40·77	25·73	7·59	0·22	16·03	1·81	2·42	1·65	1·57	3·79	2·73	
Horizontal Cirm. of the Head.	47·39	15·80	22·52	10·18	15·52	3·65	6·09	9·31	1·92	4·85	0·01	4·92	19·47	0·74	
Sagittal Arc ..	15·23	4·71	1·83	0·14	0·61	34·79	30·82	8·68	10·76	0·31	6·28	0·77	0·00	0·63	
Transverse Arc ..	8·90	2·35	20·19	7·60	1·85	9·80	4·33	7·36	4·36	3·36	10·95	6·59	2·58	0·66	
Length Breadth Index.	33·43	23·87	45·46	25·61	1·80	76·17	0·27	4·86	7·91	9·89	41·12	29·70	9·12	0·68	
Length Height Index	21·41	0·42	32·23	30·65	1·76	13·22	0·11	3·18	0·18	35·02	6·89	5·58	0·31	3·57	
Breadth Height Index	0·24	7·34	0·25	2·22	0·18	7·79	0·24	0·01	2·20	52·52	4·92	2·70	6·42	1·38	
Trans. Fronto-Parietal Index.	3·51	0·17	22·28	4·34	0·85	3·08	1·95	8·77	0·19	3·01	12·64	0·05	5·06	2·41	
Orbitonasal Index ..	10·09	0·15	14·00	0·33	0·27	6·81	1·78	1·32	1·60	0·24	6·46	16·83	3·77	2·73	
Nasal Index ..	37·01	26·67	15·10	26·05	28·15	1·50	6·78	7·09	0·21	0·45	1·65	0·70	3·49	1·63	
Nasal Elevation Index.	13·91	12·73	2·62	0·71	3·93	4·02	7·47	3·26	2·21	2·30	3·39	0·00	0·12	0·61	
Upper Facial Index .	2·39	7·75	14·46	0·36	0·20	7·23	17·66	11·76	4·00	1·14	0·17	0·08	1·96	5·71	
Total Facial Index ..	1·98	10·05	0·39	1·31	5·58	4·90	16·88	4·79	5·62	4·76	0·88	0·01	15·80	7·98	
Trans. Cephalo-Facial Index.	17·11	12·83	0·12	2·23	3·88	42·97	1·04	1·70	2·47	7·75	52·43	38·17	4·24	10·34	
Vertical Cephalo-Facial Index.	11·50	2·38	0·04	0·15	9·33	2·76	4·47	0·40	1·45	12·26	3·63	12·33	1·52	0·28	

TABLE XLV.

Kanarese Brahmin with other races.

Bania-Jain.	Chitpavan Brahmin.	Desastha Brahmin.	Saraswat Gour Brahmin.	Maharatta.	Nambudiri Brahmin.	Iluva.	Tamil Brahmin.	Kala.	Telogu Brahmin.	Nair.	Kadar.	Bhil.	Khasi.	Characters.
6·13	8·40	3·64	0·98	3·28	2·38	4·54	3·87	13·29	5·93	44·41	42·88	0·12	24·39	Stature.
0·34	0·44	0·72	3·53	0·36	11·65	1·16	7·90	0·03	3·09	7·85	0·80	17·59	10·16	Auricular Height.
1·35	2·74	0·26	5·00	1·53	76·75	22·32	11·46	12·75	23·68	46·15	2·81	2·38	6·36	Max. Head Length.
8·35	2·78	1·04	0·80	3·13	11·40	22·02	0·03	6·51	10·31	6·08	123·11	48·31	1·02	Max. Head Breadth.
1·05	0·28	0·09	1·60	0·83	10·81	22·13	5·72	18·78	8·74	6·67	27·46	17·59	24·62	Min. Frontal Breadth.
22·25	2·52	2·04	0·77	1·99	0·08	15·35	2·60	0·00	0·20	0·08	36·72	1·26	1·86	Max. Bizygomatic Breadth.
18·33	3·93	15·24	0·74	12·37	0·98	0·10	1·65	7·27	0·91	4·25	6·23	4·36	69·08	Bigonial Breadth.
18·42	4·67	15·83	1·16	5·01	3·54	5·87	1·07	6·33	4·45	4·06	2·59	2·26	2·23	Inter-Orbital Breadth.
0·03	11·81	15·45	0·43	26·24	0·00	3·12	2·89	4·56	0·25	0·02	88·64	23·39	30·51	Orbitonasal Breadth.
0·00	0·07	0·90	0·04	4·67	9·81	1·58	4·52	11·16	0·46	1·93	23·42	5·84	53·66	Orbitonasal Arc.
7·69	0·92	0·27	0·24	0·09	0·31	8·84	0·07	8·22	0·01	1·09	28·34	18·94	13·89	Nasal Length.
3·40	1·22	3·48	0·38	1·45	1·75	0·78	0·38	2·27	5·35	4·85	45·98	14·13	7·42	Nasal Breadth.
0·00	10·76	10·24	1·46	9·30	7·29	7·80	0·06	5·87	0·15	1·87	88·50	20·72	121·14	Nasal Height or Depth.
0·04	2·44	1·64	0·74	2·03	3·47	3·61	0·70	1·53	0·29	3·71	8·41	20·88	1·78	Upper Facial Length.
3·44	0·02	1·18	4·24	0·86	9·30	0·02	2·64	0·01	0·07	13·89	37·74	4·66	4·78	Total Facial Length.
3·67	1·53	1·94	1·57	0·25	18·39	0·17	4·96	0·02	4·36	9·59	163·59	9·82	1·52	Horizontal Cirm. of the Head.
0·07	7·77	3·07	0·00	12·96	42·19	16·39	10·54	0·39	4·07	17·67	94·49	12·11	2·33	Sagittal Arc.
0·34	9·61	0·48	0·80	4·37	0·93	1·64	1·04	1·68	0·68	4·96	623·35	43·89	0·02	Transverse Arc.
3·31	7·46	2·12	5·97	0·70	79·13	57·51	6·35	23·96	3·97	47·03	90·00	31·06	8·33	Length Breadth Index.
1·36	2·67	1·24	0·26	0·32	1·85	11·39	0·69	2·94	0·80	0·83	2·70	9·98	1·99	Length Height Index.
5·34	0·20	0·01	4·49	0·63	26·71	4·63	10·29	3·15	13·38	15·79	71·72	0·81	12·10	Breadth Height Index.
5·30	1·69	0·83	0·03	1·17	0·84	1·41	3·54	6·82	1·01	0·24	64·67	18·22	9·09	Trans. Fronto-Parietal Index.
0·03	18·44	10·65	1·03	8·79	17·84	0·25	0·93	4·52	0·12	4·07	12·91	5·03	15·57	Orbitonasal Index.
0·65	3·21	3·71	0·00	0·90	0·68	8·91	0·29	12·67	3·48	0·83	112·94	47·14	26·48	Nasal Index.
1·29	9·54	14·17	1·66	10·35	2·56	8·87	0·01	8·71	0·92	0·02	126·02	34·06	119·00	Nasal Elevation Index.
5·75	5·39	3·89	1·51	2·89	3·35	0·08	2·50	1·20	0·57	2·54	0·20	13·31	0·13	Upper Facial Index.
19·56	0·67	3·07	5·81	2·85	8·80	5·24	6·13	0·02	0·00	10·20	3·94	1·75	8·53	Total Facial Index.
0·93	14·06	6·75	0·02	12·29	18·01	4·42	2·51	11·11	13·38	12·27	77·45	68·51	7·27	Trans. Cephalo-Facial Index
0·68	0·36	0·00	0·00	0·02	0·31	0·57	1·09	0·06	2·24	0·16	21·36	2·07	15·02	Vertical Cephalo-Facial Index.

TABLE XLVI.

Values of $\frac{N_s \, N_s'}{N_s + N_s'} \left(\frac{M_s - M_s'}{\sigma_s} \right)^2$ for

Characters.	Red Kaffir.	Pathan.	Uzbeg.	Tadjik.	Khos (Lower Chitral).	U. P. Brahmin.	Bengali Brahmin.	Bengali Kayastha.	Bengali Pod.	Orissa Brahmin.	Malva Brahmin.	Rajput.	Nagar Brahmin.	Audich Brahmin.	Kathi.
Stature	6·70	0·16	0·35	3·38	0·79	1·59	12·58	9·64	1·24	0·06	0·07	24·07	0·68	0·53	6·14
Auricular Height ..	12·87	0·10	12·44	5·71	6·94	9·14	1·92	0·38	10·38	5·21	17·59	13·00	10·70	26·56	6·33
Max. Head Length ..	23·13	5·58	11·36	21·45	0·10	11·68	2·38	7·79	11·15	24·75	1·18	0·01	8·57	15·05	0·30
Max. Head Breadth	0·17	0·72	52·66	22·58	2·07	19·36	1·15	11·99	7·36	13·70	24·13	8·14	18·87	0·41	15·79
Min. Frontal Breadth	30·52	2·87	28·83	36·13	11·21	2·27	4·18	12·63	0·21	0·03	0·01	2·08	28·46	12·71	5·14
Max. Bizygomatic Breadth.	40·18	15·35	117·65	82·51	30·33	4·08	3·45	18·80	0·70	0·72	3·92	14·85	27·19	16·21	60·24
Bigonial Breadth ..	32·53	5·93	33·65	21·46	16·25	3·87	6·01	10·50	3·69	5·93	8·00	2·75	3·20	1·56	3·60
Inter-Orbital Breadth	3·48	27·06	39·42	27·20	13·40	0·29	0·45	0·00	0·40	44·75	18·15	3·01	21·10	24·11	15·29
Orbitonasal Breadth	50·50	40·47	7·14	20·70	49·22	12·46	2·07	1·08	37·48	38·18	24·00	48·91	16·41	19·13	4·97
Orbitonasal Arc ..	20·59	32·68	32·17	24·31	48·26	6·89	0·81	1·27	24·28	29·54	8·78	13·99	8·01	10·47	1·04
Nasal Length ..	49·96	36·65	30·99	34·32	24·80	9·33	14·52	25·40	0·07	0·39	0·17	3·39	6·10	0·69	20·11
Nasal Breadth ..	5·28	3·13	0·43	3·60	8·37	0·38	0·17	0·28	0·08	0·91	1·50	0·08	0·66	2·06	0·30
Nasal Height or Depth	7·01	8·00	4·77	0·04	15·29	8·59	8·59	7·12	3·09	4·67	1·38	0·00	0·00	0·01	1·37
Upper Facial Length	10·41	12·78	34·70	20·35	5·33	5·75	15·50	18·02	0·10	0·09	0·01	0·21	0·60	6·14	3·68
Total Facial Length	7·19	11·92	30·87	21·85	10·44	1·28	9·21	4·52	0·08	0·18	0·12	0·39	14·73	12·28	0·98
Horizontal Cirm. of the Head.	18·59	3·05	7·93	0·71	2·00	0·10	0·06	0·23	13·06	24·12	4·69	0·13	3·31	2·82	6·58
Sagittal Arc .	0·02	1·16	18·19	14·41	8·41	7·03	5·31	0·64	0·00	11·50	33·08	21·38	14·31	20·24	37·97
Transverse Arc ..	17·32	6·52	13·23	2·83	6·34	17·24	1·12	2·35	9·67	9·47	18·75	14·05	0·18	3·92	0·01
Length Breadth Index	8·31	5·60	83·62	59·48	2·29	38·55	3·99	26·13	0·09	0·01	15·16	6·46	35·44	4·19	16·15
Length Height Index	31·24	2·18	25·06	21·75	5·14	19·95	0·25	0·68	1·56	24·60	11·94	11·02	2·31	8·02	4·23
Breadth Height Index.	10·57	0·10	2·65	1·05	9·83	0·16	3·61	7·05	0·83	20·14	0·03	1·24	28·25	15·16	20·44
Trans. Fronto-Parietal Index.	16·39	5·24	9·60	0·01	1·48	13·22	0·24	0·62	5·39	16·15	29·58	3·80	0·00	13·66	5·34
Orbitonasal Index ..	4·22	0·35	21·65	2·56	2·63	2·68	0·13	0·00	0·09	0·48	2·48	8·90	0·66	0·30	1·06
Nasal Index ..	44·94	32·51	19·47	32·14	34·98	3·10	0·87	10·78	0·01	1·76	0·56	2·12	6·22	3·57	15·19
Nasal Elevation Index	14·86	13·53	2·37	0·92	4·44	4·47	8·08	3·73	1·90	1·92	3·00	0·01	0·22	0·82	1·88
Upper Facial Index ..	0·08	1·45	0·04	1·14	1·82	1·23	6·87	2·68	0·18	0·73	1·38	2·39	10·50	17·57	5·08
Total Facial Index .	2·11	0·48	2·47	2·13	0·20	0·07	2·67	0·45	0·01	0·70	2·37	8·87	47·02	31·91	32·24
Trans. Cephalo-Facial Index.	35·60	26·71	3·12	9·93	14·20	66·26	0·32	0·00	9·96	22·22	77·90	64·14	0·04	25·25	10·64
Vertical Cephalo-Facial Index.	21·13	6·69	1·30	2·20	17·97	7·33	9·98	3·55	5·06	5·23	8·70	5·37	0·02	2·95	1·46

TABLE XLVI.

Tamil Brahmin with other races.

Bania-Jain.	Chitpavan Brahmin.	Desastha Brahmin.	Saraswat Gour Brahmin.	Maharatta.	Nambudiri Brahmin.	Iluva.	Kala.	Kanarese Brahmin.	Telegu Brahmin.	Nair.	Kadar.	Bhil.	Khasi.	Characters.
0·04	0·38	0·15	0·96	0·06	0·22	23·56	3·21	3·87	0·22	21·24	78·54	2·66	50·79	Stature.
14·61	15·40	17·04	0·87	12·24	0·29	15·12	6·08	7·90	1·11	0·02	5·81	49·06	0·01	Auricular Height.
7·51	5·18	11·89	1·32	22·65	28·04	1·79	0·14	11·46	2·19	10·61	32·00	24·30	1·55	Max. Head Length.
9·57	2·40	0·66	0·52	2·52	10·22	20·40	5·69	0·03	9·21	5·21	118·56	45·89	0·36	Max. Head Breadth.
14·29	5·04	6·23	1·28	2·50	0·70	5·35	4·32	5·72	0·32	0·01	172·45	3·25	5·30	Min. Frontal Breadth.
43·24	11·95	10·97	0·54	9·54	1·86	5·32	2·40	2·60	1·35	3·89	17·34	0·24	9·95	Max. Bizygomatic Breadth.
7·83	0·24	5·77	4·62	4·75	0·11	0·94	2·20	1·65	0·11	0·52	0·97	0·64	47·35	Bigonial Breadth.
30·04	11·27	26·87	4·44	10·97	8·63	11·93	12·17	1·07	9·86	9·56	7·96	6·42	4·91	Inter-Orbital Breadth.
4·50	29·26	34·98	5·54	47·48	3·51	12·00	13·97	2·89	4·84	3·61	130·27	42·72	54·97	Orbitonasal Breadth.
5·82	4·86	11·77	3·74	19·12	0·91	11·44	28·56	4·52	7·85	0·69	56·77	20·62	93·87	Orbitonasal Arc.
9·51	0·41	0·04	0·57	0·00	0·69	7·31	6·82	0·07	0·04	1·76	28·34	16·66	11·74	Nasal Length.
1·29	0·15	1·33	0·00	0·32	0·48	0·07	1·19	0·38	2·89	2·44	36·72	9·90	4·17	Nasal Breadth.
0·07	12·68	12·13	2·10	10·89	6·02	9·21	7·02	0·06	0·02	1·25	93·92	22·98	127·12	Nasal Height or Depth.
1·38	6·42	5·10	0·00	5·27	1·01	7·49	4·10	0·70	0·09	1·10	15·09	29·24	0·16	Upper Facial Length.
13·91	3·07	8·89	0·19	6·85	1·92	3·17	2·72	2·64	3·57	4·12	64·88	14·33	15·95	Total Facial Length
0·00	1·82	1·46	0·95	7·94	4·03	3·42	4·97	4·96	0·02	0·59	237·46	28·74	0·10	Horizontal Cirm. of the Head.
12·12	42·95	30·71	10·37	48·69	10·06	0·64	5·94	10·54	1·51	0·66	183·29	45·25	0·54	Sagittal Arc.
0·36	18·37	3·55	0·02	9·94	0·01	5·30	5·11	1·04	3·41	1·34	686·86	58·47	0·70	Transverse Arc.
22·31	0·04	2·20	0·01	3·19	39·90	25·65	6·35	6·35	14·28	17·86	42·55	9·32	0·01	Length Breadth Index.
4·50	6·75	4·84	0·10	0·09	4·88	17·68	6·23	0·69	2·98	3·17	0·45	15·91	0·25	Length Height Index.
25·57	5·41	8·38	0·07	2·80	7·41	0·06	0·23	10·29	1·61	2·19	32·02	2·22	0·73	Breadth Height Index.
0·02	12·14	9·66	2·96	9·24	8·07	9·41	0·76	3·54	8·35	6·04	104·62	37·86	0·85	Trans. Fronto-Parietal Index.
0·89	10·03	4·53	0·00	3·82	10·43	0·22	9·28	0·95	1·75	1·01	6·04	1·63	25·36	Orbitonasal Index.
2·04	1·37	1·69	0·31	0·15	0·01	5·99	9·32	0·29	1·76	0·12	99·91	40·05	20·69	Nasal Index.
1·02	8·77	13·23	1·39	9·64	2·93	8·23	8·12	0·01	0·72	0·00	123·15	33·68	116·36	Nasal Elevation Index.
17·32	17·27	14·58	0·12	11·20	0·05	1·68	6·69	2·50	0·68	0·00	2·00	27·35	1·95	Upper Facial Index.
52·96	13·62	21·57	0·01	18·19	0·19	0·04	6·22	6·13	6·13	0·37	23·99	14·44	32·21	Total Facial Index.
7·81	31·24	19·80	3·02	26·57	34·41	13·61	23·31	2·51	27·49	27·60	113·76	97·28	20·18	Trans. Cephalo-Facial Index.
0·15	3·28	1·49	0·98	0·91	0·26	3·25	0·54	1·09	0·21	2·22	11·51	6·17	7·44	Vertical Cephalo-Facial Index.

TABLE XLVII.

Values of $\frac{N_s \, N_s'}{N_s + N_s'}\left(\frac{M_s - M_s'}{\sigma_s}\right)^2$ for

Characters.	Red Kaffir.	Pathan.	Uzbeg.	Tadjik.	Khos (Lower Chitral).	U. P. Brahmin.	Bengali Brahmin.	Bengali Kayastha.	Bengali Ped.	Orissa Brahmin.	Malve Brahmin.	Rajput.	Nagar Brahmin.	Audich Brahmin.	Kathi.
Stature	0·13	2·01	1·10	0·02	7·98	0·36	2·41	0·71	8·10	3·61	2·40	6·31	1·64	1·78	0·43
Auricular Height ..	0·27	4·74	31·23	23·22	0·09	0·15	1·35	4·96	0·33	24·12	2·21	0·29	0·04	4·07	0·00
Max. Head Length ..	16·19	3·42	12·64	22·44	0·52	8·08	3·36	9·08	12·43	25·19	1·97	0·26	9·89	16·18	0·78
Max. Head Breadth	9·54	2·50	82·29	48·27	15·07	3·11	11·52	34·92	0·03	0·34	5·05	0·00	45·42	4·32	36·39
Min. Frontal Breadth	55·83	13·50	48·94	60·94	29·80	0·43	16·03	31·89	2·71	5·26	4·01	1·04	53·39	31·75	17·00
Max. Bizygomatic Breadth.	16·91	4·60	80·04	47·51	11·44	0·13	0·04	5·10	3·24	1·13	0·10	3·28	9·33	3·98	39·09
Bigonial Breadth ..	12·95	0·66	17·59	7·78	4·35	0·14	0·68	1·74	0·11	0·22	1·40	0·02	0·00	0·25	0·15
Inter-Orbital Breadth	4·97	2·01	8·07	1·53	0·25	15·96	16·99	16·02	0·61	4·03	0·28	5·52	0·07	0·41	0·16
Orbitonasal Breadth	5·48	5·10	0·68	0·13	5·47	0·38	5·68	8·61	4·14	1·54	0·81	5·00	0·27	0·02	2·05
Orbitonasal Arc ..	3·62	0·00	0·35	0·94	0·23	8·23	20·19	25·18	0·49	1·80	6·50	6·67	12·14	8·90	16·85
Nasal Length ..	90·36	69·21	58·75	67·60	56·80	30·15	38·49	58·18	5·56	13·48	8·96	21·77	27·73	13·70	45·32
Nasal Breadth ..	10·12	6·75	2·13	7·57	13·85	0·12	1·73	0·32	1·41	3·91	0·05	1·71	3·29	5·64	1·96
Nasal Height or Depth.	29·76	28·25	0·09	6·68	11·02	29·30	29·30	29·97	0·98	1·34	2·38	8·92	9·04	9·38	13·13
Upper Facial Length	27·93	29·12	56·44	40·28	19·40	18·38	32·92	38·79	5·41	4·51	3·68	7·40	2·54	0·00	14·01
Total Facial Length	18·94	24·04	46·05	37·28	18·63	7·37	20·34	14·74	1·92	2·45	1·76	1·67	2·78	1·96	0·39
Horizontal Cirm. of the Head.	42·50	15·02	22·05	9·76	14·44	3·73	6·03	8·82	1·39	3·50	0·04	4·83	17·87	0·88	20·69
Sagittal Arc ..	8·45	2·03	3·49	1·02	0·00	24·38	21·25	4·09	6·09	0·05	8·91	2·30	0·52	2·07	12·49
Transverse Arc ..	1·66	0·02	30·34	15·54	0·04	2·74	10·62	15·87	0·45	0·02	3·32	0·82	8·81	0·49	4·99
Length Breadth Index.	0·04	0·08	120·84	97·27	17·78	11·12	19·38	57·60	5·03	8·51	1·33	0·25	70·25	22·30	38·46
Length Height Index	5·50	1·22	49·36	48·74	0·47	2·94	4·10	12·93	1·74	55·09	0·58	0·06	2·08	0·03	0·17
Breadth Height Index	6·09	0·61	1·25	0·21	5·65	0·73	1·72	3·67	0·14	22·07	0·10	0·24	19·09	9·47	14·71
Trans-Fronto-Parietal Index.	7·61	1·65	14·00	1·02	0·02	6·53	0·17	2·95	1·73	7·08	18·10	0·67	1·10	6·01	9·12
Orbitonasal Index ..	28·70	6·20	2·85	2·86	3·59	21·07	11·47	12·10	11·05	8·86	20·41	38·68	17·85	15·36	16·90
Nasal Index ..	93·49	71·04	48·47	72·37	79·15	22·22	36·19	42·28	9·80	23·43	5·52	23·14	33·55	26·80	43·49
Nasal Elevation Index.	46·23	39·84	1·21	15·05	26·37	23·45	30·56	25·18	2·40	4·45	1·48	11·05	13·60	16·27	16·02
Upper Facial Index ..	7·14	13·84	4·62	2·91	2·67	13·18	25·58	19·80	8·89	5·21	2·18	2·26	0·00	0·97	0·10
Total Facial Index ..	2·20	9·91	0·56	1·54	5·60	5·05	16·26	4·87	5·73	4·81	1·09	0·01	12·21	5·96	9·12
Trans. Cephalo-Facial Index.	0·00	0·00	7·13	4·37	3·58	8·10	18·46	29·80	3·44	1·95	12·20	3·76	32·61	0·57	2·21
Vertical Cephalo-Facial Index.	11·73	2·91	0·18	0·39	9·71	3·31	5·04	0·83	1·92	8·69	4·19	1·73	0·92	0·60	0·20

TABLE XLVII.

…il Kala with other races.

…lia- …n.	Chitpavan Brahmin.	Desastha Brahmin.	Saraswat Gour Brahmin.	Mahratta.	Nambudiri Brahmin.	Iluva.	Tamil Brahmin.	Kanarese Brahmin.	Telegu Brahmin.	Nair.	Kadar.	Bhil.	Khasi.	Characters.
	2·16	5·82	7·36	4·31	5·16	31·98	3·21	13·29	1·82	6·06	104·96	11·10	73·94	Stature.
	0·67	0·98	3·00	0·56	9·15	1·44	6·08	0·03	2·18	5·95	0·38	17·11	7·70	Auricular Height.
	6·43	13·11	2·14	23·61	21·09	0·78	0·14	12·75	1·04	7·08	32·03	25·26	2·47	Max. Head Length.
	1·85	3·91	2·92	0·96	0·33	3·51	5·69	6·51	0·23	0·11	53·39	16·02	3·46	Max. Head Breadth.
	19·75	21·95	9·87	13·21	1·78	0·01	4·32	18·78	2·39	4·33	210·69	1·44	0·19	Min. Frontal Breadth.
	2·06	1·66	0·73	1·68	0·09	13·86	2·40	0·00	0·20	0·06	31·67	1·18	1·53	Max. Bizygomatic Breadth.
	1·52	0·27	12·31	0·26	3·34	5·74	2·20	7·27	3·23	0·75	0·63	0·53	22·81	Bigonial Breadth.
	0·75	–0·64	2·25	0·25	0·64	0·05	12·17	6·33	0·28	0·53	1·99	1·21	0·12	Inter-Orbital Breadth.
	0·56	1·41	2·31	6·73	4·66	0·22	13·97	4·56	2·77	4·42	38·85	5·87	7·82	Orbitonasal Breadth.
	1·64	8·68	12·41	2·05	40·39	4·65	28·56	11·16	7·30	2·28	0·67	1·13	9·92	Orbitonasal Arc.
	5·66	7·34	11·06	7·17	11·88	0·00	6·82	8·22	7·78	15·67	3·64	1·53	0·10	Nasal Length.
	0·48	0·00	0·86	0·19	0·09	0·45	1·19	2·27	0·45	0·25	20·46	4·15	0·77	Nasal Breadth.
	0·08	0·03	1·65	0·12	25·12	0·04	7·02	5·87	7·73	14·45	34·77	3·50	57·52	Nasal Height or Depth.
	0·00	0·05	4·19	0·00	9·09	0·31	4·10	1·53	3·06	9·56	1·57	9·43	6·76	Upper Facial Length.
	0·07	0·75	4·24	0·56	8·92	0·00	2·72	0·01	0·02	13·08	30·67	3·68	3·63	Total Facial Length.
	1·67	2·06	1·72	0·11	17·34	0·26	4·97	0·02	4·40	9·23	135·98	7·98	1·66	Horizontal Cirm. of the Head.
	10·81	5·44	0·32	16·19	29·86	10·19	5·94	0·39	1·64	10·86	93·96	15·25	1·07	Sagittal Arc.
	1·93	0·72	4·59	0·38	4·99	0·01	5·11	1·68	0·27	11·82	362·42	24·48	0·66	Transverse Arc.
	9·28	18·12	6·71	18·36	11·34	5·00	6·35	23·96	1·09	1·81	9·75	1·30	7·21	Length Breadth Index.
	0·19	0·87	4·82	5·25	0·22	2·15	6·23	2·94	0·75	0·85	12·19	1·60	10·09	Length Height Index.
	2·58	4·53	0·05	1·16	9·29	0·06	0·23	3·15	2·80	3·55	33·35	0·86	1·73	Breadth Height Index
	4·97	3·51	0·56	3·80	3·17	4·08	0·76	0·82	3·43	1·96	70·56	24·29	3·29	Trans. Fronto-Parietal Index.
	40·94	29·76	9·53	24·88	37·78	6·78	9·28	4·54	3·24	16·37	33·30	18·07	1·78	Orbitonasal Index.
	5·74	5·27	12·77	7·83	8·17	0·56	9·32	12·67	3·24	8·09	32·63	8·48	0·78	Nasal Index.
	0·25	0·01	3·01	0·00	20·41	0·02	8·12	8·71	4·20	8·61	48·51	6·88	47·76	Nasal Elevation Index.
	0·81	0·32	5·08	0·21	8·05	1·86	6·69	1·20	3·27	6·94	2·80	5·50	2·37	Upper Facial Index.
	0·33	2·07	5·91	0·27	8·65	5·37	6·22	0·02	0·02	10·00	2·72	1·18	6·47	Total Facial Index.
	0·11	2·00	10·18	0·03	0·34	1·82	23·31	11·11	0·01	0·03	18·37	19·02	1·26	Trans. Cephalo-Facial Index.
	0·71	0·08	0·04	0·02	0·07	0·92	0·54	0·06	1·34	0·41	15·81	2·59	11·15	Vertical Cephalo-Facial Index.

TABLE—XLVIII.

Values of $\frac{N_s\ N_s'}{N_s + N_s'}\left(\frac{M_s - M_{s'}}{\sigma_s}\right)^2$ for

Characters.	Red Kaffir.	Pathan.	Uzbog.	Tadjik.	Khos (Lower Chitral).	U. P. Brahmin.	Bengali Brahmin.	Bengali Kayastha.	Bengali Pod.	Orissa Brahmin.	Malve Brahmin.	Rajput.	Nagar Brahmin.	Audich Brahmin.	Kathi.
Stature	4·20	0·01	0·03	1·82	2·02	0·63	9·49	6·58	2·50	0·10	0·05	19·06	0·08	0·04	4·16
Auricular Height ..	5·61	0·56	19·46	12·22	2·08	3·88	0·11	0·36	4·71	12·24	9·88	5·72	4·19	15·65	2·33
Max. Head Length ..	9·61	0·78	21·48	38·31	4·00	3·75	9·14	20·25	23·22	45·93	6·59	3·24	21·68	31·00	3·78
Max. Head Breadth	15·36	4.77	96·92	63·18	23·81	1·86	16·86	48·54	0·11	0·00	3·52	0·42	62·03	7·94	46·73
Min. Frontal Breadth.	38·15	5·10	33·68	43·62	16·19	0·89	6·80	17·69	0·01	0·25	0·24	0·63	35·91	17·70	7·84
Max. Bizygomatic Breadth.	24·96	7·59	93·94	61·77	17·54	0·74	0·48	8·96	2·04	0·33	0·67	6·30	14·90	7·29	49·5
Bigonial Breadth ..	37·02	7·67	36·30	24·83	19·44	5·29	7·75	13·14	5·08	7·98	10·00	4·18	4·69	2·66	4·89
Inter-Orbital Breadth	3·17	4·26	11·82	3·65	0·01	13·52	14·53	13·52	0·07	8·22	1·26	3·57	0·88	1·77	0·90
Orbitonasal Breadth	20·86	17·32	0·49	5·00	20·43	5·85	0·58	1·28	15·38	12·26	7·34	19·82	2·23	3·47	0·02
Orbitonasal Arc ..	1·64	8·50	9·83	3·93	14·22	0·03	3·61	4·45	4·52	4·11	0·03	0·26	0·19	0·00	2·64
Nasal Length ..	46·86	34·40	28·46	32·03	22·71	8·21	13·12	23·25	0·21	0·16	0·05	2·63	5·06	0·38	18·54
Nasal Breadth ..	18·18	12·04	4·59	13·60	23·24	1·19	4·45	2·06	3·89	9·14	0·23	5·01	7·79	11·39	4·62
Nasal Height or Depth	6·25	7·24	5·19	0·12	0·04	7·80	7·80	6·29	3·60	5·43	1·72	0·03	0·03	0·00	1·08
Upper Facial Length	12·75	14·97	36·97	23·23	6·98	7·25	17·90	21·02	0·37	0·00	0·03	0·63	0·19	4·59	4·83
Total Facial Length	23·64	28·52	51·18	44·38	28·85	9·11	24·23	18·55	2·59	3·52	2·40	2·42	2·69	1·82	0·62
Horizontal Cirm. of the Head.	20·02	3·56	8·44	0·99	2·47	0·03	0·15	0·41	12·07	22·48	4·10	0·04	3·93	2·31	16·17
Sagittal Arc ..	2·54	0·02	9·81	6·26	2·27	15·06	12·49	0·38	1·60	3·59	20·45	10·27	5·55	9·59	25·04
Transverse Arc ..	4·20	0·51	27·22	13·12	0·18	5·33	8·42	13·41	1·60	0·70	6·19	2·62	6·57	0·02	3·3
Length Breadth Index.	2·27	2·00	152·89	136·63	33·63	5·91	33·36	89·78	12·15	20·47	0·01	3·32	107·15	40·39	57·4
Length Height Index	12·96	0·06	41·84	42·00	0·10	7·50	1·51	7·96	0·23	48·36	2·98	1·76	0·24	0·75	0·1
Breadth Height Index.	22·24	0·90	7·43	5·57	20·02	0·75	10·03	16·97	4·74	9·14	2·08	6·65	34·09	28·49	32·6
Trans. Fronto-Parietal Index.	0·58	0·36	31·44	8·83	4·25	0·56	5·77	17·00	0·32	0·26	6·50	1·92	11·70	0·17	25·3
Orbitonasal Index ..	12·85	0·54	11·79	0·04	0·02	8·75	2·83	2·40	2·61	0·84	8·35	20·30	5·51	4·20	6·4
Nasal Index ..	67·73	49·42	30·58	49·95	65·07	9·55	19·98	23·20	1·99	8·67	0·34	8·94	16·32	11·59	26·5
Nasal Elevation Index.	23·36	20·47	0·60	3·43	9·41	8·77	13·61	8·46	0·28	0·13	0·78	1·16	2·12	3·50	4·7
Upper Facial Index..	0·52	4·11	0·29	0·04	0·17	3·74	11·88	6·71	1·55	0·02	0·12	0·35	5·20	10·58	2·1
Total Facial Index ..	2·05	10 05	0·39	1·31	5·58	4·90	16·88	4·70	5·62	4·76	0·88	0·01	1·58	7·98	11·1
Trans-Cephalo-Facial Index.	0·08	0·01	8·26	5·56	4·74	8·39	21·90	36·45	4·36	2·79	12·83	3·82	39·90	0·91	2·8
Vertical Cephalo-Facial Index.	26·20	9·23	2·39	3·50	22·58	9·98	13·04	11·78	7·29	3·12	11·57	8·06	0·16	4·08	2·6

TABLE XLVIII

Telugu Brahmin with other races.

Bania-Jain.	Chit-pavan Brah-min.	Desastha Brah-min.	Saraswat Gour Brah-min	Mah-ratta.	Nam-budiri Brah-min.	Iluva.	Tamil Brah-min.	Kala.	Kanarese Brah-min.	Nair.	Kadar.	Bhil.	Khasi.	Characters
0·11	0·01	0·88	2·09	0·52	0·90	19·24	0·22	1·82	5·93	16·98	88·58	4·40	58·47	Stature.
6·81	7·31	8·41	0·02	5·82	2·61	8·05	1·11	2·18	3·09	0·94	1·38	35·43	1·58	Auricular Height.
19·78	15·94	26·80	6·92	39·69	14·29	0·02	2·19	1·04	23·68	2·93	54·73	41·08	8·35	Max. Head Length.
43·46	4·24	7·46	5·37	2·47	0·01	2·19	9·21	0·23	10·31	0·79	53·57	13·98	6·56	Max. Head Breadth.
19·63	8·42	9·95	2·87	4·70	0·07	3·05	0·32	2·39	8·74	0·26	3·27	1·53	2·80	Min. Frontal Breadth.
27·40	4·44	3·82	1·84	3·53	0·03	12·04	1·35	0·20	0·20	0·57	30·60	0·45	3·46	Max. Bizygomatic Breadth.
10·13	0·77	7·79	3·30	6·38	0·00	0·40	0·11	3·23	0·91	1·14	1·90	1·29	52·58	Bigonial Breadth.
3·48	0·08	2·30	1·07	0·00	0·08	0·10	9·86	0·28	4·45	0·04	0·76	0·37	0·00	Inter-Orbital Breadth
0·17	8·16	11·19	0·02	21·17	0·24	1·40	4·84	2·77	0·25	0·16	77·47	18·80	24·67	Orbitonasal Breadth.
0·67	1·09	0·02	0·76	2·12	14·62	0·34	7·85	7·30	0·46	4·39	18·15	3·03	43·20	Orbitonasal Arc.
8·22	0·74	0·18	0·32	0·05	0·41	8·36	0·04	7·78	0·01	1·27	30·76	18·24	13·23	Nasal Length.
0·68	2·49	0·70	2·89	1·45	1·09	2·04	2·89	0·45	5·35	0·05	16·48	2·09	0·02	Nasal Breadth.
0·17	13·85	13·27	2·52	11·86	5·35	9·00	0·02	7·73	0·15	0·95	96·88	24·32	130·60	Nasal Height or Depth.
0·70	4·80	3·67	0·10	3·96	1·71	5·97	0·09	3·06	0·29	1·85	12·52	26·15	0·53	Upper Facial Length.
2·41	0·20	0·60	5·39	0·42	11·02	0·01	3·57	0·02	0·07	16·01	34·04	3·60	3·59	Total Facial Length.
0·05	1·41	1·09	0·70	7·15	4·63	2·84	0·02	4·40	4·36	0·84	232·44	27·27	0·05	Horizontal Cirm. of the Head.
4·28	20·29	16·86	3·96	32·48	19·63	4·12	1·51	1·64	4·07	4·40	146·24	30·23	0·01	Sagittal Arc.
2·33	4·61	0·07	2·95	1·53	3·27	0·21	3·41	0·27	0·68	9·51	577·96	33·68	0·26	Transverse Arc.
82·44	20·95	34·78	14·80	37·70	5·99	1·65	14·28	1·09	3·97	0·08	4·32	0·53	16·95	Length Breadth Index.
0·02	0·35	0·00	1·99	2·22	0·20	6·14	2·98	0·75	0·80	0·00	7·29	5·11	5·74	Length Height Index.
42·61	14·43	19·15	2·37	8·89	2·03	2·27	1·61	2·80	13·38	0·02	17·36	7·61	0·29	Breadth Height Index.
11·98	0·02	0·07	1·37	0·00	0·01	0·03	8·35	3·43	1·01	0·31	47·27	10·65	17·09	Trans. Fronto-Parietal Index.
0·34	22·08	13·48	1·86	11·08	20·98	0·73	1·75	3·24	0·12	5·68	16·06	6·75	12·56	Orbitonasal Index.
8·76	0·14	0·06	3·54	0·99	1·18	1·25	1·76	3·24	3·48	1·07	71·12	25·00	9·43	Nasal Index.
[illegible]·00	3·91	7·01	0·11	4·94	6·65	4·09	0·72	4·20	0·92	0·73	102·04	24·57	96·98	Nasal Elevation Index.
8·76	10·23	8·16	0·22	6·19	1·12	0·22	0·68	3·27	0·57	0·65	0·20	19·41	0·23	Upper Facial Index.
[illegible]9·56	0·67	3·07	5·81	2·85	8·80	5·24	6·13	0·02	0·00	10·20	3·94	17·50	8·53	Total Facial Index.
[illegible]·57	0·26	2·80	12·29	0·09	0·25	2·42	27·49	0·01	13·38	0·10	20·24	21·33	1·89	Trans. Cephalo-Facial Index.
[illegible]·82	5·46	3·05	2·07	2·02	0·94	5·06	0·21	1·34	2·24	3·85	8·19	8·62	4·98	Vertical Cephalo-Facial Index.

TABLE XLIX.

Values of $\frac{N_s N_{s'}}{N_s + N_{s'}}\left(\frac{M_s - M_{s'}}{\sigma_s}\right)^2$ fo

Characters.	Red Kaffir.	Pathan.	Uzbeg.	Tadjik.	Khos (Lower Chitral)	U. P. Brahmin.	Bengali Brahmin.	Bengali Kayastha.	Bengali Pod.	Orissa Brahmin.	Malve Brahmin.	Rajput.	Nagar Brahmin.	Audich Brahmin.	Kathi.
Stature	10·35	0·76	0·01	5·63	0·14	3·11	16·81	14·06	0·33	0·69	0·54	31·46	1·97	1·67	8·84
Auricular Height	18·68	0·73	9·70	3·55	11·09	13·19	3·82	1·59	14·72	2·99	23·34	18·89	16·06	35·16	9·46
Max. Head Length ..	1·44	8·28	66·14	106·90	40·66	3·23	47·26	81·77	75·90	136·24	41·05	39·15	85·43	101·64	30·60
Max. Head Breadth	17·21	5·41	104·64	68·05	26·34	1·70	18·42	53·18	0·18	0·01	3·35	0·60	67·83	9·05	49·89
Min. Frontal Breadth	44·58	6·62	38·62	49·75	19·76	0·49	8·59	21·56	0·14	0·71	0·57	0·26	42·15	21·50	9·64
Max. Bizygomatic Breadth	24·19	6·92	9·58	61·35	16·73	0·49	0·28	8·20	2·66	0·65	0·43	5·61	14·09	6·58	48·93
Bigonial Breadth ..	39·34	7·99	4·26	26·06	20·56	5·50	8·07	13·92	5·29	8·49	10·42	4·41	4·96	2·80	5·06
Inter-Orbital Breadth	2·24	5·70	14·35	5·07	0·17	12·17	13·15	12·06	0·00	10·94	2·02	2·65	1·67	2·85	1·51
Orbitonasal Breadth	27·90	22·56	1·34	7·90	27·24	8·79	0·08	0·35	20·29	17·88	10·63	26·68	4·48	6·17	0·38
Orbitonasal Arc .	33·01	46·34	13·91	36·83	68·09	13·27	3·53	5·17	35·99	46·28	15·91	24·20	16·35	19·63	3·75
Nasal Length ..	40·03	28·80	24·35	26·38	17·51	5·27	9·43	17·93	1·22	0·14	0·17	0·87	2·48	0·01	14·42
Nasal Breadth ..	10·12	6·28	1·64	7·19	14·26	0·01	1·24	0·07	0·95	3·40	0·31	1·20	2·74	5·20	1·47
Nasal Height or Depth	0·01	0·19	19·37	7·80	5·75	0·30	0·30	0·01	18·00	27·66	13·34	8·27	8·41	7·38	1·24
Upper Facial Length	4·65	7·03	26·08	12·72	0·64	2·10	9·13	10·29	0·47	2·41	1·26	0·49	3·94	13·77	1·03
Total Facial Length	1·33	4·61	19·62	11·12	3·05	0·05	2·95	0·34	2·79	4·61	3·01	5·10	31·24	27·10	5·37
Horizontal Circm. of the Head.	4·46	0·05	1·18	1·57	0·70	5·44	3·10	3·40	32·57	57·08	17·84	7·31	0·23	16·26	0·53
Sagittal Arc ..	12·49	18·26	51·27	51·88	43·72	0·21	0·66	20·43	9·85	55·03	82·07	71·63	58·26	68·59	86·02
Transverse Arc ..	17·65	6·42	14·26	3·28	6·27	17·39	1·35	2·81	9·62	9·54	18·94	14·25	0·27	3·80	0·0
Length Breadth Index.	19·19	15·16	222·62	212·53	76·94	0·00	69·89	159·40	36·19	59·27	5·43	22·36	133·84	87·69	100·8
Length Height Index	10·21	0·49	49·85	50·65	0·03	5·58	2·88	11·73	0·87	59·12	1·76	0·73	1·05	0·15	0·0
Breadth Height Index.	42·54	5·74	16·59	15·39	40·20	5·34	21·77	34·90	13·34	2·14	8·40	18·65	75·37	50·90	51·4
Trans. Fronto-Parietal Index	0·76	0·25	32·23	9·62	3·97	0·78	5·49	16·97	0·22	0·45	7·42	1·68	11·52	0·31	25·3
Orbitonasal Index ..	2·69	14·69	57·86	25·45	28·71	2·41	8·18	13·93	8·57	21·97	2·56	0·45	8·68	9·85	2·9
Nasal Index ..	52·37	37·34	22·45	37·31	41·08	4·32	12·18	13·74	0·13	2·93	0·24	3·32	8·39	5·13	17·9
Nasal Elevation Index	3·94	4·21	9·53	0·67	0·05	0·20	1·43	0·00	0·74	12·54	12·14	3·57	2·32	1·07	0·0
Upper Facial Index..	0·29	1·01	0·15	1·75	2·67	0·83	6·01	2·03	0·04	1·32	2·01	3·39	12·84	20·70	6·2
Total Facial Index ..	3·95	0·08	3·93	3·78	0·90	0·49	1·52	1·41	0·29	1·92	3·99	12·63	56·85	39·48	38·1
Trans. Cephalo-Facial Index.	0·45	0·33	11·60	8·59	7·83	6·02	27·73	45·83	6·95	5·42	9·94	2·03	49·90	2·40	4·7
Vertical Cephalo-Facial Index.	17·23	4·57	0·51	0·97	14·35	5·12	7·42	1·82	3·21	8·71	6·30	3·24	0·54	1·41	0·

TABLE XLIX.

budiri Brahmin with other races.

Chitpavan Brahmin.	Desastha Brahmin.	Saraswat-Gaur Brahmin.	Mahratta.	Iluva.	Tamil Brahmin.	Kala.	Kanarese Brahmin.	Telegu Brahmin.	Nair.	Kadar.	Bhil.	Khasi.	Characters.
1·41	0·02	0·28	0·06	13·88	0·22	5·16	2·38	0·90	23·68	73·91	1·44	45·17	Stature.
21·90	23·97	2·23	17·16	20·41	0·29	9·15	11·65	2·61	0·49	9·79	59·40	0·24	Auricular Height.
72·98	95·96	41·88	108·18	15·40	28·04	21·09	76·75	14·29	4·85	147·10	106·39	50·52	Max. Head Length.
4·97	8·56	6·06	2·91	2·03	10·22	0·33	11·40	0·01	1·01	55·56	13·96	7·20	Max. Head Breadth.
10·88	12·71	3·98	6·23	2·33	0·70	1·78	10·81	0·07	0·63	2·44	1·01	1·99	Min. Frontal Breadth.
3·83	3·23	0·38	3·01	13·78	1·86	0·09	0·08	0·03	0·34	34·10	0·75	2·87	Max. Bizygomatic Breadth.
0·80	8·25	3·48	6·67	0·43	0·11	3·34	0·98	0·00	1·18	2·00	1·33	53·56	Bigonial Breadth.
0·00	3·58	0·61	0·11	0·36	8·63	0·64	3·54	0·08	0·01	0·33	0·12	0·05	Inter-Orbital Breadth.
12·40	16·46	0·42	27·36	3·18	3·51	4·66	0·00	0·24	0·01	94·08	24·55	31·22	Orbitonasal Breadth.
11·52	21·79	8·61	30·04	19·51	0·91	40·39	9·81	14·62	3·44	79 44	31·40	118·76	Orbitonasal Arc.
2·67	1·41	0·00	0·80	12·93	0·09	11·88	0·31	0·41	0·24	42·04	25·07	19·33	Nasal Length.
0·16	0·13	0·48	0·02	0·18	0·48	0·09	1·75	1·09	0·77	29·52	6·37	1·71	Nasal Breadth.
42·84	42·05	15·49	35·30	30·90	6·02	25·12	7·29	5·35	2·02	166·99	54·15	200·54	Nasal Height or depth.
14·38	12·38	0·97	11·59	14·51	1·01	9·09	3·47	1·71	0·00	27·12	42·79	0·49	Upper Facial Length.
11·76	22·20	0·89	17·05	10·30	1·92	8·92	9·30	11·02	0·40	99·32	27·69	31·22	Total Facial Length.
13·99	13·05	9·04	24·84	15·01	4·03	17·34	18·39	4·63	1·72	334·96	56·17	2·90	Horizontal Circm. of the Head.
109·73	89·45	41·83	109·47	5·53	10·06	29·86	42·19	19·63	6·18	315·08	101·15	8·56	Sagittal Arc.
18·75	3·43	0·00	9·93	5·18	0·01	4·99	0·93	3·27	1·62	727·85	60·01	0·62	Transverse Arc.
50·41	80·50	40·88	70·83	1·28	39·90	11·34	79·13	5·99	5·18	0·57	10·18	47·40	Length Breadth Index.
0·01	0·20	3·55	3·94	4·38	4·88	0·22	1·85	0·20	0·24	10·97	3·51	8·72	Length Height Index.
31·20	38·38	8·99	20·51	8·79	7·41	9·29	26·71	2·03	1·78	6·84	18·03	4·52	Breadth Height Index.
0·08	0·02	1·17	0·03	0·09	8·07	3·17	0·84	0·01	0·20	52·30	11·95	16·58	Trans. Fronto-Parietal Index.
0·26	2·58	10·14	1·86	13·76	10·43	37·78	17·84	20·98	5·53	1·70	3 69	75 18	Orbitonasal Index.
0·78	1·03	0·71	0·01	4·97	0·01	8·17	0·68	1·18	0·01	99·98	38·47	18·64	Nasal Index.
25·59	33·30	8·52	24·67	21·60	2·93	20·41	2·56	6·65	3·31	182·11	58·54	163·05	Nasal Elevation Index.
20·44	17 45	0·33	13·29	2·38	0·05	8·05	3·35	1·12	0·08	2·88	30·80	2·74	Upper Facial Index.
18·39	27·79	0·25	23·05	0·39	0·19	8 65	8·80	8·80	0·03	30·16	13 59	38 55	Total Facial Index.
1·19	5·30	16·55	0·68	4·37	34·41	0·34	18·01	0·25	0·72	15·97	17·72	3·75	Trans. Cephalo-Facial Index.
1·62	0·44	0·25	20·39	1·77	0·26	0·07	0·31	0·94	0·99	16·88	4·14	11·22	Vertical Cephalo-Facial Index.

TABLE L.

Values of $\frac{N_s \; N_s'}{N_s + N_s'}\left(\frac{M_s - M_s'}{\sigma_s}\right)^2$ for

Characters.	Red Kaffir.	Pathan.	Uzbeg.	Tadjik.	Khos. (Lower Chitral.)	U. P. Brahmin.	Bengali Brahmin.	Bengali Kayastha.	Bengali Pod.	Orissa Brahmin.	Malve Brahmin.	Rajput.	Nagar Brahmin.	Audich Brahmin.	Kathi.
Stature	7·07	17·60	11·97	8·06	38·91	10·83]	0·82	4·46	33·29	30·00	18·82	0·04	20·95	20·77	3·06
Auricular Height ..	13·29	0·04	14·19	7·01	6·95	9·15	1·73	0·25	10·46	6·64	18·05	13·46	11·00	28·14	6·21
Max. Head Length ..	1·65	0·62	40·52	38 48	16·66	0·10	23·70	45·96	45·48	87·77	19·29	15·33	48·54	62·01	13·15
Max. Head Breadth	9·71	1·94	90·74	54·77	17·17	5·35	11·56	40·30	0·30	1·26	8·11	0·12	53·46	3·83	39·33
Min. Frontal Breadth	35·51	3·43	31·71	40·92	13 53	2·21	4·92	14·97	0·16	0·01	0·00	2·05	33·22	14·99	5·94
Max. Bizygomatic Breadth.	19·46	4·50	90·80	55·48	12·70	0·02	0·00	5·23	5·06	2·41	0·01	3·15	10·26	3·94	43·67
Bigonial Breadth ..	27·11	3·33	28·82	16·82	11·84	1·78	3·39	6·73	1·66	2·86	5·00	0·84	1·08	0·24	1·68
Inter-Orbital Breadth	2·72	5·48	14·18	4·86	0·10	13·35	2·11	13·54	0·01	10·86	1·84	3·19	0·15	2·64	1·36
Orbitonasal Breadth	28·20	22 51	1·18	7·66	27·48	8·55	0·16	0·54	20·20	17·94	10·40	26·93	4·23	5·92	0·29
Orbitonasal Arc ..	14·35	26·40	26·38	18·45	40·91	3·64	0·01	0·05	18·61	22·75	5·12	8·95	4·08	6·08	0·08
Nasal Length ..	35·30	24·96	21·06	22·52	14·03	3·47	7·04	4·56	2·59	0·97	0·82	0·16	1·11	0·43	11·67
Nasal Breadth ..	18·23	11·63	4·23	13·28	7·93	0·85	3·96	1·61	3·41	8·78	0·08	4·52	7·35	11·07	4·13
Nasal Height or Depth	2·25	3·37	10·53	10·85	0·76	3·78	3·78	2·31	8·72	13·68	5·48	1·77	1·80	1·41	0·03
Upper Facial Length	4·79	7·19	23·70	13·12	1·53	2·11	9·30	10·69	0·52	2·67	1·37	0·56	4·28	14·74	1·02
Total Facial Length	0·22	2·48	15·66	7·62	1·18	0·72	1·30	0·02	5·38	8·88	5·69	9·26	41·93	36·70	8·61
Horizontal Cirm. of the Head.	13·47	1·11	4·99	0·01	0·37	1·21	0·27	1·56	23·65	38·47	9·18	1·64	1·04	7·11	3·78
Sagittal Arc ..	0·62	3·75	26·34	1·33	16·03	3·83	2·54	3·26	0·61	21·47	46·51	34·31	24·82	32·53	51·36
Transverse Arc ..	33·35	14·64	7·50	0·29	15·98	30·21	0·00	0·07	19·42	22·38	32·28	28·46	0·86	11·82	0·98
Length Breadth Index	3·61	3·08	174·30	157·83	41·71	5·10	39·84	107·70	15·37	26·82	0·02	5·10	128·15	49·75	66·26
Length Height Index	14·76	0·06	45·61	45·92	0·13	8·32	1·58	8·79	0·23	5·40	3·34	20·55	0·24	0·89	0·22
Breadth Height Index	26·85	1·31	80·43	6·97	25·18	1·12	11·98	20·70	5·89	9·16	2·75	8·51	54·65	33·98	37·08
Trans. Fronto-Parietal Index.	1·99	0·01	28·92	7·33	2·37	9·21	3·80	13·82	0·01	1·54	10·38	0·66	8·82	1·16	22·17
Orbitonasal Index ..	1·01	2·62	32·52	7·49	8·23	0·50	0·39	1·32	0·48	0·70	0·42	3·95	0·10	0·33	0·16
Nasal Index ..	56·58	39·76	23·77	39·96	44·39	4·80	13·19	15·16	0·19	1·85	0·18	3·83	9·37	5·79	19·18
Nasal Elevation Index	17·00	14·97	2·46	1·08	5·12	5·00	8·98	4·33	1·99	1·84	3·17	0·02	0·29	0·98	2·10
Upper Facial Index ..	0·05	1·72	0·02	1·12	1·85	1·47	7·81	3·26	0·24	12·72	1·37	2·47	11·38	19·13	5·25
Total Facial Index ..	5·07	0·01	4·67	1·73	1·37	0·78	1·21	2·03	0·51	0·34	4·90	7·41	63·99	44·69	41·87
Trans. Cephalo-Facial Index.	0·08	0·06	7·45	4·57	3·76	11·18	20·88	36·36	3·47	7·16	16·48	5·98	40·07	0·42	2·10
Vertical Cephalo-Facial Index.	9·78	1·47	0·02	0·00	7·70	1·70	3·28	0·06	0·74	0·30	2·53	0·50	3·63	0·01	0·02

TABLE L.

Nair with other races.

Bania Jain.	Chitpavan Brahmin.	Desastha Brahmin.	Saraswat. Gour Brahmin.	Mahratta.	Nambudiri Brahmin.	Iluva.	Tamil Brahmin.	Kala.	Kanarese Brahmin.	Telegu Brahmin.	Kadar.	Bhil.	Khasi.	Characters.
26·78	23·69	34·66	31·69	25·62	23·68	72·78	21·24	6·06	44·41	16·98	223·13	39·82	161·45	Stature.
15·20	16·07	17·87	0·71	12·44	0·49	15·43	0·02	5·95	7·85	0·94	5·79	51·59	0·06	Auricular Height.
45·14	39·12	56·67	19·87	70·42	4·85	3·46	10·61	7·08	46·15	2·93	98·25	70·64	24·74	Max. Head Length.
85·42	1·29	3·41	2·35	0·52	1·01	5·92	5·21	0·11	6·08	0·79	78·22	22·97	2·91	Max. Head Breadth.
18·25	6·16	7·56	1·60	3·04	0·63	5·43	0·01	4·33	6·67	0·26	6·33	3·23	5·46	Min. Frontal Breadth.
21·77	1·81	1·38	1·45	1·39	0·34	19·18	3·89	0·06	0·08	0·57	46·06	2·13	1·24	Max. Bizygomatic Breadth.
4·52	0·11	2·88	8·78	2·36	1·18	2·99	0·52	0·75	4·25	1·14	0·03	0·01	41·70	Bigonial Breadth.
4·81	0·01	3·37	0·79	0·12	0·01	0·26	9·56	0·53	4·06	0·04	0·49	0·20	0·00	Inter-Orbital Breadth.
0·00	12·26	16·20	0·31	27·46	0·01	2·95	3·61	4·42	0·02	0·16	97·21	26·56	32·40	Orbitonasal Breadth.
2·51	1·85	7·05	1·41	13·80	3·44	7·29	0·69	2·28	1·93	4·39	49·18	15·29	86·37	Orbitonasal Arc.
2·95	5·05	3·21	0·29	1·62	0·24	17·22	1·76	15·67	1·09	1·27	52·53	31·24	26·11	Nasal Length.
0·39	2·03	0·40	2·44	1·08	0·77	1·64	2·44	0·25	4·85	0·05	20·90	2·97	0·16	Nasal Breadth.
2·50	25·96	25·24	6·91	21·41	2·02	18·37	1·25	14·45	1·87	0·95	135·47	37·48	173·17	Nasal Height or depth.
6·13	15·43	13·30	1·06	12·28	0·00	15·28	1·10	9·56	3·71	1·85	29·03	44·88	0·57	Upper Facial length.
40·07	18·07	31·09	2·48	23·65	0·40	15·12	4·12	13·08	13·89	16·01	120·82	46·11	42·23	Total Facial Length.
0·78	5·47	4·83	3·20	14·13	1·72	7·15	0·59	9·23	9·59	0·84	299·43	40·56	0·72	Horizontal Cirm. of the Head
21·55	62·62	46·93	17·44	66·67	6·18	0·00	0·66	10·86	17·67	4·40	236·10	61·44	1·70	Sagittal Arc.
3·96	34·99	11·41	1·67	20·41	1·62	12·73	1·34	11·82	4·96	9·51	855·55	83·64	2·69	Transverse Arc.
99·11	26·90	43·49	18·54	39·53	5·18	1·21	17·86	1·81	47·03	0·08	3·53	1·07	21·73	Length Breadth Index.
0·03	0·43	0·01	2·10	2·86	0·24	6·82	3·17	0·85	0·83	0·00	8·08	5·69	6·25	Length Height Index.
50·45	17·75	23·33	3·10	10·78	1·78	2·98	2·19	3·55	15·79	0·02	18·03	9·21	0·41	Breadth Height Index.
9·10	0·64	0·15	0·44	0·38	0·20	0·56	6·04	1·96	0·24	0·31	63·30	15·74	13·96	Trans. Fronto-Parietal Index.
4·73	4·74	1·15	0·92	1·00	5·53	2·23	1·01	16·87	4·07	5·68	2·00	0·11	41·41	Orbitonasal Index.
3·71	0·68	0·93	0·86	0·00	0·01	4·86	0·12	8·09	0·83	1·07	104·17	39·17	19·43	Nasal Index.
1·07	9·66	14·66	1·45	10·40	3·31	8·81	0·00	8·61	0·02	0·73	138·38	36·39	128·99	Nasal Elevation Index.
19·45	18·86	15·91	0·10	11·90	0·08	1·69	0·00	6·94	2·54	0·65	2·07	29·22	2·00	Upper Facial Index.
71·04	21·46	31·96	0·46	26·08	0·03	0·65	0·37	10·00	10·20	10·20	35·22	20·94	44·56	Total Facial Index.
9·45	0·02	1·96	11·18	0·00	0·72	1·70	27·60	0·03	12·27	0·10	26·67	26·44	1·19	Trans. Cephalo-Facial Index.
1·79	0·03	0·22	0·21	0·30	0·99	0·15	2·22	0·41	0·16	3·85	29·06	1·22	20·51	Vertical Cephalo-Facial Index.

TABLE LI.

Values of $\frac{N_s N_s'}{N_s + N_s'} \left(\frac{M_s - M_s'}{\sigma^s}\right)^2$

Characters.	Red Kaffir.	Pathan	Uzbeg.	Tadjik.	Khos. (Lower Chitral).	U. P. Brahmin.	Bengali Brahmins.	Bengali Kayastha.	Bengali Pod.	Orissa Brahmin.	Malve Brahmin.	Rajput.	Nagar Brahmin.	Audich Brahmin.
Stature	53·59	20·20	11·89	37·84	14·11	23·74	58·45	61·41	8·92	27·39	18·98	92·79	31·31	29·20
Aurcular Height	0·83	12·83	48·91	41·99	3·15	0·75	6·27	15·01	0·44	45·87	0·10	0·78	1·57	0·53
Max. Head Length ..	10·65	1·05	20·83	36·49	3·38	4·32	8·31	18·81	21·88	43·62	5·88	2·68	20·17	29·23
Max. Head Breadth	31·69	13·44	127·33	90·33	43·02	0·02	31·21	75·29	3·25	3·19	0·16	5·58	92·16	20·31
Min. Frontal Breadth	67·15	16·04	55·22	71·28	36·05	0·65	18·97	37·73	3·44	6·90	4·98	1·50	64·41	38·39
Max. Bizygomatic Breadth	81·03	38·75	166·49	132·48	65·97	18·72	17·33	48·98	4·17	13·34	18·37	42·45	62·38	44·32
Bigonial Breadth ..	46·53	11·59	44·41	31·94	26·31	8·62	11·60	18·90	8·35	12·94	14·42	7·71	8·44	5·55
Inter-Orbital Breadth	4·51	3·06	10·23	2·50	0·06	15·93	17·02	16·31	0·34	6·17	0·65	5·07	0·31	0·94
Orbitonasal Breadth	9·65	8·40	0·17	0·82	9·54	1·33	4·11	6·71	7·07	3·85	2·11	8·96	0·00	0·18
Orbitonasal Arc ..	0·12	5·45	7·06	1·89	9·69	0·57	6·15	7·73	2·39	1·75	0·18	0·02	1·22	0·38
Nasal Length ..	103·81	76·68	63·63	75·73	64·71	33·14	42·43	66·59	5·92	15·33	9·66	24·62	31·53	15·33
Nasal Breadth ..	6·82	4·17	0·80	4·77	10·46	0·12	0·46	0·05	0·30	0·44	0·91	0·35	1·27	3·05
Nasal Height or Depth	37·84	34·36	0·27	8·96	14·68	35·59	35 59	38·09	1·63	2·35	3·47	12·14	12·33	12·67
Upper Facial Length	40·80	39·85	69·43	54·63	29·30	26·38	44 55	54·85	9·33	9·18	6·89	13·09	5·81	0·42
Total Facial Length	22·43	27·38	51·03	42·88	27·54	8·47	23·18	17·49	2·26	3·04	2·07	2·04	3·12	2·18
Horizontal Cirm. of the Head.	41·17	12·74	19·73	7·64	12·11	2·27	4·26	6·67	3·21	7·26	0·12	3·06	15·53	0·16
Sagittal Arc ..	0·59	3·52	24·83	21·52	14·51	3·43	2·26	2·99	0·59	19·07	42·94	30·80	22·27	29·30
Transverse Arc ..	2·26	0·06	32·37	16·85	0·01	3·43	11·29	17·57	0·65	0·07	4·11	1·19	9·59	0·42
Length Broadth Index	8·81	7·28	186·59	170·07	52·65	1·31	49·86	120·09	22·76	37·06	1·37	10·93	14·04	61·17
Length Height Index	0·54	7·44	76·66	82·58	6·25	0·07	13·72	32·28	8·73	96·32	0·56	2·36	11·38	3·82
Breadth Height Index	8·86	0·31	2·00	0·60	8·22	0·41	2·76	5·67	0·45	22·68	0·01	0·71	25·39	13·13
Trans. Fronto-Parietal Index.	0·26	0·61	34·03	11·09	5·13	0·32	6·66	18·75	0·56	0·09	5·62	2·54	13·16	0·04
Orbitonasal Index ..	6·74	0·02	17·93	1·22	1·19	4·44	0·69	32·33	0·59	0·01	4·18	12·42	1·84	1·17
Nasal Index ..	90·82	66·41	43·49	67·98	75·52	17·72	31·24	37·32	6·40	18·54	2·90	18·34	28·54	21·92
Nasal Elevation Index	51·37	42·86	1·04	15·83	28·72	24·84	32·61	27·49	2·23	4·45	1·29	11·65	14·51	17·44
Upper Facial Index..	1·48	6·25	0·93	0·09	0·02	5·79	15·36	9·84	2·95	0·52	0·02	0·00	2·99	7·36
Total Facial Index ..	1·52	0·78	1·97	1·60	0·05	0·01	3·31	0·21	0·01	0·37	1·83	7·63	44·07	29·54
Trans. Cephalo-Facial Index.	2·91	2·19	2·32	0·52	0·17	19·81	9·77	17·99	0·29	0·05	26·39	14·06	20·31	0·67
Vertical Cephalo-Facial Index.	6·36	0·62	0·21	0·17	4·85	0·83	1·86	0·04	0·21	19·02	1·33	0·06	4·95	0·11

TABLE LI.

…va with other races.

Chit-pawan Brah-min.	Desastha Brah-min.	Saraswat-Gour Brah-min.	Mah-ratta.	Nam-budiri Brah-min.	Tamil Brah-min	Kala.	Kanarese Brah-min.	Telegu Brah-min.	Nair.	Kadar.	Bhil.	Khasi.	Characters.
28·85	19·31	9·74	16·22	13·88	23·56	31·98	4·54	19·24	72·78	16·34	6·10	6·60	Stature.
0·34	0·17	8·74	0·27	20·41	15·12	1·44	1·16	8·05	15·43	4·67	9·71	19·12	Auricular Height.
14·66	25·10	6·19	37·85	15·40	1·79	0·78	22·32	0·02	3·46	52·29	39·29	7·46	Max. Head Length.
14·27	19·89	14·42	9·68	2·03	20·40	3·51	22·02	2·19	5·92	31·11	5·10	17·70	Max. Head Breadth.
24·29	26·98	11·84	15·88	2·33	5·35	0·01	22·13	3·05	5·43	250·09	0·26	0·07	Min. Frontal Breadth.
37·62	36·06	9·25	30·12	13·78	5·32	13·86	15·35	12·04	19·18	2·11	7·82	32·71	Max. Bizygomatic Breadth.
2·61	12·48	1·39	10·16	0·43	0·94	5·74	0·10	0·04	2·99	4·52	3·13	63·33	Bigonial Breadth.
0·42	1·33	1·81	0·08	0·36	11·93	0·05	5·87	0·10	0·26	1·53	0·85	0·04	Inter-Orbital Breadth
1·93	3·50	1·24	10·80	3·18	12·00	0·22	3·12	1·40	2·95	53·87	9·44	12·69	Orbitonasal Breadth.
2·96	0·27	2·10	0·73	19·51	11·44	4·65	1·58	0·34	7·29	12·74	1·35	35·14	Orbitonasal Arc.
6·22	8·70	11·97	7·75	12·93	7·31	0·00	8·84	8·36	17·22	4·60	1·90	0·18	Nasal Length.
0·01	0·70	0·08	0·08	0·18	0·07	0·45	0·78	2·04	1·64	32·94	8·26	3·03	Nasal Breadth.
0·0(	0·00	2·52	0·02	30·90	9·21	0·04	7·80	9·00	18·37	37·49	3·09	62·41	Nasal Height or depth.
0·41	0·88	7·62	0·31	14·15	7·49	0·31	3·61	5·97	15·28	0·44	7·13	11·88	Upper Facial Length.
0·10	0·82	4·90	0·58	10·30	3·17	0·00	0·02	0·01	15·12	35·54	4·02	4·06	Total Facial Length.
0·59	0·94	0·72	0·85	15·01	3·42	0·26	0·17	2·84	7·15	176·00	12·52	0·90	Horizontal Cirm. of the Head.
56·01	41·96	16·17	61·02	5·53	0·64	10·19	16·39	4·12	0·00	209·70	56·68	1·67	Sagittal Arc.
2·61	0·65	4·74	0·58	5·18	5·30	0·01	1·64	0·21	12·73	552·30	28·56	0·59	Transverse Arc.
30·82	54·72	26·42	49·77	1·28	25·65	5·09	57·51	1·65	1·21	0·32	4·04	30·76	Length Breadth Index.
5·20	7·98	15·11	16·38	4·38	17·68	2·15	11·39	6·14	6·82	31·50	0·05	26·19	Length Height Index.
4·21	6·85	0·00	2·04	8·79	0·06	0·06	4·63	2·27	2·98	35·25	1·57	1·24	Breadth Height Index.
0·01	0·22	1·82	0·02	0·09	9·41	4·08	1·41	0·03	0·56	44·46	9·51	18·77	Trans. Fronto-Parietal Index.
13·77	7·16	0·26	5·96	13·76	0·22	6·78	0·25	0·73	2·23	9·05	3·05	20·29	Orbitonasal Index.
2·79	2·43	9·00	4·66	4·97	5·99	0·56	8·91	1·25	4·86	50·65	15·06	3·33	Nasal Index.
0·13	0·08	2·85	0·01	21·60	8·23	0·02	8·87	4·09	8·81	59·66	8·61	57·71	Nasal Elevation Index.
7·02	5·31	0·90	3·99	2·38	1·68	1·86	0·08	0·22	1·69	0·01	15·47	0·00	Upper Facial Index.
12·06	19·58	0·02	10·56	0·39	0·04	5·37	5·24	5·24	0·65	21·88	13·05	29·88	Total Facial Index.
1·71	0·02	3·81	1·73	4·37	13·61	1·82	4·42	2·42	1·70	40·04	38·12	0·15	Trans. Cephalo-Facial Index.
0·07	0·77	0·66	0·81	1·77	3·25	0·92	0·57	5·06	0·15	30·31	0·47	22·10	Vertical Cephalo-Facial Index.

TABLE LII.

Values of $\frac{N_s \; N_s'}{N_s + N_s'} \left(\frac{M_s - M_s'}{\sigma_s} \right)^2$ for

Characters.	Red Kaffir.	Pathan.	Uzbeg.	Tadjik.	Khos. (Lower Chitral).	U. P. Brahmin.	Bengali Brahmin.	Bengali Kayastha.	Bengali Pod.	Orissa Brahmin.	Malve Brahmin.	Rajput.	Nagar Brahmin.	Audich Brahmin.	Kathi
Stature	133·93	57·25	46·91	93·44	53·92	72·77	122·58	148·12	34·69	90·34	54·96	20·33	92·06	86·00	87·
Auricular Height ..	17·64	0·19	13·73	6·47	9·62	11·71	2·64	0·68	13·26	6·13	22·18	17·86	14·86	35·54	8·
Max. Head Length ..	49·97	14·98	6·64	15·15	1·19	26·44	0·22	3·02	6·10	18·23	0·00	1·93	3·59	9·03	0·
Max. Head Breadth	2·13	0·02	73·82	38·71	6·83	16·62	4·02	24·93	4·85	11·10	22·60	5·41	36·47	0·05	26·2
Min. Frontal Breadth	84·11	17·52	61·41	85·07	43·55	0·39	20·92	47·44	3·22	7·58	4·89	1·20	80·97	46·63	21·4
Max. Bizygomatic Breadth.	12·60	14·33	81·59	47·19	6·96	0·83	1·19	1·51	11·90	9·50	0·91	0·45	4·93	0·84	35·9
Bigonial Breadth ..	2·79	17·41	0·09	4·48	11·82	22·03	17·27	20·46	22·51	36·36	13·95	40·39	39·72	44·87	18·4
Inter-Orbital Breadth	1·36	1·97	6·41	1·60	0·00	6·72	7·21	5·75	0·05	3·07	0·56	1·56	0·32	0·69	0·4
Orbitonasal Breadth	0·47	0·11	12·64	7·71	0·39	5·19	33·81	53·10	0·37	5·23	3·71	0·67	18·43	13·89	19·8
Orbitonasal Arc ..	41·64	11·09	5·18	22·77	11·39	45·82	75·44	107·17	17·71	37·15	40·87	53·26	72·14	59·37	62·4
Nasal Length ..	151·59	103·21	81·55	105·08	95·23	46·55	58·74	99·24	9·77	26·72	15·03	39·13	49·51	25·15	65·8
Nasal Breadth ..	26·21	16·08	6·19	18·61	32·83	1·86	6·23	3·40	5·50	14·19	0·46	7·71	11·74	16·59	6·2
Nasal Height or depth	276·61	207·91	55·46	139·03	187·38	211·24	211·24	277·38	86·84	144·63	99·41	183·35	187·36	181·01	138·71
Upper Facial Length	10·59	12·76	36·47	21·64	4·78	5·13	15·80	19·66	0·00	0·77	0·28	0·00	1·94	11·12	3·0
Total Facial Length	62·59	61·35	90·49	90·68	70·71	27·57	54·29	54·36	13·57	21·75	13·07	16·65	0·16	0·47	6·9
Horizontal Circm. of the Head.	9·70	2·36	5·64	0·81	1·58	0·01	0·24	0·42	4·83	7·37	1·41	0·01	2·27	0·56	4·6
Sagittal Arc ..	0·78	0·00	5·99	3·31	1·23	6·66	5·47	0·07	0·57	6·19	10·69	4·80	2·68	4·56	13·7
Transverse Arc ..	3·19	0·89	12·01	3·98	0·57	4·23	2·47	3·52	1·77	3·65	4·75	2·31	1·35	0·02	0·71
Length Breadth Index	10·46	6·49	100·11	77·05	3·40	46·51	5·32	36·31	0·06	0·00	18·02	8·08	49·29	6·06	20·1
Length Height Index	48·44	4·50	24·50	21·60	9·93	29·21	1·10	0·12	3·50	25·48	18·43	19·15	5·47	14·42	7·2
Breadth Height Index	22·29	0·25	7·33	4·19	20·69	0·17	8·64	16·35	3·43	16·70	1·09	5·25	50·36	29·34	32·5
Trans. Fronto-Parietal Index.	33·63	12·02	6·57	0·75	6·15	24·65	2·14	0·04	12·27	35·16	48·56	11·34	1·11	28·61	2·8
Orbitonasal Index ..	71·03	19·10	0·46	12·66	16·28	46·89	29·45	36·92	28·67	32·22	45·48	90·91	49·60	43·08	37·09
Nasal Index ..	175·28	118·57	76·61	5·70	147·67	42·34	64·68	86·04	21·52	55·48	13·82	51·25	71·02	57·18	72·4
Nasal Elevation Index	304·29	221·32	59·62	158·21	227·77	172·63	194·52	231·47	66·66	151·67	78·51	171·45	186·74	190·61	133·2
Upper Facial Index ..	1·84	7·43	1·02	0·08	0·01	6·92	18·60	12·82	3·47	0·64	0·01	0·01	4·27	10·13	1·3
Total Facial Index ..	26·47	41·57	10·39	19·39	37·82	28·98	56·11	36·60	30·92	40·38	15·72	11·40	1·13	0·04	0·9
Trans. Cephalo-Facial Index.	2·40	1·66	3·86	1·42	0·80	21·11	14·68	38·55	0·87	0·04	28·70	15·34	32·14	0·27	0·3
Vertical Cephalo-Facial Index.	72·19	31·01	13·04	20·68	63·82	32·51	38·42	29·24	27·02	0·44	35·61	34·83	9·90	26·55	14·8

TABLE LII.

Khasi with other races.

Bania-Jain.	Chitpavan Brahmin.	Desastha Brahmin.	Saraswat Gour Brahmin.	Mahratta.	Nambudiri Brahmin.	Duvas.	Tamil Brahmin.	Kula.	Kannarese Brahmin.	Telegu Brahmin.	Nair.	Kadar.	Bhil.	Characters.
0·18	132·67	68·02	36·48	52·17	45·17	6·60	50·79	73·94	24·39	58·47	161·45	2·39	28·25	Stature.
19·98	21·13	23·40	1·27	15·80	0·24	19·12	0·01	7·70	10·16	1·58	0·06	8·32	60·77	Auricular Height.
3·83	1·29	6·21	0·00	16·32	50·52	7·46	1·55	2·47	6·36	8·35	24·74	25·64	17·96	Max. Head Length.
20·80	0·50	0·00	0·00	0·86	7·29	17·70	0·66	3·46	1·02	6·56	2·91	136·71	45·14	Max. Head Breadth.
50·99	29·09	32·64	12·66	17·59	1·99	0·07	5·30	0·19	24·62	2·80	5·46	0·00	0·09	Min. Frontal Breadth.
14·65	0·04	0·00	5·46	0·02	2·87	32·71	9·95	1·53	1·86	3·46	1·24	76·48	0·81	Max. Bizygomatic Breadth.
26·19	60·26	31·45	85·94	22·87	53·56	63·33	47·35	22·81	69·08	52·58	41·70	53·78	35·88	Bigonial Breadth.
1·36	0·05	0·88	0·56	0·00	0·05	0·04	4·91	0·12	2·25	0·00	0·00	0·34	0·20	Inter-Orbital Breadth.
41·49	7·29	4·73	23·01	0·00	31·22	12·69	54·97	7·82	30·51	24·67	32·40	17·37	0·02	Orbitonasal Breadth.
78·06	84·16	61·46	56·84	27·76	118·76	35·14	93·87	9·92	53·66	43·20	86·37	9·75	21·51	Orbitonasal Arc.
59·06	11·58	15·57	18·22	12·74	19·33	0·18	11·74	0·10	13·89	13·23	26·11	3·93	1·24	Nasal Length.
1·29	4·06	1·33	96·93	2·28	1·71	3·03	4·17	0·77	7·42	0·02	0·16	20·68	2·12	Nasal Breadth.
175·14	90·63	94·41	93·39	66·26	200·54	62·41	127·12	57·52	121·14	130·60	173·17	6·76	35·33	Nasal Height or depth.
3·39	11·75	9·72	0·14	9·01	0·49	11·88	0·16	6·76	1·78	0·53	0·57	25·26	41·17	Upper Facial Length.
0·23	7·86	1·98	20·04	1·58	31·22	4·06	15·95	3·63	4·78	3·59	42·23	19·97	0·05	Total Facial Length.
0·12	0·27	0·19	0·13	2·55	2·90	0·90	0·10	1·66	1·52	0·05	0·72	89·55	11·65	Horizontal Cirm. of the Head.
2·12	11·69	7·59	2·27	16·08	8·56	1·67	0·54	1·07	2·33	0·01	1·70	61·24	15·59	Sagittal Arc.
0·25	3·45	0·10	0·56	1·69	0·62	0·59	0·70	0·66	0·02	0·20	2·69	344·12	49·93	Transverse Arc.
31·04	0·10	3·35	0·03	4·39	47·40	30·76	0·01	7·21	8·33	16·95	21·73	56·28	10·96	Length Breadth Index.
9·06	12·69	8·91	0·72	0·71	8·72	26·19	0·25	10·09	1·09	5·74	6·25	0·02	23·82	Length Height Index.
46·00	13·54	18·86	1·32	7·49	4·52	1·24	0·73	1·73	12·10	0·29	0·41	29·48	6·20	Breadth Height Index.
0·91	26·61	22·46	8·03	19·20	16·58	18·77	0·85	3·29	9·09	17·09	13·96	168·64	60·27	Trans. Fronto-Parietal Index.
24·40	95·28	74·18	25·76	55·89	75·18	20·29	25·26	1·78	15·57	12·66	41·41	81·67	41·56	Orbitonasal Index.
50·60	17·23	16·35	26·65	18·86	18·64	3·33	20·69	0·78	26·48	9·43	19·43	36·58	6·20	Nasal Index.
138·79	92·66	79·95	89·76	61·59	165·05	57·71	116·36	47·76	119·00	96·98	128·99	0·13	18·77	Nasal Elevation Index.
10·30	9·80	7·48	1·03	5·24	2·74	0·00	1·95	2·37	0·13	0·23	2·00	0·00	19·52	Upper Facial Index.
2·61	6·71	2·34	31·39	1·38	38·55	29·88	32·21	6·47	8·53	8·53	44·56	1·65	2·10	Total Facial Index.
4·48	1·18	0·07	6·38	1·22	3·75	0·15	20·18	1·26	7·27	1·89	1·19	47·58	41·94	Trans. Cephalo Facial Index.
13·63	28·62	22·14	14·54	15·13	11·22	22·10	7·44	11·15	15·02	4·98	20·51	0·29	29·78	Vertical Cephalo-Facial Index.

TABLE LIII.

Values of $\frac{N_s N_s'}{N_s + N_s'}\left(\frac{M_s - M_s'}{\sigma_s}\right)^2$ **for**

Characters.	Red Kaffir.	Pathan.	Uzbeg.	Tadjik.	Khos. (Lower Chitral).	U. P. Brahmin.	Bengali Brahmin.	Bengali Kayastha.	Bengali Pod.	Orissa Brahmin.	Malve Brahmin.	Rajput.	Nagar Brahmin.	Audich Brahmin.	Kathi
Stature ..	1·44	87·00	68·55	137·60	90·97	107·05	169·86	220·92	57·07	150·38	84·00	293·45	147·36	135·84	121·82
Auricular Height ..	2·34	4·21	36·77	29·80	0·15	1·31	0·61	4·87	1·90	34·09	6·35	2·43	1·25	12·40	0·45
Max. Head Length ..	170·27	71·15	10·85	0·27	40·92	93·62	14·76	12·11	3·00	1·32	19·18	47·32	11·38	4·04	21·08
Max. Head Breadth	195·51	97·78	308·60	302·96	221·23	32·67	147·56	317·53	59·27	96·88	26·13	97·37	365·83	153·65	214·04
Min. Frontal Breadth	96·87	19·62	64·37	95·04	50·12	0·51	23·37	54·92	3·74	9·26	5·62	1·55	93·56	53·68	23·64
Max. Bizygomatic Breadth.	172·34	76·94	251·45	236·57	140·77	42·77	40·29	112·49	14·84	45·05	42·14	99·94	139·44	101·63	174·6
Bigonial Breadth ..	35·52	3·52	32·73	20·27	14·72	1·76	3·59	8·17	1·62	3·31	5·47	0·76	1·03	0·13	1·62
Inter-Orbital Breadth	1·30	10·86	21·96	10·44	1·37	11·93	13·05	12·62	0·31	24·07	4·79	1·70	5·10	7·38	3·60
Orbitonasal Breadth	26·65	15·47	45·90	46·22	24·71	35·79	94·53	152·17	17·76	53·85	31·19	28·14	85·81	70·07	63·54
Orbitonasal Arc ..	13·48	0·69	0·00	4·80	0·17	19·86	41·95	62·25	3·08	9·49	16·49	21·08	34·27	25·73	33·53
Nasal Length ..	239·62	154·82	118·27	16·27	158·78	79·47	96·13	167·08	25·06	63·83	33·64	79·18	95·82	56·16	101·60
Nasal Breadth ..	107·82	66·25	35·30	77·27	118·47	28·51	42·77	46·56	40·70	88·54	21·34	61·41	74·19	83·55	38·72
Nasal Height or depth	234·51	169·42	34·22	103·49	147·15	172·60	172·61	235·28	58·11	105·02	69·10	142·90	146·61	140·94	106·
Upper Facial Length	78·56	65·41	100·12	91·96	56·91	44·95	72·48	102·94	1·81	22·43	14·07	28·91	15·06	2·60	33·
Total Facial Length	177·76	146·75	174·45	203·58	187·73	88·05	135·09	159·65	59·71	106·21	58·59	84·07	27·36	29·00	39·
Horizontal Cirm. of the Head.	599·17	304·99	269·66	308·81	411·10	226·13	246·26	386·21	124·55	205·86	165·49	346·02	466·34	273·26	295·
Sagittal Arc ..	286·65	150·65	46·18	99·78	160·05	277·46	264·01	247·32	184·35	191·37	45·90	119·11	147·88	116·42	29·
Transverse Arc ..	737·58	538·48	708·75	910·81	803·73	454·76	753·65	1178·55	508·61	980·93	445·89	766·05	111·17	858·41	590·7
Length Breadth Index	19·70	13·99	254·58	264·73	94·56	0·60	78·71	210·25	38·18	75·57	3·78	23·65	246·39	109·53	113·
Length Height Index	61·63	5·79	25·96	23·63	13·16	35·04	1·58	0·05	4·57	29·19	22·38	25·05	7·62	18·86	8·
Breadth Height Index	122·92	27·91	44·91	53·44	114·62	26·90	62·26	106·86	45·25	1·30	34·35	70·52	190·64	136·93	108·
Trans. Fronto-Parietal Index.	57·19	57·34	146·55	122·91	115·20	36·11	93·38	183·01	56·77	71·86	15·35	3·08	163·42	60·26	146·
Orbitonasal Index ..	0·21	9·92	54·31	20·71	24·62	0·29	4·14	9·01	4·46	17·59	0·36	0·51	4·18	5·23	0·
Nasal Index ..	432·49	278·89	184·39	309·69	375·53	145·60	187·41	271·91	101·85	231·04	83·13	201·31	245·48	209·66	188·
Nasal Elevation Index	344·93	237·84	60·61	171·01	254·65	184·53	208·48	260·81	89·83	173·10	82·09	191·67	209·94	212·68	139·
Upper Facial Index ..	1·94	8·00	0·99	0·06	0·00	7·38	20·22	14·52	3·64	0·63	0·00	0·04	5·42	12·43	1·
Total Facial Index ..	17·87	32·65	5·87	12·31	28·38	21·06	46·48	27·14	22·76	30·43	9·54	5·31	6·46	1·26	4·
Trans. Cephalo-Facial Index.	32·18	21·06	51·23	58·76	65·92	1·20	100·05	173·26	48·37	67·88	0·08	9·62	185·59	44·23	37
Vertical Cephalo-Facial Index.	99·63	41·39	17·69	29·42	87·58	43·25	50·52	43·09	36·44	1·72	47·07	50·56	16·64	39·02	30

TABLE LIII.

Kadar with other races.

Bania-Jain.	Chit-pavan Brah-min.	Desas-tha Brah-min.	Saras-wat Gour Brah-min.	Mah-ratta.	Nam-budiri Brah-min.	Iluva.	Tamil Brha-min.	Kals.	Kana-rese Brah-min.	Telegu Brah-min.	Nair.	Bhil.	Khasi.	Characters.
125·15	139·69	113·51	59·48	82·57	73·91	16·34	78·54	104·96	42·88	88·58	223·13	48·25	2·39	Stature.
3·37	3·80	4·83	1·73	2·71	9·79	4·67	5·81	0·38	0·80	1·38	5·79	33·93	8·32	Auricular Height.
12·44	17·44	7·56	18·54	0·09	147·10	52·29	32·00	32·03	2·81	54·73	98·25	0·02	25·64	Max. Head Length.
299·82	137·33	160·49	100·88	9·39	55·56	31·11	118·56	53·39	123·11	53·57	78·22	8·54	136·71	Max. Head Breadth.
58·95	33·94	38·11	14·24	19·91	2·44	250·09	172·45	210·69	27·46	3·27	6·33	0·14	0·00	Min. Frontal Breadth.
179·65	91·25	89·02	25·28	65·50	34·10	2·11	17·34	31·67	36·72	30·60	46·06	22·46	76·48	Max. Bizygomatic Breadth.
5·30	0·37	3·24	12·34	2·44	2·00	4·52	0·97	0·63	6·25	1·90	0·03	0·00	53·78	Bigonial Breadth.
11·66	0·52	9·11	0·12	0·95	0·33	1·53	7·96	1·99	2·59	0·76	0·49	0·02	0·34	Inter-orbital Breadth.
130·01	54·59	47·14	74·35	14·69	94·08	53·87	130·27	38·85	88·64	77·47	97·21	13·89	17·37	Orbitonasal Breadth.
39·11	43·57	26·37	27·91	7·58	79·44	12·74	56·77	0·67	25·42	18·15	49·18	4·91	9·75	Orbitonasal Arc.
109·05	33·88	41·44	38·60	31·30	42·04	4·60	28·34	3·64	28·34	30·76	52·53	0·28	3·93	Nasal Length.
36·51	49·74	38·00	36·72	32·83	29·52	32·94	36·72	20·46	45·98	16·48	20·90	5·57	20·68	Nasal Breadth.
13·51	57·43	60·53	63·81	39·67	166·99	37·49	93·92	34·77	88·50	96·88	135·47	21·74	6·76	Nasal Height or depth.
10·97	2·69	4·10	15·29	1·86	27·12	0·44	15·09	1·57	8·41	12·52	29·03	6·12	25·26	Upper Facial Length.
27·46	61·22	40·39	73·35	29·04	99·32	35·54	64·88	30·67	37·74	34·04	120·82	12·99	19·97	Total Facial Length.
61·66	306·15	318·85	203·45	167·03	334·96	176·00	237·46	135·98	163·59	232·44	299·43	82·92	89·55	Horizontal Cirm. the Head.
51·64	73·84	100·23	95·11	35·70	315·08	209·70	183·29	93·96	94·49	146·24	236·10	31·68	61·24	Sagittal Arc.
06·12	742·06	935·49	679·13	573·10	727·85	552·30	686·86	369·42	625·35	577·96	855·55	296·42	344·12	Transverse Arc.
95·55	70·06	101·78	43·73	81·57	0·57	0·32	42·55	9·75	90·00	4·32	3·53	8·60	56·28	Length Breadth Index.
12·20	16·91	12·11	1·09	1·10	10·97	31·50	0·45	12·19	2·70	7·29	8·06	28·71	0·02	Length Height Index.
76·17	99·74	116·36	35·71	62·52	6·84	35·25	32·02	33·35	71·72	17·36	18·03	54·91	29·48	Breadth Height Index.
80·91	69·55	79·47	67·76	52·10	52·30	44·46	104·62	70·56	64·67	47·27	63·30	9·53	168·64	Trans. Fronto-Parietal Index.
17·71	0·85	0·16	5·79	0·07	1·70	9·05	6·04	33·30	12·94	16·06	2·00	0·93	81·67	Orbitonasal Index.
2·36	120·49	119·47	113·31	102·08	99·98	50·65	99·91	32·63	112·94	71·12	104·17	6·52	36·58	Nasal Index.
4·13	101·76	87·49	94·27	64·37	182·11	59·66	123·15	48·51	126·02	102·04	138·38	18·26	0·13	Nasal Elevation Index.
2·72	12·14	9·36	1·00	6·27	2·88	0·01	2·00	2·80	0·20	0·20	2·07	22·43	0·00	Upper Facial Index.
0·57	2·08	0·08	23·24	0·07	30·16	21·88	23·99	2·72	3·94	3·94	35·22	0·19	1·65	Total Facial Index.
3·84	38·82	60·54	74·34	26·18	15·97	40·04	113·76	18·37	77·45	20·24	26·67	0·87	47·58	Trans. Cephalo-Facial Index.
1·75	42·43	33·81	20·74	21·92	16·88	30·31	11·51	15·81	21·36	8·19	29·06	39·87	0·29	Vertical Cephalo-Facial Index.

TABLE LIV.

Values of $\frac{N_s \; N_s'}{N_s + N_s'} \left(\frac{M_s - M_s'}{\sigma_s}\right)^2$

Characters.	Red Kaf-fir.	Pathan.	Uzbeg.	Tadjik.	Khos (Lower Chitral.)	U. P. Brah-min.	Bengali Brah-min.	Bengali Kayas-tha.	Bengali Pod.	Orissa Brah-min.	Malve Brah-min.	Rajput.	Nagar Brah-min.	Audich Brah-min.	K
Stature	19·98	4·10	4·18	12·62	0·92	8·36	26·80	24·85	0·03	4·86	3·56	46·07	7·41	6·70	1
Auricular Height ..	20·29	44·86	95·50	95·23	28·16	15·85	31·58	55·83	14·30	7·20	7·90	20·08	23·83	7·95	1
Max. Head Length ..	110·27	53·16	1·05	0·31	27·75	69·66	11·47	8·41	2·53	1·05	14·77	31·37	7·86	3·03	1
Max. Head Breadth	67·84	35·09	176·83	141·14	83·16	5·64	61·54	127·33	16·50	20·03	3·47	24·69	149·53	50·16	10
Min. Frontal Breadth	57·83	12·21	48·66	62·50	29·43	0·09	14·78	31·74	1·81	4·03	2·96	0·40	55·22	31·53	1
Max. Bizygomatic Breadth.	33·33	11·76	108·36	73·41	24·52	2·34	1·87	14·22	0·57	0·06	2·22	10·81	21·57	12·03	58
Bigonial Breadth ..	22·82	2·67	25·87	14·36	9·74	1·36	2·72	5·36	1·25	2·09	4·11	0·54	0·71	0·11	1
Inter-Orbital Breadth	1·13	7·12	16·15	6·50	0·62	9·44	10·28	8·86	0·11	12·99	2·98	1·42	2·70	4·08	2
Orbitonasal Breadth	0·19	0·03	9·97	5·41	0·16	3·68	25·99	37·68	0·17	3·16	2·57	0·31	12·57	9·49	15·
Orbitonasal Arc ..	0·57	1·38	2·63	0·02	3·24	3·67	13·25	16·96	0·15	0·01	2·49	2·23	6·03	3·74	10·
Nasal Length ..	138·78	102·72	84·76	103·08	92·30	50·86	62·28	95·10	14·52	31·29	20·13	42·95	52·12	30·11	69·
Nasal Breadth ..	35·17	24·16	11·96	27·13	41·73	6·42	12·64	9·63	11·69	22·88	3·69	15·27	20·01	25·24	12·
Nasal Height or depth	66·95	58·08	4·37	23·46	33·94	59·66	59·66	67·27	9·21	33·32	13·11	30·41	30·90	30·97	32·
Upper Facial Length	89·67	80·68	114·77	104·04	71·23	60·93	87·31	110·01	32·77	39·43	28·03	44·90	30·44	13·62	48·
Total Facial Length	49·72	52·37	79·76	74·95	56·56	24·16	46·50	42·21	12·29	17·50	11·86	14·02	0·32	0·66	6·
Horizontal Cirm. of the Head	110·28	50·52	67·71	42·08	56·13	25·45	31·38	44·47	3·05	2·59	10·22	34·05	64·95	19·57	58·0
Sagittal Arc ..	62·75	31·94	3·00	10·78	22·34	87·96	81·57	48·51	45·70	23·02	0·95	9·88	16·35	10·07	0·0
Transverse Arc ..	21·77	25·94	109·31	94·63	37·84	12·21	75·77	107·39	20·59	38·83	11·00	25·82	86·82	45·44	53·3
Length Breadth Index	0·42	0·47	14·08	119·37	24·77	9·96	25·51	74·61	7·62	13·25	0·71	0·97	90·39	30·57	47·5
Length Height Index	0·97	6·31	73·32	58·75	5·08	0·23	12·17	29·51	7·50	91·49	0·29	1·65	9·74	2·92	2·9
Breadth Height Index	2·34	3·27	0·09	0·29	2·10	3·57	0·17	0·88	0·34	38·54	1·74	0·37	12·83	4·83	9·71
Trans. Fronto-Parietal Index.	9·34	14·93	73·69	43·23	33·19	6·33	32·10	62·27	14·68	11·89	0·51	26·57	52·10	10·94	65·79
Orbitonasal Index ..	0·34	3·49	31·66	8·65	9·42	0·13	3·40	2·10	0·97	5·03	0·09	2·28	0·45	0·83	0·01
Nasal Index ..	196·30	144·72	101·11	151·99	171·35	65·44	89·68	112·16	41·10	81·55	31·16	76·80	97·20	82·94	97·29
Nasal Elevation Index	111·48	89·89	13·21	49·94	75·46	62·70	74·73	74·50	19·59	32·27	16·57	46·26	52·21	56·59	4
Upper Facial Index ..	33·15	41·38	10·99	19·68	20·99	40·17	61·64	58·93	31·91	30·37	16·44	20·19	8·11	3·14	[illegible]
Total Facial Index ..	8·62	20·19	3·28	6·44	14·91	12·51	29·50	13·80	13·63	14·38	5·11	1·98	5·93	1·73	4
Trans. Cephalo-Facial Index.	29·39	22·05	49·39	52·09	54·98	2·97	86·47	129·29	44·99	53·18	1·08	11·42	136·72	38·74	3
Vertical Cephalo-Facial Index.	2·99	0·01	1·15	1·28	2·02	0·05	0·46	0·97	0·06	26·58	0·22	0·30	9·15	1·23	[illegible]

TABLE LIV.

...hil with other races.

Baia-hia.	Chit-pavan Brah-min.	Desas-tha Brah-min.	Sara-swat Gour Brah-min.	Mah-ratta.	Nam-budiri Brah-min.	Iluva.	Tamil Brah-min.	Kula.	Kana-rese Brah-min.	Telegu Brah-min.	Nair.	Kadar.	Khasi.	Characters.
4·35	6·28	2·28	0·43	2·13	1·44	6·10	2·66	11·10	0·12	4·40	39·82	48·25	28·25	Stature.
18·08	17·66	16·40	36·87	13·93	59·40	9·71	49·06	17·11	17·59	35·43	51·59	33·93	60·77	Auricular Height.
8·65	11·87	5·32	14·29	0·14	106·39	39·29	24·30	25·26	2·38	41·08	70·64	0·02	17·96	Max. Head Length.
116·86	40·93	50·35	36·67	29·83	13·96	5·10	45·89	16·02	48·31	13·98	22·97	8·54	45·14	Max. Head Breadth.
34·30	18·80	21·14	8·59	11·93	1·01	0·26	3·25	1·44	17·59	1·53	3·23	0·14	0·09	Max. Frontal Breadth.
36·13	8·35	7·51	0·06	6·65	0·75	7·82	0·24	1·18	1·26	0·45	2·13	22·46	8·81	Max. Bizygomatic Breadth.
3·31	0·19	2·15	8·70	1·81	1·33	3·13	0·64	0·53	4·36	1·29	0·01	0·00	35·88	Bigonial Breadth.
6·82	0·18	4·95	0·18	0·46	0·12	0·85	6·42	1·21	2·26	0·37	0·20	0·02	0·20	Inter-Orbital Breadth.
19·20	4·73	2·95	17·50	0·01	24·55	9·44	42·72	5·87	23·39	18·80	26·56	13·89	0·02	Orbitonasal Breadth.
7·96	9·30	3·50	6·81	0·12	31·40	1·35	20·62	1·13	5·84	3·03	15·29	4·91	21·51	Orbitonasal Arc.
60·[illegible]7	16·75	20·79	23·41	17·79	25·07	1·90	16·66	1·53	18·94	18·24	31·24	0·28	1·24	Nasal length.
6·20	10·61	6·36	9·90	7·33	6·37	8·26	9·90	4·15	14·13	2·09	2·97	5·57	2·12	Nasal Breadth.
27·74	4·00	4·47	11·20	2·84	54·15	3·09	22·98	3·50	20·72	24·32	37·48	21·74	35·33	Nasal Height or depth.
25·59	13·99	16·44	29·48	11·09	42·79	7·13	29·24	9·43	20·88	26·15	44·88	6·12	41·17	Upper Facial Length
0·00	6·97	2·07	17·80	1·74	27·67	4·02	14·33	3·68	4·66	3·60	46·11	12·99	0·05	Total Facial Length.
38·37	23·74	25·51	19·24	7·61	56·17	12·52	28·74	7·98	9·82	27·27	40·56	82·92	11·65	orizontal Cirm. of the Head.
18·26	1·57	5·35	12·30	0·00	101·15	50·68	45·25	15·25	12·11	30·23	61·44	31·65	15·59	Sagittal Arc
67·52	21·03	49·61	56·56	23·06	60·01	28·56	58·47	24·48	43·89	33·68	83·64	296·42	49·93	Transverse Arc.
67·95	12·61	25·51	9·80	24·64	10·18	4·04	9·32	1·30	31·06	0·53	1·07	8·60	10·96	Length Breadth Index.
6·13	4·12	6·63	13·47	14·62	3·51	0·05	15·91	1·60	9·98	5·11	5·69	28·71	23·82	Length Height Index.
11·22	0·36	1·34	1·49	0·02	18·03	1·57	2·22	0·86	0·81	7·61	9·21	54·91	6·20	Breadth Height Index.
32·51	13·35	16·61	19·64	11·30	11·95	9·51	37·86	24·29	18·22	10·65	15·74	9·53	60·27	Trans. Fronto-Parietal Index.
5·84	2·84	0·41	1·52	0·39	3·69	3·05	1·63	18·07	5·06	6·75	0·11	0·93	41·56	Orbitonasal Index.
76·09	38·12	37·09	47·34	38·39	38·47	15·06	40·05	8·48	47·14	25·00	39·17	6·52	6·20	Nasal Index.
32·28	14·23	9·85	21·37	8·61	58·54	8·61	33·68	6·88	34·96	24·57	36·39	18·26	18·77	Nasal Elevation Index.
3·27	3·66	5·23	23·80	4·39	30·80	15·47	27·35	5·50	13·31	19·41	29·22	22·43	19·52	Upper Facial Index.
8·49	0·51	0·04	13·94	0·10	18·50	13·05	14·44	1·18	1·75	17·50	20·94	9·19	2·10	Total Facial Index.
73·52	34·27	49·93	66·02	26·08	17·72	38·12	97·28	19·98	68·51	21·33	26·44	0·87	41·94	Trans. Cephalo-Facial Index.
6·16	1·15	2·83	2·24	2·59	4·14	0·47	6·17	2·59	2·07	8·62	1·22	39·87	29·78	Vertical Cephalo-Facial Index.

PHYSICAL OBSERVATIONS.
Tables LV to LIX.

TABLE LV.
Physical Observations.
United Provinces, Central India, Bengal and Orissa.

Races.	Skin Colour (von Luschan.) — Forehead.													Upper Arm.								
	10	11	12	13	14	15	16	17	18	23	25	26	27	9	10	11	12	13	14	15	16	17
1. Bengali Brahmin—Male—50. Percentage ..	..	..	2·00	12·00	34·00	28·00	..	20·00	..	4·00	..	..	..	..	..	6·00	..	18·00	38·00	26·00	..	12·00
2. Bengali Kayastha—Male—100. Percentage ..	3·00	2·00	6·00	13·00	26·00	16·00	3·00	26·00	1·00	4·00	..	..	..	1·00	3·00	1·00	10·00	12·00	26·00	29·00	..	17·00
3. Bengali Pod—Male—50. Percentage ..	..	..	..	..	6·00	24·00	..	38·00	4·00	22·00	..	2·00	4·00	..	..	..	..	..	2·00	10·00	6·00	16·00
4. Orissa Brahmin—Male—143. Percentage ..	..	..	1·39	7·69	22·37	15·38	7·69	13·28	25·87	..	0·69	5·59	..	..	..	..	1·39	1·39	15·38	22·37	2·79	15·38
5. U. P. Brahmin—Male—50. Percentage ..	..	..	2·04	8·16	18·37	36·73	..	28·57	4·08	2·04	..	..	..	..	..	..	4·08	6·12	18·37	42·86	..	24·49
6. Malve Brahmin—Male—50. Percentage ..	..	2·04	2·04	20·41	26·53	26·53	..	20·41	..	2·04	..	..	..	2·04	..	2·04	12·24	24·49	32·65	12·24	2·04	10·20
7. Baghel Rajput—Male—50. Percentage ..	..	2·00	..	8·00	26·00	26·00	..	26·00	..	8·00	..	..	4·00	..	..	2·00	..	8·00	30·00	28·00	..	26·00
8. Miscellaneous Rajput—Male—50. Percentage ..	..	..	2·00	6·00	22·00	34·00	..	22·00	2·00	8·00	..	..	4·00	..	..	..	6·00	16·00	24·00	24·00	..	24·00

Races.	Skin Colour (von Luschan)—*contd.* — Upper Arm—*contd.*							Breast.													
	18	22	23	25	26	27	28	9	10	11	12	13	14	15	16	17	18	23	25	26	27
1. Bengali Brahmin—Male—50. Percentage ..	..	..	..	..	..	..	..	..	..	..	2·00	22·00	28·00	24·00	2·00	16·00	6·00	..	..	..	..
2. Bengli Kayasatha—Male—100. Percentage ..	..	..	1·00	..	..	..	..	1·00	3·00	1·00	10·00	13·00	23·00	23·00	7·00	17·00	1·00	1·00	..	..	..
3. Bengali Pod—Male—50. Percentage ..	16·00	2·00	32·00	..	2·00	14·00	..	..	..	..	..	..	4·00	4·00	2·00	16·00	26·00	32·00	..	2·00	14·00
4 Orissa Brahmin—Male—143. Percentage ..	34·26	..	..	0·69	6·29	..	..	..	..	..	1·39	1·39	..	25·17	2·79	15·38	34·26	..	0·69	6·29	..
5. U. P. Brahmin—Male—50. Percentage ..	2·04	..	2·04	..	..	..	..	..	..	..	4·08	8·16	18·37	28·57	8·16	8·16	22·45	2·04	..	..	..
6. Malve Brahmin—Male—50. Percentage ..	..	..	..	..	..	..	2·04	..	..	..	..	..	..	..	..	..	..	..	..	..	..
7. Baghel Rajput—Male—50. Percentage ..	..	..	2·00	..	..	4·00	..	..	..	..	..	..	..	..	..	..	..	..	..	..	..
. Miscellaneous Rajput—Male—50. Percentage ..	2·00	..	2·00	..	..	2·00	..	..	..	..	..	..	..	..	..	..	..	..	..	..	..

TABLE LV (a).

Physical Observations.

United Provinces, Central India, Bengal and Orissa.

Races.	Hair.															Beard and Moustache.			Body Hair.			
	Colour Nos. (Fischer).						Character			Quantity.						Quantity.			Quantity.			
	3	4	5	6	27	Grey.	Straight.	Wavy.	Curly.	+	++	+++	Shaved.	Bald.	+	+ +	+++	+	++	+++	*Nil.*
1. Bengali Brahmin—																					
Male—50.																					
Percentage ..	...	12·00	..	..	76·00	12·00	72·00	24·00	4·00	6·00	82·00	..	..	12·00	20·00	80·00	..	64·00	28·00	8·00	..
2. Bengali Kayastha—																					
Male—100.																					
Percentage ..	1·00	26·00	1·00	1·00	67·00	4·00	44·00	43·00	13·00	6·00	83·00	1·00	..	10·00	41·00	58·00	1·00	62·00	33·00	1·00	4·00
3. Bengali Pod—																					
Male—50.																					
Percentage ..	..	4·00	..	..	92·00	4·00	60·00	40·00	..	8·00	90·00	..	..	2·00	52·00	48·00	..	68·00	22·00	..	10·00
4. Orissa Brahmin—																					
Male—143.																					
Percentage ..	..	3·49	..	..	84·61	11·88	62·22	34·96	2·79	9·09	83·91	0·69	2·79	3·49	46·17	43·35	10·48	54·53	18·88	1·39	25·17
5. U. P. Brahmin—																					
Male—50.																					
Percentage ..	..	10·00	..	..	74·00	16·00	90·00	10·00	..	..	42·00	..	44·00	14·00	28·00	72·00	..	68·00	32·00	..	..
6. Malve Brahmin—																					
Male—50.																					
Percentage ..	..	40·81	2·04	..	36·73	20·41	82·22	15·56	2·22	2·04	57·14	..	28·57	12·24	28·57	67·35	4·08	87·76	12·24	..	..
7. Baghel Rajput—																					
Male—50.																					
Percentage ..	..	44·00	6·00	..	46·00	4·00	72·00	28·00	..	..	88·00	..	8·00	4·00	42·00	54·00	4·00	92·00	6·00	..	2·00
8. Miscellaneous Rajput																					
Male—50.																					
Percentage ..	..	55·10	..	..	40·81	4·08	70·83	29·17	..	..	80·00	..	4·00	16·00	40·82	57·14	2·04	85·71	14·29	..	..

TABLE LV(b).

Physical Observations.

United Provinces, Central India, Bengal and Orissa.

Races.	Eye												Supra Orbital Ridge.			
	Colour Nos. (Martin)							Form.			Epicanthic fold.					
	1	2	3	4	5	6	7	Round.	Oblique.	Slanting.	+	++	+	++	+++	Not marked.
1. Bengali Brahmin— Male—50. Percentage	6·00	30·00	54·00	8·00	..	..	2·00	100·00	..	..	*Nil*	*Nil*	62·00	10·00	..	28·00
2. Bengali Kayastha— Male—100. Percentage	6·00	40·00	44·00	7·00	2·00	1·00	..	98·00	2·00	..	1·00	1·00	72·00	20·00	1·00	7·00
3. Bengali Pod— Male—50. Percentage	4·00	60·00	36·00	..	..	..	..	90·00	10·00	..	4·00	..	68·00	4·00	2·00	26·00
4. Orissa Brahmin— Male—143. Percentage	39·16	38·46	14·68	2·79	0·69	3·49	0·69	86·01	..	13·98	5·58	1·38	95·85*	4·13*	..	—
5. U. P. Brahmin— Male—50. Percentage	6·00	30·00	38·00	16·00	4·00	2·00	4·00	98·00	..	2·00	2·00	..	72·00	10·00	..	18·00
6. Malve Brahmin— Male—50. Percentage	..	34·69	53·06	10·20	..	..	2·04	91·84	8·16	..	4·08	..	69·39	16·33	..	14·29
7. Baghel Rajput— Male—50. Percentage	..	18·00	52·00	20·00	4·00	4·00	2·00	96·00	4·00	..	4·00	..	86·00	8·00	..	6·00
8. Miscellaneous [?]Rajput— Male—50. Percentage	..	24·00	64·00	10·00	..	2·00	..	94·00	6·00	..	4·00	..	72·00	18·00	..	10·00

*Observations based on 121 subjects only.

TABLE LV(c).

Physical Observations.

United Provinces, Central India, Bengal and Orissa.

Races.	Nose. Nasal Depression (Root). +	++	Nose Form. Flat.	Medium.	Prominent.	Very Prominent.	Convex.	Lips. Thin.	Medium.	Thick.	Chin. Pointed.	Medium.	Broad.	Face. Shape. Long.	Pear.	Round.	Square.	Prognathism. +	++
1. Bengali Brahmin— Male—50. Percentage	6·00	..	2·00	18·00	64·00	10·00	6·00	14·00	80·00	6·00	8·00	70·00	22·00	38·00	2·00	34·00	26·00	6·00	..
2. Bengali Kayastha— Male—100. Percentage	2·00	..	3·00	26·00	48·00	13·00	10·00	6·00	69·00	25·00	17·00	62·00	21·00	31·00	16·00	32·00	21·00	6·00	..
3. Bengali Pod— Male—50. Percentage	14·00	..	18·00	28·00	54·00	..	..	4·00	80·00	16·00	10·00	62·00	28·00	22·00	24·00	26·00	28·00	24·00	..
4. Orissa Brahmin— Male—143 Percentage	17·47	1·39	22·38	22·38	51·72	2·80	0·70	0·83*	88·33*	10·83*	27·26	61·53	11·18	28·66	29·36	8·39	33·56	15·29	2·09
5. U. P. Brahmin— Male—50. Percentage	14·00	..	8·00	16·00	64·00	12·00	..	22·00	74·00	4·00	32·00	48·00	20·00	28·00	26·00	16·00	30·00	2·00	2·00
6. Malve Brahmin— Male—50. Percentage	30·61	..	12·24	36·73	38·78	..	12·24	22·45	71·43	6·12	10·20	73·47	16·33	28·57	24·49	8·16	38·78	10·21	..
7. Baghel Rajput— Male—50. Percentage	12·00	..	6·00	30·00	50·00	..	14·00	24·00	72·00	4·00	4·00	68·00	28·00	20·00	26·00	14·00	40·00	*Nil.*	*Nil.*
8. Miscellaneous Rajput— Male—50. Percentage	16·00	2·00	8·00	30·00	52·00	..	10·00	18·00	72·00	10·00	10·00	76·00	14·00	26·00	26·00	24·00	24·00	6·00	..

*Observations based on 120 subjects only.

TABLE LVI.
Physical Observations.
Guzrat and Kathiawar.

Races.	Skin Colour (von Luschan). Forehead.														Upper Arm.											
	10	11	12	13	14	15	16	17	17D*	18	22	24	27	28	9	10	11	12	13	14	15	16	17	17D*	27	28
1. Nagar Brahmin—Male—105. Percentage ..	3·81	9·52	15·24	18·10	22·86	23·81	..	5·71	0·95	..	..	..	..	..	6·67	3·81	18·10	14·29	21·90	22·86	6·67	..	4·76	0·95	..	..
2. Audich Brahmin Male—93. Percentage ..	..	2·15	6·45	13·98	22·58	31·18	1·08	18·28	1·08	1·08	1·08	1·08	..	..	..	..	3·45	9·68	22·58	23·66	16·13	3·23	18·28	..	..	..
3. Brahma— Kshatri Male—31. Percentage ..	3·23	6·45	22·58	32·26	19·35	12·90	..	3·23	..	..	..	..	..	..	3·33	..	36·67	13·33	30·00	6·67	6·67	..	3·33	..	..	..
4. Kathi—Male—40. Percentage ..	..	..	5·00	12·50	45·00	27·50	..	..	7·50	..	..	..	..	2·50	..	..	2·50	10·00	22·50	35·00	20·00	..	2·50	5·00	..	2·50
5. Bania—Jain—Male—99. Percentage ..	..	2·02	5·05	6·06	23·23	33·33	..	24·24	5·05	..	..	..	1·01	..	..	..	7·07	5·05	23·23	26·26	18·18	2·02	16·16	1·01	1·01	..

*D represents deeper shade.

TABLE LVI(a).
Physical Observations.
Guzrat and Kathiawar.

Races.	Hair. Colour Nos. (Fischer)								Character.			Quantity.				Beard and Moustache. Quantity.			Body Hair. Quantity.		
	4	5	6	7	27	28	Grey.	Black.	Straight.	Wavy.	Curly.	+	++	Bald	Shaved.	+	++	+++	+	++	Nil.
1. Nagar Brahmin—Male—105. Percentage ..	35·24	5·71	0·95	..	36·19	0·95	16·19	4·76	73·33	21·91	4·76	4·81	87·50	7·69	..	38·10	59·05	2·86	93·33	6·67	..
2. Audich Brahmin—Male—93. Percentage ..	35·49	12·91	2·16	1·08	18·28	..	16·13	13·98	69·89	29·03	1·08	6·45	89·25	4·30	..	44·09	54·84	1·08	93·55	6·45	..
3. Brahma—Kshatri—Male—31. Percentage ..	25·80	9·68	3·23	..	38·71	..	19·35	3·23	67·74	25·81	6·45	19·35	77·42	3·25	..	16·13	83·87	..	83·87	16·13	..
4. Kathi—Male—40. Percentage ..	10·00	..	..	..	47·50	..	42·50	..	80·00	10·00	10·00	12·50	67·50	17·50	2·50	2·50	97·50	..	80·00	20·00	..
5. Bania—Jain—Male—99. Percentage ..	36·46	6·26	..	..	42·71	..	12·50	2·08	70·71	26·26	3·03	11·11	81·82	6·06	1·01	50·51	49·49	..	91·92	7·07	1·01

TABLE LVI(b).

Physical Observations.

Guzrat and Kathiawar.

Races.	Eye.															Supra-Orbital Ridge.		
	Colour Nos. (Martin).											Form.		Epicanthic fold.				
	1	2	3	4	5	6	7	8	9	10	11	Round	Oblique	+	++	+	++	Nil.
1. NAGAR BRAHMIN—Male—105. Percentage ..	24·04	30·77	28·85	11·54	0·96	1·92	..	0·96	0·96	..	..	93·33	6·67	..	0·95	85·71	14·29	..
2. AUDICH BRAHMIN—Male—93. Percentage ..	26·88	34·41	27·96	7·53	1·08	..	1·08	1·08	..	..	..	93·55	6·45	1·08	2·15	75·27	23·66	1·08
3. BRAHMA—KSHATRI—Male—31. Percentage ..	13·33	20·00	43·33	16·67	6·67	..	..	..	..	..	..	100·00	..	*Nil*	*Nil*	77·42	22·58	..
4. KATHI.—Male—40. Percentage ..	8·10	37·80	37·80	8·10	8·10	..	..	..	..	..	..	95·00	5·00	*Nil*	*Nil*	62·50	37·50	..
5. BANIA-JAIN—Male—99. Percentage ..	34·34	36·36	23·22	5·05	1·01	..	..	..	..	..	1·01	86·87	13·13	4·04	2·02	84·85	15·15	..

TABLE LVI(c).

Physical Observations.

Guzrat and Kathiawar.

Races.	Nose.							Lips.			Chin.			Face.					
	Nasal Depression (Root).		Nose Form.											Shape.				Prognathism.	
	+	++	Flat.	Medium.	Prominent.	Very Prominent.	Convex.	Thin.	Medium.	Thick.	Pointed.	Medium.	Broad.	Long	Pear.	Round.	Square.	+	++
1. NAGAR BRAHMIN—Male—105. Percentage ..	18·09	..	10·47	26·67	51·43	3·81	7·61	21·90	76·19	1·91	13·33	76·19	10·48	13·46	29·81	25·00	31·73	..	1·92
2. AUDICH BRAHMIN—Male—93. Percentage ..	17·20	2·16	11·83	35·48	51·62	1·08	..	8·60	83·87	7·53	9·68	79·57	10·75	12·90	44·09	10·75	32·26	7·53	..
3. BRAHMA—KSHATRI—Male—31. Percentage ..	3·23	..	3·33	3·33	93·33	..	..	16·13	77·42	6·45	16·13	80·65	3·23	22·58	38·71	16·13	22·58	*Nil*	*Nil*
4. KATHI.—Male—40. Percentage ..	7·69	..	10·00	22·50	67·50	..	..	10·00	75·00	15·00	12·50	62·50	25·00	7·50	35·00	20·00	37·50	..	2·50
5. BANIA—JAIN—Male—99. Percentage ..	15·63	..	18·34	33·67	46·94	..	1·01	23·23	69·70	7·07	13·13	77·78	9·09	15·15	32·32	24·24	28·28	12·12	..

TABLE LVII.
Physical Observations.
Maharashtra.

Races.	Skin Colour (von Luschan.)															
	Forehead.											Upper Arm.				
	10	11	12	13	14	15	17	17D*	23	26	27	9	10	11	12	13
1. Chitpavan Brahmin— Male—103. Percentage	0·97	3·88	24·27	28·16	26·21	13·59	2·91	..	..	..	..	1·94	1·94	26·21	22·33	31·07
2. Desastha Brahmin— Male—107. Percentage	0·93	0·93	3·74	11·21	29·91	32·71	17·76	0·93	..	0·93	0·93	0·93	0·93	5·61	8·41	24·20
3. Prabhu— Male—55. Percentage	..	1·82	9·09	18·18	41·82	20·00	7·27	1·82	..	..	..	1·82	..	16·36	14·55	30·91
4. Karada Brahmin— Male—48. Percentage	..	..	8·33	18·75	45·83	18·75	8·33	..	..	..	..	..	..	6·25	14·58	37·50
5. Mahratta Brahmin— Male—59. Percentage	..	..	1·69	6·78	23·73	20·34	22·03	6·77	..	3·39	15·25	..	..	1·69	6·78	10·17
6. Saraswat—Gour Brahmin— Male—50. Percentage	..	..	..	10·00	26·00	36·00	20·00	2·00	6·00	..	..	..	..	..	4·00	22·00

Races.	Skin Colour (von Luschan)—contd.															
	Upper Arm—contd.							Breast.								
	14	15	16	17	17D*	22	27	11	12	13	14	15	16	17	17D*	22
1. Chitpavan Brahmin— Male—103. Percentage	10·68	3·88	..	1·94	..	..	..	..	..	..	..	..	..	..	..	..
2. Desastha Brahmin— Male—107. Percentage	25·23	25·23	1·86	6·54	0·93	..	..	..	..	..	..	..	..	..	..	..
3. Prabhu— Male—55. Percentage	23·64	10·91	..	..	1·82	..	..	..	..	..	..	..	..	..	..	..
4. Karada Brahmin— Male—48. Percentage	20·83	12·50	..	8·33	..	..	..	..	..	..	..	..	..	..	..	..
5. Mahratta Brahmin— Male—59. Percentage	25·42	15·25	1·69	25·42	8·47	..	5·08	..	..	..	..	..	..	..	..	..
6. Saraswat—Gour Brahmin— Male—50. Percentage	38·00	22·00	6·00	4·00	2·00	2·00	..	2·00	2·00	22·00	40·00	22·00	4·00	4·00	2·00	2·00

*D represents deeper shade.

TABLE LVII(a)
Physical Observations.
Maharashtra.

Races.	Hair.																Beard and Moustache.			Body Hair.			
	Colour Nos. (Fischer).								Character.				Quantity.				Quantity.			Quantity.			
	3	4	5	6	27	28	Grey.	Black.	Straight.	Wavy.	Curly.	Wooly.	+	++	Bald.	Shaved	+	++	+++	+	++	+++	*Nil.*
1. CHITPAVAN BRAHMIN—Male—103. Percentage ..	..	32·04	4·85	2·91	37·86	..	18·45	3·88	85·44	13·50	0·97	..	0·98	54·90	24·51	19·61	45·63	54·37	..	93·20	5·83	..	0·97
2. DESASTHA BRAHMIN—Male—107. Percentage ..	0·93	34·57	1·86	..	42·99	..	16·82	2·84	89·72	9·34	0·94	..	0·94	66·98	16·04	16·04	33·64	66·36	..	92·52	7·48	..	..
3. PRABHU—Male—55. Percentage ..	..	29·09	1·82	1·82	40·00	..	27·27	..	78·18	20·00	1·82	..	1·82	70·91	21·82	5·45	29·09	70·91	..	92·73	7·27	..	..
4. KARADA BRAHMIN—Male—48. Percentage ..	..	33·33	2·08	..	41·67	..	16·67	6·25	83·33	10·42	6·25	..	2·08	54·17	25·00	18·75	41·67	58·33	..	93·75	4·17	..	2·08
5. MAHRATTA BRAHMIN—Male—59. Percentage ..	..	32·20	..	..	50·84	..	13·56	3·39	83·05	13·56	3·39	..	..	67·63	15·25	27·12	44·07	55·93	..	91·53	8·47	..	..
6. SARASWAT-GOUR BRAHMIN—Male—50. Percentage ..	..	28·00	12·00	..	60·00	2·00	..	..	54·00	44·00	..	2·00	6·00	86·00	4·00	4·00	42·00	56·00	2·00	64·00	28·00	6·00	2·00

TABLE LVII(b).
Physical Observations.
Maharashtra.

Races.	Eye.													Supra-Orbital Ridge.			
	Colour Nos. (Martin).									Form.			Epicanthic fold.				
	1	2	3	4	5	6	7	8	9	Round.	*Oblique.*	Slightly slanting.	+	+	++	+++	Not marked.
1. CHITPAVAN BRAHMIN—Male—103. Percentage	3·88	21·36	36·89	9·71	9·71	10·68	3·88	1·94	1·94	94·17	5·83	..	0·97	81·55	8·74	0·97	8·74
2. DESASTHA BRAHMIN—Male—107. Percentage	16·98	35·85	37·74	7·55	0·94	..	0·94	..	..	92·52	7·48	..	4·67	74·77	3·74	..	21·49
3. PRABHU—Male—55. Percentage	5·45	32·73	50·91	1·82	5·45	3·64	..	..	..	98·18	1·82	..	1·82	81·82	3·64	..	14·55
4. KARADA BRAHMIN—Male—48. Percentage	16·67	22·92	50·00	10·42	..	..	..	..	..	100·00	..	..	*Nil.*	68·75	8·33	..	22·92
5. MAHRATTA BRAHMIN—Male—59. Percentage	10·17	35·59	45·76	8·47	..	..	..	..	..	94·92	5·08	..	1·69	72·88	6·78	..	20·34
6. SARASWAT-GOUR BRAHMIN—Male—50. Percentage	32·00	44·00	16·00	4·00	..	..	2·00	..	2·00	96·00	..	4·00	*Nil.*	86·00	10·00	4·00	..

TABLE LVII(*c*).

Physical Observations.

Maharashtra.

Races.	Nose.							Lips			Chin.			Face.					
	Nasal Depression (Root).		Nose Form.											Shape.				Prognathism.	
	+	++	Flat.	Medium.	Prominent.	Very Prominent.	Convex.	Thin.	Medium.	Thick.	Pointed.	Medium.	Broad.	Long.	Pear.	Round.	Square.	+	++
1. Chitpavan Brahmin—																			
Male — 103.																			
Percentage	27·45	2·94	4·85	47·57	34·95	0·97	11·65	15·53	73·79	10·68	11·65	78·64	9·71	13·72	32·35	27·45	26·47	7·77	4·85
2. Deshastha Brahmin—																			
Male — 107.																			
Percentage	23·36	1·86	5·60	48·60	34·58	0·93	10·28	14·95	72·90	12·15	13·08	69·16	17·76	15·00	29·91	24·20	30·84	6·54	0·93
3. Prabhu—																			
Male — 55.																			
Percentage	14·29	..	5·46	49·09	27·27	..	18·18	12·73	69·09	18·18	12·73	81·82	5·45	21·82	36·36	30·91	10·91	1·79	..
4. Karada Brahmin—																			
Male — 48.																			
Percentage	37·50	6·25	8·33	47·92	31·25	8·33	4·17	12·50	77·08	10·42	14·58	79·17	6·25	14·58	50·00	10·42	25·00	18·75	2·08
5. Mahratta Brahmin—																			
Male — 59.																			
Percentage	44·07	..	5·08	57·63	28·81	..	8·47	5·08	84·75	10·17	3·39	86·44	10·17	11·86	33·90	27·12	27·12	13·56	3·32
6. Saraswat—Gour Brahmin—																			
Male — 50.																			
Percentage	16·00	..	14·00	34·00	36·00	14·00	2·00	4·00	80·00	16·00	16·00	56·00	28·00	24·00	32·00	22·00	22·00	20·00	

TABLE LVIII.
Physical Observations.
Southern India.

Races.	Skin Colour (von Luschan) — Forehead. 12	13	14	15	16	17	17D*	18	22	23	23D*	24	25	26	27	28	29	Upper Arm. 11	12	13	14	15	16	17	17D*	18
1. Nambudiri Brahmin—Male—55. Percentage ..	7·23	21·82	34·55	18·18	1·82	14·55	..	..	..	1·82	..	..	..	..	..	..	..	1·82	5·45	20·00	38·18	16·36	1·82	12·73	..	1·82
2. Nair—Male—60. Percentage ..	..	3·33	6·67	20·00	1·67	30·00	8·33	1·67	..	20·00	5·00	..	..	..	3·33	..	..	..	..	3·33	16·67	15·00	..	41·67	6·67	..
3. Illuva—Male—50. Percentage ..	..	6·00	8·00	16·00	6·00	30·00	2·00	..	..	6·00	2·00	..	2·00	2·00	16·00	2·00	2·00	..	2·00	4·00	8·00	22·00	..	26·00	6·00	4·00
4. Tamil Brahmin—Male—50. Percentage ..	..	8·00	26·00	36·00	..	22·00	4·00	..	..	2·00	..	..	..	..	2·00	..	..	..	6·00	6·00	46·00	16·00	..	18·00	4·00	..
5. Tamil Kalla—Male—40. Percentage ..	..	..	..	..	..	2·50	..	2·50	..	20·00	45·00	5·00	..	..	17·50	2·50	5·00	..	..	..	..	..	..	..	..	2·50
6. Tamil Chetti—Male—50. Percentage ..	..	2·00	10·00	12·00	..	22·00	6·00	..	..	10·00	14·00	..	..	..	22·00	2·00	..	..	..	..	12·00	10·00	..	24·00	6·00	..
7. Telugu Brahmin—Male—50. Percentage ..	..	8·00	16·00	32·00	..	24·00	..	6·00	2·00	6·00	..	..	..	2·00	2·00	2·00	..	..	..	10·00	26·00	22·00	..	26·00	4·00	6·00
8. Telugu Non-Brahmin—Male—50. Percentage ..	..	..	..	8·00	..	28·00	..	2·00	6·00	14·00	4·00	..	..	..	24·00	14·00	..	..	..	..	2·00	10·00	..	30·00	12·00	..
9. Kanarese Brahmin—Male—50. Percentage ..	2·00	4·00	6·00	14·00	8·00	26·00	..	20·00	..	20·00	..	..	..	..	..	..	..	..	6·00	8·00	6·00	40·00	..	34·00	..	2·00
10. Kanarese Non-Brahmin—Male—50. Percentage ..	..	..	2·00	..	..	16·00	..	14·00	..	36·00	..	..	..	..	24·00	8·00	..	..	..	2·00	..	12·00	..	44·00	8·00	..

*D represents deeper shade.

TABLE LVIII.

Physical Observations.

Southern India.

Races.	Skin Colour (von Luschan).																									
	Upper Arm—*contd.*								Breast.																	
	22	23	23D*	25	26	27	28	29	11	12	13	14	15	16	17	17D*	18	22	23	23D*	24	25	26	27	28	29
1. NAMBUDIRI BRAHMIN—Male—55. Percentage ..	..	1·82	..	..	..	..	..	..	..	3·70	14·55	36·36	21·82	1·82	14·55	..	5·45	..	..	1·82	..	..	..	..	..	..
2. NAIR—Male—60. Percentage ..	..	6·67	5·00	..	1·67	3·33	..	..	..	..	3·32	15·00	13·33	3·32	30·00	6·66	10·00	..	8·30	5·00	..	..	1·66	3·32	..	..
3. ILLUVA—Male—50. Percentage ..	..	..	4·00	2·00	4·00	16·00	2·00	..	..	2·00	6·00	4·00	22·00	..	16·00	6·00	16·00	..	..	4·00	..	2·00	4·00	14·00	2·00	2·00
4. TAMIL BRAHMIN—Male—50. Percentage ..	..	2·00	2·00	..	..	..	..	..	..	4·00	2·00	34·00	34·00	..	12·00	4·00	3·00	..	..	2·00	..	..	..	..	..	..
5. TAMIL KALLA—Male—40. Percentage ..	..	7·50	15·00	..	..	60·00	10·00	5·00	..	..	..	..	..	..	..	..	2·50	..	5·00	20·00	2·50	..	..	55·00	10·00	5·00
6. TAMIL CHETTI—Male—50. Percentage ..	..	10·00	18·00	..	2·00	16·00	2·00	..	..	..	..	6·00	12·00	..	20·00	4·00	10·00	..	8·00	12·00	..	..	2·00	24·00	2·00	..
7. TELUGU BRAHMIN—Male—50. Percentage ..	..	4·00	..	..	2·00	..	..	..	..	..	6·00	28·00	18·00	..	22·00	4·00	16·00	..	4·00	..	..	..	2·00	..	..	..
8. TELUGU NON-BRAHMIN—Male—50. Percentage ..	4·00	10·00	4·00	..	..	26·00	2·00	..	..	..	..	2·00	10·00	..	26·00	16·00	4·00	2·00	14·00	2·00	..	..	..	22·00	2·00	..
9. KANARESE BRAHMIN—Male—50. Percentage ..	..	4·00	..	..	..	..	..	..	2·00	4·00	4·00	10·00	32·00	..	38·00	2·00	8·00	..	..	..	..	..	..	..	..	..
10. KANARESE NON-BRAHMIN—Male—50. Percentage ..	..	20·00	..	..	..	12·00	2·00	..	..	..	2·00	..	10·00	..	40·00	6·00	6·00	..	20·00	..	..	..	..	12·00	4·00	..

* D represents deeper shade.

TABLE LVIII (a).
Physical Observations.
Southern India.

Races.	Hair.													Beard and Moustache.			Body Hair.				
	Colour Nos. (Fischer).					Character.			Quantity.					Quantity.			Quantity.				
	4	5	27	28	Grey.	Straight.	Wavy.	Curly.	+	++	+++	Bald.	Shaved.	+	++	+++	+	++	+++	++++	*Nil.*
1. NAMBUDIRI BRAHMIN— Male—55. Percentage ..	16·36	1·82	60·00	5·46	16·36	60·00	23·64	16·36	3·64	70·91	5·45	18·18	1·82	16·36	70·91	12·73	34·55	32·73	18·18	5·45	9·09
2. NAIR— Male—60. Percentage ..	10·00	15·00	66·67	3·33	5·00	50·00	33·33	16·67	1·67	90·00	..	6·67	1·67	18·33	75·00	6·67	40·00	41·67	16·67	..	1·67
3. ILLUVA— Male—50. Percentage ..	26·00	16·00	54·00	..	4·00	36·00	48·00	16·00	2·00	90·00	..	4·00	4·00	50·00	48·00	2·00	48·00	36·00	6·00	..	10·00
4. TAMIL BRAHMIN— Male—50. Percentage ..	55·10	6·12	34·70	..	4·08	74·00	18·00	8·00	..	68·00	..	10·00	22·00	44·00	56·00	..	64·00	28·00	..	..	8·00
5. TAMIL KALLA— Male—40. Percentage ..	52·50	..	47·50	..	..	57·50	40·00	2·50	2·50	90·00	..	2·50	5·00	62·50	37·50	..	67·50	10·00	..	..	22·50
6. TAMIL CHETTI— Male—50. Percentage ..	48·00	..	40·00	8·00	4·00	74·00	18·00	8·00	..	72·00	..	18·00	10·00	58·00	42·00	..	50·00	26·70	6·00	..	18·00
7. TELUGU BRAHMIN— Male—50. Percentage ..	24·00	14·00	54·00	..	8·00	72·00	24·00	4·00	4·00	88·00	..	2·00	6·00	32·00	66·00	2·00	52·00	40·00	4·00	..	4·00
8. TELUGU NON-BRAHMIN— Male—50. Percentage ..	24·00	14·00	42·00	..	20·00	68·00	28·00	4·00	2·00	90·00	..	4·00	4·00	40·00	58·00	2·00	74·00	22·00	2·00	..	2·00
9. KANARESE BRAHMIN— Male—50. Percentage ..	24·00	12·00	60·00	.	4·00	78·00	18·00	4·00	..	70·00	..	2·00	28·00	34·00	64·00	2·00	58·00	34·00	2·00	..	6·00
10. KANARESE NON-BRAHMIN— Male—50. Percentage ..	10·00	18·00	68·00	..	4·00	70·00	28·00	2·00	..	78·00	..	8·00	14·00	42·00	58·00	..	66·00	24·00	2·00	..	8·00

TABLE LVIII (b).

Physical Observations.

Southern India.

Rates.	Eye.												Supra-Orbital Ridge.			
	Colour Nos. (Martin).							Form.			Epicanthic fold.					
	1	2	3	4	5	6	7	Round.	Oblique.	Slanting.	+	++	+	+ +	+ + +	Not marked.
1. NAMBUDIRI BRAHMIN—Male—55. Percentage ..	29·09	40·00	29·09	..	..	1·82	..	98·18	..	1·82	*Nil.*	*Nil.*	85·45	10·91	..	3·64
2. NAIR—Male—60. Percentage ..	35·00	45·00	18·33	1·67	..	..	..	96·67	..	3·33	1·67	..	78·33	20·00	..	1·67
3. ILLUVA—Male—50. Percentage ..	26·00	46·00	22·00	4·00	2·00	..	..	88·00	..	12·00	10·00	..	72·00	22·00	..	6·00
4. TAMIL BRAHMIN—Male—50. Percentage ..	16·00	62·00	10·00	6·00	..	4·00	2·00	96·00	..	4·00	*Nil.*	*Nil.*	74·00	2·00	..	24·00
5. TAMIL KALLA—Male—40. Percentage ..	17·50	57·50	17·50	7·50	..	..	..	90·00	..	10·00	7·50	..	75·00	5·00	..	20·00
6. TAMIL CHETTI—Male—50. Percentage ..	24·00	52·00	20·00	4·00	..	..	..	92·00	..	8·00	2·00	..	58·00	12·00	..	30·00
7. TELUGU BRAHMIN—Male—50. Percentage ..	20·00	50·00	26·00	2·00	2·00	..	..	90·00	..	10·00	4·00	..	80·00	10·00	2·00	8·00
8. TELUGU NON-BRAHMIN—Male—50. Percentage ..	36·00	58·00	4·00	2·00	..	..	..	88·00	..	12·00	2·00	2·00	78·00	8·00	2·00	12·00
9. KANARESE BRAHMIN—Male—50. Percentage ..	12·00	60·00	18·00	8·00	2·00	..	..	94·00	..	6·00	6·00	..	94·00	6·00	..	..
10. KANARESE NON-BRAHMIN—Male—50. Percentage ..	20·00	46·00	26·00	4·00	4·00	..	..	90·00	..	10·00	4·00	..	74·00	24·00	..	2·00

TABLE LVIII (c).

Physical Observations.

Southern India.

Races.	Nose.							Lips.			Chin.			Face.					
	Nasal Depression (Root).		Nose Form.											Shape.				Prognathism.	
	+	++	Flat.	Medium.	Promi-nent	Very Promi-nent.	Convex.	Thin.	Medium.	Thick.	Pointed.	Medium	Broad.	Long.	Pear.	Round.	Square.	+	++
1. Nambudiri Brahmin— Male—55. Percentage ..	3·64	..	12·73	14·55	29·09	27·27	16·36	16·36	74·55	9·09	25·45	56·36	18·18	41·82	20·00	29·09	9·09	1·82	..
2. Nair— Male—60. Percentage ..	16·67	..	20·00	26·67	23·33	15·00	10·00	20·00	75·00	5·00	15·00	70·00	15·00	33·33	10·00	35·00	21·67	15·00	..
3. Illuva— Male—50. Percentage ..	12·00	2·00	14·00	48·00	..	30·00	18·00	18·00	70·00	12·00	16·00	58·00	26·00	20·00	34·00	16·00	30·00	28·00	2·00
4. Tamil Brahmin— Male—50. Percentage ..	8·00	..	4·00	32·00	46·00	2·00	16·00	12·00	80·00	8·00	30·00	56·00	14·00	24·00	24·00	44·00	8·00	12·00	..
5. Tamil Kalla— Male—40. Percentage ..	27·50	..	30·00	47·50	17·50	2·50	2·50	12·50	82·50	5·00	7·50	35·00	57·50	20·00	25·00	10·00	45·00	12·50	..
6. Tamil Chetti— Male—50. Percentage ..	8·00	..	14·00	46·00	34·00	2·00	4·00	8·00	74·00	18·00	24·00	50·00	26·00	10·00	34·00	36·00	20·00	16·00	..
7. Telugu Brahmin— Male—50. Percentage ..	20·00	..	12·00	42·00	36·00	..	10·00	18·00	76·00	6·00	14·00	54·00	32·00	20·00	28·00	34·00	18·00	16·00	..
8. Telugu Non-Brahmin— Male—50. Percentage ..	48·00	..	30·00	44·00	18·00	2·00	8·00	4·00	76·00	20·00	14·00	72·00	14·00	34·00	34·00	26·00	6·00	..	..
9. Kanarese Brahmin— Male—50. Percentage ..	14·00	..	10·00	20·00	44·00	4·00	22·00	20·00	74·00	6·00	8·00	70·00	22·00	26·00	28·00	18·00	28·00	10·00	..
10. Kanarese Non-Brahmin— Male—50. Percentage ..	22·00	..	18·00	32·00	34·00	6·00	10·00	10·00	88·00	2·00	4·00	72·00	24·00	16·00	18·00	36·00	30·00	8·00	2·00

TABLE LIX.
Physical Observations.
Tribal Group.

Races.	Skin Colour (von Luschan). Forehead. 10	12	13	14	15	17	18	19	20	21	22	23	23D*	24	27	28	33	Upper Arm. 10	12	13	15	16	17	18
1. Khasi— Male—81. Percentage	1·23	1·23	12·35	1·23	23·46	41·98	1·23	..	..	..	..	9·89	1·23	..	6·17	..	..	1·23	1·23	12·35	27·16	..	48·15	..
2. Chenchu— Male—23. Percentage	..	..	..	..	..	..	..	..	..	..	..	4·35	17·39	4·35	43·48	26·09	4·35	..	..	..	..	..	..	..
3. Nicobarese— Male—122. Percentage	..	..	..	..	..	0·82	5·74	2·46	15·57	36·89	30·33	5·74	..	2·46	..	..	..	..	..	..	..	4·10	4·10	12·30

Races.	Skin Colour (von Luschan). Upper Arm—contd. 19	20	21	22	23	27	28	33	Breast. 10	12	13	15	17	18	19	20	21	22	23	23D*	24	27	28	33
1. Khasi— Male—81. Percentage	..	..	..	..	4·94	4·94	..	..	1·23	1·23	13·58	24·69	44·44	..	..	..	..	..	8·64	..	..	6·17	..	..
2. Chenchu— Male—23. Percentage	..	..	..	..	..	47·83	43·48	8·70	..	..	..	..	..	..	..	..	..	..	..	4·55	..	50·00	36·36	9·09
3. Nicobarese— Male—122. Percentage	39·34	25·41	9·02	5·74	..	..	..	..	..	..	..	..	0·82	6·56	2·46	16·40	38·53	28·69	4·92	..	1·64	..	..	..

* D represents deeper shade.

TABLE LIX (a).

Physical Observations.

Tribal Group.

Races.	Hair.												Beard and Moustache.			Body Hair.	
	Colour Nos. (Fischer).						Character.			Quantity.			Quantity.			Quantity.	
	4	5	25	27	Grey.	Black.	Straight.	Wavy.	Curly.	+	++	Bald.	+	++	*Nil.*	+	*Nil.*
1. KHASI— Male — 81. Percentage	1·23	..	1·23	95·06	2·47	..	96·30	3·70	..	25·00	62·50	12·50	50·62	3·70	45·68	40·74	59·26
2. CHENCHU— Male — 23. Percentage	4·35	21·74	..	65·22	8·70	..	13·04	78·26	8·70	..	100·00	..	69·57	30·43	..	69·57	30·43
3. NICOBARESE— Male — 122. Percentage	0·82	..	..	99·18	..	..	99·18	..	0·82	..	100·00	..	46·72	..	53·28	..	100·00

TABLE LIX(b).

Physical Observations.

Tribal Group.

Races.	Eye.								Supra-Orbital Ridge.			
	Colour Nos. (Martin).			Form.			Epicanthic fold.					
	1	2	3	Round.	Oblique.	Slanting.	+	++	+	++	+++	Not marked.
1. KHASI— Male — 81. Percentage	4·94	77·78	17·28	45·33	..	54·67	32·10	30·86	37·50	18·75	..	43·75
2. CHENCHU— Male — 23. Percentage	4·35	86·96	8·70	100·00	..	..	..	..	60·87	34·78	4·35	..
3. NICOBARESE— Male — 122. Percentage	..	100·00	..	41·80	58·20	..	88·89	11·11	98·98	1·02	—	—

TABLE LIX (e).

Physical Observations.

Tribal Group.

Races.	Nose.								Lips.			Chin.				Face.					
	Nasal Depression (Root).			Nose Form.												Shape.				Prognathism.	
	+	++	+++	Flat.	Medium.	Promi-nent.	Very Prominent.	Convex.	Thin.	Medium.	Thick.	Pointed.	Medium.	Broad.	Receed-ing.	Long.	Pear.	Round.	Square.	+	++
1. Khasi—																					
Male — 81.																					
Percentage ..	17·28	38·27	17·28	62·96	28·40	6·17	2·47	..	29·63	69·70	2·47	24·69	64·20	9·88	1·23	28·40	30·86	20·99	19·75	16·05	3·70
2. Chenchu—																					
Male — 23.																					
Percentage ..	82·61	4·35	4·35	39·13	47·83	8·70	..	4·35	8·70	56·52	34·78	8·70	65·22	26·09	..	8·70	47·83	26·09	17·39	52·17	8·70
3. Nicobarese—																					
Male — 122.																					
Percentage ..	100·00	..	..	5·06	94·94	..	..	..	..	..	..	..	..	..	..	57·38	1·64	11·48	29·51	91·30	8·70

M53CC—1,225—11-6-34—GIPS

Plate No. I.

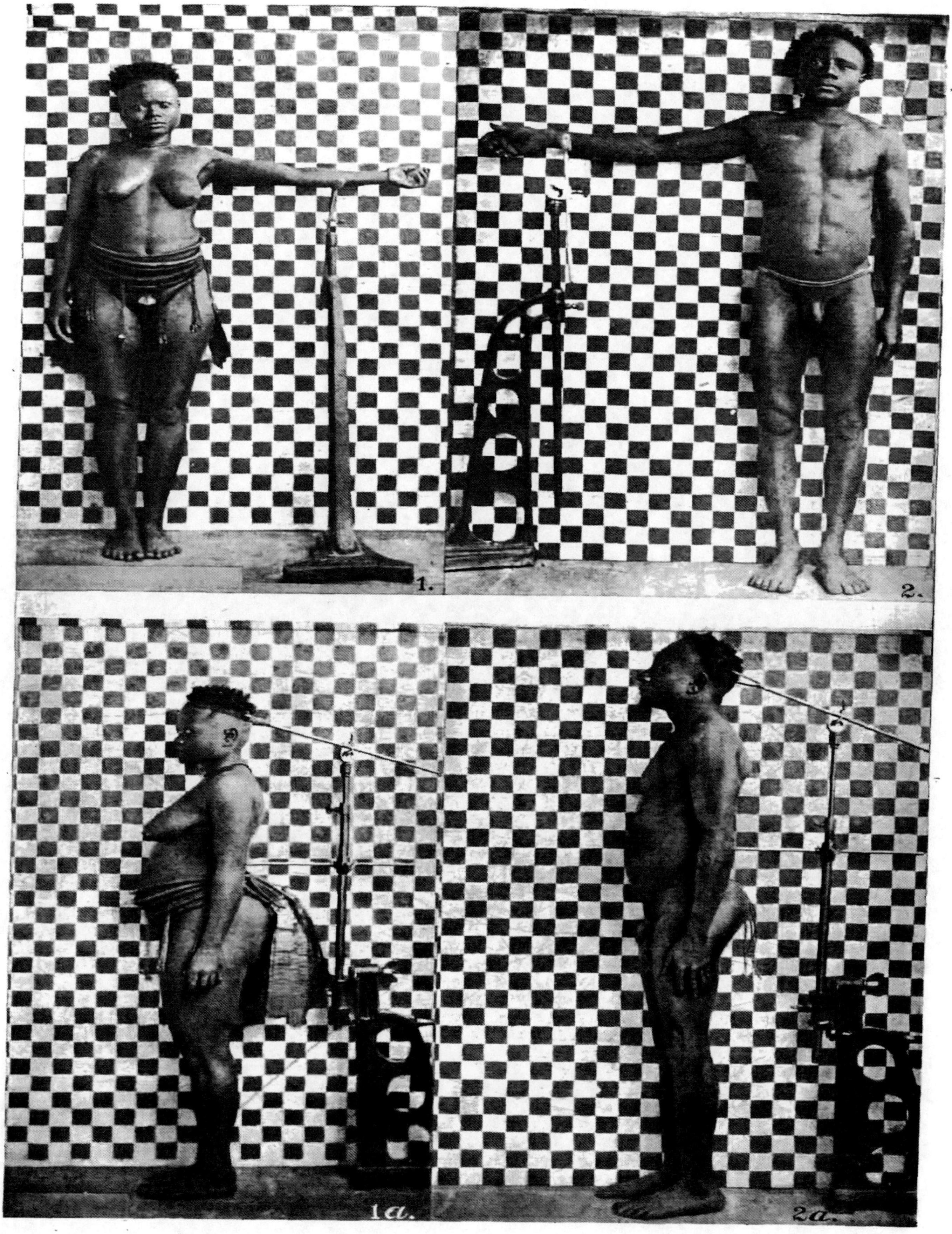

PLATE No. 1.

—	—	Sex.	Stature.	C. I.	N. I.	Skin colour.	Eye colour.
Fig. 1 ..	Front view—Andamanese	♀	..	..	..	..	..
„ 1a ..	Side view—Same.						
Fig. 2 ..	Front view—Andamanese			..	..	..	..
„ 2a ..	Side view—Same.						

Plate No. II.

			Sex.	Stature.	C. I.	N. I.	Skin colour.	Eye colour.
Fig.	1	Front view—Kadar	♂	1489	74·30	83·33	33	2
,,	1a	Side view—Same.						
Fig.	2	Front view—Kadar	♂	1504	72·78	79·17	33	1
,,	2a	Side view—Same						
Fig.	3	Front view—Kadar	♂	1545	77·35	84·00	29	2
,,	3a	Side view —Same.						
Fig.	4	Front view—Bhil	♂	1632	80·59	86·36	28	2
,,	4a	Side view—Same.						
Fig.	5	Front view—Kol	♂	1504	73·54	95·50	27	2
,,	5a	Side view—Same.						
Fig.	6	Front view—Gond	♂	1620	76·22	95·65	27	2
,,	6a	Side view—Same.						
Fig.	7	Front view—Chenchu	♂	1705	66·67	92·50	23	3
,,	7a	Side view—Same.						

Plate No. II.

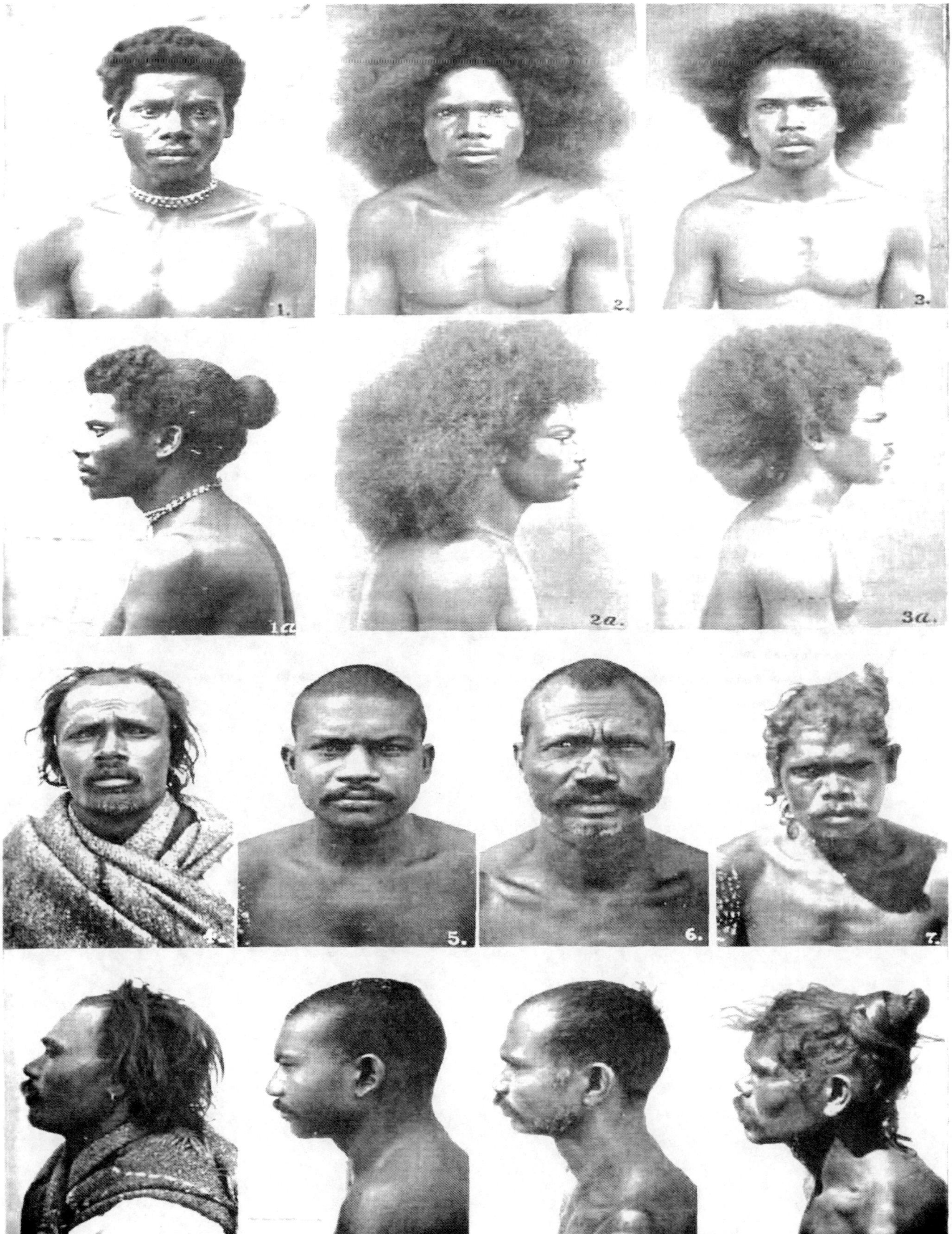

Plate No. III.

			Sex.	Stature.	C. I.	N. I.	Skin colour.	Eye colour.
Fig.	1	Front view—Gujrati Jain	♂	1638	80·43	65·52	17	2
,,	1a	Side view—Same						
Fig.	2	Front view—Rajput (Parmar)	♂	1717	82·32	65·45	15	2
,,	2a	Side view—Same.						
Fig.	3	Front view—Rajput (Baghel)	♂	1716	82·78	67·27	13	3
,,	3a	Side view—Same.						
Fig.	4	Front view—Kanarese Vekkaliga	♂	1631	90·48	62·96	27	1
,,	4a	Side view—Same.						
Fig.	5	Front view—Bengali Kayastha	♂	1658	85·31	61·40	18	3
,,	5a	Side view—Same.						
Fig.	6	Front view—Bengali Vaidik Brahmin ..	♂	1729	83·24	56·45	13	3
,,	6a	Side view—Same.						

Plate No. III.

Plate No. IV.

—	—		Sex.	Stature.	C.I.	N.I.	Skin colour.	Eye colour.
Fig.	1	Front view—Gujrati Nagar Brahmin ..	♂	1704	88·59	72·7	10	3
,,	1a	Side view—Same.						
Fig.	2	Front view—Kathi (Kathiawar)	♂	1775	88·24	71·93	15	3
,,	2a	Side view—Same.						
Fig.	3	Front view—Gujrati Audich Brahmin ..	♂	1674	81·77	66·67	14	3
,,	3a	Side view—Same.						
Fig.	4	Front view—Chitrali (Khos)	♂	1579	81·32	66·10	12	5
,,	4a	Side view—Same.						
Fig.	5	Front view—Tadjik (Badakshan)	♂	1662	82·29	58·33	10	5
,,	5a	Side view—Same.						
Fig.	6	Front view—Brahui (Baluchistan)	♂	1654	82·49	68·52	Brown.	Light brown
,,	6a	Side view—Same.						

Plate No. IV.

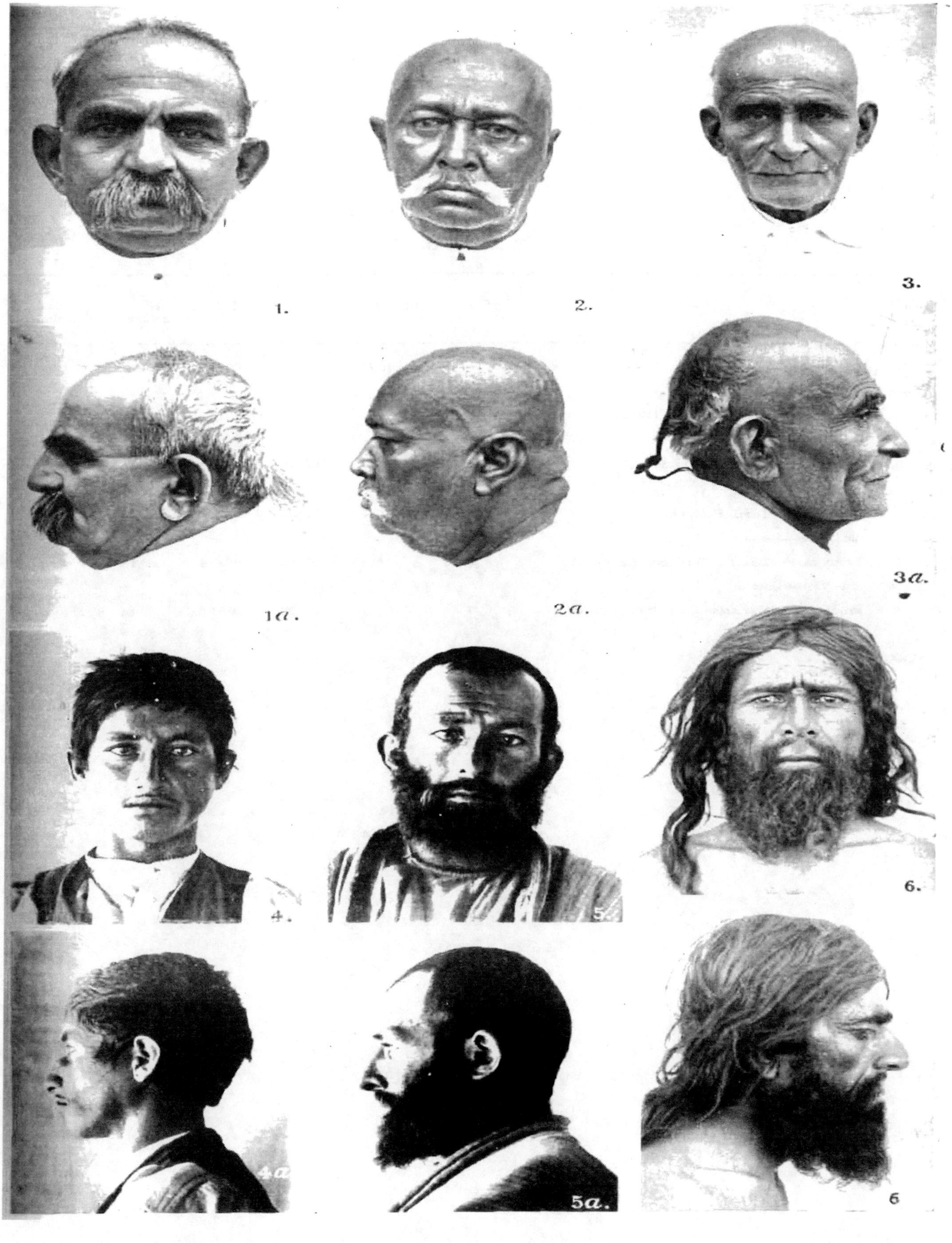

Plate No. V.

—	—		Sex.	Stature.	C. I.	N. I.	Skin colour.	Eye colour.
Fig. 1	Front view—Saraswat Gour Brahmin	..	♂	1585	84·27	60·71	15	9
„ 1a	Side view—Same.							
Fig. 2	Front view—Mithil Brahmin (Behar)	..	♂	1667	89·57	69·09	17	3
„ 2a	Side view—Same.							
Fig. 3	Front view—Bengali Brahmin Vaidik	..	♂	1687	82·26	64·00	15	2
„ 3a	Side view—Same.							
Fig. 4	Front view—Tamil Brahmin ..	..	♂	1685	81·77	74·07	15	3
„ 4a	Side view—Same.							
Fig. 5	Front view—Desastha Brahmin (Marathi)	..	♂	1625	91·86	78·43	15	..
„ 5a	Side view—Same.							
Fig. 6	Front view—Kanarese Brahmin ..	..	♂	1615	91·30	[illegible]·96	14	2
„ 6	Side view—Same.							

M53CC

Plate No. V.

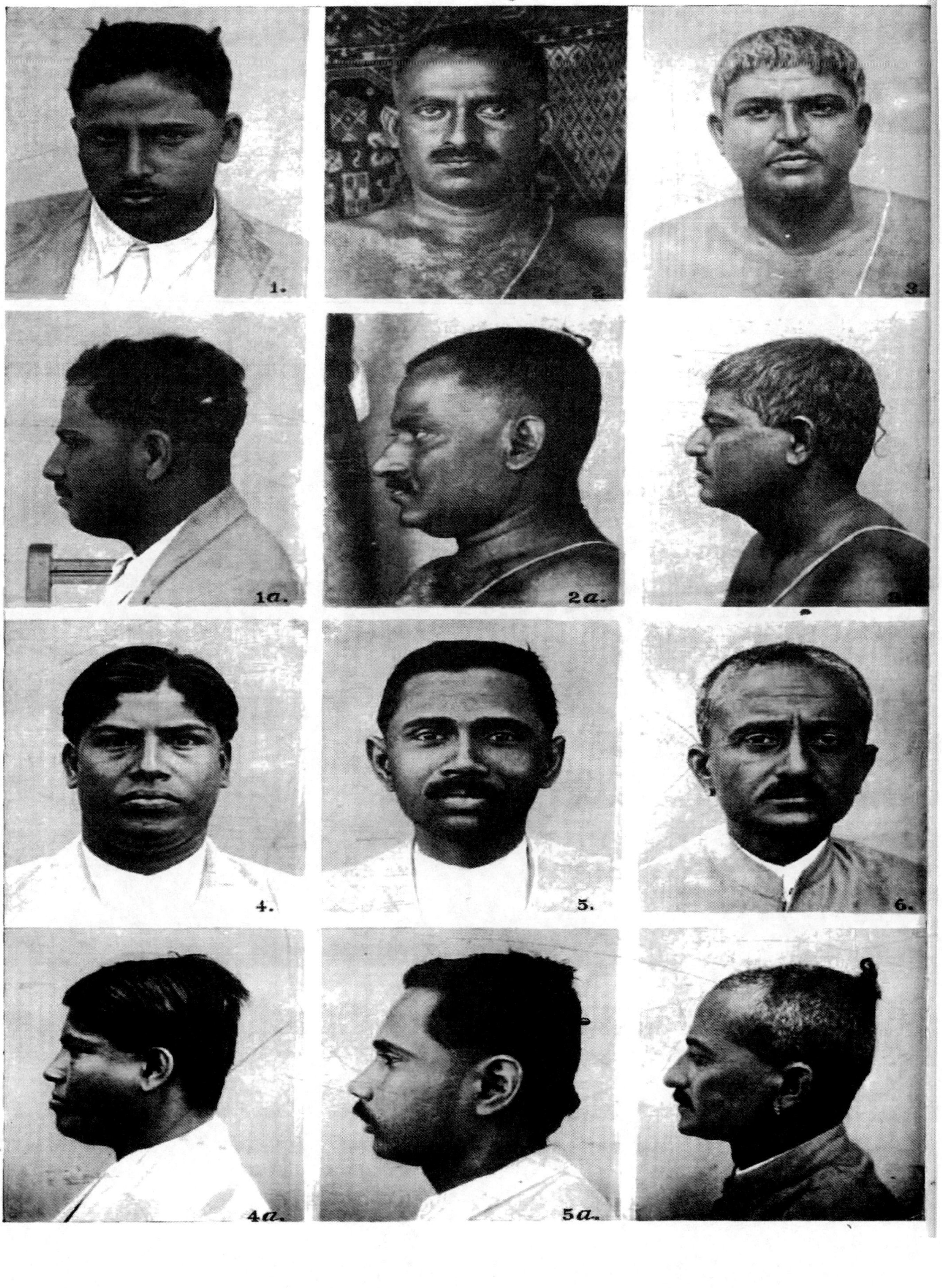

Plate No. VI.

—		—	Sex.	Stature.	C. I.	N. I.	Skin colour.	Eye colour.
Fig.	1	Front view—Sikh	♂	1707	73·87	67·80	14	3
,,	1a	Side view—Same.						
Fig.	2	Front view—United Provinces Brahmin ..	♂	1765	71·07	64·41	15	7
,,	2a	Side view—Same.						
Fig.	3	Front view—Nambudiri Brahmin (Malabar) ..	♂	1676	71·78	60·71	14	7
,,	3a	Side view—Same.						
Fig.	4	Front view—Chitpavan Brahmin (Marathi) ..	♂	1611	74·24	69·09	13	7
,,	4a	Side view—Same.						
Fig.	5	Front view—Tamil Brahmin	♂	1601	75·51	72·92	15	3
,,	5a	Side view—Same.						
Fig.	6	Front view—Telugu-Brahmin	♂	1621	76·19	73·08	15	1
,,	6a	Side view—Same.						

Plate No. VI.

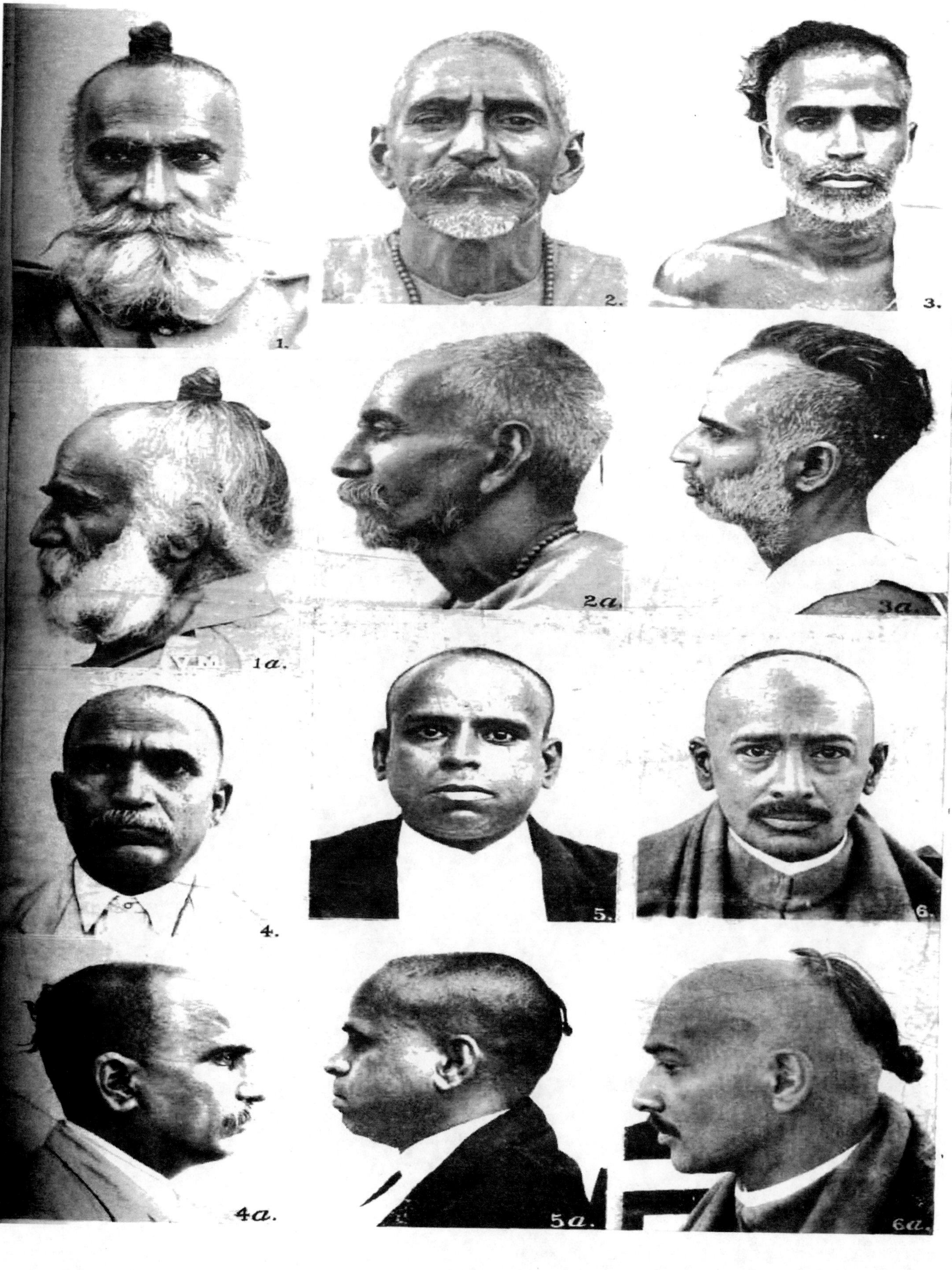

PLATE No. VII.

			Sex.	Stature.	C. I.	N. I.	Skin colour.	Eye colour.
Fig.	1	Front view—Hunza (Gilgit)	♂	1731	74·26	71·43	12	7
„	1a	Side view—Same.						
Fig.	2	Front view—Afghan—Gilzai (Afghanistan) ..	♂	1745	72·96	73·08	12	4
„	2a	Side view—Same.						
Fig.	3	Front view—Shenwah—Chitrali (Khos) ..	♂	1670	72·68	66·67	10	10
„	3a	Side view—Same.						
Fig.	4	Front view—Pathan—Bajour	♂	1596	76·80	62·26	10	14
„	4a	Side view—Same.						
Fig.	5	Front view—Red Kaffir (Kaffiristan) ..	♂	1714	70·44	50·00	10	7
„	5a	Side view—Same.						
Fig.	6	Front view—Khalash (Rambar)	♂	1589	73·54	64·81	9	12
„	6a	Side view—Same.						

Plate No. VII.

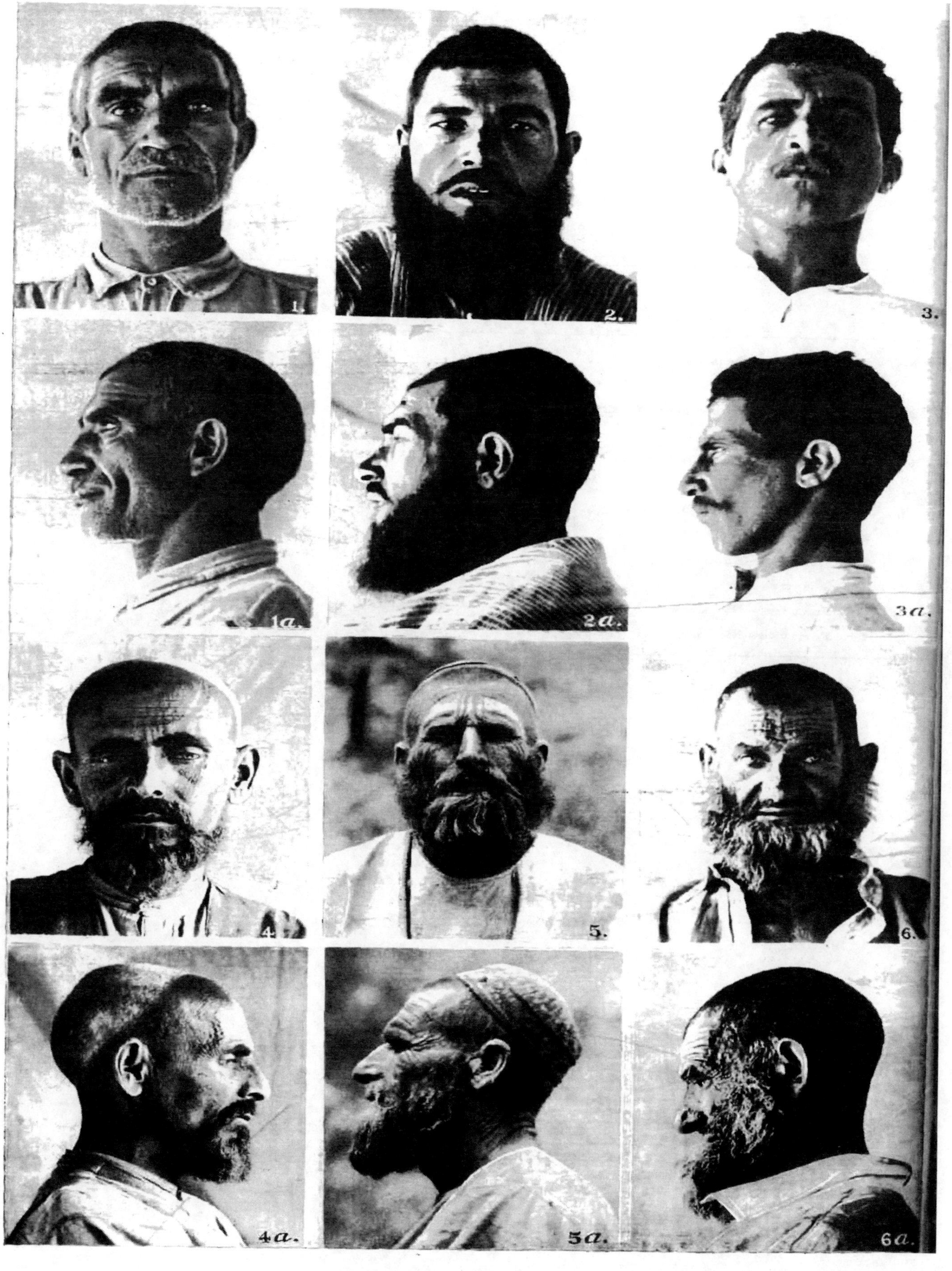

Plate No. VIII.

—		—	Sex.	Stature.	C. I.	N. I.	Skin colour.	Eye colour.
Fig.	1	Front view—Sema Naga	♂	1643	76·37	75·42	17	2
,,	1a*	Side view—Same.						
Fig.	2	Front view—Turki (Chinese Turkistan) ..	♂	1715	88·40	71·43	11	5
,,	2a	Side view—Same.						
Fig.	3	Front view—Uzbec (Tashkhand)	♂	1625	84·07	70·59	10	3
,,	3a	Side view—Same.						
Fig.	4	Front view—Tadjik (Badakshan)	♂	1668	81·82	67·27	0	6
,,	4a	Side view—Same.						
Fig.	5	Front view—Khasi (Assam)	♂	1676	76·58	77·46	5	2
,,	5a	Side view—Same.						
Fig.	6	Front view—Nicobarese	♂	1578	77·66	78·43	21	2
,,	7	Front view—Nicobarese	♀	1543	77·19	74·42	20	2

* **Note.**—The first illustration in row 2 should read 1*a* instead of 2*a*.

Plate No. VIII.

Plate No. IX.

		—	Sex.	Stature.	C. I.	N. I.	Skin colour.	Eye colour.
Fig.	1	Front view—Marathi Saraswat Brahmin	♀	1469	78·98	65·91	14	1
„	1*a*	Side view—Same.						
Fig.	2	Front view—Malayali Nair	♀	1590	76·50	73·91	13	2
„	2*a*	Side view—Same.						
Fig.	3	Front view—Marathi Karada Brahmin	♀	1579	76·24	59·26	11	4
„	3*a*	Side view—Same.						
Fig.	4	Front view—Malayali—Ambalavasi	♀	1550	71·88	57·14	14	1
„	4*a*	Side view—Same.						
Fig.	5	Front view—Malayali—Illuva	♀	1480	75·98	88·10	27	1
„	5*a*	Side view—Same.						
Fig.	6	Front view—Kadar	♀	1382	76·79	92·50	27	1
„	6*a*	Side view—Same.						

Plate No. IX.

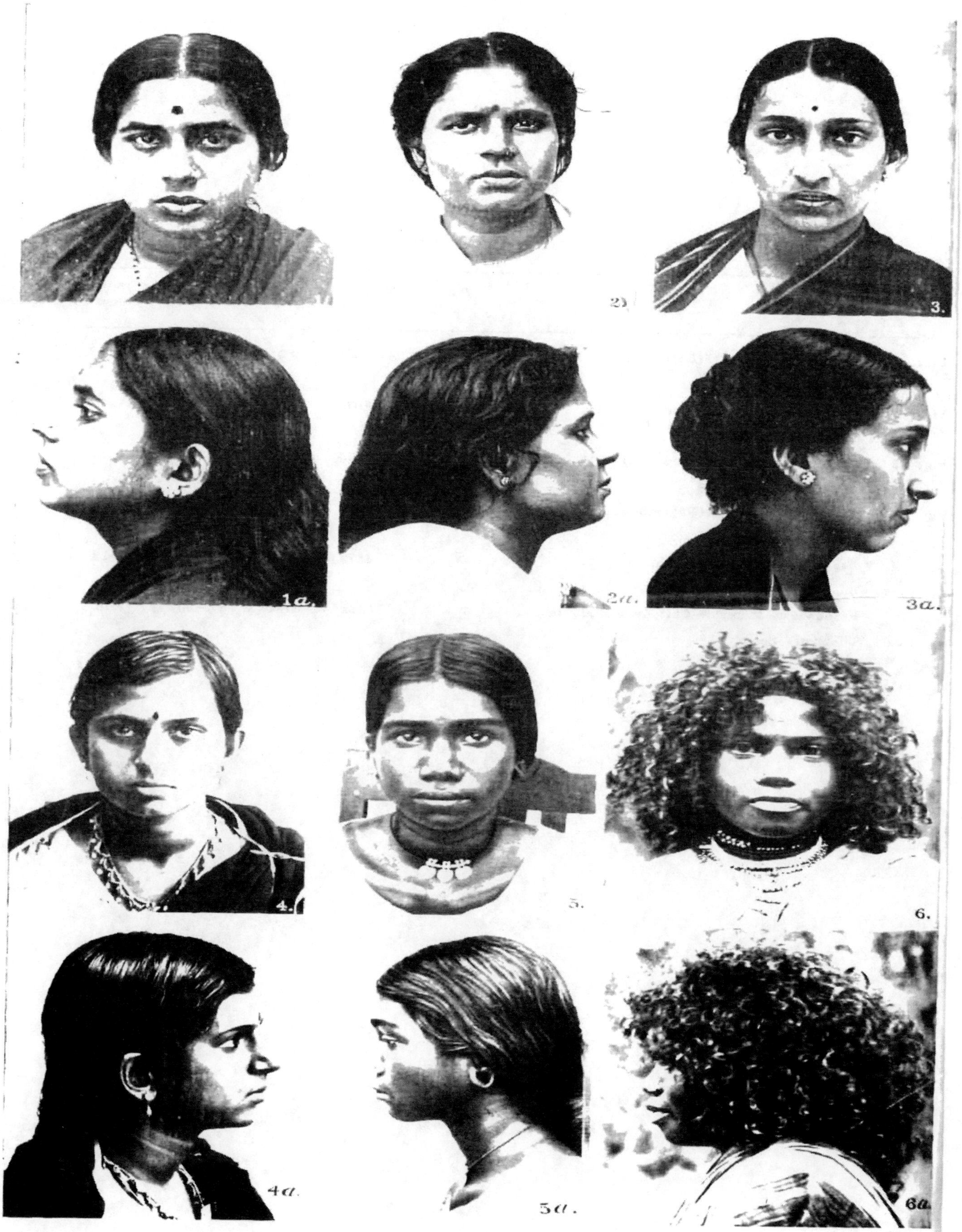

Plate No. X.

			Sex.	Stature.	C. I.	N. I.	Skin colour.	Eye colour.
Fig.	1	Front view—Gujrati (Rajput)	♀	1693	80·68	64·15	12	4
”	1a	Side view—Same.						
Fig.	2	Front view—Bengali (Vaidya)	♀	1676	82·02	63·93	10	1
”	2a	Side view—Same.						
Fig.	3	Front view—Parsi (Ahmedabad)	♀	1475	86·13	53·85	13	2
”	3a	Side view—Same.						
Fig.	4	Front view—Gujrati (Nagar Brahmin) ..	♀	1447	82·66	62·00	12	2
”	4a	Side view—Same.						
Fig.	5	Front view—Bengali—Brahmin	♀	1572	97·52	60·38	13	3
”	5a	Side view—Same.						
Fig.	6	Front view—Marathi—Chitpavan Brahmin ..	♀	1524	81·14	75·00	9	8
”	6a	Side view—Same.						

Plate No. X.

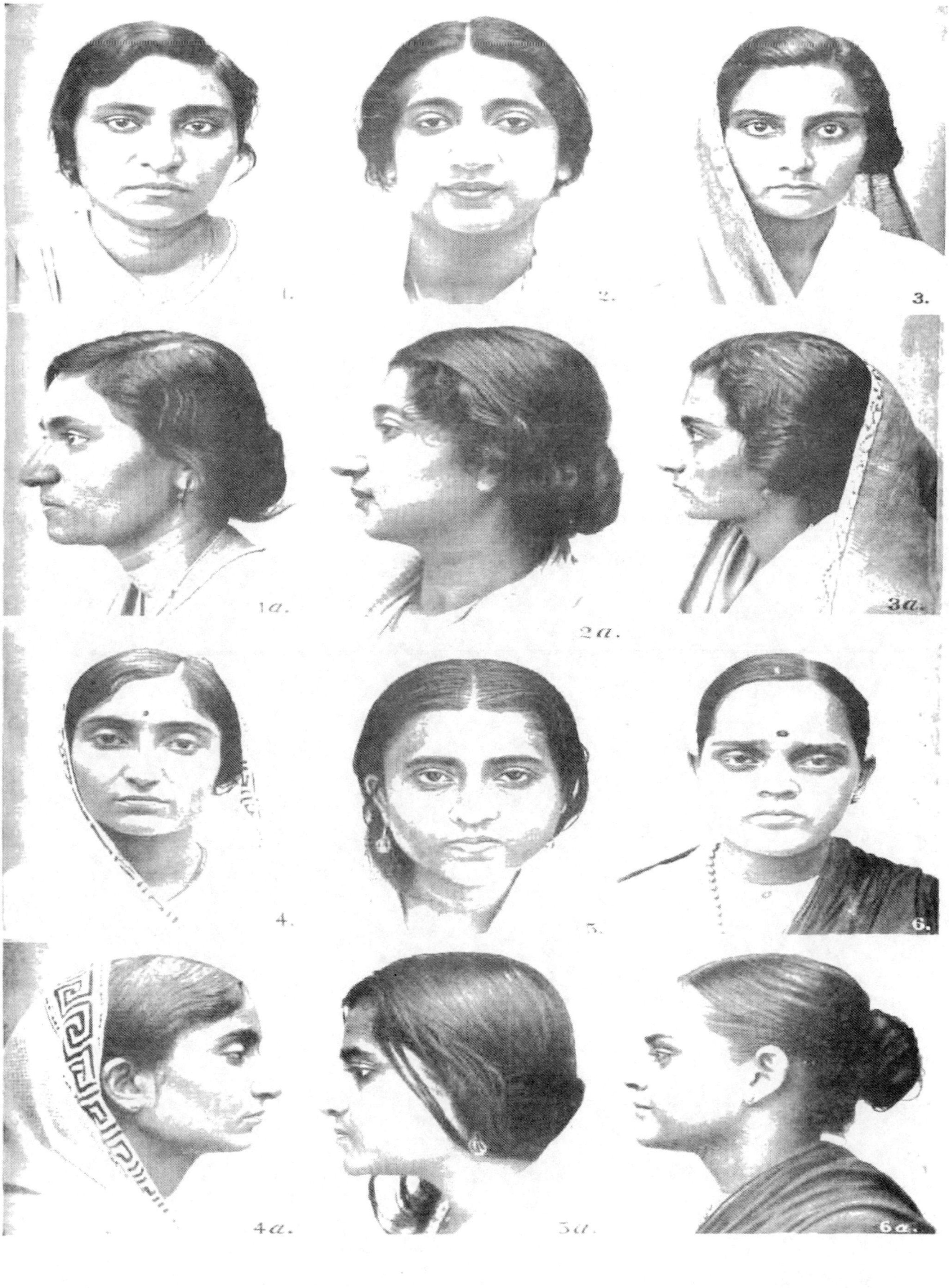

PART B.

Ethnographic Notes by various hands.

Edited by J. H. Hutton.

B.

LIST OF CONTENTS.

ILLUSTRATIONS.

Tour Notes of the Census Commissioner for India.

i. Bhils.

ii. Chota Nagpur.

iii. Gonds.

iv. Madras Agency Tracts (Kondhs, Sawaras, etc.).

v. Hyderabad (Chenchus).

vi. Mysore.

vii. Cochin and Travancore.

viii. Andamanese.

ix. Nicobarese.

I.—Bhils—(July 1931).

The Rajputana village festival in which a large boulder is annually dragged round the village is known as the *Ghas-Bavji* and the stone is apparently regarded as the god of grass and vegetation.

The Bopa is a witch-finder caste of Bhil. He conducts ordeals and foretells the future.

Physically the Bhils appear to be a mixed type entailing Caucasian and Australoid elements and sometimes features which rather suggest a touch of the Mongolian though their heads appear markedly long. The nose shows decidedly greater glabial depression than that of a Rajput.

Nearly all Bhils refused to have their houses numbered at the census at any rate in Mewar State on the ground that whatever is numbered is reduced. The houses themselves, where they have not been changed by contact with more civilized community appear to be made round and with an umbrella-shaped roof, and some such houses may still be seen in the neighbourhood of Udaipur, though most houses there are built of stone and tile. The umbrella-shaped roof is apparently made like a basket and then thatched over, the shape obviating the necessity of a central pole at any rate in small structures. The same roof is used everywhere for small field houses generally in conjunction with a flat roofed extension very much suggesting the southern India pointed temple and flat *Mantapa*. This suggestion is carried still further by the commonness of stone platforms usually built round ficus trees but occasionally, it seems, roofed in at the sides like a regular morang. The stone platforms are to be seen both square and circular, and over the gates of the Bhil quarters of villages a wooden carved superstructure is put up when weddings take place, rough wooden peacocks being made perching on the steps of this superstructure. Inside the house, the house-god is accommodated in a sort of painted design on the mud wall, which, like the peacock, is extremely suggestive of the Sawaras. They told me that the gods worshipped in this way were *Bheronmátá* and *Ganesh*. I noticed in one case a ficus tree which had been trained to drop an arm on to a stone platform built at some distance from the main tree. Menhirs and wooden memorial posts are put up by the Bhils in Banswara but no longer appear round Udaipur.

Persons who die of small-pox are buried but all the other dead are said to be burnt and in the case of some Bhils only the first victim of the small-pox epidemic is buried the rest being burnt as if they had died of some other disease—a sign one must suppose of the impending total disappearance of the burial for any reason at all.

Bănds and irrigation channels are to be seen in this country, the latter often made of stone and the normal method of sowing is by dropping the seed into a funnel of bamboo adjusted so that the seed drops into the furrow behind the plough, the funnel being attached to the frame of the plough. The man guides the plough and the woman walks alongside dropping in the seeds.

II.—Chota Nagpur.

On the 23rd June 1930, I visited a Santal village 20 miles from Hazaribagh and it was interesting to observe that the influence of the Congress was shown by the villagers having taken at their instigation to wearing a sacred thread and getting rid of all their chickens. They also told me that they have broken up their bows and arrows as they were no longer going to eat flesh, but this proved to be not strictly true, as some of the older men at any rate had kept their weapons. When, however, I asked them about their religion, they stated quite definitely that they do not follow the Hindu *dharam* but their own *dharam* and they pointed out the *manjhisthan* as the focus of their religious life. This, I take it, means that they should be returned as of tribal religion and not as Hindus.

Oraon.

From Hazaribagh I went on the 24th June with the Census Superintendent to Ranchi and on the 25th I went out in the morning to see an Oraon village 13 miles from Ranchi. I noticed that they used a shouldered hoe not unlike the Khasia hoe except for the method of fastening the handle to the tang. The village had a *Dhumkuria* in which obviously the interior decoration preserved the style of a former thatched building as the posts were quite unnecessary to support the roof which rested on the mud walls. A wooden camel on which the headman rides at the Rath festival is kept at the Dhumkuria. Each village has some different animal. They will not allow a stranger even, they say, if he be an Oraon, to approach their cooking vessels, except in the case of Christians. This practice, which so much suggests the caste system with its taboo of commensality is probably the result of fear of the magical danger from a stranger and is perhaps one of the contributing factors to the original institution of caste. The important tree to the Oraons is the Sal and a festival is performed at the foot of a sal tree which is surrounded by a thread and anointed with vermilion and the blood of chickens. As all sal trees have fallen down, substitutes are now used, one of which was a pipal tree chosen because it had been epiphytic on the sal which had formerly stood in the spot where the pipal stands. At the time of transplantation a ceremony is also performed on a stone called *Phulkhi* which was formerly erect, but in this case had been prostrated by a falling tree. *Chandi* that is the god of war is worshipped triennially in the month of Falgun, *i.e.*, about March by the young men. He lives in a stone, or his symbol is a stone, which is also deposited at the foot of a sal tree and now at that of a tree which grew out of a hollow of a deceased sal. The dead are burnt on a circular stone platform and the ashes are thrown into a local stream. Bad deaths are not burnt but buried. No one is burnt between the sowing and the harvest and persons other than bad deaths, who die between those two periods are temporarily buried and after the harvest exhumed and burnt. I noticed a vertical well lined on all sides with wooden logs down which the women climbed to a very considerable depth to get their water.

Munda.

In the afternoon I visited a Munda village 40 miles in the opposite direction from Ranchi. Very little of the tribal culture remains but a flat stone is still placed over the grave. Two generations ago it was the custom to (?) exhume their dead and bury them in a pot under a flat stone supported by smaller ones at the sides. For persons killed by a tiger a single upright stone was set up and a good many such stones appeared to be set up for people who had not been killed by tigers but had died in the ordinary way, and I was unable to get any information as to why some persons had an upright stone while others had a recumbent one. The bow is drawn with the second and third fingers, not with the finger and thumb. I noticed the practice of making a well by sinking a tree trunk after the manner of the brine wells in Assam.

III.—Gonds.

On the 21st June 1930, I visited the Gond village of Singarama, 14 miles from Pachmarhi. It was disappointing from an ethnological point of view, as the Gonds have very little of their own material culture to show. I noticed that the village god takes the form of a wooden lingam and the dead are all buried with their heads to the east and their feet to the west, lying on their backs, and the earth is rammed in immediately on the top of the body and stones piled on the grave, it is said, to keep off the wild animals from digging. When the deceased has died on his bed, the bed, probably because it is infected with death, is placed on the grave, but normally unless he is a very rich man he is lifted on to the floor to die. I am told that in other parts of the Central Provinces wooden posts are set up for the dead by Gonds but there were none here.

Notes taken in Bastar State.

March 1931.

Raj-Gonds.—In one zamindari at least the head of the family is buried standing having been kept in that position before burial by tying the corpse under the arms to a post in which position it was kept till the arrival of the next-of-kin. After burial in the same position a stone lingam is put up on the grave.

Mariyas.—The prevailing custom is to burn and then bury the dead. In the case of an important man a stepped grave is made surmounted by what are probably fertility symbols of some kind. Nearby, where passers-by will see it, is put up a tall post topped more or less in lingam fashion but otherwise square and containing carved panels representing the activities of the deceased and various animals.

The Mariyas have some blacksmiths of their own as well as professional ones imported to work in villages where Mariya blacksmiths are absent. The Mariya smiths use a bellows made of two flat wooden pans covered with a hide top the centre of which is attached by a hide thong to spring sticks stuck in the ground behind. The blower depresses the skins with alternate heels while the springs at the back raise them and admit air again.

They smelt their own iron, using a furnace with similar bellows into which they feed mixed iron ore and charcoal from which the molten iron runs to the bottom. Bachelors' houses are used. The facial type appears to be prevailingly leptorine with frequent aquiline noses of rather Papuan type, but the Dravidian and Mongolian types are also very frequent. On the whole, the people remind me more of Kachha Nagas than anything. The women put spots of tattoo in lines on the forehead and the chin and sometimes elsewhere on the face. Daos are rather suggestive of Assam types. Stones are put up as cenotaphs for the dead. Bad deaths, *e.g.*, by small-pox or tiger, are buried instead of burnt. Curly hair is fairly frequent but much disliked.

IV.—Madras Agency Tracts (Kondhs, Sawaras, etc.).

Kondhs.—Kondhs build their villages in streets and I saw a sort of degenerate dolmens under ficus trees apparently used as *mingethung*. Stones in dolmen form are placed in the middle of the village under this tree and used for the headman to sit upon. They told me the *meriah* victim was tied up under this tree and it is probable that one of the dolmens under this tree also represented the village god. In a plains Kondh village the village goddess (apparently the presiding deities of all Kondh villages are feminine) was represented by a small upright stone smeared with vermilion in front of two or three low stones set to make a wall. There were five upright stones in front of this " wall " which were named. They were all female and in front of them were the remains of leaves and egg-shell and blood from offerings. The Kondhs " dive " as an ordeal. Their musical instruments include the kettle-drum played in combination with a hide gong and flutes made in pairs, the second being made to play exactly in tune with the first by an experimental process of making one note after another. The pair of flutes is then played in unison. The Jew's harp and the *vina* were known, but I did not see specimens. The former is called *goöni*. In the plains Kondh villages near Russelkonda the Kondhs are absolutely Hindu, giving their children Oriya names, speaking Oriya as well as Kondh and consulting Brahmans as well as the village priest known as *janni*. The *janni* acts also as the first sower and the first reaper. He says he eats the same food that other people do. In one such village I noticed a small clay altar containing a basil plant. The plains Kondhs have given up tattooing but the hill Kondhs tattoo the faces, arms and legs of their women. This tattoo is sometimes put on by Kondh " bhindani " women, *i.e.*, women of the artisan families. Kondh craftsmen are known as *bhindhanis* and prefer to marry into other similar families, but are not bound to do so by any rule similar to that of caste. The tattoo of the women consists of three straight lines down the nose, three from the lower lip down the chin and lines in rectangular forms on the forehead and to each side between the eye and the ear. On each side of the three lines below the chin there is a circle and dots, and three dots are found between the eyes and a circle and a dot at each corner of the forehead. The tattoo is far more becoming to a Kondh face than I have noticed it on faces of women in the Assam hill tribes and the three straight lines down the nose seem to give the effect of a straight nose to features whose nose would otherwise be less prominent. Many possess a leptorrhine and almost aquiline nose slightly hooked at the point but with some glabial depression. The effect of leptorrhiny is often given where such a nose actually did not occur and the tattoo as a whole is distinctly becoming. The women are good looking, more so than the men, and of a more pronounced Melanesian type I think. The old story about tattoo is found, putting it down to a king who kept taking their women as a result of which they had to tattoo them to make them look ugly, and I found that the local Deputy Collector, who was Sub-Divisional Officer in this part of the Agency, had actually forbidden them to practise tattoo, alleging that they really wished to give it up. I think that this is not the case. I think that his opinion that it is disfiguring and that they themselves regard it so is decidedly open to question. The tattoo when not done by their own people is done by *Erragollas* who do it a great deal better, I think, than the local operative. They make the tattoo deeper and more incised than any I have seen in Assam, reminding me of the tattoo on Maori heads. Curly hair is very common among the Kondhs and a few have Mongolian features and some recall the Angami, though in some of the men there is practically no glabial depression. There seems to be little prognathism except perhaps in the children. Most are inclined to be leptorrhine though some are definitely pre-Dravidian in type. They use a long narrow iron hoe blade into which the handle fits in a socket. The blade is slightly curved and the hoe must be used with both hands as it is heavy. One old bhindhani whom I found in Kalingia village made carved doors which he worked with a very fine twisted, almost runic, rope design and geometrical patterns. He was also a worker in iron and in silver. Among the old men the hair is twisted into a knot on the forehead and pinned there with a double silver hair-pin. The women use long silver pins for the knot at the back of their head which is tucked under the hair as by Telugu women. The women seemed to me a more constant type than the men in features. Weaving and pot-making near the plains are done by other castes—Panos and Kumhars living in, or at the edge of, a Kondh village—but they told me that inside there were both weaver and pot-maker Kondhs, but in the case of the pottery at any rate this needs confirmation. Where these alien castes live in the village they are not allowed to intermarry with Kondhs, and Kondhs do not take their food though they take Kondh food apparently. In the case of the Panos they commonly exchange their cloths for Kondh rice which they take to market and sell, the Kondh being a bad bargainer and too independent to haggle.

A flat stone is laid over the grave of a woman who dies in child-birth before delivery, probably in order to prevent the return of ghost.

I feel very doubtful if any safe distinction can be drawn between Kondhs and Gonds, particularly Mariyas.

Sawaras.—This type again lives in streets and is different in many respects from its neighbours whether Kondh or Gond, if indeed these two be not the same thing. The women are tattooed with a simple line down the nose, or the nose and chin, though some had a very much larger number of lines on the forehead and the cheeks. Like the Kondhs the fossa of the antihelix is bored for ear-rings and as many as 14 holes are made from the top of the ear to the lobe. In the case of the Kondh spikes are put through these holes by unmarried girls which are replaced by rings when married, but I did not notice any such distinction among the Sawaras. Houses are built in the form of a street and the place for the village god consists of a sort of mud, wood and thatch *chabutra* made four-square with a pointed roof on which a carved bird sits representing a peacock. Other carved birds are found inside on the rafters under the thatch. A stone step more or less dolmenic affords an approach to the altar plinth, in one corner of which there is a round raised circular disc in which a notched upright carries a horizontal piece of wood carved on the front with the " enemy teeth " design and used for placing offerings to the presiding deity in the form of leaf cups of liquor and probably flesh and rice. The leaf cups of the Sawaras, as by Kondhs, are made on the Angami system but turned up and pinned at both sides; sometimes they are doubled. The human form is represented in drawing by two triangles with the points together at the waist. Proposals of marriage are brought in the form of an arrow through a woman's bracelet. Curly hair is common and the features, sometimes slightly negroid, are more

Mongolian than the Kondh and compare with them as a Khasi with a Sangtam. The Sawara use shouldered adzes, the simple bamboo bow with a bamboo string, arrows with iron heads, which apparently they sometimes make themselves, and a special arrow for shooting thieves which has no barb and sometimes has no iron tip. They also have the spear and as the arrow appears to be degenerate from the Gond form it is possible that the bow and arrow have replaced a spear as the typical Sawara weapon. Like all their neighbours their principal weapon at present is the *tangi*. They wear a *lengla* in the form of a perineal band the two ends of which hang down from the waist in front and behind and are covered with thick fringes of red cotton. Their hair is done like an Angami with a circular parting, at the back of the head above the *choti*, more marked than that of their neighbours, whose hair at present resemble very closely that of the Mikirs. Fire is made by a drill in a hearth in which a notch has been made to let in air to the drill tip but they told me that they were also acquainted with the saw method which was used with bamboos and could be used with dry wood as well. They use small wooden pillows for the head. Their musical instruments include the hide gong and the kettle drum, a small two-stringed *vina*, a bamboo zither exactly like that of the Khasis and an oboe exactly similar to that of the Kacharis, a horn of buffalo horn affixed to the end of a reed at the other end of which is a separate wooden mouthpiece, the Jew's harp and a flute on the lines of the penny whistle but with an indirect blast. They count by twelves as far as 20 (12 *plus* 8) and then by scores, the intermediates being taken from those from one to 20. I noted the following words :—

stars	tuitui
house	tsuung
fire	toge
water	da
dog	kincho
hen	kansim
egg	anresim

I happened to strike in one village their festival corresponding apparently to the Sekhrengi, as it was intended to secure a successful year and apparently purified their implements. All their musical instruments, which included some *vinas* with the ends beautifully carved in a conventional peacock form, and all their implements of agriculture were laid in a heap with offerings in front of the white painted figure of a horseman or rather a mounted deity painted on the wall of the main room of every Sawara house. A dance was going on outside in which music was being played in absolute jig time and a buffalo had been cut up for distribution. They told me that certain parts of the head were reserved for certain persons and the rest of the animal was completely cut up into small pieces which were all mixed together, as indeed I could see from the preparations, and then dished out in equal quantities to the participants in the feast, each getting in this case his double handful of all sorts of bits as they came. When dancing they have a trick of putting the knuckle of the first fingers into the mouth and producing a shrieking whistle. They also waved their arms over their heads when turning in the dance. In sacrificing the buffalo I was told that two upright poles were placed and then a horizontal pole on which the buffalo head was put and then another horizontal placed across so that he could not withdraw it. The form suggested to me the incisions on the stones at Kasomari. They are subject to some taboos, *e.g.*, one on crossing a stream under certain conditions, probably those of mourning, between the reaping and the sowing of a crop. All the dead throughout the year are propitiated with offerings until the *guar* ceremony of stone placing is performed at which the spirits of the year's dead are introduced to those of the previous village dead and certified so to speak as genuine members of the community, for whom a vertical stone is added to the pile at the foot of the tree after which no more attention need be paid to these particular dead. The *guar* ceremony coincides approximately with that of sowing and seems never to be performed after the rice is transplanted and I infer from this that the *guar* ceremony marks the transition of the soul into the crop which along with the previous dead it probably helps to fertilize. It may be noted that when a body is burnt, for the Sawaras like all their neighbours burn their dead, a thatched hut at the burning-place is used to accommodate a rough wooden figure (the one I saw was purely conventional but clearly female and a question elucidated the fact that the last person to die had been a woman) which serves to accommodate the soul until the *guar* ceremony. After the cremation of a body is over the burning party shoot off a couple of arrows at random as they leave. There is intense necessity for bringing back to the family burial-place the bones of anyone who may die at a distance. Persons going to Assam to work in the tea gardens are brought back to the family burial-place in this way, and their bones are reported to be buried not at the cremation ground but at the actual place at which the *guar* stones are set up and to be the only bones buried at this place.

There seem to be three exogamous groups of Sawaras one of whom is reported to supply the civil head of the village and another the religious head. It is possible perhaps that the latter body represents the older inhabitants who would supply the village priest as being acquainted with the gods of the country. It may be that the third is servile or a survival of some dual organization. At any rate the existence of three groups recalls very strongly the arrangement so common among Naga tribes. It is a point on which much more information is needed.

Notes taken in Jeypore.

23rd and 24th March 1931.

Gadabas.

Gadabas call themselves Gutob. In the section known as Bodo Gadabas, the women have the face tattooed with spot on the forehead and on the chin, two horizontal lines at the outer corner of each eye and a spot on the right-hand side of the nose below the right eye. They say this is never balanced by a mark on the opposite side of the nose. Many individuals show curly hair and they say that they use black beads made of plantain seeds. The women wear large brass ear-rings round their heads and do their hair in the form of a circular door knocker at the back. In the small of the back they wear a sort of bustle called Kundalo. The only explanation they can give of this was that it was "to give support". They say that it is taken off at night. It appears to be, in the form in which I saw it, a mere survival of a very much larger article of wear, and is made of strings wound tightly together. The people were dolichocephalic apparently and very small in size. They claim to be autochthonous. They cremate their dead except in cases of death in child-birth ; no stone is put up, nor any post erected, so they say. Mr. Rama Das tells me that at the Guotar festival they feed bulls on rupees, given them in other food, which rupees are described as "given to the donor's sister". These rupee-fed bulls are then chased with axes and hacked to death, as they run, for the sake of pieces of meat and the rupees that may be obtained from the stomach. He also tells me that they have a class of men called *bedzus* who dress as women (it is not clear whether they are actually castrated or not but probably not). Persons of this class act as priests at a festival called Balijatra at which nine sorts of seeds, grown in nine separate pans, are worshipped, this eunuch priest swinging himself and offering to swing others on a swing the seat of which is made of thorns.* He states that the Gadabas are fond of sites by rivers, that fish is given at marriages and at funerals. The Jhodia Porajas, who appear to call themselves Bareng Jhodia, tattoo their women like those of the Bodo Gadabas, except that the spot on the forehead has a semi-circle beneath it and the spot on the right-hand side of the nose is balanced by one on the left. In addition, the upper arms and legs of the women are freely tattooed with a pattern apparently derived from the human form, or possibly from the tree and circles. The complete leg is covered with tattoo from below the knee to the ankle except for a narrow band about two inches broad a little above the ankle. No tattoo may be put on after a woman has borne a child. They claim to be related to the Sodia Porajas as servant is to master but speak a different dialect and eat beef which the Sodias do not.

I visited the Jhodia village of Bagra near the Kolab falls. I found there memorial stones put up for the dead, important dead that is, in the form of a semi-circular *tahuba*. Inside the upright stones is a platform of recumbent ones. On these stones the old men sit while the young dance within the semi-circle. At the back and ends of the upright stones a fresh stone is erected for the death of each important man. On the back of the stone there is a sort of bamboo splayed out at the end recalling a very degenerate form of the universal Indonesian bamboo altar and fastened to the stone by a long strip of cloth and by a cord. Facing the semi-circle is the village goddess who inhabits a heap of stones fenced round under a big ficus tree. I noticed men also here tattooed on the wrist and forearm and a number of small dolmens in front of and about the houses. A shouldered hoe is used, which is made for the Jhodias by Kamars living in Jhodia villages, who smelt their iron themselves. A Dom is kept as a village watchman and messenger.

Bonda Porajas.

This tribe appears to speak of themselves as Bundo or Bundolog, though the term Bonda Porajas is explained as meaning 'naked Porajas' in Telugu. The women wear a very narrow strip which serves as a petticoat almost identical with that worn by the Konyak Nagas in Assam, the ends barely meeting at the top on the left thigh. These petticoats are woven at home out of the fibre of a forest tree. Girls wear a fillet of beads and of palmyra leaf and an enormous quantity of beads and neck ornaments extremely like those worn by many Konyak women. Otherwise the women wear nothing, but the men dress with a *pagri* and cloth, like any other local villagers. These people do not tattoo. The women shave their head entirely and resemble facially the slave clan of Konyak villages, but the men do not particularly resemble Konyaks, though one of those whom I saw reminded me of the dwarfish inhabitants of Aghching and Saochu. The village god lives in a heap of stones under a large tree outside the village. They say any large tree will do. For a memorial to a Naik, or an important man, they say a stone heap is put up. The dead are burned ; a Bachelors' hall is found ; fire is made with bamboos (apparently by the saw method which seems to be universal here). Their weapons are the *tangi* and the bow.

Bunda.	*English.*	*Gutob.*
da	water	da
suno	fire	sunwal

*One is reminded of the worship of Adonis and other fertility gods of Western Asia or Mesopotamia by eunuch priests who have dedicated their virility to the god.

Bunda.	*English.*	*Gutob.*
inya	sun	si
arke	moon	arke
momoto	stars	forting
kitung	sky	tirip
aron	fish	
biti	salt.	

The Bundas could not give me any numerals other than Oriya.

Khonds.

I visited a small *Khond* village in which I noticed several dolmen stones and a separate house for the cowherd who was of a different caste. I noticed curly hair. The houses are built in streets facing each other and it is said that the bachelors' hall, when provided, is placed at the end of the street looking down it. The Khonds hang on to a rope in child-birth—a method which is said also to be described in Telugu folk-songs. Some Khonds from another village came to see me and I noticed large curly hair, some Mongolian features, some Papuan noses. The women are dwarfish. They practise *podu* (jhum) cultivation, use the bow and arrow, burn their dead and put a heavy stone recumbent over the spot. They were described as Dongria Khonds. *Dongria* (apparently=*Taungya*) means mountainny—*pahari*.

Of the other local castes who came in, the *Rona* claim to have originated, as most of the local tribes do, from Nandapur, that they are Hindus, wear the sacred thread, are cultivators and generally village officials. In appearance they were largely pre-Dravidian and are probably of mixed origin. The *Holwas* are also Hindus, many of them very prognathous, generally pre-Dravidian in appearance. They claim to have come from Bastar three or four generations ago and to have declined in social position, having taken since then to eating fowls. (? Holwa = Halbi). The *Bhatra* in Jeypore speak Oriya. Pre-Dravidian in type ; cultivators ; eat pig but not beef ; are Hindus and wear the thread. *Dombus* came in, of two groups. Andhiyan, who use *Buwa* = father and *Aya* = mother. This group came from Bastar. The other group, spoken of as Oriya Dombu, claim to be local in origin and use *Bapa* and *Ma* for father and mother. *Bhumiya* of two groups also came. They are described as Bar and Suno Bhumiya. They do not intermarry. Suno eat in the houses of Bar but not the reverse. They use long drums beaten at one end with both hands, as well as the smaller ones, beaten at each end in dancing and also a curious iron rasp from which a sound professedly musical is extracted, while some of the dancers carry huge ram-daos made of wood.

Many Jain relics are said to be found in this neighbourhood suggesting that the Jain religion was at one time in the ascendance here.

Mr. Rama Das tells me that an annual ceremony is still performed in the Jeypore Fort at which a human victim is provided and his sacrifice represented by causing him to disappear through a hole in the floor.

V.—Hyderabad.

Close to Hyderabad itself there are four areas in which there are large numbers of pre-historic graves. These consist of a ring of about two dozen boulders, in the centre of which is a stone cist covered by a cap-stone below the surface of the ground, above which a quantity of broken stone, a good deal bigger than road metal, is piled in to form a barrow within the boulders and above the cap-stone. I saw another specimen of one of these cemeteries near Jedcharla. As in the case of one of the Hyderabad cemeteries the ring graves were accompanied by a single upright menhir. Nea- Jedcharla also I noticed what appeared to be cist graves from which the earth had driven away leaving the cist and cap-stone exposed. There was no ring of stones and no metal. On making enquiries from the adjacent village we discovered that such cists are still in use. They are never used for cultivators but when artisans (carpenters and goldsmiths were specified in particular and smiths also were said to be similarly treated) are not burnt which is considered a more respectable treatment and therefore preferred, they are still buried in stone cists of this kind or else in a grave with a menhir at the head and another at the feet, and as a matter of fact a modern cemetery in the outskirts of Hyderabad contains a very large number of such menhir graves. It rather suggests that the original users of the pre-historic s one cist graves were immigrant craftsmen by occupation as distinct from the indigenous cultivator.

Mr. Tasker, who had recently visited the Gond country, tells me that in one village in which he made enquiries people there are practically possessions of the Sahukar. At harvest time the Sahukar turns up, has all the grain reaped or thrashed in front of him. This is halved, one half being taken away by him the other half retained for the benefit of the village. It is sealed in a granary. The approximate needs of each household are worked out and the grain is issued at fixed periods according to the needs of each household for as long as it lasts. When it is finished, if it should not last till the next harvest which is perhaps unusual, the Gond has to live on roots or anything he can get. The villages naively remarked to Mr. Tasker that obviously the Sahukar could not be expected to lend them anything he had not received. In this condition of making over half their crop to the Sahukar whenever it is harvested the wretched villages continue indefinitely.

In many respects Hyderabad retains in its old world seclusion conditions that have passed away elsewhere. Some Chenchus looked at the perfectly good coin I gave them and asked what manner of a rupee was this. They had never seen a British India rupee before, though they knew the Hyderabad State coins. Only recently the Inspector General of Police, a British officer lent by Bengal, was approached by a Pardahi who had a representation to make and who represented his abject condition by appearing before the Inspector General of Police with his mouth full of hay as being no better than one of the beasts of the field. Apparently it is an ordinary expression of Telugu abuse to ask a man what he eats implying that he grazes.

Chenchus.

On June 21st I visited two villages of Chenchus near Farhabad in the Nizam's Dominions. The first one was called Vatvellapalli. They appeared fairly sophisticated, more so than I had expected, and were not in the least shy. Their houses are conical, rather slight in structure made of bamboos sloping to the central point and covered with a thinnish layer of thatch. At the bottom, walls of bamboo about 3 feet high. Outside this every house is surrounded by a circular fence. They have very little indeed in the way of material effects, the scanty clothes they wear, consisting of a langoti and a cloth in the case of the men and a short bodice and a petticoat in the case of women, being practically all besides a few cooking pots and a basket or two which perhaps sometimes contains grain. They have a bamboo drying shelf half way up inside the house covering part of the roof only. They keep cattle and goats, and in this particular village do a little cultivation, elsewhere subsisting on honey and forest produce which they sell. They told me they found where the bees nests were by watching their visits to water and the direction in which they flew away and taking a bee-line on that direction. The grubs are eaten. There was no bachelor's-house. When a boy is old enough he marries (apparently at about 15 or 16 years old) and has a house built for him separately. I noticed that the ears of dogs were all cut; the reason given was to avoid picking up ticks. I was told that the custom was prevalent among all people locally and it was said to be a preventive of disease. Tamarind fruit is eaten mixed with the ashes of its own bark which is reported to neutralise the acid in the fruit. The Chenchu is clearly musical and several houses possessed string instruments. The dance tunes were very suggestive of Sawara tunes and one or two approached a jig or reel in time. As by Sawaras and Kondhs a hide gong is used. The women's dance suggested more that of the Porajas but they had another dance which I have not seen elsewhere in which they sang and clapped their hands in time clapping their palms against the palms of each neighbour (the dance is circular) alternately between the claps of their hands. The village goddess is resident in a stone which is one of five or six (suggesting the five Pandavas and their mother worshipped by the Kunbis in the Deccan). These five or six stones are arranged inside a horseshoe pile of bits of stone with three flat stones in front of them. Water is poured over them or turmeric smeared on them when it is desired to propitiate them. When I saw them water had recently been poured on them on the occasion of the sale of a buffalo to another village. At Farhabad, however, the principal deity resided in two wooden lingams nearly decayed by the weather and there seemed to be a number of small stones put up in couples or singly in the neighbourhood.

The dead are buried under heaps of stones, families being grouped together closely and a son is named after his grandfather which suggests that they believe in reincarnation. The language spoken appears to be a slightly corrupt form of Telugu. The features suggest decidedly mixed origin. The Australoid type prevails and some of them are very highly Australoid with very prominent brow-edges and a deep glabial depression. Others have leptorrhine features more suggestive of the Korku or the Bhil and a few have decidedly woolly hair (in all others the hair is wavy or curly) and features suggesting the Negrito, which would perhaps explain what appeared to be, as far as one can tell without measuring, a distinct tendency to brachycephaly. The stature is generally low and the colour dark and the hair is done with a knot at the back and a flea-walk like a Konyak Naga or a Deccani Brahman, which appears to be the usual style locally.

VI.—Mysore.

I visited Mysore on 24th June 1931. Going by road to Mysore State it struck me as being considerably more prosperous and well cared for than the area further north through which I had passed before reaching Bangalore. The village culture in Mysore is particularly suggestive of that to the north-east corner of Assam. The place of the field morung, so familiar in the Naga hills, is taken by a *mantapa* consisting of a flat stone roof laid across monolithic pillars. The sitting platform so familiar alongside all roads and paths in the Naga hills is represented by the *nagakatte* a rectangular stone platform, or an earth platform enclosed by stone walls, in the middle of which are usually two or three monolithic stones carved with snakes. Very often, but by no means always, this platform is built round a pipal tree. In the *horekallu*, or burden stone, one finds an exact parallel to the platforms put up on a way up from fields by Nagas for people to rest their loads upon as they come back from their cultivation. The difference here, however, is that the load is carried on the head and not on the back so that the *horekallu* usually consists of a simple trilithon with the top stone at head height. Sometimes, however, it is walled in at the back with solid seat in front and often has a stone seat in addition to the stone for burdens.

Roadside shrines were often made in dolmen form consisting of monolithic supports on three sides and the figure of the "god", usually Hanumān, carved in stone and leaning against the middle of the three, the fourth side being open. Obviously too, I think, the temple form of these areas is derived from a dolmen with a menhir, as the temple normally consists of a pointed building which might be described as a rectangular, or sometimes a square, cone accompanied by a low *mantapa* of the pattern already described as used for field morungs.

On my way into Mysore I also noticed a house the posts of which projected through the thatch over three feet or so and were themselves thatched on the top. Mr. Iyengar stated that he had seen a few specimens of this elsewhere but did not know the reason. The only reason we could get for this was that the contractor had supplied poles which were too long but I feel some doubt as to whether this statement was not a mere guess made by one who did not know why a house should be so built. It seems much more likely that poles supplied too long would be shortened than that they should be carried through the roof and thatched at the top, which would involve considerably more labour. In any case the Konyak dodge, of building a house with poles which project through the roof and have to be thatched over in order that they may be later let down when the white ants have eaten the bottom, is forcibly brought to mind. I saw also a good deal of terraced cultivation fed by ancient channels from the various rivers, kings of old apparently being frequently credited with the construction of fresh irrigation channels. It may be added with regard to *mantapas*, burden stones and *nagakatte* that these are erected both by village enterprise, in which the community combines, and by individuals desirous to acquire merit by providing a useful work which is also monumental.

It may be noticed that westward flowing rivers are sacred and that town and village names end in "ur"; both the termination and direction suggest Mesopotamia.

In the Vishnu temples there is always a *mantapa* for the marriage of Vishnu and Lakshmi. Vishnu is apparently regarded as the all-pervading life principle and Lakshmi is described as the female aspect of Vishnu, popularly his consort, embodying the principle of mercy towards men and thus of prosperity and wealth. It seems possible that this conception of an all-pervading principle, with a special manifestation for human prosperity has developed from the more primitive idea of a material life essence which is particularly required for the prosperity of human beings and particularly manifested in the prosperous ones.

On my way from Vellore to Madras I visited the monolithic temples at Seven Pagodas. They recall the monolithic temple in Cachar, though of course are of far finer workmanship and very much more elaborate. At Vellore to which I went from Bangalore they had excavated for me two pre-historic graves both of which under enormous capstones contained not a stone cist but a baked clay cist with 4 points at the corners as if on a basket-work model. In the cists, which had no lid, were fragments of iron weapons, bones and broken pots; while outside one of them were three inverted pots containing earth different from that in the surrounding grave. Each cist was like the Hyderabad graves, surrounded by a circle of boulders the filling in between, however, being earth and not stones. The absence of stone cists was possibly due to the local material being unsuitable for splitting off in slabs, resulting in the substitution of pottery. No conch shell beads were found though this was the site on which Mr. Richards had previously found in his excavations different shell beads and ornaments exactly similar to those used in the Naga Hills to this day. The size of the earthenware cist was 2½ to 3 ft. long ×20 to 24 inches wide. A considerable space of earth intervened between the cist and the capstone which was in the centre of the circle of boulders and flush with the ground. The villagers had no traditions about these graves at all and had not recognised them as being burial places until a forest officer detected them as such and started excavation more than 15 years ago. The area in which they are found is a valley surrounded by forest clad hills in which an old culture might survive surrounding changes on account of its isolation. The remains of iron implements found were probably hoes and I have noticed in Mysore the use of a hoe made in wood exactly like the Naga hoe on a larger scale, which is represented now in Vellore and in the surrounding areas by a wood and iron hoe in which the iron blade is attached by a long elbowed shank attached by a ring to the end of a straight wooden handle requiring to be used in precisely the same method as the wooden crook hoe.

Hoe seen in Mysore.

Vellore hoe.

VII.—Cochin and Travancore.

I visited Cochin on the 21st August 1931. Nambudri Brahmans are reported to grow their hair and nails in mourning, and likewise lower castes of Malayalis, though in increasing periods as the castes get lower; this custom is not observed where the deceased has died a "bad" death, *e.g.*, by suicide, drowning, cholera or tiger.

The Armenoid type seems very marked in Syrian Christians and Tamil Brahmans.

A typical Nayar house is built round a central court into which the roofs drain and a pillared verandah runs round the court with the rooms opening on it, but outside the back is an altar containing basil and a light which is put before it every night at sunset ; a special room in the inside contains family gods. The hair of all castes is often cut straight round as by Nagas in Assam ; generally, but not necessarily, it is grown long and tied into a knot at the side.

The jungle tribe known as Nayadi uses large crescent shaped ornaments in mother of pearl.

I saw a number of Malayans and Kadars. Among the Malayans the men have, in many cases, quite good features, inclining to a Mediterranean type, whereas the women are distinctly australoid ; among Kadars, on the other hand, the men seem to be more australoid, while many of the women are more or less orthognathous and the hair of both the sexes is much more curly. The Kadars file their teeth—both men and women—or rather chip them to a point, but not universally.

Dolmens are reported to exist in the hills in a series opening into another by round holes. These are said to be accompanied by traces of irrigated cultivation, water channels and tanks and undoubtedly there is much terraced cultivation on the western slopes of the ghats, where at lower elevations it is still in use.

Cochin.

In Cochin itself there is a colony of White Jews, dwindling in numbers, who marry among themselves and have consequently preserved the purity of their race, the absence of pigmentation is very marked indeed and has perhaps been accentuated by inbreeding. I noticed a small girl with very decided Jewish features and an absolutely white skin curly flaxen hair and light eyes—either blue or hazel. The White Jews claim to have settled early in the Christian era or a little before, having come to Craganore first, from which place they were expelled by Portuguese and moved to Cochin. The men run very much to the same physical type, and among those I saw, the deviation from the mean can be very little. Among the Black Jews, on the other hand, the deviation from the mean must be very great, as the type is very much mixed, and, though some are fair enough, others are quite dark ; they claim also to have come the earlier of the two, and say they came to Southern India soon after the first distruction of the temple and the dispersion among the Gentiles, by way of Persia. I asked a Black Jew whether he had any connection with the Jews in Bombay ; he replied at once that they were accepted in their synagogue and intermarried with Bombay Jews. When however I mentioned the Beni-Israel, he said he had no connection with the Beni-Israel, who are regarded as socially much inferior. The Beni-Israel, however, are similarly divided into Black and White Jews.

Cochin contains a palace built for the Rajas by the Dutch, outside which is a temple dedicated, however, not to a god but to a goddess, who has clearly preceded everywhere in importance the present male deities, and one of the frescoes inside the p lace showed a goddess riding upon a bull, a goddess herself probably having preceded Shiva in the position of the most important deity ; her position on the bull was rather suggestive of the legend of Europa.

The indigenous bedstead here is hung swinging by four chains, a practice very suggestive of the Nicobar swings which are hung under the house in the form of a swinging platform. As there has certainly been some immigration from Indonesia to the Malabar coast this may be a point of cultural connection.

The following note is supplied by Mr. Sankara Menon *à propos* of my first paragraph above :

The highest caste—Nambudiri Brahmans—observes pollution for *ten* days. The Kshatriyas have *eleven* days' pollution. Some of the Ambalavasis have *twelve* and others *fourteen* days. The Nayars too observe *fourteen* days' pollution. Here the castes are arranged in descending order and it will be seen that the lower a caste is the longer its period of pollution lasts. The observance of pollution is not compulsory (the Sastras do not require it) where the deceased has died a " bad " death, *e.g.*, by suicide, drowning, snake-bite, attack of wild animals, etc. A Brahmachari (living with his preceptor and pursuing the study of the vedas,) has no pollution. (It is therefore argued that the observance of pollution is something in the nature of a quarantine arrangement.)

The period of mourning is one year for *all.* (The period of mourning is confused with the pollution period in paragraph 1 of the tour notes). It is not strictly mourning. Some of the funeral obsequies are continued for one year by the sons of the deceased (nephews in the case of a male deceased of the marumak-kathayam communities) or/and younger brothers. The *pinda* (ball of rice) is daily offered to the departed spirit during this period. Those who observe this ceremony grow their hair, nails, etc. They cannot live with their wives or mingle with others, but should lead an ascetic life. This one year's observance is gradually dying out. It is almost dead among the Nayars. The Ambalavasis too are giving it up. It is much less rigid than of old among the Kshatriyas. And even the Nambudiri is not as strict as of old.

(Reference : Chapter on Castes, Cochin Census Report, 1901, and the Cochin Tribes and Castes, Volume II, by L. K. Ananthakrishna Ayyar. Full details of these customs will be found in these books.)

Travancore.

From Cochin I went through by land or rather by water for half the way to Trivandrum in Travancore State. There struck me as being in the west coast a very strong African element and a very decided suggestion of Madagascar, in addition to the Arab element which is obvious in patches and from the facial type, particularly in the neighbourhood of Muslim settlements; Eickstedt says that the Arab type is evenly distributed among all classes, but my observation was that it was much stronger in patches and not evenly distributed. But it is true that the type is apparent in Hindu as well as Muslim castes.

The small children wear a very tight perineal band made of palm leaf and one frequently sees types that suggest the Melanesian element, and it may be noted that there is a tradition among Tiyyans and some other castes of immigration from Ceylon which rather suggests that there may be on the west coast a number of Indonesian elements which might easily account for a suggestion of Madagascar, if taken together with African elements from the opposite direction.

The type of building is very markedly different from anything to be seen anywhere else in India. The houses even when built of stone or brick, retain the sloping roof, which is probably necessary in that very rainy district, but this roof is in itself characteristic, the ends of the gables being raised above the level of the centre of the ridge* and the opening of the projecting gable is closed with carved wood and very often bears the name of owner or the date of erection. The lower part of the roof is flattened down towards the edge rather like that of the superior Madagascar houses. This particular style of building with its very characteristic gables is said to be now going out of fashion in Malabar, but there are plenty of indications that it will still last some time. The interior of the house is built round an atrium or perhaps one should call it an impluvium, a sort of open tank into which the inner slopes of the roof drain and which is surrounded by a pillared verandah; one room is set apart for the family gods and the the whole scheme rather suggests the ancient Roman house; each house is built in its own compound which is entered by a lychgate very characteristic of the country and again suggestive of the Indonesian Archipelago.

I noticed a heavy cross-bow by the road, and in Travancore museum I saw a pointed spear butt, exactly like those used in the Naga hills, Madagascar and other parts of the Indonesian area, which had been dug up; spears seem to be no longer in ordinary use; the piston bellows are said to be used also, but I did not see a specimen. For pounding rice a pestle and mortar is used exactly as in Indonesia generally including Madagascar and Assam. Enquiries made later failed to elicit any information as to the cross-bow, but the one I saw was unmistakable.

Among the staple crops is tapioca, which is largely consumed by the poorer classes, but that appears to be an imported plant and not indigenous, as also the Traveller's Palm, a specimen of which I noticed in Travancore.

As typical of the mixture of religion, language and blood in this area, I noticed a signboard passed by on the road advertising the services of

Sosamma Abraham

Lady Dentist

this is also typical of the status of women in Malabar where they are more educated than in any part of the Peninsula, west of Burma, and as far as English education goes they are far ahead of the Burmese. The first name be it noted was spelled with a double M and not N, *Amma* (mother) being a typical south Indian termination for a female name.

The Nambudri Brahmans are said to follow the Rig-veda excluding the others and they are probably dolichocephalic, or one would see more signs of brachycephaly among the Nayars; it is very apparent among both Tamil and Konkani Brahmans, who can usually be picked out with ease by the very different shape of their heads.

Among the hill tribes there are a number of elements which suggest the Indonesian area—seclusion at puberty, tree houses, bark cloth (*maravidi*), which however is apparently not treated after being stripped from the tree, the scissors snare for small game and the use of *acacia intsia* bark as soap. The matrilineal system is prevalent at any rate as a survival, and a very strong one, though inheritance in the hill tribes is usually on the *makkathayam* system, the couvade appears to be extended to the menses so that when a woman is in her monthly period her husband is also sick and to a certain extent secluded, though for the women themselves one tribe at any rate builds seclusion huts outside the village. The winnowing fan of the ordinary type is used and called *kotta*—a carrying basket much like that in use in Assam or the Philippines is used by the hill tribes, who call it *puni*, and the sling (*kavani*) is used by both Ulladans and Malayarayans. This sling is used with a loop round the little finger and the stone used as a missile is of considerable size. Though adjoining villages commonly seem to be occupied by different tribes, they all seem to speak the same language, a dialect of Malayalam, but do not intermarry.

* It has been stated that this style is also found in Nepal, but all the photographs of the latter which I have seen show a level roof tree with the corners of the gable slopes turned up at the end in Chinese or Burmese style, quite a different thing.

The Malabar ox-cart is distinctive. The pole that carries the yoke runs right through to the back of the cart being fixed transversely to the axle tree. Both this pole, the axle tree and the back of the cart are carved with geometrical patterns and the front of the pole has a carved nose which acts as a support to keep it from the ground when the cattle are unyoked. *This type of cart is very strong and handsome ; the hood is made of woven bamboo.* Elephantiasis is very prevalent on the coast, particularly among the cocoanut groves, which are very similar in appearance to those of the Nicobar Islands, where likewise elephantiasis is very prevalent, no doubt as a result of similar conditions of life in both cases, though in the case of Ernakulam it is put down to something in the water, and as a matter of fact the carrier is a mosquito.

Separate chapels and separate cemeteries are used apparently for the depressed classes when converted to Christianity, though they say that after two or three generations they become merged in the earlier converts and no longer regarded as depressed.

With regard to the hills many have the appearance of having been forest land destroyed by jhuming. The proto-australoid type appears to be less marked as one goes further south. One may notice a high percentage of dwarfish stature particularly noticeable among Kadars and Malayarayans, though their headmen seem taller and fairer than the general run of the tribe. The type is obviously mixed, the basic element in most of the hill tribes being probably proto-australoid.

Travancore Hill Tribes.

The *Kanikars* are apparently proto-australoid with probably some Negrito admixture, having very curly hair and being by no means pronouncedly prognathous. They use the bow, releasing the arrows between the thumb and the forefinger. The arrows are feathered. Fire is made by flint and steel with the fluff of the sago palm used as tinder. The immature appeared in some cases to be brachycephalic, but all the adults that I saw were decidedly dolichocephalic. Tattooing is done by women who use lamp black mixed with human milk ; the patterns put on are usually restricted to a mark on the forehead analogous to a caste mark. They use a musical instrument consisting of an iron tube, opened on one side, with an iron pin fastened to it by a chain exactly like the instruments used by the Khonds, from which an untuneful scraping noise is produced ; they appear to have no other musical instruments.

The *Parayas* appear to be much less proto-australoid. They are orthognathous but apparently very mixed in type, which possibly points to their being derived largely from higher castes who have lost caste. They use cowries as ornaments and appeared to me to have noticeably small hands and feet.

Ulladans.—These people dance in a double chain, the two chains moving in opposite directions. They hold a baton in each hand and the opposing dancers strike on each other's batons alternately or simultaneously according to the figure.

Besides the flint and steel method of making fire they use a drill method which is spoken of as *woral wolaka* meaning 'mortar and pestle'. Palm floss is again used as tinder and a notch is made at the base of the hole in which the drill is inserted to let the spark out.

The *Malayarayans* dance round a lighted lamp which is worshipped as a god in much the same way. They are decidedly a finer physical type than the Ulladans and appear to be much less australoid. Both these tribes use the sling.

Uralis.—This tribe seems to me to suggest the Negrito quite as much as the Kadar does. The height of the men is about 5 feet, the hair is very curly but is also harsh and in some individuals crisp and kinky. The features suggest that the basic type is proto-australoid with some admixture of Negrito and perhaps Mediterranean. Permanent seclusion huts are built for the women in their monthly periods outside the village ; they amount to a little more than rough breakwinds. Fire is made of flint and steel but the drill is also used and that on an improved system ; a cocoanut shell covers the top of the pestle, which revolves inside it, the revolutionary and counter-revolutionary motion being obtained by a cord run round the pestle and pulled lathe fashion from alternate ends. Tree houses are built as well as the ordinary houses on the ground, but generally speaking, a platform house appears to be preferred and some houses are built high up on piles.

Mannan.—This tribe would appear to contain the same elements as the *Uralis*, but with the Mediterranean element a very great deal stronger. At any rate, there is much absence of the australoid type. The features are orthognathous but the hair is very curly, the nose is sometimes depressed at the root, more often it is not. I found the scissors snare used by these people and also the pellet-bow and they are said to be very musical. They tattoo a single line down the nose of the women which seems to have the optical effect of obscuring the depression, if any, at the root of the nose.

Palayans.—This tribe is markedly australoid, but there is probably much admixture present, the brow ridges are generally very marked. They cover themselves with ashes (? as a disguise) when hunting in the streams for crabs, which they say will otherwise not be taken. They use a drum and an oboe, and they dance with shouts suggestive rather of the Konyak Naga and the Sawara, a different type of dancing to that of the Ulladans and Malayarayans. Their music is decidedly suggestive of the Sawara approaching reel or jig time and tune. Their method of hair dressing, presumably copied to some extent from that of the Tamils, again suggests the Angami or the Konyak Naga, as the hair in the front of the head is kept instead of being shaved off. The women, moreover, dance with cloths in a manner very suggestive of the Kaccha Naga and of some tribe in the Vizagapatam Agency, I think the Gadabas. Apparently their only implement or weapon is a digging stick about 5 feet long with a point hardened by fire with which they dig up yams which may be 6 feet below ground.

Kallan.—The Kallan are a plains tribe with apparently remarkable features and very numerous, running into hundreds or thousands, but treated as a criminal tribe, having a species of bull baiting which consists in jumping on to the back of a charging bull and hanging on by the hump until they have obtained a cloth fixed on the horns which are specially sharpened for the occasion and frequently inflict severe wounds. Success in this sport is apparently regarded as a qualification for marriage in the same way that head-hunting is in the Naga Hills. They are said to have many distinctive customs ; for instance, parties of pilgrims or traders going through their country used, perhaps still continue, to pay blackmail to a Kallan chief, who would then provide a Kallan girl to accompany the party as a guide ; so long as they were so accompanied no other Kallan will touch them.

In the Palni hills there are a number of dolmens (of which an account has been published by the Archæological survey) which seem to consist of long cist graves which possibl contained not the body but a wooden image of the body, the real body, or ashes perhaps, possibly having been buried in a cist tomb under-ground. I make this suggestion because, as pointed out to me, the dolmen tombs all seem to have been built in exposed sites on the tops of the hills and some of them, at any rate, not to have been buried at all. This is the opinion of Fathers Anglade and Newton of the Jesuit College at Kodaikonal who have investigated a large number of these dolmen graves. In some cases, however, possibly in many more, there is found near an exposed site a grave under-ground in a sheltered site ; the one shown to me had two chambers the dividing stone between which had a round hold in it ; a similar hole appeared at the end of the stone and may possibly have led into another chamber beyond it, and it was stated to me in Cochin that in the hills there, there are a series of stone graves opening from one into another. Another feature about the Palni dolmens is that they are in groups surrounded by a stone wall ; in some cases each rectangular cist appears also to be accompanied by a small circular chamber constructed separately. Another feature which seems to me unfamiliar is that the cists in the exposed site were all floored with stone, a single slab being used for the floor as well as for each side. I suggest that they contained wooden effigies of the deceased, because it is still the custom, or till recently was the custom in one local tribe, I think the Malayarayans, after the cremation of their dead, to place a metal effigy of the deceased person in a miniature stone dolmen cist on an elevated site and to worship this effigy annually. This suggests a degenerate form of some culture involving an erection of stone cenotaphs containing a statue of the dead. It is possible in this case that the original method was to bury the dead in the stone lined grave, and that, that gave way to the exposed stone cist in which a figure was laid when the practice of cremation came in. This would account for the existence of both types of stone cist since the very heavy underground stone chamber would be likely to give way to the much lighter and more easily erected surface structure when disposal underground became no longer essential and there was no body to be buried but merely a figure acting as receptacle for the soul of the deceased.

I noticed in the plains a large number of Christian graves with what I took to be small stone or brick dolmens placed on them. In this I was wrong, for it appears that these are merely receptacles for lights and probably not to be associated at all with the dolmen culture except by accident. What did strike me, however, was the existence among the dolmen country of irrigated terracing on a considerable scale, while the following tribes in that locality also cultivate on dry terraces :—

Mannadi, Mudaliar, Asuri, Marava, Chaliar and others. Pumbari village in particular, I noticed, surrounded by terraced fields containing temples of some local deity served by Karnam Brahmans.

The Muthuvar in the Palni Hills use blowguns made from a local bamboo sometimes of a considerable length and apparently entirely indigenous. There seems to be no possibility at all of these blowguns having come in from the Malay Peninsula, though Mr. Foulkes, who is my informant and who very kindly obtained specimens, said that he had seen on the Madras Coast blowguns which were admittedly imported from Malay Peninsula.

One of the temples at Tanjore contains among other ancient Hindu effigies carved on its walls, an effigy of an unmistakable European. The local explanation is a cock and bull story about the sculptor having had a prophetic vision of European occupation in years to come, but Mr. Foulkes tells me that he has seen a carving not only identical in style but representing the identical features of this European on a temple in Canton where it is admitted a contemporary carving of Marco Polo, as Marco Polo visited this neighbourhood ; the obvious inference is that the effigy at Tanjore is a representation of that eminent traveller. Yule mentions in his introduction to his edition of Marco Polo the existence of the carving at Canton and states

1.

2.

3

4.

1. **Andamanese harpooning dugong.**

2. **People of Great Andaman.**

3. **Great Andamanese male and female (beside a European).**

4. **Woman of Little Andaman.**

(For photographs 1, 3 and 4 acknowledgments are due to Mr. M. C. C. Bonington for two and to Mr. C. S. Cutting for the other tw

that from what he has heard, the theory that it represents Marco Polo is nonsense. Cordier gives a representation of this figure in the 3rd edition of Yule's book and gives it the title of 'The Pseudo Marco Polo at Canton'. If Mr. Foulkes is right in identifying the Tanjore with the Canton figures, it seems just possible that Yule and Cordier may have slipped up, as they have done over the oxen of the province of Bangala "as tall as elephants". Yule's note runs, "The breeds of Upper India are very tall and noble animals, etc........but...... in Bengal.....the cattle are poorer and stunted", having failed to recognise that Marco Polo is referring to *bos frontalis*, common enough in the hills dividing Bengal and Assam from Burma which is the part of Bengal with which Marco Polo's informants were likely to be most familiar. The Canton "Polo" appears there as one of the 500 arhats, but who his associates are in the Tanjore temple I do not know. If they are also the 500 arhats, though this is not likely as the temple is Hindu not Buddhist, the inference would be that it was the traditional effigy of some particular arhat and not Marco Polo after all.

VIII.—Notes on the Andamanese.

The dugong when harpooned by the Andamanese is obtained by means of a long pole at the end of which is a detachable barbed head. The harpooner stands on the prow of the boat and, when the dugong is seen, he points his harpoon in the direction which the animal takes, changing it as the animal changes direction, his companion paddling in the stern and directing the canoe accordingly. As soon as he can get within reach, he throws himself with the harpoon at the animal which makes off with the detached head, to which a cord is fixed, while the harpooner climbs back into the boat and attaches a fresh head to the same shaft and then again pursues the animal to attach it by a second cord. Ultimately the canoe is brought alongside the exhausted animal and the occupants of the canoe dive overboard and first attach the hinder flukes to the canoe by a thick rope. They then tie the fore flukes to the animal's sides, swimming round it and under it with the ropes in their hands. When hauled ashore it is despatched precisely in the same method as that used for killing a *mithun* by the Sema Nagas. An incision is made in the skin behind the shoulder into which a pointed stick is inserted, the stick being driven home to the heart, killing the animal instantly.

Turtles are harpooned in exactly the same way, but one harpoon is enough and the harpooner does not usually jump in with the harpoon, but goes in after it to catch the turtle's hind flippers to make sure of it. The turtle is despatched by piercing the brain with an arrow through the eye.

The Andamanese boys play at putting the weight. The men assured me that the pastime is indigenous and not introduced by foreigners and this indeed appears to be likely as other games do not seem to have been introduced.*

In dancing, the procedure consists first of a recitation by the composer of the party, followed by stamping on the sounding board, while the women, who sit with their legs stretched out in front of them, clap their joined hands on their two thighs and the men dance a stamping dance, arms outstretched in front of them and one finger held in the opposite hand. As the periods in the recitation are reached, the women sing as a refrain the last phrase of the composer's verse, after which another spasm of recitation follows and so on. The songs appear to be topical.

In a Jarawa village, which was founded recently, a phallic symbol in wood carved out of a tree trunk *in situ* was found and brought back.

The Jarawas use a very broad bark belt of the nature of a cuirass protecting the abdomen and the lower part of the torso in fighting, like the hide belt-cuirass still used by trans-frontier Semas.

The outrigger of the Andamanese canoe, the smaller variety that is, for the larger are used without outriggers, must, I think, have been copied from the Nicobarese pattern. The method of attachment is exactly the same. The Nicobarese always use outriggers apparently, but the fact that the Andamanese use it only in the smaller canoe rather suggests that their original custom is to have no outrigger.

I noticed that the Onge Andamanese when drinking in the jungle put their mouth down to the water.

Some of the women, those whom I noticed were all youngish married women, are fantastically obese, excessively steatopygous and with breasts falling to the waist. One such, fatter than the rest, was obviously regarded by herself and by others as a beauty. She reminded me of nothing so much as an Aurignacian "Venus".

They use red ochre and the women smear it on their faces, necks and shoulders. White clay is used by both sexes, who paint their bodies in geometrical patterns.

The yellow dried skin of a dendrobium orchid is used for decorative purposes both by the Onge and the Jarawa, as in the Naga Hills.

* *Cf. The Angami Nagas*, pp. 102, 103.

The skulls of the Onge appear to be deformed and look as if they have been artificially flattened. Mr. Bonnington considers that it is due to the carrying of loads from very early childhood and points out that the hair of women is often worn across the top of the head for the same reason. This explanation is perhaps a possible one, as the loads are carried by a band which does not pass, as in the case of most people who carry loads on their head, across the brow, where the skull is hard, but right across the middle of their head where the sutures are joined at a late date*.

The hybrids whom I saw had harsh frizzly hair clearly distinguishable from the closely curled soft woolly hair of the pure Andamanese.

Obviously the Andamanese are very highly temperamental, which, as they have been inbred for so long, is perhaps natural and comparable with the nervous disposition found in racehorses and thoroughbred greyhounds for instance, like which too they are very delicate and susceptible to disease. Their temperamental disposition was illustrated by three Onges whom Mr. Bonnington brought with him on the *Shahjehan* to visit the Nicobars, intending after that to take them to Port Blair in order to study their language for a time. The men came willingly and in Kar Nikobar Island fraternized at once with the Nicobarese who fed them all the morning on anything they could stuff inside themselves, walked about with their arms round their necks, etc. While we were at lunch one of these Onges strolled towards the jungle. The other two followed him. Some one remarked they are running away. The Nicobarese set up a wild shout (it is their custom to shout on the least provocation). The Andamanese took fright and ran away into the jungle. One we did not succeed in recovering at all. The other two were recovered trembling with emotion and were glad to get on board the ship again. One of them was sick later, but that may have been due to a stomach overloaded with strange fare. That night one of them jumped over board and the other was with difficulty restrained from doing so. He perpetually made signs that he wanted a knife apparently to cut his wrists and neck, but ultimately we got him safely back to his island. He was then reluctant to go ashore, and, having gone, plunged into the jungle, while the sad story was being made known to his fellows. The latter said nothing but trembling violently hurried after him into the jungle. We saw them returning half an hour later to take away our presents but whether the returned voyager was with them or not we could not say [see *Andaman and Nicobar Island Census* (1931), p. 17.]

IX.—Notes on the Nicobarese.

The tree, *Barringtonia speciosa*, is used by the Nicobarese for stupefying fish as other trees are in Assam and elsewhere.

Ownership is marked by a coconut at the top of a stick or similar sign known as *takoia* and constituting a prohibition against the abstraction of coconuts or other produce.

The houses have circular rat protectors† at the tops of the piles on which they are built and are extremely well made in the form of a dome, windowless but with a floor of open work cane matting which allows the air to percolate freely and enables all dirt or refuse to be swept down. The hearth is placed to one side of the centre opposite the trap door used for entrance, and consists of 3 or more stones bedded into a rectangle of earth let into the floor on boards. The villages are beautifully clean within the area of actual building ; outside that scavenging is effectively carried out by pigs and hermit crabs.

I noticed swings in use for rocking children to sleep.‡ The head-gear, both the "dog's ear" head-band and the more elaborate mitre of the *mafai* are very reminiscent of Konyak Naga head-gear,§ with two forms of which they are virtually identical.

The dead on Kar Nikobar are buried with capstan-like posts put up over them, and in the top of one I noticed a paddle decorated with flying strips of coloured cloth erected blade upwards. In some cases a rounded or painted waterworn stone seems to be substituted for the "capstan" post. Later the bones are dug up and the bulk of them thrown into the sea, or, in some cases, apparently into bushes, while the skulls of worthies are reburied. There is said to be a bone heap at the edge of the beach to the south-east of the Mus cemetery.|| It is possible that it is the reburied skulls over which the stones are put up as distinct from posts, but little information was obtainable in the short time at my disposal and the matter is clearly one for careful investigation. At Chaura the dead are buried in front of their houses for three days.

* The shape of the Onge head reminded me of that of the Marken head in Holland, where the skull was regularly deformed unintentionally by the use of tight caps in infancy.

† This device is found in Saghalien (Ainu), Formosa, the Philippines, the Shan States, Assam, Borneo, New Guinea, New Britain and Madagascar (*vide* Peal, *On the Morong, etc.*, S. A. I. XXII 251, McGovern, *Headhunters of Formosa*, 176 ; Cole, *The Tinguian*, 394 and plate LV ; Hose and McDougall, *Pagan Tribes of Borneo*, I, 53 and plate 40 ; Ellis, *History of Madagascar*, I, 302 and an unpublished diary of General Woodthorpe's).

‡ Colonel Sewell tells me that they also use swinging platforms big enough to hold three or four people. These platforms are swung underneath the huts and take the place of a *punkah*.

§ *Two Tours East of the Naga Hills* (M. A. S. B. XI. i) plates 9 & 10.

|| Colonel Sewell remarks that in rare cases the skulls are placed in a fork of the tree, and he saw two such skulls at Mus. The Headman insisted that these should not be touched though there was no objection to his removing the others provided they were not taken through the village. *Cf.* paper No. 17 (*c*) and (*d*) below.

They are then dug up and exposed in the heavy forest at the edge of the beach, each body in a canoe or in part of a canoe which is raised over the ground on a pair of forked wooden Y-shaped post. They are there left to rot and I saw many skulls lying about the ground, but owing to the fact that I could only go on board again in a Nicobar canoe and had nothing to conceal them in I was unable to abstract any. This canoe cemetery appears to be on the east of the island and to be the only one on the island, very obviously suggesting that the canoe builders entered Chaura from the east by sea.

The Nicobarese use a cane noose with a running knot at the end of a long bamboo for catching little pigs with. They make broad-bladed spears for hunting wild cattle and wild pig. They make fire by the saw method splitting a piece of dried stick into two (the tree used closely resembles the elder, but is actually one of the *verbenaceæ, Premna integrifolia*, L.). One man holds the one half while another saws across it with the edge of the other half igniting the pith in less than 30 seconds. They are amazingly muscular. The hearth is spoken of as female and the saw as male. It takes two men, however to make fire, suggesting that the other Indonesian method of sawing round under the hearth, instead of over with a cane or bamboo thong, is a derivative of the cruder method used by the Nicobarese, and has been evolved owing to the necessity of individuals to be able to make fire alone, for in the thong method the hearth can be held by the foot. At Champen village in Nankauri island I noticed automatic bull-roarers erected on trees and masts placed out in the sea in front of the village. I am told they move them round in the opposite directions when the monsoon changes and, though they told me that they were erected merely as playthings for the children, I find it very difficult to believe that a device over which so much trouble is taken is not more than a toy. Their version, however, was to some extent confirmed by the fact that one, which I had extracted from under a house was promptly claimed as his by a small boy. On the other hand it is the Nankauri people who go in systematically for scare-devils to a greater extent than the other island and I cannot help thinking that these are really intended to keep away the evil spirits. They are formed of a narrow plank to which a slight screw effect has been given by twisting and cutting so that they revolve in the wind about a central pin. At each end of the plank and facing in opposite directions is a node of bamboo the open end of which is partly blocked by rubber or wax. The result is that the revolving wood produces a very deep and loud booming noise identical with that produced by a bull-roarer. Among the familiar scare-devils* of the ordinary type I noticed that birds are very prominent, one in the form of a seagull or a hawk being very well represented. Kloss says that it represents the white sea eagle ; from the form which it has, it might equally well be a frigate bird. When there is sickness in the house the scare-devils, which during the south-west monsoon are kept indoors and not, as in the cold weather, set out along shore, are dressed in frills and hangings of young green coconut leaves and I noticed in Chaura that a man-headed post, with a slightly forked top,† was to be found outside many houses and that also in some cases similarly dressed.

Big Chinese jars are used for drinking water and very popular apparently. They are probably obtained from the Chinese who come to fish for shell, and are perhaps full of spirit when obtained.

The dead in Nankauri are buried with a sort of soul figure in the form of post on a grave which is dressed in the clothes of deceased and hung with fruit, weapons, etc. After a period which I was unble to determine, (it is possible that it depends on some festival for harvest or planting), the dead body is dug up, the skull is fêted and then re-buried. It seems to me fairly clear that in these three burial customs we have an indication of two different people inhabiting the Nicobars. I suggest that the original inhabitants buried their dead in or near their houses and dug them up again to fête the skull as is done by the Yimtsungr of the Naga Hills, and others in that area. Those who came later must have come to Chaura in the first instance and brought with them the practice of exposing the dead in canoe coffins, presumably in order that their souls may return by sea to the land of origin further east. In Kar Nicobar we seem to have a compromise between the two customs, the dead being first buried (by the sea shore in this case and not to landward as in Nankauri), and then their bones thrown into the sea. This supposition is borne out, I think, by the fact that all canoes have to be bought in Chaura or else have to be "shown the way " there ; while pottery is only obtainable from Chaura as if the new comers had not only brought in the use of the canoe or of a better form of canoe but also that of pot making. It is noticeable moreover that scare-devils, a very prominent feature in Nankauri, seem to be comparatively absent in Kar Nicobar and more so still perhaps in Chaura suggesting

---

* Human figures of various sizes generally with an upraised arm and a hole for a spear through the raised right hand, are the commonest, perhaps. Colonel Sewell noticed and photographed one human figure erected cross-legged like an image of Buddha.

† A photograph taken by Colonel Sewell shows top-hatted figures whose head-gear is developed at the top into curved almost hornlike prongs exceedingly reminiscent of the skull-retaining horns to be found on the soul statues of certain transfrontier Naga villages (*vide Two Tours East of the Naga Hills. M. A. S. B., XI., 1.*)

that the new-comers' influence has been stronger in Kar Nicobar than in Nankauri and strongest of course in Chaura.

Canoes, if not bought in Chaura cannot go there until they have been " shown the way ", for which a very heavy fee is payable to the Chaura people who steer and conduct it. Until the canoe has been " shown the way " it may not visit Chaura, and an annual visit is always paid, and other visits are made to buy pots which can only be got from Chaura.

I saw at Kar Nicobar a canoe race in two of the big outriggers which resembled very closely the Malay or the Bornean *prahu*. The racers first take a formal meal together discarding for the occasion their oddments of foreign clothing. They wear collars of young pale green coconut leaves, very becoming, and hang up similar decorations on their canoes and on the chief's house in which they feast, the hangings at the door being sprinkled with the blood of an offering. They first drink toddy and sing together the canoe songs with solos and parts, very inspiring and melodious, even if a little harsh on the part of the older men. The domed hut acts as a resonator increasing the effect of the sound. Kloss' statement that there are only four notes used seems to be entirely wrong, but it is possible that the singing of the Kar Nicobar missioners may have influenced range and composition since Kloss wrote. Obviously the Nicobarese are a musical people, their canoe songs being composed from time to time and it being the duty of one village to invite another village to a common feast with them and be taught a new canoe song annually. After the singing, rice and pork are served, the rice being obtained from traders. A piece of the pork is thrown out through the trap-door of the hut for the spirit of the canoe and promptly eaten by the dogs below. On the prow of the canoe a little live pig is tied together with live chickens, in order, it is said to propitiate the canoe. The racing takes place in the sea outside the reefs and we estimated speed at 6 knots, as they covered a mile (verified on a chart) in nine minutes on the occasion on which I watched them.

Wrestling is the favourite form of sport among the Nicobarese and every evening young men, boys, and children wrestle on the sand. The method is similar to, though not identical with, that used in Borneo and in the Naga Hills.

In appearance the Nicobarese are Negroid in feature as well as Mongolian, but the frizzly hair which one would expect to find is strangely absent, though I did see a certain number of specimens. Many of them have prominent brow ridges and I observed one specimen in which the brow ridge was excessively marked and was accompanied by a low and retreating forehead. It is possible that one would see more frizzly hair if it were not the practice of the men to cut their hair as short as possible making individual patterns round the edge above the ear with a razor. But I must admit that I noticed that most of the women seem to have quite leiotrichous hair, though it has a tendency to curl at the end which was denied to be artificial, and which made it differ from the typical dead straight Malay hair. Colonel Sewell has pointed out to me that the prognathous appearance of the Nicobarese is artificial, caused by betel chewing, and is absent in the children, but I cannot entirely agree with him. I certainly observed one or two children and one adult in Kar Nicobar, who had not the chewing habit, the lower parts of whose faces were emphatically prognathous from the glabella downwards, giving them that doglike appearance sometimes seen in the Garo and perhaps to be associated with their dog descent as is their winged white pith head-band, their perineal tail and their amazing " fig-leaf " (I use the word for want of a better term), consisting of a blue bag covering the testicles and penis and prolonged by a piece of different cloth into a long red point. As regards their reputed descent from a man and a bitch who got afloat on a raft, this descent is on record in the Naga Hills in Assam,* where it is ascribed to Europeans, and I think is also recorded of a Burma tribe†. The Nicobarese reminded me a good deal of the Manipuri or the Ao Naga, but more of the Garo in appearance, and it is possible that the Negroid looking features are derived from a pre-Dravidian rather than an Oceanic Negro strain. There is, however, something about their canoe culture which is very suggestive of Melanesia. There is a long-standing association with Moulmein in Burma which taken with the Nicobarese language may argue a Talaing connection.

Their language is Mon-Khmer and their women seem able to hold and to devise property, but the laws of inheritance are obscure. No one seems to know much about them, and as the principal property is in cocoanut trees not in land, while personal valuables are buried or thrown into the sea with the owner, inheritance in land is of minor importance. Nothing seems to be known, either, of clan or exogamy, and marriage laws are reported to be almost non-existent. At any rate no one could tell me what they were, and as no existing European in the Nicobars knows any Nicobarese at all, it is not surprising that there is much ignorance of their customs. For ordinary business affairs so many Nicobarese know a little Malay, Burmese, Hindustani or English that a knowledge of their own language has not hitherto been found essential to administration.

---

* Butler *Rough Notes on the Angami Nagas*, J. A. S. B., 1875.

† " The Peguans ascribe......their Religion to a Dog and a China woman, which escaped shipwrack ", Purchase, *His Pilgrimage*, V, v.

2. Caste in the Kumaun division and Tehri-Garhwal State.*

By A. C. Turner.

Broad divisions. The population of Kumaon and Tehri-Garhwal State may be roughly divided into three broad classes :—

(1) The Silpkars (formerly known as the Hill Doms or Hill Depressed classes) who appear to be the descendants of the aborigines of the country.

(2) The Khasiyas (or Khasas), the descendants of an Aryan or Scythian invasion† prior to the advance of the Vedic Aryans into the north of India.

(3) Aryans of pure descent who have subsequently from time to time immigrated to this country from the plains of India since the occupation of Northern India by the Vedic Aryans was completed.

I.—*The Silpkars.*

Their origin. It seems to be generally agreed that the Silpkars are the remnants of an aboriginal race who inhabited the Himalayas before the advent of the later conquerors and immigrants. It has been remarked by several writers that they are of darker colour than might be expected of a hill tribe, in this respect resembling the corresponding classes in Kashmir, Jammu, Naga and Chilas (Atkinson, *Gazetteer of the Himalayan Districts,* Volume II, page 370). They probably represent the *Dasyus* of *Vedic* times—the people whom the Aryan invaders found in occupation of northern India and either drove out or subdued. The *Vedic* scriptures speak of two varities of *Dasyus,* the fairer red-haired people of what is now the Punjab, and the darker aborigines who probably owed their origin to a more southern source. The Silpkar it may be supposed belongs to the latter variety. Some writers have mentioned negroid characteristics of the Silpkars, but more careful observation does not support this view. They are certainly smaller and darker than the Khasiyas and other inhabitants of the hills, but cannot be said to have woolly hair or other features which have been rather fancifully attributed to them. Their own traditions seem to support the theory that they were the aborigines of the hill country. They are found all along the Himalayas from Nepal to the Punjab and beyond, wherever the Khasiyas and their related races are found, living with them even now in a state not far removed from serfdom. Crooke says,‡ " In the Himalayan districts of these provinces the Dom has long been recognized as a descendant of the *Dasyus* of the *Veda,* who are supposed to have held upper India before the advent of the Naga or Khasiya race ". In earlier times they were kept in strict subjection. They were in fact the slaves of the Khasiyas and Brahmans, and were passed from hand to hand like chattels, or were attached to the soil like the serfs or *adscripti glebae* of feudal Europe. In prehistoric times the forest-clad mountains of Kumaun and Garhwal were doubtless occupied by these tribes of a low type of culture like the Kols and Gonds of Central India, who lived by the chase, or on the edible roots, herbs and fruits that are so abundant which still form no small part of the food of the people. They may possibly have practised a rudimentary agriculture, consisting in burning down a patch of forest and sowing a few grains of millet, then passing on to fresh ground leaving the former to lie fallow for six or ten years as is still done in the *tarai* and other places by wandering tribes. The Silpkars are the descendants of this race which have left no memorial of their early occupation of the land, unless some curious cupshaped markings on the rocks at Debidhura and elsewhere in the province may be attributed to them.

How the name Dom became associated with this race is unknown. In hilly Himalaya West where the bulk of the population depends on agriculture for its subsistence and villages are far apart and connected by narrow hilly-paths, each village community has to be self-contained as regards at least its primary requirements. On the Doms fell most of the hard work and every village had its own artizans and others who performed their own allotted work for the village community. In this way the Doms became split up into numerous occupational groups, which by contact with the Hindu caste system have come to be regarded as sub-castes of their tribe. Those of each sub-caste in a village were virtually considered the property of that village community, and even to this day in Tehri-Garhwal State if an Auji (drummer, who also supplies music at marriage parties and on festivals) or a Daliya (one whose function is to prevent damage to crops by hail and other calamities by means of magic or certain *mantras*) of one village goes and settles in another village the result is invariably a quarrel between the two villages which, although there is nothing in law to prevent the migration, sometimes leads to protracted litigation. Again, if the Auji or Lohar (blacksmith) of one village has a case in court against his counterpart in another village the matter becomes a village struggle and each party is stoutly backed by the village headman (*padhan*) and *panchayat,* who regard it as a case between the two villages. If a Dom is fined the people of his village often collect the sum among themselves and pay upon his behalf.

Organization and occupation. As will be seen from the brief account given above the present sub-castes among Silpkars are purely the result of the fact that they were kept by their conquerors the Khasiyas in a complete state of subjection and each man was allotted his work and kept to that profession, the sub-divisions hardening by reason of contact with Hinduism into occupational sub-castes. Below I give a list of the sub-castes found at the present day—

(1) *Agri* or *Agari.*—Ironsmiths and cultivators. (Probably connected with *ag,* fire, *cf. agyari,* kindler of fire at time of devotion). These were formerly attached to the mines as serfs by the Rajas, but have exchanged that ill-paid and dangerous avocation for road-making and other more profitable work. Now-a-days they do not extract iron from mines in Kumaun—there were some at Ramgarh and Sânudiyar and other places—but they use imported iron brought from Bombay.

(2) *Auji, Auzi* or *Bajgi.*—Drummers, found everywhere. Tehri-Garhwal State returned approximately 11,600 (males 5,900, females 5,700). In Almora some are tailors. The Auji is one of the most indispensable members of the village community. At all functions, religious or social, he plays

*For the information in this Appendix I am indebted chiefly to E. S. Oakley, Esq., of Almora, Pandit Tara Datt Gairola, Rai Bahadur, Advocate of Pauri; Pandit Bhola Datt Pant, B.Sc., LL.B., M.B.E., Deputy Collector, Garhwal; and Pandit Uma Datt Dangwal, B.A., LL.B., Sub-Divisional Officer, Tehri-Garhwal State. A. C. T.

†More likely, I think, Mediterranean or Armenoid or both, and likely to have been Dravidian-speaking. The snake cult, the use of stone, both as seats of honour and memorials, and the very obvious traces of a matrilineal system all suggest to me affinity with southern India and the eastern Mediterranean and the probable culture of the Madhyadesha before its penetration by the Pamiri Alpine or the Rigvedic Aryan invader.—J. H. H.

‡Crooke's *Tribes and Castes of the North-Western Provinces and Oudh,* pages 331-2.

the leading part with his *dhol* (drum). On the first day of every Hindu month and on all festival days he must beat his drum and *damaun* (a smaller hemi-spherical drum) before every door in the village. Every morning he has to perform what is locally called *naubat*. At every religious service, whether it be a *pandavas* dance or worship of the village god, the Bajgi's *dhol* and *damaun* plays the predominant part. Marriage parties and even parties on local pilgrimages, are led by the Bajgi.

A Bajgi is higher in rank than a Dondi, Hurkiya or Nagari.

If a Bajgi takes up the profession of a Beda or Bedi and gives up his *dhol* and *damaun* for a *dholak* (a smaller drum used in dancing only) he is called Dhaki. *Saraswathi Bhagawathi* is the chief goddess and the *pandavas* are the chief gods of the Bagji.

(3) *Athpaharia*.—Found in Garhwal District and Tehri-Garhwal State. They used to beat drums at the palace-gate of the Hindu Rajas of Garhwal at the end of each *pahar*.

(4) *Badi* or *Beda*.—Found everywhere. They are professional dancers and singers; the comedians of the hills (from Sanskrit *vadi*, a speaker, talker, disputant). In Tehri-Garhwal State at least one Beda in a family consecrates his hair to his chief god *Mahadev* and must perform *bedwart* before he can get his head shaved. If the yearly harvest diminishes continually for some years, if rats do abnormal damage to crops, if blood comes out of a cow's udder in place of milk, if the share of a plough strikes against a snake or if an unusual number of snakes appear in the fields, such calamities are taken to be the manifestation of *Mahadev's* displeasure. If *babla*, a kind of local grass, grows within the temple of *Mahadev* it is regarded as a sure sign of his wrath and the only remedy is for someone to perform *bedwart*. The Beda whose hair is consecrated to *Mahadev* is the chief functionary in the ceremony. The whole thing is grand in preparation and thrilling in performance. Months before the actual ceremony takes place the whole villages in which *bedwart* is to take place begins to collect food, provisions and money contributions to meet various expenses, such as food for the invited guests and ornaments, clothes, etc., for the Beda who is to do *bedwart*. Besides those who are invited, a large number of spectators also come from far and near and make an imposing gathering. A small *bazar* is established, *charkis* are erected and all the paraphernalia of a regular *mela*.

The main part of the ceremony is that a huge rope of *babla* grass is stretched across a valley or along the slope of a hill by fastening one end of the rope on a strong tree or rock on the top of the hill and the other end on the other side or at the bottom of the hill as the case may be. A wooden saddle is mounted on the rope at the upper end and the Beda is made to sit on it with his legs hanging down in the air. The Beda is balanced on the saddle by hanging a weight to his legs. A fall would mean instantaneous death. Thus balanced, the Beda is left to slide down the rope to the other end. As soon as the Beda reaches the end of his journey, the villagers and spectators who are gathered in readiness at the lower end of the rope, fall upon him and snatch away the hairs of his head. His hairs are considered to be those of *Mahadev* in whose name they were preserved for so long, and no evil or trouble is said to visit a house which possesses these hairs. The rope on which a Beda is to slide is generally made or twisted by the members of his own family for two reasons. They make sure that the rope is strong enough and they take great care to watch it day and night, for it is believed the moment a rope (or *bart* as it is called) is left unwatched, it turns into a huge snake and creeps off into the interior of the earth. Before a Beda is made to slide he is workshipped as *Mahadev*, is bathed in milk, dressed in new garments and ornaments, and is taken on the shoulders of the *padhan* all round the village and the fields. He is also given some cash money as fee after the ceremony is finished. In one or two instances accidents have happened and the Beda has fallen to his death. Latterly the State has prohibited any *bedwart* to be held without explicit permission. Such permission is given very sparingly. This practice used to be common in Kumaun but has long since been abandoned.

(5) *Bairi*.—Basket-makers. These live at Dhamas village near Almora and in Danpur. The Danpur Bairis make *chitai* or bamboo matting wich they bring for sale to the Bageshware fair. The name is derived from Hindi *beri*, the basket used when irrigating fields.

(6) *Bakhriya*.—Found everywhere, now ploughmen and menial servants. They were probably the grooms of olden times and they have been so named from Hindi *bakhar*, a house, as they were men who worked in and about the house.

(7) *Barai*, *Barhi* or *Barhai*.—Found everywhere. They are masons and carpenters. Orhs are also masons but sometimes in Tehri-Garhwal State Barhis who work as masons are also loosely spoken of as Orhs.

(8) *Baura or Bora*.—Sack-makers from Almora. They cultivate hemp and make coarse cloth and rope from the fibre. The name is derived from *bora*, a sack.

(9) *Bhat*.—Found everywhere. Bards and genealogists as in the plains. They are similar to Hurkiyas but their women do not dance as the Hurkiya women do.

(10) *Bhul, Teli or Baria*.—They were formerly oil-pressers and used to press oil-seeds for the village. Imported oil is now so cheap that it does not pay the Bhuls to press it, so they have taken to field work.

(11) *Chamar*.—Found everywhere. They skin dead animals and cure and tan the hides.

(12) *Chanel*.—Shoemakers in Almora. The name possibly came from *chamrel* a corruption of *chamra* (leather).

(13) *Chunera*.—Found everywhere. They are turners and make wooden vessels with a lathe driven by water power.

(14) *Daliya*.—*Dal* is a hill word for a hailstorm or violent rainstorm. Daliyas profess to know the magic or *mantras* by means of which they can divert or stop a hailstorm and thus prevent injury to the standing crops. When a hailstorm appears the Daliya goes to the top of a house or some elevated place and throws rice in all directions meanwhile reciting certain words or chanting *mantras*. By the time he finishes his magic which he can no doubt prolong or shorten according to the duration of the storm, the storm must end and so he never fails to demonstrate successfully the efficacy of the magic which naturally preserves his job. As his service is not for one individual

only but for the benefit of the whole village, the whole village contributes to pay him *dadwar*. In Tehri-Garhwal State Daliyas are chiefly found in the Narendranagar and Kirtinagar sub-divisions, where hailstorms occur more frequently than anywhere else in the State. They are also found in Garhwal district.

(15) *Darji* or *Darzi*.—Found everywhere. Tailors, from Persian *darz*, sewing, a seam. In Tehri-Garhwal State they are counted higher than the Bajgi as they do not eat buffalo flesh whereas a Bajgi does.

(16) *Dhaloti*.—Smelters of bronze in Tehri-Garhwal State. The name is said to come from *dhalua*, to cast. They make *hukkas* by casting molten bronze in *hukka* moulds. Their chief goddess is *Bhagwati Jawaladebi*, the goddess of fire incarnate, the same as for Lohars, Tamtas and Agris, but they are reckoned as lower than Lohars.

(17) *Dhanik*.—Cultivators and basket-makers in Almora. The name possibly originated from *dhanuk*, a bow. They may have made bows at some early period.

(18) *Dhobi*.—Orignally washermen. In Almora most of the present-day *Dhobis* have come from the plains and the original sub-caste of the Doms are nearly all cultivators.

(19) *Dholi*.—Drummers in Almora (from *dholak*, a small drum). Some are tailors now.

(20) *Dhoni*.—Sandwashers in Tehri-Garhwal State, whose chief occupation is washing for gold. They are very few in number now-a-days.

(21) *Dhunia*.—The word generally signifies a carder or cleaner of cotton, the monotonous noise of which operation is familiar in an Indian *bazar*. Some in Almora are now weavers and others have taken to cultivation.

(22) *Dhuniyal*.—Fishermen and ferry-men. In Almora sometimes called *Dhewar Dhimar* or *Jali* (from *jal*, a net).

(23) *Dom*.—In Tehri-Garhwal State there are still some Doms who have, unlike their other professional brethren, not yet taken to any special occupation and are content with the title of their old parental stock. A Dom is like a serf, either traditionally attached to some old *thokdari* family from generation to generation or bound to serve a money-lender in lieu of interest on the money which has been borrowed from the money-lender to get a wife. Generally the pay fixed is so low that it barely covers the interest and so the Dom becomes a life-long slave to the money-lender unless some other money-lender comes and makes a bargain with the former one, in which case the Dom only changes masters. Generally the wife and children of the Dom also work along with him for his master. They all get cooked food from their master's house and also clothing once or twice a year. Male Doms often work as *haliyas* (ploughmen) and the women and children do such work as weeding, carrying manure to the fields, and bringing grass, fuel, etc., to the master's house. The greatest number of these Doms is found in the Jaunpur sub-division and the next greatest number in Kirtinagar sub-division. In the Jaunpur sub-division there are 149 males and 119 females and in Kirtinagar sub-division 80 males and 70 females.

(24) *Dondi*.—Similar to Hurkiyas in Tehri-Garhwal State. Their name is derived from the small drum (*dondi*) they play. Very few in number.

(25) *Dondiya*.—Formerly this sub-caste, found in the Tehri-Garhwal State, were all beggars. They workship *Narsingh* and are sometimes called Dondiya-Narsingh. It is said that Dondiya was a great devotee of the god *Narsingh* of Synasu, a village in Bist *patti*. His descendants call themselves Dondiyas and are also beggars in the name of *Narsingh*. Many of them have now given up begging and have taken to cultivation.

(26) *Gadoi*.—There is a temple of the goddess *Bhagwati* named Dewalgarh in paragana Dewalgarh of Tehri-Garhwal State, which derives its name from the temple of the same name in British Garhwal. The musician or the drummer belonging to this temple was called Gadoi and so all his descendants are called Gadois though they are no longer connected with the temple. This has become a caste name now.

(27) *Hobyara*.—Trumpeters from Jaunpur in Tehri-Garhwal State.

(28) *Hurkiya*.—The lowest sub-caste in the drummer group. A *hurki* or *huruk* is a very small drum shaped like an hour-glass and played with one hand only. Hurkiyas are Garhwali bards who sing and extol the deeds of the Garhwali pre-historic warriors called Bhars. They recite the genealogies of the Garhwali Rajas and many legends connected with their lives. In olden days, every warrior was accompanied by a *Hurkiya* when going into battle. The latter's function was to encourage his master by singing spirited songs in his praise. Champa Hurkiya figures in all battles. The Hurkiyas are the repositories of local folklore, and can recite a surprising number of stories, full of minute detail. It is to be regretted that the old race of Hurkiyas is fast disappearing. The new generation have become *Mirasis* and only know *desi* songs. (*Mirasis* are singers who follow their profession from generation to generation, from *miras*, inheritance.)

(29) *Jagri* or *Jagaria*.—These are sorcerers or exorcists. If a person is in trouble the idea is that he or she is possessed of or is being tormented by some malevolent spirit or enraged deity. The Jagaria causes the sufferer to be seated before him and then beats time with two sticks on a bronze plate meanwhile challenging the evil spirit or deity to proclaim himself and the cause of his anger. The sufferer usually proceeds to dance and weep and mutter incoherently from which the Jagaria alleges he can decide who the spirit or deity is and how to appease him. This ceremony is known as *jagar* or *ghariyala*. In Almora the spirit is supposed to enter the Jagaria himself. Another function they perform is to sing the praises of certain gods and invoke them to possess devotees. The name appears to come from *jigar*, the liver or vitals, *cf. jigarkhur*, *jigar-khar*, an enchanter, sorcerer.

(30) *Jamaria*.—Cultivators, found in Almora. The name may be a corruption of *zamindar*.

(31) *Koli*.—Found everywhere. Originally they were weavers. Until about 40 years ago a dwarf variety of cotton (about 6 inches tall) was grown in the hills, from which a poor kind of cloth was woven by the Kolis for local use. This industry has completely died out and the Kolis have mostly given up weaving altogether and have turned to cultivation, trade, etc.

In Tehri-Garhwal State many Kolis despise their traditional calling and consider it beneath their dignity to admit that their forefathers were weavers. As a rule the Koli is far more well-to-do than other Doms who are still mostly without lands and are partly dependent on begging or *dadwar*.

A special note on the Kolis in Tehri-Garhwal State appears below.

(32) *Kumhar*.—Potters. In Tehri-Garhwal State there are Kumhars also who are not Doms (known as Bith-Kumhars). In Almora this sub-caste is known as *Hankia* from *handi*, an earthen pot. The Hankias work chiefly in the Patiya valley near Almora, and in Kali Kumaun.

(33) *Lohar*.—Ironsmiths, blacksmiths : found everywhere. In Tehri-Garhwal State they practically confine their work to agricultural implements. Lohars are higher than Tamtas, Dhalotis and Agris, though they all worship *Bhagwati Jwaladebi*, the goddess of fire incarnate.

(34) *Mistri*.—Carpenters.

(35) *Mochi* or *Badi*.—Found everywhere. In some parts of Uttar Kashi (Tehri-Garhwal State) he is called *Mochyata*. He is a cobbler and shoemaker. In Almora he deals in hides but never tans them. He does not interdine with Chamars. A Badi will sometimes take a Chamar bride but will not give his daughter to a Chamar. When a Chamar girl is married to a Badi she is not allowed to dine with her Chamar relatives. If any Badi inter-dines with a Chamar he is outcasted by the Badi *panchayat*, and can be re-admitted only if he gives a feast and a goat to the *panchayat*. (Some Lohars whose caste is considered to be higher than that of the Badis have begun to marry daughters of Badis, but they also do not allow them to dine with their Badi relatives). Their chief deity or goddess is *Jwaladebi*, whom they generally propitiate every third year besides on many other occasions, by offering a sacrifice called *ashtabali*, which includes one he-buffalo and one she-buffalo, one goat, one pig, one fowl, one *bhujela* (a kind of white pumpkin), one *gendara* (a kind of tuber), some cooked rice and curry. On such occasions a Brahman is employed to worship the deity and to perform the ceremony.

(36) *Nagari*.—Drummers who beat the *nagara*, a one-sided drum. They are sometimes called *Nagarchis*. A few are found in Tehri-Garhwal State.

(37) *Nai*.—Barbers.

(38) *Nath* or *Jogi*.—Beggars, found in Garhwal and Tehri-Garhwal. They call themselves followers of Guru Gorakhnath, pierce their ears and wear heavy glass or wooden ear-rings. Many of them have taken to cultivation as well for a living.

(39) *Orh*.—Found everywhere. They are masons but the name seems to be inter-changeable with Barhai and is often applied to carpenters as well.

(40) *Pahri*.—Found everywhere. In Tehri-Garhwal State he is a village orderly and assistant to the *padhan* (headman). If the village *panchayat* is to meet it is the business of the Pahri to call the villagers together. If an official comes to a village it is the Pahri's duty to look after his needs and to carry out his orders.

In Almora they are the servants of cultivators and *malguzars*, and are said originally to have been watchmen. They are village messengers, etc., corresponding to the Chamar village watchmen in the plains. (From *pahri* or *pahara*, watchman, Sanscrit *praharin*). Mr. Stowell wrote (*Land Tenures of Kumaon*, page 136) " The *pasban* or *pahri* are generally village servants, watchers, messengers and assistants to the *padhan*, they carry Government orders or the *patwari's* messages from one village to another, do a little *chaukidari*, convey the *padhan's* orders for coolies, etc. They are usually Doms and are remunerated by a payment of one *nali* of grain from each family in the village at each harvest."

(41) *Patar*.—Found in Almora. They supply leaves for use as plates at feasts on the occasions of marriages, births, etc. The name is derived from *patta*, a leaf.

(42) *Pauri*.—Found in Almora. They formerly served in temples of the lower order as *pujaris* (ministrants) and musicians. They then became potters and are now nearly all cultivatos. Their name may have come from their first occupation as door-keepers of the temples from *paur*, a door.

(43) *Pummi*.—Cotton carders, a few were found in Tehri-Garhwal State.

(44) *Raj*.—Masons, found in Almora. The name is probably derived from *raj-mistri*, a master-builder.

(45) *Raunsal*.—Cultivators, found in Almora.

(46) *Ruriya* or *Ringaliya*.—Found everywhere. Makers of baskets, mats, boxes, sieves and other articles from reeds and bamboos. The correct name is probably Baruriya possibly from *baru*, high jungle grass or reed.

(47) *Sirdalia*.—Masons and cultivators found in Almora.

(48) *Sonar*.—Goldsmiths. In Tehri-Garhwal State there are also Bith-Sonars who claim to be Rajputs.

(49) *Tamta*.—Found everywhere. Makers of brass and copper vessels (from *tamba*, copper). They form a large and on the whole flourishing community. Some have taken to agriculture though few possess land. Some are also becoming educated. (See also Nos. 1, 16 and 33 *supra*).

(50) *Tirwa*.—Sword and knife sharpeners (from *tir* arrow). They are found in Almora and were probably arrowsmiths in olden times.

(51) *Turi*.—Originally trumpeters in Almora (from *Turi*, a trumpet or clarion consisting of three pieces fixed into one another). They are now mostly cultivators.

Besides the above sub-castes there are others not based on occupation but called after the names of persons or places. This is not uncommon also in the case of Khas-Brahmans and Khas-Rajputs. Such names arise when migration occurs or when the members of the community have no fixed occupation. For instance, in Asthal Dhaneri *patti* (Tehri-Garhwal State) there were found two males and six females who said their caste was *Madiyata*. Asked what the caste-name represented they explained that one Madiya came from some other village and settled in Asthali and his descendants were called *Madiyatas* irrespective of their real origin. In the course of time this nick-name became their caste name. Similar instances are the *Chiwans* said to be called after one Channu, and *Kutiyatas* after one Kutta and *Bhairoyatas* after one Bhairu.

The chief point about these sub-castes is their essentially functional origin, totally unconnected with race. They are almost without exception based on hereditary occupations, and in the past the divisions have been very clearly defined. Until quite recently each sub-caste inter-dined and inter-married only among its own members and would not take food or water that had been touched by anyone belonging to a sub-caste lower in the social scale than their own. Roughly the order of social precedence of the larger sub-castes is Koli, Orh, Lohar, Tamta, Pahri, Ruriya, Athpaharia, Chunera, Auji, Badi, Hurkiya, Dhaki, Badi, Dhunar and Chamar. The Koli is considered the highest class among Silpkars and in Garhwal and Tehri-Garhwal State at any rate, food cooked by them can be eaten by any of the other sub-castes. These sub-caste restrictions are disappearing in Kumaun, though it is a fact that the lower sub-castes, *viz.*, Naths, Badis, Hurkiyas, etc., are still looked down on by the other sub-castes, and form a separate community the members of which inter-dine and inter-marry among themselves. In Tehri-Garhwal State on the other hand the sub-castes are becoming more strictly endogamous and exclusive in the matter of *hukka-pani*, and in some parts Lohars will now not take food and water from Kolis. Hypergamy is found in some cases among the Kolis, Orhs and Lohars in Tehri-Garhwal State, and sometimes between Lohars and Badis, but in all such cases the girl after marriage is not allowed to mix with her relatives again.

In most parts Orhs, Lohars and Tamtas inter-dine and inter-marry, so generally do Badis, Hurkiyas and Dhakis. Aujis do not favour inter-marriage with Badis and if an Auji marries a Badi girl he is called a *Hadi* and is regarded as socially degraded. Pahris and Ruriyas inter-dine and inter-marry, so do Nats and Bhats. In Tehri-Garhwal State Aujis, Darjis and some Bedas can inter-marry. The general rule there now-a-days is that if one sub-caste can smoke the *hukka* of another sub-caste or can drink water touched by that sub-caste they can inter-dine and inter-marry, but restrictions on inter-dining are increasing and so perforce on intermarriage.

In Kumaun there is now-a-days a general tendency towards the amalgamation of the sub-castes and a growing inter-mixture of occupations. In Almora with the exception of the Hurkiyas and Badis who are classed apart, the other sub-castes are rapidly leaving their traditional occupations. Lohars or Tamtas may become masons or carpenters though they are still called Lohars or Tamtas. Some occupations denoted by the names are now obsolete in the hills, *e.g.*, Kolis no longer follow the weaving trade, but do field work as *sirtans* or hired ploughmen. Many Telis have turned to basket-making. Lohars and Tamtas often practise agriculture. The discontinuance of mining in the district of Garhwal is attributed partly to the Mines Act and partly to the cheapness of imported metals, on which the Agaris and Tamtas now depend.

Tailoring, once confined to Darzis and Dholis, is now practised by some of nearly every sub-caste (and even by Rajputs and Brahmans) as a lucrative profession. The most common occupation taken up by a Dom leaving his traditional sub-caste occupation is agriculture. Those who have kept to their hereditary calling in the villages still subsist on the consideration they get for their services to the village community in the shape of *dadwar*. This is a fixed proportion of grain that every family has to give at every harvest.

The wages earned by Doms have been vastly raised in recent years. Less than 40 years ago the daily wage of a mason in the town of Almora was four annas a day. A carpenter used to get eight annas, but now gets a rupee a day or even more. Their dwellings and surroundings in town and village have been improved and made more sanitary.

The great curse of the Doms at the present time is said to be debt, and on this account so many of them remain mere *haliyas* or dependents of the agricultural class, kept in much the same servile condition as of old. The Co-operative Banks, of which four have been started among the Tamtas, are said to be doing considerable service in freeing the people from their indebtedness.

Social position.

In Tehri-Garhwal State it is said that although the Dom is regarded as of low caste he is not untouchable to the same extent as the untouchable of the plains. He sits with Khas-Rajputs, smokes from the same *chilam* (earthen pipe) and can touch without polluting *ghi*, sugar, grain, fruit, oil, and such other foods as are not mixed with water. The only ban on him is that he may not touch the *hukka* (mouth-piece of pipe) and water or any cooked food of the Khasiyas or high caste Hindus nor enter their houses. In Garhwal the Biths (higher classes including Khasiyas) will not take water touched by Doms much less inter-dine or inter-marry with them. Their touch is still considered to pollute. In the past a Dom was not allowed to touch the dwelling house of a Bith, even his shadow conveyed pollution, which was removed only by sprinkling water over the person. Doms were not allowed to wear shoes, nor use an umbrella in the presence of a Bith, nor wear ornaments of gold or silver. They were not allowed to use the same springs, nor were they allowed to ride a pony or to carry a bride or bridegroom in a *doli* or dandy at their weddings. Doms were bought and sold. But now the position of the Doms has greatly improved. They are gradually adopting the social customs of the higher castes and have begun to rise in the social scale. Some have been converted to Christianity and Islam, others have become Aryas and claim social equality with the Biths. They resent being called Dom, Bairshawa, *Tali-jati* (low caste) or *Bahar-jati* (out-caste) and have adopted the name Silpkar (artizans). Still the Doms continue to be very backward and depressed class. Their dwellings are in the most squalid parts of the villages, quite apart from the houses of the Biths. They are mostly landless. They are only given land by the Biths on service tenure as *sirtans* or *khilars*. They still cannot use the same springs as the Biths. They still may not carry a bride or bridegroom in a *doli* or dandy. They have to remove the carcasses of dead animals for the Biths, and carry fire for the cremation of their dead. But in other respects the treatment of the Doms by the Biths has considerably improved. The other old *tabus* are gradually disappearing.

In the proverbial lore of Almora district the Doms are invariably spoken of with contempt and dislike. Hard measure is certainly dealt out to them in this respect. "The marriage of a Dom simply pains the eyes", *i.e.* the Biths take no part in any ceremony or festival of the Doms, and their merry-making is felt to be rather offensive than otherwise. "The Dom is too lazy to plough or manure, but at dinner-time is envious," is used as an admonition to lazy people. The Doms eat the morsels and leavings of food given to them by people of higher castes. This is referred to in the proverb, "The Dom's vessel says, When shall I go to the dwelling of Biths ?" This is applied to the desire of low class people to be connected with the higher castes. "The singing of a Dom with a goitre on his neck is no singing at all", is an allusion to a common complaint in some parts of the province, and is a saying used by one who finds that his work is not appreciated by his superior. "No one thinks of a Bith being poor, or notices the death of a Dom". Scorn could not go further than the following, "The bear was killed and the Dom's house was burnt down, both good things", originating from a story of a bear who once entered the house of a Dom after honey in a hive (a hole in the wall), and set fire to the place by stirring up the embers. So in the judgment of the Biths, two birds were killed with one stone. *Balda bhyol paro bhali bhai: Dum kuriag lago bhali bhai.* (See *Proverbs and Folklore of Kumaun and Garhwal* by the late Pandit Ganga Datt Uprety, R.B.)

Marriage, birth and death ceremonies.

Marriage customs are very lax and no actual ceremony takes place. Bride-price is invariably paid to the parents or guardian of the bride and is usually between Rs. 100 and Rs. 300. The prohibited degrees of marriage are normally seven from the common ancestor.

Divorce, locally known as *chhut*, takes place by mutual consent of the husband and wife.

No birth ceremonies are performed but for eleven days after a birth all the members of the family are considered impure. On the eleventh day the child and its mother are bathed, and molasses or other sweets are distributed among the *biradari*.

The dead are usually burnt on hill-tops, though now some well-to-do Silpkars take their dead to the Ganges for cremation. Formerly a gourd (*tumri*) filled with water was hung on a tree near the place where the dead body was burnt, to quench the thirst of the departed spirit, but the practice is now obsolete. The relatives of the dead shave their head and are considered impure up to the 11th day. After a month the *pitrora* ceremony takes place, in which a small stone representing the spirit of the deceased is placed among the other stones which represent the spirits of the other departed relatives of the deceased. (This custom has by contact been adopted by the Biths or upper castes in Garhwal.) On this occasion the *biradari* is feasted, and a goat or pig is killed.

Religion.

The religion of the Doms is largely animistic and demonistic. Crooke wrote* " It is the Doms who preserve to the present day the pure demonism of the aborigines, while the Khasiyas temper it with the worship of the village deities, the named and localized divine entities, and furnish from their ranks the priests." The Doms have always believed in the power for evil of the ghosts of injured persons and in *karma* (re-incarnation), and as Mr. Burn (now Sir Richard Burn) pointed out† these two beliefs, which are shared by many Khasiyas, were not without considerable effects on practical morality, one result of which is seen in the fact that hardly any police are required in the hills." The fact seems to be that the lower elements of Kumaun Hinduism as a whole, as we might expect, are due to the Doms, who appear always to have specialized in impersonation of deities (good and bad), fortune-telling, devil-dancing, divination, and the like, and, as not infrequently is found to be the case, the religion of the lower subject race has had considerable influence on that of the classes above them in the social scale.

The majority of the Doms of the present day in Garhwal worship demons of various sorts, chief among them being *Masan Bhut, Khabish, Kalinka, Achheries, Gorel.* But their principal deity is *Nirankar.* The worship of this God is performed with great solemnity and the whole family fast and keep vigil at night singing songs in honour of the deity. The ceremony lasts for three days, and ends with a feast to the *biradari* and killing of goats and swine. The priest who officiates at the ceremony is a Dom. The worship of this God is also prevalent among some Biths of southern Garhwal. Next to *Nirankar* is *Kali* or *Kalinka.* The worship of this goddess is also performed with much ceremony. Male buffaloes, swine and goats are freely sacrified in honour of this goddess. The Doms ascribe any kind of ailment or calamity to the wrath of one or other of their godlings. Such is their faith in these godlings that Doms will spend large sums, even selling or hypothecating their property and incurring heavy debts in order to propitiate them.

Some observers in Almora remark that the Doms seem to look on the whole subject of religion from a secular aspect. With the exception of the after-death ceremonies and the *sraddha,* which they do perform and regard as incumbent on them, their other so-called religious customs have a decided tinge of secularity, though the Doms appear to retain a kind of ancestor-worship. Many or most of the local gods and godlings described by Mr. Atkinson with such wealth of detail in his *Himalayan Gazeteer* must originally have been worshipped by the Doms more especially. The Doms still have their own gods and temples and their gods in Almora are *Bholanath, Ganganath, Haru, Shiam, Gwala, Nirankar,* etc. Some of them (as described in the *Himalayan Gazeteer*) were persons who committed flagrant crimes and whose ghosts have to be propitiated, or who suffered some great injury or were murdered, and whose spirits often possess and torment people. The sorcerers of the Doms (*Jagarias*) declare which god has possessed or is afflicting their clients; singing and dancing is performed and offerings presented; the spirit of the god or gods comes into the sorcerer and he informs the sufferer what offence he has committed and how he is to propitiate the offended spirit. Even the higher castes sometimes participate in such rites and give credence to them.

Now-a-days in some parts of Kumaun Silpkars are imitating the marriage and funeral ceremonies of the more or less orthodox Hindus, but no Brahman officiates, his place being taken by either a son-in-law, or a sister's son‡. They are ignorant of the orthodox rites and the *mantras,* and the whole affair is but an imperfect imitation. In the hill *pattis* of Naini Tal district quite a large proportion of Silpkars returned themselves as Aryas at the last census and a few on the southern borders of Almora and Garhwal. These include some who are but imperfectly converted but who call themselves Aryas in an attempt to improve their social status. On the other hand, they include many who are learning and practising to the best of their ability and opportunity the rites of orthodox Hinduism. It is said that between 8,000 and 10,000 have put on the sacred thread (*janeo*),§ but no instance of inter-marriage with the higher castes has come to my knowledge. The movement is, however, making for their social uplift, and in small ways it can be seen that in Kumaon the attitude of the higher castes towards the Silpkars is under-going change. In Almora formerly the higher castes did not allow Doms to have a flag at a wedding, nor the bridegroom's basket containing valuables and eatables for the bride, but now both these bans have been removed. Similarly Doms were allowed to perform the *sraddha* ceremony only on the last day of the *sraddha* period, but now they follow the orthodox calendar and do not have to wait till the last day.

A steady though perhaps not very large influx of Doms into the Muslim fold takes place owing to the Muslim practice of taking Dom women as wives or concubines, the children of course being brought up in the religion of their fathers.

* Crooke's *Tribes and Castes of the North-Western Provinces and Oudh,* Volume II, page 333.

† United Provinces Census Report, 1901, Part I, Page 77.

‡ From Garhwal it is reported that sometimes a Brahman does now take the place of the son-in-law or sister's son.

§ Quite recently the Sauns (an offshoot of Doms) in Agar *patti* were invested with the sacred thread by a Hill Brahman. The Bauras of Athigaon near Berenag were anxious to be so invested and were prepared to pay handsomely for it. Unfortunately for the Brahman who was to profit by the venture, he was thwarted by his *biradari* who threatened to ex-communicate him if he performed the ceremony. In some parts it is said that Arya Samajists take a rupee or two per head for such an investiture.

Other Doms have become Christians. Here again some are imperfectly converted and have adopted the new faith with a view to raising themselves socially. Others have received education and have fully embraced their new religion and are said to be respected by good caste people.

In Garhwal district it is alleged that Silpkars fear to embrace Christianity or to become Aryas lest they be excommunicated from their *biradari*.

The sub-divisions of Koli Doms in Tehri-Garhwal State.

Kolis divide themselves into two classes, *viz.*, (1) Gaikriya Koli, (2) Dom Koli. The Gaikriya Koli claims to be a non-Dom and as such, claims for himself a place somewhere between Khasiyas and Doms. He feels offended if he is called a Dom either by a Rajput or a Dom and will even file a defamatory suit against him. Up till now only one case seems to have gone as far as the Hazur Court, the final court of justice in Tehri-Gahrwal State, in which the punishment of fine on the accused was upheld on the ground that the word Dom was, under the circumstances of the case, definitely used with intent to insult and to provoke the complainant Koli. But a decree purporting to declare the status of the Koli as a non-Dom, has not been given so far by any court.

A Gaikriya Koli does not take food or water touched by a Lohar or any other Dom, while all Lohars and Hill Doms take food and water from the hands of Kolis. But as already mentioned the Lohar has now begun to desist from taking food or water from a Koli's hands on the ground of Lohars claiming equal status with Kolis. A case recently happened in which a Lohar, who was settled in a village in which Kolis lived, refused to take cooked food and water from a Koli's hands, which they say he used to take before. This was taken up as a challenge to the alleged superiority of Kolis over Lohars. The Koli concerned, whose food was refused, went to court and filed a defamatory suit against the Lohar. The case has assumed great importance for both the castes and the issue involved has become communal.

The word *Gai-kriya* literally means " swearing by the cow ", and the justification of the Gaikriya Koli's claim to higher status than that of other hill Doms is that he holds the same respect and reverence for the cow and the Brahman as any other high caste Hindu. The second argument is that they do not eat the flesh of pigs and domestic fowls whereas all other Hill Doms do. They say their fore-fathers never ate cow's flesh while the fore-fathers of other Hill Doms, they contend, did so.

The Gaikriya Koli observes many Hindu ceremonies—such as untouchability of a woman for 11 days after child-birth, *garhapuja* or propitiating the stars, and the keeping of horoscopes. Some Kolis have even performed *sraddha* ceremony and some have married their daughters according to the Brahman form of marriage, which is the highest form of marriage among Hindus. *Nag Raja*, the snake god, is the chief god of all Kolis whether they be Gaikriya Koli or Dom Koli. Many of them have made small temples to *Nag Raja* in their own homes and worship there daily.

In the bigger temples of *Nag Raja* only Brahmans are employed to offer *puja* or worship. They all have their Brahman *purohits* who perform ceremonies for them such as the purification of the woman 11 days after child-birth, *garha puja*, comparing horoscopes, making of horoscopes and officiating at the *sraddha* ceremony and at such marriages as are performed according to Brahman form.

The Gaikriya Koli caste is an endogamous group and is one caste, but shows signs of breaking up into exogamous sub-castes within itself.

Though as yet there are no sub-castes generally recognized by outsiders among Kolis, the following is a list of such sub-castes as Gaikriya Kolis say exist among themselves. One common feature noticeable in the majority of the stories of their origin is that their descent is traced from some high caste Hindu who lost caste through his relations with a Koli woman.

(1) *Bagyal Koli.*—Bagyal, is a sub-caste among Rajputs. A Bagyal Rajput once kept a Koli woman and so became a Koli. Bagyal Kolis trace their origin from him.

(2) *Bantwan Kolis.*—They say that *Oneswar Devata*, a form of the god *Mahadev*, made himself manifest in their family. They established a temple in his name. They consequently possessed the *banths* or shares of lands belonging to that god and were known as Banthwans, *i.e.*, share-holders of Oneswar's lands. Their descendants are still known as Banthwans.

(3) *Chokiyals.*
(4) *Kalyatas.*
(5) *Kurlatas.*
} They are named after the villages Chouki in Bangarh, and Kalda and Kurna in Bist *patti*. They all left their original villages and settled elsewhere.

(6) *Kadwans.*—Their ancestor lived in Kadduguru in Kaddukhal, a place between Kanatal and Dhanolti. *Kaddu guru* was the *pujari* of *Surkand Devi*. They are called Kadwans after the name of *Kaddu guru*.

(7) *Khonchyatas.*—*Khonch* in Garhwali means the back part of the knee. There was a Rajput Ramola,–whose *khonch* was bent to such an extent that he appeared lame. He kept a Koli woman. The descendants of this Ramola are known as Khonchyatas. Khonchyatas are found in villages Gwar, Raika and Okhal. The are strictly exogamous and call themselves Khonchyata Kolis.

(8) *Kuslwans.*—Kuslwans say that their ancestor was a Patwal Brahman who kept a Koli woman.

(9) *Masani Koli.*—The origin of this sub-caste is not from a high caste Brahman or Rajput but from a female ghost. The story runs thus. There was a Koli of village Khandal who one evening went to Tippri, a village about three miles from his home. As it was very late in the evening the villagers of Tippri detained him there for the night. At about midnight the Koli believing that the dawn was near, left Tippri and started for his village. On the way near a bridge named Khandhal ka Pul he saw a party of ghosts dancing near the Bhilanganga river. The Koli went and joined the dance and took hold of a female ghost. As morning approached all the other ghosts disappeared and the Koli then took this remaining ghost to his home and made her his wife. Masani Kolis trace their descent to these parents. They live in Khandhal village.

(10) *Nath or Jogi Kolis of Jyundasu.*—Their ancestor was a Dhamwan Rajput who was out-casted for keeping a Koli woman. He then became a Nath and so they are called Naths.

(11) *Semman Kolis.*—A Brahman woman had a liaison with a Koli. According to Hindu custom she was permanently out-casted, for a high caste woman who once gets mixed up with a person of any low caste can never be purified by any penance or *chandrayan*. Thus failing to secure re-admission to her caste she was permanently kept by her paramour. After some time the Koli died without leaving any issue. A Semwal Brahman, whose name was Harrariya, having no

wife, began to reside with this woman and gave descent to the present Semwal Kolis. They live in Kangsali village. It may be observed that this story goes a step farther than those which allege origin from some higher caste on the father's side only.

(12) *Bayalas*
(13) *Jagratyas*
(14) *Kirwals*
(15) *Manswans*
(16) *Mengwals*
} Are other sub-castes the stories of whose origin are not known.

Kolis who have intermarried with other Doms and eat the flesh of pigs and fowls are still called Dom Kolis. The majority of Dom Kolis in the State are still weavers.

II.—The Khasiyas.

Their origin.

For a brief account of past references to the Khasiyas the reader is referred to the introduction to Dr. L. D. Joshi's *Khasa Family Law* (published by the Government Press, Allahabad in 1929).

References to them are found in the *Puranas, Mahabharata* and other early literature including the *Rajtarangini* or Kalhan's famous chronicle of Kashmir written in the 12th century, but few details are mentioned about them.

It seems to be generally accepted that they invaded the country extending from Kashmir to Nepal in the long-forgotten past. The ancient name of the country now comprising the districts of Kumaun was *Khas-des* (*i.e.* the country of the Khasiyas). They subdued the Doms and reduced them to slaves. It is not known whether this took place before or after the migration of the Vedic Aryans, but it was probably before. There are a few traces of an ancient civilization in the present-day dense forests of the *tarai* at the foot of the hills.

Atkinson wrote * "as early as several centuries before the Christian era the shrine of Badari (in Garhwal) was celebrated as a seat of learning and as the abode of holy men."

Mr. Oakley † thinks that Kumaun and Garhwal were probably included in the great Kosala kingdom in the sixth or seventh century B. C..

Feristha, probably quoting a legend, tells us that the Raja of Kumaun named P'hoor (Porus) fought against the Greek King Alexander and was killed. (Greek writers said that he was only wounded).

From such evidence it seems safe to conclude that the occupation by the Khasiyas took place long before the Christian era.

The earliest ruling dynasty known to authentic history is that of the Katyuris. One of their inscriptions on stone in Bageswar temple is supposed to be 1,500 years old. Feristha tells of the defeat of the Raja of Kumaun "who inherited his country and crown from a long line of ancestors that had ruled upwards of 2,000 years", between the years 440 and 470 A.D., by Ramdeo Rathor of Kanauj.

After the decline of the Katyuris the Chand dynasty reigned for several centuries in Kumaun. The present-day Khasiyas include the descendants of this original Khasa race and the descendants of later immigrant high caste folk and the Khasas with whom they intermarried. The name Biths originally applied only to the Khasiyas but now-a-days has been extended to the more recent immigrant Brahmans and Rajputs of pure Aryan stock. The Khasiyas include those known as Khas-Brahmans and Khas-Rajputs, and those of Kumaun represent the purest Khasa blood. The Garhwal Khasiyas are more mixed, though the difference is scarcely noticeable.

The majority of Khasiyas are Khas-Rajputs and these include the original Khasiyas and also the descendents of any subsequent Rajput immigrants who intermarried with the Khasiyas.

The origin of the Khas-Brahmans is not so clear. Some think they are the descendants of mixed marriages between subsequent pure Brahman immigrants and the Khasas, but as they form nearly 90 per cent. of the total Brahmans in Kumaun this does not seem to be the only explanation, especially as Khas-Rajputs form practically the same percentage of all Rajputs in Kumaun and Garhwal. It is possible that they originated in much the same way among the Khasas as did the Brahmans among the Vedic Aryans who invaded Northern India, by becoming specialists in religious matters and learning in general and so gradually forming their separate community, which was no doubt subsequently added to by mixed marriage.

Panchayats.

The early Khasiya tribes lived in different villages or *pattis* (glens) or *garhis* (forts). The Doms were their slaves and did all menial work. Groups of villages were banded together under a tribal chief who led them in war against the neighbouring tribes. Each village community was regulated by its own village *panchayat* presided over by the *thokdar* or *padhan*‡ (in Jaunsar-Bawar of Dehra Dun district he is known as the *siana*). Some account of these *panchayats* and their methods will be found in paragraph 334, page 345 of the 1911 Report *census of the United Provinces.* Formerly each village reserved a large stone slab on which the *thokdar* used to sit in the *panchayat*. This custom has disappeared now, but the *panchayats* are still very powerful though owing to improved communications and the spread of learning their judicial authority and in fact their authority in general is decidedly on the wane.

In Tehri-Garhwal, the State has taken over some of the former functions of *panchayats*. For instance if a Bith (including Brahmans and Rajputs of pure descent and also Khas-Brahmans and Khas-Rajputs) smokes from a *hukka* which has been touched by a low caste man or takes food touched by such or has sexual intercourse with a low caste woman, he is out-casted and in such cases the State carries out the normal functions of the *panchayat*. Such a Bith can be readmitted to his caste only by undergoing a penance called *chandrayan* which is prescribed and conducted by the *dharmadhikaris,* who are appointed by the State. The usual procedure in such cases and in all other cases in which the *Shastras* enjoin purification, is that either the man himself reports his offence to the State and applies for purification or, if he omits to do so, the *padhan* of the village in which the offender lives informs the State about the offence. It is not only a social obligation upon the *padhan* or villagers but a legal obligation on them to give such information to the State.

Such applications or reports are then sent to the local Sub-Divisional Officer for inquiry. If the breach or offence is proved the whole file is sent to the *dharmadhikaris* for their opinion, which is generally based on *Yagnyanbalk-Smṛiti* and the *Manusmriti*. When the *chandrayan* ceremony has been performed according to the prescription of the *dharmadhikari* the State gives a purification certificate (*sudhi patra*) which serves as a

---

* Atkinson's *Gazetteer,* XI, 274.

† Oakley's *Holy Himalaya,* page 132.

‡ The *thokdar* appears also at one time to have been a farmer of revenue (for the upkeep of the army).

passport for the man's re-admission to his community. He does not have to give a feast to his *biradari* nor pay any fine but has to defray the costs of the purification ceremonies. Until he performs the purification ceremonies the offender remains an out-caste by order of the State.

Religion. By contact with the Doms the religion of the Khasiyas became almost purely animistic, which was not surprising in view of the inaccessible nature of the country they came to occupy. Dr. Joshi writes*—

" Fear caused by solitude in the midst of huge forests, high mountains and roaring rivers is likely to induce nature worship and belief in supernatural powers, and the conquered Doms also seem to have contributed to the religious outlook of the Khasas." He goes on to show that as a result of abandoning their orthodox religious beliefs and practices they came to be regarded as degenerate from the Brahman point of view.

Mr. Atkinson† gave a description of the various gods, goddesses, ghosts and spirits which they recognized and worshipped (or propitiated.)

" Mountaineer "‡ gives a faithful picture of the present day religious beliefs of the majority of the Khasiyas. Writing of the *pahari* in Garhwal and Tehri-Garhwal State (the remarks apply equally to Almora and parts of Naini Tal) he says their religion is a simple form of Hinduism. They speak of divinity not as such and such a god, but as the god of such and such a place.

" Almost every remarkable hill has also an individual protector, and the small lakes and ponds are considered as particularly favourite places of the deity's abode. The principal sylvan deity is the *Nag Raja*, a god supposed to clothe himself in the form of a serpent. The spirits of the departed are believed to revisit the scenes of their mortal career and to possess the power of afflicting individuals of the family of which they were once members. The great characteristic of *pahari* worship is the number of sacrifices made and the manner of making them ; sacrifice indeed is the universal and almost sole method of manifesting thanks for benefits received, or making supplication to avert calamity. To see a *pahari* family sacrificing in the forest, the sheep or goat for a victim, the pastoral appearance of the people, the fire, and the rude altar of rough stones, carry one back at once to early ages of the world. Sacrifices are made to the *depta* (god) of the village, to the divinities of particular places, to the fairies, demons and spirits of the departed."

In case of illness a goat or sheep is led round the sufferer and killed at the spot. Oracles are consulted by enquiry of the *depta* and the divinity is conjured up for the purpose. In Kumaun snake worship is not common now, but there are temples and places to show that it must have been practised extensively at one time.

A common form of sacrifice, the *athwār* ceremony to propitiate some deity or ward off the displeasure of some evil spirit, was as follows. Huge crowds gathered (including Biths) and many goats were sacrificed, but the important part was the sacrifice of a he-buffalo. The first blow was dealt by the headman of the village and the animal was then made to run the gauntlet of the crowd who were armed with *lathis* or sharp weapons, accompanied by the beat of drums, until it was beaten to death. The carcase was then taken off by the Doms to feast upon. Present-day legislation has almost extinguished this form of sacrifice.

In Garhwal the sun and moon are regarded as gods and the Great Bear and other constellations as *Rishis* The sun is considered as male and the moon as female. The sun is considered as driving in a chariot of seven horses, going down to the lower world (*patal*) in the night. The Great Bear is known as *khat khatula* (a cot) and a few groups of constellations are known as *gurmuli*. A galaxy is called *gorgat* or *gorginda* (cattle path). Markings on the face of the moon are considered as marks of leprosy. The story about this is that the moon being proud of its beauty, insulted the sun which cursed it and so leprosy marks appeared on its face.

The common belief is that the whole earth rests on the head of a snake, known as *Sheshnag* and whenever it shakes its head there is an earthquake. As regards the cause of eclipses the legend is that the sun and moon had once to borrow money from an untoucheable (*chandal*), but the interest swelled to such an amount that it could not be paid. The *chandal* worries them sometimes and throws a skin on their face. Owing to this belief people generally bathe when an eclipse disappears. As regards the rainbow, the belief is that it is the bow of the god *Indra* and when one end of it is seen on the ridge of a mountain and the other on a river bed the belief is that there will be normal rainfall, when both the ends are seen on a river bed there will be continuous and heavy rainfall, and when both the ends are seen on the ridge of a mountain there will be a drought. It is not considered as a bridge by which the souls of the dead reach the sky.

There is universal belief in the transmigration of souls. Each soul has to pass through 84 lakhs of forms including animal and insect. Messengers of *Yama* take the souls before the *Dharamraj*, who keeps a record of all good and evil actions performed in this world and gives a judgment.

Among Pabela Khasiyas there is custom of making near a public thoroughfare a *chabutra* (terraced platform) on which is placed a single upright stone on which the name, parentage, residence and age of the deceased are engraved. This serves as a monument and is used by travellers as a place of rest.

Stone and wood are used for building houses. The only restriction in the ease of wood is that oak, cactus, and *khina* wood are considered inauspicious for dwelling houses.

Formerly the Doms were not allowed to wear velvet, silk or other costly dresses nor to build *pakka* houses. But such *tabus* do not exist now. The women folk of the Pabelas wear a particular kind of dress known as *tyankha* made of hemp or wool.

But increasing contact with more advanced Hinduism and the gradual spread of education is slowly affecting the religious beliefs of the Khasiyas and they are slowly returning to more orthodox beliefs and ceremonies.

The name Khasiya is considered derogatory and Khasiyas now claim to be either Rajput or Brahman pure and simple. As far back as 1901 Mr. Burn (now Sir Richard Burn) noted that the Khasiyas were beginning to put on the sacred thread and were claiming connexion with the Brahmans and Rajputs of the plains in order to better their social status. This movement has now spread very considerably especially in Naini Tal and Almora, where we have already seen that even the Silpkars are affected.

The Khasiyas are freely assuming Brahman and Rajput surnames. Their social position has much improved since the War when many rendered meritorious service. The military exploits of the Khasas are enshrined in the records of the 39th Royal Garhwal Rifles. Wherever they have been tried they have proved themselves brave men and in every other quality of a soldier may challenge any portion of the Indian army,

* Dr. L. D. Joshi *Khasa Family Law*, Introduction, page 24.

† Atkinson XI, Chapter IX.

‡ Mountaineer ", *A Summer Ramble in the Himalayas*, pages 187-9.

for "each of these simple mountaineers has hidden away within his inner consciousness that little spark, perhaps dulled by disuse or oppression, which represents the fiercely burning flame of military ardour that burned in the breast of some old ancestor."—*Historical Records of the 39th Royal Garhwal Rifles*, 1923, page 8.

Marriage customs of Khasiyas.

The sub-division of both Khas-Brahmans and Khas-Rajputs are legion, usually being named after some place of former residence or some ancestor. The only rule seems to be that no man may marry in his own *gotra*. The present day sub-castes are neither endogamous nor exogamous. Mr. Atkinson* gives a list of 250 septs of Khas-Brahmans. A list of no less than 1,025 sub-castes of Rajputs (mostly Khas) was sent me from Tehri-Garhwal State†.

Among the Khasiyas marriage has no religious significance. It is merely an institution to regulate sexual relationship and an arrangement for bringing up children. Marriage among the Khasiyas is a simple affair—a mere question of purchase and sale of the girl. Bride-price is invariably taken and no religious ceremonies are essential. Some-times *Ganesh puja* is performed when the bride is taken to the house of the bridegroom.

Among the Pabelas there is a custom of making some payment known as *mamadam* to the maternal uncle of the bride. The presence of the bridegroom is not essential. When the husband is unavoidably absen tthe bride is formally married to a pitcher of water as representing him. This is called *kumbh biyah*. An image of a god may be substituted for the pitcher of water and then the name is *pratima biyah*, or she may be married to an *ak* tree in *arak biyah*.

Levirate.

It is reported from Garhwal that there are two practices of this nature. In the first the widow (even if not childless) continues to live in her deceased husband's house and her brother-in-law goes and visits her there with her consent and that of the other reversioner. The second form is the common practice of taking to wife the widow of a deceased brother. The widow in this case leaves her own house and comes to the house of the brother-in-law as his permanent wife. The children of such a union are considered legitimate. This custom is confined to the inferior sub-castes of Brahmans, Rajputs and Khasiyas.

Ghar-baitha.

The practice of a man going to live with a widow whom he marries is also found among the Khasiyas. The man is known as a *kathela* or *takwa*.

Ghar-jawain.

Succesion among the Khasas is strictly agnatic. Mr. Pauw notes "It is the custom for a man who has no son to marry his daughter to a son-in-law who agrees to live in his house and who is known thereafter as the *gharjawain*. In such a case the daughter takes her father's inheritance but should she go into her husband's house the inheritance usually descends to the nearest male heirs of the deceased. Even in the case of a *gharjawain* the relatives frequently make a strong fight for the property, especially if the marriage has been arranged by the widow after the death of her husband. In such case it is not uncommon for the widow to go through the form of selling the land to the *gharjawain* on the pretence that the sale-proceeds are required to repay him the cost incurred in settling her husband's debts." Sometimes no marriage ceremony is performed, but the essential condition is that the son-in-law must live in the house of his father-in-law. The *gharjawain* institution is analogous to that of an "appointed daughter" in early Hindu law. Sometimes a deed of gift is executed in favour of the daughter and *gharjawain*, but it is not an essential condition. A *gharjawain* does not lose rights in his paternal estate. If a son be subsequently born to the father-in-law, the son and the *gharjawain* share the property equally.

Adoption.

Adoption is against the Khasiya instinct and is not very frequent, though it is now obtaining a footing. An adoption among the Khasiyas has more a secular purpose than a religious significance, no religious ceremonies of adoption are observed. The boy is simply brought to live with the adoptive father. He may be married or unmarried.

A sonless male owner can appoint an heir to his estate. A widow can appoint an heir with the consent of the reversioners. The large majority of successions among the Khasiyas are of non-agnates. Adoption among Khasiyas is really a simple appointment of an heir, who will help a man in his old age, look to his cultivation and after the appointer's death perform his funeral ceremonies and pay up his debts, if any. As a return for services rendered, the adopted son gets the inheritance.

Jhatela.

If a man marries a divorced woman or a widow and she brings with her a son by her former husband such a son is called *jhatela*. Mr. Atkinson notes that the "children by a first marriage who follow the mother to her second husband's house lose their paternal inheritance but are entitled to succeed to their step-father's property equally with their stepbrothers, his children of the second marriage". Backward Khasiyas would regard a *jhatela* succession as a matter of course, while more advanced Khasiyas wish to be rid of antiquated practices and explain equal inheritance as a concession rather than a right.

Sautiya bant.

The custom of *sautiya bant, i.e.*, division *per stirpes*, was originally connected with the Khasiya law of inheritance, but is now disregarded by courts. All sons get an equal share.

Jethon.

The custom of giving a bigger portion to the eldest son when the family property is divided was fairly widespread among the Khasiyas, but is becoming obsolete now. The customary right of *jethon* is not enforceable in law.

A daughter's rights.

A daughter is not considered as an heir to her father. Formerly the courts recognized the right of a daughter to succeed her father when such a custom was alleged, but now daughters are excluded from inheritance and so are their descendants. A daughter takes the estate only when her husband is accepted as a *gharjawain* or when a special deed of gift is executed by the last male owner.

Various influences on the Khasiyas.

The Brahmans and Rajputs brought to *Khas-des* by the Katyuri and Chand Rajas had considerable influence on the religious and social outlook of the Khasiyas, but more modern contacts have had far greater effects. During the early part of the nineteenth century after the British occupation of the hill districts, a large number of tea estates and colonies were formed by the East India Company and other Europeans in Kumaun for working which Doms and Khasiyas were recruited on a large scale. Some mines were also worked, *e.g.*, the Dhanpur gold mine, for which also a large number of labourers was recruited. The labourers had to live away from their homes and being cut off from their tribal associations for a considerable time imbibed new ideas. Since the British occupation communications have considerably improved. The great improvement of the pilgrim routes to the sacred shrines of Kedarnath, Badrinath, Gangotri, and Jamnotri now attract great numbers of pilgrims from the plains, social contact with whom has affected the older social organizations. Within the district itself the peoples of the different and formerly inaccessible parts have been brought closer together owing to improved communications, with the result that the old tribal, social and linguistic differences are disappearing. It is also true that owing to the improvements in communications narcotics such as *charas* are imported on a large scale; while cholera and other epidemics and crime are also increasing.

* *Gazetteer*, Volume XII, pages 421—428.

† The list is given at the end of Appendix C to Chapter XII *of the Census Report on the United Provinces*, 1931.

Formerly higher education in the hills was confined to Brahmans. Hence primitive tribes were not much influenced by Brahmanical civilization and adhered to their own tribal customs. But modern universal education is levelling down society, with the result that the people are giving up their family or tribal vocations and entering service. This often makes them unfit for and discontented with their social environments. The people are also borrowing foreign customs in the matter of clothes, houses, and drink with the result that their standard of living has considerably risen, while their income has not kept pace with it. This is more particularly noticeable among the Garhwali soldiers who went to Europe during the Great War. Their outlook on life has changed and they find themselves out of their element in their old homes and villages. They look down upon their neighbours and have no definite purpose in life.

An increase in the taking of intoxicants is thought by some to have contributed to an increase in disease, especially consumption. This disease is said to have been rare in ancient times. My informant remembers having heard from old people in his childhood that in olden days if a person suffered from consumption he was taken to a forest and made to walk over a pit covered with slender branches and leaves. The patient fell into the pit and was burned there. This shows how dreaded that disease was then.

Legislative and administrative measures have also greatly interfered with and modified primitive social customs, such as the sale of Doms as slaves, the customs of offering human sacrifices to deities, the custom of *beda* (or *bedwart*) or rope-riding, etc.

Christian and Arya Samaj proselytizing has also had its effects, for those who have come under such influences leave their folklore, music, games and festivals and often leave their former professions.

The modern uplift movement has resulted in more and more Khasiyas donning the sacred thread and styling themselves Bhandari, Negi, Bist, Rautela, etc. Under the old Hindu Rajas there was little possibility of a Khasiya rising to be a Brahman or Rajput. The new immigrants from the plains saw to that. But in modern times it is by no means uncommon to find that by acquiring education and more especially wealth a man manages to pass from Khas-Brahman to Brahman or from Khas-Rajput to Rajput. Some of the more orthodox resent such transformations but they are occurring with increasing frequency nevertheless. It seems to be a fact that when the later more cultured and orthodox Brahmans came to Kumaun in the time of the Chand Rajas they proceeded to proselytize the population of Khasiyas to a considerable extent, and gave some the sacred thread. The idea was to bring all such men within the pale of the caste system and Hindu religion as far as possible. Some of the later immigrants were so strict that they would not allow fuel to be taken into their kitchens by the low castes without its having been washed, and they would never take water from the hands of those who did not wear the sacred thread. Whether the putting on of the sacred thread can make a person a " twice-born " is a question that will be answered differently according to the outlook of the person questioned. But it is certain that the *sanskar* purification does not end there, it carries with it certain duties and obligations. The whole course of conduct and life of a " twice-born " is supposed to be strict and orthodox in every way. Study of the *Vedas*, the performance of *yagnas* or sacrifices and rituals, the imparting of instruction to others, piety and the acceptance of no gratifications were imperative. An interesting catalogue of the qualifications of the Brahmans who were to be invited to the *yagna* performed by Raja Dasrath with a view to securing male offspring is given in the *Ramayan* of Valmiki. It may, however, be argued that many Brahmans of today have fallen from such an ideal and yet are still regarded as " twice-born ".

Whatever be the point of view taken it is, however, certain that this movement to adopt the sacred thread is a healthy sign of a desire for social uplift which is all to the good.

III.—The Brahmans and Rajputs.

The third class consists of the descendants of the later Brahman and Rajput immigrants from the plains after the Aryan invasion of Northern India. Their ancestors were mostly brought to this part of the land by the Rajas of the Katyuri and Chand dynasties, by whom they were employed as preceptors or soldiers They were given villages for their service. The descendants of many of these old families in Almora still have in their possession copper plates on which the fact of the original grant was engraved. Such grants were confirmed by the Nepalese Government in the time of the Gurkhas domination of Kumaun and again by the British Government since. *Some of these families know whence their ancestors originally migrated.* The *leading* families of Joshis in Almora say they came from Jhusi (Allahabad district). Pants say they came from Maharashtra, Pandes of the Gautam *gotra* from Kot Kangra in the Punjab and Pandes of the Bharadwaj *gotra* from Kanauj (Farrukhabad district), and Tewaris from Gujarat. The Rautelas claim to be descendants of the Chandrabansi Rajas of Kumaun. Padyars claim solar descent. Gusain (which means master) represents a descendant of some family of feudal overlords. Negis were military officials : the word also signifies a leader. Rawat in common parlance means a big man. The Rawats were also military officials. One account says their ancestor Rawat was a former king of Donakote in Kali Kumaun. **Origin.**

The sub-divisions of both Brahmans and Rajputs in Kumaun are innumerable. Of the Rajput clans the more inportant, who are incidentally now classed as *sayanas*, are the Bangaris, Bists, Dangwals, Kathyats, Manrals, Padyars, Rajbars, Rautelas and Rawats. These have all been very powerful families in the past and even at present many of them enjoy a privileged position in society. **Sub-castes of Brahmans and Rajputs.**

Pandit Ganga Datt Upreti accepted 26 sub-castes as near and real kinsmen of Kashttriya or reigning Rajas and hence called *Jankari* or real Rajputs.

I quote below from a note by Pandit Uma Datt Dangwal, B.A., LL.B., Sub-Divisional Officer in the Tehri-Garhwal State. **Brahmans in the Tehri-Garhwal State.**

" There are about 380 sub-castes of Brahmans in the Tehri Garhwal State, most of whom derive their names from the villages in Garhwal in which their progenitors originally settled. Some are named after their forefathers.

Broadly, the Brahmans of Tehri-Garhwal are divided into two classes, *viz.*—

(1) Brahmans of pure descent, who have pure Aryan blood in them, and

(2) Brahmans who are descendants of mixed marriages between Brahmans and Khasiyas and are sometimes called Khas-Brahmans.

The first group is again divided into two sub-sections, *viz.*—

(*a*) *Sarolas*, and

(*b*) Non-*Sarolas*.

I have purposely avoided using the most common epithets of *Gangari* and *Nanagotri* in the above-mentioned classification for, besides their having more than one implication in different ways, they have become so much the subject of bitter controversy that it is better to avoid them when the purpose of ethnology can as well be served without their use. As a matter of fact I received reports from several persons complaining against their being entered as *Gangaris* or *Nanagotris* in the census records.

The various meanings that are attached to these disputed words will be given later.

Sarola.

Sara is a Hindi word which means the top or peak of a hill. *Sara ka Sarola, gadka Gangari* is a very common saying in Garhwal, which is advanced wherever the origins of the words *Sarola* and *Gangari* are considered. The saying means, that those who lived at the top were called *Sarolas* and those who lived at the *gad, i.e.*, near the river were called *Gangaris*. So far as the origin of the *Sarola* community is concerned part of the saying seems to be based on the fact that the primary twelve clans of *Sarolas* derive their names from the twelve villages all of which are found in Chandpur, the historical residence of Raja Kanakpal,* the founder of the dynasty of the rulers of Tehri Raj. Like many other social customs or distinctions that trace their origin from the advent of Raja Kanakpal the *Sarola* community also dates its origin from that time. It is said that the clan of Nautiyals was one of those which came to Garhwal with the Raja. The first twelve sub-castes of *Sarolas* above referred to are :—

(1) Nautiyal,
(2) Dimri,
(3) Khanduri,
(4) Semalti,
(5) Maithani,
(6) Raturi,
(7) Thapliyal,
(8) Semwal,
(9) Gairola,
(10) Chamoli,
(11) Hatwal, and
(12) Lakhera ;

which derive their names from the villages of Nauti, Dimmar, Khandura, Senalta, Maithana, Ratura, Thapali, Sema, Gairola, Chamola, Hatwalgaon, and Lakherigaon respectively.

The Brahmans of these villages, owing to their being close to the capital somehow or other exerted more influence both in the court and in the palace than any other community, and so by virtue of their continued enjoyment of certain privileges came to be regarded as a distinct community in course of time. Since the time of Raja Kanakpal, the Nautiyals and Khanduris of village Raturi in British Garhwal have always been the *Raj gurus* (religious preceptors) of the rulers of Garhwal and, until the expulsion of the Gurkhas in 1815, the Khanduris were also the hereditary *kanungos* of Garhwal (since then the office has undergone several changes). But final shape and consolidation was given to this community by Raja Ajaipal, who, in order to remove the commensal difficulties of his standing army, which included numerous sub-castes, ordered the army to take food from a common mess if it was cooked by a Brahman of the community to which the Raja's cooks belonged.

This ordinance gave the final shape to the *Sarola* community as we find it to-day and this is the only difference between the *Sarola* and non-*Sarola* Brahman. As a group the *Sarola* community is an endogamous group and its sub-clans are exogamous. But the whole group is so small and offers so many difficulties over marriage that some of the exogamous groups have split up into still smaller groups in order to give them a wider choice of brides and bride-grooms. For instance the Nautiyal sub-caste is again divided into six other sub-castes, *viz.*, Dhangan, Palyal, Manjkhola, Gajaldi, Chandpuri, and Bousoli all of which call themselves Nautiyal but inter-marry among themselves. The origin of these smaller sub-castes, seems to be that their progenitors all belonged to the same parental stock of Nautiyals, but settled in different villages after which they became called. As has been said above there were only twelve original sub-castes of *Sarolas* but now there exists a far greater number, for instance, Bijalwans, Dyundis, Kotiyals, Dobhals and so on. How and when these later clans were added to the primary stock is not definitely known except in the case of Dobhals, but it is most probable that the reason which led to the splitting of Nautiyals also led to the formation of these later sub-divisions.

There is only one family of Dobhal *Sarolas* in the whole of Garhwal and that family is in the State. This is the latest addition to the *Sarola* group which took place as follows. There was a Dobhal Brahman, who as such belonged to the Chauthoki class of the non-*Sarola* group. He had no issue and so adopted a *Sarola* boy who belonged to the Chamoli sub-caste, because there is nothing to prevent a non-*Sarola* from adopting a *Sarola* boy. The boy adopted the sub-caste of his adoptive father but retained his *Sarola* status.

The status of a *Sarola* is not affected by his marriage even to a Khas-Brahman girl, nor by being adopted by a person of any other Brahman caste, so long as he observes the caste rules of food.

The *Sarolas* have always found it difficult to procure wives among themselves and this has lead to a very common custom among them of inter-marrying with non-*sarolas*, and in some cases they also keep Khasiya women as concubines. The husbands, as already observed can preserve their *Sarola* distinction, but the offspring born of such mixed marriages are not entitled to the designation of their fathers, and are called *Gangaris*.

The inevitable result of this custom is that the number of *Sarolas* is continually decreasing. In the family of Lakheras there are only two *Sarolas* in the whole State. There are only 11 Hatwal *Sarolas*, 12 Raturi *Sarolas*, 2 Thapilyal *Sarolas* and so on in the State. The total number of *Sarolas* at present is 735 (401 males and 334 females).

Gangari.

We have to go back to the same saying, *Sara ka Sarola, gad ka Gangari* to find the meaning of the word *Gagari*. Literally the word means an inhabitant of *gangari, i.e.*, of the regions lying on the bank of the Ganges. As these regions by the side of the Ganges are generally low in the valleys and much warmer, the word came to mean any inhabitant of a low-lying valley or of a warm place. It is in this literal sense that the word is still used in Rawain and Jaunpur parganas and in Taknaur. Jads of Taknaur Nelang call all people living below Harsil *Gangaris* : the people of Rawain and Jaunpur call all people living on the eastern side of the State *Gangaris* whether they be Brahmans or Rajputs or even Doms. People of Fatehparbat and Panchganin call even the inhabitants of lower Rawain *Gangaris*, for the latter region is comparatively much warmer than the former on account of its being on the bank of the Jumna. But the word when used for Brahmans only as compared with *Sarolas* loses its original meaning just as the word *Sarola* no more means an inhabitant of the top or peak of a hill. In its latter sense the word *Gangari* only serves as a term to contrast all other Brahmans from the *Sarolas*. Another theory is that this word *Gangari* was invented by the *Sarolas*. Just as a Jad of Nelang calls any man who lives below Harsil a *Gangari* no matter whether he be a Brahman or a Rajput or even a Dom so the *Sarola* living on the top of Chandpur peak contemptuously called all others living elsewhere on the banks of the Ganges *Gangaris*, and if a *Sarola* married or kept a woman of any other caste than those at the top, the offspring were given the name *Gangari*. It is on this ground that several Brahmans of Tehri based their objection against the application of the term *Gangari* to them. Thus it will be seen that the word *Gangari* is ambiguous.

* According to the State archives he ascended the throne 5 *Baisakh, Sambat* 745, *i.e.*, April, A. D. 688.

Nanagotri.

The use of the word *Nanagotri* is also not free from difficulties for like the word *Gangari* it also is given two interpretations differing widely from each other. *Nana* in Hindi means mother's father and *Nanagotri* means one who traces his descent through his mother or through his mother's family. It may be that the word is a remnant of the promiscuous days before Sewetketu, son of Uddalak, introduced the institution of marriage.

Another interpretation is that the word *Nana* in Sanskrit means 'many' and a *Nanagotri* is one whose *gotra* is traced to one of the thousand *Rishis* who were born after the first ten *Rishis* were born of Brahma. If the latter interpretation is correct it is difficult to see why *Sarolas* and other Brahmans of the first rank are not called *Nanagotris* when their *gotras* descended from Bharadwaj, Shounak, Kasyap and Koundiya who were among the thousand *Rishis* born later.

Whatever the real meaning, the fact appears to be that many Khas-Brahmans are also called *Nanagotris*, and a *Nanagotri* Brahman is generally considered much inferior to a *Sarola* or a *Gangari* Brahman ".

Again I quote from Mr. Dangwal's note :—

Rajputs in the Tehri-Garhwal State.

" The Rajputs of Tehri-Garhwal may be divided into three classes, *viz.*,—(1) Thakurs, (2) Rajputs higher than Khas-Rajputs, and (3) Khas-Rajputs.

Thakurs are the kinsmen of the Tehri Raj family and are among the descendants of the dynasty of Raja Kanakpal.

Rajputs of the higher order include those who claim descent from the petty chiefs who ruled in Garhwal before they were brought under the consolidated rule of Raja Ajaipal and his descendants, those who claim to have descended from the ruling family of the Katyuris of Kumaun, and those who claim to have come along with Raja Kanakpal as his courtiers, etc.

Khas-Rajputs, who form the majority of Garhwali Rajputs, are said to be either mixtures of the higher Rajputs and Khasiyas or are pure Khasiyas who have come to be known as Rajputs. The old saying *Kedare Khas Mandale* indicates that Kedarkund, which is another name for Garhwal, was a stronghold of the Khasiyas before Brahmans and better class Rajputs immigrated into Garhwal. The name Khasiya has now become a derogatory term and is resented by all Khas-Rajputs. *Khas kahe to Khas pare larne ko ho jaya, ek bar Negi kahe lot pot ho jaya* is a very significant saying which is commonly used. It not only explains how a Khasiya grows offended at being called a Khaisya but also hints that the sub-caste of Negi has become an all embracing sub-caste in which Khasiyas usually try to gain admission. The saying means " Call a man a Khasiya and he will get angry and will quarrel, call him Negi and he will become exceedingly happy and glad". (*Lot pot ho jana* literally means to laugh to such an extent that one falls down.)

Now-a-days the distinction between a real Rajput and a Khasiya is fast decreasing and the word Khasiya is disappearing from common use. The War, in which many Khasiyas served, is largely responsible for this ".

How numerous are the Rajput castes, especially among Khas-Rajputs, is seen from the fact that at the recent census no less than 1,025 sub-castes were returned from the 2,918 villages of the Tehri-Garhwal State.

Religion.

The religion of the higher Brahmans and Rajputs of the hills has, to some extent, been affected by contact with the animistic beliefs of the Khasiyas and Doms. But modern tendencies are rapidly purifying it of these accretions, though the attitude of the high castes towards Khasiyas and Doms is slowly relaxing.

IV.—Miscellaneous.

Besides the above three major communities there are miscellaneous immigrants of other castes and races from the plains and elsewhere.

Of these mention may be made of the Vaishyas. Many of these are the descendants of families who were attracted to *Khas-des* when the Katyuri and Chand dynasties were in power. They are much sub-divided as would be expected from the nature of their arrival. The names of their sub-divisions are often derived from the places in which they first settled, *e.g.*, the Gangolas of Gangoli, Kumayans of Kali Kumaun. The most important of their sub-castes are Gangola, Jagati, Kawa, Kholbhitiya, Kumayan, Okhaliya, Salamgahiya, Syal and Tantri.

Then there are the descendants of immigrants from Tibet known as Bhotiyas who are now claiming to be Rajputs.

3. (a) Untouchability as observed by the Caste Hindus in their own families.

By R. Y. Chitnis.

1. Now that the question of untouchability amongst the Hindus has come to the forefront, if one were to take a survey of all the Hindu communities and observe their daily practices carefully he will find that untouchability is not confined to the Depressed Classes alone.

2. The religious preceptors amongst the Hindus have framed certain rules of conduct and enjoined their strict performance by the caste Hindus in their daily routine. As a result of these religious injunctions it will be seen that untouchability, to a certain extent, is observed by the caste Hindus in their own households with respect to their mutual behaviour with each other.

3. The religious injunctions relating to untouchability are based, it seems, on certain hygienic principles which are enforced in practice in the name of religion.* Thus both Hygiene and Religion are, as it were, mixed up together and are inseparable from each other.

4. In order to be able to ascertain clearly the incidence and extent of untouchability as observed by the caste Hindus, it is desirable to grasp the exact meaning of the following terms, which are of frequent occurrence in the writings of Hindu religious preceptors and which indicate the composition of a Hindu family.

5. *Sapindas* or blood relations are of two sorts :—(1) *Gotraj Sapindas* who belong to the same Gotra or family as the deceased. They are all Agnates connected with the deceased by an unbroken line of male descent, and (2) *Bhinna Gotra Sapindas* who belong to a different Gotra or family from the deceased. They are all cognates, that is persons related to the deceased through a female and they are called *Bandhus.*

6. Under Gotraj Sapindas come :—(*a*) *Sapindas* proper. They include blood relations to the 7th degree only reckoned from and inclusive of the deceased and (*b*) *Samánodakás.* They are those male relations of a Hindu to whom he offers oblations of water while performing the Shradha ceremony and include all his Agnates from the 8th to the 14th degree. Those coming after the 14th degree up to the 21st one are simply classed as *Sagotrás.*

7. Bhinna Gotra Sapindas or *Bandhus*, as they are called, comprise three groups of persons—(1) *Atma-Bandhus,* (2) *Pitri Bandhus* and (3) *Matri Bandhus.* Persons designated as *Atma-Bandhus* include :—(1) father's sister's son, (2) mother's sister's son and (3) mother's brother's son. In the same way *Pitri Bandhus* and *Matri Bandhus* include the same aforesaid relations of one's father and mother respectively.

8. The composition of a Hindu family being known it is not difficult to understand the incidence and extent of untouchability to be observed by different groups of persons.

9. On the occasion of a birth or a death in a Hindu family the members composing it are required to observe untouchability in a prescribed manner. The period prescribed to be observed by different members of the family varies according to their propinquity. Generally speaking *Sapindas* are to observe untouchability for full *ten days* from the date of birth or death ; while the *Samánodakás* are to observe it for *three days* only. *Sagotrás* may observe it for a *single night* or they are relieved from its observance by a purification bath.

10. There is also a difference in the degree of untouchability according to its incidence either as attached to a birth or to a death. In the former case *i.e.,* in the case of *Jananáshauch* untouchability is not observed in all its rigour. Sapindas and others can have, then, free intercourse with each other but they are to abstain, during the period prescribed, from performing their daily worship and such other acts of a religious nature. *Jananáshauch* is thus distinguishable from *Mritáshauch* during which period Sapindas and others are both untouchables and ineligible to perform their daily practices of a religious character.

11. In case of a birth in a Hindu family the burden of observing untouchability with all its implications falls solely and wholly to the share of the mother. If an abortion takes place during the 5th or 6th month of her pregnanacy she has to observe it for as many days as the number of months she may have carried. But the father and other Sapindas have to observe *Jananáshauch* for *three days* only. Delivery from and after the 7th month necessitates the observance of Jananashauch, by mother, father and other Sapindas to the 7th degree, for full *ten days.*

---

* The underlying principle is clearly tabu, but tabu itself can no doubt be described as often due to a desire to escape infection and therefore perhaps as hygienic even when based on completely erroneous principles.

J. H. H.

12. The general rule as to the observance of *Mritáshauch* is given above in paragraph 9. The Mritashauch to be observed by particular members of a Hindu family is given below in a tabular form :—

Mritáshauch to be observed.

For whose sake.	By whom.	Period for which and circumstances varying the same.
1. Father and mother	Son who may or may not have undergone thread ceremony.	10 days from the date of death or from the date on which the death is known.
	Daughter (unmarried) ..	Ditto.
	Daughter (married)	3 days (if the death is known within first 10 days).
	Ditto	1½ days (if the death is known after the first 10 days).
2. Son (who may have undergone thread ceremony.)	Father and mother	10 days.
Ditto ..	Ditto	3 days (if the death is known after the first 10 days).
Son (who may not have undergone thread ceremony).	Ditto	3 days.
3. Daughter (unmarried) ..	Father and mother	1 day (if not more than 6 months old).
	Ditto	3 days (if more than 6 months old till marriage.)
Daughter (married)	Ditto	3 days (if the death occurs either at her parents' or at her husband's).
	Ditto	1½ (if death occurs at a distant place).
4. Brother (who has undergone thread ceremony).	Sister (married)	3 days (if death takes place at his sister's).
	Ditto	1½ days (if death takes place elsewhere in the same village).
	Ditto	1 day (if death takes place at a distant village).
5. Sister (married)	Brother (who has undergone thread ceremony).	3 days (if death takes place at her brother's).
	Ditto ..	1½ days (if elsewhere in the same village).
	Ditto ..	1 day (if at a distant village).
6. Husband	Wife	10 days (even if the death is known after the first 10 days).
7. Wife	Husband	Ditto.
8. Father-in-law and mother-in-law	Son-in-law	3 days (if the death takes place at the residence of the son-in-law).
	Ditto	1½ days (if death takes place at some other place).
	Ditto	1 day (if death takes place at a distant village).
9. Son-in-law	Father-in-law and mother-in-law	3 days (if the death takes place at the residence of the father-in-law).
10. Maternal uncle	Sister's son and daughter ..	3 days (if the death takes place at the sister's son's house).
	Ditto ..	3 days (if sister's son was under his maternal uncle's obligations).
	Ditto ..	1 day (if death occurs at a distant village).
11. Maternal Grand-father ..	Grand-son or grand-daughter ..	3 days (in the same village).
	Ditto ..	1½ days (if death occurs at a distant village).
12. Maternal Grand-mother ..	Ditto ..	1½ days.
13. Maternal aunt	Sister's son and daughter ..	3 days (if the maternal aunt dies at their own residence).
	Ditto ..	1½ days (if death takes place elsewhere).
14. Paternal aunt	Brother's son and daughter ..	3 days (if death takes place at the brother's son's house).
	Ditto ..	1½ days (if death takes place elsewhere).

3. (b) The custom amongst the Hindus of Bombay of initiating their children as Fakirs during the Moharum festival.

By R. Y. Chitnis.

Origin of the custom.

The *Taboots* or *Tazias*, which are installed everywhere at the beginning of the Muslim celebration of the Moharum each year, are the symbolical representations of Hasan and Hussain, the grandsons of the Prophet. The Hindus, by their close association with their Muslim neighbours, began, in course of time, to look upon them as worthy of veneration and used to mix up freely with the Muslims in celebrating the annual Moharum festival. The issueless amongst them even went so far as to take a vow of installing *Taboots* in their own house and at their cost and also of initiating their children as Fakirs, if by the grace of these prophets they are favoured with progeny. Habit being a second nature, the custom observed by their ancestors in the bygone days has become prevalent and is still followed by the members of many a caste amongst the Hindus especially amongst the agricultural and artisan classes.

Initiation ceremony and its essentials.

Whenever anybody desires to initiate his child as a Fakir he is required to give the child a fresh bath and after covering it over with new garments suitable to the occasion to take the child to anyone of the *Taboots* installed in the neighbourhood of his residence on or after the 5th day of Moharum. Before he proceeds there he must take with him some coloured yarn to be worn over the new garment by the child as a garland on the breast and as wristlets on the wrists. The yarn is coloured in significant colours to indicate the fact that the two brothers—Hasan and Hussain—had to take up the cudgels on behalf of their subjects on the eve of their marriage—an auspicious day in their life but which, in the end, proved fatal to them. A Mohammedan priest who officiates is present at the Taboot installation at all times of the day. Upon the production of the child and on the wish of getting it initiated as Fakir being duly expressed and on the production of the necessary materials, *e.g.*, yarn, incense and other articles of worship the priest burns some incense before the *Taboot* and fumigates the yarn over it and by muttering some prayers invokes the Prophet's protection for the child. Then the child is asked to wear the yarn, as aforesaid, as a blessing from the Prophet and to distribute some alms to the poor.

Observances during the initiation period.

As an humble believer in the spiritual powers of the Prophet the child is required to beg alms from door to door from the time of his initiation till the 9th day of Moharum which is looked upon as the day of the massacre. Rice and pulse mixed together is usually given as alms to this newly initiated Fakir whenever he goes abegging. With whatever cash received as alms, he is to purchase flour, ghee and *gul* or raw sugar and prepare sweet balls out of the same. All the alms collected—whether raw grain or cooked food—after partaking of the same is meant to be distributed in charity and so on the 9th day of Moharum before midnight it is handed over to the officiating priest at the Taboot installation for such distribution amongst the poor and destitute Fakirs. The whole collection at each Taboot installation is so distributed generally on the 3rd day after the immersion ceremony. On the 10th day of Moharum and before the immersion ceremony takes place the yarn worn by the initiated child is thrown over the Taboots. After the yarn is thrown over the Taboots the child has to bathe again and after this bath it is supposed to be free from pollution.

There is a great scarcity of water in the sacred places of the Muslims and this fact accounts for the reason why the child is not allowed to bathe during its initiation period. By undergoing this initiation ceremony the child is not supposed to have become a convert to Islam but by humble supplication it simply becomes a believer in the spiritual powers of the Prophet and while doing so it remains all along in the pale of Hinduism.

4. (i) Note on Moghias.

By H. G. Waterfield, Assistant to the Agent to the Governor General in Central India, Criminal Branch.

The generic name of the tribe, commonly spoken of now as the Moghias, is not Moghia but Baori and the tribe, with its name, according to its own traditional history, was brought in to existence in the following manner.

About 360 years ago, probably in the time of the Emperor Akbar, a Rajput Chief of Gujerat had to send a princess of his house to Delhi to enter the harem of the Emperor. Naturally she was escorted by a large armed force which consisted of Rajput Thakurs, servants of her father's Raj and in her company were many servants male and female of all conditions and castes. At one halting place the camp was situated round a large stone well (*baoli* or *baori*) into which, owing to some insult offered her or because of her shame at the thought of entering the harem, the Princess threw herself and was drowned. This well is variously stated to have been in Alwar or Jodhpur territory. The escort, with its convoy, now dared neither to go forward to Delhi nor to return to Gujerat and halted where they were until all their food supplies and funds were exhausted. By this time their encampment had become a permanent village and they took to looting travellers and committing dacoities and robberies all round about them. The Rajputs having taken to wife the various servant girls and female attendants of the late Princess raised families which of course were outcasted by other Rajput but which, amongst themselves, kept up the caste distinctions of their fathers and so have handed down to their descendents the same caste names and distinctions as exist among real Rajputs; the camp followers married such women of the surrounding country as they could obtain and one and all became known as the Baoliwalla or Baoli and finally Baori tribe of robbers and dacoits.*

As last the community grew too large for maintanence in one place and their leaders decided to break up into parties and go in various directions. One party made for Delhi near which they settled and gained the title of Delhiwal Baori amongst themselves and that of Badhuk amongst the people of the country. This name is said to have been derived from '*Bad Karm*', '*Bad Kar*' and then Badhuk which means executioner or murderer from the Sanskrit *Badh* or *Wadh* to kill and so murder.

Here again they had to take lower caste women of the country as wives with the consequence that their children fell in caste. Owing to increase in numbers parties had again to emigrate and did so, principally towards Oudh where eventually they formed large settlements in the 'tarai' and finally became so powerful that they committed very heavy dacoities on treasure and even attacked treasuries and went down quite close to Calcutta on their expeditions so that eventually military operations had to be undertaken against them in the early forties when their strongholds in the tarai were destroyed and themselves scattered. One section of the refugees appears to be that now known as Baoris who are settled at Muzaffernagar and Gorakhpur in the United Provinces, and who are certainly connected with another which came down into Gwalior and Bhopal and are now chiefly settled round Raisen in Bhopal and at Mungaoli in Gwalior and are still known as Delhiwal Baoris and Badhuks, and often call themselves Byragis. Baoris of the United Provinces have often, when they have absconded, stopped amongst the Badaks around Raisen and they can be recognised at once by Bhopal Badhuks and have apparently the same 'slang' language'.

Another portion of the Delhiwal Baoris or Badaks came down into the Karrauli State and are now known as Karraulia Badaks. They intermarry with the Bhopal Badhuks and many many of them, owing to famine have come down at various times into Central India, where several families are now located at the Gwalior Settlement at Mirkabad, Mungaoli. These people too keep up connection with the United Provinces Baurias.

The remaining large branch went back into Rajputana and became known as Baori, Bagri or Moghias according to the localities in which they finally settled.

The name of Bagri, must not be confounded with the similar name of an apparently aboriginal tribe who are merely hunters and are in no way connected with the Baori Bagri. The latter are Baoris and are only called Bagris because they originally happened to settle in that parts of Rajputana called Bagur from which this name, which most Baoris repudiate, is said to be derived as also other names of the same branch such as Bagora, Baguri or Wagri, the last being now generally known as Takinkars in the Berars and the Deccan.

The Baoris who remained in Marwar and all their descendants who migrated South and East are to this day called Baori, except a Division of them which got the name of Moghia, now so often used as a general name for all sorts of Baoris in the following manner :—

A Colony of Jodhpur Baoris lived near the borders of Mewar (Udaipur) the Chief of which State employed then against a band of truculent Bhils or Minas (accounts differ) who had defied his authority, whom they so successfully exterminated that the Maharaja, in his gratitude held a Durbar at which he took the whole colony into his service gave them land and said they should be to him as precious as the '*Moongas*' *i.e.*, coral beads, of his nacklace.

* This story seems to be widely spread among criminal tribes.—J. H. H.

Thus this Band came to be called the Moongias and finally Moghias and they settled down around Chittorgarh whence they spread southward into Malwa and the States bordering that country, losing, in the operation, touch with their Jodhpur Brethren and forming a new branch of the family with new divisions, such as Marwara, Kherara, Malwi and God-wara, and because they were the first to be brought under regulations, gave their name to the department which eventually was formed for the control of themselves and their kinsmen in Rajputana and Central India. From the connection of the department so called whole of the branches of the tribe in Rajputana and Central India became known generally as the Moghia Tribe, a title which the majority of the sects do not acknowledge.

Such is the tribal history handed down from generations past ; but the real origin of all branches of the Baori tribes would appear to be identical with that of the Sansi or Sansiya, who also claim Rajput descent and have the Rajput gotes or sub-divisions. The Sansi have a mythical ancestor 'Sans Mull', from whom sprang the Haburahs, Badhuks, Bagris, Baoris, Kungars, Gidias, Kecchaks, Bauriahs, Moghias and other tribes who are all professional thieves who will eat, drink, smoke and some times commit dacoities together but who will not intermarry. These again must be all connected with the supposed descendants of Sans Mull's younger brother, Mullsnoor, from whom the Beriahs, Kolahties Domes and Domaras, Nath Bediyas and Binds trace their descent, so that the majority of tribes now known as the Criminal Tribes in the northern half of India have probably arisen from a common stock, a proof of this theory being the great similarity of their 'slang' or thieves talk, which except in their own brotherhood, has its roots in Gujerati and is very similar for all tribes, even though these tribes now have names so dis-similar to each other and varying according to the country they inhabit.

The Sansi were originally Bhats to the Jat races, but as they increased in numbers and found it impossible for all to live up on the Jats, they scattered over Marwar and Mewar and then on South and East over Malwa and the valley of the Narbudda to Nagpur and Hyderabad and gradually broke up into separate branches with distinctive names which lost touch of each other and wandered farther and farther over India. Soon after this happened, each tribe according to its surroundings invented for itself a better ancestory and history and so cut itself still further from its parent stock until, in the course of time, some of the tribes came to be no longer recognised as being connected with the main branch of the Sansis which still flourishes as a separate tribe.

The Baori portion of the tribe under various clan names and with a certain amount of clan cohesion became settled in Rajputana as Baoris, Bagris and Moghias—

In Central India as Badaks (Delhiwal and Karraulia), Baoris, Bagris and Moghias.

In Berar, the Central Provinces and the Deccan, Wagris or Takinkars and Baoris with various local names.

In Bombay as Bagodi, Takri and Phanspardi.

In the United Provinces as Badaks, Habudahs, Baurias, Gidias, Kecchaks, Aruks.

In Bengal as Kecchuks and Badaks, Bagdis and Baoris.

In the Punjab as Bauriahs or Baoris, Delhiwal Badaks and Dhanderia.

In Gujerat as Baoris (who go in for coining).

That these sects of the tribe do keep up a certain amount of touch with each other and recognise relationship is evident from the fact that members settled in Northern India, as for instance those of the United Provinces (known as Bauriahs) and in Central India (known as Badaks and Baoris) when they abscond generally go south and remain away for years at a time, amongst their clan brethren of the locality they visit. Muzaffernagar Bauriahs have often visited the Badaks round Raisen in Bhopal and there have been cases in which some of them have been arrested in the Central Provinces and Bombay through Badak informers. In the same way Bhopal Badaks have stated that absconders of their settlement have gone upto the Muzaffarnagar Bauriahs, while very many of them have stopped for years with Baoris, *i.e.*, Wagris or Takinkars and other tribal relations in the Berars and the Deccan.

All of these tribes keep up a pretence of Rajput descent and their caste sub-divisions or 'gotes' are those of the Rajputs, *viz.* :—

1. Chohan, 2. Powar, 3. Rathor, 4. Solanki, 5. Dabi, 6. Charan, 7. Dhamdhara, and some later added ones, such as Bhariara Bhatti, and their marriages are arranged according to the rules of these castes amongst the Rajputs, while the birth and death ceremonies are likewise governed by Rajput customs with local variations which will be noted later.

Settlement and control under the Criminal Tribes Regulations has done much to break this large brotherhood, which practically stretches right across India, of its criminal proclivities, more or less according to conditions, but in almost all its sects the propensity to crime is still inherent and is easily brought to the surface.

Time and distance have caused greater or less severance of kinship between the various branches and when the 'Moghia' Department was instituted the only Baoris that came under its operations were those of Rajputana and Central India and consequently these have come to be generally known as 'Moghias' and are considered as distinct from various sects of their original tribe which are now known under new local names which have obliterated the memory of their descent from and kinship to the Badaks, Baoris and their original ancestors the Sansis.

The first attempt to bring the Baoris or Moghias under rules was made in 1869, when the Political Agent in Mewar proposed a set of rules which he had drawn up and which many years afterwards, developed in to the rules laid down for the guidance of the Moghia Department and eventually became embodied in the rules for the control and reclamation of Criminal Tribes for the guidance of the States in Rajputana and Central India, issued by the Government of India. The members of the tribe affected by these regulations and now generally referred to as Moghias (instead of Baoris which should be their distinctive title) are, in Rajputana and Central India known under the following tribal names :—

Merwara Baoris, Bagoras or Bagris.

Kherara Baoris or Bagris.

Karraulia Badaks and Bagris.

Badaks or Delhiwals.

Godwara Baoris.

Malvi Baoris.

Moghias.

In Central India, the Moghias, who at the close of the year 1906 numbered 2, 293 registered members, were shown in the census of 1901 as totalling males and females of all ages 6,381, and are of the Badaks, Karraulia, Godwara Kherara, Marwara, Malvi and Moghia sects.

Of these the Kheraras are the most numerous and are to be found in the states of Indore, Gwalior, Dhar, Dewas, Rutlam, Sailana, Sitamau and Jaora, Maksudangarh, Khilchipur, Narsingarh and Rajgarh, in that portion of the Agency known as Malwa. All these are named after the country in which, as Baoris, they originally settled and from which they spread, *viz.* :— the tract lying between Kotah and Jhalrapatan in Rajputana to a line passing about 40 miles East of Gwalior and Jwad in the Bhopal Agency.

Next come the real Badaks, known as Delhiwals and Karraulia Badaks or Bauris who are to be met with in the States of Bhopal, Gwalior, Pathari and Rajgarh east of a line running due North and South of Bhopal ; of these the Gwalior State members have now all been colonized at Mungaoli.

The Marwaras who next come in numbers are more scattered over the Agency than all others and are to be found from West to East in the States of Indore, Gwalior, Jaora, Sitamau, Rutlam, Sailana, Garha, Bhopal, Dhar, Tonk (Sirong Pergana), Narsingarh Rajgarh, Khilchipur and Maksudangarh and Kurwai. They and the Kheraras are frequently to be found together and though mortal enemies on some points, the two sects more generally live and work together than any other two sects of the tribe.

The next in order, as regards numbers, is the Godwara sect which take its name from the country of its origin, *viz* :—the tract lying on the frontier of Marwar south of Pallu and stretching from Mahairwara on the North East to Sirohi on the South-West and Mewar on the East.

Members of this sect are to be met with in the States of Rutlam, Narsingarh, Gwalior and Pathari.

The Malvis come next and are, as their name implies residents of Malwa proper and to be found only in the Piploda, Thakurata, Jaora, Rutlam and Sailana, Bhangarh of Indore and a portion of Bhopal lying in the Malwa country and in the Neori Pergana of Gwalior.

Finally there are members of the tribe descended from the Udaipur Monghias or Moghias and answering only to the name of Moghia (not Baori) who are settled in the Malwa portion of Gwalior.

All these sects are devided into the gotes of Bhati, Chohan, Solanki, Rathor or Charan, Dhandal, Powar, Dhamdara, Pidiara, Mahawana, Jadov, Soorj Bansi, Gailote, Dabi and Kulmi.

Of these Rathor or Charan are most numerous, while the Bhati, Solanki, Chohan and Puar come next in order and the numbers of the other gotes are all very few in comparison.

Birth, marriage and death ceremonies are all carried out more or less according to those of the true Rajputs of the corresponding gotes.

The Baori or Moghia in Central India has now practically given up dacoity as a profession though the Marwara and Kherara is still prone to break out in this form of crime if at all hard pressed by scarcity.

The Badak or Karraulia very rarely now goes in for dacoity but is one of the most expert of burglars : all goes in heavily for this form of crime.

The Godwara will join the Marwara or Kherarā, if he is allowed, in either dacoity or burglary but is not an expert and seldom works on his own.

The Malvi is now scarcely to be called of a criminal class. He has gone in for business and in many cases has proved most successful and as a community the Malvi Baoris are better off than those of all other sects.

The Moghia has very much the proclivities of the Marwara and Kherara but is less bold and expert than either.

INDORE ;

November 1907.

4. (ii) The Bhantus a criminal tribe of India.

By C. J. Bonington.

The Bhantus are one of the many wandering gipsy tribes of India who subsist by organized robbery and dacoity and who are for this reason proscribed by the Indian Government as criminal tribes. They are found in North and Central India. branches of the tribe also existing in Eastern India where are known as Karwal Nats. Their area of operations even extends as far as Burma, but they are not distinguishable there from the other Indians because they do not wander about in gangs. Being a proscribed criminal tribe, and probably the most dangerous of all such tribes even in India, the Bhantu invariably covers his identity by adopting an *alias* such as Kanjar. Sansia, Habura, Beria, Chaparband, Kuchband. etc., with which he has no connection whatsoever as a tribe.

For years the Government of the United Provinces has tried to confine them to settlements under the care of the Salvation Army, where they have been taught industries, but it is with great difficulty that they have been secured and confined within the limits of the settlement. A large gang of Bhantus in 1926 voluntarily came to the Andamans from Indian jails and from free Bhantu settlements. These were settled on the land under the care of Staff Captain Sheard of the Salvation Army, and their wives and children were allowed to accompany them. In the Andamans their conduct has been good and the colony comprises 285 individuals. Here they cultivate the land, the younger men and boys also being employed in the saw-mills and on coolie labour in various other industries.

Owing to their antecedents as a criminal tribe, there is very little information available about these people, except that found in police records. Hollins in his " Criminal Tribes of the United Provinces " gives an account of their activities, but it is obviously difficult to obtain correct information, because they usually have a past of hitherto undetected history. or being good Bhantus, and there are few such, they do not wish to have their identity known, owing to the stigma attached to the name. In the Andamans no such concealment is necessary because their previous history is known, and they themselves are intimately known to the Salvation Army Officer in charge, who has been connected with them for many years. It is due to the latter's co-operation that I have been able to place on record some data on their tribal organization, habits and customs.

Adjutant Sheard supplied most of the information in reply to a questionnaire. which I set, and spent several months verifying it. his experience obtained by daily contact with them for many years being unique. The writer is extremely grateful to him for his care and willingness and for the thoroughness of his replies to the questionnaire.

Origin.—The Bhantus claim descent from the Chauhan Thakur clan of Chitorgarh, which they regard as their mother city. Ethnologically they are perhaps of Dravidian origin*, being a branch of a great nomadic race. According to tradition, most of the clan perished when the state was raided by Musalmans many years prior to the advent of the East India Company. Those who were fortunate enough to escape took to the jungles, becoming wanderers, and thus started their gipsy form of existence. Legend has it among them that the sacred threads of the Brahmins who were butchered in this particular Muslim raid weighed seventy-two maunds or 5,760 lbs.

As far as one can judge, the Bhantus probably have an ethnological connection with the Sansias, Haburas, Kanjars, Karwal Nats, and Jats ; but the present day members of the tribes named differ considerably. Prior to their proscription it was usual for the Bhantus to meet every rainy season on the plain of the old ruined city of Nuh-Khera to the north of Jalesar in the Kheri district of the United Provinces for the settling of disputes and marriages. No definite information can be obtained as to the etymological meaning of the word Bhantu, but one villager suggested that it is might have sprung from the practice of villagers and others, who, on seeing strangers on their land, invariably yelled out, *Bhag-tu*—" Run away ", obviously an aetiological derivation. Hollins is of the opinion that the term comes from " Bhante " in the sense of " broken " and that the name implies that the tribe is composed of various mixed elements, which is perhaps supported by its tradition of Rajput origin.

Gots.—The Bhantus are said to be divided into some thirty-six *gots* or clans but only the names of twenty-four have been ascertained. Almost every *got* differs in the observance of customs relating to worship, marriages, burial, etc.. of a few of which differences mention will be made later. Information with regard to this must be taken with a certain amount of reserve as most of the Bhantus themselves had no idea there were so many *gots*. One man on being questioned gave the information that there were twelve and a half *gots*, explaining that eunuchs were given half a *got*, which is called the *Hijara Got*.

As far as has been ascertained the system. of marriage is exogamous with the exception of one *got*. the Bhanswale. No particular explanation is offered as to why the names of the *gots* were chosen, many of them being selected from words in every day use. Several of the *gots* I have been able to identify with those mentioned by Inspector Baldeo Sahai's report on the origin, habits and customs of the wandering tribes, which he classes as Khanjars and Behrias inhabiting the Agra district in 1875. The Behrias usually marry Bhantu women and the difference from the Bhantu is therefore merely in that they follow a different profession while the Sansias, Haburas, Kanjars, and Karwal Nats may have a common origin with the Bhantus. The Mahe *got* is referred to as one of the three principal Kanjar *gots* and the Dhapo *got* has a distinct affinity with the Dhapu mentioned by Baldeo Sahai. who refers to it as one of the 'Puckas' of the five *gots* which claim their descent from Bidhu, one of the three persons whom legend ascribes to have been born in the west at a place called Garwar.

---

* W. Crooke's " *Tribes and Castes of the N.-W. Provinces* ".

The Kanjar is more of a hunter than a criminal, but Kanjars have been known to work with Bhantus as the local adherents of a raiding party. It is probable that owing to the continual adoption of aliases, confusion has arisen as to the identity of the *gots* as well as that of the various criminal tribes as a whole.

The names of the *gots* ascertained are as follows, a description following later in a tabulated form of the essential differences between the more important :—

1. Sade.
2. Dhapo.
3. Chareli.
4. Chanduwale.
5. Gadho.
6. Mahes.
7. Gehla.
8. Bhanswale.
9. Chhede.
10. Koran.
11. Timachi.
12. Marwarie.
13. Dhaneke.
14. Rorke.
15. Pophat.
16. Mataike.
17. Ghasive.
18. Dholive (High).
19. Dholive (Low).
20. Mire.
21. Range.
22. Gange.

General Appearance.—The Bhantus are experts in all kinds of dacoity and robbery, and are skilled in the use of fire-arms. They are of good physique and are reputed to be good runners. The women are strong and handsome and are gifted with exceptionally strong voices. They are clever and intelligent and are well able to take care of themselves and their families when the men of the clan are away on raiding expeditions.

Dress.—They wear the "*lenga*" or pleated skirt. This consists of some twenty to forty yards of material. The two ends are sewen up and a hole is made at one edge through which a cord is threaded. When the cord is drawn tight the skirt is "kilted". An edging of contrasted material is sewn on the bottom edge to make it hang properly. Women who are not suckling children wear coloured "armlets": a shirt made similar to a man's and of any kind of cloth is worn loosely and hangs down over the *lenga*, a white or coloured cloth completing the dress. Girls wear clothes on the same lines. The men and boys have no distinctive dress. Jewellery is also freely worn by the women, and the men invariably wear some small gold ear-rings, and occasionally a small necklace of gold ear-rings. On the whole the women are far more distinctive as a type than than the men, both in their dress and physical appearance; they are completely different to other Indian women, a stout Bhantuni is not usually met with, while the men would pass easily for ordinary villagers. The women however are very "gipsy' in appearance and are dirty and untidy in their habits owing no doubt to the fact that they lead a nomadic life, and are always on the move leaving their filth behind. They also tattoo each other with an ink of burnt *akaua* leaves in oil. The Bhantus possess no particular physical quality peculiar to themselves and the fact that they never oil their hair, a custom which is a direct contrast to that throughout India, is no doubt due to the fact that they are wanderers and unable to carry oil about or resort to the barber, but there is no special tabu on the use of hair oil except in case of children in certain circumstances (See paragraph on *Child-birth*).

Internal Administration.—The Bhantus lead their nomadic life in gangs consisting of a dozen families, keeping as far as possible away from villages when they camp; men from different gangs, would however combine in the event of a raiding expedition. The system of internal administration of the clan is communal, all disputes being dealt with by the Panchayat or council of elders. In theory this may be composed of any five members of the tribe called together to settle any particular dispute, but in practice certain persons by reason of their knowledge of tribal laws, etc., come to be regarded as the Panchayat of any particular gang. Age has little to do in deciding who shall sit on the Panchayat. On a dispute arising, the parties concerned appear before the Panchayat, each party having its own advocate to state its case and wrangle for it. The whole however has the appearance of a debate more than anything else, for others (including women and children whatever the nature of the enquiry may be) attend, and most have something to say in the matter. Generally speaking the Panchayat aims at reconciling parties rather than punishing them. They have however considerable powers to inflict punishment, usually in the shape of pecuniary fines, some of the fines becoming the Panchayat's perquisite. Besides disputes, all manner of offences against tribal custom such as incest (marriage within a *got* is so regarded), divorce, adultery, etc., are dealt with by the Panchayat, not to speak of trials by ordeal, settlement of marriage-prices, and questions of general importance affecting tribal life; for their services they may also charge from ten to fifteen rupees.

Crime.—As has already been said, the Bhantus prior to being confined to settlements lived entirely by crime. A few were ostensibly engaged in agriculture but this only covered up their real activities. Their nefarious practices found most scope in dacoity or robbery by violence, but being a community organized for crime nothing came amiss to them.

On deciding to commit a dacoity in any particular locality spies would be sent out to select a suitable victim, study the general habits of the villagers and the distance from any effective aid, and enumerate the number of men and firearms. Inspector Baldeo Sahai also asserts in his report "That they have been known to travel very great distances in disguise by rail for the purposes of committing thefts, robberies, and dacoities, never committing offences of any kind near their encampment". The raid usually took place at midnight. Acting on the information given by the spies, men would be posted at various points in the village, and by firing off their guns attract attention from the main gang which would attack the particular house or houses previously appointed. The gang would usually consist of some thirty to forty men and would not be over-scrupulous in their methods. If resistance was shown they were merciless, indeed, the particular gang sent to Port Blair had committed over fifty murders in one series of outrages. As they were working against time, cruel and violent methods were often adopted to compel the victims to reveal the hiding place of their treasure, such as forcing women to sit on burning charcoal, etc. Rape was common. The traditional weapon of attack was a short hard stick, thrown with tremendous force, while the lathi was used for defence. In more recent years, however, guns have been adopted and khaki worn. Having secured their plunder, they buried it immediately in the vicinity to avoid any incriminating evidence and dispersed. In the event of a murder being committed. no serious action is taken, though it is regarded as *pap* or sin, and if a stranger has been murdered, the murderer distributes *gur* among the brotherhood. This costs Rs. 1-4-0. Should one of the tribe however be murdered the offender must give a feast costing Rs. 101. When the whole affair has blown over, the plunder is dug up and given to the women who dispose of it to the goldsmiths who act as receivers.

It is essential to emphasise the great part played by crime in the general life of the clan. A boy is initiated into crime as soon as he is able to walk and talk. No doubt the motive is practical to a great extent, in so far as it is always better to risk a child in petty theft, who, if he were caught would probably be cuffed, while an adult would immediately be arrested. An important part is also played by women, who although they do not participate in the actual raids have many heavy responsibilities. Besides disposing of most of the stolen property, they are also expert shop-lifters thus participating in the material support of the tribe. They also arrange for the legal defence of arrested men, as well as supporting and visiting relations in jail.

A raiding party is composed of men who only operate at some distance from the district in which the rest of the gang containing old men and women and children have camped. Thus in the absence of the men on a raiding expedition, the women are responsible for the camp and the main body is in the charge of a woman and may be known by her name. It is no doubt this, which induces Hollins to remark that "A feature of the tribal organization is that many gangs are led by women". Mr. Sheard informs me that he has never heard of an active gang being under the leadership of a woman or women while actually engaged in dacoity or raiding. Quite recently a number of Karwal gangs wished to come to the Andamans, and in every case a woman's name was given as the leader of the gang; he was convinced however that this was merely for ease in reference to any particular gang and had no connection with leadership in crime. It is also apparently legitimate for a Bhantni to use her womanly wiles in the advancement of the tribe's criminal activities, but such aid cannot be termed prostitution.

W. Crooke in his "Tribes and Castes of the North-Western Provinces and Oudh" (pages 136—139) refers to the Bhantu as "one who lives by stealing and thieving cattle". With the exception of stealing goats for food, cattle thieving is not indulged in. The Bhantu is essentially a highway robber and dacoit, and the difficulties and risks incumbent on the disposal and transport of cattle would be too great; besides this, beef as an article of diet is forbidden.

Morality.—The Bhantus, have a tribal code of morality which is strictly enforced. The moral standard is high and any offence is severely dealt with by the Panchayat. Many writers have ascribed to this tribe a very low state of sex morality, due no doubt to the confusion regarding the identity of the tribe owing to the adoption of *aliases*, such as Behria, the morals and discipline of which tribe are notoriously lax.

Promiscuous intercourse before or after marriage is condemned. It is usual for Bhantus to marry Bhantus, but union with Behrias is common. A strict rule is maintained to prevent marriage with blood relations, that parties should not marry within the same *got*, there is however one exception, that of the Bhanswale *Got* who may marry within their own clan. Should it accidentally happen that two persons within the same *got* marry one another, they are brought before the Panchayat and fined Rs. 100. Where intercourse or adultery between two people of the same *got* is proved, the parties are guilty of incest, a serious offence, mention of which is made later.

Marriage.—The ceremony and arrangements for marriage differ greatly according to *gots*. Beneath follows a description of marriage according to the Sade *Got*, all essential differences between *gots* being mentioned in the tabulated form appended. A system is in force throughout the clans whereby it is incumbent upon certain clans to intermarry according to certain rules; for instance a boy of the Dhapo *Got* marries a girl from the Chireli *Got*. A Dhapo boy may not marry a girl of the Dhapo *Got* but may marry a girl of the Chireli *Got*, provided there is no blood relationship with the grandmother, *i.e.*, the marriage system is patrilineal and exogamous, and the female line is barred for two generations. He may however marry a girl of any other *got*.

Formerly the age of marriage for both a man and a woman was from 20—23, but latterly, prior to the Sarda Act, young children could be married at the age of the ten with consummation on puberty. Much depended on circumstances and the ability to pay the money demanded. In the Sade *Got* the parents of the boy send male friends to the parents of a suitable girl. If the prospects are favourable the Panchayats and the father of the boy call on the girl's parents and in their presence two pigs are killed. The spilling of some liquor on the ground seals the engagement (*mangni*). These preliminary arrangements are called the *baithak*. Two or three days later the price to be paid is settled at the *bol* when one or two more pigs are given. The price generally accepted is according to *got* and this varies considerably. The terms are settled by the Panchayats and vary according to circumstances. For instance Behrias have paid as much as Rs. 1,500 for a Bhantu girl, whilst the lowest price is paid in the Timaichi *Got*, *viz.*, Rs. 280. This price may be lowered for any or all of the following reasons, (*viz.*) :—

	Rs.
Lameness	140
Squint	140
Broken teeth	25
Unchastity.	60

These items may cost more or less according to *got*. If the girl has not had small-pox and dies before giving birth to two children, the parents will refund the money paid for the girl. Should she die from small-pox after giving birth to two children nothing can be claimed from the parents. Questions are also asked as to whether the performance of any acts of worship have been promised in the name of the girl.

A few days later, the third and last of the preliminaries known as *mokhan* is settled. A pig is killed and prior to killing it, the following recited :—

"*Ai Maharaj Sri Thakur Ji, Karan kisi ka nam pahile tera nam. Hamare Pir Purke ke nam, jaise bap dadonki jat men hota aya hai ham waise hi karte. Tumhari larki ki ham shadi karte hain. Achchhi tarah se rakhna, Donon taraf achei tarah rakhna*", "O Maharaja Sri Thakur Ji (or any other Deity named) no matter in whose name we do this, thy name is taken first. In the name of our ancestors and as our fore-fathers have done in our tribes before us, so do we. This is your girl. We are arranging her marriage. Be kind to her and to both parties in this contract".

The pig is then killed by a pointed stake being inserted behind the shoulder piercing the heart. On the day of the Khatmi Shadi, the boy is dressed in clean clothes and is decked out in borrowed jewellery. The women paint round both his eyes with black and white, and when all is ready escort him to the house of the bride singing songs and abusing any relations of the bridegroom they may meet on the way. A coloured shawl or *Chadar* is held over the bridegroom's head by two women who lead the procession.

On arrival at the house of the bride, the boy enters but is stopped by two females who hold up a curtain and demand money before he can see his bride. When this has been given he is permitted to push under the bottom edge of the curtain a small bowl containing a mixture of water and *gur*. The girl touches this with her lips. Meanwhile the mother of the bride having smeared her right hand with *haldi* slaps the bridegroom on the back, leaving the impression of her hand on his clothes. She also stamps a grain of rice (steeped in *haldi*) on his forehead. Presents are given, the curtain is taken down and the bridegroom is free to take his bride home. The next morning, the near male relations of the bride meet at the bride's house and are given liquor. A basket or bowl is put under a *chadar* placed in the centre of the circle of squatting men and as the liquor is passed round a present of money or jewellery placed in the bowl by the men and is afterwards given to the married couple. This is termed *piyale chelti.* The Panchayat also receive their fee at this gathering.

It is a custom for portion of a sum demanded for a bride to remain owing. This is called the *baqaya.* Should the girl be given trouble or be illtreated payment of the *bagaya* is demanded. Until this sum is paid, the parents of the girl have a right to interfere in the affairs of their daughter. "*Maje ne mal mol liya hai, tere ko kya ?*" "I have bought this property ; mind your own business", is the answer of a husband to any interference when the *baqaya* has been paid. Exchange weddings are very popular as the expense is much less. A brother and sister from one family will marry a brother and sister from another family. Should however one girl be illtreated by her husband, her brother, will promptly give his wife trouble although, otherwise, he may have no cause to do so. As a rule the eldest son in a family is married first, but should he be in jail or absconding when a suitable girl is available she may be married by proxy to another brother, who may with the elder brother's sanction take her to his house. On the return of the elder brother he may either take his wife or marry someone else. Should, however, the elder brother claim his wife, any children born while living with the younger brother remain with the younger.

Divorce.—Divorce is permitted by the clan, but not looked upon with favour. The Panchayat deals with the matter and decides how much of the original purchase price shall be refunded by the family of the girl. No particular ceremony is performed. A divorced woman may remarry, but a reduction is made in her original price of Rs. 60-80 according to *got.* If at the time of her husband's death a woman has a grown up family, she may please herself whether she remarries or not. She may live with the family of her brother-in-law, nearest in age to her husband, preferably the next brother in age below. In the event of a man's first wife failing to give him a son, he may, if he can afford it, take a second wife ; this is however as a rule uncongenial to the rest of the tribe.

Child-birth.—In child-birth a woman is considered unclean for six days after the birth of the child and during this time is not permitted to touch any of the family cooking utensils, she also keeps apart from her husband for between two and three months. In the event of the mother dying within the unclean six days, she is considered to have died a "bad death" and is said to return and take possession of members of the family. This possession takes a form of mental affliction, for which the sole remedy is a good beating administered with a shoe by the *bhajat.* For persons of either sex to die in their teens unmarried is considered as a "bad" death and they are termed *Shaitan* because of the trouble they give their relations ; convulsions of children are supposed to be due to their influence. A person secretly committing incest and subsequently dying is held to have died a "bad death", his ancestors having caused the fatal sickness. In all bad deaths however, no difference is made in the treatment of the corpse, but the spirits of those who died are likely to cause troubles.

The ghost or *bhut,* that is the spirit of one who dies a "bad death" is confined to the district in which the person dies and can never enter a community. The *bhut* of a virgin is called *balai* while that of a woman who dies in child-birth is known as *churel.* This exclusion of the *balai* and *churel-bhuts* from the spiritual *biradari* or brother-hood, makes them most unhappy and particularly jealous of a child which appears to be well-fed and cared for. It is therefore dangerous for this child to enter their *hadd* as they are apt to cause it to be possessed. If ever this happens they can only be driven out by a *bhajat.* Should there be a suspected case of possession, or should a child be attacked with convulsions, all the children in the vicinity are given old clothes to wear and their hair is left unoiled and untidy, children remaining at home being immune. Sometimes, when driving out a *churel* the *bhajat* beats himself on the back with a *chamte.* This is an iron ring about three inches in diameter, from which are hung two chains on the ends of which are thirty-six pieces of sharpened iron *phale.* The whole weighs two and a half seers. More often than not the back of the *bhajat* is not cut. He also cuts his tongue and spitting the blood into some liquor, drinks the lot.

Incest.—Mention has been already made of the severity with which incest is treated by the Bhantus. The commission of incest involves *pap.* Should any member of a particular *got* be found guilty of incest in his own *got,* the whole *got* is debarred intercourse with the rest of the clan until the parties have been restored. In addition to a fine the culprits undergo a purification ceremony. Part of the fine is used in buying materials for a feast, which as a rule no adults but children alone attend. The culprits are kept apart from other members of the tribe in the charge of one of the Panchayat and must fast for twelve hours. The next morning the man and woman bathe and the Panch give them two pieces of khaddar. The man wears one as a *dhoti* and the woman the other in *sari* fashion. In front of the assembled tribe, the pair walk three times around a fire of *kundi,* two men (usually of the Mahes *Got*) throwing the same burning *kundis* at them. These however cause no serious damage. Wine and the blood of either a goat or a pig is also sprinkled over them. The hair of the woman and the moustache of the man together with the eyebrows are shaved off and hung up in the village as a warning to others.

Religion.—The Bhantu religion is a form of Animism inter-mixed with ancestor worship. In a sense they are Devi worshippers and many of them consider themselves low-caste Hindus, but they neither visit Hindu temples nor use Brahmins in any ceremony.

The Bhantus believe that after death the spirits of the departed meet again as Bhantu communities in the spirit world and that the spirit can only enter such communities after the prescribed number of feasts have been given to the tribe by the living members of the family. Until the whole of these feasts have been given, the spirit is said to be *bhandha* and is regarded as an outcast in the spirit world. Poor families often neglect to provide or else delay the provision of these feasts, so the spirit chafes at the delay and worries the family by causing some member to fall sick.

When any member of the tribe dies in peculiar circumstances such as in jail and the body is burnt by strangers, as soon as is possible an effigy is made of the deceased by his relations. This they proceed to bury or burn with all the ceremony usual in cases of death. In time of epidemics it is often impossible to deal with the dead according to custom, so it is permissible to get rid of the bodies as convenient and to perform the customary rites only when able to do so. The *putli* or effigy may be made of old or new cloth or even of an old quilt. It is merely roughly shaped by being partly rolled at both ends. One roll makes the arms and the head, the other the legs, while the middle portion is gathered together to make the trunk. Occasionally a shirt and pants are stuffed with straw and servo as the *putli*.

Ancestor worship plays a considerable part in tribal life. The spirits of the ancestors are supposed to be familiar with the doings of individual members of the tribe and in fact are regarded as a species of "guardian" spirit. Ancestors of three or four generations are known as *Purkha* or *Pir Purkha* while those of older generations are known as *Devta*.

Should there be a case of an individual committing an offence against tribal morality, such as adultery, the spirit community show their displeasure by outcasting the ancestors in that family. These vent their displeasure on the living members of the family by causing some member to fall sick. Whenever a Bhantu falls ill, the question arises as to the cause; certain members of the tribe are known as *bhajats* or mediums, who profess to receive communications from the spirits, and so the sick invariably seek their advice.

After squatting on the ground, the *bhajat* fills his huqqa and enquires as to the symptoms. When these have been described he sits smoking a while, then putting aside his huqqa, he commences the peculiar oscillations which appear necessary for him to get in communication with the spirits. The practice varies a little with individuals but it may generally be described as a rhythmical shaking of the head accompanied by forceful ejaculations of "Hu" "Hai" which gradually work up to a necessary frenzy. After a little while the sick one who sits in front of the *bhajat* with clasped hands will say to him "*Ai Maharaj, main ne kya kasur kiya ki mijh ko satata hai ?*" "Oh Maharaj, what is my fault that you are troubling me ? "The Bhantus are not very clear whom they address, although while using a term which to them indicates God, they address themselves to the spirit of the departed but first take the God's name. The *bhajat* then replies in somewhat the following manner. "*Main Devta hun tu 'ne hamara puja qabul kiya aur abhi tak tu' ne nahin kiya*" "I am a godling. You promised to perform a sacrifice for me, and you have not yet done so", to which the sick one replies. "*Main fulana din zarur kadunga*" "I will certainly peform it on such and such a date" and receives the assurance that "*Ab men tujhe chhor deta hun, meghe ainde men mat bhulna*". When the message has been delivered, the *khel* stops abruptly and the *bhajat* takes to the huqqa. He does not take any payment for his services but when the *puja* is celebrated, he receives a goodly portion of the food and drink ! Many reasons are ascribed for a person taking ill, chief among them being the failure to perform the yearly *puja to Nagarkot Devi* or to do a *Puja* to *Parvati Devi* as thanks giving for the safe delivery of a child. The *bhajat* however is supposed always to be able to trace the cause of sickness.

Feasts of the Dead.—There are three feasts required for the dead, they are—

1. *Khuta*—given to those who attend the funeral.
2. *Teiya*—given to the tribe.
3. *Jagha*—a set quantity of provisions divided among those who attend the feast.

The *Teiya* Feast. When the party has assembled, the pig (which has been fastened up since the previous evening) is brought to the gathering. Taking up heavy sticks one of the male members of the party fractures the right hind leg of the pig with a heavy blow. The blood drawn as a result of the fracture of the skin, smeared over the utensils used in the feast. If blood is not drawn the *puja* is abandoned and performed at some other time. The pig is next laid on the ground and following declaration is made :—

"*Ai Maharaj Sri Thakur Ji Tere nam ahile, jaise bap dadon men hota hai waise hi karte, Yih apna manzur kare. Mari ki roti ham karte hain ; hamare ghar par taklif na dena, bal bachhon par mehrban ho, ek roti rahgayi hai woh bhi ham karenga, aur isko jat biradari men jane do*". "Oh Maharaj, thy name shall ever be first. As our ancestors have done so do we. Accept this. We are giving the feast for the dead so do not give any trouble to our households. Be kind to our children. One feast remains that also will be given. Allow the departed one to enter his brotherhood". The pig is then killed, and the four men who bore the deceased at the funeral, make a *chappati* and break it up in *karna* oil at the fire-place. Each then takes a little and puts it on the ground, the following declaration being made by the *tapnewale* : "*Ai Maharaj, is ke rote karte hain. Khandan par mehrban ho, aur jo Jagha rahgayi hai woh phir karenga. Ise chhor do. Jat biradari men jane do*". "Oh Maharaj, we are giving the death feast of the deceased. Be kind to our families. We shall also provide the feasts that remains. Let him go. Allow him to join the brotherhood". Four *pindi* or balls consisting of rice, wheat and gur are then given to the four men who partly eat it and throw the remainder into a hole which has been dug in the ground. The *tapnewale* gives *chappaties* to five women who dip them in gravy and throw them untouched into the hole. A large *nand* earthen pot is then filled with food. First a layer of rice is laid in the bottom of the *nand*, then follow successive layers of *lentils*, coconut, sugar, pork and sweetmeats. The process is repeated seven times. On the top of this the broken leg, the heart, kidneys and liver of the pig are placed. A small quantity of dried earth is sieved on to the ground and is covered over with a wooden bowl. The spirit is said to leave a mark on the dust under the bowl if the feast is acceptable to him. The food is distributed and when all has been consumed the earthen vessels are broken, thrown into the fireplace, and the whole party walk round the debris seven times. The broken leg, etc., are not eaten but are left in the empty *nand* for the dogs. The provisions for the feast consist of wheaten flour, ghee, sugar, and one pig, rice, etc.

The "Jagha" feast.—Chappaties are baked and then mixed with ghee and gur. The pig (*hink te*) is then killed, a similar declaration being made as in the "*Teiya*". After the hair has been signed off the pig, a small portion of ground is cleared of grass and on this a small mound of earth is built. The right side of the carcase is then skinned, the head is cut off and after being wrapped in the skin is placed on the top of the mound together with a *pindi* of food. A small piece of skin is chopped up fine and scattered on the ground in front of the head and over it wine is poured. As this is done, the head of the family says "*Ai Maharaj, tumhare Jagha ham karte hain aur hamare upar kuch haqq nahin rahe, ab usko chhor do take*" "O Maharaj, we are providing the *Jagha* feast so there is now no further responsibility upon us. Let him go and enter the brotherhood. Be kind to our families". One member of the party who has been fasting since the night before (the '*Nina*') is then given some wine, meat and other food, and when he has finished it the rest of the party eat the remainder of the food. The men only are given a portion of the skin which was wrapped round the pig's head. The mound is broken down and the head eaten by the men. Finally the whole party walk round the fireplace seven times and disperse.

Besides giving feasts to the dead, certain *pujas* are performed at various times of the year to various *Devtis*. The Bhantus say that the *gupta puja* has no reference in their case to human sacrifice but indicates that when a person ostensibly performs a *puja* to one *Devti* he really intends the puja for another.

In the case of an individual who has committed a secret sin for which he is being worried by his *Pir Purkhe* and which he is anxious that the rest of the tribe should not know about, he performs what is known as *gupti, or gupta puja*. The intention expressed is that relief should be obtained from the *Pir Purkhe* and at the same time the matter be kept from the knowledge of the rest of the tribe. Ostensibly a *puja* is performed to one *Devti*, but mentally it is offered to another.

In order that dark nights may accompany the commission of a particular dacoity, a *puja* is promised to the *Kalka Devi*. In performing this *puja*, the *bhajat* cuts off the head of the pig, and drinks a quantity of the blood mixed with liquor.

Superstition.—As a whole the Bhantus are superstitious and omens play a large part in their daily life, raiding expeditions, dreams, etc. Any enterprise or work is invariably put off should any of the following circumstances occur at the commencement of it :—

1. *A single sneeze*—More than one is regarded as a good omen.
2. *A corpse if met on the right hand.*—If on the left it is a good sign.
3. A water pot if carried so that the inside can be seen. Whenever possible a raiding party will always include at least one *bhajat* or medium. As the spirits of the dead are believed to remain in the locality in which they die, it is customary for the *bhajat* to enquire from any ancestor of the tribe who may have died in the vicinity whether the intended raid has any prospects of success. Should a *bhajat* be not available a small *lota* of water is suspended by a string held by one of the members. If the *lota* swings in a circle, the omen is a bad one, but if it swings backward and forward the omen is good. The cry of a female jackal, the lowing of a cow, a snake crossing the path ahead or to the right of a raiding party is considered a bad omen. If however behind a party, the prospects are favourable.

No superstition is current with regard to any days of the week or month being particularly auspicious for raids, etc., nor is an individual credited with possessing supernatural or magical powers. Methods of divination, such as the consultation of grain current among the Haburas, are unknown, but the *bhajat* is often appealed to should property be stolen, cattle lost, etc. Dreams however have a peculiar significance. To dream of anything flying such as a bird, is very bad for women, who fear becoming barren and they invariably seek the aid of the *bhajat* to prevent this. A barren woman is always considered to have a bad influence and is supposed to possess the power of preventing conception. This power is exercised by tearing a piece of cloth belonging to another woman. Formerly it was not uncommon for a barren woman, to be "lost" in the jungles, and no questions to be asked. To dream of death denotes death, but not in the family of the dreamer, while to dream of marriage denotes death in the family. Dreaming of one's own death is a good omen. To dream of shallow water in a small stream is good, but a deep river means trouble. Eclipses are considered dangerous to the unborn, while earthquakes and comets note the death of a king. In the event of a man's going blind a *puja* of a simple nature is made to the sun (*Surya Narain Devta*) while it is rising.

Decision of cases by Ordeal.—In the event of the inability of the Panchayat to prove a charge of which they are doubtful it is usual to impose a "*gasam*" on the suspected person, who may depute a "Champion" to undergo the ordeal for him. This man receives Rs. 5 if he is successful, but only Rs. 2-8-0 if he fails. Those ordeals are of three kinds, the fire ordeal, the water ordeal, and another ordeal to pick out a "pice" from a *lota* of hot oil, but for obvious reasons this is seldom resorted to ; the fire test is the more popular.

Fire Test.—The suspected person or his champion is placed in charge of the Panchayat at the night previous to the test At day-break the man bathes and puts on a piece of *khaddar* and a piece of thread over his shoulder. A level piece of ground is chosen for the test, a *gudali*, *i.e.*, an iron hoe blade about a foot long and one and a half inches in diameter, is made red hot in a fire of *kundies*. From a point near the fire and with the back facing the sun, seven paces are measured off. The one taking the test stands on the starting line. Seven pipal leaves are then spread over his outstretched hands and fastened on with cotton thread. When all is ready and the iron is red hot, the head of the Panchayat with arm upraised, makes the following declaration. "*Sri Maharaj hamne insaf kiye par thik nahin hua. Ab tere pas ate hain. Jhuth ko jhuth, sach ko sach*". He then takes the iron out of the fire, and balancing it on two sticks, lays it on the hands of the accused who carries it for the seven paces and throws it down. Should there be no burn he is considered innocent. The slightest blister is sufficient to leave him guilty, his hands being carefully examined by the Panchayat after the test. As the leaves are full of sap, there is little fear of the accused being burnt, provided he keeps his nerve. The Bhantus hold that should the person be guilty the fire will burn through the leaves at once, a miracle being worked to prove guilt and not innocence.

Water Test.—The water test is undertaken under similar circumstances. A pool or tank about 4 feet in depth is chosen. From the edge of this a course of 100 paces is measured, the test being taken as soon after day-break as possible. A bamboo is stuck upright in the tank near the side, and the man to be tested stands in the water holding the pole with one hand. When all is ready the head of the Panchayat claps his hands three times and as the accused sits down on the bottom of the tank with his head under water, a man starts to run the course from the tank, to the spot 100 yards away where one of the Panchayat stands. After taking a small stick from him the man rushes back to the tank and, jumping into the water, lifts up the accused from the bottom of the tank. If the accused is able to remain under water until lifted out, he is proved innocent.

It is to be noticed that the pipal tree, the leaves of which are used in the fire test has a peculiar significance. It is regarded as a sacred tree and an oath sworn while touching it, is regarded as binding. An oath may be taken with reference to either past or future conduct. One is supposed to make a true statement when touching either pipal or the *akaua* tree. In cases of suspected theft the head of a cock is cut off and some of the blood, with salt and liquor are mixed in an empty coconut shell. A representative from each family dips his or her finger in the mixture and swears the following "*Agar main ya hamare khandan ke admion ne yih kam to jaise yih murga waise he hamare chandar*".

Should the leaves of the pipal not be large enough at the time of the fire test, *akaua* leaves are resorted to.

Disposal of the Dead.—As has been said, the Bhantus burn or bury their dead according to *got*. A description follows of both methods as used by the Dhapo and Dholiya *gots*, respectively. *Dhapo Got-Cremation.*—If it is seen that a person is about to die a *kande* is lit and kept burning until the pyre is fired. The body is lifted from the bed and laid on an old blanket or rezai spread on the ground. Knives are stuck in the earth at the head and feet and removed later when the body is taken away. The following articles are then procured to clothe the body :—Two-and-a-half yards of white cloth, cloth for a shirt and pagri and also a little thread. When the body has been clothed and while still on the ground a pice and a needle are placed on the mouth and a *pindi* of wheaten flour in the right hand. The right side of the bed is partly chopped through and is then broken by the relations with a blow from a heavy stick. The cot is immediately turned over and the broken side quickly repaired with rope. Having placed the body on the inverted bed four men carry it to the burial ghat. As this is neared, the *pindi* is taken from the hand of the corpse, is placed under a bush and is covered with a piece of cloth torn from the shroud. On arrival at the ghat the body is placed on a wooden pyre, which is lighted after the chief mourner has circled it three times with a small torch of burning grass lighted at the *khundi*. Some *gots* in the meanwhile break the skull. When the burning is finished the party walk round the spot seven times and then go to bathe in the nearest stream or pond. The chief woman stands in the water and makes the following declaration.

"*Ai Maharaj, jo kuchh us ke upar bandha tha aur gubula thar agar wuh zinda rahta to ham puja dete, ab wuh margaya ishiye us ke sang chale jao*". "Oh Maharaj, whatever *puja* or sacrifice has been promised in the name of the deceased would have been given if he had lived. Now he is dead, all these promises go with him." A little water is then thrown forward seven times. On the return of the party to the village, the relations and others gather in front of the house, and a small piece of unbaked chappati, wrapped in *akua* leaf is given to each. This is bitten and spat out on the ground. After partaking of food the party is sprinkled with water and disperses.

Dholiya Got-Burial.—After death the body is laid on the ground. Knives are struck in the ground at the head and the feet and the body is dressed in dhoti, shirt and pagri. A pice is put in the mouth but the needle in this case is put in the cloth and not in the mouth, as in the Dhapo *got*. Nothing is put in the hand. The bed side is broken (this must be broken at one blow otherwise an extra pig will have to be sacrificed), the bed turned over, repaired and the body placed on it. On leaving the house an earthen pot full of water is dashed to the ground. Three times during the journey to the burial place, the bed is put on the ground and a pice and cowri are placed in a small hole in the ground and covered up. If the family are able to afford it, money is thrown in front of the party while the body is carried along. The grave is made after the arrival of the party and is usually about 5 feet deep, and when possible the sides and bottom are boarded. The body having been lowered into the grave (no women attend) the men take a little earth and throw it into the grave saying as they do so "*Aj tumhara nam gaya khuda ke pas,*" "To-day your name has gone to God". The grave is then filled and a lathi left lying along side it. All bathe and a similar declaration is made as in the Dhapo cremation. On arrival at the village they are sprinkled with water three times, the party lifting up their hands while this is being done. Assembling in front of the house, thin chappaties are cooked, wheat meal being boiled in water and served in different portions for men, women and children. A bottle of liquor is split on the ground while the head of the house says *Ai Maharaj, rish tadaran ne laya, is ko mano am hamara pir purkhe milke pijawe.* "On Maharaj, the relations have brought this, accept it and drink it with our ancestors". On the third day a young pig is purchased and swung round three times by one leg in the room where the death took place. After being killed, a portion of the right flank is cut off and finely chopped up and scattered on the ground while the following is repeated :—*Sri Thakur Maharaj tum lena phir pir purkhe am hamare bap dada khale*—"Sri Thakur Maharaj, take this and eat it with our ancestors". The rest of the pig and other food is then consumed by the party.

Tabus.—Bhantus abstain from fish, beef, fox and duck but usually eat pig, goat, porcupine, *guil* and jungle cat. The Bhansware got however, which is regarded as the lowest *got*, and intermarry within their own clan, eat anything.

Dialect.—The Bhantus have a dialect which is peculiar to their tribe. *Tapi* is the term used for this dialect, which is not understood by the other criminal tribes such as Doms, Sansias, and Haburas, except when they come in contact with them in the settlement. There is an apparent relationship to Hindustani, which can be noticed from the list of words given below with the corresponding vernacular terms. Apart, however, from the actual changing of the words, they further mutilate their Hindustani by speaking somewhat in this way :—for *Kidhar ja rahe ?* They will ask, *Kitar Jasi* or *Kidhar jahgre*. *Engra* and *Agra* is apparently a suffix attached to many words and is apt to be confusing. It is not unlike a schoolboy's idea of producing a foreign language saying "Whera you arago gorogoing" for "where are you going". The whole is species of thieves' slang which however the settlers in Port Blair are rapidly losing, particularly the younger ones. Young women of the tribe often have a habit of speaking among themselves in this way. For example for *Kitna kam baqi hai.* They will say *Kamitha karam bawaqi hai ?*

English.	Hindustani.	Dialect.
Bhantu	Bhantu	Chantu.
Woman	Aurat	Chintani.
Boy	Larka	Bohra.
Girl	Larki	Bohri.
Police officer	Daroga	Khagra.
Constable	Siphai	Chivra.
Stranger	Ajnabi	Kaja or Teha.
Mohr (Gold)	Mohr	Piskare.
Rupees	Rupiya	Kupaiya.
Cloth	Kapra	Richara.
Boots	Jute	Gonia.
Abuse	Gali	Rani.
Oil	Tel	Nel.
Ghee	Ghee	Rehuta.
Village	Gawn	Raun.

English.	Hindustani.	Dialect.
Dog	Kutta	Bhokara or Rutta.
Goat	Bakri	Beri.
Wheat	Gehun.	Risu.
Water	Pani	Cheni.
Sweetmeats	Mithai	Kaddu.
Wine	Sharab	Kallu or Karu.
Run away	Bhag jao	Binti jao.
Have a smoke	Hukah pineko	Bukhta lo.
Earthenware pipe	Chillam	Nillam.
Arrested	Giriftar ho gaye	Chekra geya.*
Father	Bap	Dapap.
Mother	Ma	Maoti.
Sister	Bhain	Chaen.
Gun	Banduq	Tihari or Nanduq.
Revolver	Tamancha	Namancha.
Bed	Palang	Rahat.
Chair	Kursi	Rursi.
Grain	Anaj	Khanaj.
Sugar Cane	Ik	Rania.
Molasses	Gur	Ṛurcha.
To go to sleep	So jana	Luni jana.
Drink	Pijao	Toge le.
Strike, Don't run	Maro, Bhago Mat	Lirpo Binto Mat.
Stop him and strike	Rokh ke maro	Koke se maro.
The enemy is upon us, run	Dushman a rahe, Bhago	Tiare aye binti jao.
Drink milk	Dudh Pio	Nud toge lo.
Hand	Hath	Khot.
Head	Sir	Nhir.
Eyes	Ankhen	Konke.
Ears	Kan	Ran.
Fingers	Ungli	Kongre.
Feet	Pair	Gone.
Spear	Ballam	Kallam.
Fire	Goli chalao	Nahr.
Stop them	Unko roko	Kirped.
They will run away	Wuhe bhag jaenge	We sab hinte jagre.
Severely wounded	Gehra gahow ho gaya	Rahra rahow ho gaya.
I have been caught, come	Pakra hua ajao	Mujh ko nurai lepo.
Take no heed	Fiqr mat karo	Rogan de.
Jewellery	Zewar	Newar.
Speak	Kahna	Kogna.
Shut up	Chup chap baitho	Thonke jao.

Note I—

Gots.—There are supposed to be some thirty-six *gots* but only the names of twenty-two have been ascertained.

1. Sade. Marry into other *gots*. Burn dead. Feast of either *Roti* or Sweatmeats. Second day after death collect bones and bury in earthen pot. Marriage Rs. 500.

2. Dhapo. Burn dead. Leave bones unburied until relatives do a "Puja". If the bones are also consumed in the fire, the ashes and earth from the "Ghat" are buried. Marriage Rs. 500.

3. Chareli. Burn dead. At the funeral feast *Roti* is only part baked and is afterwards taken by the members, baked again and eaten. Marriage Rs. 500.

4. Chandu-wale. Bury dead. Clothe male corpse in shirt, a female in *Lenga*. Prepare boiled rice for the feast.

5. Gadho. Bury dead in Pyjamas and bind up the head. Feast as in Sadi *Got* except that when possible the body is kept overnight and a live pig is fastened near the house. In the morning the principal woman takes a heavy stick and stretching one of the pig's legs over a stone, recites the following :—"*Siri Thakur ji,*

*P for *Pakar giya.*

tere nam ki sath ki jaija. Ae Maharaj iske ham kaj kiriye karte hain. Ae Maharaj, ise jat men shamil karde, hamare balbachche khaisala rakho."

The legs of the pig is then broken by a heavy blow of the stick, and the pig is immediately killed to be eaten at the feast. Marriage Rs. 500.

6. Mahes. Burn dead. When fines are inflicted by the Panchayat for any reason, any member of this *got* who may be present is asked to purify the money by touching it. When fire is thrown on offenders in a purification ceremony, the first to throw are members of this *got.* Marriage Rs. 500.

7. Gehla. Similar to Sade Got.

8. Bhanswale. Burn dead. Eat beef and jackal's flesh. Use rice in funeral feast. Can marry in own *got.* Marriage Rs. 600.

9. and 10. Chhede and Koran. Similar to Gadho.

Others. 11 Timaichi, 12. Marware, 13. Dhaneke, 14. Rorke, 15. Pophat, 16. Matiake, 17. Ghasive, 18. Dholive (high and low), 19. Mire, 20. Range, 21. Gange.

Note III—Bibliography—

1. Crooke—*Tribes and Castes of the N. W. Provinces and Oudh.*

2. United Provinces Police Report, 1911.

3. Inspector Baldeo Sahai's Report on the origin, habits and customs of the wandering tribes known as Kanjars and Behrias inhabiting the Agra district. Agra 1875.

4. *Criminal Tribes of the United Provinces.*—S. T. Hollins.

5. *Report on the Ferrargunj colony for the year 1929.*—E. Sheard.

6. Mr. Sheard's reply to a questionnaire on the cultural anthropology and ethnology of the Bhantus.

C. J. B.

4. (iii) A.—The Sathiyas.

By Khan Bahadur D. F. Vakil, Census Officer of Ratlam State.

The Sathiyas are a wandering tribe and form one of the depressed classes though not untouchable They keep moving from one *hat* (weekly market or fair) to another with their animals, cattle and bullocks. They buy young bulls cheap and castrate them and sell the bullocks at a higher price. It is considered unlucky, if not a sin, to have one's cattle castrated; for, after castration, should any calamity befall in a family, the superstitious people attribute it to this practice. The peasants and farmers part with their bulls cheaply because of the difficulty and danger in controlling them, and exchange them for, or buy, bullocks from the Sathiyas who, though Hindus, have no scruples or compunction about this sort of practice and traffic, and who generally do castration themselves.

As the Sathiyas have no settled homes, they move about with their families, women and children, like the Gadulia Lohars or itincrant blacksmiths, also Hindus, who move about with their families in quaint bullock carts carrying their bellows, hammers, etc., with them; and who collect old and broken iron vessels und forge them into useful articles like tongs, *khurpas,* (ladles), scissors, hoes, etc.

These Sathiyas perhaps were once Rajputs, forced by circumstances to this sort of wandering life. But unlike the criminal Moghyas they carry on honest trade in bulls and bullocks. The Sathiyas are hard topers, both men and women indulging in country liquor. They quarrel constantly among themselves, hence the phrase "Sathiya jaise larna". Especially through the influence of liquor the quarrel takes place among them over most trivial affairs and is accompanied by blows of lathis and fists and often stones, which lead to profuse bleeding and render them unconscious for hours; sometimes grievous hurt is also caused to them. Inspite of these quarrels they never go to any court of law and after the incident they forget and forgive each other and do not retain any revengeful spirit or grudge.

On enquiry it is understood that these Sathiyas came originally from Hadoti district (Jhalrapatan) in Rajputana. This is evident from the dialect which they speak and which contains a few mutilated words of Hadoti language. They have no special language but their dialect is Malwi generally.

The Sathiyas are superstitious and hold the pipal tree sacred and take their oaths in the name of this tree. They believe in spirits and minor gods of the Hindus and offer prayers to them, when anyone in the family is taken ill.

No restriction of age exists among them for marriage; their system of marriage is very simple and common. Among them exists a peculiar practice, *viz.*, that of mortgaging their wives, daughters of other female members of their family to moneylenders—Sathiyas only from among their own class—for the debts contracted by them. To the creditor or to a person who stands surety for a Sathiya for a debt or for the performance of some engagement usually in a caste dispute, the Sathiya makes over his wife or any other female relative till she is redeemed on payment of the debt or on fulfilment of the obligation. The usufructuary right in this human "chattel" is recognised and if the woman conceives during the period of her transfer the natural child is claimed by and left at the house of the temporary or substitute husband. No shame or immorality is attached to the woman or her husband who has thus to pledge her. This does not mean that Sathiya women are of no account. They generally assist in managing animals and in driving bargains, etc.

The Banjaras, another well-known wandering tribe have a better sense of morality and tneir women are very chaste. So are the women of the Khanabadosh Iranis, who wander over the whole country and were once a terror to the country side. They are wrongly called gypsies; for they are really Persians, speaking among themselves excellent Persian. They say that they had come to India with Nadirshah's army, but did not return to Persia with him. These people never go to law courts, but their Jamadars or Sardars settle the disputes of their respective Kaflas or gangs. The chastity, alluded to above, among their women folk is perhaps due to the memory of the old punishment of Sangsar, that is, pelting the guilty one with stones.

These Iranis are Shias and swear by Ali and Panchtan. But they drink liquor and gamble. They used to live by horse-dealing but now-a-days they have no ostensible means of livelihood and they cheat or steal but are not known to commit burglaries. Their women pretend to make money by retailing knives and scissors, or locks and beads which they buy from a Bohra's shop when they go to some town in their wanderings. They travel by rail almost free like Sadhus and faqirs, one or two tickets being considered quite enough for a whole gang.

4. (iii) B.—The Bargundas.

By D. F. Vakil.

The Bargundas in Ratlam form one of the so-called depressed and untouchable classes, and their main occupation is the making of mats, brooms, etc., of date palm leaves and baskets of palm (*khajur*) sticks. They are not to be confused with Ganchhias, who split bamboo sticks and make bamboo baskets (*tokras*); nor with Kuchbandas who make *moris*, cords (*sikas*), etc., of *san* (hemp fibres).

From the dialect which the Bargundas speak among themselves it appears that they originally came from the Tamil Districts of Southern India and perhaps they belonged to some wandering tribes. The dialect is not pure Tamil but a strange mixture containing words of Tamil origin and possibly of Kanarese and Telugu also, in a corrupted and unintelligible form. They have forgotten many words of their own tongue and have substituted local words for them. They are not aware exactly what language they speak but they call it Bargunda 'Parsi'. Any peculiar or unknown dialect used by a tribe is called its 'Farsi' by the illiterate people.

In the Census Report of the Ratlam State for 1911 on page 4, there is the following reference to Bargundas :—

"The couvade custom, it is generally believed existed formerly among Bargundas. But on being questioned about this belief, they explain it away by saying that the story originated in the incident of a Bargunda's evading the service of a subpoena by pretending that according to the custom among his caste he had to take to his bed for some days as his wife had given birth to a child."

None of the local Bargundas is able to tell how when and where from they came and settled in this part of the country; but the old persons think that about 12 generations have passed since they came here. So some 300 years ago about the time the city of Ratlam was founded a band of these people appear to have migrated either through necessity or natural inclination to this part, dividing themselves into several batches and settling in Nemar in the Central Provinces and in Indore State, and in Malwa (Bhopal, Ujjain, Ratlam, etc.). In these various parts over which they are scattered they have become naturalised and have adopted the mode of living, dress, customs, manners and accent too of the indigenous tribes of similar type. They are very poor in condition and have forgotten the songs or traditions peculiar to themselves. They can sing only local (Malwi) songs and speak the local language. Their womenfolk go to the cities and villages carrying articles made by them and dispose of them generally for cooked food or leavings.

The Bargundas eat flesh of every kind except that of the cow as it is held sacred and they consider themselves superior among the classes who eat refuse of food thrown away, for they do not eat flesh of dead animals as Chamars do. The Bargundas are expert in catching *goyara* (not to be confounded with *gho*) a kind of large lizard, believed to be very poisonous. They eat goyaras or ghos as the Kalbelias are said to eat the snakes they catch. It is believed by ignorant people that lightening falls on a tree or a building when a *goyara* is on the top of it. The marriage ceremonies of Bargundas last for 3 days only, the females attending to all the functions. Remarriage of widows is allowed among them with the restriction that a bachelor is not permitted to marry a widow but a widower may marry a widow or a maid as he chooses. They worship lower orders of deities of the Hindu pantheon and believe in *bhuts*, devils and other evil spirits and take their oaths in the name of Ganga, Tulsi and other Gods. They burn their dead and observe mourning for three days only. On the 3rd or 4th day they perform 'nukta', *i.e.*, they invite their relatives and caste fellows and feed them as their means permit.

In the accompaniment to this note are recorded some words and sentences in the Bargundi dialect from the mouth of Bargundas themselves with their Tamil equivalents with the kind assistance of Mr. R. Y. Acharya of the Darbar Office.

D. F. VAKIL, *Khan Bahadur*,
Census Officer, Ratlam State, Ratlam.

The Bargundi Dialect.

Below are recorded some words and sentences in the Bargundi dialect from the mouth of Bargundas themselves with their Tamil equivalents.

	English transliteration of Bargundi.	Tamil.
I go ..	Nān pugāke	.. Nân pogirên.
We go ..	Nāng hadanu pugāko	.. Nângal pogirôm.
Thou goest ..	Ni pugarā	.. Nî pogirây.
You go ..	Ni hadanu pugāgāv ..	.. Nî po (singular) Nîngal pogurigal plural).
He goes ..	Ād pugāk	.. Avan pogirân.
They go ..	Ayā hadanu pāk ..	.. Avargal pogirârgal.
I shall go ..	Nān pogarevade ..	.. Nân povên.
We shall go ..	Hadanu pogarom ..	.. Nângal povôm.
Thou shalt go	Ni pogaravade ..	.. Nî povây.
You shall go ..	Hadanu pogarān ..	.. Nîngal povîrgal.
They shall go	Hadanu pogaron ..	.. Avargal povârgal.
He shall go ..	Vande pugar .	.. Avan povân.

	English transliteration of Bargundi.	Tamil.
I went ..	Nā pohane	.. Nân ponên.
We went ..	Nūng poyanom ..	.. Nângal ponôm.
Thou wentest	Nī poyanā	.. Nî ponay.
You went ..	Nīng poyanāng ..	.. Nîngal ponîrgal.
He went ..	Ad payadīs	.. Avan ponân.
They went ..	Ayā pohasu	.. Avargal ponârgal.
Speak ..	Pesa	.. Pêsu.
Sit	Koohabuk	.. Ukkâr.
Beat ..	Adhī	.. Adi.
I sit on a horse	Kodar ṃele kocharū ..	.. Nân Kudiraimêl utkârugiren.
He sits under a tree.	Ad seḍ uḍache kochabuk	.. Avan marattu aḍiyil utkârugirân.
Policeman has caught a thief.	Ulaged tirūde kopīḍachī	.. Polêskâran tiruḍanai pidittirukkirân.
The house has caught fire.	Udako nīrapu vudos ..	.. Vîttil nerruppu vilundadu.
A child has fallen into a well.	Vonḍ gōt ganḍarako udos	.. Kulandai kinarril vilundirukkiradu.
Put mangoes into the basket.	Māngāya bītako vachahu	.. Kuḍaiyil mâmpalam vai.
The ḍog barks	Nāh kol chāk .. .	.. Nâi kulaikkiradu.
Kill the hen ..	Kojake khand poḍung	.. Kôliyai kol.
Cook flesh and eat it.	Karī pukungo pīn tīnang	.. Kariyai samaittu sâppidu.
Water ..	Tanī	.. Nîr.
Air ..	Kās	.. Kâttu.
Fire ..	Nīrap	.. Neruppu.
Earth ..	Tar	.. Man ; tarai.
Red ..	Rātā	.. Sivapppu.
White ..	Vāle	.. Vellai.
One ..	Ond	.. Onru.
Two ..	Hareḍ	.. Irandu.
Three ..	Munḍ	.. Mûnru.
Four ..	Nal	.. Nângu.
Five ..	Ānj	.. Aindu.
Six ..	Ār	.. Âru.
Seven ..	Yeg	.. Êlu.
Eight ..	Et	.. Ettu.
Nine ..	Onmbaj	.. Onbadu.
Ten ..	Pat	.. Pattu.
Eleven ..	Padaonḍ	.. Padinonru.
Twelve ..	Panḍarund	.. Pannirandu.
Thirty ..	Murat	.. Muppadu.
Forty ..	Nālod	.. Nârpadu.
Nose ..	Muk	.. Mûkku.
Ear ..	Šārh	.. Kâdu.
Breast ..	Nenj	.. Mârbu.
Leg ..	Kāl	.. Kâl.
Arm ..	Ke	.. Kai.
Stomach ..	Varang	.. Vayir.
Wood ..	Nug	.. Maram.

	English transliteration of Bargundi.	Tamil.
Iron	Haram	Irumbu.
Brass	Pital	Pittalai.
Donkey	Ked	Kaludai.
Tiger	Pul	Puli.
Monkey	Bāndaron	Kurangu.
Bird	Pharejanāvar	Paravai.
Crow	Kāgalo	Kâkkai.
Coat	Āngad	Sokkâyi.
Pagri	Talavāt	Talaippâgu.
Sword	Āhad	Vâl.
Knife	Chakkū	Katti.
Pulse	Beḍ	Paruppu.
Sugar	Khānḍ	Sakkarai.
Milk	Pâl	Pâl.
How many children have you got.	Tine adankarakā adamasīrū	Unakku ettanai kulandai.
She cries	Ad angāsī	Aval lalugirâl.
The moon is full	Nelā purāvalasī	Mulu nillâ.
He laughs	Adī sīrachā	Avan sirikkirâu.
This is a wheat field.	Had godamen kolasī	Adu gôdumai vayal.
That is a cotton field.	Ad pherate kolachī	Idu parutti vayal.
God	Devar	Kaḍavul.
Heaven	Melak	Param.
Hell	Narak	Narkam (Sanskrit); kîl (classic Tamil).
Good girl	Vichake lalīsī	Nallappen.
Bad woman	Kulajāmārā nārāk	Keṭṭaval.
Stick	Kahakol	Kôl.
Basket	Mābuch	Kûdai.
Bamboo	Bāmsakol	Mûngil.
Beggar	Kīdako tīngār	Piccaikkâran.
Woman	Kulajāmārā	Pen.
Sister	Tangach	Udan pirandaval.
Brother	Tem	Udan pirandavan.
Mother	Gam	Tây.
Father	Gav	Tâgappân.
Father-in-law	Amān	Mâmanâr.
Mother-in-law	At	Mâmiyâr.
Sun	Chauk	Magan.
Daughter	Pichaker	Magal.
King	Rājo	Arasu.
Queen	Rāsīyāt	Ráni.
I see a snake on the ground.	Ṫaramele panmapāte	Nilattin mêl pâmbai âpparkiren.
When will you eat.	Yapo tingarā	Eppoludu sâppadu girây.
What will you drink.	Nīkudaoharā	Enna kudippây.
Which girl is good looking.	Lali pīchakaḍī yatanesī	Enda pen nalla alagu.

5. A.—The Sidhis of Kanara.

By H. T. Sorley.

Origin.

This community appear to have been imported into India by the Portuguese towards the end of the 17th century presumably as slaves.

It is not clear what numbers of this community are still to be found in Indian Portuguese territory but they are now to be found in scattered groups in Kanara, Mysore.

Religion.

It is curious in view of their origin that they show no strong tendency to retain the habits and practices of the African races and it is still more singular that they appear to have no desire to segregate themselves into compact groups, nor do they draw together under pressure and present a united front to the world. They may be divided into 3 groups.

(*a*) Those who practise Christianity.

(*b*) Those who are converts to the Hindu religion.

(*c*) Those who are adherents of Islam.

The Christian group, as may be expected, are members of the Romish faith, but it is admitted by their own priests that they are a difficult people to handle and not zealous in their obedience to the tenets of their faith. Both men and women change their partners frequently, often both dispensing with and ignoring the marriage tie. Not infrequently sanctification of a union is sought years after the couple have lived together as man and wife. Hindu and Muhammadan converts have identified themselves completely with the habits and practices of the religions which they have entered and Muhammadan Siddhis will cheerfully take sides with their co-religionists against either Hindu or Christian Siddhis. Similarly they appear to have lost all knowledge of their original mother tongue and speak exclusively the local vernacular dialect.

They are hardy, of robust appearance, and fearless in disposition. They are a long lived race. They are not untruthful and apparently not particularly superstitious. Both sexes are addicted to alcohol. A percentage are strongly Negroid in feature possessing blunt noses, crinkled hair, thick lips and a blank complexion, but the majority are of mixed descent and in some cases, are barely distinguishable from the castes among whom they live.

Formerly the whole clan were inclined to criminal practices but during the last 20 years they appear to have settled down to peaceful pursuits and the majority are engaged in agricultural labour generally in the capacity of tenant farmers. They are excellent shikaries and range the forests at will. They, however, are unable to settle in one place and constantly change the sites of their huts without apparent reason, they also frequently change their landlords after a period of 3—5 years, often merely for the sake of cultivating a new holding. Personal names show small trace of their African descent. Both the women and men are unchaste.

As a rule, regular marriages are contracted within the tribe and this may account for the general fact that families are usually small in number, the usual number of children per union being about two. So far as I was able to ascertain infant mortality is specially low among Siddhis but I must point out that this observation is based on too small a percentage of the total population to be of value.

Their numbers in the Kanara District are as follows :—

Ankola Taluka	224
Yellapur Taluka	791
Haliyall Taluka	1,126
Mundgod Peta	103

5. B.—Note on the Aboriginal and Hill Tribes Found in the Bombay Presidency.

By H. T. Sorley.

A reference to section 8 of the Chapter on Religion (*Bombay Census Report, 1931*) will show that the total number of these Tribes in the Bombay Presidency is 24 and that their probable strength to-day is in the vicinity of 1¼ milions. Of the total number of 24 Tribes the following 7 account for slightly more than one million of the total estimated population :—

Name.	*Recorded population.*
Bhil	536,491
Tadvi Bhils	8,241
Varlis	139,691
Dublas and Talavia	138,662
Thakurs	105,856
Dhodias	92,806
Katkaries	76,421
	1,098,168

Bhils.

This clan, which consists of a series of tribal groups, is for by far the largest unit among the Aboriginal and Hill Tribes and is possibly the most interesting. For their early chronology, their present habitat and composition and their general social system, a reference is invited to the remarks made by Mr. R. E. Enthoven in his publication entitled "Tribes and Castes of Bombay". Considerable controversy has taken place over the vexed question whether Bhils should be regarded as Hindus or Animists. The Reverend Enoch Hedberg, a missionary who has spent many years among the Bhils of West Khandesh, is of opinion that they should be regarded as Hindus but the reasons advanced by him in support of this view are not particularly convincing. However whether, the bulk of this clan should rightly be regarded as Hindu by religion or not it is less well known that a small group of Bhils scattered along the forest line on the southern slopes of the Satpuras, from Burhanpur to Chopda, are Muhammadan by religion. During the reign of the Emperor Akbar, a number of villages was granted to local Bhil chiefs as service grants for keeping the hill roads through the Satpuras clear of robbers. The attention of the Emperor Aurangzeb was apparently directed to this irregular police force and it is not impossible that in some cases at least the continuance of their grants of land was purchased by the holders at the cost of a change of religion. Since then their descendants have continued to ensure safe conduct to travellers through the passes of the Satpuras and in many cases these grants of land have been confirmed by the British Government, who still call upon the holders to perform minor police duties. The Emperor Aurangzeb appears also to have stiffened the local levies by adding a certain number of north country Muhammadans and posting them at selected points. These individuals were compelled to procure their womankind locally and the descendants of these Muslims and their Bhil wives and also the local converts are known in this Presidency as Tadvi Bhils. It is a curious fact that on the northern slopes of the Satpuras another group, also known locally as Tadvi Bhils exist, but these are one and all Hindu.* Thus we have two distinct sets of persons both known by the same designation, but differing in religion, residing in areas almost parallel to each other, at a distance of barely 50 miles apart and separated only by a single mountain range. *It is not clear whether the majority of the converts reverted to their former religious belief* but such an explanation fits the circumstances and cannot be regarded as extravagant.

*See below 6. B. *The Bhils of Central India* § 32.

6. A.—The commemorative monuments of the Bhils of the Satpuras.

By C. S. Venkatachar.

The Bhils cremate their dead. When a man is killed in a fight or by a wild animal away from his home, a stone monument is erected at the spot where he died. A man on horseback is generally carved on that stone. Such monuments are common in the Bhil tracts to the north of the Vindhyas.

Among the Satpura Bhils—the Tadvis mainly—memorial stones to a person of importance are common, and as this particular one shows it is erected in memory of a women. In the Bhil settlements in the Satpuras such monuments are dotted over more frequently than in any other place that has come to my notice during the course of my enquiry. The one which is chosen to be photographed was situated just at the foot of the hills.

The commemorative monument is usually of stone but wooden ones are also found. If stone is unavailable for any reason wooden monument is erected.

The most distinctive feature of these monuments is the wooden 'Zulla' (swing) as the Bhils call it. *It is placed just in front of the stone monument as shown in the photo. This* so-called swing is not to be found in any part of the Vindhyas and as far as my present information goes it is localised in the Satpuras. When questioned the Bhils told me that the swing is for the soul of the departed. It comes and perches on the swing and enjoys itself.

On the 2 wooden parts in figures, sometimes another cross piece of wood is placed. It was explained that food and offerings are left, presumably for the spirit of the departed. As regards the last stone slab I could get no particular information.

The spirit of the departed is invoked in times of distress and trouble and it is believed that a childless woman will be blessed with progeny by offering prayers at the monument.

MEMORIAL STONE ETC. ERECTED BY BHILS IN THE SATPURAS

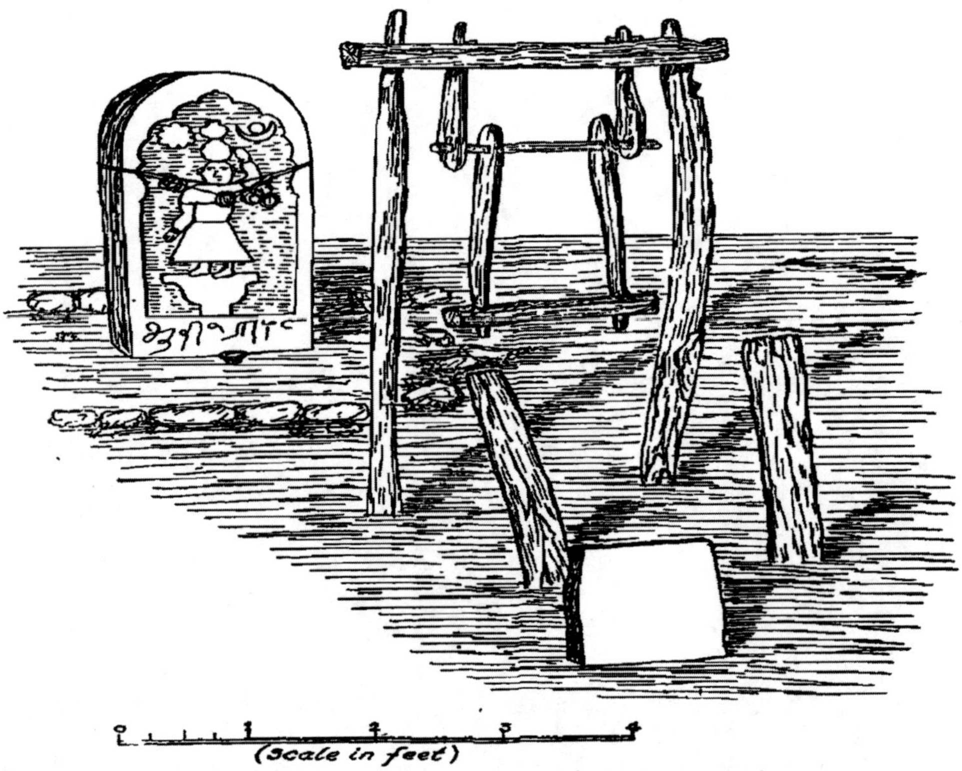

NB. The swing is drawn to scale, the rest is in perspective

6. B.—An Ethnographic Account of the Bhils of Central India.

By C. S. Venkatachar.

SECTION A.

The Bhil Tribe.

[NOTE.—The only detailed account of the Central Indian Bhils is that contained in a monograph entitled *the Jungle tribes of Malwa* which formed the second volume of a series of an uncompleted ethnographical survey of the Central India Agency by the late Colonel C. E. Luard, C.I.E., who for three successive decades from 1901 was in charge of the Agency Census. The materials for this monograph were collected by him in connection with the 1901 Census and published a few years later. So far as I know only two copies of this monograph are extant. As there was a danger of the valuable information contained therein being lost, I have reproduced it in the following pages, rearranging the matter and considerably abridging certain unnecessary details, supplemented here and there by fresh materials collected in the course of the present Census. The specimen of Bhil songs has however been reprinted *in extenso* without any change. I am also indebted to Mr. R. M. Puranik, M.A., LL.B., Census Officer of Dhar State and to the Roman Catholic Mission at Jhabua for placing useful notes at my disposal. It should be pointed out that no attempt has been made in the notes to distinguish the matter extracted from Colonel Luard's monograph from the supplementary notes.]

1. *Strength and distribution.*—According to the Census (1931) returns there are 363,124 Bhils in Central India Of these 144,836 returned themselves as Hindus and the remaining 218,288 retained their allegiance to their tribal religion. The true strength of the Central Indian Bhils has hitherto not been estimated. Certain tribes allied to the Bhils are paraded under different labels in the Caste table as separate castes or tribes. The strength of the Bhil group of tribes is considerable if we amalgamate, as we should, the figures for a number of the allied tribes. As far as it could be ascertained the following statement gives the composition and strength of the Bhil group :—

Bhil group.	Hindu.			Tribal.		
	Persons.	Males.	Females.	Persons.	Males.	Females.
1	2	3	4	5	6	7
1. Bhil	144,836	73,939	70,897	218,288	109,666	108,622
2. Bhilala	187,145	94,926	92,219	6,630	3,363	3,267
3. Barela	38,517	19,647	18,870	108	59	49
4. Mankar	20,430	10,058	10,372	49	26	23
5. Nihal	11,529	5,766	5,763	702	350	352
6. Patlia	8,268	4,280	3,988	11,140	5,812	5,328
7. Rathia	37,260	19,028	18,232	..	..	..

The Hinduised section forms 6·8 per cent. of the toal population and the Tribal section 3·6 per cent. Thus the Bhil group constitutes one-tenth of the total population of Central India. The tribes enumerated above are exclusively found in western Central India. Only few stray Bhils have been enumerated in the eastern parts of the Agency. In the west their real home is the Vindhyas and the Satpuras. The bulk of them have been returned from the States of Ratlam, Sailana, Jhabua, Dhar, Ali-Rajpur, Barwani and Indore.

2. *Name.*—It is commonly held that the word Bhil is derived from a Dravidian word for a bow (Tamil and Kanarese *bil*) which is the characteristic weapon of the tribe. The ancient Tamil poets termed certain savages of the pre-Dravidian blood as Villavar (bowmen) who 'may possibly be identical with the modern Bhils.'* If that be so, the name may have been given to the Bhils by the Dravidians. In common with the various Munda tribes, such as the Kols, Santals, etc., the tribal name, is not used by the members of the Bhil tribe among themselves. They employ the usual titles of relationship or position such as Bap (father), Tarvi (headman), Nahal or Naik (an honorific term). When addressing entire strangers the polite prefix *da* is added, as Da Rupa, Da Walji, etc. When the Bhils came in contact with the Aryans, they again figure in the Sanskrit literature. Thus the word Nisada which occurs in the early Vedic literature is sometimes held to mean a Bhilla or Bhil, though others hold that 'the word seems to denote not so much a particular tribe but to the general term for the non-Aryan tribes who were not under Aryan control.'† In the later system, the Nisada is the off-spring of a Brahman and of a Sudra woman‡. According to Mr. Enthoven the earliest mention of the word Bhil occurs in *Katha Sarit Sagara* of Gunadhya§ wherein mention is also made of a Bhil chief opposing the progress of another king through the Vindhyas. These references show that the Bhils are one of the earliest races in India and they have been brought into contact with all the great racial migrations into India.

3. *Origin.*—In the present state of our anthropological knowledge we cannot say whether the Bhils are autochthonous or not. At best we can only surmise and hazard some views leaving it to further scientific research to prove or disprove them. There is no doubt they represent a race which inhabited India earlier than the Aryans and the Dravidians. Very possibly they are a proto-mediterranean race who spread far and wide when a climatic crises occured in the grass steppes of Sahara and it is this race which is responsible for the industry associated with the final Capsian culture in the Vindhyas. The Bhils are one section of the great Munda race which occupied the pre-Dravidian India and had for its home the central regions across the peninsular India with possible extensions into the Gangetic plain. The home of the Bhils has been the western Vindhyas and it is perhaps in contact with the Dravidians on the other side in Gujarat they acquired their present appellation. If we accept the view which is gaining ground in recent years, that the Dravidians, a branch of the Mediterranean race, entered India through north-west then it is reasonable to suppose that Gujarat was on the way of the immigrant Dravidians in their march towards the Deccan and the south. Gujarat was a Dravidian tract before it was Aryanised. It is again significant to note that the home of the Nisadas as shown in the map in the Vedic Index exactly fits in with the historically known habitat of the Bhil tribe. There the Nisadas are shown as dwelling south-east of the Aravalli hills between the Banas and the Mahi rivers and up to the Chambal. The position shown is no doubt approximate but its significance cannot be underrated. The Bhils lay on the path of the conquering and the migrating Aryans towards Gujarat and Malwa. The impact of the Aryans must have caused the displacement of the Bhils along the Vindhyas and into the Satpuras but any such movement was restricted because they were flanked by the presence of other tribes of the Vindhyas and the Satpuras. In these hills the Bhils have maintained considerable independence, glimpses of which we get when we read of a Bhil Chief in the Sanskrit book already quoted and also of the forest king who assisted the Emperor Harsha in the search of his sister in the Vindhyan forests of Malwa. The

* *Cambridge History of India*, Volume I, page 595.

† *Vedic Index*, Volume II, Nisada.

‡ *Vedic Index*, Volume II, Nisada, foot-note.

§ *Tribes and Castes of Bombay*, Volume I, Art. Bhil.

Bhils, however, never appeared to have become effectively masters of the plain because Malwa was colonised in very early times and in spite of political convulsions, civilization never so fell as to facilitate the extension of tribal rule. Malcolm records that, according to the Bhil tradition, their home is in the country to the north-west of Malwa from where they were ousted when the Rajputs began to conquer their country. This again meant a further displacement of the Bhils along the Vindhyas. The tradition of the Bhils in Malwa points to immigration from a western home but the story of their change of habitat does not appear to have clearly survived. The Jhabua Bhils still retain some dim and incoherent outlines of their migration. Their story is that the first Bhils were the Damor. Another section of the Bhils were the Warkrya who were living with the Damor. One Warkrya committed violence on the daughter of a Damor as a result of which war sprung between the two people. The Damors fared badly in the struggle and they had to migrate. They stopped at a place called Dholka in Kushalgarh State (Rajputana Agency). This is supposed by the Bhils to be their original home and other tribes are said to have sprung from the Damors. The Bhils have their own traditions of their origin. One relates that a dhobi who used to wash his clothes in a river was one day warned by a fish of the approach of a great deluge. The fish informed him that as he had always fed those of his species he had come to give him this warning and to urge him to prepare a large box which would enable him to excape. The dhobi prepared the box and got into it with his sister and a cock. After the deluge Rama sent out his messenger to inquire into the state of affairs. The messenger heard the crowing of the cock and so discovered the box. Rama then had the box brought before him and asked the man who he was and how he had escaped. The dhobi told his tale. Rama then made him face in turn north, east and west, and swear that the women with him was his sister. The dhobi remained firm in asserting she was his sister. Rama then turned him towards the south, upon which the dhobi contradicted his statement and said she was his wife. Rama then asked who told him how to escape and on hearing at once had the fish's tongue cut, and since then that kind of fish has been tongueless. Rama then told the dhobi to set about repopulating the world, and he therefore married his sister by whom he had seven sons and seven daughters. Rama presented the first born son with a horse but the recipient of this gift, being unable to ride, left the horse on the plain and went into the forest to cut wood, he and his descendants becoming foresters and starting the Bhil tribe.

Another tale relates how on the creation of the Bhil, five men went to see Mahadev. Parvati seeing them approaching, said to her spouse, "Here come five of my brothers to ask *dahej* (bride-price) of you consequent on my marriage with you." Mahadev gave them a feast and then explained that except for his bull Nandi and his Kamandalu he had nothing to give. They therefore went home. In order to give them something, however, Mahadev placed a silver stool in their way, but they were incapable of seeing this. Parvati noticing how they had missed the gift, sent for them and told them what had happened, pointing out that as they were not able to see the stool, there was little hope of their prospering, but she would do what she could, and so informed them that they must be very careful of the Nandi whose hump was full of wealth untold. On reaching home one of the five suggested slaying the Nandi and obtaining the wealth, the others demurred, but he prevailed. No wealth was found in the hump and the five were dismayed. Parvati now appeared and told them that they should have yoked the bull to the plough and thus gained wealth from mother-earth, but that as they were so foolish as to slay the sacred animal she would never look on their faces again, and left in high displeasure. For thus killing the sacred animal the Bhil has ever lived a miserable existence and been of no caste.

The Puranik origin of the Bhils traces descent from the thigh of Vena, son of Anga, a descendant of Manu Swayambhuva. Vena was childless and the Sages therefore rubbed his thigh and produced "a man like a charred log, with flat face, and extremely short". He was told to sit down (Nishada). He did so and was known as Nishada, "from whom sprang the Nishadas dwelling on the Vindhyan mountains, distinguish by their wicked deeds."*

The Rajputs have had a very long connection with the Bhils. Forced by circumstances to make an alliance with the denizens of the Vindhyan hills, the Rajputs did not hesitate to take women from the tribal ranks and this was responsible for the disintegration of the Bhil tribes into various hinduised sections, such as Bhilalas, Patlias, etc. The infusion of Rajput blood has led in some instances to a distinction among the Bhils. For in some places the Bhils are split up into *Ujale* or pure and *Mele* or impure with a third or lower status the *Madalye* who are musicians and singers by profession. The *Ujale* and *Mele* Bhils are separate endogamous groups with septs which are exogamous.

4. *Caste and Tribal sub-divisions.*—The Bhils consequently are a very mixed lot at the present day Besides the Bhil proper, the other tribes are Bhilala, Barela, Mankar, Nihal, Patlia and Rathia. The description given in the following paragraphs relates to the Bhils as a whole. The other tribes are described briefly at the end of these notes. The divisions or the septs are very variously given and no two lists agree. They are summarised in a tabular form in a separate section. The usual reverence appears to be paid to any object which is regarded as a sept totem, it being never destroyed or injured, nor is its effigy ever tattooed on the body.

5. *Marriage : General.*—The Bhil tribe being an endogamous group no Bhil can marry without it. The septs again are all exogamous and no member of a sept can marry another from the same sept. This prohibition is extended for 3 generations to any sept into which a man has already married. A man cannot also marry into the sept from which his mother came for 3 generations as the members of this sept are held to be the brothers and sisters of such man. The same rule is extended to the septs of grandmothers, maternal and paternal. A man can marry two sisters but the exchange of daughters between fathers is not usual. Certain occupations are now looked upon with askance, due to Hindu influence, and certain families are inclined to reject marriage with a family which has taken up the following professions :—manufacturing of winnowing fans, and sieves, of a butcher, of a tanner, of a professional mendicant, of a *Rawal*, or dancer and singer. Sometimes, though it is not a formal restriction, the village Bhil does not like to take a wife from among the Bhils living near the bazar or in the town. The rural Bhil has a low opinion of the town dweller and he does not think much of the morals of the bazar Bhil girl.

Marriage is adult and infant marriage is non-existent unless Hindu ideas have overpowered the tribal practice. The earliest age for marriage of girls is 12 years, while most are married between 15-40. Puberty has no place in determining the age at which the girl is to be married. In accordance with the Hindu ideas, the parents settle the marriage, and courtship, though apparently by no means uncommon, is not in general vogue.

Where pre-nuptial sexual intercourse takes place with the affianced husband, no penalty is incurred, except that the regular marriage ceremony is omitted, the girl being simply made over to the man. If the the sexual license is indulged by the girl with another than her fiancé, she is, if the fiancé still desires it, made over to him but the support of the child born of the irregular intercourse is borne by the real father.

* *See Mahabharata, Vishnu Puran, Hari-Vansa, etc.*

6. *Marriage ceremonies.*—Four persons from the boy's side go to the girl's house to settle the betrothal. If the girl's guardians are willing a sum of Rs. 7 is paid to the *panches* who purchase *gud* and wine and entertain the caste people. The betrothal then becomes irrevocable. When means permit some persons from the boy's side go to the bride in the company of some guests and entertain the members of the caste with wine and *gud* worth Rs. 9. The party is then entertained by the girl's father and thus end the rites of *Badi Sagai*.

When marriage preparations begin a party consisting of 5 to 25 guests starts for the bride's house. After mutual entertainments the boy's father pays Rs. 41 for the dowry and the celebration of marriage is settled. The party then returns home.

The boy and girl in their respective houses are anointed with oil and turmeric. This marks the commencement of marriage ceremony which is known as "*Bana Baithana.*" This ceremony is performed at the bride's house on the day next to that on which it is performed at the boy's. They are daily taken in procession at their own residences when their relatives give money varying from an anna to a rupee. As soon as these *Banas* have finished the marriage shed is erected. Four poles are located in the ground and the shed is covered with *jamun* leaves. It is decorated on its sides by the hangings of mango leaves. One post is fixed in the *mandap* which crosses the roof and goes high above the house with leaves of Jamun tied to its top. Four unmarried boys and girls first dine under the Mandap and then the whole caste is entertained with "*Makka Thuli.*" The relatives then give clothes to the members of the family which is called "*Perawain.*" The bridegroom is attired in marital costume of red and white. Round his waist a scarf is tied. He takes dagger and sword in his hand. Well clad and ornamented, he puts on his head the marriage crown of imitation pearls and stands under the *mandap* where his mother moves rice-pounding pestle, arrow, and grain thrasher etc., round his face and throws 4 cakes in four quarters, this ceremony being called *Padachhana* ceremony. Placing a coconut at the feet of *Mata*, the wedding party starts at night for the bride's village and stops at that place where fire is kindled for them by the bridge's people before the dawn.

The bridegroom then touches the ornamental hanging on the door with the sword he carries and is seated under the booth. A pair of cloths and shoes, and a bodice are presented to the girl early in the morning. The bride is bathed and dressed in those clothes. The same "*Padachhana*" ceremony is repeated here by his mother-in-law. A long piece of cloth is put round his neck and his mother-in-law draws him on to the picture of their family deity, by holding the ends of that cloth.

No sooner does the bridegroom reach that place than the bride extinguishes the lamp burning there. The boy again lights it and worships the *Mata*. The ends of the upper garments of the couple are knotted and the bride's brother joins their hands. Subsequently he separates the hold and is given some *gud* for his service. A caste dinner is given after which the whole party goes to a stream or river to clean their hands and mouth, the females dining at home. The auspicious "Kankan," and copper ring are tied round the wrist of the bridegroom there. After the party returns from the stream the cloth of the couple is knotted and the couple seated on a piece of cloth. The hand of the one is locked in that of the other and this is called "*lagan.*" A Brahman or any caste member in his absence, assists in the performance of "*hom,*" in which oblations of ghee, oilseeds, etc., are offered. With their hands joined the couple give 7 turns round the nuptial fire. Then follows *Kanyadan.* Some cloths, silver ornaments and cash varying from one to five rupees are given. The hold of the hands is separated.

A few days after that the members of the bride's family come to the boy's house to fetch the bride. When they come they ask the boy's parents whether they are asleep or awake. When the boy's father hears this he brings a cock or a goat, which is killed by the bride's party. The guests are then entertained and the bride taken to her parent's house. The same custom is observed when the boy's party goes to fetch the bride. These rites are called "*Ana*" rites. Generally one rupee is paid to the Government as a marriage fee.

7. *Other forms of union.*—The description given above applies to the orthodox form followed by well-to-do and the completely Hinduised section of the Bhils. The Bhil knows to his cost that the adoption of Hindu customs is extremely expensive. The whole series of the marriage customs amount to a total of at least Rs. 350, which is a minimum. Many boys cannot afford such a sum of money. So sometimes after formal betrothal they take away their betrothed by surprise, by force or by mutual secret consent. They thus save a great deal of money and incur few expenses. Sometimes the girl of her own accord goes to the house of a young man and declares her intention to remain there. The union is regularised by the recognition accorded by the *Panchayat.* When a man has not enough money to perform a solemn marriage he searches for a girl whose price is cheaper. A girl who has had a child or a rejected girl, would be his likely bride. She is given a '*Lugra*' and '*Ghagra*' and some money. The girl becomes his wife without any further ceremony.

8. *Ghar Jamai.*—The payment of bride-price by means of personal service is often met with. Where the girl's father is well-to-do the young man undertakes to serve a term for his future father-in-law. This is commonest where the girl has no brothers to assist the father in his work. The usual term of years is seven. It is reported that in recent times it has become the practice of making him serve for 9 years. Though not seldom, the Ghar-jamai often escapes with his wife after 2-3 years. Ordinarily the two live as husband and wife but cannot leave the bride's home until the period of service is complete. If the two live amicably but after 2 years have no issue, the father-in-law has them anointed as if for a regular wedding and they are made to do 7 '*Pheras*' as in ordinary marriages. The father-in-law provides the young couple with means to start their own home.

9. *Marriage by capture.*—Marriage by capture or *ghiskarlejana,* is still common. The usual time for abducting a girl is on the *Bhagoria* festival, the day before the *Holi* is burned. The young man assisted by his friends enters the village and makes off with the girl. Occasionally the union is regularised by going through a short ceremony which is also performed in the case of a girl who falls in love and goes off with the man of her choice.

10. *Re-marriage of widows.*—The remarriage of widows is permitted. There is, however, no obligation for her to marry any particular person such as her husband's younger brother (*dewar*). When the consent of the lady is known the suitor goes to her village with some clothes as presents and attended by four or five friends. He pays seven pice to the widow's brother's wife (*bhabi*) or to her paternal aunt (*phuwa*), provided they have husbands living. A general drink is then indulged in, in which the Tarvi of the widow's village takes part, and the ceremony is complete. This re-marriage is always done by night. The widow never enters her new home by day, as this will, it is believed, produce famine. Any person who accompanies the man marrying a widow is bound to carry out this duty seven times.

The widow, and children by the re-marriage, have no interest in the property of the first husband after re-marriage.

In a case where she marries her deceased husband's younger brother, should there be already a son by the first husband, children by the second have no rights in the property of the first husband. If, on the other hand, there was no child by the first husband, children of the second inherit the property of the first husband.

11. *Divorce.*—Among the Bhils divorce is frequent. The man who keeps a woman who has left her husband has to pay her former husband whatever expenses the latter has incurred in marrying her. Any reason is sufficient for a divorce. To effect a divorce the injured man calls together his village *panchayat* and in their presence tears off a piece from the end of his turban which he hands to his wife, stating that finding that her conduct was bad he is divorcing her and that from this day forth she will stand to him in the relationship of a sister. The divorcee takes the piece of cloth and hangs it carefully on a rafter of her father's house for a whole month.* This shows that her former husband has no further rights over her and she can re-marry.

The Bhils are very suspicious of their women folk, and not without reason as the majority of criminal cases which are brought by Bhils concern their women. This is a reason why they do not build their houses close together.

12. *Funeral ceremonies.*—The Bhils cremate their dead. They bury young babies whose teeth have not yet appeared, lepers and persons dying of small-pox and of suicide. All these are buried in sleeping position. An ascetic is buried in the sitting position. On the occurrence of death notice is given by firing off guns before the deceased's house, while the village dhobi sounds his drum. The corpse is bathed in cold water and dressed and in the case of unmarried adults some turmeric is thrown on the dress. It is placed on a bier with the face upwards and covered with a cloth. Two coconuts are hung at the head of the bier. The eldest son or a near relative, if there is no son, takes an ignited cake of cowdung in his hand and the corpse is carried to the cremation ground, the man with the fire leading the way. Sometimes music played softly, accompanies the bier. The corpse is always carried so as to lie north and south, the feet pointing to the south. In the meanwhile, in the deceased's house a small lamp is placed upon the spot where the person died, sprinkled with maize and covered with a bamboo basket.

On coming to a *ber tree* (Zizyphus jujuba) the corpse is set down, while all the persons present proceed to take up stones with which a heap is made. A piece of cloth is then torn off the dead man's garment and thrown over the tree. The corpse is then picked up, those formerly at the head going to the feet. Tradition has it that the rest under the *ber* is made for this reason. Once the son of an aged dame died. The old women carried his corpse as far as a *ber* tree but could not go on further. She then decided to appeal to the gods by fasting, for the restoration of her son's life, and sat for three days fasting beneath the tree. This was not the fruit season, but seeing her piety the gods gave the tree fruit, and also caused hunger to attack her. She could bear her pain no longer and rose to seize the fruit. Suddenly the tree grew and raised the fruit beyond her reach. At length she propped the corpse against the tree and standing upon it reached the fruit. She had broken her vow and the village people took and cremated the corpse. To avert any such evil each corpse is now halted under a *ber* tree, and a piece of the garment is offered to the gods. The earthen vessel containing water to wash the corpse is taken and broken under this tree on the heap of stones.

Burning ghats are situated anywhere near a stream or tank. The body is placed on the pyre with its head to the north and burnt together with the man's bow, club, etc., and in the case of a woman some favourite ornament. The unconsumed bones are carefully collected from the pyre and separated from the ashes. The bones are placed in an earthen vessel and buried near the house. There they remain till the 12th day ceremony is performed. If there is no chance of carrying out the ceremony they are thrown into the nearest river, usually the Narbada. The deceased is provided with food and drink on the 3rd day, the provisions being placed under the *ber* tree where the corpse rested. The stones heaped up there are scattered.

13. *Belief in a future life.*—The Bhils have some definite ideas about the future of the departed soul. The flour round the lamp is examined and by the shape of the marks, it is determined what animal the spirit of the dead will next inhabit. If it is like a human footprint a man is his next abode ; if like a hoof, a horned animal ; if like a bird's foot, a bird ; if like a scorpion or snake, one of these animals. It is also believed that Yama comes from the south and carries the soul of the dead man to the north. On the way the soul passes over a thorn-strewn plain. Hence shoes are given as gift on the day of the funeral feast or else his spirit suffers greatly. He then passes between two heated pillars ; the spirit then encounters a *bhatyari* (keeper of cook shop) who offers him hot cooked food. He then reaches a river. A cow is given as a gift. It is supposed this animal providentially appears and by treading on its tail, the departed gets across, otherwise he suffers agonies and is half drowned. On reaching the end of the journey Yama determines which of the three hells (lit, kunds or tanks) he is to enter, one being full of nectar, the others of varying degrees of foulness (worms, blood, etc.,) until he is born again. Those who die a violent death become inimical spirits (*bhut*), so do Badwas or medicine men ; others become Khatris, who however cannot harm human beings but only animals, and others *Deos* who are beneficent spirits. A sinner is also believed to be transformed into an insect.

14. *Memorial stones to the dead.*—When a man is killed in a fight or by a wild animal away from his home, a stone monument is erected at the spot where he died. A man on horse back is generally carved on the stone. Such monuments are common in the Bhil tracts to the north of the Vindhyas. Among the Satpura Bhils—the Tadvis mainly—memorial stones to a person of importance are quite common. The commemorative monument is usually of stone but wooden ones are also found. If stone is unavailable for any reason wooden monuments are erected. These Satpura monuments are somewhat elaborate. First of all there is an upright stone monument of about 3½ feet high on which the figure of the person in whose memory it is erected is carved *i.e.*, a man or a woman. In front of it are two wooden posts, 4½ feet high with a bar placed across them on the top. Suspended from this bar is a small wooden swing. This is followed by two small wooden posts, not more than 2 feet in height and finally there is a small stone slab of about 1 foot high and 9 inches in breadth. The most distinctive feature of these monuments is the wooden swing. This is meant for the soul of the departed. It comes and perches on the swing and enjoys itself. On the smaller wooden posts, a cross bar is placed on which food and offerings are left for the spirit of the departed. In times of distress and trouble the spirit is invoked and it is believed that a childless woman will be blessed with progeny by offering prayers at the monument.

15. *Religion.*—It is difficult to describe precisely the religion of the Bhil. He has been in contact with Hinduism for a long time and in spite of his preference for Hindu gods and godlings, his outlook is essentially animistic. The Bhils call themselves Hindus, invariably asserting that they are the followers of Mahadev and they have appropriated all the well-known gods of the Hindu pantheon. *Baba deo* is a generic term for the village tutelary deity. In *Shrawan* he is specially worshipped. All the village collects at the forest where he is making his abode and offer liquor, grain and fowl. Many other forest, woodland and mountain deities are worshipped. Local gods vary with almost each village.

* Somtimes for half a month only.

Brahmans are not as a rule employed for religious or ceremonial purposes. The Badwa or the medicine man is an important person in their tribal life. He evokes spirits and tells them the results. On such occasions the Badwa or witch is supposed to be possessed and goes through a performance consisting of various contortions of the body and rapid movements of the head, the eyes roll in their sockets while the nostrils are distended and in the excitement the few rags worn are often thrown off. The possessed being then half incoherently blabbers out what the spirit has told him, and soon after calms down and for a time becomes as helpless as a child, doubtless owing to the exertion he has undergone.

In casting out disease or an epidemic from a village, after a sacrifice to the principal deity, the Badwa will visit all the sacred spots within the precincts of the village, chanting in a droning tone some invocation, followed by drummers ; at each spot he will offer a little red ochre and a piece of coconut, while at the principal entrance into the village limits, he will show by various antics and rapid gestures of hand and body with his back turned to the village, that the spirit to which the disease was due has been cast out into the adjoining territory. Another form of casting out an epidemic is to sling some baskets, that have contained corn, and earthen pots that have been used for water, on a bamboo pole which is carried on the shoulders of men who run along the main road shouting at the top of their voices *todka* ; *todka*. On hearing the shouts, the next village sends out men to meet the procession at the boundary and these take over the burden and so the process is repeated. Thus the epidemic is carried away often to great distances, until eventually it is thrown into some stream or river which stretches across the path or is deposited in the forest. If no one from the next village is present to meet the procession at the boundary, the bearers are at liberty to deposit their burden in the village precincts. Sometimes a young he-goat is similarly carried on the shoulders of men or tied on to a light bier. The origin of Bhilat Deo worshipped by the Rathia Bhils is as follows :—

Bhilat Deo was the son of Ruparela Gaoli and his mother's name was Mheinda Rani. He was a great simpleton when young, and in consequence was always being chaffed and made fun of by every one. Accordingly disgusted of life, he left his country and after wandering far and wide arrived in Gaur Bengal where he met a spirit Karanda Jogan by name who taught him magic. He studied the art to perfection and then returned to his native place to pass the remainder of his days. On one occasion while many people were collected together, he took his harp and began playing when a snake came out of a mole-hill. The snake was so huge that the earth vibrated beneath the lashings of his tail. Bhilat Deo, however, caught the snake and took it to Indar Raja (Indra) who was greatly pleased to see his marvellous strength and power and ordered the people to reverence him as a Deo (god) in future ; thus, his worship started. Indar Raja gave him Bheru Deota for a personal attendant, and also presented him with some cows as a reward of his merit. Bhilat Deo selected a spot under a tree on Mangalawri hill near Sendwa in Indore State, to settle. His cows increased daily in number, so much so, that he employed 900 cowherds to look after them, each man taking up his abode with his cows on a separate hill. Thus each of these spots represents the site of Bhilat Deo, the gods being kept under a tree or under some rude cover or in a small temple.

The Bhils have great reverence also for hill tops difficult of ascent, as being the abode of spirits which must be propitiated during sickness or calamity or to obtain offspring. In such cases, after the usual offering the forest is often set alight.

16. *Charms and witch-craft.*—Sometimes a newly-born baby has an elongated skull which may be due to the pressure of a too narrow opening of the womb. But the superstitious Bhils, seeing that the baby has a queer head believe it is an evil spirit and kill the baby at once, or if the newly-born baby looks queer and is queerly shaped, it is also killed thinking it is an evil spirit. It is reported that such murders are not rare.

The belief in magic and witch-craft is universal. Should any person fall sick without clear cause the Badwa is called in to exercise the evil influences at work and discover the origin of the illness. With care he can usually discover some wretched old beldame who lives in the sick man's village and falling into a trance describes her accurately to the inquirers. The witch would be placed on one end of a yoke with cowdung cakes on the other in a pond. If she sank she was a witch. If she swam she was innocent. Red pepper would be put into her eyes ; if no tears came she was a witch. In cases of serious illness it is almost invariably considered to be due to a witch taking possession of the patient's heart. A Badwa's charms are the only remedy. The sick man is often subjected to fumigation with the leaves of plants, a charmed thread is tied on his neck while a special dance in which the gods are invoked, is performed round him. He is then often carried from village to village. A few grains of *jowar* mixed with a copper coin are passed round the sick man's body and then sent to a Badwa. The Badwa then places over them a leaf of the Butea frondosa and floats the whole collection on water. He then picks out the grains and slowly drops them one by one into the water saying *bhut, deo, dakini* (witch), successively. When a grain floats he is thus able to determine which of these evil influences is at work, by the name which fell to the grain which floated. If it is determined to have been caused by a witch, he then repeats the process calling out the names of all the witches known to him. Should no grain float, the sickness is put down to natural causes. Another process is to take a handful of grain, chips of wood or leaves and throw them away counting each piece or grain as it falls and repeating this process for every known witch until an odd number falls to one of the names ; the name so determined is that of the offender.

The belief in witch-craft is not only common amongst the Bhils but is widespread from the highest to the lowest classes. An excellent account of its prevalent in former times in Central India will be found in Sir J. Malcolm's *Memoirs*.* A reported case of witch-craft occurred nearly 45 years ago. In 1888 a Kachhi called Rata complained that his mother Issa had been, by order of the Rao of Bhatkheri, mounted on a donkey by a scavenger, beaten and turned out of the village as a witch ; had then been made to drink water offered by a mochi, and beaten. The woman died from this treatment. Her body was burnt and the complainant's house broken into and Rs. 2,000 taken away. Complainant was away at the time, and on his return was told to leave the village.

Inquiry followed, on which the Rao admitted that Issa had been thus treated because she was a witch, and had caused the death of the wife and son of a rich Bania. Issa was 'named' as a witch and driven out of the village. She, however, came back and was seized. It was alleged that on being seized she was said to have asked for a leopard to ride on but as no leopard was forthcoming they put her on the donkey, blackened her face, made her eat from a scavenger's hand and expelled her from the place. The Rao stated he himself heard her barking like a dog, and saw her making attempts to bite like one, and that after her expulsion she remained outside Bhatkheri for some days barking and flying at passers-by like a dog, till she died.

17. *Oaths and trial by Ordeal.*—Trial by ordeal is common, though in places it is now dying out. Some of the forms employed were the swallowing of live coals in the hand, piercing the palm of the hand with an arrow, eating poisonous herbs or fruits etc. The simplest form consists in making the man take a solemn oath and

* II, 212-217.

then waiting for seven days. If (within this period) any mischance befalls him, or his family, or possessions, he is considered to have perjured himself, and the case goes against him. One common form of oath in such cases is this. The man is brought before the *Sarkari Gaddi*. This is simply a chair in the nearest Tahsil office. A clean white cloth is thrown over it and it is placed in full view. This represents the ruler of the State and is in fact the emblem of authority. The man touches the chair with both hands and swears by *Barabij*. The Tarvi, who is administering the oath, turns to the east, and draws a circle on the ground with the point of a sword, commencing on the east and passing round by the north and west. Within this circle two lines are drawn joining north and south and east and west. The sword is then placed in the circle with its point to the east. The Tarvi then turns to the man and says: "if your cause is a good and true cause, raise Bhavanimata in your hand (*i.e.*, the sword)." The man does so exclaiming "Barabij visit me with evil within seven days (or other period) if I swear untruly." He then lifts the sword, bows and replaces it. The Barabij are the twelve *bij* or second day of each mouth, on which the new moon is usually first visible, and is a day held in reverence. Other oaths are laying the hand on a son's head and swearing; taking up one of the village gods (image) in the hand and swearing; in boundary disputes a goat is beheaded and then skinned and the skin placed on the man's head, who with his face to the east, swears his cause is good, and then drags the skin along the line of the boundary. Certain oaths are inviolable. One is that of the dog. A Bhil swears with his hand on a dog's head calling out that the curse of the dog should fall on him if he swears falsely. It appears that the dog as the companion of the god *Bhairon* is specially looked up to.

18. *Omens.*—These are very numerous. Some are given in the table below :—

A list of common omens observed at starting from the house.

No.	Omans.	Auspicious.	Inauspicious.	Time.
1	Beda-pani calls	On the left	On the right	Any time.
2	Cry of the Devi-Chiriya	Left	Right	Day.
3	Caw of a crow	,,	,,	,,
4	Cry of the Chiwara	Right	Left	Night.
5	A deer crossing the path	Left to right	Right to left	Day.
6	Call of the Sara	Right	Left	,,
7	Cry of the Saras	Left	Right	,,
8	Cat crossing path	Left to right	Right to left	Any time.
9	Snake crossing path	In either direction	..	,,
10	Cry of the Kanahari	Right	Left	Day.
11	Braying of a donkey	Left	Right	Any time.
12	Bellowing of a bull	From either side	..	,,
13	Lowing of a cow	,,	..	,,
14	Hooting of an owl	Left	Right	Night.
15	Howling of a jackal	,,	,,	,,

If a peacock cries before dawn on the third *Vaisakh* his cries are counted as it is believed there will be as many months of rain as there are cries. This is considered a most reliable omen. The appearance of a lark, calling just before rain is due, is a good sign. When sparrows constantly bathe in the dust, rain, even if just commenced will soon cease. The croaking of frogs is another sure prediction of rain The calls of certain birds are held to fortell success in the pursuit of game. Again when starting on an errand if a horse should neigh on the right side, it bodes success : if on the left side, failure. It is usual to seek knowledge of the return of a member of the family. This is done by going to an old women versed in such lore, who takes a winnowing fan which she balances on the little finger of her two hands, 5 grains of wheat or maize being placed on it. She then addresses the fan asking if the wayfarer will return. If the fans moves in answer all is well.

In former times when the Bhils seized a whole herd they sometimes offered a human sacrifice to the *Mata* of the thieves. They then killed the shepherd near the *Mata* as a sacrifice. The sacrifice was also conducted in another way. The shepherd was taken to the top of a steep hillock. His legs and arms were tied and he was rolled down the hill. These practices have been abandoned now. A common vow taken in honour of the *Mata* is to burn seven hills or to burn seven houses. When the grass in the jungle is dry they set fire in seven different places so as to destroy a great amount of grass in every one of these seven places. These acts are done presumably to obtain help of the *Mata* or to thank her for the success of a plundering expedition.

Appearance and character and social rules and customs.

19. *Physical type.*—There is a classic description of the Bhil attributed to the much maligned Bengalii Babu! "The Bhil is a black man but more hairy. When he meets you in his jungle, he shoots you in the back with an arrow and throws your body into the ditch. Thus you may know the Bhil."* Malcolm describes the plundering or wild Bhils who reside in the hills, as a "diminutive and wretched looking race whose appearance shows the poverty of their food: but they are nevertheless active and capable of great fatigue †." The typical Bhil has a broad nose, thick lips which are 'opened' and the upper jaw is somewhat strong and prominent. He is dark but owing to much intermixture there are varying shades of darkness among the Bhils of different localities. Their hair is black but not woolly, and straight but not wavy. Many men, especially the young ones, like to keep long hair. The eyes are straight and usually black.

20. *Character.*—The Bhils in villages and in more settled parts have lost much of their suspicion of strangers and live like the lower castes. In the wider and inaccessible parts they are still very timid. They vacate a village on the least provocation such as sickness or a rumour of probable harsh treatment. Though they have given up their predatory habits, the propensity to take to plunder is still lurking in them. Some of them are enlisted in the Malwa Bhil Corps where they have proved faithful and loyal. They are capable of great endurance and it is recorded in 1858 some women of the Malwa Bhil Corps walked over fifty miles without once stopping, most of the way lying through heavy jungle. They are truthful unless spoilt by being 'civilised.'

* Sir Michael O'Dwyer, *India as I knew it.* † *Memoir* ii, 179.

21. *Admission of outsiders.*—A Chamar or Bhangi is not admitted to the caste. Others if eligible are admitted. Under Hindu influence, a ceremony has been devised for such admissions. The man is called before a panchayat. He then prepares a *tirth* as it is called of cowdung and Ganges or other holy water in a dish. This is presented to the Patel or Tarvi presiding. The patel drinks it, and the same ceremony is then performed with the members of the panchayat. Rice boiled in goat's blood is then presented and eaten. A payment of four or five rupees to the Patel concludes the ceremony ; save for the inevitable carouse which winds up all Bhil ceremonies. Social position is determined by food, admittedly an importation from Hindu ceremonies. Thus the too near approach of a man of the sweeper or Gachha caste to food which is being cooked defiles it. If a man of these castes touches a Bhil's clothes they must be washed.

Balais and Chamars, " whom " it is naively remarked " we must have about us to do the village work," are allowed to take water from the village well, but not Gachhas or sweepers. It is amusing to note the Bhil observe untouchability. The high caste Hindu does not consider a Bhil an untouchable.

22. *Panchayat.*—Before the organisation of a judiciary in the States, the *panchayat* used to decide cases of all natures. The *panches* now try and decide such cases as pertain to the caste. Petty disputes are settled by the *panches.* The tribal constitution however appears to be disintegrating in recent times according to the report of some observers. The charge of the headman, the Tarvi, remains hereditary. The Nat Patels in former days exercised considerable authority but the tendency now is to reject their authority. Nobody seriously obeys the decision of the *panchayat.*

23. *Tattooing.*—This operation is generally performed at ten to twelve years of age on girls, on the cheeks, forehead, arm below the elbows, chin and wrists, and the calf of the leg and feet. Men are tattooed between 8 and 9, on arms, wrists and chests. Men operators tattoo men, women and girls. The object of tattooing is said to be this. After death each individual is asked whether he has been pricked by thorns in the jungle ; the presentation of these tattoo marks is considered as affirmative answer, without this they would have to be pricked with thorns in after life*. Designs are numerous and are made to the fancy of the person operated on. Boys, it should be added, are in the habit of burning marks on each other on the back and wrist in either five or seven distinct places. This is done with a piece of smouldering cloth or the match of a match-lock. The custom is called *dhamla* and appears to have the same object as tattooing. Females are never branded in this way.

24. *Occupation.*—The Bhil always states that agriculture is his original occupation. If so, he can scarcely be credited with much recollection of it, as at this day he does but little cultivation even when every endeavour is used to induce him to settle and he is given land and pecuniary assistance. Tradition has it, however, that the Bhil at his creation was given by Mahadev a plough, sickle, harrow and a pair of bullocks and was promised that if he sowed two *Seers* of cereals he should reap two *Manis.* Gradually the States are getting the Bhils to settle and become regular cultivators and many now hold leases from the Darbar like ordinary agriculturists but as a rule on very easy terms. Where regular settlements exists the Tarvi or headman generally contracts for the revenue of the village making what he can out of the inhabitants. Cultivation is often done by outsiders who are paid a share of the produce. Sometimes a man agrees to work for 3 days for another, cultivating his own land on the fourth day. Hindu ideas as to propitious days, etc., have become general, with some modifications, in the observances followed. Thus before sowing a cultivator sets up a stone at the top of his field and anoints it with red lead breaking a coconut over it ; this stone represents Ganesh. The evil eye is averted from crops thus. Two sticks are planted in the ground with a piece of conspicuous coloured cloth tied to them or heaps of stones are raised and whitewashed. The onlookers' gaze thus falls first on these objects. After the reaping is is completed, the evil spirits are appeased by the offering of a cock and liquor. Before a well is sunk a stone is set up and anointed with red lead and propitiated with offerings, the stone standing in this case for the water deity of the locality.

Except in the case of such few who have taken to cultivation, the Bhils are still a wandering population and as a rule have no fixed village. Without migrating far away, they keep wandering within certain limits in the States of the Vindhyas. Many find occupation in reaping the harvests on the uplands of Malwa from March to April. If the Bhils were encouraged to build *pacca* houses they would become less wanderers. Many of them, every third or fourth year desert their village and settle elsewhere. So long as they have the spirit of *wander-lust* they will never become good agriculturists. Some take up the work of village watchman and a great many are addicted to plunder and theft. One observer who has 22 years' experience among the Bhils writes that the majority of them go in for theft. A hundred years of peaceful rule in Central India has not completely reformed them and weaned them away from their former habits. They are no longer turbulent as they were in the days of unsettled rule in Malwa. But still they remain low and degraded. Malcolm wrote " that the common answer of a Bhil when charged with theft or robbery is 'I am not to blame ; I am Mahadev's thief '. In other words my destiny as a thief has been fixed by God ".†

25. *Inheritance.*—Tribal custom determines inheritance. Of the property half goes to the youngest son, who is responsible for the payment of all expenses incurred on his father's *nukta* (the feast given after his death, usually on the 12th day after). He has also to make provision for his sisters. The other half is divided between the elder sons. If they all live together, a very rare occurrance, they share equally in the property. In the case of the deceased being a Tarvi or headman, his position is assumed not necessarily by the eldest son, but by the most fit, who is chosen by the *Panches.* He then becomes entitled to the usual rights pertaining to the position, as well as its responsibilities, such as entertaining strangers of position, etc. In the case of a Tarvi dying childless, his successor is chosen in the family. A widow is mistress of her husband's property for life, provided she conducts herself properly. It is not uncommon, however, to divide the property in order to prevent disagreeable quarrels. A daughter can under no circumstances inherit her father's property. Only those who are *sagotra* (of the dead man's sept) can inherit. If there are no heirs, the *Panches* consider the case, and no relatives being traceable, the property goes to the Darbar.

26. *Festivals, music and amusement.*—The Bhil observes the principal Hindu festivals. A mock marriage of two dolls representing the deities who control the rain is sometimes performed. Just before the *Holi* a great fair called *Bhagoria hat* is held. The men put on their best clothes and carrying bows and arrows dance in a circle ; women cannot take part in it. If it can be called so, the drum is their chief musical instrument. On this three predominant notes are used ; for Joy, Grief, and Fear. For Joy the drum is beaten at both ends, for Grief only at one, the end being previously muffled by rubbing it over with moistened *Urad* flour. In the case of alarm it is beaten at both ends a continuous loud note being emitted while screams often add to the commotion. This note is at once picked up by the next village and in an incredibly short space of time the whole district

* C. E. Luard, *Tattooing in Central India,* Indian Antiquary, 1904.

† *Memoir* i, 526.

is aroused, all gradually collecting at the spot where the first alarm was sounded. Cymbals of brass or pewter and bamboo flutes are also used. Dancing and singing form part of all important ceremonies such as weddings and other festive occasions. In all mixed dances men and women dance in separate circles. Dancing is always performed in two groups, men in one group and women in the other. The movements are rhythmic and in many cases accompanied by the beat of sticks in time to the somewhat monotonous chant to which the dance is performed. A special performance takes place in *Holi*. A man is blackened with charcoal and dressed in a blanket and is called Budelya, another man dressed as a woman being called Raiyi. These two dance while all sing obscene songs, much liquor is drunk and practically all present gradually become inebriated.

27. *Language*.—The Bhils speak Bhili and other cognate dialects which are detailed in Imperial Table XV. Whether the Bhils had a language of their own is now difficult to say. The Bhili dialect is mainly derived from Gujarati and is influenced by Malwi, Nimadi and other dialects of Malwa in accordance with the proximity of these to the Bhil tracts. Sir George Grierson is of the opinion that Bhili shows 'traces of a non-Aryan basis which are too few to be certainly identified. The basis may have been Munda or it may have been Dravidian—perhaps more probably the former—but has been completely overlaid by an Aryan superstructure'.* It is now thoroughly an Aryan language. The same authority assumes early Dardic influence in the Bhil languages.

28. *Bhilala*.—The Bhilalas are closely related to the Bhils, Patlias and other tribes which inhabit the Vindhyas and Satpuras. They have a considerable admixture of Rajput blood in them. They claim Rajput descent and are considered to be of higher status than their neighbours. The name of the tribe is said to be derived from Bhilara (or Bhilala), *i.e.*, those accused of being Bhils from *ara* a fault. They consider this appellation derogatory. They always style themselves Thakur, Bhumia, Rawat, Patel, Mukhui, etc.

The traditions of the tribe state that their Rajput ancestors lived at Delhi, and were Chauhans, members of the family of Prithviraj, the last Hindu king of Delhi. When the Chauhans were finally driven out by the Muhammadans† 200,000 of them migrated to Mewar and settled at Chitor in Udaipur State. On the capture of Chitor by Ala-ud-din in 1303 a large number fled to the Vindhya hills for refuge. Here they formed marriage connections with Bhil women and so lost caste. Their superior status is always admitted and they form the local aristocracy of the Vindhyas, the Raja of Mandhata, as he is called, being the head of the clan. Malcolm says that in his day the Bhilalas and Sondhias were the only robbers in Malwa whom no traveller could trust, as no oath, however sacred, restrained them.‡ He concludes with the remark that they combine "with the pride and pretensions of Rajputs the cunning and roguery of the Bhils," while they are destitute of any of those feelings of chivalry which occasionally redeem the vices of true Rajputs. In the beginning of the 19th century some members of the clan rose to importance during the confusion which the Pindari depredations caused in Central India. Nadir Singh, a Bhilala of Jamnia village near Mandu, assisted Jaswant Rao Holkar in his compaign to recover the family estates. Nadir Singh Bhilala's name soon became a terror in southern Malwa. By 1818 he had collected a body of 200 horse and 700 foot, and his power was such that Hate Singh, a Khichi Rajput, Thakur of Naulana, actually consented to dine with the Bhilala Chieftain, in order to save his estate fom ravage. When Sir John Malcolm asked Hate Singh about this, he replied that his having dined with Nadir ringh did not degrade him, but raised the Bhilala. There are now ten estates held by Bhilalas under the British guarantee and others held without a guarantee, from Dhar and other Darbars.

The tribe is divided into two main sections but no marriage distinctions are made, the *Badi* and *Choti Jats* only differing as regards eating and drinking, the septs in the *Badi jat* never eating fowls or drinking liquor. In marriage relations they are on the same footing as the septs in the *Choti jat*. As regards septs the usual difficulty has been experienced in obtaining a list. No two persons ever give the same name or the same number of septs. Lists are given in another section. From these lists it will be seen that practically no septs are now traceable to totemistic origin, though possibly there were totemistic reasons for many names; others are Rajput names; and many local.

The Bhilalas form one big endogamous group divided into 42 septs which are exogamous. No two members of the same sept can marry. Sexual license before marriage is not recognised at all. Where connection has been made with a man of superior caste, such as Rajput, Brahman or Bania, the children may be admitted to the Bhilala caste but not if the girl has lived with a low caste man. The marriage ceremony is like that of the Bhils, with greater importation of Hindu customs. The practice of *ghar jamai*, abduction and the choice of husband are also in vogue. Widow re-marriage is recognised among the Bhilalas but the higher classes now prohibit it owing to Hindu influence.

They cremate their dead. In matters of religion they consider themselves Hindus. And though they undoubtedly have as much claim to be considered so as members of the lower classes of the recognised Hindu community, they borrow a certain number of the more animistic practices of their Bhil neighbours. They consider the deity Onker Mahadev, on the island of Onkarnath in the Narbada, as their special tutelary god, while they accept all the other members of the Hindu pantheon. They also reverence the tombs of Musalman saints. In fact they are in all essentials Hindus and they are admitted to be so as shewn by their being allowed to enter temples and generally take part with Hindus in all religious ceremonies. Priests are not necessarily employed by them, although when possible Brahmans are engaged, particularly by the well-to-do such as the Bhumia land-holders. An elderly and respected member of the family can always act as *Pujari*.

Once they were as predatory and turbulent as the Bhils. They are now peaceful agriculturists and their position more and more approximates to that of the lower Hindu castes. The land-owners have considerable pretension to be ranked as Rajputs and are slowly transforming themselves into well-known Rajput clans.

29. *Patlias*.—The Patlias are principally found in Jhabua State and in small numbers in Ali-Rajpur, Dhar and other minor States of the Southern States Agency. They are almost on the same footing as the Bhilalas and have an admixture of Rajput blood in them. In appearance there is little to distinguish them from Bhilalas. The name Patlia is derived from *bitle* or "polluted" owing to their being outcasted.

The tradition connected with the formation of the caste is this:—

Originally the caste being a section of the Paramara clan dwelt at Abu, but were driven by famine to migrate to Gujarat and settled at Pavagarh in the Panch-mahals. Here one day at the Navaratri festival the goddess Kali joined the women of the clan in chanting *garbhas* (songs) in praise of Devi. The great beauty of the goddess struck a barber who at once rushed off to the chief of Pavagarh, Parthi (Prithvi) Singh, and informed him of his find. The Raja fired by the account hurried to the spot and without beating about the bush at once advanced to the lovely dancer and requested her to become his wife, offering her the rank of *Patt-rani*. The goddess was highly incensed and cursed the Raja and his people, vanishing as the last words of her curse fell on the Raja's ears. From this moment misfortune dogged the steps of the clan, a severe famine enentually forcing

* *Linguistic Survey of India*, Vol. I, 178-179. † By Muiz-ud-din in 1192 A. D. ‡ *Memoir* i, 425, ii, 126.

them to migrate once more. They retreated to Nalwai village in the Dohad district. Here one of the clan driven by hunger killed a *roz* (*nilgai, Bos elephas trago-camelos*) which they ate. This act of sacrilege outcasted this section of the clan and they were stigmatised as impure (*bitle*) becoming known ultimately as Patle or Patlia. They were forced to leave Nalwai and took to the hills. Another tale narrates how, when thus driven into Gujarat, they accepted food of the Tentiya Rajput clan, of spurious origin, and hence lost caste. Apart from the legend, there is no doubt that they came originally from Gujarat as the connection with this district is still kept up, serious caste matters being to this day referred to the Patel of Gangedi village in Gujarat.

The Patlias form a single endogamous group or tribe divided into exogamous septs. Nearly 12 sept names have Rajput appellations with local affixes such as Pipria Parmar called after Pipria village in Baria State, Tandia Parmar called after Tanda village in Amjhera district of Gwalior and so on. This supports their Paramara descent.

Their marriage customs are like those of the Bhilalas. The practice of *ghar jamai* is prevalent. It is not uncommon for a man to work for his bride acting as the servant of his father-in-law. Seven years is the usual period. No payment is made for the bride in this case. After 7 years the couple are given a separate house and means to cultivate whereas up to then clothing and food only are given. If no child is born after twelve months from their taking up a separate residence the usual marriage ceremony is performed at the expense of the girl's father. If the couple elope before the seven years is complete, the man has to pay a bride price. Abduction and elopement are also common in obtaining a wife. The re-marriage of widows is practised. All ancestral property is divided equally between the sons. In the case of joint family, even where one individual is a larger contributor, the total earnings or belongings are held to belong equally to all. In the case of a hereditary Patel or Tarvi the son (if any), best qualified, becomes Patel and receives the customary dues and also any *inami* land which belongs to the Patelship ; these things are not considered common property. A widow with no male heir is sole mistress of the property which passes on her death to the nearest of kin. In cases where she has a son, who is living apart from disagreement, the widow is held to be a son for the purposes of inheritance and gets an equal share with her son or sons. Daughters have no rights of inheritance. Where there is no next-of-kin the property passes either to the Darbar or the *Panches* of the village.

Oaths, omens and charms followed and practised are similar to those of the Bhils. These are carried out by the Badwas who become "possessed" under favourable conditions and foretell the future ; the exercising of deities of disease is one of their special functions. In the case of cholera the *rogta* procession or procession of health is practised. The Badwas are called in and all collect at a central spot in the village. After a time they become "possessed" and heave and sway about and commence to chant songs in praise of the goddess continuing to sing throughout the night. Early in the morning they take some parched gram and some balls of dried gram flour and a thread of many colours, a *tiki* (the piece of tinsel worn on the forehead by women) and some boiled wheat and the head of the freshly killed cock. These are placed in an earthen jar broken into two halves. Some liquor is poured over these objects and they are placed in a small wooden toy cart. This is dragged to the border of the village, the Badwas following dancing and twisting and heaving under the influence of the goddess. At the border the cart is taken by men from the next village and similarly passed on to the next. When dysentery becomes epidemic, another process is followed called *totka*. Every case has an inverted earthen jar full of burning cowdung cakes placed on a brass dish put below the patient's bed. In the case of an ailing child the mother makes a leaf dish and in it puts a few hairs from her own head, some salt and chillies, and a small lamp of flour. Cowdung cakes sometimes take the place of the leaf dish. This dish is then carried up to the sick child and passed down seven times over it from the head to the feet ; it is then taken at once out of the house and put down in a spot where three thoroughfares meet. Another cure consists in placing the hair, salt and chillies with some wheat in the fold of her head-dress passing this over the child. Another method is to make two dolls of coloured cloth, swing these above the child and then cast them into a running stream. When a child suffers from the evil eye, an earthen pot is made red hot and put into a dish half full of water, mouth downwards, the bubbing and steaming which ensues carries off the evil effects.

In all important ceremonies Brahmans are employed. The Patlias worship the Hindu deities but in particular Kalika Devi. The reason for this is that at Abu they were special worshippers at her shrine and they believe that it was through her the Ponwar (*i.e.*, Paramara) Marathas got Dhar. The minor deities are identical with those of the Bhils but they have two warrior gods, Nahar Singh and Makua Paramara who are much revered. They were certainly former leaders of the tribe. The dead are cremated and the usual ceremonies are observed.

The Patlias are prone to wander and cultivate only to a small extent. Like the Bhils, dancing, singing and a good deal of liquor-drinking are their chief recreations. They appear to join in Bhil games to a certain extent. The recitation of the past glories of the tribe is done by their special Bhat who comes over from Gujarat yearly. He will not feed with them or take food prepared by them.

30. *Rathia.*—The Rathias are a section of the Bhil tribe. They have been exclusively returned from Barwani State, numbering 37,260 (19,028 males and 18,232 females). They appear to have acquired their appellation owing to their long sojourn in the Rath country which now forms a great part of Ali-Rajpur State. The Rathias of Barwani date their advent from more than a century and half when one Bhima Patel and others came from Rath and settled at Pati in Barwani State in the time of Rana Chandra Singh. Then the country was full of forests and suited to Bhil immigration.

Marriage ceremonies are simple. At the time of betrothal the boy's father with some relatives goes to the girl's house and presents a small amount to the girl. Then they eat and drink together. At the time of marriage the bridegroom's father accompanied by his male and female relatives goes to the bride's house and pays Rs. 50—60 to her parents. The bride and bridegroom are made to sit together, while the men and women sing and dance to the strains of Bhil music. No elaborate ceremony is performed. Re-marriage of widows is permitted.

Brahmans are not employed for ceremonial purposes. A casteman of the tribe performs the ceremonies. Their religious beliefs, etc., have been noticed under the Bhils. They are indifferent agriculturists like the Bhils. Some work as labourers. They are usually distinguished by their rude dress. The peculiar usuage in respect of dress is the loin cloth which is allowed to hang low down behind almost to the knees and flap in the wind like a tail. They are always armed with bows and arrows.

31. *Mankar.*—The Mankar Bhils have been principally returned from the States of Indore, Dhar and Barwani. A class of Bhils famous as trackers, they now form a separate group. The Mankars are also called Dhankawas by other Bhils but are amongst themselves styled Nahals or Naik. The name Mankar is an occupational term, these men being under the orders of the village headmen ; the term Dhankawas is from Dhanukh, a bow. The term Nahal means simply 'one of mean appearance'. The title of Naik was conferred on them by the State authorities in early days. They say they are the descendants of Rajputs and Bhil or Bhilala

women. They form two endogamous groups with twelve exogamous septs, the Chokaria (or superior), Mankars and the Nahal Mankara. Some of the septs are totemistic. Thus :—

Mori.—Called after peacock. The sept worship the peacock and never injure it.

Sanyar.—Called after a goddess of this name whose temple is at Bal-Kuwan village, eight miles from Barwani. The goddess rides on a cat and this animal is reverenced and never injured by them. Any vessel from which a cat has drunk is at once put aside as sacred and never used again.

Soliya or Khas Soliya.—Called after a bird of this name. This bird is never injured and is worshipped. Any injury done is believed to be punished by the blinding of the man doing the injury.

Semlia.—Called after the *semal* tree (*Bombax malabaricum*) which they reverence and never injure.

32. *Tarvis.*—The Tarvi (or Tadvi) Bhils of Barwani do not return themselves as Tarvis and hence the Caste table does not contain them. Two septs of these Bhils came into Barwani. One from the Rath and another from Dohad in Bombay Presidency. The Rathvi Tarvis speak Rathvi ; the others Bhagori, a corrupted form of Gujarati. They are divided into two endogamous divisions, Tarvis and Natra-Tarvis. Many of the septs are totemistic. Marriage must take place within the division but outside the sept. Marriage with a girl of the maternal uncle, maternal aunt, mother-in-law or sister-in-law is prohibited. Exchange of daughters is practised. Sexual intercourse before marriage is tolerated, is not considered disgraceful, and is often encouraged. Marriage ceremonies are simple. As soon as the girl is found the man proceeds to the girl's house and takes a pitcher of liquor with him. Omens are carefully considered and a bad sign on the road is sufficient to break off the wedding. When the betrothal takes place a feast is held of all relatives. The day for the marriage procession is settled and the wedding is celebrated with much singing and consumption of large quantities of liquor. Widows are allowed to remarry and divorce is a simple matter.

They do not employ Brahmans. They do most of the ceremonies themselves. Badwas are requisitioned when necessary. Like other Bhils the Tarvis are animistic in their beliefs. Hanuman is their tutelary village deity and they observe Hindu festivals. They cremate their dead.

33. *Barela.*—The Barelas have been exclusively returned from Indore State. A detailed account of them could not be obtained from the State authorities. *It is hoped the gap in the knowledge will be made good before* the next Census.

34. A list of 122 Bhil and 42 Bhilala septs with notes as to origin stories and totemistic observances will be found in the Census Report for 1931 on the Central India Agency.

6. C.—Migration of Castes and Tribes into Central India and their distribution.

By C. S. Venkatachar.

I.—*Introductory.*

1. *Area defined.*—The Central India Agency is an arbitrarily constituted administrative unit for the purposes of political control and we cannot restrict the area to the present day political boundaries. The best way to define the area for our purposes is to imagine a triangle with the Narbada and Son for its hypotenuse and having for one side the valley of the Ganges and for the other river Chambal and the Chitor hills. Let us assume that the region round about Gwalior is the apex of this triangle. Then the area comprised within this triangle will include the Central India Agency as at present constituted, the state of Gwalior, the British Bundelkhand districts in the United Provinces and the valley of the Narbada lying in the Central Provinces.

2. *Physical features.*—To understand the ebb and flow of migration, into the area so defined, a knowledge of its physical features is absolutely essential. These have already been briefly touched upon in Chapter I of the Report and for the sake of convenience we may recapitulate them here. The most important of them is the range of the hills spreading from the borders of Gujarat to Rajmahal. The Vindhya rage together with its offshoots and the Satpuras lie entirely in our region and to their north lies a table-land which gently slopes away to the Gangetic basin. The Vindhya wall has served as an effective barrier across peninsular India and it has set the limit to every migration from the north to the south. Though in the centre the Vindhyas might have proved a formidable barrier, there are gaps at either end. Thus in western Malwa the Vindhyan gap easily lends a passage to Gujarat and its sea-ports. The eastern portion of the Vindhyas was crossed at Mahisatti (identified with Onkar Mandhatta on the Narbada) in early Buddhistic times when it was a recognised route from the Deccan to the northern parts. It is however doubtful whether any large scale migration took place through this route.

3. *Main currents of migration.*—The main streams of migration to this region have come from the Indo-gangetic plain, from the region beyond the Chambal on the western side and from Gujarat. Evidence also points to the fact that there has been considerable movement in early times through the corridor along the Narbada valley from the Gujarat littoral. Migration from the area beyond the Chambal, probably dates from the time of the rise of the Rajput clans and there is evidence to believe that Malwa was colonised very much earlier than that part of the country. The connection between Gujarat and Malwa was well established, as far as we know, in Buddhistic times. Ujjain had then become a prominent place and Malwa was on the highway. In considering the migration from the northern parts we have to bear in mind the following few facts :—

(1) The contiguity of the Central Indian table-land to the densely-peopled parts of the Gangetic-doab, the centre and seat of ancient culture and civilization.

(2) The absence of any physical barrier from the northern plains to the table-land till the Vindhyas are reached.

(3) The fertility of Malwa and hence a coveted possession for strong and powerful Rulers.

(4) The Central India regions have possessed low density. Being sparsely populated they have always sucked in people but have sent out very few.

(5) We have also to bear in mind one important fact which is apt to be lost sight of. The waves of migration did not flood all the parts as we may be tempted to suppose. Civilization rose and fell according to the political fortunes and convulsions in the Gangetic plains. When there was anarchy in the northern regions, in parts of Central India the forests advanced and there was an extension of tribal rule.

(6) In Malwa itself we have again to recognise two regions as was done from the earliest times, *viz.*, western Malwa (*Avanti*) and eastern Malwa (*Acara*). The former may be approximately described as lying between 77° North and 22·5° East. (This may historically be not quite exact). Western

Malwa has at all times been far more exposed than eastern Malwa or the eastern parts of Central India. It has received some share in all the racial incursions that have taken place into the northern plains. It has been subjected to the Scythian and the Hun invasions of the early historical times.

(7) Lastly, practically the whole region lying to the east of western Malwa has been for a long time a partially opened up tract in places and entirely unopened area in other parts. In one of his works Crooke wrote that the Central Indian jungle with its occasional patches of brushwood or coarse grass is rather a copse than a primeval forest. It is true that it stands no comparison with the forests of the Himalayas and neither has it the abundant and luxuriant foliage of the great forests. But the denuded and poor forests of Central India of to-day must have been different in the days gone by. They have undoubtedly suffered at the hands of the colonizers and its primitive in habitants and probably also on account of climatic changes. We have very little information so far on the last point. A reference in the Arthasastra reveals the fact that Avanti was a region of considerable rainfall and the precipitation for this region is given as 23 *dronas*. Only four centuries ago there were thick forests in eastern Malwa and further east it is recorded that the forests in Orchha were so thick that it occupied the Moghal armies several days in cutting away through them.*

4. *Factors of migration.*—We have next to consider what lies behind the movements of people. The causes are various and with the scanty material at our disposal it is often difficult to disentangle the various factors that have governed the movements of men. In the early times climatic changes, dessication of certain regions setting in motion movements of nomads, pressure of population, disturbed political conditions, conquest and colonisation, have all played their part in varying degrees. In more recent times, famine, religious persecution and colonisation have influenced migration. Generally all movements are primarily due to food. The task of isolating one or more of these factors is by no means easy and before we assay to do so and set up some kind of rough frame work within which we can get some glimpse of the movements of people, we must first deal with the baffling question of those primitive tribes who are inhabiting the hills and forests of these regions.

II.—*Early racial drifts and migration.*

5. *The present day primitive tribes.*—The important primitive tribes of this region are Bhil, Gond, Korku' Kol, Baiga and Saharia (Sonr). There are various offshoots of some of these tribes. Who are they and whence have they come ? All the primitive tribes have the tradition that they have been the inhabitants of these regions from time immemorial and they are unable to point out to any migratory movement. The Gonds say they come from south which so far as our regions are concerned practically means Gondwana and they are an overflow into Central India from that part. The Bhils of the south-western Vindhyas have some tradition of movement but that is merely a displacement from one place to another along the Vindhyas. The Gonds speak a language which is classified as Dravidian. The Korku and the Kol (with whom we may associate the Baiga and the Bhil) once spoke a language which is classified as Austric. Linguistic considerations may go to suggest more than one racial drift. But it would be dangerous to assert any such movement on linguistic grounds alone.

6. *Defective knowledge about them.*—Much of their history is still in the realms of uncertainty and will remain so till expert investigators make an intensive and concentrated study. The four broad tribal belts have yet to be regionally surveyed and the Bhil area has to be split up and separately studied in the Satpuras, in the Vindhyas and further west in Mewar. A systematic exploration of the pre-historic archæology of the Vindhya-Kaimur system has to be undertaken. An extensive field work is necessary in the remoter parts of the Central Indian hills especially in south Rewa to secure ethnographic and anthropometric data. The materials obtained by these different studies are bound to form a valuable clue to many problems in the racial and cultural history of these parts.

7. *The pre-Dravidians.*—In the meanwhile, we may consider the problem, however unsatisfactory it may be, in the light of the few materials known or available so far. In doing so we shall not speculate whether early man arose in India or not. The early home of the modern types of men has not yet been satisfactorily located but let us assume that it is to be provisionally placed along what is now Sahara, Mesopotamia and Arabia. Man and vegetation flourish easily in temperate or tropical zone and it is believed in the glacial epoch of the Pleistocene period, a belt of cyclonic storm lay over these zones. Sahara, now a vast desert, was then a grass land. Peake and Fleure believe that the early type of man spread from these regions. "Among the people who retain the unlengthened head with the ancient prominent jaws and with spirally curved hair, we may mention the Andamanese.... : these are all very short, and very dark with broad flat noses."† If we construct the distribution of land and water with the coast line at the present 100 fathom or thereabout, Sumatra, Java, Borneo, Palawan would form a hooked peninsula attached to farther India and this will help us to understand their spread to these regions.‡ Whether they spread from the supposed 'cradle' of modern man or not, we start with a dim perception that several millenia before recorded history there was a dark negroid race of low culture characterised by a physical type of very short stature, low forehead and flat face and nose. This race we may term pre-Dravidian.

8. *All great racial migrations into India are from the West.*—If there is one fact which impresses upon us strongly in connection with the migrational history of India, it is this that all the great racial movements into India from the dawn of history up to the modern 18th century have been from the regions to the west and north-west of the Indian peninsula and they have been into India and not out of India. Its physical formation has been such that along the great plains, or in its coastal regions or in its highlands, the floods of invasions have spread themselves out in the vast area enclosed on three sides by the sea and closed on the northern side by the impenetrable mountain barrier. But India has always been a centre of secondary dispersion of culture and civilization towards east and further east. It is therefore to the west we look for the migration of races into India unless stronger evidence is forthcoming to abandon this view. We have reason to ascribe that several migrations took place into India from the western direction.

9. *Migration of the Proto-mediterranean race.*—It may be hazarded as a point of view worth consideration that one of these took place due to sudden climatic changes. An important crisis occurred in the early history of man when the northern ice cap over Europe retreated and the climatic belt that lay over Sahara followed it. The grass-land of Sahara began to dry up. This resulted in the migration of the animals to more favoured regions and the hunters who hunted them followed them. These hunters spread towards the Nile and later

* *Imperial Gazetteer of India*, Central India, page 51. † *Corridors of Time*, iv-184. ‡ *Ibid.*

on appear to have extended up to the Vindhyan hills in India and even to Ceylon.* These people largely lived on small game, shot with their bows and arrows and supplemented their diet by digging up edible roots with hoes of flint.† These people we may designate as the proto-mediterraneans. They conquered or blended with (whatever process took place if it did at all) the early pre-Dravidian element in these parts. Nothing very definite, however, is so far known about the presence of a Negrito element in the aboriginal population of India in general and in the primitive tribes of Central India in particular. These proto-mediterraneans consitute the first of the racial strata in the central parts of India and it is these whom we call the Munda tribes. They have at the present day everywhere been submerged by the later invasions and are mere remnants of a vanished people in the hills of Central India, represented by the Baiga, Kol, Saharia, Sonr, Korku and Bhil tribes. The Austric family of languages should be associated with these people and the Munda branch of this family still survives in island patches in the central regions.

10. *Their culture.*—Their long contact with the culture of the plains has modified their primitive culture to a very great extent and what little is left of it is difficult to reconstruct. They remain inspite of agriculture being compulsorily forced on them, hunters and food-gatherers by instinct. The art of cultivation has never been seriously acquired by them. The Baiga is an inveterate 'dhaya' (shifting) cultivator. So is the Sor in Bundelkhand who is a wretched cultivator. 'He sows his Jowar by jabbing the seeds in with a pointed stick.'‡ Before the Korku became a wretched village drudge his life in the mountain haunts was not far different from the early hunters and food-gatherers. He practised shifting cultivation if it suited him. That was a precarious job but he had nothing to despair. Nature was bountiful in the forests. He would live on edible roots, wild yam, bamboo seeds, supplemented by the flesh of wild animals and by fish obtained by poisoning the pools.§ The Bhil who has been for long in contact with the Hindus has become so to say civilized but some of the Satpura Bhils are still very backward and live mostly on roots and berries and were formerly practising shifting cultivation. Of their material culture, the details are sadly lacking. The custom of erecting small upright stones as monuments to the dead among the Bhils, and of tattooing, belief in a soul as being born as an insect and certain ideas regarding metempsychosis, go to suggest that their culture was part of a wide-spread one.

11. *Possible distribution.*—It would be interesting to attempt some kind of distribution of this submerged people. We have good reason to assume that they were far more widespread than in their present day mountain homes. Linguistic evidence goes to shew that in the Himalayas the Munda survivals are most apparent. Dr. Sten Konow believes that the Kolarians at one time occupied the vast area of northern India ; that the existence of Korku tribe in the heart of India seems to point to the conclusion that people of a similar descendency have occupied a large territory in central parts of the country and probably also in the Deccan.¶ The same authority holds that they influenced the germs of art, religion and philosophy.** Judging by their present day distribution it would appear that from Gujarat across Malwa along the Vindhyas were the Bhils. Further north in Malwa were the Saharias or Savars stretching from the borders of the Jumna-Chambal system across the peninsula to the north-east of the present day Madras Presidency. 'The most southern forms of Munda speech,' says Sir George Grierson, 'are those spoken by Savaras and the Gadabas of north-east Madras. The former has been identified with the Suari of Pliny and the Sabarae of Ptolemy. A wild tribe of the same name is mentioned in Sanskrit literature even so far back as in late Vedic times, as inhabiting the Deccan, so that the name can boast great antiquity.'†† Thus this branch covered a wide expanse of territory though now separated and confined to the jungles of eastern Malwa or of Bundelkhand. Cunningham says "Indeed there are good reasons to believe that the Savaras were formerly the dominant branch of the great Kolarian family and that their power lasted down to a comparatively late period, when they were pushed aside by other Kolarian tribes in the north and east and by the Gonds in south. In the Saugor district I was informed that the Savaras had formerly fought with the Gonds and that the latter had conquered them by treacherously making men drunk."‡‡ To the east of the Savara belt were the Kol, Baiga and other allied tribes in the Kaimur-Vindhyan hills, with a great extension towards Chota Nagpur and possibly even beyond. We have also some good evidence to believe that some of the offshoots of these tribes were in occupation of the northern Gangetic plain either before or at the time of the Aryan invasion into India. They have now passed into oblivion and possibly merged into the lower castes. The memory and tradition of at least three peoples are preserved. They are the Bhar, Cheru and Seori. The Census caste table does not show them. It is believed that the Hinduised tribal caste of Bharia returned from Rewa and other Baghelkhand States are descended from the ancient Bhars of whom Crooke says "The most probable supposition is that the Bhars were a Dravidian race closely allied to the Kols, Cherus and Seoris who at an early period succumbed to the invading Aryans. This is borne out by their physique and appearance which closely resemble that of the undoubted non-Aryan aborigines of the Vindhyan-Kaimur plateau."§§ There is no doubt that the Bhars were once a widespread race. They were in north Rewa before the Rajputs displaced them and once a wide tract in northern India from Gorakhpur to Saugor was under their sway. They were very powerful in Oudh and in portions of the Gangetic doab.|||| They have again a claim to antiquity as a tribe mentioned by Pliny in his list of the Indian races as the following quotation from McCrindle's Ancient India as described by Megasthenes and Arrian would show :—

"There is a very large island in the Ganges which is inhabited by a single tribe called Modogalingæ. Beyond are situated the Modubæ, Molindæ the Uberæ with a handsome town of the same name", etc. The Modubæ (says an explanatory foot-note) represent beyond doubt the Moutiba, a people mentioned in the *Aitareya Brahmana* along with other non-Aryan tribes which occupied the country north of the Ganges at the time when the Brahmans, established their first settlements in the country. The Uberæ must be referred to the Bhars, a numerous race spread over the central districts of the region spoken of and extending as far as to Assam. The name is pronounced differently in different districts and variously written as Bors or Bhors, Bhowris, Barrilas and Bharhiyas, Bareyas, Baoris, Bharais, etc. The race though formerly powerful is now one of the lowest classes of the population."

---

* *Corridors of Time*, III, 8.

† *Ibid.*

‡ *Damoh district Gazetteer.*

§ Forsyth. *Highlands of Central India.*

¶ J. A. S. B. 1925, No. 3, p. 315, quoted in *Pre-Musalman India* by Mr. V. Rangacharya, Huxley Press, Madras, page 67.

** *Ibid.*

†† *Linguistic Survey of India*, volume I.

‡‡ Quoted in *Castes and Tribes of the Central Provinces*, Art Savara.

§§ *Castes and Tribes of the Central Provinces*, Art Bharia.

|||| Sherring *Hindu tribes and castes.* The Bhar tribe.

The Cherus were also a powerful race and were the masters of the soil in the eastern Gangetic plain. Buchanan noticed a peculiar custom among them of appointing a Raja for every five or six families who is created in the Rajput fashion by the application of a mark or *thika* to the forehead. From all accounts these people appear to have advanced in their material culture more than their brethren who remained or preferred to remain in the inaccessible hills but they could not withstand the onslaught of the invading Aryans or the later invaders speaking Aryan languages. Their languages were strangled, their culture destroyed and in course of time not without struggles and set-backs on either side, they finally succumbed and perished.

12. *The Dravidians—a branch of the Mediterranean race.*—Subsequent to the migration of the proto-Mediterraneans, at a later period, there was another racial drift. Due to climatic changes or to the pressure of population, possibly from the area which Peake and Fleure call the Fertile Crescent, a branch of the Mediterranean race—the Dravida speaking people, passed through Baluchistan and the Indus valley, down to Gujarat the Deccan and the southern regions. Linguistic consideration shows that Sanskrit has been much modified by a good many Dravidian features and it has been well-established now that the Brahmi script itself from which all the Indian scripts have been derived is to be derived from the pictographic signs used by the people of the Indus valley civilization.* If that is so, the Dravida speaking people must have settled in the Gangetic valley also. It is extremely doubtful if they ever occupied the Central Indian plateau. It is also not possible that the invading Aryans could have driven them south. No such movement was possible through the Vindhyan barriers. The movement of the Drávida-speaking people to the south must have been along the west coast or even by sea. In the south their culture was influenced by the cultural migrations from Egypt and Mesopotamia. It is recognised the Mediterranean race possessed a higher culture and its migration led to a more pronounced advance in civilization and the Dravidian civilization of the south is believed to have drifted to farther East. To the north-west, in the Indus valley, a distinct and elaborate culture was also thriving. Whether this culture had a provincial form in the Gangetic valley or in the borderland of our parts or even in the central regions, whether the Dravidian man was responsible for it and whether that culture materially affected the aboriginal population of Central India are all questions for which we have to wait for an answer till further light is thrown by investigations which are yet in progress. If the orgin of the god now called Shiva or Mahadeva, could be traced to the Indus valley civilization it is worth noticing that the Bhils, Savaras and the Korkus—all trace their origin to Mahadeva, though it is possible that the tradition may be a latterly acquired Hindu idea.

13. *The problem of the Gonds.*—We may at this stage deal with the problem of the Gonds and other allied tribes who speak a Dravidian language. They have made a wedge in the different parts of our region. The fact that the Gond speaks a Dravidian language no more proves that he must be a Dravidian (so called) by race than the Baiga who speaks a corrupt form of Bagheli is an Indo-Aryan. The Gonds and the Oraons have a tradition that they came from south and their immigration into the Central Provinces is held to have occurred in more recent historical times.* The Gonds may be the pre-Dravidians of the south on whom the Dravidians imposed their language and due to some causes in the regions of north-east Madras, there must have been a large scale displacement of the tribes into the interior of the central regions.

14. *Alpine race.*—We have to mention another racial drift though it does not appear to have reached these parts so far as we know. Along the west coast of India, there is a concentration of what is known as the brachycephalic Alpine type. The same type is dominant in Bengal where the 'main concentration is in the southern or deltaic region with gradual decrease towards the north and the east'.† The older view which sought to explain this type as due to Scythian influence in the west coast and to Mongolian infiltration in Bengal has been abandoned in favour of the belief that the broad headed element is descended from an Alpine race which intruded into India in the pre-historic times long before the Scythians invaded Gujarat and other parts of India. There is no reason to warrant so far that the broad headed element pushed its way across Central India. The path of the intruder was effectively blocked by the forests and the mountains and by the presence of the various Munda tribes. It is more probable the Alpine element reached Bengal by some other land route.

III.—*Migration in historical times.*

15. In the previous section we have noted the present day distribution of the primitive tribes and suggested some possibilities of their migration. We can carry the migration history into the historical times more satisfactorily if we can fix certain arbitrary periods in the history of Central India. They may be set down as follows :—

1. From the time of the Aryan invasion of India to the rise of Buddhism.
2. Mauryan epoch to the invasion of Huns and other foreign hordes.
3. The rise and fall of Neo-Hinduism.
4. The Rule of Islam up to the downfall of the Moghal power.
5. Recent times.

16. *Period I.*—The last of the pre-historic migrations was that of the Aryans who according to the commonly accepted views entered India from the north-west, occupied the Punjab first and then in the Gangetic diab evolved the complex Indo-Aryan culture and civilization. It is certain the Rigvedic Aryans did not migrate into Central India. The Central Indian rivers and the Vindhyas are not mentioned in the early Vedic literature. The identification of the Bhils with Nishada is not quite certain. In the later Vedic period it a appears that a tribe called Chedi had occupied the present-day Bundelkhand. Later on we find that the Rajputs who rose in the third period appear under the name of the Chedis and a large tract of the country lying in the Narbada valley was designated as the land of the Chedis. Malwa was certainly colonised by the Aryans from the doab and in the early Buddhistic times the kingdom of Ujjain was one of the 16 Aryan tribes ruling in different parts of northern India. With the rise of Buddhism Ujjain was connected with Magadha by way of Sanchi and Vidisha (modern Bisanagar) in eastern Malwa and Bharut now in Nagod State in the Baghelkhand Agency. The colony of the Aryans was perhaps dotted over all these regions surrounded in the midst of the non-Aryan population. From the list of Megasthenes we read of another tribe of uncertain affiliation, called Charmæ who have been identified as residing in Charmamandala and are believed to be represented by the Chamars of Bundelkhand and the parts adjacent to the basin of the Ganges.‡ By a process of enslavement or by degradation or of mixed marriages or by other causes, the lowest elements in the caste composition of the present day, were formed. At least the process of formation started in this early period and their ranks have been reinforced for ages till the caste system obtained a fixity and rigidity. Of such castes mention may

* This has been pointed out to me in a private communication from the Census Commissioner.

† B. S. Guha. *Some anthropological problems in India. Modern Review*, Calcutta, August 1928.

‡ McCrindle's *Ancient India*, 150-151 and foot-note.

be made of, Basor, Balai, Chamar, Kotwar, Arakh, Dhanuk, Dahait, etc. They have no tradition of migration. Excepting the Basor and the Chamar, the rest are generally employed as village menials and watchmen from time immemorial. They are the authorities on village boundaries and the *Arthasastra* which in main depicts the pre-Buddhistic India lays down that the interior of the kingdom should be watched by archers, hunters, chandalas and wild tribes.* The penetration of the Aryans to the different parts of Central India seems to have been achieved in the post-Vedic and the early Buddhistic period. Thus the Son (Sanskrit Suvarna or 'gold'; also called Hiranyavata, possibly corrupted to Erranoboas of Arrian), the Ken (Sanskrit Karavati, the Kainas of Arrian), the Dhasan (Dasharana, possibly the Dasaron of Ptolemy), the Betwa (Sanskrit Vetravati) and the Chambal (Sanskrit Charmanvati) received their names in the Indo-Aryan language and possess the earliest historical mentions.

17. *Period 2.*—Perhaps in the Mauryan epoch arose the complexity if not the rigidity of the caste system and the association of caste with craft thus paving the way for the formation of the various occupational and functional castes. Castes were also forming owing to the interaction of the old four divisions. In the dark period between the collapse of the Mauryan power and the rise of the Guptas, very little is known about the movement of people. It is tolerably certain that the eastern parts of Central India passed under tribal rule with the weakening of the authority of the Aryan Rulers. Western Malwa was ruled by the Sakas or the Scythians. Political subjection by the Sakas or the Huns need not necessarily always mean a migration and settlement of them in large numbers in tracts which according to history were ruled by them. It is not quite safe to assume the Scythic or the Hun element necessarily modified the composition of the population by the nature of the political rule. At the same time we have to take note of the fact that the Sakas ruled western Malwa from Ujjain and further north were the tribal republics of the Malavas and the Abhiras. It is supposed that the former have given the name to Malwa though as a distinct people they have disappeared or merged with the general population. The Abhiras from whom the modern Ahirs are said to have descended were a widespread people and they have given the name of Ahirwara to the country between Gwalior and Jhansi. According to the *Khandesh District Gazetteer*,† the Abhiras were on the North-West Frontier before the Christian era. In the third century A. D. they were in lower Sindh and north Gujarat and next they appear to have passed down the Tapti valley into Khandesh. It is very probable these tribes were the advance guard of the vast migratory hordes that poured into India in the first few centuries of the Christian era. After the fall of the Guptas, there was again an inroad of the barbarians known to history as the white Huns. Malwa was ruled by their chief Mihirakula, a Hun tyrant. The rule of the Huns was terminated by a local rising under a Raja of Central India. After a brief spell of the vigorous rule of Harsha, there followed a very considerable adjustment in the Hindu society and a great stir in the migration history of these parts. Before we consider the nature of this stir, we note two small points which are of some significance. Compare the empire of Asoka, of Samundragupta and of Harsha on a map of India as given in say Vincent Smith's early history of India. The country to the west of Central India (the present day Rajputana) and to the east (the present day eastern Central Provinces districts) are practically *terra incognita* in the time of the Mauryas, the Guptas and even of Harsha. The western boundary of Central India has always been the Chambal as it is even to-day. Secondly the western regions in Harsha's time began to be peopled and already places like Bhilmal and others attract attention.

18. *Period 3.*‡—In the time of the Mauryas and the Guptas the seat of civilization was Magadha but with the downfall of their power, it shifted to the Doab. Kanauj took the place of Pataliputra as the radiating centre of ancient civilization. The eastern parts of Central India which now and then were brought under the sway of a powerful northern Ruler again came under the rule of the primitive tribes. In this period two other movements are seen at work. One is the growth of neo-Hinduism which appealed to the people at large and which in course of its evolution absorbed a good deal of the non-Aryan cult. It became broad-based and not exclusive as the Vedic religion of the Aryans. The second is the process of absorption into the fold of this neo-Hinduism of the foreign elements that were present in India at that time as well as the aboriginal element in the existing population. The classification of society no longer proceeded on racial lines but on occupations. "The higher the caste the more numerous and more honourable the occupations open to it."

There is a difference of opinion as to the rise of the various Rajput clans and a certain amount of fiction still persists that the Rajputs are descended from the ancient Kshatriyas. It requires some stretch of imagination and credulity to believe that the Rajputs of Malwa are descended from the Kshatriya kings of Avanti of the early Buddhistic times, ignoring all the kaleidoscopic changes of more than two millenia. The generally accepted historical view is that some of the renowned clans like the Parihars, Solankis, Chauhans and the Paramaras have a foreign origin. In the early history of India, three definite irruptions of the foreign barbarians have now been recognised. They, in order, are of the Sakas, the Yuechi or the Kushans and the Huns. It is not known definitely how far the first two have contributed to the composition of the Rajput clans but the Huns together with the allied swarms decidedly have. The aristocratic sections amongst the foreigners became the ruling clans while the others in course of time became the cultivating classes like the Jat or the Gujar. The foreigners established their kingdom in the early medieval times and one of them was at Bhilmal and the ruling dynasty belonged to the Prathihara (Parihar) clan of the Gurjara tribe. The familiar legend of the Agnikula Rajputs, the Pawar (Paramara), Parihar, Chauhan and Solanki is perhaps a convenient allegory to explain their purification and absorption into the Hindu fold. The country to the west and north of Chambal became the home of the early clan settlements. Some of the other clans to the east of Chambal, like the Chandel, Bundela, Gaharwar, etc., are supposed to have sprung from the Hinduised aboriginal elements. The Gaharwars are associated with the Bhars and the Bundelas and the northern Rathors are associated with the Gaharwars.

The rise of these clans is a most important period in our discussion. They were a restless and a vigorous people constantly seeking for new settlement. This movement has gone on for several centuries till the establishment of British power in India. The quest for settlements set in train a widespread migration of clans over a large part of upper India. Kanauj was a great focus from which the migrations spread and from these a dispersal of people took place to reinforce the distant colonies and settlements. It is even believed that the functional and occupational castes migrated from there to different parts of western and eastern India.

The distribution of the important clans by locality is enumerated below :—

The Solankis were the rulers of Gujarat and Kathiawar and their capital was Anhilvad Patan. The Chauhans, a powerful clan occupied the whole country from Mount Abu to Hissar and from the Aravallis to the northern tracts of Bundelkhand. The Kachhwahas held Gwalior and Narwar while the Tomars occupied Hissar and the country round about Delhi.

* *Arthasastra*, translated by Dr. R. Shama Sastry, Bk. II, Chapter I.

† Volume XII (1880), 39.

‡ This section and a portion of the next one are entirely based on Vincent Smith's *Early history of India* (1914), Chapter XIV and on J. Kennedy's brilliant essay in Chapter VIII of the *Imperial Gazetteer of India*, Volume II.

Excepting the Kachhwahas, the above-mentioned clans were to the west of the Chambal. Of the clans settled in Central India, the most famous of them were the Paramaras of Malwa who appear to have migrated from a vicinity near Mount Abu. Further east in the Narbada valley were the Kalchuris, who are also known as the Chedi or the Haihaya or Haihaivansi Rajputs. It is likely they were descended from one of the early Scythian or foreign tribes. Their first capital was Maheswar on the Narbada which is now in Indore State. Later on the Kalchuris appear to have extended their power into the heart of what is now the Central Provinces possibly being subjected to the pressure of the growing powers of the Paramaras of Malwa. The Chedi country was divided into two kingdoms, Western Chedi or Dahala with the capital near the modern Jubbulpore and Eastern Chedi or Mahakosala with its capital at Ratanpur. In the recurrence of these classical names of the Epic period we observe how the newly absorbed elements took upon them the old mantles and as the saying goes that history repeats itself, several centuries later when the Great Moghal was dead, we see the same process at work when every power that rose was appropriating to itself the tattered and torn mantle of the Moghals. Such has been the strength and vitality of tradition and the strange influence of fiction on Indian thought in its long evolution.

To the north of Narbada and up to the Jumna, in the Bundelkhand area, were the Chandels. Before the Chandels, the Parihars, allied to the Gurjara—Prathihars of Rajputana were settled and their capital was at Mau-Sahaniya, now a small road-side village between the cantonment of Nowgong and Chhatarpur. The Chandels who are believed to have been Hinduised Bhars overthrew the Parihars and subsequently rose to great fame and have left imperishable monuments in the temples at Khajuraho now in Chhatarpur State. To the north beyond the Ganges, particularly towards the east of Allahabad, the Bhars and other tribes held the country and at Benares were the Gaharwars who are also associated with the Bhars. The clan settlements were wider still but the distribution is restricted to the central regions. There was incessant struggle between these various clans which occupies a great portion of the history of this period. It may be, as Vincent Smith holds, that there was a secular struggle between the foreign Rajputs and the indigenous Rajputs. What-ever it may be, the Paramaras, the Chedis and the Chandels disappeared after the struggle and the Bundelas who are descended from the Gaharwars did not rise into power till the 15th century.

19. *Period 4.*—The incursion of the northern barbarians—this time professing a militant religion—set in motion further migration in a helter skelter fashion. Delhi and Kanauj fell to the invaders. Islam dealt a final blow to the warring Chauhans and the Chandels and the Rajput clans were 'scattered on the face of northern India'. The Solanki power in Gujarat was shattered and Anhilvad Patan destroyed. These again resulted in a different distribution of the clans.

When Kanauj fell the Gaharwar clan migrated to the deserts of Marwar in Rajputana and in later history came to be known as the Rathors. In the Muhammadan times a branch of these Rathors carved out principalities in western Malwa. The Kachhwahas driven away from north Gwalior later rose into power in Amber and they have left small colonies in Central India. The Tomars built up their power in Gwalior when the Muhammadans were fighting amongst themselves. In Malwa the Paramaras sunk into insignificance when reduced by the Solanki and Chedi confederacy and after a rule by the Tomara and Chauhan clans, Malwa passed into the hands of the Muslims. The Chedis disappear from their habitat towards the end of the twelfth century. They were supplanted by the Baghels. On the question of the migration of Baghels the *Rewa State Gazetteer* which tries to give an account of their history according to the Baghel tradition, is somewat confusing. The Baghel clan is a branch of the Solankis and it appears that they migrated from Gujarat and founded the State of Rewa. The Solankis were in touch with the Chedis through Malwa. It is more probable they migrated from Gujarat through the Narbada valley and first occupied southern Rewa than that they came from northern India and conquered the Rewa territories. According to the Baghel account the Baghel chief Karandev married a daughter of the Haihaya chief of Ratanpur and the fort of Bandogarh was given in dowry to the Baghel chief. The probabilities are the Baghels supplanted the Haihayas, first extended their rule to the wild country below the Kaimur and later on to the plains to the north of the Kaimur range. The Kalchuris are now found in small numbers in few of the Rewa villages and their cranial measurements have been taken by Dr. Guha of the Zoological Survey of India. Small colonies of Chauhans were planted in central and northern Malwa while the eastern parts of Central India received a contingent of Chauhans and other clans from the tracts round about Kanauj.

Driven everywhere from the fertile plains by the victorious onslaught of the forces of Islam, the Rajput clans had perforce to seek shelter in inhospitable and inaccessible places and this led to their closer contact with the primitive tribes in the Vindhyas. It is often thought that the Aryans were responsible for the subjugation and degradation of the pre-Aryan indigene. That was perhaps true in the plains but in the less accessible parts the latter maintained a good deal of independence and as we have seen previously they again and again extended their rule and power over those portions from which they were dispossessed. Further it is doubtful if the Aryan conqueror ever waged incessant struggle against them. The conqueror was soon absorbed and a mixed culture arose with the Aryan characteristics predominating. We should rather look to the period of Rajput settlement for the disintegration of tribal areas, for the disappearance of certain aboriginal tribes and for the formation of the Hinduised aboriginal castes. This was almost inevitable for the Rajputs could no longer maintain an independent existence in the fertile plains and they had to carve out principalities in the desert, mountain and forest regions. In the Vindhyas Rajput colonies were planted after dispossessing the Bhils from their possessions. The Bundelas rose into power by displacing the Khangars and further east the Bhars, Cherus, Khairwars and others were annihilated after an incessant struggle against the Rajputs.

It would appear that the migration of many of the principal castes took place in the Muhammadan period. Malcolm wrote: "These provinces were amongst the most early subjected to Muhammadan power; and it would appear from their present population, that a great proportion of Hindus of all tribes and classes, followed the conquerors from Hindustan. Subsequent invasions from Gujrat poured another tide over their plains and almost all trace of their original inhabitants is lost."*

20. *Period 5.*—In recent times the Mahratta invasion of Malwa is the only outstanding event in the migration history of these parts. It is recorded that the Andhras—a southern people penetrated into Malwa after the fall of the Mauryan power. Except for this isolated incursion, no movement has taken place from the south of the Vindhyas. The political migration of the Mahrattas is therefore unique in the traditional history of Central India. They were the last to add one more strand to the diversified composition of the Central Indian population.

* *Memoir*, ii, 3.

IV.—*Race composition.*

21. *Racial types of the population.*—A few words may be added, not so much by way of elucidation as of drawing attention to the snares involved, with regard to the question of the race composition. Into what physical types should the population be distributed—Pre-Dravidian, Munda, Indo-Aryan or Aryo-Dravida? Before we pin our faith to any of these labels, it is best to remember the frequent migrations and the consequent changes in the population that have ceaselessly gone on for ages. While culture, custom and social organisation have been evolving the racial stocks who have been handing them over from generation to generation need not necessarily have remained constant in type. Waves of foreign elements have been absorbed in the earlier days and they have modified the composition of the population. No one would therefore be disposed to disagree with the excellent dictum of Boas " that a people may remain constant in type and language and change in culture ; that it may remain constant in type but change in language ; or that it may remain constant in language and change in type and culture ".* The presence of an Aryan strain in the population of Central India may be admitted but it is not predominant as a type. It has been overwhelmed by the non-Aryan elements everywhere but the culture and the languages are thoroughly Aryan in derivation and they have completely submerged and overlaid the pre-Aryan elements. In many cases when we use the label Aryan at the present time, we are really connoting the speakers of the Aryan tongues and the possessors of the Aryan culture rather than the physical type of the Rigvedic Aryans. " The lasting gift bequeathed by the Aryans ", says Mr. Gordon Childe, " to the conquered people was neither a higher material culture nor a superior physique but that which we mentioned in the first chapter—a more excellent language and the mentality it generated. The physical qualities of that stock did enable them by the bare fact of superior strength to conquer even more advanced peoples and so to impose their language on areas from which their bodily type has almost completely vanished. This is the truth underlying the panegyrics of the Germanists : the Nordics' superiority in physique fitted them to be the vehicles of a superior language."† The truth of this sober but accurate estimate is apparent when we consider the origin and spread of the resent day population in Central India.

These desultory notes which I have set out are merely a foot-note to the study of vast and interesting problems concerning the people of Central India. Such a study is beyond the scope of a Census Report and it is moreover the work for a trained expert. My object is mainly confined to draw attention to few points. One great need is the study of human geography and the control exercised on man and his movements by such geographical factors as climate, relief of land, and the distribution of flora and fauna. Secondly, wherever necessary we should cease to be bound by the present day arbitrarily constituted political boundaries. Such areas like Central India are mere geographical expressions without any precise meaning and they are heterogeneous. Thirdly, to speak of Rajput or Brahman or any other caste without reference to locality in Central India is misleading and is specially to be borne in mind when securing anthropometric data. Nothing is so fatal to the accuracy of the statistics of the physical types of the living population as an ignorance of the tradition, history and the regional distribution of the types chosen. Lastly, there are innumerable questions which one may be tempted to ask. What for example is the affiliation of the lower castes to the existing hill population. What causes a great variation in the different sections of the popultion though groups of them possess the same culture—forms such as traditions, customs and beliefs. How far cultural and regional variations stand in the way of the fusion of similarly scattered groups. What are the racial types, as distinct from the ethnic labels in current use, in the population and how far are they as an individual and separate factor responsible in influencing the capacity to develop or to retard the culture and civilization of the different peoples. In relation to all such and other enquiries the Census statistics attain considerable value.

V.—*Some migration data.*

22. Before setting out the data for some castes and correlating them with the Census figures as regards their present day distribution, the more important castes may be arranged as in the table below. The list is incomplete as there are some castes about which out information is indefinite or lacking. The primitive tribes are excluded from the list.

Castes for which some tradition of migration exists. 1	Castes known to have no tradition for migration. 2	Mixed Rajput castes. 3
1. Ahir.	1. Balai.	1. Bagri.
2. Banis.	2. Basor.	2. Banjara.
3. Brahman.	3. Chamar.	3. Bedia.
4. Dhangar.	4. Dhanuk.	4. Dangi.
5. Gadaria.	5. Dhangar.	5. Dhakad.
6. Gujar.	6. Dahait.	6. Deswali Mina.
7. Jat.	7. Kotwar.	7. Kir.
8. Kachhi.	8. Arakh.	8. Kirar.
9. Kayastha.		9. Moghia.
10. Khati.		10. Charan.
11. Kunbi.		11. Sirvi.
12. Kurmi.		12. Sondhia.
13. Lodhi.		
14. Maratha.		
15. Rajput.		

23. *Brahman.*—It is a very interesting fact that the Brahmans in Central India are all migrants, though they have now become localised in the different parts of the Agency and form separate endogamous groups. The main classes are Malwi, Nemari, Bundelkhandi, Marwari, Dakshani and Mewari. The last three are migrants as their names themselves would suggest. With the exception of the Dakshani Brahmans who came with the Marathas in the 18th century, the Brahmans of Malwa, Bundelkhand and Baghelkhand are early settlers but none can go very far back. There is sufficient reason to hold that Malwa received the Brahman

* Quoted in the article on Aryans in the *Encyclopædia Britannica*, 14th edition.
† Gordon Childe. *The Aryans* 1926, 211-212.

immigrant population earlier than the eastern parts which were under the rule of the primitive tribes for few centuries after the dispersal of the Rajputs from northern India. The immigrants to Malwa have mostly come from Gujrat and Rajputana while the eastern parts have received the Brahman population wholly from the **Gangetic** *doab*.

The details for the immigration of the Brahmans to Malwa are set out in the caste chapter of the 1901 Report of this Agency. For the sake of convenience they are summarised here briefly. Malwi Audumbar (Panch Dravid), Chawise (Panch Dravid) of whom ten families are said to have come into Malwa, Jambu (Panch Dravid), Audumbar Potachor (Panch Dravid) and Audumbar Rodwal (Panch Dravid) all these have come from Gujarat. The Malwi Audich (Panch Gaur) came from north of India originally the parent stock being found near Delhi. Moolraj, Raja of Gujarat settled some of these Brahmans in his country and the Malwi section is sprung from the Gujarat section which is known as Sahasra as 1,000 families were brought into Gujarat.

The Gujar Gaur Malvi Brahmans (Panch Gaur) originally came from northern India but the Malvi group appears to have come from Gujarat. The Tiwari, Mewari and Mewari Shrigaud (Panch Gaur) have come from Mewar. The Naramdeo Brahmans on the banks of the Narbada appear to be a purely local group.

Of the eastern Brahmans, the Sanadhyas (Panch Gaur) came originally from the country round about Muttra. The Bhagors derive their name from the place of residence. The original home of the Jijhotias of Bundelkhand is the country between the Ganges and the Jumna. They were introduced into Central India by Jujhar Singh, Raja of Orchha, who gave them grants of land. The Sarwarias are mainly found in Baghelkhand and have come from Gorakhpur and other eastern districts of the United Provinces.

Migration from Gujarat side and the west of Central India is due to famine or religious persecution. Several casts in Central India give out also that they came to Malwa, which has been a proverbially favoured region, owing to famine elsewhere.

The following table shows the distribution of the main Brahman sub-classes according to the three territorial divisions :—

Brahman sub-classes. 1	Total. 2	Malwa. 3	Bundelkhand. 4	Baghelkhand. 5
Bhagor	11,167	4,043	7,029	95
Dakshani	18,890	17,999	391	500
Jijhotia	48,879	4,452	43,562	865
Kanaujia	44,565	8,990	32,529	3,046
Sanadhya	33,192	15,688	16,456	1,048
Sarwaria	299,022	1,622	24,167	273,233
Shrigaud	9,834	9,432	270	132

24. *Bania.*—So far known there are very few local groups of the Banias in Malwa. Tradition has it that there were very wealthy mercantile classes in the days of the Paramaras but there is no authentic information. In Malwa, they are all settlers in recent times either from Gujarat or from Rajputana. Ujjain perhaps had the oldest colony : their settlement in Indore is not more than a century or a century and a half old. The larger influx of the Banias from Rajputana dates from the time of the Maratha rule. The former opium trade in Malwa attracted a considerable colony of mercantile classes. The Agarwals are from Delhi and Hissar side. The Oswal, Porwal and Mahesri Banias have come from Rajputana. In the east the main divisions are Gahoi, Golapurab, Kasundhan and Kesarwani. The original head-quarter of Gahoi Banias is said to be Kharagpur in Bundelkhand. Some of these classes are local groups while others like Kesarwani may have come from the trans-Jumna tracts. The distribution of the Bania sub-castes is given below :—

Bania sub-castes. 1	Total.* 2	Malwa. 3	Bundelkhand. 4	Baghelkhand. 5
Agarwal	23,684	14,918	4,517	4,249
Gahoi	14,687	1,093	13,052	542
Golapurab	2,835	35	2,800	..
Kasaundhan	6,373	21	315	6,037
Kesarwani	14,286	186	308	13,792
Mahesri	9,952	9,908	5	39
Oswal	25,255	23,192	1,376	687
Porwal	23,285	15,548	6,688	1,049
Saraogi	4,346	3,840	506	..

25. *Rajput.*—The distribution of the Rajputs closely follows the migrational history which has already been set forth in a previous section. The Bundela Rajputs have no tradition of migration.

26. Certain main castes.—*Ahir.*—As already mentioned the word Ahir is derived from Abhira—a tribe of great antiquity. The Abhiras were once a widespread people in nothern and Central India and also in the Deccan. They had perhaps also a southern extension for according to the *Cambridge History of Ancient India* 'a race of uncertain affinity was the Ayar, who in many respects resembled the Abhiras of Northern India and seem to have brought into the south the worship of the herdsman god Krishna '. The tract to the east of Malwa and west of the Betwa river including Jhansi, Sironj, etc., is still known as Ahirwara. The Ahir population is found in these parts and has spread further east but not towards the central Malwa plateau. The line runs from Bhopal to Orchha, Bijawar, Chhatarpur, Panna, Maihar and Rewa. The marginal table gives figures for the northern Gwalior districts which have returned the bulk of the Ahirs from that State. In Indore 13,845 Ahirs out of the total strength of 23,830 have been returned from the Nimar district to which place the Ahir element has spread from the Khandesh side.

District. 1	Strength. 2
Narwar	26,505
Isagarh	37,373
Bhilsa	10,563
Bhind	15,163
Gird	15,774
Shajapur	7,051

M53CC

27. *Gujar.*—Historically a well-known people and it is not necessary to mention their origin here. The Gujars have spread into Central India from the west of Chambal. They are found in Malwa and northern Gwalior. In Malwa they are less in evidence in the western and south-western Malwa. In the east they have not spread at all. In the Central Provinces they are found in the Hoshangabad and Nimar districts, and are supposed to have migrated in the 16th century from Gwalior. Their distribution in Gwalior and Indore is given below :—

Gwalior State	119,314	Indore State	47,103
Ujjain	10,686	Rampura Bhanpura	14,021
Mandsaor	12,766	Mahidpur	8,281
Shajapur	27,162	Nimar	17,942
Tonwarghar	27,162	Nemawar	4,847
Narwar	10,835		

The fact that they have not colonised central Malwa but the Narbada valley shows that they have migrated in earlier times to the more unopened parts below the Vindhyas and have spread on either side of the Narbada.

28. *Gadaria.*—They are spread everywhere though they are concentrated in Bundelkhand. In northern Malwa they say they have come from the East. Nothing is known about their movements.

29. *Jat.*—This caste appears to have migrated originally from the west of Chambal, the country round about Bharatpur. It entered Hoshangabad district of the Central Provinces in the 18th century, migrating from Bharatpur and halting in Marwar on the way. The Jats in northern Malwa have also a tradition that they migrated there from Bharatpur owing to famine. This appears to be borne out by their present day distribution. In north Gwalior they are found in small numbers. But in the Malwa portion of Gwalior more than half are found in Ujjain and Mandasor districts. They are chiefly found in central Malwa in this Agency. They appear to have reached the Narbada valley through the Nemawar district of Indore and Bhopal.

30. *Kachhi.*—The Kachhis are mainly to be seen in the east and in Bhopal. They are concentrated in north Gwalior and have not spread to Malwa. The Bundelkhand Kachhis have a tradition that they migrated east from Narwar after the fall of the Kachhwaha Rajputs.

31. *Khati.*—This caste is distributed in the Bhopal Agency, Indore and the Dewas States. They have a tradition that they were brought into Central India by the Muslim Rulers. They are concentrated in central Malwa. The bulk of the Indore Khatis are settled in the Indore district. They have not spread to any other part of Central India.

32. *Kunbi.*—The Kunbis have migrated from Gujarat. They are to be found in the Malwa and Southern States. They appear to have migrated to Malwa and thence to Khandesh which part they also colonised through the Tapti valley. According to the chronicles of the Rewa Kunbis they arrived about the 11th century in a large body in whose vanguard alone were 2,000 carts. It seems not unlikely that this account is correct and that the Kunbis were forced to leave Gujarat by the encroachment of Rajput tribes.*

33. *Mixed Castes.*—The settlement of the Rajputs in Rajputana and Malwa has given rise to many mixed castes in the medieval and later periods. Such are the Charan, Dhakad, Dangi, Kirar, Sondhia, Banjara, etc. Some have arisen locally and others have migrated from Rajputana and are now settled in Central India. The Dhakad and Dangi castes are mainly found in northern Malwa and they have migrated from Rajputana. The Dangi is mainly found in the Saugor district of the Central Provinces and the bulk of the Gwalior Dangis are returned from north Gwalior. According to the *Central Provinces Castes and Tribes* the Dangis migrated there in the 11th century. Their distribution shows they have migrated through northern Malwa and Bhopal. The Kirars are exclusively found in Bhopal and in the Central Provinces it is recorded they left Gwalior about 1468 A. D. under two of their leaders and settled in Hoshangabad district. In 1931 the Kirars in Gwalior numbered 75,897, the bulk of whom were enumerated in the northern districts of that State and very few in the Malwa districts. Their distribution seems to corroborate this tradition.

34. *Loda.*—In north Malwa they claim to have come from Lohargarh in Rajputana. After the fall of Prithvi Raj they went to Lohargarh and then migrated to Malwa. In the Betul and Hoshangabad districts of the Central Provinces they are considered to have immigrated there from Central India in the fifteenth century. In Central India they are now exclusively found in the Bhopal Agency. The Lodhis, a much more numerous group, are largely found in the east to which place they have spread from the Gangetic plains.

35. *Kayastha.*—We have the authority of Malcolm that the Kayasthas were brought into Malwa by the Muslim conquerors. Some of the families trace their settlement from the earliest Muslim conquest; many are of more recent date.

The following table shows the territorial distribution of certain main castes.

Caste. 1	Total. 2	Malwa. 3	Bundelkhand. 4	Baghelkhand. 5
Ahir	233,782	51,931	102,609	79,242
Gujar	84,813	79,396	5,146	271
Jat	28,135	27,358	755	22
Gadaria	98,350	36,500	46,730	15,120
Kachhi	224,212	44,803	113,562	65,847
Khati	64,649	64,649	..	..
Kunbi	42,182	32,188	..	9,994
Kurmi	205,371	64,219	37,810	103,342
Loda	19,226	19,224	2	..
Lodhi	135,554	48,147	80,669	6,738
Kayastha	37,092	13,090	15,124	8,878
Dangi	45,064	38,899	6,062	103
Dhakad	34,283	34,256	1	26
Kirar	32,822	30,151	2,664	7

* *Khandesh District Gazetteer* (1880), page 39.

7. The Aboriginal Tribes of the Central Provinces.

By W. H. Shoobert.

A.—The effect on the tribes of contacts with civilization.

There are, as stated in chapters XI and XII of this report, over 4,000,000 members of aboriginal tribes in these Provinces. Of these 1,969,214 were returned at the census as following tribal religions, and the remainder were stated to have become Hindus or Christians. The number of Christianized tribesmen is in fact negligible except in Jashpur State where there are 47,479, almost all Oraons. In the British districts of the Central Provinces and Berar the number of aborigines is about 3,000,000 of whom over 1,600,000 were returned as followers of the Hindu Religion. Change of religion is of some importance as an indication of the influence upon the primitive tribes of contact with a culture foreign to their own, but how slowly that influence has worked will be clear from a study of books by earlier observers, such as Forsyth, and comparison of their notes with those taken quite recently by various officials in the more remote tracts of the country. Some of the latter are reproduced below. It would, however, be incorrect to class the Hinduized aboriginal with the ordinary Hindu villager of the Central Provinces for, although, after centuries of varying degrees of contact, each may have assimilated ideas and customs from the other, their cultures are most obviously distinct. This is a fact which, while the Census Report was in Press, was recently stressed in the columns of an influential local periodical. The test of religion is in itself very fallible and the difficulty of obtaining accurate returns of those retaining their tribal creeds has been explained in chapter XI of the Census Report on the Central Provinces. The position was briefly defined by Mr. Stent in his report upon the census of the Amraoti district :—

" During the recent census the tendency of all enumerators was to record all aboriginal tribes as Hindus, and it was found almost impossible to induce them to question the members of these tribes regarding their religion. The majority of enumerators no doubt assumed without question that persons who were not Muhammadans, Parsis or Christians must be Hindus ; but some of them were certainly animated by the conscious desire to extend the scope of Hinduism. It is significant that the Korku Revenue Inspector of the Dharni tahsil, in his report on this subject, remarks that all Korkus are followers of the Hindu religion. As a matter of fact few, if any, of the Korkus in the Melghat can be accurately described as Hindus. Those men who have settled in the plains have to some extent adopted Hindu Gods and customs in addition to their own, but the dwellers in the Melghat retain their ancient beliefs."

The difficulty was accentuated because many of those tribesmen, who are more closely associated with the cultivators of the plains, themselves deliberately returned Hinduism as their religion, considering that such a return would elevate them in the social scale, while to the more simple of them the term Hindu does not convey any connection with religion but merely indicates a race. The actual returns of religion are not, however, necessarily material to any discussion of the effects upon the tribes of contact with cultures other than their own. The bare fact is that the descendants of the original inhabitants of the Province, who before repeated invasions withdrew to the hills and forests where they have lived their own lives and for centuries developed upon their own lines, form more than 20 per cent. of the population. The extension of communications and the development of mechanical transport has increased their association with villagers in the plains, and a considerable proportion of them are now indistinguishable from the ordinary cultivator. The majority are however distinct in appearance, interests and custom from their more civilized neighbours, and it is therefore not improper, without touching upon the forbidden subject of politics, to comment upon the fact that according to the recent Communal Award only a single seat in the Reformed Legislature would be granted to the aborigines of the Province. Those who wish to do so will of course have the opportunity of voting in general constituencies but few have the necessary qualifications and it can be asserted without danger of contradiction that in the more backward tracts, where education even if available is frankly disliked by the people of the forests, the number of such voters would be entirely negligible. The contrast between the treatment given to the depressed classes and to this other great non-vocal community is obvious and that there is, in certain circumstances, a definite danger of exploitation of the aborigines has been proved in the recent past.

The results of the contact of races in the Central Provinces are not so obvious as in some other parts of the world or in some other parts of India—Assam for instance. Possibly this is because different races have mingled together in the past, and different cultures have existed side by side for many centuries. The differences between the descendants of Aryan invaders and the true autochthonous stock in fact became stereotyped long years ago. There was much in the religion of each which could easily be assimilated to that of the other. As already stated the aborigines generally withdrew to the forests and hills before a new civilization, where they were protected by natural obstacles and by malaria, from frequent disturbance, and for this and various other reasons, so far from the race dying out as has happened to the aborigines in other parts of the world, it has continued to form the most fecund element in the Provinces. In recent times occasional contact with Europeans has had no appreciable effect upon the tribes. The devastating results of the activities of traders and mission workers upon the ancient cultures of the Pacific and elsewhere, which have recently occupied the attention of many distinguished ethnologists, have only a very dim reflection in Central India. Perhaps this is due to the policy of official toleration which has, in regard to the customs and religion of the people, been followed by the Government of the country for a very long time. In general it may be said that in most tracts no deliberate attempt has been made to supplant the old culture. It is true that education, missionary zeal—whether Christian or Hindu—and mere casual contacts in *bazaars* must have their effect, and that ordinary laws are often unsuited to the primitive tribes—but it would not be fair in any way to draw a parallel between the condition of the aborigines of this province, and, for example, that of the disappearing tribes of the Pacific, of whom Capt. Pitt-Rivers has written :—

" The inevitable result of destroying all the old culture forms and an environmental conditions in the endeavour to impose too dissimilar a culture upon a people specialized by a long process of adaptation to particular conditions is actually to exterminate them." (*The Clash of Culture and Contact of Races.*)

It has already been observed in my Report that the motor-horn will sound the death-knell of the aboriginal tribes as such. Facts and statistics all point to their gradual absorption in the Hindu fold. When they themselves claim inclusion in it, their object as mentioned above is to attain social uplift. It is, however, rather doubtful whether that object is generally achieved. The Gandas and Pankas, aboriginal people who have lost their identity and are not included in the list of primitive tribes, are regarded as untouchable almost throughout the Province. The Kolis, who have all become Hindus, both in religion and in custom, are included among the depressed classes in several districts where they are numerically important. The Pardhans, Ojhas and Nagarchis are also treated as impure particularly in the west of the Province. The inference is obvious and remarks recorded by Mr. C. U. Wills, I.C.S., regarding the position of the primitive tribes in Chhattisgarh twenty years ago are still relevant :—

"There is evidence to show that the present social organization in these open *zamindaris* has been substituted in comparatively recent times for the more archaic semi-tribal form which still persists in the hill estates, and that this change has taken place owing simply to the natural facilities for immigration offered to the *khalsa* castes. Thus a tradition is recorded by the Settlement Officer of 1868 that the whole Mungeli tahsil was at one time held entirely by Gonds. This we can well believe, for there were in the Rajput and early Maratha days Gond *Zamindars* not only in Pandaria but also in Nawagarh and at Mungeli itself. At the present time the Gonds form an altogether negligible fraction of the population in the west of the district, being found in any numbers only in the hills to the north of Pandaria towards the Mandla border. A similar phenomenon is found in the Raipur estates of Bhatgaon and Bilaigarh-Katgi. Here, too, though the *Zamindar* of Bilaigarh-Katgi is himself a Gond, his tribesmen are found nowhere but in the fringe of forest villages along the Phuljhar border in the southern hills. One inference from these facts is obvious, that in the more accessible estates the mere presence of an aboriginal *Zamindar* has afforded inadequate protection to his fellow tribesmen against dispossession at the hands of the more forceful *khalsa* immigrant Brahmins, Kshatris, Kurmis, Telis and Chamars. Granted a facility for immigration and at once the *khalsa* people have begun to drive off the earlier settlers to the hills.

"This introduces an important problem of future *zamindari* administration. Every year sees greater inducements and fresh facilities offered for immigration to the wilder portions of the district, the present stronghold of the aboriginal tribes, and past history shows that this new factor, if uncontrolled, will mean their steady, if gradual, displacement by traders and agriculturists from the open country. Is it incumbent on the Government to check this natural movement, or should it stand aside and allow free play to the competing forces, letting the weakest go to the wall ? The chief peculiarity of the hill estates is the large predominance of the non-Aryan peoples—Kanwars, Gonds and the like, who are racially distinct from the people of the plains, and represent an earlier stage of social development. Their institutions are still predominantly tribal and, though the influence of Hinduism and the Hindu caste system has modified the line of separation between, say the Kawar in the forest and the Kurmi in the open country, yet they are still sufficiently distinct to require in many respects differential treatment. The need for a definite policy of protection for the local indigenous tribes of the Satgarh is a matter which requires to be specially emphasized in the course of this report, not only because it has hitherto not received the attention it deserves but because the view has been advanced in certain quarters that such protection is unnecessary in the interests of the aboriginals themselves, and undesirable on a consideration of the general welfare of the tract. Against any policy of antagonism to the indigenous inhabitants or even of *laisser faire* where their interests clash with those of the Khalsa people who press upon their borders, I would enter a serious protest. Such a policy would be foreign to the traditions of our rule. The Land Alienation Acts of other Provinces, our own policy in the Melghat taluk of Berar, the gift of a statutory status to the tenancy of these Provinces, are all indications that the play of free competition among the conflicting interests of a simple agricultural people is recognized as being fraught with grave dangers to the welfare of the country.

"The displacement of the aboriginal is an accomplished fact practically over the whole of the open country estates. Interest in their preservation therefore must in this district be centred on the seven northern estates, the Satgarh, in which the aboriginal is still socially predominant but where there are already signs that his predominance is being undermined. A brief discription of the social organization of this tribal stronghold, and a reference to the recent census enumeration and to the inferences that can be drawn therefrom will show clearly how matters stand at present, and will serve to emphasize the importance of protecting this primitive people until they have had time to adjust their own defence against the new forces they have now to meet.

"With a view to disclosing the general division of the population of these seven estates into immigrant on the one hand and what may be loosely called indigenous on the other, and to show how far in the last 45 years the latter have yielded to the former, an abstract was prepared showing the population of these zamindaris, caste by caste, for 1866 and 1911. In Pendra the percentage of the indigenous castes has fallen from 79 to 68, in Matin from 88 to 78, in Chhuri from 86 to 75, in Khenda from 88 to 76, in Pandaria from 32 to 21, in Kanteli from 32 to 16 and in Champa from 51 to 37. The fall in the other estates is not so marked (figures for Bhatgaon and Bilaigarh are not available).

"It is apparent at once that the local tribes have during the past half century lost considerable ground. They have lost more relatively in the open country, where the process of displacement is nearing completion than in the hills where it is only just commencing. But, what is a more serious matter from the point of view of their social predominance, they have lost village headships in the same proportion as their numerical superiority has decreased. From statistics abstracted from the Settlement records it appears that in 1868, 87 per cent. of the headmen in the Satgarh were aboriginals. The percentage now is 79. In the other five estates 22 per cent. of the headmen were of indigenous origin in 1868 but only 12 per cent. were so recorded in 1911. This shows that the dispossession disclosed by the general figures of population is genuinely affecting the social influence of the older inhabitant. The significance of this will only be fully apparent to those with some close acquaintance with a forest tract. The removal of a headman will not infrequently mean the departure of a very large section, perhaps the whole of the tenantry, who would rather follow the fortunes of their old leader than risk suffering from the want of sympathy of an alien lessee. It was just this substitution of foreign for local headmen in the adjoining Province of Chhota Nagpur which led to the Kol rebellions of 1820 and 1831, and although the process is in Bilaspur far too gradual to awaken violent opposition among the people yet they recognize the threat to their social supremacy offered by the gradual increase of outside influence, and express their dislike for the *khalsa* immigrant in many ways." (*Report on the Land Revenue Settlement of the Bilaspur Zamindari estates, 1912.*)

Mr. Wills was not opposed to the improvement of the aboriginal tribes by contacts with civilization, but only urged that they should be given breathing space and a fair opportunity of adapting themselves to new conditions. This is clear from what he wrote of the Kawars :—

"By their partial acceptance of the Hindu creed they indicate their desire for social advancement. The Paikra Kanwars, a very numerous, well disposed and prosperous community in all these seven northern zamindaris are an instance of what Hinduism can do to teach primitive people social decency and self-respect, carrying with it lessons of thrift, industry and self-restraint ; and what is true of the Paikras is true to a less extent of all the other component classes in the superior social stratum of these estates. They are now rapidly improving their standard of living and this means greater industry, greater credit and greater agricultural stability. Nor is social improvement through Hinduism confined to the better class of aboriginal. Even the low class Panika has in these estates an important Kabirpanti shrine at Kudurmal in the Korba Zamindari, and though their social practice is not on a par with the more exalted level of their religious tenets (as the Hindu expresses it, their *karm* is defective though their *dharm* is good), yet the influence of religious precept is not altogether lost as is proved by the abstention of many Panikas from intoxicants in deference to Kabirpanti doctrine. When in addition to these signs of social advancement it is possible to point, as will be seen hereafter, to remarkable agricultural developments, thousands of acres brought under new cultivation year by year and land embanked at such a pace that it is a difficult task to keep the field survey work up-to-date, it is clear that we are dealing with a people suited to their environment, vigorous, capable of being developed into excellent agriculturists, and at least worthy of encouragement and protection sufficient to enable them to work out their own salvation, unhampered for a time by undue competition from outside."

It was many years after the remarks above had been recorded that the Central Provinces Land Alienation Act was passed and applied to certain districts in order to protect aboriginal proprietors from unfair exploitation by adventurers. Mr. Lillie's observations upon this subject in his report on the recent revision of the Land Revenue Settlement of Mandla district are interesting :—

"The Act has certainly served the purpose for which it was passed. The ground lost by the aboriginals since settlement in small shares, is 15 mahals approximately, largely previous to the passing of the Land Alienation Act. The process which the Act interrupted is readily discernible in the Dindori tahsil, where it is usual to find in villages owned by Gond Malguzars, one or two small shares that have passed to non-aboriginals, generally Banias resident in Mandla. Since 1916, this process by which ultimately the whole village passes to non-residents has been materially checked. Whether the Gond malguzar is good or not for the general prosperity of his village is a question on which two opinions are possible. But to my mind the fact that he is invariably a resident cultivator, and is on friendly terms with his tenants, whom he treats well, far outweigh his defects of improvidence and intemperance. In any case, whatever view be taken of his value to the community, nothing can be said in support of those to whom his villages usually pass, through usury, deceit and trickery. They are nearly always oppressive Banias, who treat their villages on the most strict commercial lines, levy all sorts and kinds of illegal dues, and have no regard whatever for tenants' rights and interests. The men to whom such villages would pass if the Act were not in force, are those to whom the small shares have already been transferred, and neither I nor any revenue officer with experience of the district, would hesitate to describe them as worst possible landlords."

Mr. Lillie's statement is true of many districts besides Mandla. There are in fact various ways in which in the past the ordinary laws of the land have operated unfavourably to the aboriginal tribes. The custom of human sacrifice has, of course, disappeared with the substitution of an animal for the victim, and the earlier savage ritual is not missed, but this custom which was well-known among the Kondhs, and probably also among the Marias and Gonds is recalled almost every year in the evidence in murder cases in Chanda district or Bastar State and several apparently genuine instances of resort by individuals to human sacrifice in times of extreme difficulty have come to notice. The murder of wizards or witches, alleged to have cast spells over the accused, is comparatively common, and often appears to command the sympathy of the people in the more backward tracts. That civilized law should punish offences of this kind is now recognized in the most remote places—but the prohibition of marriage by capture, shifting cultivation and distillation of liquor by a beneficent Government is not so cheerfully accepted.

Rai Bahadur Hiralal states :—

"Among the Gonds, particularly in the wild tracts of Chanda and Bastar, marriage by capture was formerly the rule. But the magistracy treated this social custom as an offence against the penal code, and inflicted punishment upon the so-called wrong-doers. This alarmed the simple forest people, who had to invent a device for following their time-honoured custom, without offending a code of laws foreign to their ideas. This device was to make the capture merely a formal ceremony, after settling the marriage between the man and girl.

"Another great check upon the freedom of the tribes was the prohibition of cultivation by the *dahia* or *bewar* process. It was the habit of these wild people to cut down trees, burn them and sow seed in the ashes, instead of ploughing the land. When Government found it expedient to limit this extravagant mode of agriculture, the people in forest tracts regarded it as a great grievance.

"Lastly according to ancient tradition the gods of the tribe required offerings of liquor distilled by the family worshipping them. The excise rules now prohibit such distillation, and the majority of the tribesmen yield to the law and now offer to their gods liquor purchased from a licensed shop, but many continue stealthily to distil their own and to satisfy their gods and godlings as their forefathers did."

Rai Bahadur Hira Lal also mentions the decay of the authority of the tribal panchayat, and its revival in a different form, as another example of the disadvantages suffered by the primitive tribes under the ordinary code of laws and administration. The opinion of selected Deputy Commissioners upon the same subject is worth quoting.

The Deputy Commissioner, Amraoti.—"Under the present excise policy of the Central Provinces Government the progressive increase in the duty rate in pursuance of the policy of gradual prohibition has put Government liquor beyond the purse of the poor Korku inhabitants of the Melghat. In consequence those who live within easy reach of the Betul border smuggle Government liquor from the low-duty shops in the Betul district. Last year some 10 Korkus living in a village only two or three miles from one of these low-duty shops in the Betul district were fined sums varying from Rs. 25 to 50 for smuggling liquor from that shop, though the nearest Government liquor shops in this district were 20 miles away. I reported the case to the High Court and had the fines reduced to Rs. 5 and Rs. 10. In fact I was informed that the original fines had completely impoverished the village and forced several of the accused to sell their property, or cattle, or to have recourse to the money-lenders who lend in this area at exorbitant rates of interest. This difficulty has now been solved by putting the majority of the forest villages in the Melghat area in the same low-duty area as the neighbouring parts of Betul. The ryotwari tracts and Chikalda alone remain at a high rate. In this district it has not been found that Korkus resort to any degree to illicit distillation as Gonds in similar circumstances do. There is no doubt however that the high price of Government liquor does operate very harshly on all these aboriginals. The use of liquor is still regarded as a necessity in marriages and other tribal ceremonies.

"I regret I have been unable to obtain any definite instances of the operation of other laws. In general it is reported that the ordinary law of contract operates harshly owing to the poverty, ignorance and honesty of the Korkus. Being illiterate they are unaware of the terms of the bonds into which they enter for repayment of loans. They are generally inclined to trust the *Saokars* to be as honest as they are themselves. They will always pay whatever is demanded to the utmost of their power. The money-lenders of course take advantage of their ignorance to impose exorbitant rates of interest, to put down more in the bond than was actually advanced, and so on. The Usurious Loans Act does not give much protection because the Korku debtor will not plead it and as he is unable to calculate the amount of his interest he accepts the money-lender's word as to the amount he owes him.

"It has been reported to me that the restricted tenure of land also has occasional ill-effects but on the whole I am of opinion that it is a necessary and desirable protection. I have not come across any other particular instances of disabilities suffered by the aboriginals from the ordinary laws."

The Deputy Commissioner, Hoshangabad.—"I think it is true to say that the aboriginal is handicapped in the courts by the system of law and procedure of which a rich man can reap the advantage which a poorer man, because of his poverty, cannot. A rich man can brief pleaders who by means of the rules of procedure can frequently defeat justice. This a poor man cannot do, and an aboriginal is a poor man. How many poor men (including aboriginals) are acquitted of a murder charge? On the contrary, how difficult it is to convict a rich man of murder. For one thing, the rich man is able to buy up prosecution witnesses and suborn defence witnesses.

"On the civil side, what a small chance a poor man has against an unscrupulous money-lender? These considerations are so notorious, that it is unnecessary to quote instances."

The Deputy Commissioner, Balaghat.—"The existing laws in some respects operate harshly upon some aboriginal tribes, particularly Gonds, who in accordance with their religious ideas and practices must have liquor at certain social functions and the price of the liquor being high, they are sometimes forced to resort to illicit distillation even knowing well the consequences."

The Deputy Commissioner, Raipur.—"The Land Alienation Act has not been extended to any part of the district. Attention is, however, invited to paragraph 304 of the Excise Manual, Volume I, which contains a general provision for not imposing sentences of imprisonment on the aboriginals for petty cases of illicit distillation. The strictness of the excise administration no doubt is strongly opposed to aboriginal sentiment but no special orders have been issued in this connection for lenient treatment of members of aboriginal tribes in this district."

The Deputy Commissioner, Nagpur.—"The Excise laws of course are the hardest in their application to Gonds. For many festivals the Gonds require liquor for offering to their gods or for their tribal feasts. Traditionally the liquor should have been distilled beforehand for the occasion. The prohibition policy of Government has operated very harshly on the Gonds with the result that many are driven to illicit distillation, while when illicitly distilled liquor is not available they cannot afford Government liquor and so are driven to offering their gods a mixture of sugar and water. This is undoubtedly having its effect in promoting the decay of rites and ceremonies and adding to the general depression in the Gond villages in the district.

"The land revenue policy of Government adopted in the sixties was ill-considered so far as Gonds were concerned. Their tribal system is naturally one of a village headman and ryotwari tenure, the village lands being regarded as the property of the community rather than of individuals. A limited number of Gonds were given proprietary rights in the sixties, but ever since their numbers have steadily fallen owing to their ignorance of the civil laws and the ease with which they have become a prey to money-lenders. For no sound reasons the Land Alienation Act was not extended to the district and there are now only half a dozen Gond malguzars, leaving out of account the Gond Raja of Nagpur. At the present time the tendency is also to expropriate Gond tenants. In nearly every Gond village in the Deolapar tract the Gonds are dissatisfied with their Hindu or Moslem malguzars, and many of the Gonds are abandoning their tenancy land rather than put up with alien landlords. Several of them go to the forest villages, where they are fairly happy, but most are degenerating into landless labourers. Outside the Ramtek *tahsil* practically all Gonds are landless labourers, except in a portion of Saoner.

"I have not had time to study the effect of the ideas of Hindu law on Gonds in the district; nevertheless they appear to be degenerating into a low caste on the borders of Hinduism. Hindu ideas of succession are gradually affecting them to the detriment of the old idea of succession by the senior efficient member of the family.

"The sections of the Indian Penal Code dealing with offences against marriages are utterly unsuited even now for Gonds in this and all other districts. The vast majority of Gonds ignore them however and leave such matters to the decision of their own panchayats. From time to time however if dissatisfied with the panchayat's decision or if the case is one that it is not likely to succeed before the panchayat, bad Gonds do bring complaints in a Criminal Court. There is much to be said for a simplification of the Penal Code and the Criminal Procedure Code in its application to aboriginals, as in the Madras Agency tracts and the Assam Hills. The Gond however of the Nagpur district is probably too advanced for this, but there can be little doubt that it would be a sound measure in the Plateau districts and considerable parts of several other districts of the Province."

In considering the opinions recorded it may be recalled that when the Reformed Government was constituted certain tracts in this Province were excluded from the area of the constituencies of the Legislative Councils. These were the Sironcha tahsil of Chanda district, the whole of the Mandla district and various zamindaris of the Chanda and Chhindwara districts and of the Chhattisgarh Division. Three of the latter—Chandrapur, Padampur and Malkharoda—were enfranchised in 1923 and Mandla district was enfranchised in 1926, but it is doubtful whether many of the real aborigines qualify for a vote or use it.

Regarding the general subject of the effect on the primitive tribes of contacts with civilization something has been recorded in chapter XII of the Central Provinces Report, and more particularly, in chapter VII, Mr. Grigson's note at the end of which is especially suggestive. It cannot be denied that the development of communications while it has immensely facilitated, internal trade has undoubtedly spread disease. Owing to official control distilled liquor has generally taken the place of rice-beer, a comparatively innocuous beverage: and when liquor cannot be obtained the substitution of opium and other harmful drugs is the obvious alternative. Clothing, of which the aboriginals cannot have sufficient to change with the variations of climate, and which they will not generally wash because the process causes wear, is a source of dirt and disease. The prude who tries to teach them that clothing has any useful purpose except as a protection against the weather is one of their worst enemies.

It may be argued with considerable justification that the benefits bestowed upon the aborigines by the march of civilization more than balance the loss of many features in their own culture, and that the administration of an ordered Government is far more favourable to them than the autocratic rule of the chiefs and zamindars of the past and its attendant *begar* (forced labour) and oppression. There is however a very reasonable answer to such argument. The primitive tribes were allowed the freedom of the forest with little disturbance in the past; the system of *begar* was well suited to this Province until very recent times, and it has to be remembered that many of the most noble buildings in India, monuments of her ancient civilization, were constructed almost entirely by this form of labour, to say nothing of the numerous useful local forts and water tanks, which protected and benefited not only the lord of the village but also the peasants by whose hands they were built. The remarks in paragraph 25 to chapter VIII of my Report are relevant to this subject.

Enough has been written in this appendix and elsewhere in the Report to give a fairly-clear idea of the results of the contact of the Aryan invader and the primitive tribes. Even now the methods of cultivation of many of the latter are almost unbelievably primitive; in some tracts plough cattle are unknown and the attitude to the modern luxury of riding in a cart to which reference is made in paragraph 46 of chapter I is not confined to Bastar State. This part of the appendix may be closed by another interesting quotation from Mr. Grigson's notes regarding Bastar State:—

"There has been little change in the style of house construction. From the experience of wide touring for four years in the State I can say that the best and cleanest aboriginal houses are those in the Abujmar hills. There the cleanliness is due to the practice of shifting the village site every fourth or fifth year when the adjacent hill-slope or *penda* cultivation is exhausted, or for some purely superstitious reasons. A hill Maria village in the last year before its shifting is a dirty affair, but for the first two years at all events it is a sanitarium in comparison with many of the settled Parja, Bhattra or Muria villages even close to Jagdalpur. The huts in the settled villages are generally smaller than those in the shifting villages.

"The hill tribes and wilder aboriginals have no hesitation about killing and eating cattle, and in fact there is very little meat that they will not eat, whether the animal has died a natural death or has been killed four days or more before by a tiger. Around Jagdalpur, Murias and Bhattras have largely given up beef eating, and actually out-caste persons who take beef. In one case, a witch caught walking naked in a cremation ground at night was forced to eat beef as a preliminary to being out-casted. Even the Dandami Marias in the Jagdalpur tahsil and the Marias of the Abujmar Hills on the Dantewara side are being affected by the Hindu ideas about beef eating. The latter now say that they only eat beef when it has been sacrificed to their clan god, or is sacrificed and eaten at the ceremony of erecting a monolith in honour of the dead; they declare that they have given up eating the flesh of dead cattle. The Dandami Marias have in their villages a place generally on rocky ground set apart for killing, cooking and eating beef. There are occasions even now when beef is felt to be a necessity, but instead of killing their own cattle, they often employ the professional thief of the village to steal an animal from the nearest non-Maria village. Jagdalpur Jail usually has at least 40 Dandami Maria cattle thieves convicts, and though they are very reticent about the complicity in their crime of their fellow-villages, they are often compensated by village subscription for their period of detention. Most of the Hindus in the State are to some extent meat-eaters on occasions, goat and chicken being the usual meat. The buffaloes sacrified at Dashera are eaten by Halbas and Mahras and other low castes. But in general it may be said that as the population becomes more Hinduized, it eats less meat. The physique of the more Hinduized aboriginals is certainly inferior to that of the wilder ones. It would be unsafe to attribute this entirely to meat-eating, as the wilder tribes have generally four meals a day, *pej* or gruel twice and *thal* twice a day as compared with the two meals normally taken amongst the average population of India.

"Lastly, the imitation of Hindu marriage custom has not persisted far in the State, pre-puberty marriage is practically unknown amongst the aboriginals though there are signs of a tendency to introduce it amongst the more Hinduized Dandami Marias."

B.—Notes on fifteen tribes.

These notes are selected from a large number which I recorded during the course of my own tours and from others kindly collected by Mr. M. Ikramullah, I.C.S. in Mandla district, by Mr. Amir Khan, Superintendent of Udaipur State, Khan Sahib Abdul Gaffar Khan, Superintendent and Mr. M. N. Ghosal, Assistant Superintendent of Jashpur State. Most of the notes upon the people of Bastar State were written by Mr. W. V. Grigson, I.C.S., to whom I am greatly indebted. Ethnologists must look forward eagerly to the publication of his book on the tribes of Bastar. I have endeavoured to exclude as far as possible anything which has already appeared in the late Mr. Russell's great work, or in other local ethnological literature. The photographs of the Bison-head Maria dance and wedding and the woman and child were kindly lent by Mr. Grigson. The others are my own.

Little has been recorded in the past regarding some of the tribes mentioned in the following pages; in the case of others the object of the notes has been merely to supplement existing knowledge. It must be observed that many customs, particularly in connection with wedding and funeral ceremonies vary not so much from tribe to tribe as from tract to tract. Naturally each tribe is bound to assimilate ideas from its immediate neighbours. It will also generally be found that the village Baiga (Bhumia or Goonia) propitiates certain universal gods on behalf of a village or group of villages—and these are quite distinct from the separate gods of the tribe, or clan or household. In the Chhota Nagpur States images of the gods were not usually forthcoming in the villages which I visited, and it was stated in most cases that no emblems for them existed.

The Korkus, Bhils and some other people of numerical importance are not mentioned in this part of the appendix because I had no opportunity of making a special study of them. Lack of time and space has in fact rendered it imperative to include articles on a few tribes only and much of the material available has of necessity been omitted. For the same reason six or seven notes at the end of the series have been reduced to a very summary form and are merely reproduced to give a rough idea of the culture of the tribes described.

1. The Baigas of Mandla and Balaghat.

The difficulty of identifying tribes in different parts of India, on account of the changes which their names undergo from tract to tract, and owing to the fact that, in the past, various clans have from time to time broken away completely from the parent tribe has often been mentioned in ethnological literature. In Table XVIII (Central Provinces) separate figures are shown for Baigas, Binjhwars, Bhainas and Bharia-Bhumias. Although in many places members of the Binjhwar clan return themselves as belonging to the Baiga tribe, in Chhattisgarh as pointed out by Russell the Binjhwars have successfully cut themselves off from the original tribe and boast many subtribes of their own. It is however generally acknowledged that the Chhattisgarhi Binjhwar and the Baiga are most probably of the same stock. Mr. Lillie, who, as Settlement Officer of Mandla, was familiar with the Baigas, was surprised in Raipur to find them passing under the name of Bhumias. There were few returns of either Baiga or Bhumia from Raipur district at the Census and it is highly probable that these Bhumias gave their tribe-name as Binjhwar to the enumerators. "Bhumia is the name of an office, that of the priest of the village and local deities, which is held by one of the forest tribes. In the tract where the Baigas live, they, as the most ancient residents, are usually the priests of the indigenous gods; but in Jubbulpore the same office is held by another tribe, the Bharias. The name of the office often attaches itself to members of the tribe, who consider it as somewhat more respectable than their own, and it is therefore generally true to say that the people known as Bhumias in Jubbulpore are really Bharias, but in Mandla and Bilaspur they are Baigas." (*Tribes and Castes of Central Provinces*, Volume II, page 78). There is also a group called Bharia-Baigas in Mandla and so the difficulty of correctly classifying each entry in the census records is obvious. It was clearly only possible to show the returns under the tribe-name given in each case. Another wild tribe, the Bhainas of Bilaspur and the surrounding country, who have now a very distinct organization, is supposed to be descended from irregular unions between the Baigas and the Kawars and lastly the Bhuiyas or Bhuinhars of the Chhota Nagpur States, whose tribal name is etymologically the same as Bhumia and means roughly "aboriginal", have by some authorities been identified with the Baigas, alleged to be the branch of the Bhuiyas which settled in the Central Provinces. The tribes named are now all sufficiently distinct to have been treated separately by Russell. His article on the Baigas is full and available for reference to all who read this Report. In the following notes recorded by Mr. M. Ikramullah, I.C.S., Assistant Commissioner, there is, however, some interesting additional information regarding them which has not hitherto been published.

"The Baiga *Chak* is a small block of Government Forest in Karanja range where a special reserve for Baigas has been created. Its area is 20,000 acres. Baigas used to practice *Bewar* cultivation whenever they were found but this was stopped by Government and they were settled in the '*Chak*'. Here they are allowed to practise *Bewar* cultivation and live their own lives. I was rather disappointed when I visited the place because I found them wearing more clothes than I liked. In fact they are getting civilized. I missed the fine physique which has been described in Russell's book. They have started regular cultivation side by side with *bewar*. They are, however, still a very amiable set of people, jolly and inquisitive. They would insist on having a ride in the car !

"Baigas are scattered in small groups all over the South Mandla Forest Division. In some cases they appear to be just like the Gonds. My note should be read with Russell's chapter on Baigas.

"*Clans*. These Baigas state :—"We are all *Bharotia* Baigas. *Binjhwar* and *Bhaina* Baigas are not found in this District. We do not interdine with them. Nor have we anything to do with *Bharia* Baigas who eat beef. We do not eat beef. All Baigas originally came from Deonaori and Sumer Pahar. We do not know where these places are situated. So far as we know we have always been speaking the same language as you hear from us (corrupt Chhattisgarhi). We have no language like the *Parsi* of the Gonds who live round about Ghugri.

"*Tribal Legend*.—Bhagnan had a Guru. His name was Baba Vishisht Muni. Kari Nagin used to look after him and wash his loin cloth. One day she found a little semen on it. In spite of her repeated efforts to clean it she could not. So she thought of removing the spot by licking it. The moment she licked it, the cloth was purified but she became pregnant. She gave birth to Naga (probably Nanga) Baiga. We are all descended from Nanga Baiga. He married Nangi Baigan. Nangi Baigan was also known as Bhinj Baigan. Their son was Urgan Baiga. Urgan Baiga's son was named Pargan Baiga.

"Kari Nangin's younger sister was Ranmat. We do not know the name of her husband. From her was born Ravan Bangi who is responsible for the birth of all the Gonds.

"Kari Nagin had a third sister whose name we do not know. Nor do we know whom she married. Her son was Nanga Jogi. It is from him that all 'Jogis' have descended.

"It was Burra Deo who taught us how to cut trees and do *bewar* cultivation. He also taught Gonds (locally known as Kisans) how to cultivate land—(*vide* page 79, *The Tribes and Castes*, Volume II).

"*Sub-Tribes*.—We have many sub-tribes among Baigas. A few have already been mentioned above. These sub-tribes are endogamous. If any one marries out of his sub-tribe he is out-casted.

"*Septs*.—We have many septs in each sub-tribe. These septs are exogamous. Members of the same tribe can marry into various other septs but not in their own septs. Our septs are :—(1) Tataria, (2) Sadia, (3) Daria, (4) Nadia, (5) Sararia, (6) Rathoria, (7) Mudakia, (8) Bararia, (9) Ghangaria, (10) Lamothia, (11) Chandronia, (12) Kusaria, (13) Devadia, (14) Pangaria.

"These various septs are merely branches of the same family and all are equal in status. The septs like Markam, etc. (*vide* page 81, paragraph 2, *Tribes and Castes*) are not our septs. They are Gond septs.

"*Religion*.—Burra Deo and Dulha Deo are the same. Other gods are Narayan and Thakur Deo. We have only these gods. They are all equally powerful. Dharti Mata (the earth) is married to Thakur Deo, who lives in a saj tree.

"*Methods of worship*.—Have been correctly described in *The Tribes and Castes*, page 85.

"No Gond can ever be admitted into the Baiga fold. Nor can a Gond woman (even a virgin) marry a Baiga. Those who say that they can are not proper Baigas.

"*Marriage*.—One cannot marry in his own sept but he marries in the same sub-division, which worships the same gods. A boy can marry his father's sister's daughter but not his father's brother's daughter because those two will be in the same sept. The sept is continued through males only.

"The marriage is always between adults. The parents of the boy and the girl have to consider beforehand if he or she would like to marry a particular person. Marriage takes place only when the boy or the girl do not object to each other. Such enquiries are not made directly but through others. A girl sometimes selects the man she wants to marry and informs her parents of the choice. If she is married to a person whom she has not herself chosen she generally runs away.

"The boy's parents have to pay Rs. 5, 7 or 9 to the girl's parents. If they are too poor to pay the boy has to work for his father-in-law, sometimes for three years. If a man seduces another's wife, the husband is entitled to compensation.

"The day the choice of the bride is confirmed the boy's father has to produce two bottles of liquor. Some is given to Burra Deo and the rest is served among all those present. The ceremony is known as *Sagai*. A fortnight later the bridegroom's party goes to the bride's house with four bottles of liquor. A feast is given by the girl's parents and a date for the marriage is fixed. The ceremony is known as *Barokhi*. The girl's parents get at least 10 days to make arrangements for the marriage. After that the groom's party goes for the wedding. No women accompany them as women are not supposed to go to another village. The party starts on a Tuesday and generally gets to the girl's village on the same day. The girl's party feed them and all dance the night through. Liquor is provided by the girl's parents. The boy's parents take only two bottles of liquor with them. Next day *Bhanwar* takes place in the afternoon. A '*pandal*' is erected for the purpose and a pole is fixed in the ground round which the boy conducts the girl five times. Then the party leaves for the boy's house, the father and the mother of the girl accompanying their daughter. There is another *pandal* and a pole at the boy's home and the boy and the girl have to go round it seven times. It is followed by a feast and a dance at the boy's house.

"The boy does not ride the improvised 'elephant' mentioned in the *Tribes and Castes*. It is only the girl's brother who rides it. He is given some liquor. Sometimes he gets a rupee or two. Parched rice or *maka* (Indian corn) are thrown by the bride and bridegroom at each other. After this the boy puts a brass or copper ring on the small or ring finger of the right hand of the girl and the boy and girl have their feet washed by their elders. They are taken inside the girl's house and fed separately. The anointing of the girl takes place on Tuesday evening. After they have been fed they are taken out and *Bhanwars* take place as mentioned above.

"The elder brother cannot marry a younger brother's widow. Nor can the younger marry his elder brother's widow.

"*Naming.*—See page 83 of the *Tribes and Castes*.

The naming ceremony of a child takes place 15 or 20 days after its birth and the name is selected by an old man.

"*Burial.*—A man or woman who dies within five days of illness is buried—others are burnt. Sometimes a coin is put into the mouth of a dying person. It is taken away after the death and is made into a ring.

"*See page 85 of Tribes and Castes.*—The tail of the pig is cut off and it is castrated and left alone for three years before it is sacrificed to Narayan Deo.

"*See page 86.*—Flowers are offered to Nag Deo. If the unmarried die they become *bhuts* (ghosts), but married persons become good spirits after death. Good spirits can be driven away by burning *Ral* (Sal resin).

"No one in a panchayat can contradict an elder. He declares what action to be taken. They have wooden seats in their houses but elders sit on them.

"They do not know what the sun, moon and the stars are. The dark spots in the moon are a black-buck."

Enquiries which I made personally at Supkar and Piprawada in the Balaghat district among Baigas of the Binjhwar clan, apart from small local differences, confirmed information already recorded by Russell and supplemented by Mr. Ikramullah's notes. There is no room to deal with purely local customs here but it may be noted that—

(1) the Baigas have no bachelor's quarters;

(2) they state that they bathe every three or four days;

(3) the Binjhwar clan burns its dead when it can be afforded, but those, for instance, who have no relatives are buried—with their feet to the south. Stones are placed to cover the whole body at the spot where a man is burned or buried;

(4) the Binjhwars do not eat cow or bison or buffalo;

(5) when a field is first sown a young cock is sacrificed, but there is no worship at harvest time.

2. The Gonds.

In "*The Castes and Tribes of the Central Provinces*" Russell included among Gonds—Agarias, Ojhas, Pardhans, Parjas, Koyas, Bhatras, Marias and Murias, although separate articles were written in that work upon the Agarias, Pardhans, Parjas and Bhatras. It is a pity that information regarding the Marias and Murias also was not separately recorded, for their customs are in many details distinct from those of the Gonds and the arrangement of the matter dealing with these various tribes or sub-tribes is somewhat confusing. In chapter XII of my Report it has been pointed out that physically the Marias (and also the Murias) appear to the casual observer to but differ from the Gonds in many ways. Hislop's description of the Gonds, quoted by Russell is anything flattering although it is accurate enough but the Marias are on the whole good-looking people. As already observed the leptorrhine type is commonly met among them and aquiline noses are not infrequent. (There were many in the group of Chanda Marias shown in the illustrations). Such contrast with the Gonds might suggest intermarriage with some Aryan stock yet the Marias are the most retiring and primitive people of the Province. I do not propose to rush in where angels fear to tread and pit my inexpert observation against seasoned ethnologists, but I feel that the fact of the existence of contrasts which are striking to the amateur fully justified the separation of Marias and others from the Gonds in this report. It may be mentioned as a further justification that, as far as I have ascertained, the Marias and Murias do not worship Burra Deo, the universal deity of the Gonds, and their treatment of the dead differs in some details from that of the various sub-tribes of Gonds. In these Provinces there are more than 2,260,000 true Gonds, who form over 12 per cent. of the population and are incomparably more numerous than any other tribe or caste. One hundred pages were devoted to them by Russell. The following notes regarding those who live in the States of Khairagarh and Jashpur indicate variations in tribal names, and customs in different parts of the country, and changes in the last twenty years due to Hindu influence.

Khairagarh State.—Lachhna and surrounding villages.—There are three sub-tribes in the State, Raj Gond, Dhur Gond and Gaitiya (Gotte) Gond. I saw no Gotte Gonds, but the Raj Gonds and Dhur Gonds are obviously becoming Hinduised. They call themselves Hindus and do not eat the flesh of the cow. They do however eat all other kinds of meat, including that of the bison if they can get it. They worship Burra Deo, Devi and Dulha Deo and for the sake of safety are willing to acknowledge gods of all denominations. Bhagwan (Mahadeo) is to them the great God whom all the world worships but Burra Deo is the great special god of the Gonds. The Raj Gonds of the state do not appear to retain many traces of animism in their religion and do not worship the spirits in streams or trees, but the Dhur Gonds do worship streams. The Goddess Devi (whom they seem to identify with Kali or Durga) is apparently the same as the Hindu deity. She is worshipped periodically in the months of Chait or Mang and is specially propitiated when there is an outbreak of small-pox. Dulha Deo is worshipped in Chait and after weddings "to prevent his worrying people". Prayers may be offered to the sun, whom they know as Suraj Narayan. It was also stated that the moon is worshipped in Mang, but the statement was made with hesitation. Offerings of *malida* (wheat cakes reduced to powder and mixed with molasses and *ghee*) are also made to the Hindu Bhagwan (Mahadeo). These Gonds are agnostic regarding the after life. They do not wear the sacred thread.

Treatment of dead.—The dead are burned, if they have been married, but virgins of both sexes are buried—head to south and feet to north. The body is laid on its back, naked. A mound of earth is made where a body was cremated, but there is no such mound over a person who has been buried. If a man dies on a cot, it is left at the place of burial or cremation because his life went out on the cot and people are afraid of his ghost. After a funeral a goat is sacrificed by a *samdi* (connection by marriage) of the deceased and thereby the spirit of the dead man is held to be amalgamated with that of Burra Deo. This is simply in the nature of a sacrifice.

Weddings.—Marriages are performed by the Baiga who is responsible for other ceremonies also. The ceremony is of the usual tribal type influenced by Hindu ritual. The two bridal parties come from the house of the bride's father and from the house of the bridegroom's father; they meet half-way between the two and exchange gifts. The final rite is when the bride and bridegroom go seven times round the sacred object, which in the case of the Gonds of this tract is stated to be water. Dancing is popular especially after weddings, and when liquor is available. There are four dances, the *dhanda* (stick) dance, the *beohar* and two others.

Septs.—There are the following *gotras* in the tract around Lachhna:—Chegarya, Tekam, Maday, Kunjawan, Pusam, Masram, Nakmutta, Balaiyi, Markam, Korappa and Kusram. People obtain information as to their *gotras* exclusively from their own *Bhats*, who form a kind of local college of heralds, and belong to the Pardhan tribe. Marriage with a person of the same *gotra* is forbidden. Sons of course take the *gotra* of their father. The *gotra* names of the Dhur Gonds and of the Raj Gonds are the same and a Dhur Gond may give his daugher to a Raj Gond in marriage but a Raj Gond will not lower himself to give his daughter to a Dhur Gond. It was stated that there are 12½ sub-divisions among the Gonds, but I am doubtful of the accuracy of this statement. 12½ has a double meaning. It is considered unlucky throughout the State to use the number 13, but the 13th sub-division of the Gonds is said to consist of eunuchs and hermaphrodites and is therefore reckoned as only half a division. In regard to the superstition about the number 13 a member of one of the leading families of the state quoted an amusing couplet, to show that the superstition is supposed to have arisen from the similarity of the words *tera* (thine) and *terath* (thirteen), since it is unlucky for a thing to belong to someone else:—

"*Tera kouri tere pas*

Tera bahin mere pas."

which may mean "You have thirteen pieces of money and I have thirteen sisters", or changing the translation of *tera* may have three different meanings.

Panchayats.—Tribal councils are called to give decisions in small matters, field disputes, etc. All adult men sit in these councils to deal with purely tribal matters. To settle extraneous disputes the *mukaddam* (head-man) of the village may also be invited to be a member of the Council, whatever his caste or tribe may be. Such panchayats of course deal also with cases of conjugal infidelity. The price of a wife is regarded as from Rs. 50 to Rs. 60. About Rs. 10 is given to the *panchayat* and the wife is then retained by her seducer.

The Gonds in this part of the world are regarded as the true aborigines. They are certainly the most primitive people of the tract but it is doubtful whether they are the real *autochthones*.

Gonds of Jashpur. (Chetba and Chirora villages).—The Gonds of Jashpur are immigrants from Phuljhar Zamindari in the Raipur district. They are divided into six classes—

(1) Maharaj Gonds, that is those belonging to ruling families.

(2) Raj Gonds, those who were Sardars or Dewans of the rulers.

(3) Pachasi Gonds, who were followers of the Maharajas.

These three classes are superior to the others. They eat goats, birds, fish, fowls and eggs but do not eat pigs, rats, snakes, bats, ravens, tigers, etc.

(4) Badi Gonds, those born of mixed parentage. The tradition is that the Phuljhar Gonds had gone to invade Delhi. After they were repulsed there, if their women had illicit connection with men of any other tribe or caste the children were known as Badis. Their profession is tattooing. In Udaipur State I found that the Badis were regarded as an entirely separate tribe and claimed to be unconnected with any other caste or tribe. Reference to various authorities regarding this apparently new tribe, gave no clue to their origin, and only the fact that they worship Burra Deo was in any way significant. It was after obtaining information regarding the Gonds of Jashpur that I was able to identify them.

(5) Thukel Gonds, who on return from the Delhi invasion were driven away by superior Gonds spitting in Their face. They do tattooing work and deal in cattle.

(6) Dokhar Gonds who when repulsed fell at their conqueror's feet and apologised. They deal in cattle and mill-stones and do tattooing work.

The last three classes of Gonds are scattered all over the State, there being one or two houses of them in each village. They are regarded as untouchable by the higher classes, who will not take even tobacco from them. They can of course take water or cooked food from the three superior divisions. Maharaj Gond males will eat any food cooked by male Raj Gonds, whether it is from an earthen vessel or a brass one; and male Raj Gonds will eat food cooked by male Pachasi Gonds, but only from a brass vessel. The women of a superior class will not however eat any food cooked by a women of an inferior class. Raj Gonds and Pachasi Gonds of both sexes will eat any food cooked by a person of a class higher than their own.

Tattooing.—All Gond women are tattooed, generally on the chest, forearms, legs, shoulders and ankles, by women of one of the inferior classes, but they never have their foreheads tattooed. This is a contrast to other tribes and castes in the tract and to the Marias of the south who have their foreheads tattooed also. There is no particular design peculiar to the tribe, and tattooing is not compulsory. It is generally done after the age of 8 years.

Septs.—Members of the following septs are found in the State:—

(*i*) Marpachi (tortoise)—these will not eat tortoises. (From Lanjhigarh).

(*ii*) Jaghat or Goha (Gecko), who will not kill the gecko. (From Chandagarh).

(*iii*) Kana—a kind of fish with a sensitive tail. It is callous to a touch on any other part. Members of the *gotra* will not eat this fish. (From Hiragarh).

(*iv*) Bagh (tiger)—They will not eat tiger flesh. A member of the sept who sees a tiger killed will throw away one of his earthen pots and fast for one meal. (From Sumergarh).

(*v*) Marai (Cobra)—who will not kill cobras. (From Garh-Mandla).

(*vi*) Baisia (Hawk) who will not use hawks for catching birds. (From Bairagarh).

The six classes of Gonds all have the same septs which are exogamous. (The children of sisters and brothers can marry since they belong to different septs.) *The tradition regarding these *gotras*, which are more clearly defined and more obviously totemistic than in most places, is that when the Gonds were migrating from Phuljhar they found the Gondki river in flood. Each group selected a different animal to take it across the river, and these were adopted as the totems of their gotras. Eventually they settled in various places, each being called a *garh*, and the members of each different *gotra* all settled in a separate *garh*.

Customs.—Marriage is performed by a Brahman, thus indicating Hinduizing tendencies. Some of them wear the sacred thread also. There are separate bachelor's quarters for boys and for girls in each village. (The Gonds in other parts of the Province have not this custom, although the Marias of Chanda and Bastar have. It is significant that the custom is common among the Oraons and Pandos of the tract.) Marriage is at any age. The Gonds of the tract worship Burra Deo as their principal deity. Khan Saheb Abdul Gaffar Khan has described the rites in the following words :—

" All the tribe gathers and proceeds to the forest. There a small platform is constructed which is completely covered by cloth. The *Pujari* brings two iron *sujas* (thin pointed arrows about a foot long) which he had previously kept in the hollow of a tree. A new earthen pot full of water is placed upon the platform and the *sujas* are washed in this. The feet of *Bharaos* (people familiar with spirits) are also washed in the same water. One *suja* tied with *chirobin* (a kind of forest grass) is given to each *Bharao* and the latter hold them and begin to shake their bodies and hands. Five seers of *ghee* and 12 seers of milk are poured over the *Bharaos* who proceed to shiver and wave the *sujas* above their heads until they are tired out, when they sit down. The *Pujari* then sacrifices five he-goats (not castrated) before these *Bharaos*. The cost of the goats is subscribed in the village. All Gonds who come to this sacrifice bring with them either a fowl or a goat or a cocoanut. Animals are killed by *Balwas*, each man cutting the throat of his own offering. The offerings are all collected on one side and the *Bharaos* are seated upon the platform. After this ceremony the *Pujari* prepares a meal of rice and of the flesh from the heads of the five goats in the enclosure. Outside the enclosure his brothers cook the remaining flesh of the goats. At a little distance the other Gonds prepare a meal from the remaining sacrifices. When the *Pujari's* feast is ready he calls upon others asking whether they will eat the sacrifices of Burra Deo. The reply is of course in the affirmative. They then sit down to the feast in which only males, adults or children join. No female is allowed to partake of it. If anything is left over it is put into a pit and burnt and taken back to the village. When the feast is complete the *sujas* are washed by the *Pujari* and replaced in the hollow of the tree from which they were removed. All the six classes of Gonds join in the worship of Burra Deo who is the only principal god of the Gonds. Ancestor worship is unknown but the village Baiga performs ceremonies in honour of Mahadeo to which the Gonds as well as all other local castes and tribes make their contribution." (It may be mentioned that according to the statement of Khan Saheb Abdul Gaffar Khan no girls take part in the dances of this tract.)

" *Treatment of dead bodies*.—The dead are buried whether male or female. They are buried face upward, head to the north and feet to the south in the clothes in which they died with a new cloth spread over the body. The body is not washed before burial. The ritual is as follows :—The eldest son of the deceased after bathing fetches a pot-full of water and then burns a bundle of dried grass with his back to the grave, pulls it apart with his hands and then drops the burning grass over his head and behind his back into the grave. Water is poured on the burning grass and the corpse is covered. At the head of the grave a small quantity of paddy and cotton is placed. This of course indicates the agricultural occupation of the deceased before his death. Cotton and paddy are also dropped along the path on the way to burial. All the dead are buried in a single *marghat*. Those who accompany the funeral party take a bath before returning home. All the Gonds in the village on the day of death, give one handful of rice to the bereaved family. On the same day all the earthen pots in the house are thrown away and until the third day of the death the food of the family is cooked in brass pots. On the 3rd day a ceremony known as *tirni or pitagi* is performed. The Gonds of the village gather at the house of the bereaved family. The nearest male relative (son, or failing that a brother's son) shaves his head, moustache and beard. Other relatives and members of the tribe shave only their beards and foreheads. They then go to a stream to bathe. There one of the Gonds takes a lota of water from the stream and distributes to all others. It is first given to the senior member of the bereaved family. All take water in the palm of their hands and suck it. This is called the *Bisar Pani* ceremony. Its significance could not be explained. When the gathering returns to the house of the bereaved family one of them fetches new earthen vessels from the potter and gives them to the family. The price is paid by the bereaved family. There is also a tenth day ceremony when another bath is taken and a feast is given at the house of the bereaved family. On the same day the local Brahman is given a meal and other charity and then immediately is driven away. It is believed that if a man dies before marriage he becomes a ghost and haunts the house whenever this occurs. *Matis* or people who know the proper charms are called to drive the ghost away."

Gonds of Mandla. (*Notes by M. Ikramullah, I.C.S.*).—There are the following clans among the Gonds :—

(*a*) The Jhalarias, who do not cut their hair.

(*b*) The Porabias who live in towns.

(*c*) The Surajbansis who do not eat beef or chickens.

(*d*) The Ravanbansis, who eat both beef and chickens. They are however giving up the habit under the influence of Hinduism.

These clans are endogamous and there are exogamous *gotras* within the clans.

A poor Gond generally wears a *bandi* (half-sleeved waistcoat) and a *dhoti*. The rich wear a *saluka* (full-sleeved shirt) and a coat with the *dhoti*. They all now wear turbans, and their favourite colour is red. Black is the colour for Ahirs and Pankas and yellow for Pankas and Patharis.

The sun is female and the moon is male because the moon is absent for a day in every month—but the sun is ever present. The black spots on the moon are because of the blackbuck. The sky is nothing but a cloud. There are three kinds of clouds—white, black and blue. Stars shoot when they die. A comet is known as a " broom-star ", and when it appears many people are " swept away ". The rain-bow is called the " *ghora* " (horse). When the clouds are full of water they contain waves. The thunder is merely the noise of those waves.

Children and young persons are buried, and also those who die of cholera or plague. Older men and women are burned. Those who die of disease cannot be burned because it is thought to spread infection. (The ritual is much the same as elsewhere). On the top of the grave stones are placed a layer of thorns to

* Compare the similar traditions given by Russell and in the appendix to French's Gondi Grammar.

prevent wild animals digging up the body: if they do the deceased must have been a sinner. Graves disappear during the rains, but for persons of importance a piece of timber is sometimes set up by the roadside and all persons passing by are expected to place a stone near it; the accumulation of stones forms the Ghuri of the dead man, a sort of memorial.

Gonds of Nagpur.—A note regarding the household gods of the Gonds has already been included in this Report as an appendix to chapter XI. It is of interest to quote again from Mr. Grigson's notes regarding the festivals of the Gonds of Nagpur:—

"The first takes place in Chait (April) when coconuts are offered to Bhimsen at the festival of Mata Devi. The God is represented by an oval stone by which three dancing sticks (*saila*) are buried in the ground. Matadai is the sister of Bhimsen, who is a Maravi by clan. Men and women join in this festival which is held under a *bar* tree; a *mandap* is made of nim leaves. The goddess is given bits of yellow cloth, thread, bangles and combs. The stones and *trisuls* are given offerings of vermilion and coconuts. There is also a sacrifice which is always of both a he-goat and a nanny goat. The nanny is first sacrificed to Matadai by the Bhumka who belongs to the Kokodia clan, and then the he-goat is sacrificed to 'Gariwan' (the driver). The Matadai stones must always be on the east side of the tree and the 'Gariwan's' on the north, or in front. All stand up and as the goats are sacrificed urge Matadai to bless them during the next year and look after their wives and children. The Bhumka cuts off the head of the goat with a sacrificial knife kept in his house for the purpose. First he washes the feet of the animal and sprinkles water on it. He then sets its feet in the direction of the goddess, praying her for a good year, waits for the goat to shiver and sacrifices it by cutting the throat upwards. The Kumri clan reverences goats and on their behalf the Bhumka sacrifices a hen to the goddess and a cock to Gariwan. The bird does not shiver but is made to eat a grain before it is killed. While the goats are being sacrificed all members of the Kumri clan go to a *Mahua* tree for if a goat merely touches a Kumri's *handi* (pot) on this occasion it has to be broken.

"The tradition of this sacrifice is that originally a man of the Kumri clan was sacrificing a Brahman boy. His parents came in pursuit and he prayed the goddess to save him. She substituted a goat for the boy and so now the goat is regarded as a boy. (*Compare the Jewish legend of Isaac and the Muslim version regarding Ishmael.*)

"(The Bhumka's wife *leeps* the sacrificial platform with mud every Tuesday. Tuesday and Saturday are the special days of the goddess and of Bhimsen.)

"After the sacrifice the goats are cooked and eaten inside the *mandap*, except by the Kumris who are defiled by goats' blood and eat their fowls outside. Clans do not sit together. Before the goats are skinned the Bhumka cuts off their right forelegs and hangs them to the roof of the *mandap* to show all who come that the ceremony is over.

"There is no dancing at this festival. At Til Sankrant there is no ceremonial hunt but all go out hunting and slay a male animal which is eaten in the home. This has no religious significance.

"The second festival is Sanjari Bidri in the month of Asarh before the rain falls. This takes place before the shrine of Bhimsen. He is given vermilion and coconuts and the malguzar supplies grain of all kinds which the Bhumka offers to Bhimsen, afterwards giving a few grains in a leaf cup to each cultivator who mixes it with the seed which he has with him for sowing in the coming season. Then all cook the grain which they have brought and have a vegetarian feast. After this festival sowing begins and the dancing season commences.

"Liquor is never offered to Matadai but it is offered to Bhimsen when it can be afforded. People who are ill offer to Matadai a *Koraberi* (a sort of handcuff) which they first place on their hands and then, bowing before the goddess leave at her shrine.

"The third festival is in Baishakh the *Nawa Tindana* (*Nāyā Khānā*) or *Gara Nawa*. This takes place in the house and the Bhumka has no part in it. The kernel of fresh *mahua* fruit is extracted and is burned in *ghee* on the *Hom* fire. Before this if a man has in his house a *gadwa pen* or *sanāl** *handi* (vessel containing the ghosts of his ancestors) he adds to it new *tora* oil prepared for the purpose. In Diwali month new *tilli* oil is poured into the *gadwa* pot. If it has been broken a penal offering of a goat has to be made at the threshing floor of the gods. Coconut, vermilion and dried fruit are given to the household gods at Diwali and Phag, although these and one or two other festivals observed are not truly Gond."

Bastar State.—The Raj-Gond zamindars of Bhopalpatnam are buried standing, having been kept in that position before burial by tying the corpse under the arms to a post. It must remain like that until the arrival of the next-of-kin. After burial in the same position a stone lingam is put up on the grave.

3. The Marias.

The Marias who number 181,095 or 1·01 per cent. of the population are the most attractive people in the Province, and some of the bravest. It was only a few years ago that the life of the Divisional Forest Officer of South Chanda, who was picked up and carried off by a man-eating tiger, was saved by a Maria. The latter was awarded the Albert medal, the only resident of this province who has received that honour. When the late Sir Frank Sly went to decorate him with the medal he found that he could not pin it on as the hero was dressed in only a loin cloth. The Marias are noticed in Chapters XI and XII of the Central Provinces Report, where the distinction and relationship between Marias and Murias has been discussed. It was explained there how much the objects of their worship vary from village to village—and so notes from various places reproduced here could perhaps be contradicted from other tracts. Those now collected should however give some idea of the general organization and customs of the tribe. The distinction between the Bison-head Marias (called by Mr. Grigson Dandami Marias) and other Marias in Chanda and Bastar must be mentioned.

The Marias of Amarelli (Chanda District).

As stated in Chapter XI, 7 gods are worshipped in this village.

(1) *Chikatraj*, to whom offerings of rice boiled in milk are given to ensure good health, good crops, etc.

(2) *Bhane Ghare*, a goddess who must be propitiated to ward off disease from cattle. Her worshippers dance all night and sacrifice to her goats and chickens.

(3) *Edmari*, to whom chickens are sacrificed before the crop is reaped.

(4) *Ura Marad.*—The worshippers sacrifice chickens and goats to this deity and dance before him in order to avert devils.

* Bastari *hanal*.

Marias of Chanda district.

A bison head Maria.
(Bastar State.)

Dihari Korwa women.

Pandos. (Udaipur).

Korwas. (Jashpur).

Pahari Korwas.

Temporary huts of Pahari Korwas.

(5) *Bhumi Siradu*, the most important god of all to whom goats and chickens are sacrificed when there is a scarcity of rain. The Marias also dance before him.

(6) *Ghuntelpoo*.—The other object of worshipping this god is to avert tigers. Goats and chickens are sacrificed to him.

(7) *Radelpoo*, to whom sugar and *dal* are offered in order to keep away from the village anyone suffering from an epidemic.

Some of these names indicate Kanarese influence.

Enquiries in Bastar State disclosed that only Chikat Raj was a well-known deity over the border, but possibly some of the others appear with altered names. Something has been recorded of the gods in villages near Jagdalpur in Chapter XI. In Amarelli village the gods are all worshipped once a year on a particular day and also at other times of adversity or need. If in any year the crop is not good in the following season a pig is killed at the altar of the god Bhumi Siradu. Its blood is mixed with paddy and thrown on the boundary of the field which is to be sown. A chicken is always sacrificed before a field is sown and at the time of harvest chickens are again sacrificed.

Marriage ceremonies.—Marriage takes place when the girl is mature. She is chosen by the bridegroom, who makes arrangements with her father and mother and she has no say in the matter. The ceremony takes place at the house of the bridegroom, to which the bride is brought by her father and mother. No god is worshipped at the time of marriage, but a goat is killed and liquor is distributed to caste-fellows. Marriages may be arranged between a man's son and his sister's daughter, but marriages between those of closer connection, for instance, the children of brothers, are not permitted. (Exogamous septs were not named, but undoubtedly exist.) Alliances outside the tribe are extremely rare, but a Kapewar Patwari in this tract has taken a Maria woman as his wife. He has to cook food and she takes it from him. She now wears clothing like a Kunbi woman and the marriage is said to be happy.

Disposal of the dead.—Important men are burned and poor men are buried. The ashes of those who are burned are left where they lie and corpses are buried with feet to the west and the head to the east, face upward, flat on the back. The burial-place is close to the public path. A stone is fixed at the head of each place where a person is buried or burned, its size varying according to the status of the deceased. Notes regarding the treatment of the dead in Bastar State are given separately below but it may be mentioned that near Jagdalpur the custom appears to be to burn and then to bury the dead. In the case of an important man there a stepped grave is made surmounted by what are probably fertility symbols of some kind. Nearby where travellers will sit is placed a tall carved post often more or less like a lingam at the top but otherwise square and containing carved panels representing the activities of the deceased and various animals.

Dress.—Men generally wear a single cloth round the waist with a flap coming down in the front. They also have necklaces of beads and when they dance put cock's plums and peacock's feathers in their turbans. Unmarried girls wear a tri-coloured cloth of red, green and white as may be seen from the photograph. They purchase these from weavers from Sironcha tahsil headquarters and normally wear nothing above the waist. Married women are generally clothed in a white cloth. All of them have toe-rings of brass or white metal and masses of beads of all colours round their necks. Most of them also wear bracelets of scrolled brass and necklaces of some white metal. Ear-rings are very popular. Some of them are of German silver and others of plain brass. All of them are obtained in neighbouring bazars as a rule in exchange for rice and other grain. Many of the girls wear ordinary collar-studs in their ears, purchased at one pice each. They are profusely tattooed, especially on their faces, and some of them on their legs as well. The type of tattooing is said to be according to the taste of the individual and it is done with thorns and needles. On ceremonial occasions the unmarried girls bind their hair with a snood of red cotton as shown in the photograph, with bunches of pompoms of red and blue colour behind. In their hair many of them stick the feathers of jungle cocks and their heads are also adorned with combs of wood and tin and brass. The wooden combs are made by the Marias themselves and the brass ones are made by blacksmiths. The men wear their hair long or short or with a long scalp lock only according to their individual taste.

Household customs.—In sacrifice a knife is used and the men have axes which they purchase from the *bazars*. But the Marias of Amarelli have no other weapons. They used to carry spears until Government prohibited the custom. Axes and knives were prepared by a Maria blacksmith at the village of Jinghi but as he is dead they are now purchased from Sironcha. Earthen pots are generally used, which are brought from the *bazars*, but those who can afford them use brass pots. Meals are eaten from the leaves of the Pallas tree unless the family can afford earthen plates. Hunting horns made of cast brass are found in most villages.

Food.—In summer the staple food is the fruit of the Mahua tree and in winter it is maize. In March, April and May people live largely on toddy and also eat the fruit of the toddy palm and other forest fruits. This diet is supplemented with *kolta* and minor millets. Rice is consumed only at special feasts. Except in the hot weather meals are taken morning and evening. The Marias will eat any kind of flesh which they can get but find it difficult to obtain meat from the jungle now-a-days.

Houses.—The houses stand in large enclosures very far apart, that is to say, 50 to 100 yards, unlike the houses in an ordinary Indian village. They are built of bamboo wattle and mud and thatched with palm leaves. Inside they are very neat. On pegs set in the walls there are hung small rounds of rope for carrying pots on the head, wooden instruments for pounding, hollow gourds, wooden spoons, etc. Bundles of *bhuttas* (Indian corn) are also in evidence and hollow bamboos for holding oil. Earthen pots, etc., are hung up in nets. In the verandahs of the houses which I entered, I found bundles of bamboos tied together for use when tapping toddy. A false roof of palm leaves forms a loft and store. Big baskets for holding grain, etc., *bhuttas* and small pots, some full and some empty, are kept there. The *chulha* or hearth is inside the main room generally with an earthen pot simmering on the fire. Usually the huts have two rooms. In one house which I entered the inner room was a kind of store and in another both were used for living. The cattle shed is separate in the houses of the more substantial people. At one place in the village all the cattle of the neighbouring village, which had been sent to graze, were kept in a pen. The villagers sleep on the floor of their houses and the bachelors sleep outside in the open. In other places the Maria bachelors have separate quarters. One man was living in the jungle all alone, about half a mile from the village. The tract is infested with man-eating tigers and two head of this man's cattle had been taken away by them. But he stated that if he was destined to die it was merely a matter of fate.

Marias of Bastar State.—In Bagmundipanera village the Marias belong to the Mami *gotra* and state that they will eat almost anything except the flesh of tigers, horses and bears. Chickens are eaten but not wild birds. In the *Gotra* only one god is worshipped. He is Kosa Deo, to whom pigs are sacrificed once a year. Girls wear white clothes except when there is a dance on and then they wear coloured clothes. The dead are burned except those who die of small-pox or in child-birth or are killed by tigers. The head is set to the east and the feet to the west. In Bastanar village the Marias are of the same *gotra* as those of Bagmundipanera. Three gods are worshipped. (1) Mata Deo, to whom a goat is sacrificed or a promise made that if no goat is available one will be sacrificed next time. This happens on a Monday every three months and the god is also propitiated at the time of sickness. (2) Anda Deo, to whom a pig is sacrificed each year in the month of Chait to avert great calamities from men, cattle and crops. (3) Kosa Deo, to whom a pig is sacrificed in Chait to avert illness. Brass rings are also given to this god.

I noticed that the men in the Bastar villages wore their hair in buns and the women were tattooed in various parts of their bodies. A separate menstruation hut is kept for women. The following notes of Mr. Grigson give most interesting details regarding Marias and Murias of the State :—

Notes on the Marias (and related tribes) of Bastar State.

By W. V. Grigson, I.C.S.

In the following notes the terms "*dadabhai*" and "*akomama*" relatives are often used. The distinction is based on the rules of exogamy. All members of clan A are related as "*dadabhai*" to their fellow-clansmen and to members of other clans from which they may not take a wife ; they are related as "*akomama*" to clansmen of clans from which they may take a wife.

(i) A Dandami (bison-head Maria) wedding, at Massener, Dantewara tahsil, Baster State (May 1930).

We went first to the house of the girl's father. There a smallish crowd had gathered. The girl had gone to the *Munda* (tank) to be bathed by her sister and her brother's wife. The bridegroom was there, walking about and talking to his friends. A few drums sounded, but no men were wearing any *Tallagulla* (bison-horn dancing head-dress). Around the door of the sleeping house some 30 women were standing shoulder to shoulder swaying to and fro, singing the most obscene things they could, led by a laughing Gondin in the centre, whom they answered in chorus, with a refrain of *Kokolin-Waya* ! Another band of women hurled abuse at them, and each leader tried to out-Billingsgate the other.

When the girl had been bathed, she emerged with a cloth over her shoulders and was dragged into a closely-linked (arm in arm) chain of girls dancing and singing, while the bridegroom, also with a cloth over his shoulders, was pushed into another chain. These circled and gyrated in and out seemingly inextricably mixed up together, only to disentangle miraculously and weave themselves into fresh spirals and circles, singing abuse at each other. All the while the standing group of girls went on swaying and singing at the door. They caused great laughter by improvising a refrain warning all girls to be careful that night, for the Diwan, the Tahsildar and the Circle Inspector were watching them and who knew what might happen after dark ?

Before we arrived the boy's party had arrived with the "bride-price" consisting of one slaughtered pig, one living pig, five *handis of landa*, fermented rice gruel) four yards of Mahra cloth for the girl's mother, five *pailis chanwal* (rice), one rupee. Then the sister of the girl's mother came out and displayed the girl's "going away" presents—a *Masni* or sleeping mat, a little basket with a *paili* or so of rice, a *handi of landa*, while they also sent for her to her new house a young bull calf newly weaned.

After dancing and singing to a loud accompaniment of bamboo flutes and drums, the boy and girl arrived together, with the girl's father and the boy's elder brother holding the hands of the girl and boy. Then the old father held up his hand for silence, and started a long speech, asking the boy's brother :—"Have you come willingly for this flower ? Will you wear it and cherish it ? It is fresh and tender, and will not bear rough handling. Know you not how witless women are ? If she is a poor housekeeper, pardon her. If she cooks badly, pardon her. If she speaks to other men, do not take it amiss, but pardon her," etc., etc., to all of which the brother of the bridegroom replied "yes". (*N.B.*—The boy was 19 years of age ; the girl probably 20). Then the father took the girl, who took the boy's right hand, pulled off a ring from her little finger and placed it on the boy's little finger. He then did the same from his other to her other hand, cloths held the while over their heads. Then the boy took off another ring, which the girl's elder sister received in her outstretched cloth, while she said "From now onwards you must not touch me or utter my name till I am dead. If you do so, all will laugh at you and your brethren will fine you." (At death he will take a ring off her little finger and wear it on the middle finger of his right hand.) He also gave a ring to his wife's younger sister which he put on her fingers, for he can touch her and talk of her. Then the boy's brother touched the old man's feet, and the old man touched his. Then each placed his hands on the other's shoulders, and leaned forward, first on his right, then on his left shoulder. Each then salaamed the other with both hands and said *Juhar*. Then they did the same to all other near relatives (*Saga*) and important guests. I came in for my share of it ; it was not a sweet-savoured performance.

Then the girls started singing again, telling the bride that she must leave them and go to her man, and that her lot would be hard and that if she did not like her husband she should make up her mind to leave him. Meanwhile the boy slipped off over the fields to his father's house to be ready there to receive his wife's bridal party.

Then the procession formed up led by 30 women, singing and side-stepping along the narrow jungle-path in the gathering darkness. After them walked the elders, then a party of drummers, followed by the bride pretending to struggle against the cluster of laughing girls pushing her to Massenar the bridegroom's village. All danced as they went, beating their jangling dancing staves on the ground in tune with the drums and the steps of the dance. It took two and half hours for them to cover the two miles to the boy's father's house.

There a multitude of other girls and men received them, all in the traditional dancing costume, with a thundering roll of drums and dozens of explosions of "*patakas*" of gunpowder and rice chaff. The full moon beat down on a sea of tossing plumes or shone back from the glistening horns of the head dresses, till the whole courtyard seemed full of rampaging and fantastic movement. The boy and girl were seized by 50 girls and made to sit with them in front of the house, where they were later to live, packed as closely as sardines, all swaying to and fro on their hips as they sat, and singing foul obscenities in full-throated chorus while the hapless boy and girl with cloths over their heads were plucked at and prodded all over their bodies by the jostling girls, who did not spare their most intimate members.

I returned to the scene at midnight. The crowd had swollen and every forest path was thronged with eager men and women, with drums and dancing kit, hastening to join the dance. Some came from 25 or 30 miles, but showed no sign of fatigue. Around the dance many were lying already drunk, for 60 large *handis of landa* were provided for the guests. And now and again an excited boy and girl left the dance, but not to

A Bison-head Maria Dance.

A Bison-head Maria woman.

A Bison-head Maria wedding.

Marias of Bastar State.

Tattooing on an Oraon woman. *Bust and foot.*

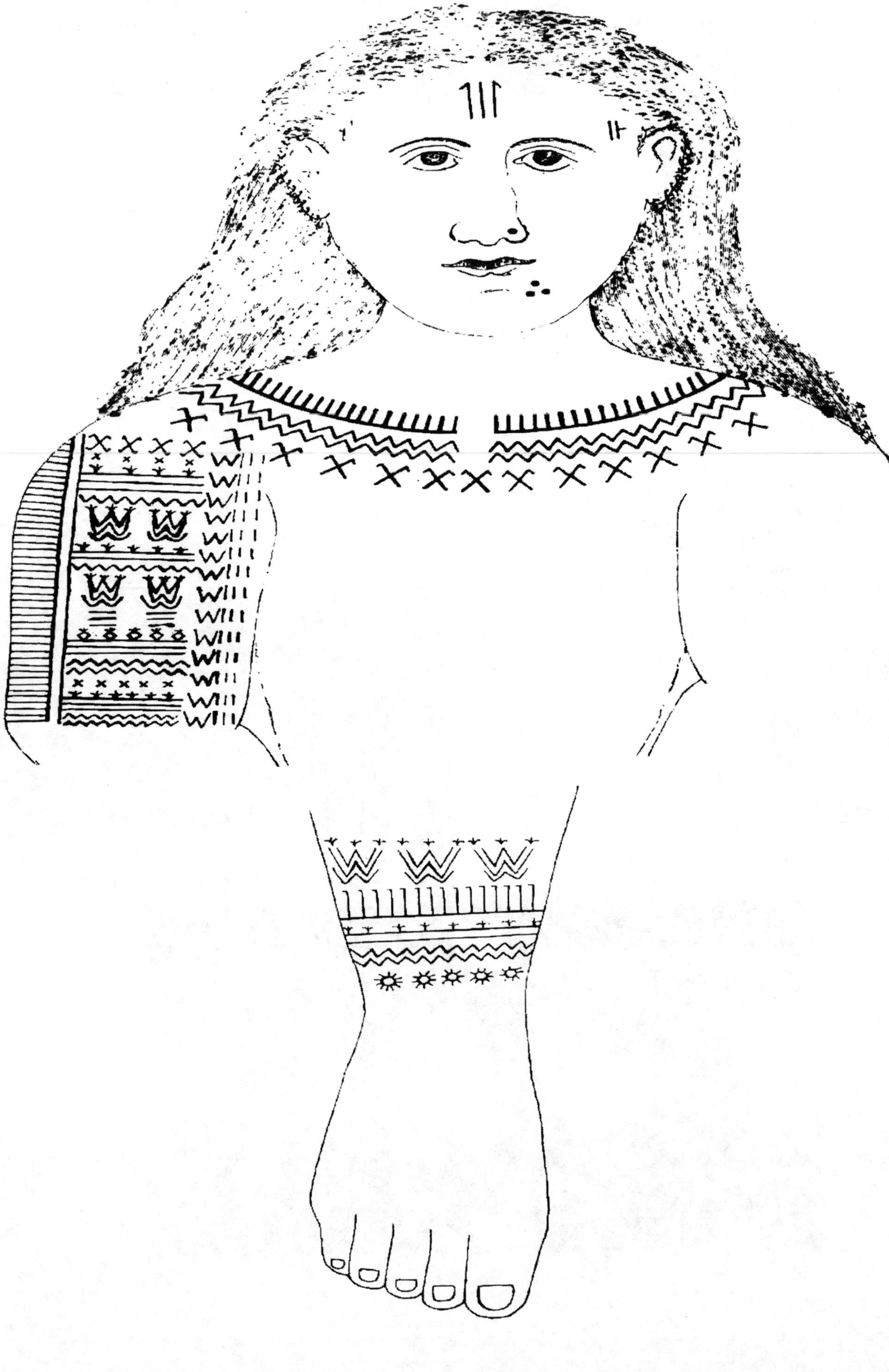

sleep. In the end there must have been over 2,000 dancing men. They were still dancing, or lying drunk or resting with piled drums and headdress, when I again returned at 7-30 A.M. Now many men with horrible black gourd masks and hair and beards of bear's fur carrying staves, dummy guns and nets rushed in and out among the dancers, making the most suggestive and obscenest imaginable gestures with their staves at the dancing or watching girls, to the general amusement. Looking for the bride and bridegroom, I found them still covered with the same cloths, riding " piggy-back " on the shoulders of their sister's husbands in the middle of a long chain of girls with outstretched arms and hands linked, who headed off all the efforts of the " steeds " to break out of the circle of dancers.

The fathers of the couple now decided that the time for the final ceremonies had come : the sun was getting hot, and *landa* supplies low, for dancers continually left the dance for a drink and a nap before the maddening beat of the drums called to them once again. A hurdle was placed in front of the opened door of the hut where they were to pass their married life. To this the boy and girl were led, and freed at last from the cloths which they had had to wear over their heads for 12 hours, were stood up together, hand in hand, on the hurdle. A man, the girl's father's brother, climbed on to the eaves of the roof, and from there suddenly tipped a large *handi* of cold and dirty water over the couple, whereupon amid general laughter the boy seized the girl, and they rushed together into the house where the door was closed upon them. But they had only ten minutes privacy " to discuss what they would do that night " as the old man explained, and even then the din of the dance, which never ceased for a moment, not even when the water was poured over them, cannot have let them hear each other speak. After 10 minutes the bride reappeared, surrounded by the girls of her own village, who in unison sang to her advice on housekeeping and leaving her husband and returning to them if he ill-treated her, while she provided a chorus of simulated wailing. They took her off to a room and sat all the morning and afternoon with her, where all had their food, while the guests finished the *landa*, and slowly dispersed, beating their drums, along the forest paths. At 5-30 P. M. the new husband entered his house alone. His younger brother went to the house where the bride had spent the day, and cried, " Come sister-in-law, it is time you were bedded ", caught her by her hand and tried to drag her off. She screamed and feigned resistance, when he called 4 or 5 other lads to help him, and between them they pulled the girl to the door, opened it and pushed her in, barring the door from outside. Then they stole a cock from the bridegroom's coop, and plucking its feathers as they went and scattering them along the path, took it to a forest clearing, cooked and ate it with the girl's attendants, and all dispersed.

(ii) The organization of the Bachelors' quarters. (Khairkatta village—February 1931.)

The Murias call the boy's quarters *chelik gotul* and the girls' *motiari gotul*. The *Gotul* ranks in order of precedence were stated to be as follows :—

Boys.	*Girls.*
1. Silledar.	1. Jhaliyaru.
2. Subedar.	2. Lahari.
3. Laharsi.	3. Manjoro.
4. Ramsu.	4. Suliaro (Suliyaro).
5. Jhaliyarsi.	

The Silledar is the *Leyur-Gaita* (boy's headman) and head of all, including the *Jhaliyaru* and girl officials.

The Subedar's work is to arrange for the boys and girls to collect small pieces of wood for burning as torches.

The Laharsi's duty is to call boys and girls to the *gotul* to dance after supper. If any boy or girl is absent on any day, he enquires if sick, etc. Any *chelik* or *motiari* absent for 2 days without good reason is expelled from the *gotul* and only readmitted on payment of a fine of tobacco to the *Silledar* who divides it among the *cheliks*, if the absentee is a *chelik*, or to the *Jhaliyaru*, in the case of a *motiari* absentee, whose fine is divided among *motiaris*.

The Ramsu's work is to see that the girls keep the verandah and compound clean. Expulsion is the penalty for slackness on the part of a girl.

The *Jhaliyarsi* has to arrange for the supply of fire-wood, deputing the smaller boys to fetch a log from each house in the village. The boys are punished if slack by extra " fagging " or expulsion from the *gotul*. Girls do not collect fuel. There is no penalty for a householder who refuses to supply a log.

The *Jhaliyaru* is the head girl and sends girls home after the night's *gotul* round of dancing, etc. (Hereabout the girls do not sleep at night in the *gotul*, but each in her own home).

The *Lahari* fetches the girls in the evening to the *gotul* to dance.

The *Manjaro* is responsible for bringing girls to *leep* and sweep the *gotul* : but obviously she has some other function, as my informers were all very reluctant to describe her duties.

The *Suliyaro* supervises the work of the girls brought by the *Manjaro* at the direction of the *Manjaro*.

There are various minor punishments for slackness and breaches of *gotul* discipline. The most common is a fine of a bottle of liquor.

Other ranks stated later, for which no function could be assigned or was admitted, nor could the names be explained :—

Boys.	*Girls.*
6. Laharu.	5. Nirosa.
7. Jalka.	6. Jhelo.
8. Jolsai.	7. Saiko.
9. Jolu.	8. Gujaro.
10. Joria.	9. Piyosa.
	10. Belosa.

All dormitory boy officials are chosen by a *panchayat* of all the boys and girls. The senior boys always hold office. There are no insignia of office.

Admission into Gotul.—There is no initiation ceremony for boys or girls : there is no *handi* for urination, and no spitting ceremony. At *Taroki* Gotul I was told that when a boy enters the *Gotul*, he offers the *Silledar* a bottle of liquor and prays for admission into the fraternity.

Relations of sexes in Gotul.—Each *chelik* pairs off with a *motiari* and the attachment lasts till either of the two leaves the *gotul* on marriage. The idea of infidelity among *gotul* couples was absolutely unheard of and so there are no penalties prescribed.

It was readily admitted that the *cheliks* and *motiaris* by mixing in the *gotul* learn the meaning and functions of sex, and co-habit. There are no ceremonies on the attainment of puberty such as the insertion of a boy's penis in a cleft stick among the Oraons. But when a boy is " old enough to work a plough " one of his elder companions teaches him how to copulate, demonstrating, with him as a girl, how to take a girl by her breasts, lay her on the ground, place her legs round his thighs, catch her by the shoulders, and have intercourse with her.

A *Chelik* and his *Motiari* must not co-habit in the *gotul-ghar*, but outside in some secluded spot. In theory a *Chelik* should pair off only with a *motiari* who is of an *Akomama* clan whom he could legally marry. Of course illicit unions between *dadabhais* do occur, but the penalty is out-casting "; the child, if any, of such a union is given to the father.

It is wrong for a girl in the *gotul* to become pregnant, but it is worse for her to try to secure abortion. If she is found to be pregnant, she is told to name the youth responsible, and goes and takes him by the hand. He always, they say, admits his fatherhood, and then takes the girl to his house. He has to celebrate a wedding by *tikka* with her, even if owing to poverty they have to wait 2 years to collect the wherewithal. They will be married by having water poured over them as in all Bastar Gond marriages, but from the eaves of his house, not of a special marriage *mandap*, as for a regular wedding.

Marriages often result between the boy-friend and girl-friend of *gotul* days ; but in many villages all the children are of the same clan, and *dadabhai* to each other, so that there is no *akomama* girl available to be *gotul* girl-friend and subsequent marriage is thus out of the question. Moreover there is a general idea that a young man should marry a girl from another village, as then there will be a three-days " *beano* " in that village before the wedding. But when a girl or youth is going to marry a spouse other than the *gotul* companion she or he takes a formal farewell of the *gotul* companion, at which they say that there is no ill-feeling shown, and exchanges gifts such as bead necklaces. They stated positively that after such a farewell there is never any further connection between *gotul* companions, and that they had never heard of a girl running away from her husband with her former *gotul* " boy-friend ".

Three days before a wedding the bridegroom-elect or bride-elect, as the case may be, gives a farewell feast to the *gotul*-gudi of a pig, a fowl, a goat, rice and liquor.

During *gotul* days each *motiari* among the Murias around Koilibera and Partabpur regularly attend on her " boy-friend " after the night's dancing, when they massage their arms (not their legs) and waists and comb their hair. The boys do not reciprocate this service. Each *motiari* regularly makes bead necklaces earring tassels, hair bead chains, etc., for her *chelik* with the beads supplied by him, and a good *chelik* makes wooden combs for his *motiari* to wear in her hair.

The Marias of Chhote Mar (Tapalibhum), Bare Mar (both formerly in Paralkot Zamindari) and Sonpur parganas told me in February 1931 that their *gotuls* are strictly reserved for unmarried youths and boys that girls are not allowed in them, that there is no kind of training in them, and that there are no *gotul* ranks or special names. Dancing, they said, was learnt by nightly practice on the village dancing ground (*Endanna-Kara*). Yet they admitted that the girls string bead ornaments for the boys and youths, and that girls and boys co-habit freely from puberty onwards till marriage, if only with *akomama* partners ; they are out-casted for co-habiting with *dadabhai* partners ; in such cases the child, if any, of such " incestuous " unions goes to the father, who can be received back into the clan on the payment of the usual penalty. The girl, however, remains beyond the pale unless she subsequently marries an *akomama* spouse. These admissions, coupled with the clearer description of *gotul* life in Padaldesh, Nurbhum and Tapalibhum given me by Padalis and Tapalis at Koilibera in May 1932 show that the *gotul* life of the Murias of North Antagarh and the Marias of adjacent parganas (Padaldesh, Nurdesh, Baremar, Chhotemar, Tapalibhum and Sonpur) is practically the same ; at least the northern Marias are copying the northern Murias.

Amongst the Antagarh Marias and Murias and Jhorias I can find no case at all in which boys and girls sleep together in the *gotul*. Yet this is common among the " Marias " of Kondagaon Tahsil : anyone can see on any night boys and girls sleeping together, as I saw at midnight on 27th February 1931 some 28 boys and girls fast asleep higgledy-piggledy over the floor of the *gotul* in the Jamkot-para of Kondagon itself, each boy paired off with his girl, often sleeping in each other's arms. (The Jamkot *gotul* had only one door, like a hutch-door, window-size and window-height above the ground. There were no windows.) This practice is known to some Antagarh Marias and Jhorias and condemned by them as wrong.

Religious and magico-religious observances.—There is nothing at all corresponding to the ceremonies described in Roy's Oraons of Chhota Nagpur, *viz.*, the provision of each new *chelik* with 3 new earthen jugs, and their magical water-filling and the final sacrifice of the contents of the jugs to the *chandi* spirit. There is no naked ritual and no magic ceremony for increasing strength ; the only things done at any stage of childhood to secure strength or beauty are the bathing by mothers of babies with warm water, the rubbing of their bodies with mango kernel oil and the manipulation of their soft skulls to make them shapely and symmetrical.

There is no ceremonial hunting among the *cheliks* ; they do not hunt at all but occasionally *cheliks motiaris* go together to catch fish for their *gotul* feasts. Nothing like the Oraon micturation ceremony takes place.

Training in social duties.—The *gotul* is really a school for training Maria-youth in social duties and the lore of the clan, and the *gotul*, officials are little more than prefects and monitors. The *Gaita* and cultivators of the village often ask the *Silledar* and *Jhaliyaru* for the help of *cheliks* and *motiaris* respectively in field work. The owner of the field has to feed them and pay wages for their work to the *Silledar*, who spends the money on a *gotul* feast for *cheliks* and *motiaris*. They may be similarly hired for other forms of labour, such as thatching houses, etc. At weddings *cheliks* and *motiaris* have to build the wedding *mandap*, collect fuel and leaves for fuel and leaves for plates and cups, and to serve the feed to the guests ; but they are never employed as cooks though the *motiaris* make rice cakes in the *gotul* for wedding feasts but do not get any special rice as their wages, nor is there any singing or merriment while making the cakes.

The *gotul* has no funeral functions and is not employed at funerals.

At the village festivals they have to collect fuel and leaves for plates and cups, and have to dance.

The *cheliks* commonly, in fact invariably, have to attend the camp of any important state official as *begaris*, preparing the camp beforehand, fetching and carrying, beating for game, sleeping around the camp, and collecting supplies. They carry food supplies for their elders ; if the camp lasts for 4 or 5 days, fresh supplies are brought by women and *motiaris* ; and it is always considered the right thing for the official to celebrate at least the last night in camp with a dance, the dancers among the Marias of Antagarh, the Jhorias and the Murias who have only recently ceased to be Marias being invariably *cheliks* and *motiaris* ; among the Murias, *e.g.*, of Amabera, Antagarh pargana and parts of Kondagaon married men and occasionally wives join in the dance.

Dancing is in fact learnt in the *gotul*, purely by imitation. On every fine night the *cheliks* and *motiaris* dance. From the first day of admission into the *gotul* the novice may drink and dance. There is no rule that dancers should be ranged in order of age, eldest to the right and youngest to the left. They also play various games in the *gotul*, such as *koko*, hide-and-seek (*Wikachha* in Halbi, *Kork karsana* Gondi), *Dudu* and blind-man's buff (*Andu Andakarsana*, Gondi). They learn the seasonal songs and the *gotul* song.

(iii) Tiger-netting by Marias (1932).

The purpose of our Koilibera camp was to kill man-eating tigers. For this purpose, inter alios, 140 Barsur Dandamis had been called with their tiger nets. These they arrange on a line about 5 feet off the ground propped on two bamboo poles leaning lightly against each other, one on each side of the net. Any animal driven by the beaters dashes into the nets which fall on the animals. About 20 paces behind the nets they make little shelters of leaves, and wait there with spears. As soon as an animal is entangled they rush forward. The first man spears and holds the animal down, while the others also blood their spears. The first spear gets the right hind leg from buttock to knee as his portion, and the *peda* (headman) the saddle, and the *waddai* (clan-priest) the liver (the portion always reserved for the *hanal*, spirits of the dead). I saw several barking deer, four-horned antelope, and a panther and a tiger netted. The panther was badly entangled, the net being in high grass which added to the entanglement. This made it seem to me very safe behind the nets, and so I was there with a group of Dandami spearmen on the afternoon of the 6th May when a tiger, shot at twice but missed from the *machans* in front, hurled itself at full gallop into the net 20 yards on my right. It fell over at once, entangled in the net ; but the net was an old and dry one, fixed over rocky and ungrassed ground, and the tiger's huge weight and velocity smashed the sustaining rope and burst a hole in the net. There was a brief vision of a mighty right forearm sweeping aside the encumbrance and the tiger was free, and rushed roaring just past the next group of spearmen so close that it could have been touched. Wisely no one tried to do so, but as soon as the tiger passed the line of spearmen a shot rang out from the back *machan*. Whether this hit the tiger or not we could not find out but the tiger swung round and started to charge back. I fired, the Chief Forest Officer, the Tahsildar and a friend of the Chief Forest Officer fired as soon as the tiger was safely out of the line of spearmen but only one of our bullets hit the tiger passing through and breaking its left forearm. The headman of the netmen (the Barsur *pargana* had an old 12-bore gun, patched with iron bands and wire and as loose in the breach and stock, as a gun could be. Yet he saved the situation by firing and hitting the tiger in the neck with a contractile bullet which killed it outright. It was a bulky 9 feet 5 inches tiger.

All four tigers were drummed back to camp by Murias and Marias to the beat U U—, U U—. The Marias broke into a dance over a tigress which I shot at Partabpur, advancing and retreating before the dead tiger to the same anapaestic drum beats. As usual the women everywhere held ropes across the road to bar our entrance to their villages after shooting tigers.

At Jiramtarai, where a man-eater shot had 10 days before killed the village shikari, there was on the wall of the *gotul* a clay relief of a large tiger painted with black and white stripes, killing a *Sambhar*, while two naked shikaris pursued, one firing a gun with a tripod hanging from the barrels, and the other, in front, with an axe raised above his head to strike. Both men were shown naked, the marksman with erect penis of which the tip and testicles were coloured with vermilion. The other wall had rude drawing in red ochre and white of deer and a horse and black " cup markings ".

The dead shikari's remains had been burnt in the jungle where he was left by the tiger. They refused to perform further obsequies or to " bring back " his soul, for fear of their bringing a tiger back also.

Another unique event in a tiger-beat at Partabpur was the presence in the beat of both a tigress and six red dogs, which barked at her and snapped round her hind quarters. She was shot, and I shot one of the red dogs, the leader who had left the pack and started by my *machan* to call them with a peculiarly liquid, clear bell-note, like a single note of a bird, of particular intensity.

Maria treatment of the dead.

In the heart of the Abujmar Hills burial is the usual thing, but there are exceptions ; thus at Tondabera (Neghalur Tondabera) the Neghalur cremate all their dead. At Lakka (Lanka) at the foot of the hills on the Kutru side they ordinarily bury their dead ; but there and in the next village of Bodel they burn the bodies of men of standing, such as Gaitas and Pedas and their old wives and mothers.

When a person dies, there is no beating of a drum to announce the fact : the statement in Russel (*iii*, 89) to that effect is not true of Marias but only of Dandamis, who have in the past not been distinguished from other Marias. The custom of beating a drum is however now creeping into Abujhmar from the Dantewar and Bhairamgarh sides, where the Dandamis predominate, and has reached Lakka and Karangul, but is reserved for men of higher status. The drum used is the Turam drum ; it is beaten by boys of the village continuously from death till the body is buried or cremated, day and night. There is no special village drum for the purpose ; but in the smaller villages usually the only Turam drums are village property and are kept in the *gotul*.

News is sent to all the *dadabhai* and *akomama* relatives in other villages, and to friends as well. The funeral takes place when they arrive, on the 2nd or even the 3rd day. All the women of the village assemble and weep and wail in and around the house where the body is lying. They never let a dying person die on a cot, but lift him on to the ground—this does not apply to women, who in any case are not supposed to lie on a cot, but they say they only do this because they do not want him to fall off the cot in any death convulsion. They close the eyes, and straighten out the corpse, which is lifted on to a bier. It is burned or buried with the loincloth that was on it at death and all the jewellery. If other clothes are in the house which the deceased wore, they are taken to the grave for burning or burying with the corpse, or for hanging up around it. All his dancing clothes and ornaments, his axe (not his bow and arrows) his *godari* (*korki*, digging tool), but not spears, are buried with him or burnt with him ; in the latter case they are often picked up by passers-by after a few days and taken into everyday use. No money is ever buried with the body.

The corpse, which is not washed or otherwise prepared but is carried out just as it was composed after death, is carried out on a hurdle. The work of carrying it may be done by anyone, except a Waddai (clan-priest), whether he be a relative or not. The hurdle goes first, followed by all the relatives and villagers, all wailing and beating their breasts.

If the death is due to cholera or small-pox, or to suicide, the corpse is not buried in the regular burial ground (or burned in the regular cremation ground) but in another spot at some distance away. Persons killed by tigers are *burned* where they are found, or where they are after the inquest, and should not be touched, logs are piled under the remains and kindled. They have no *marmangal* or *kotokal* stone, are given no food at cremation, and only have burned with them whatever is found with the body or at the spot where it was attacked; no dancing dresses or other property are brought from the deceased's house to be burned with him.

Both for burial and cremation most Marias place the body in the grave or on the ground with the head face upwards towards the east and the feet towards the sunset; the Usendis of Orcha and other villagers however reverse this. The *Waddai* ordinarily goes as a spectator, just like any one else there; but he must not touch the corpse.

If there is no doubt as to the cause of death, the following ceremony is omitted. But, if, *e.g.*, a young man or woman dies suddenly for no obvious reason, then the bearers halt on the path just by the grave or burning place, and stand there with the hurdle on their shoulders. The *Waddai* takes 7 *saja* leaves, and places them in a row on the ground some 7 or 8 yards paces away from the corpse. One leaf represents the Earth or *Bhum*, standing for death through the displeasure of the Village Mother; the second represents death from sickness: the third death through the displeasure of gods and ghosts (*pen-hanal*): the fourth death through the magic of a fellow villager; the fifth from magic a man whose enmity has arisen from a quarrel or exchange of abuses; the sixth death from the magic of a wizard, witch or *sirha*; and the seventh normal death. The *Waddai*, or, if there is none, the *Gaita* or *Peda*, strikes the earth three times with an axe, and calls on the corpse to disclose the cause of its death. The corpse then impels the bearers to rush to one of the leaves and stand on it; or else the *Waddai* first excites the corpse by scattering rice over it, till it moves its bearers to one of the leaves. Then the bearers leap away some 8 or 9 paces from the leaf, and behind their backs the order of the leaves is changed, and the former process repeated. If in 3 or 4 tests the same leaf is always indicated, they are satisfied that the cause of death has been revealed. If it is witchcraft, nowadays they do not proceed immediately to hunt for the witch; but a seed of suspicion has been planted that will grow in the dark jungles of their mind, and will sooner or later lead to assault or murder. If the corpse makes several mistakes, they do not waste further time, and assume that the death was natural. They admit that in old times in which witch craft was pointed out as the cause of death, the corpse was next asked by the *Waddai* to point out the magician among these present at the funeral, or in the dead man's village or an adjacent village.

Then, if it is burial, the bearers bring the corpse up to the grave, which is shallow, only waist-deep, lift it off the hurdle and into the grave, with feet towards the sunset and face upwards. The senior near *dadabhai* relative then throws a clod of earth on the corpse's head, and says "This is all I can now do for you, and I give you my portion". He is followed in turn by each of the *dadabhai* close relatives who throw clods all over the body; after them five elders of the village, who are distant *dadabhai* kin, do the same, and after them any *akomama* relatives who happen to be present; in the absence of any near *dadabhai* relatives, the 5 *dadabhai* elders take the lead in the ceremony. Then earth is shovelled in from all sides. His wife's brother (*erramtogh*) will have carried all his property to be buried with him from the house to the grave, and placed it in the grave by the head of the corpse as soon as it has been laid in the grave. Over the heaped earth leaves are strewn, and over these logs. Then carved wooden posts are set up; they are called *hanal-gutta*, and there should be four smaller ones at each corner of the actual grave and two larger ones in front. The posts have roughly carved wooden peacocks on the top, and have been made ready beforehand by the villagers in the jungle near the burial or burning ground, from saja wood, at the time of digging the grave. These posts having been set up, at the foot of the two front posts a little stone cromlech, known as *hanal-garya* (ghost's throne) is set up by the dead man's *erramtogh*. (If a woman is being buried, it will be her brother but not her husband's kin). The *erramtogh* then pours a little mahua liquor on the ground near each post, and lays some rice on the headstone of the cromlech, on which also he has poured a little liquor. He then takes a cock, and twists its neck, breaking the skin as though to *halal** it with his nails, so that blood may be sprinkled on to the rice; he leaves the cock there, and no one eats it. Then he drinks some liquor himself, and after him all the *akomama* relatives present, then the *dadabhais* and then others present. The *erramtogh* also offers rice and *kosra* in a little basket to the *hanal* and an empty *handi*, small in size. The food and drink are paid for by the dead person's *dadabhai* kin. Before the drinking of the liquor, but after the sacrifice of the cock, the *erramtogh* ties a piece of his own cloth and pieces handed to him by other relatives and others who wish to honour the dead to the boughs of an overhanging tree. A bamboo fence is then made round the grave except the two front wooden posts.

For a cremation the ritual is much the same. The pyre is prepared beforehand, and the corpse laid on it; no wood is placed on the corpse, in the manner of Hindus. The *erramtogh* brings from the deadman's house a burning log, and with it he kindles the pyre; and then *dadabhais*, village elders, and other *akomamas* each place a small piece of wood on the head of the corpse, just as in a burial they throw clods of earth, using the same formula. They do not pile any leaves or wood over the ashes, but leave them there in the open, with a fence around them; and then the usual *hanalguttas* and *hanalgarya* are set up.

In some places, particularly on the Narainpur side of the country no *hanal-guttas* are set up, or only one. Also the mahua liquor ritual differs; after the earth, leaves and wood have been piled over the grave and the *hanal-gutta* (if any) and the *hanalgarya* (if any) set up, the *erramtogh* takes a leaf-cup of liquor, pours a little from it over the earth above the head of the corpse, and drinks the remainder; this is done after him in turn by the *akomama* men, the *dadabhai* men, and then by the women present.

It is probably evening by the time that all this has finished; but at any rate the next ceremony must take place at evening. Most people proceed direct to it from the burial or cremation, but a few forget their offering of rice and have to return to fetch it. All proceed to a spot by the roadside near the entrance to the village, and there the senior *akomama*, the *erramtogh* or next nearest *akomama* relative, builds a cairn of stones from 1½ to 2½ feet high, surmounted by a flat cap-stone; this cairn is called a *marmangal*. Then he and each of the householders present places a pinch of rice or *kosra* grain on the capstone, addressing the dead man's *hanal* by his name, and saying that he gives him this grain to eat. Then they go home.

* Cut its throat.

A house or a portion of a house where a death has occurred should be shut up and not inhabited. It is not pulled down, but it is not repaired. It is considered that so long as it stands it will be a memorial of the dead.

If man is rich enough to put up a stone to the dead in the *kotokal*, without waiting to collect sufficient funds, he should do so after four days ; in any case mourning is observed for four days, and no one goes to work. On the day after the funeral the house and the *angan* are cleaned out, and the floors are leeped.

If on the fourth day the son or heir of the deceased cannot afford to set up a stone in the Kotokal, he goes to the graveside, and bows before the *hanalgarya*, and tells the ghost he is sorry, but cannot afford yet to put up his stone, and begs him to be patient to forgive him for the delay and not to harass him.

When he has enough grain and money collected to pay for the food and drink required, he calls together his friends and relatives and they all go off into the jungle to look for a suitable stone. There is no ritual for selecting one ; they just take whatever stone they think suitable, and one which will require only as many bearers as they can afford to provide with food and drink. The highest that I saw in Abujhmar were in Lanka, where several were from 6 to 10 feet in height. They drag out the stone and place under it several cross pieces of wood, the stone lying between two long and stout poles, to which the cross-pieces of wood are lashed ; the stone lying is then lashed to the cross pieces, and the poles are lifted on to the shoulders of the bearers, up to 20 or 25 or even 30 in number, and the journey to the *Kotokal* begins. At intervals they stop to drink, as mahua gives them strength to bear the burden. They are given a meal on the way by the dead man's heir. So they arrive ultimately at the *Kotokal*, and deposit the stone on the ground at the selected spot. A hole is dug in the ground at one end of the stone, and then the stone, if small, is pulled upright by willing hands, and held there while the earth is shovelled in. If it is large and heavy, ropes are lashed round its far end and used to pull it to a vertical position, while 10 men or so on each side hold poles across the top of it to prevent it falling over while stones and earth are rammed round its foot. When the stone has been erected at its foot a "*hanalgarya*" cromlech is made, about 1 foot high. Around the *Kutru* side of the Abujhmar hills the heir then comes up to the *hanalgarya*, and squats down with his back to the stone. He takes a small 8 or 9 days' old chicken and holding it behind his back and never looking at the stone, *halals* it with his hands and nails, sprinkles blood on the capstone of the cromlech and then pushes the body of the chicken under the stone ; next he places an offering of rice or grain on the capstone. As he makes the offerings to the ghost, saying "whether you were killed by magic, or by any angry *hanals* or gods, or died naturally, I know not. But now I have put up this stone for you, and you must wander no more. Stay here in peace for ever, and do not worry us, your descendants". He then runs off, with his back still to the stone, which he must not see, to the nearest water, where he and all who have been present at the ceremony wash their hands and legs, and disperse to their homes. Men and women are present at the ceremony, but no one must look at it ; all sit with their backs to the stone. This finally lays the ghost, and no further funeral ceremony takes place.

But until the stone is erected in the *kotokal*, the *hanal* must be fed every year at the *Nawakhani* festival at the *hanalgarya* at the grave, not at the *marmangal*.

Around Karangul and Lanka they say they do not erect the stones brought to the *Kotokal* for women and children, but leave them flat on the ground.

Everyone believes that these stones increase or decrease in size according as the *hanal* is satisfied or not.

Around Orcha, Hikpulla, Ader, etc., a cow or pig is sacrificed in the village, and portions of the flesh cooked are placed under the *hanalgarya*, while the tail and sometimes a hoof, are fastened by a cord from the top of the stone. There is also a regular feast, in the village afterwards at which the rest of the beef and pork are eaten, and there is dancing and liquor. Needless to say this is a far more expensive procedure, and many *hanals* there have to be content with *marmangal* cairns, which they say frankly they put up if they cannot afford a *kotokal* ceremony.

I could find no separate ceremony for "bringing back the soul"; obviously it is hardly necessary if there is a *kotokal* ceremony. If a man dies in a village other than his natal village or if a woman dies in a village other than her husband's natal village, or, rather than natal village, the traditional village of his *katta*, then the stone is erected in the traditional *katta* village, not in the village where he died. The Usendi woman who had just died at Tondabera (Naghalpur) when I visited the village was to be buried at Tondabera, but her *marmangal* cairn was to be put up just outside the Usendi village of Orcha, where her husband's *katta* live.

The whole ceremony seems to be one of re-uniting the *hanals* with *Bhum*, the earth and universal *hanal*, which also they will occasionally say is their *Bhera Pen*, their *I spural* and their Village Mother.

NOTE.—In a separate description of burial customs Mr. Grigson has remarked that the Dandamis (Bison-head Marias) do not burn their dead but bury them unless killed by tigers or dying from cholera, small-pox and women dying in child-birth. Among them the *kotokal* of the Abujh Marias is known as *Uraskal*. In some tracts he found that no *Uraskal* stones had been erected within the last 10 or 15 years because of the expense. Since the ceremony involves killing at least one goat, two bullocks and the provision of three or four *Khandis* of grain as well as rice gruel and mahua liquor, it is of course expensive, but in Mr. Grigson's opinion it is being abandoned more because the Dandamis as they raise themselves socially are forgetting their Maria customs than on account of the cost since the same people will entertain a thousand guests at a wedding. In connection with this a reference may be made to the remarks regarding the title "Marias" in Chapter XII of the Central Provinces Report.

[The following note is taken from a letter from Mr. Shoobert :—

> "In connection with the customs of the Korwas and Pandos of making a separate door in their houses for use of women during their period of menstruation, Grigson informs me that this custom is also very strictly followed by the Marias. He gave to me a most interesting description of the sort of dog kennel in which women are confined at such times in some Maria villages. Apparently these special menstruation huts cannot be entered except in a stooping position and there is a sliding door near which the food is placed. Women are not allowed to go out of them at all except after dark and then for purposes of nature have to go outside the village area."

It may be noted that separate menstruation huts set apart from the main village are used by some of the hill and forest tribes of southern India, *e.g.*, by the Uralis of Travancore. J. H. H.]

4. THE PANDOS OF UDAIPUR STATE.

Returns of a Pando language in Udaipur State led me to undertake some enquiry regarding the people speaking it. State officials reported definitely that this language or dialect was spoken only by the tribe of the same name, with which no other tribe in the state could be identified, and it was classed by Rai Bahadur Hira Lal as a broken dialect of Chhattisgarhi, mixed with tribal words, some of which resembled Korwa and some Oriya. Nowhere in ethnological literature is any reference to the Pandos to be found. They were amalgamated at the 1921 census with Bhuinhars, who also speak a broken dialect of Chhattisgarhi, but no information is forthcoming to show the reason for this amalgamation and they will not themselves acknowledge any connection with other tribes in the Chhota Nagpur Plateau. Physically they were some of the finest men, whom I have met in this Province. They did not in any way resemble the Bhuinhars of the same tract. Their custom of maintaining bachelors' quarters is, however, according to Risley and Russell, observed also by the Bhuinhars or Bhuiyas (although those residing in villages near the Pandos do not follow that custom) and it is possible that the god Boram mentioned by Dalton as one of the gods of the Bhuiyas is the same as the Pandos' god Baraihan. Rai Bahadur Hira Lal has suggested that the Pandos are akin to Kawars the descendants according to a tradition of the Kauravas of the Mahabharat, whose cousins were the Pandortas a theory which is not supported by my notes regarding their customs. There is, however, a marked similarity between the Pandos and the Korwa whose photograph appears in Crooke's Tribes and Castes of the North-Western Provinces and Oudh and there are certain other resemblances between Pandos and Korwas. But until further evidence is forthcoming it is, clearly only fair to treat the Pandos as quite a separate community. The notes recorded below are taken from statements made by the Pandos themselves.

Social divisions.—The tribe is found in the Smopur, Kandro, Tejpur, Rairumakhurd and Guttri-Gogra villages of Udaipur State and probably elsewhere. There are branches in Surguja with whom the Pandos of Udaipur intermarry. The Pandos acknowledge relationship with no other castes or tribes, but there are two sub-tribes known as Utarha and Surgujiha. They have exogamous divisions or *gotras* and gave me the following names of them :—Jau, Takey, Naupan, Jissey, Karwayhan, Kanhariya, and Jannoo. Additional names of other *gotras* found in various villages were Baren (fig tree), Ithi (an insect), Kirketta (a bird), Gohity (a gecko) and one or two others, Naupan is, it appears, a name of a village. Many of these *gotras* are evidently totemistic in their origin, but the history of the names of some of them is unknown. People of the *baren gotra* will not eat figs, those of the *gohity gotra* will not eat the gecko, those of the *kirketta* will not eat the kirketta bird and so on. Information regarding *gotras* is given to the tribes by their Baigas or Goonias (priests).

Religion.—They worship one God Baraihan and also venerate their ancestors. The form of ancestra worship is to get resin from the saray (Sal) tree and burn it over the fire. Whilst it is being burnt a praye is made to all ancestors not to trouble them and to protect them. There is no shrine but *chour* (rice) is spread on the ground while the worship is being made. It takes place in the month of Phagun and at the Dassehra—that is at the time of harvest. The worship of Baraihan is in the nature of a sacrifice. A goat is killed in the yard of any house in which a goat is available at Dassehra or in Phagun. The head is consumed in the *gotra* of the family making the sacrifice but all the Pandos in the village are given the meat. There is no special shrine to the god. If no goat is available, an offering of rice is made.

They venerate the Sun, that is, salute it occasionally but they do not worship it. Worship of Mahadeo is performed by the village Baiga, and not actually by members of the tribe. Pandos themselves do not become Baigas ; the latter are drawn from different tribes, Majhis and so on.

Food.—Cows are not eaten nor are she-goats but he-goats, pigs and other ordinary kinds of flesh are eaten.

Disposal of the dead.—The dead are buried (" We cannot afford to burn them "), head to the north, feet to the south. New clothes are put on the corpse and other clothes and the personal effects, axe, etc., of the dead man are put in the grave. Three big stones, 2 or 3 feet high, are put at the grave at the top, bottom and in the middle. I was unable to inspect a grave because the village which I visited was newly settled. No rice is put into the mouth of the corpse but *dhan* is thrown over the grave and water is also sprinkled on it so that the soul of the deadman may have rice and water with it wherever it goes and when it goes into a new body. " Souls pass into the bodies of those born in the same *gotra*. Baigas who are Goonias tell us—we do not know about it ".

Marriage customs.—Before marriage the bachelors live in a separate house called the " Bhangra ". The unmarried girls also live in a separate *Bhangra* or *Derwa Kuria*, generally with some elderly widow as chaperon, but both girls and boys feed with their father and mother. I was allowed to inspect these *Bhangras* although the Pandos would not allow me to go into houses where they did their cooking. They were small and clean huts capable of holding about six people each and the two which I saw, one for men and one for girls, each had a couple of cots of wood and bamboo fibre in them. There were several bachelors' quarters in the village because the huts were not very large. If a boy is absent from his quarter for five consecutive nights a *panchayat* is held to enquire into his conduct. The girls marry at ten or twelve ; the boys from 18 to 20. The mother and father arrange the marriage. If two young people run away together, they are subsequently allowed to marry and if a girl has a child by a man, he is forced by caste custom to marry her. The marriage ceremony leads up to the common custom of circling seven times round a pole set up for the occasion. Dancing is performed at any time. They take wine when they can get it.

Dress.—Nearly all the men have the front of their head shaved and allow the back hair to grow long. Those who do not are said to be copying other castes. In the day time they wear a single loin-cloth of scanty dimensions. The women wear a cloth round their waists reaching almost to their feet and looking like a skirt. They also wear separately a loose cloth wrapped round their shoulders and over their head in which they sling their babies if they have any, *i.e.*, their dress is by no means of the nature of one piece *saree*. The men have bows and arrows made of bamboo. The bow string is of bamboo fibre and the arrows are balanced by peacock feathers. The heavy iron barb is made by a blacksmith.

The village.—The village which I saw was very well built from stout timber with thick mud walls unlike many other aboriginal villages where no mud is applied on the wattle at all. The outside of the house was *leeped* and in some cases done over with white clay and ornamented with a wavy pattern. The houses were built all round a centre square which was very clean and levelled. The inhabitants made their living principally by making baskets from peeled bamboos. They complained that they preferred *Dahia* cultivation by breakihg up the jungle which the State forbids them to do. They are a very well set up and cheerful looking lot of people. Utarha Pandos have only one door to their houses, but Surgujiha Pandos have two, the second for the exclusive use of women during the period of menstruation.

Another group of Pandos from Maheshpur village gave similar general information regarding the tribe, but stated that they worship only Dulha Deo and their ancestors. This is an instance of the way in which the name of the " Great God " alters from tract to tract, and of how often the matter is influenced by the custom of all the tribes of a village rather than of a single tribe. It may be noted that the Pandos of Maheshpur like those of Sonpur, etc., etc., maintain bachelor's quarters for both boys and girls.

5. The Korwas.

Risley, in the Tribes and Castes of Bengal, stated that the Korwas appeared to be divided into four sub-tribes, the Agaria-Korwa, probably a cross with the Agarias, the Dand-Korwa, the Dih-Korwa, settled in regular villages, and the Paharia-Korwa. Russell mentioned the principal sub-divisions as the Diharia Korwas and the Paharia Korwas. It is these two divisions which are now found in Udaipur and Jashpur.

They will not intermarry and the Diharia Korwas will not take food or drink frotmhe Paharia Korwas, although the Paharia Korwas, who are still a very wild community, will take food and drink from the Diharias. On the Surguja border there is a third division known as the Bhadiya Korwas, who will not intermarry with or eat with the Diharias. The notes regarding the two principal sub-tribes are given separately. (The Khoraku division is not found in Jashpur or Udaipur and is apparently confined to Surguja.)

(a) *Pahari Korwas or Hill Korwas.*

Social Divisions.—The following exogamous groups, or *gotras*, are found in Udaipur and Jashpur—Hansdwar, Edigwar, Mudhiyar, Samat, Ginnur and Rehla. The members of the tribe do not seem to know anything about totem taboos in relation to these gotras.

Religion.—Russel wrote :—" The Korwas worship Dulha Deo, the bridegroom god of the Gonds, and in Surguja their principal deity is Khuria Rani, the tutelary goddess of the Khuria plateau. The hill Korwas of the Khuria zamindari of Jashpur State, however, worship no gods. They sacrifice only to the spirits of their ancestors. It may be mentioned that Colonel Dalton found only ancestor worship among them in Surguja also, while Risley stated that it was in the Jashpur Zamindari that Khuria Rani is the object of veneration. The explanation is that religious custom varies considerably from tract to tract. At Jaldegar (Udaipur State) Mahadeo is the name under which the tribal deity is honoured. The Pahari Korwas of Kardhana (Jashpur State) worship Mudhkhuri and Barenda Bhut as their principal gods and claim to have done so from time immemorial. Perhaps Mudhkhuri is a local name for Khuria Rani, changed in the course of migration. In this village they worship also Dulha Deo. Mudhkhuri is the wife of Barenda Bhut. The names are being handed down from father to son and nothing is known of the origin of these gods. They are worshipped for general welfare and in particular for the purpose of obtaining good harvests. No images or emblems of any kind are kept to represent the deities. Similarly the veneration of Dulha Deo has been handed down from generation to generation. No legend concerning him is known. All these deities are especially worshipped in Kartik (October) and in Kuar when the new corn is eaten. The latter is the Nawa festival celebrated throughout the tract. (The Deothan feast mentioned by Russell is also observed in some villages). Ancestors are all worshipped at these times along with the gods. As many heaps of *chour* (husked rice) are made as there are *Bhuts* to be worshipped. Two fowls are brought and fed on these heaps of grain. It is not considered necessary that these fowls should be of any special colour. (This is mentioned because very often for similar ceremonials the colour of the sacrificial victim is important). When they have eaten, the throats of the fowls are cut, and the name of the *Bhut* to be worshipped is called. " This worship is done for you—keep the family happy ". At the same sacrifice ancestors are included in the invocation. Their separate names are not mentioned but the head of the family says :— " *Mara masan, leo* ", meaning " Dead people take this." There is no regular shrine in the house on which this sacrifice is made, but before it is performed the place is *leeped* with cow-dung. The same form of worship is followed at each of the two festivals, and it takes place in every house. Afterwards the birds are cooked and eaten by the family and neighbours.

The sacrifices at the festivals may be on different days in different houses. After the chicken has been killed a little rice-beer (*Handia*) is poured as a libation and the tribesmen also consume some. The feast is enjoyed by men, women and children together and after if there is dancing. Men and women all dance together whether they are married, unmarried or widowed.

At times of illness there are special forms of ceremonials for which the *Dewars* are responsible. Those *Dewars* are of the Korwas' own community. They know the *Bhuts* who are unknown to the people in general When anybody is sick, the *Dewar* puts rice into a basket and begins to winnow it. He mentions the name of a *Bhut* and says " If you have come upon this sick person you must go away ". If he hits upon the name of the particular *Bhut* responsible, the *Bhut* is duly driven out. A chicken is then sacrificed on a heap of rice and the name of the *Bhut* is invoked. The head of the chicken and the rice are thrown into the jungle and the *Bhut* is warned not to come again. The rice and the chicken is eaten by the *Dewar*. Apart from this method of allaying diseases, the Korwas use various forest herbs as medicines. Curiously enough in Kardhana village they have never had any small-pox, and so no special mode of propitiating a small-pox goddess is prescribed.

They do not have a *Baiga* for the tribe but there is a *Baiga* in a neighbouring village who performs certain ceremonies of worship on behalf of all the tribes of the tract and the Korwas take help from him also. Apparently he performs his worship in the village where he lives and as he is concerned with the welfare of the whole tract, the Korwas as well as others contribute chickens for the performance. The *Baiga* keeps these chickens until the time comes for the ceremonies. This system is said to save trouble. The Korwas of Kardhana do not go to this *pooja* nor do they know the names of the gods whom the *Baiga* worships.

Disposal of the dead.—The dead are buried with heads to the north and feet to the south, on the back. If the family can afford it, the corpse is wrapped in a new cloth, but otherwise it is buried in the clothes which were worn at the time of death. Some water is put into the mouth of the corpse before burial so that he or she may not be thirsty. Anything made of iron which belonged to the deceased is buried with him and his ornaments, waist-band and the dishes from which he ate and drank are also generally deposited in the grave. The usual custom is, for one of those who go to the burial, to throw a handful of earth on the grave commencing with the nearest relative of the dead person. Sometimes a handful of paddy is thrown at the head of the grave. Babies who have not yet commenced to eat cooked rice are taken to be buried by their mothers and no funeral rites are performed for them. The mat of leaves on which the deceased had slept is thrown away but old clothes are kept for family use. Stones are put upon the grave to keep away animals. Those who are left behind fear the ghosts of the dead, but they have no special fear of the ghosts of a murdered man or of a woman dying in child-birth or of children like some other tribes ; and all are interred in the same burial ground. There does not appear to be any belief in after-life, but when a child is born the soul of a deceased ancestor is supposed to enter into it. The ghosts of the dead remain in the burial ground awaiting the opportunity of such a birth. There is a feast after each funeral on the 9th or 10th day in the case of the death of adults and on the 7th day in the case of children. All the relatives gather together, the male members of the deceased's own household shaving their heads, beards and moustaches and others shaving only their heads and beards. All then bathe, smearing their bodies with oil and turmeric and drink rice-beer. This is regarded as a method of purification.

Marriage customs.—The Pahari Korwas do not have bachelors' quarters. Marriages are generally performed when both the bride and bridegroom are adult. A boy who is ready to marry goes with his relatives to the house of some suitable girl and arrangements are made. How soon the marriage takes place depends generally upon his means. Persons of one *gotra* cannot of course intermarry. The actual form of wedding ceremony varies slightly in detail in different villages. The day before the wedding the bridegroom and his relatives go to the bride's father's house with gifts, among which a suitably large quantity of rice-beer is prominent. If the pot in which rice-beer is being taken to the house of the bride is by any chance broken the mishap is considered most inauspicious. Throughout the night before the wedding the couple are anointed by unmarried girls with oil or, in some villages, with *haldi*. In the most backward places the actual ceremony is very simple. The bride and the bridegroon are seated cross-legged under a *mandwa* (shelter) made of leaves. Their mothers or maternal uncles anoint their foreheads with oil and rice-beer is given to them in a cup of leaves. The groom drinks first and a portion is left for the bride. She drinks and still leaves a little which is given to the bridegroom. (It is a tribal custom for a wife generally to set aside a portion of her meal for her husband.) Meanwhile the rest of the party supply music. The married couple salute their relatives and the ceremony is complete. In some villages the unmarried girls come with vermilion and oil, singing as they approach the *mandwa*, in which the bride and bridegroom are seated on stools on long grass, and it is the bridegroom who applies this once with his finger to the forehead of the girl, while she in return applies some to his throat. In some places vermilion and turmeric are used, in others they are not. It all seems to depend largely upon taste, expense and local custom, and small differences in ritual are unimportant as those in a Christian wedding service performed at St. Margaret's Westminister, contrasted with that in the village church. Divorce is easy. A man dissatisfied with his wife can say :—" Go, I will not keep you." She then goes to her parents and can marry anyone else. The husband finds another wife. A woman, of course, has no power to divorce. Widow remarriage by *sagai* is usual. The procedure is simple. The bridegroom goes to the woman's parents with rice-beer, and asks for their daughter. He takes her as his wife before witnesses.

Other customs.—In each hut there is a small opening at the back for the special use of women during their periods of menstruation. At that time they are not allowed to enter the house by the front door for five full days. The object of this is to avoid the danger of their touching any man and thus polluting him. During that period they never do any cooking. When the time is completed the women are purified by taking a bath.

After child-birth the mother is impure and is not allowed to do household work or to cook food for about two months. Then the feet of both the child and the mother are washed with rice-beer. The mother drinks rice-beer and pours a libation of a few drops in the name of the child.

The women are not tattooed.

General.—The following information has been supplied by Mr. B. N. Ghosal, Assistant Superintendent of Jashpur State.

" Five years ago Pahari Korwas were to be found only in the thickest forests on the hills. Families lived separately from each other often at great distances in isolated huts and it was never their habit to visit villages on the plains. But whenever they found that the need of food or clothing was serious they used to form gangs and go on plundering expeditions into the plains. They had no land or plough cattle or proper agricultural implements. They carried bows and arrows and axes for cutting wood. All the cultivation which they knew was what is known as *beora*, that is to say, they used to fell trees on the slopes of the hills and burn them. Then, when the monsoon broke they would just scratch the surface of the ground with small iron implements and sow millets known locally as *madua, rahir, bendey, sutru*, etc."

Owing to their habits the Pahari Korwas were regarded simply as a wandering gang of looters and so the State authorities compelled them to come down from the hills and settle down in villages. They were supplied with land and plough-cattle and seed grain. Mr. Ghosal states further that they generally pass the whole day roaming about on the hills and in the forests and still live on the edible roots which they collect there. They also eat any kind of meat which they can get including that of the cow although it is said that they are beginning, no doubt under Hindu influence, to give up this habit.

(b) *Dihari Korwas or village Korwas.*

The Dihari Korwas are noticeably cleaner than the Pahari Korwas, especially the women. Their customs, however, vary very little from those of the sub-tribe living in the hills except that, of course, they are not so primitive. The exogamous groups have generally the same names as those of the Pahari Korwas, but the Hansdwar *gotra* is regarded as superior to the others and in some villages men of this *gotra* will not dine with those of others.

Religion.—Religious observances are slightly different to those of the Pahari Korwas. The principal creed is ancestor worship. Dulha Deo is also an object of veneration and Mahadeo is propitiated through the agency of the village *Baiga*. The principal festival of the year is at the *Nawa Khana* when Dulha Deo and the family ancestors are worshipped on the same day. The worship is done by placing a small heap of new rice on a specially cleaned spot in the house. A brown* coloured hen is set to feed on this rice. If it refuses its life is saved and nothing is offered to the ancestors in that year. If the hen eats the rice the father of the family calls out " Good parents and grand parents, here are our offerings to you. Please take them and keep the family in good health." Then the victim is killed by blows of the fist and further offerings of cooked rice and *dal* and rice-beer are made. Later in the festival a similar ceremony is performed in the name of Dulha Deo, but for this a red coloured hen is the victim. The prayer pronounced is " Good Dulha Deo, here is our offering. I am bowing to you. You are our ancestral god. Keep our cultivation prosperous and the members of our family in good health." The throat of the hen is then cut with a knife. This form of worship takes place once only in the year. For the propitiation of Mahadeo each household gives a small hen and handful of rice to the village *Baiga* annually. No other deities or ghosts are separately worshipped by the Dihari Korwas but the *Baiga* is responsible for the propitiation of the village *Bhuts*, of whom the principal are *Path Bhut* and *Kunth Bhut*. Bhuts exist in every corner of the village. In some villages sacrifice is performed only to ancestors and not to Dulha Deo. In most places the *Sohraid* is observed when the horns of the village cattle are smeared with oil and their feet washed with rice-beer. The cattle are also given rice to eat on this occasion. It is not customary for anybody to sow his field until the *Baiga* has sacrificed the hens collected from the villagers and has first sown his own. (The significance of the selection of a bird of a certain colour for sacrifice is not known but is regarded as important in almost all Dihari Korwas villages. Among other tribes goats which are sacrificed at certain festivals are also required to be of particular colours.) In the case of any epidemic appearing in the village an offering, in which the fruit of the castor plant and fowls from the principal part, is made by the *Baiga*, who thus keeps evil spirits out of the village.

Burial and marriage ceremonies.—Dead bodies are disposed of in practically the same way as among the Pahari Korwas. An interesting rite is described as follows by the Korwas themselves :—

" Near the head of the grave we generally keep small quantities of paddy, millet, cotton, etc., and water in an earthen pot, the brim of which is invariably slightly broken. We also place there sticks used for cleaning the teeth. The number of the sticks depends upon the number of days which are to elapse before the final funeral ceremonies. (*This custom is observed also by the Bhuinhars of this tract.*) For boys and girls

*Probably the colour of a painted partridge.

these are performed 5 days after death, for young men and women 7 days after death and for grown-up persons 10 days after death." Females are generally buried with their faces upwards and males with their faces downwards, the head, as in the case of the Pahari Korwas, pointing to the north."

In some villages it is considered that a pregnant woman will become an unfriendly ghost after death but in others this belief appears to be non-existent. The details of funeral ceremonies, like those of wedding ceremonies, vary considerably from village to village.

When negotiations are being made for a wedding it is considered extremely unpropitious if a fox crosses the path of the bridegroom's party. The actual wedding ceremony is in some particulars very similar to that of the Oraons, Rautias and other tribes in the same tract. By the side of *Mandwa* post a grindstone is placed on the ground and upon it five small heaps of rice are placed separately. On one heap a copper pice is laid, on a second a piece of *haldi*, on a third a betel nut. The bride stands in front of the bridegroom with a winnowing basket in her hands. Her younger brother places some fried paddy in this (winnowing basket) while the bridegroom holds the hands of the bride from behind. They then move round the *Mandwa* five times shaking the winnowing basket until all the rice falls on the ground. Each time as they circle the mill-stone the bridegroom catches hold of the leg of the bride and knocks over one of the heaps of rice. The usual anointing with oil or signing with vermilion of course follows. This form of ceremony is observed in Pandhrapath and other villages, but in Kardhana, which I visited, the most important part of the wedding ceremony appeared to be for the bridegroon to stand with his left foot upon the right foot of the bride, who remained in a sitting posture, and to anoint her head five times from a leaf full of oil his hand being guided by an elder relation. Upon completion of this ritual all the spectators cheer loudly and a similar ritual is performed by the bride.

6. Chiks of Jashpur (Kharsoda).

1. Cannot eat or drink with Gandas or Pankas, but do the same work. Where Gandas and Pankas are found Chiks are not. Consider themselves Hindus but do not wear the sacred thread.

2. Worship only their ancestors. The village *Baiga* propitiates Mahadeo on their behalf.

3. Eat most kinds of flesh, but not cow, rat, snake, cat or monkey.

4. The marriage ceremony is much the same as that already described for the Dihari Korwas of the tract and followed also by the Rautias and Oraons.

5. Dead buried head north, feet south flat on back. No food is put in the grave or in the mouth of the corpse, but unhusked rice is scattered from the house of the deceased to the burial ground and all that remains is left with the basket at the head of the completed grave. No memorial is erected. There is a caste dinner from 5 to 10 days after death according to the age of the dead person. No belief in after life.

7. Nagasias (Udaipur State).

1. There are no sub-tribes, but there are at least twenty-four *gotras*, each one named after a different kind of snake.

2. The Nagasias will not dine with nor take water from Nagbansis, who mark their foreheads with vermilion and whose bodies are tattooed. The Nagasias have neither of these customs. Their women wear bangles of brass and wear white clothing. Nose rings and coloured clothing are not allowed. Their tradition is that they came from Nagpur (presumably Chhota Nagpur) and that they are descendants of Shesh Nag, who was white.

3. The wedding ceremony is the usual mixture of tribal and Hindu ritual. There is no sacrifice of an animal or bird, but after a ceremonial bath in the river, the bridegroom shoots an imaginary deer seven times with a bow and arrow. At the seventh attempt the *Bhanto* (sister's husband) of the bridegroom, who conducts most of the marriage rites, runs away with the arrow. The bridegroom pursues him and if he cannot catch him has to pay a fine of one anna.

4. The objects of worship are Nag Deo, the cobra or snake god, the Sun, the Moon, Dulha Deo, Bhagwan (presumably Mahadeo) and ancestors. Ghosts and spirits of trees, etc., are not worshipped. For snake worship an idol representing the cobra is prepared from kneaded flour. No other images are made. In times of illness the *Baiga* is summoned to propitiate Shitala Devi.

5. Dead are generally buried, head north, feet south. Paddy and cotton are scattered on the way to the grave. A pot of water is placed by the grave. A little water is sprinkled in the mouth of the corpse with some mango leaves, first by his next-of-kin and then by other relatives. Stones or logs of wood or thorns are placed over ordinary graves to keep off wild animals, but for an important man a monument of plastered mud is made with a fence. The cot on which he died or was carried to the grave is left there. The remaining ceremonies resemble those of other tribes in the neighbourhood.

6. There are very definite contrasts between the Nagasias of Udaipur and the Nagasias of Jashpur, who are known locally as Kisans. The latter have two sub-tribes the Senduria and the Teliha, the former of whom use vermilion and possibly correspond to the Nagbansis of Udaipur. The Teliha Nagasias of the Khuria hills who were questioned stated that they had no *gotras* at all. Ancestor worship is really the only form of religion, the ordinary festivals of the tract are observed and at the *Nawakhana* chickens are sacrificed to the spirits of the dead with ritual very similar to that followed by the Korwas of Jashpur. Dulha Deo is not venerated, but *Baigas* perform ceremonies for the village gods and ghosts. In some villages the dead are burned, in others they are buried head north and face upwards. On a cremation pyre females are laid upwards and males face downwards. The funeral ceremonies and wedding ceremonies resemble those of other tribes in the same tract.

8. Nagbansis.

Russell mentions Nagbansis only as sub-tribes or clans of Rajputs, Daharias and Gonds. I have been unable to identify them definitely but those in Udaipur and Jashpur certainly do not appear to be either Gonds or Daharias. They state, in fact, specifically that they are not Gonds. It appears likely that they are merely a division of the Senduria Nagasias mentioned above or a branch of the Kharias who have a Nagbansi division. The following is briefly the information obtained from them :—

(1) Their *gotras* are :—Kumar, Baghin, Dudhkanra, Sukra, Manakhia, Baranga, Kherwar, Bagaria, Kansar, Lohra, Samrath, Kutuwan, Bhuiyan, Pradhan, Baiga, Manjhi and Rajpuria. These are exogamous

septs. After a girl is married she will take no food cooked in the vessels of her parents but she will eat food cooked by her brother in metal and not earthen pots. She will not eat food cooked by her brother's wife even in metal pots.

(2) Mahadeo and Dulha Deo are worshipped in a month of Kartik when a goat and coconut and spices are offered to them. There are no special shrines but Dulha Deo is worshipped within the house and Mahadeo outside the house after *leeping* the place where the sacrifice is to take place. A *Baiga* is called to officiate at the ceremony to Mahadeo.

(3) The dead bodies of well-to-do persons are burnt but others are buried with the head to the north and feet to the south. No monument is erected.

(4) The Nagbansis say that their ancestors came from Nagpur (presumably Chhota Nagpur) and that they are named after Nag, the snake. They eat all kinds of flesh except the cow, the pig and other unclean meat. They regard themselves as Hindus and assume the sacred thread when they are married but not earlier. It would appear that they are Hinduized Nagasias or Kharias.

9. Rautias of Jashpur State.

These notes are additional to those to be found in Russell's *Castes and Tribes*.

1. Three sub-divisions—Baraik, Naik and Parap. The order is that of their precedence. They consider themselves Hindus and the first two sub-divisions wear the sacred thread. The sub-divisions are exogamous.

2. There are the following exogamous septs :—Kirketta (Kirketta bird), Aind (eel), Nag (cobra), Bagh (tiger), Singh (lion), Dandwa (Dandwa fish) and Barwa (wild dog). They are totemistic and the sept animal is duly venerated.

3. Near Jashpur both Dulha Deo and ancestors are the object of worship, in the Khurai hills only ancestors. No images for worship are kept in the house or in the village. The ritual is almost exactly as described for the Dihari Korwas. The *Baiga* of a group of villages as elsewhere performs the ceremonies for the village gods and the spirits of hills and corners (*Khunta pat*). The *Baiga* calls on many names but in Champa Toli village the people remember only Sri Pat. In Sitonga village two rivers have their source—Sri and Bonki. From the day they rose the spirit Sri has been worshipped through the *Baiga*, who is a Nagasia by tribe.

4. There are no bachelors' quarters. The marriage ceremony in the Khurai hills is the same as that already described for the Dihari Korwas in many details. When a bride is being sought it is most unlucky to see a partridge or a *sui* bird. The following is the description of the worship of Dulha Deo at a wedding given to me by Rautias in Champa Toli village :—The girl is taken in a sort of palanquin to the wedding which in some villages, is borne by Oraons. After completion of the marriage ceremony a heap of rice is made and a goat of *khasia* colour (reddish colour with black markings) is brought and fed on this rice. It is then killed outside the house by a blow of an axe on the back of the neck. The blood is brought into the house and sprinkled on the rice and Dulha Deo is invoked three times, first when the rice is heaped, next when the goat is fed and last when the blood is sprinkled. The prayer is for the happiness of the husband and wife. Afterwards the rice is thrown into the stream and the flesh of the goat is eaten by the family and the guests. Other details of the ceremony are similar to those of other tribes in the neighbourhood but on the second day a mango tree is worshipped by a barber who may be either male or female. The bridegroom is carried to any mango tree where resin is burnt and he has to sprinkle *ghee*, flour, molasses and resin on the fire. A thread is tied round the tree and a branch taken from it or from any other mango tree to be fixed in the ground under the bride's *mandua*. The barber then takes the bride to perform the same ceremony. The usual ritual of applying vermilion to the face and throat of the newly married couple follows and after this has been done the barber distributes rice to all the guests and sprinkles water with the mango leaves first upon the bridegroom and then upon the bride. He also ties together the clothes of the bride and bridegroon. The ceremony at the mango tree is said to have been handed down according to the tradition of their ancestors.

5. In the Khuria hills those who can afford it burn their adult dead. Children and those who die unnatural deaths are buried. Nearer Jashpur the tribe generally buries its dead—head north, feet south, flat on the back. No implements or ornaments are buried with the body but paddy is scattered from the house of the deceased to the grave and some is left at the head of the grave. No memorial is erected.

6. Forms of tattooing and style of dressing the hair are a matter of taste. But the *choondi* (long scalp lock) must be left. The women wear earrings of rolled leaves like the Dihari Korwa women of the neighbourhood shown in the illustration.

10. Bhuinhars.

Much will be found about the Bhuinhars or Bhuiyas in Risley and Russell. The process of time has however brought about a good many changes.

1. The Bhuinhars of the neighbourhood of Pathalgaon in Udaipur State stoutly deny that they are the same as Bhuiyas, who live in Gunpur and Raigarh. These Bhuinhars claim to have come from Garha Mandla.

2. Around Pathalgaon the following exogamous *gotras* are found. They are definitely totemistic, Dumen (*the dumen tree*) Murhi (*a vegetable*), *Sali* (*a tree*) Nag (*cobra*), *Sukra* (*spear grass*), *Maji*, *Chitki*, *Raki* and *Ali*. In Jashpur State the *gotras* seem to be different. The following were found :—Ahind (eel), Harhuria (*a species of snake*), *Kirketta* (*a species of bird*), *Goha* (*Gecko*), *Beng* (*frog*), Thithio, Tope, *Saras* (*various kinds of birds*), and Chorant (spear grass). Veneration of the totem is observed in various ways, for instance people of the *Chorant gotra* take a ceremonial bath if there is a forest fire. It may be noticed that in Jashpur the totem names are the same for many neighbouring tribes.

3. Ancestors are worshipped especially at the *Nawakhana* festival. In Jashpur chickens are sacrificed but not in Udaipur. In villages of both states resin is burned as a ritual. Around Pathalgaon (Udaipur) the Bhuinhars separately worship also the sun and the moon. Mata Devi is propitiated for small-pox.

4. The dead are buried, head north, feet south. In the Khuria Zamindari males are interred face downwards and females on their backs. Other ritual is similar to that among various tribes in the tract (including the custom of placing sticks for cleaning teeth on the grave). Logs and stones are placed on graves to keep off animals.

5. Other ceremonies vary little from those already described as common in the Chhota Nagpur States. In the Khuria hills rice-beer is used freely in their performance.

6. Bhuinhar women are tattooed on their arms and ankles, but there are no particularly distinct forms. The Khurai Bhuinhars stated that there are also Munda Bhuinhars and Sonjhara Bhuinhars from whom they will not take cooked food.

11. Birhors.

Russell has a very brief note upon this tribe, but a full account of it will be found in Rai Bahadur Sarat Chandra Roy's book "The Birhors". Colonel Dalton's description of the tribe was "a *small dirty* miserable looking race, who have the credit of devouring their parents", and the physical characteristics of those whom I saw in Udaipur bore out the first part of this description. They still wear their hair long and matted and often hanging over their faces.

2. There are no sub-tribes in the tract of Udaipur around Rairooma Khurd. The exogamous *gotras* there are :—Sunwani Bandi, Barih, Kasondih, Goira, and Chenga. None of these names appear in Rai Bahadur S. C. Roy's list of the totemistic clans of which he had information. Marriage is adult and is performed almost exactly according to the ritual of the local Kanwars and Gonds.

3. The dead are buried, head north, feet south on the back. (Roy states "head pointing south".) For important men a *chabutra* (platform) of mud is raised over the grave, and some roofing is put up over it. The cot on which a man died—if he did die on a cot—or his bier is left near the grave, and also an earthen pot with a little rice in it. No rice is scattered on the way to the burial ground. A purification ceremony is performed from two to eight days after the funeral according to the time which it takes to collect the kinsmen for the feast.

4. Mahadeo is the object of veneration. These people seem to have forgotten the gods or spirits worshipped by their ancestors. A day is set apart for a ceremonial sacrifice in the month of Kartik. There is no image or shrine, but the place where the offering is to be made is *leeped* with cow dung and water. Coconuts and betel nut are offered after "Hom" has been burned. There is no animal sacrifice to Mahadeo. The Birhors do not consider themselves to be Hindus.

5. There are certain special birth ceremonies. As usual among almost all tribes the navel cord is cut by the mother. It is buried, not, as generally, in front of the entrance to the house, but at the place where the birth takes place. Seven days after a birth a chicken is sacrificed to the ancestors of the family. The feet of the child are washed with milk, and water is poured into an earthen pot. The names of individual ancestors are called in turn, and as each is called a grain of rice is dropped into the pot. When one of these grains floats the child is given the names of that ancestor and it is thought that the soul of the latter has returned in the new-born child. This ceremony, which is exactly the same as the naming ceremony of the Oraons described by Father Dehon, is generally performed by the head of the house but occasionally a *Baiga* is called to do it. In times of illness the *Baiga* is called to propitiate Mata.

6. Almost every kind of meat is eaten except cows, cats, snakes, dogs, rats, crows, tigers and bears. They eat monkeys but have had none for six years. The monkeys are snared in a net, cut up like a goat and curried ; the flesh is rather tough. These Birhors have no recollection of having eaten human flesh.

7. There are bachelors' quarters for both sexes in Birhor villages, known as the "Derwa Ghar". Boys live separately from the girls.

8. The Birhors are bi-lingual, speaking their own language and Chhattisgarhi. They work as labourers and also follow their traditional occupation of making rope from creepers. The women are tattooed, if they can afford it.

9. Dalton held that the Birhors are a sub-tribe of Kharias. Those in Udaipur resemble the Kharias very little. The latter have in fact become largely Hinduized and their customs are similar to those of others Hinduized tribes in the tract. They have totemistic *gotras*:—the Kirketta bird, the dhum dhum fish etc. In this tract Dulha Deo is their god : otherwise they still follow the description given in Russell.

12. Majhwars (Ududha, Udaipur State).

They claim to have no connection with the Majhis or with any other tribe, and have no sub-tribes. They have the following exogamous *gotras* (which do not correspond to the list in Russell) :—

Sunwani (Suwar is a title), Khunta (a peg), Jhingri (tree frog), Dhuma (a flower), Murhi, Sitar and Chhengga (meanings not explained).

2. Mahadeo alone is worshipped. (Russell says Dulha Deo.) There is a platform for him in every house but no image. A goat is sacrificed to him once or twice a year, at sowing time and at Holi. Chickens are not sacrificed. Betel nut and rice are also offered up. Marriages are performed according to common rites by the *Baiga* and panches.

3. Dead are buried, head north, feet south—lying on the right side. The personal effects of the deceased are placed on top of the grave. For important men a small temple or house (Matt) is erected over the grave.

4. Dancing is popular. They begin ceremonial dances in Chait and finish in Phagun, before sowing. They also dance at weddings and have the Karam Raja dance as described by Russell.

13. Saontas (Semipalli, Udaipur).

This tribe or sub-tribe offers a curious example of degradation due to economic reasons. They state that they are really Kisan Majhi who migrated from Sirguja, where there are large numbers of their relatives They have taken to basket work and are therefore classed with the low caste Turis, and have changed their name to Saonta. They are related to the Majhis of Chiro village and intermarry with them. The title Manjhi, "village headmen," is invariably adopted by the Santals (Saontas) in some tracts (see Russell's short note). The Saontas dine with Majhis, but not with Majhwars, which confirms the claim of the Majhwars that they are distinct from Majhis.

2. Exogamous *gotras* are :—Murhi (a species of vegetable), Baiha Sua (a parrot), Tuchsi Sua (a different species of parrot), Koksa (a kind of fish), Paridhia and Doma. The totems are respected in the usual way.

3. Mahadeo and Dulha Deo are worshipped in Phagun, and at sowing time. There is a small shrine of Dulha Deo in each house and a covered shrine of Mahadeo for the village. Ancestors are also worshipped.

4. They do not eat cows, pigs, cats, dogs, snakes, frogs, crocodiles, etc., but eat other kinds of flesh.

5. Dead are buried head north and feet south, on the back, with new and old clothing in the grave. A handful of rice is thrown on the grave. There is no memorial stone.

6. The marriage ceremony is ordinary. Two young unmarried girls take a leading part in the ritual.

7. Like all the tribesmen of Chhota Nagpur the Saontas are great dancers. I noted that their great drums were larger than those of any other tribal dancers in the neighbourhood.

14. Oraons.

The customs of these cheerful and prolific people vary from tract to tract in Chhota Nagpur, but most of them will be found detailed in the works of Father Dehon or of Rai Bahadur S. C. Roy, or in Russell's *Tribes and Castes of the Central Provinces.* The god Dharmes (Dharmesha) mentioned by those three observers was known only in certain villages in Udaipur State. Elsewhere in the Central Provinces the Oraons except of course the Christians, worship principally their ancestors, and Dulha Deo and Burra Deo (equivalent presumably to Dharmes), whilst the village *Baiga* as usual propitiates Mahadeo, Mata Devi, etc. Every where they have their own *Dewars* who know magic and are called in time of sickness and to lay evil spirits. These may belong to any caste or tribe.

2. The various local ceremonies of sacrifice, marriage and burial are according to ritual already described for the Korwas, and other tribes of the same tract. Squirrels are inauspicious to Oraon wedding parties in some villages. Dead bodies are burned by those who can afford it. Others are buried head south, feet north on the back. Ornaments are buried with the dead. No monuments are raised. There seems to be little difference between the ritual performed in Udaipur, the Khuria hills and the Jashpur plateau.

3. The exogamous *gotras* are named after various totems—animal, vegetable or mineral. There is no social precedence and Oraons throughout Chhota Nagpur appear to be permitted to marry into any *gotra* other than their own.

4. The bachelors' quarters, known as the *Dhumkuria* are separate for boys and girls. As mentioned in the Report the Christian Oraons still retain a bachelors' dormitory and continue the ceremonial of cicatrization. It is said that they also often perform weddings according to tribal rites after the church ceremony.

5. The tattooing of Oraon women is rather distinctive—and is generally profuse. The illustration is prepared from a diagram kindly sent by the Superintendent of Udaipur State. Tattooing is shown on one arm only because the pattern on each arm is generally the same. There is no definite custom that it should be done on either arm or on both arms.

6. On the Jashpur Plateau where most of the Oraons are Christians, they are contented and fairly industrious cultivators and labourers distinguishable only from other castes and tribes by their physical characteristics. Of those in the Khurai Zamindari Mr. Ghosal writes :—

> " Both males and females are very ill-clad. The women do not generally cover the upper part of their body when they move about among their fellow villagers, but conceal their breasts when they see a stranger. They usually wear a cloth only from their waist to their knees."

7. The Oraons are great dancers and must be ranked with the Marias, Murias and Parjas as the leading exponents of the art in these Provinces. They are of course extremely fond of *handia* (rice-beer).

15. Gadabas.

I met a few Gadabas in Bastar State, the census total is 395 only and the tribe is not found elsewhere in these Provinces. The younger people speak only Bhatri, but the old ones know their own language, which is quite unlike any other in the tract. They say that they are the hereditary palki-bearers of the State. They consider themselves like the Murias and will eat food cooked by Murias although the latter will not take anything cooked by them. In the houses inspected, which were constructed of bamboo wattle and mud, they had a separate room for a kitchen " because of the heat ". They bury their dead on their backs, naked, head to east and feet to west. It is stated that stone slabs are erected as memorials—where sacrifices are offered occasionally. The men wear their hair in buns behind and shaved in front. I missed in Bastar the dress which I had seen Gadaba women wearing some years previously in the neighbouring district of Vizagapatam. Evidently the Bastar Gadabas belong to either the Ollar, Bodo or Parangi section of the tribe, who do not wear the dress peculiar to other sections. The latter is so remarkable as to merit a summary of the description from the Vizagapatam Gazetteer :—

" The dress of the men is ordinary. Women have round their waists a fringed narrow cloth woven by them on primitive handlooms, the warp being hand spun fibre of different jungle shrubs, the wool cotton dyed at home with indigo and *morinda citrifolia* and arranged in stripes red, blue and white. Over or under this is a bustle made of some 40 strands of stout black cloth woven from other shrubs and tied together at the ends, Round the upper part of the body is another cloth similar to but smaller than the waist-cloth. On the right forearm from wrist to elbow are a number of brass bracelets. Over the forehead is a chaplet of cowrie shells, white *kusa* grass seeds, or the red and black berries of *abrus precatorius*. In the ears are enormous coils of thick brass wire (one specimen was found to be 8 inches across and contained 20 strands), which hang down on their shoulders and in extreme cases prevent them turning their heads except slowly and with care. Details of the costume vary locally. The reason for the bustle is that a goddess incognito visited a Gadaba village and asked a woman leave to sit on a cot. She was told that the floor was the proper place for beggars and therefore decreed that all Gadaba women should wear bustles to remind them of their churlishness.

I endeavoured to get photographs of these picturesque people in Jeypore on several occaions, but although they frequently work on Public Works Department road construction they were shy of the ordeal.

The Chuddur Penk (small Gods) or Household Gods of the Gonds and the Phara Pen or Clan God, by W. H. Shoobert.

The religion of the Gonds has been dealt with very fully in Volume II of Russell's Tribes and Castes of the Central Provinces, pages 97 to 118. In that article a distinction has been drawn between the village gods, the tribal gods and the household gods. Some description of these household gods is given in a note by Mr. J. A. Tawney, sometime Deputy Commissioner of Chhindwara, included in the Central Provinces Census Report for 1881, in which he observed :—

> " I may mention that it is somewhat difficult to get a Gond either to confess that he has any household gods or to show them. The best way is to send off the father of the family on some errand and then to ask his unsuspecting wife to bring out the gods. You generally get them on a tray and some of the villages will help her to name them."

Mr. W. V. Grigson, Deputy Commissioner, Nagpur, recently made some enquiries in Gond villages in the district regarding the existence of Chuddur Penk there now. The following description has been put together as far as possible in his own words from rough notes which he most kindly made available to me :—

" The Chuddur Penk are worshipped often in the house and especially at Jiwati festival. I was shown them by an old *Partiti* (six-god) Gond of Mundepar. He was very reluctant at first, but on hearing me described as proficient in Gond legends and lore, agreed : he first washed his hands and feet and then bade me sit on the threshold of his verandah from where I could see into his ' Pen kholi ' or ' god-room ' through the door D shown in the rough plan of the house reproduced below.

ROUGH PLAN OF GOND HOUSE SHOWING PENKHOLI

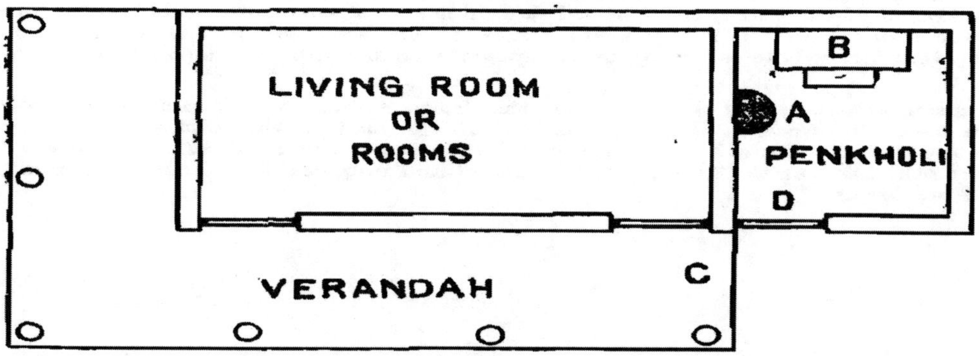

The gods were tied in cloth inside two *handis* (earthen pots) called the *Penk Atka*, suspended from the roof above the *chabutra* (platform) at B. This *chabutra* is used for their worship and is known as *Bina*. At A there was another small breast-shaped *Bina* on which there was a small offering of juari bread, because this *Bina* contained the ghosts (*Sana* equivalent to the Bastari *Hanal*) of the Gond's father and mother, who were dead but whose ghosts had not been united with the dead of the *Pari* (clan) in the *Penkara* (clan god's threshing floor) at some place in the Balaghat district, near Katangi, for lack of money, although the *Pengadwa* (custodian of the clan god) had actually summoned my informant to go there. The latter said that the trip would cost him Rs. 40, which he could not afford.

The smaller *handi* contained only five Chuddur Penk, made of wood and shaped like *phalloi*, coloured with vermilion and *sendur*. These five out of the six household gods are made for a six-god Gond by his *Samdhi* (Soyera), maternal cousin, or some other close connection on his wife's or mother's side. The sixth god, I was informed, had flown away, but was a piece of *ling*-shaped iron. My informant had not had a new one made, because he was old and poor and without heirs. But if he did want one, the Gond Lohar and his wife would make one for his *Samdhi* working both stark naked by night, as when they forge a new *Pharapen* (clan god) for a *Penkara*.

Besides the Chuddur Penk this man had in another big *handi* what he and all the Gonds there described as Mahadeo—a double image about two inches tall with small emblems erect in front—and another image of Parbati. These were collectively described by all as Mahadeo but had no other Gondi name. This deity, all the Gonds said, had nothing to do with the *Phara pen*, confined to the Pari (clan) god of the *Penkara*, but was a purely domestic god to be worshipped in the *Penkholi* of the house along with the Chuddur Penk. The images were of roughly cast brass, and were stated to have been made at Badamba, two miles beyond Deolapar and a mile east of the Great Northern Road, by a Gond Kasar. One of the emblems, a little white excrescence, in front of the Mahadeo, is intended to represent a conch shell, and is known as Narayan Deo. The worship appears to consist of washing the image and the Chuddur Penk. As the old man was likely to die soon and is childless I enquired the fate destined for his Mahadeo and Chuddur Penk. It was unanimously stated that Mahadeo and Chuddur Penk would be thrown into the river after a funeral ceremony. If a father has three sons, on his death the house Mahadeo and Chuddur Penk pass to the eldest. The families of the younger sons ordinarily remain joint with that of the eldest son and so they do not have separate gods in their own houses. To demand separate gods is a sign of feud destroying the family unity, or sometimes of amicable partition of ancestral property.

From enquiries made in a number of places I found that the *Penkara* of various septs of six-god Gonds and seven-god Gonds were situated at different villages often quite remote from their own places of residence. A good Gond will go to his *Penkara* twice a year on the occasions of *Gara Nawa* and of *Wanjeng Nawa*. He then pays Rs. 2 or Rs. 2-8-0 to the *Pengadwa*, and the god is washed. Such visits are also paid to the *Pengadwa* to offer what are fees or fines (they use the Hindi word *dand*, or the Gondi *badai*, such as wedding fees (*marming badai*), cradle fees (*ukar badai*) and fines for getting maggots into a wound (*phara rota dand* or *bara deo ka dand*), or for being handcuffed, whether any subsequent trial results in acquittal or not. A Gond who visits the *Penkara* must be shaved all over and give a dinner after offering a goat at the *Penkara*. He takes with him three companions of his own *pari* and has to pay all their expenses.

For the offence of fornication with a man of her *pari* a woman is never forgiven. A man may be if he turns away the woman with whom this offence has been committed, and pays a *panchayat* fine and *penkara dand*. Women are never allowed inside the *penkara* because they would become mad if they entered it.

The ceremony of entrusting the soul of a dead man to the *Pengadwa* is described as follows. The maternal first cousin of the dead man's heir slays a he-goat by striking it on the skull with an axe. It is then eaten by all the *panches*. This is done at the house of the deceased. His daughter-in-law, or, if he has none, some girl of a clan in which his son could marry, and his daughter then drag the head of the goat to a place appointed for the *Guddi* (betrothal of the ghost) where it is buried in a hole dug by the maternal cousin (*Soyera*) of the man, all those present dropping on it earth and mohua juice. The *Bhagta* (Shaman, man possessed by a familiar spirit) is then possessed by his *deo*, looks up to the sky and claps his hands together. When he opens his hands a wet grain of rice is found which is considered to be the dead man's soul. This is wrapped up in cotton and a new cloth. The maternal cousin (*Soyera*) leeps the spot selected for the *guddi* and lights the ceremonial *dips* (saucer-like utensils in which small wicks float in oil). The heir then provides a *pailli* of juar or gram which his wife, that is the dead man's daughter-in-law, has brought and left at the *guddi*. This grain is taken away by the dead man's daughter, who, being married, belongs to another clan or *pari*. This is considered as the *paring*, or bride price. If, however, the heir has not enough money to provide the bride price and to take his father's ghost to the *Gadwa* the daughter of the dead man looks after the '*Jiwa*' (ghost) which the *Bhagta* has found in the grain of rice until the heir has procured the money necessary for the ceremony. She plasters mud round the cotton wool in which the grain of rice is wrapped and keeps it in the ground under the floor of the front verandah of the house. The place is leeped over and every day the woman offers a little of her food to the *Jiwa*. It is in return for handing this grain over to him when he is ready to take it to the *Gadwa* that the bride price is given by the heir to his married sister. The grain is kept in the house of the heir and not in that of his sister. It is interesting to note that at the *Guddi* or the ceremony of the betrothal of the ghost, the married daughter and the daughter-in-law go in procession round the *Guddi* behind the *Bhumka* of the village seven times if they are seven-god Gonds and six times if they are six-god Gonds, etc. The whole ceremony is as expensive as a wedding except for the difference in the bride price.

When he has sufficient money the heir takes the *Jiwa* or ghost, wrapped as it is in cotton wool and new cloth, to the house of the *Gadwa*. The cloth is tied on the back of the *Gadwa* and he goes through a full marriage ceremony with his own wife passing seven times round the usual *salai* or *mohua* pole. The *Gadwa* then opens the cloth, takes up the grain, places it in oil and empties it into the *Gadwa* pot, so re-uniting the soul with the *Pari* or clan".

SKELETON MAP
OF
THE CENTRAL PROVINCES & BERAR
Scale 1 Inch=64 Miles
30 0 50 100 Miles
CENTRAL INDIA AGENCY
CENTRAL INDIA AGENCY
BOMBAY PRESIDENCY
BENGAL
MADRAS PRESIDENCY
NIZAM'S DOMINIONS
SAUGOR
DAMOH
JUBBULPORE
NARSINGHPUR
HOSHANGABAD
CHHINDWARA
SEONI
MANDLA
BETUL
NIMAR
BALAGHAT
KAWARDHA
BILASPUR
KOREA
SARGUJA
JASHPUR
UDAIPUR
RAIGARH
NAGPUR
BHANDAR
AMRAOTI
WARDHA
BULDANA
AKOLA
YEOTMAL
CHANDA
DRUG
RAIPUR
KANKER
BASTAR
KHAIRAGARH
NANDGAON
REFERENCES
C....Chhuikhadan.
N....Nandgaon.
K....Khairagarh.
M....Makrai.

8. The Kurmis of Chota Nagpur.

By W. G. Lacey.

Mention has been made in Chapter XII of the Bihar and Orissa Report of the claim to Kshatriya status advanced by the Kurmi caste. It was at first supposed that this claim was confined to those Kurmis who reside mainly in Bihar proper and in the United Provinces and whose traditional pursuits are cultivation and domestic service. For census purposes it has always proved impossible to distinguish this community from the *Kurmi Mahtos* of the Chota Nagpur plateau, as their habitat is not in all cases a reliable guide; in the census tables therefore they all appear together simply as "Kurmis". It has, however, generally been assumed in previous census reports that the Kurmi Mahtos are a semi-aboriginal people, whose ancestors were allied to the Santal and Bhumij tribes. Instructions were accordingly issued on the present occasion that a return of Kurmi-Kshatriya might be accepted in the case only of the Bihar community. These instructions gave rise to a flood of protest. The "All-India Kurmi-Kshatriya Association" took up the cudgels on behalf of the Kurmi Mahtos, and stoutly affirmed that "they and the Kurmi-Kshatriyas of the western provinces are the same, proofs of which, if necessary, can be produced before the Government." It must be confessed that, when invited to produce these proofs, the Association showed no great eagerness to respond and eventually took refuge in the following generalities which, besides being unsupported by evidence or illustration, would undoubtedly be contested by many persons who have considerable experience of the Kurmi Mahtos:—"(1) The sections and sub-sections are similar. (2) The occupations are the same. (3) The habits and customs are similar." But the favourite authority of those who maintain the kinship of the two communities is Dalton's *Descriptive Ethnology of Bengal* (1872), in which the following passages occur:—

"In the Province of Chota Nagpur the ancestors of the people now called Kurmis appear to have obtained a footing among the aboriginal tribes at a very remote period, and in more than one part of Manbhum have supplanted them. There are traditions of struggle between them and Kolarian aborigines of these regions, and, though the latter generally managed to hold their own, we find in some places Kurmi villages established on sites which, we know from the groups of rude stone pillars or cenotaphs still conspicuous, were once occupied by Bhumij or Mannas, and in others vestiges of ruined temples appertaining to Hindu or Jaina settlements, both most likely belonging to successive generations of Kurmis, amidst villages that have for ages been occupied by Bhumij. . . . .

"Though the Kurmis include so many noble families, their social position in Bengal is not high. They are not even *jalacharaniva* or a tribe from whose hands a Hindu of the higher castes would drink water, but in Bihar this honour is accorded to them. The social customs and religious observances vary much in different districts. Where they are found in common tenancy with non-Aryan tribes, they conform to many usages which they must have acquired from the latter, and, following their examples, swerve considerably from orthodox Hindu practices. The Kurmis employ Brahmans as priests in all ceremonies except marriages."

Finally he describes them as "unquestionably Aryan in looks" and thinks it probable that they are the descendants of some of the earliest of the Aryan colonists of Bengal.

2. An entirely different view was taken twelve years later by Risley in his *Tribes and Castes of Bengal.* In his opinion Dalton's remarks about their physical appearance "referred only to the Kurmis of Bihar, and the caste bearing the same name in Chota Nagpur and Orissa belonged to an entirely different type." He found them to be "short, sturdy and of very dark complexion. . . . . . . .closely resembling in feature the Dravidian tribes around them. . . . . In Manbhum and north of Orissa it is difficult to distinguish a Kurmi from a Bhumij or a Santhal, and the latter tribe, who are more particular about food than is commonly supposed, will eat boiled rice prepared by Kurmi; and according to one tradition they regard them as half brethren of their own sprung from the same father, who begot the Kurmis on the elder and the Santhals on the younger of two sisters. The distinct and well-preserved totemism of the caste is noticed at length below." After finding that "the sections in use among the Kurmis of Chota Nagpur are purely totemistic and that a large portion of the totems are capable of being identified," he comes to the conclusion that "the Chota Nagpur Kurmis are derived from the Dravidian stock and are perhaps a Hinduised branch of the Santhals."

3. In Volume V (*ii*) of his *Linguistic Survey of India* Sir George Grierson writes that the Kurmis of Chota Nagpur "are an aboriginal tribe of Dravidian stock and should be distinguished from the Kurmis of Bihar who spell their name differently with a smooth instead of a hard *r*. These two quite distinct tribes have been mixed up in the census." Many of these people speak a language of their own, commonly known as *Kurmali*, although, as Sir George Grierson points out, in Manbhum this language is not confined to the Kurmis alone but is spoken by people of other tribes also. In Bamra state, where it is spoken by undoubted aborigines, it is known as *Sadri Kol*. This language is a corrupted form of *Magahi*, but, to quote again from Sir George Grierson, "in this belt Maghahi is not the language of any locality. It is essentially a tribal language"—just as *Mal Paharia*, a corrupted form of Bengali, is the language of the aboriginal tribe bearing that name. With regard to the spelling of Kurmi with a hard *r*, it has been verified from the local officials that this differentiation is observed still. It may possess real significance, but the general tendency in Chota Nagpur to make the *r* hard is a circumstance that should be borne in mind.

4. In the District Gazetteer of Manbhum (1910) Mr. Coupland writes that the distinction between the Kurmis of Bihar and those of Chota Nagpur, "which is now generally accepted, is exemplified in this district by the fact that marked traces of the characteristic Kolarian village system remain, the *Mahto* or village headman of the Kurmis corresponding exactly with the *Manjhi* of the Santhals, the *Sardar* of the Bhumij and the *Munda* of the Ho races." The Kurmi Mahtos are included among the tribes exempted from the Indian Succession Act. By a printing error the name appeared in the original notification (issued about 20 years ago) as "Kurmi, Mahto" and in the revised notification which was issued very recently the word "Kurmi" only is retained. There is no doubt that, until quite recent years, the two communities were agreed in repudiating any connection with one another. The Bihar contingent would commonly allude to their namesakes of Chota Nagpur as the "Kol-Kurmis," and the latter were no less spirited in asserting their independent identity. Not only inter-marriage, but interdining was entirely out of the question. Even to-day, although it will presently be seen that these restrictions have been formally abolished by resolutions passed in solemn conclave, and although it is probably true that the Kurmis of Chota Nagpur no longer take the same pride in their ancestry that they used to do, no authentic case has come to notice of inter-marriage between the two peoples. The Superintendent of the Leper Hospital at Purulia writes that "a Kurmi constable from North Bihar at present resident in this hospital was very scornful when I suggested his eating with our local Kurmi patients." The same correspondent states that, in spite of Risley's observations about the (then)

prevalent totemism of the caste, he himself had for years been unable to find a Kurmi with a totem name "Within the last few months, however, at a village 21 miles from here I was assured by a fairly educated villager, very proud of being a Kurmi, that his name was *Bok* (paddy bird)—obviously a totem name."

5. The question at issue has in late years been agitated in courts of law. In the case of *Ganesh Mahto* v. *Shib Charan Mahato*, which was taken to the High Court (A. I. R. 1931 Patna, 305), both parties were Chota Nagpur Kurmis and they both admitted that they were aboriginal by race, the dispute being in regard to the succession law by which they were governed. It was eventually held that, where parties to a suit admitted that originally they were aboriginal but their families had subsequently become Hindus and had adopted the Hindu religion, it was upon the party alleging that they were not governed by the ordinary Hindu law of inheritance and succession to prove any special custom or rule of custom prevailing among, *e.g.*, the Kurmi Mahtos of Chota Nagpur. This ruling, while of considerable interest in itself, clearly does not help to establish the kinship between the two Kurmi castes. More pertinent to this question is the decision in *Kritibash Mahton* v. *Budhan Mahtani* (6 P. L. T., 604, 1925) that the term *aboriginal* in Chota Nagpur denotes race only and implies nothing as to religion ; on the other hand, the term *Hindu* has in Chota Nagpur reference only to religion. There can be no question but that the Kurmi Mahtos are completely Hinduized and have been for many years. They are in general much better educated, much more prosperous and enterprising, than the other aboriginal tribes or the low-caste Hindus, and they have succeeded in retaining their self-respect in a degree which is uncommon among primitive tribes converted to Hinduism. It is doubtless this circumstance which is now leading them not only to identify themselves with the Hindu caste which happens to bear the same name but also to join with that caste in affirming their Kshatriya origin.

6. Whatever the motives may be, there has certainly been a great deal of agitation in this behalf during the last decade. In the year 1923 caste *sabhas* were held in more than one centre of Manbhum district and various resolutions were passed. It was decreed that Kurmis should no longer eat chickens or drink wine ; Kurmi women should work not as casual labourers for persons belonging to other castes ; they (the women) should wear a second garment, and should not go to the *bazar* by themselves but should always be accompanied by menfolk of their own caste ; when a Kurmi died, his *sradh* ceremony should take place on the twelfth day after death, as with the Kshatriyas of Bengal, instead of on the tenth day as heretofore. The 17th session of the "all-India Kurmi-Kshatriya conference" was held at Muzaffarpur in the year 1929, and three delegates from Manbhum were present as representatives of the Chota Nagpur Kurmis. "There it was settled that there is no difference between the Kurmis of Chota Nagpur and the Kurmis of Bihar proper. The three delegates returned home from the conference after taking the sacred thread." This was followed in the same year by another large *sabha* at Ghagarjuri in Manbhum, which was attended by a representative of the Kurmis of the United Provinces, and on this occasion "it was settled that the Kurmis of Chota Nagpur and Kurmis of United Provinces and Behar are akin to each other and there will be inter-dining and inter-marraiges among the said Kurmis ;" also that "the Kurmis of Chota Nagpur would join closely with the *all-India Kurmi Kshatriya Association* and will be guided by the directions of it." At this gathering "it was explained that the Kurmis are Kshatriyas and they have right to wear sacred thread, and some fifty Kurmis wore the sacred thread in the conference with the help of genuine Brahman priests." The correspondent from whom the foregoing extracts are quoted, himself a Kurmi Mahto and a member of the legal profession, adds that "thereafter the Manbhum Kurmis began to take *jangupabit*, though less in number." His ingenuous narrative continues :—"The Kurmis' conference caused a great sensation among the Kurmis, and the caste got the courage of raising their status. And there was such wonder in the mind of the non-Kurmis of Manbhum that Panchet raja, having come up from the ancient Kshatriya royal family of the district, accepts the Kurmis as Kurmi Kshatriyas. The Panchet raja took great interest in the upliftment of the Kurmis. He advised the social leaders of this community to carry out the resolutions passed in the Ghagarjuri conference, and he gave them power in writing for the purpose, and the mass carried out the resolutions of the Ghagharjuri conference to a great extent." In 1931 the session of the all-India Kurmi Kshatriya conference was held in Manbhum, and was signalized by the adoption of the sacred thread by more of the local Kurmis—the estimates vary from two hundred to a thousand. The same correspondent notes that "some orthodox Kurmis residing in Para and Barabhum P. S. made protest meetings against the use of sacred thread by Kurmis, but the use of sacred thread is increasing day by day in all parts of the district of Manbhum."

7. It may be questioned whether this movement is calculated to promote the best interests of the Kurmi Mahto community. As aboriginals, they receive the benefit of a special measure of protection from the revenue laws of Chota Nagpur ; for instance, the transfer of their holding to non-aboriginals is not permitted. It may be that the true position in this respect is not appreciated by many of them. On the other hand they may be prepared to forego such privileges for the greater honour and glory which they believe will accrue to them in their new status ; and it is quite true that, in view of their material prospectity, they do not stand in the same need of protection as the other aboriginal tribes of the locality. As already stated, it is not possible to give accurate statistics of the Kurmi Mahto community, but something over 660,000 "Kurmis" were enumerated on the Chota Nagpur plateau, and the overwhelming majority of these (about half of whom were found in Manbhum district) would undoubtedly be Kurmi Mahtos.

Note by the Census Commissioner for India.

It is suggested in view of what Dalton says, and after all he is the earliest authority, that the Kurmi-Mahtos represent an amalgamation of the brachycephalic Pamiri stock which it has been suggested in the Report preceded the Rigvedic Aryans as invaders of northern India. This would account for the traditions found by Dalton and for the existence in Kurmi-Mahto villages of rude stone monuments which may have been the remnants less of expelled Kolarian tribes than of the Kolarian ancestors of Kurmi-Mahtos amalgamated with an intrusive stock itself partly assimilated to the aborigines in the course of time.

There is still time to clear up the point. Careful measurements with coefficients of racial likeness, and blood tests, should show in what respects the Kurmi-Mahto differs from the plains Kurmi, and also from the Munda, Santhal and Oraon. If it be found that he has a definitely higher degree of brachycephaly and a definitely higher proportion of B blood group than is found in the Kolarian tribes without reaching the standard of the plains Kurmi in these respects the hypothesis I suggested will be fairly established, and the Kurmi-Mahto a clear monument of the Alpine migration into India and the process of its absorption.

J. H. H.

9. Notes on the Santals and other Chota Nagpur Tribes.

(i) The Santals.

By W. G. Lacey.

The number of Santals enumerated in Bihar and Orissa at the present census was 1,712,133. They are easily the largest of the primitive tribes found in the province, and they outnumber every Hindu caste except the Goalas and the Brahmans. They are of course most numerous in the district which bears their name : rather more than one person out of every three in the Santal Parganas is a member of this tribe. Over the province as a whole there has been an addition of 234,662 (or about 16 per cent.) to the number of Santhals enumerated at the last census.

2. The early history of the tribe is still wrapped in mystery. Some hold that they, along with other Munda peoples, entered India from the north-west, and have steadily moved in an eastward direction ever since. A later theory, which is perhaps more generally favoured by present-day investigators, holds that they came originally from the east and penetrated to a point a little beyond Benares before they began to turn back again. The views that have from time to time been advanced on this subject are reproduced more fully in the District Gazetteer of the Santhal Parganas, which also contains a most interesting account of their traditions, tribal organization, religious beliefs, social customs and other characteristics.

3. There is no doubt that by the beginning of the nineteenth century the Santals had established themselves on the plateau of Chota Nagpur. Hazaribagh, Palamau and Singhbhum appear to have been their especial strongholds at the time, but they were already beginning to make their way towards the district which is now known as the Santal Parganas. It was in the middle of the century that their migration to this particular locality took place on a grand scale, and it has been suggested that many of the persons shown as immigrants into the district at the census of 1901 were the survivors of those who had taken part in that movement. But by that time they were already on the move again. " The Santals," wrote Mr. (now Sir Edward) Gait in 1901, " are spreading north and east, and the full effect of the movement is not exhausted in the districts that adjoin the Santhal Parganas, but makes itself felt even further away, in those parts of Dinajpur, Rajshahi and Bogra which share with Malda the elevated tract of *quasi*-laterite known as the Barind. These wanderings of the Santhals have hitherto been confined to a laterite soil, and they are said to be averse to the payment of rent. In what direction they will spread when they have finished their work of reclamation in the Barind it is impossible yet to conjecture. The future alone can show whether they will then accept the inevitable and settle down as permanent rent paying cultivators, or move further afield, overcoming their dislike to alluvial soil, or retrace their steps and rove once more in the infertile uplands of the Chota Nagpur plateau."

4. The table below shows the strength and distribution of the Santhal tribe in Bihar and Orissa and in Bengal at the time when the above words were written and the variations that have occurred at each subsequent census :—

Locality.	Actual number of Santals.				Percentage of total population.			
	1931.	1921.	1911.	1901.	1931.	1921.	1911.	1901.
1	2	3	4	5	6	7	8	9
Bihar and Orissa : ..	**1,712,133**	**1,477,471**	**1,407,346**	**1,298,347**	**4·0**	**8·9**	**3·7**	**3·6**
Santal Parganas ..	754,804	676,450	608,149	670,535	36·8	37·7	35·6	37·1
Purnea	46,995	34,995	21,023	6,843	2·1	1·7	1·1	0·4
Bhagalpur ..	30,799	33,503	25,249	26,632	1·4	1·6	1·2	1·3
Monghyr	26,742	23,080	20,479	19,857	1·2	1·1	1·0	1·0
Hazaribagh ..	129,103	98,738	93,269	78,379	8·5	7·7	7·2	7·7
Manbhum ..	282,315	238,747	232,296	195,400	14·6	15·4	15·0	15·0
Sighbhum ..	108,890	94,381	88,241	77,363	11·7	12·4	12·7	12·6
Feudatory States ..	309,540	261,791	247,791	211,937	6·7	6·6	6·3	6·4
Elsewhere ..	22,981	15,777	11,377	11,500	·09	·07	·05	·05
Bengal	**796,656**	**712,040**	**670,689**	**570,727**	**1·6**	**1·5**	**1·4**	**1·3**
Dinajpur	130,338	120,211	110,244	110,101	7·4	7·0	6·5	4·7
Malda	72,145	72,140	66,520	52,126	6·8	7·3	6·6	5·9
Bogra	5,351	7,182	5,836	4,533	·5	·7	·6	·5
Rajshahi	25,591	21,300	14,145	4,858	1·8	1·4	1·0	·3
Jalpaiguri ..	27,859	23,988	32,641	10,895	2·8	2·6	2·5	1·4
Birbhum	64,079	57,180	56,087	47,738	6·8	6·7	6·0	5·3
Burdwan	101,522	79,090	65,978	46,533	6·0	5·5	3·3	3·0
Bankura	114,577	104,912	115,017	105,722	10·3	10·3	10·1	9·5
Midnapur	169,750	152,751	161,523	148,391	6·1	5·7	5·7	5·3
Hooghly	38,013	34,963	23,992	9,966	3·4	3·2	2·1	·9
Murshidabad ..	22,725	18,401	14,393	12,556	1·7	1·5	1·0	·9
Elsewhere ..	24,716	19,913	15,314	23,308	·07	·06	·05	·08

During these thirty years the total strength of the tribe in the two provinces combined has increased from 1,869,074 to 2,508,789. This represents an increase of over 33 per cent. in a single generation—a rate of growth just double that achieved by the population of this province as a whole, and a striking indication of the hardy, prolific character of the tribe.

5. The first decade of the century witnessed an acceleration of the outward stream of migration from the Santal Parganas. At the census of 1911 the number of persons born in that district and enumerated elsewhere was no less than 321,283, an increase of 95,000 over the figure recorded ten years earlier. Not all of this vast army of emigrants were Santals, but it is safe to say that the great majority of them were. For, although conditions during the decade had been generally favourable for a rapid increase of population (particularly on the Chota Nagpur Plateau, where the average rate of growth was as much as 14 per cent.), there was an actual decline in the number of Santals enumerated in their home district. The flow into the Barind was still strong, the districts of Dinajpur and Rajshahi being the recipients of most of the fresh emigrants to this part of Bengal. Further to the north-east the tea-garden districts of Jalpaiguri and Darjeeling absorbed a substantial overflow, while some 59,000 Santals were found still further afield in the province of Assam. But his decade saw also the beginning of a new movement into the purely alluvial tracts of Purnea and Hooghly districts. Moreover, the Santals were now showing signs of retracing their steps in a southerly and even in a westerly direction. The increase in their numbers during this period (1910-11) in Manbhum, Hazaribagh and the Orissa States is too great to be ascribed entirely to natural growth. In the two first-named districts the coalfields were the main attraction, and the partiality of the Santal for labour of this kind was responsible also for a marked rise in Burdwan district.

6. During the next decade the eastward current of migration was very much less pronounced. The total number of emigrants from the Santal Parganas in 1921 was less by about 23,000 than it had been at the previous census, and, despite the ill-health and economic distress of 1918—20 which prevented the population of the province as a whole from registering any progress, the number of Santals residing in the Santal Parganas was greater at the end of the decade than it had been at the beginning. This circumstance is the more remarkable because agricultural scarcity had compelled many who would not otherwise have left their homes to emigrate to the tea-gardens of Assam, and over 84,000 Santals were enumerated in that province in 1921, as compared with 59,000 in 1911. Very few fresh emigrants found their way into the Barind, but the thrust into Purnea and Hooghly continued, and there was a temporary movement across the north-western border of the district into Bhagalpur.

7. The present census does not record the number of persons born in the Santal Parganas and enumerated outside the province. Emigrants from that district to other parts of Bihar and Orissa are almost, but not quite, as numerous as they were ten years ago, but there must have been a heavy decrease in emigration to Bengal and Assam. It is significant that in this province the strength of the tribe has increased since 1921 by 16 per cent., while in Bengal the rate is barely 12 per cent. In practically none of the Bengal districts, except the colliery areas of Burdwan, is the increase in numbers out of proportion to the natural growth of the tribe; and, although of course it is not suggested that all the Santals who were enumerated in Bengal in 1921 have remained there ever since and multiplied in the ordinary course of nature, the figures do indicate that there are nowadays very few fresh emigrants who are making a permanent home in that province. In Assam statistics of Santals were not compiled on the present occasion, but there has been a decline of just over 1,000 in the number of persons speaking Santali as their mother-tongue, and it is therefore probable that the number of Santals has fallen also. Within the province of Bihar and Orissa there has been a further development in the streams of migration to Purnea. Hazaribagh, Manbhum and the States. The present indications, therefore, are that the movement of this tribe to the north-east has been definitely checked for the time being, and that a great number of them are settling down in their own district as permanent rent-paying cultivators. Such migration as is now taking place is not governed by any fixed principle but is the result of ordinary economic pressure, and its direction is determined by the availability of land (whether laterite or alluvial) and the scope for labour of a kind which appeals to the Santals, such as work on tea-gardens or in coal-mines.

(ii) Notes on the Santals.

By P. O. Bodding.

The Santals are as a people endogamous, but divided into twelve exogamous septs of which one is reported lost. Marriage between persons belonging to the same sept is forbidden. Persons who break this custom or rule are outcasted, if they belong to the same subsept. The septs referred to are divided into a number of subsepts, theoretically in twelve in each sept, in reality sometimes more, sometimes not so many. Marriage between persons of the same sept, but of different subsepts is not looked upon as quite good, but such ones will not be outcasted. These subsepts have possibly something to do with a wish to find a way out of the difficulties in finding wives. It should be remarked that in counting relationship the mother's side is not taken into account, except for the nearest relatives. Their traditions tell that during their ancestors' stay in a country called Champa their 'kings' belonged to the Kisku sept, the Nurmu sept were priests, the Soren sept were peadas or soldiers, the Hembrom sept were 'princes', a kind of nobility, the Tudu sept were musicians and workers in iron and the Baske sept were merchants or traders. There is, however, no precedence among the septs at present, but some of the septs are theoretically inimical, in this way, that most septs will not intermarry with persons of especially two septs. I am under the impression that people of these despised septs may, where not known, have declared themselves as belonging to one of the other septs.

The organization is democratic, interwoven with patriarchal strains. In a genuine Santal village there are five officials, a headman and his deputy, a *custos morum* and his deputy, and a man who is the headman's messenger and often the most influential village official, wherefore he is nicknamed the 'big headman.' Besides they have two priests, the *ato naeke*, village priest, who has to worship (sacrifice to) the national godlings, and the *kudam naeke*, lit. the priest of the place behind the house, who has to attend to the worship of the spirits supposed to reside in the neighbourhood. As a rule the positions may be called hereditary, especially so far as the headman is concerned; but the village people may depose any village official and elect a fresh one. So far as the headman is concerned, they have to get the deposing and the electing sanctioned by the local head of the district. In this connection a very curious custom should be mentioned. The month of Magh is with the Santals a month of importance; during this month the servants leave and fresh ones are engaged. Then the village people after having had a sacrifice to the national godlings eat and drink, whereupon they all surrender their positions and lands into the hands of the village, the headman his office to the village people, and these their lands to the headman, only reserving for continued possession their old sites and their huts. The Santal expression is explained as meaning " their wives." All the officials do the same as the headman, also the priests. A week or so afterwards the headman calls the village people together and gives them plentifully of beer to drink and offers his services again as headman and is accepted as the only possible good headman ; afterwards all the other officials do the same, and also the village people receive their lands back. It is now looked upon as a pretext to come together and drink during the off season ; I have mentioned it, because it is an indication of how Santal society in former times has managed the community. The village is practically ruled by the headman and his deputy ; nothing of a socially binding character can be done without the headman being a party to it. he as the representative of the village. In villages where there is no regular headman the Santals will appoint one of their number to be what they call a ' beer-headman ' (because beer is an integral part of their social function) who functions as their representative and leader in all social matters. As will be understood, their social system is a democracy with chosen leaders to which responsible authority is given. In all social matters, and also in other matters that they do not wish to bring before a court, the village council, called the Five men, probably a name adopted from the Hindus, will pass judgment. Any one may go to the headman and complain ; the headman sends the *godet* to call the village people together at a certain time and a suitable place. The headman will act more or less as the president ; everybody may be present and also speak ; the contending parties may bring somebody or other, even several persons to assist, Santals who are known to be able to talk well and are supposed to know the Santal customs and ' law '. There may be endless talk, but in the end they generally manage to do what is right, although the opposite may also happen, especially when some of the council have been bribed by money or by beer, or some other strong influence has been able to make itself felt. It is not, however, often to hear complaints. One peculiarity should be mentioned in this connection a village council will generally not pass judgment, until a guilty person has confessed ; many devices are resorted to and much time is spent in attempts to bring this about, when the council are convinced. In cases where the inhabitants of more than one village are concerned a combined meeting is arranged, generally under the presidency of a parganait or a so-called Des-manjhi. It should, however, be mentioned that this old method of adjudicating matters is now getting more or less out of vogue. Instead of parganaits they have got sardars in many places and these hold more or less regular meetings having a more official character. The village councils, however, continue ; one might be tempted to style them peace-making councils, or an institution to restore normal conditions in the community. They try to do away with all causes of social disturbances. To give one, otherwise rare example. When a case of social scandal has been settled and the guilty party fined they dig a small hole in the ground. Into this the complainant, the one punished and a representative of the village council each put a small ball of cowdung and another of earth into the hole, whereupon the hole is filled up with earth and a stone put on it, and it is said, that if any body should mention the matter now settled and buried, he will be punished and will have to pay the double amount of what the guilty party has paid. It is symbolic action.

The highest national council of the Santals is the hunt-council. From the middle of April the men of the country-sides have great hunts. They hunt during the day through a forest and assemble in the evening at a place previously agreed on, called *gipitic*, *i.e.* ' assembled lying down '. Here they spend the night partly in merry-making, but so far as the more mature men are concerned in judging any matter brought before this council that represents the whole people, *e.g.*, outcasting is decided on by this council and the judgment is enacted the day following or the next. At the hunt council the village officials have no more standing than anybody else, a servant boy is equal to a parganait, they say. The place is dark and the meeting is presided over by the hunt-priest, a Santal who is elected for this purpose and who decides the time and place of the hunt, performs sacrifices in connection with the hunt, in fact everything. I have been present and have been much impressed. I am sorry to be obliged to add, that I have heard reports of the doings of these meetings during later years having become somewhat degraded.

We have to do with democracy. The Santal loves his individual independence and is liable for this reason to break away from individual authority, but is loyal in connection with the decisions of his village council, which he will not disobey, but in some very rare cases he may appeal to the hunt-council, or, it must be added, may run away from the village, because the people would have no desire to let him mix with themselves in all social matters ; the communal feeling is strong in a Santal.

I have not said anything about the patriarchal strain. It is not much different from what may be found elsewhere.

The Santals have a number of traditions, some with a good many details, describing the wanderings of their ancestors. They begin with the creation of the world and of the first human pair, describe how these were holy, until a being, indentified with the present principal godling, called Marang buru (lit, the big mountain, and whose real name is said to be Lita, a name found in their name for the rainbow, Lita's bow) presented himself to them as their grandfather and taught them to brew beer and induced them to drink ; they became drunk and during this state had intercourse with each other and thus lost their sanctity. The traditions further tell, how humanity became depraved and God decided to destroy mankind, which he did, except that he shut a good pair up in a cave in a mountain called Harata. While they were there God destroyed all others by rain for seven days, whether it was fire-rain or other rain, the gurus say they have forgotten*, but in one of their songs "fire-rain" is used, and in what is told in stories about what happened when the pair came out from the cave, destruction by fire is pre-supposed. All present mankind are the descendants of this pair. They wandered together, until they came to a large plain called Sasang beda, lit, a turmeric plain along a river. Here they were divided into races, and the Santals into septs. From here the ancestors wandered towards the East, until they reached their present home. When recited, as is done at least twice in the life of a Santal the traditions are brought up to the moment of recitation. It will be seen that the earlier parts of the Santal traditions are heard like a corrupted edition of the first chapters of Genesis. According to the traditions the Santals and their ancestors have been wanderers from one country to another, sometimes staying for generations in one country, but when moving always more or less moving towards the East; and when emigrating at the present time the main direction is towards the East, not to the West.

All their traditions maintain the same direction and all present day Santals believe that they have come from the West. Some gurus, however, commence their recitations by stating the 'birth' of the race was towards the rising sun. This may or may not point in another direction. The traditions also tell that the first human pair were created of earth, but on the water. Here we very likely have some details introduced from foreign sources†. The traditional story is as follows :—

"Thakur" made the first human pair of earth; but when he was going to give them soul (life) the "Day-horse" came down and kicked them to pieces. Thakur was grieved and said, he would not make them of earth; he would make birds. So he created a pair of swans (*hås-håsil*) having taken (*kair*) from his breast. He kept this pair in his hand and breathed on them, and they became alive and flew off. But as they did not find any place to alight, they came back to Thakur.

Then the day-horse came down along the gossamer thread to drink water. When doing this he spilt and left some froth; this floated on the water.

Thakur now told the two birds to alight on the froth. They did so and were floating about all over the sea. But they had nothing to eat.

All was covered by water, and Thakur called upon a number of animals to bring up earth; none of these succeeded until the earth-worm was asked; but he promised to do so, provided the tortoise would stand on the water. The earth-worm had his tail on the back of the tortoise, ate earth with his mouth and let it come out on the back of the tortoise. (It is this part that I have taken to be borrowed.)

Now Thakur harrowed the earth, thereby producing hills and valleys. The froth mentioned adhered to the earth and Thakur sowed different seeds of grass and trees at last all kinds of vegetation. The birds made their nest in a clutch of Sirom grass (*Andropogon muricatus*), the seed first sown. Here they laid two eggs, and from these a boy and a girl were hatched out. Thakur instructed the birds how to feed them. They should let the juice of what they themselves ate fall on cotton, and this they should put in their mouth to suck. The next trouble was to where they should keep these when they grew up. They again implored Thakur, who told them to fly and find a place. They fly towards the setting of the sun and found Hihiri Pipiri, and at Thakur's order they took them there flying with them on their backs. This was the place where the first human pair lived. What happened to the two birds afterwards is not known, they say.

One thing more should be kept in mind. The Santals have a number of folk-tales dealing partly with witchcraft, partly with ojha-dom—the ojhas are their medicine-men—, partly with some fabulous beings. What is heard in these stories reminds one of Eastern matters. The man who according to their traditions first taught the ancestors medicine was a man, undoubtedly a Hindu, named Kamru. They also tell, that at one time their country and Kamru's country were bordering on each other; this might point towards a time when the ancestors were living near the present Oudh—they have folk-tales that mention their stay in these parts in so many words. On the other hand they have folk-tales that mention the Kamru country, and I have often been wondering whether this is not the old Kamrup.

It is not possible to be absolutely certain. The present day Santal language has in its vocabulary a large number of words that are related to words found in many of the languages spoken all over Eastern Asia and on the Pacific islands. There does not seem to be any question of relationship, only whether the connection has been in the East or in India or even before the ancestors of the present-day Santals came to India. I may mention, that some scholars are at

---

* *Cf.* Part I, Chapter XII. One Santal account definitely describes the rain as one of fire.—J. H. H.

† The Santal story of the creation of human beings out of mud has many parallels in Assam, Burma, Indonesia and Oceania. It is shared by the Korkus of Central India.—J. H. H.

present trying to make out a relationship between the Munda languages and the Finno-ugrian group of languages, and if this could be proved, it would influence our ideas to a certain extent.

In connection with rice the Santals have terraced cultivation. I do not remember to have seen the ridges revetted with stones. The slopes may be fairly steep, but never anything like what is seen in the Hills.

I have never been able to discover traces of megalithic stones or dolmens, etc., among the Santals. The cause of this may be, that the ancestors at one time deliberately gave up certain old customs and adopted new ones under Hindu influence, as the traditions expressly state. Among the customs given up was burial of the dead for which cremation was substituted with an addition that the bones—generally only two or three small ones—are taken to the Damuda river and immersed there at certain ghats.

The old way of building a house was to fix poles in the ground close together and plaster the walls with earth. Or the poles might stand somewhat apart the spaces between being filled up with branches kept in position by saplings. At present very many Santals during the dry season build walls of earth and fix a roof on these ; this they have learnt from the Bengalis. The roof will be mentioned below.

The following is a description of how a Santal would go about building a house for himself some fifty years ago ; for smaller houses the practice is followed now also. The man brings timber from the forest He fixes nine poles in the ground in three rows, three poles on each side and three higher ones in the middle and fixes three beams on the top of each of the three rows of poles. Next he fixes cross beams in pairs one pair at each end and one in the middle. Next he puts the roof rafters into position with three rows of saplings tied on one row at the top, one in the middle and one row at the eaves. Thereupon he makes a ramework of thin branches or split bamboo tied to the rafters and finally thatches the roof, using preferably a wild grass, called *sauri* (*Heteropogon contortus, R. & S.*) Thereupon he prepares the walls, filling the side walls with branches and plasters this, *i.e.*, his wife does all the plas ering and earth work. Inside in one corner a low partition is put up, to separate a small space for the ancestors, called *bhitar*. The centre pole is called *Kham Khunti*, the principal supporting pole.

Stones do not play any role in Santal house-building.

Above description refers to houses with a two-gabled roof, by the Santals called *bangla orak* Another form is a house with four-sided roof, by the Santals called *catom orak*, lit. umbrella house. Now-a-days all Santals may have houses of either description, but some must have the *bhitar* in a house having a two-gabled roof, or in the umbrella-roofed house and not in another. It depends on the rules of the sept to which the man belongs.

So far as houses are concerned there is outside a village headman's house, provided he is a non-Christian, a so-called *manjhi than*, a place for the original headman, by many Santals considered to be the first man. As a rule it is a small square place with a four sided roof rest ng on four poles, one in each corner and one pole in the middle ; sometimes one sees only a pole corresponding to the above mentioned central one. At the foot of this a small stone is placed, representing the spirit of the original headman. Here sacrifices are made to his spirit. Instead of the stone one sometimes may see a head of wood, the only sculpture that the Santals have, probably borrowed from the Hindus. The *Manjhi than* is generally erected in the village street on the side opposite the headman's house. People frequently meet here for talk.

Widows frequently wear only white clothes and no ornaments. This is likely something adopted from the Hindus, as it is not compulsory, and widows frequently remarry.

The sun, moon and stars are considered to be animate beings, the sun being the male, the moon female and the stars their children. A shooting star is called a star-excrement,* a comet a tail-star. Ursa major is called *Budhi parkom, i.e.*, the old women's bedstead, only, however, the four stars. The three stars, the shaft, are called *bursi kombroko*, the fire-pan thieves ; the star furthest out from the bed is always kept so far away, because he is always laughing. The three stars of the belt of Orion are called *arar ipilko*, the yoke stars, and three small stars close to the yoke are called *arar lalakko*, the yoke cutters or dressers. The Pleiades are ca led *sorenko* ; what *soren* means, I am not at present prepared to say, but it may be mentioned, that one of the twelve Santals septs is called *soren*, and *soren sipahi*, 'the soren soldier', is a very frequent combination. Two small stars near Vega in Lyra are called *potem bele*, the dove eggs. The milky way is called *hat dahar panjar dahar*, lit. the market place way, the rib way. They have a few other names, but as I am not sure of what they represent, I shall not mention them now. Of the planets Venus is as a morning star called *Bhurka ipil* and as an evening star *sukar*, this borrowed from the Hindus. One of the planets, rising in the morning, is called *angak ipil*, the dawn star ; the same is also called *adratia*, lit. the half-night star, and *cor kheda* the thief pursuing star, because it is believed that when thieves see this star they cease thieving and return home†. This star is generally Jupiter, but may also be Venus. As regards eclipses they have a couple of explanations, partly possibly borrowed‡. The most common is that once upon a time the sun or the moon or both together

* So the Kuki in Assam.—J. H. H.

† So the Angami calls the Evening Star the Thief-watcher.—J. H. H.

‡ Close parallels are found in Assam. See *Assam Census Report, 1921*, appendix B, and *Folk-Lore*, XXXVI No. 2 (June 1925). *Some Astronomical Beliefs in Assam.*—J. H. H.

stood security for humanity, when they had to borrow food from the Dusad, a certain godling. As the men are unable to pay back, Dusad now and again catches hold of the sun or the moon to get his dues ; this happens during an eclipse and the Santals call out and beat their kettle-drums to make the Dusad let his hold go. To explain the moon's phases they have a story. Formerly the sun and the moon had many children, the boys were staying with their father the sun and the girls with their mother the moon. On account of the terrible heat of the sun and his sons, all stars, it was felt as if all on the earth should be burnt up. The moon then suggested to the sun, that they should eat their children, and the sun said to his wife, that she should eat her daughters first ; if this was not sufficient, he would also eat his sons. Then the moon—a woman, we know their trickish nature, the narrator adds—put all her daughters under a large bamboo basket and hid them, whereupon she went to her husband and said, that now she had eaten all her girls, and still the heat was just as bad ; if he did not also eat his sons, mankind would perish. The foolish husband then really ate his sons, all the day-stars. When it became night, he saw that all the girls were there. He became very angry, took a sword, pursued his wife, the moon, and reaching her cut her. He might have destroyed her entirely, but as the moon gave him two of his daughters, he was somewhat comforted and left her. But every month he remembers her deceit and pursues her and cuts her, and the moon has very little rest, except for a couple of days. The two stars are Venus and Jupiter, that may be seen during day time.

As regards thunder and lightning : all natural phenomena are considered the acts of the Supreme Being " he rains, blows, thunders ", etc. They have several names for thundering, all probably, onomatopoeic, except one descriptive expression, literally translated " cloud-sound ". Like a number of other peoples the Santals believe, that the stone implements found in the ground are thunderbolts, *ceter dhiri*, lit. " stroke-of-lightning-stone "; *ceter* is their name for a stroke of lightning. The tale of Rama's shooting is heard among them ; I have, however, the impression that the Santals deem this only a story—some Santals may try to guard themselves against the lightning by keeping an arrow on the bowstring in aim against the threatening cloud.

The Santals have a ceremony called *caco chatiar*, when a child or a youth is given the full social rights of a Santal ; it is possibly a ceremony of purification and may be gone through at any age from say four to twelve years of age. Without having been through this no Santal may be married or cremated, but having been through this every Santal is burnt, with the exception of those mentioned below. The cremation is performed generally near some water ; the pyre is built so that it stands North and South. After a number of ceremonies have been performed the dead body is placed on top with the head turned to the South. All clothes, ornaments, etc., are removed and a branch with leaves is placed on the body to cover its nakedness. The nearest male heir is the one who has to set fire to the body. When the body is burnt, the heir washes the bones and pours turmeric water and milk on them and puts these small bones in an earthen pot, *viz.*, a bit of the skull and two bits of the collar bone. On the mouth of the pot a pot-sherd is put with a hole to let the dead one breathe through it, and in the hole they put a certain straw (*Rottboellia perforata*, Roxb.) by which the dead one may go out and in*. There are a good many ceremonies in connection with the cremation, and also the cleaning of the place and the doing away of what may not have been burnt. The above details have been mentioned, because they show some connection with the Munda practices. After cremation there are many ceremonies, the last one being an—according to means—large festival with sacrifices to the dead ones.

Santals who have not been through the *caco chatiar* are buried ; these are only very small children and they are buried without any ceremonies, so far as I have heard, in the forest, in a river bed, etc. Besides, those women who die during pregnancy are buried, if the foetus is not cut out after death ; I have heard that this has been done. While they who die and are cremated become bongas, spirits of the ordinary kind, women who die pregnant become a kind of spirits called *curin*†, and all who die either in the foetus state or before having the *caco chatiar*, become what is called *bhut*. A *curin* is supposed to be a spirit with a large head with hair standing out, and a *bhut* is very small. They are all considered dangerous.

A person dying from cholera is first buried and after a couple of months or so dug out again and cremated. The body is laid in a shallow grave, covered with branches, and the earth is filled into the grave. There is no coffin or anything.

Christians bury. The body is placed on a bedstead covered with a white cloth. When lowered into the grave some beams are placed above the bedstead in the two sides, strong enough to carry first a number of thick sticks and branches and the earth filled in.

There is no exposing of the dead body.

The Santals believe in the continued life of the soul. At death the soul leaves its hut. At the last funeral ceremonies the dead one is formally sent over to the dead ancestors with a request to these that the dead one may not be kept at the back of the house, *i.e.*, outside the community.

* *Cf.* the precisely similar custom of the Kacharis of Assam (Endle, The Kacharis, p. 47), the Kukis of the same province, the Kayans of Borneo, the sea Dyaks of the same island, and the Betsileo of Madagascar.—J. H. H.

† Hindustani *churel*.—J. H. H.

The ancestors have, according to the gurus, been told that God sends man to this world, and that He at birth gives every one by measure what he will need of food ; when there is no more left, he dies ; as will be understood, the Santals have a kind of predestination theory. They believe that God takes man away to the other world, judges him according to his deeds in this world ; a good man gets a good place, a bad one a bad place. The spirits have no power over the good ones, but they torture those who were bad. The ideas of good and bad are naturally to a certain degree dependent on the thoughts of Santal society ; the punishments in the other world are often thought to be always to be exposed to the sight of what they desired most here in this world, but without possibility of getting it. Certain sins are punished by the sinner being put in a mire of excrement. A man who dies without having paid his debts is called on to pay in the other world, and as he has nothing to give, they flay his back and sow salt in the sore, and when it heals the act is repeated. I do not think, the Santals ever combine this idea with what they owe to the Hindu money-lenders. I am under the impression, that the ideas mentioned play no large role, if any role at all, in the daily life of the Santals.

One may sometimes hear a Santal express a wonder whether they may become a lizard or a grasshopper after death ; they have some tales, that presuppose a belief in the soul of a living man being able to come out through the mouth in the shape of a small lizard. I do not think that the Santals have any real belief in transmigration.

The complexion is brown, rarely very dark, never black like that of Negroes, and often fairly light. Eyes are dark brown. I have seen two instances of something resembling a kind of blue. Hair is generally coarse and straight, black, in individuals sometimes a little bleached to a peculiar reddish brown colour by the Santals believed to be due to exposure to the sun. In individuals the hair may be wavy and frizzly and somewhat curly, never however like what is seen in Africa. Formerly both men and women kept their hair long, tied in a knot at the back of the head, the men's knot a little different from that of the women. Now-a-days men generally cut their hair. Women use plaits of the long hairs of the tail of a cow to assist in tying their hair knots. Eyes are straight, generally dark, but the iris is never quite black. The nose is generally broad and flat ; but they admire and wish to have a high-ridged and narrower nose. The head may have nearly all shapes, but by far the most common is the mesocephalic form. The Santals are generally sturdy, straight limbed and strong ; the height varies much but as a rule it is a little lower than what is seen among the neighbouring Aryans. Dr. Hrdlicka once wrote me that he thought that many Santals he had seen on tea gardens, to him seemed to be Negritoid ; I have myself often thought the same, my principal objection to this theory being that the Negritoid races are somewhat shorter in height than the Santals.

To get all necessary facts it would be most desirable to have the Santals scientifically measured ; it is not satisfactory to rest one's opinions only approximate observations.

I may add that the present-day Santals are not an unmixed race. During the last generations certainly, perhaps also formerly there must have been admixture of other blood, especially Aryan, perhaps also Mongolian. It should not be stressed, but it is a fact that the so-called Mongolian marks are found among them in certain families.

Rice is sown in beds the seedlings being transplanted—one kind of very rarely cultivated rice is sown where it is to grow—millets are sown broadcast ; the same is the case with most other cereals. Maize is planted each corn separately in the furrows by a man or woman following the ploughman. It should be remembered that the Santals have apparently learnt most of their cultivation from other races and are still learning ; they are among the best clearers of jungle in India, but must learn a good deal to become really good agriculturists. The most primitive and certainly oldest implement of the Santals is a wooden bar used for digging out roots, making holes, etc. Formerly it was a bar of hard wood ; now-a-days a flat piece of iron is fixed in one end. The plough is made a log of bent or bent-fashioned wood with an iron ploughshare fixed in a grove on the front upside portion. There are several shapes of the handle ; the plough has a beam that is fixed to the yoke. They have further a hoe or pickaxe with one narrow more or less pointed blade ; an implement called *kudi*, a 'kodali', the most spade-like implement they have consisting of a blade a little curved or concave, having a handle stuck through an iron shaft, some four inches high, fixed vertically in the middle of the one end of the blade ; the handle runs parallel with the blade, is just a little longer than the blade and has a top end sufficient for the user to take hold of when digging. The *kudi* is worked towards the user, not like our spade. They have also another hoe, having a flat piece of iron fixed at the end of a handle in the same way as the above mentioned pickaxe. All iron implements are made by semi-Hinduized blacksmiths. European made implements are coming in.

To level the earth and to carry earth for making a ridge, etc., they have a kind of large wooden shovel called *karha* ; a *karha* is a piece of flat wood, three to five feet long and ten to fifteen inches broad and some three inches thick tapering towards an edge ; a handle is fixed in the middle. At each end, or in some forms in the body of the *karha* near each end, a comb is cut (the Santals call it *nakic*, a comb), *i.e.*, part of the wood has been cut away leaving a big tooth standing ; a ring, at the end of the shafts or chains, is fixed here, the other ends in the yoke. When worked a man keeps the 'shovel' more or less upright by the handle and the earth is dragged along. When the place where the earth is to be left is reached, the man lets go the handle, the *karha* automatically turns over forwards leaving the earth there, and the bullocks drag the *karha* back to the starting point. There are several kinds of *karha* having different details but the principle is the same. They have a similar implement called *raksa*, used for levelling the surface of a rice field. The *raksa* is much longer and has a narrower wooden board with two holes cut through. The rings mentioned above, or rather the chain attached to them, are taken through these holes and something put through the rings to prevent them from slipping through.

They have further an implement called *ărgon*, a clod-crusher. It is a piece of wood some six to nine feet long and some six to eight inches broad and thick, with a beam to which the yoke is fixed ; some have two beams and some no beam at all, only holes through which chains are run. This is used for levelling the earth after ploughing or after the seed has been sown.

The Santals are a musical people. They have a flute with six holes and one hole for blowing. They are now-a-days generally bought from low-caste Hindus, but some Santals know how to make them. They have also some small pipes blown from the end, manufactured by themselves. They have a one-stringed fiddle also their own make, with a hollow ' breast ' as they call it, covered with a piece of skin, often of an iguana or some large snake. It is played kept in front of the operator, the string being turned away. They have a couple of other string instruments, one a hollow piece of wood or pumpkin, covered at the one end with a bit of skin, through which a double string is run. It is kept in the left armpit, the left hand stretching the two strings with a small bit of wood tied to the strings. It is only used when the disciples of the ojha go begging. It makes a marvellous sound. Another kind used for the same purpose and with similar sound is a bit of bamboo, often an old flute, to which pins are fixed and to these again two strings. At the middle of the bamboo an empty, hollowed out piece of a pumpkin is tied. When this is played, the pumpkin is kept against the stomach, while the playing is done with a wooden pin. They have a dancing drum, of earthenware, covered at the ends with skin, and strengthened with leather thongs, running round the body, conical in shape, *i.e.*, narrower at the one end, and also running lengthwise. They have further kettle drums of several shapes. They also have some instruments the sole aim of which is to make noise, generally for the sake of fun. They also have cymbals. They have a horn, made of the horn of a buffalo cow, with one hole for blowing. They have also other blowing instruments, but all got from others. It should be noted, that flutes and horns are always made in pairs with the same pitch. This serves a double purpose, they will know where the parties are, when hearing the sound, and if lost or stolen they are able to identify a flute or a horn. Dancing drums are also made in pairs. The flute, the horn and the fiddle are likely the original Santal instruments. The Santals use bows and arrows. The bow is generally made of bamboo, but also of some other resilient wood. The string is mostly of hemp, but is also often of bamboo. The string is always fixed at one end permanently, at the other upper end it is loosely tied so as not to get off. Here there is a loop and when the bow is to be used, this loop is slipped on to the bow end. Until this is done the bow is more or less straight and could not be used. With the string properly fixed, the bow is flexed and ready for use.

They have a large assortment of arrows, suitable for special different purposes. The arrows are mostly made of the *sar* grass (*Saccharum Sara*, Roxb.). *Sar* is the Santal name for an arrow. As a rule the arrow has cut feathers fixed to its end ; the arrow flies straighter with this. At the end there is a notch cut just deep enough to take the string. Arrows without the feathers are called naked. To shoot birds or small animals the arrow is blunt, having a bit of wood fixed some three inches long. To shoot animals they have arrows with iron heads. These heads vary very much in shape and size ; I have seen some twenty different arrowheads. They also have one arrowhead for shooting fish ; the head of this is not a point, but a curved blade.

They have also a pellet-bow with which to project small stones. Of spears they have had several kinds ; but these are not found any more. Battle-axes are found in a very few houses ; they are of different shapes and are now used for sacrificial purposes.

The Santals have a number of hunting implements and fishing nets, etc. They are all proofs that the Santals have studied the nature of the animals, birds, etc., that are to be caught, and have fashioned their implements accordingly.

The Santals are not head hunters and have not had any fight with others, so far as is known, where any practice of this kind has been observed. It might in this connection be mentioned, that they keep certain hairs and claws, etc., of leopards and tigers killed, and even eat the flesh of these in the belief that such eating will give them some of the qualities of these animals.

The Santals as they are called by outsiders, are not by any means what they were some time generations ago. They have during the past been developing and altering ; at the present time they are in a transitory stage, and I believe I am right saying, that their very existence as a separate people will depend on, how they manage to work their way through the present times.

The Santals have some very interesting traditions that start with the creation of the world and the first human pair and with the development of mankind, until they were divided up into races and the ancestors of the Santals were divided into septs, a story that seems to be a bad edition of the first eleven chapters of the Genesis. The traditions further tell of the wanderings of the ancestors, always apparently towards the east, a direction that the Santals follow in their migrations up to this date. They tell, how they tried to live in certain countries, and how they went away, apparently often to save themselves as a people from being 'defiled' by others. In India they have been in contact with Hinduism. I am inclined to think, that a good many of the low caste Hindus, or so-called semi-Hinduized aborigines of Northern India have originally belonged to the same people as the ancestors of the Santals; they have been absorbed by, or rather they have themselves originally attached themselves to Hindu society. The present day Santals are exposed to similar happenings. The Mohammedans have, on the other hand, apparently not been able to influence them.

The traditions tell, that at one particular time the ancestors deliberately decided to give up some old customs and adopt instead Hindu customs. Formerly they buried their dead ones; from that time they commenced to cremate. Their marriage customs were altered to suit many Hindu ideas, and so on.

They have been under the influence of Hinduism in many ways. They have seen the superiority and have felt some desire to become equal to them. Still when one get down to their innermost heart, one sees, there is much hopelessness; they have a feeling, that they some day will be bereft their all by the Hindus. Hinduism is at the present time influencing the Santals; it is not what is good in Hinduism that influences them, but specially what is grotesque or down right bad; a good many attend the Hindu festivals, not to worship, but to see (as they themselves call it) : and they furnish most of the din and noise. They are naturally influenced.

They were formerly a truthful and thoroughly honest people. They have learnt to lie from the others; they have seen, how the others manage to gain their purpose; they try to imitate. As yet they have not learnt to stick to the lie; it is not difficult to find them out. They are, I have been told, especially lying when they use not their own, but the Bengali or the Hindi language. It is a pity that they have to learn a foreign language to get a little education.

I shall not say more on these points; I have said so much to try to make the position of the present day Santals clear.

They have been struggling to keep themselves ntact, but have, as mentioned adopted a good deal not originally Santal.

If we look at their language we are struck by certain peculiarities. Their grammar is systematically pure; their vocabulary shows an immense number of words borrowed from Aryan language, especially Hindi and during the last two or three generations also from Bengali; but we also see, that every borrowed word has to be adapted to the phonetic peculiarities of the Santal language. It might be said, that the language provides safeguards, so that what is adopted must become fit for use; it may in this way help in developing without spoiling. The present-day schools are not very helpful in this respect. I suppose it cannot be altered, but it is not encouraging to see, how school authorities write Santal names and words.

As regards the special problems mentioned I have the following to say :

The exploitation of forests is undoubtedly influencing the Santals. The local zemindars have been selling the forest trees to raise money; there is apparently no law to prevent all trees from being cut; the land has in this way been made bare in many places, where there only a generation ago were good forests. This naturally deprives the Santals of the opportunity of bringing and using many things found in the forests and used by them in their households or for other purposes. On the other hand, the Santals themselves are far from good foresters; although they have been living in the forests and have had from these much of what they have needed for support, they have not thought of preserving forests. They apparently consider it their birthright to cut down any trees that have been of any use to them. To clear jungle is one of their strong points. When there is no forest they will have to take to agriculture and in this respect they have much to learn.

The Santals have cleared most of the country round here; but they have been deprived of their lands in many cases through running into debt and through not knowing, how to get the most out of their lands; I am sure, it is well enough known, how these matters are managed by the money-lenders and their debtors, so that I shall not say more about it. In parenthesis I shall add, that in order to teach the people to get more out of their fields it is necessary to let them see how it is to be done and to see the results; talk only has no effect.

A good many Santals work in the coalmines; they are well paid, too well, I am told. They do not know, how to spend money properly, if they have more than is sufficient for their wants. They will either start lending out money (which they have not as yet learnt to do in a sensible way) or they will use their money for drink or for women, with disastrous results. I have been told that Santals working in the coalmines earn enough by two days work to live (according to their standards) luxuriously the five remaining days of the week. There is another difficulty in connection with coalmines and teagardens or similar working centres. As a rule no questions are asked about the workers, and these places have often been refuges for people who have left wife and children at home and gone here with some other women. This is the dark side; there is naturally also another side. The people are taught to work and much else.

The influence of aliens is in many cases deplorable. All Santals living in these parts now daily see the other races and see that they in many ways are better off than the Santals; this cannot otherwise than influence them in their general outlook. The village authority is not what it has formerly been. The money lenders have a baneful influence, the shopkeepers also. One of the worst alien influences is perhaps that which affects their attitude towards truth; they see that lies may help others to gain their ends, why not try the same?

Very few Santals use narcotics, and always taught by aliens. They drink beer and partly country liquor; a Santal drinks to become drunk, in order for a short while to forget the troubles of life; to make the beer quickly intoxicating they add vegetable poisons, some of a dangerous nature. Santals who take to country liquor very soon become habitual drunkards and are spoilt.

As to diseases; the Santals tell that up to the Santal rising against the mahajans in 1855 they had no tuberculosis, leprosy or venereal diseases. It is likely a too sweeping statement; but these diseases have spread much among them during the last generations. A good deal of the venereal diseases is likely due to contagion from aliens.

Santals are not criminals, but they have learnt to do things, that they have not done formerly. In many cases I should be inclined to think, that they are not awake to the criminality of certain acts; this is naturally dangerous.

Very much might be said about the influence of education. As it is carried on at present I am afraid the results are not always desirable. The language used above the infant stage is foreign; this naturally to a great extent handicaps them, not only in competition with those who have the school language for their mother tongue, but a good deal of the imparted instructions will be either not understood or only partly understood and not digested. This use of a foreign language naturally has a deteriorating influence on the selfesteem of the people; the deduction is that what the others have is better and more suitable; the future is not for them in their own language, beside all that may be deduced.

Further, the school syllabus is not in all parts happy for the Santals. The syllabus may be good enough for those who intend to continue their studies up to matriculation; but except for certain parts it has not for its goal to make the Santal boys and girls better fit to tackle the daily problems and difficulties of village life.

It would be of the greatest and real benefit to the Santals, if they could get schools where they were taught in their own language, and got education in matters that would be of use to them in their village life and also in their intercourse with others. This would be a gain, not only to themselves, but also to others.

If anybody should want to get a higher education, he should have to use English. This would naturally help the Santals to see, that they were on the same level as the others and not inferior.

I may add, that so far as common sense is concerned, the Santals are in no way inferior to the other races here, that is to say, when they are not sidetracked by the others.

When the Santals live in their own villages, there does not seem to be much influence from others. The way in which their villages are built may be said to be fairly sanitary, much more so than what is found among other races in their neighbourhood. Their houses are not, however, sanitary; they are dark, without windows and only small holes to let smoke out and some air in; their houses are partly storehouses, partly houses for accommodating their fowls and often small pigs. During the hot and rainy season they will as much as possible sleep outside. They have much to learn in connection with their houses, but not from most of their neighbours.

Schools might have some influence in these matters, also by instructing people how diseases are spread.

Foreign customs are likely gradually creeping in especially what is seen with the Hindus, not with the Mohammadans who have very little influence on the Santals.

I do not think that much can be said as to law. There is naturally the influence of the laws as administered by the courts. There are some matters, that are criminal in acc. with the Penal Code, but that the Santals do not considered to be much so, and *vice versa.* Much has been done for the Santals, that they appreciate. One of their great difficulties is to save themselves from the money-lenders. A Santal may be said to understand the value of things, but very little of the value of money. He may understand the value of a pice, but not of a rupee, consequently he will take as much on credit as any one will let him have; but he has little thought of what it will cost to pay it back. If only something could be done to prevent the people from running into hopeless debt, and prevent the mahajans from running small original debts into large sums.

In one respect the Santals have shown a really good wish to better their state ; they are anxious to get the status of their womenkind bettered, so as to prevent these from being left defenceless and at the mercy of distant male relations when their parents die.

I shall not say anything about other missions that may have a practice different from the mission to which I belong. It has been our desire not so much to get Santal Christians as to have Christian Santals. We have so far as possible let our Christian Santals keep their social customs when there is nothing in connection with them that is immoral or combined with their spirit worship.

We have been obliged to set our face against drink, for the reason stated above, that a Santal drinks to become drunk ; anything that does not quickly intoxicate is considered worthless.

We have also been obliged to prohibit certain dances among our Christians ; the Christians themselves say that they feel ashamed, when they hear the dancing drum. Their most common dance, practically the only dance seen or heard in the villages on ordinary nights, is what is called *lagre* ; the dance itself is ordinarily innocent enough to look at, except the suggestive movement of the girls' bodies. What is especially objectionable in connection with this and some other Santal dances is the opportunity they give the sexes of meeting at night ; the opportunity is very frequently used for illicit intercourse. Some of the Santal dances are horribly obscene.

It has always been our wish, that the Santals should be kept as Santals, all our work has had this as a background. Personally I am of opinion, that if the Santals continue to be exposed to the influence of the Hindus, they will some day be found again as a new low caste that has attached itself to Hindu society, of little use to themselves and a danger to the country where they live, incidentally also a political problem. So far as I can see, they may be saved and become useful, even very much so, if they are helped in the proper way, and treated as deserving to be kept as Santals.

The present-day Santals are a virile race. There is, so far as I know or have observed, no reason to think that they are indifferent to the propagation of their race, rather quite the opposite. It is not to this side that the Santals problem shows itself.

Education has not in our mission led to discontent, perhaps because we have not as yet gone in for any higher education than Middle English.

I believe it would be advantageous for all, if the village councils could be given some more power and work, naturally with certain safeguards so that their work could be controlled. I believe, it is a fact, that a good many cases are brought to court that a Santal would never dream of beginning in his own village. He goes to the court as a speculation, thinking it may be possible to gain his end by the help of a pleader or by the lack of knowledge on the part of an alien judge.

(iii) (a) Other notes on the Santals, etc.

By F. Rowat.

(English Missionary since 1888.)

Santals are divided into eleven exogamous clans.

Several clans like Kisku or Murmu are considered better than other, their kings were chosen from the Kisku class and their priests from the Murmu class.

The chiefs or Parganaits are drawn from all the clans.

The order seems to be democratic. The people being represented by chosen headmen of villages, desh Manjhi, desh Parganait, etc.

Much different opinion expressed, and traditions quoted regarding origin from N. W., N. E. or S.; probably from the S.

No existence of terraced cultivation before them. Jungle lands and slopes have been prepared and made into rice fields by these settlers.

No traces of megalithic monuments as in the Khasia hills. Stone for seats not used.

Materials used for building include walls of mud sometimes, a little stone, sal wood for rafters, bamboos for lathes, thatch of grass (*souri*) or straw (paddy) sometimes palm leaves and the leaf of the sugarcane are used for thatch. String made from *saboi* or *babai* grass. Certain kinds of trees such as bael or banyan never used as timber in a roof.

Social position is not indicated by shape of their houses or colour of the clothes they wear.

It is held that any extension of a house should not be towards the S.

Ideas as to the sun. The sun is regarded as Masculine Gender referred to as Babba (father) the moon is a wife, therefore feminine and the stars are called the children of above. They have names for the different constellations the " milky way " is called the elephant's way or path. The seven stars are referred to as seven brothers and sometimes called the old women's bed.

The sun is worshipped as a God, thakur, and a goat is sacrificed to the sun (not annually) but after 3 or 5 years. This is said to preserve the worshippers from disease and is faithfully performed by the majority.

Earthquakes are said to be caused by the moving of a tortoise. According to the Santal tradition a worm raised or created the Earth on the back of the tortoise, the earth thus became established on the back of a tortoise, and the moving of it is said to be the cause of earthquakes.

Rainbows are said to be the bow of the mythical hero Lita. It is generally believed that neolithic stone adzes fall frequently during severe storms accompanied by thunder and lightning.

Eclipses of sun and moon.—The shadow on the sun or moon is said to be the hand of a money lender wishing to seize it for arrears of debt. The Santals respond by beating the alarm drum used for assembling the clans, when danger is threatened by the approach of an enemy or wild beasts. During the eclipse a fast is observed, a woman with child must not be observed, presents of rice must be brought out of the house. The money-lender is urged to relinquish his hold on the sun or moon. The sun is always referred to as an animate object.

Methods of disposal of dead.—Cremation is the rule, except during epidemics of influenza or cholera, when the body is disposed of by burial. Sometimes after three days or when the epidemic has passed the body is exhumed and cremated.* This is a bad practice and should be punishable as it is often the cause of a fresh outbreak.

Lepers are not cremated but accorded decent burial. A bone from the breast and one from the head are taken from the body and carried to the Damodar river for disposal. The departed are called upon not to return to the village to cause sickness and death. Offerings of pice, etc., are buried in the sand of the river.

Beliefs abode of dead.—Transmigration is not believed in. They say the departed has gone to be a shepherd of crocodiles, or to become a Churin, *i.e.*, female god or evil spirit. Animism is believed by all.

(b) Notes on the Santals.

By W. N. Hearn.

Santals marry only with Santals of a clan other than their own. Santal tradition says there were originally 12 clans, but only 11 are known to exist now ; and all are now co-equal, although in olden time the several clans had distinct functions to perform, such as " Kisku Raj ", Soren-Sipahi, etc.

Santals have over-chiefs called pergannaits a position of honour which is usually hereditary. Village organization is democratic being invested in a council of five persons, *viz.*, Manjhi, Parganait, Jog Manjhi, Naek, Godet, the Des Manjhi acting as caller, Chairman and acclaimer of decisions and rewards.

Santal traditions mention northern Orissa, Chai champa and Chaibasa as their original home.

Santals have no monuments of any description. Stone seats are often found in Santal villages ; but such are for the use of all in common.

It is a matter of common belief by Santals, that the sun is male and the moon is female. They believe the sun to be the creator and sentencer of the world and community sacrifice is made to it periodically.

The stars are supposed to be the offspring of the sun and the moon, but possessed separately and not jointly ; and an eclipse is supposed to be the result of one attempting to devour the other, on account of unpaid debt incurred on behalf of their family, and during such occasions Santals bring out their stores of grains into the open and with much shouting offer to pay the debt if the devourer will release his or her victim.

Santals burn their dead excepting victims of cholera which they bury ; they also bury all children for whom the " Chatiar " ceremony has not been performed ; which is both a ceremonial *cleansing* and a ceremonial admission into all the privileges of the tribe. No marriage can take place with a person for whom Chatiar has not been performed.

Santals believe in a future existence in a human form a reward of peace for the good, and punishment for bad.

Recruitment for labour on tea estates, coal fields and in railway construction, has taken large numbers away from their village homes and has greatly demoralized them, and has made their one time simple honesty and truthfulness conspicuous by its absence.

A primary education does not appear to unfit them for their ordinary village life and social customs ; but the lack of it which is all too prevalent, leaves them an easy prey to the wiles and dishonesty of their non-Santal neighbours and money lenders.

* *Cf.* below, 11, viii, Khasis—J. H. H.

(c) Dr. Macphail of Bamdah contributes the following notes :—

The Santal tribe is divided into 11 exogamous septs. There are said to have been 12 originally, but only 11 are now in existence. Even among Christian Santals, marriage never takes place within the sept.

Each village chief is hereditary, descended from the founder of the village, but this office is not the prerogative of any particular class or sept.

The village is governed by the Chief, with the help of his panchayat. There are also hereditary *Parganaits* or district chiefs, and a *Dihri* for each large district, who is responsible for calling the annual hunt, and who presides over the Santal "High Court" on the night which intervenes between the two days' hunting........................

There is terraced cultivation, generally in flat valleys or on gentle slopes. I have sometimes seen it revetted with stone........................

According to Santal tradition, the sun is male, and the moon female, the stars being their children. These are all daughters, staying with their Mother, except the morning and the evening star, which are sons. There used, according to their traditions, to be a number of day stars, shining by day, but the moon persuaded the sun by subterfuge to do away with them, on condition that she would also do away with daughters—a condition which she did not fulfil.

Eclipses.—After an eclipse of the sun (*gahna*) a nephew goes to his maternal uncle and says to him : "I have come to release the *gahana*." The uncle makes him a present of anything from a fowl to cow. After an eclipse of the moon, the uncle goes to his nephew and is presented with something of a like nature by him. *Constellations* have the following names in Santal :—

The Great Bear=*Budhi Parkom* (*i.e.*, the old women's bed). Pleiades=*Sorenko*—this is the totem of the Soren sept. Orion's belt (the three stars of)=*Arar* (*i.e.*, plough). Scorpio (four stars of, three in line and one at apex of a triangle)=*Argom* (*i.e.*, a harrow). Lyra (two stars close together in)=*Potam bele* (*i.e.*, a pigeon's egg), Milky Way—*Hat dahar* (*i.e.*, the road to market). *The Rainbow* is called the bow of Lita, a traditional hero, who by teaching the first man and woman to brew rice beer was responsible for their fall from innocence. [This rather suggests the influence of some prohibitionist mission. J. H. H.]

Santals give to all natural phenomena a personal signification—*i.e.*, they do not say "it is raining" but "he is raining", "he thunders", etc. From this it may be deduced that they look on such phenomena as the activities of a heavenly being or beings, but apart from this I do not know that they have any specific explanation for various phenomena.

The dead are cremated. The skull and collar bones are retrieved from the pyre, and at some suitable future time taken to be committed, with certain ceremonies, to the waters of the Damuda River........................

The bow and arrow, and a rounded shield with a sharp point projecting from it, for purposes of attack, seem to be the chief weapons.

(d) Notes on Santals.

By Drs. Dempster & Kitchen.

"Of late, a new invasion of Santal customs has occurred in the form of congress and Hindu propaganda calculated to persuade the Santals to abandon their age-long customs and take to purely Hindu customs, such as the adoption of the sacred thread and vegetarianism. A bitter cleavage exists between those Santals who have taken the sacred thread (*janeo* or *suta*) and those who have not, resulting in social boycott and the insistence of the adoption of the 'suta' before intermarriage is allowed.

There is a tendency among the Janeo-dhari Santals to regard themselves as socially superior to their more conservative brethren.

The Parganaits seem to form a chiefly class ; they belong to all 'Paris'. The tribal organization is democratic. In the Santal system the village community is a unit, managed by a headman known as the Pradhan, who is, so to speak, the intermediary between the Santal community and the outside world. Disputes are settled by Panchaits and the public opinion of the community suffices to discourage dishonesty and untruthfulness. This system works very well in the Santal Parganas, but where the Santals have come more in contact with other more advanced civilizations, their system has tended to crumble, and their strength to decay.

There is a tradition among Santals here that Mount Parashnath is the Sinai of the race, where the ancient law-givers gave the Santals their laws. Their tradition is that they are the original inhabitants of the country.

Terraced cultivation exists both in the valleys and on slopes but not, as a rule, revetted with stones........................

The sun is a ball of fire, and the moon is his consort, and the stars their progeny. The Milky Way is a primrose path down which the sun and moon take their pleasurable walks. The markings on the face of the moon are due to ditches. Earthquakes are due to the tremors of a tortoise on which the earth rests. Eclipses are due to the harassments of a Dusadh from whom the sun and moon have borrowed money. The Rainbow is a bridge from white ant hill to white ant hill, along which the souls of the dead reach the sky. Thunder and lightning are the manifestations of an angry Deity, when out to kill.

The dead are burnt, although little children are buried and a heap of stones placed over their graves."

No. 3605 C. R.

(e) Notes on the Santals and Kherias of Manbhum District.

By Rai Bahadur C. C. Mukherji, O.B.E.

The following primitive tribes of forests or hill tracts are found in this district :—

(1) Oraons (2) Mundas (3) Santals and (4) Kherias. The population of these tribes in this district as reported in the census of 1921 were :—

	Hindus.		Animists.	
	Male.	Female.	Male.	Female.
Oraons	1,577	1,369	144	75
Mundas	1,148	1,070	48	17
Santals	104,274	105,271	14,767	14,222

The population of the Kherias in this district is small, *i.e.*, less than 1 per mille of the provincial population and it is not given in the Census Table XIII part IA of 1921 but I have included them in the list owing to the local importance of this tribe.

Kherias.—From the list above it will be seen that the number of Animist Oraons and Mundas is very small in this district. So I do not deal with them in this report.

Kherias.

The exogamous clans are :—

1. Sahar Bhuian.
2. Chang Bhuian.
3. Jati Bhuian.
4. Taru.
5. Budda.
6. Hemra.
7. Tesa.
8. Tiring.
9. Ubusanr.
10. Salgulgu.
11. Kauri also called *Dharma bandha Kauri*

and others (which could not be definitely stated by any Kheria).

The last named No. 11 are said to be the lowest in social position because they are said to have tied the bull of Lord Siva and wanted to kill it the next morning but the expected day never dawned.

There are two classes of Kherias. The Savar Kherias and Paharia Kherias. They do not intermarry. There is no definite order of social precedence. Each class thinks itself higher than the other class. There is no chief class or clan.

The organization, on social matters, is democratic. The decision of the Panchayat (in which the representatives of the families living in the village or villages concerned, sit) if not obeyed ensures expulsion from the community.

According to their traditions the Kherias, who are descendants of Angad, the Monkey Hero of Ramayana, came from the Nilgiris, when Ramchandra killed Bali the Monkey Hero by unfair means, Angad, the son of Bali was much grieved. Sri Ramchandra, however, told Angad that one of his descendants would kill Sri Ramchandra at his incarnation.

This tradition appears to have been borrowed from the Hindu Mythology.

Cultivation is done both on flat valleys and on slopes. On steep slopes terracing is not done, on slight slopes the fields are terraced.

The dead are either buried or burnt. At the time of burying, the small finger of the right hand is cut and kept in a small earthen pot which is buried under a dolmen on the 10th day after the death. If burnt a small bit of unburnt scalp is kept in for burial on the 10th day after death.

It is buried in the ground after placing it in a small earthern pot and a dolmen (one flat stone supported by 3 upright stone pillars) is erected so as to protect this pot from sun and rain. In the case of children and infants a single upright stone serves as the monument.

Each family has a separate place outside the village site for these monuments.

They believe that the dead go to Indrapuri (heaven) where judgment is delivered after counting the good and evil deeds done by the deceased.

The Kheria's ideas about the Sun is that he is Dharma and he is a male. They have no definite idea about the moon, stars and comets. At least one pigeon or cock has to be sacrificed by a Kheria yearly. The names of the different constellations are :—Pleides—*Sat Khatila* or *Sat Bhaiya*. The seven stars are believed to be seven brothers who are taking their parents for cremation.

Earthquake.—The earth rests on the heads of Vasuki a big snake with many heads. When one head of Vasuki gets tired she shifts the earth to another head and this causes earthquake.

The markings on the face of the moon are due to hares dwelling in it.

The eclipses are due to *Rahu's* eating the sun and moon. No explanation of the rainbow is given. The Thunder and Lightning are said to be caused by a piece of iron falling from the clouds to the earth. This piece of iron of which the size is that of a small ploughshare has never been seen by anybody.

They have no tradition about the treatment of heads taken from their enemies.

NOTE.—It will be seen that there is difference in some points between the accounts given in Colonel Dalton's Ethnology of Bengal pp. 158-161 and in Risley's Tribes and Castes of Bengal Vol. I, pp. 466-471 and the account given above.

Santal.

The different exogamous groups are :—

1. Kisku. 2. Murmu. 3. Soren. 4. Hansda. 5. Turu. 6. Hemrom. 7. Mandi.

The two main groups in which the Santals are at present divided are (1) the Deswali Santals who returned themselves as Hindus at the Census and (2) Tharua Santals who returned themselves generally as animists. Inter-marriage is prohibited between these two main divisions.

The order of social precedence amongst Tharua Santals is 1st Kisku, who is the highest in order, 2nd Murmus who are the Gurus or purohits and are generally called the "Thakurs" and 3rd Sorens, who were the fighting class.

The chiefs are drawn from the Kisku class. The father must be a Kisku.

The organization is not exactly democratic in social matters. There are *desh-mondal* (Heads of certain defined areas) who generally decide social questions.

Origin.—The account as given by the Tharua Santals is that they came from the West where in olden times a drake and a duck came and the duck layed two eggs on a karam tree. From these two eggs a man and a woman were born. They begat seven sons and seven daughters. The man went away with his seven sons for hunting and the woman went away with her seven daughters to pluck vegetables. The seven daughters after plucking vegetables near a pond were amusing themselves by swinging themselves on swing bars. The seven sons who came to the pond before the daughters after hunting and had drunk water from the pond were playing on their flutes at some distance. The mother of the seven daughters asked them to see who were playing on the flutes. The seven daughters went to see and they eloped with the seven sons. Then the parents whose names were Pilchu Haram and Pilchu Burhi went to the place where their sons and daughters were staying and Pilchu Haram gave Pilchu Burhi some grains of "Sama" grass and asked her to cook same. Then Pilchu Haram brought some roots of plants and asked Pilchu Burhi to grind these and put some ground roots and the juice of some roots into the pot containing the cooked grains. Then the parents left the place for four days instructing their children to drink the liquor of the cooked grains.

The children after drinking the liquor became intoxicated and lived as man and wife, and the parents on their return were pleased at the conduct of their children. One Tharua Santal said that they came from Sekharbhum.

The Deswali Santals have no tradition of their origin. The tradition of the division of the Santals into Deswali and Tharua as given by a Deswali Santal is that the original Santal had two sons one of whom was 'Kana' (blind) and the other 'Uja' (not blind). The descendants of the Kana's sons are the Deswalis and those of the other are the Tharuas.

Terraced cultivation of paddy exists on valleys. On slopes which cannot be conveniently terraced, rabi crops are grown.

A man can build his house with the materials he chooses and wear the cloth he chooses. The only difference between a Kisku and Murmu on the one hand and the remaining septs on the other is that the Kisku can use the palki (palanquin) and the Murmu the *Chaural* at the time of marriage for carrying the bride or bridegroom, whereas the other septs cannot use these.

The sun.—Dharma. He sits on judgment of all deeds of a dead person. He is a male.

The moon.—Bhagaban (a female).

The stars are the sons and daughters of the moon (Chando Bonga).

Comets.—They do not know what a comet is, but it is known that if it falls on the earth it will cause destruction. They have no name for Orion's Belt, the Hyades, Castor and Pollux, Hydra, Cassiopeia, the Great Bear, the Milky Way or Sirius. Pleiades is called "Sat-bhaiya".

The idea is that out of the seven stars six stars represent six sons of a deceased female carrying the dead body of their mother for cremation, and the seventh star is the seventh son following with a lighted *barh*. As the mother earth is not allowing any space for burning the dead body, the sons are carrying the deadbody for ever. The explanation of the markings on the face of the moon is that there is a tree in the moon.

Earthquake.—The earth rests on the back of a tortoise and when the tortoise moves any of his limbs the earth quakes.

Eclipse.—The sun and the moon, in order to maintain their children on earth, borrowed much money and other things from a *Mahajan* but could not pay up. This Mahajan catches the sun and the moon at times and eats them.

The Rainbow.—The idea is that it resembles Lakshman's (brother of Sri Ram Chandra) bow.

The idea about thunder and lightning is that Sri Ram Chandra and his brother Lakshman fire their guns.

The deadbody is either buried or burnt. If burnt a remnant of the burnt skull (a small piece) is kept in a new and stainless small earthen pot of which the mouth is tied with a piece of cloth dipped in turmeric solution. If buried the grave is dug on the 9th day of the burial and a piece of the skull is taken out and burnt and then kept in a new earthen pot as stated above. This earthen pot is kept hanging generally in the cow-shed. On the appointed day this bit of the skull is taken out and wrapped in a small new cloth and thrown into the Damodar river. In the case of the infants and children of tender age these ceremonies are not performed. The body is buried. There is no tradition regarding the treatment of the heads of enemies. The customs in regard to some of the above points are different in the case of the Deswali Santals (who call themselves Majhis).

There is no order of social precedence, and no chiefly clan. The organization is democratic in social matters. The decision of panchayat must be obeyed or the party will be expelled from the community.

There is no tradition of origin except that stated above in point 5 about the division into Deswali and Tharua from the same ancestor.

The remains of the dead are not taken to the Damodar but those who can afford take it to the Ganges.

Earthquake.—The earth rests on the head of the Bhuin-Champa Nag (serpent) and when this serpent moves, the earth quakes.

Thunder and Lightning.—Lightning is a piece of stone which falls from the clouds. But none has seen this stone.

The dead are either buried or burnt. Some stones are laid on the grave but no cairn is raised. No coffin is used. No monument is raised.

NOTE.—It will be seen that there is difference in some points between the accounts given in Colonel Dalton's Ethnology of Bengal pp. 207—218 and in Risley's Tribes and Castes of Bengal Vol. II, pp. 224—235 and the accounts given above.

(f) Notes on the Sauria or Maler Paharias.

By Radharaman Ghosh.

I have collected as much information as possible from a cursory perusal of such literature as is available in my office library dealing with the Rajmahal Paharias and from hasty local enquiries made at Sahebgunj and Mandro.

The Rajmahal Paharias or as they are better known Sauria or Mal Paharias belong to a race distinct from the Mal Paharias of the South. The district Gazetteer divides the Paharias into two branches, *viz.* (1) The Maler or Male or Sauria Paharias and (2) The Mal Paharias. According to some authorities the two branches are quite distinct in race, history, forms of worship, etc. The Sauria Paharias are a "Dravidian" race and in the District Gazetteer we find the following "A clue to their origin is found in the tradition of the Oraons that their original home was in the Carnatic, whence they went up the Narbada river and settled in Bihar on the banks of the Sone. Driven thence by the Muhammadans, the tribe split into two Divisions. One of these, now represented by the Oraons took possession of the North-Western portion of Chota Nagpur. The other following the course of the Ganges settled in the Rajmahal Hills and were the progenitors of the Maler." According to some the tradition of the Oraons is not reliable and while their descent from the Dravidian stock is maintained they are said to be the original settlers in the Rajmahal Hills even prior to the Aryan invasion.

I have not been able to find out any existence of groups or classes amongst the Sauria Paharias.

There is no chief class or clan from which Sirdars, Naibs or Manjhies are drawn. Their posts are generally hereditary.

Violation of social, matrimonial and religious customs and petty disputes are settled by the Manjhies, Naibs or Sirdars with the help of villagers. Otherwise there is no democratic organization amongst them.

Terraced cultivation exists in some hills but the main is the *kurao* by the process of Jhooming on hill sides. Plough is rarely used. The process is described in Mr. Day's Settlement Report.

There is no megalithic monument in existence. The Sirdar, the Naib and the Manjhi or the Chief of a hill are only privileged to sit on a stone. The Sirdar is however given the precedence if he is present. The Naib in the same manner is given the precedence over the Manjhi.

A paharia uses only bamboo and straw in making his home. A hut with two or three entrances is generally made. The roof is generally made in one piece of whole bamboo and split bamboo pieces bent down to form a semi Circle and thatched with straw while the walls are made of wattled bamboo and grass. The Paharia huts are always erected north and south, all in rows about 10 feet apart.

The Sauria Paharias, as Mr. Bainbridge in his " Saurias of the Rajmahal Hills ", pay regard to the sun and the moon as visible representatives in the heavens of Ber or Beru Gosain and Bilp Gosain which they worship along with other deities such as Laihu Gosain, Darmare Gossain and Jarmatre Gosain.

The sun is regarded by them to be a male with Surji as his wife. The Paharias, so far as I have been able to ascertain have no ideas of their own about the constellations. Their explanation of the eclipses of the sun and moon is that when these deities are angry with the human beings they hide their faces to them. I do not know if they have any explanations regarding earthquakes, etc. None could enlighten me in this matter.

The Paharias bury their dead. The ancient custom is interment. The corpse is placed at the bottom of the grave over poles and leaves with its head towards the North. The grave is then filled in. Stones are some times put on the top. The area is fenced and in some cases, as Mr. Day, in his final report on the Survey and Settlement of the Sauria Paharia hills, says, hut-like structures of all sizes with thatched roofs and bamboo-latticed sides are erected over the graves. A man or woman dying of small-pox or cholera is not buried. The body is covered with thorns or wood and left in the jungle. The Paharias whom I have questioned could not say anything regarding their beliefs as to the ultimate abode of the dead. They have no idea of their own about the transmigration of the soul. One Paharia however told me that the ghost (*Pauri*) of the dead person lives in the grave and sometimes comes out.

I quote below a very interesting description of a Sauria Paharia given by Mr. Bainbridge.

" The typical Sauria is short of stature, light of build, wiry and capable of undergoing considerable fatigue. Pale complexions are not uncommon ; but the characteristic colour is a chocolate brown, sometimes merging into black ".

There is another description of these Paharias given by Captain Sherwill and quoted in Mr. Mcpherson's settlement report. " The hillman, ' he says ' is much shorter than the Santal, of a much slighter make is beardless or nearly so........... ......his hair fastidiously combed, oiled and ornamented ....".

The following description is given in the Gazetteer.—

' The Maler is short of stature and slight of make, with limbs long in proportion to his low stature. His complexion is a light brown, his nose is not prominent but flat and broad at the base ; and his eyes have the peculiar beady look of the Dravidian. His hair is long and ringleted, and he keeps it well oiled and combed in a knot on the top of his head....................The nasal index.................. closely approaches the proportions ascertained for the Negro ".

The Paharias, except where they have terraced cultivation, seldom use the plough. They choose the hill sides to jhum and with iron-shod staff, or a pointed stick hardened by charring, make holes in the soil and drop seeds in them.

Bows and arrows were and are to some extent even now their weapons while the *Tangi* continues to be their principal weapon. They also use *Tetha* or a staff with a pointed iron piece at one end.

(g) Notes on the Tribes of Palamau.

The following notes on the tribes of Palamau district have been described by Mr. M. S. Mukherjee, the Khas Mahal Officer, Palamau. He arranges the aborigines in the following order of social precedence.—

1. *Chero, Ghatwal and Rautia.*
2. *Bhumij and Mundas.*
3. *Kherwar and Bhogta.*
4. *Oraon.*
5. *Kurmis, Santals and Hos.*
6. *Tamaria.*
7. *Parahiya.*
8. *Korwa, Birjia, Asur and Malar.*

Numbers 1 and 3 he regards as having the same origin. He states that the three mentioned under No. 1 are "to all intents and purposes one class". These five tribes now claim to be Rajputs and are Hinduised, the other tribes are partly Hinduised, partly tribal in their beliefs, and of the Oraons some are Kabirpanthis and some Christians. With regard to No. 5 he regards these three tribes as originally identical, though the Kurmis have now become Hinduised, whereas Santals and Hos have not. These Kurmis of course refer to hill tribes known by that name and are not to be confused with the Kurmi cultivating caste of the plains. The Tamarias he describes as sub-class of Bhumij and Munda at present separated and degraded though Hinduised. Korwas and Birjias follow tribal religions. Asurs "generally extract iron ore and prepare agricultural implements". They also follow their tribal religion. "Malars" prepare brass utensils.

Terraced cultivation is found in flat valleys or plateaus. All tribes burn their dead except where they have died of cholera in which case they are buried. Munda, Bhumij, Ho and Tamaria erect monoliths in memory of their dead.

The following trees are tabooed for house buildings :—

Jamun.	Siris.
Tamârind.	Nim.
Plum.	

Small wooden seats called *pirha* are only used, and another contributor mentions that the Santals are fond of sitting on stones.

Mr. Mukherjee continues "The sun and the moon are worshipped by some of these aboriginals. They believe that the spot in the moon is the shadow of a *Kadam* tree under which an old woman is spinning. They also believe the existence of another world after the present one. Earthquakes, they believe, are due to the turning of the back of the "sesnag" (snake) on which the Earth rests. They believe that the sun and the moon have taken loans from the Doms (Rahu) and when they are unable to pay the loan on demand, they are overshadowed (eclipsed) for some time as a sort of punishment. The *Rainbow* is termed *Panshokha* or *Barhboha*. One that rises in the east is called *Pansokha* while one that rises in the west is called *Barhboha*. The former is supposed to cause a slight rain by its appearance while the latter indicates heavy rainfall. Some of these aboriginals believe that the thunder is the angry voice of God.................... Bones of the dead are sometimes preserved and buried under a stone as a mark of respect to their memory.

They believe in the transmigration of the soul into creatures and insects though generally no special creature or insect is specified. They believe also that the soul passes into heaven ....

They all use bow except Cheros and Kherwars who use swords, Tangis, Dhals (shields) as their weapons. They generally hide the heads of their enemies in some hilly place after offering them first to their gods".

(h) Further notes on the tribes of Palamau are contributed by Qazi Nazir Hussain, sub-Deputy Magistrate, Daltonganj.

"All the classes of the aboriginals that are found in this district claim to have descended from one great man Fame Jhukut Rai. The classes or groups are arranged below in order of social precedence :—

1. Cheros, 2. Kharwar, 3. Mundas, 4. Oraons, 5. Bhuinhars, 6. Bhuinyas, 7. Koro or Korwas, 8. Birhors, 9. Kharia, Agaria, Kisans and Ghasis, 10. Kawas, Kawars, Cherwa. The last named are low class labourers from Sirguja or South Mirzapur.

The Sub-Divisions among the Cheros are—

(*a*) Bara hazari and (*b*) 13. Tera hazari from the number of forces (12,000 or 13,000) sent by the Chero Rajas to fight the army of the Moghal Emperor advancing on the Palamau Fort.

Kharwars are sub-divided into two classes "Dowal bandha" and "Birbandha".

The "Dowalbandhas" live in decent houses after the manner of the Hindus and are superior to the "Birbandhas" who are labourers living in jungly houses (from Bir *i.e.*, Jungle). Kharwars claim to be Kshatriyas, as well as "Gurus" or Priests of the 12 sects of the Santals, Bhogtas and Ganjhus who form a lower division of the Birbandhas.

Mundas are of 21 "Kilis" or classes, *viz.*:—(1) Kachua, (2) Topu, (3) Bhengra, (4) Sandi gura, (5) Dungdung, (6) Lipi—from a singing bird of Munda form and tradition. (7) Houre, (8 Han, (9) Kundir, (10) Kirkita, (11) Barla, (12) Puti or Tudi or Tudu, (13) Hemrora, (14) Kongari, (15) Sanga, (16) Kujri or Kuju, (17) Soi, (18) Kiru, same as Tudu, the 7th Paris of Santals, (19) Ugu, (20) Oria, (21) Purti. All these 21 Kilis are again subdivided into various sects according to the work they do.

Birhors in the district are subdivided into 12 Paris or classes, *viz.*:—

(1) Hasdas—being the descendants of the 1st son of "Pilchu Heram" (1st Grand old man—Adam) "Pilchu Budha" (1st. Grand old woman—Eve).

(2) Murmus from 2nd son of Pilchu Budha.

(3) Kiskos from 3rd son of Pilchu Budha, who became the Raja family of all Birhors.

(4) Hembroms from 4th son of Pilchu Budha.

(5) Barki from 5th son of Pilchu Budha.

(6) Sorem from 6th son of Pilchu Budha.

(7) Tudu from 7th son of Pilchu Budha.

(8) Barki, (9) Birsa, (10) Peereas—or Pauro cloth wearers.

(11) Kari or Kora children of Mundas and Santal (Kora means a child), (12) Bedia an advanced class, given to tatooing.

Oraons are a class of the Kolarian division of the aboriginals. They were originally divided into 7 main classes :—

(1) Mundas—agriculturists (Some Mundas are claimed as Oraon).

(2) Turis—Bamboos workers.

(3) Ghatias—Drummers.

(4) Goulias—Bird catchers.

(5) Kharwars—agriculturists.

(6) Birijias—Honey collectors.

(7) Badias—Tatooers.

Later they were subdivided into 12 Paris, of which two Paris appear to have been lost. The remaining 10 are—

(1) Mijwar, (2) Tapwa or Topuo like Topu of the Munda Kili. (3) Bek or Hozo, or Hor of the Santals. (4) Bara, (5) Khes, (6) Lakra, (7) Jugo, (8) Khalkhwa, (9) Kujar or Kuju of the Munda "Kili" (10) Tirkia, like Tirki of the Asur clan.

Marriages at present are not confined to the same Paris but a man of one "Pari" can marry a girl of an other Pari of Oraons.

Other classes mentioned above have probably no subdivisions. They are of the lowest ranks amongst the aboriginals.

Each class has a chief of its own.

The villages in the district of Palamau, inhabited by the aboriginals, have purely democratic system of organization. They select one old and intelligent Munda or Oraon to be their head in all matters secular. He is called Mahto. Matters relating to religious festivals and worship of village Gods are entrusted to the Bhogtas or Ganjhus, a sect of the aboriginals who are called village Pahans. These two offices are strictly hereditary. On the death of the village "Mahto" and village Pahan the eldest male heir is selected by unanimous agreement of the villagers and appointed on the "Sarhool", festival day in the month of Baisakh. These posts are recognised for administrative purposes by the village zamindars, and village disputes are referred to them for decision.

Mundas, Oraons and Cheros all came in succession from the west. Mundas were the first arrivals, followed by Oraons and others. They stayed for a long time in "Chaichampa"—(modern Azamgarh) where they have left their relics. Later, they moved on to Rohtas and eventually they came to this district.

Those of the aboriginals who are reported to have emigrated from Surguja and Jaspur Feudatory state to this district are—

Savars or Sabers of Sarguja.

Birjias.

Dhemars.

Kharias.

Kesans.

Koza and Korwa.

Badis.

Cherwas.

Semarlokas, a class of Ghasis in Sarguja.

The aboriginals put up a rough stone slab at cremation places to guard the mortal remains of their ancestors. This rude stone slab is called "Gajhath". Stones are piled up in heaps in a village to guard the village from the evil spirits.........................

Every kind of wood is allowed for building purposes, except neem wood which is not permitted. This wood is supposed to be the destroyer of wealth and therefore is discarded for building purposes.

Imli wood being sour is also looked upon as inauspicious.

Khour wood produces *khour* or destruction and so does *Riri* a black wood, and both are therefore discarded.

Pipar and *Bar* is scarcely used by them, in imitation of their Hindu neighbours.

Stones are largely used in foundation and for decoration on walls.

Belounjan wood is a good material for building purposes and more specially for making bedsteads. It is supposed to expel evil spirits.

The social position of a Munda or Oraon is generally indicated by the number of Machans called " Mochas " for stacking of hay on them which he possesses.

Oraon women are identified by the peculiar way in which they carry their children on their back, and attire themselves with small breadth sari. The males use " *Bharia* " and females " *Depli* " for carrying articles and not *vice versa*. The aboriginals hate carrying baskets on their head like their women.

The Oraon and Munda make a peculiarly constructed house which differs from the houses of other aboriginals. It has no enclosure but a main house facing towards north, and other small houses or verandas on three sides with exit doors at the corners.

Mundas and Oraon are the only classes of the aboriginals to be identified by an odd number (usually 5 or 7) of brand marks on the left hand called " Sika " marks.

According to their traditions, the sun is " Sen Bonga " worshipped by all aboriginals, as the " Sun " of prosperity. The moon is the sister of the sun, and the stars are the children " Renga " of the moon.

Acording to the Oraon traditions there were formerly seven brothers as Suns—Complaint when to the moon that the whole world was melting from the heat of the suns, unless she took measures to stop it. The moon began to eat a Bel fruit in presence of the sun. The sun asked his sister what it was that she found to be such good taste, as he also wanted to eat it. The Moon replied it was nothing but one of her own " Rengas " the stars her children, and suggested to the sun to boil the flesh of his own brothers, and to use them in this way which would give similar taste. The Sun killed his brothers accordingly but when he began to eat them it gave a different taste and smelt differently. The sun thinking that he was cheated by his sister rushed towards her with open word to make away with her. The moon instantaneously concealed herself into the hollow of a Bar tree and thus escaped death but had a slice of her body cut off by the sun. Since that time there is only one sun. The moon gets eclipse twice a year and has a black spot which represents the hollow of the Bar tree.

Regarding the Great Bear, their belief is that the seven stars were " Rishis " and owing to regular worship were changed into stars.............................." Arundhati " she is a female small star attached to the end of the fifth bright star of the Great Bear [Pleiades ? J. H. H.]. The belief is that any one who cannot see this star will die within six months.

Tin Dandia—a cluster of 3 stars in a line [Orion's Belt ? J. H. H.], who were Rishis originally, for guiding the travellers in jungle. After their death, they were changed into stars.

" Kachbachia " [Pleiades ? J. H. H.]. They are believed to be the daughters of some Rishis and born of aboriginal women.

All stars are Indra's eyes and so " Indra " is called " Poorandar " or " Shahasra Netra " having thousand eyes.

A Comet is " Ketoo " the year of its visibility is the year of destruction. It is the biggest of the 9 destructive " grahs " and makes an " Ahar " or meal of a lac of maunds of grain. It has only head, without body.

The belief of some advanced Mundas of O. S. Balumath is that all the stars are agricultural " *Nichattras* ", they are all 27 in number with thousands of other small stars to help them in producing varieties of crops.

Earthquakes are believed to be the shaking of *Ses Nag* or of 4 Diggaj elephants on North, South, East and West, that keep the earth on their heads.

The belief about the rainbow is that the two ends of the Rainbow which appear to touch the earth, collect scorpions. [*Cf.* No. 11, (*i.*) J. H. H.]

Thunder and lightning are believed by the aboriginals to be bajjar thrown by clouds to break boulders of stones, and other elevated rock for formation of good soil. Some samples of these *bajjar* [*i.e.*, stone celts ?] called *Cheter Dheri* are still kept preserved in the families of wealthy aboriginals. They are kept as amulets and are used by aboriginal women at the time of delivery.

The Milky Way is believed to be a *Chhour* or a path on the sky for the passage of buffalos for grazing.

Shooting stars are believed to be the " Kôochal " " Choogal " or back-biters in this world, who after, death go to hear the talk of Rishis at Indra's Darbar and are punished with fire. Obviously these astronomical and astrological ideas borrow largely from the Hindu ideas.

They dispose of the dead bodies by cremation and throw the remains into River Koel. Some times they have to travel long distances to approach river Koel. In contact with the Hindus the aboriginals are now imitating Hindu methods of the disposal of the dead.

The belief as to the ultimate abode of the dead, now in vogue is the same as of the Hindus, a *dut* of Jamraj comes up suddenly who takes the soul to Jamrajpuree, where it is dealt with according to the deeds good or bad, done in this world.

Good souls are given to the "Dharamraj" whose duts take them to "Dharampuri", *where* they pass through various phases, and, most of them return to this world to live in peace. The best souls are absorbed in " *Niranjan Jot* " divine light and have no transmigration at all.

The souls of Tana Oraons who worship cows are transmigrated into cows. But those souls do not return to the earth. They remain in the heavens as cows. [*cf*. the Ao Naga belief in the souls (*tiya*) of men being the cattle (*gaur*) of the gods—Mills *The Ao Nagas*, page 224. J. H. H.].

The souls of sinful men in Jampuree or Jamlok are subjected to punishment of 84 kinds. The souls of the Oraons and other low sects, of the aboriginals haunt a big tree in the village which is often worshipped by the surviving relatives. Bodies of women dead during confinement are disposed of by driving nails, needles and thorns into the palms of their legs, to prevent them from becoming evil spirits. Children of low castes are buried and not cremated. Cholera corpses are also buried................ Both sexes wear a circular iron band round their head.

10. Notes on the Peoples of the Chittagong Hill Tracts.

(*Bengal Census Report, 1931.*)

The essay here printed is by Mr. J. P. Mills, I.C.S., now Honorary Director of Ethnography in Assam, and is based on the notes which he made during a short stay in the Chittagong Hill Tracts in 1926. Mr. H. R. Wilkinson, C.I.E., I.C.S., at one time Deputy Commissioner of the Hill Tracts, makes the following comments :—

"My recollections date from the years 1920-1922 and must be regarded merely as the impressions of a layman. Where they differ from Mr. Mill's statements, the latter should for obvious reasons be preferred.

The district known as the Chittagong Hill Tracts has more in common with the neighbouring Lushai Hills than with the Chittagong District. But its generous river system provides natural means of communication with Chittagong and the sea. The tendency therefore has been for these hill people, especially those living anywhere near the big rivers, to come more and more into contact with and thus assimilate the customs of the people of the Regulation District. This tendency has been aggravated and accelerated by the inclusion of the district in Bengal; the Commissioner is at Chittagong and for administrative purposes the people look to Chittagong. Although pleaders are not allowed in the Hill Tracts, the people have easy access to the legal profession at Chittagong and the influence of the litigious spirit which prevails in Chittagong District cannot but begin to make itself felt among the hitherto unsophisticated people of the Hills. This is particularly the case with the Chakmas, partly because of their geographical situation but also because the Chief himself would appear to have encouraged the imitation of Bengali habits.

Originally the Chiefs were tribal and not territorial but now they exercise whatever power they have over the Circles called after their names and corresponding now to the three subdivisions. The Chakma Circle is served by the Karnaphuli and its tributaries, which are navigable to the small boats in use in most parts of the Circle. Motor boats now ply regularly between Chittagong and Rangamati and can go a good way beyond that. The Chakma Chief has house property in Chittagong Town and, like the other Chiefs, land in the district. The natural approach to the Hill Tracts is through the Collectorate.

The Chakmas are fair of complexion and to me show distinct traces of Mongolian origin. I am surprised at what Mr. Mills says about their language and religion. I thought that they had a definite language of their own but that it was gradually merging itself into Bengali—Chittagonian Bengali. Similarly I should have said that they were officially Buddhists though with decided animistic tendencies and had always been so, and that contact with the people of the plains and the efforts of the Chief to ape the manners of the educated Bengali had resulted in a certain tinge of Hinduism being noticeable in their attitude. The establishment of a High School in Rangamati has created a demand for professional employment.

In times of famine and distress they are extremely reluctant to take up any relief work, and for the ordinary Public Works Department road work a staff of Sonthal coolies has to be regularly employed. I think it is pride rather than laziness, which prevents them from taking to this kind of work. Similarly, I think I am right in saying that the Forest Department find it very difficult to obtain the services of Chakmas in Forest villages. My impression also is that it is the Chakmas who have taken most kindly to the imported plough cultivation in place of the indigenous system of *jhuming*; but this of course is due in part at least to the fact that they are more likely to occupy land suitable for plough cultivation.

I came across the Mros very little as I was not long enough in the Hill Tracts to visit their area in the south-east of the district and they themselves are very retiring and clannish. They show very little effect of the influence of the plains."

Mr. C. G. B. Stevens, I.C.S., who succeeded Mr. Wilkinson was assassinated before Mr. Mills' essay was shown to him, and it is consequently impossible to give his comments. Some notes are added however, which were put together by Babu S. S. Chaudhuri, B.J.C.S., and footnotes marked A. S. H. are details supplied by Mr. A. S. Hands, I.C.S., who succeeded Mr. Stevens.

Notes on a tour in the Chittagong Hill Tracts in 1926.

By J. P. Mills, I.C.S.

The Chittagong Hill Tracts form the hinterland of the District of Chittagong, the long boundary between the two districts following the base of the hills. Marching with the Hill Tracts to the North is the State of Tripura, and to the East of and behind them are the Lushai Hills and the Arakan District of Burma. Even since the days of the Mogal conquest the inhabitants of the Hill Tracts have paid tribute, first in cotton and later in money to the paramount power which held the coastal belt of plains. Indolent and unwarlike however they were never able to protect themselves from Lushei and Kuki raiders and in order to safeguard those from whom we received tribute we took on and administered this hinterland from 1862. It now forms a district of the province of Bengal. Its administration has always presented peculiar problems and it was while on deputation in connection with one of them that I was able to record the notes on which this paper is based.

Save where it borders on the Lushai Hills and Arakan the district contains no hills of even a respectable height, and the bulk of its inhabitants are valley folk, hugging the rivers which provide their chief means of communication. The ranges which run through the district are low and remarkably straight, often only a few hundred feet in height and rarely exceeding two thousand. All are of soft sandstone and laterite and there is no supply of stone such as could be put to any cultural use. Many of the valleys are so broad and flat that as one looks across the rice fields one might almost imagine oneself in the plains of Bengal. Others are a mere jumble of laterite and sandstone hillocks, with here and there a few plots of ground level enough for the plough. The rivers, save where they emerge from the higher ranges, meander over sandy beds. The Karnaphuli, for instance, the main river of the district is navigable for Bengali boats for 85 miles from Chittagong up to Subalong. Here some short rapids where the river runs over a low outcrop of rock form an obstacle. Above them again the stream is navigable for many miles. The scenery, as one travels by river, is varied. Sometimes high banks of mud are all one sees on either side. In other places, steep, heavily wooded cliffs of sandstone run down to the water. The rainfall is heavy and the climate exceedingly unhealthy for much of the year.

In this area the Lushei-Kuki tribes from the North and races of Burmese origin from the South have met face to face. The result has been continual contact and intermingling, and the consequent culture-borrowing has resulted in great uniformity throughout the area. Besides this the long plains border and the rivers which have always given the Bengali trader easy access to the very heart of the district have laid a thick layer of foreign culture over the Indonesian substratum. Yet each tribe still presents its own peculiarities if one looks for them. When I entered a Kuki or Mro house I could imagine myself in the Naga Hills; in the house of an educated Chakma I was in Bengal; in the house of a Southern Magh I was in Burma.

Few areas offer a richer field to the ethnologist but we still await the detailed accounts we long for. Such accounts can only come from those who have lived among the people. A casual visitor like myself can only record what the eye sees ; beliefs and social systems must remain hidden from him. It is in this area that the cultures of Assam and Burma meet and such monographs as those published by the Government of Assam would supply many invaluable links. Two officials at any rate, Captain Lewin and Mr. Sneyd Hutchinson, have in the past gained some knowledge of the people by long residence among them, but the books of both only leave us asking for more. Dr. Riebeck is the only trained ethnologist who has ever visited the people of the Hill Tracts and he lacked both knowledge of the language and capable interpreters and did little more than collect specimens of handicraft.

Save the Lusheis, Chaks and Kukis I saw a little of all the tribes inhabiting the Chittagong Hill Tracts. For the sake of brevity I will confine myself to my own observation and refrain from quoting information already available in the few books on this area. For the paucity of the information I can give I am not entirely responsible. Partly, it is true, it is due to the hurried way in which I had to tour. But partly one can justly blame the goods of the Bengali trader which, brought by river almost to the doors of the Hill Tracts folk, have ousted almost every indigenous article. This process is aided by the almost unbelievable indolence of the people. The cotton crop in an unfailing source of cash and I have even known hillmen buy baskets from Bengalis rather than make them from the countless bamboos near at hand ; while the highest ambition of a Chakma is to obtain a grant of land and immediately sublet it to a plains man, living himself in complete idleness on a share of the crop. As the Maghs and Chakmas are the most numerous of the Hill Tracts tribes I will describe them first.

Maghs.—These are essentially valley folk and I saw no village which was not on the bank of a stream. They are almost certainly of Tai origin, their ancestors being the Tai Long (Greater Tai) who were driven out of China towards the south and south-west.* The earliest home, however, of which they have any definite traditions is Arakan, whence they migrated early in the 17th century into what is now Cox's Bazar subdivision. There they split up. Some migrated further into Bengal proper, while two bodies entered the Chittagong Hill Tracts. The first to arrive were the southern Maghs, under the leadership of the Chief of the Phru family of the Ragretsa clan. They occupied the territory drained by the Sangu and its tributaries in the south of the Chittagong Hill Tracts District. Later the Northern Maghs, under the Chiefs of several clans of which the Palangsa was the most important, moved north along the coast, and settled for a long time on the Sitakund range, to the north of Chittagong. Having *jhumed* that country out they turned east, and crossing a narrow belt of plains, entered the low hills along the Tripura border in the north of the Chittagong Hill Tracts District. There they settled, finding the country empty save for a scattered Tippera population. This migration did not come to an end till early in the 19th century, and the longer sojourn of the Northern Maghs on the coast of Bengal has caused them to lose many of the Burmese characteristics which the Southern Maghs still retain.

Magh villages usually contain from about 10 to fifty houses, but are generally small. They are invariably built on the banks of streams. The houses are flimsy structures of bamboo on bamboo piles and consist of two main rooms, each with a separate door opening out on to the big sitting out platform, and a small store room at the back. The climate is too hot for a fire even to be necessary for warmth, and for cooking a hearth is built in the corner of one of the main rooms. It consists of a bed of clay and three clay cylinders on which the cooking pot rests. These are obviously substitutes for hearth stones in a country where nothing but laterite or soft sandstone is to be found. The eaves of the house are low and stretch far out over the sitting-out platform, which invariably faces the East. It is under these eaves that the family sits during the day, retiring inside at night to sleep on mats in the breeze which blows through the thin bamboo matting walls of the house. The stting-out platform is railed round and the only approach to it and so to the house is up a notched log, which is either pulled up or reversed at night.

In villages in which the houses are arranged to form a street there is often at one end of it a roofed platform on which the men sit and talk. This is probably a survival of the *morung* found in Assam. In one Northern, Magh village (Maischari) I saw on the ground near one or two of the houses rough, low, strongly built huts, just high enough for a man to crawl into. I was told that they were used as shelters during hurricanes. Most villages boast of a little Buddhist temple, which is always built well apart from the other houses.

On the site on which it is proposed to built a new house a pole is set up, and to the top of it is fixed a model of a bow with an arrow on the string and pointing skywards, the idea being that evil spirits are thereby frightened off.

Though the Maghs are now Buddhists they admit that they were once head-hunters. Only faint memories of those days remain and I could learn no details. They say that after the heads were brought in they were welcomed by the women and were then buried, but where and in what position I could not ascertain.

The tribe is divided into endogamous clans (*Osa* or *Sa*) with descent in the male line. A clan is usually named after the stream or place near which the original ancestor is said to have lived. The Northern and Southern Maghs each contain their own group of clans, and a village, unless big, is usually inhabited by the members of one clan only. A man may marry any woman of his own clan who is not a near blood relation. Marriage outside the clan used to be strictly forbidden and I was told that members of different clans would not even eat together in the old days. Now, however, these restrictions have been greatly relaxed and marriage outside the clan is by no means uncommon.

The language is Arakanese, a dialect of Burmese. There are slight differences of dialect between the Northern and Southern Maghs. Burmese characters are used. In figures the Magh is short and sturdy. The face is broad and rather Mongolian and the complexion a sallow brown. The men usually have a straggling moustache and occasionally a beard.

By the men of the Northern Maghs Bengali *dhoties* are now worn, but most of the Southern Maghs wear Burmese dress—a silk *lungi*, a jacket and a white *puggaree*. Often instead of a *puggaree* a man will twist a jaunty piece of coloured silk round his head. The dress of a women varies little throughout the tribe. She wears a long silk skirt, striped horizontally, of which the predominating colour is usually red. When there are no strangers about this is often the only garment of both young and old, but in public a piece of lined, homewoven silk is bound over the breast or tucked into a black string tied round the body about them. A dark coloured jacket is also worn by some. A white *puggaree* is worn, sometimes with embroidered ends.

Many individuals of both sexes have the teeth blackened with a certain sap but the custom is not universal. Tattooing is commoner among the Southern Maghs than among the Northern. Men are tattooed on their arms and women on the backs of their shoulders and of their hands. The only "patterns" I saw

* *Vide* Le May *An Asian Arcady*, page 4.

were words in Burmese characters. The operation is done by Maghs learned in the art who come up from Cox's Bazar in the cold weather, and the instrument used, I was told, is a little bamboo holder into which three ordinary needles are fitted like a nib. The word to be tattoed is marked on the skin and pricked over with the tattooing instrument. This is operated by the right hand and guided against the side of the forefinger of the left. The sap of a certain tree is finally rubbed into the perforated skin.

Popular though the recently introduced plough is among the Maghs, *jhuming* is still carried on. The method, which is the same among all the tribes I saw in the Chittagong Hill Tracts, differs somewhat from that with which I am familiar in Assam. The jungle is cut in the early spring and is burnt as soon as it is dry. Three crops are then sown simultaneously in drills—vegetables, rice and cotton. These come to maturity in that order and are gathered in turn. Land is only sown once and is then abandoned for a term of years, instead of being sown twice as in Assam. During the hot weather the villages of the valley tribes are abandoned and the whole population moves up to the *jhums* till after the rice harvest. The grain is stored in round matting bins in the houses and not in separate granaries. For hoeing little adze-shaped hoes of Bengali manufacture are used. Nearly all Mags use the Bengali husker, which is worked with the foot. Only in one or two villages did I see rice being husked by hand with a pounding pole in a cavity hollowed out in the end of a short log, bobbin-shaped and set up on end on the ground near the house. A single Bengali pounder is usually shared by several households and is kept in a shed specially built for it. The houses are too flimsy for any pounding to be done in them. The winnowing fan is a circular tray of bamboo matting.

Lungis and jackets are usually bought, but skirts and head cloths are woven at home. Silk thread is bought but cotton thread is home-spun. The cotton is seeded in a machine with little rollers working reverse ways, indentical with that used by Thado and other Kukis in Assam. It is then ginned with a bow, the string of which they twang not with the finger, as Nagas do, but with a smooth piece of wood shaped like a penholder with a blunt end. This bow-twanger I found used by all the tribes I saw in the Chittagong Hill Tracts. In Assam I have only seen it among the old Kukis. After being ginned the cotton is rolled into "sausages" round another thin piece of wood and the thread spun with a simple spinning machine. This machine, too, I found throughout the Hill Tracts, save among the Mros. The loom is of the simple tension type, and boat-shaped shuttles of wood or horn are used.

Though no Magh blacksmith was at work in any village I visited I was told that *daos* and knives are still made in a few places. The bellows, my informant told me, are of the type found in the Naga Hills, and consist of a pair of upright bamboo cylinders, with pistons padded with feathers laid with their tips downwards. Handsome silver pipes are made by Maghs. Wood-carving appears to be a lost art. The only good specimen I saw was an old musical instrument called a "crocodile harp", which was carved in the shape of that reptile.

When matches are not used fire is produced by the method used by the Kacharis and Old Kukis in Assam and all the other tribes I saw in the Chittagong Hill Tracts. A piece of bamboo about a foot long is split in two. On the outside and near the middle of the half used a notch is cut deep enough to perforate it. A thong of bamboo or cane is pulled backwards and forwards across this notch by the operator, who meanwhile holds the piece of bamboo firmly on the ground with his foot. The friction against the edge of the hole scrapes a fine dust off the thong. This dust is forced through the hole and lies in the trough of the inner side of the bamboos. As the heat increases it smokes and finally glows.

The Maghs nowadays have no weapons save guns and *daos*. Tradition definitely states however that they used to have both crossbows and upright bows, as well as spears. I was also shown an ancient square-leather shield. For killing birds pellet bows are used and long blow guns. Nooses are used for snaring. Fish traps are generally of the Bengali pattern but conical traps lined with cane thorns are still occasionally to be seen. The only toys I saw were stilts, used by little boys.

The feathers of the Great Indian Hornbill were used as fans and ornaments in the old days. I never saw any carving of this bird. The earth from its nesting hole is, however, used as a medicine. Another medicine one sees in houses is a species of fungus which is dried and ground up and made into an ointment for sore nipples.

The official religion is Buddhism and yellow robed priests are to be seen everywhere, especially among the Southern Maghs. But many primitive elements remain. The belief in evil spirits is strong and charms are plentiful. On the outer walls of houses are put little saucers inscribed with texts in Burmese. Inside the houses, over and on either side of the inner doors, are pointed pieces of bamboo marked with transverse black lines. These are known as "crocodile teeth." Exactly similar charms are put outside their doors by the Nagas of the unique village of Semkhor in the North Cachar Hills, and very similar wooden ones by Kachha Nagas of the Maruongmai group in the same area.

When a man falls ill it is often thought that an evil spirit has captured his soul and is holding it to ransom. A small offering to appease the spirit and buy the soul's release is then made on the path, as among Nagas. To cure headache a little grid of bamboo strips is set up on a stick outside the village.

When a child is born the naval string is cut with a bamboo knife. Steel may on no account be used. Nor may the mother, during the days of her uncleanness, use any spoon other than a gourd one. The afterbirth is buried in the clay of the hearth and dug up again after three days. A small portion is then kept in a hollow bamboo and the rest thrown away. These customs are most strictly observed even in the household of the Bohmaung, the Chief of the Ragretsa clan and leading Magh of the district. Nor the least enthusiastic followers of ancient ways are his sons, graduates of Calcutta University.

The bodies of the dead are burned on the banks of streams. For their spirits lamps are lighted under *pipal* trees and offerings made for seven days. These offerings are made on the anniversary of the death till the heirs get careless. All offerings to the dead must be made with the left hand. I saw two types of what might be called funeral monuments. One, of which I saw several examples, is a mound of earth in tries, like a wedding cake, revetted with bamboo matting. On the top are placed some pots and a lamp. Another type I saw at Patag in the Northern Magh country. In a field in front of a little Buddhist temple was an area of beaten earth fourteen yards square and fenced round. In this were set up thirty high poles, each of which was surmounted by a pagoda-like ornament of paper with hanging decorations of pith. There was a lamp at the foot of each pole and another at the top attached to a pulley by which it could be lowered to be lighted. Above the pulley was a roughly carved wooden bird, which I was told was a paddy-bird but which looked remarkably like a hornbill. The lamps are lighted in honour of the dead, to whom offerings of rice, milk, etc., are made for a period of thirty days while the crops are ripening—clearly a fertility rite.

The bulk of the property of a dead man goes to his sons. One-half goes to his eldest son, one-eighth to his daughters and the rest to his other sons equally.

Chakmas.—All the tribes of this area resemble each other so closely in many points of culture that having dealt with the Maghs at some length I shall be able to describe the other tribes more briefly.

If a Chakma be asked the origin of his tribe he either denies all knowledge of the matter or repeats like a parrot an incredible and purely modern story of descent from an ancient and noble Hindu race. Kalindi Rani, the great chieftainness who flourished in Lewin's time, knew only of some half-dozen previous chiefs. The present chief, second in succession after her, signs himself "45th Chakma Raja", so greatly has the length of his ancestry increased in recent years. To describe how the Raja reached his present position would be of no interest from the ethnological point of view. Suffice it to say that a supreme chief has no place in the ancient polity of the tribe, and that he is nothing but the descendant of tax farmers aggrandized by the paramount power.

The name "Chakma" is derived from the Maghi word *chaok*, meaning "of mixed origin", and the Chakmas are undoubtedly in the main the descendants of Maghi women and Mogal soldiers. There is a small tribe known as Chaks in the southern portion of the Chittagong Hill Tracts. Unfortunately I had no opportunity of visting them and of ascertaining how they are related to the Chakmas proper.

Despite their mixed origin the tribe is now very uniform and presents several features that merit description. They migrated from what is now Cox's Bazar subdivision in Chittagong towards the end of the 18th century and now inhabit the middle reaches of the Karnaphuli. They are by far the most Bengalised tribe in the district. Even their language is a dialect of Bengali, though one section of the tribe is said to have spoken Maghi till recently. The script in common use is Bengali, but the ancient script, which is still used by the more conservative members of the tribe, is of the Burmese type and is considered by Sir George Grierson to be closely allied to the ancient Khmer script.

In appearance they resemble Bengalis and their features show little trace of their partially Mongol origin. The dress of the well-to-do men is Bengali, but the poor men often merely wear a rag pulled between the legs and tucked into a string round the waist in front and behind. The dress of the women is distinctive. They wear a long dark blue skirt to the ankles, with a broad red band near the edge. Till puberty the upper part of the body is bare. Latter a broad strip of embroidered silk is usually worn over the breasts. Bengali ornaments are worn in the nose and ears, and silver rings on the ankles. A flat silver band is worn round the neck. The hair is done in a bun at the back.

All the villages I saw were on the banks of streams. A few rich men have brick houses after the Bengali style, but the ordinary houses are exactly like those of the Maghs, with the platform similarly facing east. The villages are small and often contain members of more than one of the many clans (*goza*) into which the tribe is divided. In the old days each *goza* was endogamous and was under the control of a headman, called in the modern dialect a *dewan*. In order to increase their own power however the chiefs set out, about a hundred years ago, to lessen that of the *dewans*, by making all relations of *dewans* into *dewans* and so turning an office into a class. This tended to break up the clan system, a tendency which was accelerated when Government, for purposes of administration, divided the country into *mauzas* with fixed boundaries, each under a headman. These headmen have been steadily acquiring the power which the *dewans* used to have, and the tendency is for an endogamous *mauza* to be substituted for an endogamous clan. That is to say a man may now-a-days marry any girl of his own *mauza* not nearly related to him, but is expected to provide an extra lavish marriage feast by way of a fine if he marries a girl of another *mauza**.

In so far as they can be said to have a religion at all the Chakmas are now Buddhists. In the 18th century many of them adopted the religion of the Moguls to whom they paid tribute and the chiefs of that time had Muhammadan names. Then a reaction towards Hinduism seems to have set in, bringing with it the Hindu names which are now almost universally adopted. The Hinduism prevalent was however of a very half-hearted type, and Kalindi Rani decided that something definite must be done. After considering the advantages and disadvantages of various creeds she is said to have given orders that the tribe was to adopt Buddhism. Buddhists they therefore are to this day, though I must confess that I only once saw a priest in their country.

The chief's womenfolk and those of one or two other families are kept purdah. This custom only originated in the time of Kalindi Rani, who went purdah one day herself in order to avoid an interview with Lewin on the morrow. It is not in accordance with Chakma tradition and is much disliked by the better elements among the people.

Underlying their Buddhism is a belief in animism. One often sees offerings to spirits on little platforms, and on one such platform at Toyichakma I noticed little squares of thread exactly like those placed on Angami women's graves. They also release scape-goat chickens for illness, just as the Semas and other Nagas do. They swear on a tiger's tooth, a stream or withering leaves, and they told me that they sometimes settle disputes by the diving test.

Their method of cultivating and preparing rice is exactly similar to that of the Maghs, save that I never saw a rice husker other than of the Bengali pattern. The women weave their own skirts and breast cloths on an ordinary Indonesian tension loom. Shuttles are rarely used. The only one I saw was of a type found both among the Tipperas of the Chittagong Hill Tracts and the Kolang Kukis of the North Cachar Hills. It consisted of a piece of bamboo prettily ornamented with a pattern scratched on it and open at one end only. In the side was a small hole for the thread to pass through. At first sight the problem of getting the thread through this small hole from the inside is a difficult one. In reality it is quite simple. You unwind about a foot of thread and put the bobbin with this loose end into the shuttle. Then you blow hard in the open end and the pressure of air forces the thread through the hole. All the other instruments of spinning and weaving are exactly similar to those of the Maghs.

The children play a game with the seeds of the sword bean similar to the Naga game, and pellet bows are very popular.

Tipperas.—At least two very different sub-tribes of the district are classed under the general name of Tipperas. Many inhabit the Mong Raja's circle, which marches with Hill Tripura. It is a country of low hills and sluggish streams, and until the Maghs came the Tipperas were apparently the only occupants. They are very Bengalised, the men wearing *dhotis* and *puggarees*, and the women dressing exactly like Chakma women I saw very few in the old fashioned dress—a piece of cloth pulled through a string round the waist, long hair and leaves in the ears. A home-spun cotton cloth, with broad white and dark blue stripes is occasionally worn.

---

* At Nauyarchar, 20-7-28.—System of marriage by which a Chakma who cannot pay the price of a wife, gets another man to buy one for him agreeing that after marriage they will live at the benefactor's house and serve for a period of years. This case was an agreement to work for five years to repay marriage expense of Rs. 300, *i.e.*, one month's work equals Rs. 5. The period and the rate may vary in different cases. The price of the girl in this case was Rs. 60, ornaments Rs. 90 odd, drummers Rs. 8 and the balance for clothes for the girl and a general feast. It is analogous to the *gharjamai* system, but I could not find that it had any special name. The married couple have broken this agreement by bolting after doing 6 months' work.

(A. S. H.)

The houses are exactly like Chakma houses, and the villages, which are small, are sometimes on the top of the ranges and sometimes in the valleys. The religion is Hinduism and no stranger may enter their houses unless he removes his boots. A conspicuous feature inside is the main post with bunches of ears of rice, tied to it, being the first fruits of successive years. In every way their material culture appears to be identical with that of the Chakmas. They seem to know few folk tales, but they believe that the marks on the moon are trees.

A more primitive and interesting section of the tribe is scattered about the Banderban circle in the South of the district. They are said to be the descendants of Tippera slaves taken to Arakan long ago. The men wear white waist clothes of which the black embroidered ends are left hanging down at the side. The corners are decorated with cowries. Above they wear white home-spun jackets. Their heads are shaved at the sides and back like those of Nagas and small *puggarees* are worn, with the ends hanging down over their right ears. In the lobes of the ears are cylinders of bamboo, from which hang crescent-shaped ornaments of silver. Small blue and white beads are immensely popular, and both men and women load their necks with strings of them. The *dao* is carried pushed through the waist-cloth at the back.

The women wear a skirt of black and gray, with brown and black edges. Before marriage they usually cover their breasts with a narrow, tight strip of red and brown cloth, with cowries at the corners. The hair is worn in a big bun at the back. Armlets of black beads are often worn above the elbow. Through the top of the ear a spiked ornament of silver is worn, and through the lobe a crescent-shaped ornament.

Though nominally Hindus they readily admit strangers to their houses, which resemble those of Kukis. A house consists of one big room, with sliding doors and a narrow verandah at either end.

Their methods of cultivation and their industries are identical with those of the Maghs. For weaving they sometimes use a tubular shuttle of the Chakma pattern. Birds are shot with a short blow-gun.

The Khyengs.—The chief home of the Khyengs is in Arakan, and of the few there are in the Chittagong Hill Tracts I was only able to see the two small villages of Arachhari and Kukiyachhari, close together on low, steep hills at the Northern end of the Bandarban Circle. I was very much struck by the negroid features and curly hair of some of the men, but from such scanty evidence it would be unfair to draw any inference. They claim to have inhabited the country from time immemorial. Those whom I saw had long been under Magh and Chakma influence and their culture presented few distinctive features. *Dhotis* are now common, but the more conservative men still wear a narrow white cloth with red ends, pulled through a string round the waist. The hair is done after the Mro fashion, that is to say in a bun on the left side of the head, with a bone pin stuck in it. The women wear a skirt and breast cloth of white with narrow red lines, and a large white *puggaree*, with red embroidered ends. The houses are on piles, and each consists of one large room with a kitchen at the back. By religion they are Buddhists and, unlike Chakmas and Maghs, are divided into exogamous clans. All property goes to sons, the youngest of whom gets the greatest share. Their relationship terms seem to show traces of a former dual division.

Kukis.—In the Southern portion of the district only Bonjugi Kukis appear to be found, but in the Northern portion the majority are Pankhos, with a few Bonjugis. As their villages are invariably on the top of the ranges, where my work did not take me I was unable to see nearly as much of them as I could have wished.

Mr. Rowlands in a private note, says that the Bonjugis came from a village called Daun on the Koladan, while the Pankhos came from Pankhua, three miles from where the Lunglet-Thaka track crosses the Koladan. Some figured memorial stones are said still to exist there, which would probably well repay investigation. The two tribes are closely akin and will inter-marry, often even inhabiting the same villages. They speak slightly different dialects.

The Bonjugi men wear a narrow white waist cloth, a white jacket, and a very narrow white home-spun *puggaree* with embroidered ends. The hair is done in a tight bun on the top of the head and ornamented with a metal pin. Strings of small cornelian beads are worn and also enormous beads—sometimes dark red, and sometimes yellow—of a very light substance which is said to be amber. The women wear a white skirt with red lines in it, and, when strangers are about, a cloth of similar pattern thrown over the upper part of the body.

I was able to visit Basanta, a Pankho village containing a few Bonjugi houses, near Subalong in the Northern portion of the district. The men wear a small white apron and a white coat ornamented with a little embroidery round the bottom at the back. Some men do their hair in a bun at the back, while others—usually young men—pile it up over the forehead into a sort of horn. Into this horn a well-dressed man pushes, base down, a small triangular ornament of steel pins, embellished with a red tassel at the "apex." The beads worn are similar to those of the Bonjugis. Women wear a white skirt with narrow red lines and usually leave the upper part of the body bare. Round the waist they wear strings of beads and rings of brass wire. The latter may once have been their sole dress, as very small girls wear such rings as their only garment. Large plugs of bone or bamboo are worn in the ears.

The houses are on piles and are big and well built. There is one main room, with an open porch in front and a sitting-out platform at the back. A man who has sacrificed *mithan* (*gayal*) sets up in front of his house a large forked post with a *mithan* head carved on it. The skulls of animals sacrificed are exhibited on a rack propped up against the centre post of the living room.

The loom is of the ordinary Indonesian type, and for a shuttle a stick with an enlarged conical head is used. Both Pankhos and Bonjugis have bamboo flutes, but not, apparently, the gourd "bagpipes" found among Thados and other Kuki tribes in Assam.

The Mros.—Of all the tribes I saw the Mros interested me most. They are often spoken of as Mrungs, a term which is not only erroneous, but liable to lead to serious confusion, as it is properly applicable to one of the Tippera clans.

The Mros say they are immigrants from Arakan. Those I saw inhabit the Southern portion of the Bandarban Circle in the South of the Chittagong Hill Tracts, where their villages are hidden away in a tangle of low steep hills drained by the Sangu and its tributaries, some situated on low spurs just above the streams and others on the tops of ridges. The people, especially the women, have the reputation of being very shy, but I found no difficulty in taking such photographs as I wanted. Certainly they are suspicious of strangers and keep themselves very much to themselves, and to this and an innate conservatism may be attributed the remarkable way in which they have retained their primitive characteristics, in spite of their proximity to the plains and their constant contact with Bengali traders.

They are of medium height and light built and one is struck by the almost entire absence of Mongolian traits in their features. Their costume is of the lightest. The men wear a narrow white or red cloth, which is wound round the waist, pulled between the legs from the front and tucked in at the back. In addition a homespun coat is sometimes worn. The hair is done in a bun on the left side of the head and through the bun a bone pin is stuck. A *puggaree* is sometimes worn. Large rings of white metal are worn through the lobes of the ears. Young men often wear round the waist a narrow girdle of beads very prettily worked in a flower pattern. The teeth are often stained black. The women wear nothing by day but a very short dark blue skirt, edged with white beads. This reaches half way down the thigh and is open down the left side. It is tucked into a narrow silver girdle, and over it a belt of scarlet beads is worn. At night both sexes wear very thick cotton cloths.

All clothes are removed for bathing, and both sexes bathe together unembarrassed and with perfect propriety, the left hand providing such covering as is required.

The villages usually contain between ten and twenty houses.* These are large and well built. The roofs are slightly hog-backed. They are on piles and the only approach is up a notched log. Inside they consist of one large room and a store room at the end. This latter is regarded as the women's room and no stranger may enter it. There is a sitting-out platform at the end of the house.

A man who has given the full series of feasts of merit may built an extra large house and may set up by the side of it four or five long bamboos. Forked posts are not put up. The series of feasts is (1) fowls, (2) a pig, (3) a dog and (4) bulls, buffaloes or *mithan* (*gayal*) up to three in number. A plain upright post in the middle of the village marks the place of sacrifice. In some villages, but not in all, a small pointed stone is set up at the foot of the post for every animal sacrificed. In one village I passed through, the sacrificial post was very high, and was surrounded at a distance of some feet by a circle of lower posts notched at the top. When a feast is to be given rafters are fitted from these side posts to the centre post and the whole roofed over, so that the ceremonies can take place under cover.

A Mro if asked his religion will say he is a Buddhist, but to the observer the only traces of Buddhism visible are charms occasionally placed on houses and the practice of burning the dead. Their real religion is animism. The religious affairs of a village are run by an old man called a *sera*, who may be of any clan and who also acts as exorcist. For epidemics a pig and a dog are sacrificed and a series of sabbaths called *to-ung* observed for the nine days of which no one may descend to the ground from the verandah of his house†.

Hutchinson (*Account of the Chittagong Hill Tracts*, page 165) says the tribe is divided into five "septs," the Dengua, the Premsang, the Kongloi, the Naizar and the Gharoo Gnar, meaning respectively the cultivated plantain tree, the cockscomb plant, the wild plantain tree, the jack tree and the mangoe tree. I am afraid I omitted to make enquiries on this precise point, but I was told that the tribe was divided into a number of clans—evidently subdivisions of Hutchinson's septs. They are exogamous, but not mutually so. For instance in Bali village I found the following clans—Shimlung, Chingnao, Nirincha and Shitnma. All are exogamous, but, though a Shimlung man may marry a Chingnao woman, a Chingnao man may not marry a Shimlung women. For this I could obtain no explanation at all. Large clans are divided into sub-clans, called *kuchis*. In such cases a man may marry a woman of his own clan provided she is of a different *kuchi*. Property descends to the sons, the youngest getting the largest share.

At birth the naval cord is cut with a steel knife and never with a piece of bamboo. The baby is immediately laid on a plantain leaf. The funeral customs show clearly, exactly as they do at Semkhor in the North Cachar Hills, that the practice of burning the dead is a comparatively modern one. Every village has its burning place near a stream and usually close to a pipal tree. The body is burned and the calcined bones are removed and placed in a little house on piles a few yards further back from the stream. To the sides of the house are fastened bamboos festooned with tassels of bamboo shavings, and in the house are put with the bones, food, drink, pots, and bits of rag for clothes. All vessels, whether of pottery or brass, are broken. The finer ashes, left where the man was burned, are also treated as if the spirit of the dead man were there too. Over them is laid a piece of cloth. This is pegged down at the edges and on it are laid a *dao*, a hoe, etc. Over this another cloth is laid and by them are placed pots of food and drink. Finally a little lean-to shelter is built over the heap, with the open side towards the east.

As far as I know the method of cultivation is identical with that of the other tribes of this area. The winnowing fan, however, is of the sugar scoop type that Nagas use and not of the round type used by all the other tribes I saw in the Chittagong Hill Tracts. I saw no Bengali *dhan*-pounders. All were of the primitive round type.

The loom is identical with that found among the other tribes of the district, but the Mros alone spin against the right thigh after the Naga fashion.

The tribe must take a heavy toll of jungle animals and birds. For leopards and tigers boxtraps with drop doors are made, identical in pattern with those found in the Naga Hills. Very long fences are built across the line which rats must take going backwards and forwards between the cleared fields and the jungle. These fences are impenetrable save at the gaps which are left every few yards. In each gap there is a fall trap. Birds are both speared with nooses and caught in nets stretched between bamboo poles on saddles which they are in the habit of crossing.

The Mros are a musical race and use both bamboo flutes and "banjos" made by cutting out and lifting thin strips of the outer layer of a piece of bamboo. The favourite instrument however is a gourd "mouth-organ" which closely resembles that made by Thado Kukis in Assam. The instruments are made in pairs, of which the two harmonise. The players walk at the head of a procession of dancers. The step is very slow and solemn and the feet are pointed as they touch the ground. This is the only dance the tribe has, and there is only one tune for it, and that a singularly monotonous one.

---

* 6-12-28—*Tain valley.*—I found some Mro forest houses at Amtoli (Tain valley). The Mros call them *liku*. They are put up for taking refuge in when there is a storm. They do not appear to be kept up permanently, but are put up when it looks as though there is dirty weather coming. The ones I saw were made two months ago. This strikes me as curious because the Mro houses are the most solidly built of all, the support being of stout logs instead of bamboos and much of this fencing being made of whole bamboos. Of course the Mro village is usually perched on an exposed ridge, but then so are *jhum* houses very often. The peculiarity of Amtolipara (Lengsa Karbari) is that it is right down on the level bank of the Tain. The *liku* were out in a sheltered grass space outside the villages. They say that for villages on the hills, the *liku* are erected in a sheltered place at the foot of the hill. (A. S. H.)

† The Mros do not do puja at the funeral house of a woman who has died before her child is 3 years old. The Khumis make no such distinctions. (A. S. H.)

Notes on the Chaks.

Compiled by Babu S. S. Chaudhuri, B.J.C.S.

The Chaks trace their previous abode at Chakyandong in Koladain hill in Arakan, where there were, it is said, about 11,000 families who lived under a chief of their own. There were signs of 10,000 houses made of bamboo and 1,000 houses made of wood at Chakyandong for a long time. When the Chakmas, another hill tribe, migrated to Chittagong Hill Tracts from Burma, they also came with them and settled in Nakhyongchhari side of this district (Chittagong Hill Tracts). The Chakmas advanced further towards the north and they were left behind in these places. Little is known of their migration previous to this. There is a story as to how the Chaks were left behind by the Chakmas which runs as follows :—

When the Chaks began to cook their curry with *Chingri* fish they were asked to follow the Chakmas who were ready beforehand. But as the *Chingri* fish, which turns red by cooking, could not be made white, they thought that the cooking was not complete as the fish still contained blood, so they cooked the curry on and on but the fish did not turn bloodless, *i.e.*, white. The Chakmas seeing their delay left them behind and they settled in these places.

At present there are only a small number of Chaks, not more than 100 families in the district, who are found in Nakhyongchhari, Baisari, Pagali (near Reju) and Bakkhali mauzas. Thus it appears that the Chaks came from the south to this area.

The following are stories current amongst the Chaks :—

Earthquakes.—There were 4 disciples under a priest who used to cook their food. These disciples were so selfish that they always took the best curries for themselves while the priest was supplied with all the remaining bad things. After their death the 4 disciples went into hell and as punishment they had to bear the earth on bamboo poles on their shoulder. They were placed on the four directions north, south, east and west. As they cannot bear the earth on the same shoulder for a long time they are required to change their shoulder. And it is at the time of changing their shoulders that earthquake begins.

Rainbows.—Once there was no water in the locality anywhere except in the house of a blacksmith. A brother and a sister being very thirsty went to the house of the blacksmith to drink water. When they asked for some water, the blacksmith told them that if they could live like a husband and wife he could give them water. In order to quench their thirst they were compelled to live as husband and wife and then drank water and died soon afterwards. After their death they became rainbows and appear in the sky occasionally. Still now two rainbows are seen at the same time. The bright one is the sister and the faint one is the brother.

Eclipses.—Tha-O the great Snake gave a half-pice to the sun. As the sun did not repay it the great snake began to devour him and when the sun promised to repay it he was allowed to go. Hence the origin of the eclipse of the sun.

Note on the Maghs of Cox's Bazar.

Regarding the Maghs of the Cox's Bazar subdivision, Babu Manindra Kumar Sen, district census officer, Chittagong, has furnished the following notes for information supplied by Rai Sahib Bipen Bihari Rakshit :—

They live in raised huts or wooden houses built very close to one another. Groups of houses form one *mahalla* with one elected *mahalladar* at its head. This *mahalladar* is an aged and respectable person and wields autocratic powers and his wish is regarded as law by every one residing in his *mahalla*. All disputes between themselves are decided by *mahalladars* and they hardly resort to the law courts, except at the express direction of the *mahalladar*. Inter-*mahalla* affairs are settled by the *mahalladars* of different *mahals* concerned. By nature they are meek, peaceful and ease-loving and are terribly afraid of the law and its agencies. All of them belong to the same sect, with Buddhism as their common religion. They maintain several *Keyangs* (temples of Buddha) which are occupied by celibate priests and their disciples who live on cooked food, sent to them by the villagers. Each *Keyang* situated in a solitary place contains a good many images of Lord Buddha. Some of the images are adorned with costly ornaments. The celibate priests are recruited from the villagers after the performance of a ceremony called the *Maishang* ceremony. The family feels proud and happy if it can supply a *Maishang* in the *Keyang*.

Polyandry or polygamy is not in existence. Widow-remarriage is in vogue. Divorce is rare and its incil dents are governed by the Burmese Buddhist law which is in force in Lower and Upper Burma. No sexua- indulgence with outsiders is allowed before or after marriage. System of courtship is unknown. Marriage is generally settled by the parents of the parties in consultation with their relations (numbering on each side not less than 7 persons). Consent of the bridegroom or the bride is not essential. The marriage ceremony is simple and does not entail much expenditure. The bridegroom's party will visit the bride's house with some ornaments and sweets and in presence of the invited-gentlemen of both the sides, the guardians of the bridegroom will make them over to the guardians of the bride; this will mean an engagement or preliminary contract for marriage. On the day of marriage the priest will go to the bridegroom's house and bless him with some *mantras*. The same priest will then visit the bride's house and bless her with similar *mantras*, and on the same day the priest will again bless the couple in the house of the bride in presence of their grand-father or grandmother or grand-uncle or grand-aunt. This being over the bridegroom and the bride will take a meal from the same dish. After the meal the wife will walk round the husband seven times saluting him as her husband on each round. They will then live in the bride's house for seven days as husband and wife and on each of those seven days the husband will present flowers to the wife. On the eighth day the newly-married couple will visit the *Keyang* and there they will take a vow before the priest that they will never separate. Thus the marriage is completed. No document of any kind is required.

A note on some of their festivals and social customs is given below :—

(*a*) *Boat festival.*—This takes place on the full-moon night in the month of Aswin. They make religious offerings in the *Keyang* during the daytime and at dusk they flock to the bank of the river. They prepare small toy boats with pieces of wood and cloth and paper and gorgeously decorate them with lace and coloured papers. Inside the boat they carefully place lit candles and get them afloat in the water. They shout, sing and clap their hands as those toy boats float down the stream with the current. It is Lord Buddha, they say, sailing through the dark world with light.

(*b*) *Water festival.*—This takes place on the last day of Chaitra. It is a gala day for the youths and children. They (both male and female) come out in the street in batches with buckets and syringes and throw water at one another ; one batch fights the other with water, running, chasing, retreating, attacking ; shouts of joy and loud laughter ring through the air. Other people than the Maghs are also attacked with water when passing along the street. Every one takes it in good spirit. This resembles to certain the extent *dol jatra* of the Hindus. Seniors rarely take part in this festival.

(c) *Buha Chakra.*—This comes off on the full-moon day in the month of Magh. Of all the festivals this seems to be enjoyed most by the Maghs. It lasts for 3 or 4 days. A *buha* (labyrinth) is constructed of bamboo fencing on fairly large block of land, with two gates, one of entrance and the other of exit. Once you enter the labyrinth, you have to go round and round by several zig-zag ways laid between bamboo fences and the labyrinth is so skilfully constructed that you cannot come out of it unless you have traversed the whole area of the land enclosed. Inside the labyrinth there are 4 or 5 pedestals on which are placed beautiful images of Lord Buddha. In course of moving along the labyrinth the people halt before each image and salute it and place a lighted candle at the foot of the image invoking the Lord's blessings. The gate of entrance is dark and the gate of exist is well lighted. During this festival there are pantomine and puppet shows, and *watcha* dances (dance of the Buddhist professional girls) are also performed.

(d) *Phungyi burning ceremony.*—This is perhaps the most expensive ceremony of the Maghs. When a Phungyi (a priest of high class) dies they preserve the dead body in a bier in the *Keyang* for a period of one year. During this time all the *mahallas* contribute money and big wooden cannons are prepared and loaded with gunpowder. On the appointed day all the Maghs of all the *mahallas* flock to the cremation ground and arrange the cannons in a row with a flag of each *mahalla* flying over its cannon. With pomp and ceremony, in a well-adorned bier, the dead body is brought into the cremation ground in procession, followed by the Magh musical concert party. The bier is then placed on a well decorated hut built high up in the air like the Persian tower of silence. Cannons are then discharged from a distance of about 400 yards towards that hut amidst shouts and uproar. The cannon-ball that touches the hut or passes very close to it receives tremendous cheers and the fortunate *mahalla* to which that cannon belongs, feels itself proud and happy. They run up to the cannon and bring the empty cannon back dancing and singing round it all the while. After all the cannons have been discharged one after the other, the hut is set on fire with various combustible substance and with the bier is soon burnt into ashes.

The Maghs, except the poor and children, are burnt with pomp and ceremony. The corpse is placed in a beautiful coffin and is carried along the street in a big procession of both sexes followed by a musical party.

The Maghs have very little contact with the people of other religions. They live secluded among themselves. They are very conservative in manners and habits and are still unaffected by Western civilisation. The males often take to trading and brokery. The poor Maghs catch fish in the sea and live on fishing. Some of them, like so many drones, live idly at home upon the income of their wives who earn a good deal by weaving silk cloths and *lungis* which they send to various trade centres through brokers. The women are active and industrious like ants and work from morning till night, weaving, cooking and doing sundry other works. They do not like cultivation of any kind.

Most of the Maghs, males and females, learn the Maghi language. Very few are reading in high English schools and colleges and they do not seem very anxious for English education. By nature they are truthful, simple and sincere and seldom litigate against one another. They distrust other communities and resent outsiders meddling with their affairs.

11. Notes on some Assam Hill Tribes.

(i) Notes on the Lakhers (N. E. Parry).

(ii) Notes on the Western Rengmas (J. P. Mills).

(iii) Notes on the Hill Kacharis (J. H. Crace).

(iv) Notes on the Biete Kukis (J. P. Mills & A. H. Fletcher).

(v) Notes on the Khelma Kukis (J. P. Mills & A. H. Fletcher).

(vi) Notes on the Lushei (N. E. Parry).

(vii) Notes on the Garos (G. D. Walker).

(viii) Notes on the Khasis and Syntengs (Hari Blah).

(i) Notes on the Lakhers

By N. E. Parry.

The Lakhers are divided into the following groups, the Tlongsai, the Zeuhnang, the Sabeu, the Hawthai, the Lialai, the Heima, and further into a number of clans.

At the present time neither the groups nor the c'ans are exogamous. Marriages either within or without the group or clan are equally permissible. Most of the clans are found among all the different groups, though a few of the numerically weaker clans appear only to exist in certain villages.

The clans are divided into three classes.—

(1) Royal clans, Abeiphang.

(2) Patrician clans, Phangsang.

(3) Plebeian clans, Machhiphang. There is a definite social gulf between the three classes. The women of higher clans have higher marriage prices than those of lower clans.

Each group has a chiefly clan, thus the Saiko Tlangsai's chief's clan is Mara Hleuchhang, the Siaha Tlangsai's, Khichha Hleuchhang, the Zeuhang's, Bonghia, the Sabeu's, Lialai's and Heima's, Changza, the Hawthai's, Nonghrang.

It is not necessary for a chief to belong to a chief's clan by both parents. Chiefs usually do marry into either their own or another royal clan but it is not obligatory for them to do so.

The organization is not democratic. A village is ruled by the chief assisted by the village elders or Machas.

There is no very clear tradition, but a vague tradition that they came from the north does exist. It can be definitely stated that they moved into their present home from Haka, *i.e.*, from the north-east.

No terraced cultivation exists.

The following stone monuments are found.—

Longphei.—A flat stone laid on the grave and supported on all four sides by four stones of the same length planted on their sides.

Phura pachang.—A pyramid of stones six or seven feet high erected in memory of chiefs or wealthy nobles outside the village. Only erected for men.

Longdong.—A square enclosed by four stone walls about three feet high erected on the path leading to the village, gaps being left for the path at each end. Erected in memory of men or women.

Social position is not indicated in the shape or material of houses except in one small point. A particular kind of round wooden door called pako is reserved to chiefs. The doorway consists of a round opening cut in the plank wall, the door itself is of wood, swings on wooden hinges and can be bolted on the inside.

To some extent social position is indicated by clothes, the embroidered cloths called cheulopang, cheunapang and sisai ahnang are only worn by members of chiefly familes or rich people. There is no definite prohibition on other people wearing these clothes but in practice they do not do so. Chiefly, I think, because they cannot afford to make them.

A head-dress of the feathers of the siasi bird can only be worn by men who have given a housewarming feast on building a large new house.

A head dress consisting of goat's hair dyed scarlet and called *chheutlia* or *rabon* is worn by persons who have taken human heads.

The sun is a woman, she is married to the moon by whom she had a child. The moon formerly was bright and hot like the sun, but his light was so fierce that one night it killed a widow's child, which was sleeping on the platform in front of her house. The widow got very angry at this, killed the moon's child with a spear and threw the refuse out of her beer pot into the moon's face thus making it dirty and reducing its light. The sun has a house in the east where she is guarded by a race of black dwarfs* called Nangchhikhawpa, who open the door every morning to let her out. The sun walks along all day holding her hand a solder walking stick, at night she shines in Atikhi, the abode of the dead, after which she goes home, takes her food and is then released by the Nangchhikhawpa for another day.

A halo round the sun is believed to foretell the capture of a chief by the foreigners.

Eclipses of the sun and moon are due to these orbs being swallowed by one of the dogs owned by Nateu, who lives where the sky meets the earth. One dog is red and the other black. If the reflection of the sun in water is red the Lakhers seize a red dog and beat it in order to make the red dog's brother in the sky spew out the sun. If the sun's reflection in water is black, a black dog is beaten.

Parhelia known to the Lakhers as Sawmachupa are unlucky and portend an unnatural death.

Venus as an evening star is known as Thlaseu, as a morning star as Deiva. Both Thlaseu and Deiva were men who were turned into stars at the great darkness. Deiva who spent a long time feasting does not come out till about 4 A.M. Thlaseu who only enjoyed a much short feast comes out early in the evening.

Orion's belt is Vothawlapiapa. Two men were going along carrying a pig, as they were doing so the great darkness began and they were turned into stars.

Orion's sword is Nongsawthaimangchhangpa. This represents a mother teaching her daughter to weave, a tiger that came to eat them and the young men who gathered to protect them.

The planet Mars is Awsichakeipa, the tiger star.

The Pleiades are Aswsicharu, the six stars. There were six men who were sitting gossiping when the Great Darkness fell and they were turned into stars.

The Milky Way is Sonatachhiarari, meaning " rains and dry weather boundary ".

The Plough is Keulachongpa. Keulachongpa got killed in a raid, his slayers took his head and his left leg, but before his relatives could carry off his corpse, the great darkness fell and he was turned into a constellation. Four stars form his body, two his thigh and his leg, the smallest star is a chicken which was killed for him as *Riha.*

The following are stars which I have not been able to identify.

Latlang and *Labeu.*—A husband and wife, of whom the wife died first. The husband Latlang used to visit her in the abode of the dead but finding this unsatisfactory deliberately annoyed his guardian angel (*Zang*) who consequently caused his death. Latlang then joined Labeu in Atikhi and after a while they were turned into stars. Lusheis call these two stars *Nufa thembu in chuh* and say that they are a woman and her daughter quarrelling over a spindle.

Aphilu.—Constellation of four stars representing the corners of a piece of matting which was being made when the great darkness started and was turned into stars. This is possibly the Square of Pegasus.

Sohlu vang araipa.—A constellation of five stars formed by four men and a flying fox's skin that they were stretching out to dry when the great darkness started. Possibly Cassiopeia.

Lodo pazo adongpa.—A constellation of about ten stars representing men catching rats in a rubbish dump near a jhum house. This is the same as the Lushei *Khiangte zong zim,* which means the Khiangtes catching rats and is identified by Lorrain and Savidge as a group of stars in Taurus near Aldebaran.

Sahruatong.—A constellation of three stars representing a threshing floor, which was being made when the great darkness started.

---

* So also the Chang Naga.—J. H. H.

Shooting stars are star dung. Comets are regarded as heralds of disease and famine. Thunder is caused by God rolling stones about; another explanation is that it is caused by a python beating its tail on the floor of heaven. Lightning is said by some to be God striking steel, by others to be caused by thunderbolts striking against each other in the air. Thunderbolts are hurled by God at a lizard called Pachichariapa who swells up his throat and then blows out the air which goes up to heaven and hits the son of Khazangpa on the posterior thereby annoying Khazangpa.

The Rainbow is the tail of a celestial red cock which comes down after rain to catch crabs in the streams. Its tail spreads out over the sky and forms a rainbow. It is unlucky to point at a rainbow. It is believed that the finger which points at the rainbow will get cut accidentally off. The Lakher name for a rainbow is Meisokupa.

Hurricanes are caused by fights between Khisongs (the abodes of spirits). Ordinary winds are the breath of spirits of men and animals.

There are two beliefs as to the cause of earthquakes. Some say that earthquakes are due to the matrimonial intercourse of the sky and the earth, who are husband and wife. As this only takes place shortly before the death of some great chief, earthquakes are believed to portend the death of a chief. Others say that when a chief dies his spirit flies through the cords by which the earth is attached to the sky and as it passes the spirit cuts through one of the cords with its dao thus causing an earthquake.

Exceptionally high floods are called Tisaitlong and are due to Spirits of the mountains and rivers changing their abodes and causing the Kolodyne to swell so as to make a road for their passage. Landslips which always follow these floods are caused by the lesser spirits coming to greet their lords who present them with ear-rings.

The dead are always buried. Coffins are never used, the body is merely wrapped in a cloth.

Chiefs and important persons are buried in their family vaults which consist of pits lined with stone and with a stone as a doorway. Valuables are often buried with the dead person and taken out when the next corpse is laid in the vault. These valuables then become the property of the person who opens the vault, who must be the sister or the sister's son or, failing these, the daughter or daughter's son of the person to be buried. When a vault is opened to receive another inmate the person who opens it collects the head and the bones of the person last buried, wraps them in a cloth and lays them on one side of the vault; she then sweeps all the debris on the floor of the vault into a corner and the new corpse is then placed inside. Vaults are known as *thlapi* or *longang*. Corpsse are nowadays buried in vaults in a prostrate position. An ordinary grave is called *thlata*. It consists of a pit 5 ft. long × 2½ft. wide × 5 ft. deep, at the end of which a hole is excavated just wide enough to hold the body, which is pushed into it feet first. This hole is closed with a stone and the outer pit is filled in with earth. It does not matter in which direction the head lies. The head is never disposed of separately.

In the case of bad deaths, *i.e.*, *sawvaw*, an unnatural death and *thichhi* death from certain loathsome diseases, graves are always made outside the village to the west. This kind of grave is known as *Thlachhi* and is dug differently. Instead of the actual resting place of the corpse being made at the end of the grave it is made at one side. The body is placed in this alcove and enclosed by a log of wood or bamboos. The grave is then filled up. A flat memorial stone called *Longphei* is usually placed over the grave.

The abode of all ordinary spirits is *Atikhi*, lit. the dead men's village. Here life goes on much the same as in this world, the rich remain rich and the poor remain poor. People who have married several times in this world marry their first wife or their first husband as the case may be in Atikhi. After long residence in Atikhi a spirit dies again, when this spirit's death occurs a chief's spirit turns into heat mist and goes up to heaven and vanishes. A poor man's spirit becomes a worm, which gets eaten by a chicken and so ends finally.

Over a certain spring near Longchei village which is said to be the dead men's water supply, the spirits of the dead are said to hover in the shape of a swarm of flies.

Lakhers believe that just prior to death a dying man's soul sometimes enters a pig or a tree and only returns to its human habitation to leave it finally for Atikhi.

Those who have died bad deaths, *sawvaw* or *thichhi*, are not allowed in Atikhi, they have to go to an abode of their own called *sawvawkhi*. The Chhongchhongpipa, the guardian of the gates of the abode of the dead, sees that they go to their right place.

Yet another abode of the dead is Peira or Paradise, to which only the spirits of those who have killed certain wild animals can ever attain. Peira is the happiest abode as it is nearest to Khazangpa. A man who attains Peira takes his wife and children there also when they die.

It is believed that the spirits of children can sometimes be re-born in the person of a younger brother or sister and I have been given definite instances in support of this belief. In certain cases the parents of a dead child have smeared its ankle or its cheek with lamp black and when another child was born it was found to have black mark in the same place as the lamp black had been applied to the body of the dead child. From this the Lakhers say that the dead child's spirit has been born again in the body of the newly born baby.

The only implements used in cultivation are the hoe (*atu*), the dao (*takong*), the axe (*ahrei*). All three tools are made in the village forge, the handles being made of the root of *melocanna bambusoides*. The dao is described under weapons. The hoe and axe are both fixed into a hole made in the handle, the spike at the base of the blades being run through the hole and protruding an inch or two on the other side of the handle.

Musical Instruments.

I. Instruments imported from Burma.

Dawkhang, large Burmese gongs six to ten spans in circumference.

Viadaw, similar to Dawkhang but smaller.

Dawchheu, pairs of small bell metal gongs.

Ladaw, pairs of small brass gongs.

Chiami, brass bugles.

Photla, brass cymbals.

II. Lakher home-made instruments.

The Khang, a drum made out of a hollowed log of *aveu* wood (*Gmelina arborea*, Roxb.).

The membrane is made of the skin of barking deer or serow, and so are the thongs to hold the membrane in place. The skins are soaked in water and then stretched over the ends of the wooden cylinder, where they are held in place by the thongs.

The Tangta, a one-stringed violin made out of a hollow gourd the top of which is cut off and covered with leaves of *chaihna* (*Phrynium capitatum, Willd*). The string is made of palm fibre, the bridge out of a bit of gourd. The neck of the instrument is made of a bit of split bamboo which is passed through holes in the gourd made to receive it. The instrument is held at the neck with the left hand, the fingers of which make the notes by pressing on the string, while the bow which consists of a thin piece of split bamboo is plied with the right hand.

The Siaramang Chapawpa, a bamboo flute, closed at both ends. At one end a hole is cut in the side to blow down at, the other two holes are cut by placing the fingers on which notes are produced.

The Siaramang Chanongpa, another kind of bamboo flute, open at both ends. One end is notched for the lip to fit the mouthpiece, at the other four holes are made for producing notes. The performer blows down the mouthpiece and makes the notes with his fingers.

The Tlaipi, a bamboo zither. It consists of a joint of hollow bamboo closed at each end by a node. One side of the bamboo is shaved away so as to leave two thin bamboo strings, under which small bamboo wedges are placed and slid up and down to increase or reduce the tension of the strings as desired. The instrument is held in the two hands, the strings being twanged with the thumbs.

The Chaei, a Jew's harp. There are two kinds of bamboo *chaei* and an iron *chaei* has recently been introduced from Arakan. The oldest form of *chaei* is a small straight piece of bamboo hollowed out so as to leave a tongue in the middle. At one end is a loop of string which goes round the little finger of the left hand at the other end near the base of the tongue, is a rather longer bit of string. The instrument is held so that the tip of the tongue of the harp is opposite to the player's mouth and the string at the base of the tongue is jerked continuously to cause the tongue to vibrate. Unless the string is pulled, merely blowing on the tongue of the harp produces no sound.

The newer form of bamboo *chaei* is on the same principle but is shaped like a small cricket bat. The iron *chaei* made in Arakan is a bit of umbrella spoke bent into the shape of a key handle with a thin steel tongue.

Weapons of offence, guns, bows and arrows (now obsolete), daos and spears.

Weapons of defence, shields, panjies (*seu*), stone shoots (*longpa*).

Guns, these are practically all flintlocks, most of them being Tower muskets dating round about 1815. The stocks are often lacquered black or red.

Bows, the cross-bow is unknown to the Lakhers. The plain bow consists of a bamboo stave about 5 ft. long with a string made of the bark of *Hibiscus macrophyllos*. The whole bow is called *li*, the stave *libow*, the string *liri*.

Arrows are of two kinds, bamboo headed and steel headed. They are not feathered. When shooting a bracer is used called *hneuthli*.

Pellet bows are used for killing birds.

Spears, these were always carried to war and are still always carried when out hunting. They are used both for thrusting and hurling. The shaft is made of the wood of *Caryota urens*. The heads are either made in the village forge or bought in Lungleh or Haka. They are lozenge shaped, quite plain and without barbs. The head is fixed to the shaft with lac as is also an iron spike at the butt used for sticking into the ground when the spear is not in use.

Daos, the ordinary dao is the *takang* which is made left-handed or right-handed as the case may be. [Because the cutting edge is plano-convex and can only be used effectively from one direction.—J. H. H.]. The blades are made in the village forge. The handles from the root of *Melocanna bambusoides*. The blade is fixed into a hole made in the handle with lac. The *takang* was always carried to war and is now used for every kind of work, agriculture, carpentering, etc.

The Vaina, a special ceremonial dao, carried to war and also in the ceremonial dances performed after taking heads. The handle is of brass and ornamented with a tuft of scarlet goats' hair. The blade is curved and about 17 inches long. At the handle the blade is two inches wide, it widens out to a breadth of 4½ inches and then tapers down to the point. About 2½ inches from the end of the blade is a small sharp protuberance opposite to the cutting edge.

The Zozi, a ceremonial sword with a brass handle and a brass scabbard lacquered in red or black. It was carried to war and worn by Chiefs as a sign of their position. They are brought from Haka.

The Chaizoang, a small double-edged knife used for skinning animals, chopping up meat, slicing bamboos, etc. This knife is made in the village forge, the tang fits into the handle which is made of the wood of *Brehmeria regulosa* (Wedd.) and fixed in with lac. The knife is provided with a sheath of soft wood.

Shields (*Veupho*), are quadrangular and are made of three or four layers of mithun hide. The upper half of the shield is covered with brass discs, from the bottom row of brass discs hang tufts of scarlet goat's hair and a long tuft of scarlet hair hangs from each of the top corners.

Panjies or *seu* are sharp bamboo stakes planted in the paths along which a raiding party is expected. These pierce the feet and legs and cause nasty wounds.

Longpa or stone shoots are booby traps consisting of rocks and stones placed so that by cutting the creepers and bamboos which hold them in place they can be precipitated on to an enemy travelling along the path below.

Treatment of heads, taken from an enemy.

Heads were hung up on trees and left there till they fell off and disappeared in the jungle. Among the Hawthai and Sabeu heads could not be brought inside the village at all and were hung up on trees immediately after the return home of the raiding party. For the Ia ceremony, which must be performed over all heads to ensure that the dead man shall be the slave of his slayer in the next world and also to prevent the dead man's ghost (*saw*) from harming his slayer, the Sabeu and Hawthai used imitation heads made out of a gourd. The Tlangsai and Zeuhnang had no objection to bringing heads inside the village and did so for the Ia ceremony after which they hung them up. Heads taken for *Machhipaina*, that is to end the mourning which must be held after the death of a chief, were placed on the memorial posts above the chief's grave. This was last done by the Zeuhnang who hung up the heads of some Khumis they had slain in 1917 on the memorial posts over the grave of the late chief Hmanglai.

(ii) The Western Rengma Nagas.

By Mr. J. P. Mills, I.C.S.

1. The tribe is divided into a southern and a northern group, speaking different dialects. The groups intermarry. The southern group in turn is divided into (1) the big exogamous Kentennenyu clan and (2) the Azonyu group of clans. The Azonyu group in turn is divided into three exogamous groups of clans. The northern group is divided into some six exogamous groups of clans. Descent goes in the father's line.

2. There is no definite order of social precedence. In the southern group the Kentennenyu clan is vaguely regarded as senior, with the Sampinyu as the senior subclan of the Azonyu division. In the northern group the Mhatongza clan is vaguely regarded as senior.

3. There is no chiefly class.

4. The organization is democratic and very bad. Old men and men of position are listened to to a certain extent, but there is very little discipline in a village.

5. It is believed that the tribe was originally one with the Lhotas and travelled with them on their migration from Kheza-Kenoma to the south as far as Therugu Hill on the southern edge of the present Rengma country. There the main body of the tribe split off, though certain clans joined them later both from the Semas to the east and the Lhotas to the north. Some sixteen generations ago a body split from the village of Kitagha and travelling away to the east, became the present Eastern, or Naked Rengmas. Another section split off about three or four generations ago and settled in the Mikir Hills.

6. There is a certain amount of terraced cultivation in some of the southern villages. The art was learnt from their Angami neighbours. Terraces are built on steep slopes and revetted with stone.

7. Megaliths are of two kinds : (1) A rectangular stone platform is made near a path and on it is set up a monolith for the performer of the ceremony, a slightly smaller one for his wife, and a little one for each of his children. A son may set up one of the monuments in the name of his dead father if he has had a series of bad harvests. The Kentennenyu clan of the southern group, and the Mhatongza of the northern group do not put up these monuments.

(2) Alignments are very rare. One was set up in Phesinyu in 1929 by one Gwalu in honour of his father. It consists of 18 monoliths 9 to 18 inches high and represents the deceased Hongpung with his wife and children and all who owned him as master. In the past such alignments have been set up by childless people who wish thus to distribute their wealth at a feast and leave some memorial.

8. Circular, or, more usually, semi-circular, stone seats are made by the sides of paths. Upright stones help to strengthen the wall. Sometimes a man makes one during life as a memorial to himself, and sometimes a widow or a son makes one as a memorial to a dead man. It is particularly common for a son to make one as a memorial to his father if he has been having bad crops, as these seats are believed to recapture the lost fertility of the parents. Any one may sit on them.

9. Houses are of wood, bamboo and thatch. Planks for the front wall and porch may only be used by a man who has given the first of the feasts of merit.

10. (*a*) The shape of the front porch of the house varies according to the distance the owner has progressed in the series of feasts of merit. In Tesophenyu a man who has completed the series put up " house horns " of the Angami pattern, but smaller.

(*b*) A man who has given the feasts of merit wears a dark blue cloth with white bands and red lines at the edge. His daughter may wear a body cloth ornamented with circles of cowries.

11. It is very vaguely believed that the sun is male and the moon female. Both were once equally hot, but God (Songinyu) saw that men were troubled because they had no means of telling night from day and planted a ficus tree (*urembi*), and a plant with long leaves (*alaphatung*) on the moon. These shade it and are the marks we see on the moon now. Orion represents men trying to attack a village. The belt itself is *Terison keyenyu* (the sentries) and the dagger *Byenyu* (the strangers, *i.e.*, attackers). The Pleiades are called *Shenyu Pempi Kepenyu* (the star of the pounding table carriers). There are believed to be seven, but most people can only see six. Any one who can see seven will be very happy in his married life. A pair of stars (Castor and Pollux) is called *Letung* (girl's stick) and represents a young man cutting a stick for his mistress. Venus, both as a morning and an evening star, is called, *Shepfu* and is believed to influence the crops. There is a separate name for each fork of the Milky Way. The big fork is called *Zule* (the Diyung River), and the small fork *Serizu* (the Tulo stream in the Sema country). They had a quarrel over the killing of a mithun and parted. Shooting stars are merely falling stars.

An earthquake occurs when the sky has connection with his wife the earth.

Neolithic stone adzes are called *tsamphara duding* (axes fallen from the sky). They are believed to come down with lightning. It is lucky to find one and the finder keeps it as a charm. They are hurled down by god (*Songingu*) on any tree which he claims and wishes to fell. Thunder is the voice of god and in whatever direction it is heard most the crops will be best. The rainbow is the breath of a spirit. It rises from damp, haunted spots. If you point your finger at it you get ill.

An eclipse of the moon happens when a tiger tries to eat it. The sun is eclipsed when a great man dies.

12. The dead are buried in the village. Sometimes a man will ask to be buried outside the village, and if so, his wishes are complied with. The head is not separately treated. The grave is covered with a slab of stone, and if on a slope stone slabs will be used to support the sides and make a flat top. Ordinarily a burial is made alongside a former burial, till large paved platforms are formed. If a grave is made in the rains a shelter is built over it.

13. The soul of the dead man remains in the village till the Ngada ceremony which marks the beginning of the next agricultural year. Very occasionally a dead man goes to a home in the sky, but the vast majority go to the Land of the Dead under the earth. The Kentennenyu clan go to Sihama, a village to the west, and enter the Land of the Dead at a spot there which is not known. All other clans use the cave on Wokha Hill used by the Lhotas. All meet at the same destination. Including the present life a man has seven lives in worlds one below the other, each being an exact repetition of the one before. Finally, those who can sing become crickets, and those who cannot, butterflies.

14. The complexion is sallow. The hair is black, and usually straight, but occasionally slightly wavy. It is shaved all round the head. The heads of girls are entirely shaved till they are betrothed, when their hair is allowed to grow. The eyes are brown and slightly oblique. The nose is rather long. The head appears moderately round (no measurements have been recorded).. The physique is strong, but slight.

15. Seed is sown broadcast and a spoon-shaped digger used to cover it. The hoe is an iron hoop derived from the primitive bamboo hoe.

16. A simple bamboo flute with two holes, one of which is used for the mouth and other for the production of notes. Also jew's harp.

17. Weapons used are *dao*, spear and cross-bow (now almost obsolete). A few specimens exist of a short, heavy club which was used as weapon of offence in riots, and, held in the left hand to ward off *dao* blows, as a weapon of defence in serious fighting. Raw hide armour, consisting of cuirass, leg pieces and arm pieces, also used to be used.

Enemies' heads were kept for one night on the shelf of the carved post of the Bachelors' Hall to which the taker belonged. Next day they were hung from bamboos which were leant against the head-tree.

(iii) The Hill Kacharis.

These notes by Mr. J. H. Crace, I.P., Political Officer, Sadiya, and formerly Sub-Divisional Officer, North Cachar Hills, describe some of the traditions and customs of the most old fashioned and least spoiled villages in the North Cachar Hills.

1. A son may not marry into his mother's clan, nor a girl into her father's clan.

2. In the pre-Dimapur days there were only 7 male clans. Of these, the oldest clans were the Bodosa, the clan which had formerly been royal, the Thaosengsa, which was then the ruling clan, and the Hasyungsa, the royal collaterals but not ruling. The other clans were the Langtasa, Jigidingsa, Haflongphongsa, Shengyungsa. After the tribe left Dimapur there were 40 clans.

At Dimapur there were 13 clans of women. Certain clans had functional names :—

Female—Sagaodi—The clan of the Raja's mother.

Phraidi—The clan of the Prime minister's wife.

Male—Songyabsa—The royal cooks.

Nobidasa—The professional hunters.

Female—Siadima—The hereditary washers of the royal rice.

Anujiya—Hereditary ayahs to royalty.

Male—Bengyasa—Servants, slaves and menials to royalty.

Ngablaisa—Fishermen to royalty.

The Bodosa and after them the Thaosengsa were the royal clans. The Raja's mother might belong to any clan. When she was sent to the royal harem she was entitled to be called Makhamgupujik, signifying that she was as beautiful and satisfying as the finest rice.

3. The organization of the tribe used to be autocratic but now-a-days it is democratic. There is a headman to give the final orders, a minister for land to advise the headman on all matters concerning lands and cattle, a head boy to keep the youngsters in order, and a head girl for the girls. None of these are hereditary offices.

4. Endle's Book on the Kacharis gives a story of an origin from the north-west. The legend I have is as follows :—

"We lived in a land called Ilasaw Kamruli in the very high mountains of dazzling brightness. We lived in big villages of stone. Not far away was a river in a great valley which flowed from the west. We were driven out and got across on a raft fixed to a rope which ran from side to side. We got to a place called Khundilo where the river comes out of the mountains into a sandy plain. Here we settled at a place called Phrapdisari Prappongsari after a great tree. We were driven from that place by the Shengphongsarao who had long swords in wooden sheaths." Here the story continues as in Endle's book.

5. Houses are built entirely of bamboo with wooden posts and a thatched roof. Some houses have a small earthern plinth if the site is not level and this may be either stone or plank or faced with wood. Stones are used as seats, but their use is not privileged.

6. When a man dies, his neighbours and relations enter his house and his widow or, if he had no widow some old woman kills a cock (for a woman a hen) at the head of the deceased. She then says "father and mother who have died, take your child away." Then the corpse, which has been washed, is carried to a stream near the village and placed on a pyre of 12 layers of wood, and is burnt, the head to the west. The ashes are then thrown into the stream, and the people go back to the house. The widow, or old woman, puts a piece of gold or silver into a little bowl of water and with a leaf sprinkles on those assembled one by one saying—"I have sprinkled, go." Clean clothes are then put on. In the evening, if there is any rice in the house, the married youths and maidens collect wood and leaves and the rice is spread on a mat and pounded. A little is distributed to each house in the village where it is cooked ; next day it is brought back to the house of the deceased. When all are assembled pigs, goats, cocks, hens and tortoises are killed, and a feast follows. The next day all go to where the corpse was burnt and scatter rice, then they go back to the house and get water which they sprinkle on the burnt-out pyre after which they return to the house of the deceased, where drink is supplied.

The married men then proceed to build a model house outside the village. The house is about 2½ feet high including the comparatively tall *chung*. There is a notched stick up to the little verandah by way of a ladder, and at the foot there is a little dug-out. On the verandah is a small wooden seat and often a cloth. Several scarlet and black woollen squares are hung from the roof to frighten away evil spirits.

7. Sowing is broadcast. The implements of agriculture are generally short-handled and small-bladed ; they consist of narrow bladed hoes, small trowels and an elementary sickle.

8. The bow is still used, and sharp as well as blunt arrows are used for hunting. I have found no trace of any practice of taking heads.

(iv) The Biete Kukis of the North Cachar Hills.

By Mr. J. P. Mills, I.C.S., from information supplied by Mr. A. H. Fletcher, I.C.S.

1. There are four clans—Chungal or Nampui, Darnei or Thanglei, Ngamlai and Kiete. A fifth clan, called Klangpa, is now extinct. Strictly speaking, the clans are endogamous, but marriage between clans is not infrequent, the woman being received into the clan of her husband. Marriages between members of the Chungal and Darnei clans are common, and these two clans less frequently intermarry with the other two clans.

It is forbidden to touch the comb and hair oil of a member of another clan. If a man marries outside his clan he receives his wife into his clan by anointing her head with some of his own oil.

2. The Chungal and Darnei clans are definitely regarded as superior to the other two.

3. The Chief (*Khalim*) of the tribe is chosen from the Chungal and Darnei clans alternately. He holds office for life. Both his parents must be of the same clan.

4. Each village is run by a headman acting with village elders.

5. They point to the Lushai Hills to the south as their place of origin. They were undoubtedly pushed north into their present home by the Lushei invasion of the Lushai Hills in the 18th century.

They belong to the old Kuki stock.

6. The megaliths which abound in some parts of the Biete country were not set up by them, but by previous inhabitants. As far as is known the Bietes never set up megaliths, but the closely allied Khotlangs on very rare occasions set up small, slender monoliths to commemorate feasts, and the Bietes may have done so in the past.

7. Houses are of wood and bamboo, and are thatched. Stone and planks are not used.

8. People dress as they like, save that a *Khalim* wears a silver or brass bracelet on each wrist and ear ornaments of a special pattern.

9. The sun is female and the moon male. Once the moon (which was the sun then) became so hot that it scorched the earth. It was therefore turned into the moon, and the then moon became the sun. How this change was effected is not known. The sexes were not changed.

Orion's Belt is called *Sijuchoi* ("Rat holes stars"). Orion's sword is *Sivajoun* ("Bhimraj stars"). The Pleiades are *Sirup* ("Six Stars"). Three bright stars close to the Pleiades are *Nunei numan thorkhuol* ("Widow fencing a brinjal plant").

An eclipse occurs when the sun or moon faints for lack of water. They used to come down to earth to get water, but the dogs drove them away and now they dare not come.

Lightning is caused by a snake, which lives in a river, firing a gun.

The rainbow is searching for fish in streams.

10. The dead are buried. No coffin is made. A small platform is built over the grave and offerings of food and drink for the dead put on it.

The land of the dead is Ithikuo. No soul can reach it till the proper charm has been uttered by Kuolsam, an old man whom the soul meets half-way. Nothing is known of the life of the soul.

11. Sowing is usually broadcast. The agricultural implements used are the "dao", a small narrow triangular hoe, an adze and sickle.

12. The following are the musical instruments used :—drum, bamboo flute and lute with silk strings.

13. The true bow, as distinguished from the Naga crossbow, was once used but is now obsolete. The modern weapons are spears and *daos*.

Enemies' heads used to be stuck on poles in the village. A man had to bring in a head before he could marry.

(v) The Khelma Kukis of the North Cachar Hills.

By Mr. J. P. Mills, from information supplied by Mr. A. H. Fletcher, I.C.S.

1. The tribe is divided into thirteen, or possibly more, clans. Descent is reckoned from the father. The clans are strictly speaking endogamous. Though marriage with a person of another clan is frequent it is definitely regarded as entailing defilement. A man contracting such a marriage cannot perform the funeral rites of his parents. Each family therefore sees to it that one member at least marries within the clan.

A woman is not received into her husband's clan on marriage and cannot touch his comb and hair oil if she is of a different clan. In such cases her husband's sister has to be called in to do her children's hair. All clans are socially equal.

2. The organization is democratic. The head of each clan is known as the *Khalim*. The *Khalims* settle matters of importance.

3. The tribe belongs to the Old Kuki stock. It points to the Lushai Hills to the south as its place of origin. Thence it was driven north by Lushai expansion of the 18th century.

4. Houses are of wood, bamboo and thatch. There are no restrictions.

5. A Khalim wears ear ornaments of a special pattern. Otherwise there are no distinctions in dress.

6. The sun is female and the moon male. The Pleiades are called *Sirup* ("Six stars"). Orion's Belt is *Jubarjon* ("Jar carriers"). Men are carrying an earthen jar home from the "jhum". Orion's sword is *Saidanchu* ("Rice basket pulling"). Three brothers are fighting over a rice basket. Venus as a morning star is *Sikovar* ("dawn star"). Venus as an evening star is *Koloi*. *Koloi* was a man whose head was taken when he was returning from a distant village with his bride. That evening he appeared in the west as a bright star. A shooting star is a star going to be married. The Milky Way divides the hot and cold halves of the sky. In the hot weather it is low in the sky; but in the cold weather it is overhead.

An eclipse is caused when the sun and the moon take the same path across the sky. Though there are ten different paths they sometimes make a mistake and meet.* A rainbow means that tigers and bears are likely to be particularly dangerous. Earthquakes occur when a race of evil beings living beneath the earth have a battle.

7. Poor people are buried and the rich cremated. No monument is erected. A tall bamboo with a piece of white cloth at the end is put up by a grave. If a man dies a violent death the cloth is red.

8. The souls of the dead go to *Marsi*, which lies above the earth. They travel on foot up a very steep path called *Marsithung*. A man called Pangam was once taken to his dead wife in heaven, hanging on to a wild cat's tail. He looked at the dead dancing, though she told him not to, and was sent back to earth; he related that the dead live in happiness, without hunger or thirst. They call bamboo leaves fish and rotten wood flesh.

9. Seed is sown broadcast. The implements are a narrow triangular hoe, a *dao*, axe and sickle.

10. Musical instruments are bamboo flute, Jew's harp and drum.

11. Weapons are the bow (now obsolete), spear and *dao*. Enemies' heads used to be hung up in the Bachelor's Halls. Now-a-days no heads are taken and no Bachelors' Halls are built.

(vi) Notes on the Lushei.

By Mr. N. E. Parry, I.C.S.

1. The Lushais are divided into numerous clans details of which will be found at pages 125-127 of Colonel Shakespear's book "The Lushei Kuki clans". One of the most striking characteristics of the Lushais is their capacity for absorbing other races. This process began before they came under British rule and has continued ever since. Most of the tribes in the Lushai Hills district have been strongly influenced by the Lushais both as to their customs and their language and it may be said that the only villages which have maintained their tribal customs free from Lushai influence are the Lakhers and to a lesser degree the Chin villages in the Lungleh sub-division. The Fanais, the Paihtes, the Thados and other Kuki tribes have all come very largely under Lushai influence and before many years have passed will be practically indistinguishable from the Lushais. This is partly due to the special gift for rule which characterises the Sailo chiefs and partly to the fact that the language taught in all the schools in the district except in the Lakher villages is Dulien, the language spoken by the Lushais. The absorption of the Raltes had begun and made great strides prior to the advent of British rule and now-a-days Raltes can only be distinguished from other Lushais by their excessive love of talking and their litigious propensities.

None of the Lushai clans are now exogamous, nor do they appear to have been so within recent times. Among the Sailos the favourite marriage is of first cousins and at one time it was usual for a Sailo always to marry a Sailo. Now-a-days however the younger chiefs have begun to take their wives from almost any clan, though if a suitable Sailo bride is forthcoming she is usually preferred. It can be stated quite definitely however that a young Lushai whether a member of the Sailo clan or not has the completest freedom in his choice of a wife and is bound neither by exogamy nor by endogamy. The position seems to have been much the same when Colonel Shakespear wrote in 1912, *vide* "The Lushei Kuki clans", page 50. The marriage of a brother and sister however is incestuous and is believed to ruin the village crops. I have known of two such marriages.

2. Practically the only social distinction that exists is that conferred on persons who have performed the Thangchhuah feasts. As these feasts are, I fear, becoming rapidly obsolete, even these distinctions will shortly cease to exist. There is no marked division into classes with a definite order of social precedence and in this the Lushais differ markedly from the Lakhers. The Sailos, the chiefly clan, are universally looked up to and given precedence socially; apart from this however there is practically complete social equality among the people. That this state of affairs has existed for a long time, and is not merely a result of British rule, is shewn in Colonel Lewin's book "The Hill tracts of Chittagong and the Dwellers therein". Such distinctions as do exist seem to be due more to wealth than to birth. People who are well-to-do are often spoken of as "mitha", while poor people are referred to as "michhia". For all practical purposes however social distinctions among the mass of the people simply do not exist at all. There are it is true a few clans like the Panchhuao which formerly used to regard themselves as of a superior status and to demand higher marriage prices for their daughters. These distinctions however have practically disappeared. The tendency has been for the marriage price to become the same for all Lushais irrespective of clan, the Sailos alone retaining a higher rate. The return of the labour corps from France led to temporary but marked rise in marriage prices as the returned labourers had money to burn and were ready to pay any exorbitant price that the parents of the girls they fancied demanded. Thus, contrary to all customs, a girl's price became more dependent on her looks and the greed of her parents than on her birth and the customary rate of price. The chiefs highly disapproved of this breach of custom and as soon as money got scarcer a reaction occurred and a more or less definite rate of marriage price, based on the most prevalent old rate, was fixed for all girls.

3. The Sailo clan is the chiefly clan. This clan is descended from Sailova, great-grandson of Thangura to whom all members of the clan trace back their genealogies. The early Sailos were gifted rulers who crushed out practically all the then existing chiefs again, excepting the Lakher and a few Chin chiefs in the south-east of the district, and established themselves all over the hills. To this day the Sailos are for the most part capable rulers and their villages are far better conducted than the few to which for one reason or another members of non-chiefly clans have from time to time been appointed as chiefs by Government. Formerly Sailos married practically entirely within the clan, though there does not appear to have been any definite rule compelling them to do so. Now-a-days however much less importance is attached to this by the younger generation, who are apt to marry any girl they fancy whether she be a Sailo or not, and there are quite a number of chiefs who have married non-Sailo wives. This seems to be due partly to the fact that Sailo brides are much more expensive and partly to the fact that in the past many chiefs kept concubines belonging to other clans. Failing legitimate issue, the children of these concubines have in some cases become chiefs, and being themselves of mixed parentage do not feel so strongly the necessity of finding Sailo brides. The fickleness of a Lushai's affections and the ease and frequency with which he can change his wife may also have had an effect, as the Sailos share this characteristic with the rest of the tribe. Still the fact remains that other things being equal a Sailo chief still prefers to marry a Sailo.

4. The Lushais have no indigenous terraced cultivation and attempts to introduce it have met with little or no success. I know of no genuine terraced cultivation carried out by Lushais. The only places where wet rice cultivation is carried on to any extent are in the broad Valley of Champhai and to a lesser extent

*It is difficult to believe that vague rumours from a Mission School have not given rise to this explanation.

at North and South Vanlaiphai, Lailiphai, Tuisenhnar and a few other places where there are similar but less extensive valleys. Prior to the advent of the British no wet rice cultivation at all was carried out, the only method of cultivation known to the Lushais being *jhuming*. Lushais were taught wet cultivation at Champhai by Santal coolies imported for the purpose.

5. Stone monuments are not common, the usual memorial being a wooden platform (*lungdawh*) made of logs. Stone memorials (*lungphun*) are however put up for chiefs and formerly were erected for persons who had taken heads. The word for a memorial "*lungdawh*" which means literally "stone put" seems however to indicate that at one period the usual monument erected was of stone. The stone memorials consist either of a pile of stone (*lungdawh*) with a large upright stone (*lungphun*) in the middle, or of a single erect stone (*lungphun*). The upright stones often have carvings of mithun's heads, gongs and guns showing the number of mithun slain by the deceased for the Khuangchawi feasts and the number of gongs and guns that he possessed. On the wooden platform are hung up the heads of all the game shot by deceased in his lifetime. One stone monument on the path from North Vanlaiphai to Farkawn has a carving of a man holding four heads in each hand. I could not find out its history. Near Champhai are a number of these stone memorials the best known being Mangkhaia's *lungdawh*. which is illustrated in Colonel Shakespear's book. Near Tachhip village is a large memorial stone to a Palian chief called Sibuta known as Sibutalung. Memorial stones are generally erected on the side of a path though I have seen them in the middle of a village and they may be erected anywhere that the person erecting them pleases. Now-a-days Christians often erect stone or wooden crosses in memory of their dead either by the side of path or over the grave. Another new custom is to erect a stone in memory of a hunting dog with an inscription extolling the animal's virtues and a list of the game he was instrumental in bringing to the bag.

6. Stone seats are but rarely found. There is however no objection to men using stone seats. Women never use stone seats as they believe that woman who sits on a stone seat will give birth to a hone. This is known as "*Falungtat*", lit. "child hone".

7. The materials used in building are wood, bamboo, cane, and for roofs thatch and palm leaves or if the two former are not available bamboo leaves, while now-a-days in Thakthing the Aijal village as many as can afford it use corrugated iron for roofs. Wood is used for the posts and crossbeams and bamboos in one form or another for all the rest of the work. The whole framework of the houses is of bamboo and the floors and walls are of bamboo matting. Neither stone nor wood is ever used for walls, floors or roofs but there is no particular restriction on the use of these materials. The steps leading up to the houses are made of wooden logs laid like steps not merely of one wooden log with steps leading up to it.

8. The only social distinctions are those conferred on people who have performed the *Thangchhuah* feasts often loosely spoken of as *Khaungchawi* and consisting of the following parts. *Chawng, Sedawi-chhun, Zan khuang, Mithirawplam, Sedawi-in-a-tlip, Khuangpui, Sedawi-in-a-tlip, Khuangpui vawihnihna, Sedawi-in-a-tlip, Zawh-zaw-zo.* Persons who have performed these feasts can wear a special striped cloth known as a Thangchhuah cloth and a turban of the same cloth with a headdress of king-crow's feathers. Men who had performed the feasts as far as *Mithirawplam* were allowed to assume these distinctions, though to attain real merit it was desirable to perform the whole series. In addition to the distinctive dress, those who had performed the feasts were allowed to make a window in the side wall of their house and to have a small verandah at the back of the house called bazah. Now-a-days the feasts are very rarely performed partly owing to the spread of Christianity and partly owing to their great cost. I do not know one of the younger chiefs who has performed the whole series and only a few who have begun it. Chiefs whether they have actually performed the requisite feasts or not wear the *thangchhuah* cloths and the headdress of king-crow's feathers on formal occasions. The restrictions on the use of windows is no longer strictly observed and bazahs are rarely seen.

There were two other distinctive headdresses now completely obsolete. The *chhawndwal*, a plume of goat's hair dyed red worn by a warrior who had, taken a head and the *arkeziak*, which were plaits of red and black cotton made by the girls and tied round the hair knots of the men who had taken heads when they returned from a raid.

9. *The Sun.*—The Sun is a female and being but a timorous woman is afraid to wander abroad at night, while the moon who is a man has no such fears and is consequently seen at night.

The marks on the face of the moon are accounted for as follows.

In the middle of the moon is a huge Ficus tree (Bungpui) and the marks on the moon's face are its branches in which is seated a headless monkey. If any one sees this headless monkey he is sure to die. Lushais therefore avoid staring at the moon lest they should see the headless monkey and so come to an untimely end.

Madmen get worse with the waning moon, their wits vanishing as the moon disappears.

Eclipses whether of the sun or of the moon are caused by a mythical animal called an "awk" said to be the spirit of a Poi chief trying to swallow the moon. There are said to be two clans of Poi chiefs but I have not been able to find out which clan is responsible for the "awk". Whenever an eclipse of the sun (*Ni-awk-lem*) or of the moon (*Thla-awk-lem*) occurs, Lushais beat gongs and drums and make as much noise as they possibly can in order to frighten away the "awk" and prevent him from swallowing the orb. They fear that if the "awk" really swallows the orb there will be another darkness or "*Thimzing*" during which all human beings will be turned into monkeys or other animals as happened once before. Many of the animals we now know were human beings before the last Thimzing.

At lunar eclipses if the moon reappears from the shadow exactly opposite the spot where it first disappeared this is believed to portend an outbreak of cholera within the month.

The Stars.—Venus as an evening star is known as *Chongmawii*, as a morning star as *Hrangchhuana. Hrangchhuana* is *Chongmawii's* lover and is always pursuing her, sometimes he catches her up and they love one another and on these nights a Lushai lover is sure to attain his heart's desire. The story of these lovers is as follows :—

"While their respective villages were at war, *Hrangchhuana* and *Chongmawii* were in love with each other and *Hrangchhuana* used to visit *Chongmawii* every night. Each night when he left *Chongmawii Hrangchhuana* used to slay one of the young warriors of the village, but one night he got killed himself. As soon as *Hrangchhuana* was killed his slayer called out "whose lover is this youth, it is he who has killed so many of our young men." *Hrangchhuana's* body was laid out just outside the village fence and as they wanted to find out whose lover he had been, the chief sent round the village crier to order all the girls to go down to the fields that morning. Accordingly, all the girls went down to the fields and on the way passed *Hrangchhuana's* corpse

Chongmawii's father was very proud of *Chongmawii* but *Chongmawii* was very afraid of passing her lover's corpse and hung back till the very last. She could not refuse to follow the others however and had to come along in her turn. When she reached the corpse however *Chongmawii* was unable to pass it and knelt down by it and wept bitterly. When *Chongmawii's* father saw this he himself slew her by the side of her lover and after this *Hrangchhuana* and *Chongmawii* were turned into stars and still meet occasionally at the appointed season."

The *Plough* is called *Zangkhua* and represents a man who was killed in war. His slayers carried off his head and left leg and before his relatives could rescue his remains they were turned into stars. Four stars form his body and three his thigh and leg.

The story of Zangkhua is as follows :—

There was once a chief called Zanga and in his village there dwelt a man called Kawlawia who went on a visit to his maternal uncle in another village. While he was on this visit Kawlawia had a very bad dream to the effect that he was killed in war. Kawlawia told his uncle of this evil dream and the latter scarified a chicken and performed "thlahual" to call back and soothe Kawlawia's soul as he attributed the dream to Kawlawia's soul having wandered away from him. Kawlawia then uttered the following words :—

"Pu te vang Khua ah va zin ila tawn mang ah chhia, i tih ding emaw. Bawh ar in ran thla zuk hual ila thlafam tur serh khua a kham emaw."

When Kawlawia returned to his village, his maternal uncle accompanied him and escorted him to a point close to his village from which they could see the village memorials. At this point his uncle said "nothing can happen to you here" and left him and returned to his own village. Near the place where the escort turned back was a saddle called Berva Kawn and at this saddle a party was lying in ambush. They slew Kawlawia and cut off his head and one of his legs and thighs and carried them off without Kawlawia's uncle and friends knowing anything about it. Presently the Tlaiberh (bulbuls) began calling in the village 'Kawlawia is dead, Kawlawia is dead" and the villagers asked them "where is he ?" to which the Tlaiberh replied "on Berva Kawn". The villagers said "perhaps he really is dead, let us go and see", so they went out to see and found Kawlawia's remains on Berva Kawn and then the remains were turned into stars and can be seen to this day.

Orion's belt and *sword* are known as *Chhohreivung*. There are eight stars which represent an owl, a rat's nest and six rat's holes. The owl used to sit just above the rat's front door and catch the rats as they came out. One day however the mouse said to the rat "you are very foolish, why do you not have a back door as well as a front door as we do, and then the owl will not be able to catch you". The rat accordingly made a back door as advised, but as soon as he had finished it the great darkness called the *Thimzing* started and the owl and the rat's holes were all turned into stars.

A variant of the story relates that after the rats had found how to avoid the owl, their home was discovered by some men who proceeded to dig the rats out. While they were doing this however their chief found that he had forgotten his tinder box and went home to fetch it but on the way was eaten by a tiger. The villagers surrounded the tiger but it escaped from the rings and ran away and is now the star called *Sikeisen*, which is the planet Mars. The chief's tinder box has given a name to another star which I cannot identify but which is known as *Simeitalh*.

The Pleiades are called *Siruk*, meaning the six stars.

The Milky Way is *Thlasik Kong*, meaning the cold weather road.

The North Star is *Hmar Arsi Sen*, meaning North Star Red.

Cassiopeia is called *Dingdi Puan Tah*, which means Dingdi is weaving.

Dingdi was a girl who was being taught to weave by her mother, when the great darkness fell and they were turned into stars.

There are two stars called *Nufa Thembu In Chuh*, which represent a mother and her daughter quarrelling over a spindle.

Sikawikap consist of seven stars which represent a chief and two commoners playing at the Kawi game with the beans of *Entada Scandens*. The great darkness fell in the middle of the game and the players and their beans were all turned into stars. These stars are probably the Square of Pegasus and part of Orion's belt.

Si Chakai means the Crab Star.

Khiangte Zong Zim meaning the Khiangtes catching monkeys, is a constellation of about ten stars representing a number of members of the Khiangte clan who were all turned into stars at Thimzing while they were chasing monkeys. This constellation is identified by Savidge and Lorrain as a group of stars near Taurus in Aldebaran.

Pukula Thang identified by Savidge and Lorrain as the constellation of Grus represents a deer trap set by a mythical character called Pukula.

Si Rokhuai is a constellation formed by the conversion into stars at Thimzing of a long bamboo with a wild cat's skin hanging from it to dry.

Vandui Saihrua meaning the Sky Bow is formed by a number of stars including Castor and Pollux, Sirius and Procyon.

Si Vawk Bawm means literally Star Pig's Basket. I cannot identify it. Nearly all the Lushai names for stars refer to persons or things that were turned into stars at the great darkness called Thimzing. Shooting stars are known as *Arsithlawk*.

Comets are called *Simeikhu* or the star with a fiery tail. "Once upon a time there was a man called Chawngthanga who was very ill and about to die. Before he died he said "before burying me if you look up to the sky you will see that I have turned into a comet." On the night that Chawngthanga died his friends looked up to the sky as he had told them and saw a comet, as Chawngthanga said they would do.

Parhelia are known as *Sarzam*. When seen in the east they are lucky and portend the taking of a head or the shooting of some large animal. When seen in the west they are unlucky and portend an unnatural death. It is unlucky to point at a *Sarzam* as he who does so will get broken fingers.

The Rainbow is known as *Chhimbal.* It is made by a gigantic Spirit who stands up in a river bed and then bends over to drink. It is unlucky to point at a rainbow as the finger which points will drop off. The danger to the finger can be averted if after a person has pointed at a rainbow he at once points at a hen basket. If one end of a rainbow is seen just over a house, it is believed that the owner of the house will die prematurely. Earthquakes are caused by the beetle called *Pawngeklir,* which collects dung from the road to take home with him. Sometimes as he is rolling his ball of dung along he by mistake lets it roll over the edge of the world and thereby causes an earthquake. The edge of the world is the horizon which the Lushais call Kawlkil.

An alternative explanation of an earthquake is that it is caused by the sexual intercourse of the earth and the sky.

Another version of the beetle story is as follows. "The beetle having collected his ball of dung rolls it along over the earth until he comes to the sea. He enters the sea with his ball of dung and without letting go of it swims over to the other side of the sea and there presents himself before the creator of mankind and of the world and says: "All the people on the world have died and I have inherited their property" and shows to the creator the ball of dung that he has brought with him. The creator in order to see whether all the men in the world have really died or not shakes the earth which causes an earthquake.

Lightning is *Tlumtea chem vilik* which means the flashing of Tlumtea's dao. Tlumtea is a mythical figure.

Thunder is *Puvana Thlegnpui Hnuk Ri* which means the noise made by Puvana moving about a big plate. Puvana whose name means literally "old man in the sky" is the same as Pathian, which is the Lushai name for God.

A *Chhawifa* is a light like a meteor which is said to fly through a village burning brightly. A Chhawifa always starts from a house and is believed to be the spirit of a dying person. It is believed that the owner of a house from which a Chhawifa starts will shortly die.

10. The dead now-a-days are nearly always buried, the grave being made in front of the house. The body is wrapped in a dark blue cloth known as *puandum* and laid flat in the grave. Coffins are not used. Some personal articles such as a pipe, a bag, or possibly a *dao* are often buried with the body. Christians are generally buried in cemeteries instead of in front of the deceased's house. People who have died bad deaths "*sarthi*" having been killed by a wild animal, drowned or killed by a fall from a tree, died of cholera or in childbirth must be buried outside the village. If the first child in a family dies soon after birth it is known as "*hlamzuih*" and is buried in an earthenware pot generally under the house. *Hlamzuih* are buried usually by the father and must on no account be buried by an unmarried person lest his future children should die in the same way.

There is one other way of disposing of the dead, which now-a-days at any rate is only followed by the chiefs because of its great expense, though formerly it seems to have been followed by all true Lushais. The body is placed in a coffin made by hollowing out a log, the opening being closed with a plank of wood. The coffin is placed against the wall in the deceased's house and a special hearth is built close to it. From a hole in the bottom of the coffin a bamboo tube is run through the floor and down into the soil below the house. A fire is lit on the hearth and is kept burning day and night until the corpse has been entirely dessicated, the coffin being turned round at intervals to ensure that the corpse is dried through and through. After about a month the coffin is opened to see what progress has been made and it is not until all the flesh has been dried off which may take three months or more that the skull and larger bones are taken out and placed in a basket which is kept on a shelf near the hearth. The smaller bones are placed in an earthenware pot and buried. When the collection of bones in the house becomes too large they also are placed in an earthenware pot and buried. While a body is being dried the widow is supposed to sit by it and a chief who is drying his wife's body is not supposed to leave his house until the process has been completed, though there is no formal "*hrilh*" the breach of which would entail penalties. The tube which is run from the coffin into the soil is to allow the decaying matter and gases given off by the corpse to escape into the ground. The job of keeping up the fire and seeing that the corpse is properly dried is an unpleasant one and the young men who help to do this have to be liberally supplied with food and drink. During the process the deceased's friends and relations come to condole with the survivors bringing with them zu and animals to be killed to accompany the dead man's spirit to the next world, which incidentally afford a feast for the living. Vanphunga is said to have taken six months to dry his wife's body. Thuamluaia who also dried his wife's body a few years ago only took about two months over it.

11. There are two abodes of the dead, *Mithikhua* and *Pialral.* To Mithikhua which means "dead men's village" go the spirits of all ordinary persons, while to Pialral, which means "across the Pial river" and corresponds to our Paradise, go the spirits of certain privileged mortals who have specially qualified for admittance. Thus the spirits of persons who have performed the Khuangchawi feasts and are known as Thangchhuah go to Pialral. The spirits of men who have been especially successful with women, those who have enjoyed three virgins and those who have enjoyed seven women whether virgins or not, are also admitted to Pialral. The last class of spirits that can claim admittance to Pialral are those of men who have killed a man and also one of each of the following animals:—elephant, bear, wild boar, wild mithun, sambhur, barking deer, hamadryad, flying fox and eagle, men who have killed these animals are also counted as Thangchhuah. No women are admitted to Pialral. The guardian of the lower world is Pupawla the first human being to suffer death, Pupawla, who may be compared with the Lakher *Chong chhong pipa,* shoots with a pellet bow at all the spirits on their way to the lower world, but is not allowed to shoot the spirits of those who are qualified for Pialral by any of the tests already described. All other spirits however, including the spirits of all women, he is able to shoot and all the spirits that he shoots must go to Mithikhua. Those who are bound for Mithikhua first of all pass over the Hringlang hill, cross the Lunglo river whose waters are the waters of forgetfulness, pluck *hawilo* flowers (*Impatiens Chinensis*), which remove all desire to look back to the world, and enter Mithi-Mithikhua.

In spite of the fact that both Lushais and Lakhers believe that there are definite abodes to which spirits must go after death, it is none the less clear that both tribes believe to a great extent in the omnipresence of the spirits of the dead. Thus among the Lushais as well as among the Lakhers I have come across the belief that the spirits of dead children are sometimes born again in the bodies of their younger brothers or sisters. Lushais believe that spirits may migrate into hornets while Lakhers believe that they be flies. The Lakher sacrifice of *Laliachhia* is essentially a sacrifice to the spirits of their dead relations, while the Lushai feast called *Mimukut* has the same *raison d'être.* Again the Lushai *Mithirawplam* which is one of the series of Thangchhuah feast is held in the honour of the ancestors of the giver of the feast. When a woman's husband dies, she has to set aside a small portion of each meal for her husband's spirit for three months after his death. This is known as *Mithichawpek* and if during this period the widow misconducts herself with any man she is liable to all the pain and penalties of adultery as during this period she is held to be as strictly bound to her husband as if he were still alive. After every feast a Lushai has to set aside a small portion of meat, rice and zu for the spirits; this is known as *rawchhiak*. Lushai also used to place a little of the first fruits of every crop under the eaves of the house as an offering to the spirits of their dead parents. This offering is known as *Mithichhiah*. Lushais also believed that the spirits of the deceased come to watch the *Chapchar Kut* ceremonies. With the spread of Christianity these beliefs are gradually dying out but they still linger on among the more conservative. Among the Lakhers, however, the old beliefs have not yet been displaced. Lakhert place eatables on a grave until the memorial stone and post have been erected, also on newly planted memorial posts and again once a year at Laliachhia. Lakhers also believe that woman's childlessness may be due to the fact that the spirits of her dead parents or of her husband's parents are displeased with her. All these examples, pointing as they do to a modified form of ancestor worship, show that though both Lushais and Lakhers believe that definite abodes are allotted to the spirits of the dead, they at the same time believe that the spirits of the dead can revisit their old haunts and exercise influence over living being.

12. *Heads of enemies killed in war.*—The heads of enemies killed in war were brought back to the village and the *Ai* ceremony was performed over them. The purpose of this ceremony was to ensure that the ghost of the man slain's should be the slave of his slayer in the next world. After the *Ai* ceremony had been performed the head was hung up on a tree outside the house where it could be seen. Any kind of tree was regarded as suitable for this purpose but a tree on which a head had been hung up was henceforth known as *Sahlam*. Once the head had been hung up on a tree no further notice was taken of it and it was allowed to fall down and decay. Heads were never buried. A young man who had taken a head was known as a *Huaisen* or a *Pasaltha*. Both of these terms may be translated as "man of valour." Persons who had taken heads were entitled to wear the headdresses known as *Lenchhawn* and *Chhawndawl*, the latter being reserved for specially heroic warriors.

(vii) Notes on the Garos.

By Mr. G. D. Walker, I.C.S.

1. Throughout the Garos and their cogeners the Lynggams (Megams) there is a division into two great exogamous groups. These are called Sangma and Marak. Among the Chisak tribe of Garos in the north-east part of the Garo Hills and among the Garos and Lynggams in Goalpara, Kamrup, and Khasi Hills, the Marak group is frequently called Momin. In the same locality Sangma is replaced, but to a much smaller extent, by Areng and one or two other smaller clans. (Even among the Koch people, on the edges of the Garo Hills, a similar division exists though the names used are not the same. The Tintiki clan of Koch use Sinchung and Ajum for Sangma and Marak. These Koches are Garolike in origin, but have drifted a small way towards Hinduism. The Rabhas also have exogamous clans but have no generic names for them. They have subdivisions in two groups anyone of one subdivision being restricted in choice of a mate to a subdivision of the other group).

The strictness of the Sangma-Marak division has been loosened of recent years, especially under the influence of contact with Christian missions. While it is still uncommon for a Momin to marry a Marak yet the temptation to avoid social ostracism has induced Garos to treat Momin as a separate exogamous group. The missionaries have not actively encouraged the breakdown of the old exogamous system, in fact modern missionaries respect it, and discourage union between Sangma and Sangma, but the solvent is at work nevertheless. To a Garo, for a Sangma to marry a Sangma is equivalent to incest, and a man who has married within his clan is called "Madong," meaning "one who has married his mother", an epithet which never fails to raise a laugh among the bystanders. It may be said therefore, that in spite of modernising influence, the exogamous division of the Garos is very strict.

There are many subdivisions of each group. From careful enquiries carried on for a number of years I compiled a list,* which differs in many ways from the list given in Appendix A of *the Garos* by Playfair.

2. There is no definite division into groups or classes with a definite order of social precedence as between these classes. Any man who has acquired social status is called a "*nokma*," anyone else is an "ordinary man," (*ramram mande*). The husband of the owner of the village land is called nokma. So also is one who has given the necessary feasts, which entitle him to wear certain badges—among Chisaks in the north-east *jaksils* (elbow rings), and red silk turban. Among Chisaks the standard of feast required is very low, and nokmas abound. In the rest of the hills only the very rich can give the elaborate feasts required. In some parts only a genuine nokma (*i.e.*, one who has gone through the expensive ritual of feasts and is called a *ganna nokma*, 'ganna' having the same force in this case as 'genna' in the Naga Hills) can adorn his house with certain carved boards, and with a criss-cross pattern of bamboo slates in the walls at the fore-part of his house.

3. There is no chiefly class or clan among Garos.

4. The organisation of the Garos is more or less democratic. When a matter is in dispute, all concerned, including the women, assemble and debate, with feasting proportionate to the gravity of the issue. Generally the chair is taken by the *nokma*, if it concerns only one village, or by the *laskar* (a petty magistrate appointed by Government, generally on election by the *nokmas* of the charge), or even by the *mauzadar* (salaried Garo official who checks the assessment, to house tax for a group of *laskars*).

5. *Traditions of origin.*—In *the Garos* by Playfair a tradition is given of migration from Tibet through the plains of Assam. This tradition is known only to the Chisaks (of the north-east of the Garo Hills and the plains of Goalpara and Kamrup). The vast majority of Garos have other traditions, but with education and the potency of the printed word, the Chisak tradition is getting wider credence.

Nearly all Garos say they came from the east. Within the Garo Hills the movement in the last 15 to 20 generations has been westwards up the higher valley of the Someswari (Simsang) and out into the low hills south and west of the main range of hills. The Rabhas and Koches and Garo tribes with Koch-like affinities appear to have been driven to the edge of the plains by the more active hillmen, the Abengs and the Matchis. As the foot-hills on the north of the Khasi and Jaintia Hills district are said to have been inhabited by† "Garo" in descriptions of Assam less than a century ago, it would seem that the Khasis on the one side and the plains people on the other gradually squeezed the Garos westward. That a portion of the Garos in their wanderings may have tried to obtain a footing in the Bhutan Hills is quite credible; but I scarcely think that any but a very few travelled so far. For a nomadic tribe, given time and unbroken jungle, there is nothing incredible in that tradition.

*Not printed.

†It must be remembered that the earliest generation of British in Assam used "Garrow" as a term for all hillmen and applied it even to Kukis and Lushais.

6. There are no megalithic monuments in the Garo Hills, with the possible exception of the stone *rang* (gong) near Sokhadam (upper valley of the Krisnai). It is a font-shaped block of sand-stone. If ever it stood as a basin it has been completely overturned. It is half-buried in the earth on a hillside, mouth downwards, and it is difficult to inspect it. I was baffled by the tradition that the local god would be annoyed and bring bad luck to the village if the *rang* were disturbed. The basin is almost perfectly hemispherical, 12″ deep and 16″ in diameter. The thickness of the lip various from 8″ to 12.″ It seems to have been a freak of nature, embellished by art ; possibly a stone containing a " pot hole " worn out by the stream, and the rock containing it trimmed and shaped to facilitate its removal. I was not able to get any tradition as to how it came to be there.

I do not know if the " *asong* " or " *Khosi* " are " megalithic," because none of the stones are very large, though probably the largest obtainable. Every old village, and every new one which wants to acquire a separate status, has in a grove on the village land, often a long way from its present site, a group of small flattish boulders planted upright in the ground. Originally it appears that the head of an enemy was buried at the place, and a stone put in the ground over it. Inside a village such groups of stones are occasionally met with, and each stone, originally at least, was set up when a head was brought in from a raid, but new ones, if any, added now-a-days, commemorate some big feast given by a *ganna nokma.*

Every year before seed-time each village has its commemoration of the *Khosi,* called in some parts the " *asong-tata* " ceremony. No one from another village may be present. If a new stone is to be added to the group it is done at this ceremony, being dragged by the *nokma* and his men from the river-bed, usually no great distance. Whether a new stone is added or not, all the existing stones are decorated with a criss-cross band of bamboo-strips to represent the " *khadisil* " or fillet with brass-inset which adorned the brow of the warrior who brought back a head from a raid.

7. Stone is not used for seats. The only use of which it is put, except for *khosis,* is as a lid over the hole in the ground into which the ashes of the dead are put in the midst of the village. They are not sacred, every one walks over them, and unless pointed out would pass unmarked.

8. The Garos use no stone in building. Whenever they can they use *sal*-wood for the main posts of their houses and granaries. The poorer villages have to contend themselves with bamboo. Thatching grass is nearly always available but in some places bamboo leaves are used for roofing. There are no social distinctions in the choice of material. In the mode of using it, bill boards and lattice work, there is a distinction as mentioned in paragraph 2.

9. (*a*) A *gannani nokma* can show his rank in the appearance of his house. For example in the front wall and the flank walls of the front verandah ordinary people have the slates horizontal and vertical, but the nokma may place these cross-wise, whether in the open work window ventilation (*Mikchiwena* or *mikchiwata,* literally, that which gets rid of tears) in the upper part of the front gable, or in the close woven wall proper. I have found on occasion ordinary people using this mode, but they had to do an annual sacrifice (with feast) for the privilege.

In house of Gobang (Abeng), a nokma of high standing, I found carved beams, across the front verandah and also across the main room. In the house of Raising (Natchi), regarded as of still higher eminence, there are no carved beams, as he says it is not the custom in that part of the country. [Raising has a *danil* (round leather dancing shield) and jaksils (elbow rings), but Gobang has not.]

Every man who is a ganna nokma may wear a red pagri. This is of silk with a fringe, and yellow embroidery, and is woven by the Khasis. Such pagris are common in the Chisak country where nokmas are three a penny, but very rare in the rest of the hills. The Chisaks alone among Garos wear *jaksils* when of the rank of nokma. These are plain bronze or brass hoops worn just above the elbow.

In the old days when the coloured loin cloth or *gando* was decorated with beads, as it rarely is now-a-days, only one who had taken a head could sport a fourth row of beads. Now anyone who has given the requisite feasts is at liberty to do so.

Only great land-nokmas are allowed to keep yak's tails in the house, and on bringing one in the nokma has to perform a sacrifice called *gurerima* (holding a horse) but this is confined to Chisaks.

10. Some Garos hold that the sun and moon are brothers, called *Saljong* and *Susime.* The moon is the elder. Others make them sisters, the sun being older. Some make the sun female. The moon is now less bright because the sun threw cowdung in his face. As the moon comes out only at night he (or she) has no chance to wash his (or her) face.

About the stars I have had difficulty in ascertaining to what stars certain names apply. For example, *Walsal,* meaning night-light, was Jupiter on some occasions, Sirius on others. And *Ja-manggot,* the moon's walking-stick, " because it is always seen near the moon," may possibly be Mercury, at least Mercury was once pointed out to me as *Ja-manggot,* but on other occasions I got only vague answers.

There is no doubt, however, about the Milky-way which they call " *matma rama,*" the track of the buffaloes. Orion is " *wakripe,*" the carrying of a pig, the bright stars in a quadrilateral being the carriers, and Orion's belt being the pig. It is also called " *churipe,*" the carrying of the chu or rice beer. The belt is also called " *donggipeng-donggro* " (dwells north, dwells south), suggesting that Garos are aware that the belt at rising and setting divides north from south. The Great Bear is " *mangripe* and *mangganchi,*" Alpha, Beta, and Gamma being " *mangripe* " (the carrying of the corpse, and the other four-stars being the " *mangganchi* " (or *delang*) the altar (of bamboos) on which the ashes of the dead are placed. These four stars are also called " *mangjabak,*" (four stakes as used in making a stack of fuel).

The Milky Way, Orion and the Great Bear are all associated with the myth of Susime's mother, a person held in great awe. The story is detailed, but consists mainly in a description of her funeral to be taken, presumably, as the prototype of all funerals.

The Pleiades are called *dosadiphil* which means a group of chickens ; and the Hyades are called *dosuthat,* which means fighting cocks, or *chekechet,* a Hajong fishing net ; Venus is called *pringphang* when it is the morning star and *athamphang* when it is the evening star.

An eclipse is said to be due to the sun or moon being swallowed by an evil spirit or *nawang. Goera* is the god of thunder and lightning, and the flash is caused by the glittering of his *milam* or sword when he flourishes it. Celts (neolithic stone adzes) are called *Goera gitchi* which means hoes of the lightning, as they are supposed to be of meteoric origin.

11. The Garos normally dispose of their dead by burning, either on the evening of the death or on the following evening at the latest. The ashes (bones as they call them) are put in a small hole in the ground at the place of cremation which is generally in the courtyard, in front of the deceased's house. A flattish stone is placed over this hole in the ground, and over the place a structure of bamboos is made in the form of an altar. At the four corners are set up *khimas* or curved wooden posts and a broken *rang* (gong) is hung up with rough models or miniatures of implements used by the deceased in his life-time. The *rang* (gong) is broken for the purpose and is never used again. A small scoopshaped winnowing tray is placed upside down on the altar. In it a hole is broken to enable the spirit of the deceased to escape in due course. Offerings of food to the dead are placed by the altar for seven days ; and at the next the harvest, small sheaves of ripe grain are hung from the poles at the corners of the altar. In the following spring about the time when the village ceremony is performed the altar and everything it contains is burned up. It appears that the Garos believe that the spirit of the dead resides in or near the altar, but the final burning drives the spirit away for good and no further sacrifices are made on its behalf. In the case of death from cholera, *kala azar* or leprosy, the body is buried in a remote part of the village land. The body is placed in the grave lying on its back. *Kala azar* is a disease recently introduced into the Garo Hills. When it first appeared, people buried the victims in the courtyard but this was held to spread the disease, so *kala azar* cases are treated like those of cholera and leprosy. Anyone killed by a tiger is burned at the place where the corpse is found and not in the village. The idea appears to be that the tiger might attempt to follow the corpse to the village.

The Garos have no strong belief about the ultimate abode of the dead. When the final burning of the altar is over the spirit has departed, whether few Garos trouble to consider. They have, of course, an old wives story that the spirit of the dead finds its way ultimately to the hill Chutmang ; but that hill is in no way sacred or regarded as haunted.

12. A head taken from an enemy used to be brought in and after a night of feasting taken to the place of the *khosis* and boiled. The flesh was put under a *khosi* and the skull taken and hung up in the latrine of the house of the *nokma.* One old man told me that there were 30 skulls in his father's house. When the enemy ran away, sometimes the fingers and toes of the dead were taken, but the whole body was never taken. If there were no time to take the head, at least an ear was cut off if it could be done.

Another account says that warriors on their return used to march around the village square with the head. The head was boiled and the flesh was put in the ground in the village open space and a *khosi* was put over it. One *khosi* was put up for each head taken.

(viii) Notes on the Khasis and Syntengs.

By Mr. Hari Blah, Extra Assistant Commissioner.

1. The Khasis are divided into the following groups :—

Khasis, Syntengs or Pnars, Wars, Bhois and Lyngngams and into an immense number of exogamous clans and sub-clans which are mostly to be found among the Khasis and the Syntengs. The above groups are not strictly endogamous nor are they strictly exogamous but generally Syntengs more often marry Syntengs than Khasis and *vice-versa.* But marriages within the same clan or sub-clan belonging to the same group or to different groups are strictly forbidden, for instance a Khasi of the Diengdoh clan is forbidden to marry a Khasi of the same clan and a Synteng of the Lalu clan is forbidden to marry a Khasi of the Diengdoh clan as their first ancestress is traced to the same person and they thus belong to the same clan.

2. The clans are generally divided into the following classes with a slight variation in the different States :—

(1) Royal clan—Ki Siem (Kings).

(2) Priestly clan—Ki Lyngdoh.

(3) Minister clans—Called the Mantris ; the chief Mantri or Governor being called a Lyngskor.

(4) The plebeian clans.

There is a definite order of precedence between the above classes in public and State affairs but there is no definite social gulf between them as inter-marriage between the different clans is not prohibited.

3. Each State has a chiefly clan, generally a royal clan or priestly clan, from which all chiefs are drawn. The chiefs are styled Siems or Lyngdohs. Heirship to the siemship or lyngdohship lies through the female side and not through the father's side. It is necessary for the chief's mother to belong to the chief or royal clan but the father need not be of the royal or lyngdoh clan. In one of the States the actual head of the State is a female who delegates her temporal powers to one of her sons or nephews who thus becomes siem or lyngdoh. A siem is succeeded, unless disqualified, by the eldest of his uterine brothers ; failing such brothers, by the eldest of his sister's sons ; failing such nephews, by the eldest of the sons of his sisters' daughters ; failing such grand-nephews, by the eldest of the sons of his mothers' sisters, and failing such first cousins, by the eldest of his male cousins on the female side, other than first cousins, those nearest in the degree of relationship having prior claim. If there were no male heirs, as above, he would be succeeded by the eldest of his uterine sisters : in the absence of such sisters, by the eldest of his sister's daughter's ; failing such nieces, by the eldest of the daughters of his sisters' daughters ; failing such grand-nieces, by the eldest of the daughters of his mother's sisters, and failing such first cousins, by the eldest of his female cousins on the female side, other than first cousins, those nearest in degree of relationship having prior claim. A female Siem would be succeeded by her eldest son and so on.

4. The organization is not democratic. A Khasi State is a limited monarchy, the chief's powers being much circumscribed. The States are ruled by a chief assisted by a darbar of their Mantris and Lyngdohs.

5. The tradition of origin is vague. According to one tradition the Khasis had some connection politically with the Burmese to whose King they used to render homage at one time by sending him an annual tribute in the shape of an axe as an emblem merely of submission. Another tradition indicates the North as the direction from which they migrated and Sylhet as the terminus of their wanderings from which they were ultimately driven back into their present hill fastnesses by a great flood after a more or less peaceful occupation of that district. It was on the occasion of this great flood, the legend runs, that the Khasi lost the art of writing, the Khasi losing his book whilst he was swimming at the time of this flood, whereas the Bengali managed to preserve his. The general tradition, however, is that they come from the East.

6. Terraced cultivation exists in flat valleys only. The bottoms of valleys are divided up into little compartments by means of fairly high banks corresponding to the Assamese *alis* and the water is let in at will into those compartments by means of skilfully contrived irrigation channels, some times a mile or more in length.

7. The following stone monuments are found :—

(1) *Mawlynti* or *mawkjat* stones which are erected to serve as seats for the spirits of departed clansfolk on their way to the tomb of the clan, *i.e.*, when their remains are carried by their relations to the clan cromlech. These generally consist of 3 upright stones, the tallest being in the centre and a flat table stone being placed in front. Some clans, however, erect more than 3 upright stones. The upright stones are not as a rule more than 3 or 4 ft. high and are to be found in great numbers all along the roads or paths which lead to the clan cromlechs.

(2) Stone cromlechs or cairns which serve the purpose of ossuaries. These cromlechs contain the bones of the dead and are built of blocks of stone, sometimes on stone platforms and sometimes resting on the ground. They are frequently of considerable size and are opened by removing one of the heavy stone slabs in front. They are generally square or oblong but are sometimes in circular shape also.

(3) *Mawumkoi* or *Mawtyrut.*—These are erected to mark the sites of purificatory tanks, which have been dug so that the remains of deceased persons may be cleansed from the impurities attending an unnatural death and to counteract the adverse influence of *Ka Tyrut* or the goddess of death upon the clan. The stones consist of a flat table-stone and in some cases upright stones also are erected.

(4) *Mawbynna* are stones erected to commemorate deceased ancestors on the female side of the family and consist of 3, 5, 7, 9 or, in an exceptional case, of 11 upright stones with flat table-stones in front. The upright stones are called male-stones and the flat table stones female stones. It frequently happens that there are 2 flat table stones in front of the upright stones, the one on the left being the first ancestress and the one on the right being the grand-mother of the actual family to which the memorialists belong. The flat table-stones are some 2 to 2½ ft. from the ground. Sometimes immediately on either side of the large central upright stone there are 2 much smaller stones called *Mawksing* or the stone of the drum and *Mawkait* the stone of the plantain ; the drum being used in all religious ceremonies by the Khasis and the plantain relating to their custom of feeding young children on plantains.

(5) *Mawnam* are stones erected to commemorate the father and his brothers or nephews. These consist of 3 upright stones and one flat table-stone in front. The large central stone is called *U Mawthawlang* or the stone of the father, and the upright stones on either side are meant to represent the father's brothers or nephews. The flat table-stone is the grand-mother of the father and not the first grand-mother of his clan.

8. The following stones are used for seats but their use is not privileged in any way—

(1) *Mawshongthait*, or stones in the uplands upon which weary travellers sit, are to be found along side all the principal lines of communication in the district. They consist of upright stones of uneven numbers of great height standing sometimes over 20 ft. above the ground and flat table-stones in front of them. These flat stones or dolmens are sometimes very neatly hewn resting on stone supports, the top of the uppermost plane being some 2 to 2½ ft. from the ground. This flat stone in a certain case near a bazar measures as much as 28½ by 13¾ ft. and is a foot or more in thickness.

(2) *Ka kor.*—These are stone walls upon which weary travellers also sit and are to be found only in the War countries to the south and west of the district along all the principal lines of communication in those villages. These walls are either square or rectangular and are about 10 or 15 ft. square in some cases. They are built on the paths which pass through the middle of these squares. The outer wall is higher than the inner wall which is used for seats on both sides of the path. The same kind of wall or seat is to be met with in the Kacha Naga country which is called "*rnei.*"

9. Building materials consists of wood, stone, bamboos, reeds, canes, thatch, slate and palm leaves. Posts are of wood and walls of stones or planks. It was tabu in ancient time to build a house with stone walls on all four sides, to use nails in building a house and to use more than one kind of timber in building the hearth.

10. (*a*) The social position of individuals is not indicated in the shape or material of their houses except that the Chiefs' houses are usually bigger than those of ordinary villagers and in some cases chiefs erected sacred houses called *Lingsad*. It was considered tabu to build a house with resinous timber which only the Siem's family can use.

(*b*) Social position is indicated to some extent in the pattern and colours of the clothes they wear. Only members of chiefly families or rich people on ceremonial occasions put on a silk turban called "*spong khor.*" The chiefs sometimes use this kind of silk for their dhuties also. A scarlet broadcloth indicates authority as such cloths are usually presented by, at least the Siem of Cherra, to his Mantries at the time of his coronation. There is no prohibition on other people wearing these clothes but in practice they do not do so as they cannot afford them.

11. The Sun (*Ka Sngi*) is a woman while the Moon (*U Bnai*) is a man.

They are two out of the four ch ldren of a rich gentleman.* The moon was as bright as the sun but he was a wicked young man for he began to make love to his elder sister Ka Sngi. When the sun became aware that U Bnai harboured such an incestuous and wicked intention towards her she was very angry and covered his face with ashes. Since then the moon has given out a white light only as his former brightness was covered with ashes.

A halo round the sun or the moon is believed to foretell some pestilence or other calamity.

Comets are called *Khlur dih duma* smoking stars and portend the death of Kings or some great personalities.

The Milky Way represents the trade communication, *i.e.*, trade will prosper in the direction it runs.

---

*What of the other two ? Is it possible that they are represented in the shadows, sometimes regarded as a dark material orb. which eclipse the sun and moon respectively ? The Palaung of Burma, another Mon-Khmer tribe, describe the sun, the moon, and the dark orb which passes in front of them as three brothers.

J. H. H.

An earthquake is supposed to be a gigantic giant who when he moves his small finger only a slight shock is experienced but when he moves all his fingers, a severe shock is felt. The severity of the shock depends on the force with which he moves his fingers. Eclipses of the sun and moon are due to these orbs being swallowed by a toad (*Hynroh*). On such occurrence tins and other articles are beaten and other noises made in order to make the toad in the sky spew out the sun or moon.

Lightning (*Ka Leilieh*) is the sword of a god called *U Pyrthat* and thunder is the noise made by this god. The god generally strikes dangerous snakes and centipedes and also those people who commit incest (*sang*) with this sword. Oaths are sometimes taken on *U Pyrthat*.

Hurricanes are caused by a devil called U Kyllang.

The Rainbow is called *Sim Pylliem* and is supposed to fish in streams.* It represents a fishing rod.

12. The Khasis burn their dead. As soon as death is certain the body is bathed in warm water from three earthen pots and is reverently laid on a mat where it is dressed in a white cloth. The waist cloth and turban being folded from left to right and not from right to left as in the case of the living. An egg is placed on the stomach of the deceased and nine fried grains of *riew-hadem* or Indian corn are tied round the head with a string. A cock is sacrificed, the idea being that the cock will scratch a path for the spirit to the next world. A sacrifice of a bull, or of a cow in case the deceased is a woman, follows. A small basket is hung up over the head of the corpse, the basket containing pieces of the sacrificed animals and a dish containing eatables and betel-nut and a jar of water are placed near the head of the corpse by way of offering refreshment to the spirit of the departed. Food is given each morning and evening that the corpse remains in the house and each night the corpse remains in the house guns are fired, drums are beaten and flutes are played. If it is intended to burn the body on a masonry pyre a bull is sacrified. If the body is placed in a coffin a pig is sacrificed and if it is intended to adorn the pyre with flags a fowl is sacrificed. The corpse, which is wrapped up in mat or placed in a coffin, is laid on a bamboo bier called *Ka krong*. Cotton or, in the case of a rich man, silk cloths are tied cross-ways over the bier if the deceased is a male and in the form of a parallelogram if it is a female. The funeral procession is preceded by various purificatory ceremonies. On nearing the pyre the dead body is exposed to view and laid on the pyre, inside the coffin, if one is used, with the head to the west and the feet to the east. Logs of wood are placed around the body and the egg is broken by being thrown on the pyre in the direction of the feet of the corpse. Fire is applied to the pyre first by the *Kur* or members of the clan and then by the children, if any, of the deceased. After another fowl is sacrificed three arrows are shot from the bow, one to the north, another to the south and a third to the east. [*Cf.* the Sawara custom, B, 1, iv., of this volume. J. H. H.]

When the body has been thoroughly burnt the fire is extinguished with water and the bones are collected by the relatives in three trips. The bones thus collected are carefully wrapped in a piece of white cloth by the female relatives and the party sets out to the bone repository called *Mawshyieng*. On reaching it, a sacrificer washes the bones three times and then places them in an earthern pot tying up the mouth with a white cloth. He then places them inside the cairn and shuts the door. The bones are eventually taken out and placed in the common stone sepulchre of the clan, the removal thither being an occasion of much feasting and dancing which continues often for several days. A coffin is called *Ka Shyngoid* (manger) and in former days used to be hollowed out of the trunk of a tree. In the case of the disposal of the corpses of the Siems of Cherra State this coffin is enclosed in an elaborately carved wooden shell called *Lynkhasan* which was placed on a bier and on top of it was placed a large conical canopy resembling in shape a Muhammadan *tazia*. In Mariaw and Nongstoin States a large wooden coffin is used, painted white, with ornamentation on the outside and standing on four legs. This coffin is not burnt on the funeral pyre. The bones and ashes of the dead in Shella are in some cases kept in a cavity hollowed out of a post made of the heart of the jack-fruit tree and erected for the purpose. The bones and ashes are afterwards removed to a cromlech as is done among the Khasi uplanders.

The only cases in which dead bodies are buried are cases where persons have died of cholera, small-pox or other such infectious or contagious disease. The bodies are dug up again and burnt with all the customary rites when fear of infection or contagion is over [*cf.* Santals, B. 9, iii (*a*) of this volume. J. H. H.] The head is never disposed of separately from the rest of the body.

13. It is believed that the spirits of the dead, whose funeral ceremonies have been duly performed go to the house or garden of God ; hence the expression " he who is eating betel nut in God's house." The spirits of those whose funeral ceremonies have not been duly performed are believed to take the forms of animals, birds or insects and to roam on the earth ; but this idea of transmigration of souls, has been probably borrowed from the Hindus. The spirits of the wicked go to a place called *Ka Nurok ka ksew* (dog)—a place of punishment.

14. The following agricultural implements are used :—

A shoulder-headed hoe called *mohkhiew*, an axe for felling trees called *u sdie*, a large dao for felling trees called *ka wait lyngun*, two kinds of billhooks called *ka wait prat* and *ka wait khmut*, and a sickle called *ka rashi*. All the tools are made in the village forge. The hoe is fixed into an iron head-piece provided with a wooden handle while the axe is fixed into a hole made in the wooden handle the spikes at the base of the blade being run through the hole and protruding an inch or two on the other side of the handle. The dao, the billhooks and the sickle are fixed into a hole made in the wooden handle to which are attached one or two woven bamboo rings called *ki ksah*.

15. *Musical instruments* :—

Ka nakra which is a large kettle drum made of wood having the head covered with deerskin.

Ka ksing kynthei which is a cylindrically shaped drum which is beaten when women dance.

Ka padiah a small drum with a handle made of wood.

Katasa a small circular drum.

All these drums are made of wood.

Ka duitara is a guitar with murga silk strings which is played with a little wooden key held in the hand.

**Cf.* the Santal story that it is catching scorpions (called " the crab's mother " in most Assam hill languages), the Lakher description of it as the tail of a celestial cock that comes down to catch crabs in streams after the rain and the Biete kuki account. J. H. H.

Ka maryngod is an instrument much the same as *Ka duitara* but is played with a bow like an violin.

Ka marynthing is a kind of guitar with one string played with the finger.

Ka tangmuri is a wooden pipe, which is played like a flageolet.

Ka kynshaw or *chakuriaw* are cymbals made of bell metal.

Ka sharati is a kind of flute made of bamboo and played at cremation ceremonies only.

Ka shingwiang is a flute made of bamboo.

Ka singdiengphong a zither made out of reed.

Ka mieng, a Jew's harp made of bamboo.

16. Treatments of heads taken from an enemy—

Heads taken from an enemy used to be fixed to the top of wooden shafts in some public place round which an altar was built. The warriors then danced round the altar. The heads and shafts were later on planted outside the village near some public road or outside the village gate on the main village path.

The Syntengs or Pnars.

The Syntengs or Pnars are very closely allied to the Khasis. In language, religion and customs the differences are extremely slight and the same may be said of their general cast of features.

The following differences may be enumerated :—

2. The clans are generally divided into the following classes :—

(1) Royal clans—Ki Siem.

(2) Priestly clans—Ki Lyngdoh.

(3) Officers' clans—Ki Doloi and Patons.

(4) Plebeian clans.

There is a definite order of precedence between the above classes in public and State affairs but there is no definite social gulf between them as intermarriage between the different classes is not prohibited.

3. There is only one chiefly clan of family from which all the Siems and Rajas of Jaintia are drawn. The chief's mother or sister must belong to the royal clan as in the case of the Khasis. A Kongor or a husband for the Siem's sister is selected from the other clans or classes.

4. The upright stones and the flat table-stones at Nartiang are called "*Ki maw jong Siem*" and it is said that in the days of the Jaintia Kings only the Raja could sit upon the great flat stone.

5. Orion's belt is called *Ki Rah bhar i.e.,* carrying loads with a bamboo piece over the shoulder as is done in the plains [*cf.* Santals, 9, *(ii)* above. J. H. H.]

The Pleiades are called a "*Tharu Syiar*" *i.e.,* a fowl cage with chickens inside.

Face of the moon. It is said that an old man pounding paddy in the moon can be seen on a clear moon.

A bright star appearing on the outer side of a young moon is alleged to portend death during childbirth while a bright star on its inner side portends the death of a person by being eaten by a tiger.

The rainbow is called "*Ka Sain thylliej,*" *i.e.,* a snake with a tongue.

6. A plough (*Ka Lyngkor*) and a harrow (*Ka iuh moi*) are used in the Jaintia Hills. The land is made into a thick paste in the Jaintia Hills by means of the plough. Droves of cattle also are driven repeatedly over the paddy fields until the mud has acquired the right consistency. The seed is then sown broadcast in the wet mud.

7. Heads taken from an enemy were treated in the same way as among the Khasis but skulls of famous enemies are preserved. It is said that the skull of the Siem of Malngiang—an enemy—was mounted with silver and preserved in the house of the Jaintia Rajas for many generations.

(ix) Northern Sangtams.

1. The Northern Sangtams are divided up into different exogamous groups of clans. The groups are *Tongre, Chingre, Lebitongre, Mongsarre Lemkitongre and Anarre.*

2. No clan takes precedence over any other clan.

3. There is no chiefly clan or class from which all chiefs are drawn. The founder of a village becomes a chief.

4. Like a Chang village a Sangtam village is run by the chief and a council of elders. The elders hold office for life, and may be deprived of their office by the chief. The number of elders depends on the requirements of the village.

5. The Sangtams claim to have emerged from the earth near a stone at *Chongliyimti,* in the country they now inhabit. This is also the reputed place of origin of the Ao tribe. All the clans were born together.

6. Terraced cultivation is not in existence in the Sangtam country.

7. One monument is known in the Northern Sangtam country, consisting of two monoliths curving in towards each other.

8. Stone is not used for making seats.

9. The houses are of bamboo, with wooden posts. Stones and planks are not used.

10. Performance of the full series of feasts of merit entitles a man to have carved posts in his house, and wear body cloths of a special pattern.

11. The sun is male, and the moon is female. The marking on the moon is said to be cowdung, thrown at it by an old man, because it was coming too near the earth.

Earthquakes.—The earth is held in the hand of God, and whenever he wants to do something or other, he lets it go, and the earth shakes.

Eclipses.—The Sangtams say the same things as the Changs. That is that the moon is being eaten by the spirit of a tiger.

Rainbow.—The rainbow is said to be the fumes issuing from some bad place. The rainbow is never pointed out to another man, lest the finger which is pointed at the rainbow drop off.

Thunder and Lightning are explained by the story of the brothers who go to do battle with the wind.

12. The Sangtam either bury their dead, or expose them on platforms. The choice of method appears to be optional. They do not sever the head. They built shelters over graves, on which are emblems of the dead man's achievements.

13. Dead men's souls go on a long and arduous journey. After a time they enter the earth and become dust.

14. The Sangtams' complexion is light; the hair is straight and is cut in a circle round the head, just above the ears. Eyes straight, occasionally a man with definitely oblique eyes may be seen. The nose is stubby. The shape of the head is round. Physique is generally poor.

15. Rice and millet are sown broadcast. Job's tears are sown seed by seed.

16. Musical instruments are—

(1) Jew's Harp.

(2) Two holed flute.

(3) Horn.

17. The weapons are—

(1) Spear.

(2) Dao.

(3) Cross Bow.

(4) Shields.

The heads of enemies are first placed in a shrub in the village, specially grown for the purpose. When the flesh has rotted and fallen off, they are hung in the Bachelor's Hall (*morung*).

(x) The Changs.

1. The Changs are divided up into five exogamous groups of clans. The groups are Chongpho, Bilashi Lomo, Kangsho and Ung.

2. There is no evidence to show that any clan takes formal precedence over any other, though the Chongpho clan is generally considered to be superior to other clans. The Ung clan corresponds to the Ang clan of the Konyaks. Certain religious duties can only be performed by members of this clan. It is however rather looked down on and only one chief belongs to it.

3. There is no clan from which all chiefs are drawn. Any man founding a village, becomes chief of that village. It is usual, for a man of the Ung clan to go to the new village with the founder.*

4. A Chang village is run by the chief and a council of elders. The number of elders varies with the size of the village. The elders are appointed by the chief, and can, if the chief thinks fit, come from the same clan. An elder holds office for life, but if the chief disapproves of him, he can be turned out of office. The more recent the foundation of the village the greater the power of the chief. In old villages the branches of the founder's family are so numerous that no one can exert any effective power and the village becomes a democracy.

5. The Changs trace their origin from the North East.

6. Terraced cultivation does not exist in the Chang country.

7. No evidence has been found of the existence of megalithic monuments.

8. Stone is not used for seats.

9. Houses are built of bamboo, with wooden posts. Stone and planks are not used.

10. The general shape of rich men's houses are the same. But only rich men and men of renown in war are allowed to decorate their houses with carvings, and to build sitting out platforms. Social position is also indicated by the pattern and colour of cloths.

11. The sun is male and the moon female. The markings on the moon are said to be cow dung thrown at it to drive it away. The Changs account for earthquakes by saying that two brothers challenged the wind to combat and that the wielding of one of the brother's shields causes the earth to quake. Eclipses are explained by the fact that a tiger wishing to eat the moon prays so hard for his wish to the fulfilled that his "ghost" goes up to the sky and eats the moon.

The Changs have very vague ideas about rainbows. They say that they spring out of crabs' holes, and associate them with spirits. Thunder is accounted for by the slapping of the shields of the brothers, who fight the wind, against their legs, and the lightning is said to be the flashing of the brothers' daos as they go on their way.

12. The Changs dispose of their dead either by putting them on machans, or by burying them. The customs is not fixed and the heirs of the deceased person decide upon the method of disposal. A person much loved is usually buried within the house. A person who dies of a deadly disease is put on a platform in the branches of a tree a long way from the village. Rich men and men famed in war are buried in coffins decorated with hornbill heads. Poor men are wrapped up in a cloth and buried. If the corpse is buried outsid the house a shelter over the grave is built, and kept up for one year. Bodies placed on machans are take

*The Ung clan probably represents the chiefly clan of an older stock which has taken an inferior social position as a result of invasion by later comers.—J. H. H.

down the year after death. The bones are then carefully counted and buried and the skull is put in an earthenware pot in a secret spot or a cliff reserved for the dead man's clan. This separate treatment of the head illustrates one of the many similarities between Chang and Konyak custom.*

13. After an arduous journey the Chang reaches his paradise, and there he receives a fresh life, but never returns to this world. This paradise is said to be somewhere beneath the surface of the earth.

14. The complexion of a Chang is brown with a reddish tinge, the eyes are straight, and brown. Nose straight, head small. The men are of very fine physique—broad chested, slim-waisted, and very long in the body.† The calves are usually small.

15. Rice and millet are sown broad cast and Job's tears seed by seed.

16. The Changs have three musical instruments—

(1) Jew's Harp.

(2) Flute.

(3) Horn.

17. The Chang weapons are—

(1) Spear.

(2) Dao.

(3) Crossbow.

(4) Shield.

The head of an enemy is placed in a certain tree in the village. After the flesh has rotted it is put in the Bachelor's Hall (*morung*).

(xi) The Thendu Konyaks.

1. The Thendu Konyaks are divided up into groups of clans, all of which, except the Ang clan, are exogamous.

2. They are divided up into four groups of clans with a definite order of social precedence. The Ang clan is the senior and is sacred.

3. The chief (Ang) of a Thendu Konyak village must come from the Ang clan, and both his parents must belong to that clan, a unique instance of endogamy in a Naga clan.

4. A Thendu village is run by its Ang. His prestige is enormous, and his position is almost that of a divine autocrat.

5. The Thendus claim an origin in the North East.

6. Terraced cultivation does not exist.

7. A monolith is always erected in front of the house of the Ang. At the foot of it enemies' heads are laid when first housed in.

8. Occasionally huge stone seats are made for the Angs and the use of these seats is restricted to Angs. These seats are not common.

9. Stone is not used in the construction of houses.

10. There is no indication of social position in the general shape or materials of a Thendus house, nor in the patterns of cloths, except in the case of a man who has taken a head. A member of the Ang clan is entitled to wear a band of pale blue beads below the knee.

11. The sun is male, and the moon is female. The markings on the face of the moon are explained by the saying, that once upon a time, a man desiring the moon sent a monkey up to the sky to bring it down. The moon seized the monkey and kept him there. The markings are traces of the monkey.

Earthquakes are said to take place on the death of an Ang. When the Ang dies he hovers between this life and the next. Now this life and the next life are held together by a rope. When the Ang is going to the next life he has to cut this rope. If his dao is sharp the rope instantly parts and there is no trembling, but if his dao is not sharp the rope is agitated in the cutting and the earth quakes.

Eclipses are said to be the act of sexual intercourse between the sun and the moon.

Rainbow is said to be a God who has come to look for crabs. It is never pointed out, lest the finger of the indicator drop off.

Thunder is the voice of God.

Lightning is the flash of his gun. Both thunder and lightning are held in very great awe by the Thendus.

12. The dead of the Thendus are disposed of on machans. The coffin of an Ang is decorated at each end with carvings of the heads of hornbills and is invariably placed in the branches of, or under, a ficus tree. When the flesh has rotted the head of the corpse is wrenched off, and is put in a stone cist or earthenware pot outside the village. The face of the head is put facing the path. After the harvest, the face is turned round, the front of the cist or pot closed up, and the dead man has gone for ever.

13. Thendus say that their souls go back to the birth place of the tribe.

14. Complexion fair, the hair is straight. It is parted near the crown. The front portion is brushed straight down to the forehead and the back portion is drawn back and is done up in a bun. Their eyes are brown and straight. The shape of the nose is straight. Their physique is on the whole good.

15. Rice seed is sown by the broadcast method, and also by separate placing of seed. The nature of the sowing depending on the kind of seed to be sown.

---

*Exposures with separate disposal of the head is to be regarded as the more ancient and indigenous custom, burial as intrusive and later.—J. H. H.

†I should say rather very long in the thigh. J. H. H.

16. *Musical instruments*—

Flute.

Horn.

Jews Harp.

Xylophone (drum).*

17. Weapons—

Spear.

Dao.

Cross-bow.

Shield.

The heads of enemies are cleaned of the flesh and are hung in the house of the Ang. The heads of very bitter enemies are insulted and tortured by the placing of chillies, *etc.* in the eye sockets and mouth "to make them smart" after which they are placed on shelves either outside the Ang's house or in the bachelors' morung.†

(xii) The Thenkoh Konyaks.

1. The Thenkohs are divided up into exogamous groups of clans.

2. They are divided into four groups of clans with a definite order of social precedence, the Ang clan being the chief.

3. The chief (Ang) of a Thenkoh village must be drawn from the Ang clan, and both his parents must be of the Ang clan.

4. The village is nominally run by the Ang, but he is often a figure head, the real power lying with the young men of the "morungs."

5. They claim an origin from the North East, but often assert that they descended to the plains in the course of their wanderings and re-entered the hills by the Dikhu valley.

6. Terraced cultivation does not exist.

7. *Small monoliths of a characteristic curved shape are often set up in front of the morungs.*

8. There is no restriction as to the materials used for buildings.

10. No indication of social position is given by the shape or materials of a house. A man who has performed the full series of feasts of merit wears a heavily embroidered cloth, and his wife an embroidered skirt.

11. The Sun is male, and the Moon is female. The Thenkohs have the same story about the markings in the moon as the Thendus.

Eclipses.—The same as the Thendus.

Rainbow.— Ditto.

Thunder.— Ditto.

Lightning.— Ditto.

12. They dispose of their dead by placing them on *machans*. The Angs are disposed of in the same way as the Thendus dispose of their Angs. The head is treated in the same way as among the Thendus.

13. They believe that their dead go back to the birth place of the tribe. The birth place of the Thenkohs is in the same place as the Thendus.

14. Their complexion is fair, the hair is straight and is kept long from the crown to the forehead. At the crown it is parted, one half being brushed straight down to the forehead, and the other half worn in a tail, which may be of considerable length. The eyes are straight. Physique, usually small and sturdy.

15. Rice is sown broadcast and other seeds separately.

16. Musical instruments—

Flute (two holes).

Jews Harp.

Horn.

Xylophone (Drum).

17. Weapons—

Spear.

Dao.

Cross-bow.

Shields.

Heads are hung for a time on a tree outside the village fence, and are later deposited in the *morungs*.‡

**I.e.*, "Canoe drum" a dugout wooden gong without membrane and often of great size and length.

†After a preliminary exposure on a small stone table by a pile of small monoliths erected on a mound, planted with euphorbea, on which the accession of each fresh head is marked by the addition of another small menhir.—J. H. H.

‡They are sometimes in the first stage hoisted high on bamboos attached to phallic monoliths and associated with *euphorbia* trees, orchids and other fertility emblems. When there are several the jaws are sometimes hoisted above and the skulls pegged to a wooden plank across the top of more than one monolith. In any case the jaw is hung separately from the skull.—J. H. H.

12. Notes on the effect on some primitive tribes of Assam of contacts with civilization.

The Effect on the Tribes of the Naga Hill District of Contacts with Civilization.

By Mr. J. P. Mills, I. C. S.

The conditions obtaining throughout the Naga Hills district being fairly uniform, to deal with each tribe separately would entail much unnecessary repetition. I will therefore note on the district as a whole, drawing my examples from the Angami, Sema, Ao, and Lhota Nagas, and the Thado Kukis.

In this area contact with civilization is brought about in two ways—by the visits of tribesmen to the plains lying along the base of the hills, and by the penetration of foreigners into the hills. The latter is by far the most important. Foreigners residing in the hills influence the culture and mode of life of the indigenous inhabitants in numerous ways—by administration, by missionary propaganda, by the innate tendency to imitate foreigners who display a culture in some way regarded as "higher", by objects of trade imported from without, by the introduction of disease, by medical work, by communications that make travelling everywhere easy and safe, by the presence of an armed force strong enough to suppress any rising or inter-tribal war, and by countless subtle influences that react on the mentality of the villages, usually to the detriment of their pride in their customs and history.

There has been little or no exploitation of forests, minerals or agricultural land, but the future cannot be held to be secure as long as the ruling of Government stands that *jhum* land, which the owners have bought or inherited as immovable property which can be validly held by an individual or a clan, is all unclassed State forest at the absolute disposal of Government, on which there is no liability to pay compensation in the event of its being taken over.

There is no systematic recruitment of hillmen for work in the plains. Gangs, especially of Semas and Aos, go down in the cold weather to work on tea gardens in order to earn cash for their house tax. They come back none the better for the journey. Women do not go down with the men in any large numbers, but when they do go girls are not infrequently lured into a career of prostitution by the prospect of an easy life, being unable to distinguish between the easy-going moral code of their own villages and the systematised vice of the plains, with their so-called higher culture. The men are apt to waste money on rubbish they see displayed in the shops, and on distilled liquor for which they acquire a taste. Gangs going year after year to the same garden are paid regularly and well, but those working for petty contractors are cheated of their earnings with regrettable frequency. They cannot bring suits in the plains—the expense, the distance and the endless adjournments are all against them. When they find that Government is prevented by its own legal methods from settling their claims equitably and quickly their respect for it naturally suffers.

Improved communications, while they have immensely facilitated internal trade, have undoubtedly spread disease. All Nagas assert definitely that since their country was taken over illness has increased. Not only have specific diseases, such as venereal disease and tuberculosis, been introduced, but epidemics spread more quickly. In the old days of war and raiding villages remained more or less constantly segregated Nowadays people travel freely everwhere and disease spreads quickly. Tuberculosis is definitely established. So far its spread has been slow, but the time may come when it will become rampant and the Nagas and Kukis of these hills will follow other primitive peoples into oblivion.

The national drink of the hill tribes of Assam is rice beer. Foreigners have brought in distilled liquor, and its effects are evil. The casual labourer working away from his village, himself the product of contact with civilization, has no wife with him to brew his rice beer and buys spirits instead. Later he comes to regard distilled liquor as a necessity. Nagas are fully aware of the evils, and certain Angami villages have sworn oaths that no member will indulge in it.

Opium is only consumed in certain areas. The Konyak Nagas are inveterate opium addicts, having acquired the habit from plainsmen, with whom they have been in close contact for a very long time. A limited number of Ao Nagas have also taken to the habit. A few years ago a village founded by the American Baptist Mission as a Christian village contained more opium addicts than the whole of the rest of the tribe. The reason was that the Mission had forbidden alcoholic liquor and their converts had taken to opium as a substitute. I believe things are much improved now. In the rest of the district there are few addicts except detribalised Nagas living in Kohima bazaar. With them the vice must be directly put down to contact with foreigners.

The opening up of the cart road to Manipur has undoubtedly led to an increase in prostitution. Except to a limited extent among the Eastern Angamis, prostitution, in the sense of women selling themselves for money to all and sundry, is not an indigenous Naga or Kuki custom. In many tribes girls before marriage allow their lovers every privilege, but this is very different from a commercial transaction. Foreigners coming into the hills by the cart road often demand women, and where there is a demand a supply is apt to be forthcoming. Some women even visit the cart stands and offer themselves to the bullock drivers.

While the extension of communications has led to the introduction of much foreign rubbish and cheapjack ware it has also stimulated genuine Naga trade. For example in the old days the supply of ivory armlets was very limited, as they could only be obtained from the very few elephants killed by Nagas themselves. Now Angamis bring large numbers up from Calcutta and trade them through the hills. Similarly, Naga ornaments which are only made in a few places, such as the baldricks made in the Sema village of Seromi, are far more easily distributed. I have no doubt more Naga ornaments are worn now than were worn in the days before the hills were taken over, and for this peace and easy communications are responsible.

Before the hills were taken over the important villages of Khonoma, with insufficient land to support its population, raided far and wide for heads, tribute, loot and prisoners they could hold to ransom. Now they have substituted trade for raiding, and landless men wander right into Burma selling beads. The prestige of the village enables them to keep almost a monopoly of this trade.

I have mentioned above the increase in prostitution due to the cart road. Far more serious in this respect is the presence in Kohima of a large number of unmarried foreigners, including the unmarried men of a battalion of Assam Rifles, and of Naga subordinates living away from their villages. A population is growing up of persons with no tribe or customary law and religion, and their settlement is a plague spot. Any girl who quarrels with her parents in a Naga village and can bolt to this sink of iniquity can find an old hag ready to take her in and start her without delay on a career which can only end in disease and misery.

Education of the type which is given has been on the whole an evil rather than a good. Some men have withstood its evil influence and have remained good Nagas, with something else very useful added. Not so the majority. Very rarely indeed does a Naga regard education as something which is going to make him more fitted for his ordinary life; he regards it as something which will fit him for a very different life, and he expects that life to be offered to him in the form of a Government post—aptly described to me once as a "sitting-and-eating job". When boys apply to me for scholarships my custom is to ask them what they intend to do when they have finished their education, and the reply almost invariably is "I hope Government will find me a job". The result is a surplus of half-educated youths, unwilling to go back to the village life of their fathers and looking in vain for employment which they consider suitable to their talents. The situation is especially bad among the Aos. A few educated Angamis have ventured into commerce, usually with disastrous results, borrowing money wildly and expecting that somehow their education will bring them enormous profits.

Foreign dress is spreading slowly, but steadily. For this the blame must fall both on certain departments of Government, who allow their employees to wear it, and on missionaries whose active encouragement has not always as yet been reduced even to connivance. It is certainly definitely connected in the Naga mind with education, and a smattering of superficial knowledge is considered to entitle the possessor thereof to a pair of shorts, while a suit complete with watch-chain and trilby hat almost corresponds to a doctor's robes. The custom is bad from every point of view. It entails waste of money where money is hard to find. It encourages dirt, since no Naga can afford the changes he ought to have in the damp heat of Assam. It spreads disease in two main ways. Adults become more liable to chills and phthisis since they do not change their wet clothes, and children who are carried against wet "shirt waists" instead of against their mothers' warm backs suffer as a result. From the artistic point of view it is especially and utterly to be condemned. To substitute soiled and poor quality western clothes, or more often a caricature of them, for the exceedingly picturesque Naga dress is an aesthetic crime. More of the body is covered up, but I have yet to find that this leads to stricter morality.

Nagas who have taken whole-heartedly to foreign customs often build houses resembling the worst type of "shack". A Naga house, as all fittingly built houses should, seems to have grown out the landscape. The corrugated iron roofs of the "foreign" houses are blots upon it. They are expensive and stuffy. The fashion has been encouraged, I fear, by the Baptist chapels, which as artistic productions are execrable, and, widely spread as they are, tend to kill the Naga's unconscious but innate sense of architectural fitness.

Only two ancient customs have had to be put down by Government—the sacrifice of mithun by cruel methods, and head-hunting. The suppression of the first is wholly good, and more humane methods of killing can be substituted without detriment to the rites. The suppression of head-hunting, though necessary in any area which is fully administered, has probably not been for the benefit of the tribes. The very fact that, far from being an honour, it is a disgrace to be killed in war, makes all Nagas very careful of their own safety, and their wars were singularly innocuous affairs. In a war between two big villages each side might lose one or two men a year. The number of lives saved by the suppression of the practice is therefore negligible, and is far more than balanced by those lost through the spread of disease made easy by safe travelling everywhere. In addition to this there is a very real loss in virility and keenness. Unbroken peace is no better for Nagas than it is for any other race.

Realising that on the preservation of customs developed exactly to fit the environment and tested by centuries of use depends the whole fabric of tribal society, Government has been at pains to preserve them to the utmost limit possible and to ensure that such change as must inevitably come shall not be destructive in its suddenness. In strong contrast has been the attitude of the American Baptist Mission. As religion plays a part in every Naga ceremony and as that religion is not Christianity, every ceremony must go. Such ceremonies as the great Feasts of Merit, at which the whole village, rich and poor alike, is entertained, and of which the religious aspect is far less important than the social, have not been remodelled on Christian lines, but have been utterly abolished among converts. This has been the fate, too, of all village sacrificial feasts. The place of these is not adequately taken by small parties meeting to drink tea. The suppression among Baptists of the ancient feasts in which all joined is not only a loss to the would-be hosts, but to the village as a whole, and not least to the poor, who always get their full share of good cheer at Animist festivals. To abolish these feasts is to do away with the very few occasions on which the awful monotony of village life is broken. They are, too, the natural Naga and Kuki way of distributing wealth. I have heard a Baptist teacher boast that his granaries were so full of the store of years that some of the grain was black with age. Had he been an Animist that grain would not have been left to rot uselessly but would have been eaten by his fellow villagers.

To any one who unable to reject some of the most hallowed passages in Scripture, regards fermented liquor in moderation as not only harmless but beneficial, the strong prohibition policy of the Mission cannot but seem a grave mistake. Few of its advocates attempt to justify it from Scripture. They use the arguments which brought the Volstead Act into being. Such an obsession has abstention from fermented drink become among converts that teetotalism is often regarded as the outstanding mark of a Christian. Among the Aos "teetotaler" and "Christian" are used as synonymous terms in ordinary conversation. The substitution of opium for rice beer is probably rare among Christians now, but as in America, secret drinking goes on, with results that are morally evil.

It is at the big feasts that singing and dancing are indulged in and full dress worn. These have been entirely suppressed among the Ao, Lhota and Sema Christians, the men of whom wear no ornaments at all, having stripped their beads from the necks, their ivory armlets from their arms and even the cotton wool from their ears. The women are more conservative and still often wear their beads, though I doubt if a girl would actually wear her ornaments at a Mission school. Angami men too are difficult to dislodge from their ancient ways. The best of them do not give up their picturesque dress and are quite ready to put on all their finery and take part in the ceremonial singing parties which are such a feature of their village life.

Of the material arts in these hills wood-carving is the chief. It is displayed on the houses of those who have given the great Feasts of Merit, on the "Morung" posts of the Aos, Konyaks and Lhotas, and on the big xylophones of the Aos. This is doomed to extinction as the power of the mission increases. Feasts of Merit are forbidden among them, and no attempt is made to induce rich Christians to decorate their houses in the old way. No Christian boy is allowed to go through his time in the "Morung" and they are not built any more in Christian villages. In such villages, too, the old xylophones can be seen rotting in the jungle.

The suppression of the wearing of all ornaments or tribal finery, of dancing, of singing (except hymns), of village feasts and of all artistic outlet is spreading an unspeakable drabness over village life. Old songs and old traditions are being rapidly forgotten. Told year in and year out that all the past history, all the strivings, all the old customs of his tribe are wholly evil, the Naga tends to despise his own race, and no night of the soul is blacker than that.

The suppression of the "Morung", in which young Animists learn to be useful citizens is unwarranted by any good reason that I have ever heard. It is part of the tendency to abolish old things just because they are old, and substitute for the strong communal feeling which has enabled the tribes to survive for so long an individualism which is really foreign to them. Not only is this individualism wrapped up with the strong emphasis on personal salvation; it is also the direct and natural reaction against the destruction of all the old things that mattered in village life and all the old expressions of the artistic and social genius of the tribe. "My tribe has erred hopelessly" says the convert "all through the centuries it has tried to work out its destiny, I will work out mine, and mine alone". An Animist puts his village before himself. A Baptist puts himself before his village. No Semas are as prone to disobey their Chiefs as Christian Semas, and Christian Aos have often refused to take the part in village government to which their years and experience called them. A "Civilized" Naga is apt to call customary discipline restraint, and many of them are eager to leave their villages and live free of all control.

Times are changing and new influences and tendencies are appearing. Tribes and villages acting as units will be able to judge of them and resist them if need be. Individuals will find them too strong. Will the time come when these hills will be inhabited by scattered families, without pride in the past or hope for the future, without arts and without recreation, dressed in nondescript garments as drab as their lives, and busy only to win from the steep, rocky slopes enough sustenance to enable them to beget children and die?

Julian Huxley in one of his articles which he quotes in the introduction to his book *Africa View* sums up the exactly similar problem of that continent as follows :—"On the top of all this variety of nature and man there impinge western civilization and western industrialism. Will their impact level down the variety, reducing the proud diversity of native tribes and races to a muddy mixture, their various cultures to a single inferior copy of our own? Or shall we be able to preserve the savour of difference, to fuse our culture and theirs into an autochthonous civilization, to use local difference as the basis for a natural diversity of development?"

The effect on the Lushei of contacts with civilization.

By Mr. C. G. Helme, I. C.S.

1. It may be said in general that contact with civilization has made little or no difference to life into ordinary Lushei village. For the important purpose of trade the Lushei Hills are not really in effective contact with civilization at all. They produce very little that has any exchangeable value and difficulties* of communication make the marketing of surplus produce practically impossible. Thus the ordinary effects of contact with civilization—the stimulus to produce, the ability to exchange, the rise in the standard of consumption are almost entirely absent. Domestic life, methods of cultivation, village habits and customs, food and drink, amusements—all with a few exceptions to be noted below remain as they were half a century ago. It is only in the relations between village and village, and between the Lushei Hills and the outside world, in religion and in education that any marked difference can be observed.

2. The introduction of settled government has not only prevented the Lushei from raiding the inhabitants of the plains on their borders, but has dispelled the constant fear in which they themselves lived of similar raids upon their own villages either from their neighbours or from more powerful tribes further inland.

3. The first Missionaries arrived in the Lushei Hills in January 1894, and the spread of Christianity has been extraordinarily rapid. I estimate the number of professed Christians at about one half of the population of the district. Conversion to Christianity operates as a powerful solvent of ancient customs which are gradually falling into neglect and disrepute. The new religion—adopted mainly in the form of Calvinistic Methodism—is effective chiefly in field of ritual observance. The standard of morality which was never low, remains the same.

4. The influence of Christianity has been strongly re-inforced by the fact that education has been left entirely to the Mission, and, except in two respects, education in general has had no influence apart from Christian teaching. The two exceptions are (1) Most Lushei, Christian or non-Christian, are now able to read and write.

(2) Higher education in these hills as elsewhere breeds a dislike for manual labour, and its growth and spread are increasing the number of unemployed and discontented youths.

5. These are the results in general of the contact of the inhabitants of these hills with civilization. Minor results are tabulated below :—

(1) In a few suitable localities, the Lushei have adopted the system of wet rice cultivation.

(2) The cultivation of fruit, coffee, tea has been introduced and taken up with avidity, and in this respect there has been a slight rise in the standard of comfort. The drinking of tea in its turn is leading to the general use of milk, formerly looked upon as excrement by the Lushei. The use of milk is said to be effecting a considerable reduction in the rate of infant mortality.

(3) The use of quinine in combating malaria is now universal.

(4) There is an obvious tendency to adopt clothes of European style, and to cut the hair short.

(5) European games, especially football and hockey have been taken up and are played with great enthusiasm, alike on the part of the players and, in the towns of Aijal and Lungleh, of the spectators.

* There are no motorable roads in the Lushai Hills—only bridle paths.

13. General description of the Naga Tribes inhabiting the Burma side of the Patkoi Range.

By the late T. P. Dewar, O.B.E., of the Burma Frontier Service.

[The similarity of the Nagas on the Burma side of the Patkoi to some of the tribes to the east of the Naga Hills District in Assam is very noticeable in this account. Some of the tribes described suggest the Yimtsungr, Sangtamr and Chang tribes of central Nagas, while others are clearly very closely akin to the Konyak Naga tribes of the northern and eastern groups. Some account of the Assam Naga tribes is to be found in the series of tribal monographs published by the Assam Government and a few notes on the tribes above-mentioned are appended to the volume on the Angami Nagas, though the parallels will be much more apparent if a reference be made to Memoir No. 2 of Volume XI of the Asiatic Society of Bengal, published in 1929, describing two tours to the east of the Naga Hills District in Assam and fully illustrated by photographs. Mr. Dewar's notes are of considerable importance as indicating what the practises were in the custom of human sacrifice and as having been collected at a time when the knowledge of custom was still fresh since it had only recently been prohibited by the Government of Burma. J. H. H.]

Nagas of Burma.

These notes deal with the Nagas inhabiting the Burma side of the Patkoi Range, whose villages are established in those mountain systems lying roughly within the following bounds :—The Namhpuk Hka, the Tanai Hka, the western edge of the Hukawng Valley and the inhabited ranges to the north of these limits up to the Patkoi Range. The whole of this area consists of lofty mountains and low hills, whose altitudes range from nine thousand to a few hundred feet above the plains. The chief range is the Sangpan Bum, which lies due east of the Namhpuk Hka, and runs from north to south. It is round the southern base of this great mountain that the Namhpuk flows to join its parent stream the Tanai or Chindwin River. In the north the range breaks into two, one range connecting it with the Patkoi, and the other running in an opposite direction, gradually breaks up into subsidiary spurs which cease at the Tarung Hka, one of the main tributaries of the Tanai River. The summits of this T are the source of those streams, which divide the spurs and subsidiary ranges. The chief streams are the Tarum, Tawa, and Namyung. The beds of the valleys are very low, particularly in the vicinity of the Sangpan Bum, where often the drop from hill top to stream bed is as much as three thousand feet.

Except for large tracts to the west of the Sangpan Bum, where intensive "taungya" or hill cultivation, practised by successive generations of Naga tribesmen, has converted the once luxuriant big tree forest into long grass and stunted tree growth, the whole area is densely covered with tropical ever-green forest. Further to the west of the Namhpuk similar grass-covered hills and mountains were visible, bearing evidence of the systematic hill cultivation practised by the Nagas to eke out an existence. This area west of the Namhpuk Hka is densely inhabited by the Naga Tribes, who have been cut off from expanding to the east by the lofty precipices and rocky ridges, which are a marked feature of the southern half of the Sangpan Range. The western mountains are un-mapped, and unexplored, and extend up to the Patkoi Range. The chief streams are the Namhkao and Namcharing, tributaries of the Namhpuk equally large if not larger than that river. Such tribes as have crossed to the north and east, have done so within the past three, four or five generations.

At the higher altitudes the forests were of the same density as that in the lower hills, the place of many species of tropical trees being taken by oaks, a few stunted pines and a reed-like bamboo. The boughs and boles of the bigger trees were covered with moss and festooned with lichen. Of flowering plants, the scarlet rhododendron, white primula, violets, orchids, and several species of the most beautiful red and purple berries grew along the paths.

At night heavy damp mists formed in the lower valleys, the higher ranges and the ridges being free, where the cold was sharp yet bracing and the atmosphere clear. Rarefied air, always so very trying to laden coolies was experienced as low down as six thousand five hundred feet. The rainfall on the west of the Sangpan Bum appears to be considerably less than that on the east of the range, which in its turn is less than that which falls throughout the winter months over the low-lying Hukawng Valley. December, January and February are the finest months, in March the weather breaks up, and from April onwards the climatic conditions are practically the same as the monsoon. Over the open lands the rays of the sun are very powerful, even during the cold weather. The forests abound with several kinds of monkeys, sambur, barking-deer, porcupine and wild pig, while leopards, tigers and bison [gaur] are not uncommon. The rocky ridges and precipitous hill sides are the homes of the serow or goat-antelope. Of game birds there are several species of pigeons, the black pheasant, great peacock pheasant and jungle fowl. Ordinary bird life is plentiful, and gaudy butterflies were seen in large numbers. A bird named in vernacular *Ja Wu*, bird of gold, which from its description appears to be the beautiful Monal pheasant,* is said to be found at certain spots on the Sangpan Range. Regarding this bird a curious story is attached. It is said that those who snare or kill it invariably die ; such appears to have been the fate of those few persons who have taken its life in the

* Probably Blyth's Tragopan, which is found at heights above 6,000 ft. on the range separating Assam from Burma. I have heard, I think, the same superstition on the Assam side of the range.—J. H. H.

past. The superstitious fears of the tribesmen have thus preserved this bird, which may be unknown to science. In the main streams the chief sporting fish taken were the black mahseer, barralus, bola and chilwa. At several places in the Naga Hills small Kachin Settlements existed till quite a recent date, in fact at the time of writing a few households are living on the south-west of the Sangpan Bum in the Namhpuk Valley and also in the north in the Tarung Valley. The original history of how these Kachin families entered the Naga Hills is unknown. That they exercised considerable influence over the Nagas is abundantly proved in the present day, by the descendants of the original families, who, although they live outside the Naga Hills, exercise a a loose control over the Naga clans in their neighbourhood, and also over several of the more distantly situated clans. It is probable that the Kachins in the zenith of their power pushed ahead into the wider and more favourable of the valleys, occupying the best sites, expecting an influx of their race which never came, and being gradually surrounded by the Nagas, were cut off from returning, and were obliged to exercise such influence as they had acquired, craft and tact to exist in their foreign surroundings. In the course of years, owing to internal strife the colonies gradually became weaker and weaker and eventually were obliged to leave the hills and return to their ancestral homes. Such is the history related of eight or nine households of Kachins, who with their slaves occupied a wide reach of the Namyung Valley above the confluence of its tributary the Tahkam Hka. It is said that these Kachins quarrelled amongst themselves, the weaker having to leave the hills, and seek refuge with relatives and friends either in Assam or the Hukawng Valley. Eventually the few remaining households, distrusting the Nagas whose power was increasing, left the site fearing extermination. Early in the year 1926 a family of Kachins, called the *Laika Ni* living in the Namhpuk Valley were attacked by their enemies the Htangan Nagas and, although they repulsed the attack with a certain degree of success, were obliged to return to the homes of their forefathers in the Muengyi country, south-east of the Hukawng Valley a distance of about one hundred and fifty miles.

Kachin Settlements.

With an illiterate race like the Nagas who have no written language and documents on which dependency could be placed for their origin, we are dependent for the origin and migration of the clans on the statements of the tribal elders now living, that is on knowledge which has come down to them from their ancestors, handed down from father to son through successive generations. The most distant date they go back to is about ten generations, a period roughly calculated at 250 years. Several of the clans maintain that they formerly lived in the Hukawng Valley, mentioning sites now occupied by the Kachins and situated in that part of the Hukawng lying to the west of the Tarung Hka and north of the Tanai Hka. It is said that the exodus took place from these sites, two routes being mentioned, one up the Tarung Valley towards the Patkoi Range, and the other down the Tanai River, through its upper and lower gorges and thence round the southern base of the Sangpan Bum into the Namhpuk Valley. The Hkalak Nagas declare that they occupied their present sites on leaving the Hukawng, but they appear to be the only exception, for the hills and mountains due east of the Sangpan Range have with few exceptions been occupied within the past three or four generations by the surplus Naga population from the Namhpuk clans, who give two main reasons for leaving the Namhpuk Valley. The first is that they were starving, the second that their enemies the Htangans were constantly attacking them. The Pangaw and Pyengoo Nagas, who reside in the hills lying north and east of the confluence of the Namhpuk and Tanai Rivers, were the first to leave their ancestral homes at the headwaters of the Namhpuk. They migrated about ten generations ago, occupying their present sites with the permission of the Kachins, to whom according to the Kachin tribal custom they gave presents. The Pangaw Nagas have intermarried freely with the Kachins, and but for a few households, who in appearance, dress, habits and customs are practically the same as Kachins, may in the present day be considered an extinct clan. The Pyengoo Nagas, chiefly that is the men, have almost entirely adopted Kachin dress, but they still observe many of the habits and customs of their ancestors. The validity of their long residence in their present hills is amply proved in their appearance, the familiarity with which they speak the Kachin dialect, and the statements of their neighbours in the Dalu Valley the Shans and Kachins. If further testimony of this exodus from the congested Namhpuk Valley is required, it may be obtained from some of those clans, who in the present day occupy sites on both sides of the Sangpan Range. Those on the west still retain their national costume, whereas those on the east have borrowed articles of dress from their more civilised neighbours the Kachins and Shans.

Origin.

It is only in certain of the localities visited, such as the Namhpuk Valley and the northern hills, that the Nagas have permanent villages ; they generally move to suit the lands they cultivate, new villages being established when all cultivable land in the vicinity of a site has been worked out, a period which may extend from two to eight or more years. Probably the main reason for these shifting villages is that there are extensive lands to cultivate, and that the best results can be obtained by cultivating fresh lands annually. In the course of years with an increased population permanency in the occupation of sites is likely to follow. A Nat ceremony

Villages.

is invariably performed at the establishing of a village, but since these temporary villages are moved on sudden sickness appearing, not much importance is attached to this ceremony, which is entirely dispensed with by some of the clans. The highest peaks are selected to build on; consequently very few villages were found sheltered in the valleys.

The sanitation of a Naga village is primitive in the extreme. In fenced villages the pigs are depended on to act as scavengers. The droppings from cattle and pigs are every where. The refuse from houses is thrown just outside where it remains to gradually fall to decay. The narrow rocky ridge, on which many villages are built is generally the main street. Houses however are not erected with any order or system, and are jotted down where and how it may please the owners to build them. Building material is plentiful in the neighbouring forests, except at some of the villages in the Namhpuk Valley, where bamboos are scarce and have to be brought from long distances. In such treeless tracts houses are thatched with long rush-like grass, which grows abundantly where once evergreen forest existed. Paddy granaries are erected on the outskirts of most villages, and are used for the storing of valuables, such as gongs, dahs, spare axes, etc. In the southern villages east of the Sangpan Range very frequently the granaries are built hidden away in the forest, close to the hill cultivation, and are subject to depredations by monkeys. Periodical visits are paid to such granaries, paddy and other edibles being removed sufficient for the requirements of the household for a stated time. The grain is made into loads, securely packed and bound, before being placed in the granary, in order that it may be moved and hidden elsewhere should occasion arise.

Domestic Animals.

The chief animals kept by the Nagas are cattle, buffaloes pigs and goats, and in certain villages mithun. An old bull mithun fetches from 100 to 120. The buffaloes are short and sturdy and do not compare favourably with the animal from the plains. No use is made of any of these animals which are kept solely for the purpose of offering to the spirits worshipped by the tribesmen. Each family generally keeps a few fowls but no ducks were seen throughout the area visited.

Fortified Villages.

In the Namhpuk Valley certain villages subject to attack from the west Namhpuk Naga tribes have defences erected round them. Perhaps they do not envelop the whole village perimeter, the Naga considering a steep hill side or low wall of natural rock sufficient protection against attack. Such features are by no means uncommon, as the village site is carefully selected as a stronghold, and is generally built on a rocky or shaly knife-like ridge, or cone-shaped peak. The defences although not very stable are kept in a good state of repair. Where easy of approach a low wall of rock is built and above it is erected a palisade of stout stakes, interlaced with rushes, brushwood and spliced bamboos; the latter have their ends sharpened with the points sticking outwards. Such defences may be still further strengthened by a shallow trench on the outside, and inside the defences for several yards branches of trees up to four feet high are irregularly planted with all their offshoots pointed and sharpened. This second internal defence barrier needs to be carefully negotiated during the hours of darkness. The gateways are narrow and high with roughly hewn wooden doors, of substantial thickness revolving on simple primitive hinges. At the sides and above the gateways especial care is taken to strengthen the defences as much as possible. On the inner sides the doors have two protuberant knobs carved from the natural block; these are bored, and when closed for the nights a stout bar passed through the holes in the protuberances effectively secures the doors against being opened for a stealthy ingress. The village precints are kept thoroughly cleared of undergrowth and scrub; all trees left standing have their lower branches lopped off up to a height of from twenty to twenty-five feet above the ground; thus the bole of the tree is kept clear and allows no cover for a skulking foe. A central house is invariably used as a look-out, and from it the various approaches to the village are visible. The village paths in the vicinity are highly planted with bamboo panjis, and on these tribesmen are mainly dependent against a sudden night attack.

Naga Houses.

Except it be in the more permanent villages the Naga does not seek for either durability or comfort in the construction of his house. Saplings and bamboos are used for house posts and cross beams; walls and floors are made from split bamboo, and being so badly put together afford no protection against the elements. The roof is either of thatch, palm leaf, or the leaf used by the Kachins and known as "*shinglwe lap*", according to the produce most easily obtained in the neighbourhood. In the south houses are small and fragile, consist of one room with two entrances, in front and at the back, and are built on piles three to four feet above the ground. In the northern villages the houses are larger and more stable in structure, with stouter house posts. One half of the house length from front to back is divided into compartments, from three to six or more according to the number of families in residence. The other half is an open verandah or enclosed with bamboo walls, all rooms opening on to it. There are no windows and but two entrances, the front and back. In each a family lives. The fire-place is in the centre of the room, a few logs are always kept burning or smouldering, and round these crouch those members of the family engaged in cooking meals or other indoor occupations.

Even on the brightest day the interior of the house has a dull and gloomy appearance, rarely free from acrid smoke. The long room or verandah has shelves for implements of husbandry with other articles hanging from the roof. In this room many of the women pound the paddy in the wooden mortars raised a few feet above the floor. Others use the front porch, here also the mortar is raised well above the ground to suit the floor of the house on which the women stand when pounding the paddy. The reason given for not pounding the paddy on the ground, is that it is very cold. These houses are also built on piles, which are of various lengths to suit the slopes of the hill sides or ridges on which they are built. All these houses have porches of varying depths to suit the size of the house. It is in this porch that the men sit near an open fire, either talking, consuming opium, or working on making ropes, fashioning dah handles, etc., etc. The Naga is not too hospitable to his guests, and considers he has done sufficient for his visitors' comfort by permitting them to occupy this porch during the period of their visit. The porch is also used for storing baskets, etc., and it is here that the skulls of victims and horns of animals offered at sacrifices or killed in the forest are hung from the roof or affixed to the house posts. Too often the front stairs is but a notched tree trunk. A Nat ceremony is held at the building of a new house, but this custom is not observed by all Naga clans.

When the head of a family dies the room is vacated and fireplace removed, the widow and children, if any living, go elsewhere.

Religion.

The Nagas are animists or spirit worshippers, the chief spirits feared are: 'Mu' (the heavens), 'Ga' (the earth), 'Bum' (the mountains) and 'Sawn' or 'Jawn', the Nat of Hades said to have power over life and death.* To such spirits altars are erected either at village sites, at lonely places along the sides of roads, at the entrances to villages, or at the crossings of high unfrequented passes. The altars are frail in structure and, being uncared for after the sacrifice to the spirit has been made, soon fall to pieces. It is however to be noted, that at some remote passes the altar site is maintained, some passing traveller erecting a new altar by the side of the old one, so that frequently one sees at such places, several altars in various stages of ruin. The spirit of the mountain is generally appeased by the traveller placing an egg as an offering on the altar, while more often than not a twig plucked *en route* suffices. In many of the villages there is a Nat House, at which the community sacrifice to the communal spirits. Some clans hold these communal sacrifices at fixed times during the year, and other clans only when occasion arises, such as once in two or more years. In villages where there are no "Nat Houses" the communal sacrifices are held at some recognised house or particular spot in the village. These "Nat" ceremonies are held to ward off and cure sickness or disease, for a fruitful harvest, welfare of the village cattle, pigs, etc. The animals sacrificed vary amongst the different clans; some sacrifice only cattle, pigs and fowls, others include buffaloes, dogs and goats; in addition to the above some clans included human beings, or only the parts taken from the corpse of a sacrificed human, and still others used the head, arms and legs of enemies they had killed to propitiate the spirits. At a deserted village site a 'phallic' worship stone, planted three to four generations ago was seen. It was said that the offering used to purify houses in the village at which women had died at child-birth, generally human flesh, was placed before the stone to fall to decay.

Nat Ceremonies.

The Nagas are dependent almost solely on the success of the crops they cultivate for their subsistence, and, being a superstitious and uncivilised race, make sacrifices to the spirits they worship for a plentiful harvest. At these Nat sacrifices, which are held at fixed periods, they strive to appease the spirits with the blood of animals in the hope that the land will be blessed and be fruitful. They also recognise the necessity of a sacrifice after or about the time of the harvest, as a thank offering for the fruits of the land. The most propitious times at which these ceremonies are held are as follows:—At the clearing or cutting of the annual hill cultivation, at the time of preparing the land, or just before sowing the grain, and again after sowing, or when the grain is sprouting. Later when the crops are about a foot high, or just prior to the forming of the ears of grain, or at the reaping of the harvest, or after its gathering winnowing, etc. In some clans these are communal sacrifices, in others partly communal and partly independently offered by each household or house-owner. At some of these ceremonies which last three days there is general rejoicing, when the village community indulges in feasting, drinking and dancing. At other ceremonies, which last a day or so, only the spirits are appeased and liquor drunk. There is no rejoicing. Opium, a recognised necessity, is consumed at all these ceremonies. The Longri clan spend a month or more rejoicing every year after the hill cultivation has been cut. It is their custom for each house-owner to appease the spirits independently, and to hold a feast to which all the villagers are invited. The next day is observed for rest, and on the third day another house-owner makes a sacrifice and gives a feast. This procedure is carried on till every house-owner in the village has made a sacrifice and held a feast. It is said that throughout this period no work of any sort is undertaken. Rather a curious sacrifice is held by the Mawshang Nagas. It is said that when a tribesman acquires wealth, he entertains his relatives and connections by giving them a big feast at which he provides all the animals for sacrifice, accepting no assistance from others.

* These words like many of the customs described are forcibly suggestive of the Chang Nagas on the Assam side of the range. In Chang *mügh*='sky', *gau*='earth' and *sou*=the ghost of a dead man.—J. H. H.

To perform their religious ceremonies and approach in the orthodox manner the numerous spirits which they worship, the Naga makes use of Diviners, Praying Priests, and Mediums.

Priests, etc.

Some clans have no Mediums and employ only Diviners and Praying Priests. Although the Diviner officiated when the promise to sacrifice a human was made, and a token affixed to the house posts, it was the Praying Priest only who was employed at the final ceremony when the human was offered, and it was he who later hung the skull, arms and legs from the house roof. The Diviner's business is to discover the correct offering which will appease the offended spirit and remove the primary cause of the sickness, ill-health, etc. For his art he makes use of a species of bamboo or leaf, as is done by his neighbour, the Kachin. The Praying Priest supplicates the offended spirit, and blesses the offering before it is sacrificed in order that it may be found acceptable. The Diviner may receive no payment for his services, the Praying Priest generally receiving the hind leg of a buffalo at a big Nat ceremony. The mediums claim to possess the power of metempsychosis during the period of their temporary trance, when they enter the form of a tiger and discover what is taking place at long distances. For these services they receive a small present in money or in kind. It is said that the proof of these supernatural claims are exemplified in the tiger's foot-print which has five distinct toe impressions, exclusive of the pad of the foot, the ordinary foot-print having but four. Such belief is not uncommon amongst the Kachins as well.*

The custom of sacrificing humans was not practised throughout the area visited. It was confined to the central and northern villages, where live the clans of Haimi and Rangpan

Human Sacrifices.

Nagas. Two stories are given as to why this custom was initiated by these clans. The first is, that the Nagas and Kachins were neighbours, inhabiting the Majoi Shingra Bum, and from there came down together to the southern ranges. The Kachins were successful with their cultivation; not so the Nagas who finding their crops a failure consulted the Mahtu Mahta Nat, and were advised by this spirit to sacrifice a *Ningrau Chinga* (the sloth monkey).† As advised by the spirit the sacrifice was duly performed, but without any success. A second application was made to the same spirit, who suggested the offering of a human. The advice was again taken, a human procured and sacrificed, the result being that the crops were a success, the health of the people and cattle improved, and the Nagas attained wealth. After that humans were sacrificed when all else had failed. The second story is that originally the clans sacrificed *Woi* (the small red monkey‡) to the spirits, to cure sickness, for a successful harvest, welfare of the cattle, etc. It was found in the course of time that the offering was not acceptable, as the results for which the ceremony was held were never obtained. At this stage a human hand is said to have dropped from heaven, and those who witnessed this remarkable occurrence proclaimed that it was a sign from the spirit, clearly pointing out that if humans were sacrificed they would find favour with the god. From that date the sacrifice of humans was introduced and the spirit appeased.

The sacrifice of a man was the chief form of Nat ceremony held by the Nagas, and was only performed when the blood of cattle, pigs, etc., had failed. Thus in the present day it might be regarded as the Nagas' last resort to cure some lingering malady, an epidemic amongst men and cattle, or successive years of poor harvests. When such misfortunes occurred a diviner would be consulted, and he, divining with a species of leaf and bamboo, would declare the sacrifice of a human essential to appease the offended spirit. The diviner would very rarely have declared the sex of a human to be offered but would have made a general statement that a human had to be killed. So soon as the wishes of the enraged spirit were made known through the diviner, a minor Nat ceremony was held at which a pig was killed and a promise made to the spirit that a human would be sacrificed at some future date. At the time that this promise was made a token would be affixed to one of the main house-posts. The token was generally a small piece of iron, a dagger or a dah. It was only after the human had been killed that the token was removed and caused to disappear, that is, it might be thrown away, or buried at the base of the sacrificial posts, with certain parts of the head, etc. When removed from the post, the *Tumsa Wa* (praying priest) informed the spirit that as a human had been asked for, a promise had been made which had now been fulfilled. The sacrifice had to be held once a promise had been made, and the token affixed to the house posts, no matter what length of time it took the family concerned to collect sufficient money to purchase a victim. It very often happened that in cases of sickness the person making the promise died, this did not affect the ceremony which was held by his son or relatives. As a general rule such sacrifices were held within from five to 10 years after a promise. The victims offered did not belong to any particular tribe, they came from villages some distance west of the Namhpuk Hka, close to the foot of the Patkoi Range, where the country is inhabited by several Naga tribes declared to be constantly at war with one another. From the south to the north and east the victims were transported by middlemen, living in a chain of villages up the Namhpuk Valley, and connecting the suppliers of slaves with the human sacrificing clans. The victims who were sold were

* And is general in the Assam Naga Hills.—J. H. H.
† *I.e.*, the slow loris, *nycticebus coucang*.—J. H. H.
‡ Probably a macaque.—J. H. H.

either slaves, prisoners of war, captives taken in raids, or persons seized and sold for bad debts, etc.; in one case a woman was sold by her husband because she was an inveterate thief. The price of a slave for sacrifice ranged from Rs. 300 to Rs. 500; this included the charges paid to agents and others employed to convey the human to the purchaser's village. The purchaser might pay the price of the victim himself but should he not have had sufficient money or goods, he was helped by his relatives. In consideration for such assistance these relatives received parts of the bone and flesh of the human sacrificed, with which they performed minor Nat ceremonies at some subsequent date. An advance payment for the slave might be made through agents, but this was not essential, and very often a purchase was made direct from middlemen in possession of a victim and moving in the vicinity of the human sacrificing area looking out for a purchaser. When agents were employed they brought the slave to the purchaser's village where they acted as warders, and only handed the victim over to the purchaser after full payment had been made. After being feasted and receiving gifts from the purchaser they were allowed to return to their homes. Sometimes as many as six persons were engaged to convey a slave to the purchaser's village. The victim might be of any age or sex, there being no appreciable difference in price for a mere child or person of mature years.

Captivity might last for months prior to delivery at the house or village at which the victim was to be killed. Here the confinement might be in stocks for both arms and legs or for only one leg or for the arms only; all depended on the nature, sex, and age of the victim. A child might only be watched, and allowed to play about with other village children. A woman might be allowed the liberty of moving about the village, with only one leg in a stock, and yet a grown man might have both arms and legs in stocks, and be confined to some unfrequented part of the house. The confinement might last in the owner's house for just the period necessary to make all preparations to hold the ceremony, that was about ten days, and then again the time might be extended for several months, should there be no immediate haste to hold the ceremony. As a rule victims were not kept long; they were never manumitted, and having been purchased for a special purpose it was necessary that they should be killed. In the few cases where an owner developed feelings of pity and kindness for the victim, he might not sacrifice the victim himself but sold him to some one else for a sacrifice, purchasing a new victim for his own use. Such occasions however, were very rare. Provided a victim made no efforts to escape, the treatment was neither harsh nor unkind. He was not unnecessarily restrained; his food was sufficient and of the same quality as that eaten by other members of the household. The victims had however, to eat their meals separately, and when confined in stocks for both arms and legs, ate their food from a basket placed in front of them. The older victims knew that they were meant for a sacrifice and had to be carefully watched to prevent them from committing suicide.

The duration of the human sacrificing ceremony might last up to seven days, the period changing with the clan to which the person holding the sacrifice belonged. Generally the first two or three days were devoted to making preparations for the sacrifice such as collecting the sacrificial posts from the jungle, leaves for wrapping food into packets to serve the guests, jungle ropes to bind the cattle to the sacrificial posts, the erection of altars, etc. On the next day a pig was offered and killed, and the victim feasted on the flesh of this animal. The day following the victim was killed, and the next day the guests departed to their homes. The following procedure, given by a member of the Lokai Clan of Haimi Nagas, is typical of the way in which a human sacrifice was conducted :—

"*Ru Gawk*".—*The first day.*—The ropes to tie the cattle and buffaloes are procured from the jungle, liquor being distributed freely amongst those present.

"*Nap Tawk*".—*The second day.*—*Lahpaw* leaves are collected from the jungle. These leaves which are broad and long, resembling the canna leaf, are used as wrapers for making food into packets. They also serve as plates.

"*Bandak*".—*The third day.*—Sacrificial posts are cut and fashioned in the jungle and brought to the village, where they are ornamented with black and white paint, the pattern being on one side of the post.

"*Bai Hkung*".—*The fourth day.*—The sacrificial posts and altars are erected, a pig is offered and killed, and the victim feasted on the pork. Later, if the victim was in stocks they were removed, and the victim taken to various houses in the village where liquor and food were given. He was then brought back to the house and carefully watched at night. At this stage all those invited have arrived at the village.

"*Dahkang*".—*The fifth day.*—Early in the morning the victim was killed, and that night the guests danced round the house seven times, the butcher carrying the head, arms and legs.

"*Ngatang*".—*The sixth day.*—All the buffaloes, cattle, pigs, fowls, etc., are offered and killed, they are then skinned and cleaned and cut up.

"*Rungan*".—*The seventh day.*—There is a general feast after which the guests return to their homes.

The last night of captivity the victim was handed over to the guests, who acted as warders and were responsible for seeing that the victim did not escape. It is said that as a rule he was not ill-treated, and that he had to be well feasted, otherwise the crops were a failure. So long as the victim remained in a submissive and meditative mood he was not beaten, but any refusal to conform with the wishes of the warders being met with brutal treatment. One tribesman said it was necessary to beat the victims to such an extent that they should lose their minds—"*Myit shamat ra ai*". This may have been the custom of his clan. The same result could have been obtained by stupefying the victim with liquor and opium. In fact many persons declare that the victim used to be quite drunk when led out to be killed. The slave-o vner did not know how the warders were treating his slave as they guarded the slave in a different part of the house to that occupied by the owner on that night. It is said that the victim was beaten only with the open hand, and and that it was wrong to inflict open wounds causing a flow of blood. It is rumoured that pounded chillies were placed in the eyes to cause blindness, but this was denied by those interrogated. On his last night the victim was not allowed to sleep.

The victim might be killed in any one of the following ways :—The victim was led to a stake planted about ten yards in front of the house, where the butcher struck off the head with a stroke of the sacrificial *dah*, the whole skull or only part of the frontal bone was affixed to this post, where remaining uncared for it would fall to the ground and disappear. Amongst some of the clans who killed their victims in this manner the arms and legs were not cut off and kept. In other clans the victim was led to the head of the front stairs, there the head was cut off, and the headless trunk pushed down the stairs, on falling to the ground the arms and limbs were lopped oft. The skull was then thoroughly cleansed and divided into two. The front part was retained by the house owner, and the back given to the butcher, a close relative of the person holding the ceremony. The arms and legs were either retained by the owner, or given to those who had assisted to purchase the victim, or sold, or given away to friends and relatives. They were used for minor Nat ceremonies. The *Tumsa Wa*, or praying priest, hung up the parts of the skull in the houses of the owner and butcher. These parts were said to retain supernatural powers and to act as talismans to ward off evil influences from attacking the members of the household, the cattle, pigs, fowls, etc. A few clans used to spear their victims at the head of the stairs, and when they fell to the ground others struck off the head, arms, and legs. These were cleaned and smoked and hung up in the houses, as was the custom with other clans.

After the human offering had been killed, the butcher cut open the body and removed small parts of the heart, liver, and spleen. These were offered to the spirit by the praying priest, who in his supplication informed the spirit that since a human had been asked for and a promise made, the same had now been fulfilled. The token was then removed from the house posts, and either thrown away or buried at the base of the sacrificial post with the cleanings of the head such as the lips, ears, eyes, flesh, etc. Other parts from some of the internal organs, and flesh from the body were also removed, and used later for minor Nat ceremonies, or sold to other tribesmen for such purposes. The major portion of the trunk was removed to some distance from the village, in order that the village dogs and pigs should not eat of the flesh of the offering. It was disposed of in one of the following ways :—either hidden in the jungle, or put into the hollow trunk of a tree, or placed on a specially prepared bamboo platform, built in a tree some height above the ground, where it soon fell to decay.

Perhaps the most important Nat ceremony performed with the parts of a victim, was the purification of a house in which a woman had died in child-birth. This ceremony was held even by those clans who did not practise human sacrifices themselves, and were therefore obliged to purchase the parts of a human they required for an offering from some neighbouring clan who sacrificed human beings. With some clans the offering used was thrown three times over the house, from the front to the back, ba k again to the front, and for the last time from the front to the back. The offering was then thrown away, the priest later washing his hands with clean water. Pigs and fowls were then sacrificed and at the same time the house was declared pure, and once again fit for habitation free from evil influences. Houses were purified at the same time as a human sacrifice was made. The necessary parts, having been removed from the human corpse, were rubbed over the floors and walling of the house by the priest, who in performing these rites declared the house free of the evil influence with which it had been contaminated.*

The Wanga Nagas, a clan who did not themselves practise human sacrifices, purchased the human offering they required for the purification of a house, generally a piece of human flesh, and with it propitiated the spirit and declared the house pure. After this ceremony was over the offering was removed to the "*Namshang*" (*Nat* house), where it was stuck up for a short while in the first instance, and later thrown away. Such an offering cost Rs. 10. Other clans who used the bones of the hand for the purification ceremony, paid approximately Rs. 15 per hand.

* It should be understood that the original significance is undoubtedly not to purge from an evil which has attached to the house but to supply a deficiency from which it suffers. The real principle underlying all head-hunting and human sacrifice in the Naga Hills area is that of the supply of life-matter to living organisms or even to material substances which are shown to be deficient in vitality.—*See* part I, Chapter XII *passim*.—J. H. H.

The sacrificial *dah* was retained by the butcher after he had committed the dreadful deed. Some clans considered it lucky to carry this *dah* after use. In cases where the sacrificial *dah* was affixed as a token at the time the promise to sacrifice a human was made, the *dah* was only removed from the house post at the very last moment just prior to the decapitating of the human offering.

Stocks.

Amongst the human-sacrificing Naga clans stocks were used to prevent victims from escaping during the period of their captivity. One stock was used for both arms, but for the legs separate stocks were used. The stock for the leg was about four feet long and ten inches in diameter, tapering slightly towards the ends. The leg was placed in the stock, and to secure it and keep it in position a false piece of wood was inserted and kept in position by a wooden pin. For the arms the stock was about eighteen inches long and six inches in diameter, the hands were placed in the stock one in front of the other, the stock lying along the front of the body, a false piece of wood was inserted, whilst a wooden pin secured it and kept the arms in position. The stocks were made from solid, durable wood and were quite heavy. The duration of captivity depended on the urgency or otherwise of the sacrifice, and might last for any period from ten days, to three, four or more months.

Appearance.

In general features the Naga resembles the Kachin of the neighbouring tracts. He is more of the Aryan type, the features being pronounced, the nose longish and in many cases inclined to be aquiline. Physically he is built on a slimmer mould, and in stature there is not much to choose between the two races. In cases where he still wears the tribal costume, the waist is contracted from earliest youth, with the result that the abdomen is frequently pushed upwards, and gives the body an un-natural bulge over the waist band.

The women are much shorter than Kachin women, have a stouter build, are well developed, and over a great part of the country are decidedly fairer with regular pronounced features. The hair is inclined to be wavy, very dark brown or blackish, with a decidedly reddish tinge easily distinguishable in certain lights. The scalp is well covered, and even in advanced years there does not appear to be any tendency towards baldness, although the growth may become scanty. Over large areas both men and women wear their hair long; in some clans the women shave the poll, and the men wear a short crop. In the Namhpuk Valley the head dress of the males may briefly be described as follows :—

" The head is shaved to about an inch above the ears, and round the back of the skull. The front part of the remaining tuft is allowed to fall as a fringe, the back is kept much longer, is twisted into a bun and twined round a bone ornament, which rests across the nape of the neck. The bun is frequently further decorated with a strip of red cloth, or goats hair dyed red ". Some of the women part their hair in the centre but do not plait it and in the remoter villages the hair is allowed to fall in matted unkempt locks. The eye is generally a very dark brown, but the shape varies. Some Nagas have large roundish eyes with the lids well opened, and the eye-lashes long , in others the eye is narrow, and the inner corner almost covered by the Mongolian fold, the eye-lashes being scanty. Little hair is grown on the face, and such males as cultivated a beard had a very scraggy growth.

A very large percentage of the men in the villages nearer to civilization, and along the route to Assam have adopted the style of dress worn by their immediate neighbours, such as the Shans and Kachins, and may briefly be described as follows :—

Dress.

A tartan waist cloth, a jacket or shirt, white or coloured, sometimes both, a stripped *gaung baung* or turban, and the *hkamauk* (Shan hat). In the northern villages frequently a heterogeneous collection of garments, borrowed from both the west and east of the Patkoi Range is worn. A large white puggaree tied in the Indian fashion, still further enhanced the incongruity of this adopted dress. The *Gyi* string is worn in the remoter villages, and the person of the male, when resting on a cold day, envèloped in a cotton blanket. These blankets, generally black, dark blue, or a dirty white, rarely striped, are coarse in texture and are woven by the Naga women. The blankets are sometimes decorated with cowrie shells stitched on to form a border, or cross lines over the surface on one side. Frequently a jacket or shirt is substituted for the blanket. The *gaung baung* is worn by some, entirely discarded by others and very often its place taken by the Naga helmet, or the *hkamauk*. A rectangular piece of cloth about a foot long, and four to six inches wide, of the same coarse material and colouring as the blanket cloth, is worn suspended from the *gyi* string waist band and falling immediately in front of it. This sporran like garment is known in the vernacular as a *shingup*. On festivals and gala days the *shingup* may be adorned with a highly polished small brass gong, worn over the generative organs. The protuberance in the centre of the gong is pointed and hollow, and from it may stick out a tuft of coloured goats hair, generally red, or may be suspended a few blue beads. On such special occasions may also be worn, the front entirely covered with cowrie shells, a *shingup* of coarse material.

Like the men in the villages nearer to civilizing influences the Naga woman has borrowed a few articles of dress from her neighbours, the Kachins. Chief of these are gaudy strip of cloth or tartan, wound carelessly round the head to represent a turban, and the Kachin *ningwawt*, or breast covering, a piece of cloth about eighteen inches wide, wrapped round the body and neatly tucked in over the bosom. Those of the women, in the habit of visiting the Shan and Kachin villages in their immediate neighbourhood have also taken to wearing the Burmese *aingyi* or jacket; such women however are considerably in the minority. The woman's skirt is two narrow pieces of coarsely woven and very durable cloth stitched roughly together to form a width of about sixteen inches, and of sufficient length to just go round the hips and allow a few inches of overlap. This garment is affixed at the top end by one or more safety pins, but where these are not available sharpened bamboo pins hardened in fire or large jungle thorns are substituted. The split of the skirt is on either side, and slightly to the front. In different parts of the hills the colouring of the skirt changes. In the northern hills it is of a greenish hue with narrow red, blue, and white stripes, while in the central villages very dark blue, black, or once white skirts are worn. Amongst the southern villages on the eastern side of the Sangpan Bum a more elaborate skirt is worn. The outer side is raised like a huckaback, with a distinct pattern of greys and blacks, or it may be of one uniform blackish colour, relieved with orange and green stitches worked on to it by hand at distant intervals. Amongst many of the clans no clothing is worn above the waist. When resting or on cold windy days the women envelop themselves in a coarse cotton blanket similar to that used by the men. The blanket is generally discarded when performing outdoor pursuits or travelling between villages. In all the northern villages two broad pieces of cloth suspended from the shoulders or neck and falling to within a few inches of the knees, are also worn. These are generally of the same material and colour as the skirt and are often decorated with brightly coloured strips of cloth stitched on to the surface at regular intervals, or are still further beautified by having the lower edges hung with similar strips of cloth or coloured cords. In addition to this chemise-like garment the women often wrap round their bodies large cotton blankets.

Children up to the ages of eight or ten go about naked, or with only a strip of cloth worn round the loins. In the more distant villages, until adolescence is reached, the bigger girls cover themselves with a blanket. It is said that the older boys do not wear the *shingup* and *gyi* string until they have attained puberty.

Necklaces.

Both men and women wear necklaces. Those worn by the women consist of long strings of large beads, blue, yellow and white being the three colours most favoured. The women also wear a necklace of finely woven cane strips, into which are worked small glass beads of various colours, a similar necklace to this is worn by the men and fits the neck loosely. A hollow brass moulded necklace, which has along its front effigies representing the human skull, gongs and knobs, stiffly sticking out from it on slender bars, is much favoured by the males. It is said that the representation of the human skull is not emblematical of victims of raids, heads taken in war, etc., but solely for the sake of beauty and decoration. These effigies are also worn by the men suspended from a close fitting necklace of the large blue beads strung on coarse cord.

Cane Rings.

A cheap and neatly finished ring made from strips of cane of various widths and coloured red, black and yellow is worn by both men and women below the knee and above the calves. Black is the colour most favoured. Not many rings are worn and some people have them on one leg only. A more substantial ring, also made from cane to which small cowrie shells are affixed, appears to be exclusive to the males. Some of the women also wear large number of these rings round the hips just above the skirt line. Not meant to support the skirt they fit the body loosely. In the Namhpuk Valley at Sanka Village a man was seen wearing about fifteen black cane rings round his waist. These rings were about half inch wide and quarter inch thick.

Ear-rings.

In a few clans the women wear two narrow circular welded coils of brass about three inches in diameter. Amongst such women from years of constant use the ear lobe becomes deformed and is dragged down several inches, the ornament eventually resting on the chest above the bosom. Perhaps the commonest ear-ring favoured by the men in certain localities is made of brass, similar to the cog-wheel of a clock, but considerably exaggerated. The body of the wheel fits into the bored ear lobe, this hole often being large enough to admit a tube half an inch in diameter. A piece of brass wire, coiled at one end like a watch spring, or formed into a circle with a few beads strung on it, or even the bone of an animal, or a tuft of dyed goats hair is used to ornament the ear. Such ear ornaments are common to both men and women. In addition to the ear-ring suspended from the ear lobe, men still further decorate the ear by wearing a second ear-ring at the top.

Armlets and Wristlets.

The women wear both armlets and wristlets of brass and of some whitish metal which resembles aluminium in colour. The wristlets worn by the men are generally of brass, but neither as heavy nor as large as those worn by the women. A narrow band woven from the hairs of the tails of the pigs offered at sacrifices is also worn by both men and women. In several clans these hair wristlets are symbolical that the wearers are married. They are also worn by many as charms to ensure good health. In the locality some men wear a few red cane rings round the wrists.

Tattooing.

Tatooing of the body is not practised to any great extent. No tatooed women were noticed. Some of the men were tatooed with five parallel lines from the angle of the chin downwards on either side of the neck. The upper body is tatooed with lines down the front and sides of the chest abruptly halting at the waistband where the marks are more conspicuous than elsewhere. On the legs the only marks seen were coils, which looked like representations of snakes. The tatooing is done in early manhood, no tatooed male children were noticed.

Fear of attack from the Htangan Nagas.

In many of the villages in the Namhpuk Valley, the tribesmen lived in constant terror of of attack from their enemies the Htangan Nagas. All the village pigs, cattle, etc., enter and sleep within the defences at night. A watch is kept, the fighting men sleeping with their arms by their sides ready for immediate action. Travelling after sundown is rarely undertaken and then only in a large party. No one leaves the village defences in the morning until the sun is well in the heavens; there is always fear of a lurking foe. The cultivation of the land and hewing of wood is performed by parties sufficiently large for some member to detect an enemy in the vicinity. On the least alarm being raised such parties return to the village defences with as great haste and little delay as possible. It must be remembered that the Htangan Nagas were a head-hunting race, who made no discrimination and killed men, women, children and even infants, taking the head, arms and legs of their victims to offer to the communal Nats for the purifying of houses and villages in which a woman had died at childbirth, welfare of the crops, health of the community, etc., etc.

Method of Fighting.

On the war path the Naga depends chiefly on surprise for a successful issue. When in large numbers he may attack in massed formation discarding all precaution and coming boldly forward. On arrival at close quarters the spear is cast and, should it take effect, the attacker rushes on his enemy kills him with the dah and cuts off the head, arms and legs, which are immediately placed in the basket carried for the purpose. An attack is of very short duration, and over almost as soon as it has begun. The shield is held in front of the body slightly to the left, and struck against the left knee from time to time with a sharp tap, while the brave hops and prances, at the same time shouting execrations and yelling defiance to distract his foe. While retiring he rapidly plants bamboo panjis in the ground in the hope that an attacker rushing carelessly forward may be spiked and go lame. Attacks on villages generally took place in the quiet hours of the night or a few hours before dawn, in order to give the attackers an opportunity of gaining safe territory before a pursuit could be organised. To lie in wait at some lonely part of a road, first spear and then kill travellers, be they men, women, or children, was a method frequently resorted to in the southern Namhpuk villages. When a party was on the war path, the main body generally lay up in some lonely spot, a few scouts going out to spy out the land and later bring in information on which the attack was carried out.

War Drum.

At certain of the fortified villages west of the Sangpan Range, where the tribesmen lived in constant dread of attack from their enemies, a hollowed out trunk of a tree is generally placed on the ground at some central spot in the village. The one at Kawlum is about twenty-five feet long, and three feet in diameter. When heads had been taken in a raid, or while resisting an attack, the victory was celebrated as follows:—The heads were placed at the bow, the braves who had assisted to procure the heads lined up on either side of the drum holding in their hands wooden stakes or paddy-pounders. With these they pounded the drum together, with regular uniform strokes, at the same time chanting their song of victory and shouting loudly. It is said that the sound carries very far, from five to six miles, and could be heard in the enemy villages across the Namhpuk Valley. At the conclusion of the celebration the heads were removed and permanently affixed to a tree trunk in the vicinity of the village. During the course of the year, from time to time the braves were said to dance before the skulls, thus reviving memories of the victory gained.

Naga Helmet.

The tribal headdress of the Naga male is a cone-shaped helmet, still worn in those remoter villages where the tribesmen have not been influenced by their more civilized neighbours living in the plains. The foundation of the helmet is made from cane strips about quarter of an inch in width. Except for two triangular shaped patches on the sides, the hole is covered by finely woven cane mats dyed red with a pattern in yellow ochre picked out in front and behind. Similarly on the side mats small circles are picked out at regular intervals. A narrow binding with yellow cane* strips, disguises the junction of the mats, and gives the helmet the appearance of being covered by an unbroken surface. The helmet is ornamented with the tushes of the wild boar, both in front and behind, a feather or two from the tail of the great hornbill, falcon, or

* Not cane but the dried stem of a dendrobium orchid commonly used for decorative purposes in the Naga Hills of Assam and in the Andaman Islands. The stem dries a brilliant, and permanent, yellow.—J. H. H.

drongo, and sometimes a strip from the pelt of a bear, a few inches wide, stretched across the top of the helmet from side to side. A similar decoration made from goats' hair and dyed red is also used. Other decorations are flat circular pieces of brass, three to four inches in diameter, polished, and affixed to the sides of the helmet. One man had these brass plates in the shape of an old English battle-axe. The Headman of one village still further decorated his helmet with the scalp hairs of two of his enemies, who he said had killed one of his sons. Some hats are made of hide, fit the head more closely, and resemble a Roman helmet. Some wear a chin-strap of woven cane or string, and all helmets have a loop of woven cane at the top for carrying in the hand, or hanging up in the house when not in use . The hats worn by the braves are of interwoven cane and fit the head more closely, like a skull cap. They are not dyed or coloured and are adorned like the helmets, including scalp hairs from the head of some previously killed enemy.

Dah.

Over a large part of the area visited the Naga has adopted the dah and scabbard of the Kachin. The tribal dah resembles that of the Kachin but is not so long and is carried by a belt round the waist, lying up the back with the handle protruding over one or other of the shoulders and always ready for immediate use and the downward cut. The scabbard is a flat piece of wood, about ten inches long and five inches wide. The dah slips into a depression carved out of the block, and is kept in position by narrow strips of brass or steel let in cross-wise above the depression. On either side of the depression and at the foot the scabbard is decorated with fine strips of brass hammered into the wood. The sides are generally carved with some simple pattern, such as lines and ziz-zags. The waist-band may be of hide or of closely interwoven cane or of finely woven cane strands dyed red. On either side of the scabbard are affixed either part of the tine taken from a sambur's antler, or serow horns, or imitations of these carved from wood. One end of the dah belt is permanently affixed to the horn or tine, the other is looped and slipped over the second horn or tine, when the dah is worn. The dah handle is of plain wood, or bamboo and is rarely ornamented, though often bound with fine strips of cane, or a band of steel. A very much larger dah, with a longer handle is said to be used by warriors and on feast days ; there is no scabbard ; it is carried in the hand. Dahs are manufactured chiefly by the Risa and Rangsa Nagas, the blacksmiths sometimes decorate the blades with a simple pattern hammered on to it when forging the iron.

Arms.

There are not many guns, and those seen were chiefly flintlocks. The large cross-bow with poisoned arrow is not known in the country visited, it is said to be used by the western Naga Tribes living across the Namhpuk Hka. The feathered spear is manufactured by the western Naga Tribes though here and there in the villages visited men may be found who have learnt the art from their neighbours. These spears are given as gifts at marriages, used on ceremonial occasions, and when paying visits of importance. A similar spear without the feathers is used to spear cattle offered at sacrifices, etc. One two or even three lighter spears are carried by the braves on the war path, they can be thrown up to thirty yards on the flat but considerably further downhill. A small cross-bow is often used to shoot birds. The shield is of tough hide, about three feet long and two feet wide, with handles about midway on the inside. To these handles are attached quivers which hold bamboo panjis, or the panji quivers may be suspended from the waist belt. The panji is about twelve inches long, made of bamboo, with both ends sharpened ; it is hardened by scorching with fire. To the dah belt hangs an open work bamboo basket, which is worn during a raid or resisting an attack. It is meant to carry the head, arms, and legs of an enemy.

Industries.

The ginning, spinning and weaving is done by the Naga women, who use rude and primitive appliances. The resulting cloth although rough is very strong and lasts for years. The dyes are obtained from jungle herbs and roots. The men weave hand fishing nets, snares, etc., the twine used is made from the fibres of the *Lakwi* (Kachin) tree, and is pliant, strong and durable. Over the central area the forging of dahs is a well known industry. Spear heads and shafts are made at all villages where there is a blacksmith.

The brass ornaments referred to elsewhere, are manufactured at Hkamla, a distant Naga village west of the Namhpuk River. The chief trade is with the low-lying Shan and Kachin villages, where dahs, fishing nets, and Indian corn wrappings (*kawpa lap*) used in the manufacture of cigars, are brought down by the Naga tribes from distant villages, to be bartered for salt, ready cash, or other commodities. Amongst themselves the Nagas chiefly trade in paddy which is exchanged for ornaments and beads.

Cultivation.

Throughout the area the tribesmen practise "taungya" or hill cultivation only. These lands may be cultivated two or more years in succession, according to the fertility of the soil. Generally a fresh cultivation is cut every year, but where an old one is cultivated for the second year in succession, the new cultivation is cut over smaller limits merely to supplement the produce from the old field. The hill clearings are generally within a few miles of the village. Daily visits are made to the fields for the purpose of protecting the crops, from destruction by wild animals. When the paddy is ripening in many areas monkeys are very troublesome, the fields being watched night and day. No cultivations are cut higher than at an altitude of 6,000 ft. After the jungle is cut it is allowed to dry, and then burnt, the ashes so formed being worked into the ground to fertilise the soil. The chief crops grown are paddy, maize, beans, yams, red and white pumpkins and cotton. The poppy is also cultivated chiefly in the vicinity of the villages and in between the house sites within securely fenced in areas. Amongst some of the clans precedence is given to the headman's fields, which are sown and reaped first. Some clans cut all the fields in one place, others split into groups, and yet others clear lands where they please. In congested areas families have recognised fields which they work in rotation. The limits of these areas are bounded by natural features, such as minor water-courses, subsidiary ridges, rocks, etc., etc. Disputes over lands are settled by the headman and village elders, according to the customs of the clans concerned.

Roads.

Throughout the area the custom is for the several clans to clear and maintain annually only those roads which lead to the hill cultivation. As the hill cultivation sites change almost annually, new paths have to be made; or where old fields are being re-cultivated, after a rest of several years to give the jungle an opportunity to grow, an old path is but cleared and renovated. In the course of years the hill sides and minor ridges are interlaced with overgrown footpaths, needing but to be cleared. Thus this customary duty does not fall hard on the tribesmen. Inter-village roads are never cleared, and consequently the worst part of a path connecting two villages will be found, on either side of the recognised boundary between the two places.

The habit of only preparing the road to the hill cultivations, has led to the adoption of a linear measure used frequently by the tribesmen, it is :—One hill cultivation distant, "*Yi lam mi*" in Kachin. From what has already been written it is clear that no reliance can be placed on this measure of distance which may be anything from a few furlongs to two or more miles.

Marriage and Courtship.

Throughout the area visited the Naga marries at an early age, the men between the ages of twenty and twenty-four, and the women between the ages of sixteen and twenty. Prior to marriage there is invariably familiarity between the sexes, and for this purpose separate houses are set apart at most villages, frequented nightly by the young people. In the larger villages there may be two or more houses for each of the sexes. These houses are also utilised to perform indoor occupations, for it is here that the young women gin, spin and weave, while the men fashion dah handles and scabbards, make snares, and weave fishing-nets. The men visit the maidens' hut during the night where the young couples spend the time talking, working and making love to each other. The lovers also meet in some widow's house, granary, while the women are pounding the paddy, or while performing outdoor pursuits. Amongst some of the clans, such as the Rasa and Kumga Nagas, once a woman has been promised to a man, the couple sleep at the same fireplace as the girl's parents and her younger brothers and sisters; the house is a large room with one fireplace only at which the entire family sleep. One of the headmen when referring to this custom, declared, "We Nagas know no shame", and another said that any remonstrance by the girl's parent is met by the couple replying, "When you were young, you did the same". Amongst other clans it is considered shameful to make love in the presence of a relative of the opposite sex, and to avoid this happening in the larger villages several huts for the sexes are built. At a Rau village in the Namhpuk Valley established on an exposed conical peak, at an altitude of over 6,000 ft., where the cold was intense, the maidens' hut was a hole in the ground, eighteen feet long, fifteen feet wide, and five feet deep. A dome shaped roof of branches, twigs and clods of earth making it watertight, snug and warm. The entrance, a small opening on one side, had a direct drop to the floor. The furniture consisted of a few roughly hewn planks, of an average width of one foot six inches, raised on trestles a couple of feet above the ground. The young people meet at this rendezvous after dark and disperse before dawn. There appears to be no marriage ceremony, the custom is for agents to go on behalf of the man and ask for the bride, she comes to the bridegroom's house the same day and a feast is then held, after which the couple live together as husband and wife. Amongst some clans wristlets are woven from the tail hairs of the pigs killed for the marriage feast and worn by the newly married, or the tail hairs may be suspended from a wristlet woven from the fibres of the *Lakwe* (Kachin) tree. It is said that amongst the Longhkai and Mawshang Nagas, the newly married should they not have known each other before marriage, very often after union live for months under the same roof without either talking to each other or sleeping together. But for the one exception of Htangan Nagas living at the south-eastern base of the Sangpan Range, dowry is always delivered, either before, at the time of, or after union; or partly before and partly after union. In some clans there is a fixed scale, amongst others it varies according to the social standing or beauty of the bride, while some clans have adopted the Kachin custom of giving dowry throughout life. The Pyengoo Nagas give dowry once only amounting to three buffaloes, the bridegroom may help his wife's people by assisting at the annual clearing of the hill cultivation, for one or more years before marriage, and occasionally even after marriage.

With the Punlum clan a cotton blanket as worn by the tribesmen (ornamented with a large number of cowrie shells), four or five pigs and some fowls are considered sufficient dowry. With the Rasa Nagas no dowry is delivered until the children from the union have grown up, when they give as many as three buffaloes to their mother's relatives. The only time amongst this clan when a man pays dowry is when the woman is barren, he then delivers a cow or its value. The Hkalak Nagas have adopted the Kachin custom, and in addition the bridegroom presents his wife's elder sisters with Rs. 10, and her younger sisters with Re. 1 ; should there be no sisters the money is given to the parents. Some of the other clans have adopted a similar custom substituting small presents for money. Generally with the agents sent to ask for the bride presents and opium are sent ; should the marriage offer be declined by the woman's relatives, then the man has to bear the loss of the gifts sent, invariably opium consumed at the time of the agent's visit, or money spent in purchasing liquor. The Saukrang clan, however, reverse this custom claiming a debt amounting to twice the gift sent by the agent, when the parents refuse to give their daughter in marriage. The Tulim clan deliver dowry to the third generation for their brides, their neighbours the Longri clan varying the custom by delivering dowry of one kind at the birth of each child in the family descended from the union unto the third generation, a custom which cripples those families where sons only are the result of the union. The Sangche clan, who give a fixed dowry for their brides, are obliged to give part of the dowry delivered for their daughter to their wife's relatives. Here also a custom which hits those families hard where daughters prevail, as no assistance appears to be given by the wife's relatives when dowry is given for a bride for a son in the family. Amongst the Mawrang Nagas, where the scale of dowry is on the exorbitant side like the Tulim Nagas, very often a poor tribesman, unable to satisfy the claims for dowry, makes over a marriageable daughter to his wife's people, who give her in marriage and accept the dowry delivered for her in settlement of that due for her mother. These Nagas refer to their women folk as being of great value.

The Nagas marry with certain recognised families, thus reviving every second or third generation connections by marriage originally established by their ancestors, any breaking away from this custom leading to a debt case with the family from whom the bride should have been asked. After marriage the newly married may build their own house, or occupy a separate room in the house, setting up an establishment independent of their parents.

Polygamy, Divorce and Widowhood.

Polygamy is practised only by the Pyengoo, Kuku and Myimu Nagas, who generally have two wives, very rarely three. Amongst the Lakai Nagas polygamy is extended to the headmen, but denied the tribesmen, this curious distinction and perquisites of office has come down to them from their ancestors. Its origin is unknown. Some of the clans allow a married man to "collect" the widow of a deceased relative ; she is not regarded as a second wife.

Divorce is recognised and permitted for various causes. In some clans a change of affection suffices, provided the fickle one is willing to pay the other compensation according to a fixed scale. In other clans it is permitted, but is not obligatory, for the offence of adultery only, and with still others no divorce is allowed, no matter how grave the offence may be. Amongst the Htanghkaw and Macham Nagas, where after marriage there is a change of affections, the party seeking divorce gives the other a small gift. For instance, a woman desiring to divorce her husband gives him a spear and a dah, and should the man wish to divorce his wife, he gives her a pair of bracelets. The Hkangchu Nagas have a similar custom but with them the compensation to be paid amounts to fifty rupees. The Tulim and Longri Nagas only divorce their wives after adultery has taken place and the co-respondent unable to pay the heavy damages recognised for this offence has been killed. Regarding the custom governing an unfaithful husband's conduct the tribesmen are silent. Amongst the Sangche, Langshin and Myinmu Nagas either party may divorce the other for the offence of adultery. When the husband is unfaithful and is divorced by his wife, he has to suffer the loss of all dowry he has delivered for her. When the wife is at fault and is divorced by her husband, the dowry he has given must be returned in full.

Widows are generally taken to wife by a near relative of the deceased husband ; with some clans it is immaterial whether the man doing so is married or unmarried, with others only an unmarried relative of the deceased husband may take the widow to wife. The custom of the Longri clan is unique, for only a widower, a relative of the deceased husband, may take the widow to wife and where there is no such widower relative she is compelled to remain single. Where no relative takes the widow, some clans maintain that she must remain single ; others hold that her relatives may give her in marriage elsewhere and accept further dowry for her. A few clans declare that any man can enter and live with a widow who has not been collected by a relative and is obliged to live alone, provided he acts towards her as a husband should. The custom amongst the majority of the clans regarding misconduct with a widow, who has not been taken to wife by a husband's relatives, is that it is an offence, the debt incurred being appeased by varying scales of compensation, the greatest being that in which the full dowry given for the woman, has to be returned *plus* one extra kind, the least being some small amount. The widow is generally collected by a husband's relative within a few months after she has become a widow, the time however may be extended.

Amongst the Nagas where familiarity between the sexes is recognised before marriage, the birth of illegitimate children is a common occurrence. The general rule is for a union of the parties in such cases, but here also there are exceptions which vary according to the customs of the clans concerned. Where union is not obligatory, a stigma generally rests on the woman who is the mother of an illegitimate child. In such cases a debt is claimed, the scale of damages varying with the clans to which the parties belong. Generally the damages to be delivered are of one, two, three or more kinds, custody of the child invariably remaining with the mother, and only being handed over to the father on payment of further compensations. With the Kumga Nagas the sum to be paid is extremely small, only Rs. 2 this however gives the man no claim on his offspring, which should he desire, can only be attained by payment of a further sum of Rs. 20. Amongst the Risa and Hkangchu Hangas no debt is claimed ; if, after the birth of the child, the parties do not care for each other, they merely separate, the woman returning to her parents' home taking the child with her. Where one of the parties still cares for the other, and that person's feelings are not reciprocated, the other party has to deliver compensation, which may amount to Rs. 100, according to the social status of the person jilted. It is thus obvious that inconstancy is not favoured by these clans, who consider it deserving of what is to them quite severe punishment. In some clans where, by the payment of certain compensation, the father attains custody of his child, which, being too young to be parted from its mother, has to remain with her, he is obliged to pay her extra for nourishing and tending it until the child is old enough to be weaned and come to him. When the mother of an illegitimate child gets married at a later date, should the father not have taken custody, the child does not necessarily follow its mother to her new home, it invariably remains with the woman's relatives. Pregnancy before union is always a time of grave anxiety on the part of the two concerned. Amongst some clans the man builds a hut for his mistress and cares for her until the child is born, in other clans child is born in the house set apart for the unmarried women. Death at childbirth is always greatly feared by the man as it necessitates the payment of very heavy compensation to the woman's parents or relatives. In some cases the house has to be purified, and invariably the man has to arrange for the burial and pay all the funeral expenses. It sometimes happens that the man accused by the woman denies all liability, and unless before her death, she can prove him to be the father of her unborn child, the responsibility for her burial rests on the community, who are obliged to make the necessary arrangements and bear the consequent expenses.

Birth of Illegitimate Children and Adultery.

Adultery is always punishable, and as with other offences the scale of compensation varies with the clans. In most clans the co-respondent is held to blame and has to pay the compensation fixed for the offence. Amongst the Rangsa, Ranghku, and Longhkai clans the erring ones are beaten, it is said sometimes so severely that they succumb to their injuries ; compensation also has to be given. Amongst the Tulim, Sangtai, and Longri Nagas, this offence is regarded very seriously, the scale of compensation being fixed in the vicinity of Rs. 500, which if not paid leads to the death of the woman's lover. The Saukrang Nagas declare that the man must be killed, the woman is pardoned and continues to live with the husband. Amongst the Mawrang clan the wronged husband not satisfied with the beating he gives the man, and the large compensation he receives, visits the man's house, and declaring that as the man has disturbed the peace of his home, he also will ruin him, cuts the house with a dah, symbolical that he has killed the house spirit, overcome the house owner and all the inmates of the house. A deed which is a grave offence, and which if committed under different circumstances could only be settled by the payment of heavy damages.

A feast is generally held at the naming of infants which takes place at varying periods after birth, according to the customs of the clan to which the parents belong. Amongst some clans, the periods vary for infants of different sexes. For instance, the Sangche and Myimu clans, hold their ceremony for male and female infants three and two months after birth respectively. With them, as with several other clans, the infant's head must be either shorn or shaved. Where no distinction is made according to the sex of the infant, it is named from five days to a month after birth. With some clans the infant is named by an elderly relative, such as a grandparent, uncle, aunt, etc. ; with others the parents, either one or both, name the child. Amongst the poorer members of the clans, who cannot afford it, a feast is dispensed with and the infant simply named. The Sangtai Nagas sacrifice fowls only at the naming ceremony, holding that should pigs be killed the child dies. Generally only pigs and fowls are killed at this ceremony, but the Risa Nagas sometimes include dogs.

Naming Ceremony of Infants.

Except in the case of a few clans whose customs are noted separately, the dead are invariably buried, either under or in front of the houses or at the Nat house in the vicinity of the village. As a general rule amongst such clans women who die in childbirth, and persons who die by violence and accident, or are killed by wild animals, are buried in the jungle. Regarding such deaths there are also exceptions. For instance, the Tulim Nagas do not bury such corpses but hide them in the jungle, where they are at the mercy of the denizens of the forest. The Longri clan who occupy a site a few miles from Tulim, make a unique exception by burying the corpse of the woman who dies in childbirth, with her infant, should it not survive, under the house. After

Death Customs.

the disposal of the corpse there is merry-making, when such animals as are obtainable are sacrificed the same night and a feast held. A few clans keep the corpses for a day or two before burial. The Pyengoo Nagas hold what they call the "Kawk-wa-bawk" ceremony from three months to a year after the corpse has been buried. At this ceremony the spirit of the deceased, which is declared to be hovering in the vicinity, is despatched to the ancestral home of the tribe. The ceremony lasts two days; there is feasting and dancing both inside and outside the house. With the corpse are buried articles of daily use such as dahs, spears, etc., with males; and necklaces, baskets, weaving implements, etc., with female corpses. The Mawshang Nagas, living in the north near the Patkoi Range, have customs different to all other clans. They only bury the corpses of those who die from epidemics under the houses. Other corpses are cremated, those who die ordinary deaths in front of the houses, and those who die by violence, accident, etc., or women who die in childbirth, in the jungle. They bury the epidemic corpses at once, but cremate the others the day after death.

The Kuku Nagas, who are a mixture of Haimis and Htangans, observe two forms of disposing of the dead. One is practically identical with the general custom already described; the other is totally different. Briefly the rites observed may be described as follows:—After death the corpse is preserved by being smoked over a slow fire. It is then placed in a wooden coffin, and conveyed to a charnel-house built close to the village. At a fixed date in the year, the heads from all the corpses for the preceding year are cut off, and thoroughly washed and cleaned with hot water. The cleaned skulls are then taken by certain members of the clan to a secret shelving rock, and there deposited with the skulls of previous years. The site of this shelving rock is kept secret, and disclosed to only a few members of the clan.* At this secret 'golgotha' the collection of human skulls must be considerable, as Kuku or its immediate neighbourhood has been inhabited by the tribe for the past ten generations, roughly 250 years. The headless trunks are said to remain undisturbed in the charnel-house, where they gradually fall to decay. The Htanghkaw and Macham Nagas who also belong to the Htangan Tribes, wrap the body after death in a mat, and place it in a small hut just sufficient for the corpse; there it rapidly falls to decay, uncared for in its flimsy grave. These charnel-huts are built in one place by the village entrance.

Naga Graves.

The grave site is either in front of or under the house, and owing to the rocky and shaly nature of many of the village sites is shallow and difficult to excavate. The site is enclosed by a low open-work bamboo fence, having a roof of thatch. The graves seen were partially filled in, the mats in which the corpse had been wrapped and covered, being kept exposed. It would appear that the grave is filled in at some later date. The sites of long established villages, such as exist in the Namhpuk Valley, are neither more nor less than cemeteries. In front of the house the deceased's property is stretched on a frame-work of bamboos and sticks to gradually fall into decay. The following were noticed near a new grave site:—Naga helmet complete with boar tushes, feathers, etc., dah and scabbard, clothes, cross-bow, spear, haversack, etc.

Headmen.

Amongst many of the clans the post of headman is hereditary, in others it is entirely by selection, and in some clans goes to a younger brother of the deceased headman, and should he have no younger brother then to a son or near relative. Headmen as a rule dispose of the more petty disputes which take place in their jurisdictions either themselves, or with the help of tribal elders; for such they may or may not receive a fee; it is a recognised custom to pass a loving cup of liquor round at the close of a case, and to consume opium during the discussion. In some clans the tribesmen help their headman to clear, sow, and harvest his lands; in others such assistance is only rendered when the headman makes arrangements to feed his tribesmen on the days they will assist him. Certain other perquisites are attached to the office, such as part of the flesh of an animal killed in the forest, or sacrificed at a Nat ceremony, or some small gift at marriages, etc. These, however, are not recognised by all the clans. In a few clans the headman has the power of punishing the tribesman who disobeys his orders, such punishment taking the form of chastisement or the imposition of a small fine. It is the headman, accompanied generally by a few tribal elders, who represents the clan on important occasions.

Criminal Offences, Blood-feuds, etc.

Crime amongst the Naga clans is invariably settled by the payment of compensation, this is even in the cases of blood-feuds, which have originated over some petty trouble and extended over a period of many years. With the settling of the bigger debt cases in this manner, the appeasing of certain of the tribal and family spirits have to be taken into consideration, and for this purpose, perhaps in addition to the recognised scale of award, some animal has to be given to appease the Nat offended. A few instances may be quoted: for the offence of theft from another's granary, amongst some clans the thief has to give a young boar for a sacrifice to the offended Nat, and thus purify the granary which has become contaminated by the intrusion of a person, not a member of the household to which the granary belongs. Similarly, amongst some clans, a woman

* *Cf.* the similar customs followed in Tuensang, the principal village of the Chang Naga tribe on the Assam side of the main range—*vide* M. A. S. B., XI, No. 1, page 49.—J. H. H.

may have to purify her body after the birth of an illegitimate child, should her lover not marry her, and she be obliged to return to the home of her parents. A buffalo for sacrifice is generally awarded in such a debt case.

The more serious offences are :—Murder, confinement, incendiarism, theft, rape, and adultery ; while those of a less serious nature are :—trespass, and the working of another's lands, mischief by cattle destroying standing crops, simple hurt and the like. For each of these several offences the scale of compensation varies, and the amounts to be awarded may take the form of ready cash, or animals, or goods, such as guns, gongs, dahs, spears, wearing apparel and the like. Perhaps there is no such offence as rape of an un-married woman, though once a woman is married, or has been left a widow, rape is a recognised offence and punishable by the delivery of compensation to the person injured, be he husband of the woman or close relative of the widow. Theft is always considered a very serious offence especially if it is from a house or granary, no matter how small and trivial the article stolen is. The Sangtai Nagas declare that the price of a slave, approximately Rs. 400 has to be given as compensation for breaking into another's granary. It may be that this clan has considerably exaggerated the scale of compensation, it being out of all proportion to the scales given by members of other clans. However that the offender is often very harshly dealt with is exemplified from the details of human sacrifices collected, where one of the victims, a woman, was sold by her husband for a sacrifice because she was an inveterate thief. The reason for such severe punishment is not hard to find. The Nagas are a poor race who cannot afford to keep servants ; their occupations are often of such a nature that they are away from their homes for several hours each day. It is therefore essential that during these periods of temporary absence from home their property should remain unharmed ; hence the tribal law which imposes a severe sentence.

A few particulars were collected regarding some of the bigger blood-feuds which exist in the Namhpuk Valley. In one case the debt originated between parties who were related by marriage : a bride refused to return to her husband ; this led to a claim which not being fully satisfied resulted in attack and counter-attacks. In another the theft of a gong from a granary was the original cause, and in yet another several Trans-Namhpuk clans united and attacked a Naga village because they held the tribesmen of this village responsible for an epidemic of small-pox, which broke out shortly after the return of tribesmen who had visited Assam.

Hunting, fishing, etc.

Owing to the depredations which are perpetrated on their standing crops in many areas by wild animals there is constant warfare with the denizens of the forest. Many and varied are the traps set by the tribesmen, and so skilful are they in this art, that even such animals as the serow, sambhur, barking deer and pig are taken in the traps. Once the animals have been noosed they are speared or shot on the spot, the meat is removed and the skull brought in as a trophy and put up in the front porch. Smaller animals and birds are generally snared in the vicinity of the hill cultivations during hours of idleness, and such traps may be seen near the paths and fences of the fields.

The Pyengoo Nagas keep many decoy parrots, by means of which when parrots are flighting during the rains, large numbers up to a hundred or more are netted at a time. The net by which the birds are taken is stretched across a cutting made in the jungle, at some prominent ridge, or head of a stream, over which the wild birds are in the habit of passing in their daily flight. The decoys are placed in the trees by the side of the cutting, by their calls they attract a passing flock, which swoops down, gets entangled in the net, and by their weight bring it down to the ground. They are then easily despatched by the snarers who are in hiding in the jungle close by. The flesh of these parrots is considered a delicacy. Sometimes other flighting birds are also accidentally taken in the net and meet the same fate.

Monkeys are caught in an ingenious trap made in the form of a cage, with the trap door on the top. The bait is usually a yam placed on the ground inside the cage. From the trap door a string trails to the ground, close to the yam. The monkey jumps into the cage, takes the yam and to get out naturally endeavours to swing himself up by the string, this releases the trap door and makes him a prisoner.

The usual form of fish trap used is to erect a weir across a steam, with openings in two or more places at the entrances to which are placed funnel shaped bamboo tubes. Fish swimming down stream enter these tubes, in which being too narrow for them to turn, they must remain until removed by the fishermen. At one end of the weir may also be erected a shute of bamboo and cane, down which the fish swim into shallow water, where they are easily taken by the waiting fishermen. Hand and drag nets are also used, in most of the larger streams. The fish taken in a weir are generally shared amongst those who have helped to build it. Amongst one clan it is said that the catch is always shared with other members of the clan, who for various causes have been prevented from accompanying the members of the fishing excursion.

Hunting and fishing are permissible within the village bounds, but these rights as a rule do not extend to an adjoining clan's lands, where permission must first be obtained and the spoils of the chase shared with the neighbouring tribesmen.

14. The Pau Chin Hau Movement in the Chin Hills. (*J. J. Bennison.*)

This movement originated about the beginning of the present century but there is no mention of it in the *1911 or 1921 Census Reports. Pau Chin Hau is a Sokte Chin about 60 years of age and now lives at Mwelbwem*, a village not far from Tiddim in the Chin Hills. The origin of the movement is best described in Pau Chin Hau's own words :—

" From the year 1888 to 1902 I suffered from a long and severe illness.

From the year 1900 onward in dreams and visions I received a series of communications which I hold to be divine and are the foundations both of my alphabet and my religious teaching.

The first of these was in 1900 when in my dream I saw a twisted rope suspended between the heaven and the earth. Many people were trying to climb it but no one was successful. I knelt in prayer and ascended the rope as far as the thirtieth heaven, then descended to the earth and still by means of the rope, which had penetrated the ground, descended deep into the heart of the earth.

A year later I heard the voice of God calling me by name and commanding me to look forward to the future when many mysterious things would occur. I saw visions of railway trains, steam-ships and other Western inventions although I had never been away from the Hills and had no knowledge that such things existed. There were visions of great battles, of stone-clad horses and horsemen. There were English, Indian and many unknown nations engaged in the struggle. I saw amongst other things the unknown nations falling dead and disappearing from view while my own people who were with me, though still alive were left cowering in the valleys between the hills, covered with dust and rubbish. I tried to cover my face with my hands but in spite of myself I I had to continue gazing into a mirror held by an Englishman so that the vision remained in my mind's eye for three days and three nights.

In 1902 I had another dream. In this dream I saw an Englishman who appeared to me to be divine. He wanted me to learn lessons, taught by means of stones in the shape of letters, which put together formed a book. I tried to learn the same and eventully succeeded and my eyes then opened.

When I got up from sleep my passion for learning and teaching the symbols and sounds of the alphabet was so great that I could not sleep either day or night until I had written them out on paper. Though the Deputy Commissioner of the Chin Hills advised me to have my invention printed I was not satisfied with it and revised it more than once the third and last revision being carried out in 1931.

As above stated, during the period of those visions I was still suffering from severe illness which was not cured during the year when I had seen the letters. In the following year, however, in another vision I saw many races of people flocking together in a huge plain. Then there appeared a being who came riding the sun as a horse, the bridle and other trappings of which glittered like gold. Then I shouted 'Behold and obey the order of God' and while all bowed themselves to the earth he called me by name twice in succession 'Pau Chin Hau, Pau Chin Hau, will you worship me ?' I said 'who are you ?' and he replied, 'The Lord who made heaven and earth, men and animals, the sun, the moon and the stars and who has power to cure all sickness.'

I had faith in him and in a moment was cured from my illness of fifteen years. During those years for the cure of that illness I had paid the sum of Rs. 400 in making sacrifices of various kinds of animals to the nats or demons. The cure of God was complete and cost nothing.

I stood alone in my faith for three years during which time the members of my own family, even, reviled instead of encouraging me but gradually as my neighbours and even people from distant villages saw me still enjoying sound health my religion began to spread until after six years people from all parts of the hills became my fellow worshippers.

Our Chin ancestors worshipped various kinds of Nats such as House Nat, Forest Nat, Water Nat, etc., altogether fifty-four in number. Those who have believed and wished to enter my religion came from far distant villages and invited me to visit them. Together with a little band of disciples I made it my custom to accept their invitation and on entering a house or village after praying to God would destroy completely the articles used for making sacrifices to the Nats and whereas sufferers had previously, like myself, had to pay large sums for such sacrifices our only charge was a nominal sum to cover travelling expenses. Sometimes it seemed as though some of my more hasty or unintelligent followers were themselves possessed by demons after such visits but after praying to God they speedily became normal again.

Further some of my followers, either through reluctance to destroy completely ancestral customs or through fear of specially powerful Nats, have retained in part their Nat Worship. I have declared that this was not the will of God and many, like myself, are now entirely freed from such practices.

One wholesome effect of my teaching is that where formerly many who had nothing went into debt to obtain sacrificial offerings and so could neither afford to buy food nor pay their taxes, my followers being free from such expenses are in much better circumstances.

Among other results I should mention that the old custom of the Chins of retaining a corpse in the house for many days, until it stank and bred corruption and disease, has now been abolished amongst the villages which accept my teaching.

Another old custom of the Chins was that of attempting to discover the particular Nat which caused an illness by feeling the pulse or reading the countenance of the sick person. The Nat, when discovered, was propitiated and petitioned. We now pray to the One God.

Again according to Chin belief the soul of a man may leave his body and as it wanders afar be seized on by one of the numerous Nats resulting in illness or death of the owner. To make the spirit return to its home it was necessary to sacrifice an animal. We retain no such belief. A particularly difficult disease to deal with was supposed to be caused by the injection of a foreign substance into the body through sorcery or witchcraft and in this case it was considered necessary to make a compound of turmeric and other roots, ground and steeped in water, to be drunk as a libation while calling upon the name of the king of Nats. We, ourselves, call upon the name of God.

Amongst all the Festivals observed by our Chin forefathers we have retained but one, the Festival of the Separation of the Years (New Year Festival). It is now, however, called the Festival of God and each year after the completion of the merrymaking we meet in church and offer prayers to God.

As regards the organisation of my religion—as I am myself unable to go to every village into which the religion has entered I have appointed an elder connected with the religion in each village. Further, not long after the birth of this religion certain prophets termed either 'seers' or 'interpreters of the word of God' arose, some of whom were able to show wonderful and miraculous doings. Others, alas, have gone astray and are opposing the simple faith.

Given under the hand of Prophet Pau Chin Hau at Nwelbwem, on the 25th May 1932."

The following information regarding the religion has been furnished by the Assistant Superintendent, Tiddim Sub-division, Chin Hills District :—

"Any household wishing to adopt this religion has to pay Rs. 3 as initiation fees. This money is not taken by Pau Chin Hau but is taken by the person who converts the household. No other payment is made. On New Year's Day, English calendar, a collection is made in his churches. This money is spent on a big feast. Drinking in moderation is not observed by any of the followers, nor is it observed by Pau Chin Hau himself.

In the churches are kept earthenware pots. People who are ill go and pray into these pots and ask for divine help. If the person is unable to go as far as the church he may do so in his house, or some other person may do so on his or her behalf. The spirit addressed is called 'Pa Chiem.' This is the Chin word for 'GOD'. During service in the Church a glass of *zu* is handed round to those present which is said to be the outward sign of thanks to God for the food and drink given.

The religion has many amusing parts in it. There are men known as 'Pa leik-thas' (Policemen), who also go by the name of 'Kut-dom-pas' (men who feel the pulse). These men sport a uniform in the shape of a red head dress. These Pa-leik-thas were introduced into the religion, because as all bad characters are said to shun the police, so in the same way all evil spirits will shun the sick person, or the society of any person as long as there is a Pa-leik-tha present in his red head dress. No Nat is ever said to 'pet' (bite or cause illness to) any 'Pa-leik-tha', so long as he is in uniform, but as soon as the 'Pa-leik-tha' removes his red-head dress and adorns a white one he is liable to attack at any moment as the Nat is no respector of persons who are not in uniform."

The Pa-leik-tha number from 3 to 6 per village. There are also commissioned officers amongst them. These men are known as 'Botair' (meaning an Inspector, Jemadar, or Subedar). Whenever a person falls ill the ordinary policeman is sent for. Should his prayers and presence cause no relief, the next highest in rank is called in and so on until the patient recovers or dies. There are quite a number of patients who suffer in silence until the pain they bear becomes unbearable and these men, some very intelligent, will tell one that directly they utter the words "Pa-leik-tha sam in" (call the commissioned officers) their disease or the pains would leave them.

Apparently Pau Chin Hau himself does not favour *Nat* sacrifices but he admits that some of his followers still carry them out. According to the Deputy Commissioner, Chin Hills District, drinking is not forbidden by the Pau Chin Hau rules nor is there anything specially laid down in regard to drinking to excess. Presumably Pau Chin Hau realises that it is too much to expect his followers to give up their former customs entirely. He himself drinks and has admitted that he may occasionally get drunk. The Christian Mission working in the Chin Hills is the American Baptist Mission and it is presumably this liking for alcoholic liquor which prevents them from being accepted as Christians.

Unfortunately, when the census was taken, the Census Superintendent was not aware of the existence of this movement and the followers of Pau Chin Hau were all recorded in the enumeration schedules as Animists. The Deputy Commissioner of the Chin Hills District has estimated the number of followers in his district at 35,700 (26,000 in Tiddim Sub-division and 9,700 in Falam Sub-division) but there are also followers on the other side of the frontier.

A copy of the script mentioned by Pau Chin Hau will be found in Chapter X [of both Burma and India Reports].

2. Among other religious sects peculiar to Burma may be mentioned the *Silein* and *Kleebo* sects, which are off shoots from Christianity. Mr. Grantham gives particulars of the *Silein* sect in paragraph 84 of his Report [Burma, 1921]. At the 1921 census 102 persons were recorded as belonging to this sect but it was not recorded at all at the 1931 census. The origin of the Kleebo sect is also described in paragraph 84 of the 1921 Census Report. The following has been kindly furnished by the Rev. W. Sherratt :—

"The origin of Thomas Pellakoe's movement seems to have been due to the translation of the Hebrew word 'quesheth' [which according to the lexicographers means both 'bow' (the weapon) and 'rainbow'] in Genesis ix v. 13 etc., by the word 'klee' which means the ordinary crossbow, instead of by the word 'terkwai' meaning an arc, in the Karen Bible.

It was stated at the time that Pellakoe, himself an ordained priest or deacon of the Church of England heard a sermon by one of the Missionaries in which the promise of Genesis ix. v. 13 'I do set my bow in the cloud' was explained as being a prophecy of the coming of the Christ transliterated 'kree' in the Karen language.

Pellakoe seems immediately to have come to the conclusion that the word 'klee' was identical with the word 'kree', indeed that the latter was a mistaken pronunciation of the former, which led, by an easily understood development, to the substitution of the 'the shooting of the bow' for 'baptism' as the initiatory ceremony of the Thomas Pellakoe, or as it soon came to be known, the Kleebo Sect.

So far as the movement is still alive this rite of bow shooting is observed."

There were some adherents of this sect in the Delta at the 1921 census but apparently they were not recorded as such (see paragraph 84 of the 1921 Census Report). The number recorded in 1931 was only 10 (in Thaton District) but no information is available as to whether this is a correct estimate of their number or not. They have been treated as Christians in the tabulation.

15. Lahu and Kaw Marriage Customs (Burma Census Report, 1931).

By J. H. Telford.

The following account of the marriage customs of Lahus and Kaws (Akhas) of the Lolo-Muhso group has been kindly furnished by the Rev. J. H. Telford of the American Baptist Mission, Loimwe :—

" Formerly, it was customary for Lahu young people to do their 'courting' in the house and in the presence of their elders. The lovers would sit, one at either side of the fire-place and would engage their time singing love songs to each other as follows :— The young man sings to the girl these lines ; for there is among the Lahus a standard language of courtship :—

While I was in my house
Lying down on my bed
The light of you was so bright
As it came in through my door.
I thought it was the light of the moon
I thought it was the light of the morning star
I thought it was the light of the sun.

The love poem is of great length, so long that it is only desirable here to give the substance of it in which we shall observe in the mutual fears expressed by the lovers, subtle allusions to animistic thought and beliefs. The lover goes on to say that—

He lifted his hand to his eyes
To shade them from the light
And whirling around three times on his heel
He observed that the light was the light of his love.

The poem represents the young man as saying that he has a village " Hkasheh " or chief and he has obtained the permission of the 'Hkasheh' to visit his lady friend. He also has parents and they have given him permission to go on his journey of love. The song pictures the young man starting out and he passes through the lonely and dangerous jungle towards the village where the girl lives. He follows the rays of light and as he pursues his journey on the path before him he sees a pair of quail and upon seeing them his heart sinks ; for he thinks the quail are the spirit of his lover who has suddenly died. Here the young woman speaks a word of encouragement and tells him that he should cause the quail to fly away ; for the quail are not her spirit at all. She further says that he is not a cowardly man. Continuing his love adventure he comes up against other discouraging circumstances. He meets another pair of birds, a pig with a yellow tooth, a bear, a wild fowl, a crow, a big log of wood, a marble house and then seven big rivers and seven mountains. At one river there was a big and fearsome dragon that was shooting out its tongue at him. At the sight of all the different birds and animals his heart becomes fearful, for he interprets each in turn to be the spirit of the girl he loved. When he arrived at the big log he walked around it three times and felt it very difficult to separate himself from it. He wanted to take his axe and cut it up and from the wood build a house. When he saw the marble house, he said that if he were not permitted to live in it he would buy an axe from the blacksmith and with its aid he would build a house of marble. If his hands and feet should not be sufficiently strong to build a marble house, he would certainly build one of wood. Then the girl responds and says to the young man that the quail, the pair of birds, the pig with the yellow tooth, the bear, wild fowl and crow are not her spirit. Those birds and animals, she says, because they have no ground to cultivate and no stores of food are compelled to search for food wherever they can find it. You had better take your axe and from that log you saw prepare timbers and build the house. As regards the marble house, she says, if you do not live there I will not live there and her final word assures him of her acceptance of him, when she says, " Take the iron which god has created and cut down the trees and build a house and then come for me. The threatening dragons that you saw, if those made you afraid and caused your soul to flee from your body, I will take the cocks and the hens and call your soul back.

Lahu marriages are arranged by mediators or 'go-between,' and the marriage ceremony is conducted by the village priest or by some responsible elder of the community. A large pig is killed and the whole village feasts on its flesh. The neck of the animal is always reserved for and eaten by the " go-between ". The bride and bridegroom, with their faces covered with sheet of thin white cloth, sit in the presence of the village elders and priests. The young couple are given candles and each of them lights two and sets them reverently before the elders. The priest fills a cup full to the brim of cold water and gives it to the groom to drink and when he has drunk all of it, the same cup is again filled to the brim with water from the same jug and this second cup is given to the bride to drink. Extreme care must be taken by both of them not to spill a drop of the water ; for if on this occasion water is spilled, no children will be born to the young couple. When they have both finished drinking the water, the priest invokes a blessing upon them and it is significant that the request of the priest is addressed to 'G'uisha' or 'Awpa G'uisha' which means, " Father God."

'Our Father, God, to-day these two children of thine are a pair like the sun and moon, like the stars and meteors. Let their children be plentiful as the fruit of a tree ; make their life as unending as the river and rock ; let the cattle under their house increase ; prosper their fields and in their search for food let them discover the eternal food.'

The mating season of the Kaws is during the months of December, January and February. By the end of November their crops have been harvested and during the three months immediately following the harvest the young couple have much leisure time. This three months period, so far as weather is concerned, is the best time of the year, for there is no rain. It is the winter season, when the mornings and evenings are cold and crisp and in the day time the heat of the sun is less fierce. Favourable weather conditions permit and encourage frequent visitation by the young people to all the Kaw villages in the district.

The Kaws mate early in life and it is their custom to allow promiscuous sexual intercourse between the sexes before the establishment of the marriage relationship. There is a public courting place in every Kaw village which is called the 'Deh Hkawng'. There the young people of both sexes meet at night and play and sing love songs to each other. Little house sheds adjacent to the parents' houses are set apart as places in which the young people can meet privately and the young couples repair to those houses at the close of the more public meeting at the 'Deh Hkawng'. A Kaw man while visiting in a village other than his own particular village is not allowed to court as above mentioned ; he may do so only within his own village group. In the daytime, outside the village, at work in the jungle or when going to or returning from market, the young folk meet and sing love songs to each other and when distance divides them they shout their love songs across the hills and the valleys.

Kaws can marry without the consent and approval of their parents. Marriage by elopement is not by any means an uncommon thing among the Kaws. However there must be no compulsion of the girl ; for if the girl does not of her own will freely consent to run off with the young man and should he by force carry her off, the marriage would not be recognised and the young man would be fined by his village chief. On the other hand, as sometimes happens, a young Kaw couple are returning together from the Shan market place and they fall in love with each other. Should they decide to elope, the young man is quite free, according to Kaw custom, to immediately take the girl to his own home and village. Friends of the young couple go to inform the girl's parents that their daughter has gone off to get married. Should the parents desire to prevent the marriage under such circumstances they may follow in hot pursuit of the elopers ; but if the young couple have had time to cook and eat an egg together in his house, before the arrival of the girl's parents, they cannot prevent the marriage from taking place. Sometimes marriage by elopement is prevented by fond parents by their promising a big wedding feast, provided the marriage is consummated according to regular marriage custom.

Kaw marriage ceremonies always take place in the village of the bridegroom and the bride is conducted to the village by her friends. She takes with her a hog's head which the Kaws look upon as the price of the bride. The rest of the pig is prepared and fed to the members of the village which she is about to leave. The bride receives no presents ; the bridegroom and the elders are the only parties who receive gifts. The girl upon entering the groom's village does not go directly to the house of the groom but to the house of some elderly woman, and while there the bride adorns herself in white clothing. Having so attired herself, she proceeds at once to the house of the groom. There her first duty is to carry through a ceremony of pretension during which she plays at drawing water and carrying wood. With water jugs in a basket slung over her back she makes a hurried trip down the ladder-steps of the house and goes through the motions of drawing water. While she is doing so and while making a hasty retreat inside the house, the young people standing at the foot of the steps fling lumps of cow manure at her. They do so again when she decends the step a second time, on this occasion to pretend that she is chopping firewood. This besmirching of the bride with manure, the Kaws say, is to secure for her good luck and great blessing. After she has changed her clothes the bride is now ready for the marriage ceremony which is performed by the village elders. Meantime the marriage feast is being prepared by the younger members of the community, though before anyone partakes of the food, part of it is offered by the elders to the "Myicha Ne" in the house of the groom's parents. The newly married couple are allowed to retire in peace and are left undisturbed in their own little house which is adjacent to the house of the groom's parents. A Kaw girl virtually becomes the slave of her husband, in the sense that the village law prescribes that she cannot visit the home of her own parents for more than three days in the entire year. All her time must be devoted to her husband and to the affairs of her own household. Frequently Kaw men are opium smokers and when such is the case the burden of the work falls upon the Kaw woman.

Winning a girl by magic is sometimes accomplished by the Kaws. If a Kaw girl does not want to marry her suitor but he wants to marry her and her only, such a man may resort to magic in order to win her. A wax from two different kinds of bees which live in the same hollow of a tree is collected by the Kaws. This is taken and magically blown upon while a formula is recited. Part of this magically treated wax is stealthily rubbed or concealed on a garment of the wanted girl. When this is done it is impossible for her to keep away from the young man. If she does not see him, she is restless and impatiently longs to see and meet him, and though she does not love him, she finds it impossible to resist his attentions. Such marriages when consumated, the Kaws say, are neither happy nor prosperous and if children result from the union of such people, they do not live.

If a young unmarried Kaw woman becomes pregnant, the whole countryside is advertised to secure for her a husband. However, in such cases where the girl can point out to the young man whom she claims as the one responsible for her pregnant condition he must marry the girl. Where responsibility cannot be located and there is no husband in sight for the girl soon to become a mother, everything is done to try to secure a husband for her ; for it is considered a disgrace among the Kaws for a child to be born out of wedlock. Such unfortunate girls are compelled to take any kind of Kaw or man of another race who offers to become her husband. She has no say in the matter, if she knows not the person responsible for her condition.

After years of married life if a Kaw wife has not borne any children, two means are resorted to in order to make her become a mother. The first of these two methods I have already mentioned ; with regard to the second means, the Seer consults the spirits and afterwards announces to the barren wife that her sterility is occasioned by the river in the spirit-world becoming blocked with leaves and weeds which prevents the waters of the stream from flowing freely. Therefore to remove the cause of barrenness the soul of the Seer goes to the river in the spirit-world and takes away the obstructions and when this is done the sterile woman is able to bear children ; but never more than two children can be borne by this supernatural or spiritual aid of the Seer. There are occasions when a Kaw husband must refrain from sexual intercourse with his wife. On all occasions when offerings are being made to the 'Myicha Ne' as for example, at paddy planting time, during the growth of the crops, and at harvest time. When on those occasions the village priest sends forth his soul to the spirit-world to discover what spirit has been offended, he must stay separate from his wife. The successful hunter upon his return from a hunting expedition must not sleep with his wife for a period of seven days. The same rule pertains when villagers return from a fishing expedition. After a child is born in a Kaw family, the husband must refrain from sexual intercourse with his wife for ten cycles of time. One cycle is twelve days. If during that time the husband should disregard this-not-too-strictly-adhered-to law and if the wife were to report the case to a responsible village elder, the offending husband would be fined one pig. This one hundred and twenty days prohibitive period is largely because of physical reasons, namely, to prevent the wife from getting what the Kaws call 'Napaku', which is a condition of health when the colour of the face is bad ; the mother becomes thin and loses vitality. While many Kaw men have just one wife, it could not be said of the Kaws that they are a monogamous race ; for many of them have two wives and others have three. The Lahus, their close neighbours, are a strictly monogamous race".

16. A Note on the Indigenous Races of Burma.

By Captain J. H. Green, F.R.A.I., I.A.

Up to the present time, language has been the only basis of classification of the races and tribes of Burma. Linguistic evidence, valuable as it is, when used as the sole basis is liable to, and in the case of the races of Burma, has, I think, led to many errors in our racial classification. A linguistic connection definitely proves only a possible connection between the races, or the ancestors of the races in question or a connection between them and a third race. Language, however, does give us a hint regarding the probable migration of races as migrations of people and cultural waves are normally inclined to follow the paths of least resistance which are so often the paths of language affinities.

Some of the races or tribes in Burma change their language almost as often as they change their clothes. Languages are changed by conquest, by absorption, by isolation and by a general tendency to adopt the language of a neighbour who is considered to belong to a more powerful, more numerous or more advanced race or tribe.

To obtain more accurate knowledge of the inter-relationship and culture of our tribes, a study of ethnology, anthropology, and folklore is of the greatest importance. Unfortunately, practically nothing, so far, has been done in this respect, and races are becoming more and more mixed, and the threads more and more difficult to disentangle.

The large number of languages and dialects has, I fear, frightened would-be students. The variety of dialects and the resultant complex classification has tended to exaggerate our difficulties. If instead of searching for language similarities we had concentrated upon searching for similarities in body measurements, customs, laws, arts, and religious beliefs, etc., etc., we would find that the classification of our tribes into stages of cultural evolution would be considerably simplified. Such a classification would help the administrator and might indirectly save considerable friction and some punitive expeditions which are so often due to mis understandings. For the administrator, a general knowledge of the culture of the people is, perhaps, of even greater importance than a knowledge of their language. I know of at least two cases where officers, who spoke the language of the people, got into trouble which finally necessitated punitive expeditions. Had an officer been transferred direct from the Colonial Service in Africa—where a training in anthropology is compulsory and had he realised what state of culture the people had reached, such misunderstanding would probably not have occurred, although he knew not a word of the language.

The unreliability of the language test for race has again become apparent in this census. Atsis, Lashis and Marus appear to have decreased, whereas it is more probable that they have declared themselves to be Kachins. The H' amti Shans who have migrated from Hkamti Long to Myitkyina have declared themselves as Shans. Many small tribes of the Shan States are recorded as Shans.

The classification of the indigenous races has been further complicated as the names now applied to them are not their own names, but those given to them by their neighbours. In many cases these originated as terms of abuse. The words "Kachin", "Chin" and "Karen" appear to be derived from three different pronunciations of the original Burmese word for the wild hill tribes—"Kakhyen".

The Shans, in the presence of the hill tribes, often politely call them "Tai-Loi" or "Hkun-Loi"—which means "Hill Shan". They refer to the Kachins, however, behind their backs as "Kang"—Savages. The Kachin passes the same word "Kang" on to the Chins. The Kachins call the Lachikaw "Lashi"—which name we have adopted, whilst the Nungs call the Yawyin "Lashi".

The Nungs call the Shans "Muwa", whilst the Kachins call the Chinese "Muwa", and so it goes on. In hardly any case are the people called by their own generic names. Generic names in some cases, however, do not exist.

Racial Classification.—During the last fourteen years, I have spent considerable time studying and living amongst the wild tribes of Burma. On our eastern frontier, I have visited almost all the tribes from Tibet to Tennasserim and on the west many of the tribes on the Assam border. I have measured several thousand tribesmen and have particularly interested myself in their customs, arts and crafts and their physical peculiarities. I realise that I have been merely scratching the surface: for what is fourteen years' spare time amongst about seventy tribes where one hundred and forty years' whole time employment would be none too much?

All along the eastern frontier, I have been impressed by the Indonesian character of the people (*see* Plates V and VIII) with undulating black hair often tinged with red, and with many cultural connections with the tribes of the Dutch East Indies, Malaya, Indo-China, Melanesia and the Philippines. So strong has been the evidence, that I doubt if Southern Mongol blood does preponderate in Burma, although it is certainly a strong element. I think it probable that at any rate, the tribes of the Shan States, the Nmai Valley, the Salween Valley and the Naga Hills are far more closely connected with the people of the south-east than has hitherto been considered to be the case.

The Nagas, the Nungs (Lolo-Muhso Group), the Nmai Valley tribes (Burma Group), the Bhamo and Shan States Kachins appear to me to be all related (*See* Plates I to XVIII). They all lie along a line of cultural migration. The House Horns, Types of Dance Poles, the Indonesian Loom, the Neck-tie Hoe, the Thorn-lined fish trap are prominent amongst many peculiar connecting links. Their physical characteristics are similar. They are all lighthearted people and very different from the Chins and Hkahku Kachins (*See* Plates XIX to XXIII), who are inclined to be sullen and are totally different in appearance. Culturally, I would also put them into the same category as the Kaws, Lahus, Was, Palaungs and Hill Karens.

In the case of the Kachins, I am of the opinion that the Hkahku Kachins from the Triangle, the Hukong Valley and from west of the Irrawaddy are a very different people from the Bhamo and Lashio Kachins although they all speak the same language. The two types of Kachins have often been described; one as being markedly Mongoloid, the other a taller type with long, oval face, pointed chin and aquiline nose. These types are to some extent mixed south of Mytkyina but are separate people further north. The former are the tribes of the Nmai Valley and the latter the Hkahku Kachins (Compare Plates III and XXII).

The Nung is, in appearance and character, identical with the Maru. The Maru has been put in the Burma Group because their language shows a close connection with Burmese; few tribes are, however, less alike.

Plate I.
MARU FROM NMAI VALLEY.
Shows Indonesian Strain. (Not typical.)

Plate II.
MARU GIRLS FROM NMAI VALLEY.

Plate III.
KACHIN GIRLS FROM SHAN STATES.
Typical of Bhamo and Lashio Kachins.

Plate IV.
NUNG HIGH PRIEST.
Upper Nmai Valley.

Plate V.

YOUNG NUNGS FROM UPPER NMAI VALLEY.

Plate VI.

PADAUNGS FROM KARENNI.

Plate VII.
BREK YOUTH.

Plate VIII.
WA.

Plate IX.
MIAOS FROM SOUTHERN SHAN STATES.

Plate X.
MIAO FROM INDO-CHINA.

Plate XI.
KAWS (KENGTUNG STATE).

Plate XII.
KAW GIRL.

Plate XIII.
LAHU GIRL (KENGTUNG STATE).

Plate XIV.
BLACK LISU (LISAW).
From Ahkyang Valley.

Plate XV.
YAWYIN (LISAW) FROM HPIMAW.
Shows Caucasian Strain.

Plate XVI.
BLACK LISU (LISAW) FROM AHKYANG VALLEY.
Shows Caucasian Strain.

Plate XVII.
YAWYIN (LISAW) FROM BHAMO HILLS.

Plate XVIII.

LISAWS FROM SOUTHERN SHAN STATES.

Plate XIX.

KUKI CHINS.

Plate XX.
NGORN CHIN GIRL.

Plate XXI.
HAKA (LAI) CHIN.

Plate XXII.
HKAHKU KACHIN FROM TRIANGLE.

Plate XXIII.
HKAHKU KACHIN GIRL.

Plate XXIV.
PWO KAREN GIRL.

Plate XXV.
HKUN (TAI).

Plate XXVI.
SHAN.

The Hill Karens are another group which, I suggest, has been misplaced (Compare Plates XII and XXIV). Again in appearance, physique, and character they are very different from the Sgaw and Pwo, and, I think are related to the Yangsaks and Yanglaws with whom they are probably survivals of the Lawa tribes which once peopled the Shan States. Mr. Taylor's explanation—that both the Brek Karens and the Was have possibly absorbed a pre-Dravidian stock represented by the Veddas of Ceylon and the Sakai of Malaya—would also meet the case. The fact remains that, in spite of any small language connection with the plain Karens, for all practical purposes the majority of the small Hill Karen Tribes appear to be more closely related to the Palaung-Wa Group.

There also appears to be a close connection between the Nmai Valley people, the Bhamo and Shan States Kachins, and the Palaung-Wa Group and also some of the tribes of the Lolo-Muhso Group such as the Kaw and the Lahu. This connection, which is to me obvious, may also be accounted for by the same explanation—that they have all absorbed elements of another stock, possibly pre-Dravidian.

A Caucasic strain appears amongst some of the Lisus and the Nungs (*See* Plates XV and XVI).

In the case of Chins, a distinct change in appearance and general characteristics appears to take place south of the Haka Sub-division.

To sum up, I think the following classification would be nearer the true racial classification judged by physical appearance, body measurements, culture, customs, technology and the temperaments of the tribesmen. Language connections have been considered and have been rejected only when, in my opinion, other evidence is overpowering.

Suggested Grouping of some of the Indigenous Races of Burma.

There is a strong element in common between all these races.

- Naga Group.
- Mishmi Group.
- Nmai Valley Group.
    - Daru.
    - Nung (Plate V).
    - Tangsir.
    - Khwinpaung.
    - Atsi.
    - Lashi.
    - Maru (Plate II).
    - Bhamo District Kachins.
    - Shan States Kachins (Plate III).
- Palaung-Wa Group (Plates VI to VIII.)
    - Hill Karen Tribes.
    - Pyin.
- Malay Group.
- Mon Group.
- Man Group (Plates IX and X).
- Lolo-Muhso Group.
    - Kaw (Plates XI and XII).
    - Kwi.
    - Ako.
    - Lahu (Plate XIII).
    - Lisaw.

Some connection is apparent.

-
    - Lolo (Plates XIV to XVIII).
- Kachin-Chin Group.
    - Dulengs.
    - Hkahku Kachins (Plates XXII and XXIII) Kachins from west of Irrawaddy.
    - Singhpos.
    - Other Kachin Tribes.
    - Northern and Central Chins (Plates XIX to XXI).
- Southern Chin Group.
    - Chinbok and other Southern Chins.

- Karen Group.
    - Sgaws.
    - Paku.
    - Pwo (Plate XXIV).

Taungthu—Doubtful. They may belong to the Palaung-Wa Group.

- Tai Group (Plates XXV and XXVI).

Some of the Tai races show a connection with the first seven suggested groups (Naga, Mishmi, Palaung-Wa, Malay, Mon, Man and Lolo-Muhso.)

NOTE.—The letters and the numbers given above refer to the racial classification given on pages 242 to 245 in Part I of Imperial Table XVII.

17. Extracts from the Census Report on the Andaman and Nicobar Islands, 1931.

By M. C. C. Bonington.

(a) Early References to the Andamans and Nicobars.

Owing to their central position along the trade routes of India, Burma and the Far East, many mentions of the islands are found in ancient history. Their excellent harbours served both as a refuge in the monsoons as well as a place to replenish water supply. Like the Nicobars the islands are mentioned by Claudius Ptolemy (2nd Century) as Agmatae* while the Arab travellers of the 9th Century mention them as Angamanain, by the Chinese Buddhist Monk I'Tsing (672), Marco Polo (1286), Friar Odoric (1322) and Nicolo Corti (1430). The earliest mention of the islands and their inhabitants has been seen by some in the Ramayana of Hindu Mythology which is regarded as indicating the inhabitants of the Andaman by its references to the 'Hanuman' or 'monkey peoples', the aboriginal antagonists of the Aryan immigrants in India. According to Temple (Census Report, 1901) the Malays refer to them as 'Handuman' a corrupt form of 'Hanuman' which has been carried down to them in story and tradition. Malays for many centuries used the islands for piratical purposes and for a trade in Andamanese slaves. These slaves found their way to the courts of Siam, Cambodia, and Indo-China for many a century, thus naturally bringing about the deepest distrust and hostility on the part of the aborigines to all visitors to the islands.

Owing to their situation in the middle of the Bay of Bengal, the Nicobars were along the ancient trade route to the East. The earliest mention of them is that made by the famous Chinese traveller and Buddhist monk I'Tsing in 672 A. D. who refers to them as the land of the 'Naked people' (Lo-Jen-Kuo) and this seems to have been the recognized name of for them in China. Yule however identifies with the Nicobars the islands referred to by the Buddhist monk as 'Nalo-kio-chen' (*i.e., Narikel-dwipa* or coconut islands) where the men are 3 feet high and had beaks like birds, no cultivation, and lived on coconuts. The beaks might be taken as an allusion to the protruding mouths developed by the betel-chewing habits of the Nicobarese. In A. D. 607, the Empress of China, Yang-ti, sent an envoy to Siam who reached the Nicobars, spoken of as the country of Rakshasas—meaning demons. He reported that the inhabitants were very ugly, having red hair, black bodies, teeth like beasts and claws like hawks. Sometimes they visited Linyih (Champa) but traded at night, by day they covered their faces.

The Nicobarese have also been identified with the "Lankhabulus" "Langa balus" or Najabalus (Sanskrit *nagna, nanja*-naked) of the "Arab Relations" 851 A. D. In Pinkerton's Voyages and Travels, Volume 7, page 183, appears "an account of the travels of two Mahomeddans through India and China in the ninth century" translated by the Abbe Renaudot from the Arabic. The Nicobars here referred to as "Najabulus which are pretty well peopled; both the men and the women there go naked, except the women conceal their private parts with the leaves of trees". Mention is also made that ambergris and coconuts are bartered by the inhabitants for iron. Gerini has fixed on "Maniola" for Kar Nikobar and "Agathodaimonos" for Great Nikobar among the *Satyrorum insulae* of the 1490 edition of Ptolemy. Apparently Ptolemy however regarded "Agathodaimonos" and the "Maniolæ" as an entirely different group. He mentions ten islands as called "*Maniolae*". As to the *Satyrorum insulae* he mentions that the inhabitants are said to have tails like those with which Satyrs are depicted. The Nicobar Islands also appear in the Great Tanjore Inscription of 1050 as "Nakavaram" or land of the Naked†.

S. Krishnaswamy Iyengar, Ph. D., in his contribution to the Journal of Indian History describes the overseas expedition of Rajendra Chola II and includes among his conquests the Nicobars, Kar Nikobar appearing as Kardipa, Great Nicobar as Nagadipa, the whole being the islands of Naccavaram. This invasion has been fixed at the beginning of the 11th century. The name appears as Nocuveran, and Nicoveran in Marco Polo (1292) and Friar Odoric (1322) respectively. In the 15th and 16th century the islands are referred to as Nacabar and Nicubar by the Portuguese pioneers who attempted to try and evangelize them by means of missionaries who had their headquarters in the neighbouring Mergui Archipelago.

* *Note by Census Commissioner for India.*—"Agmatæ" is a variant reading probably to be preferred to the more usual "Aginnatæ" an obvious emendation on the variant readings is "Agmnatæ", which brings us very close to the Arabic dual Angamanain for Great and Little Andaman though in point of fact it is the islanders not the islands whom Ptolemy described as *Agmnatæ*. Yule however suggests a similar identification for the island next mentioned by Ptolemy—*Agathou daimonos*, for which he would ingeniously read *Agdaimonos Nesos*, getting thus still nearer to our "Andaman". Apparently the Agmnatæ islanders are to be regarded as inhabiting both *Agdaimonos Nesos* and the adjoining five *Barussæ* islands, which Yule identifies with the Nicobars under their name of *Lankha Balus*.

† The Nicobars have always been identified with *Lankhabalus* of the Arabs, *Nakavaram* of the Hindus and Marco Polo's *Necuveram*. The name no doubt survives in Nankauri. One is tempted to identify them with Ptolemy's *Nagadipa* (as the island of the Naked, *Nanga*, not of Snakes) east of Ceylon, but the traditional identification is with the *Satyrorum Insulae Tres* 'the inhabitants of which are said to have tails as the Satyrs are depicted,' a reference perhaps to the tailed girdles worn by the men. Even the comparatively recent Swedish navigator Koeping reported the Nicobarese to be gifted by nature with anatomical tails (1647). An alternative identification is with Ptolemy's five Barussæ islands (inhabited, of course, by *anthropophagi*), which may be taken to correspond well enough to Teressa and the other islands of the Central Group (*vide supra*, page 5.)——J. H. H.

(b) The Aborigines of the Andamans.

The Negrito race is surmised to have been the earliest people to inhabit the continent of South Eastern Asia and of this race the Andamanese and the Semangs of the Malay Peninsula represent to-day perhaps the purest type. In the Philippines the Aetas are of the same origin but less pure in type, while traces of their race inbred with other tribes are represented in Malaya and are perhaps to be found in Assam and in the hills of Southern India. The chief characteristic of these peoples, a characteristic which is the key-note of Andamanese life, is, that they are naturally, "collectors of food, and not cultivators........ The social units is the family, and they move in family groups, where game, fish and wild yams are easiest to obtain." The many anthropological similarities of customs, religion, weapons, treatment of the dead, etc., point clearly to the definite relationship of the Andamanese to the aboriginal race inhabiting South Eastern Asia which is mentioned in Hindu Mythology.

It is only owing to their unique position and complete isolation from the rest of the continent that their survival can be accounted for.

The Andamanese are of two types :—(*a*) The coast tribes of South Andaman and all the tribes of Middle and North Andaman. (*b*) The Önges of Little Andaman, including the Jarawas of South Andaman and the Sentinelese of North Sentinel Island.

The difference between these two types is distinct, both in features, mode of dress, structure, of bows and languages. Sir R. Temple in his Census Report, 1901, divided the first group into two sections. The Yerewa or northern section containing the Chariar, Kora, Tabo, Yere and Kede tribes. The southern or,

Bojigngiji section containing the Juwai, Kol, Bea, Balawa, and Bojigyab tribes. This first group is however no longer an actuality. Its members have lost all cohesion since some of the clans have entirely died out, while the remaining individuals marry irrespective of tribe, with however no contact with the Önge-Jarawa group, who keep to themselves.

Fortunately valuable historical, anthropological and ethnological data of this group have been recorded by Man. Temple, Portman and Brown, so no further mention need be made of them.

The Southern group or Önge-Jarawa group is the only one which is still intact. These inhabit the whole of South Andaman, Rutland, Little Andaman and North Sentinel. In addition there was a fourth clan of Jarawas on Rutland of which nothing has been seen since 1907. In that year a boy of the clan was reported to be staying with the Önges, but he escaped before he was seen by the authorities. A small communal hut belonging to those people however was seen. The hut was of the same type as that built by the Önges but quite different to the Jarawa communal huts ; nevertheless the Önges called them Jarawas and did not claim any relationship with them. This is interesting in view of the fact that the fourth clan of the Southern group has not been again recorded, through Portman mentions that the Rutland Jarawas were distinct from South Andaman Jarawas.

Portman further opines that the Jarawas and Önges, were originally one people consisting of *eremtaga*, *i.e.*, forest dwellers and *aryoto*, or coast dwellers and these tribes were the first to come in contact with Blair's settlers from 1789—96 and that contact with civilization reduced the group so considerably that they could no longer hold their own against the Aka-Beas. Thus the Önges, coast-dwellers, retreated to Rutland and Little Andaman, while the Jarawas, forest dwellers, retreated to the interior of South Andaman. This theory is possible but it is doubtful whether the separation took place as recently as 1789-96, for though there are many points of similarity between the Önges and Jarawas which entirely separate them from the other Andamanese of Great Andaman, there are nevertheless distinct differences in dialect, custom, wearing apparel, house construction, etc., which makes one believe that they have been separated for more than a hundred years.

Cultural Differences, Bows.—The Jarawa, Önge and Sentinel islander's bow is a curved long bow, while that of the remaining Southern tribes is S shaped and the North Andaman bow though also S shaped is somewhat different from that of the Southern Andamanese and is invariably inverted when unstrung. The Jarawa bow though considerably longer, broader and heavier is similar to the Önge bow. The Jarawa and Sentinelese bows have similar patterns marked on them, while the Önge bow has no special markings.

Baskets.—The Önge-Jarawa baskets have a pointed bottom and are coarsely woven while the rest of the Andamanese make a basket with a "kink" in the bottom and finely woven. A basket found on North Sentinel in 1927 was of very fine workmanship.

Wearing Apparel.—The Önge-Jarawas do not wear the bustle (*bod*) on their posteriors as the coastal Great Andamanese do. They do not wear leaves in the front as the Bojigngiji, but long tassels of fibre ; the Jarawas and Sentinel islanders wear a short tassel and have also been found quite naked.

Canoes.—The outrigger canoe of the Önges differs from those of the two Northern groups ; the prow from which the turtle are harpooned is according to Portman of recent origin and copied from the Great Andaman pattern. The Sentinelese have a different type of canoe altogether turning upwards and cut off short at both ends, which is not a good sea boat, and could only be used on the shallow reefs surrounding the island. The Jarawas have no canoe but build rafts for crossing the straits.

Huts.—The Jarawas and Önges construct large communal huts though differing in shape. The Önges sleep on raised cane platforms in the huts, while the Jarawas and Sentinelese sleep on the ground. The remaining groups have no communal huts now but ordinary thatched lean-to shelters.

Remains of Ancestors.—The Önge, Jarawas and Sentinelese have never been found to carry the complete skulls of their relations about with them, but part of the jaw-bone and other small bones. The other groups preserve the entire skull. It has however been found that the Sentinelese bury their infants in their huts placing a Nautilus shell and other smaller shells over the grave. The same has been recorded of the other groups.

Dancing.—The Jarawas and Önges do not use specially scooped out pieces of board for beating the time upon when they assemble for dancing, although a Jarawa woman has been seen using a hollow tree to dance on.

The dances of the Önges and Jarawas are quite distinct from one another. The Jarawas usually dance in their communal huts where they always keep a large number of bundles of small leaf branchlets for the purpose. The Coastal Great Andamanese usually use similar bunches of leaves with which to strike the ground, in their turtle dance, hopping all the time on both feet in a bent down attitude with the knees thrown forward. The Önges dance in the open, men and women standing opposite each other bending their knees forward at the same time lifting their heels. Such dances have a sexual inspiration.

Arrows.—The Önges and Sentinelese use multiple-headed arrows for shooting fish and birds. In the case of the Sentinelese, they use arrows barbed with small splinters of pigeon-bone. Specimens taken at North Sentinel showed they had been mainly used in shooting pigeon as they had a large number of small feathers adhering to the prongs. Perhaps part of their diet consists of such meat, for the number of pig on so small an island must be limited. On a visit to the island a few pig were however seen.

Marriage.—The Önges marry while young, the girls being ten or eleven years old and not even developed. This is not to be wondered at for Önge children seem to know all about sex matters which is perhaps . . due to their living together in communal huts as well as to the actions exhibited in their dances. With the Önges there seems to be no elaborate ceremony as with other Andamanese. Men on a casual visit from distinct villages are very often given a young girl* by an elder merely placing the man's hand on the girl's wrist, no word being spoken. The girl is quite docile and goes along but should the man let go, she will escape into the jungle and he has to go home without her. Nothing is known about the Jarawas.

Greeting.—The Önges unlike the Great Andamanese are completely silent when they meet. The residents of a village when meeting friends sit on the sand and the visitors sit on their laps ; thus they embrace each other for several minutes without saying a word and pass on from one person to the next until all have been embraced, both men and women. Nothing is known about the Jarawas or Sentinelese.

* It is probable that these marriages have been arranged on previous visits.

From general observation of the customs of the clans of the outer group, the Önges of Little Andaman and the Jarawas of South Andaman may be classed as closely related. They are known to understand each other, whereas none of the friendly Great Andaman tribes understand either the Önges or the Jarawas.

The Jarawas of South Andaman and the Sentinelese are apparently very closely allied ; possibly the latter are Jarawas, who while, crossing Macpherson Straits on a raft were drifted out to sea by the tide and landed on North Sentinel Island.

Portman also mentions the existence of an *eremtaga* clan of Önges on Little Andaman. This information was derived from some Andamanese who were left on Little Andaman for a short time. They had told him of men coming from the south who had larger bows than the Önges, and of similar length to the Jarawa bow. A considerable portion of Little Andaman both in the Northern and Southern parts of the island has been surveyed by the writer, but no indication of a separate *eremtaga* clan was found. Its existence is therefore doubtful. Possibly the people belonged to a neighbouring sept, which had larger bows, for it happens that particular septs make larger bows when they are at enmity with another sept. On the other hand the island has not been completely explored, and the existence of an inland sept may still be found.

Conclusion.—Von Eickstedt, a German anthropologist who recently visited the Andamans, was also of the opinion that the Önge-Jarawas and the remaining Andamanese represented two different layers of the primitive Negrito race. He further mentioned that he noticed among the Önges of Little Andaman somatic influences of Arab and other alien origin whereas the Great Andamanese possessed a considerable mixture of Burmese and other elements. These elements he opined were due to shipwrecks. Von Eickstedt's views and opinions require confirmation. It is however of interest to note that Portman found hereditary syphilis to be present among the race. Dr. Hutton suggests that Portman mistook yaws for syphilis, but the writer has not noticed among the Önges the distinctive features of this disease which is frequent in the Nicobars. Further investigation is necessary to confirm either view.

Of those Great Andamanese that the German anthropologist saw, a very considerable number must have been half-breeds who differ from the pure-blooded Negrito both in facial features and in stature. The most noticeable difference between the hybrid and the pure Negrito lies in the hair, which is distinctly frizzly like that of the Papuan whereas the pure Negrito hair is curly and short, growing in what appear to be at first sight separate and as it were insulated tufts. This is especially remarkable in a few half-bred civilized women (of whom one is at school in Rangoon) who have allowed their hair to grow long, while those who retain their primitive life keep it short. It is this feature of the hair and height of stature mainly which does not seem noticeable among the Önges in the somatic strain, so named, of von Eickstedt. Among the Great Andamanese, only one instance came to notice of a girl with undoubted Burmese features, but with the hair and skin of an Andamanese, while one Önge was seen with frizzly hair.

Dr. Hutton has suggested the aquiline nose noticed by von Eickstedt among the Andamanese may be the result not of an Arab mixture but of Papuan strain since the aquiline nose arising from a glabial depression is a typical Papuan feature. Since both Papuans and Negritos are branches of the Oceanic Negro family, an early connection between the two is not impossible and the hair in that case would probably conform to the negroid type. In connection with von Eickstedt's remarks of difference in features among the Önges leading him to suspect somatic influences, it may be mentioned that similar difference, were noticeable among the Andamanese when these tribes were still pure and numerous. These differences exist also among the Jarawas.

In 1905 the writer of this report brought 3 Önges to Port Blair where they stayed for 3 or 4 months enabling a vocabulary of some 350 words and some of the grammar to be recorded. Since that time relations have always been friendly. Parties have regularly landed on Little Andaman and presents have been freely distributed. With the exception of isolated cases they have shown no signs of their former animosity. Occasionally a few individuals visit Rutland and come in contact with the Settlement but this is avoided as much as possible.

In September 1930 three Önges from Hut Bay were persuaded to accompany the writer to Port Blair *via* the Nicobars. They showed no alarm until they were frightened by the Nicobarese at Kar Nikobar. One man ran into the jungle and has never since been seen. As a small canoe disappeared at the same time, it was suspected that he tried to return to Little Andaman.

The other two men could thereafter only be kept on board by restraint. During the night one successfully eluded the police and Andamanese guards and jumped overboard at sea, and must have been drowned. The third man also tried to jump overboard on several occasions and had to be locked up until taken back to Little Andaman. Their whole behaviour after first being frightened showed a very highly strung temperament. On subsequent visits it became apparent that news of the incident had spread all round the island, but the people were friendly and recognized that the officials were not to blame.

It appears, however, that the wives of the two missing men were subsequently put to death by order of the headman of their sept. They are said to have been drowned by the other women of their own sept.

Tribal Distribution.—Portman while at Little Andaman indentified six Önge septs. The other six mentioned below are those which were found among the Önges who came to Rutland and the inhabitants of the west coast of Little Andaman.

1. Ekdi.
2. Palalankwe.
3. Tokynia.
4. Tambebui.
5. Titaije.
6. Tobechelebe.
7. Totamadale.
8. Quingandange.
9. Quananame.
10. Yantige.
11. Tugalange.
12. Chetamale.

N.B.—There may be several unknown septs, in the interior, but nothing definite has ever been found.

Cultural Anthropology.—Little is really known about the cultural anthropology of the Önges, no doubt on account of their comparative isolation and natural timidity. The few superficial cultural differences have already been remarked on, but a vast field of research awaits the anthropologist of the future.* Portman was able to collate a vocabulary of some hundred words of their language, but their psychology, morals, superstitions, religious beliefs, or mythology have not yet been discovered and as a result are excluded from the following resumé of their cultural developments.

* Provided, that is, that the Önge survives long enough.—J. H. H.

Government and Tribal Communities.—Little Andaman is divided between various septs, the names of which are found under the heading " Tribal Distribution". Each sept possesses a stretch of territory or hunting ground which has definitely recognized boundaries. Any intrusion on to this hunting ground is regarded as a sufficient occasion for the outbreak of inter-sept warfare, even though the different septs may be related by marriage.

Habitation.—Each sept occupies a large circular communal hut which is generally built on the sea-shore, but it is not unusual, when the coast is exposed to the full force of the monsoon or in the season for collecting fruit and honey, for all its occupants to take to the jungle. These huts are ingeniously made, with a frame of circular cane-work rising to a point. Over this thatching is neatly bound. Around the hut are a series of small raised cane platforms used for sleeping purposes. Trophies of the chase by way of ornament are suspended from the roof of hut. Buckets made of logs and sometimes of giant bamboo are found suspended in the huts as well as nets and baskets. The bamboos are collected on the shore, having drifted there from Burma.

Tribal Government.—There is a nominal chief, but to use Man's words while describing the Andamanese system of internal government " Communism modified by authority " holds sway ; a feature common to most primitive tribes. The elders of the sept undoubtedly possess an authority almost equal to that of the chief.

Marriage.—Marriage is usually exogamous, sometimes the wife goes and lives with the sept of the husband and at other times the husband joins the sept of the wife. One or two cases are on record where man and wife are both of the same sept. The Önges marry quite young being perhaps only ten or eleven years old and not fully developed. The writer has on several occasions witnessed a marriage. The ceremony was very simple and consisted in an elder of the sept taking the wrist of his daughter and place it in the hands of the young man of the visiting sept. The girl then became his wife and he was free to take her away provided the girl did not release herself and run away in the interior, in which case she was free to go back to her sept. This actually happened in the writer's presence much to the annoyance of the would-be husband. Consummation of the marriage and pregnancy likewise appear to take place before the bride attains maturity, and a woman may be a grandmother when she is 30 years old or younger. The average age attained by the healthy is perhaps not much more than 40 years, and persons known to the writer 30 years ago as children have within his knowledge declined and died when they were about 40 years old.

Divorce.—To leave a wife appears to be a breach of tribal morality. The writer came across a case where a man deserted his wife and went to live with another sept. On his return to his own sept to live with his former wife he was much scolded by an old woman of the sept and was told to go away again.

Death and Burial.—Nothing is known about the burial ceremony. They preserve the jaw-bones of deceased relatives, which is not unlike the Great Andmanese custom.

Ornaments and Attire.—The Önges possess no broad tasellled belts as common among friendly tribes of Great Andamanese, and their women-folk wear a tassel of yellow fibre in front in the place of the leaf worn by the women of the Great Andaman coastal tribes. The yellow dried skin of a dendrobium orchid is used for decorative purposes, while white clay is smeared by both sexes on their faces and body sometimes in ornamental patterns.

Greeting.—The Önges are completely silent when they meet. The residents of a sept meeting friends sit on the sands and the visitors sit on their laps, thus they embrace, each other for about a minute without saying a word and pass on from one person to the next until all have been embraced, both men and women.

Food.—Portman mentions the staple food of the Önge to be the seed of the mangrove boiled, as he always found it in their huts. Artocarpus fruit is eaten after roasting it on hot stones. Since their acquisition of dogs they have been able to obtain more readily the wild pig which have always formed their staple food. They are fond of turtle but not all know the art of using the harpoon. Turtle are much appreciated as presents. Their eggs are to be found on the long stretches of sandy beaches and are often seen in the huts hanging up in nets. The women catch fish almost daily in hand nets and these are dried and stored. Portman argues that this is probably due to alien influence which " they must have been in contact with at some previous period ".

Canoes.—The canoe-culture of the Önges is in a much lower standard than that of the Great Andaman tribes possessing neither the technique or the finish. The canoe is of the outrigger type like that of Great Andaman, from which it has been copied, since formerly, as recorded by Portman, their canoe had no prow.

Bows.—The Önge bow resembles the European type of long bow but is much smaller and flatter. It is generally made of ***Mimusops littoralis*** and the string is made of fibre.

Arrows.—For shooting fish and birds a multiple headed arrow is used, similar to that used on North Sentinel. The Sentinelese arrow is however barbed with small pieces of the wing bones of pigeons.

Dancing.—The Önges dance in the open, men and women standing opposite each other bending their knees forward at the same time lifting their heels ; sexual thoughts are connected with such dances.

Conclusion.—The Önges undoubtedly belong to the *Eremtaga* or Jungle dwellers division in contrast to the *Aryoto* or Coast-dwellers. They do not possess the skill and dexterity shown by the coast tribes of Great Andaman in fishing and turtling. As a type von Eickstedt places them as being the " best representatives of the old type of Negrito, being the least affected of all the tribes by changes due to contact with the outside world." Despite their lack of contact with the outside world the Önges like the other Andamanese are undoubtedly a dying race. Estimated figures for the last thirty years are unfavourable.

	Estimated.
Census 1901	672
Census 1911	631
Census 1921	346
Census 1931	250

A decrease of about 63 per cent. is hence shown in the last thirty years.

Experience has shown that the aborigine as a type is dying out whenever he comes in contact with civilization. In Little Andaman conditions are better than in Great Andaman owing to greater isolation from alien destructive influences, yet the numbers decrease year by year mainly from infections such as influenza introduced at times of contact with civilization. Some septs have almost completely disappeared during the last 30 years.

The Önges have not assimilated the vices of civilization in the same way as the other Andamanese and every effort has been made by the local administration to keep them in their isolation.

Note by Census Commissioner for India.—The disappearance of aborigines is perhaps not an invariable concomitant of contact with a more advanced culture. Such contact probably leads in all cases to a serious decline at first, but provided the tribe in question can be saved from extermination for a period long enough to enable it to adapt itself to the change in its contacts and environment, the period of decline seems to give way again to one of increase. The Tasmanian is extinct but the Maori is at last reviving. In the case of the Andamanese the period required for adaptation is likely to be abnormally prolonged on account of the exceedingly long period during which these islanders have been isolated in a peculiar environment of their own to which they have become specially adapted. They appear incidentally unable to survive if without the shelter of the forest to which they have become accustomed (*vide* Portman, *History of our Relations with the Andamanese*, page 875).—J. H. H.

Report on the blood grouping of the Andamanese.

COPY OF A MEMORANDUM NO. 3005, DATED 18TH MARCH 1932, FROM THE SENIOR MEDICAL OFFICER, PORT BLAIR, TO THE SUPERINTENDENT OF CENSUS OPERATIONS, PORT BLAIR.

The bloods of the Andamanese and others tested here showed that they all fell in group I, indicating that standard sera with which the tests were carried out were probably inert. Therefore sera of the following Andamanese were sent to Pasteur Institute, Rangoon, to have the tests carried out with the cells of known donors. The results are as follows :—

1. Kin. Great Andaman .. .. Group III of Jansky.
2. Dundey K. Gasay of Little Andaman .. .. Group I of Jansky.
3. Female Bora. Great Andaman .. .. Group IV of Jansky.
4. Charaman of Great Andaman .. .. Group I of Jansky.
5. Ukla. Little Andaman .. .. Group III of Jansky.
6. Ta Kie Keay Ganay. Little Andaman .. .. Group III of Jansky.

Note by the Census Commissioner for India.—Colonel R. B. Lloyd, I.M.S. the Imperial Serologist, tells me that Jansky's group I corresponds to international group O. His II to international A, his III to international B, his IV to international AB. Group A is therefore not yet reported from the Andamans, but as group AB is present, it may be assumed to exist. Mydlarski working on Polish soldiers has correlated different groups with different head forms. Group A with meso-or sub-brachycephalic heads, group B with brachycephalic, group O with dolicho-and mesocephalic heads. Kossovitch interprets these groups as corresponding to Nordic, Mongolian and Mediterranean races, and points out that although the anthropoids may belong to any group, orangs and gibbons appear inclined to groups B and AB, and gorillas and chimpanzees to groups O and A (*Reveu anthropclogique*, June 1931). The Andamanese according to Risley are all meso-or brachycephalic.—J. H. H.

Numbers of the Aboriginal Population.

Of the aboriginal population only the friendly Great Andaman tribes were counted, while the Önges, Jarawas and Sentinelese were estimated.

The following table gives the figures for the various friendly Andamanese tribes of Great Andaman as they stood at the beginning of 1931 :—

	Men.	Women.	Boys.	Girls.
Yere	9	20	4	1
Half Bred	2	2	6	2
Kora	6	12	2	4
Kede	..	1	..	..
Half Bred	1	..	..	..
Chariar	4	4	..	..
Half Bred	..	..	..	1
Balawa	..	..	..	..
Half Bred	1	..	1	..
Bojigyab	1	..	..	..
Tabo	1	5	..	..
Total Pure Bred ..	21	42	6	5=74
Half Bred	4	2	7	3=16
	25	44	13	8=90

The total is only 90 against 209 in 1921 or a decrease of 57 per cent. During the preceding decade the decrease amounted to 54 per cent. The causes for the decrease have been explained in the chapter on the Andaman Home. It is certain that very few pure blooded Andamanese of the friendly Great Andaman tribes will survive another decade. Most of these Andamanese have lost tribal cohesion but they nevertheless often cling to some extent to their territory. For instance the writer failed to persuade a solitary couple at Port Cornwallis to join the remaining friendly tribes at Havelock in order to be able to give them some medical attention, while a few Chariars from Landfall island could only be persuaded to live at Havelock during the monsoon on the promise that they would be taken to Landfall after the monsoon. It was desirable to bring them away from Landfall as some suffered from diseases which required medical treatment.

Table showing the estimated population of Önges, Jarawas, and Sentinelese :—

	1921.	1931.
1. Önges	346	250
2. Jarawas	114	70
3. Sentinelese	117	50

The Önges.—The Önges were estimated in 1921 at 346 persons. In the present census they were estimated at 250 persons only. There has been a considerable decrease in this population mainly from deaths due to influenza and malaria which caused several septs on the south and west coast almost to disappear while most of the children at Jackson creek were found to suffer from enlarged spleens so badly that they could only walk with difficulty. The present estimate may however be on the low side and it is hoped to verify it in the coming cold weather.

The Sentinelese.—Very little is known of the number of aborigines, which inhabit Sentinel Islands. Like the Jarawas they are entirely hostile. The present estimate of 50 persons is made on conclusions arrived at from several visits during the last decade and after counting the number of huts found and the sleeping places. Though the previous census showed 117 persons there has not necessarily been a decrease in the population, as even for that census no accurate data was available. It is believed that the population is stationary for the Sentinel islanders have been kept free from direct contact with civilization.

The Jarawas.—The Jarawas have been estimated at 70 persons only while the previous census showed 114. It is assumed that there has been some decrease in the Jarawas because quite a number of adults were killed or seriously wounded by Captain West's party in 1925. Apart from this the population like that of the North Sentinel is probably stationary. It does not necessarily follow that there has been a reduction in numbers of 44 persons during the decade, because the number estimated depends a great deal on individual opinion. The writer has often been through their territory and counted the huts and sleeping places and on this the present estimate is based.

Note by Census Commissioner for India.—Mouat in 1858 computed the number of Andamanese on Great Andaman alone at 5,000. Homfray in 1867 put it at 3,000 and considered that the race was becoming extinct. The earliest estimate of the total Andamanese population on which any reliance can be placed is that of E. H. Man who estimated their number in 1883 after "the ascertained ravages of certain epidemics" at a maximum of 3,500 of which 2,000 were accounted for by the coastal tribes of Great Andaman and the remaining 1,500 (or possibly 1,000 only) by the Jarawa or Önge tribes of the interior of Great Andaman, of Little Andaman and of North Sentinel island. Portman writing at the end of the century after many year's intimate acquaintance with the Andamanese, put their total numbers in 1858 at the date of their first contact with the British at 8,000. This estimate was regarded by Sir Richard Temple as too high and in his census report on the Andamans in 1901 he estimated the total normal population of the islands up to 1858 at not more than 5,000 and the reasoned considerations on which he based that estimate will be found in chapter I of his 1901 Census Report. His estimate has been criticised by A. R. Brown, but as this writer had no experience of the Andamans remotely comparable with that of Portman, Man or Temple his criticisms in this respect carry little weight. Accepting therefore Sir R. Temple's conservative figure for the Andamanese population in 1858, we arrive at the following comparative numbers :—

Tribe.	In 1858.	In 1883.	In 1901.	In 1911.	In 1921.	In 1931.
Chariar	100		39	36	17	9
Kora	500		98	71	48	24
Tabo	200		48	62	18	6
Yere	700		218	180	101	46
Kede	500	2,000	59	34	6	2
Juwai	300		48	9	5	0
Kol	100		11	2	0	0
Bojigyab	300		50	36	9	1
Bea	500		37	10	1	0
Balawa	300		19	15	4	2
Önge	700	1,250	673	631	346	250
Jarawa	600		585	231	231	120
Total	4,800	3,250*	1,882	1,317	786	460†

This devastating fall in the numbers of the Andamanese in less than 75 years of contact with administration paralyses comment, but it is impossible not to agree with von Eickstedt's view of the 'Andaman Home' policy. The relations with the Önges prove that the method was not without alternative.—J. H. H.

* The intermediate figure between Man's maximum and his minimum.

† Of whom 16 Great Andamanese are half-bred.

(c) Anthropology of the Nicobars.

Owing to territorial distinctions the Nicobarese are divided by customs, manners, physical and linguistic characteristics into groups. These groups are :—

I.	Kar Nikobar	Northern group.
II.	(a) Chaura	Central group.
III.	(b) Teressa	Central group.
	(c) Bompoka	Central group.
IV.	(d) Nankauri	Central group.
	(e) Kamorta	Central group.
	(f) Trinkat	Central group.
	(g) Kachal	Central group.
V.	(a) Little Nikobar	Southern group.
	(b) Pulo Milo	Southern group.
	(c) Great Nikobar (coastal tribes)	Southern group.
	(d) Kondul.	Southern group.
VI.	The Shompen of the Interior of Great Nikobar.	

Anthropologically and ethnologically the Nikobarese have many points of affinity with the Indo-Chinese Race as distinguished from the Tibeto-Burmese and Malay tribes, and their manners and customs point to an eastern rather than an Indian origin.

S. H. Roberts in his Population Problems of the Pacific mentions waves of migration which took place towards the Pacific, in the fifth and thirteenth centuries from Indonesia. Undoubtedly, there were even earlier migrations from the main land to the islands and it is not improbable that such migrations took place from the Penang Peninsula in the fine weather of the north-east monsoon for which the Nikobars would be a natural destination. All the Nicobarese are excellent sailors and build large seaworthy outrigger canoes comparable with Hawaiian, Tahitian, Fiji and Maori types in which Cook in 1777 found Tahitians as far as 200 leagues from home.

There can be no doubt that the Nicobarese of the different islands have various mixtures of foreign blood which has been introduced at a date considerably later than the migration. In the people of Chaura, possibly, the purest type is represented, on account of their exclusiveness and isolation. In them the highest form of Nicobarese culture is found as well as a tribal and economic organization superior to that of the other islands. This exclusiveness is due to their refusal to allow any foreigners to remain on their islands and even within the last 40 years they are known to have killed two large canoe crews of Nicobarese who had come for pots and could not leave owing to a change in the monsoon. Although this never had come to the notice of the administration, it is admitted by the Chaura people and substantiated by John Richardson, the Nicobarese Honorarary Tahsildar of Kar Nikobar, whose father was one of the massacred crew.

Owing to their position the Northern group as exemplified in Kar Nikobar appears to have assimilated a certain amount of Burmese blood while in the south the influence of the Malay is very noticeable. Pere Barbe in his monograph on the Nicobar Islands in 1846 states that the natives of Kar Nikobar have a tradition that they are Burmese, who owing to rebellion were forced to fly from Tenasserim and seek safety in the Nicobars. This theory has very many supports both anthropological and philological to bear it out.

The Kar Nicobarese hold themselves to be descended from a man and a bitch, who got afloat on a raft. Dr. Hutton has recorded a similar belief in the Naga Hills, where such an origin is ascribed to Europeans, and points out that in Purchas' *Pilgrimage* (Volume V, Chapter V), " The Peguans ascribe................. their origin to a dog and a China woman, which escaped shipwrec . ". The stories are of the same nature and are probably of the same source, and were no doubt taken by a branch of the Mon race to the Nicobars together with the Mon language which is still spoken. Young Kar Nikobar women when dressed in Burmese costume can hardly be distinguished from Burmese or Talaings. The Talaings speak a Mon language and are not identical with the Burmese by race, though now much mixed up with them, but there is evidence of later migration by the Burmese race proper for in Kar Nikobar, there is a village *Oung Chun*, Burmese for coconut island, the inhabitants of which are said to have arrived about 100 years ago ; the Kar Nicobarese indeed assert that they killed several of them as they were cruel and obnoxious generally.

The " dog's ear " head band of the Kar Nicobarese is supposed to represent the canine ancestress' ears and the long end of the loin cloth her tail. Dr. Hutton mentions a resemblance between some forms of Konyak Naga head-gear and that of the Nicobarese. The Chaura people assert that the reason for the Kar Nicobarese being averse to dog's flesh is their presumed descent from a man and a bitch. In contrast the Chaura people themselves eat dog's flesh which suggests that they and the Kar Nicobarese claim a different origin.

The strongest link which binds the chain of Nicobarese affinities to the Indo-Chinese group is that formed by the philology of the Nicobarese language. Various grammars and vocabularies have been prepared in the past by missionaries, officials, and others of the Nankauri dialect of the Central group. So far the Rev. G. Whitehead is the only person who has collected that of Kar Nikobar.

Among the many differences which exist between the islands the chief one is linguistic. Some six distinct dialects are in existence, though four of these, those spoken in Chaura, Teressa and the Central and Southern groups might be regarded as one, though there are distinct differences, due no doubt to the operation of " tabu " on words which here, as in various other regions where scattered communities exist speaking an unwritten language, and having infrequent means of intercourse and communication, has effected constant changes in the languages.

The best attempt to reproduce the dialect is E. H. Man's dictionary of the Central Nicobarese language 1889. This has been identified by the great philologist Pater Schmidt and by Sir G. A. Grierson, as having " affinities with the Indo-Chinese language as represented now-a-days by the Mon or Talaing languages of Tenasserim and Malay Peninsular and Khmer languages of Cambodia amongst civilized peoples, and by a number of uncivilized tribes in the Malay Peninsula. Philologically the language is invaluable, as owing to isolation and inconsiderable miscegenation, it is the ' true probable basis for the philology of the languages of the Indo-Chinese family ". Lieutenant-Colonel P. T. Gurdon in the " Khasis " (1914) quotes Pater Schmidt that " Khasi possesses many words in common with Mon or Talaing, Khmer, etc........................and to a lesser degree with those Malacca and the Nancowry language of the Nicobar Islands."

The Central Groups.

Traces of miscegenation in the Central group are most noticed at Teressa and Nankauri. In Teressa South Indian influence is predominant, the features and general physiognomy of some of the people pointing to a strong South Indian mixture at some period. The top tuft of hair, the " tiki " of the Hindu, is usually worn by males from childhood. They powder their head with a red powder and apply a concoction of turmeric to their body for medicinal purposes. It is possible that this has originated from Hindu customs, besides the general cast of feature and colour of the skin of some of the youths is such that they would not be distinguished from others on the streets of Madras.........There are undoubtedly traces of old Hindu colonization in the Nicobars which is stated to have existed 900 years ago when King Rajendra Chola II invaded Sumatra and the Nicobars, *vide* S. Krishnaswamy Aiyangar, Ph. D. " Journal of Indian History " *Rajendra, the Gangaikanda Chola.*

At Nankauri harbour anthropometrical measurements were taken which induced Dr. Naidu to believe that a mixture of nordic blood was present. According to history, the Nicobars were at various times during the last 300 years visited by European vessels, Dampier in particular giving a long and interesting description of his visit there in 1688. It is possible that the nordic shape of head noted in Nankauri may be accounted for by the former presence of a Danish garrison. A legend is current among the people of Teressa that the people of Nankauri are descendants of Malays who visited the islands on a fishing excursion and lost their boats.

The Southern Group.

The diverse differences between the inhabitants of the Northern, Central and Southern groups have given rise to a number of theories as to whether the Nicobars are inhabited by two different peoples, or the original inhabitants and an invading race or whether they are one people who have changed owing to successive influences of foreign blood. Boden Kloss advances the theory in his " Andamans and Nicobars " " that the islands were originally peopled by a race of Malays who were gradually driven south by the immigration from the coast of Burma of the Indo-Chinese settlers, but that, in the process, there was a certain fusion of races which would account for the Malay element in the Nicobarese of to-day ". The Shompen* or inland tribe of

* *Vide* below.—The Shom-Pen.

Great Nikobar are the last element of the Malay race, who were enabled to hold off the invaders, and maintain a separate existence in the dense forests of the interior of that island. Kloss also mentions a possible mixture by immigration in remote times from Southern India, to account for the dark skin, and curly or wavy hair met with among the Shompen. He further substantiated this by pointing out that the skull is brachycecephalic with marked prognathism; the type of people approaches very nearly to that described by Herr Baelz as typical of the Japanese of the lower Malay type, *i.e.*, Pithecoid.

This is supported by E. H. Man who notes that the differences are both racial and linguistic between the coastal and Pen tribes though the Shom-Pen are fairer than Malays. He holds that the Shom-Pen were the original inhabitants of Great Nikobar and that at a later date they were driven into the interior by aliens, more powerful than themselves, who were wrecked on their coasts. Sir R. Temple in his 1901 report, page 200 contradicts this, stating that there is no radical difference between a Shom-Pen and other Nicobarese. The differences are merely such as exist between islands and as are to be expected among people living an almost isolated existence.

During the visit of the Census party to Great Nikobar, a Shom-Pen village on the Alexandra river was visited and anthropometric measurements taken of a dozen individuals. As a type they appeared to be totally different to other Nicobarese and the men possessed distinct features. Some resembled the Papuan while the women had Mongoloid features and often the epicanthic fold. Several male children on the other hand showed features very suggestive of South Indian blood.

While the coastal tribes of Great Nikobar exhibit all the characteristics of a mongrel Malay race, the Shom Pen with their more primitive culture and nomadic habits are distinct and differ from the remaining groups and are really not part of the social economic group either. They alone of all the groups do not use Chaura cooking pots, while the " hentas and hentakois " and other signs of spirit propitiation and devil scarers common in the houses of the coast dwellers are absent in the crude huts of the Shom-Pen.

With the exception of Chaura there is a considerable mixture of Malay, Chinese, Pre-Dravidian and even Indo-European blood in the Central and Southern groups. At the present day Chinese influence is most apparent in the south and in parts of the Central group, where possessing most of the trade, the Chinese have families of hybrid stock.

The different ossuary practices prevailing on the islands of Kar Nikobar, Chaura, Teressa with Bompoka and Nankauri with the Southern group, indicate however the possible presence of different original stocks. Further details are given in the section on Ossuary Practices. Dr. Hutton has suggested that the practice of ancestor-worship and of preserving the bones of the family in little coffins in the dwelling houses, as prevails in Teressa and Bompoka, has Melanesian associations. Anthropological researches in the Pacific and Melanesia, *e.g.*, *Argonauts of the Western Pacific* by Malinowski, etc., reveal an environment and culture presenting many similarities to those found in the Nicobars, and point to a possible former connection.

During the Census some 200 anathropological measurements were taken, which were sent to the Calcutta Museum, and have been analysed by Dr. Guha as follows :—

> " Though the Nicobarese are generally known to belong to the Mongolian stock, accurate information regarding their somatic characters was lacking due to the absence of definite metric data. The measurements of 121 males and 50 females on which the present analysis is based will go a great deal in removing this want.

> " The mean stature of 121 males is 1589·25 which places the Nicobarese among the short-statured people, though not quite so short as the Andamanese. The proportion of the breadth of the head to the length is 76·76 and the auricular height is 127·14. The above figures show that the Nicobarese are not brachycephalic as is commonly supposed, but mesocephalic with a relatively high head. The nose verges on platyrrhiny, as the mean basal index of 83·87 indicates, with a sunken bridge (mean orbito-nasal index 111·81). The face is low but broad, the mean total and upper facial indices being 82·08 and 48·05 respectively. The maximum bixygomatic diameter is as high as 138·31 and the bigonial breadth 102·26, showing that the face is of the square shape."

The Shom-Pen of Great Nikobar.

Contact with the Shom-Pen or inland tribe of Great Nikobar has been of an extremely desultory nature. With the exception of Mr. C. W. B. Anderson's exploration of Great Nikobar in 1905, no prolonged stay has ever been made among the people. Visits have always been short, limited to a day or two, and in reality little is known of their customs and habits, leaving an important field of research for the anthropologist of the future.

History.—The existence of an inland tribe in Great Nikobar was first mentioned by Paster Rosen, a Danish missionary in 1831. In 1846 Admiral Steen Bille paid the first recorded visit. When the islands were annexed by the British Government Mr. de Roepstorff, officer in charge, paid three visits finding a temporary encampment, and was accompanied on one occasion in 1881 by the Chief Commissioner, Colonel Cadell. Mr. Man first visited them in 1884 and was subsequently much in contact with them. His researches together with those of Boden Kloss and Anderson afford the only available data.

The Shom-Pen are divided into a number of small communities or septs, each sept living within its own territory and rarely leaving it except when bent on a raiding expedition. Constant feuds have been maintained for generations between the coast people and these inland tribes, and have resulted in the evacuation of the East Coast of Great Nikobar by the Nicobarese. Ethnologically the Shom-Pen are a problem. They differ from the coast tribes both racially and linguistically, and among themselves present several distinct types. The researches of Boden Kloss show a dark skinned people with curly or wavy hair, indicating a Malay type with possible pre-Dravidian miscegenation. Man holds they were in no way allied to Negritos, being fairer than Malays. Observations made by the Census party, which encountered a village community on the Alexandra River, found no signs of curly or wavy hair, but a dark skinned people, with features among adults reminiscent of the North American Indian, and features of young boys suggestive of possible pre-Dravidian affinities. Again on the Bagmar River, fair Shom-Pen were found with curly hair.

Concerning the internal organization of the Shom-Pen very little is known, but as far as could be judged the same communal spirit exists which is so marked among the other Nicobarese. In their habits they are as nomadic as the Andamanese and move from one place to another directly the supplies of game and fruit in their vicinity are exhausted ; yet they keep strictly within the territories of their sept.

Habitations.—Huts are of a far more primitive and coarser type than those found in the rest of the Nicobars. There are two species. The first a lean-to of the pent roof type, raised three or four feet from the ground and thatched with long leaves of the areca palm. These are only constructed when a stay of a short nature is intended. The second, of a permanent nature, consists of an erection on posts some eight or nine feet from the ground, access to which is obtained by means of a ladder. The village community found on the Alexandra river had thatched theirs with long leaves of the areca palm, but Man mentions in his monograph on the Shom-Pen that roofing is often made of the spathe of the bark of the *areca augusta*. In 1905 Anderson noticed that the sites for permanent habitation were always well chosen for defensive purposes and were surrounded by a slight stockade, which fact affords evidence of inter-sept warefare among the Shom-Pen who would never have worried about the possibilities of an attack by the coastal Nicobarese on the inaccessible villages in the interior. A third type of hut is also found built in trees and was noticed on the Dagmar river and by Boden Kloss on the Galathea River.

There is no segregation of sexes in the huts or at meal times. Within the huts reed mats were observed and short lengths of wood which probably served as pillows. All cooking is done either within the hut or in a neighbouring shelter constructed for the purpose. The cooking pot is made of stout bark, later identified by Dr. King as *Calophyllene*. Lengths of bamboo (*bambusa gigantia*) with pierced inter-nodes are used for the storage of water. Beneath the hut a species of fencing is often erected to act as a cage for any wild pig captured, but of recent years owing to greater contact with the coastal people, domestic pig and dogs have found their way into Shom-Pen encampments.

[" The family cooking pot of the Shom-Pen is ingeniously constructed from large strips of bark of two distinct kinds. One strip is folded lengthwise with the rough surfaces outwards to form a large trough, the folded ends being inserted into split stakes. The sides are then built up with the other strips, in pairs, and the open ends also inserted into split stakes, and the whole tightly bound, strips of cane being passed round from stake to stake, along the overlapping edges as well. The stakes are driven into the ground such a distance apart as to cause a bulge in the bark. The edges are bound with the leaves of *sterculia*. A small cane basket inserted into the bottom of the vessel completes the structure and serves the purpose of more easily lifting out the contents when cooked."—C. W. B. Anderson *Exploration of Great Nicobar*, 1905.]

Dress.—Both men and women are now in possession of loin-cloths obtained from the trader through the coast inhabitants, but formerly both sexes wore a species of bark-cloth around the loins. The bark of '*celtis vestmentaria*' is obtained and subjected to repeated blows with a large stick. The substance is then immersed continually in water till all the hard substances are removed. When thoroughly pliable, it is stretched out to dry, presenting a fine tissue. The length of the bark used by the women as a skirt is from 6 ft. to 8 ft. long and from 2 ft. to 2½ ft. broad—(*Women of the Mintira Gunong Burmen*, Jour. Indian Archipelago, 1847, page 253). The holes of the ear are pierced and enormously distended, as strips of bamboos as much as 5″ in circumference are inserted, and act as a receptacle for betel leaf and other odds and ends. Bead necklets, and armlets are also much worn. A spathe band or piece of cloth is bound round the head to keep the hair in position.

Cultivation.—Cultivation is of an extremely crude and primitive type, reminiscent of that of the Tapiros of New Guinea. A sharp stake with the point hardened in the fire, serves as the sole agricultural implement.* Yams, edible roots, a coconut tree or two, pandanus, areca and plantain trees are planted, small fences being erected around the yams and edible roots to protect them from the depredations of both wild and tame pig. Betel is much chewed by both sexes, causing a prognathic deformation and blackening of the teeth. Lime is obtained by burning shells collected on the sea-shore.

Death.—The dead are buried in a sitting posture with the hands lashed together near the mouth in which pulp of pandanus is placed. The body is not subsequently disinterred as among other Nicobarese. According to Anderson, a year later a large feast accompanied by dancing is held, lasting some six to eight days to which all neighbouring septs are invited. The camp is immediately deserted and never occupied again, all septs being informed of the fact, it is however re-visited so that any ripe fruit from the plantations may be collected.

Marriage.—Very little is known about customs relating to marriage, religion and death. Anderson mentions the existence of a '*meluana*' or witch doctor, which he ascribes to the influence of the coast people Marriage as a rule is arranged by the parents, and the girl is handed over to the parents-in-law after she is weaned. This lends great support to information gathered by the Census party that the Shom-Pen sell their children to the coast people for a dah and three fathoms of cloth per child. The child grows up with the family but assumes the position of a servant and in most cases subsequently marries into the family.

Canoes.—The Shom-Pen have small canoes made by themselves from 6 to 10 ft. in length, but they only use them on the rivers and never venture out to sea. Occasionally they help the coast people in the construction of a canoe. The canoes are roughly made possessing neither the technique nor the finish of those made by the coast people.

Weapons.—Neither the bow nor the Nicobarese cross-bow is known amongst the Shom-Pen. The only weapon is a wooden pointed spear (*hin-yuan*) of areca wood which is notched on the upper parts to serve as barbs. Of late years iron has been obtained to make these spear heads, and dahs are also obtained by trading. The chief diet of the Shom-Pen is turtle, snakes, frogs, birds, lizards, crocodiles, fresh-water fish, shell-fish, honey, yams, bulbs of the *caladium*, spathes of the areca, fruit of the *nipa* palm, plantain, pandanus, coconut and above all wild pig. Pigs are either staked and speared or hunted down with dogs, while birds such as the megapod are snared. Fish are either speared or caught by means of a network of bamboo placed across the stream at low tide, enabling the fish to be easily secured. Another very common method is to poison the water with the bruised bark of a forest climber, thus stupefying the fish. Anderson was told that bird-lime was used for catching birds.

Relations with the Coast tribes.—As has been said the constant feuds between the Shom-Pen and the coast tribes have caused the latter to evacuate the east coast of Great Nikobar; of recent years however no attacks have come to the notice of the Administration, although the inland tribes are to be trusted at no time. The aggressive party were always the Shom-Pen who came to the coast in search of iron and cloth, attacking any village when the menfolk were away, killing the remaining inhabitants, and plundering the huts. Each village is however on friendly terms with some sept of the Shom-Pen with whom they barter for rattan and obtain permission to make canoes in the jungle.

* This is also the case with some of the (?) proto-Australoid tribes in the hills of Southern India, whose sole implement is a digging stick with its point hardened in the fire.—J. H. H.

In this they are often helped by the inland sept who expect both payment for their labours and an extra present for the permission to make the canoe, this present being a form of royalty. The rattan is purchased in bundles from the Shom-Pen and form the chief export of Great Nikobar not only to the rest of the Nicobars but to Penang and Singapore where it commands a high price. The practice of selling their children has caused the tribes to come much more in contact with the coast people of recent years, and it is not unusual to find several *Shom-Pen* at *Kondul* and in coast villages of Great Nikobar. The children appeared to be quite happy and beyond having to perform numerous domestic duties are treated as one of the family. There is however a danger of their being exploited, as the Chinese captain of a junk at Nankauri said he could easily procure them.

Conclusion.—So far there is very little known either of the economic prospects of Great Nikobar or of the anthropology of its inland tribe. An untouched field of research awaits the future investigator, who, by staying among the people for many months, might be able to learn their language and record a great deal of valuable anthropological data.

Internal Government and Social Organization.

The Nicobarese are divided in their various islands into a series of communities or clans which find expression as a unit in the village. To borrow a phrase from Sir R. Temple " Government is in fact simple democracy bound by customs ". Though there is this detribalization, which finds expression in the complete independence of the individual, yet there are customs and uses which form unwritten tradition, to which the individual must bow. Throughout the islands, with perhaps the exception of Chaura, the govenment of the village lies essentially in the hands of the elders of the village rather than a head-man. The headman is usually an individual who owing to his superior wealth, symbolised in the number of his pigs and the size of his plantations, has reached a position of influence within the community. This position of influence is almost invariably hereditary. He is in most cases nothing more than *primus inter pares* who acts as the mouthpiece of the elders of the village. As an individual, his personality and wealth alone will increase or decrease the practical value of his position.

Within the clan or village a patriarchal family system holds sway. Owing to the procedure of inheritance, a number of individuals are economically dependant on the owner of the land and plantations ; thus a whole village consists of a number of households, each head of a household having a large number of dependents both male and female. In return for their sustenance, these individuals are at the beck and call of the head of the house, performing all domestic duties for him, such as feeding his pigs, cultivating his plantations, building his huts, preparing his canoes, etc. The whole is remarkably akin to the feudal system except that the sustenance of the individual replaces the land tenure.

The prestige and influence of the headman has always been encouraged by the Administration, which presents him with a flag (' Union Jack'), a letter of appointment and a book in which all vessels and visitors can record their visits.

Each head of a family has a recognized position within the community as an elder, and it is before a council of these elders that all questions of weight and inportance are decided which concern the general welfare of the community at large. The elders can also hear disputes and possess certain primitive powers, mention of which is made under " Tribal Law and Justice ". In Kar Nikcobar, and to a lesser degree in the other islands excepting Chaura, tribal administration in the general run of community life, has lost its former power whereby the interests of the clan were safeguarded. Contact with the trader and civilization seems to be eliminating those economic and social qualities which are such an essential factor in the existence of a primitive race in its fight against the forces of civilization symbolised in a superior culture.

Owing to its position and size, which involve no commercial possibilities, Chaura has never really come in direct contact with the administration, or under its influence. The people being the purest of the race, have an intensely rigid and complicated tribal organization, in which the authority of and dependance on the Chief or Captain of the village stand out. All points and decisions are referred to him by the community, and he settles all disputes deciding what the punishment of the individual should be.

The appointment of an Assistant Commissioner at Kar Nikobar has of late years induced the Kar Nicobarese to refer disputes and general offences to the local court. In other islands offences against morality, customs and tradition are still referred to the elders of the clan who resort to punitive powers, in the shape of fining an individual so many pigs, or physical correction in the shape of a good beating. On Chaura the individual is brought to the Captain who in conjunction with the elders inflicts a fine on him of at least one pig.

This is immediately seized and the rest of the community participates in a feast at the culprit's expense.

Should the accused be a dependent, the elders approach the head of his family and obtain the pig from him.

In the cases of disputes on Chaura, both parties, in the presence of the Captain, select a man each to assist them, thus with two men, a side they proceed to fight with quarter-stayes. The party which is adjudged to have been worsted, no real serious injury ensuing, loses the dispute and at the same time makes over a fee in the shape of a pig which is consumed by both parties.

Sir R. Temple in his Census Report mentions the settlement of quarrels by parties attacking each other at night, armed with quarterstaves, wearing coconut husk helmets and smearing their faces with blood. No serious harm ensued, and the idea expressed appears to be the moral retaliation for any offence suffered. This custom appears to have died out on the Northern group, but is no doubt still current in the South and Central groups.

Devil Murders.—Until recent years " Devil murders " were current in Kar Nikobar, Chaura and Teressa. The idea involved seems to have been the desirability of ridding the community of individuals who were dangerous to the general welfare of the village and in many respects is a primitive exposition of the modern lynch-law of the United States. Many cases appeared before the Administration, records of which will be found in Appendix D Census Report, 1901, which deals with this matter in detail. The murders appear to havd been committed solely for the public benefit after a more or less open consultation of the elders of the village. The general cause appears to have been that the victim was possessed of an evil spirit and hence was both harmful and dangerous.

The causes of the murders proved to be—

(1) Possession by an evil spirit.
(2) Witchcraft to the public harm.
(3) Danger to the community.
(4) Homicidal proclivity.
(5) Threat on the part of the victim to kill.
(6) Failure to cure (by a " doctor ", *menluana*).
(7) Theft.

In recent years owing to the powerful influence of the Administration and realization on the part of the Nicobarese that severe retaliatory measures would be taken, these murders have entirely ceased and are no longer a cause for anxiety and constant 'surveillance'. The orthodox method of killing a victim is very cruel. The legs and arms are broken or dislocated to prevent the individual's fighting. He is then strangled and thrown into the sea with a heavy stone around his legs.

Among the Nicobarese boys attain puberty at about 14 and girls at about 13. They attain full growth at about 22 and 21. At an early age they are initiated into sexual life, no doubt as a result of the practice of a man's living with all his dependents in a communal hut. This feature of "free love" is however the rule rather than the exception among primitive peoples, and in no way offends their sense of morality. Among the young people games of hide and seek are played in the evening which are little more than opportunities for sexual intercourse.

The usual age for marriage is sixteen in the case of a girl and twenty-two in the case of a man. Girls are always free to choose their own husbands. Marriage is usually the outcome of some long-standing affection for a particular youth. The consent of the parents or head of the family is however necessary. In Chaura, before couples are able to marry, either the boy or the girl must possess at least three pigs which are given by their parents or the head of the house. To obtain a bride, the suitor must always give a present which differs with the clan status of the bride's father. In the case of a wealthy parent it would be ten pigs, 20 fathoms of cloth, 20 rupees, 2 large silver spoons and 1 bundle of silver wire. Should this indemnity be too much for the suitor or should he be a poor man, he can enter the house of his father-in-law and work as his dependent, and should he possess a small coconut plantation this becomes the property of his father-in-law and stays for ever within the latter's family.

Although there is no ceremony or rite associated with marriage, a large feast is invariably held to which the whole community is invited. They are expected to bring presents for the newly married couple so that at some time they may set up in a new home. Pig and toddy form the chief attraction in the feast wherein the partakers invariably leave thoroughly intoxicated. It is usual for the woman to come and live in the man's house and though the opposite sometimes takes place it is rare.

The status of women socially is every whit on a par with that of men. Far from being inferior they exercise considerable influence in the councils of the men and are at complete liberty. On them also the majority of the work, both domestic and otherwise, devolves.

As a rule after a couple have married infidelity is rare. Marriage however is by no means binding on either party in the Nicobars. Should a husband and wife fail to get on well they just leave one another to look elsewhere for a mate, no malice being borne on either side. Adultery is rare, but is good cause for divorce. It is treated as an offence against the community, and the delinquents are both fined three pigs each. On Kar Nikobar and other islands it is not unusual to beat severely both the man and the woman. Should there be any children they are divided between the couple. As an actual moral offence adultery is not regarded in a serious light, but the husband and sometimes the injured family get pecuniary compensation for the alienation of his wife's affections. A case happened a few years ago where the co-respondent had to indemnify the brother of the woman with whom he had committed adultery; the brother in anger over his sister's conduct had destroyed his own racing canoe. The co-respondent was unable to pay for it and had to hand over a part of his coconut plantation as compensation.

Ownership of land.—Throughout the Nicobars recognised proprietary rights exist in land. R. F. Lowis in Appendix G of his Census report gives an able and clear exposition of the rules as to ownership of land in Kar Nikobar.

Kar Nikobar.—Tradition and usage has vested ownership of land in Kar Nikobar in the person of the village chief or headman as his personal property. Hence all land, jungle, or otherwise in Kar Nikobar is the property of some village headman. In the course of time the headman has made grants of land to all families of his village. This land has either been cultivated or sown with coconuts, and is now the scene of thriving vegetable and yam gardens as well as fine coconut plantations. The headman would naturally keep the major part of the land for his own family to enable them to acquire greater prestige by the number and size of their plantations, and the number of their pigs, for it is by wealth alone that a family can show its importance.

All land therefore on Kar Nikobar is either unplanted, in which case it belongs to the headman who owns the timber growing on it, or has been allotted by him to various families. The usufruct of this allotted land belongs to such a family, and remains with them as a family rather than as individuals, but not the soil itself. Thus in the Nicobars it will be found that a plantation has descended in a family for generations never changing hands. This considerably enhances the unity of the family which in turn strengthens the village and community, the tribal unit.

The headman has also powers to sell land to members of neighbouring villages, and sometimes even to make them free grants, but to such alienation the consent of the elders of the village is always necessary. It also often happens that plantation land in one village is exchanged for garden land in another, and in most cases of this nature there is usually trouble over the land alienated to other villagers and many of these cases are brought into the local court every year.

Throughout the Northern and Central groups of the Nicobars, the jungle is interspersed with large open spaces of *lalang* grass. This grass is used to form the thatching of the beehive huts and is the common property of all individuals, every villager having the right to cut and use it. The boundaries which divide the lands of one village from that of another one are recognized by certain marks; a young coconut stuck on top of a stick is one such and constitutes a prohibition against the picking of coconuts.

Tribal custom allocates the land and the forest growing on it to certain villages and when the inhabitants of other islands wish to cut down trees for canoes they have to pay royalty to the owner. In Great Nikobar before attempting to cut down a tree in the jungle for canoe-building permission is always obtained from the Shom-Pen who expect certain presents in return. Judging on inferences, it is concluded that the land in Great Nikobar is divided up by boundaries into the hunting grounds of the various groups or tribes, who would naturally retaliate at any attempt to encroach on their land.

Chaura.—The whole island is split up into numerous holdings, consisting of jungle and cultivated land. Contrary to the custom at Kar Nikobar, this land is the property of the owner of the trees upon it. A chief, of whom there are but five, has no rights over the land belonging to the members of his village. Comparably to the old English village land system, an individual owns strips of land all over the island, cultivated and otherwise, which have come into his family by inheritance or marriage. Even the conspicuous hill on Chaura, (which is supposed to be the resort of maleficent evil spirits, and is shunned by the inhabitants, and can only be climbed with one's person devoid of ornaments and wearing a white loin cloth for fear a snake should bite or the spirits seize one) is split up into a series of holdings from which individuals at certain times of the year cut fuel. All wells are the property of certain villages.

With the exception of Chaura, the only property that goes by inheritance in the Nicobars, are coconut trees, canoes and sometimes huts. Whoever has planted a tree is the owner of it and his heirs after him. The land, as has been shown is not claimed, only the trees.

According to the primitive laws of inheritance current in the Nicobars, all real property, coconut and areca trees and gardens, will descend to the surviving members of the family which lives in the village. It remains with them as family rather than as individuals as has been explained. Each village community is divided into a series of families, each family consisting of a number of individuals who have a right to be sustained from the plantations which are in reality their common property, though the head of the family assumes a despotic position. All persons both male and female have equal rights to the property. Should a son marry in Kar Nikobar he can either bring his wife to live in his own village, or he may go and live in her village with her relations. By doing this latter he renounces all claims to his own family inheritance, and thus virtually becomes a member of another family group. The same is the case with a daughter who leaves *her family. For inheritance is communal to the family. Each individual has an unspecified but effective* right to part of the produce of the plantation. It supports each member of the group it belongs to, and they can supply themselves at will. Should a family completely die out the plantation will of necessity go back to the chief who owns the land. He can either keep it for himself or allot the same to some other member of the community.

In Great Nikobar and in the Central Group where communities are smaller, the possession of coconut palms, that is of the source of all wealth, is usually vested in the headman and the eldest son succeeds to the inheritance, or the daughter if there is no son. Occasionally a man or woman will hold property in several villages, is contrast to the usage in Kar Nikobar.

The distintegration of the lands of a village would result in the breakdown of the community. Thus the land is never alienated to traders.

Organization of labour.—In the organization of labour, the family, clan, village community, and ultimately the whole island are the groups which co-ordinate for the accomplishment of their various tasks throughout the Nicobars. The duties which a dependent owes his family, and which the family owes the village community, are united to undertake the task. The building of huts, canoes, and plantation are economic factors which are undertaken by the various family groups. In these any member of the village may take part and as a reward or recompense will join in the large feast given by the owner who organizes the task. At the great ossuary feast which takes place at Chaura every three monsoons or eighteen months, the whole island community resort to the *al panam* or village near the shore. This contains 32 specially built large communal huts which house the whole population, and are vacant at other times of the year. All the pig in the island are driven into specially cleared areas surrounded by fences and are then killed and eaten at the feast which lasts a month. Some 1,280 pigs are eaten at the feast as 40 jaw bones of pigs stained red are hung in orderly rows in each hut. These are cleared just before the next feast takes place. This naturally exhausts the complete stock of pork on the island, so a new era of work and trading commences to replenish the stock before the next 18 months.

Pottery.—The importance of the pot to Chaura has been stated. In it are displayed the industrial qualities of the women. The clay is procured from Alheun village at the northern end of Teressa where it is obtained in the hill side. Clay was at one time procurable on Chaura but the Chaura people say it is of poor quality and very brittle. Each man is only allowed to take the equivalent of 2 cubic feet of clay every season from Teressa, much to the annoyance of the Chaura people who make it a subject of complaint. Thus Teressa controls the output of Chaura pots.

Prior to making pots the Chaura women sprinkle themselves with pig's or chicken's blood, in order, they say, to prevent the pots cracking, and wear collars of young banana leaves. The pots are handmade. The process adopted is that of coiling. Starting from the base, long pencils of clay some 9" in length are coiled one on top of the other until the size required is made. This is then smoothed into the shape of pot with a spatula of wood. Before it is fired it is left to harden in the shade under the hut for a day or so, so that any blemish or crack may be easily discerned. After firing, black stripes 2" in width are painted on it. The paint consists of resin extracted from the husk of the coconut boiled over a fire.

A woman on Chaura is supposed to be able to make 2 large pots in one day. Each pot can be identified, as its maker leaves her special mark on the outside just below the rim.

Economic Wealth.—Dependants and children in the Nicobars are an economic asset, as from the age of ten till they reach manhood they do most of the domestic work around the house such as fetching fuel, drawing water, feeding the pigs, climbing coconut trees, etc. Owing to their extreme usefulness in this way an orphan is never without some support to fall back on, as any family are willing to adopt him or her as a depandant and as a mainstay in their old age when all of the hard work falls on the younger people.

On Great Ni obar several Shom-Pen children were found with the coast Nicobarese who said they had bought them for 1 *dah* and 2 fathoms of cloth from their parents. These children are in the same position as the remaining dependants of the community and are quite happy in their new surroundings.

In a rich man's household often as many as three hundred coconuts are consumed in one day. Some two hundred of these are used in feeding the family's many pigs in the jungle. One by one the pigs are brought to a large wooden trough filled with the contents of fresh coconuts. Each pig being given an allowance in accordance with its size.

Inter-Island Trading.—The trading season of the Nicobars opens with the fair weather but usually not before February. This is marked on Chaura by the many short journeys to Teressa to fetch clay, and under every hut women and children are seated the whole day preparing pots. The men gather round their large canoes, up to 70 feet in length, which have been drawn up during the s. w. monsoon and covered with coconut palms to prevent cracking. They prepare for the ceremony of burning the canoe, wearing necklets of young banana leaves, their bodies covered with pig's blood. The canoe is charred all over and then shaped and chipped with adzes and axes to make it lighter in the water. New rattan lashings hold new outriggers in place, and new pennants are fixed on the canoe, the whole accompanied by singing, toddy drinking, and general feasting by the men engaged. After all village canoes are ready, canoe racing takes place in the evenings to watch which the whole of the community line the shore criticising the merits of the various canoes. At night feasting, dancing, and singing of canoe songs take place. Canoe songs usually have sex as a theme, and are either composed on the island or have been imported from Kar Nicobar. With the coming of the full moon the canoes set out for Kar Nikobar, Teressa, Bompoka, Nankauri and Kachal laden with pots. In return all islanders come to Chaura where they stay for a few days with their friends to trade and feast. As many as ten Kar Nicobar canoes will arrive in the fine weather to purchase pots and canoes, and put up in the empty huts of the *al panam* being fed by the Chaura community.

Culture.—All canoes in the Nicobars, are made either in the islands of the Central or of the Southern Group, manufacture being completely "tabued" on Kar Nicobar, Chaura, Teressa and Bompoka. Besides there not being a large number of trees available for the purpose, there is a legend current in Chaura, that a chief once attempted to make a canoe from the wood obtained from the tabued hill ; immediately his plantations were destroyed by pigs, his hut burnt down, and misfortune followed him in whatever he undertook.

All canoes made in the Central Group are either cut out by parties sent from the various northern islands or are bought direct from the inhabitants. If bought direct the equivalent in pork, lime and general trade goods of 1,000 pair of nuts is given per fathom of canoe, otherwise if personally cut by the Chaura people for instance, a royalty is charged on the tree by the island owners. All Kar Nicobarese must either purchase their canoes through Chaura, or failing to do so must give the equivalent of the price they paid at Nankauri to any Chaura man. Most of the Kar Nicobarese have a friend or agent on Chaura to whom they pay this money, and will stay with him in the event of their visiting the island. Unless this price has been paid a canoe may never visit Chaura and as a pilgrimage to Chaura is as important as the *haj* to Mecca the necessity for it can be realized. The journey of a youth from Kar Nicobar to Chaura by canoe, is the first step in initiation to manhood. The price usually paid for a large racing canoe, if bought on Chaura by the Kar Nicobarese, is roughly Rs. 100, 20 fathoms of cloth, 20 pigs, 100 spoons, 10 large spoons, 3 or 4 empty tin boxes, silver wire, *dahs*, and betel boxes.

Navigation.—Primitive charts and drawings are not existent in the Nicobars. To go north from Nankauri to Chaura, or from Chaura to Kar Nikobar, the North Star or Plough is followed. To go south the Southern Cross is used as a guide. The Nicobarese have names for some of the more prominent stars.

Southern Group.—A few canoes find their way north from the Southern Group, but the outturn is not as great as in the Central Group. Most southern canoes are brought from either Kondul or Pulo Milo. To make a canoe in Great Nikobar, permission must be obtained from some friendly tribe of Shom-Pen. These will assist in cutting down the trees and hollowing out the log, and in return will receive a *dah* or two, some cloth and other trade articles. Besides coconuts the chief export of Great Nikobar is cane or rattan. The coast villages of Great Nikobar trade for this with the Shom-Pen, and although the major part falls into the hands of the Chinese traders, a considerable amount goes north to be exchanged for Chaura pots, for Bompoka and Teressa tobacco and for general trade goods and to be used as canoe lashings and in hut building. For one tin of rice two large bundles of cane are obtained, while on Chaura, two large pots are exchanged for one bundle.

Tobacco.—Both Bompoka and Teressa grow excellent tobacco which is valued by the leaf in Chaura, Kar Nikobar and the Central Group. 600 leaves were obtained by the Census party in return for a bag of rice, while on Chaura it is sold at the rate of 40 leaves for one medium sized pot.

Lime.—Throughout the Nicobars the natives are much addicted to the chewing of betel nut from the areca palm mixed with lime, which is responsible for the hideous deformation of the lips and blackened appearance of the teeth. One of the steps of initiation to manhood is the permission given to chew betel nut. Both men and women are very fond of it. Lime is obtained by the burning of *tridacna* and other shells. On Chaura and Teressa this is "tabued", so that the Chaura people resort to Nankauri for their supply of lime while the Teressa people obtain it from the neighbouring island of Bompoka. Owing to the weather of the s. w. monsoon which prevents travel, it is necessary for the Chaura people to lay in a good supply of lime to last over the s. w. monsoon. For this purpose a whole canoe load of men go to Nankauri and will be charged at the rate of one pot per man if they wish to burn lime. While there, they are fed by the local community and in return are expected to help in the general duties of domestic life.

It can be seen how great a part the inter-island trade system plays in the daily life of the Nikobarese. It has an important place in their tribal economic activities which necessitates much work, and considerably engages the minds of the people. Its destruction would create a void in their lives, leaving them without interest or occupation.

As the religion, magic, ossuary practices, etc., of Kar Nikobar have been fully described in Appendix A by the Rev. George Stevenson, the contents of this chapter deal purely with the Central and Southern Groups which have similarities with the general customs of Kar Nikobar in fundamentals but differ considerably in details.

The religion of the Nicobars is animistic and consists in the propitiation or compulsion of evil* spirits, which are credited with possessing power to cause sickness, damage property, and generally harm individuals. To discover and frighten away these *iwi* (evil spirits), the Nicobarese erect "scare-devils" which differ considerably in form and number in the Northern, Central and Southern Groups. In the north, they are marked by either simplicity and adherence to two patterns only, while in the Central and Southern Groups, they are noticeable by their numbers, elaborateness and general talent shown in their execution.

On Chaura, only two types of scare-devil are found, the first consisting of a man-headed post, with a slightly forked top, hung round with lalang grass and young banana leaves, found in every village clearing, the second an elaborately carved model canoe which is hung up inside the huts. Besides this on building a new hut or clearing a new plantation area, young coconuts are hung up on sticks to propitiate the good spirits or *iwi ka*.

---

* *Note by Census Commissioner for India.*—The conclusion is, I think, unavoidable that these spirits are not vague malicious Earth spirits but definitely ancestral spirits in a bad temper. The Chaura "scare-devil" posts to which Mr. Bonington refers seemed to me to take indubitably the form of the soul figure of a defunct ancestor, as the slightly forked top of the head suggested at once a vestigial survival of such a device as the prongs of a Naga soul-post intended to hold the skull in place during the downward transition of the soul into the wooden figure prepared for it [*vide* M. A. S. B. XI (1929), p. 19 and pl. 3]. This view is confirmed by photographs taken by Colonel Sewell of a so-called "scare-devil' on Teressa showing the headgear developed in just such curved hornlike prongs, and by Mr. Bonington's subsequent discovery on Teressa and Bompoka of the figure itself actually bearing the skull (see *Man.*, 1932, 133). Clearly the purpose of the man-headed post is to provide a local lodging for the fretful soul of a troublesome ancestor, while the miniature canoe hung up in the house is probably to provide for his return to the ancestral land overseas.—J. H. H.

The medium through which the Nicobarese communicate with the spirits is the *menluana* or witch-doctor, who is credited with powers of smelling out evil spirits and driving them away. These people are suppose to possess considerable powers, even to the extent of causing a person to become ill and die. This can however be countered by using the services of some other witch-doctor to counteract the former's evil influences On all occasions of sickness the witch-doctor is immediately sent for, he smells out the offending evil spirit and drives it away, at the same time making a new scare-devil for the benefit of the patient, this being their peculiar privilege on Chaura.

At the annual feast of spirits the fundamental idea underlying the whole festival is the propitiation of the spirits with pork, toddy, coconuts, etc., so that the island may have good trade for the next two years, that their pots may not break, that the plantations may thrive and that general prosperity may come to the community.

Every canoe is supposed to be guarded by *iwi ka*, who are always propitiated when the canoe has been racing or has undertaken a long journey by large pieces of pork, young coconuts and fruit being placed inside it. The pennants which are always found on the bow and the stem of the canoe, besides being there for purposes of ornamentation are supposed to frighten away the evil spirits by their constant flapping in the wind, thus ensuring a successful voyage.

Central and Southern Groups.—The scare-devils of the Central and Southern Groups are marked by their variety, and their aggressive theory symbolised in the forms they take. At Nankauri three types are found :—

(1) *Henta.*

(2) *Henta Koi.*

(3) Automatic bull roarers and bamboos with bushes of grass erected in the sea in front of the village.

(*i*) *Henta* are paintings worked on areca spathe screens or boards with considerable skill and a fineness amounting almost to art. On each screen some four to eight pictures are found depicting a man (probably representing an anthropomorphic conception of God, perhaps acquired from missionaries), the sun and the moon, domestic scenes, fishes, etc.

(*ii*) *Henta Koi* are carved wooden figures, animals, birds, crocodiles, fish and human beings, often monstrous and showing considerable skill and talent in creation, found both in the Central and Southern Groups. These are always aggressive in character so that the evil spirits may be readily scared.

(*iii*) *Automatic bull-roarers.*—These are found in the Central Group on the sea front, being attached to trees and poles often 40 to 60 feet in heigh, and are thus described by Dr. Hutton :—" They are formed of a narrow plank to which a slight screw effect has been given by twisting and cutting so that they revolve in the wind about a central pin. At each end of the plank and facing in opposite directions is a node of bamboo the open end of which is partly blocked with rubber or wax. The result is that the revolving wood produces a very deep and loud booming noise identical with that produced by a bull-roarer " (*Tour notes in the Nicobars*).

When there is illness in the house, the *henta koi* are decorated with young nuts, leaves, lights burning in *tridacna* shells, and these together with young coconuts adorn the interior ; strips of pork and fowls are placed about to propitiate the spirits, their subsequent disappearance being ascribed by the people to consumption by the spirits. In Great Nikobar, *henta koi*, which are on wheels, are trollied about the gardens. Should these be of no avail, the *henta koi* are thrown away and new ones are made.

Burial customs vary greatly throughout the Nicobars. Dr. Hutton, Census Commissioner for India, in his tour notes of August 1930 has propounded a theory as a result of his enquiry. He came to the conclusion that the three forms of burial customs current indicate that the Nicobars are inhabited by two different peoples (*a*) the original inhabitants who buried their dead in or near their houses and dug them up again to fête the skull as is done by the Yimsungr of the Naga Hills ; (*b*) those who came later, to Chaura in the first instance, and brought with them the practice of exposing the dead in canoe coffins, presumably in order that their souls might return by sea to the land of origin further east. In Kar Nikobar there is a compromise between the two customs, the dead being first buried (on the sea shore and not to landward as in Nankauri) after which their bones are thrown into the jungle at the edge of the sea.

Since the Census Commissioner for India's tour, a visit to Teressa and Bompoka, where he did not touch, revealed that on these islands ancestor worship is current, the skull of a revered personage being preserved and placed on a life size wooden body in a sitting posture. The body is hollow and fitted with a door, the remaining bones of the deceased being inside the figure. Not only are the bones of important people kept but all the bones of the deceased family were found kept in little hollowed logs about 1 foot in diameter and 3 ft. long, as many as ten being found in one hut besides the wooden figure of a woman with a skull fixed into the head, who was said to be the mother of the present headman. Ram Kishen, the headman of Malakka in Nankauri harbour, also keeps the skull of his father in his house but it was ascertained that this custom had been brought from Teressa where Ram Kishen was born.

After death, a man on Teressa is buried with his head to the west and his feet to the east, near the village. " A soul figure in the form of a post "* is then placed over the grave which post is covered with cloths, and general belongings of the deceased such as spears, ornaments, silver wire, spoons, in fact all his personal property as well as the head dress of his wife worn on festive occasions and the skulls of pigs which he had killed and which were hung up in his life time as ornaments within the hut. It is customary for all relatives and friends to attend the funeral and bring pieces of cloth in which to swathe the dead. The body is then buried at sundown so that no shadows (*i.e.*, spirits) of the attendants shall fall into the grave. This method of interment is common throughout the Central and Southern Groups. Bodies of unimportant poor people or orphans are placed in canoes as on Chaura. At Nankauri and in the Southern Group it is usual that a great feast should be given in honour of the deceased and that before burial certain expenses should be undertaken to procure silver wire and cloth to wrap around the dead man before interment. Should the children not possess the wherewithal with which to provide these, it is customary for a friend or relative to undergo the expense and in return seize all the landed property and plantations of the children, which circumstances may have prevented their turning into ready money for the funeral. The children then become the dependants of the new owner but completely lose their inheritance.

---

* Dr. J. H. Hutton.

Beyond the real estate of the individual nothing is left by him after death, as all his portable property is destroyed by being left to rot; on the island of Kar Nikobar the huts too are burnt should the man not die in the *al panam*. One exception there is however to this general rule which makes the Chaura people unique in the Nicobars. They do not destroy any of the personal wealth of an individual but rather preserve it, avoiding the condition found in the rest of the Nicobars, where wealth only stays in the family during the life time of the deceased. By their preservation of all the property of the dead man, they accumulate wealth. On Teressa and Bompoka, after the bones of the relatives have been disintered, cleaned, preserved, sometimes after many years, which has allowed the people to collect many pigs, a large feast, is held to which the whole community is invited, particularly those individuals who gave presents of cloth for the wrapping up of the corpse, all bones are then thrown into a common ossuary near the sea shore.

Chaura.—On the death of an individual on Chaura, the whole community ceases work for several days, the length of time varying with the importance of the man. Singing, fishing, dancing or any type of communal labour is forbidden. The body is then taken and washed and prepared for burial near the village. In the case of a man, he is buried with the top of his head pointing west and he lies on his back with his legs towards the east. This signifies that he has been on a long journey through life and like the sun constantly crossing the sky reaches the west after much travel; a woman is always buried in the opposite direction*. As a sign of respect to the deceased it is customary for the whole village to shave their heads, which operation is performed with a sharp *dah* by the women.

After the corpse has been in the ground for three days, it is disintered; when this takes place the community may again resume the domestic routine and duties of tribal life. The corpse (*canopa*) is then put into one of the deceased's canoes which has previously been sawn in two, and placed in the ossuary (*laich*) in the jungle near the sea shore on a pair of forked wooden Y shaped posts, from four to six feet from the ground. The body is then left to rot, and in time owing to the breaking up of the canoe, falls to the ground, which is covered with the skulls and bones of many generations and there it stays, the bones being partly consumed by the village pigs. After disinterment a feast is given by the relatives to the whole village community and one of the trees of his coconut plantations, which lapse to his heirs, is ceremonially cut and burnt as a sign of his death. A cut is also made either in the floor or in one of the posts of his hut to mark his death, many huts being found covered with such marks.†

On the death of an individual it is customary to "tabu" his name to the whole community, while in the Central and Southern Groups certain forms of food and drink are "tabued" for a time as a sign of respect to the deceased.‡

The comparative isolation of the Nicobars has so far rendered the islanders immune to alien influences. The islands with two exceptions are in a thriving condition. The appointment in recent years of an officer at Kar Nikobar with magisterial powers is tending to break up the tribal system of Government, as it causes the Nicobarese to bring all complaints of a petty nature to the local court, instead of adjusting them within the tribe. The former policy of the Administration, in maintaining a Government Agent without magisterial powers, was to pursue an indirect form of Government through chiefs and elders, and only interfere in cases of violence, and it seems not unlikely that such a policy is sounder than that which involves direct action through British courts.

Education.—For many years past, a Mission has been established in Kar Nikobar, to educate and Christianise young Nicobarese, who are either orphans or who have been placed in the Mission by the parents. This is in a flourishing condition and is a source of much good, especially through a hospital which is kept up with the assistance of Government. The outlook of those who have been brought up in the mission from infancy is however changing and there is danger of this becoming inimical to the welfare of the race; for instance the younger generation thus brought up is inclined to treat tabus as superstitious customs. These tabus are however an important factor in the life of the people. The inter-tribal trade, indeed the whole social and economic life of the Nicobarese, is built up on them.

In this connection, it may be noted that experience in the Oceanic Islands of the Pacific where conditions of environment and culture bear a great resemblance to that of the Nicobars, depopulation has been rapid mainly owing to similar causes. "Destruction of tabu and its consequent interests, destroys the sociology of primitive tribes, and their minds are left a perfect blank."§

As the same writer proves in his book, destruction of the interests of the natives of Tahiti caused them to relieve themselves in endless dissipation ending in decimation of the population.

In order not to leave those who are the products of the Mission standed between two worlds it is therefore of some importance to link up any form of education to their tribal environment and thus inculcate the necessity of keeping up tribal customs, tabus and economics. It is also desirable for their welfare to confine lessons in missions to part of the day only, allowing the afternoon to be spent by the children at their ordinary occupations at home under the care of their parents or the elders, thus making them fit for their future place in Nicobarese society. The necessary ground and support will then be found against the blighting effect of a superior culture and alien influence which will never meet an inferior culture half-way, but completely destroys it.

Trade.—Although the trader may be classed as a necessary evil, it is possible that he favourably affects the adaptability of the race through a slow process of miscegenation. Prior to the annexation of the islands, the Nicobarese protected himself against the influences of the trader by murdering the crow and plundering the vessel in cases of dispute. It was mainly to put a stop to this that the British Government assumed possession of the Islands at the same time affording the trader complete protection. Left without their natural means of protecting themselves, the Nicobarese, in the course of years, steadily came under the influence of the trader, until it was found in 1915 that the natives were in debt to the extent of 29 millions of nuts, a sum representing the total output of 4 years crops. In several cases, the debtor was found to be without plantations

---

* *Note by Census Commissioner for India.*—This difference in the treatment of male and female corpses seems to me to go some way to confirm my theory of the immigrant nature of the Chaura burial customs. If male navigators from the east landed on Chaura and introduced the canoe and pottery cults, which Chaura controls, and Kar Nikobar tradition (*vide* Census Report of 1921, p. 49) very definitely ascribes the introduction and use of pots to Chaura, what more natural than that the men should be buried so as to face east and the women, who may be supposed to have belonged exclusively to the indigenous inhabitants, laid to face the other way. Similarly one may suppose that disinterment was originally followed by the preservation of the skull and bones in a wooden soul-post, for which treatment canoe exposure was substituted as a result of the immigrant culture.—J. H. H.

†"P. Hamilton (1801) reports this to be a vicarious sacrifice of one of the widow's finger joints, inferring a survival of the actual sacrifice of the finger joint". (R. C. Temple.)

‡ There is no tabu on the forms of address adopted by an individual to any of his relatives, maternal, paternal or "in law". An individual is always addressed by name, be she wife, daughter, sister, mother, etc., a father or mother are always addressed by name by their children.

§ S. H. Roberts, *Population Problems of the Pacific*.

and was consequently reduced to a state of serfdom, as he worked without remuneration of any nature. To solve the problem Government decided that the traders should be allowed five years grace to collect debts, and at the end of the period closing March 31st, 1920 the total debts outstanding were to be written off. At the same time traders were forbidden under the terms of their license to grant further credit to the Nicobarese.

Owing to the peculiar economic position of the Nicobarese whereby his total wealth is vested in the land and can only be gradually drawn on, it was found necessary that the Assistant Commissioner should allow credit to certain individuals in certain circumstances. The death of the member of a family necessitates the realization of this wealth. Lack of tangible assets necessitates obtaining credit to procure cloth and silver ware for the deceased as well as giving feasts to all comers. In the Central Group, should the heirs be unable to provide the necessary provision for the deceased it is usual for some wealthy relative or friend to provide it, but at the same time, all the plantations of the deceased fall to this benefactor, leaving the heirs without support and causing them to assume the position of dependants in his household.

Owing to lack of control in the Southern Groups, it is difficult to gauge whether the rule regarding debts is adhered to. The Census party received the impression that the Nicobarese were heavily in debt as no goods were seen in the shops of the trader, but piles of nuts were collecting daily in his yards, giving the impression that the score of past debts had not yet been paid off.

Medical Treatment.—With the exception of the hospital at Kar Nikobar and a compounder at Nankauri, the islands are without medical supervision. Distances prevent cases being brought by canoe to these two stations. Mention has already been made of the presence a yaws on Teressa and Bompoka, and of syphilis throughout the Southern Group. It would be highly beneficial to the people if the services of a Sub-Assistant Surgeon were procured to visit the islands regularly and keep down the ravages of these diseases which are a danger to the fertility of the race. A small oil-driven schooner costing about Rs. 35,000 would possibly solve the question of inter-island communication, and at the same time enable the Assistant Commissioner and Sub-Assistant Surgeon to visit the islands, and allow of a judicious supervision of the Central and Southern Groups which are at the moment in a state of isolation except for the very occasional visits of the Station Steamer.

(d) Religion of Kar Nikobar.

By the Rev. G. Stevenson.

With the exception of a small body of Christians and some Moslems and Buddhists the people of Kar Nikobar are animists.

People who write about them tend to say that they have no conception of a Supreme Being, but during one of their festivals in which the witch-doctors *to-milno-no,* who deal with the spirits of the dead and the evil spirits, take no part at all unless as laymen. On the day of "taking food", *kia-la,* in all the houses offerings of food in pots, coconuts and fruits of several kinds are hung up and the people make supplication: "Let our houses be always supplied with plenty to eat; let us have many things to eat from other villages; let there come new girls to our villages; grant us to be happy."

Their conception of a Supreme Being may be very vague and undefined, but this supplication seems to be addressed to some being or beings apart from the spirits of the dead and the evil spirits and who supposedly can hear prayer*.

Origin of the Kar Nicobarese.—What might be called the Kar Nicobarese Creation Legend is as follows: "There was once a great flood in the land and all the surface of the earth was covered by water. One man was lucky enough to swim to a big tree which was not entirely covered by the water. He lived among its branches until the floods went down, existing on coconuts and dead animals that were floating by his tree. When the waters were dried up he found no other living human being at all, but in the branches of another tree he found a bitch with her ear spiked to the tree by a great thorn. He climbed up the tree, released the animal and made her his wife. They lived together and had offspring that were human. So in these parts the people copy the dog in wearing the *ki-sat* (a very narrow loin-cloth with the ends hanging down behind) for it has tails hanging down like dog's tail. The head-dress worn by the man (*ta-chokla*—a band made of the spathe of the betel-palm with its ends crossed) is symbolic of the ears of their first mother and all dogs are treated kindly and are never beaten."

There is hardly much reason to suggest that this tale is a remnant of former missionary teaching; it is more likely a form of the Flood legend which is common over Indonesia.

NOTE.—Prehistoric Egyptian chiefs sometimes wore as a war dress a short kilt and a tail, said by the British Museum to be jackal's tail.

"The Khamis in the Arakan District of Burma have villages in the plains opposite Kyauktaw and elsewhere but they are a timid naked people and the population fled from the only village I entered as soon as they saw me. Khami women wear only a very short skirt and a triangular bit of cloth over the left breast—the breast specially dedicated to the husband. The men wear nothing but a quite inadequate waist band of very narrow cloth, and are said to regard nakedness as a sign of manhood. The ends of the loin-cloth hang down before and behind like tails and for this reason the Arakanese have corrupted the name Khami into Kwe-mi (Dog's tail)." From *A Burmese Wonderland*, C. M. Enriquez.

The Mono-Alu of the Solomons have a tale of a chief who married a bitch's daughter. The Angami Nagas have a story of descent from a white dog and a woman who floated away on a raft, while according to Purchase's *Pilgrimage* the Peguans ascribe their origin to a dog and a China-woman who escaped ship-wreck. The Ao-Nagas again have a dog clan, the Azukamr, who claim relationship with and the characteristics of dogs.—J. H. Hutton.

Spirits.—The Kar Nicobarese have an intense belief in evil spirits *sio-ta-choich,* who are the unseen enemies of mankind. They never bring happiness or prosperity but only sickness and misfortune of all kinds.

The spirits of the dead *ma-a-la-ha* are distinguished from these evil spirits. The spirits of the dead maintain to a great extent the kindly temperament that they had in life and are ready to do good services to those who are still alive. Many of them, however, miss the friends and companions of their life on earth and this desire for their company will cause them to bring sickness to these friends so that they too may die and join the spirits in the spirits' world. So this friendly intentioned sickness has to be guarded against as well as the sickness caused by the evil spirits.

When a Kar Nicobarese dies his spirit is seized by the evil spirits and is carried about with great rejoicing. The spirits of the dead then intervene and there is a struggle for the dead man's spirit. The struggle always ends in the victory of the spirits of the dead, who rescue their fellow and take him away to the Spirit world, a place, *El-ki-tel-ko-re,* which means "Mid-air", and there he lives on, very much as he did when alive on the earth.

Though those spirits of the dead live in "Mid-air", they can localize themselves and every village in Kar Nikobar has a place near it—avoided by all except the witch doctors called *panam-sio* (the place of the spirits) and there the witch doctors claim that they can meet and converse with the departed spirits.

* All the same it is probably a spell rather than a prayer, and magic rather than religion.—J. H. H.

Every year in July after the driving away of the evil spirits from the island the living provide food and clothing for the spirits of their relatives. When a man dies his belongings should also be destroyed as he will need them in the spirit-world, but often a pretence at this is enough.

The Driving away of the Evil Spirits.—Twice a year, in July and in November, the evil spirits are driven out of the villages.

During the day bamboos are got ready and decorated with bunches of leaves tied on them and all are daubed with soot and red paint. In the evening these are erected on the beach (*el panam*) and after sunset the people meet in the "Village Hall" and sing *ma-a-fai* songs; the lights are turned down and shaded with the spathe of the giant palm, because the evil spirits dread the light. The witch doctors then spear the devils with their magic spears made of a light, brittle wood—the devils squirm and squeak, making a noise such as one could make with a leaf between one's lips and drawing in one's breath. The captured spirits are tied up with a kind of creeper common in the island. The people help the witch doctors in wrestling and capturing spirits, after these are speared. This goes on for three nights, if necessary, until all the spirits possible are captured, and on the fourth evening the doctors go round all the houses in the village, and those on *el-panam*, spearing and capturing until no more can be caught. Meanwhile by day rafts have been got ready by the young men and women, as many in number as will be necessary to ship away the captured spirits. These rafts are equipped with sails of palm-leaves, dry palm leaf torches and bunches of evil-spirit-expelling leaves.

NOTE.—The Malays, who regard diseases as caused by spirits have the custom of setting a boat afloat sometimes with a man in charge and loaded with eatables apparently to take away the disease, and in Borneo the soul of the dead with an effigy of the dead man, and formerly sometimes a female slave fastened to the raft, is set afloat, while in Oceania generally the custom appears sporadically, sometimes having taken the form of sending the embalmed body of the dead adrift in a canoe. This again is clearly associated with the use of canoe coffins and inasmuch as it is frequently the spirits of the dead who cause the disease these treatments of evil spirits and of the ghosts or souls of the dead are probably intimately connected.—J. H. H.

The tied-up spirits are placed on the rafts, and each raft is put in charge of a spirit of the dead, represented by a leaf-made figure about four feet high. The rafts are towed out beyond the breaking surf, those engaged in this task keeping the spirit-expelling leaves in their hands, and finally with great rejoicing the rafts are carried off by wind and tide.

The bamboos are then taken down and any evil spirits that happen to have been over-looked before are speared and thrown into the sea.

After this follow the feasts for the dead, referred to above. This feeding and clothing of the departed spirits is done partly because they will need these things in the spirit world and partly because they have helped in the driving away of the evil spirits.

Another expulsion of the evil spirits takes place in November but this time they are thrown into the sea only and not placed on rafts, as the winds is from the north-east, neither is there any feast for the dead.

At other times when an accident happens such as a man falling from a coco-palm and killing himself, the evil spirits in the place of the accident are driven down to the beach and deported or thrown into the sea.

Marriage, Birth, etc.—There is no marriage ceremony. The young man who desires to marry a girl makes friends with her family, helps her in her daily work and sleeps for a time in whatever house she may occupy.

During the night he seeks the girl, who will be sleeping among other girls, and by blowing on the lighted end of a cigarette he obtains light enough to discriminate. If the girls does not care for him she will resist with blows and scratches.

This will continue for several nights until, if she is willing to have him for a husband, she yields herself. When they begin living as man and wife both live with the girl's parents and he works for them. No dowry is given and no marriage settlements made. Formerly it was a crime punishable by death for either to commit adultery, but now a fine of three pigs is the penalty.

When the wife is pregnant—during the last two months—both parents must abstain from certain foods and certain kinds of actions as also for some time after birth. When the mother-to-be goes down to a birth-house on *el-panam* her husband goes with her. The birth of a child must take place in birth-house for if it took place in a ceremonially clean house, that house would have to be destroyed.

When the young mothers living on *el-panam* (the parents of a child do not usually go back to their houses until three months after its birth) hear that the labour pains have come, they will arrive to massage the woman and the inexperienced will be taught the art of midwifery by the experienced. If the delivery is delayed it means that the child is being held back by something closed or knotted about the house and though care has been taken beforehand to see that no belongings of the parents are boxed up or knotted in any way, a new search is made and care is taken that the door of the hut and the lids of any boxes are left open so that the delivery of the child may not be hampered in any way. The men will lift up the racing canoes of the village an inch or two and let them down again, and if there are any logs or heavy articles lying about they will turn them over.

While the woman is pregnant neither she nor her husband must make anything tight such as nailing a board or tying knots, for fear the spirit of the unborn-child should get fastened up in these and delivery be rendered impossible.

After the birth of the child the mother and baby are rubbed over with saffron and their clothes dyed with it. The mother is for some time ceremonially unclean and may not feed herself nor touch her food with her fingers.

The husband looks after the mother, supplying all her needs and he may not do any heavy work nor walk in the sun nor bathe in the sea until the child is a month old, so that it may not get sick.

Another reason for his not walking in the sun is given also. If the child is born light-skinned the husband may not go in the sun without an umbrella, lest the child's skin should become dark.

When the child is two or three months old it is well rubbed over with fowl's blood mixed with certain crushed leaves supplied by a witch doctor or other experienced person and also with the crushed shells of young coconuts and saffron. This is repeated monthly until the child can walk.

When the baby is three months, and in some cases not till it is six months old, the parents and child will return to their village but they must leave behind them all cooking pots, clothing, mats, etc., which they have been using for these are ceremonially unclean and will render unclean any house they are brought into.

The child's first food, other than its mother's milk, will be the tender part of the green coconut—the part nearest the shell. This is mixed with pandanus paste and warmed over a fire. It may not eat fish until it is over five years old.

If there are in the parent's opinion too many children in the family they will often give one away to another husband and wife who have too few children or are childless. Children handed over in this way are rarely claimed again.

If twins were born one of the twins used to be killed. A child born deformed was put to death also, as births of this kind (twins or deformities) were regarded as entirely abnormal, in fact contrary to nature. This is not done now, but the parents and those in attendance are horrified when such birth takes place.

The child, if a boy, as he grows up looks forward to the time when he can go to Chaura. This happens usually about the age of six or seven, and when he has done this he has won his spurs and can regard himself as a man.

Death and Burial, etc.—Death is feared among the Kar Nicobarese and even the word will not be mentioned. When a man is about to die he is usually brought to a "Death house" on the beach (*el-panam*) and there is left to die, the leaves which are said to keep away evil spirits having been placed around his bed.

When he is dead each group of houses in his village provides two yards of red cotton cloth and two yards of white in which the corpse is wrapped after having been washed with coconut water. If the deceased is wealthy he may be adorned with silver wire and necklaces of coins. When the time for the funeral comes the corpse is lifted by two men and brought down the ladder in as upright a position as possible to the relatives waiting below, where it is bound to pieces of old canoe to make it rigid and easier to carry to burial. The relatives weep and wail and pretend not to want the corpse buried but brought back to his own house in the village. The rest of the community wish it to be buried, so there is a struggle about the corpse (which sometimes suffers in the struggle), the relatives trying to take it towards the village, the others towards the burial ground.

It never reaches the village partly because those for burying are in the majority and also because if brought into the village it would render it ceremonially unclean.

When the burial ground, also on *el-panam*, is reached the corpse is put into the grave prepared for it, the wrappings over the region of the heart of the deceased are pulled aside and chickens and sometimes young pigs are stabbed and the blood allowed to drip on the body over the heart of the deceased.

These are then thrown into the grave and buried with the corpse. All the bedding, wraps, etc., used by the deceased while sick are burned and vessels, etc., are broken in pieces and the ashes and pieces are thrown into the sea.

A feast is then provided by the people living in the same group of houses as the deceased used to live in. The mourners rest next day and after a certain number of days—there seems to be no special number of days except that the number must be odd not even, there is a purification of the deceased and a chicken is burnt over the grave. Until this ceremony has been performed the mourners must not sing or laugh or dance, nor eat any fruit except coconut and bread-fruit (pandanus). Those who have handled the corpse are unclean for a month or two and may not touch their food with their fingers or hands, though they may use a small skewer. They may not to do any "clean" work, such as that concerned with the preparation of food or building, nor may they enter any house. When this period of uncleanness is over they may return to their work and houses without any purification ceremony.

At the purification festival mentioned above the memorial post of the deceased is set up. This is a round log about a foot in diameter buried until about two to three feet of it is above the ground. A short distance from the top there is a hole cut through and while the feast is being kept a stick is put through the hole and spoons and forks are hung on the stick. These spoons and forks are removed later, but sometimes other spoons and coins are nailed on the post and these are not removed. There is a feast also at this purification festival held generally in the "Village Hall" after sunset, and a basket of pork is provided for the deceased and hung up for the night in the door of the house. Next morning the basket and its contents are thrown into the sea and the memorial post is set over the grave. Again there is a feast in the village hall in the morning and this finishes the whole burial ceremony.

Nowadays some of the richer people have coffins for their dead relatives, an imitation of European custom and sometimes the body is carried to the burial ground in a canoe, which is said to be an old custom at the burial of rich people. The canoe is afterwards cut up and broken to pieces.

After the burial ceremony the name of the deceased is not mentioned and if another man in the same village has the same name as deceased he will change it, or if the deceased bore a name like fire or water the relatives will henceforth use a synonym for this when mentioning it.

Feast for the Dead.—Once in 3 or 4 years a feast for the departed is held in a village. The villagers some ten months beforehand have agreed on the time about which it will be held and preliminary invitations are sent out to other villages. After these invitations are sent out, a tree of about 60 feet high is cut down and holes are bored at intervals all along the stem after the branches have been removed, and pegs are driven into the hole. When this has been done the post is set up in an arranged spot, with posts fixed alongside it, to which it is tied in order to steady it. A man climbs the post with the end of a rope in his hand. Fruit, baskets of pork, etc., are drawn up by this rope and fastened on the pegs, until sometimes there is a great array of food.

If the villagers are poor this post may not be set up. Bamboo cages able to hold about a dozen pigs are made in the village about the same time. Canoes are decorated and set up in front of their own houses. The graveyard on *el-panam* and part of the beach around it are tidied up and kept tidy. All this takes about three months and during that time no pigs may be killed in the village. Then the date is definitely fixed and special invitations are sent out saying that on the day after tomorrow the houses will be decorated, on the third day the pigs will be put into the cages and on the fourth day they will be killed.

This date may fall at any time of the year except that for convenience's sake the wet seaon is avoided and the months of November and December are chosen which are cold.

Pigs are brought into the village from outside having their legs tied to a pole and they are carried round the village before being put into the cages.

Soon after the special invitations are sent out the nearest visitors begin to arrive. These visitors will dance all night by the group of houses where the post with the food on it has been erected. Next morning the post is cut down and the food, putrid or fresh, is thrown into the jungle. A pig is taken and sacrificed and the intestines and some of the flesh are placed on coconut leaves over the place where the post stood.

Then the pigs for the feast are slaughtered near the village and singed over the flames of palm leaf torches. After a mid-day feast the visitors all receive a portion of pork. Every part of a pig except the lungs and lower jaw bone is given away. After this distribution some of the visitors return home, though many wait for the pig-wrestling*. Some of the most savage pigs are let out of the cages in the late afternoon and men who are skilled in the sport seize these pigs by the ears and hold them. Sometimes a man is bitten or gored by the tusks of the pigs; any pig that injures a man is speared at once. Young folk may not eat the flesh of such a pig, only the older people. No reason is given for this except that it is the custom. After this is over more of the guests will return home.

Next day the fat pigs are reduced to lard, which is stored in coconut shells. There will be dancing through the night by the villagers and any visitors who have stayed on.

On the following days preparations are made for digging up the bones by the deceased's friends. Water is drawn from wells and covered over with leaves. The women squat by the memorial posts at the graves and lament. A fence of palm leaves is made right round the burial ground, except for one exit near the unclean place in the jungle where the bones are thrown away.

Then the bones of those who have been dead for two years or more are dug up, a witch doctor standing by each grave and keeping evil spirits away by waving a bunch of the leaves that keep away evil spirits. If by chance the bones are found to have flesh on them they are put back and covered over again to await the next festival. Otherwise the skull is wiped clean by hand, wrapped in white calico and placed on a spathe of palm. The other bones are taken out one by one and placed on the same spathe. This is then carried to the Dead House on *el-panam* and placed on top of big yams that are scattered under the Dead House for this purpose.

Then this spathe containing all the bones is wrapped round with white and red calico. When all the digging is completed and the bones wrapped up, the bundles containing the bones of more important people are reinterred in the grave from which they were taken, the others are carried to the unclean place in the jungle and the bones are scattered there and the cloth torn to rags.

After all this the grave diggers go down to the sea and wash their hands and legs or bathe.

Witch Doctors.—In Kar Nikobar only of these islands is there a novitiate to the School of Witch Doctors These novices are called *ma-a-fai* and they may be of either sex, though female applicants are very rare. If a man or boy is of a sickly nature the witch doctors usually want him as a novice and at night will throw into the house where he resides some leaves such as they use for their charms and perhaps one or two chickens with their legs tied together. When these are found the sickly man's friends know that the spirits are calling him and he must become a novice. A day is fixed for his novitiate and just before sunset the witch doctors and friends of the man or boy thump the ground under the house with stems of the coconut leaf, each one holding in his hand a bunch of evil-spirit expelling leaves.

The novice is meanwhile lying on his back on the floor of the house. Then the people all go up and spread over him several large banana leaves. To each leaf several wing feathers of a fowl are festened and singed. Soon after the leaves are removed and a witch doctor finds several small lizards which are presumed to have come out of the novice's body and to have been the cause of his sickness.

Early next morning the novice is decked out with the jewellery of the witch doctors as well as with other jewellery lent by friends. His arms and legs are covered with silver wire and round his neck are necklets of two-anna pieces. A throne is made for him on which he is seated and he is given a magic spear and a sceptre. In this chair he may afterwards be carried from village to village, though this is rarely done.

After a few days he goes with his friends to the edge of the jungle where *pa-nam sio* (the place of the spirits) is. The friends remain behind and he goes with the witch doctors and is introduced to the spirits.

Then all go to the novice's house where dancing takes place and songs are sung. This singing and dancing takes place frequently during the novitiate of the person, which lasts about a year. During that novitiate he may do no work of any kind and may not even touch a dah. He may remain all his life a *ma-a-fai* if he wishes, or he may resign, for which there is a special ceremony, but if he wishes to carry on he is promoted to the ranks of the *to-mi-luo-no*, and then may work if he chooses.

These *to-mi-luo-no* deal with the evil spirits that are such a terror to the ordinary man and which bring sickness and all kinds of misfortune.

Eclipses.—These may perhaps come under the head of religion, though in this case evil spirits are not the cause of the eclipse but a python who according to the Island folk-tales was a man at one time.

This python now and again starts swelling up either the sun or moon. When this begins the people collect and beat tins or anything that will make a noise and shout "Vomit it out". The python pays no heed to their calls but goes on swallowing. Then as the sun or moon is swallowed the cry changes to "Evacuate it" and to this cry the python does pay heed and the people get back their sun or moon again.

Christianity.—The first attempt to Christianise the people of Kar Nikobar was made by Jesuit missionaries in 1711, but the settlers succumbed to the effects of the climate and all traces of their work soon disappeared.

About 1834 or 1835 two Roman Catholic missionaries arrived on the island from Malacca. These were expelled from the island and went on to Teressa and Kamorta, where one died and the other left.

Captain Gardener in the Singapore Review, Volume II, gives an account of two Moravian missionaries being expelled in 1851.

"Having converted a few natives," he says, "dispute arose between them and their heathen countrymen. They were of such a serious nature that it was determined to hold a general council of delegates from every village to consider a remedy for the evil. They came to the conclusion, that, as they had always lived in love and amity with each other before the arrival of the missionaries, with their stange story of the first women stealing the orange, etc., the obvious remedy was to send them away. Accordingly the missionaries were waited upon and told respectfully that they must leave at the first opportunity, that the natives were not to be joked with, and must be obeyed.

* Similarly the Ao Nagas of Assam wrestle with the mithun (gayal) bulls which are to be sacrificed.—J. H. H.

The Mission house was then burned down and a fence erected around the spot, inside which no native will step. It is unholy ground, they say, where the devil first landed ; for until the missionaries brought him with them, he had never been in the island or knew where it was. I was told that a day is now set apart in the year when all the inhabitants assemble to drive the devil out of the island."

In 1886 Mr. Solomon, a Madrassi of the Anglican Communion, became Agent in the island. He acted also as a School master and Catechist, and under him for the first time in the island's history Christianity made some progress.

Of him, Sir R. C. Temple, the Chief Commissioner, in a lecture given in 1899 before the Indian Section of the Society of Arts said : " He is imbued with an untiring enthusiam resting on a foundation of much common sense, and by the exercise of these qualities he has acquired a remarkable ascendancy over the people, used for their good............Mr. Solomon's efforts to keep up peace and goodwill between village and village are practical''.

The first Christian to be baptized was Rose, a female, on the 24th of July 1900 and since then the number of Christians has been slowly increasing.

There is no resident Chaplain on the island. The Rev. George Whitehead lived amongst the people for some years and put their language into writing with the assistance of Mr. J. Richardson, the Nicobarese Head-master of the school, and produced a Prayer Book and some reading books comprised mainly of legends common to the people as well as extracts from the Old and New Testaments. With this exception the Nicobarese Christians as Catechist and teachers and members of the Church Committee carry on the spiritual and educational work themselves with occasional visits (about five times a year) from the Chaplain at Port Blair, who administers the small grant by the Indian Government for educational and hospital work on the island, and supervises the work of the hospital and the five schools that are there.—G. S.

ABSTRACT FROM A LECTURE DELIVERED AT THE CLINICAL SOCIETY OF PORT BLAIR ON 13TH FEBRUARY 1932.

(e) Yaws in the Nicobar Islands.

By Major A. J. D'Souza, I.M.S., Senior Medical Officer, Port Blair.

Incidence of Yaws in the Nicobar Islands is not mentioned in standard books on Tropical Medicine (Manson and Castellani). I have received reports from time to time, since my arrival in Port Blair, that syphilis is very prevalent in the Nicobars, causing severe disfiguration of the inhabitants and threatening the extinction of the race. Two typical cases of yaws in the secondary stage were noticed by me among Nicobarese who were sent to Port Blair for a trial for murder and were cured with 2 injections of N. A. B. (O. 6 & O. 9 Grams) in 1930 : and it transpired that the cases reported to be suffering from syphilis in the Nicobars may be cases of yaws. I understand that Lt.-Col. Barker, I.M.S., S.M.O. in Port Blair, in 1924 brought a case of yaws from the Nicobars and demonstrated the lesions at a meeting of the Clinical Society, but I fail to find any record of the prevalence of this disease in the Nicobars. An opportunity occurred for investigation, when the Census Superintendent for the Andaman and Nicobar islands required the services of a Sub-Assistant Surgeon to record the anthropological measurements of the Andamanese and Nicobarese in connection with his report for these islands. Dr. Naidu was deputed for this work, and after receiving preliminary instructions in the use of instruments for taking these measurements in Calcutta, he proceeded to Nicobars on 7th February 1931. I sent him well equipped with what I considered an adequate supply of N. A. B. in the hope of temporarily ameliorating the condition of people and awaiting a report from him as to any further steps to be taken to combat the disease. I may mention that the Andaman islands are free from yaws, while syphilis and gonorrhœa are common and are principally responsible for undermining the fertility of the Andamanese. Dr. Naidu worked under difficult conditions with regard to language and time limit and the discomfort of a camp life from 7th February 1931 to 18th March 1931. From his report it would appear that an interesting study of tropical diseases could be made in these islands. His time was limited for a study of the local conditions, as well as of the diseases prevalent among the inhabitants living in the various villages. The principal diseases prevalent in both the Great and Little Nikobar as well as the Central Group are yaws and elephantiasis. Altogether he treated 60 cases of yaws :—

		Nos.
Little Nikobar.—	Pulo Milo	1
Great Nikobar.—	Kondul	2
	Pulobabi	3
	Shompen camp Alexandra river	1
Central Group.—	Bompoka	4
	Nankauri	7
	Chaura	9
	Teressa	33
	Total	60

He also noticed that at Chaura, out of a total population of about 600, 35 were showing visible signs of elephantiasis. During the course of his whole journey he came across only two cases of syphilis—one contracted at Nankauri and the other at Kar Nikobar—both trading centres for the outside world with a floating population of eastern nationals. He had a large out-patients' attendance wherever he camped. The people from different islands appreciated the treatment given and expressed a desire to Mr. Bonington, Census Superintendent, and to Dr. Naidu that they wanted the whole-time services of a doctor for the island. If a doctor could be appointed for them, Teressa or Camorta would be a central place for a hospital or dispensary. As regards medical facilities for the Nicobars, a doctor appointed by the Kar Nikobar Mission (subsidised by the local Government) is stationed at Kar Nikobar in charge of a hospital and a small dispensary in charge of a compounder is established at Nankauri ; but there are no amenities for treatment at any of the other islands, unless the inhabitants can go in fine weather to either of these centres. Dr. Naidu exhausted his stock of N. A. B.

in treating cases of yaws before he returned. On receiving his report I proceeded to the Nicobars with Dr. Naidu in April 1931 with a plentiful supply of N. A. B. We took the opportunity of examining some of the cases that had received an injection two months previously. The inhabitants were so impressed with the efficacy of the treatment that more cases eagerly sought treatment and the following number was treated :—

Central Group :—	
Chaura	10
Teressa	35
Nankauri	2
Total ..	47

This number would have been considerably higher if it lad been possible to send information beforehand to the various villages of our impending visit. The cases that had received an injection in February or March had all healed up with the exception of two who still manifested latent infection and indolent sores. These were given a second injection each. We studied together the disease, local peculiarities and notions of the disease which are given under their appropriate headings in the lecture.

Injections.—Conditions under which they were given were not ideal. No previous preparation of the patient was possible and sterilization and preparation of solution and administration of injection were all performed in the centre of a group of anxious and expectant patients and their friends and relations either on the deck of the boat or on a sandy shore. *There were no accidents or ill effects and pain was negligible.* As even the three children who were given the injections did not cry nor make a noise to resent the treatment. It was useless to advise them to rest after the injections ; but they departed happily hoping to be cured of the disease in the same way as their friends were on the previous occasion.

Yaws (Framboesia).

Island.	Local synonyms for yaws.	For syphilis.
Teressa ..	.. *Aiyoke*	.. *Thannoi.*
Chaura ..	.. *Aiyak*	.. *Sakayee.*

Although they do not bear any relation to the native names mentioned by Manson or Castellani, there is a resemblance in phonation in the local synonyms for yaws in the two islands, while it is noteworthy that the names for syphilis are distinct and definite without any such similarity.

Definition.—Yaws is a chronic contagious inoculable disease of a granulomatous type with an indefinite and lengthy incubation period, which is followed by constitutional symptoms such as fever, malaise, pains in muscles and bones and joints, subsiding with the development of granuloma. In its progress there are three well defined stages, the granulomata varying in each stage in sites, number and extent.

Geographical distribution and endemicity.—The Nicobar islands may be regarded as a continuation of the chain of islands of the Malay Archipelago and is adjacent to the endemic areas of yaws, *viz.*, Upper Burma, Assam, Siam, Ceylon, Java, and Sumatra. As the sanitation is primitive and conditions are ideal for the maintenance of infection in the way of primitive huts whose floors and walls may be impregnated with infection and where human beings, dogs and pigs live together, it is easy to understand how this endemic disease may rapidly take on an epidemic form ; although it has not been possible to trace any epidemicity to this disease in any of the islands where intelligible information has been available. We have not been able to trace any cases to house infection nor to direct insect bites. We are of opinion that infection is most likely conveyed by insects, *e.g.*, flies from a yaws sore infecting a pre-existing sore such as an ordinary sore or itch pustules or scratches or breaches on the skin, which are numerous, owing to the jungle life the people lead. It is quite possible that house infection is important judging by the habits of the people but our conclusion is based on the innumerable flies we saw settling on yaws sorce and it is easily conceivable how such flies can convey the spirochoetes to pre-existing breaches of skin. Principal occupations of the people are cultivation of coconut and tobacco, pig breeding and fishing. While it has been observed by authorities on yaws that the disease has a predilection for certain native races, particularly of the negro or negrito stock, it is not known among the Andamanese who belong to the Negrito stock, although syphilis is very common among them, and yaws exists endemically within 150 miles of these islands.

Symptoms .. .. 3 stages are differentiated.

(1) Primary stage of infiltrated nodule.

(2) Secondary stage of granulomatous eruptions.

(3) Tertiary stage of deep ulcerations and gummatous nodules and bone lesions.

There is no para stage corresponding to syphilis.

Primary stage.—"Madre Buba or Mother Yaws". An infiltrated papule develops at the site of inoculation or a granuloma in an old skin lesion such as an ulcer, itch pustule or insect bite or any abrasion and scratch incidental to a jungle life. In the initial stage, they complained of intense itching lasting for about a week.

Secondary stage or stage of generalized eruptions.—The onset of this stage corresponds with the decline of constitutional symptoms and most of our cases treated were well advanced in the secondary stage. Generalised eruption is ushered in as follows :—Minute roundish papules of the size of a pin head are seen with a yellow crush at the apex usually three months after the primary lesion, lasting a few weeks and leaving when they disappear furaceous patches ; these patches are circular and show a fine sand-colored desquamation as if the skin has been dusted over with flour or atta. This condition was only noticed in one of our cases. Some papules coalesce, enlarge and skin gets proliferated or hyperkeratoid.

Tertiary stage.—This is a stage of gummatous nodules and deep ulcerative processes. The transition period between secondary and tertiary stages differs widely from that of syphilis. Instead of getting absorbed and healing, yaws may spread marginally as well as deeply and leading to extensive ulcers which may last for years. Such ulcers may ivolve deep structures producing necrosis of bone or cartilage or give rise to cicatrical contractures in the process of healing or from immobility of joints, and it is said that in such cases (8 per cent. according to Manson) typical lesions of yaws disappear and the ulcer is non-infective.

Feet, Crab Yaws and Clavus.—Yaws in the soles of feet is limited by thick skin. Like an abscess in this region, it is under high tension. It attains a large size before it bursts and is therefore very painful. When the thick epidermis gives way, yaws is converted into a fungating ulcer and although painful to the touch is not painful to the same degree as it was before it burst through skin. This ulcer, after the pent up secretion, oozes out, appears like the section of a pomagranate cut through with a knife.

"Gangosa".—This is a destructive disfiguring process with deep ulceration of the nose and pharynx and is said to commence as an ulcer of the soft palate. It spreads slowly and leads to complete destruction of hard palate, soft parts, cartilage and bones of nose; in some cases sparing the upper lip as a bridge, in other cases leading to its partial destruction. A great cavity is left with the tongue as the floor, which remains unaffected.

Bone Lesions.—These are common in the tertiary stage. As in syphilis painful nodes on the anteror surfaces of long bones such as tibia, radius, ulna and clavicle, hard, tender and painful in the beginning remain as thickenings when acuteness subsides.

The charactristic sabre-shaped deformity of long bones affecting tibia, forearms, arms, and clavicle and digits was noticed.

General Health.—Yaws is a chronic disease which does not appear to incapacitate its victims from carrying on their vocation or occupation so far as the Nicobar Islands are concerned. Perhaps the early constitutional disturbances may restrict their movements, although from the information gathered not to any appreciable extent.

In spite of their animistic ideas of religion, they appear to be grateful for western methods of treatment and need no persuasion to be injected, as they have gained faith after the first course of injections given as to the efficiency of our means of curing the disease.

They believe that it is a chronic but not fatal disease. Although at Teressa many adults are reported to have died of the disease only 3 children under 10 have died at Chaura from yaws within the last 3 years. We have to take into consideration an outbreak of small-pox which may have been responsible for the large number of deaths reported at Teressa.

Treatment.—With limited time at our disposal the only treatment tried was injections of Novarsenobillon

0·9 grams. for adults.

0·6 grams. for young adults.

0·3 grams. for children up to 10 years of age.

One injection appears to have cured most of the cases, although this needs confirmation by a second visit to the islands to examine the cases that have been injected.

Treatment adopted by the Nicobarese.—At Chaura, application of certain leaves (*rafab*) according to them appears to check the disease. At Teressa the ulcers are rubbed with sand and then washed in sea water, which is supposed to irritate the ulcers and assist cleaning, and a paste of leaves (*ramintho*) made by boiling and grinding is then applied. Ulcers are said to disappear in a few cases after a series of applications. The inhabitants appear healthy and well nourished and yaws did not affect their general health, so that the prescription of tonics, good food as general treatment was not necessary in them.

Prophylaxis.—To prevent contagion and spread of this disease, it would be necessary to isolate and segregate infected cases and give them N. A. B. injections—one, two or three according to the response and keep them under observation. House infection cannot be eliminated unless the thatched houses are burnt down, and sanitation in and around inhabited houses improved, but such measures are impracticable in an uncivilised country. In my opinion the only way of adopting prophylactic measures for the eradication of the disease is to appoint a medical officer with a steam launch at his disposal for one year so that he can visit all islands in turn periodically and give appropriate treatment where necessary. Each endemic area needs to be visited at least once in three months.

In concluding this lecture I wish to express my thanks to Dr. D. Naidu for his loyal co-operation and help in collecting statistics and local information and in treating cases under adverse conditions.

Note by the Census Superintendent.—This abstraction from a paper written by Major A. J. D'Souza, I.M.S., is of value as indicating the extent of yaws in the Nicobars. It shows that the disease is prevalent throughout the Central and Southern groups and was found to exist even among the Shom-Pen. It is particularly virulent in Teressa where out of 17 villages only one was visited in the 24 hours spent on the island while a few patients came on board from another village. Yet 68 persons were treated at Teressa. There are only 437 persons on the island so it seems not too high to estimate that about half of the inhabitants are infected with this dreadful disease which without modern treatment takes a course almost identical to that of syphilis when not treated, and as Major D'Souza says it threatens to exterminate the inhabitants. I am grateful to Major D'Souza for his kind co-operation in placing Dr. Damodaram Naidu at my disposal during my visit to these islands for without this co-operation the extent of the disease would not have come to light. Dr. Naidu having been previously in East Africa where the disease is not uncommon, recognized it at once. It is to be regretted that owing to the difficulty of keeled transport and the short time at our disposal we were unable to visit all the outlying villages of the different groups. It is however desirable that an extensive visit be made in the near future by a medical officer so that the disease may at any rate be kept within limits if not entirely exterminated. The number of small coffins with the remains of the bones of deceased relatives in the different huts, 6 to 12 in number, also indicate the high death rate, most of them had probably died within the last year or two, for it is usual for the remains to be thrown into a common ossuary periodically at the ossuary feast.

M. C. C. BONINGTON.

18. Notes on Madras Tribes.

By M. W. M. Yeatts, etc.

(a) Kuruman (Kurumba) and Paliyan.

The following notes are based on information supplied by Mr. J. Selvanayakam.

The Kurumban of the Nilgris live on the lower slopes of the hills in small groups of houses called 'Kombais.' 'Kombai' is Kanarese for sheepfold, a circumstance which points to the origin of the tribe and a former identity with the shephered Kurumbas of the Deccan and Mysore. They have two divisions, Nagar and Belagar, which operate only for purposes of exogamy ; no apparent difference survives between them. The chief man is called a mudali and succession is to his eldest son. If he has none, a new mudali is elected. Each mudali is supposed to be watchman and sorcerer to a group of Badaga villages and something like the kaval system of the plains exists here, for one of the mudali's chief tasks is to see that no other Kurumba injures the Badagas in the Mudali's charge. Tributes for puja performance and probably abstention from sorcery are paid by Badagas to Kurumbas and a common belief is that no Badaga girl can expect a peaceful married life unless the Kurumbas have been duly fed.

Every Kombai has two plain upright stones on a raised platform, one supposed to be male, the other female. These are taken to represent the ancestral abode. Huts are generally built near stone outcrops which can be used as seats. Nothing in housing, apparel or ceremony indicates social position. All feast together, old and young, male and female, and several from one leaf.

The sun they consider male and the moon female. The man in the moon is the hare which was chased by the snake ; the moon prevents the snake from swallowing the hare till the sun rises.

Marriage is easy and widows can remarry. Marital customs are distinctly free. Childbirth must not take place within the ordinary hut. The dead are generally burnt, the Mudali and his family however being buried and also small children. There is occasional variation in these details but what is unchanging is the keeping of a stone to represent the deceased. These stones are all deposited in a cave reserved for the purpose in each Kombai.

They are skilful musicians and claim that the Kotas have copied this art from them. They make their own flutes, etc.

Their Gods are Herugudian, God of sowing, Mari, Goddess of rain, Mahalinga the male God, Masani a female (*cf.* Masanagudi in Mysore) *plus* the Hindu pantheon. Their chief God, however, says my cynical informant, 'is their own belly'.

Sholagars. The Sholagars are essentially a tribe of one taluk, Gopichettipalaiyam, in Coimbatore, all but 3 per cent. of their total of 2,878 being recorded there. The 1931 total is in accord with the figures of 1891 and 1921 and is probably a close approximation. The 5,700 of 1901 and 1,900 of 1911 are inexplicably high and low and probably non-Sholagars are present in the first and Sholagars omitted from the second. Over 1921-31 the increase is 6½ per cent. and over 1891—1931 is 5·9 per cent.

The so-called '7-Kula' Sholagars are really the tribe described by Thurston as Uralis and speak mostly a form of Tamil as opposed to the true Sholagars' Kanarese patois. The two however intermarry, according to Mr. R. C. Morris, who has had Sholagars on his estate for 20 years, and is my informant on the tribe. According to Thurston there was no intermarriage, though Sholagars and Uralis would eat together. The Uralis will not intermarry with the Irulas of the Nilgiris. The Sholagars proper ('5-Kula') claim to be of higher status (so do the 7-Kulas, however) but actually no precedence is observed. The Uralis say they hailed originally from Girikarur and Arkud in the Nilgiris and the presence of an Urali temple at the foot of Rangaswami's Pillai in that district is possibly an indication of such an origin. It is an incident in their burial customs that some of the remains of the dead or a handful of earth from his grave should be taken generally 6—12 months after burial to this temple and reburied there. The Uralis usually put a small piece of jewellery such as a ring in the corpse's mouth. The 5-Kula Sholagars frequently bury a personal belonging, knife, axe, etc., with the corpse.

There are definite traces of terraced cultivation on the Biligirirangam Hills but the Sholagars deny any connection and say the terracing was done by a pigmy tribe long since vanished. They have no megalithic or other monuments and do not use stone for seats. The caste headman's house is usually larger than the others but there is nothing else to indicate superior status, either in his house or attire. The social organisation seems rather to have weakened for among the 5-Kulas only two of the five offices which used to be filled one by each Kula now survive, that of Ejmana, or caste head, chosen from the fourth and Chik-Ejmana chosen from the 5th (Surya Kula). The duties of the last named are to summon panchayats when required to preserve order at feasts and ceremonies, and quasi-hieratic functions. The Monegar, Judge and Chieftain are no longer appointed.

The 5-Kulamen are better trackers and jungle men generally whereas the 7-Kula specialise more in trapping. Both have lost the art of fire making by wood friction. The matchbox has conquered here too.

Paliyans. Paliyans live in small isolated groups all along the Western Ghats from the Palni Hills in the north down to the Tinnevelly Hills in the south. The note below by Mr. R. Foulkes, O.B.E., of Madura, covers all general matters relating to the tribe. Inevitably, however, in such circumstances of dispersion local differences arise. These are nowhere very considerable however. The Paliyans near Kuttalam in Tinnevelly declare that their ancestors fled from the persecutions of some Nawab. This may possibly refer to Tippu. Tinnevelly Paliyans seem generally to be called Karatu whereas the Madura ones are known as Kavu. Several small groups of Paliyans have diverged almost entirely from the tribal customs. In their case the effect of Christianization has been almost entire assimilation to plains types and customs. Other Paliyans ordinarily will have nothing whatever to do with their Christian fellow-tribesmen. Among Paliyans, as in other tribes, racial intermixture takes much wider range among Christians than among those adhering to the tribal faith. An interesting variation from the account given by Mr. Foulkes is from the Tahsildar of Periyakulam who declares that males are buried with face upwards but females with face downwards. This point would require however further elucidation. Among the Paliyans of the Saptur Hills, according to Mr. J. A. Vedanayakan, it is the bridegroom's sister who ties the beads round the bride's neck at a marriage, and there is a kind of banns proclamation, one man announcing in a loud voice that a marriage is in the making at a certain house and another elderly Paliyan from an adjoining group of huts calls out the community's assent in a loud 'yes.' The same Paliyans hunt sambhur with a sharpened heavy stick which they hurl with some skill like a javelin. The Tahsildar of Periyakulam reports to the same effect. Apparently the Saptur Paliyans abandon their hut on the mere occurrence of death, not only for an epidemic visitation.

It seems to be a general circumstance for Paliyans (other than Christians) to be peculiarly attached to their tribal life and customs and to be hardy and long-lived. Mr. Vedanayakan thinks there must be more than one Paliyan centenarian.

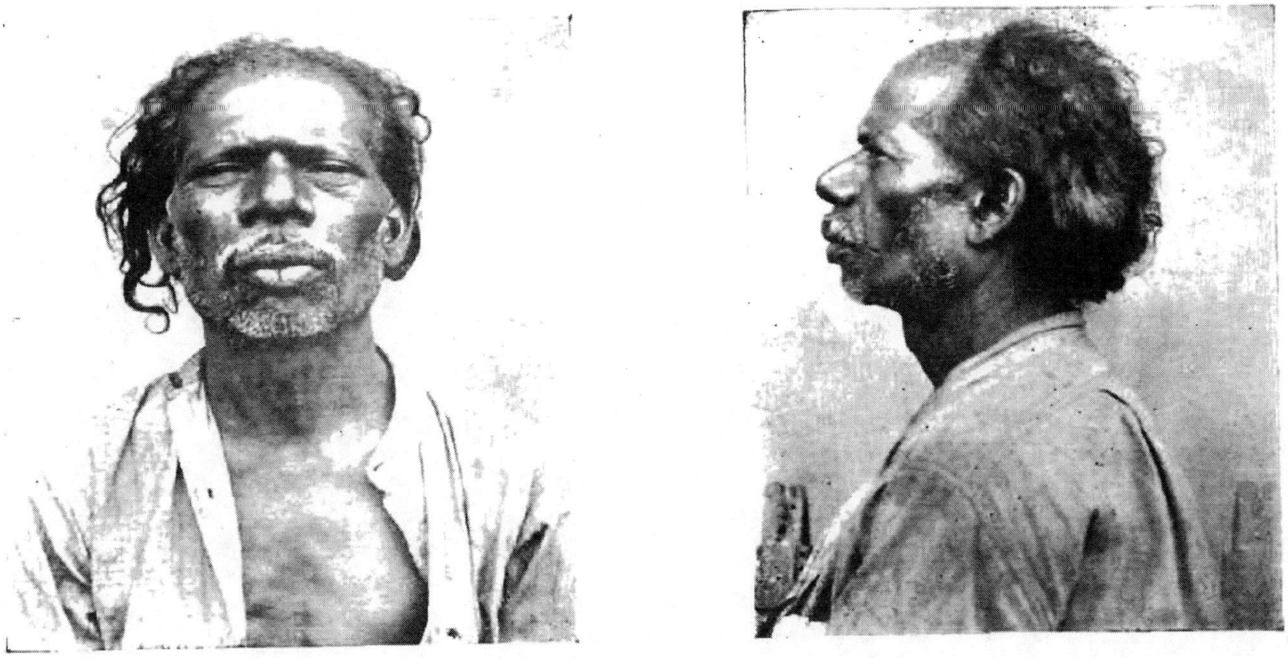

Paliyan Male.

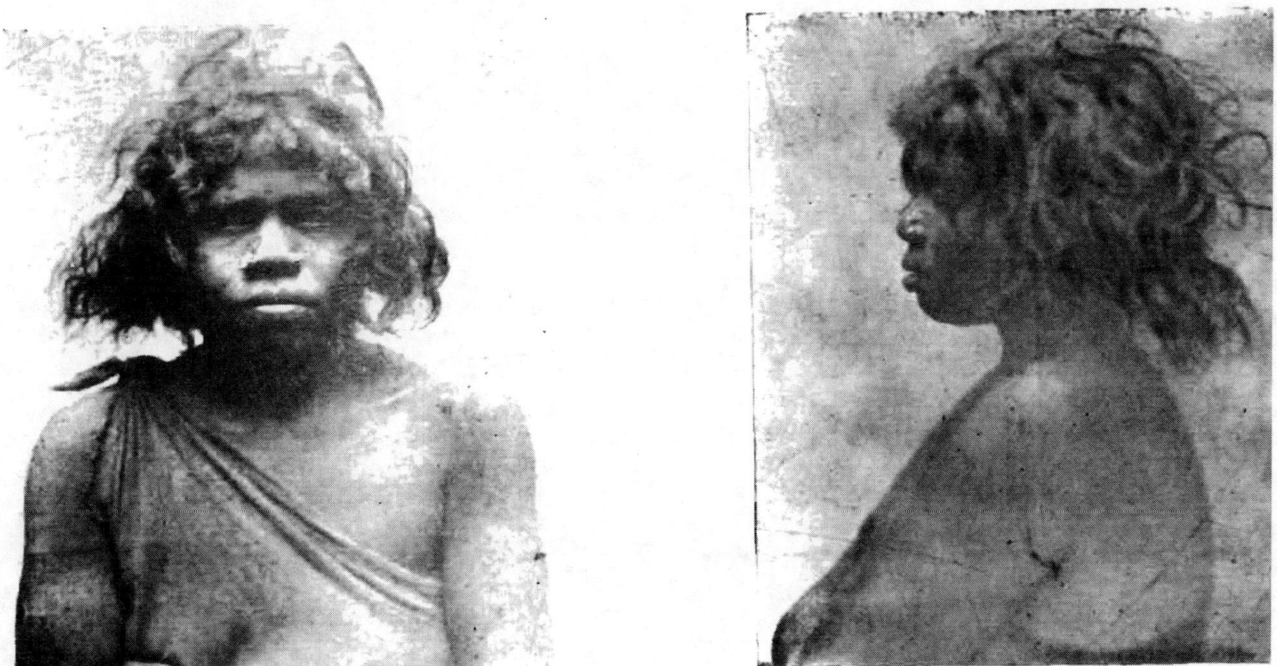

Paliyan Female.

(b) A note on the Paliyans of the Madura district.

By R. Faulkes, Esq., O.B.E.

Religion.—The Paliyans worship Palichi-Ammal (Palichi, female of Paliyan ; Ammal, the honorific). They have no knowledge of any other god or goddess. When asked, they think she must have had a husband (" Can a woman live without a husband "), but they know nothing about him. At rare intervals the whole community worships together this goddess, but each family worships her separately much oftener. One old man said communal worship occurred once in 10 or 20 years, but others said it was more frequent. They have no idea, however, of the lapse of time. For instance one of them made the statement that the original Paliyans must have come to this part of the country from they did not know where, about 25 years ago.

A few stones are set up in a row, the number being immaterial, though generally from 1 to 7, under a rock or tree. The stones are usually smooth pebbles from a stream. Each stone is painted with a figure to represent a man (or woman ?), with vermilion paste. They could not say whether it was a man or a woman. The worship consists of the offering of honey and some roots of the wild yam (Diascorea—Tamil, " Velvalli " or "Sevalli "). They then prostrate themselves on the ground before the stones and utter prayers for protection from wild beasts and evil spirits. The women are also present and prostrate. The chief performer is generally an elderly man who is called the " Thevaradi " (literally, " the dancer of the god "—or goddess—in Tamil). He works himself up to a state of ecstasy and falls into a trance. The " Sattan," another elderly man, then, acting as interpreter, puts him questions about the future welfare of the community, or of an individual and the Thevaradi, who is supposed to be inspired by the goddess, answers.

The Paliyans, apart from the above form of congregational worship, also pray privately to Palichiammal for protection against danger of any kind in the jungle. This is done mentally and without any outward ceremony. Although they evidently dread evil spirits, their ideas about them are very vague, and they cannot describe them. They do not seem to give them the shape of men or of animals. The offices of Thevaradi and Sattan are hereditary. They have no permanent temples, and the locality where the community worships is chosen according to convenience and need not always be the same. Communal worship seems to take place when the community can afford it, and that is, apparently, very rarely.

Death customs.—The dead are always buried. The body is not washed or prepared in any way, and is kept in the hut or cave where death occurred until the time of burial. Ornaments, if any, are removed, but not the clothing. The eyes are never closed, but the arms are extended at the sides. One old man said that the arms are sometimes crossed over the breast but the others denied this. The body is placed in the grave, which is only breast deep, in a recumbent position on its back. When a death occurs messengers are sent to the neighbouring habitations to announce it. All are bound to attend it, especially the near relations. As there habitations are generally far apart, it may take three or even four days before the neighbours can assemble. The body in the meantime is left unburied even though it becomes offensive. It is borne to the grave, which is always close by, by anyone, but the front bearers must be near relations if possible. A penalty is inflicted on those who do not attend the funeral. The delinquent is made to kneel, a heavy stone is placed on the nape of the neck, and he is asked to explain why he was absent. This is generally satisfactory. The offender and the chief mourner exchange a drink of water from each other's hands and the affront is thereby condoned. It was not known what happens when the explanation is not satisfactory.

On the eighth day after the death, the spirit of the departed is worshipped with offerings of roots and honey, and its protection is invoked. From that time onwards the spirit is deemed to be merged in the deity. This ceremony is absolutely imperative, and is never omitted for either sex. The dead are remembered whenever Palichiammal is worshipped, and their protection is sought together with hers. In times of great mental or physical distress, or when a Paliyan dies an unprepared death, an invocation of the spirits of the departed takes place, and they manifest themselves through a living Paliyan present who makes revelations about the affairs of the invoker. This is called ' the calling of the shadows.'

The Paliyans seem to think little about a life after death. When asked what happens to the spirits of the dead, or where they go to, they said they did not know and did not care. They also appear to make no difference between the good and the bad after death.

Marriage.—As a rule marriages are arranged for the young people by the elders of a family. But there are cases when the young couple make their own choice generally as the result of illicit sexual intercourse. Such behaviour is condoned without much difficulty and a marriage is brought about as the best solution of the trouble. Bride prices are not paid, but the bride receives trifling presents from her relations such as roots, honey, beads, etc., when the time comes for her to be taken to her husband's dwelling. The actual ceremony of marriage consists in the tying of a string of black beads round the neck of the bride, and the presentation of a cloth to her, by the bridegroom. The bride also ties a similar string of beads round the neck of the bridegroom. The woman wears hers permanently if she likes, but it is not imperative. I have seen married women without them. The man usually discards his after the eighth day, as he is too shy to wear it longer. He is also presented with a new cloth by his father.

The wedding festivities last for one day, and one meal only is given to the guests after the tying of the beads. The young couple are given a new hut and are left severally alone for some time—some said a few days, others three or four months, and others still more, until the first conception.

Widows may remarry. Adultery is not common, but when it does occur, no penalty seems to be exacted, although the act is strongly condemned.

Marriages are permitted between a man and his maternal uncle's daughter or sister's daughter. All other marriages among relations are prohibited. An alliance between interdicted relations is viewed with displeasure and is treated as concubinage, but is condoned when due apology has been made by the offending couple. Marriage always takes place soon after puberty, never before. But it is common for a girl to reside in the house of her future husband for some time before puberty, if he is her maternal uncle. There is, however, no intercourse before she attains puberty.

A woman is said to be polluted for 5 or 6 days during the menstrual period and for 15 days after confinement. No other kind of pollution is observed. After a confinement, purification is done by burning earthenware vessels and other polluted articles in a heap. The hut is also thoroughly scrubbed and washed. It is only after this purification that the woman is permitted to associate with the others.

Birth.—There seem to be no birth ceremonies besides purification. There are no midwives. The mother or some other elderly woman, does all that is necessary at a confinement. The newborn baby is plunged into the nearest stream for its first bath, and the mother also bathes immediately after her confinement and washes her cloth. For some days after delivery she and the baby sleep on a bed of ashes, probably for warmth. Oil is never administered to the baby as purgative, but a decoction of herbs known only to Paliyans is given when necessary. Other decoctions are prepared for other baby illnesses. Although this shows that the Paliyans have some acquaintance with the medical properties of herbs, no adult is ever given medicine of any kind when he is ill. They cannot account for this curious fact, except by stating that the Goddess cures them, and it is therefore unnecessary to take medicine.

General.—The staple food of the Paliyans consists of roots (the wild yam, chiefly) honey and the flesh of animals and birds. They also eat various grains (cumbu, cholam, etc.) when they can get them, either from the minor produce forest contractors, or by going down to the plains themselves. They exchange honey roots, skins, etc., for what they require. They do not eat beef. They obtain game by means of traps and they catch birds with birdlime, but they do not hunt as they have no weapons. They do not use bows and arrows, nor even blowpipes, though the latter are common among the Muthabars who inhabit the same country. They own no property (immovable), and their only possessions are an " aruval " (bill-hook) and a burnt stick sharpened to a point, which is used for digging up roots, and is called a ' Pavuttam Kombu.'

They make fire by means of two sticks, by knocking two stones together, or by a flint and steel. They shave the front of the head in the Hindu fashion by means of broken glass and with the aid of salt. The face is also sometimes shaved.

The majority of Paliyans cannot count, but a few who have had some contact with civilization, can. One old man who was sitting near me began to count his toes when asked to show how far he could count. He reached seven. Another counted correctly to 100. This man had been a village " tandal," and is referred to again below.

They know nothing of their own origin. Several told me the names of their father and grandfather, but could go back no farther. It was suggested to them that Palichiammal might have been their ancestress. They thought it possible.

They are in the habit of signalling to each other in the jungle by different intonations of a cry much resembling ' coo-ee ' in order to signify danger, pleasure, etc. They of course have no education, but they speak a Tamil which is quite intelligible and very fluent. Many of those I saw at Periyakulam were obviously not true to type but must be of mixed descent. The typical Paliyan of both sexes is rather below the average height of the natives of the Plains, has very curly (not woolly) hair, and the skin is not black. Alliances with Koravars and others seem to be common and many have quite straight hair. The expression of the face is intelligent and with a few exceptions they look healthy, but their general appearance is filthy, as they seem neither to bathe their bodies nor wash their clothes. As has been said, they take no medicine when sick, but pray to Palichiammal to cure them. I imagine that the Paliyan is rarely ill; except when visited by epidemics like smallpox. In that case, no cure is attempted. The invalid is abandoned and the whole community migrates to another place.

Their only amusement seems to be dancing, in which both sexes indulge simultaneously, but in separate groups. It is very similar to the dancing of other castes in the plain. There seem to be several different kinds of steps. They go round in a circle clapping hands or waving a cloth, occasionally uttering loud cries. The " steps " are mostly grotesque postures in the case of the men, and they make faces at one another, but the women are rather graceful. The dancing is accompanied with drums and a primitive form of music played on reed-pipes, which are not very shrill. The music consists of the repetition many times of a short phrase of a few notes. One man had a long ' snake-horn ' of brass. They frequently dance on moonlight nights, purely for pleasure and without any religious significance.

Honey plays a very important part in the lives of the Paliyans. Very largely used as a food, no ceremony can be performed without it. It is offered as a gift, together with the wild yam, to important persons and most of their bartering with the people of the plains is done with it.

Their method of taking honey is very interesting, but is similar in many respects to that employed by other jungle tribes which I have witnessed in various parts of South India.

A rope made of twisted root, fibres, or creepers is fastened to a tree or a stake in the ground a little distance from the edge of the precipice where the honey-combs are usually in considerable numbers. A Paliyan descends the rope from above, and as he swings from one comb to another he dislodges them with his ' Pavuttam Kombu,' which has been mentioned before. Other Paliyans, men and women, stand at the foot of the precipice, and catch the falling combs in baskets or cloths. When he has finished the Paliyan ascends the rope and thus reaches the top again. This performance is one of great danger and requires much courage. From the beginning another Paliyan has been posted at the top, and his duty is to guard the rope. It may be injured by animals, it may fray at the edge of the precipice, or it may be tampered with by an enemy. It is naturally of great importance who is chosen as guardian of the rope. He is whenever possible the brother-in-law of the honey-gatherer, for, in the event of the latter's death, the former would have to maintain the widow, and he is therefore unlikely to saddle himself with this burden if he can possibly avoid it. No one is allowed to guard the rope who would benefit by the death of the gatherer, so he can never be a blood-relation. I have found exactly the same custom prevalent among the pearl-divers at Tuticorin. The amount of honey collected varies, of course, from year to year and the comparative wealth or poverty of the Paliyans depends entirely on this factor. They are much addicted to the toddy extracted from the Sago Palm, which grows wild in the jungles, and I have several times come across a Paliyan lying at the foot of the one of these trees in a state of dead drunkenness.

They are, as a rule shy and timid but their confidence can be gained easily if well treated. The women disappear in the jungle like wild animals if a stranger appears. I and my men have often tried to find them when this has happened, but we have never succeeded. They live almost entirely on the hills and rarely come down to the plains with the men. A rumour that I had arranged to meet some Paliyans had spread, and a large crowd gathered from the neighbouring town of Periyakulam to see them dance, which, apparently had never been witnessed before by those who assembled.

Most of the information I have given above was obtained from a group of 40 or 50 Paliyans, about half of whom were women, and one very healthy looking baby, who had been collected together for me by the kindness of the Zamindar of Vadagarai and Mr. Santanakrishna Nayu, who live at Periyakulam. The Zamindar is the overlord of some of them and was treated with great respect. He had arranged a feast for them, which evoked many expressions of gratitude. I myself, however, at one time owned a property in the hills near Bodinayakkanur, where there were a number of Paliyans. They paid no taxes, but were bound by custom to render me service when required, but this was very rare. I generally employed Muthuvars who live in the same hills to fell jungle, etc., as they are much more skilful at this kind of work than even the Paliyans.

The group of Paliyans I met at Periyakulam were quite at their ease in a very short time. A few are now working for the Zamindar in his gardens near Periyakulam. They answered questions readily and were easily amused. One man related amid much laughter, how he had been captured by a coolie-recruiter when he was lying drunk in the forest, and had been carried off to Ceylon to work on a tea estate. He returned after three years with savings of about Rs. 50 which soon disappeared, he could not say how. He had evidently been well-treated and seemed very proud of his adventure. Another man had acted as a " tandal " (village servant) in a Government village on the upper Palni Hills for three or four years. He had apparently got this job through the " Karnam " (village accountant) who had also obtained for him 3 acres of Government land which he still owned. He was very vague as to how he got this land or why the Karnam had been so generous. The land, of course, must have cost the karnam nothing, and I suspect that he pocketed the greater part of the pay of his tandal in exchange during the period of his service. Both these men were less shy and seemed more intelligent than the others. The last named could count correctly and quickly up to 100. This is the only case I know where a Paliyan has owned and cultivated land.

The men wore a filthy loin cloth only, but the women were fully clothed like the women of the plains, in very dirty saris. They were probably ' dolled up ' for the occasion, as I have always seen them in the jungles wearing nothing but a loin cloth.

The Jesuit Priests own a coffee estate at Palamali on the Palni Hills about 10 miles from Kodaikanal A number of Paliyans work there as coolies, and have become Christians, but other Paliyans will have nothing to do with them.

(c) Porojas and Saoras.

By M. W. M. Yeatts.

The term ' Poroja ' in its Agency origin connotes the idea ' subject ' or ' subjected ' as opposed to rule and epitomizes the history of Vizagapatam Agency and its people.

What constitutes a ' Poroja ' has long been a matter of uncertainty and all that is certain is that the term covers several quite distinct tribes. Whatever may be the objections to its using as a specific name a term merely generic, the fact remains that a great number of persons in Vizagapatam Agency when asked their caste or tribe can say only ' Poroja ' and the census has perforce to make the best of what it gets. An expert anthropological inquiry would probably evolve some certainty out of the prevailing vagueness but one can hardly expect a census enumeration to produce it. **Porojas.**

The number returned under Poroja has increased largely since 1921, by 41 per cent. 1911-21 saw a decrease of 6 per cent. The increase over the last decade is much greater than any previously recorded for this tribe or for any other tribe of Vizagapatam Agency over 1921-31. Only the Konda Doras show an increase rate approaching 40 per cent. One is inclined to relate the Gadaba decrease of 6,000 to the Poroja growth, for a wide variety of Gadaba names exists and they are occasionally brought (even by the persons themselves) under the catholic term ' Poroja ' in such a way as might well mislead an enumerator unskilled in these subtleties (as practically all were). Something of this has probably occurred, but a large source of Gadaba decrease is to be found in the plains, where Porojas are almost completely unrepresented. So many variables enter the Poroja equation that further speculation is hardly justified and the numbers must be taken for what they are worth ; they do show at least that 123,000 persons not of Oriya, Telugu or other origin and not belonging to the main Agency tribes, were in 1931 found in the Vizagapatam Agency.

Poroja presence is essentially a matter of the central and higher level agency ; the four taluks of Padwa Pottangi, Koraput and Jeypore yield nearly 80 per cent. of the total and with Naurangpur, 95 per cent.

One circumstance worth mention is that the Poroja sex ratio has at this census gone for the first time above par ; there are 1,010 females per 1,000 males against 957 in 1921 and similar figures in previous years.

Porojas are by no means homogeneous but certain general characteristics can be suggested. Broad heads are more common and straight hair, though wavy and even curling hair is encountered. The complexion is usually of a copperish hue and very dark persons are definitely rare. Eyes are straight, nose platyrhine. Tall men are rare. They are more careful of toilet and more cleanly than is usual among hill tribes. This applies particularly to the women.

Any comment on Porojas is subject to the qualification that more than one distinct stock comes under the term and a consequent overlap is inevitable. The notes which follow, contributed by the Special Assistant Agent, Koraput, are of much interest but should be read accordingly. In some cases they seem to refer to Gadaba sects who, as already remarked, refer to themselves and are generally known as Porojas.

Relics of their forgotten language can be picked up from the homely talk or the songs of the peoples Puttra (a stream), Kanda (a child), Sala (region) as in Ku-sala, the place around the well, are some of such words ; " Pa " is pronounced as " ha ." There is a marked peculiarity in their intonation in pronouncing Oriya.

The Porojas seem to have been inhabiting Vizagapatam Agency from about the 2nd century of the Christian era, if not before. The words " Kanda, Sala " occur in the inscriptions of Amaravati, dated about the 2nd Century A.D. In an inscription which on palaeographical evidence can be assigned to the 9th Century A.D., the region of Nandapur, the centre of the Nandapur State of the 14th Century A.D., is said to have been located in Gond-Mandala, the province of the Gonds. A King of the Kalachuri family (Central India) bought a piece of land from a Poroja at Borigumma and gave it to the God Bhairava at that place (inscription in the temple of Danteswari at Dantawara, Bastar State). Gangavamsanucharitam, a Sanskrit poem a manuscript of which exists in the Oriental Library at Madras, was written during the 17th Century A.D. It says that a prince of the Ganga family of Orissa came southwards and established a throne at Gudari near Gunupur. This prince is said to have had an army of hill tribes. These items of evidence go to support the theory that the real sons of the soil were the Porojas and other hill tribes. The rulers were immigrants who brought along with them some Oriyas and gave them holdings of land, free of rent in some cases but mostly on feudal tenure. The Oriyas having become the lords of the land, the sons of the soil had to seek service under them, became ' prajas' or ryots. The Poroja was practically reduced to slavery. He lost his independence but the usurping ruler maintained the conditions of his original contact with the original inhabitants to observe the religious rites and festivities of the sons of the soil. The Meria sacrifice appears deprived of all its cruelties in the Dasara rites ; the festivities to propitiate the earth goddess (the Jaker) take the form of Bali Jatra celebrated in the lunar month of Bhadrapada (August-September) ; the Chaitra Parvam or the tribal hunt is only a form of the Vernal festival of the aboriginal tribes.

The Porojas are divided into twelve tribes and each tribe is called after the region in which that tribe lives. But generally they are divided into the Bodo Poroja or Sodia, the Sano Poroja, the Jodia Poroja, and Perang Poroja.

The first class do not eat the flesh of the cow or the ox. The Sano Poroja eats beef ; the third class or Jodia eats beef ; a man ties his turban with crossing belts in front and a big lump behind. The Perang Poroja eats beef ; the women wear only brass ornaments and also a peculiar ornament which sits astride on the saddle of the nose and projects upwards to the middle of the two brows.

Dress and general demeanour.—A man wears two cloths one round the loins and the other for the head. He trims his hair into any form he likes but does not adopt any one form always. A young man wears one or two metallic rings on his left wrist and some garlands of coloured beads round his neck. But it is the woman that presents the dress and ornaments typical to the tribe.

The Bodo Poroja woman combs her hair with parting in the middle on the top of the head. All the hair is collected behind and is put into a knot. She does not use hairpins like the women of the lower classes. Garlands of beads of various colours embrace the neck from the nape to the clavicles and thence hang down to the pit of the stomach. Over these are worn one or two round metallic rings. The lobes of the ears are bored and in each is worn a coil of metallic serpents. The outer-wall of the ear also is bored in several places and a thin small ring is passed through each hole. To one or two of the topmost rings of the left ears pendants of small chains are worn. On the left lower arm the women of this class wear brass rings which extend from the wrist to the elbow ; but on the right lower arm few or none. Each finger is provided with a ring topped with a coin or a round flat piece of metal. On the ankles are worn " U " shaped hollow anklets in which jingle small round pieces of stone or metal. Each toe is also adorned with a ring shaped in such a form as to suit the particular toe for which it is intended.

Any cloth of any colour is worn but the white cloth provided with red hems is the one peculiar to all classes of Porojas. It is folded lengthwise so that the two hems may form one broad band. The lower end does not descend below the middle of the thighs ; the apron part of the cloth goes from below the right arm across the trunk to over the left shoulder where the one in front and the one from the back are united in a knot. The rest of the cloth is wound in several coils round the waist, always taking care to have the red hems come one above the other.

Sano Poroja.—The women of this class wear ornaments and dress similar to those of the first class, but with some peculiarities in dressing the hair and in certain ornaments. These women comb the hair with a parting in the middle and collect all the hair behind and thrust it into a loose knot from below ; this knot hangs down below the nape of the neck. One or two hairpins with broad outer ends are put into the knot to keep it intact. Some women wear a ribbon-like garland of fine beads round the head. Round the neck the ornaments are similar to those of the first class. The rings adorning the left lower arm are of white metal. The anklets of this class are different from those of the first class. On the toes, the women of this class wear clusters of small metallic bells which make a rhythmic jingle when they walk.

The cloth is worn so as to hang down to the knees. In other respects it is worn as by the women of the first class.

Jodia Poroja.—This class of men and women also eat beef and dress like the Sano Porojas. The distinction between the two is not marked. The woman of this class in addition to the metallic wrist rings on the left lower arm, wears on each upper arm a bracelet about three inches in breadth.

The Pareng Poroja.—This class eats beef. The women wear ornaments all made of brass. Garlands of small brass beads are worn round the neck and brass rings on the lower arms. The peculiar distinguishing ornamet is a triangular brass wire which sits astride on the saddle of the nose, its apex projecting upwards to the middle of the two brows.

Village life.—Every village is enclosed with a living fence in which a gap is left to serve as an entrance. Houses are built in two or more rows leaving a broad space between. Each house is divided into a store room, a kitchen and the sleeping apartment ; a cow shed and a drinking space also form a part of some houses. All these are built separately and are enlosed by a wall or fence. In one place of the wall is left a gateway.

Two houses are built separately, one for the grown up maidens of the village to sleep in and the other for the unmarried young men. The maidens are responsible for keeping their sleeping house neat and tidy and are under the control of a head, who is also a maiden and who attains that position by common consent. Similarly the young men are responsible for keeping their sleeping apartment tidy and are under the control of a head young man. After nightfall none of the maidens is supposed to stray out, nor is any young man permitted to do so. Flirtations occur nevertheless.

The villagers are under the control of a headman who is nominated by all the villagers and approved by the zamindar. At times, the headman may be appointed by the zamindar himself and the villagers have to accept him. Yet, behind such appointment can be seen the common consent of the people. In the middle of the village is planted a banyan (Ficus indica), or ficus religiosa or a mango tree. Round the foot of the trunk a platform surmounted with stone slabs is raised. This serves as a seat for the headman when he sits in court to hear and decide the village disputes. Whenever a dispute arises in the village, he summons all the villagers and they come and sit, each on a stone lying scattered under the trees or on the ground. Women also attend but remain standing. When all men are assembled, the headman takes his seat on the platform and the question is discussed. The decision of the assembly must be accepted by all.

Marriage.—Generally the young man selects the woman he likes to marry and informs his parents who carry on the negotiations with the parents of the selected maiden. If the maiden's parents do not approve the match fails. But if they consent, the bride money is settled and the marriage day is fixed. A day previous to the appointed one, the bridegroom lurks along with some of his friends, in a place by the side of which the maiden is expected to pass alone. He then pounces on her and with the help of his friends carries her away to his home. But the maid's parents hearing of it go with friends to her relief. A small mock fight ensues between the two parties and when every one is exhausted, they all go to the bridegroom's house where they are served with food and drink.

Amongst the Porojas, there are many Gotras or totems. Bag (tiger) ; Nag (serpent) ; Phulu (flower) ; Goru (cow) ; Matshu (fish). The Poroja does not kill or eat the thing that is the emblem of his totem. The Poroja of the Phulu totem does not wear flowers ; one of the fish totem does not eat fish. Persons of the same gotra may not marry. Nor may the children of a brother and a sister or of brothers. Widow remarrige is allowed. It is compulsory for a widow to marry her late husband's younger brother. If she does not wish to do so, the man she marries must pay to that younger brother an amount fixed by the villagers. Divorces are permitted ; if a woman does not like her husband she will pay him five rupees and go away from him ; but a husband leaving his wife pays her only one rupee. If the woman while living with one man goes to another, the new one must pay her late husband a sum of money fixed by the elders of the village. The children, if she has any, are taken away by the man to whom she bore them.

Agricultural implements consist mostly of a hoe. square in shape and provided with a long handle so that a man can dig standing. A Poroja who can afford it may have a plough. The tangi or a hand hatchet is an implement which the Poroja uses for a variety of purposes and also as a weapon of offence and defence. Wherever he goes he carries it on his left shoulder.

Death ceremonies.—When a man or a woman dies in a family, the corpse is taken to a place outside the village, all the men and women following. The corpse is either burnt or buried according to convenience. Then all of them bathe in an adjoining river or pond and take along with them a flat long stone to their village and set it upright just outside the village and place another slab flat at its foot. A small rag is tied round the middle of the upright stone and a bamboo the top of which is split and formed into a trident, is placed upright behind the vertical stone. Every day or whenever the departed soul is propitiated, offerings of food and fowls are made on the flat stone at the foot of the vertical one. Generally the offerings are given on the third and the tenth days.

On the tenth day, after nightfall, food and other offerings are prepared and a man carries them to a place half-way to the cremation or burial ground. He places them there and calls by name on the soul of the dead man. Then one of those that carried the corpse on the first day, is possessed by that soul and he issues out of the darkness sounding his tangi on a hoe. Every time the departed soul is called upon, the man possessed responds with a grunt. Thus he is led to the house where the death occurred. In the house geometrical figures with flour are made and three grains are placed in the middle of those drawings and a pot put over them. The drawings are one of Yama, one of Saturn and one of the devil. The possessed man enters the house and kicks away the pot and discovers the grains. If they are found on the drawings of Yama, it is understood that the soul was taken by Yama or the God of death ; if the seeds are discovered on the Sani (Saturn) drawings the soul was taken away by Sani. It is believed that the soul became a devil, if the seeds are found on the devil drawings.

Gods and festivals.—At the entrance of the village, under a tree is kept the God called the Nisan-devata. It is a small oval stone installed on an auspicious day even before the village is formed. Over it stones are piled up in the form of a temple. It is believed that this Nisan Devata protects the village from epidemic, wild animals or other dangers.

In the middle of the village under a shed is kept the God called Thakurani, of course a female. This is represented by some wooden images under a shed. Near the foot of the hill, is installed the God called Jhakar-devata. This is also a female. She is the protectress of the crops.

In addition to these, the tiger Goddess is propitiated by offering sacrifices to her in the mountain caves. All the villagers during the dry season go to the cave, prepare food and kill a goat or a buffalo and offer them all to the tiger Goddess ; they then drink liquor and dance to the accompaniment of drums till nightfall and return to the village. It is believed that as a result of this performace the tiger will not molest the villagers during the year.

The Porojas hold feasts to propitiate all these gods. In the month of Chaitra they hold the hunting feast and all the villagers—men alone—retire into the forest for a hunt. None of the party should return without an animal. The women in the village decorate themselves in their finest and spend the time in dance and play. Young maidens are wooed at this time and the selection of brides made. When it is reported that an animal has been killed, the women of the village proceed to the edge of the forest and await the arrival of the men. The carcass, decorated with garlands of flowers and peacock feathers, is carried on a litter carried on men's shoulders and the women sing and dance in front, while drums are beaten and the Indian flute played. Thus the procession goes to the village where the carcass is flayed and quartered. If it is eatable, the flesh is divided amongst all the villagers.

The Nua-kuya.—This is eating the new harvest. This takes place in the month of " Bonda Pani " *i.e.*, Sravanam of the Indian calendar which corresponds to July-August. The leaves of the growing paddy plant and its roots are cooked together, offered to all the gods and enjoyed along with other dishes and liquor.

The Pus festival.—This is held on the full moon day of month of Pushya (December and January). They kill a buffalo in the name of all village gods, have a feast and drink and dance the whole day. This is all on the day before the full moon. On the full moon night young damsels go singing from house to house and receive doles of rice at every door. The rice thus collected is all cooked on the fire lit in the middle of the village in the early dawn of the day. After sunrise they all bathe, wear new cloths and feast.

These are the most important of the festivals observed by the Poroja tribes. Others observed are not tribal. Each family has its own traditional feasts which are restricted to its members. Association with the Oriyas has taught Porojas some of the feasts observed by their masters. The car festival (June and July) is one of such festivals that have been adopted. On the day of the Hindu Car-festivals, the Porojas make a small handy car and place it before their god, kill a fowl and a pigeon to that god and then present the car to it. The arrangement of these festivals and the fixing of these festive days is generally the duty of the Disari, the village priest.

Witchcraft and Sorcery.—The Disari or the village priest knows astronomy, medicine, witchery and sorcery. Whenever a man or a woman or a child falls ill, the Poroja consults his village Disari. At first he gives some herbs but if the illness is not cured, he comes to the house of the patient and then sits in a room alone. After a few minutes he falls senseless and remains in a trance for some time. When incense is burnt before him, he sits up and speaks as if possessed. In that state he gives out the cause of the illness and ascribes it to the existence of bones in a corner of the house, or to the failure to propitiate a certain god or to some devil or to some sorcery of an enemy of the patient or his parents. He proposes to remove the cause on some future day and orders the master of the family to keep ready certain things for that day, a fowl being one of those prescribed. On the appointed day, the Disari again goes to the patient's house and burning incense, recites some prayers in a tone and intonation deemed peculiarly suited to the occasion. Then after some time, if the ascribed cause was the presence of bones under floor of the house, he goes to that corner and digs out the bones and presents them. If the illness be due to a devil, he ties a talisman round the neck of the patient ; if it be due to sorcery, he puts some food, red and yellow cooked rice, in a bamboo dish and with a light in the middle and the whole thing is taken out of the house and left where two roads cross.

He is also capable of doing evil to others either of his own accord or at instigation. He goes to a certain plant which grows into a small shrub and binds all its branches together then holding the whole shrub in his hands he utters a prayer to the effect that the particular man should fall ill. He then bends the shrub to one side and places a stone over it. The man falls ill ; if the stone is removed and the branches are freed he gets better. If the sorcerer wishes to extinguish life in his enemy he has to root out the shrub and fling it away. As it drys and decays, the person also dies gradually.

A man is made to swell up by means of a frog ; a big frog is caught in a brook and its entrails removed. Some cooked food is placed in its stomach and the whole sewed in a cloth and buried in a place where two roads cross. Then the body of the person in whose name it is done, will swell up. If the buried thing is removed and thrown away, he recovers his health. If the sorcerer wishes that he should die, the frog is left untouched.

Many kinds of sorcery are practised and the Poroja believes in them all. The most efficacious of them is the little finger sorcery. When a still born child is buried, the sorcerer goes to the grave in the dead of night and takes out the body. Instilling life into it, he asks it to give its little finger of the right hand. The child speaks and permits the sorcerer to cut it. Having cut it, he removes the life of the child and buries it again. This little finger he uses for many purposes. He sends it to any place he likes and gets through it anything he wishes. He can kill a man or cure a patient with it. Every one in the village and also in the surrounding villages is terrified of a sorcerer possessing this finger.

The Disari knows the names of the constellations and of the planets. He makes calculations and foretells evil or good. The month is lunar and all festivals are fixed within five days either before or after the full moon. The auspicious day for performing marriage is fixed by the Disari. He performs marriages and ties the nuptial knot. At village assemblies his presence is required and his advice on every tribal question solicited.

Saoras. As mentioned in the language chapter the spelling 'Saora' has been adopted in order to indicate the pronunciation of the tribal name. The Telugu 'v' which is usually thrust in not only has no justification at all but distorts the correct sound. The second 'a' in 'Savara' is also a wrong rendering of the actual sound.

Seven thousand six hundred and forty-nine persons in Ganjam Agency and 1,865 in Ganjam Plains returned their caste as 'Sudho.' This community is claimed by some Oriyas as racially theirs, but it is certain that many of the former at least must have been really Saora and if 5,000 are so allowed for, the decade increase for the tribe would exceed 3 per cent. If all the Sudhos were classed as Saoras—not an unreasonable course—the increase would from that fact alone rise to 5 per cent.

The Saora area could be described as the basin of the Vamsadhara or 'bamboo' river. Gunupur holds most of the upper reaches of this, Parlakimedi the lower and between them these taluks contain two-thirds of all the Saoras in the presidency.

They have not roamed to the same extent as the Konds in search of podus new and their dispersion is perhaps less the results of roaming and more due to the presence of remnants in ancient homes. Saoras are found, *e.g.*, in Kodala, in the hills near the Chilka Lake, not as isolated wanderers but in a small settled clump. Eickstedt considered the whole plains population of Ganjam as evidencing clearly an original Mongol strain.

As is well known, the Saora language is Munda and their features have a Mongolian caste sometimes strong, sometimes weak, but generally present, particularly in men. Much has been written on them in the past and further study is being prosecuted by Rao Sahib G. V. Ramamurti Pantulu, his son Mr. G. V. Sitapati and by Miss A. C. M. Munro. A note by the latter two is appended. An interesting circumstance brought to my notice is that while Saora women have no particular objection to being touched on any part of the body, even the uncovered breast, they resent violently any touch on the shoulder. I am informed by Mr. H. R. Uzielli that he has heard that a somewhat similar prejudice obtains among the Kachins of Upper Burma. If the parallel is correct it is a circumstance of interest.

The precise significance of the shoulder touch may relate to some belief in the presence there of the life spirit but this is a matter for anthropologist research and enquiry.

One of the most interesting circumstances of the Madras Agency tracts is the presence in adjoining areas of so representative tribes of widely differing types as the Kond and Saora. They differ in almost every way and provide a vivid illustration of the racial differences which exist in India. Eickstedt found the Konds 'cheerful, mobile, friendly and selfpossessed,' the Saoras 'reserved, suspicious, refractory and obstinate (hartnackig).' Most will agree with that general differentiation. In general 'Mongolism' and savageness go together, he says, and the most intractable people he came across were those with most apparent Mongol traces. The Kond is open, the Saora closed.

(d) The Soras of the Parlakimedi Agency.

By Miss A. C. M. Munro and Mr. G. V. Sitapatoi.

1. There are no Totemistic groups among the Soras, although their kindred, the Mundas and the Birhors have them. The rules relating to exogamy preclude marriage among persons of the same village, except with such as are known to be new comers. Those of the same village are looked upon as brothers and sisters. Marriage with cousins and cross cousins is prohibited. Laxity with reference to this prohibition has been noted in a few instances, but fines have been imposed, in these cases.

Regarding endogamy, there are several classes of Soras, such as the Jadu Soras, the Arsid Soras, the Luari Soras, the Kapu Soras and the Sudra Soras, among whom there are no intermarriages. Exceptions have been noted, but as above, fines have been imposed.

2. In each of the endogamous classes, as noted above there are grades with reference to social precedence.

(*a*) The Gamangs. (*b*) The Buyas. (*c*) The Parjas.

The Gamang is the civil head of the village. During pre-British days he was the chief of the village. His position is now reduced to such as that of a village munsiff in the plains. All the male members of his family append Gamang to their names.

The Buya is the religious head of the village. He exercised equal authority with the Gamang in the past, and his status was in no way inferior. His power is now further reduced. Apart from the distinction he holds in the eyes of his own people the only official distinction he is given is when, equally with the Gamang, he is presented with a pair of cloths by the Agent to the Governor at the annual Bhet. In many cases the hereditary Buya does not possess the necessary powers of officiating priest. In such cases there are officiating priests, who belong to his extended family and bear the designation of Buya, but such are not hereditary or officially recognised. The officially recognized Buya is known as the Sadi Buya, *i.e.*, recipient of the Agent's gift. The practical and officiating Buya is known as the Pur-pur Buya. The perquisites of the Buya are distributed between the two.

There are intermarriages between the Gamang and Buya families generally.

The Parjas are regarded as inferior in social status. The Gamang or Buya families will take of the daughters of the Parjas as wives but will not give their own daughters to the Parjas in marriage.

The houses of these three classes are in separate groups in most villages, particularly is this so among the Jadu Soras of the Gumma and Kellikote areas. The cremation grounds are also kept separate.

3. The Gamang and the Buya must come from their respective classes and descent is *patrilineal.*

4. Organization in the past was in all probability democratic. There are indications in the folk-lore, of a free discussion of any matters of importance at open-air meetings. The forms of address used at meetings, as handed down, are, " Oh, you Gamangs."—" Oh, you Buyas."—" Oh, you Parjas." The presence of women also is indicated. The privilege of electing officers does not seem to have existed, since the offices are hereditary, but nothing of importance could be done by the chiefs without consulting the Parjas.

5. There are traditions of origin from the North. They say that their ancestors, their deities and their demi-gods came to the Ganjam and Vizagapatam Agencies from Odisa (Orissa). The frequent occurrence of the expression " Odisa-Maindura," as the original home of their deities and demi-gods would probably indicate the way by which they came to their present habitat. Maindura means Mahendra, the highest peak in their vicinity. As there are no indications along the coast, of the existence of the Soras, except for a few miles to the north of Mahendra it may be concluded that they did not come by the coastal route. It would seem that they had followed the more inland route lying to the north-west of Ganjam.

6. Terraced cultivation is found in the valleys and on the steeper slopes, which are built up with stone revetments.

7. There are no monuments in the accepted meaning of the term, but in every village at the Guar or biennial memorial for the dead, shafts of stone are set up, one for each departed soul, in the area kept for this purpose. (Guar literally means " plant a stone ".)

8. It is not necessary that seats must be of stone. Seats of stone or wood may be used accordingly to convenience. At the time of sacrifices the seat or stone used by the Kudan is privileged but at no other time.

9. Soras build with stone and mud and use thatch, or they interweave slender branches and plaster on both sides with mud. They also on the plains build with upright stakes or slabs of the sago palm. Brick and tile are taboo. If such were used the spirits would be attracted and come too often. Tamarind branches or wood may not be used, as tigers will prowl about it, they say. The use of banyan, pipul and cashewnut is also taboo.

10. The Gamangs and Buyas are privileged to wear very large coloured turbans, red, orange and blue, and if they can afford it, neck ornaments with gold beads and gold earrings. It is not forbidden to others to wear such but they are likely to be twitted about it, if their circumstances do not justify their having gold.

11. The sun is regarded as father, the moon as mother and the stars as children.

Ding-la-tujan, literally , pull-tail-star, *i.e.,* a comet. To ward off possible evil effects, a buffalo sacrifice is made at the appearance of a comet.

Junduda-tujan, a meteor. This is regarded as a male star. Literally prostitute star.

Names of constellations, etc.—

Orion's Belt.—Pangsal-tujan, lit. " take-liquor-star." At the time a proposal of marriage is made, three pots of liquor must accompany the proposal.

Pleiades.—Runkiu-tujan, lit., cluster.

Great Bear.—Sandi-tujan, lit. a cot. They recognize only the four stars.

Sirius.—Togin-tujan, lit., fire star.

Venus.—Sunkara-tujan. The one remaining child of the sun, and may sometimes be seen at midday. There is a folk-story that the moon pretended to have swallowed all her children, but had in reality tucked them into her hair. She advised the sun to swallow his. He did so but reserved one out of affection.

Milky way.—Tangtangrap-tujan.

Earthquake.—Ob-seng-lon, lit., " turn sides-earth." Auspicious. Crops will be better for this.

Eclipse.—Mo-yongan, is the solar eclipse, lit., swallow sun.

Mo-gajan is lunar eclipse, " swallow moon." Soras cry, shoot off guns and arrows at time of eclipse, to scare away the snake that has done the swallowing.

Rainbow.—Inil-bongan.

Iling bongan. Will bring good crops. Plains Soras say there will be famine.

Thunder.—Dumdum-tiran. Good as indicating rain.

Lightning.—Kilajan. Good as indicating rain.

Planets, stars, etc., are known to the Soras and called by name. They are named after animals as tiger, birds or parts of the bodies of such, as, head of tiger, tail of tiger, according to fancied resemblance.

12. The dead are now, throughout the whole Sora country, cremated. Exceptions.—Persons that die of smallpox are buried, this perhaps in imitation of the people of the plains, because the Soras believe that the disease has come to them by visitations of the Goddess of Smallpox from the Plains. In a smallpox burial the body is placed with the head to the South, while in the cremation of a body from death by another cause the body is placed on the cremation pyre with the head to the North, *i.e.,* toward the country from which they came. The idea being that the soul returns to the country of its ancestors, except in the case of the smallpox death where that Goddess has taken the soul to the Plains country.

No coffin is used. Tradition as well as the prevailing custom in the interior of the Sora country indicates that the " orthodox method of carrying the body to the cremation ground is as follows. In each village there is one man set apart to carry the dead. His perquisites are generally provided at the Guar, at which time he also has certain duties to perform." He carries the body *face upwards* over his back. In some villages, he is assisted by two others, one supporting the head, another the feet, and he himself carrying at the waist. In other villages they now carry the body, borne by four men, on a stretcher.

On the second day after burning, the remains (fragments of bone and ash) are gathered and buried in a small grave close by the cremation ground. This when filled in, is covered over with thatch and stones, or a miniature shed is erected. In some villages as at Munising (observed by Dr. Hutton, March 1931) a permanent common hut is built for the accommodation of the spirits during the period of mourning.

The Soras do not in any way mutilate the body before cremating.

When a Sora dies elsewhere than in the village of his birth, and is cremated there, the remains must be returned to his native village for burial as above, within the year.

13. The ultimate abode of the Dead is believed to be in the Land of their Ancestors. Every person is believed by the Soras to possess two souls, *viz.*, (*1*) Suda Purada and (*2*) A-Baleng Purada or Rup Rup Purada. The former, *i.e.*, Suda Purada is conceived to be the Soul which is immortal. It can leave the body at will, particularly during sleep. It possesses the power of passing by transudation. Its substance can permeate the whole body, and even the garments in contact with the body, and the shadow and the area on which the shadow falls. This Suda Purada meets with the Suda Purada of others, either living or dead in dreamland. Dreams are interpreted as the experiences of the Suda Purada. The immortality of the Soul is inferred by the Soras from such meetings of the Suda Purada of the living with the Suda Purada of the dead. The body does not perish by the temporary absence of the Suda Purada, but though the body is alive it is deprived of consciousness during such temporary absences. Soras are very careful not to arouse a sleeper suddenly, lest his Suda Purada should be absent and not have time to return.

After the death of the body, the Suda Purada leaves it, though it may if it choses, remain till the body is burnt. After leaving the body it is no longer known as Suda Purada, but as Kulba-n and may hover about in the vicinity of the grave or village or house to which it belonged. In a hamlet at Serung, two and a half years ago, a Sora named Sandu had a child. Before the child was born Sandu had a dream, during which his Suda Purada met and conversed with his father's Suda Purada (Dalima by name) which expressed the desire to be borne again in the family. So Sandu's son when born was named Dalima, after his grand-father. Last year the little Dalima died and on the same day, within a couple of hours the mother gave birth to another baby boy. The general belief of the whole hamlet is that the spirit, or Suda Purada of the dead child took up its habitation in the body of the new-born child. The Kulba-n expects the surviving members of the family to feed and care for it (symbolically) as in life, until the funeral rites are completed and it finds its ultimate abode. The funeral rites culminate in the periodical Guar, immediately after which the departed soul is privileged to take up its permanent residence and is thereafter raised to the status of a deity called by the class name Sonum.

The Guar being the final ceremony, the sooner it is done the better for the departed soul, but as it is a very expensive one it is performed at regular intervals of two years, so that it may accommodate all those who have departed this life during that period. All the families that have been bereaved combine in making preparations. They invite their relative from other villages as well as their own villagers. On the first day the Kudan invokes the members of the final abode who had originally been members of the village, to come and lead the way for these new-comers. A conversation after the following fashion between the two parties takes place, enacted by the Kudan and his assistants.

New candidates.—Won't you take s to the permanent abode and let us live with you ?

Invoked souls.—How can we do so without knowing that you belong to this village and that you are genuine Soras ?

N.C.—Make a tour of investigation about the village and find out about us. (A procession goes around the village.)

I. S.—We are satisfied. To-morrow our relatives will set up the memorial stones and then you will be at liberty to join us. We will conduct you.

The a-Baleng Purada is the life substance of the body. It resides in the heart. Rup Rup Purada is onomatopoetic, representing the heart beats. It ceases to unction after the final departure of the Suda Purada, but temporary absences do not embarrass it.

The Soras also believe in the immortality of the body, which prevailed in by-gone ages when men could slough off the worn out elements and rejuvenate. This power was later lost, but the idea is still present, "Labana-mar," which literally means "sloughman," indicates the idea of an immortal person. The benediction, "May you live long," or "live for ever" is expressed by "Jadan-a-laba-labanaba" which literally means, "Snake's slough, slough you."

The Soras also believe in the transmigration of the souls into butterflies, "Kunkudibudan" and the cochineal insect.

14. Sora babies up to ten days old are an unusually beautiful creamy yellow color, but they darken quickly due to exposure to the sun to which they are subjected from the fourth day. There is no doubt an admixture of types for the complexion of the adult Sora varies from a light yellowish tan to dark brown. Soras of a very dark complexion are rare. Hair is generally wavy, but sometimes frizzy.

Babies heads are shaved on the day of naming which falls within ten days of birth. Children, both boys and girls have their hair cut short,—shaved clean in the hot season, until about ten years of age, after which the girls let theirs grow to just above the shoulders and confine it neatly with a bandeau. After marriage they usually draw it together and tuck it in under at the right side. Boys keep their hair short but leave a goodly strand at the crown, which they twist in a coil and into which they attach feathers for head dress. The women use a brass hair pin of noticeable design which may have in former times been used as a weapon.

They treat the hair with gingelly oil, caster oil, and "karanja" oil, this latter to destroy vermin.

Eyes are generally oblique and of neutral colors.

Two distinct types of nose are noticeable, one straight and narrow at the bridge, but with strong round nostrils, another flattish and broad, with decidedly large round nostrils.

The head is generally dolichocephalic, but variations are noted. The face is usually broad with high cheek bones. The typically heart shaped face is noticable among the women.

The average height of Sora men is about five feet two inches, and the women are a little shorter, but men of six feet are not rare. Tall women are rarely seen. Excellent muscular development is a marked feature of their physique. Among women up to middle age and among children generally, pot-belly is noticeable. In walking they toe in, especially the women.

15. Except for paddy cultivation sowing is done broadcast. Implements—*vide* lists.

16. *Musical instruments*—

i. *Percussive*.—*Dollun*, a big drum, built on the lower cut from the trunk of the sago palm, in the shape of a hollow hemisphere three feet in diameter by three feet in depth, covered with buffalo hide. Used on the occasion of marriages and feasts. Beaten with the palms or leather strips.

Tuduman, the ordinary tom-tom, which is carried either over the back and is beaten by another man, or over the stomach and beaten by the person carrying it.

Dagadum, a small drum of the shape of a hemisphere, beaten with two short slender sticks.

Muringan, barrel shaped, one end of less circumference than the other. Played on both ends. About three to four feet long. Smaller end four inches in diameter, larger, about eight inches. Played with the hands.

Kadingan, circular, on an iron rim, covered with goat or buffalo skin. Slung over the shoulder and beaten with two sticks.

Sannakad rajan, Sarrakad rajan.—Twenty to thirty reeds twelve inches long, held together flat, between a pair of splints at each end. On both faces, with the exception of the marginal pair of reeds, back and front, the cane is split. On the back surface two wooden pieces serving as frets are inserted lifting the cane. On the front surface four frets are inserted lifting the cane in alternate pairs. Two loops of fibre are suspended on the back surface and held by the thumb and little finger of the left hand, with the other three fingers free to play the split cane on that side while the front is played as a guitar.

Kudan rajan.—Used by the Kudan to accompany invocations and hymns. It is used to give the key and keep the time. Consists of a hollow bamboo, twenty inches long, a carved peacock headpiece, one large gourd which is pressed against the Kudan's chest is attached towards the headpiece. Two strings of twisted sago palm fibre are strung on the outer side from the end of the bamboo to the headpiece.

Tanar jaban, Tarsa rajan.—A bundle of long reeds, tied at one end. Held upright in left hand by the tied end and the loose ends made to rattle by striking with the right hand.

Pimpingan.—Tiny brass bells.

ii. *Stringed instruments*—

1. *Dambung rajan*.—Sacred instrument. Same as Kudan Rajan described in Percussive, having two strings that stand in the relation of *b* flat and *c*. Vibrated in accompaniment to the Kudan's songs.

2. *Godgod rajan*.—Consists of sounding box made of a half coconut covered with lizard skin and stem of hollow bamboo twelve to fourteen inches long, with two strings and bridge and played with a bow made of bamboo strung with fibres of sago palm. The bow is found in all cases to be strung so that the fibres are of the exact length of the neck or stem of the violin itself.

3. *Kenken* or *Me-me rajan*.—Their only stringed instrument which is provided with frets. In construction and principle similar to the "kinneri" of the aboriginal tribes of Central and Northern India. As No. 2 corresponds to a violin, the me-me rajan corresponds to a guitar. It consists of a hollow bamboo neck eighteen inches long, on which are built up four frets made of wood and secured with bees' wax. There are two strings, one of which passes over the frets and is used to produce the melody, while the other string is at a little lower level and separated slightly from the first string. The first string is secured in a straight line passing over the frets from the key to the tail-piece. The second is slightly shorter, functions as a drone, is attached from tail-piece to key, which latter is set at a sufficient angle to spread the strings apart. This instrument has one to two gourds, the size of a large orange secured on the back at each end of the neck. These are cut out at the bottom. The instrument is held with the gourds towards the body and pressed against, or removed, to regulate the volume of sound. The keys are struck from underneath with the nails of the index and second finger of the right hand.

iii. *Wind instruments*—

1. *Tirudujan* or *Pirudujan*.—A hollow reed or bamboo of eight to twelve inches long by half an inch in diameter with five holes.

2. *Dagarapedan* is the ordinary Indian flute, probably borrowed by the Soras.

3. *Taredtedpedan*, which resembles the clarinet and is probably borrowed.

4. *Tattudu pedan* consists of a brass horn three feet in length, into the narrow end of which is fixed a mouthpiece. The horn is gently curved and graduated in diameter. Gives a bugle call.

5. *Deren-bong-pedan*, consists of a buffalo horn twelve inches long with a bamboo mouthpiece six inches long. Produces a similar sound to the conch. To sound it is taboo at certain seasons.

17. *Weapons*—

(*a*) *Bow and arrows*.—Bow is simple in construction, consisting of stave, a shaped piece of split bamboo 43—50 inches long and string 35-38 inches long. The string is made from a piece of split bamboo half an inch thick, three inches of this thickness are left at each end of the string, the rest has the wood split out leaving only the cortex. The ends have each three notches. There is also a notch at each end of the bow. With twisted fibres of the sago palm a loop is made and securely fastened, one at each end of the string, by means of the notches. One end of the string is looped tightly to the bow and to string, this end is placed on the ground, the Sora presses the belly at the centre and secures the loop over the upper horn, into the notch.

Arrows.—The shaft is 18 inches long, notched; has feather insert usually. Bird arrows have a blunt core of bamboo 3 inches long fixed to the head, or the core is split into three prongs this latter is called Rogaba. The prongs may also be made of iron. For shooting animals arrow heads of iron are usually used. These heads are secured by driving the spike into the slender end of the shaft and binding with fibre or slender thong. The heads are triangular, varying in length, the longest being three inches at the sides and an inch at the base. They are barbed; also a spike arrow and a quill arrow.

Sella, a spear used for killing bear, the head of which, made of iron, is shaped as an arrow, is twelve inches long, wings grooved, has one or two barbs at the bottom, and is set in a shaft the length of a man. There are also some barbless spears.

Knives—

1. *Kadiban*, a long slightly curved sword, thirty inches point to hilt.
2. *Nora-kiban*, same as above with protected hilt.
3. *Kandattarun*, a curved, broad, pointed blade sharp on inner edge, used also as an implement for cutting fuel, about eighteen inches blade. Short wooden handle.
4. *Kokkoran*, of the same shape as three but small, used generally to cut and peel vegetables or fruit.
5. *Kundin*, one edged dagger, of varying lengths.
6. *Suri-kunan*, double edged dagger.
7. *Anub-suri-kunan*, double edged dagger with protected hilt.

Axes—

1. *Enjuman*, head, eight inches over all, cutting face widening to three inches.

   A smaller sized one is called parsi juman.
2. *Angin*. Battle-axe. A variety of shapes.
3. Patur-ang.

NOTE.—Soras always have a knife in the loin cloth and carry either one of these battle-axes or bow and arrows. Arrows are never carried in a quiver, but gripped in the hand with the stave of the bow, even while shooting. Sheathes are provided for swords, daggers, and certain knives. For small knives and daggers sheathes are sometimes made of wood instead of leather.

Matchlocks—

1. *Modusi.*—A hollow iron tube about six inches long which is charged with powder and discharged at frequent intervals at the time of death or of Guar, to scare away the spirits.
2. *Jamiki-balan.*—A very long rudely made. Used as above and for killing birds and animals.
3. *Katturu-balan.*—A hand matchlock about twenty inches long used as No. 1.

NOTE.—Soras are not allowed to use or own cartridge guns or rifles. They are permitted to have shot guns.

Clubs.—They have oar-shaped, mace shaped and a bulging flat-headed club.

(e) Languages of the Madras Agency Tracts.

Munda tongues

The Munda Branch now contributes 50 to every 10,000 in the presidency. The variations in the contribution are shown in the margin. After a drop in 1921, the figure of 1901 and 1911 has almost been reached again. Particular efforts were made to secure as precise language returns as possible in the Vizagapatam Agency in which most risk of uncertainty in Munda languages arises. Saora gives no difficulty. It is recognized as a distinct language and returned as such. Its fellow-Mundas, however, are apt to be lost under such terms as Jhodia or Poroja. Enumerators were told not to accept such answers as Jhodia or Poroja, but to ask what particular variety of either was in question. As a result, many returns of Pareng and Bonda were received which went to swell the Munda total. Pareng is probably associated with Saora rather than Gadaba. Gutob was included in Gadaba, of which it is a form. This insistence on detail was responsible for the appearance of the Pengo form of Kond and for Dhruva. There was a large remnant of Poroja *tout court* which has had to be shown as such. This may cover elements from various languages. Jhodia has been shown separately and a similar uncertainty attaches to it. Some Oriyas say Jhodia is 'merely Oriya' but this is a glib deduction from the large number of Oriya words which of necessity appear in the speech of all Vizagapatam hill tribes of the central plateau taluks. One might as well say English was 'merely Latin'—or Greek—because of its extensive borrowings from these tongues. It is much more likely that expert linguistic survey would remove from the Oriya head some of the dialect forms now classed under it. It is unfortunate that the Linguistic Survey did not deal with Madras; a magnificent field awaits the philologist in Madras' Agency tracts. My acquaintance with the Vizagapatam Agency is unfortunately only that of a visitor but even a visitor's ear can observe the pronounced individuality of much that passes for Oriya in these areas.

	1931.	1921.	1911.	1901.
Munda ..	49	47	50	50

Agency Tongues.

Words and Phrases from certain Agency languages.

Dhruva (chiefly N. W. Malkanagiri).

A collection of typical Dhruva and Gondia word is given. For these I am indebted to Mr. Bell, who wrote in forwarding them ! 'I have examined some Dhruvas, and enclose some specimens of their language, from which it can be seen that it is Dravidian in origin, but has an Oriya superstructure, *e.g.*, all numerals above five are Oriya. They do not know any Telugu, but can all speak the local Oriya, which is known as "Holuva bhasha". They have relations in Bastar, and in one village (Gondipalle) near Malkanagiri. They are separate from the Diduva Porojas of the Kudumulagumma neighbourhood. They drink all kinds of alcohol but do not eat cowflesh.

'I also give some specimens of the Gondia language for purposes of comparison. These Gondias are really Koyyas, but as they are separated from the Koyyas near Malkanagiri, they say they have a little difficulty in understanding the real Koyya language. They do not know Telugu. They are found mainly in the Salimi mutta and Sukuma of Bastar.

It is difficult to express some of the sounds especially consonants, l and n, at the end of the word. Gondias and Dhruvas say they cannot understand each other's language, nor can they speak in it with members of any other tribe'.

Kamari (Koranat).

2. This peculiar tongue was tentatively classed with Oriya on the advice of local officers. It is doubtful however whether Oriya is the origin or merely a superstructure which has obscured a different origin. The words and phrases at the end contain a good deal that seems non-Oriya. In this as in so many other cases of these Agency tongues a longer and an expert scrutiny would be required.

Valmiki (or Thalli) (Padwa, Pottangi).

3. The sentences given at the end show both Dravidian and Oriya elements The verb 'is' resembles Oriya, but the general nature is Dravidian. Some words are identical with Telugu, *e.g.*, 'marriage', 'fifty', etc. This dialect, whatever its true associations, gives a good idea of the extraordinary mingling of different elements in a single common speech.

4. If the examples which follow seems to very in quality it must be remembered that they have been collected in answer to my requests by persons mostly quite unskilled in philology, here a revenue inspector, there a range officer and so on. They are inserted in the hope that they may throw some faint light on the linguistic variety of Vizagapatam.

	Dhruva.	Gondia.
Water	*Nīru.*	*Er.*
House	*Ollen.*	*Lōnu.*
Hill	*Konding.*	*Metta.*
River	*Kolāb.*	*Savara.*
Gedda	*Sīluva.*	*Kuyar.*
Tree	*Merku.*	*Mora.*
Father	*Tāta.*	*Bābō.*
Mother	*Iyyā.*	*Yāyo.*
Son	*Chindu.*	*Mara*
Daughter	*Mālu.*	*Maiyār.*
Dog	*Netta.*	*Nayyu.*
Cow	*Gāi.*	*Godu.*
Bull	*Badāo.*	*Konda.*
Goat	*Mēva.*	*Mekka.*
Crow	*Kākāl.*	*Kākār.*
Elephant	*Enu.*	*Enu.*
Milk	*Pēlu.*	*pālu.*
Paddy	*Vērchil.*	*Vanji.*
Rice	*Perukul.*	*Nūka.*
Ragi	*Rātel.*	*Gorra.*
Hand	*Khēyu.*	*Khēyu.*
Stomach	*Potta.*	*Potta.*
Nose	*Mūānd.*	*Mosar.*
Ear	*Kēkōsil.*	*Kēvu.*
Head	*Tel.*	*Tala.*
One	*Okut.*	*Ondu.*
Two	*Urdu.*	*Rendu*
Three	*Mūnduk.*	*Mūndu.*
Four	*Nāluk.*	*Nālu.*
Five	*Chēnduk.*	*Engu.*
Six	Etc., as in Oriya.	*Aru.*
Seven		*Sāt.*
		Etc., as in Oriya.

(1) There are four houses in my village.

Dhruva .. *E polubti nāluva olle mendāl.*

Gondia .. *Nā nāte nālu lōnu mende.*

(2) I have two wives.

Dhruva .. *Anu urdu āyārchilānu mendal.*

Gondia .. *Nāku rendu motte mende.*

(3) To-morrow I will go to the shandy.

Dhruva .. *Tōlin āt chendā ānu.*

Gondia .. *Nāru āt anumanji vattun.*

(4) He beat me.

Dhruva .. *Od ani chāditil.*

Gondia .. *Odra naku rēstor.*

(5) I have two { sons. / daughters. }

Gondia .. *Nāku* { *iruvuru marku* / *rendu māyārs* } *mende*

Gutalu.

Golgonda Agency.

(1) *Idya edo no ?* .. .. .. Did you take your food ?
(2) *Nomo karnugono ?* .. .. .. Are you married ?
(3) *Ne karnugone ?* .. .. .. I am married.
(4) *Sarmo girno gunornu ?* .. .. Have you washed your face ?
(5) *Sarmo girno genne* .. .. .. I have washed my face.
(6) *Yentha monthi yonend.* .. .. How many children have you ?
(7) *Ponbo gusso dithu ?* .. .. .. Have you a dog ?
(8) *Nonbo gusso udoya* .. .. .. I have no dog.
(9) *Yapati boma dithu ?* .. .. How many cattle have you ?
(10) *Neyapa kiltgori dithu ?* .. .. Have you a god ?

Thigh = *Billi*. Eye = *Moh*. Water = *Doy*.
Hand = *Thithie*. Ear = *Rintulu*. House = *Diyenu*.
Chest = *Nera*. Fire = *Sungala*. Horse = *Kirathe*.
Tiger = *Ghikola*.

Numerals are Telugu.

Clearly this is widely different from Telugu, despite certain evidence of borrowing. Of Oriya there is no trace. A Munda language with some apparent resemblance to Saora.

Gutob.

Palkonda Agency.

(1) *Miyya kaba dulilino ?* .. .. What work are you doing ?
(2) *Nonpai yendaruone ?* .. .. How many children have you ?
(3). *Miya kaba dililino ?* .. .. What are they doing ?
(4) *Ingomboy endaru duthupen ?* .. .. How many people of your caste are living in your village ?
(5) *Pay ingombo penukilankay endaru duthupen ?* Have you any relatives living in any other villages ?
(6) *Nom payi bhumi duthuki ?* .. .. Have you any lands ?
(7) *Nomg payiyeti kiye pati kirampingi ?* .. How much paddy do you get annually ?

Traces of Telugu borrowing appear—'*endaru*', *e. g.*,—but this is no Dravidian or Aryan tongue. *Cf.* the Gutalu from Golgonda, farther south. The resemblance is obvious.

Gutumuo.

Yellavaran taluk, East Godavari Agency.

(1) What is your village ? .. .. *Yen bōr goda.*
(2) How many children have you ? .. *Nō pā yendal vōnē ?*
(3) Four children .. .. .. *Nalluru vōnē.*
(4) Sit down on the stool (to an inferior) .. *Vulō dādā pittam bō laibāni.*
(5) Please sit on the stool (to a superior) .. *Vulō bābā pittam bō laiba.*
(6) Why did you abuse me ? .. .. *Me pailōngano ?*
(7) Is there any rice (uncooked) ? .. .. *Rukkum uttudā ?*
(8) No .. .. *Urē.*
(9) Do you eat rice (cooked) ? .. .. *Ayyam sōmānā ?*
(10) I eat (it) .. .. *Sōmāni.*
(11) Are you married ? .. .. .. *Kamu dēngō ?*
(12) I am married .. .. .. *Kamu dēnga.*
(13) Did she send the maize ? .. .. *Jonna bullukā ?*
(14) She sent (it) .. .. .. *Bullūka.*
(15) How many seers of ragi do they give to the rupee ? *Sammēl yerān jēdbēn dēlē tonka ?*
(16) Four kunchams per rupee .. .. *Tonkā pai nalgu kuncha mulu.*

Telugu numerals are used and some borrowing of words appears (stool, ragi) but this seems clearly a branch of Gadaba. 'Tonka' is Oriya.

KAMARI.

Koraput Taluk.

Nouns.	Kamari.	Telugu transliteration.
Tree	*Gatchu.*	
Watch	*Pāniyāk.*	
Man	*Dāda.*	
Box	*Pediyāk.*	
Table	*Pattāka.*	
Chair	*Kurchiyāk.*	
Wall	*Kotti*	
Verbs.		
Came	*Keruthīs.*	
Went	*Kenjāvīs.*	
Ate	*Kadalis.*	
Slept	*Kunaītō.*	
We both went to the bazar	*Diyi lōku misnūju sangai.*	
I am uneasy today	*Ebba makka bĕhām sukhuni.*	
He owes me money	*Tomak tonkā dĕbbāku achai.*	
The rate of standard gold is too high	*Sunnā vachi dattī dhara vachi achai.*	

Some Oriya influences are clear : tree, '*tonka*', 'give'. 'is', are obvious Oriya forms. Others are Telugu. There is a considerable residue which seems to be neither, a residue containing common roots and constructions.

KONDA.

Padwa Taluk.

What is your village ?	*Ima nato ?*
My (village) is Mattamputtu	*Nadi Mattamputtu.*
What is your occupation ?	*Pani kedeng ?*
I live by cultivating land	*Bhumi panikyo vundeng.*
How many children have you ?	*Yeasondar monnar buda ?*
I have five children	*Iduko manishi kodūr monnar.*
How have your crops fared this year ?	*Yevatti panta pandu vetad ?*
Formerly I used to get 10-12 pattis, now 5	*Padi patlu ani bhūmi ayidu puttlu atadi.*
Why ?	*Ennika ?*
Wind and rain brought a spate in the nalla which washed over my crops.	*Gali pirru gedda vatadal evondu ma panta doru vattad.*

Verbs.

Come = *Ra.* Lie down = *Rasunia.* *Sit* = *Basa.*
Bring = *Tasso sitha.*

Nouns.

Dog = *Nukūdi.* Cat = *Belli.* Man } *Loku.*
Cow = *Kodi.* Horse = *Gurram.* Person }

Numerals.

8 = *Yenimidu.* 12 = *Pandyandu.* 20 = *Eravai.*

All numerals are apparently Telugu and many roots, *e.g.*, come, horse, wind.

MULI.

Padwa Taluk.

(1)	*Hulo paiti kortinga*	I am doing cultivation.
(2)	*Gandagudai jamin*	I was born in Gandaguda.
(3)	*Podaman vedhaman hai*	I have wet and dry lands.
(4)	*Putek deryiputek paksa*	Yielding one or two puttis.
(5)	*Bhinga jairotho odiya sango kothaheth amor.*	I speak Oriya and our own language if I go outside.
(6)	*Kodriya boro oake moke behiba korna*	I was married at 20 years of age.
(7)	*More lechi hai*	My wife is alive.
(8)	*Goteksi beta moke hai.*	I have one son.

Oriya resemblances or borrowings appear at once, *e.g.*, *hulo, paiti, beta, kodriya.* Other resemblances are more with Hindi, *e.g.*, hai. The structure seems however to justify a classification with Kond.

PARENG.

Padwa Taluk.

(1) *Ming jaoding neru meng neru* .. .. I live by begging.

(2) *Doraputu jonmu nera raxi* .. .. I was born in Doraput.

(3) *Mingku yagloako duke gi* .. .. I have three sons.

(4) *Ming labo ao duku* .. .. .. I had lands.

(5) *Minumku kudixe puti danuluru* .. I was getting 20 puttis of paddy.

(6) *Ming amkyi kire kaduregi* .. .. My wife died.

Some resemblances to or borrowings from Oriya are evident, *e.g.*, *Jonmu* and *kudixe* but the general structure is widely different.

REMU (GADABA).

Palkonda Taluk.

Come = *Vutō*.

Go = *Vuyyā*.

God = *Kithuvōrēmu*.

King = *Mēvu*.

Mother = *Iyyām*.

Father = *Appiyā*.

Paddy = *Kērām*.

Water = *Diyya*.

I am eating = *Idiyā idini*.

What are you doing ? = *Miyāmka bādu litinō*.

VALMIKI (THALLI).

Padwa and Pottangi.

Anka vyavasayam kamu .. .. I am doing cultivation.

Anka padbe jermilai .. .. .. I was born in Padwa.

Anka doggula duvo asti .. .. .. I have two daughters.

Anka bhumulu asti .. .. .. I have lands.

Anka yabhei khandi dhanu versi jettayi .. I get 50 putties of paddy annually.

Anchi jati mansutile anchi bhasha lattabuttasi yera jati mansutile jeveinchi bhasha lattabuttasi. Among my caste people I speak my own language. Among other caste people I speak their language.

Anka yiseku versuka pendli jalli .. .. I was married when 20 years of age.

Anchi terni jeevitile asse .. .. .. My wife is alive.

19. The Chenchus.

By Ghulam Ahmed Khan.

The Chenchus are located in the south of the Mahbubnagar district of the Nizam's Dominions which the Krishna separates from the Kurnool District of the Madras Presidency. They at present inhabit the plateau of a hill range known as Nallamalai. The altitude of the hills ranges between 2,500 and 3,000 feet. The hills are densely forest clad and infested by wild animals. Until thirty years ago this part of the Nizam's territory had not been traversed by any. The Collector of the district, thirty years ago, with a view to explore the possibility of making the hills a summer resort had a track cut through the woods over the hills to the highest point which he named Farhabad. The first lap of this track has since been moorumed and improved so as to be motorable. After a hairpin turn from the first ascent you motor straight to Mannanur, wherein is His Exalted Highness' penitentiary for political prisoners and a fairly good rest house for those who seek shikar. From Mannanur the first Chenchus's penta is ten miles distant.

According to the recent Census there are as many as 53 pentas scattered over the hills and valleys. A penta consists of 15 to 25 huts. Thus they form a social compact which wander about a tract of a few miles square forming the beat, gathering honey and berries and digging roots.

Appearance.—The physique of the person living in higher altitude is distinctly superior to that of their brother in the lower regions, who are comparatively short in stature and emaciated. Handsomeness as we understand is unknown in the case of men and women. The man grows his hair as a woman does and dresses it in a knot either at the back or on the upper left of his head. He does not comb his hair but prunes it with his fingers and the falling hair is scrupulously collected, plaited and wound round the knot. The barber's razor of Sheffield make has found its way into the huts and is made a liberal use of for mowing down beards. Baldness among men or women is unknown.

Women grow their hair which is neither cut nor combed. The use of castor oil for the hair is a recent innovation, so also that of wooden nit comb for destroying lice. Women's hair is generally short and curly.

Dress and ornaments.—The men's garment is a strip of cloth about three to six inches wide according to requirements and 30 inches long. It is an abbreviated lungoti, passed between the thighs and the ends thereof are held to the waist covering the nakedness by a plant fibre. If the piece is longer, the extra length is left to flap about behind. It is the ceremonial dress and is certainly a distinct advance on the teak leaves. Occasional visitors to the hills distribute country dhoties but the men do not use them. The dhoti is slung over the shoulder when standing and put under the buttocks when sitting. The top outer edge of the left ear is bored and a few wear a brass ring with a bead in the centre. One or two men wear on their left arm above the elbow nickel armlets. This is another evidence of the slow and sure process of Civilization. Men wear a waistband of a double piece of leather crudely cut from goat's skin and sown together. They carry in this, flintstones and also stick into it knives.

The Chenchu woman's original dress was that of mother Eve's—a two piece costume of broad teak leaves held round the waist by means of fibre. Now the suggestion of wearing leaves is repugnant to the woman and is regarded as an outrage on her modesty. She is proud to wear a piece of rag which does not reach below her knee. A choli (bodice) for the upper part of the body completes her dress. The bodice is quite a recent introduction. It is given as a present of the graziers in return for the services rendered. The Chenchu woman does not know the use of the thread and needle. The Chenchu woman is as scantily clad as any poor woman of the depressed classes; but the man will never give up his langoti, which he regards as a mark of distinction. Several strings of beads adorn the neck—one worn in childhood, another at puberty and a third of two or three rows, at marriage. They are taken out only when the woman becomes a widow. Before the advent of beads women collected half dried polki seeds, pierced them with a thorn and when dry and strung them into two or three rows and worn round the neck. Glass bracelets are worn by women. The absence of them is a sign of widowhood.

Weapons.—Weapons of warfare are none. The only equipment the men have is the bow and arrow. They are seldom used except in self-defence. The stave is of a single piece of wood. It is cut, trimmed and shaped with notches at both ends. The string is made of the fibre of a plant. The fibre is cleaned, dried and twisted into a cord and greased. The centre of the cord where the arrow is placed is bound with leather. The arrow is of bamboo. Its butt end is plain. When not in use the string of the bow is released from the top notch. Iron tipped arrows are also used for shooting wild animals but no poison is applied to the tip.

Character.—The Chenchu is noted for his truthfulness and honesty. When I was recently on a visit to the hills I was informed by a Forest officer that two men were put up for trial on a charge of distilling and selling liquor. The prosecution had no eyewitness but merely relied on the accused's honesty. At the trial both the accused pleaded guilty to the charge of distilling and were sentenced to a month's imprisonment.

To visitors to their villages they are kind and hospitable. In every village there is built a guest house, a simple unfurnished hut. If it is found occupied, one of their own dwellings is cleared for the use of the visitor. He is admirably compromising in his attitude towards a wrong doer and the words of the Chief are implicitly obeyed. They detect bees nests by watching their visits to water and the direction in which they flow away and taking a bee-line in that direction.

[*Cf.* the practice of the Angami Naga in Assam who catches large hornets and ties a piece of pith to each, following the white mark and releasing another hornet when it is out of sight, thus being led ultimately to the nest and a comb of many grubs, large, fat, white and esculent. A similar practice is recorded of the Dalleburra tribe in Queensland on the Australian continent (*vide* J. R. A. I., LVII, p. 410; and *The Angami Nagas*, p. 84).—I. H. H.]

The Chenchu is fleet-footed. Though poorly fed he has extraordinary physical endurance. Carrying a load on his head he would negotiate steep and narrow gradients with greater ease and facility than one would imagine.

Cold he can't bear. Being ill clad he sits by the fireside and warms himself. He imagines that the rest of the world is much colder than his country. I offered to show the city of Hyderabad to one of the stalwart young man; but he said he was afraid he would be frozen to death if he went out. Women make dutiful wives as perhaps all women do in a lesser grade of civilisation. In their husband's absence from home the Chenchu woman would not go beyond the limits of the village. When necessary, she would seek the company of an elderly woman or her nearest female relative. Polygamy is prevalent among them and is attendant with such evils as bickerings quarrels. The woman, who is not tolerant to the other wife, is at liberty to quit the home with her children. Children are well looked after and chastised for naughtiness.

II.—*Domestic Life.*

The site of the Chenchu pentas is usually on the plateaux. I would not call the pentas as villages. They are a mere cluster of huts bearing none of the features of the Indian villages which have evolved out after a series of incursions of different races. The names of pentas, at least some of them, do not appear to have been given by them. Vittevalpalli, Mallapuram and Tapsipenta are the names assigned to the forest clearings for settlement. Tapsipenta, for instance, is the spot noted for tapsi trees. But Puli Chalma, by which name a penta goes, suggests that it was given by the Chenchus, puli meaning tiger and Chalma a pond. Communication between pentas is by means of paths across dense jungles. They are obliterated by the rains and by grass and vegetation in the winter.

The arrangement of huts in a penta is not on any definite plan. The first row of huts are arranged in a semi-circle and the others go in a straight line from the last hut. Patches of vegetable garden are at close quarters, gourd and pumpkin being the only varieties grown. The gourd plant is allowed to creep upon the hut or on a temporary support erected in front of the hut. Cattle are tethered to posts stuck in the ground in front of the hut.

The graves of the dead are about a furlong away from the penta and are marked by earth mounds overlaid with stones.

The penta is surrounded with rubbish heaps and therefore very insanitary.

The House.—There is only one type of hut found in the pentas. A well seasoned tree, six cubits long and twelve inches in circumference, at the bottom is planted. With a split bamboo or some plant fibre of three cubits in length a circle is drawn round the pole from its base and a bamboo mat three feet wide and sufficiently long to go round the circle is next fixed and secured to the ground by means of plugs. From the top of the central post bamboo rafters are laid to rest on the mat wall, and with similar material the frame work of the conical roof is completed and covered with thatch. Entrance to the hut is obtained by a rectangular opening, about two cubits high and three feet wide. The doorway of the hut may not open towards the west. A smaller hut is exactly half the size in all respects. The mat wall is mud plastered. Within the hut, a hearth of stones is made and the household utensils such as cooking and water pots, baskets, winnows etc., are kept on the left, the right half of the hut-space being reserved for sitting and sleeping. Bow and, arrows and muzzle loading guns are stuck into the roof from inside the hut. Half way up the roof they have a shelf of bamboo mat.

Fire.—Safety matches have not yet gone into this area but it is convenient for the Chenchus to make fire in the old time-honoured method, with flints. Brand is served to the neighbouring housewife when called for. Refusal would tantamount to excommunication.

Agriculture.—" I don't know how to till the ground " is the answer invariably given by men.

Livestock.—The cattle consist of buffaloes, not their own but belonging to graziers, left in their charge for a time. Goats and chickens they rear. Dogs are their pet animals. Only two names of dogs are current among them, namely, Pappy and Laddu. Both appear to have been borrowed from the Banjarras. One is distinguished from another by its colour, *Nalla Pappy* (black pappy) and Thella Laddu (white laddu). Cats are not found in the villages.

Food.—The food of the Chenchu consists principally of roots (*gaddalu*) and berries (*pandulu*). Herbs and fungi are also eaten. Tamarind fruit is eaten mixed with ashes obtained from burning the bark of the same tree. Mohwa flower is boiled and eaten. No salt is added to the cooked food, whether of roots, fruits or jawar (*Sorghum vulgare*). Pumpkins and gourds are cut into large pieces and boiled and eaten without salt. They appreciate salt but it is not available. They eat animal flesh when available. The skin is also eaten after the hair has been singed, so also the intestines after removing the filth. Small birds, squirrels, rats and mice are roasted on fire and eaten.

Drink.—Mohwa flower (Bassia latifolia) is collected and boiled and the water which is not absorbed into the cooked flower is poured off into a vessel. It is then cooled, fermented and drunk.

Narcotics.—The only narcotic generally used is tobacco. It is obtained by bartering honey or other forest produces. It is retained in the mouth and spat out again.

Dancing.—Generally when intoxicated on occasions of festivals and marriages men and women dance to the beating a circular drum. A satisfactory description of the dance is a difficult task. Dr. Hutton says that " the dance tunes are very suggestive of Sawara tunes and one or two approached a jig of reel in time. As by Sawaras and Kondhs a hide gong is used. The women's dance suggested more that of the Porajas but they had another dance which I have not seen elsewhere in which they sang and clapped their hands in time clapping their palms against the palm of each neighbour ". The dance is circular alternately between the claps of their hands. With alternate movement of limbs the body is swung aside. Women take the upper part of their saree and holding the wide ends in the hand dance. I have not yet been able to ascertain the nature of songs they sing.

Daily Life.—The daily life of the Chenchu is an uncertain one. The man rises early in the morning and goes off to the jungle in search of roots and berries for the family. Woman sweeps the floor and cooks food if any available and brings water. Young children cling to their mothers at home while the grown ups are busy doing odd jobs. Before noon men return home and are served with food. After them, women and children eat. After food, elders collect together and discuss matters of common interest.

Organization of Society.

The Chenchus can be said to be an organised body so far as it is compatible with their primitive culture. If the Penta is the basis of unit of organization it is interesting to note that it is not inhabited by one particular sept or kulam to the exclusion of all others. Except in the matter of choosing a wife, there is no occasion for accentuating clan feelings.

Exogamy.—The Chenchus are divided into five septs. Thokalu, Nimalu, Erravalu, Siggilu and Maindlu. The origin of the Kulams is indeed a matter of conjecture. Various fantastic accounts are heard but one is not without interest. Thokalu in Telugu is tail. A person was fond of eating tail in preference to any other piece of flesh and whenever an animal was slaughtered they cut the tail and reserved it for that man, saying this is for thokalavadu (tail man). His offspring came to be called Thokaluwadu. Another version and probably more reasonable is that the name has been taken after the squirrel, which in these regions is reddish brown in colour and as large as a rabbit in size with a big bushy tail. I saw one of this variety at the Zoo labelled as " Malabar squirrel ". Nimalu is the name given to the class of Chenchus who happened to live in a lime grove. The man who relishes some red roots more than any other variety came to be called Erravalu, or perhaps it may indicate a remote reference to its connection with the Mediterranean people as all fair people are generally called red by the primitive people. Siggilu is presumably a corruption of Sigiri, tender edible leaves of the tamarind tree. Maindlu's origin is obscure and worth investigating. Another assumption can be that as this clan is regarded as the more respectable one, perhaps remained free from the contact of other people—Munda means head. However uncertain their origin may be, it is clear there is some form of totemism since most of them trace their clan formation to animals and trees.

The five groups of the Chenchus are exogamous. Thokalus and Erravalus are regarded to be near cousins; so are Nimalus, Siggilus and Maindlus. The two groups therefore intermarry. A Chenchu, whichever sept he may belong to, may not marry any but the daughter of mother's brother or that of father's sister. If intentionally a man married a woman of his own totem he is charged with incest and outcasted and banished from the limits of the colony.

Relationship through the female line is seldom recognized as the Chenchu society is of patriarchal nature.

The Chenchu is not strictly a monogamist. The chief or he who has the means, marries two wives. On the ground of barrenness or sterility on the part of his wife or even on the excuse of incompatibility of temperament a Chenchu takes a second woman. Brother's widow, if childless and she is willing, is taken over by the younger or elder brother.

Property.—Property consists of the hut, earthern utensils, crude implements and mats and baskets. To the list may be added chickens and goats. On the death of a man, his first son inherits them. If the widow is childless the property of the deceased goes to the first brother of the deceased; if the man had no brother, his sister claims it. If none at all, the nearest relatives and the people of the penta distribute the belongings among themselves. No case of adoption is known to the Chenchus. Settlement of disputes is made by the headman after he has heard the case in panchayat of elders. Oath is generally taken on heaven (Akasa amma) and earth (Bhoomi amma). More reliance is placed on the evidence tendered on oath taken on trees such as Mohwa and Tamarind which provide the witness with food. It may be interesting to mention that the most sacred oath with the Gond is on the tiger skin and that of the Bhil on the dog. He who commits a breach of the settlement is fined and the fine is "eaten" by the Panch. The fine is realized by way of Mohwa flower and liquor.

Religion.—By religion the Chenchu is officially known to be animist; but as far as I have been able to enquire he has still retained his pristine paganism though apparently he is now a believer in deities which have definite names, characteristics and functions. The principal deities are Akasa Amma (Sky), Bhoomi Amma (Earth) and Amma Talli (Smallpox goddess). The sky is the supreme god. The latest addition is lingam represented by a piece of stone or wood. The sun also is worshipped. The appearance of the soul of a deceased person in any form is incredible, says the Chenchu, although he holds that a dead body should be washed in sitting posture so that the water may wet both sides; otherwise the spirit would return home. [This rather suggests that the dead are washed to prevent the spirits leaving the body, as the inability of spirits to cross water is notorious.—J. H. H.] The religious belief and observances of the Chenchus offer a wide field for a sympathetic study and I propose to take up the question early.

Birth.—As soon as pain begins the males move out of the hut and old women of the penta are called in to assist the labouring woman. Utensils and other articles are collected on one part of the hut allowing other half of the space for lying in. The expectant mother is made to squat with her legs propped up. A large stone is placed to support her back or she is held by the shoulders by another woman. A woman who has experience in attending to delivery cases sits in front of the woman and renders her timely assistance. When the woman is delivered of the child the after-birth is buried away from the hut by the woman who attends upon her. The baby is washed and laid beside the mother. Should the mother die in child-birth she is taken out quickly and buried. If the child be alive it is given to another woman for suckling; but if the child is dead both the mother and child are buried together in the same grave.

The period of confinement is six or seven days. Both the midwife and the woman are considered to be unclean. Their meal is served at the doorway. Their vessels are not touched by others. On the seventh day the woman is given bath and the stained cloth washed and dried. The midwife in the meantime sweeps the floor and plasters it with mud, and then takes her bath. She is then clean and goes out to call the husband of the woman delivered to come into the house, who during all these days had been living in another hut.

Naming of the child generally takes place after ten or twelve days. The name is chosen and given by the parents themselves and no ceremony attends the function. Lingadu, Biyadu and Guruvadu are the principal male names and Lingamma, Guruvamma and Idamma, are those of females—all derived from their goddesses.

A child is suckled for about one year or until another is born.

Puberty.—In the case of a girl, she is secluded in a hut specially erected for her. An old woman attends upon her. Both are unclean for 3 or 4 days. The girl is then bathed and her soiled linen if useless buried; otherwise it is washed and dried for further use. In their leafy days, the soiled leaves were likewise dealt with. The girl after bath is given a piece of clean cloth and a bodice and her forehead is marked with yellow powder which is supplied by the graziers. No ceremony is done on that occasion. Such grown up girls sleep in their own hut but away from their parents. Boys either sleep in a corner of the same hut or with friends of their age. But no separate dormitory or bachelors hall exists for them.

Marriage.—That a girl has attained womanhood is not published in any manner but through her parents and relatives the news goes from mouth to mouth. A lad who is in the know of things approaches his mother with a desire to marry the girl. The mother informs the father. Both father and mother then set out to the girl's house. Preliminary enquiries are first made through an old woman who acts as an intermediary. Then the mother of the boy speaks to the mother of the girl and the father to the father. The girl's consent is also obtained. If all ends well, a date is fixed for the marriage. The Chenchus are extraordinarily ignorant of time and distance. The fixing of a day is therefore not significant. It means the elapse of a few days and nights. If the bride belongs to another penta a messenger is sent there in advance to inform them of the bride groom's arrival. The parents of the boy with their relatives and friends headed by a drummer set out carrying a load of Mohwa flower and liquor. On sighting the penta the drummer beats the drum and the bride's party from that penta come up a distance to meet the guests and the bridegroom. They exchange greetings and eat, drink and dance. They next proceed to the penta spend the night. Soon after sunrise all collect together and the bride's parents provide a feast of Mohwa flower, roots and liquor. The girl is given by the lad a piece of cloth and bodice and also some strings of beads which she wears. The guests eat, drink and dance and the father of the girl then turns to the bridegroom and tells him to look after his wife kindly and well. This is all the marriage ceremony and no priest is employed to perform any rite. As a matter of fact the priest does not exist in the Chenchu society. The party then sets out on their return journey at noon. The girl reside with her mother-in-law till a separate hut is erected for the new couple. Until then the bridegroom sleeps elsewhere. In the day time, however, the young man takes his wife to the jungle where they cohabit.

Burial Ceremony.—When a man is seriously ill and on the point of death they gather a bamboo post, some dry grass and plant fibre. After he has breathed his last inside the hut, the body is brought out, propped up and washed by men. The upper garment which he may have is taken away by the brother or a near relative and the body is laid on the grass. The bamboo post is placed on the body and wrapped up and tied. Two men carry the body on their shoulders to the grave yard. Then they dig the grave, about 3 feet deep and about the length of the body, running east to west, untie the bundle, draw off the bamboo post and the body is lowered. It is laid on the stomach, head towards the west, face turned to the right and the palms of hands turned upwards. The position of the body in the grave as laid on the stomach is rather unique and I have never found any other people burying their dead in this manner. [See page 361 of the Madras Census Report, 1931. Some Chenchu appear to bury and others to burn their dead, and in the case of burial the head may be to the north or the south, the former in South Kurnool, the latter in East and West Kurnool. The face is not necessarily placed downwards and the body is sometimes covered with a shroud or with leaves; the face sometimes with a cobweb—to catch and prevent the escape of the soul ?—J. H. H.] The langoti is then drawn off and put near the feet. The grave is then filled with earth and stones are heaped over it. While leaving the grave the persons walk round the grave once and depart from the foot end of the grave.

In the case of a woman, the body is washed by women but is carried to the grave by men wrapped in grass. Three to seven days mourning is observed.

20. The Kadar of Cochin.

By K. Govinda Menon.

The name *Kadar** signifies *forest-dwellers*. They inhabit the interior forest tracts and never the outskirts or areas adjoining plains. They are invariably dark coloured, have pouting thick lips and frizzly hair and are stout and muscular. Dr. Keane, in his *Living Races of Mankind* says :

"There is good evidence to show that the first arrivals in India were a black people, most probably Negritos, who made their way from Malayasia† round the Bay of Bengal to the Himalayan foot hills, and then spread over the Peninsula without ever reaching Ceylon. At present there are no distinctly Negrito communities in the land, nor has any clear trace of a distinctly Negrito language yet been discovered. But distinctly Negrito features crop up continually in all the uplands from the Himalayan slopes to Cape Comorin over against Ceylon. The Negritos, in fact, have been absorbed or largely assimilated by the later intruders, and, as of these there are four separate stocks, we call these Negritos the submerged fifth. There is ample evidence for the submergence since they arrived, if not in the early, certainly in the Tertiary period many thousands of years ago." The Kadar have Negrito characteristics blended with those of other races and are not racially pure in any sense of the word.

Dress, ornamentation, etc.—The dress of the Kadar in old days consisted of a white or coloured loin-cloth for men and a coloured cloth and bodice for women. The latter wore glass bangles, coloured beads, couri necklaces and *oda* ear-rings. They also stick into their hair, which is tied into a knot at the back, combs of bamboo or *oda* for ornamentation. Males too grew their hair in full and did it into a knot at the back like females, smoothening it with a gloss of cocoanut or gingelly oil. Of late they get their hair cropped in imitation of the people of the plains. They have scarcely any hair on their face except a little on the chin and on the upper lip, which they never shave.

Both males and females file the incisor teeth of the upper and lower jaws. The origin of this custom is lost in obscurity and we can only make conjectures about it. The Kadar himself says that it is done for beauty.

Weapons.—Except his root-digger or *kooran-kole* and bill-hook the Kadan has no weapon at all. These two instruments meet all his requirements whether of offence or of defence. He is not much given to offence, being gentle and inoffensive by nature, and his occasions of defence are also very rare. His keenness of hearing and smell saves him from all danger. The distant approach of his enemy, the elephant, the tiger, the bear, the panther and other wild animals, is conveyed to him by his sense of smell and hearing ; and he gives a wide berth to these enemies. Casualties through wild animals coming upon the Kadar unaware are very rare. Their children shoot birds with bow and arrows and with catapults made of a forked stick with elastic traces‡ but these pastimes are not cultivated beyond adolescence. The axe has lately been introduced in connection with wood-cutting ; but its use has not yet become common.

Habitations.—The Kadar live in huts, 15 to 20 of which are grouped together to form a village. The selection of the site for the village is based on considerations of food and water supply. These huts are but temporary structures, easily improvised of readily available materials like saplings and poles of various forest growths, bamboos, *odas,* fibres of various climbers and llianes and leaves of *oda* and teak and *punna* (§*Dillenia pentagyna*). But they are very artistic and neat, and the *oda* leaf thatching lasts half a decade. The floor is sometimes slightly raised, earth being dumped in and beaten down hard for the purpose. Of furniture there is practically nothing in the modern sense of the word. Some coarse grass mats made by themselves and a few cots of bamboo posts and split bamboo rods or *thazhuthals* are the sole appurtenan ces to their dwellings. Food is cooked in a corner of the hut in earthen-ware vessels or tins.

Utensils.—It is not a matter of great concern to the Kadar to abandon their huts when they want to shift to a new area. They have but few possessions of value to take with them. A few earthen-ware vessels, mats, their carrying-basket called *pooni* made by themselves of *oda* or rattan, their bill-hooks and digging poles and their fire-making implements which they call *chakkumukki* are the only things they have to remove to their new abode. There is another utensil used for carrying water. It is a tube consisting of a few nodes of the thick bamboo (*Bambusa arundinacea*) with the internode plates knocked through. But this is a cheap and easily procurable article, so much so that it is left behind in the abandoned hut when they migrate.‖

Fire-making implements.—The fire-making implements of the Kadar comprise a piece of steel, a bit of quartz and the floss from the fronds of *Borassus flabellifer* (palmyra palm or brab tree) carried in a scooped out seed of *Entada scandens.* With these the Kadars produce fire easily whenever and wherever they want it.¶ There is no religious significance or any other kind of importance attached to this affair.

Food.—In olden days the Kadar lived chiefly on jungle roots and tubers. They are not vegetarians and they like all sorts of game and fish, but the bison and the bear are two animals which no Kadan will touch living or dead. They are very fond of honey and the honey-gathering season is accordingly a jolly time for them.

Marriage customs.—Marriages among the Kadar are usually arranged by the parents of the contracting parties ; but instances of the contracting parties themselves coming to an understanding are not rare. Exogamy is the usual custom but endogamy also is not unknown. Marriage with one's sister or her daughter or with one's brother's daughter is entirely forbidden ; but marriages between sister's or brother's children are allowed. Girls are never married before puberty and boys rarely before 25. The best marriages are those contracted between members of different villages (*pathies*) and not between members of the same village. As a token of betrothal the contracting parties through their parents or near kinsmen exchange some forest produce. Dowries consist of forest produce or articles made by themselves. Of late years money transactions also have been introduced to the detriment of the tribe. This unhappy development is to be attributed to their contact with civilization from the plains. The real marriage ceremony consists of feasting at the huts of the bride and bridegroom for a day, or two at the most. *Thali* tying which was unknown in old days has been introduced lately ; and gold chains and bangles which also were unknown are now substituted for their primitive

**Kadan* is the singular and *Kadar* is the plural in the Malayalam language. But *Kadars* is generally used as the plural on the analogy of English plurals, so that this a new singular *Kadar* (which is strictly a Malayalam plural) has also been formed.

† I do not know of any evidence to show that Negritos reached continental India from Malayasia rather than from the north or even from the west.—J. H. H.

‡Introduced about 30 years ago. Previously the sling was used.

§In his account of the Kadars in *The Cochin Tribes and Castes,* Mr. L. K. Ananthakrishna Ayyar has made several misstatements of fact. Here, for instance, he refers to the *Calophyllum Inophyllum* instead of *Dillenia pentagyna.*

‖Mr. Ananthakrishna Ayyar makes them carry this utensil also with them when they migrate.

¶Mr. Ananthakrishna Ayyar seems to think that it is a difficult process for the Kadars to produce fire and that they therefore preserve it carefully when once it is built up. The idea is wrong and misleading.

ornaments. The *marriage tie is very loose and either party is free to sever it whenever he or she wants to* do so. But instances of such desertion or divorce were practically unknown so long as the lust of civilized man from the plains was content to leave these innocent and harmless people to themselves.

Sexual intercourse.—Sexual intercourse among the Kadar is not effected within their huts but at a trysting place in the jungle agreed to between husband and wife. They go different ways and meet at the agreed place in the course of the day. After the intercourse both take a bath, completely immersing themselves under water, and return home. This custom is of peculiar significance in view of the fact that the Kadar do not bathe daily even though they have perennial streams in their midst. The males bathe every other day or even less frequently, while the females have their baths at longer intervals. The advent of men from the plains has brought about a radical change in these sexual habits of the Kadar. The former do not leave the Kadar women alone; and, according to their usage, they have connection with these women within their huts, making it a matter of daily routine. The Kadar in their original state had sexual connections few and far between as they never knew their wives in their huts. Comparisons are odious ; but one fears that civilized man does not stand to gain much when he is compared with these primitive people in the above respect.

Pregnancy and child-birth.—During the period of pregnancy the Kadar women go about their usual vocations in their ordinary dress.* The accouchement takes place in a small hut built for the purpose and removed from the usual abode. There are no professional midwives among the Kadars but elderly dames attend the lying-in. A decoction of certain medicinal herbs and roots is taken both morning and evening during the lying-in period, and they partake of the usual diet. The mother suckles the baby for as long as she cares to, after which the baby is gradually given adult's food. Though women are considered unclean for three months after child-birth, the period of actual birth pollution is limited to ten days after which the mother and baby are bathed and admitted into the family circle. The temporary abode is then consigned to flames. Likewise the monthly period also is observed by them with great strictness. The woman dwells in a small hut put up for the purpose at a short distance from the usual abode. Food and drink for her are left at some distance from the hut and she takes it. On the morning of the 4th day she bathes in the river close by, immersing herself completely under water, and sets fire to the temporary hut.

Naming ceremony.—The ceremony of naming the new born infant is usually performed on the 10th day after childbirth, but it may be postponed to any later date before the expiry of six months. Generally it is the father that performs this ceremony but sometimes it is done by the *Mooppan* (the village headman). The performer sprinkles some cold water over the baby and calls out its name three times. A feast on a small scale is usually held on the occasion. The ceremony has apparently no religious significance. The ceremonies of the ear-boring and nose-boring of the infant are also performed on the naming day but may sometimes be postponed to any other convenient date. The operations are invariably undertaken by the *Mooppan* ; but in his absence they are done by the father or by any other male member of his village. A lighted lamp is placed before the child and ancestral blessing is invoked before the operations.

Conjugal attachment.—The marriage tie among the Kadar, as stated elsewhere, is very loose. Either party is at liberty to quit the other whenever he or she likes to do so, but this privilege was very seldom, if ever, resorted to in old days. The divroced wife or husband could easily take another mate. No council of elders is called in nor does any expulsion from the community take place in connection with divorces.† The divorced party lives with his or her parents or separately according to choice, and attends to all usual vocations. If there are any children from the dissolved union, they usually remain under the father's protection.

Polygamy and Polyandry.—The institutions of polygamy and polyandry are absolutely unknown among the Kadar. During my 29 years' service in the Forest department, not a single instance has come to my knowledge of any one man keeping more than one wife or woman, or of any one woman having more than one man at a time. It is true that the marriage tie is very loose among them, but the wholesome principle of "one mate at a time" is rigidly adhered to.‡

Family life.—The father is the head of the family and he controls and directs everything. His wife and children are obedient to his behests. The work of food-gathering is shared by all. No one is a drone in the family circle except children, very old people and invalids.

Inheritance and organization.—The son inherits the father's possessions, if any. After the father's death the son or sons are bound to look after the widow so long as she remains single. Widowed girls go to the parental roof for protection. The civic life of the village is under the control of the *Mooppan* who is appointed by His Highness the Maharaja on the recommendation of the head of the Forest department. *Mooppanship* is generally inherited by the sister's son. The *Mooppan's* position carries no material advantages with it, but there are certain distinct disadvantages accompanying it. Thus manual labour is considered derogatory to a *Mooppan's* dignity and prestige and, as Kadar cannot escape starvation if they do no manual work, the unfortunate *Mooppan* finds himself condemned to honourable idleness and its unpleasant sequel. For this reason no one is willing to accept this strange honour and the tribe is now without their *Mooppan* or chief. The symbol of this dignitary's authority is a walking-stick mounted with silver bearing the Cochin coat-of-arms. When the chief's place is vacant, the stick is returned to the Conservator of Forests. In rare cases disputes among the villagers used to be settled by *Mooppans* ; but ordinarily they are taken for adjudication to the Forest department whose decision is accepted as final.

Religion.—The Kadar worship demons of various denominations, tree spirits, *Malavazhi* (hill-ruler), and *Ayyappan*. The blessings of departed ancestors are invoked in all their undertakings besides the blessings of spirits and demons. A stone set up at the base of a tree is all their temple. Offerings of various sorts are made to it. The *poojari* (priest) is usually the headman of the village and, in his absence, any male member takes the place. Priests skilled in driving off demons and spirits are got from the plains whenever their services are required. Their mundane existence is everything to them, and they have never reflected on the life hereafter. For chastisement beyond the tomb, they have not yet been willing to accept more than a marsh, where the guilty will be delivered over to leeches, but only for a time proportionate to the faults committed. They revere spirits and demons, patrons of villages, protectors of springs and dwellers in forests and caves.

Disposal of the dead.—The dead are buried with the head always towards the south. The body is washed and covered with a piece of new cloth before being taken to the grave dug some distance from the village. A handful of rice is thrown over the dead body in the grave before it is covered with earth. Near relatives and other members of the village weep when any one dies. No kind of memorial or mark is erected over the grave, nor is any article which was owned by the deceased buried with the dead body. The

*The women do not change their costume during the period as stated by Mr. L. K. Ananthakrishna Ayyar.

†Mr. Ananthakrishna Ayyar's statement to the contrary is wrong.

‡Mr. Ananthakrishna Ayyar's statement that, among the Kadars, "polygamy is indulged in with a view to increase the numerical strength of the tribe" is an egregious error and does much injustice to these people.

Kadar observe no death pollution. If the dead person happened to be an elderly male (past middle age) he will find a place in the niche of ancestor worship and his blessings will be invoked in all future undertakings. Barring this, there will be no vestige of the deceased remaining. There are many *Cromlechs* and *Dolmens* lying scattered about in the forests of Cochin, but they appear to be connected in no way with the burial or any other ceremony of the Kadar. Indeed these people have not the remotest idea as to how or when these things came into existence.

Occupation.—The Kadar are engaged in the collection of the minor produce of the forests like honey wax, cardamoms, etc. They also help in elephant-capturing operations and take part in other activities too of the Forest department. Without their help this department and the contractors who work under it will certainly find it very difficult to do their work satisfactorily. In old days the wages of the Kadar were paid in kind and not in cash, the payment being limited to the day's rations. The Forest department then did its work departmentally and only Kadar were employed for the purpose. Later on, with the introduction of the contract system of working, contractors arrived and they brought labour from the plains. The employment of workmen from the plains involved payment of wages in money ; but these labourers did not displace the Kadar altogether, for the latter were indispensable for certain kinds of work. The system of paying one set of labourers in kind and another in cash was found to be unsatisfactory ; and therefore the wages of the Kadars also began to be paid in money. The latter now claim and obtain the same rate of wages as is paid to workmen from the plains. That the Kadar have not gained by this change will be clear when we examine their present condition.

Though the Kadar are allowed by the State to cultivate forest lands free of any tax, they do not take much advantage of this concession. One reason for their apathy is that they do not like to take to any pursuit which their ancestrs did not follow. Another reason is that they have no protective measures against the damage caused by wild elephants. Cultivation on a large scale will therefore mean sheer waste of labour. And their activities in this sphere are therefore limited to a few bananas, yams and kitchen vegetables planted round their huts.

Some of the Kadar keep a few head of cattle and goats nowadays, for they are allowed free grazing of their cattle by the Government. Cattle-rearing is not, however, likely to thrive among them, for it will be very difficult for them to market their dairy products.

Relations with the State.—The Kadar are thus allowed free cultivation of land and grazing of cattle. They are also permitted to travel, free of charges, by the State Forest Tramway. And once every year during the Malabar festival of *Onam*, the State distributes presents of clothes, trinkets, tobacco, etc., to all Kadar through the agency of the Forest department. In return for these concessions and presents, the Kadars are bound to serve the State when called upon to do so. But they will be paid due wages for their services.

Games and pastimes.—Both males and females indulge in a sort of dance, but they never have it mixed. The females' dance is a sort of merry-go-round to the accompaniment of singing, drumming and a monotonous tune from a sort of flute. There is no keeping time. The body is swayed backwards and forwards with occasional clapping. The drummers and musicians are males. The males' dance is a sort of chase of game by tiger or panther accompanied, as in the females' dance, by drumming and fluting. There is no religious significance attached to either dance. The usual season for these dances is the hot weather (April and May) when the collection of honey and wax is at its highest. This is the " harvest time " of the Kadar when they get a good return for their labour from the minor produce contractor. And they generally enjoy a good feed of honey, grabbing it from the tree tops before the comb is taken to the contractor.

Contact with civilization.—We have seen how contractors and labourers from the plains arrived when the Forest department introduced the contract system of work. The opening of the State Forest Tramway not only facilitated communication between the hills and the plains but also led considerable numbers of people (working in the Tramway department) to reside up the hills. In this way the Kadar were brought into direct, almost intimate, contact with the people of the low country. Unfortunately most of the latter were labourers belonging to the lower classes. What the influence of this contact has been and how the conditions of the Kadar's life have been altered as a result of this clash between the primitive culture of the hills and the higher and more developed culture of the plains are questions that should be examined in this connection.

Physical decay.—It has already been remarked that, of old, the food of the Kadar was simple, nourishing, and natural to their surroundings and circumstances. They were accordingly a strong, sturdy and muscular set of people possessed of great powers of endurance, so much so that they could easily carry loads of substantial weight on their backs (they never carried loads on their heads) for long distances. The contact with people from the plains has wrought a most lamentable change in the Kadar. Rice was introduced from the low country and the Kadar preferred rice diet to their wholesome roots and tubers. The contractors also took with them arrack and opium to tempt the Kadar and get the most out of the poor people for the lowest possible payment. And the Kadar fell. They now drink hard and spend the greater part of their earnings in arrack and opium. Rice diet and coffee (for they have taken to coffee also in imitation of their civilized brethren of the low country), arrack* and opium have made them physical wrecks, subject to ailments and diseases which were of old unknown in their primitive domains. Cholera and small-pox have made their unwelcome appearance among them. Diabetes and albuminuria, which were powerless against the Kadar so long as they lived their old life of simplicity, activity and wholesome diet, have already cast their baneful eye on these fallen people. And the vitality of the Kadar having been lowered to a dangerous extent, they are not in a position to withstand these diseases.

The opening of a dispensary on the hills has not tended to better their condition but has, on the other hand, made it worse. They are fast forgetting their knowledge of indigenous roots and herbs and at the same time they have not much faith in allopathic medicines. If at all they attend the dispensary, it is chiefly for the surgical dressing of wounds and not for ordinary ailments.

Moral deterioration.—If the physical health of the Kadar has been undermined and ruined almost permanently as a result of their contact with the people of the low country, their moral health has been deeply tainted by the same influence. When the dark avenues of the primeval forests echoed under the tread of the greedy contractor and his assistants, and the screech of the steam engine of the Forest Tramway first reverberated through the hills and vales, *they proclaimed that the Civilized Man, the Destroyer, had set his foot* within the fair precincts of the Kadar's domains. It was observed that the lust of the people from the plains did not leave the Kadar women alone. Promiscuous intercourse for years between the new arrivals and these women has infected the whole tribe with syphilis, the first fruits of civilization. The primitive purity of the Kadar women was tainted for ever and their ideals of chastity have been brought into adjustment with those

*An arrack shop was opened in the Forest area and this aggravated the evil beyond measure. This has now been in existence for many years. Representations were repeatedly made to the Government regarding the urgent necessity for closing this shop, but no action was taken in the matter. The pittance of revenue derived from this shop is nothing when compared with the dreadful havoc this shop has played on the life of the Kadar.

of the low class people of the plains with whom they were brought into touch. Moral and physical deterioration has followed and the rising generations show mixed and tainted blood. The employment of Kadar labour in the coffee estates of the Nelliampathi hills has very much aggravated the evil. In the estates the Kadar come into contact with Tamil labourers of the lowest classes. The surroundings, food, and other influences in this new sphere are entirely different from those the Kadar are generally accustomed to. There is free scope to indulge in arrack and opium in the estates, and the Kadar try to ape the filthy ways of the dissolute Tamil labourers. The Kadar children born in the estates are all tainted and cannot be distinguished from the puny and sickly progeny of the Tamil labourer.

Discontent and changed outlook.—In other directions also the Kadar have lost heavily by their contact with civilization. Their outlook on life seems to have been affected detrimentally by this. They were one of the happiest groups of people, because they were supremely contented with their lot. For one thing, they always lived above want, and all were equally rich or equally poor so that there was no room for envy, heart-burn and the allied plagues of civilized society. No economic depression could blight their prosperity. They were free from many of the diseases that levy their daily toll from civilized regions and they had their effective herbs and other remedies for the few ailments that visited them. Their wants were few and simple and these were easily satisfied.

Now, however, they have partaken of the forbidden fruit and new desires and ambitions beyond their reach have been kindled in their humble breasts. The Kadar began to compare their habits and ways of life with those followed by people who were supposed to be superior to them, and in their simplicity and innocence they thought that progress for them lay in the direction of becoming civilized by imitating the ways of their bogus superiors. They accordingly went in for things which served only to ruin them. Thus the old simplicity in their dress began to disappear and they became acquainted with Tinnevelly saries, Benares silk banyans and Manchester twill shirts. The women wanted gold chains and bangles, gold or gilt ear-rings and rings for their fingers. They compared their lot with that of their civilized brethren and in their ignorance thought that the latter were ideally happy whereas they themselves were destined to be supremely miserable. The blessed contentment which made their life a long and happy holiday to them in days of old deserted them and with it departed their happiness. And the discomfort which rises from vague desires impossible to fulfil and from the absence of a definite purpose in life is now the distingusihing feature of a Kadar's life.

Dishonesty.—Another baneful result of the contact with men from the plains is that the Kadar have lost their primitive simplicity and honesty and taken to ways of deceit and hypocrisy. They were of old as innocent and truthful as little children. Violence and crimes were practically unknown among them, their character being essentially gentle and peace-loving. But their association with their low country compatriots has made them adepts in lying and cheating. Originally it was very difficult to get the truth from a Kadar not because he liked to prevaricate or hide it, but because he was naturally shy. He is least inclined to displease or offend anybody, so much so that his answers depended on the way in which the questions were put to him. If he were approached properly, he became frank and gave candid replies to all enquiries.

Education.—A philanthropic missionary, who had unfortunately the ideas of proselytism in his head started a primary school some years ago and the institution throve pretty well. But one morning the missionary's agent, the schoolmaster, put into the hands of the pupils a book of catechism on the Nativity, Crucifixion and Resurrection, when the pupils in a body left and never again crossed the threshold of the school, which had therefore to be closed for good. The Kadar are included among the so-called depressed classes*, and the Protector of the depressed classes accordingly opened a school for them on the hills. But the school does not appear to be worked on proper lines. It is not a knowled e of the three "Rs" that the Kadar chiefly want. If at all they are to be educated, it is vocational knowledge that should be imparted to them. The training given to them must enable them to make the best use of the raw materials of the forest. If they could be taught to convert these materials into marketable products of utility, it will benefit them as well as others. Literacy among Kadar even of the most rudimentary type is not, in my opinion, conducive to their welfare. Their education should not wean them away from their ancestral and original callings but should supplement them. Any education which is calculated to turn the Kadar's mind and inclination to paths other than those which his ancesters were accustomed to, and which he also should legitimately and naturally follow, is bound to throw him out of gear with his environment, so much so that he will become unfit for Kadan society At the same time he will not be an acquisition to any other society. In short, he will lose his Kadan moorings and will not get into any safer haven. As a matter of fact, the boys who attend the Kadan school are known to develop a dislike for their ancestral pursuits. They want to live like the officers of the Forest and Tramway departments !

Decay in numbers.—The sum total of the influences to which the Kadar have been subjected in their contact with civilization is that they have undergone an all round deterioration. A spirit of restlessness or discomfort has invaded their life. Their adaptation to their environments has been seriously impaired because the new conditions of their life are incompatible with these environments. In the circumstances they must deteriorate and decay. And what we actually find is that they have been decaying. The returns of Kadar at 3 successive censuses shown in the margin conclusively prove this. As matters stand at present the tribe is doomed, and its utter extinction is but the question of a few decades.

Year.	Actual strength.
1911	447
1921	274
1931	267

Preventive measures.—The wisest policy in the circumstances would appear to be to leave the Kadar alone. They have to be saved both from their friends and their enemies. The type of education that is now imparted to the Kadar boys must be forthwith changed. If we have nothing better to give them than the education which is given to our boys, let us at least desist from thrusting an unsuitable system of instruction on them. Let us also banish arrack and opium from the Kadar's domains. While absolute non-interference with their habits and ways of life is essential, active and stern interference is urgently required to ensure the safety of Kadar women from the ravages of the syphilis-breeding wretches of the plains. And effective medical treatment must at once be resorted to so that the venereal diseases, which are now widely prevalent among the Kadar, and which have very much lowered their vitality and fertility, might be eradicated once for all. If these or similar measures are urgently adopted, perhaps these people may be saved from their impending doom of speedy extinction, and they may once more develop their innate qualities of natural nobility and simplicity and child-like goodness, gentleness and innocence to thrive once again in their native home.

*The Kadar were in no way depressed to start with. But now they may be regarded as depressed, thanks to the arrack shop the other influences already explained.

21. The Primitive Tribes of Travancore.

By L. A. Krishna Iyer and N. Kunjan Pillai.

CONTENTS.

THE PRIMITIVE TRIBES OF TRAVANCORE.

I.—*Introduction.*

The population of Travancore, like that of the rest of Southern India, is predominantly Dravidian ...... In the introduction to "The Cochin Tribes and Castes", Volume I, by Mr. L. K. Ananthakrishna Iyer, Mr. Keane says "that in India there is no fundamental racial unity............, that, in the present amalgam, are represented five primary stocks: a submerged *Negrito* probably from Malaysia; *Kolarian, Dravidian* and *Aryan* who arrived in the order mentioned from beyond the Hindu Kush and the Himalayas; lastly the *Mongol* mainly confined to the Himalayan slopes". Mr. Keane's theory is that the *Negritos*, whom he calls the "submerged element" came from Malaysia round the Bay of Bengal to the Himalayan slopes and gradually spread over the Peninsula, probably in the early Palaeolithic times, and that in course of time they lost their original Negrito speech and became merged in the surrounding Kolarian and Dravidian populations. He holds that the Kolarian is a distinct race from the Dravidian and came to India before the latter, probably from the north or north-east, that the Dravidians came from the north-west, and that "beyond the Vindhyan Range they have nearly everywhere absorbed or replaced both the Negrito substratum and the Kolarian indigenes". From these premises Mr. Keane concludes that the low caste aborigines now found in Southern India "were not originally Dravidians, but a blend in diverse proportion of superimposed Negrito, Kolarian and Dravidian racial strata".

It must be said in favour of Mr. Keane's view that the low caste Pulayas, Parayas, Kuravas, and Vēdars living in the plains, and the aboriginal tribes found on the hills, of Travancore show traits of Negroid character, unlike the Nāyars, the Vellālas and other high caste Dravidians........... In the process of conquest some of the aborigines might have been subjugated and made serfs, while others might have receded into the hills and forests. The former, having been in close contact with their masters, might have received an admixture of the Dravidian blood, but as they were not admitted into the Dravidian society they remained as distinct classes of a low order. These are the Pulayas, the Parayas, the Kuravas, and the Vēdas, the most depressed classes of the present population. The aborigines who receded into the hills and forests lived in complete isolation from the rest of the people. They had no settled home. They were mostly nomadic hunters living on wild beasts, natural roots and berries, while some took to agriculture and raised food grains by cultivating forest lands. Till recently they had not come into contact with the people of the plains and had, therefore, preserved their primitive customs and habits more or less intact. But this is all fast changing. The civilized man has penetrated into their province, opened up forests and established plantations. The Forest Department has imposed restrictions on their movements and their methods of cultivation. These intrusions into their primitive life are bringing about rapid changes in their physical character, their economic condition, their social customs and religious ideas. By coming in contact with the civilized people they are themselves getting civilized, but in this process they are degenerating in bodily vigour and are fast dwindling down in number. The progress of civilization has not yet gone far enough to make them extinct. They are still there and many of them even now exhibit, in a marked degree, some of the primitive characteristics of the aborigines.

II.—*Geographical Distribution of the Primitive Tribes.*

The Tribes now met with in Travancore are :—

1. The Hill-Pantāran,
2. The Muduvan,
3. The Mannān,
4. The Ūrāli,
5. The Paliyan,
6. The Mala-Pulayan,
    (a) The Kurumba-Pulayan,
    (b) The Karavashi-Pulayan,
    (c) The Pāmbu-Pulayan,
7. The Vishavan,
8. The Mala-Vēdan (The Vettuvan),
    (a) The Valiya Vēdan,
    (b) The Cheru-Vēdan,
    (c) The Chinkanni-Vēdan,
    (d) The Elichathi-Vēdan,
9. The Mala-Kuravan,
10. The Mala-Aryan,
11. The Ullādan,
12. The Kānikāran,
13. The Thanta-Pulayan.

Travancore is cut off from the rest of Southern India by the Western Ghats which form its eastern boundary. This lofty mountain range contains a number of peaks of varying heights and shapes. From there the country slopes gradually towards the west down to the flat coastal plain bounded by the Arabian Sea. The highest point in the Western Ghats is Ānamudi, being 8,837 feet above the sea-level. The northern portion of this mountainous tract is the High Range District where tea and cardamoms are cultivated. The lower slopes and the foot of the mountains are covered by rich virgin forests, from where emerge several rivers which forcing their way across the country fall into the sea. It is within these forests that the primitive tribes are chiefly met with.

The Hill or Mala Pantārám, the most primitive of the primitive tribes of Travancore, lives scattered on the higher reaches of the Pampa and the Achankoil rivers and at Thalappāra and Karumpalli in the forests of Shencotta taluk. *The Muduvan* is found on the Kannan Dēvan hills in the High Range District, the *Mannān* on the Cardamom hills to the south of the Panniyār river, the *Ū'rāli* in the forests of the Periyār, Vandamet

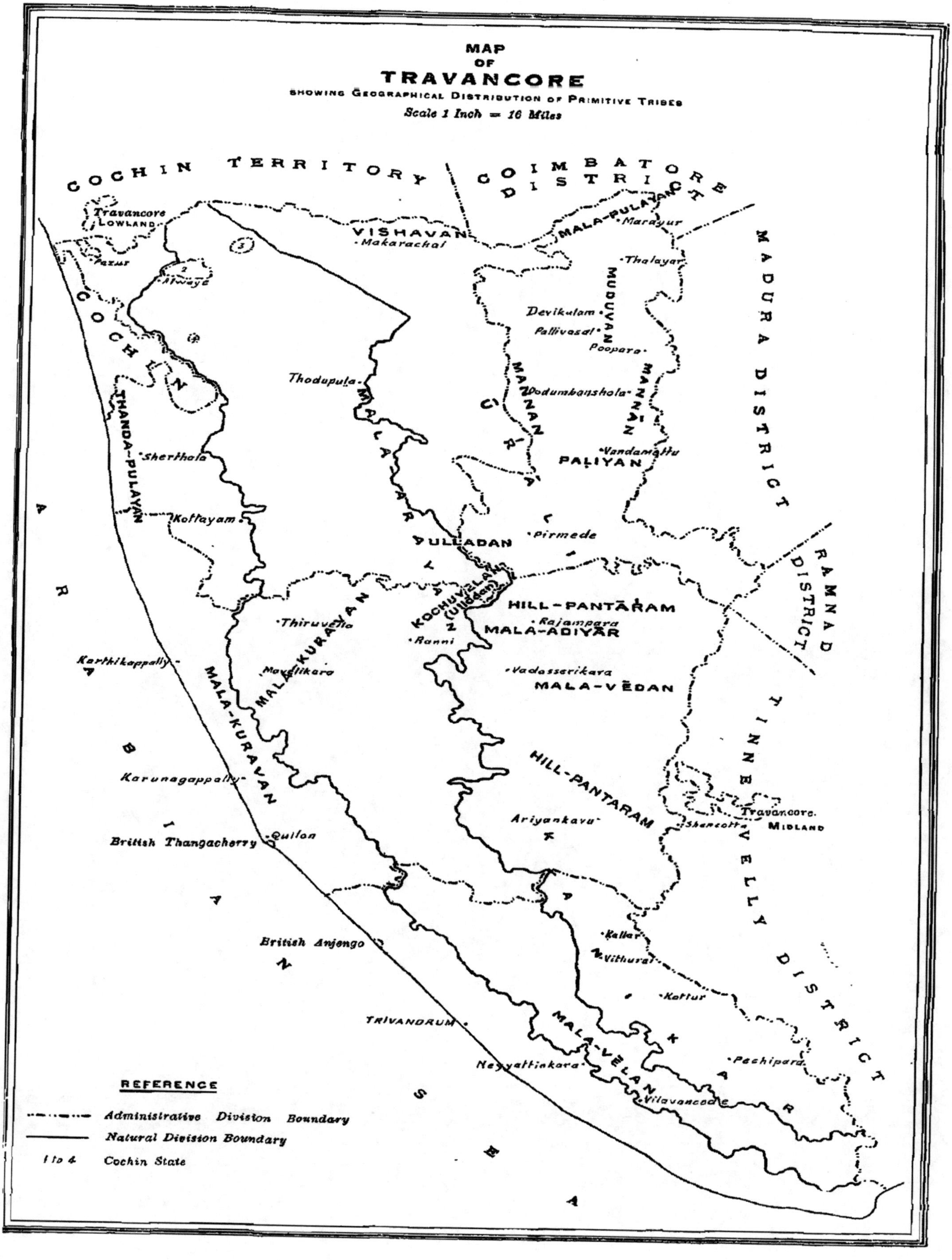
MAP
OF
TRAVANCORE
SHOWING GEOGRAPHICAL DISTRIBUTION OF PRIMITIVE TRIBES
Scale 1 Inch = 16 Miles
COCHIN TERRITORY
COIMBATORE DISTRICT
MADURA DISTRICT
RAMNAD DISTRICT
TINNEVELLY DISTRICT
COCHIN
ARABIAN SEA
Travancore LOWLAND
Travancore MIDLAND
VISHAVAN
Makarachal
MALA-PULAYAN
Marayur
Thalayar
MUDUVAN
Devikulam
Pallivasal
Poopara
MANNAN
URALI
Kodumbanshola
Vandamettu
PALIYAN
Thodupula
MALA-ARAYAN
THANDA-PULAYAN
Sherthala
Kottayam
ULLADAN
Pirmede
KOCHUVELAN (Ulladan)
HILL-PANTARAM
Rajampara
MALA-ADIYAR
Thiruvella
Ranni
MALA-KURAVAN
Mavelikara
Vadasserikara
MALA-VEDAN
Karthikappally
Karunagappally
Ariyankavu
Shencotta
Quilon
British Thangacherry
British Anjengo
KANIKKAR
Kallar
Vithura
Kottur
TRIVANDRUM
MALA-VELAN
Neyyattinkara
Pechipara
Vilavancode
Alwaye
Pazur
REFERENCE
Administrative Division Boundary
Natural Division Boundary
1 to 4 Cochin State

and Thodupula Ranges, and the *Paliyan* in the Vandamēt Range. Of the three sects of the *Mala-Pulayan*, the *Kurumba-Pulayan* lives at Pampar, Ālampatti, Karumutti and Pālampatti, the *Karavashi-Pulayan* at Kumpittānkushi, Pattatholivu, Pulikaravayal, and Nāchivayal, and the *Pāmpu-Pulayan* in the forests to the east of Chinnār. The *Vishavan* lives in the Idiyara valley in North Travancore, the *Mala-Vēdan* in the forests of near Vadaserikara and the *Mala-Kuravan* in different parts of the State. The *Mala-Adiyār* found in Koni Reserve is identical with the Mala-Kuravan. The *Mala-Arayan* lives in the forests of Changanāchery, Minachil, and Thodupula taluks, the *Ullādan* in the reserves of the Manimala Range, the *Kānikār* in the forests of Vilavancōde, Neyyāttinkara and Nedumangād taluks, the *Mala-Vēlan* in the interior parts of Neyyāttinkara taluk and the *Thanta-Pulayan* on the coastal area in Shertala taluk. The Mala-Kuravan and the Thanta-Pulayan are the only two primitive tribes living on the plains.

III.—*The Influence of Environment on Physical Characters.*

Of all the tribes, the Hill-Pantāram, the Muduvan, and the Ūrāli have been least affected by outside influences. The other tribes have been subjected to extraneous influences and have, therefore, received an infusion of fresh blood and new ideas from the more civilized people with whom they have come in contact. This is seen clearly in the Vishavan, the Paliyan, the Ullādan, the Mala-Arayan, the Mannān and the Kānīkār. Owing to the admixture of foreign blood these tribes are now approaching the composite type of civilized humanity.

The Mannān, the Muduvan, the Paliyan, and the Kurumba-Pulayan, who are found at an altitude of 2,000 to 5,000 feet above sea-level, cultivate ragi, while the Kānikār, the Mala-Arayan, the Ullādan, the Vishavan, and others who live at lower elevations cultivate rice and tapioca............ The Hill-Pantāram, is the only nomadic tribe in the hunter stage in Travancore.

The salubrity of high altitudes is favourable to man. We see it exemplified in the Muduvan, the Mannān the Paliyan and the Ūrāli. Well-developed lungs, massive chests, and large torsos of the men of the above tribes are due to the effect of the rarefied air at the high altitude at which they live.

They evince, however, an aversion to muscular effort. P. Vidal De Blache says: "As atmospheric pressure diminishes perceptably at high altitudes, atmospheric oxygen combines with blood corpuscles in the lungs more slowly. According to trustworthy observations, sluggishness and dislike of prolonged effort, muscular or otherwise, is the consequence of the slowing down of the physiological processes which act on the nervous system by means of the blood".[1]

The backwardness of tropical countries is said to be due to excessive heat. "The actinic rays of the sun are believed to stimulate the cells to greater activity, when they fall on the human body. At first it is beneficial. If it goes to excess, the cells apparently break down".[2] Intense heat of long duration, combined with a high degree of humidity, is unfavourable to human development. It brings about enervation, creates a craving for stimulants and induces habits of alcoholism. The Kānikār, the Mala-Arayan, the Ullādan, the Mala-Vēdan and the Vishavan are good examples of devitalisation caused by tropical climate.

Malaria is a disease of the tropical and sub-tropical countries, whose climate is characterised by alternate wet and dry seasons. A people devitalised by this disease cannot be expected to be energetic and active. The sluggishness of the Kānikār, the Hill-Pantāram, the Vishavan, the Ullādan, and others who live in malaria-stricken areas, is due to the baneful effect of this disease.

The Colour of the Skin.—It is said that the colouration of the skin is the conjoint effect of a number of environmental factors working through physiological processes. The pigment of the skin is found in the epidermis, and the influence of light favours its formation. In a cold climate, where the thermal action is weak, a discoloration of pigment in the skin and other parts of the body produces a kind of albinism. The Kānikār, the Ullādan, the Mala-Arayan, and the Thanda-Pulayan who live on the plains and at low elevations are darker than the Muduvan, the Mannān, and the Paliyan of the High-Ranges. Blondness increases appreciably on high slopes. "Waitz long ago affirmed this tendency of mountaineers to lighter colouring from his study of primitive peoples. This may not be entirely due to climatic contrast between mountain and plain. Economic poverty of the environment and poor food supply have also a hand".[3]

The Stature.—Darwin holds "that changes, such as size, colour, thickness of skin, and hair, have been produced through food supply and climate from the external conditions in which the forms lived".[4] "Stature", according to Semple, "is partly a matter of feeding, and hence of geographic condition"

In Travancore, the primitive peoples on the hills are generally shorter than those of the plains; and within the hilly region, it is orserved that stature is often larger at high than at moderate altitudes, a fact which has been ascribed to "the influence of a rigorous climate in killing off all but vigorous individuals".[5] Sir Arthur Keith says "that the greater activity of the pituitary gland gives the Caucasian his height of stature, bulk of body, prominent chin, strong eyebrow ridges, and pronounced nasalization".[6] The greater height of the Muduvan and the Mala-Pulayan, the Paliyan and the Ūrāli may be due to the more vigorous functioning of the pituitary gland at higher elevations. The effect of a scanty and uncertain food supply is seen on the Hill-Pantāram and the Vishavan, who are shorter in stature than others. The groups classified as short are between 58¼ inches and 62¼ inches. The average height of the Hill-Pantāram is 61 inches, of the Vishavan 61·16 inches, of the Muduvan 62 inches, of the Malapulaya 62·5 inches, of the Paliyan 62 inches, and of the Ūrāli 62·8 inhes.

The Head.—The shape of the head is regarded by most anthropologists as a constant and persistent character. According to the Frankfort Agreement of 1882, heads with a cephalic index, not exceeding 74·9, are now classed as dolichocephalic; Deniker says dolichocephaly (70 to 74·9) is almost exclusively located in Melanesia, Australia, India, and Africa. According to Risley, the prevalent type in Peninsular India seems to be long-headed or medium headed. The primitive peoples of Travancore are the modern representatives of the Pre-Dravidians. The Ūrāli is the most dolichocephalic of the hill-tribes with a cephalic index of 70·6. The Muduvan has a cephalic index of 70·9, the Kurumba Pulayan 71·1, the Mala-Arayan 72·1, the Vishavan 72·6, the Kānikār 72·3, the Hill-Pantāram 73·5, the Ullādan 73·9, and the Paliyan 74·6.

The dolichocephaly of the primitive peoples is of a more primitive type, for the vault of the head is too low and the direction of the brain backward. They occasionally shew a prognathic face, while they are generally orthognathic.

---

1. P. Vidal De Blache.—*The Principles of Human Geography*, page—173.
2. E. C. Semple.—*The Influence of Geographical Environment*, page 626.
3. E. C. Semple, *loc. Cit.*, page 39.
4. E. C. Semple, *loc. Cit.*, page 34.
5. Sir Herbert Risley.—*The people of India*, page 31.
6. H. G. Duncan.—*Race and Population Problems*, page 33.

The Nose.—The nasal idex is claimed by some to be the surest method of distinguishing racial types. The broad type of nose, according to Risley, is found in Madras, the Central Provinces, and Chota Nagpur.[1] The broad nose of the Pre-Dravidian is his striking feature. The physical configuration of the country, the vast stretches of fever-haunted jungle, the absence of roads, and the compact social organization of the primitive tribes protect them from the intrusion of foreign influence. All the Pre-Dravidian tribes of Travancore are mostly platyrhine. The average nasal index of the Vishavan is 88·05, of the Muduvan 91·05, of the Mala-Vēdan 86·6, of the Mala-Adiyār 84·6, of the Ūrāli 84·6, of the Paliyan 86·5, of the Ullādan 85·4, of the Mala-Arayan 83·1, and of the Kānikār 89·1. The Vishavan, the Muduvan, the Mala-Vēdan, the Paliyan, the Kānikār, and the Ullādan are platyrhine, while the Ūrāli, the Mala-Arayan and the Mala-Adiyār are bordering on platyrhiny.

To sum up, short stature, low forehead, flat face and nose, and dark complexion are the characteristic features of the primitive peoples of Travancore. Appendix I gives the head measurements and Appendix II the stature and the nasal measurements of some of the primitive tribes.

IV.—*Appearance, Manners and Customs of the Primitive Tribes.*

The Hill-Pantārams are found in regions where they are free from the competition and influence of other people and, therefore, enjoy full freedom for the continuance of a nomadic life. Gregariousness would be a positive disadvantage to them under such conditions. Being nomadic hunters they have no permanent habitations. Their families seldom consist of more than two or three members.

Their huts are of the simplest pattern, built of junglewood posts with a lean-to roof thatched with plantain leaves. A fire is kept going at all times to keep them warm. Fire is made by striking (*Chakmuk* in their language.)

Their clothes are scanty. They are dark-brown in complexion and short in stature. The nose is depressed at the root in the case of those living in Rani Reserve, and leptorhine in the case of those living at Pathanāpurom and Thalappāra, owing to miscegenation. Their eye ridges are prominent and the hair black and curly. The hard life they have to lead in the jungle have made the men of strong build. Nevertheless, many fall victims to diseases like small-pox and malaria, and their number is fast going down.

Girls are married both before and after puberty. Marriage is generally contracted between cross-cousins. The exchange of sisters in marriage is also practised. Marriage is celebrated at the bride's house. On the appointed day, the bridegroom is presented with a pair of cloths. The bride's father then joins the right hand of the bride with the left hand of the bridegroom and says 'I hand over my daughter to you. Take care of her'. The couple are then seated on a mat and four balls of rice are brought on a leaf. The bride hands over two balls of rice to the husband who eats them. He then gives two balls of rice to the wife and she also eats them. This completes the marriage ceremony.

When a girl attains puberty, she remains in a small shed about a hundred yards away from the hut. Pollution lasts for sixteen days. When she wants to go out, she covers her head with a cloth, and walks with her face turned downwards, led by an elderly woman. Evil will befall her if this injunction is not adhered to. When a woman is in menses, pollution lasts for seven days. During this period, the husband should not ascend a hill or climb a tree. He should keep indoors and should not handle any implements. To the primitive man, menstruous women are dangerous, and seclusion is intended to afford protection from the dreaded spiritual danger. When a woman is about to become a mother, she remains in a separate shed about 200 yards away from the hut. Pollution lasts for 16 days. During this period the husband cannot go out for hunting, for gathering food, or for any other purpose. He must remain indoors. The mother continues to be under a taboo for from three to five months if the child is a male, and four to six months if it is a female. She should not even touch the cooking vessels. A man abstains from having intercourse with his wife from the seventh month of pregnancy, and for six months after delivery.

The dead are buried. After burial the tribe deserts the locality and moves on to another place. Death pollution lasts for eight days. On the ninth day, the chief mourner gives a feast to the villagers in honour of the dead. Sons succeed to the property of the father, if any.

The Hill-Pantārams dread the jungle deities. Those at Āriencāvu worship crests of hills. The deities whom they generally worship are Sāsta and his satellite, Karuppuswāmi.

The Muduvans live at high elevations and consequently look hale and hearty. Their villages have no permanency owing to the system of shifting cultivation they follow. The huts are small, rectangular, and one-roomed with a single door in front. Their only furniture is a mat or two woven out of reeds. The fire which occupies the corner of the hut represents "that most precious luxury, the sum total of their creature comforts".

Sexual license before marriage is neither recognised nor tolerated. Unmarried youths are subjected to strict discipline. All unmarried males above ten years of age, remain in the 'Bachelor hall' at night. The unmarried girls and women sleep in a separate hut, and are in charge of an elderly woman.

The orthodox marriage is between cross-cousins, *i.e.*, between the children of brothers and sisters. The marriage ceremony takes place in the evening after 6 P.M. The bridegroom, with his best man and the bride's maid, goes to the bride's hut. The parents of the bride will then be absent from there. They should not be spectators of the ceremonial. The bridegroom presents the bride with ear-rings, glass bangles, clothes, and a comb of golden bamboo made by himself. The presentation of the comb forms the essential part of the ceremony and is always worn by the bride on the back of the head above the knotted hair. After the ceremony all the guests are treated to a feast. Marriage by capture is also prevalent among this tribe. Polygamy is allowed. The second wife must carry out the orders of the first. If they are friendly, they live in the same house. Among the Muduvans of the plateau, polyandry is also permitted, but it has become very rare in these days. Fraternal polyandry does not exist at all. The Muduvans of the Cardamom hills are purely monogamous. Re-marriage of widows is allowed, but not by the brother of the deceased husband.

When a girl attains puberty, she is lodged in a separate shed so that she might be beyond the gaze of men. Pollution lasts for three days. When a woman is about to become a mother, she is also lodged in a "seclusion hut". All the married women of the village assist in the delivery. Pollution lasts for thirty days. A child belongs to the mother's clan and is named after the uncle or the maternal grandparent. Inheritance is matrilineal. A man's property goes to his sister's son after his demise.

---

1. Risley, *loc. cit.*, page 28.

The Muduvans on the Cardamom Hills worship the forest deities, Kōttamala Swāmi and Vadaganātha Swāmi, who are supposed to have taken their abode on the crests of hills. The hills where they are supposed to abide are regarded with reverence. The influence of Hinduism on their religion is becoming visible. They worship God Subramonia, and Goddess Meenākshi Amma (*Sokuru*). They also worship the sun and the malevolent deities like Karuppu, Māriamma and Kāli.

The Muduvans are nomadic agriculturists. Ragi is their staple food. Their environment has made them hunters and trappers also. They eat the flesh of sambhar, ibex, monkey, and jungle-sheep*, and also fish. The flesh of black monkey is much relished. They do not kill the bison. The wealth of the Muduvan is locked up in his cattle which consist mostly of buffaloes. They drink milk and offer it to visitors also.

Men wear a loin cloth kept in its place by a string tied round the waist, and also a turban. A Kambli or blanket is tied up and carried on the back. It serves as a hold-all. Women wear a coloured cloth about 16 to 18 cubits long. Men wear ear-rings, silver or brass rings on the fourth finger of the right hand, and sometimes a bangle on each arm.

Those living on the Cardamom hills talk Tamil and those found near Pooyamkuty Malayālam.

The average Muduvan enjoys a better physique than most other hill-tribes. He is tall and has an aquiline nose depressed at the root. With a dark-brown skin, black and wavy hair, and a retreating forehead, his simplicity of life, his cheerfulness, and healthy look give him the appearance of a good personality. Sturdy in limbs and erect in bearing, he can endure great fatigue, and carry heavy loads at ease. His economic condition is better than that of the other hill-tribes.

The Mannāns are found mostly on the Cardamom Hills to the south of the Panniyār river up to the south of the tract of land now submerged by the Periyār reservoir. This locality has a salubrious climate and enjoys the benefit of both the monsoons.

The influence of the geographical environment of the Mannān is seen in his physical and mental characteristics, in his economic condition, and in his religious beliefs. The coal-black skin has become brown-black. The cool climate has made him hardy and long-lived, and has also imbued him with a gay and vivacious temperament. He has a long head, a flat nose, and thick lips.

The hamlets are situated on high grounds where there is a perennial supply of water and plenty of land for cultivation. Each hamlet contains five to fifteen huts. The headman alone is privileged to sit and sleep on a bamboo *thatty* (a miniature cot). All the rest sit and sleep on the floor.

Girls are married after they attain puberty. The marriageable age is between 16 to 20 for males and over 14 for females. Marriage takes place between the children of brother and sister. Before the marriage is solemnised the bridegroom goes and remains in the bride's house for a period not exceeding one year. The ceremony is conducted in the bride's house. The bridegroom bows to his parents and elders, and the bride to her parents. The couple are then seated on a mat. The *tāli* is tied round the bride's neck by the bridegroom's sister. The visitors are then treated to a feast.

The system of marriage by capture is also in vogue among the Mannāns. Should a woman refuse to return the love of a man, he forcibly takes her and stays in the forest for ten to twelve days. They are then searched for and taken to the village. The offence is condoned and they are allowed to remain as husband and wife. Elopement is also a recognised institution and takes place if parents object to the union of a man and a woman.

A man marries a second time when his first wife is sterile. Polyandry is rare, but is not altogether extinct. Widows are allowed to re-marry. A man may marry the wife of his deceased brother.

When a girl attains puberty, she is lodged in a seclusion hut for four days. On the fifth day, she returns home after a bath and puts on a new cloth. When a woman is in menses, pollution lasts for four days and during the period she remains in a sparate shed. On the fifth day, she bathes, but remains in seclusion for another four days. When a woman is about to become a mother, she is lodged in a separate hut. After delivery she continues to be there for twenty days, the period of pollution. On the 21st day, she goes to the house, but remains in a separate room.

The Mannāns are gradually getting Hinduized. They worship God Sāstha. Traces of animisim still exist among them. For example, it is believed that the clearing of jungle disturbs the spirits residing there. A portion of the primitive forests is dedicated to them and is preserved as a sacred place.

The Mannāns are nomadic agriculturists. Ragi is their staple food. In times of scarcity they eat wild fruits and roots. Fish is a delicacy to them and they also eat crabs, the flesh of black monkey, sambhar, and rats. Bison flesh is tabooed.

The Ūrālis, used to be scantily clad, but owing to their contact with the planting community they are becoming civilized and now wear a loin cloth, four cubits long and two cubits wide, shirts, coats and turbans. When they go out a blanket serves as a hold-all to carry their necessaries of life. They have long head, a flat nose, a retreating forehead, and moderately thick lips. They are somewhat fair in complexion and have dark and wavy hair.

A girl, when she attains puberty, is placed under a rigorous taboo. She is lodged in a tree-house reserved for the purpose. Pollution lasts for seven days. On the eighth day she bathes and shifts to another tree-house in the vicinity for two days. She bathes on the third day and goes home, when seven jack-leaf-fuls of cowdung water and oil are poured over her head by her uncle or brother to purify her. She then enters the hut. Similarly a woman in menstruation is confined to a distant tree-house for a few days. She then bathes and shifts to a second tree-house in the vicinity for two days. She bathes on the third day and goes home.

Marriage of girls takes place both before and after puberty. Sisters are exchanged in marriage and a man who has no sisters has only a very remote chance of getting married. Formerly an Ūrali married as many women as he had sisters, but now he does not marry more than two. Polyandry is very rare among this tribe.

The marriage ceremony is simple. The bridegroom and his father go to the bride's hut, and escort her to their home, wh[illegible]e bride's party is fed. Her dowry consists of bill-hooks, clothing and vessels.

When a woman is about to become a mother, she goes to a tree-house at a distance. She is not given any assistance in delivery. Women stand at a distance and give instructions. Even after delivery they do not approach her and render her help. Pollution lasts for 21 days. During this period, the husband refrains from doing any work. She bathes on the 22nd day and enters home.

* Jungle sheep, *i.e.*, the barking deer, *cervulus muntjac*; the bison of course is *bos gaurus*, and the ibex is the so-called Nilgiri ibex (*tahr*).

Nomadic agriculture is the occupation of this tribe. Rice is their staple food. Men avoid intercourse with women for three days after clearing the jungle, lest harm should befall them and the crop.

The Ūrālis are animists. They worship crests of hills which are supposed to be haunted by evil spirits. The ancestor-spirits are propitiated during agricultural ceremonies. There is a medicine-man called *Plāthi* who cures all diseases. The Ūralis are very orthodox in habits and do not interdine with the Paliyans and the Mannāns.

The *Paliyans* are found in the Vandamēt Range. Living as they are in the midst of cardamom ryots, they have been influenced by their contact with the low country people in their customs and manners. They have a long head, a flat nose, a retreating forehead, and moderately thick lips. They are brown-black in complexion.

When a girl attains puberty, she remains in the seclusion shed for 15 days. She returns home on the 16th day after bathing, carrying a pot of water on her head. She cooks rice and serves it to other women. Then alone is she free from pollution. During menses, she remains in the seclusion shed for five days.

Marriage takes place after a girl attains puberty. Cross-cousin marriage is in vogue. Before marriage, a man serves his uncle, who is his would-be father-in-law, for six months. Marriage is thus one of service and there is no dowry attached to it. The ceremony is conducted in the house of the bridegroom at night and lasts for one day only. The clothes of the couple are immersed in saffron water on the third day. They bathe in a stream and return home.

A man is allowed to marry the wife of his deceased elder or younger brother. Polygamy is practised, when the first wife is barren, and the second wife is invariably the sister of the first. Younger brothers are said to have intercourse with the wife of the eldest brother.

When a woman is about to become a mother, she is sent to the seclusion shed, and remains there for six days after child-birth. On the seventh day, she bathes and comes home, when a hammock made of new cloth is provided by the uncle for the baby. Sons inherit the property of the father.

The Paliyans are migratory agriculturists, and shift their cultivation annually. During sowing and harvesting they abstain from intercourse with their wives. Crops will fail, if they are not pure.

The Paliyans are animists. They worship crests of hills which are the haunt of spirits. They also worship Sāsta, Karuppuswāmi, and Māriamma. Ancestor-spirits are also propitiated.

Men wear loin cloths, 4 cubits ×2½ cubits, and also shirts, coats and turbans. Women wear coloured cloth 12 cubits ×2½ cubits. They have also begun to wear jackets.

The Mala-Pulayas are divided into three endogamous septs, the *Kurumba Pulayas*, the *Karavazhi Pulayas* and the *Pāmpu Pulayas*, in the descending order of their social status. The higher septs do not intermarry for interdine with the lower ones.

The Kurumba Pulayas are nomadic agriculturists. The Karavazhi Pulayas are dependants of the Vellālas. Ragi is the staple diet of the former, while the latter live on rice which they get in the shape of wages from their masters.

When a girl attains puberty, she remains in the seclusion shed for 30 days during which period she should not see any man. On the 31st day, she bathes and returns home, when all are treated to a feast.

Marriage takes place after a girl attains puberty. Cross-cousin marriage is prevalent. Marriage lasts for three days and takes place at the bride's hut.

Among the *Karavali Pulayās*, the boy's parents give a bride-price of forty vallams of paddy and a coloured cloth to the bride and her mother. Marriage takes place at night. The bride and the bridegroom are seated on a mat, facing east. The bridegroom ties a necklace of beads round the bride's neck. They take food from the same leaf, each giving a ball of rice to the other. All the guests are then feasted and the married couple are taken to the bridegroom's house.

Among the *Kurumba Pulayans* there is no bride-price. A cloth is presented to the bride and a string dipped in saffron water is tied round her neck. All are then treated to a feast.

An elder brother may marry the wife of his deceased younger brother and become the guardian of his children. Polygamy is practised, and man may marry the sister of his first wife. Polyandry is prevalent and even promiscuity is not uncommon. Sons inherit the father's property.

The Mala Pulayas worship Kāli, Māriamma, Chaplamma, and Katlapāramma. They abstain from intercourse with women for ten days prior to any religious ceremony they perform.

The man wears a cloth, 6 cubits ×2½ cubits, and the woman a coloured cloth, 16 cubits long. The unhealthiness of their environment is reflected in their diminished vitality.

The Vishavans are found in the Idyara valley in North Travancore. Among them a girl, when she attains puberty, is confined to a seclusion shed for seven days during which period she should not see any man. A breach of this taboo would bring harm to the hamlet. On the eighth day she bathes and goes home. A woman is not allowed to take any animal food until she is married.

Pre-marital chastity is rare. A man may clandestinely cohabit with any woman. In the event of conception before marriage, no attempt is made to cause miscarriage. Every effort will be made to legalise such unions.

Marriage generally takes place before a girl attains puberty. A man must marry outside his clan. Cross-cousin marriage is tabooed among them. Marriage lasts for a day and takes place in the bride's house. It consists merely in the presentation of cloths to the bride and her mother. Sisters are exchanged in marriage of they are of different clans. Free divorce is allowed.

Child-birth takes place in an isolated shed and no male can go near it. The mother and the baby remain here for fifteen days. On the 16th day she bathes and enters home.

A man's property goes to his nephews. Women do not inherit property.

The Vishavans are nomadic agriculturists and shift their cultivation annually. Rice is their staple diet. They supplement it with wild roots and tubers which they dig out with their digging spud. They are experts at spearing fish.

The Vishavans worship Sāsta and make offerings to the spirits of ancestors, before abandoning the land which they have cultivated.

The men wear a loin cloth, 4 cubits × 2 cubits, and also a small upper cloth. Women wear a loin cloth, 10 cubits long. They are dark in complexion, have a long head, a flat nose, a receding forehead and moderately thick lips. Eyebrows are prominent.

The Mala-Vēdans are found scattered throughout the State. They are otherwise known as *Kānaka Vēdan, Vedar*, or *Vettuvan.*

There are four classes of Mala-Vēdans :—

1. Valiya Vēdan.
2. Cheru Vēdan.
3. Cheenganni Vēdan.
4. Elichathi Vēdan.

The Cheru Vedans do not interdine or intermarry with the Valiya Vedans, but may interdine with the Cheenganni Vēdans and marry their women but the latter are not allowed to interdine with their women. If the husband dies, the wife and her children go back to her home. The Cheru Vēdans neither interdine nor intermarry with the Elichathi Vēdans. The Cheenganni Vēdans stand at a distance of 18 feet from the Cheru Vēdans and the latter stand 8 feet away from the higher castes.

Marriage is between cross-cousins. Sisters are exchanged in marriage by men belonging to different clans. Marriage takes place both before and after a girl attains puberty. It is conducted in the bride's house and lasts for a day. It consists in the presentation of a cloth by the bridegroom to the bride and the tying of *tāli* round her neck. Among the Cheenganni Vēdans, the married couple are seated on a mat, some cooked rice is placed on a plantain leaf, and both eat it.

Polygamy is prevalent among this tribe. A man does not marry the wife of his deceased brother or the sister of his deceased wife. Divorce is allowed.

A girl, on attaining puberty, remains in the seclusion shed for nine days. On the tenth day she bathes and goes home. She then makes a horizontal mark with cow-dung on the forehead of all present, and gives a bowl of rice gruel to each. Pollution then ceases.

When a woman is about to become a mother, she is confined to a room in the hut. After delivery, a decoction of medicinal herbs and charcoal powder is made and administered to her by the husband.

Among the Cheenganni Vēdans, the sons inherit two-thirds and the nephews one-third of a man's property on his demise. It is divided equally between the sons and the nephews among the Cheru Vēdans.

The Cheenganni Vēdans are dark in complexion and are short in stature. They have a long head, and a flat nose depressed at the foot. The hair is dark and curly. They have a poor physique, due to adverse circumstances. The Cheru Vēdans differ from them in having prominent brow-ridges.

The Cheru Vēdans are migratory agriculturists. Rice is their staple diet. They supplement it with wild roots and berries.

The Mala Kuravans are found in Nedumangād, Pathanāpuram, Chengannūr, and Quilon taluks. The *Mala-Adiyārs*, who are found in the Koni Reserve, resemble the Mala Kuravans in their exogamous clan system and other customs.

Marriage takes place only after a girl attains puberty. Formerly there was *Kettu-Kalyanam* (thāli tying ceremony) for girls between the ages of 5 and 8, but this has now been given up. Among the Mala-Kuravans a man marries only the daughter of his maternal uncle. He cannot marry the daughter of his father's sister. This prohibition does not exist among the Mala-Adiyārs.

Among the Mala-Kuravans, marriage lasts for a day and takes place in the house of the bride. It consists in the presentation of a pair of cloths to the bride. The bridegroom's father gives Rs. 2-8-0 to the bride's father. Without the payment of this amount, the girl is not sent to her husband's home. Among the Mala-Adiyārs, marriage lasts for two days and there is no payment of bride-price. Polygamy is practised by them. A man marries the sister of his first wife.

The Mala Kuravans are animists and propitiate the hills wherein the spirits are supposed to reside, such as, Thalapāramala, Udumpāramala, and Thevalapāramala, before they commence clearing the jungle for cultivation. Offerings are again made to them later on after the seed is sown.

The Mala-Arayans are found in the forests of Thodupula, Minachil, and Changanāchery taluks. As the name suggests, they were once lords of the hills. They claim superiority over all the other tribes. The Ullādans used to call them *Vāliānmārs* (those who rule), which evidently points to their former greatness.

On attaining puberty, a girl is confined to a seclusion shed for a day. The next day she bathes and goes to the main hut. On the eighth day she bathes in the stream, plunging three times. After the third dip she looks at the tāli-tier. The girl and the tāli-tier are taken home in procession, and there they are seated on a mat and treated to a feast.

Before girls attain puberty a tāli-tying ceremony is performed, generally for a number of girls together at the age of 3, 5, 7 or 9. Marriage takes place after they have attained puberty. The marriage ceremony is conducted at night or in the evening. The bridegroom's father gives presents to the couple. The couple are then seated on a mat, facing east. The bride's brother hands her a betel-leaf which she tears off into two halves. She gives one half to her husband to chew, and she herself chews the other half, and both spit in the same spitoon. All the guests then chew betel-leaf.

Polygamy is resorted to when the first wife is barren. Fraternal polyandry occurs rarely. Widows remarry. Sons succeed to the father's property, and in their absence it devolves on the daughters. If a man dies childless, his property goes to his brothers and, in their absence, to his sisters.

The religion of the Mala-Arayan may be described as animism or spiritism. Ancestor-worship is one of the great branches of the religion of mankind, and wide and deep traces of it are found among the Mala-Arayans. The spirits of the dead are worshipped, because they are capable of influencing the welfare of the living in a mysterious manner. The Mala-Arayans worship five hills which are believed to possess supernatural powers, but they do not distinguish the spirit from the matter. They also worship Sāsta, a sylvan deity of hoary antiquity.

The Mala-Arayans are nomadic agriculturists. They are dark in complexion, have a long head and a flat nose, depressed at the root. Brow ridges are prominent and the forehead is receding. Many have become converts to Christianity.

The Ullādans are found inside the reserved forests in the Manimala Range. There is no difference between them and the Kochuvēlans. They are also known as *kattālans.*

An Ullādan generally marries the daughter of his paternal uncle. Marriage takes place before the girl attains puberty. A preliminary *tāli-kettu kalyānam* is celebrated when the girl is seven years old. On the fourth day of the ceremony the tāli-tier and the girl bathe in a stream and return home in procession. If he so desires, he can marry her after she has attained puberty. The marriage is conducted in the bride's house. The couple stand in the marriage booth, the bridegroom presents a bundle of clothes to the bride, and she wears them. The guests are given betel-leaves to chew, and the married couple depart for the husband's house. At the latter place the guests are treated to a feast at night, and in the next morning, after another feast, the bride's party goes back.

Polygamy is prevalent among this tribe. A man may marry the wife of his deceased brother. Fraternal polyandry is also said to exist rarely.

On a man's demise, one half of his property goes to the nephews, and the other half to his sons. In the absence of nephews, the whole property goes to his sons.

The Ullādans are nomadic agriculturists. Rice is their staple food. Kochu Vēlan is the head of the Ullādans and he receives the offerings of coconuts, ghee, and cash, made by devotees of God Ayyappan at Thalapāra on their way to Sabarimala during the *Makaravilakku* festival.

The Ullādans are animists. They make an offering to Thalapāramala, Udumpāramala, and Chakipāramala annually on a Friday. They believe that they are able to live inside the forest without molestation from wild animals, under the protection they receive from the spirits residing on these hills.

The Ullādans lead a celibate life from the beginning of Dhanu to Medom (December to April), when they clear the jungle and cultivate the land. They do so, because they are then in the domain of the hill deities whose wrath they should not provoke. If a pure life is not led, Sāsta and other deities will be offended. It is said that a man who touched his wife during menses lost his eyes, when he went to hoe the soil.

The Ullādans are dark in complexion, have a long head, a flat nose, depressed at the root, and a receding forehead. Their hair is wavy or curly.

The Kānikār form a wild but inoffensive jungle tribe, inhabiting the wilds of South Travancore. According to Bourdillon, those who live in the interior are called Kānikār, while those living at the outskirts are called *Vālenmār*.

Marriage takes place both before and after a girl attains puberty. In South Travancore, marriage before puberty is not favoured because the girl will not then be in a position to assume the responsibilities of a housewife. In the Shenkotta forest division, infant marriage is in vogue and is becoming common for want of mature women.

The marriage is celebrated in the bridegroom's house in day time. A necklace of beads is tied round the neck of the bride by the bridegroom. The assembled guests are treated to a feast. The married couple sit on a mat, and take food from the same leaf. The next morning all depart, leaving the bride with the bridegroom in his house.

In Kōttūr, the husband ties the tāli round the neck of the bride, if she is an infant. His sister does it if she is grown up. A plantain leaf is placed in front of the couple and rice and curry are served. Two women hold the bride's head and press it on the bridegroom's shoulder seven times. The bridegroom then puts small quantities of rice and curry into the mouth of the bride seven times.

South of the Kōdayār, the marriage is celebrated in the bride's house. The bridegroom ties the *tāli* round the neck of the bride.

The Kānikār are generally monogamous, but if a man marries more than once his second wife is usually the sister of the first. A man can marry the sister of his deceased wife. Adultery is viewed with great abhorrence, and punishment for this offence varies in different localities. At Kulathūpula the punishment inflicted on the adulterer is this. His legs are tied to the branch of a tree with the head hanging down. Straw strewn with chillies is spread on the ground and burned. The body of the culprit is swung to and fro and he is in the meanwhile given 25 lashes with a cane on the buttocks. The guilty woman is given 15 lashes by a man who marries her, even though he may have already been married.

In Vilavancōde taluk a girl on attaining puberty is kept in the hut itself, but further north she is put in a separate shed situated about 100 feet away from the hut. Pollution lasts for six days. On the seventh day she bathes and goes home, when the medicine-man gives her some holy ash which she smears on the forehead. During the seventh month of pregnancy there is a ceremony called *Vayaru Pongal* when offerings are made to the sun. Confinement takes place in the house itself. Pollution lasts for 16 days. Abortion is common among the Kānikār women, probably due to malaria.

A man's property devolves equally on his nephews and sons. In the absence of nephews, the sons get the whole. Descent is reckoned through the female line and children belong to the clan of the mother. In Cherukara of Pathanāpuram taluk, inheritance is through the male line.

The gods of the Kānikār are a legion. Spirits of diverse kinds are supposed to haunt houses and villages They damage the crops ; they cause epidemics and famine ; they are malevolent spirits only. The propitiation of these spirits is the essence of the religion of the Kānikār. They worship Agastya and also ancestor spirits. When frightened by wild animals, they go to the *plāthi* (medicine-man) to ascertain which ancestor spirit has been annoyed. The *plāthi* takes some small pebbles and places five of them in a row in honour of Ganapathi. He then holds some pebbles in his right hand and drops them in pairs into the left. I after dropping four pairs of pebbles, an even number remains in the right hand, the *plāthi* concludes that *Echamuthan* is responsible for the incident. If an odd number is left behind, he repeats the process to find out whether *Pulichāvu* is responsible for it. In Kulathūpula paddy grains are used instead of pebbles and the operation is conducted on a wooden board. The offended spirit is propitiated by making suitable offerings.

The musical instrument of the Kānikār is the *Kokra*. It is used in all religious ceremonies. It is a cylindrical tube 9 inches long, made out of sheet iron, the lateral edges of which are serrated. A man hold it in his left hand and draws an iron pin over the serrated edges to and fro quickly. The sound thus produced is not very agreeable, but it suits the songs of the Kānikār.

The villages are rarely situated on crests of hills. They are usually built in places where there is a convenient water-supply. The huts are constructed in rows, leaving only a small space between the rows. A village is abandoned as soon as the soil there ceases to be productive. The 'Bachelor-hall' is prominent in Mōthiramala, Chembikunnu and Kōttūr. It is the home of the unmarried youth of the village, and women are not allowed access into it. Bachelors remain there day and night and go to their huts only for meals. Unmarried girls remain in a separate shed. Among the Kānikār at Arippu, Madathura and other places there is no separate shed for unmarried girls.

The Kānikār make fire by the " drill method ". A small hole, half an inch deep, is made in the centre of a piece of soft wood. A man keeps the piece in position under his big toe, takes a round stick of hard wood, 18 inches long, holds it in a vertical position keeping one end of it on the slot and turns it quickly backward and forward with both his hands. In this process a small quantity of dust is formed and the heat produced by friction ignites it.

The Kānikār also make fire by the " flint and steel method " which they call " *chakku mukki* ". It may be a comparatively recent innovation. Pieces of flint and steel and some floss of *Careya urens* are the things required. The floss is held near the flint and the latter is struck with the steel. The friction produces sparks which ignite the floss. This process is resorted to in cold weather only. The use of safety matches is now coming into vogue.

The Kānikar are nomadic agriculturists. In Kalkulam, Vilavancōde, Neyyāttinkara and Nedumangād, and in Pathanāpuram and Shenkōtta taluks they are cultivating paddy permanently on flats inside the reserved forests.

The dress of the Kānikār to the north of the Karamana river and to the south of Chembikunnu is scanty. It consists of an under-cloth held in position by a string tied round the loins. Over this is supended an apron 2½ feet long and 1½ inches wide, the loose and of which is tucked up into a girdle tied tightly round loins. The girdle is made on the takli by women, out of 17 strands of yarn or twist. A woman takes three to four days to make a girdle. The Kānikār living in places where they come in contact with the people of the plains are better clad. The Kānikār of Nedumangād tatoo their body to enhance personal beauty.

The Thanta-Pulayas live in the coastal tract in Shērtala taluk. Among them girls are married after puberty, but betrothal take place when they are seven to eight years old. The marriage ceremony consists in the bridegroom presenting a pair of cloths to the bride and tying a necklace of beads round her neck. Formerly, a thanda* garment was presented instead of cloths. Five men of the bridegroom's party are fed and *pansupari* is distributed to them. With this the ceremony is concluded.

A man may marry more than one woman, generally on economic grounds. Women work and provide food to their husbands also. Widow remarriage is allowed. The Thanda-Pulayas are matrilineal. The nephew succeeds to the property of the uncle. If there is no nephew the property goes to the son.

They worship the sun early in the morning and in the evening. They are also serpent worshippers.

In spite of their hard life, the men have a sturdy constitution. They have a long head, a flat nose, and a receding forehead. The vault of the head is low. They are dark in complexion with well-developed chests. Brow ridges are prominent.

V.—*Clans and Exogamy.*

The social organisation of the hill-tribes of Travancore is built on the foundation of exogamy. The tribe forms the outer circle within which a man must marry. Within it there are sub-divisions which prohibit the marriage of persons related through males. These are called exogamous groups or clans. The theory is that members of the same clan are descended from the same male ancestor, and are, therefore, related. Marriage is not allowed within the clan. The clan does not prohibit marriages of persons related on the mother's side, but permits the union of first cousins, provided they are not children of brothers.

The Hill-Pantārams are the least modified survival of the Pre-Dravidian race. They have no clan system, but there are two groups among them con isting of three or four families, having no distinct names. Each group is exogamous. A man marries the daughter of his maternal uncle or of his father's sister. Thus double cross-cousin marriage is practised. The exchange of sisters in marriage is also in vogue.

The Kānikār of South Travancore have a more highly developed system of exogamous clans than those in Quilon and Shenkōtta divisions. There are two clans in the hamlets of Cherukara, Madathura, Arippu and Villimala of Shenkotta and Quilon Divisions, and are known by the names of *Māttillom* and *Méni illom.* They trace the origin of the clans to the carcase of an elephant. The man who saw the haunches and hind-limbs of the carcase belonged to Mūtillom, and he who saw its trunk to the Mēni illom. The Kānikār of the present day claim to be the descendants of these two ancestors.

The number of clans is four among the Kānikār at Naravēli in Nedumangād taluk. They are *Mūtillom' Méniillom, Kāyyillom,* and *Palillom.* They are all exogamous. Members of *Mūttillom* and *Méni illom* considered to be superior to the other two clans, intermarry. There is neither intermarriage nor interdining between these and the other clans. The members of the two inferior clans are not even invited to the marriage ceremonies of the superior clans, and if they attend the ceremonies uninvited, they are fed only after the superior clans have had their feast.

Among the Kānikār of Neyyāttinkara Range, there are two distinct divisions or *Phratries*, the *Annanthambi Phratry*, and the *Machambi Phratry.* The *Anuanthambi* Phratry includes the clans of *Méni illom, Perinchillom,* and *Kayyillom* ; and the *Machambi Phratry,* the clans of *Mūttillom, Velanat illom,* and *Kurumillom.* Intermarriage between the members of the different clans of the same Phratry is prohibited.

There are interesting stories current among the Kānikār as to the origin of their clans. The ancestors of the Kānikár of Mòthiramala felt an abhorence to the promiscuous life they led in the past. With a view to evolve order out of this chaotic social condition, *Illampalli Mūthan* and *Thiruvampalli Muthan* decided that there should be a dual organization of the Kānikārs, the *Annanthambi illakārs* and *Machāmbi illakārs.* Each division was further divided into five clans, and the Kānikār of the present day are said to be their descendents.

The Kānikār of Mankutty have invented a very ingenious story about the origin of the clan system. The story is that a sambhar once did great havoc to their crops and the man who shot an arrow at the animal and killed it became *Kurumillom.* The man who sat on the hedge and saw the incident became *Velillom* and another who watched the fun at a distance *Velanāt illom.* The man who removed the sambhar's head became *Mūttillom* and one who carried the fore-limbs *Kayyillom.* Another who bundled up a small quantity of flesh in a number of leaves, which swelled its appearance, belonged to *Periman illom.* The man who removed the bowels became *Mangotillom,* and one who removed the udder of the carcase, *Palamba illom.* Lastly, a man who left a python in water belonged to *Perichillom.*

* For *thanda* or *thanta* see below under "Dress".

In the hamlets in the vicinity of Kallār in Nedumangād taluk, the clans are known by other names, and the origin of the clan system is said to be different. The *Annanthambi illom, Phratry* includes *Vellayillom, Mannati illom, Thumbara illom, Velanāt illom, Mulakōnath illom*, and *Muttillom*. The *Machambi Phratry* includes *Meni illom, Pitkayillom, Erumbiyat illom, Paramala illom*, and *Pothottillom*. Regarding the origin of these clans, it is said that once a wild elephant lay dead in the jungle, and that different parts of its carcase were appropriated by different Kānikār, from whom originated the various clans. The man who got only the earth where the carcase lay belonged to *Mannati illom*. One who carried away the genital organ became *Thumbara illom*. He who removed the heart belonged to *Vellai illom*. The man who got the lion's share of the flesh belonged to *Meni illom*. One who got only the ants that swarmed there belonged to *Erumbiyat illom*. The *Mulaikonath, Patika*, and *Pothode illoms* are named after the places called Mulaikonam, Patika, and Pothode. As regards *Pāramala illom*, it is said that a Kānikār boy and girl were found hiding in a rock cave called Pāramala and they were removed to the nearest hamlet and brought up. The children of this girl belonged to *Paramala illom*. Those who saw and enjoyed all the fun belonged to *Velanat illom*.

Dr. Edgar Thurston gives currency to the thoery that clans are named after mountains and places, such as Pālamala, Thalamala, etc. This view is not shared by the Kānikār of the present day.

The system of tracing kinship through the mother is not altogether extinct among the hill-tribes of Travancore. Among the Kānikār, the children of a man of the Kurumillon clan by his wife of the Perinchillom clan belong to the latter clan. According to the rules of exogamy, no man is allowed to marry a woman of his own clan.

As a woman's children belong to a clan different from that of her brother's children, it follows that these children, who are cross-cousins, can intermarry according to the rule of exogamy. On the other hand, children of brothers or of sisters belong to fthe exogamous clan and cannot, therefore, intermarry. Though double cross-cousion marriage is permissible, a man generally marries the daughter of his maternal uncle. A child is generally named after a member of the mother's clan, a maternal uncle, an aunt, or a maternal grand-parent.

Under the system of female descent, there was no transfer of clanship among the Kānikār. The children belonged to the mother's clan. With the introduction of the system of male kinship, came the practice of transferring a woman from her own clan to that of her husband.

The Muduvans of Nēriamangalam Range are divided into a number of exogamous clans, such as *Mēlākūttam Kānakūttam, Thūshanikūttam, Pūthānikuttam, Kanayathukuttam, Ellikuttam*. Members of the *Kanakuttam* and *Mēlākūttam* clans consider themselves to be superior to the remaining four clans, and do not intermarry with them.

Mēlīkūttam includes the *Vākās* or chieftains of the Muduvans. This clan is said to be superior to all the other clans, and members of this clan intermarry only with those of the *Kānakūttam* clan.

Kānakūttam is inferior to the Mēlākūttam, but its members alone enjoy the privilege of marriage with the members of the latter.

Thūshanikūttam.—The members of this clan are the vassals of the Vāka. The do all manual labour for him. When the Vāka visits them, a fowl is killed and cooked, and the Vāka and his followers are treated to a sumptuous meal.

Kānayathūkuttam.—The members of this clan are also the vassals of the Vāka. Their functions are identical to those of *Thushanikuttam*, but they enjoy the special privilege of putting up a *thatti* (elevated seat) for the Vāka to sit on.

Ellikuttam.—The members of this clan have their own Vāka at Kiliparambu.

Among the Muduvans at Poopara, there are only three clans, *Thūshanikūttam, Kānayathūkūttam*, and *Ellikūttam*. The *Mēl-Vāka* of *Mēlākūttam* clan is recognised as their chief, and he still receives the fines inflicted on delinquents.

The Muduvans of Kūdakād in Anjanād valley have only two clans, *Sūryanayar* and *Aryanayar*, and they are exogamous. They do not recognise the Mēl-Vāka as their chief.

Like the Kānikār of South Travancore, the children of a Muduvan family belong to the clan of the mother. The husband is responsible for the maintenance of his wife and children. The debts of his children are a charge not on the father, but on the uncle, and a man's debts devolve on his nephews. Male children are named after their maternal uncle or grandfather, and daughters after their maternal grandmother or ant. A man invariably marries the daughter of his maternal uncle.

The Vishavans of Idyara valley are divided into eight clans :—

1. Kunnikār,
2. Alappankār,
3. Maringāttukār,
4. Thonnikār,
5. Ponnēyankar,
6. Pēlatikār,
7. Pōkkankār,
8. Krāplikār.

Sir Herbert Risley classes the names of exogamous divisions as eponymous, territorial, or local, titular and totemistic.[9] The clans of the Vishavans are territorial. They are named after some village in which the members of the clan originally resided. Thus *Maringattukar* are those who came from Maringath. The *Krāplikārs* are those who came from Krāpli. Groups of Vishavans occupied different parts of the Idiyara valley, and came to be known by the name of the locality where they lived.

The *Pēlatikār* are said to be indigenous. When they began to decline in numbers, they contracted alliances with the Muduvans in Cochin State, and these came over and settled down in some parts of the Idiyara valley.

The *Pēlatikār* and *Pōkkankar* consider themselves to be superior to the other clans, and the headman is selected from these clans. This superiority does not, however, operate as a bar to intermarriages. The first three clans regard themselves as belonging to one stock and so no intermarriage is allowed among them, but they can intermarry with the remaining seven clans.

Marriage between cross-cousins is prohibited among the Muduvans. A man is free to marry any woman outside his clan and has thus a wider choice of a mate.

[9] Risley—*loc. cit*, page 161.

The Mala-Arayans of Central Travancore are divided into six clans :—

Vala illom are the descendants of the man who presented bangles to the Ambalapula Chief (Vala means bangle); *Enna illom*, of the man who presented oil to the Chief (Enna means oil); *Mundillom*, of the man who presented cloth to the Chief (Mundu means cloth); and *Pūthāni illom*, of the man who presented flowers to the Chief, (Poovu means flower.) Besides these four, there are also the *Korangani illom* and *Panthirayira illom*. The first two clans claim superiority over the others. *Mundillakārs* and *Pūthāni illakārs* are *Machambi* (brother-in-law) *illakars* to the members of the first two clans. The last two clans are the lowest in social status.

Formerly men of *Vala illom* married the women of *Pūthāni illōm*, but did not give their women in marriage to the latter. Members of *Pūthāni illom* are not allowed to serve food to those of *Vala illom* because of their lower status. These differences are now vanishing.

A Mala-Arayan is forbidden from marrying a woman of his own clan. A man's children belong to his wife's clan, and they are named after the maternal grandparent, uncle or aunt. One of the traces of the old solidarity of the clan exists in the recognition, by every member of the clan, of his duty to welcome any other member of the clan, however unrelated, as his brother.

The *Mala Vēdans* are divided into three endogamous sections, the *Cheru Vēdan*, the *Cheenganni Vēdan* and the *Eli Vēdan*.

The *Cheru Vedans* otherwise known as *Vettuvans*, are found both in the Kumaranpērūr Reserve of the Ran Range and outside. They comprise four exogamous clans :—

1. Vēnātan illom,
2. Vēndiri illom,
3. Churalayār illom,
4. Modanāthan illom.

Marriage between members of the same clan is prohibited. A man is free to marry a woman of the other three clans. A woman after marriage continues to be of her own clan and the children belong to her clan.

The *Mala-Kuravans* are divided into eight exogamous clans—

1. Mēnati illom,
2. Kara illom,
3. Kuruntadi illom,
4. Pallikal illom,
5. Thechira illom,
6. Vayana illom,
7. Venni illom,
8. Onthi illom.

The *Mēnati illakārs* consider themselves to be superior to the other clans. Men of this clan take wives only from the *Thechira, Venni, Kuruntadi, Pallikal* and *Kara* clans, and not from the remaining three clans. Marriage within the clan is forbidden. A man marries the daughter of his maternal uncle, but not the daughter of his father's sister, as she is considered to be his sister.

The *Mala-Adiyārs* of Ullinkal and Kottampāra in the Rani Range have the following clans :—

1. Kara illom,
2. Mēnati illom,
3. Pallikal illom,
4. Venni illom,
5. Plākāt illom,
6. Vayana illom.

The clans are exogamous. A woman continues to be of her own clan even after marriage, and her children belong to her clan. Owing to the similarity of their clans, the Mala-Adiyārs appear to be an early off shoot of the Mala-Kuravans.

The *Ulladans* have four exagamous clans :—

1. Kārāncheri illom,
2. Mādapalli illom,
3. Kānat illom,
4. Perakāla illom.

A woman after marriage retains her own clan. Children belong to the mother's clan and are named after a maternal grand-parent, uncle or aunt. Cross-cousin marriage is common among this tribe.

The *Ūrālis* of Periyār and Vandamēt are divided into eight exogamous clans :—

1. Kānakūttam,
2. Vettikūttam,
3. Onakuttam,
4. Thūriyakūttam,
5. Enniyārikūttam,
6. Periyilakūttam,
7. Kodiyarikūttam,
8. Vayanavarkūttam.

The story of the origin of these clans is fanciful. Those who went trudging in the *Kānam* (high forest) belonged to *Kānakūttam*. Those who went clearing the way belonged to *Vettikūttam*. Those who went easing themselves on the way belonged to *Thūriyakuttam*. Those who swept away the refuse belonged to *Periyilakūttam*. Those who numbered the cut stumps on the way belonged to *Enniyārkūttam*. Lastly those who attended a feast on Onam day belonged to *Onakūttam*.

The clans are exogamous and children belong to the clan of the mother. Marriage generally takes place by the exchange of sisters. No man can get a wife, unless he has a sister whom he can give in exchange. The result is that a number of young men remain unmarried. A man used to have more than one wife formerly but now the scarcity of women has made monogamy obligatory.

The *Mannāns* of Vandamēt have eleven clans :—

1. Aravankudi kāni,
2. Nāttumannān Kāni,
3. Anakādan kāni,
4. Thōprān kāni,
5. Edādan kāni.
6. Panikan kāni,
7. Urālian kāni,
8. Maniyāran kāni,
9. Kumblan kāni,
10. Muthukoran kani,
11. Kalkūndal kāni.

The clans are named after the localities where they live. They are exogamous and children belong to the clan of the mother.

Sir James Frazer calls Southern India " the classic home of cousin marriage ". " The marriage of cross cousins appears to originate in the simplest of economic motives, the wish and necessity to pay for a woman in kind. Formerly, the match between a brother's daugther and sister's son was most common. This is said to be a survival of the matriarchate, when a man's sister's son was his heir *".

" In Southern India, the practice of marriage with cross-cusions is thus not limited to the aboriginal tribes It is also observed by the Hindu castes, from the Nānjanād Vellālas down to the Brahmans, who adopted it to keep the family property intact within it†".

Marriage between a man and the daughter of his maternal uncle is prevalent among the Muduvans, the Mannāns, and the Mala-Kuravans; but marriage between a man and the daughter of his father's sister is prohibited. Marriage between ortho-cousins is also tabooed. Among the above mentioned tribes as well as the *Hill-Pantārams,* the *Mala-V dans,* and the *Mala-Arayans,* a father desires and claims the marriage of his son with his sister's daughter. The desire is probably based on the economic motive of reducing the marriage expenses and of keeping the family property intact. A father, on the one hand, encourages one form of cross-cousin marriage, namely, the marriage of his son with his sister's daughter; a mother, on the other hand, encourages the other form of cross-cousin marriage, namely, the marriage of her son with her brother's daughter, so that similar motives pulling brother and sister, in opposite directions balance each other and tend to produce an equilibrium between the two forms of cross-cousin marriage.

Of the two forms of marriage by barter, the exchange of sisters was earlier than the exchange of daughters by their fathers. The form of marriage considered to be quite proper by primitive tribes is that between cross-cousins. A man marries a woman who is the dauthter of his father's sister and his mother's brother, and a woman marries a man who is the son of her mother's brother and her father's sister. Husband and wife in such cases are double cross-cousins. This double relationship by blood between the pair arises from the interchange of sisters between their fathers for their wives.

The practice of exchange of sisters in marriage co-exists with cross-cousin marriage, among the Ūrālis the Muduvans, the Kānikār, the Mala Vēdans, and the Ullādans. .... Among the Vishavans of Idyara valley, the number of exogamous groups increased to eight and this was probably done to prevent the marriage of cross-cousins.

Under the system of female kinship, there was no change of clanship after marriage and both the husband and the wife retained their own clans, and the children belonged to the mother's clan. This is the case among the Kānikār, the Muduvans, the Mala-Arayans and others. With the introduction of the system of male kinship came the practice of transferring a woman from her clan to that of her husband.

In Hill-Pantārams Travancore still possesses a primitive tribe in the hunting stage of civlization, among whom children are named after the father, and descent is patrilineal.

Existence of clans from which Chiefs are drawn.

The existence of separate clans from which chiefs are drawn is a distinguishing feature of a few hill-tribes.

There are six clans among the *Muduvans.* The *Melakuttam* clan is considered to be superior to all the others, and the headman, *Mel-Vaka,* is chosen from this clan. The members of this clan are allowed to intermarry only with those of the *Kanakuttam* clan. The Mel-Vāka is the supreme lord of the Muduvans.

In the case of the *Vishavans* of Idyara valley the headman is chosen from the *Pelatikar* and *Pokkankar* who are superior to the other clans, but unlike among the Muduvans intermarriage is allowed between these and all other clans.

Among the *Mala-Arayans* of Central Travancore, the *Enna illakārs* and the *Vala illakārs* are considered to be superior to the other clans, and from these their chiefs are chosen. There is no bar against inter-marriages between the different clans.

The *Kanikar* generally have no particular clan from which the chiefs are chosen. Among the Kānikār of Naraveli alone there exist two clans, the *Mūttillakārs* and the *Mēni illakārs,* who are supposed to be superior to the other clans, and they choose their Chiefs from the two superior clans. The members of the superior and the inferior clans neither intermarry nor interdine.

VI.—*Dwellings and Materials used in their Construction.*

The primitive tribes of Travancore are found in the region of the bamboo and the reed. These grow so vigorously that they fill up all available space. They are used for a variety of purposes. There is a family likeness among all articles made by tropical peoples, and this is accounted for by the uniformity of climate and environment in which they live. The rectangular type of hut is the most common among most of the tribes.

The *Hill-Pantarams* make the simplest of dwellings. They live either in rock-shelters, or under breakwinds resting on junglewood posts and thatched with wild plantain leaves. These will accommodate two or three persons. Children over ten years of age sleep in separate dormitories. The huts are almost circular in shape.

According to Lord Avebury the Garos of Upper India and the *Kanikar* are reckoned to live in dwellings 8 to 10 feet from the ground, the object being protection from man and wild animals‡. Two such pile-dwellings exist in the Kāni settlement at Mothiramala near Pēchipāra. Each building is rectangular in shape and is 20 feet long and 15 feet broad. A bamboo ladder with two steps is used in ascending to the building which is built on posts of wood, 3 feet high above ground. There are eight of them on each side and eight in the middle. The flooring is made of bamboo *thatty* resting on bamboo cross-pieces. These two buildings are far more sanitary than other huts in which the Kānikār live. They have given up this type of dwelling as it is too difficult and costly to make.

The ordinary hut is easily built. It is 15 feet by 12 feet in dimensions, and contains only one room It is made of junglewood, reeds and bamboos. The roof is thatched with the leaves of reeds and the side walls are also covered with them. The huts are made closely in a row in the Villavancode and Kalkulam Ranges, but they are wider apart in regions to the north of Nedumangād. The floor is on a level with the ground; in some cases the side walls are made of mud to a height of two feet from the ground. These huts are very insanitary.

* Frazer—*Folklore in the Old Testament.* Volume II page 120.
†E. Thurston—*Ethnographic notes in Southern India,* page 54.
‡Lord Avebury—*The Origin of Civilization.*

Dr. Keane does not attach much importance to pile-dwellings as other ethnologists do. He does not agree with the idea that the construction of such dwellings was a custom peculiar to the non-Aryan races. It arose from such natural causes as humidity of soil and the necessity of a refuge against wild beasts and hostile tribes. Pile-dwellings are a characteristic feature of most of the tribes in Burma, Assam, New Guinea and others.

The *Muduvan's* huts are neater in appearance, but are huddled together. The floor is on a level with the ground. The huts are made of junglewood and reeds, and are thatched with grass. In the Anjanād Range, the walls are made of plaited bamboo and plastered with clay. Each hut has only one door in the front and is not provided with windows, as a protection against cold, living as the Mannāns do at high elevations.

The dwellings of the *Mala-Arayans* and the *Ullādans* are of an improved pattern. They are built far apart with junglewood, bamboos and reeds, and are thatched with grass. They have invariably a verandah in the front. The walls are made of plaited bamboo. The floor is about 2½ feet above the ground.

The dwellings of the *Mala-Pulayans* are 15 feet by 12 feet in dimensions and are two-roomed. They are made of junglewood, bamboos and poda grass. Bamboo-trellis forms the wall which is mud plastered. The floor is raised, and the huts face east. They have no windows.

The summer encampments of the *Vishavans* are on the banks of the Idara river and are of a temporary nature. They have merely a lean-to-roof, one side of which touches the ground and the other is raised by reedstakes. Here they remain from November to March, when they move on to their new clearings and put up more substantial buildings. These are two-roomed and are 20 feet long and 15 feet broad. They are made of junglewood and reeds, and are thatched with reed leaves.

The dwellings of the Ūrālis are of the same pattern as those of the Kānikār and the Muduvans, but, as they live in high jungle, they have also tree-houses where they spend the nights for fear of wild elephants. They are built upon trees as a height of about 50 feet from the ground. A single bamboo, with shoots on the sides cut short, serves as a ladder. The roof is thatched with reed leaves and the walls are made of bamboo *thatties*.

VII.—*Weapons used by the Primitive Tribes.*

The *Hill-Pāntarams,* being in the hunting stage of civilization, are the poorest in their equipment of weapons. Those living in the Rani and Manimala Ranges are in the lowest stage of civilization, and ordinarily possess only a wooden digging spud. Owing to the contact with low-country men, some of them are now equipped with bill-hooks. Dogs are their sole companions. They are ferocious animals and are helpful to them for their existence in the jungle.

The *Kānikār*, in common with other hill-tribes, use the bill-hook for a variety of purposes. It is sharpened on one surface of its cutting edge. The handle is made of wood, which is fastened to the blade by means of a pin. The Kānikār use the bill-hook for loosening the soil for cultivation, for cutting fire-wood, and for various other purposes.

They are also adepts in the use of the pelletbow, the bow and the gun. The pellet-bow is adapted for the use of pellets of stone, which are flung with great force. The stave is made of bamboo and is wider at the middle than at the ends. Two strings made of *Sterculia* fibre are tied on notches at the ends of the stave; they are kept one inch apart by a piece of reed, with a socket in the centre, one inch square, also made of *Sterculia* fibre. The stone is held in the socket by the thumb and the forefinger. A stone could be flung from the pellet-bow over a distance of 100 yards. It is used in killing small game and in driving away monkeys from the crops. Boys are taught the use of it from very early in life and by the tenth year they become experts at it. Men use it till they are 40 years old, when they give it up owing to failing eye-sight.

The Kānikār use the plain bow also. It consists of a single stave, made out of the stem of *Poliyanthia fragrans.* The string is made of the fibre of the adventious roots of Ficus, and is fastened to notches at the ends of the stave. The arrow is made of reed, and the pointed end, made of *Acacia catechu*, is fixed to it by means of wax. To steady the flight of the arrow three rows of fowl's feathers are stuck into it with gum.

The present-day Kānikār say that their ancestors were stronger than they and used to killl even big game with the arrow. They have now become weak and cannot make use of it as effectively as their forefathers did in the past.

The Kānikār get guns made for them by local blacksmiths. They are made out of the timber of *Careya arborea* supplied by the Kānikar themselves and the barrels of old unlicensed guns which the smiths manage to secure. Such guns cost from ten to thirty rupees. A Kānikār takes to the use of gun by the 15th year and kills with it the bison, the wild boar, the sambhar, the barking deer, the porcupine, the monkey, the jungle squirrel and other animals.

The *Muduvans* of the High Range use neither the pellet bow nor the plain bow; but those at Pooyamkutty use the bow, but not the pellet-bow. The stave of the bow is made of bamboo, and the arrow of reed. The string is made of the fibre of Ficus. Children are taught the use of the bow and arrow by the elders from their tenth year. The enthusiasm for the use of this weapon is dying out after the introduction of the gun. Boys are allowed to handle a gun from the 18th year.

The Ūrālis use the pellet-bow and the muzzle-loading gun. The chief weapon of the other tribes are the digging spud and the bill-hook.

VIII.—*Systems of Agriculture.*

The primitive peoples of Travancore have a clear conception of tribal lands. The Hill-Pantārams are a small nomadic hunting tribe. They generally live in families of two or three for a week in one locality and then move on to another when the food supply is exhausted. There is an understanding among them that the groups living at Achencoil shall not roam over the domain of those at Thalapāra in quest of food. Each group has its own tract for its food-supply, and, on an average, it comes to about two square miles of land per head.

Nomadic Agriculture.—Agriculture is resorted to at first as an adjunct to the chase. The Muduvans, the Mannās, the Paliyans, the Ūrālis, and the Vishavans clear the land by burning the jungle, sow the seed, rake up the soil, and reap a fairly good harvest. Shifting cultivation is the common pratice and each group takes possession of three times the area required for food production and cultivates one-third of it every year. The Kānikār, the Mala-Arayans and the Ullādans follow a slightly different system of cultivation. They cultivate a block of land for two or three years, and then take up another block, but do not change their habitation. Sedentary life adds stability to the occupation of the land. Agriculture alone enables them to live together in one place and collect the necessaries of life.

Terraced Agriculture.—The Muduvans of the Anjanād valley are the only primitive people who have resorted to terraced agriculture from remote times.

The Anjanād valley is about five miles long and two to three miles broad. Ward and Conner speak of "numberless little glades, some adapted to rice cultivation, scattered along the hilly table that overlooks the valley, whose inhabitants are never tempted to settle within this space*". Semple states that a mountain enviroment often occasions a forced development in the form of agriculture among people who otherwise still linger on the outskirts of civilization. This is true of the Muduvans of the Anjanād Valley who have been there from the second century A. D. Mountain agriculture is necessarily laborious and the paucity of arable land precludes the, possibility of letting fields lie fallow. They are constantly fertilized by cow-dung to replenish the soil depleted by denudation. Fortunately for Anjanād, the rainfall is low, and the soil clayey. The soil wash is, therefore, not appreciable, and parallel walls of stone have not been found necessary. At Marayūr and Nāchivayal, there is a vast expanse of terraced cultivation of rice. Hill slopes are cut down and made into terraces, from 10 to 30 feet broad. The terraces are irrigated by channels which carry water from the Pambanar from a distance of several miles. The terraces are so arranged that the water flows from terrace to terrace. Ownership of terraced fields is individual. The Muduvans of Kādakād divert the waters of the Manalār to irrigate their fields. The Government of Travancore have extended the scope of terraced cultivation in this area by constructing a channel called the Thalayār right bank channel about 4 miles long, along the slope of the hills, at a cost of over a lakh of rupees, thus ensuring a regular supply of water to about 1,000 acres of this area.

Terraced agriculture is commonly practised by literate peoples of Travancore in the mountainous tracts of Minachil, Thodupula, Manimala and Pirmēde. The Hindus, the Muslims, and the Christians resort to it. When food supply becomes inadequate for the growing population, artificial methods are employed to extend the area of arable land.

IX.—*Village Organisation.*

The rigidity of the village organisation of the primitive tribe is due to their long isolation, their narrow outlook on life, and close intermarriage for countless generations. They generally live in small groups of families called *Kudi* (village). Each village is even now an independent unit, and consists on an average of from 10 to 15 families, bound together by the idea of self-protection.

Among the *Muduvans* each village has its own headman and the village affairs are conducted by a council of elders. The viliage chiefs are called the *Kularan* and the *Sundarapāndi.* Above these there is the *Thalayāri* who exercises jurisdiction over a group of two or three villages. The supreme chief of all the villages is called the *Mēl-Vāka* and under him there is another dignitary called the *Muppan.* All matters which could not be settled by the village councils and by the headmen of the villages or groups of villages, are first referred to the *Muppan*, and on his decisions appeals are preferred to the *Mēl-Vāka* whose decisions are final. The offices of the *Mēl-Vāka* and the *Mūppan* are hereditary and descend from the uncle to the nephew.

When a man commits an offence, a panchayat (*Orumura*) is held in the village *chāvadi.* If he is not amenable to the discipline of the village chief, the *Thalayāri* is invited. The *Kularan* or *Sundarapāndi* (the village chief) spreads a mat and over it is placed a blanket covered by a white cloth for the *Thalayāri* to sit on. The *Thalayāri* and the village headman take their seats on the white cloth, while the other villagers sit at a respectable distance from them. The accused stands with folded hands before this council of village worthies. The complainants and the accused then state their case and after reviewing the arguments on both sides the *Kularan* and the *Sundarapandi* ask the *Thalayari* what punishment should be inflicted on the accused. He orders the imposition of a fine, which does not exceed ten rupees. The authority of the panchayat now extends over breaches of marriage laws, disputes about inheritance, and petty thefts.

The Muduvans of Nēriamangalam have a simpler organisation. There the *Mēl-Vāka* alone counts. He has nominal jurisdiction over the villages in Poopara and Anjanād also. There are two *Vakas,* called the *Mēl-Vāka* and the *Muthakka.* The latter is inferior in rank to the former. When a fine of Rs. 2-8-0 is inflicted, Rs. 1-8-0 goes to the *Mel-Vāka* and one rupee to the *Muthakka.* The *Mēl-Vāka* apprears in all his grandeur when he heads the procession annually for founding a new hamlet. Other Muduvans clear the jungles, cultivate the soil, sow the seed and obey all the orders of the *Mēl-Vāka,* in return for which he feeds them.

The *Vākās* of *Ellikūttam* are called the *Palithraka* and the *Vālathrāka* and they enjoy the same status as the *Vākās* of the other Muduvan villages.

Among the *Mannans,* village affairs are regulated by a council of elders with a headman chosen by the villagers. Chieftainship is hereditary and the nephew succeeds the uncle. The chief has a lieutenant called the *Rākshasan,* and under him there are other village dignitaries, known as the *Vāllia Elāndāri,* the *Elandāri,* the *Thandakāran,* and the *Thannipātta* in the order of their rank. The *Mannāns* build huts, cultivate the land, harvest the crops, and store them in tree-houses for their village headmen. These privileges are to some extent shared by the *Rākshasan* and the *Valia Elandāri* also. If any work has to be done, the order is issued through the *Rākshasan* and the *Elandāri,* who get it executed through the *Thandakāran.*

The jurisdiction of the village council extends over petty offences which are punishable with a fine. If a man is not amenable to the decision of the council the matter goes on appeal to the *Varayilkilu Mannān* whose decision is final. The system of village government among the Mannāns is gradually breaking down.

The *Mala-Arayans* have also their councils of elders to look after their common interests. The *Ponamban* and the *Panikan,* having equal status, are the main limbs of the councils. The office of the *Ponambān* was first conferred on a deserving member by the Poonjāt Chief, and it is not hereditary. The office of the *Panikan* is hereditary and descends from the father to the eldest son. The headman is responsible for the well-being of the people in his care.

When a man commits an offence, the council meets. The *Ponamban* reviews the offence and award punishment whcih is generally a fine ranging from 10 to 101 chackrams (A chackram is a Travancore coin worth slightly over six pies). The headman and the councils meet once a month, discuss village affairs, and depart after feasting. Each village has a common fund which is held by the headman. Loans are given to the needy and the amount is recovered in instalments. The influence of village government is weakening since the tribe has come under the control of the Forest Department.

* Ward and Conner—*Memoir of the Survey of the Travancore and Cochin States,* Volume I page 41.

Among the *Kānikār* the largest unit is the village. They are knit together by social, religious and political ties. The village acts as a unit in some matters and there is hardly room for individualistic tendencies. The villagers work jointly in clearing the jungle, in burning the debris and in all religio-magical ceremonies performed for securing a bountiful harvest.

The headman (*Mūttakāṇi*) used to wield considerable influence over his men and enjoy various perquisites. The office is hereditary and descends from the uncle to the nephew. He settles all disputes and is the final authority in matters social, religious and agricultural. He presides over the meeting of the council of elders, of which five members form the quorum. All social questions relating to marriage and divorce are discussed and settled by the council, and their decision is final. Any fine inflicted on delinquents is spent in propitiating gods. Formerly, punishment included caning and excommunication, but these are not now resorted to.

Each *Ullādan* hamlet has a chieftain called *Kānikāran.* This office is hereditary and descends from the father to the son. The villagers build the hut and cultivate the land for their chief.

Towards the end of every month, the Ullādans, meet together in a house, and settle all village affairs. The head of the household treats them to a feast. Each house has its turn. When petty cases of assault arise, the culprits are fined 10 chs., with which *pansupari* is purchased and distributed. In case of adultery, the hands of the culprits are tied to a tree, and the man is given 12 lashes by his brother-in-law and the women 16 lashes by her husband's brother.

The supreme head of the Ullādans is called the *Kochuvelan,* a title said to have been conferred by the Pantalam Raja. He is the final authority in all matters concerning the welfare of the tribe, and he alone presides over meetings of the council when the offence of incest is under trial.

The *Kurumba Mala-Pulayans* of Anjanād valley have no separate chief for each hamlet. All the hamlets recognise one common chief called *Arasan.* On his demise the office devolves on his eldest son. The *Arasan* has an assistant called *Vāriyan,* and a *Kōlkāran* to execute his orders.

Among the *Karavali Mala-Pulayans* the headman is known as *Kudumban.* He has under him a *Vāriyan* and a *Kōlkāran* to assist him in his duties. The *Kudumban* and the *Vāriyan* sit on a mat when the council meets and the *Kōlkāran* stands close by. Cases of adultery and other offences are tried by them, and the man and the woman are fined from Rs. 1-12-0 to Rs. 3 each.

The *Ūrālis* of Periyār and Vandamēt have a headman called *Kānikāran* for a group of hamlet. Each hamlet has a *Plāthi* or medicine-man and he is responsible for the good conduct of the men therein. When a dispute arises in a hamlet, the *Plāthi* informs the *Kānikārān* of it and the latter goes there, presides over the meeting of the village council and settles the dispute. No fine is inflicted on the delinquents.

The *Paliyans* have a *Kānikāran* for each hanmlet. He is assisted in the discharge of his duties by a *Valia Elandāri,* a *Veena Mariya,* and a *Thandakāran.* The first two are in charge of all unmarried boys and girls and are responsible for their good behaviour. They help the unemployed by finding work for them.

When any dispute arises in a hamlet, the village council meets and discusses the matter. The parties are admonished and the dispute is settled amicably. If a man commits an incest, he is kept in stocks for a day and then let off.

The *Mala-Kuravans* have a village council presided over by an *Ūrāli* (headman). He is also the medicine man, who cures all maladies.

The *Mala-Vēdans* have a headman called *Stāni* in each hamlet, and he settles all their disputes. The office is hereditary and descends from the uncle to the nephew. He does not exercise much influence now.

X.—*Traditions of Origin.*

The long chain of wooded hills of the Western Ghats forms the home of the hill-tribes of Travancore. How they came to occupy these hills is shrouded in obscurity. Some of them claim to be autochthonous. The Mala-Arayans believe that their original home was in Chingampāra near Karimala in the Rani Reserve, and the Ullādans think that theirs was in Kottathatti. The Hill-Pantārams also claim to be of indigenous origin.

The Kāṇikār, the Muduvans, the Mannāns, the Ūrālis, and the Vishavans entertain traditions of having come from the adjoining district of Madura or Tinnevelly. No tribe has such a wealth of traditions of origin as the Kānikār of South Travancore. These have been handed down from generation to generation in popular songs which they sing even now.

The *Kānikār* of Kōttūr in Neyyāttinkara Taluk sing a *chāttu* song on their past history. It recounts that they formerly settled down in Kalakād and Kallida-kurichi in Tinnevelly district. There were 72 Kāni hamlets under three chieftains, Vīrappen Arayan of Vīranelli Kōtta, Sithangan Arayan of Chennalur Kōtta, and Ādichan Arayan of Alantharakōtta.

In olden times the Āttingal Chief possessed rights over 'Kalakād and Kallidakurichi'. The failure of the Kāṇikār to appear before the Chief (Ponnum Perumāl) for three years led to the despatch of his minister, Māthutti Pillai, to Kalakād with a royal command, directing the appearance of the three hill-chieftains before him immediately. In obedience to the Royal call, the three chieftains went to Āttingal and made presents of honey, ivory, tiger-skin, leopard-skin, bamboo seeds, and other things to His Highness.

His Highness was so much pleased that he conferred on Vīrappen Arayan the title of Vīra Marthāndan Arayan and gave the Chiefs profuse presents. It was also ordered that that Vīramārthāndan Arayan may collect a tax from the Kāṇikār of the 72 hamlets. His Highness was about to arrange for feeding the hill-chieftains and their followers, when Vīra Mārthāndan Arayan informed him that they would themselves cook their food and that they would be satisfied if they were given provisions. These were accordingly supplied.

While they were on their way to the river to cook their food, they were accosted by Chēnnan and Chakki (Chānnāns by caste), who invited them to their home. There they ate the food given by Chakki. His Highness, who was informed of the incident said "Mannu chānnān Malayarasan" which means "By your association with Chānnāns, you have fallen in my estimation. You deserve to be only Malayarayan or lord of the hills".

Vira Mārthāndan Arayan reached Kalakād, and collected and enjoyed the tax from the 72 Kāni hamlets as ordered by the Āttingal Chief. He then decided to celebrate his installation ceremony as Chief of the Kāni-kār, and issued invitations to Adi-Pāndi Pāndiyan, Mid-Pāndi Pāndiyan, and Thala-Pāndi Pāndiyan and to others to the ceremony. Ādi-Pāndi Pāndiyan scoffed at the invitation and jeeringly sent word that he would go for the ceremony if his sister were given him in marriage. This reply provoked Vīra Mārthāndan so much that he could not take the insult lying down. He therefore decided to divert the waters of the Kōthayār, the Parliyār, the Manimuthār, and the Chembarunthār from flowing into Ādi-Pāndy by constructing a dam. Some water still trickled down to Ādi-Pāndy. The medicineman (*Plāthi*) told Vira Mārthāndan that, if the dam were besmeared with the blood of his sister, Karimpadi, no water would flow to Ādi-Pāndy. No less a sacrifice was demanded of Vira Mārthāndan, but he did not flinch from carrying out the words of the medicine man. The insult was so keenly felt that the blood of his sister was poured on the dam, and no water tricked down eastwards thence forward.

This brought famine to Ādi-Pāndy. After ascertaining the cause, the Pāndyan Chief repaired to the Āttingal Raja and sought relief. Māthutti Pillai was sent to Kalakād to break the dam with an elephant and allow water to flow eastwards, Vīra Mārthāndan dissuaded him from doing it, but his words were not heeded. When Māthutti Pillai proceeded to break the dam with the elephant, Vīra Mārthāndan discharged an arrow and killed the elephant. Māthutti Pillai committed suicide, saying "you have killed your sister and my elephant. I too shall end my life here".

This tragic event enraged the Ādi-Pāndy Pāndian and he declared war against the Kānikār. The Kānikār were defeated and their chieftains committed suicide. Some of the Kānikār escaped to Travancore and they are said to be the earliest Kāni settlers in this country. This is the tradition current among the Kānikār about their immigration into Travancore.

The history of Travancore tells us "that the famous warrior-king, Sri Mānkonda Bhutala Vīra Sri Viraladaya Mārthānda Varma conquered the whole of Tinnevelly district from the Pāndiyans about 700 M. E. (1531 A. D.), and married a Chōla princess, Chōlakula Valli, who brought with her the district of Calacaud as dowry. The dam across the Kōthayār which stands even now under the name of *Virapuli Anai* is said to be erected at the period".[20]

Kalakād witnessed several vicissitudes of fortune in later times. It now forms part of the British dominion in India. According to the tradition current among the Kānikār they were in Kalakād when it formed part of Travancore and they migrated to this country as a result of their defeat in the war with the Ādi-Pāndy Pāndiyans. The memory of Māthutti Pillai is enshrined in their religious songs, and offerings are made to him even today.

The Muduvans of the Cardamom Hills believe that they were immigrants from Madura and that they were driven to the hills owing to internal dissensions. It may possibly have been at the time when the Telugu Naickans took possession of Bodinaickanur in the fourteenth century A. D. The Muduvans who came to the High Ranges of Travancore *via* Bodinaickanur carried their children on their back when they climed up the Ghats, and hence they have come to be known as Muduvans (*Muduku* means 'the back'). This is one version. Another version is that, when they left Madura, they carried on their back goddess Meenākshi and are, therefore, called Muduvans. The Muduvan males even now carry loads on their back; and females, their babies.

The Mānnāns claim that they came from Madura to the Cardamom Hills of Travancore. Being fond of animal food, they thought that they could live comfortably on the Travancore hills, which abounded in sambhar, black monkey, and other wild animals. The quest for food is, therefore, said to be the cause of their immigration. Another version is that they were formerly dependants of the King of Madura. Owing to internecine dissensions, they were obliged to leave Madura under the leadership of a chief known as Poonjāt Raja. They entered the hills *via* Cumbum mēttu and settled down in various parts of the Cardamom Hills. They also installed their deity, Chokkanādar, on the Chokkanād peak, and Chanthiyat Amma at Ayyapancoil. It is said that they once owned a small tract of land near Cumbum. It was leased to the people of that place and the produce realised was used for temple service by the Varayil Kīlu Mannān. This land was lost through litigation.

Tradition has it that one of the former Rajas of Poonjāt nominated three Mannāns as his agents for the management of his dominion. One of them was installed at Talliāramalai with a silver sword as his badge, the second, Gōpura Mannān, was installed at Mannānkandam with a silver bracelet as his badge, and the third the Talamala Mannān, who had a silver cane as badge, was installed at Udumbanchōla. Since the Cardamom, Hills passed into the hands of the Government of Travancore, they owe only a nominal allegiance to the Poonjāt chief, who is still held in veneration by them.

The Ūrālis claim that they were dependants of the King of Madura, and that their duty was to hold umbrellas during State processions. "In ancient times many of the parts included in the Thodupula taluk belonged to the King of Madura. Once when the king came to Nēriamangalam, the ancestors of the Ūrālis are said to have accompanied him and were probably left there to rule that locality".[21] (Ūr means locality and 'āli' means to rule.)

The Mannāns are said to have held away over the Ūrālis in former times. They were a source of terror to the Ūrālis, and any Ūrāli who remained in a tree-house on the arrival of the Rāja Mannān was caught and severely chastised. The Rāja Mannān used to be arbiter of their disputes, and they paid him four chuckrams and one para of paddy annually, but, since they passed into the tutelage of the Government of Travancore, they stopped this payment.

The *Paliyans* of Vandamēt say that they were living in Madura, and a Pantāram told them that they would find it congenial to go and live on the Cardamom Hills in Travancore which were uninhabited. On hearing this, they came to the Cardamom Hills and settled down at Vandamēt.

Another tradition current from the Paliyans is that a Kallar of Madura had two wives, and that when some dissensions arose, his children by the second wife fled to Sankurandamalai, fearing molestation. Those who did not fall a victim to the marauders came to be known as Paliyans.

They came to the Cardamom Hills *via* Bodinaickanur. In memory of this connection, the Kallars of Madura refrain from doing any harm to the Paliyans. These two tribes interdine but do not intermarry. A Kallar will not allow a Paliyan guest to depart without being fed. The Paliyans pride themselves in being called *Kattukallars*. The Kallars proper are known as *Nāttukallars*.

The *Vishavans* seem to think that they are autochthonous, but the names of some of their exogamous clans indicate that they came from Adirapalli in the Cochin State: for example, the *Maringāthukārs* are those who came from Maringath near Adirapalli.

---

20. V. Nagamiah.—*The Travancore State Manual*, Volume I, page 338.

21. N. Subramony Iyer—*The Travancore Census Report*, 1901, page 350.

The traditions current among some of the primitive tribes as to their origin and their migration to Travancore hills have been described in the foregoing paragraphs ; but the people of the plains generally ascribe the colonisation of the hills of Travancore with primitive tribes to sage Agastya who came from the north. It is said "that sage Agastya repaired to Dwārka (Tamil Tuvaryppatti), and, taking with him his eighteen kings of the line of Sri Krishna, eighteen families of Vēls or Vēlirs, and others, moved to the south with the Aruvalar tribes, who appear to have been the ancestors of the Kurumbās".[22] "The Kurumbās, according to Dr. Keane, appear to be the remnants of a great and widespread people, who erected the dolmens, and form one of the Pre-Dravidian tribes of South India."[23] Agastya had the forests cleared and built up kingdoms settling there the people he brought with him. This migration may have taken place about 1075 B. C. Popular tradition supports the theory of Agastya's conquest of Southern India. The foot prints of Agastya are said to be visible at several places in his adventurous journey to the south, and the stages of his travels are marked by the little Āsrāmās (hermitages) he set up on the way. The Travancorean holds in great veneration the Agastyar peak, the highest peak of the Western Ghats, where Agastya is still believed to live, and his image is installed and worshipped at the Olakarivu waterfall on the Ashambu hills in the Kalkulam Range, at Marutuāmala near cape Comorin, at Nagercoil, and other places.

The adventures of Agastya are relevant to the extent that he is said to have played a conspicuous part in relaiming primaeval forests in Southern India, and making them fit for human habitation. Even to this day the Kānikār of South Travancore curse their enemies by swearing by Agastya, and make annual offerings to him at Agastyar Peak.

The Epic and the Purānic legends contain traditions relating to the physical characters of the aborigines (Nishadās). "The Bhāgavata Purāna describes Nishada as black like crows, very low-statured, short-armed, having high cheek bones, low topped nose, red eyes, and copper coloured hair".[24] His descendants are distributed on the hills and forests. The Ānamalai hills of Southern India form the refuge of a whole series of broken tribes. They are characterised by dark hair, short stature, and broad nose. Since these physical features characterised the Purānic Nishadās, and indicate their affinities to the so-called Pre-Dravidian, Mr. Chanda considers the dark, short-statured and broad-nosed jungle tribes as the modern Nishadās representing the old Nishada race.

At present, there are no distinctly Negrito communities in India, but in the opinion of Mr. A. H. Keane distinctly Negrito features (dark skin, short stature, and broad nose) not only crop up continually in the uplands from the Himalayan slopes to Cape Comorin, but these uplands abound in great megalithic monuments which will enable us to unravel the history of their remote past.[25]

XI.—*Megalithic Monuments.*

Dolmens are rude structures consisting of a large unhewn stone resting on two or more others placed erect. They are found scattered on the long chain of wooded hills in Travancore. They are generally considered to be "stones of the monkeys in India", but most of the primitive peoples of Travancore have no knowledge of them nor do they evince any interest in them. The people of Anjanād alone call them *Vāliveedūs* or abodes of monkeys. The Ūrālis call the dolmens *Pāndukulies*, pits or graves connected with the Pāndūs or Pāndavās, to whom ancient mysterious structures all over India are generally ascribed. They are looked upon by the credulous as sacred and dangerous. It is said that peasants in France will not take shelter under them nor go near them at night, but the Vellalas and the Mala-Pulayas of Anjanād have no such fear. They sit under them when they graze their cattle. "A dolmen in Finistière is said to cure rheumatism in any one who rubs against the loftiest of its stones and another heals fever patients who sleep under it."[28] There is a miniature menhir (3 feet high above ground) at Marayūr called *Vāthamkolli*. It is believed that any rheumatic patient who rubs his knee against this stone will be cured of rheumatism, but no one ventures to do so at present. Dr. Borlase thinks that dolmens were connected with the activities of a shady priesthood. Professor J. Dubriel has tried to connect many of the Deccan megaliths with sacrificial houses mentioned in later Vedic literature.

The earliest record of dolmens in Travancore is from the pen of Ward and Conner in 1852. They state that "the Pāndukulies or barrows, those remains of primaeval customs so common throughout the Peninsula are also found here, though they are not so numerous". The Ūrālis believe that dolmens are places where treasure is hidden, but no such treasure has been found in any of the dolmens excavated.......... In Travancore they are invariably found on the crests of hills in the Rani Reserve, and they are built of unhewn blocks of stone.

According to Colonel Meadows Taylor, the dolmens are of two kinds, those consisting of four stones, three supporting stones and one cap stone, leaving one side open ; and those in which the chamber is closed by a fourth stone ; in the latter case, the fourth stone has invariably a circular opening in it. The cap stone is ; 15′ 9″ × 10′ 9″ in one case.

Both these types of dolmens are found in Travancore. The dolmen at Kadukuthi in the Rani Reserve is rectangular and the portion above ground is 8′ × 2-1/3′ in dimensions. It has only one gallery. Lengthwise it has one single upright on one side, and two others on the opposite side. Sideways, there is one on each side. The floor is paved with a single stone slab. The capstone is 7′ × 7′ × 8″, and is rudely triangular. Boulders are lying about. This dolmen is situated on the crest of a hill. It appears to have been a dolmen of the earliest times, as it is built of unhewn blocks of stone. The existence of boulders shows that it might have been covered over with them. The dolmen appeared to have already been ransacked and excavation yielded no result.

Rev. Mateer found another type of dolmens in the mountains inhabited by the Mala-Arayans of Travancore. They stand north to south with the circular opening facing the south. A round stone in fitted to this aperture, with another acting as a support to keep it in position. The side stone as well as the stones at the top and at the bottom are single slabs. To this day the Arayans make similar little cells of stone, the whole forming a box, a few inches square.[30] The Mala-Arayans of the present day do not erect dolmens. The art has been forgotten.

Dolmens are also found at Perunthalapura on both banks of the Thalayār or Pāmbanār river, a small tributary of the Amarāvathi which flows into the Cauvery. Here on flat level rocky tableland are seen a larger number of dolmens strewn in groups of three, four or five. Around each group is a circular packing of roughly

22. M. Srinivasa Iyengar—*The Tamil Studies*, pages 45-46.
23. A. H. Keane—*Man, Past and Present*, page 169.
24. R. P. Chanda—*The Indo-Aryan Race*, Part I, page 5.
25. A. H. Keane—*Introduction to the Cochin Castes and Tribes.*
28. E. C. James, *loc. cit.* page 149.
30. Rev. Mateer—*Native Life in Travancore.*

hewn stones or boulders. These groups of dolmens are found distributed in a circle. The disposition of the majority of the dolmens is from east to west. A few are also in north to south direction. The upright stones are rectangular in shape, and are about 10 feet long, 5 feet broad, and 7 feet high. The cover-slab is 17′ × 7′ × 6″. The floor is paved with a flat stone slab 9′ × 4′ × 6″. The inner chamber is 9′ × 4′. Over some of the cover-slabs are found remnants of rubble stone packing. There is a semicircular entrance to the dolmen on one side. Most of these dolmens have four uprights, but one dolmen in some groups has only three uprights and one capstone, thus leaving one side open. The local people call them '*Vali Veed s*' and believe them to have been the abode of '*Valis*' or monkeys of the days of the *Rāmāyana*. Monuments of this kind are also found in the Bison Valley in the Cardamom Hills. At Vadattupāra in the Malayattūr Reserve there is a dolmen consisting of four uprights, but it is smaller and cruder than those found in the Anjanād Valley.

Another type of dolmen is found on the Cardamom Hills near Māttupatti. Here the chamber is formed as described above, but is buried in the earth shewing only the capstone above the ground. Dolmens of this type are said to be found on the Nilgiris and throughout Malabar. About 15 yards to the west of the above mentioned dolmen was found an alignment of monoliths or menhirs planted in the earth at almost equal distances, some small, and some very big and impressive.

A *menhir*....a tall rude stone with its base fixed in the ground....is found in some parts of North Travancore.

Geographical distribution of dolmens.—Dolmens are found from Scandinavia to Algeria and from Portugal to India and Japan. In India, the distribution of megalithic monuments follows the zones of primitive tribes in Assam, Chota Nagpur, South India, and North-West Frontier regions. "They exist over the whole country drained by the Gōdāvari, more common in the valleys of the Krishna, on both sides of the Ghats through Coimbatore all the way down to Cape Comorin". "The manner of distribution of this type of megalithic monuments has led to the theory of the existence of a migratory race known as the 'People of the Dolmens'". As Deschelette points out, European megaliths, in spite of the rudeness of their architecture, are in evident relation with the ancient monuments of the East.

Antiquarians, after careful researches, have been able to divide megalithic monuments into three classes according to their contents.

Tumuli of the Stone Period.—The tumuli of this period are considered to be the most ancient. They are often of great size and are distinguished by circles of stones and stone chambers in which are found the remains of unburnt body with objects of stone and amber. The dolmen opened by Ward and Conner at Chokkanād contained no implement and probably belonged to the Stone Age. This represents the lowest state of civilization before the introduction of metals.[31]

Tumuli of the Bronze Period.—These tumuli contain relics of burnt bodies, vessels, and implements and ornaments of bronze, which indicate that the people were in a more advanced civilization. Tumuli of this kind are rare in Kēr'aia, but it appears that Mr. Bourdillon once picked up a bronze lamp which probably belonged to one such tumulus.

Tumuli of the Iron Age.—They are the most recent and represent a comparatively advanced state of civilization. Iron implements, swords, spear heads, and highly polished vessels are found in them. In the Cochin State, all the tumuli that have been found appear to be of the Iron age, while, in Travancore, there are some that are of even an earlier period as was revealed by the excavations of Ward and Conner.

XII.—*The Disposal of the Dead.*

Burial and cremation are two common methods of disposing of the dead bodies. They are very ancient customs and there is evidence to show that both methods were practised in the Vēdic period in India. "The epithet '*agnidagdhah*'", according to Macdonell and Keith, "applies to the dead who were burnt in a funeral pyre; the other custom being burial, '*anagnidandah*' not burnt with fire". "They also refer to '*paroptah* or 'casting out', and '*uddhitha*' or 'exposure of the dead'. They add that burial was not rare in the Rig-Vēdic period. In the Vēdic period both customs appear in a modified form. A stone is set up between the dead and the living to separate them" [32].

Tamil works such as Manimēkalai, Tolkāppiam, and Poruladigāram written about the second century A. D., refer to the following methods of disposing of the dead in Pre-Brahminic period.

"1. Exposure in an open space to be eaten by jackals.

2. Cremation.

3. Throwing the corpse into natural pits.

4. Covering it with big earthen jars.

5. Burial". [33]

Most of the primitive people of Travancore bury the dead.

The *Hill-Pantārams* of Central Travancore adopt the simplest form of burial. The dead are buried where they die. After burial the tribe leaves the locality and will never again go there.

The *Muduvans* bury the dead about a mile away from the hamlet. The grave is dug waist-deep for men and breast-deep for women, the reason being that men are brave and free from danger, while women will be free from danger only if the corpse is buried deeper in the ground. The corpse is covered by a new cloth purchased by the nephew or the son, and after it is lowered into the grave, the *Chakmuk* (fire-making apparatus) and the turban are placed by its side. The grave is covered with earth and a small stone is planted at the head and feet. A thatched shed 6′ × 2′ is erected over it.

The *Ūrālis* also bury the dead about a furlong from the hut. Its depth is about the same as a man's height, for men, and a woman's height up to the breast for women. The chief mourner is the nephew. The corpse is bathed and covered in a new cloth. It is then placed over a reed mat, tied with *Kyran* fibre (*Helicteres Isora*) and carried to the grave. Billets of wood are placed in the pit and covered with a plaited bamboo mat. The sides of the grave are also covered by similar mats. The corpse is then lowered into the grave and covered by a plaited bamboo mat. The billhook and chewing materials of the deceased are placed in the right armpit. The grave is then filled with earth and a stone two feet long and one foot broad is planted at the head, feet and on one side.

---

31. Fergusson, *loc. cit.*

32. D. A. Mackenzie.—*Indian myths and Legends, Introduction*, pp. XXXII—XXXIII.

33. M. Srinivasa Iyengar, *loc. cit.*, p. 39.

The *Ullādans* bury the dead. The deceased's brother-in-law digs the grave. Before the corpse is removed from the hut the floor is swept and the sweepings are thrown on the bier so as to drive away the spirit of the dead. After burial a stone is planted at the head of the corpse.

The *Mala-Pulayās* bury the dead and place a stone at the head, the breast, and the feet.

The *Mala-Ārayans* of Central Travancore inter the dead about twenty to forty yards to the south of their habitation. The eldest son and the nephew of the deceased go round the site selected for burial thrice, strewing rice and fried paddy. They then remove three shovels of earth from there, turning their faces away from it. The grave is then dug four feet deep. The grave diggers are not allowed to carry the corpse. Wrapt in a new cloth, the corpse is lowered into the grave. All the mourners then throw earth into the grave three times, standing with their back towards the corpse, then wheel round and fill the grave with earth. Small pebbles are placed at the sides of the grave and a big stone is planted at the head and feet vertically.

The *Mannāns* bury the dead. The corpse is wrapt in a new cloth purchased by the nephew and carried to the burial ground on a bier. The grave is hip-deep in the case of men and not so deep in the case of women. The corpse is lowered into the grave with the head turned towards the south. The grave is lled up with earth and a thatched shed is erected over it to protect it from rain.

The *Paliyans* bury the dead about a mile away from the hamlet. The grave is breast-deep for women and loin-deep for men. The corpse is placed in the grave on a reed mat and is covered by it. The grave is then filled up with earth.

The *Visharans* adopt a simple form of burial. The grave is about a mile away from the hamlet and is in the east to west direction. The corpse is laid on a new mat, tied up, and carried to the grave suspended on a pole. It is placed in the grave with the head at the west and the feet towards the east end. The head is propped up so that the face looks eastwards. It is then covered by a bamboo mat and the pit is filled up with earth.

The *Kānikār* living on the northern side of the Kōthayār bury the dead. The grave diggers besmear their foreheads with holy ashes given by the medicine-man to ward off evil spirits. The son and the nephew are the chief mourners. After the corpse is lowered into the grave, the earthly belongings of the deceased are placed by the side. The grave is then filled up with earth by the son and the nephew.

The wife plays an important part in the funeral ceremony among the Kāṇikār of Kōttūr. The wife accompanies the corpse to the grave with a dishful of rice gruel, a spoon and a sieve. As soon as the corpse is lowered into the grave and covered with earth, she comes forward and deposits the above articles at the feet of the corpse.

Death pollution lasts for sixteen days among the Kāṇikār in the region of the Kōthayār, for nine days at Kōttūr, and for seven days in Kulathūppula. Those who carry the corpse have to observe pollution for twelve days.

The Kânikār living on the Southern side of the Kōthayār cremate their dead. A pit, $6' \times 2' \times 2'$ is dug and packed with billets of fuel over which the corpse is laid with the head at the southern end. Fuel is again placed over it and lighted at the head and the feet. After the body is burned small bits of bones are collected and thrown into a stream. The deceased's sister's son conducts these funeral rites. After throwing the bones into the stream he bathes and goes back to the grave with a bill-hook in one hand and lighted faggots in the other. The son of the deceased goes with him carrying a pot of water over his shoulders. They go round the grave thrice and then the nephew hits the pot gently with the bill-hook thrice and the son throws the pot backward.

The *Mala Vēdans* bury the dead about a mile away from their habitation. Before removing the corpse from the hut, the floor is swept and the sweepings and the broom are placed on the bier to drive away the spirit of the deceased from the house. The son and the deceased's sister's son are the chief mourners. After bathing, all the mourners make a mark on their foreheads with cow-dung paste.

XIII.—*Ideas as to the Sun, the Moon and some Natural Phenomena.*

Some of the primitive peoples of Travancore cherish a large number of myths and legends about the objects they see around them in Nature.

The Sun and the Moon.

The *Kanikar* call the sun, '*Bhagavan*' or '*Iswaran*' and worship him on Fridays. Early at sunrise, the Kānikāraṇ places, in front of his hut, a lighted lamp, fruits, beaten and fried rice, and while making this offering he prays, "Oh! God, pray accept what is offered to you". He and his family then partake of the offerings. The sun is looked upon as the creator and it is treated as a female.

To the Kānikāran the moon is a male and he makes his offerings to the moon on full-moon days. A lighted lamp and a quarter measure of paddy are placed in front of the hut. The rice is cooked just when the moon rises and then he prays, "Oh! Moon, pray accept this offering". The worship of the moon is intended to cure whooping cough. The mark on the moon is said to be that of a hare. The story goes that when a Kānikār and his wife were roaming in the jungle, they found the moon hiding in a stump of grass. Finding that it would make an excellent *tāli* (a neck ornament) for his wife, he made an attempt to seize it. The mark of charcoal dust on his hand left an impression on the moon, which fled away to the sky.

The *Muduvan* worships the sun both in the morning and in the evening. Praying is done in the open in the morning in some such manner—"We are in the jungle. We are ignorant. Pray guard us from mishaps". The same prayer is made at night before the Muduvan goes to bed.

The *Ūrālis* recognise the sun as the creator of the universe and the father of all souls, and the moon as the mother. The legend current among them regarding the mark on the moon is that once when the moon was serving a meal to the sun an altercation arose between them, and the sun, getting wild, smeared remnants of rice on the face of the moon. The result is that she has a spotted face. The New-moon day is believed to be the day when the moon is in menses and hides herself in the clouds.

The *Mala-Arayans* consider the sun and the moon as children of one God, the sun being the natural son born of mother Goddess, and the moon the adopted son. It is said that their mother once sent them to a feast with instructions that they should bring remnants of food served. The moon brought something of every dish, but the sun failed to do so. The mother got angry and cursed the sun, "may you be burned to a cinder", and so he became a source of intense heat. She blessed the moon saying "May you flourish with green foliage", and the moon became a source of cool refreshing light.

The Earthquake.

The *Kāṇikār* think that the earth rests on one of the horns of an ox. When the ox feels restive on account of the heaviness of the earth, it is shifted to the other horn, when an earthquake is caused.

The *Muduvans* consider that an earthquake is caused when the Goddess who bears the earth shifts it from one shoulder to the other.

The *Ūrālis* suppose that the earth is supported on the shoulders of two gigantic demi-gods (*Bhīmās*), who do their work by turn. When one Bhīmā retires, he hands it over to the other, and then the earthquake occurs.

The *Mala-Arayans* consider that the earth rests on a serpent of five heads and that the earthquake arises when it moves one of it heads.

The Eclipse.

The *Kāṇikār* consider the serpent as the parent of the moon. The moon, it seems, once refused to give pan to the serpent and consequently the serpent shrouds the moon with its hood occasionally. This is said to be the cause of the lunar eclipse, and the solar eclipse is also accounted for similarly.

The *Ūrālis* believe that, for default in payment of old debts, a serpent attacks the sun and the moon from time to time. It encircles them and attempts to swallow them up, when a part of the debt is paid and a temporary relief is obtained.

The legend current among the *Mala-Arayans* is that a hare takes shelter behind the moon when it is pursued by a serpent. The serpent gets over the moon, and then the lunar eclipse takes place.

Thunder and Lighting.

To the Kānikār of Kāllār thunder is known as *Kāttālanidi* or the blows of the *Rākshasa*. The *Rākshasa* is supposed to have a stone tied round his loins and when he sees a *maruti* tree (*Terminalia paniculata*) he strikes it with the stone, and the noise thus produced is thunder. They distinguish two kinds of thunder, *Achiyidi* and *Kuliridi*. In the case of the former, trees and grass are destroyed and in the case of the latter trees are not destroyed but only their bark is severed. Lightning is the flash of light seen when the giant strikes a tree with the stone.

According to the *Muduvans*, the thunder is caused by the Dēvās (gods) rolling a stone, and lightning by the wind and rain gods rolling a stone.

The *Ūrālis* believe that thunder, lightning and rain are caused by the duels among the *Bhīmās* in heaven. The duel takes place on a plank laid on the ground. One Bhīmā stands at each end of the plank, and in measured steps they approach towards the centre and attempt to strike each other with their swords. The rubbing of the swords causes lightning ; the sound of treading on the plank is the thunder ; and the sweat of the duellers trickles down as rain.

The *Mala-Arayans* believe that Paramēswara, the God of the earth, has a famous bow with which he keeps his enemies at bay. When he bends his bow it appears in different colours. Lightning is caused by the reflection of this bow. Thunder occurs when Dēvās fight against each other.

The Rainbow.

With the *Kānikār*, the rainbow is the bone of a Rākshasa. They distinguish two kinds of rainbow, "*palayavillu*" or old bow and "*puthiyavillu*" or new bow. The former is said to be faint, and the latter bright.

The *Muduvans* identify the rainbow with Arjuna's bow. The red line is the string and the blue is the stave.

The *Ūrālis* regard the rainbow as the bow of Rāma, one end of which is said to touch the earth.

The *Hill-Pantārams* think that rain is regulated by the rainbow. If a rainbow appears when there is no rain, copious rainfall is expected, and if it appears when it rains, the rain will cease. They also believe that excessive rain causes thunder and lightning.

XIV.—*The Clash of Culture.*

"Culture is that complex whole which includes knowledge, art, morals, law, custom, and any other capabilities and habits acquired by man as a member of society".* Environment played an important part in the cultural traits of very early and pre-literate peoples. "Life was then as it is now, and ever must be, eternal adjustment to environment. The history of human culture is the story of that adjustment".†

Environment.—The preliterate peoples of Travancore are found in the recesses of hills. Isolation according to Duncan, is the cause of the backwardness of such peoples in the race for advancement. Excessive heat in the summer burns out the energy of the Kāṇikār, the Mala-Arayan, the Ullādan, the Mala-Vēdan, and others who live in forests of low elevation, and makes them slothful. In fact, the debilitating effect of heat and humidity, aided by diseases, has reduced them to the dead level of economic inefficiency. These conditions have been aggravated by another important factor. The Kāṇikār, the Mala-Arayans, the Ullādans, and the Mala-Vēdans have been dispossessed of their former lands which were fertile and healthy, and driven to more inhospitable regions. They could not compete with the organised capitalists, and were forced into the background in most uncongenial areas. In spite of their receding into the interior forests the hill-tribes have been brought into contact with the people of higher culture, firstly on account of improvement of communications and modes of travelling, secondly through the influence of markets, and thirdly through the work of the missionaries.

Markets.—In the markets representatives of different groups meet to exchange wares. This kind of trade is advantageous to all of them and they come to be hospitable to one another. Their social environment is bereft of any other stimulation.

The Influence of Missionaries.—Ancient customs and beliefs of the primitive people are in the melting pot, and traditions are disappearing. This is due to the influence of Christianity and the infiltration of Hindu thoughts and ideals. A large number of Mala-Arayans in Minachil and Thodupula taluks have been converted by the Church Mission Society, while the London Mission Society have converted some Pailyans at Aṇakara in the Vandamēt Range.

* E. B. Taylor—*Primitive Culture*, Vol I, p. 1.
† G. A. Dorsey—*The Nature of Man*, p 83.

Insanitary Surroundings.—Sanitation is badly wanting in the hamlets of the hill-tribes. The Kānikār, the Mannāns, the Muduvans, the Paliyans, and the Vishavans do not raise the floor of the huts above the ground level. Drainage is defective and the huts are overcrowded and ill-ventilated. Living under insanitary conditions is one of the causes of the decline of the tribes. In this respect the Mala-Arayans, the Ullādans and the Mala-Pulayās stand on a higher level as the floor of their huts is raised from the surrounding ground. The Kānikār and the Mala-Arayans bury their dead about a hundred yards from their huts, but the Muduvans, the Mannāns, the Paliyāns, and the Vishavans bury the dead far away from their habitations.

Dress.—Of all the evil customs introduced by civilization, the wearing of clothes is said to be the worst. The trader and the missionary are the two chief agents in modifying the conditions of existence of the hill-tribes. Their influence first becomes visible in creating among the tribes the flesh conciousness and the virtues of concealment, the two sign-posts of higher civilization. "It is not an innate feeling of modesty that has produced clothing, but clothing which is responsible for the feeling of modesty in men* ". The trader creates in them fresh tastes and wants and is thereby able to sell his wares and make profit for himself. The Muduvans, the Mannāns, the Paliyans, the Ūrālis and the Kānikār purchase second-hand clothes on the hills. They are worn without change until they rot to pieces. The Kānikār of Kallar wear the scantiest of garments, only a front apron to cover their genital organs. The Thanta Pulaya women used to wear only a garment made of *thanta* (a water plant, called *Isolepis articulata Nees*), but now it has been replaced by a loin cloth.

Education.—The problem of education of the hill-tribes of the State is being tackled both by the Government and the missionaries. The Government have established schools for the Kānikār, the Mala-Arayans, and the Ūrālis. The London Mission Society has opened a school for the Paliyans at Aṅkara in the Vandanmēt Range, and a Roman Catholic Mission has opened another school at Thachamala in the Virapuli Reserve for the benefit of the Kānikār.

The Mission school for the Paliyans at Anākara was established about 10 years ago. Though a large number of Paliyans joined the school at first, the proselytising zeal of the Mission and the absence of other allurements have reduced the number to about 25 at present. Education undermines superstition and causes the disorganization of primitive tribes. The boys who attend the school despise manual labour. The present system of education is purely literary and not vocational. It tends to produce idlers and non-producers, and thereby causes economic waste.

Improved implements and utensils.—One of the causes of deterioration of the primitive tribes is said to be the advent of modern implements and methods. The improved implements have enabled them to save manual labour in their avocations. The Kānikar, the Muduvans, and others who have been using a wooden hoe for hoeing the soil and digging spud for digging up wild tubers and roots, have taken to the use of the axe, the pick-axe, and the mammatty. Again, the Kanikar and the Muduvans who were formerly adepts at the use of the bow, have now become the proud possessers of fire-arms. They will give anything to procure a gun, which has now become an indispensible necessity to them.

All the tribes but the Hill-Pantārams have discarded their crude utensils in favour of factory-mad-wares, and indigenous brass vessels. Kerosene lamps are driving out the reed torch which was in vogue formerly. Swedish, Japanese, and indigenous safety matches are displacing the primitive methods of making fire by friction and with the flint and steel. The Hill-Pantārams and the Vishavans alone are following the old methods.

Diet.—Changes have also come about in the food of the hill-tribes. Among the Kānikār and the Ūrālis, there has been an age-long taboo against the use of milk. A Kānikāran used to vomit and get head-ache, if he drank milk. This is the case even now ith the Kānikār of Kallār and the Urālis of Pirm de taluk. Coffee is being drunk by the Muduvans, the Mannāns, and the Kānikār, while tea is indispensable to the Ūrālis. Changed ways of life and thought have led to the unsettling of the mind of the primitive man. To procure fanciful articles, he has bartered away his heritage and retreated to more inhospitable lands. This has changed his former mode of life and deprived him of all incentive for work.

Social and Religious Customs.—Custom was a unifying factor among the primitive peoples. It regulated all details of existence, and governed politics, economics, and society. But contact with the people of the plains destroyed the complex web of customs and institutions which made up the tribal life, and in this process of disintegration the weaker went to the wall.

The control of the hill-tribes by the Forest Department has tended to the diminution of the influence and importance of the village chieftains, who are now only mere shadows of their former selves, and this has endangered the maintenance of discipline.

Frequent access to the people of the plains has weakened the taboos and the social solidarity. It has undermined the clan system and lessened the regard and respect the people had for their headman. In the words of Dudley Kidd "we are undermining the clan system right and left, and have riddled its defences through and through with explosive shells of civilization. All old restraints are removed and they have disintegrated religion and made it useless."†

Further, the opening of dispensaries is breaking down the barriers of superstition and is reducing the influence of the medicine-man. Formerly, the magical practices of the medicine-man were the only means of curing all ills. The medicine-man is now found only among the Kānikār and even among them he has lost all influence.

The Bachelor's Hall, which used to be a bulwark against malpractices, is now dwindling in importance. It has been the custom that no women could enter this hall and that all unmarried men should sleep there till they get married. This custom is still enforced among the Muduvans, but it is undergoing a slow process of silent decay among other primitive people of the State.

Use of Intoxicants.—The habit of toddy and arrack drinking among the Kānikār, the Muduvans and the Mannāns, of opium eating among the Vishavans, and of ganja smoking among the Paliyans is becoming a serious problem. On weekly market days, they buy these injurious intoxicants, and sometimes they can get them even at their very doors through the clandestine practices of unscrupulous contractors.

Diseases.—The improvement of communications has brought the primitive tribes into contact with the drugs of low-country men with the result that their morals have been affected. Lethal diseases have penetrated into the villages of hill-men, made accessible by improved means of communications. Leprosy is now

* T. A. Joyce and N W Thomas—*Women of all Nations*, p 8.

† W. C. Smith, *loc. cit.*, pp. 204-205.

found among the Kānikār of Kōttūr and Arippa, the Muduvans of Nēriamangalam and Kunjiār, and the Vishavans of Idyara valley : elephantiasis among the Kānikār at Madathura ; and syphilis among the Paliyans. Small-pox is a dreadful disease among the Muduvans, the Mannāns, and other. When a case of smallpox appears in a hamlet, the people desert it, leaving the patients to take care of themselves. The Vishavans, the Paliyans, and the Kānikār do not dread this disease so much. Barring the Muduvans, the Mannāns, the Paliyans and the Ūrālis who live above fever-level, all the other hill-tribes are subjected to malaria, to which many fall victims. There is no doubt that these deadly diseases have contributed to the decline in the population of the hill-tribes. The birth-rate has decreased and the death-rate has increased. It is seen that more children are born among the Kānikār living in the interior than among those living in hamlets more accessible. Progress in civilization has resulted in nothing but increased facilities for immorality. Opportunities to earn money by working in estates are making them less industrious and their own agriculture is consequently deteriorating.

The Psychological factor.—Pitt-Rivers speaks of the enormous influence of mind on body arising out of despair among lowly people, and says it is the basic cause of depopulation.* By the destruction of interest in life, the hill tribes are cut off from their old moorings and being ill-adapted to the new surroundings and circumstances they naturally decline. Where there have been fewer changes there the decline is not so rapid. In Travancore the Kānikār have changed most and the decline amongst them is the greatest, while it is the smallest amongst the Muduvans who have changed least.

Marriage.—Cross-cousin marriage is characteristic of all the primitive peoples of Travancore except the Vishavans. Westermarck and Duncan hold that consanguious marriages are harmful, while Pitt-Rivers and Carr-Saunders take the opposite view.

The enquiry in Travancore has revealed the fact that the existence of cross-cousin marriage among the Kānikār and the Muduvans has not decreased the birth-rates and the survival rates among them to a greater extent than among the Vishavans who forbid cross-cousin marriage. The average annual birth-rates among the Kānikār and the Muduvans are 2·3 and 3·4 respectively per 1,000 of the population, against 2·7 among the Vishavans ; and the average survival rates are 1·9 for the Kānikār, 2·6 for the Muduvans and 1·8 for the Vishavans. Coition after marriage but before the girl has attained puberty, is common among the Kānikār, the Vishavan, and the Mala-Pulayās of Anjanād Valley. Early coition is believed to be detrimental to health and fecundity. Marriage before puberty which is an ancient Aryan custom, has been adopted by some of the primitive tribes of Travancore. Carr-Saunders says that early intercourse is in urious to the general health of the mother and the off-spring. It will weaken the reproductive functions and cause abortion. This is probably the cause of the prevalence of abortion among the Kānikār.

Traces of polyandry are seen among the Mala-Arayans, the Ullādans, the Paliyans, the Muduvans, the Urālis and the Mala Pulayās. This may probably be due to the shortage of women. If polyandry is an indication of shortage of women, and if a progressive disturbance in the balance of the sexes in the direction of an ever-increasing deficit of women is an index of declining population, the polyandrous communities should have disappeared long ago. According to Westermarck, intercourse between one women and several men is unfavourable to reproduction, because of the counteracting effect on each other of the spermatozoa of different individuals. Rockhill and Sherring show that polyandry results in small families. A surplus of adult females over males is a necessary condition of the stabilization and continued vigour of human races. Among the primitive tribes of Travancore the Paliyans, the Ūrālis, and the Karavali, Mala-Pulyās show a shortage of women.

Among the polygamous groups females show a higher survival rate than males, while among polyandrous groups, the reverse is the case. Polygamous marriages produce a larger number of children than monogamous marriages. According to Pitt-Rivers, " the maintenance of polygynous institutions in an aboriginal race is one of the best indications of its preservation as a race."† The primitive peoples of Travancore are mostly monogamous.

Fecundity and Fertility.—By the operation of the various causes mentioned above the fecundity and the fertility of the primitive tribes of Travancore are getting reduced and their numbers are decreasing. Fecundity is the actual power of reproduction, while fertility is the degree of reproduction.

Most primitive tribes have but small families the number of children ranging from one to three per family. The average survival rate of children is found to be 1·6 per family among the Kānikār, 1·4 among the Mala Vēdans, 1·2 among the Kurumba Pulayās, 1·9 among the Vishavans, 1·5 among the Mala-Arayans, and 1·4 among the Ullādans. Owing to better climatic conditions in the High Ranges the number of children per family is found to be 2·7 among the Muduvans, 2·3 among the Karavali Mala-Pulayās, and 2·2 among the Cheru Vēdans.

Sex Ratio—The masculinity of the births varies among different races. The average ratio in Europe is 1,057 boys to 1,000 girls born. Among the primitive peoples of Travancore female births are in excess of male births except among the Ūrālis. The number of female births to 100 male births is 103 among the Kānikār, 105 among the Mala-Arayans, and 104 among the Muduvans, while among the Ūrālis the corresponding number is 65 only. " It is said that where food is abundant females exceed males, and where food is scarce, males exceed females."

Masculinity of children is lower among the tribes which are increasing in population than among those which show a steady decline. This is the case among the Muduvans, among whom the average birth-rate is 4·7 and the survival rate 3·8. Their sex ratio is 141 females to every 100 males. Shirley Murphy and Pitt-Rivers think that the ratio of male to female children decreases as the prosperity of different social groups decreases, so that in a group in the lowest social level the ratio of male to female children is less than that in a higher group. Among the primitive tribes of Travancore it is seen that there are more female than male children as a rule, but all the same the ratio of male to female children decreases as the prosperity of the tribes decreases. The Ūrāli, among whom there are more male than female children, is the only exception to the general rule.

Among the monogamic groups or those living in small communities, there is little difference between the number of males and females. This is true of the Hill-Pantārams, the Paliyans, and the Mala Vēdans.

There can be no doubt that a true and universally monogamic population exists in no part of the world. Polygamy is found among the Kānikār, the Ūllādans, the Mala-Arayans, and the Ūrālis. Among persons of reproductive period, *i.e.*, between the ages of 15 and 45, there are 381 females to 373 males in 327 families

* Pitt-Rivers.—*The Clash of Culture and the Contact of Races*, p. 268.
† Pitt-Rivers, loc. cit, p. 268.

of the Kānikār, 65 females to 45 males of the Mala-Arayans, and 175 females to 84 males in 84 families of the Muduvans. There is thus a surplus of women of reproductive ages among the above tribes and this accounts for their general monandry. Conditions are different among other tribes.

Infant Mortality.—Infant mortality is high among the hill-tribes except the Muduvans, the Mannāns and the Paliyans. Formerly, people were solicitous of their children and took much pains to rear them. Maternal instinct is now becoming an absent quantity and there seems to be an inherent lack of virility. According to Roberts, the dwindling in the number of the hill-tribes is part of the price paid for progress.

Size of Families.—Births are of importance in relation to deaths. The average size of the family varies among different tribes. The following table shows the average size of the family, the average birth-rate, and the average survival rate among the important tribes.

No.	Name of tribes.	Number of families.	Average size of the family.	Average birth-rate.	Average survival-rate.
1	Kānikār	91	3·9	2·2	1·7
2	Mala Vēdan	9	3·4	2·0	1·4
3	Ūrāli	49	3·9	2·7	1·9
4	Kurumpa Pulaya	12	3·3	2·0	1·2
5	Vishavan	28	3·8	2·8	1·9
6	Muduvan	84	4·8	3·4	2·5
7	Mannān	14	6·7	4·6	4·6
8	Mala-Arayan	36	4·5	2·0	1·5
9	Paliyan	7	5·5	4·6	2·3

The average survival rate will show the rate at which the population increases. " If a woman has two children who become parents in turn, the population will hold its own. If he has less than two children the population will sooner or later decrease*. Judged by this criterion, all the primitive peoples of Travancore, except the Muduvans, the Mannāns, and the Paliyans, are declining.

XV.—*Remedies for Depopulations.*

The only way to study the problem of the hill-tribes is to examine their customs and discover their bearing on the social organisation and the communal life of the tribes, and to view their morality from the standpoint of their own thoughts, without desiring to substitute something not suited to their life.

In Travancore old customs are forsaken or modified out of recognition, and beliefs which have been firmly held are quietly dropped, because the young people think that they are not worthy of credence.

In attempting to improve the condition of the primitive peoples, we must build on the tribal past through the agency of the tribes themselves. The attempt to aid and foster their development should be the concern of the Government and should not be relegated to other agencies like the Missionaries. The tribes must be enabled to control their own destiny. The advantage of this system is that it permits of unlimited growth without a break from the past. As Roberts states, " it should be embedded on the native past, and should be by natives through native institutions."† This provides openings for the bulk of the people and gives them something to occupy their minds. Macgregor insists on looking at things 'as the natives visioned them themselves.' The material and moral welfare of the tribes must be the aim, and this can best be accomplished under the guidance of the Govrnment. The scheme framed by Macgregor in regard to the tribes of Melanesia fulfils this condition and may, therefore, be considered in this connection. It contains the following provisions :—

1. Certain areas are set aside and are divided into small allotments, each of which becomes the freehold property of an individual. Communism, the enemy of initiative, has no place in the scheme.
2. Each landowner is to pay of a fixed rental and a certain duty on holdings over four mortgues in extent.
3. The control of the native affairs of each Reserve is in the hands of local boards, and councils, but is directed by an European adviser."‡

The Government of Travancore have framed a set of rules for the treatment and management of the hill tribes, but they do not come up to the level of the scheme evolved by Macgregor, inasmuch as they do not provide for the individual ownership of land and for the levy of tax on it, which alone will create in man the incentive to work and to put the land to the best possible use. Segregation in Reserves, individual ownership of property, and local self-government are the principles which should underlie the scheme intended for the uplift of the hill-tribes. The rules in force in Travancore which are given in Appendix III require revision. If the welfare of the hill-tribes is to be safeguarded efficiently they should contain the following provisions.

1. The Areas in Reserves should be divided into small blocks and assigned to individuals separately conferring on them the ownership. Communism which kills all initiative must be shut out.
2. Each hill-man to whom land is given should pay a fixed rental to the Government.
3. Village councils or local boards should be constituted for each settlement.

Education.—The spread of education is the next most important step to take in the regeneration of the hill-tribes. Education should be such as will be of practical use to them and will at the same time enable them to preserve their heritage and develop their racial qualities. Education should be vocational, agriculture and cottage industries being taught to boys and domestic science to girls. The only way to save the hill-man is to make him work and improve his economic condition. The Government should shoulder this responsibility instead of leaving it to private agencies.

Co-operative Movement.—Most of the hill-tribes are heavily involved in debts which they will never be able to discharge if they remain in their present economic condition. The plain country people who advance loans to them realise an exorbitant rate of interests, often two paras of paddy and more for a loan of ten paras for a period of six months or so. To improve their material condition, they should be prevented from incurring

* Robert R. Kuczynski. *The balance of Births and Deaths*, p. 1.

† S. H. Roberts. *Popiltation Problems of the Pacific*, p. 153.

‡ S. H. Roberts. *loc, cit.* p.

debts. Further, nomadic agriculture being their basic industry, improvidence and laziness intensify their indebtedness. It, therefore, seems desirable that adequate credit facilities should be created by Government, so that they may stand on their own legs. Co-operative credit societies should be organised for this purpose under the initiative and guidance of Government agencies.

Marketing of Produce.—Well regulated markets create in the minds of the purchasers and sellers a feeling of confidence in each other. Markets have been established in the vicinity of the Reserves for the benefit of the hill-tribes. They sell their hill produce and purchase their weekly necessaries at these markets. But the unscrupulous plain country trader often dupes the ignorant hill-man. A Kānikāran seldom gets more than 7 to 12 chuckrams (4 to 7 annas) for the produce which he sells once a week. This is hardly sufficient to meet his wants and he is, therefore, forced to lead a life of poverty. It will be a great boon to the hill-tribes if proper arrangements could be made for marketing their produce, so that they may obtain proper value for the articles. The Agricultural Department could give a lead in both these directions for the uplift of the hill-tribes.

It is said that the provision of new interests is the antidote against racial and personal despair. But the future must be built on the past. Old institutions and ancient traditions must be maintained as far as possible and development must be made in consonance with the physical environments and the mental qualities of the tribes concerned. Much damage has been done to primitive peoples by reformers who are *ignorant of their life and customs. A knowledge of anthropology will be a useful handmaid to* social reformers and administrators. It will enable them to ward off evil effects that will naturally result from the contact between a lower and a higher culture. The most important thing to do is to regulate the contact between the civilized and the primitive man, so that the progress of civilizing the primitive may be slow and general, and he may have sufficient time to adapt himself to changing conditions.

In the interests of the welfare of the primitive peoples, it may be necessary for the Government, as has been pointed out by Dr. Hutton, to follow the example of Australia, which has gone so far as even to prohibit the entry of any person into the Reserve except occasional scientists and the Administrator of the tribes. Even the opening of schools and the carrying on of missionary work among the tribes are prohibited there in order to preserve them from extermination. Dr. Hutton would welcome similar legislation in India. The problem is easier of solution in Travancore, where the Forest Department is the custodian of the primitive peoples in the Reserves.

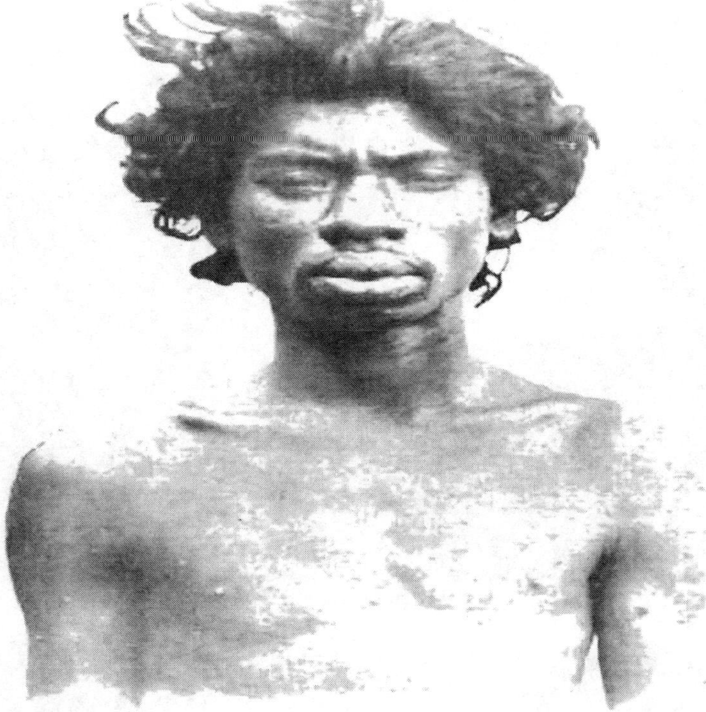

Paliyan.

Paliyan.

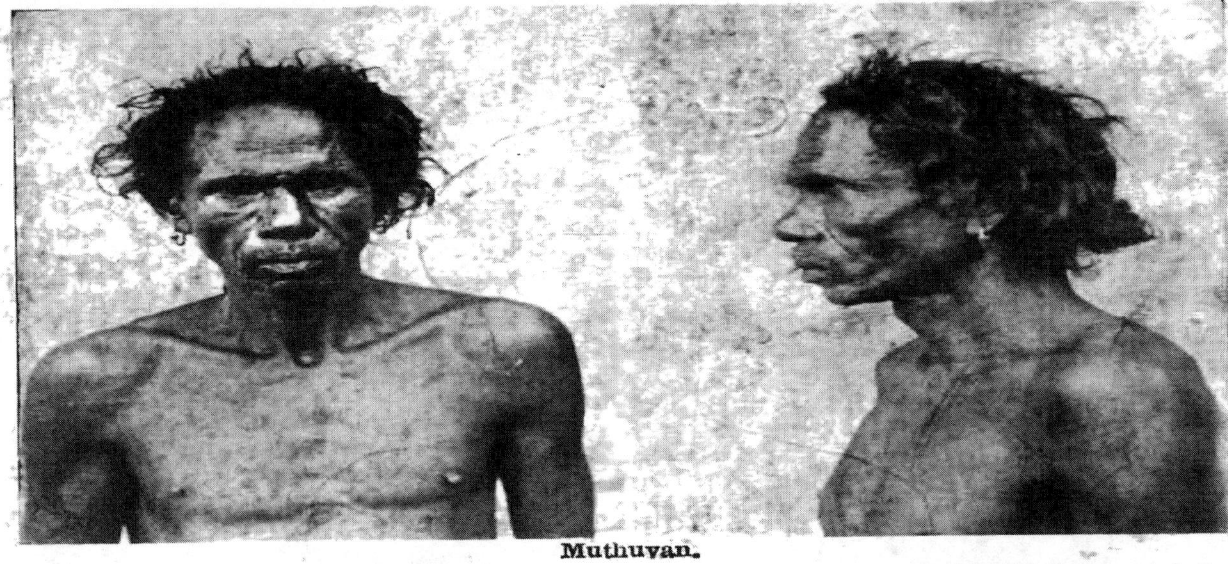

Muthuvan.

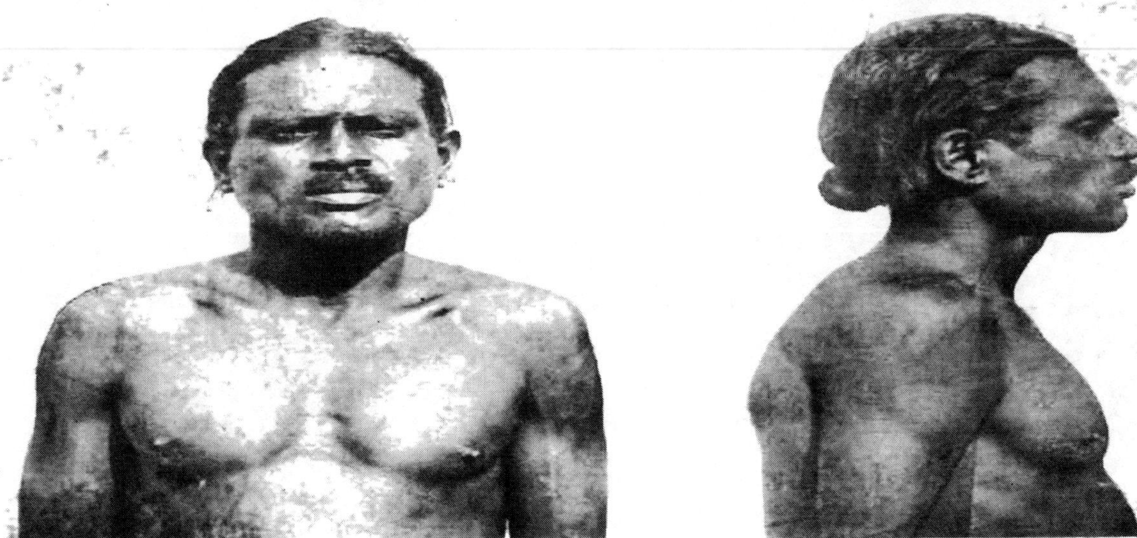

Urali.

Urali.

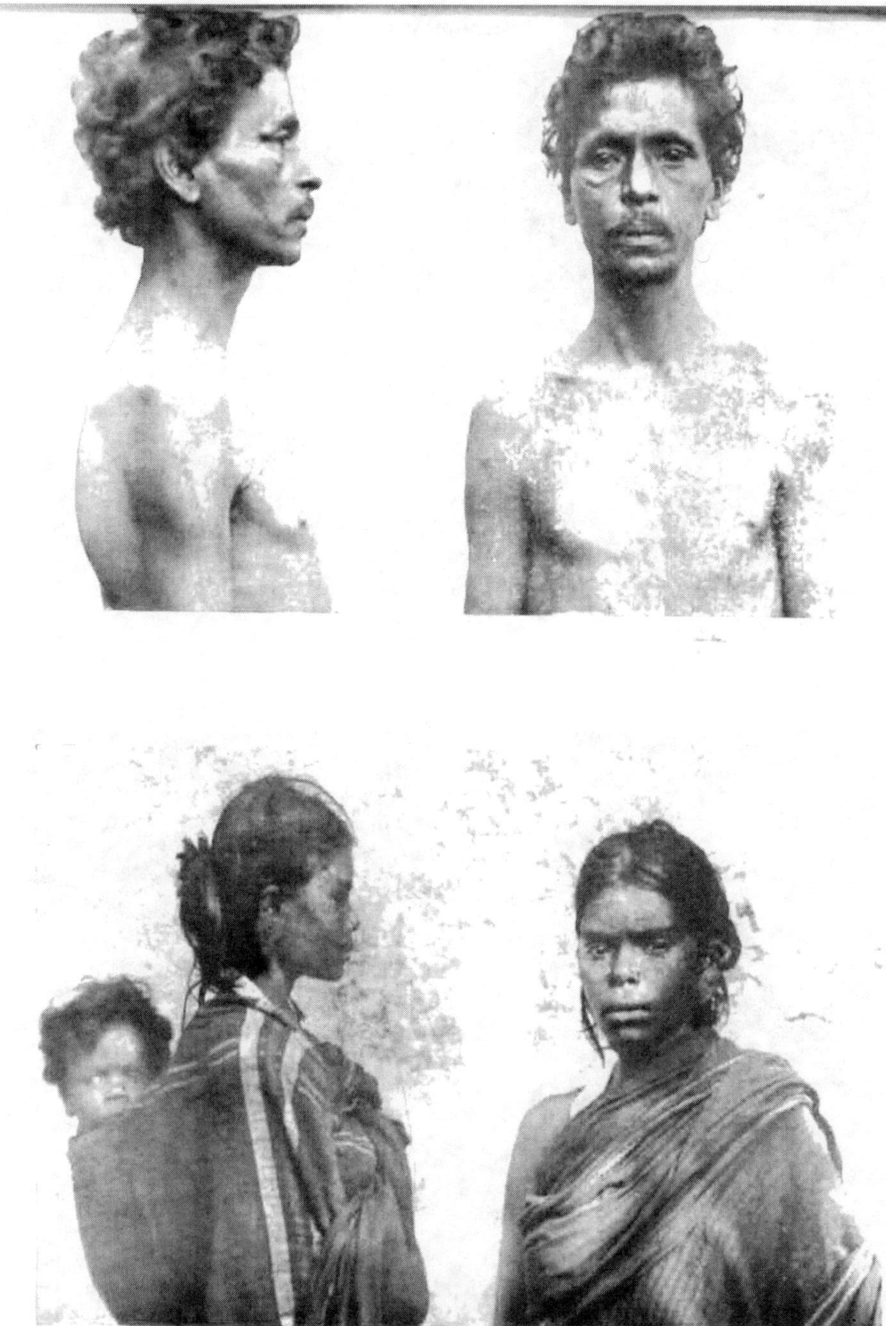

Mannan.

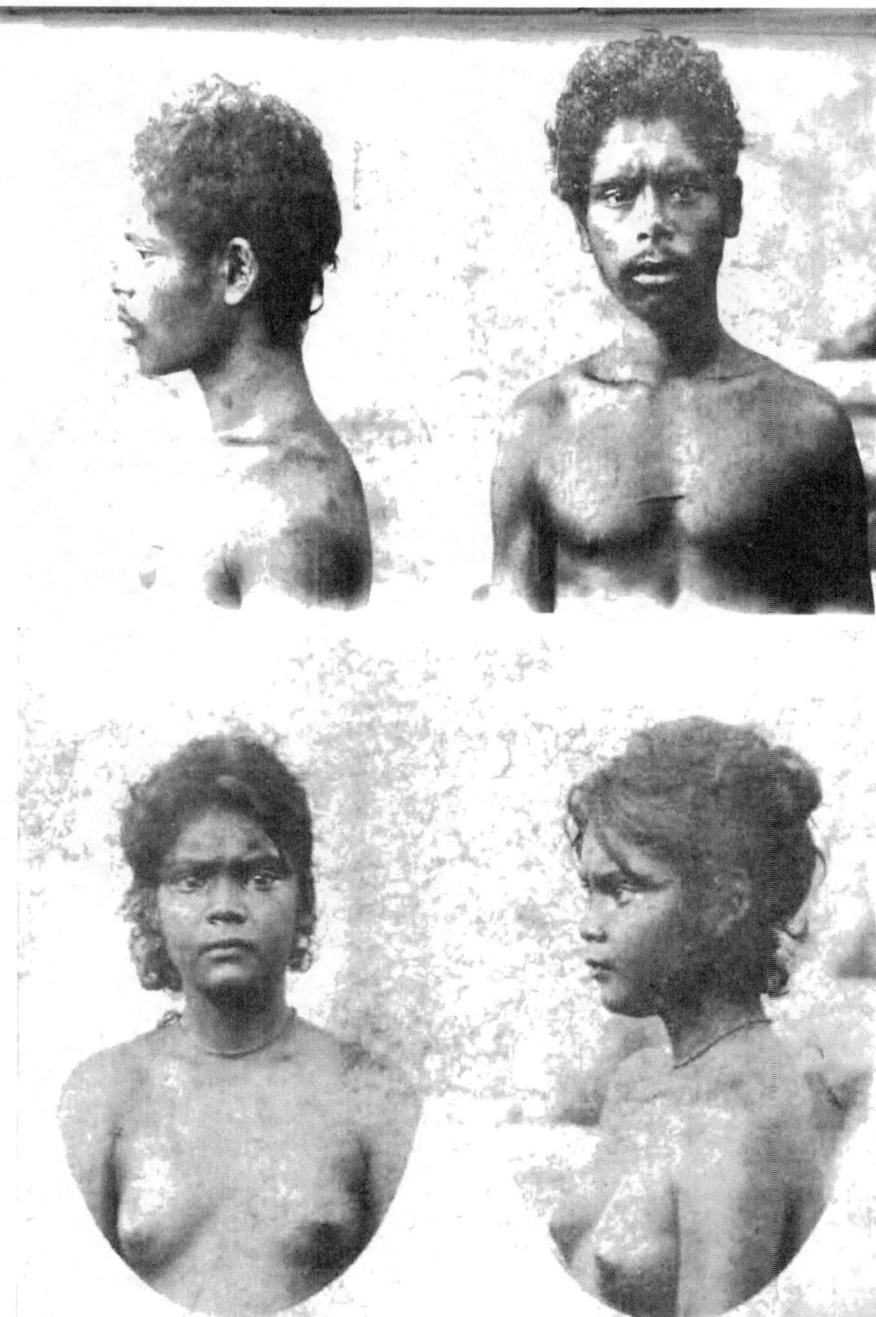

Malapantaram.

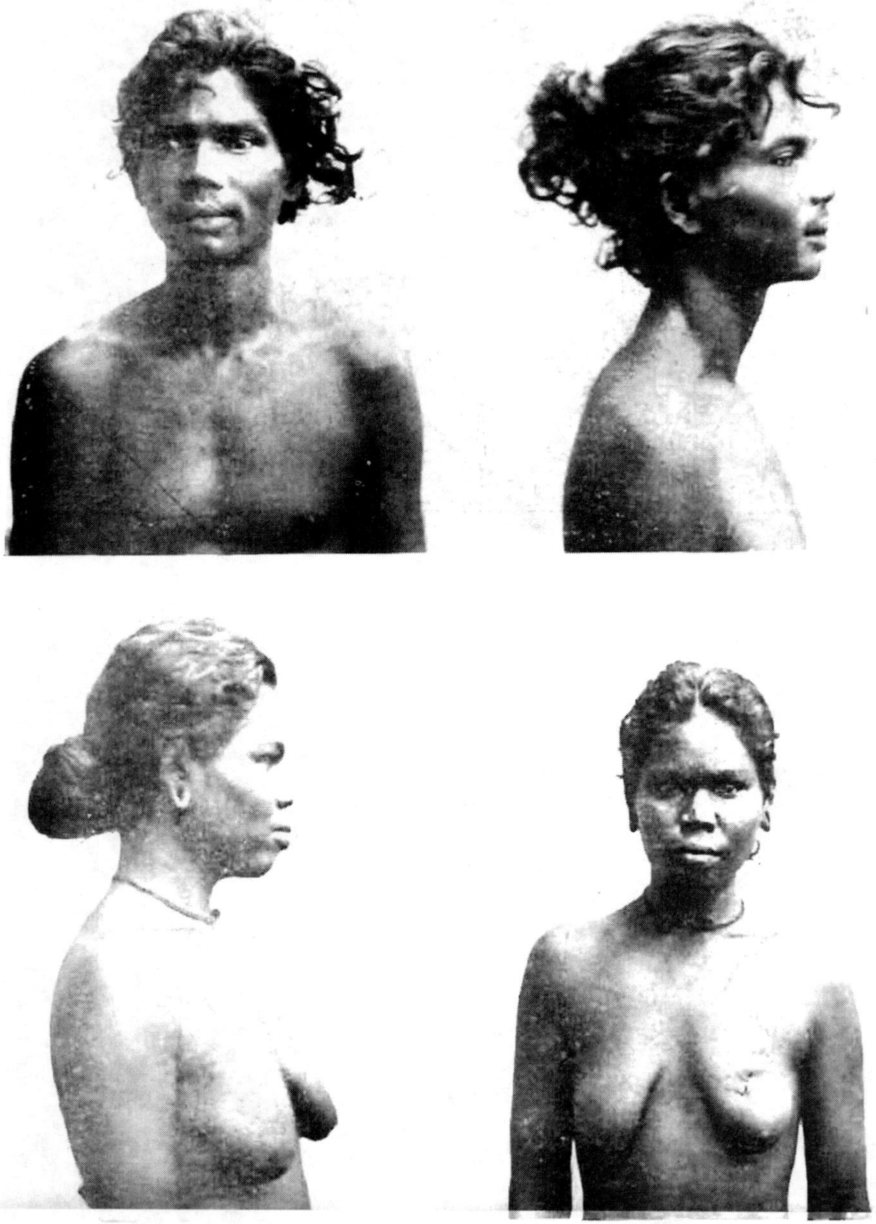

Vettuvan.

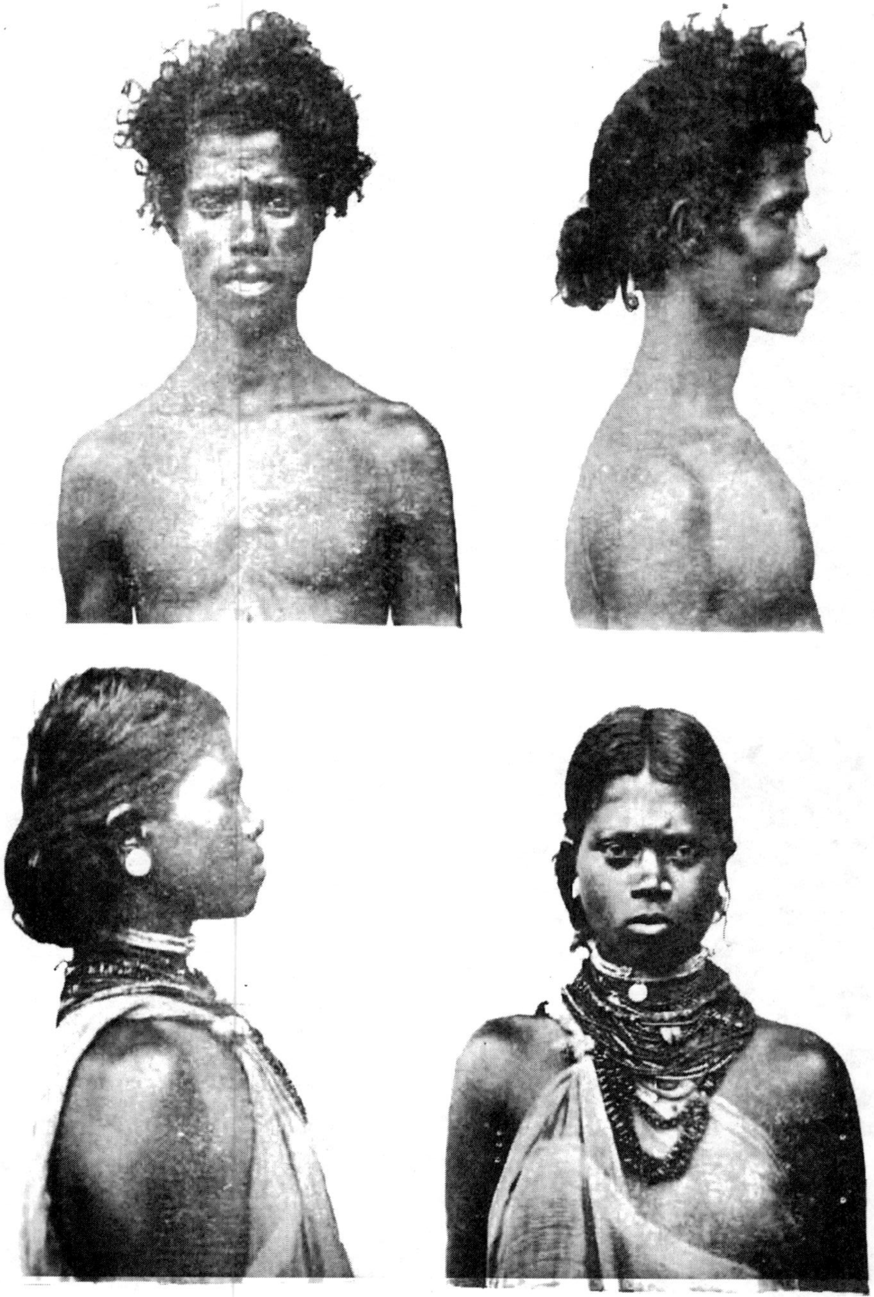

Malapulayan.

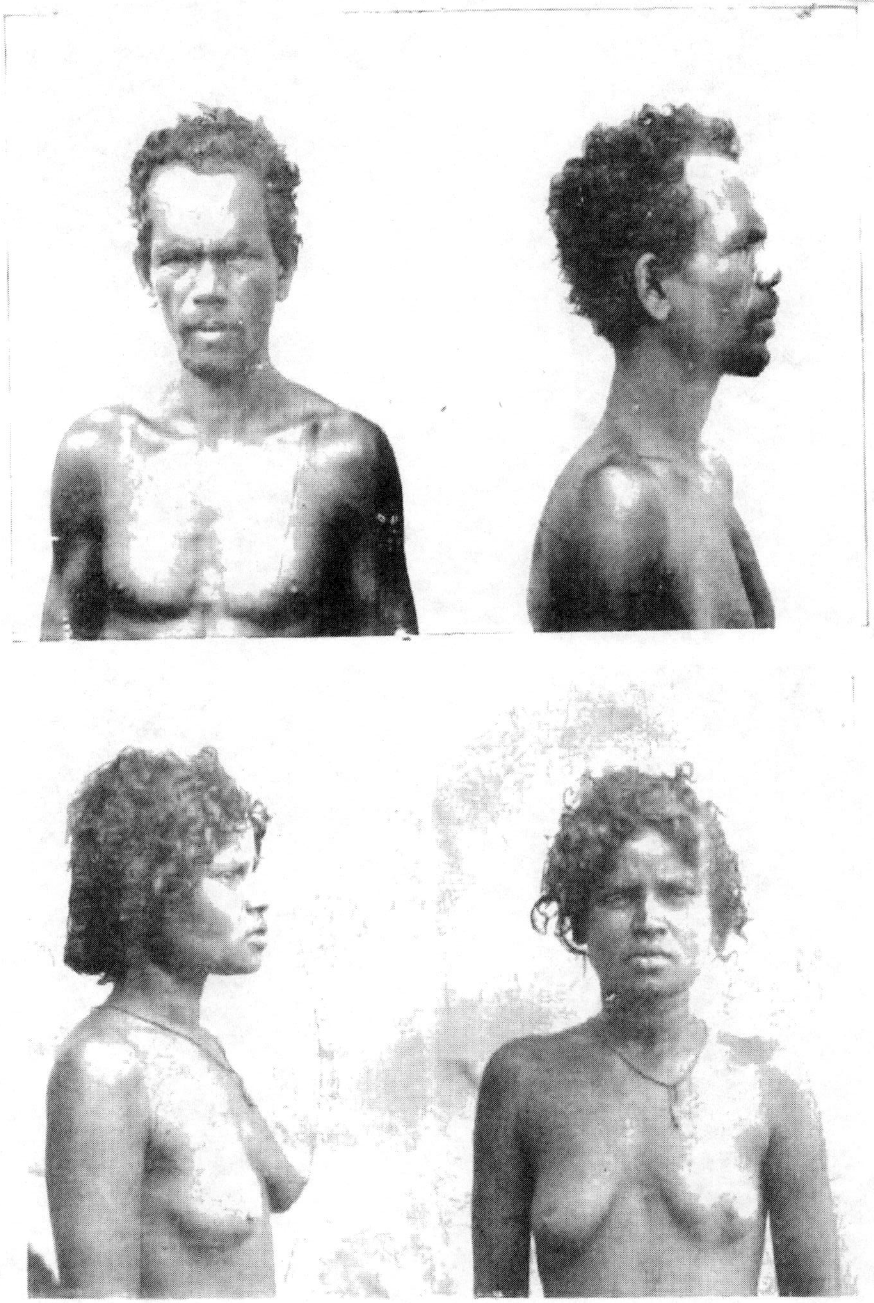

Malankuravan.

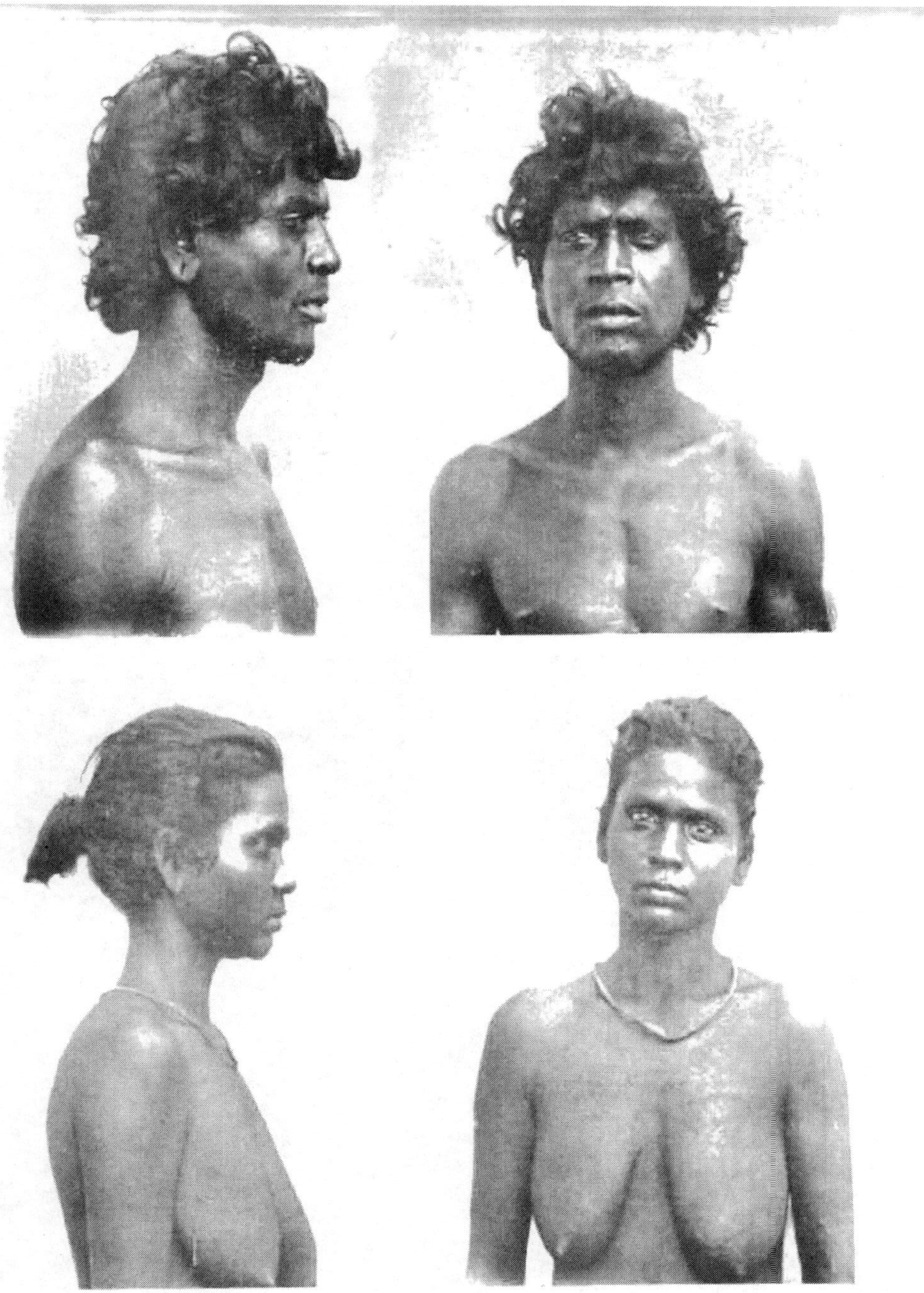

Malavetan.

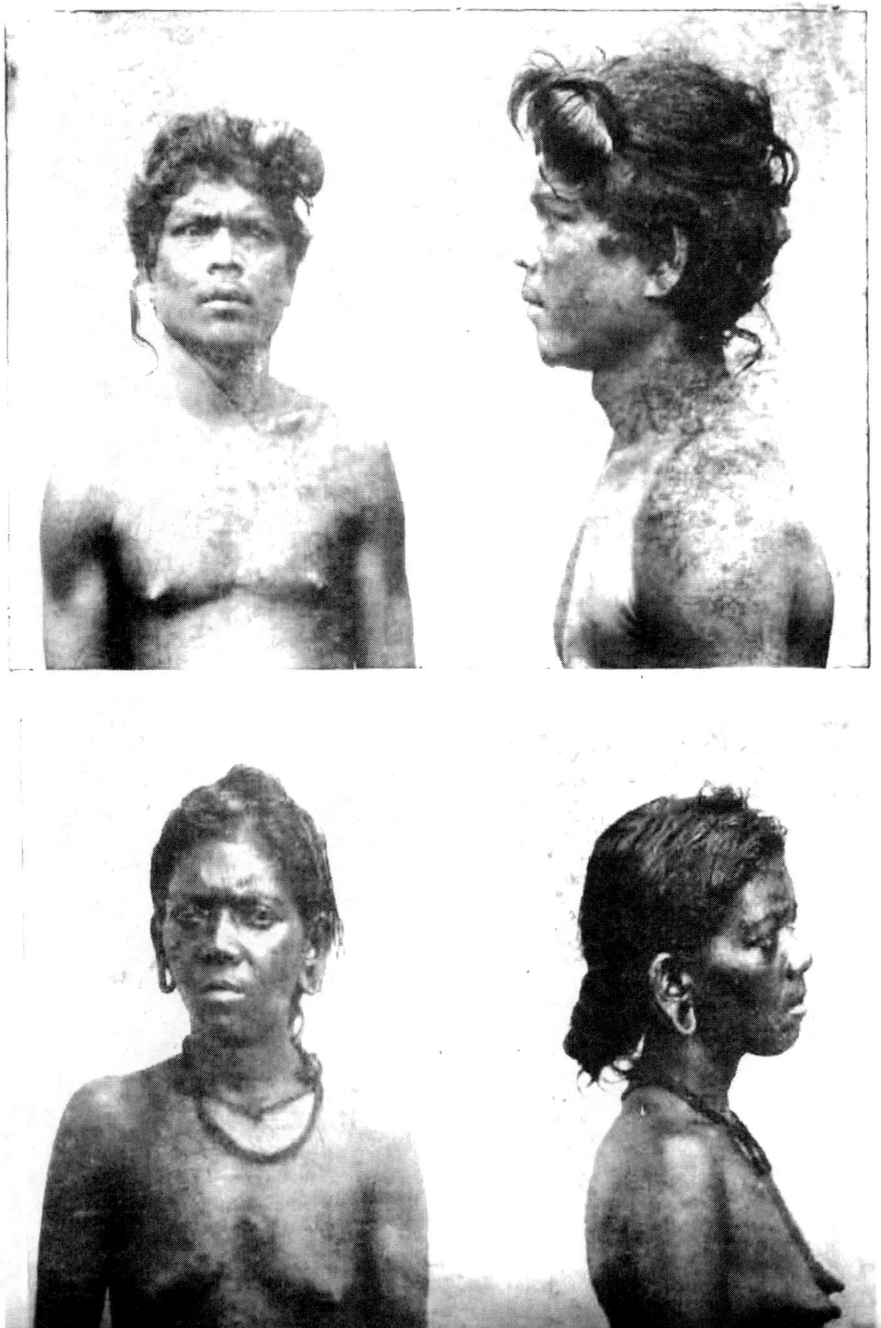

Ullatan.

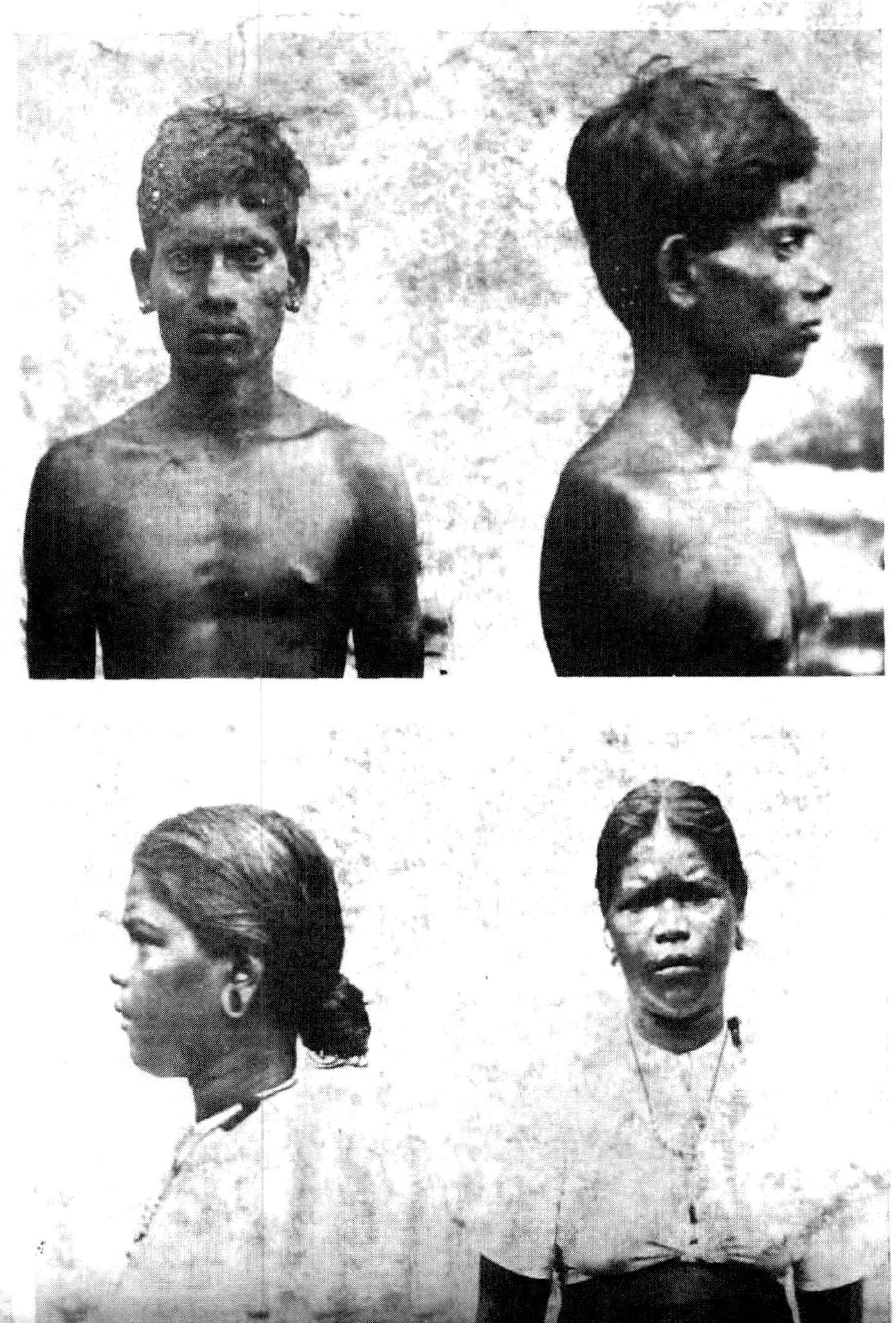

Malayarayan.

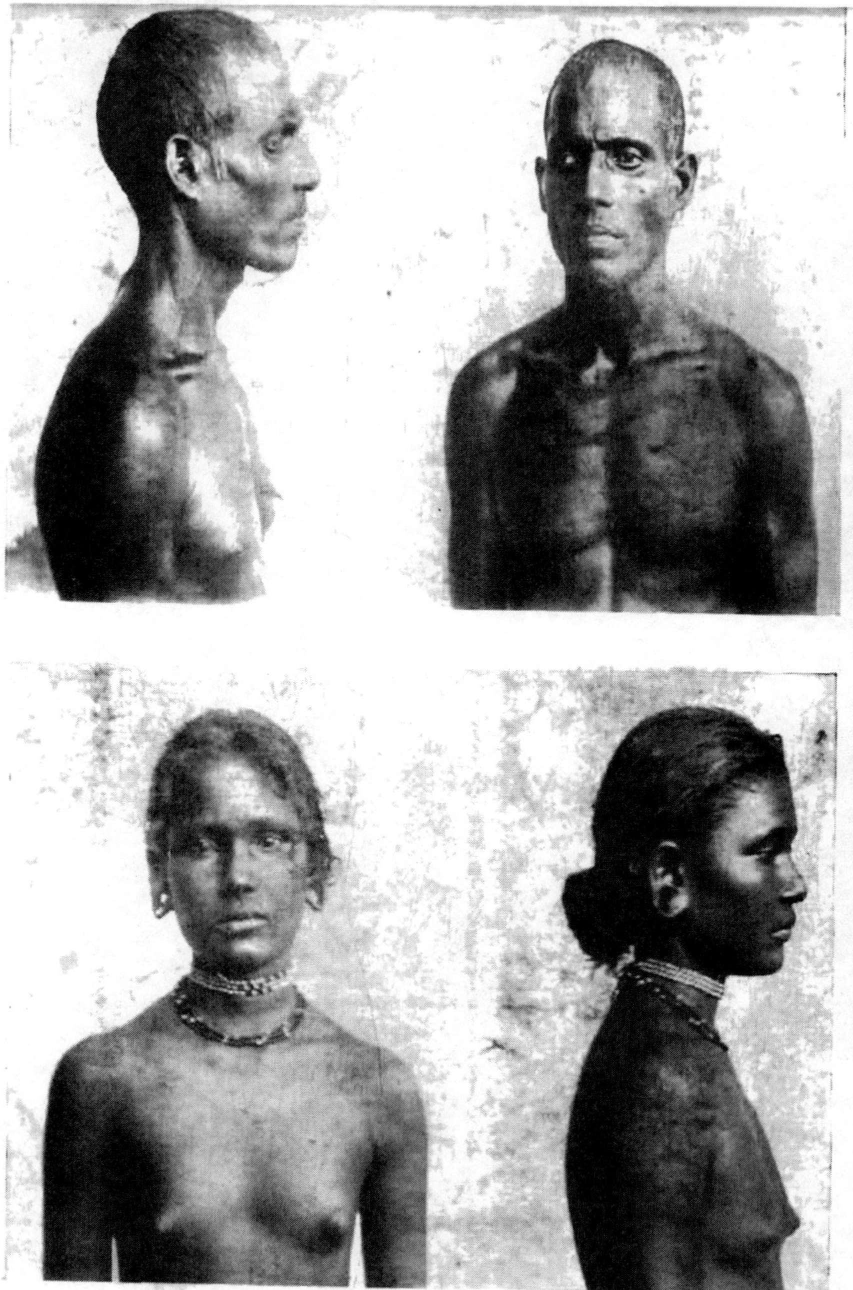

Thantapulayan.

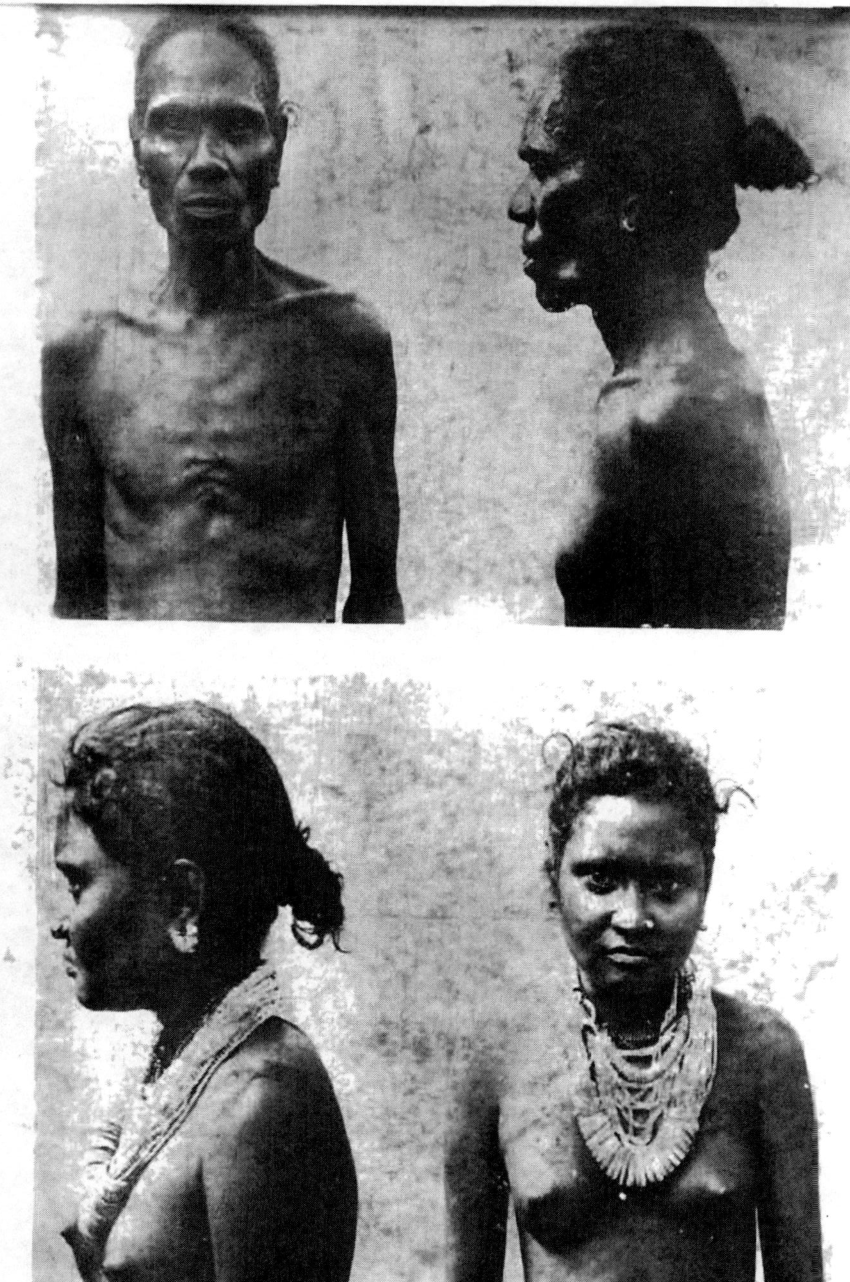

Kanikkaran.

Urali tree-house.

Malavetan chipping the incisor teeth.

Kanikkaran using bow and arrow.

Kanikkaran using pellet bow.

Kanikkaran making fire by flint and steel.

Kanikkaran making fire by friction.

Dolmens at Perunthalpara in Anjanad.

APPENDIX I.

Head Measurements of the Primitive Tribes of Travancore.

No.	Name of Tribe.	No. measured.	Length c.m. Average.	Length c.m. Maximum.	Length c.m. Minimum.	Breadth c.m. Average.	Breadth c.m. Maximum.	Breadth c.m. Minimum.	Index. Average.	Index. Maximum.	Index. Minimum.
1	Vishavan ..	25	18·1	19·0	17·5	13·5	14·3	12·7	72·6	80·2	71·7
2	Ulládan ..	22	18·6	19·6	17·3	13·7	14·5	13·0	73·9	79·1	70·0
3	Kánikár ..	25	18·6	19·6	17·7	13·5	14·6	12·5	71·5	78·9	65·8
4	Mala-Védan (Cheruvédan).	22	18·1	19·0	17·2	13·4	14·7	12·2	74·4	79·6	70·0
5	Mala-Arayan ..	58	18·7	20·0	17·5	13·5	14·3	12·6	72·1	77·7	65·0
6	Muduvan ..	22	15·6	19·0	14·0	10·7	14·3	10·0	70·9	81·2	63·0
7	Mala-Adiyar (Mala-Kuravan).	12	18·7	19·9	17·5	13·5	14·5	12·7	73·7	76·8	67·5
8	Urali ..	36	18·6	20·0	17·7	13·6	14·3	13·0	70·6	78·5	67·7
9	Paliyan ..	11	18·5	19·6	17·3	13·8	15·0	13·7	74·3	78·0	71·1
10	Thanta-Pulayan	35	18·5	19·6	17·4	13·1	15·2	12·1	74·0	81·7	63·6

APPENDIX II.

Stature and Nasal Measurements of the Primitive Tribes of Travancore.

No.	Name of tribes.	Number measured.	Stature c.m. Average.	Stature c.m. Maximum.	Stature c.m. Minimum.	Nasal Index. Average.	Nasal Index. Maximum.	Nasal Index. Minimum.	Remarks.
1	Vishavan	25	152·3	163	144	88·05	100	66·0	
2	Ulládan	22	152·8	163·1	146·5	85·4	97·2	73·1	
3	Kanikár	25	153·0	163	141·6	89·1	100	75·0	
4	Mala-Védan (Cheru-Védan) ..	22	153·7	163	144·2	86·6	100	68·7	
5	Mala-Arayan	58	155·2	173·5	146·1	83·1	100	62·0	
6	Muduvan	6	156·4	163·3	147·3	91·05	100	84·2	
7	Mala-Adiyar (Mala-Kuravan) ..	12	156·6	162	149·3	84·6	90·5	72·9	
8	Urali	36	157·0	169·0	137·6	84·6	113·5	74·0	
9	Paliyan	11	157·6	167·0	145·2	86·5	97·2	73·1	
10	Thanta Pulayan	35	152·3	161	139	78·1	91·4	67·4	

APPENDIX III.

Revised Rules for the treatment and management of hillmen in Government Forests and Reserves, passed under Clause (*e*), Section 60 of the Forest Regulation II of 1068, as amended by Regulations IV of 1071 and IX of 1085, with the sanction of His Highness the Maha Raja in supersession of those passed on 23rd September 1903, 7th Kanni 1079, and published on pages 789 and 790 of the Government Gazette, dated 6th October 1903/20th Kanni 1079.

1. The term "Hillmen" in these Rules means and includes only the following tribes who have been living in the hills from time immemorial and does not include any others :—

(1) Kānikārs residing in the hills of the Southern, Trivandrum and Quilon Land Revenue Divisions extending up to and inclusive of the Shendurni valley.

(2) Palliyārs residing on the banks of the Kallada and Achencoil rivers.

(3) Malayadiyārs on the banks of the Kakkād river

(4) Malapantārams along the banks of the Pambayār river up to Perinthēnaruvi.

(5) Kochu-Vēlans on the banks of the Pambayār river.

(6) Ullādans on the banks of the Pālaiyār river.

(7) Malaarayans living along the foot of the hills between Pambayār and Thodupula.

(8) Vizhavans at the foot of the hills on the Periyār.

(9) Ūrālis on the hills to the west of the Periyār.

(10) Palliyans on the Cardamom Hills near Vandamēttu.

(11) Mannāns on the Cardamom Hills east of the Periyār up to the foot of the High Range.

(12) Muthuvans on the Cardamom Hills, High Range and Anjenād.

(13) Mannāns in the Deviār valley.

(14) Muthuvans in the Malayattūr Reserved Forest.

(15) Hill Pulayās of Anjanād.

2. Hillmen residing in Government Forests and Reserves shall be under the control of the Forest Department.

3. Each settlement will have a headman, who has attained that position either by hereditary right or by selection or election by the members of the settlement, in conformity with the existing practice :

Provided that when a headman fails to carry out any of the duties, as hereinafter stated, the Divisional Forest Officer may call upon the adult male members to depose him and elect another competent man to take his place.

4. Hillmen residing in Government Forests and reserves shall have their numbers registered in the office of each Forest Division, and for this purpose the headman of each settlement shall report to the Range Officer concerned. Once a year or whenever called on to do so, the name of his settlement or Kāni, the number of males and females composing it, adults and children, children below three years being classed as under age.

5. No Hillman can leave his settlement or kāni or migrate to another without the permission of his headman. Appeals from the headman's decision shall lie to the Divisional Forest Officer, whose decision shall be final.

6. The settlements of hillmen residing in a Government Forest or Reserve shall be permanently fixed and they shall not be permitted to shift them from place to place, except temporarily with the special written permission of the Divisional Forest Officer in cases of scarcity of water, outbreak of epidemics, such as small-pox, etc.

7. The hillmen shall enjoy the concession of cultivating land free of tax in the Government Forests and Reserves in which they live, to the extent of 5/8 of an acre per head for every member of a settlement above three years of age.

(*i*) A compact block of land, comprising 7 times the total area required for each settlement in a year, deducting the area of wet lands permanently under cultivation shall be demarcated by the Forest Department (the hillmen concerned providing the labour free of payment) and 1/7 of that area shall be cultivated in any one year, so that the cultivation may be carried on permanently in that block on a rotation of seven years.

(*ii*) It shall be the duty of the headman to apportion the area among the several families of his settlement, subject to an appeal to the Divisional Forest Officer, whose decision shall be final.

(*iii*) In cases of trespass or encroachment in a settlement, the headman shall decide such disputes subject to an appeal to the Divisional Forest Officer, whose decision shall be final.

8. No hillman shall be entitled to the grant of patta for any land cultivated in a Government Forest or Reserve, however long his occupation of such land may be.

9. All produce of the land cultivated by hillmen in accordance with the foregoing Rules shall be the property of the hillmen and may be disposed of as they think fit, except food-grains and tobacco which shall not be sold or taken out of the Government Forest Reserve, without the written permission of the Divisional Forest Officer.

Proviso. The Divisional Forest Officer may delegate this power to such of his Range Officers as he thinks

10. The hillmen may fell and use any timber (other than of Royal or Reserved trees) and firewood bamboos, reeds, and canes, free of charge, for their *bona fide* domestic and agricultural purposes, and the last three, *viz.*, bamboos, reeds and canes, may be used by them in the manufacture of petty articles for sale, provided, however, that the Government may at any time restrict or prohibit the trade or charge a fee on the produce.

11. The hillmen may collect and use, for their own consumption or for sale or for both, any minor forest produce not collected by the Government or leased by the Government to contractors or lessees, but the sale of minor forest produce for which seigniorage has been, or may hereafter be, fixed by the Government shall not be permitted.

12. The hillmen may shoot game in wet weather from the 15th Vykāsi to the 30th Kārthigay except such animals and birds as may be prohibited by the Government from time to time, and they may catch fish, provided that the poisoning of water or the use of dynamite or gunpowder for the purpose is not resorted to. For the purposes of this rule and for the protection of person and property, each settlement may keep one gun ordinarily in the custody of the headman. The Government may, from time to time, lay down any restrictions in respect of these privileges.

13. Proviso. In exceptional cases, the Government may authorise more than one gun being kept in a settlement.

(i) Licenses to deal with the hillmen living within the Government Forests and Reserves will be granted by the Divisional Forest Officer to respectable traders, who undertake to supply articles of daily use to them at reasonable rates, provided that they bind themselves to the following among other terms by executing formal written agreements :—

(a) Not to enter into any credit transactions or to lend them money,

(b) not to sell any intoxicating liquors or drugs to them,

(c) not to quarrel with or illtreat the hillmen,

(d) not to buy grain or other articles, the sale or removal of which is prohibited by the preceding Rules or by the Forest Regulation and rules already in force or that may hereafter come into force, and

(e) to keep proper and clear accounts of all their transactions with the hillmen which accounts shall be open for inspection by the respective Range Officer or Divisional Forest Officer.

(ii) Licenses shall be liable to be revoked, withdrawn or cancelled for breach of any of the conditions of the agreement, the trader being rendered liable besides to the penalties prescribed therein.

(iii) Such licensed traders shall acquire no title whatever to lands occupied or cultivated by the hillmen under these rules.

14. The Hillmen shall work for the Forest Department, whenever called upon to do so, at prescribed rates of wages, such rates being fixed by the Divisional Forest Officer with the previous sanction of the Conservator, for three years at a time, calculated with reference to the wages paid during the preceding three years and the current market rates.

15. The hillmen shall not set fire to the Forests and they shall take all possible care and precaution to prevent fires occurring in the Government Forests and Reserves. They shall assist the Forest Officers in preventing the occurrence or commission of offences, and the occurrence of fires and in extinguishing such fires.

16. All hillmen shall assist the Police Revenue or other officers of the Government in preventing crimes, or in detecting offenders who may have sought shelter or refuge in the Government Forests or Reserves.

17. Hillmen shall not harbour, or allow to remain in their settlements, any lowland criminals or persons likely to commit any breaches of the Forest or other laws of the country, nor shall they take into partnership any outsiders, in their cultivations within the Government Forests or Reserves or in their hunting or shooting excursions.

18. They shall be further bound to deliver to the Forest Department any ivory, elephant teeth, cardamoms, wax, dammer and lac collected by them, as well as honey or any other forest produce which they may be called upon to collect and deliver to the Forest Department, in return for which they will be paid at the rates fixed in the following schedule :—

No.	Produce.	Rates.
1	Ivory	1st class (weighing 18 lbs. and above per tusk), 7 fanams. per lb.
	Do.	2nd class (weighing below 18 lbs. but above 13 lbs. per tusk), 5½ fs. per lb.
	Do.	3rd class (weighing below 13 lbs. but above 7 lbs. per tusk), 3½ fs. per lb.
	Do.	4th class (weighing below 7 lbs.) 1¾ fs. per lb.
2	Cardamom ..	with husk, 35 fs. per Thulām.
	Do. ..	Seeds 26 fs.—3chs-4c. per Thulām.
	Do. ..	Chaff with husk 6 fs. Do.
3	Wax.	45 fs. Do.
	Dammer	6 fs. Do.
	Honey — —	17½ fs. per Parah.

For articles for which rates are not prescribed in the above schedule, the hillmen will be paid an amount not exceeding one-half of the sale proceeds of such articles, with the sanction of the Conservator of Forests.

19. Any hillman found to wilfully violate, or act in contravention of these Rules, or of the Forest Regulations and Rules, shall be liable to be expelled from his settlement in a Government Forest or Reserve, temporarily or permanently, with the previous sanction of the Conservator, besides being subjected to the penalties prescribed in the Forest Laws.

22. The Kuria Muria Islands and Sokotra.

The following notes on the Kuria Muria Islands and Sokotra were obtained in 1921 through the Political Resident at Aden from the Senior Naval Officer, no subsequent information appears to be available as to the inhabitants of these islands. It will be noted that Sokotra is reported to have a peculiar language in general use among its inhabitants which is no longer written, though it may have been formerly, and that many of the inhabitants are cavedwellers.

The practice in the Kuria Muria Islands of roofing huts with fish bones is suggestive of Arrian's ichthyophagi.

Kuria Muria Islands (British Possession).

A group of five islands, 25 miles off the South east coast of Oman between Ras Sharbatat and Ras Nus, to the N. E. of Dhofar. They are of granite, and form a chain running for fifty miles due E. and W. ; they stand upon a granite ledge with very deep water immediately outside. During the N. E. monsoon they are exposed to winds from all points of the compass.

Hollaniyah the largest and central island of the group is the only one at present inhabited. It is seven-and-half miles long from East to West, and three-and-half miles broad from North to South ; one of the hills in its centre rises to a height of 1,503 feet. Water is abundant but slightly brackish. The few inhabitants are reported to speak a dialect akin to that of Murbat on the main land and resembling Mahri. They live in semi-circular huts, with walls of lose stones, roofed with sticks, fish bones and seaweed. They keep goats, and engage in fishing, but have no boats. In 1835 they numbered 23, and had increased to 36 in 1883 ; but in 1901 the island was found to be temporarily deserted. In 1835 Suda the second largest island was also inhabited ; the remaining islands are known as Jibliyah, Hasikiyah, and Gharzaut.

The origin of the English name for the islands 'Kuria Muria' is unknown. The Arabs know them as Jeza'ir Bin Ghalfan, after a Mahrah family called Bin Ghalfan, who once seized them, and in 1835 still claimed them as their property. They had been raided and the settlements depopulated, by pirates from Trucial Oman in 1818. In 1854 the Sultan of Oman, who had established a title to the group, ceded them to Great Britain and they have since remained a British possession. Between 1857 and 1859 the rich guano deposits of Jibliyah and Hasikiyah were worked out. A British telegraph station was established on Hallaliyah in 1859, but it was removed in the following year.

Sokotra Island.

Sokotra is distant about 130 miles from the nearest point of the Arabian coast, and some 500 miles from Aden. It is about 70 miles in length and 18 miles in width, and has an unbroken coast on the Southern side. The interior may be described as a tableland from 700 to 1,900 feet high (with rugged peaks rising to nearly 500 feet), surrounded by coast plain averaging from 2 to 4 miles in width ; total area about 1,400 square miles ; population about 12,000. Its principal products are gum and resin-producing plants and alloes ; the island has been famous for the latter from the earliest times. The natives look for their chief means of support to their flocks and date-groves ; melons, beans and a little tobacco are also grown. The trade of the island is small, the chief exports being alloes and ghi. The capital is Tamrida, situated on the Northern shore. The Island was formally placed under British protection in 1886 and the Sultan receives a stipend from the Government of 360 dollars, undertaking to enter into no arrangement with any foreign power without the sanction of the British Government.

The inhabitants may be divided into two different classes the Bedouins, many of whom are tall and well made, who inhabit the mountains and the high land near the Western extreme of the island, and who, there is every reason to believe, are the aborigines ; and those who reside in Tamrida, Kadhup, Kallansiya, and the Eastern end of the island—a mixed population, the descendants of Arabs, Indians, Africans, Portuguese and several other nations.

With regard to the population, so many people dwell in caves in the hills that it is impossible to arrive at anything but an approximation.

Though Arabic is spoken by the Merchants when transacting business with traders visiting the island, there is a language peculiar to it in general use amongst its inhabitants ; it is no longer a written language though it appears formerly to have been so.

M53CC—1,200—8-11-33—GIPS

APPENDIX.

POINTS ON WHICH INFORMATION WAS ASKED FOR AT THE CENSUS OF 1931 IN THE CASE OF PRIMITIVE TRIBES IN FOREST OR HILL TRACTS.

1. Existence of division into different exogamous clans or groups of clans.

2. Existence of division into two or three groups or classes with a definite order of social precedence as between these classes.

3. Existence of a chiefly class or clan from which all chiefs are drawn, and whether or not a chief must belong to that class or clan by both parents.

4. If organization democratic, how run.

5. Existence of traditions of origin from North-West, North-East, or South, etc. Possibly different clans will prove to have different traditions.

6. Existence of terraced cultivation, and if it exists whether merely in flat valleys, or built up on steeper slopes and revetted with stone.

7. Existence of megalithic monuments and whether merely monoliths (single upright stones) or alignments (rows of such monoliths) or dissoliths (one stone upright and one flat at the foot, as in the Khasia Hills) or dolmens (large flat stone supported on a sumber of smaller uprights).

8. Use of stone for seats, and whether such use is privileged.

9. Use of materials in building and what restrictions if any on the use of stone or of wood for walls or roofs.

10. Whether the social position of individuals is indicated (*a*) in the shape or material of their houses, (*b*) in the pattern and colours of the cloths they wear.

11. Ideas as to the sun, moon and stars, comets, etc., *e.g.*, respective genders of sun and moon (some tribes make the sun female); names for different constellations and the meaning of such names, particularly for Orion's Belt, the Pleiades, the Hyades, Castor and Pollux, Hydra, Cassiopeia, the Great Bear, the Milky Way, Sirius. Explanation of the markings on the face of the moon; causes of earthquakes, and of eclipses. Explanations of the Rainbow (frequently regarded as the bridge by which the souls of the dead reach the sky), and of thunder and lightning (The latter is often associated wth neolithic stone adzes.)

12. Methods of disposal of the dead—in trees, cliffs, on *machans* or by burial or by burning: form of coffin, erection of stone cairn or of any form of shelter over grave; treatment of the head (some tribes dispose of it separately from the body, wrenching it off after putrefaction).

13. Beliefs as to the ultimate abode of the dead; as to transmigration into butterflies or other insects. (*N. B.*—Contradictory beliefs may be expected to exist simultaneously.)

14. Appearance—Complexion—sallow, red or dark? Hair straight, wavy or frizzly and how treated? Eyes straight or oblique, brown or black? Shape of nose and head and physique in general.

15. Method of sowing seed, *i.e.*, broadcast or by separate placing of seed; shape of hoes used and implements generally.

16. Musical instruments.

17. Weapons—bow used or not—and treatment of heads taken from enemies—*e.g.*, buried hung in trees or kept in houses or Bachelor's Hall.

18. Methods of making fire.

M53CC—8-11-33—1,200—GIPS

Census of India, 1931

VOL. I—INDIA

Part V—Administration Report

by

J. H. HUTTON, C.I.E., D.Sc.,

Census Commissioner for India

SIMLA

GOVERNMENT OF INDIA PRESS

1933

FOREWORD.

When sending this report to the press I wish to acknowledge the fertile criticisms and suggestions of Mr. M. W. M. Yeatts, which have been particularly valuable to me as supplying that firsthand knowledge of a provincial census superintendent in which my own experience is defective. I have suggested that the mechanization of the census would eliminate the provincial sorting and compiling office. He would go even further, and taking the process to its logical conclusion, maintains that the true development of this change would be to eliminate the provincial census superintendent after the enumeration is completed. The report of the latter would then be primarily administrative, and he would not be called on to deal critically with statistics unless he happened to have expert knowledge of some particular subject covered by them. The present series of census reports would then devolve into a series of monographs by experts in the various departments to which they had reference, though designed on a common plan, certain specified subjects, *e.g.* vital statistics, might suitably be prescribed by the central authority for such treatment in each province. *Mutatis mutandis* the same principle would apply to the Census Commissioner and while the returns of age would be dealt with by the Government Actuary, or of literacy by the Educational Commissioner, those of occupation would be discussed by the Department of Industries and Labour. Figures of area, population, and community lend themselves to little treatment beyond the actual publication of the tables. Questions of fertility and civil condition need to be treated according to social rather than administrative boundaries, and, as Mr. Yeatts points out, one of the great advantages of a mechanical sort would be that it could be carried down to the smallest census unit without materially increasing costs and would thus make possible the combination of figures for areas administratively divorced but socially intimate, such as those comprising Kerala or Kannada, which can alone afford a really satisfactory basis for the study of figures of age, fertility or marital condition. At the same time village and municipal statistics could be extracted with the minimum of expense.

I admit the logical sequence of this devolution as the result of the mechanization of census procedure, and it must be added that it would bring the census of India into greater accord with the practice of other countries. It would also make very definitely for economy, and it is at least arguable that the traditional series of Indian census reports is more of a luxury than an administrative necessity. To say this involves no slight on the excellent team of Census Superintendents which I was fortunate enough to lead. It is rather that, at the risk of appearing to foul my own nest, I think it part of my business to draw attention to the necessity of keeping the census practice of India in its correct relation to the needs of a modern state. I have not however enlarged on this in the report that follows, as I have regarded that as primarily intended to treat of the census as it is, rather than as it might be or may become.

I should like to take this opportunity of once more thanking my office and compiling staff for their assistance, and for the willing way they have worked under pressure and without holidays particularly during the conclusion of the operations. Three names I have already mentioned elsewhere, and it is not possible to name them all, but at least I can here add those of my stenotypist and tour-clerk Mr. G. C. Gupta, of Mr. Sohan Lal Elhance who preceded him in that post, both of whom had the misfortune to have to decipher my crabbed manuscript, of my budget assistant Mr. Chand Kishore, whose knowledge of the subtle paths of Accounts and the horrid pitfalls of Audit was an invaluable relief to me, and of my clerks and compilers Mr. D. P. Das, Mr. M. A. P. Menon, Mr. R. K. Venkatesan, Mr. P. B. Joshi and Mr. N. M. Ananthapadmanabhan Iyer, while Mr. C. S. Kumaraswami Mudaliar drew for me most of the maps and diagrams which illustrate the Report. My chief regret in closing down my office is that so many of them must start again to search for employment in an uncomfortably competitive world.

SIMLA :
The 7th June 1933.

J. H. HUTTON.

M2CC

N. B.—The marginal references are to files in the records of the Census Commissioner's Office or to the administrative volumes of the Provinces indicated by name and refer in that case to the 1931 volume unless specified to the contrary. The Arabic numbers refer to the paragraph, the chapter being given where necessary in Roman numerals, unless pages are specifically indicated.

i.—Legislation.

Existing periodic Acts.

1. The first step in the whole Census procedure is the passing of an act to provide for the taking of a census (*vide* Act X of 1929). The legislation in this case was completed before the appointment of a Census Commissioner, and although this has not been necessarily or always the case, the legislation is in any case likely (as long as the present census procedure and system are unchanged) to take place so soon after his appointment that he will have little time to examine the provisions to be made for any modification that may seem desirable. The general experience and opinion of Census Superintendents in 1931 found that Act X of 1929 was deficient in the powers it gave for compelling municipalities to take a proper census in accordance with the code, a difficulty experienced also in 1921; in the punishments prescribed for non-compliance with the code, which, though quite adequate for the occasional delinquency of a cantankerous individual, are clearly not adapted to deal with opposition to a census on any organized scale, a danger which arose both in 1921 and 1931; and in the protection given under Section 12 of the Act. The reason why the use of the census schedule as evidence in criminal proceedings is not entirely barred is obviously in order to make its use possible in the case of deliberately false or misleading entries and in order to give control over an enumerator who might falsify as well as the enumerated. It should however be possible to use the schedule for these purposes only. As it is, a number of attempts were made to have the census schedules produced in criminal courts, not only in connection with prosecutions under the Sarda Act, but to rebut the alibi of persons accused of criminal offences. In the latter case the evidence of the census record would be very slender, as the enumerator only calls at each house to verify his preliminary enumeration and does not necessarily see more than one individual there, but there is a danger that the enumerator may claim to have been very thorough, or that the court may attach to the written record an evidential value which it was never intended to possess. In any case it is on all grounds necessary to preserve the confidential nature of the census record. It is difficult enough to get accurate information in any case, and the enumerator is, not a lawyer and can only explain in general terms the fact that returns are confidential, so that any use of them for the prosecution of the enumerated is bound to be regarded as a breach of faith. It is quite clear that a large number of persons who had married their daughters in contravention of the Sarda Act returned them as unmarried, and that the attempts to use the records for prosecutions justified to some extent their fears and false returns. Further the census record is a temporary document destroyed as soon as it is satisfactorily converted from an individual one to that of a nameless unit of the population. It seems therefore improper as well as inexpedient that the criminal law should be able to take advantage of the fact that the effective numbering of units should temporarily involve a knowledge of the names attaching to them. Sections 123 and 124 of the I. P. C. would appear on the face of them to protect the information given to census officers, but this appearance is fallacious as the Legislative Department ultimately decided that the records were to be supplied to the courts that demanded them. Fortunately however the schedules had been destroyed in accordance with the usual procedure while the matter was still under consideration. The next Census Act should be drafted to give proper protection to the information obtained.

C. P., 19, 20. Rajputana Aj. M's. 2. U. P. I.-29. B. and O., (1921) I.-21. Bombay, (1921), Pp. 5—8.

Madras, I, 9.

Several minor points on which the drafting of the Act might be amended were pointed out by Local Governments and by Census Superintendents. A record of them will be found on census file No. 12-General (Census Act of 1929) and on Home Department's file No. F.-122/29-Pub., November 1929 to February 1930.

Necessity for permanent provision.

2. The question of legislation is obviously likely to be affected by constitutional changes. In federal bodies it seems to be usual to have some constitutional provision for the taking of a periodic census. This is at any rate the case in the

United States of America, where the provision in the original federal constitution for a periodic enumeration of the inhabitants in order to determine their representation led to the growth of the permanent census department in that country. Furthermore, a census on a federal basis is likely to need provision for a more effective control over the federal units than exists at present with regard to Indian States. The existing Census Act extends to British India and the Santhal Parganas. The co-operation of the States is a matter of courtesy on their part and no legislative machinery exists, nor is it possible apparently for any to come into existence, unless some general legislative authority come into being. One of the major states at this census completely ignored at least one point on which the Government of India specially desired that information should be collected and in another point of some importance deliberately departed from the principles laid down in the Code. In order to obtain uniformity it is therefore clearly desirable that the various units contributing to the India census should be amenable to central control not only in the details of administration but also in the personnel of their census appointments. The appointment of a single slow or inefficient census superintendent in any major unit may delay the whole of the operations at the centre, and thus cause much undue and unnecessary expense to the Central Government, which must keep its organization waiting and continue to pay for it, since local delay in a single return can make progress impossible. At the same time it is essential that the responsibility for enumeration, and the cost thereof, should rest on the local unit and not on the Central Government. This point is referred to later in connection with finance.

Another point arising in this general connection is the question whether provision for a census should not be by permanent legislation as in many countries, providing for periodic census without the necessity of legislating *ad hoc* at each recurrent period. A permanent legislative provision has the advantage of being less liable to be made the subject of political 'logrolling' or of party tactics. The same point arises in connection with a suggestion that can conveniently be made at this point for a change in the general census policy. The existing method of creating a department for the taking of a census, destroying it and recreating it periodically is prodigal of effort and of experience. Continuity depends entirely on an inadequate written record and a great deal is learned at each census which is then forgotten and relearned again 10 years later. Improvements are therefore very difficult to introduce, and the whole procedure consists of organization and analysis undertaken against time, and it is therefore rash as well as difficult to undertake any change that needs to be prepared in advance. A good case in point is the introduction of a mechanical sort. This proposal was examined in 1921 and postponed for re-examination at the census of 1931. By the time it was possible to come to a very hurried conclusion against it on the score of expense it would have been too late to introduce it in any case on account of the changes in procedure involved, so that a decision in its favour would have had to be postponed again for another decade. The true solution would appear to be to amalgamate the office of Census Commissioner with that of the Director General of Statistics and Commercial Intelligence putting the two under a permanent head whose permanent office would form the standing nucleus of the periodic census department. This would involve some change in the nature of the India census and a departure from its traditional character, but it seems probable from every point of view that the time for such a change has arrived. Apart from the growing inconsistency of an attempt to deal in census reports with any matter other than purely statistical, three considerations point emphatically in the direction of such a change and it will be convenient to examine briefly each of them in turn.

When legislating for the census it might be wise to insert a clause comparable to section 4(2) of the English Census Act (1920) authorising the Census Commissioner to extract, prepare and supply to approved persons any available statistics on payment for the costs of the additional work involved. This would enable the Census Commissioner to choke off a large number of importunate persons, who write for advance figures and who want all sorts of information to be supplied, by requiring the cost in advance. Where the information is readily available the cost will be very small or *nil* and the information can be easily supplied in any case ; on the other hand the information asked for is sometime impossible or difficult to supply and may involve much extra work.

3. The first and probably the most important is the growing difficulty of enumeration by volunteers. The practice in this respect differs in different provinces, for whereas in some the greater part of the organization, including supervisors and even charge superintendents is largely voluntary; in others the real work, including the preliminary preparation of the schedules, is mostly done by revenue officers and only the actual final checking carried out by unpaid workers. It is quite obvious that a voluntary agency is a most unsatisfactory thing on which to rely, and district officers were generally very definite about the difficulty of obtaining volunteers and of getting them to carry out their work efficiently. A voluntary agency is extremely vulnerable to political propaganda, and broke down entirely in parts of Gujarat. By far the most satisfactory agency for enumeration has proved to be that of the local revenue officer, *i.e.*, of the tahsildar and patwari, wherever there is a local revenue staff as there is in most provinces of India. Under the present system however it is not possible to make use of the revenue staff for final enumeration as it is in the first place not numerous enough for synchronized enumeration, and in the second place the census invariably conflicts in several provinces with heavy revenue work, and so much so that in some cases it is impossible to utilize the revenue staff fully even for merely supervisory services. The question of a change in the date of the census to the autumn has been carefully gone into by all provinces and states at this census, and though it would enable some provinces to utilize their revenue staff to the full and would be preferable for other reasons, in most cases the change would only increase difficulties. The position can however be conveniently met by substituting a *de jure* for a *de facto* census. The census of India is at present *de facto*, that is to say it aims at a return of all persons actually found in India at a given moment. It is however unlikely that it will ever be feasible to make a census of India completely synchronous. The area is too great and too diverse, and it is possible that the development of rapid communications may increase rather than reduce the difficulties. Nor is it apparent that a *de facto* census possesses any inherent virtue which is denied to a *de jure* census. It is therefore suggested that the census should cease to be even nominally *de facto* and that a *de jure* census should be substituted such as that taken by the United States of America, that is to say that instead of recording the actual individuals found during the prescribed hours of enumeration throughout the area censused the census should record the individuals normally located in every dwelling place in that area together with all nomads who have no fixed dwelling. The latter, it is true, will have to be censused synchronously, but this presents small difficulty compared to the synchronous census of all India, and it is submitted that for an area so large and diverse as India a *de jure* census is much more likely to be suitable than a *de facto* census which is really only at its maximum efficiency in smaller countries of much greater social, climatic and geographical solidarity. The substitution of a *de jure* for a *de facto* census would enable the enumeration to be spread (as in the U. S. A.) over a longer period so that the climatic variations of each province could be met and the revenue staff everywhere utilized without interfering with their normal duties. The dangerous dependence on a voluntary organization would be eliminated as well as the anomaly of a *de facto* census which is not truly synchronous. The expense would be less than at present and the difficulties of organization would be less, as the railway and boat enumeration could be largely eliminated and the whole procedure simplified. The census would in effect approximate to the existing preliminary enumeration without the subsequent final one. Difficulties of course present themselves, as they do in the case of the existing synchronized plan. Persons living away from home, nomads and migrants will need to be provided for, but these would appear to offer less serious obstacles than the mere danger of allowing so important an undertaking as a census to depend on the precarious services of unpaid volunteers. There are also countervailing advantages from the purely administrative point of view in having *de jure* instead of *de facto* figures; I quote the following from a letter from the Census Superintendent in Madras :—

> Suggested Changes.
>
> Assam, 17 (ii). B. and O. I, 12, 47, 48. Burma, 16. Cochin, 18. Madras, I, 10. U. P. I.-15, II-2. Bombay (1921), pp. 4—9.
>
> File No. 2, Enmn.

"I received recently.........a wail from the health department that a village shown in the census with 300 people had actually 400 and they sought alteration of the figures. Here arise in a pronounced form the worse effects of a *de facto* census. The census determination was all right; it gave the facts on the night of 26/27 February 1931. About 100 people had apparently been off for the tree-tapping season or other circumstance and were absent on census night...........It seems clear that from the point of view of village figures the *de jure* total has it every time in convenience. That is one of the conclusions I wish to draw from this inc dent. The other is the very general failure to realise that our populations are all rigidly (excep in the Agencies, etc.,) *de facto* and limit themselves to the facts of a single night in ten years. Eve Collectors seem not immune from this misconception, while among such officers as health inspec tors it is rife..............it is precisely that our figures profess to give and what the genera census scheme limits them to..........A really pathetic circumstance that came out of th second case was that the health inspector, apparently in pursuance of a general district practice was extracting bi th rates per 1,000 for every village, even for one with admittedly less tha 500 inhabitants............The waste of effort and what is worse, the misdirection of effort implied are more than serious."

It is therefore suggested that future censuses should be conducted on the lines of the census of the U. S. A. and in this connection a reference may be made to *Bureau of the Census*—U. S. A. Service Monographs No. 53 (Washington, 1929).

Mechanization.

4. A further argument in favour of such a change is to be found in the growing necessity for a mechanization of the sorting, or at any rate of part of the sorting process. There can be no doubt that given correct classification of the original returns a sort by machinery is far more accurate than a sort by hand. Further while sorting by hand is likely to become—indeed has already proved to become—more expensive from census to census, a sort by machinery is conversely becoming cheaper at successive decades and is now the approved method in all advanced countries. It has the further advantage that the cards once punched can be easily stored and re-sorted by the machines at any time that any additional information is required that may be available from a combination of certain sorts of the cards but which has not been considered important at the time of the census. Thus at some previous censuses of India a sort for occupation by religion has been made. It was not made in 1931 and can therefore never be obtained for that year. Even if the sorting slips had been preserved the expense of conducting such a sort would involve the recreation of the whole sorting staff and would therefore be prohibitive, whereas if punched cards had been preserved all that would be necessary would be to pass them through the machines, and there would be no need to incur the expense of any additional staff at all, since in the case of modern census machines the very results are recorded in type by the machine itself. An investigation of the comparative costs of sorting and compilation by the present method and by punched cards and machines indicated in 1931 that the latter method would cost three times as much, but this excessive cost was due more to the necessity of classifying the very large number of entries on the present schedule than to any other cause, and it is likely that if certain suggestions made below be accepted this cost of classification could be very much reduced and a mechanized census would then be brought within the scope of practicability. If so it is obvious that it would be far more economical to centralise the sorting and to have it done on a single set of machines at Delhi than to have machines working at various provincial centres and involving either independent mechanicians or the cost of a travelling mechanical staff. A centralized sort would also be in accordance with the recommendation accepted by the Government of India that census should be a central charge except in so far as the actual enumeration and its costs are concerned.

Mechanized procedure.

File No. 3-Misc.
File No. 21-Misc.

5. As to the detailed procedure of a mechanized sort it is not necessary to enter here. Several drafts of a code of procedure for such a sort have been made, and the material for drafting a code can be found in Files Nos. 3 and 21 Misc. of the 1931 census records. It will be enough here to point out that whereas the substitution of a punched card for a written slip offers no serious difficulty at all in the case of the entries on the existing schedule which are tabulated in the margin, the first three of which would be "gang punched" in large numbers of cards at a single operation, the following entries offer serious difficulty on account of the necessity for classification before punching :—Language, Birthplace, Occupation, Industry, Caste and Religion. In the case of caste an accurate return is already unobtainable; it is doubtful if the return serves any statistical or administrative purpose; the return involves a troublesome quantity of irritating propaganda which can be a serious affliction to census officers, and I have elsewhere recommended its abolition at any rate at the sorting and compiling stages. It is submitted that the purposes at present served by the return of caste can be equally well obtained by the return suggested below to cover both caste and religion. The return of religion has already begun to give difficulty on account of persons who belong socially to a community yet do not concur with its orthodox views on religion; and who

No. of Charge.
No. of Circle.
No. of block.
Serial No. of individual Sex.
Civil condition.
Age.
Earner or dependant.
Literacy.
Knowledge of English.
Insanity, blindness, deafmuteness or leprosy

therefore wish to appear in different categories for different tables, a position very troublesome from the view of compilation when the whole scheme of classification depends on the return of religion. This difficulty is certain to increase rather than decrease. It is therefore suggested that the return of religion should be abandoned and a return of "community" substituted. This will be just as useful as a general basis of classification and will not involve any question (already resented by a few and on the face of it not a concern of the secular state) of the personal beliefs of individuals censused. It will make it possible for instance for a person to return his community as Muslim though his views on religion are completely un-Islamic without doing violence to his conscience. This particular instance is quoted because it actually arose in 1931. It will also enable each province to frame a list of those communities, including if necessary specific castes, of which a count is required by that province, and the items of such lists can be kept separate or amalgamated for India as may appear desirable. It will make it possible to obtain a return of the exterior castes as such without involving the question of the status of any particular caste. Thus if in any province a distinction were required for Hindus between Brahmans and non-Brahmans only, this could be obtained without a necessary extension to all provinces, or similarly a division into interior and exterior castes. It would then lie with the individual enumerated himself to say whether he belonged to an interior or an exterior caste, and the numbers would be determined by the persons enumerated and not by the arbitrary classification of census authorities or of any other official department. Similarly the occasionally troublesome question of whether a sect is Hindu or Sikh or what sects are Hindu or not would be met by the instruction that the census recognized certain important communities and each individual could return himself as a member of one of those communities or of some other (the latter to be amalgamated in 'Others') as he thought fit without reference to his religious views. A minimum percentage of adherents could be taken as a test by which to determine whether or not a community should be separately tabulated for a province or for India.

In any case what is proposed is that those returns which can easily be coded should be coded directly on to the enumeration schedule by enumerators, leaving the minimum amount of coding to be done in the sorting office. In some degree, and particularly if caste be excluded (a very difficult return for a mechanical sort, since so many items are involved), this principle can be extended to all columns on the schedule, subject to a maximum of numbers 1 to 5, which need not necessarily bear the same code value in each province *provided* the provincial cards are distinctive in colour or design as I suggest that they ought to be. Thus the serial numbers of the charge circle and block can be put down in their respective numbers—two or at most three digits in each case; the serial number of the individual will require at least three columns. I have elsewhere suggested that the instructions for the record of age should instruct the age to be given in years and months only where the actual date of birth is known and should otherwise be returned as age in approximate number of years. Those ages where months are given may need to go to the coder who will determine, say, to which year a person belongs who has given his age as 20 years and 7 months according to the method of grouping adopted; but 999 out of 1,000 returns, or more, will be already coded in years and will be sorted in the first instance by yearly ages, and later sorted into whatever groups are necessary for the compilation of the printed tables by means of the machine again. For male or female the enumerator will enter 1 or 2. If thought necessary a third digit could be used to cover that curious class, fairly frequently met with in India and Indonesia of males who dress in women's clothes and live the lives of women, following all their occupations except child-bearing. For civil condition again the enumerator should enter 1 for unmarried, 2 for married, 3 for widowed. The sequence is obvious and there can be little room for error. For earner or dependant again only 1 and 2 are required. For occupations, whether principal or subsidiary 1 to 5 should be entered for the following :—Rent receiver, Cultivating owner, Cultivating tenant, Agricultural labourer and Jhumiya (cultivator of shifting areas, *jhum*, *taungya*, *penda*, *podu*, *bewar*, *beora*, *dahia*, *dhaya*, etc.). Any other occupation must be entered in full, but 60 per cent. of the population will be covered by these five entries. Industry should probably form the subject of a separate statistical enquiry conducted on forms issued to factory owners and managers, but if included in the census it would probably have to be entered in full. In the column for birthplace the numbers 1 to 5 should be entered respectively for the following :—

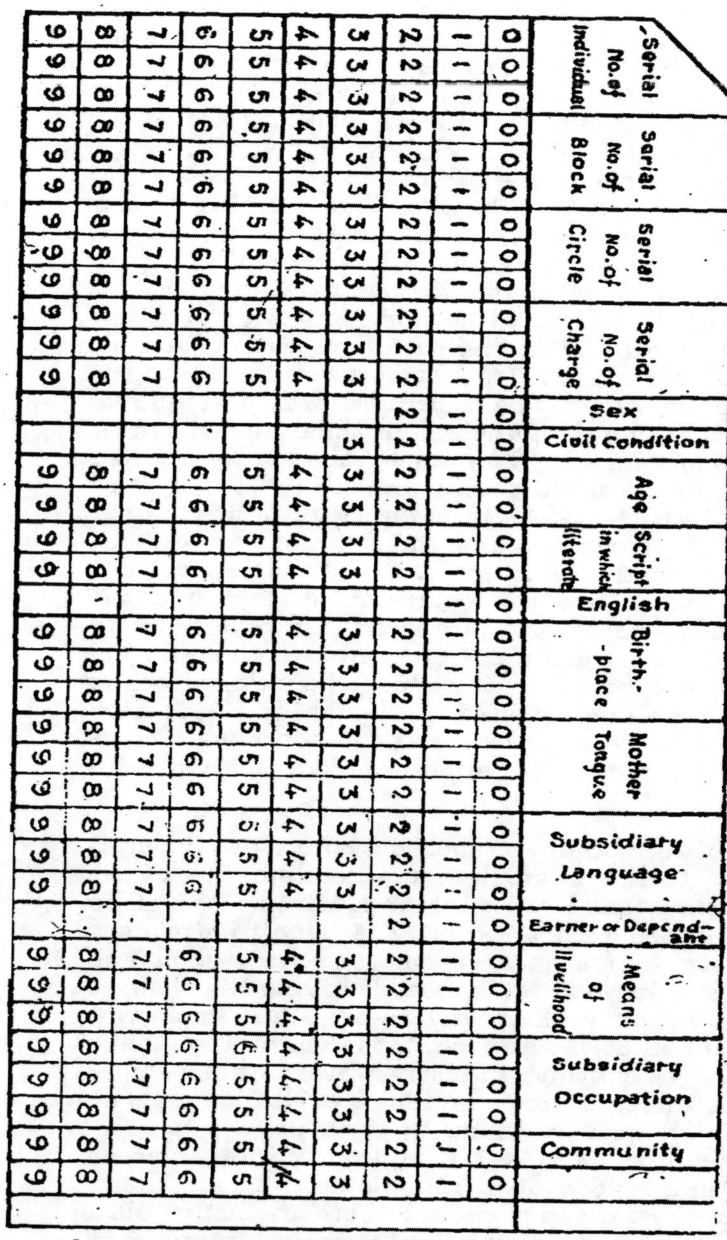

born in district or town of enumeration (1), elsewhere in the province (2), in a contiguous province (3), elsewhere in India (4), in Burma (5) ; any birthplace outside India would have to be written down in full and coded in the sorting office. This direction postulates a higher standard of intelligence and knowledge on the part of enumerators than at present, but even if the present system of enumeration and the *de facto* census be retained there would be no difficulty about the numbers (1) and (2). Similarly for mother tongue and for subsidiary language each province would have a list of five or fewer prevailing languages to be entered by the enumerator by numbers and any other being written—thus in Madras Tamil, Telugu, Malayalam, Kanarese and Hindustani would be represented by numbers 1, 2, 3, 4 and 5, all others being written down in full. Assam on the other hand might use 1, 2 and 3 to represent Assamese, Bengali and Hindustani. The central compilation office would have to sort provinces independently for language but this would offer no difficulty. At the same time it would probably not be difficult to arrange a numerical code for all languages on a geographical system such that in each province the important languages would be represented by contiguous numbers that offered little difficulty in coding. For mere literacy two numbers are enough, 1 and 0, or for script of literacy the numbers corresponding to those used for language. For English 1 and 0 again will do and for infirmities 1 to 4. Community could be dealt with on the same principle as language, using numbers 1 to 5 for Hindu, Muslim, Sikh, Jain and Christian, or for Brahman, non-Brahman, Adi-Hindu, Muslim, Christian, or for Buddhist, Muslim, Christian, Hindu, Tribal as required, all other or doubtful entries being written down in full. It is essential that the coding to be done by enumerators should be limited to the really simple points and to no more than five numbers, instructions for the use of which should of course be entered on the cover of the schedule. *By this means however all schedules could be partially coded and not less than 60 per cent. of entries could be completely coded in the process of enumeration and all that would be necessary would

* I feel that I should make it clear that the opinion of the Superintendent of my office, Mr. A. R. Chitnis, is definitely against codification by enumerators, and it is possible that others with census experience will agree with him. His view is that codification should all be done in the punching office, and that in the case of the simpler coding, which is all that could in any case be done by enumerators, the process is so rapid that little would be gained in time by having it done in enumeration, whereas much might be lost in accuracy. His opinion is based on his experience of coding for the mechanical sort in railway offices. It appears to me however that a few code numbers could be used by enumerators no less accurately than the abbreviations required by the *billets individuels* system, and that the coding in enumeration of say 75 per cent. of many millions of entries would effect a very material saving of time and therefore of money. I admit that it is probable that an extensive use of code numbers in enumeration no less than that of abbreviations in *billets individuels*, postulates enumeration by patwaris or by other village officers or by some more reliable agency than that of the casual volunteer; it probably therefore involves the substitution of the *de jure* for the *de facto* census.

be to punch the cards for the schedules. The coding would thus be reduced to about 40 per cent. of the occupation columns and a very much smaller percentage indeed of those for language, birth-place and community. In designing the card illustrated above I have cut out numbers which would not in any case be used as this will eliminate a certain number of posssible errors. This might be carried further and if, say, the maximum number of birth-places when coded was 200, all the digits above 2 could be omitted from the hundreds column. I have shown only one column for community but there is already one spare column and if necessary it would probably be posssible to utilize the columns for the serial number of the individual for some other purpose. A puncher would have cost in 1921 about Rs. 15 per month and would punch in a day many more cards than a silp copier could copy in the same time. The Hollerith estimate was 300 cards punched in an hour by one puncher, but that would only be after some practice. I think I should advocate starting the columns with 1 and ending with 0 instead of starting with 0 and ending with 9, as 0 would be much less frequently used than 1 and 2 which might conveniently start each column. The schedules which required coding would be largely completed by the time the punching of the other schedules was completed and thus no time could be wasted. The cost of the cards—at first sight a prohibitive item, would probably be more than compensated for by the absence of any necessity for provincial abstraction and compilation offices with their deputy superintendents, inspectors, compilers and sorters, and the central compiling office equipped with machines would need no greater staff tnan at present. The cards would have to be sorted as received, but the operation is very rapid and the cards would be retained in the central depot, the tabulated results only being returned to the provincial superintendent for examination and treatment in his tables and reports. Incidentally such a system would reduce the risks of bogus insertions by communalist sorters such as those detected in Bengal in 1931, since collusion between several sorters would be necessary to effect it and could more easily be guarded against than under the system by which each copyist copies all the entries on each schedule given him.

Preparation necessary.

6. It is clear however that the introduction of such a system would need very careful preparation beforehand. It also involves some modification of the existing system, and it is here suggested that by far the best solution would be to follow the example of Europe and America and have a small permanent department with a quinquennial census. At such a census the reruns should be much fewer than at the decennial one and it would be possible to ring the changes on various returns, talking more often, or perhaps invariably, the important returns of age, sex and civil (marital) condition, and perhaps community, while asking for the difficult returns of occupation and industry, returns much more expensive on account of the cost of classification, once in ten or even fifteen years, their place being taken at the intervening quinquennium by birth-place, language, literacy or script, or by new items of enquiry, *e.g.*, as to employment (as opposed to unemployment), housing, fertility, staple food or perhaps even wages. Under the present system the schedule is already overloaded though there are many points of much sociological and economic importance on which information would and should be obtained by census methods. It will no doubt appear at first sight that a change involving a permanent census department and a quinquennial (and mechanized) census would inevitably entail a great increase of expense. It is however doubtful if this would be the case. It has already been suggested that the post of census commissioner should be amalgamated with that of Director of Statistics—a permanent post already. It should also be pointed out that in any case the Census Commissioner's post and office normally last for about four years or longer out of each decade, so that its amalgamation with an existing permanent office would not necessarily involve so great an increase of expense in that direction as might appear at first sight. The increase involved by quinquennial censuses would, if the *de jure* census were substituted for the *de facto* (but not otherwise), also be largely counterbalanced by the increase of efficiency resulting from doubled familiarity, from the use of the existing revenue organization instead of one periodically created *ad hoc*, and, ultimately, from the use of machinery for sorting. The use of a greatly reduced schedule would have as its natural corollary the substitution of short statistical reports in slighter form than the present census reports and probably dealing independently with different items of the information obtained. Printing and publication could thus be cheapened and a regular output

spread over five years, of the information collected at each quinquennium would have the advantage of making possible a regular budget based on an annual expenditure instead of the financial spasm of empirical expenditure inseparable from the present decennial system, and a smaller and permanent staff would unquestionably be more efficient than one collected for the occasion whose experience is dissolved at the close of operations and must be acquired all over again by costly and preventable error at each of its ephemeral spells. In short I suggest the abolition of the phoenix as the emblem of the census and the substitution of the much more reliable if less inspiring tortoise.

It will be clear that changes such as those proposed cannot well be carried out in the short time provided for the preparation of the census when a census commissioner is appointed *ad hoc*, as at present, with only six months in which to prepare his codes and contracts before the provincial offices come into being. The question is one that needs to be considered at least some three years before the date at which the first census under a new system is to be held. It will be also clear that the changes suggested above are not necessarily interdependent. It would be possible to use machinery without making the census quinquennial or to make it quinquennial without mechanizing it. At the same time it seems likely that the most economical and efficient proceeding would be to combine the two. It is desired to emphasize here that if a census commissioner be appointed only 18 months before the date fixed for the census he will have no time to make any radical innovation.

ii.—Enumeration.

The notes that follow are made on the assumption that there will be no change in procedure, but it will be clear that many of them will be no less applicable to a changed code than to the present. They are given as far as possible in the order in which they arise in the course of census operations.

Census Units.

7. Some economy could probably be effected at the next census by combining Sind and Baluchistan for certain purposes. For enumeration Baluchistan will probably need to have its own agencies and independent control. Owing to the huge areas over which its small population is sprinkled Baluchistan enumeration is *sui generis*; it is costly but inevitably so. On the other hand the sums spent in the abstraction and compilation of the Baluchistan returns have been unconscionably high, the staff has been unduly large, and the process has been incredibly slow; the post-enumeration stages of its census could conveniently be combined with those of Sind in a single compilation office in Quetta or Karachi oa Hyderabad, which should furnish the necessary tables and subsidiary tables to the officer selected to write the report. Compilation and abstraction by Sind offices is notoriously bad, but the presence of a provincial census superintendent might do much to mend that reputation. Similarly the combined administration of Bombay with the Western India States Agency and of the Punjab with the Punjab States Agency and with Delhi might conveniently remain though a brief separate report for each Agency of this kind is probably a *desideratum*. In the case of the Madras States Agency Pudukkottai might be permitted to compile its own report and the two remaining states of Banganapalle and Sandur might be treated together in an appendix to the Madras Report, the figures being kept separate. Many difficulties were caused in the India compilation in 1931 owing to the fact that provinces amalgamated the dependent states with British districts so that it was frequently impossible to disentangle figures for States or for British territory from those of the province as a whole, and all Superintendents of Census Operations should be warned that figures for states and British territory should be so treated that *any* figure is separable at any time down to the smallest item. The need for separate figures is more likely to increase with federation than to diminish and has been much more noticeable in 1931 than it was in 1921. On the other hand collections of states dealt with by a single Agency are not administrative units in the sense that provinces are, and though full figures are required for all states the report should be very brief and enable the report and tables to be combined in a single volume. Care should be taken to have the Punjab States Agency treated as a distinct unit separate from both the British Punjab and from the Punjab states.

Date.

File No. 2. Enmn.

8. This has been partly dealt with above (under Legislation). Late February or early March is undoubtedly the best time taken all round for a synchronous census, but it does not suit Madras or Burma, and late March does not

suit Bengal or Assam (too stormy). The dates of full moon should be obtained from the Meteorological office at Poona directly the Census Commissioner is appointed; it may here be pointed out that this is unnecessary if the census is to be *de jure* and non-synchronous, as the moon will not then matter. It is important to avoid big melas and fairs, and Local Governments and Census States need to be consulted at once, as it took four months to obtain the necessary replies in 1929-30. It is also important to avoid days that are auspicious for marriages and to choose, if possible, a day followed by a holiday (assuming of course that the synchronous census is retained). As the census of Ceylon is usually made to synchronise with that of India the Director of Statistics, Colombo, has to be informed at once of the date fixed, and similar information must be given to the Straits Settlements, etc., and to French and Portuguese India.

9. The Census Commissioner at this census was appointed in October 1929. It should be clearly understood that if the time available before the census is only 18 months it is impossible to make any important departure from pre-existing procedure. An experience of census as a provincial superintendent at the preceding census should probably carry more weight in making the selection than it did on this occasion. It is a consideration of very great importance. Appointments of census superintendents were made in 1930 by the Government of India on the recommendations of the Local Governments concerned. A point to be seriously considered is the probability of communal ramps to swell unduly the census strength of one community at the expense of others. It is of the greatest importance that the Census Superintendent should be regarded as impartial. The mere fact that he belongs to one of the contending communities is liable to place the Census Superintendent in a very delicate position, in spite of the best attested probity, and to make him a target for unjust criticism. This consideration arose in 1931 in the Punjab, while in Madras a special officer (an European) had to be appointed in Ganjam on account of Oriya-Telugu rivalry. In one case at any rate a Local Government recommended an officer who very soon proved to be physically unfit. **Appointments.**

It cannot be too strongly emphasized that the physical fitness of the officer to be appointed is of the greatest importance. The duties of a census superintendent are extremely strenuous and are likely to cause a breakdown in any one of poor physique. Sufficient notice should be given to census superintendents designate to enable them to take six months leave before taking charge of their duties, and they should be encouraged to take such leave. The intellectual ability of officers to be selected is perhaps an even more important consideration than their bodily health, since the cost of the census will be largely determined by the speed with which the provincial units complete their work. The amount of work to be got through in different units varies very greatly, but generally speaking it is obvious that the more able the officer the more quickly and cheaply will he finish his work. The difference between closing a single provincial census office in September and in the following March means a difference in expenditure of some Rs. 20,000, apart from the cost that may be indirectly entailed by the delaying of the India Report. "Drive" is also an important consideration in selecting a census superintendent and comparative youth is therefore a recommendation rather than a handicap.

Another point of the greatest importance is that, once appointed, census superintendents should not be changed, interfered with, or taken away for other duties until their work is finished. Interruption is extremely detrimental to census efficiency, and in one province the appointment of a census superintendent who proved physically unfit for the work seriously jeopardized the synchronous character of the census. The Foreign and Political Department has on occasions taken liberties with personnel that would never be taken by a Local Government. During the 1921 operations the census superintendent in the Central India Agency was changed five times. Nothing quite so extravagant as this was perpetrated in 1931, but the Superintendent of Census Operations of the North-West Frontier Province was twice taken away from his legitimate work for administrative ends, and ultimately told to complete his report in Kabul. This proved impossible and a fresh officer had to be found to take his place. In Baluchistan Captain Burnett was first designated, then withdrawn and Khan Bahadur Gul Muhammad Khan appointed. At the time of writing this officer is still engaged on his report in combination with his duties as Vizier of Kalat. In Rajputana and in Central India **C. P. & B., 3, 7, 12.**

the Census Department was fortunate in having Mr. Venkatachar and Colonel Cole as Census Superintendents, of whom one was not a permanent member of their cadre and the other not on their cadre at all. It may again be emphasized that changes in administration involve inefficiency and delay and expense, and it is suggested that an effort might be made at the next census to secure that officers deputed to census should be left in their posts till the completion of operations. This should not be interpreted as meaning that officers deputed to census should be those whose services are regarded as valueless in any capacity.

Budgets.

10. In 1931 enumeration was a charge on central revenues. In accordance with previous practice the provincial budgets for the first year were framed by the Local Governments. Without suggesting that the fact that they would not have to find the sums to be expended in any way influenced the budgetting, it may fairly be pointed out that the budgets were very definitely bad, and in some cases the minimum amount of attention was given to them. One major province budgetted for the precise amount actually spent in the corresponding period of the previous decade irrespective of changes in rates of pay, etc., and another major province framed its astonishing budget not even on the actuals but on the estimate framed for the corresponding period of the preceding census and that an estimate which had proved greatly in excess of the actual expenditure incurred, to which apparently no reference had been made at all. Perhaps this estimate was a legacy of 1872.

Probably the most useful way of framing the budget for the initial year would be to make an estimate of the amount involved by any definite changes in pay or the cost of stationery, etc., which were known to have taken place since the previous enumeration and to add or subtract the resulting difference to or from a lump sum arrived at on a population basis. Thus if the total expenditure on enumeration in 1931 worked out at (say) Rs. 4-8-0 per 1,000 of the population enumerated*, to the total thus arrived at a percentage should be added for the probable increase of the population and to the sum thus reached should be added or subtracted the known difference on account of changes in rates of pay, etc., indicated above. The normal increase of the population of India in a fairly prosperous decade seems to be about 10%, but the normal increase of the province or Agency in question would be a safer guide for the percentage to be added. In the case of Madras a pretty accurate estimate of the 1931 population was arrived at by the use of the provincial vital statistics, but no other province had anything like such good vital statistics in 1933. Obviously the same principle can be applied to India as a whole and the approximate cost of the whole census similarly estimated at any rate roughly, if no drastic change in method or procedure is to be made. It must be borne in mind that many enumeration charges cannot be met till the following financial year, *e.g.*, bills for printing, T/A bills, etc., and in some cases may not be finally disposed of till the year after that, whereas only *bona fide* government adjustments, *e.g.*, printing bills against Government Presses, can be written back during the six months following the close of the financial year.

Assam, 17.
B. & O., III, 4.
Madras, III. 4.

Census Commissioner's Office.

11. At the start of operations the Census Commissioner will find two or three things essential. The first is to have a capable Financial Assistant accustomed to the Government of India Secretariat procedure and the methods of the Finance Department. Statistical knowledge is not required till a later stage. I started by appointing an assistant with statistical knowledge, but his expert knowledge was largely wasted at the earlier stages. I would recommend no appointment of a Superintendent till later, and that the staff should at the start consist of a Financial Assistant, and a tour clerk who is also a steno-typist, to whom should be added a little later a third clerk preferably with a knowledge of enumeration work in one of the major provinces—Madras, the United Provinces or Bengal. The nucleus of the office should be clerks with permanent posts to revert to, as this nucleus is likely to form also the ultimate remainder, and has less motive for unduly prolonging work and less inclination towards scamping it when the final stages are reached.

For the first three months the Census Commissioner's office should not be in the position of an attached office, but should be started as a branch of the main department. This would allow time to make arrangements for an independent

* This was roughly the average for British India for enumeration exclusive of abstraction and subsequent operations.

supply of stationery, furniture, accommodation, etc. It would obviate the necessity for a third clerk at the beginning as bills would be prepared in the main department, and it would give an opportunity for the Census Commissioner's office to learn its work before making an independent start. Much inconvenience was caused in 1931 by the creation of an independent office at the very outset when neither the Census Commissioner nor his office had any experience of Government of India Secretariat procedure and when forms, stamps, stationery and every sort of information had to be cadged or borrowed from permanent departments.

12. The first thing necessary after legislation has been initiated and the date of the census fixed is to arrange for contracts for paper for enumeration purposes (forms, etc.), in the provinces, as the quantities required and the difficulties involved by the necessity for complying with the requirements of the Controller of Stationery make it necessary to make arrangements a very long way ahead. **Initial Steps.**

Other steps which he must take are indicated in part in Chapter II of the Enumeration Code. The following may be mentioned below, but the dates of these should NOT be taken as a guide at the next census as many of them issued inconveniently late. The Secretariat is apt to take up the position that the date on which a case was dealt with in 1921 is a good guide to the correct date to deal with it in 1931, and to put the file on one side till then. This pernicious doctrine should be killed at the start.

Obtain a Resolution corresponding to No. F.-45-7-30-Pub. of the 7th June 1930.

Write to Local Governments in accordance with Education Department's letter No. 61 of the 13th July 1920 and Home Department's letter No. F.-45/8/30-Pub. of 1st May 1930. **File No. 44-Enmn.**

Arrange for the issue of instructions in accordance with Home Department's Resolution Nos. 254-270 of the 16th August 1910, and Education Department's letter No. 39 of the 22nd April 1920 and E. H. & L.'s, No. 71-L. S. G. of the 19th April 1930. It has already been pointed out that the compulsory powers given over municipalities are not drastic enough.

Obtain resolutions on the lines of Home Department's Nos. F.-45/18/29/Pub., and F.-45/6/30/Pub. of the 9th June 1930.

Obtain Resolutions and authority as in Section 7 on page 9 of the Census Code of 1921 and page 8 of that of 1931.

If the Census of Indians on the High Seas be repeated, the rules should be issued at the earliest possible date so as to enable as many ships as possible to be given schedules. Such rules should not be statutory; there is no means of enforcing them.

Obtain permission for provincial census superintendents to correspond direct with the census officers of States in political relations with the Local Government or Agency or/and with the State Durbars on all matters relating to census.

States, particularly those in Agencies, should be asked through the Political Officers to appoint State Census Officers at the earliest possible date, so that these officers *shall have been appointed* by the time census superintendents are appointed for the Agencies as a whole. **C. I. A., 12, 13. Raj. A.M., I, 1.**

Obtain the earliest possible assent of Government of India to the form of census schedule and of tabulation (including the classification proposed). It is unwise to ask for any alterations that can be avoided. If changes are asked for in the form of *existing* statistics the proposals will be circulated to all departments. This involves incredible delay in obtaining orders; it took more than 7 months in the case of the recent census. It also involves a very large number of troublesome requirements many of which will give much inconvenience to census and do no good to those that ask for them. It is very easy indeed for any one to suggest, for instance, infinite elaborations of the occupational groupings. Their practical value is doubtful as the departments that ask for them ignore Sir Edward Gait's very pertinent and true observation that "the whole (Bertillon) scheme as adapted for India is based on the axiom that a census does not supply data which are suitable for minute classification" (*vide* Volume I, part I, Section 117 of the 1931 Census Report). The best answer is that every elaboration of classification increases the difficulty, the delay and the cost of sorting. This is incontestible. The difficulty could probably be avoided if the position were adopted at the outset that any change in the occupation table would interfere with the comparative value of the figures and that it was therefore intended to continue the existing scheme of classification. Special requests for some definite change, a need for which has been felt by the department asking for it, are on a different footing, *e.g.*, E. H. and Land's request in 1931 for figures of cultivating owners, but such requests should be justified, as many proposals for alteration merely emanate from the fertile brains of someone who considers the scheme can be improved. Anyone can play at this, but it wastes much time.

Madras I, 2, and File No. 63-Enmn. of 1931.

An attempt should be made to obtain special rates from all railways for the carriage of census forms through the Railway Board. This failed in 1931 but should be tried again and, failing success, provinces with a sea-board should be told to arrange for distribution by boat wherever possible instead of by rail. The quantity of paper and forms required to be distributed and redistributed is vast, and refusal of special rates is difficult to understand as the railways depend on census figures for the knowledge of the distribution and density of population which is essential to them for various reasons.

Paper and Printing.

13. The Controller of Stationery's rules will in many cases be found inconvenient, and it was several times found necessary in 1931 to act in anticipation of his sanction. He may want paper to be bought at inconvenient places, and in 1930 he wished the paper for Bombay to be contracted for in Bengal and, as railway freight across India made this obviously prohibitive, he proposed that it should be shipped to Bombay by sea. There is no time for manoeuvres of this kind. Everything in the Census Department as at present constituted has to be carried out against time, and it is in the end cheaper to buy in the nearest market than in a distant if, at first sight, less expensive one. Delay involves great expense in the end, and every month saved in the operations is so much financial saving to Government, while at the enumeration stage a delay in the supply of paper and forms may entirely defeat the synchronization of the census. These are platitudes, but the rules framed by the Department of Stationery and Printing are probably intended for a routine supply, and not designed primarily to meet the suddenness and the haste with which census arrangements must be made *and executed* on a large scale and on a single occasion during a ten year period.

Madras, I, 2. C. P., II. Raj. A.M., I. U. P., 25.

The same applies to printing. Forms, etc., for use in the provinces must be printed there and not at Government of India presses. In the case of Bengal and Assam the Alipur Jail press is recommended, otherwise private presses will be found quicker and cheaper. Government of India presses are quite inadequate to producing the great number of forms required in the time available. Moreover they will not print in vernacular type, and (which is *very* important) they will not distribute direct to district census officers. As for Local Governments' presses, they are far more expensive than private ones and (except Madras) generally less efficient. If the Government of India has to pay for printing, private presses will be found much cheaper than those of local governments. A reference should be made to the 1931 correspondence with the Controller of Printing and Stationery and every effort made to come to an understanding with him at the start. It is very emphatically recommended that paper should be ordered before the Provincial Superintendents are appointed so that a large instalment shall be found waiting for them. Even if enumeration is entirely financed from provincial funds this arrangement should be made, as the Provincial Superintendents want quantities as soon as they are appointed and are in great difficulties if they cannot get it at once. *This involves very early arrangements on the part of the Census Commissioner.*

Powers.

14. The powers delegated to the Census Commissioner in 1931 were very decidedly more restricted than those given at previous censuses, particularly in the matter of appointments and scales of pay. This was probably the inevitable result of the general division of financial sanctions into *voted* and *non-voted*, with Assembly control over voted budgets. At the same time the necessity for a certain amount of decentralization entailed the delegation of certain similar powers to Local Governments. The manner in which the powers were delegated led to the result that in some respects the Census Commissioner was unable to exercise powers in respect to provincial offices that Local Governments could exercise, so that when the Census Superintendents themselves reverted to other employment before the complete closure of their offices, the Census Commissioner had no power to sanction, *e.g.*, honoraria for which the Census Superintendent could have obtained sanction direct from his own Local Government had he still continued in office. It was also found convenient in a number of cases to extend the powers given to the Census Commissioner in the first instance, as otherwise repeated references to the Government of India were required on very trivial matters. It will save trouble in the end if the powers with which Census Commissioner is invested are a little wider at the outset. For the whole subject of Census Commissioner's powers generally see file No. 6-Accts., which will show the subsequent additions made to the original powers of sanction. The rules for audit give a good deal of trouble. Thus the Census Superintendent of Bengal paid a sweeper a small allowance for sweeping out his office in addition to his other work, which was the cheapest method possible. This allowance was paid as a contingent charge, but after passing it for six months audit objected and the matter had to go to the Government of India for sanction. This is only one instance of many similar cases.

Circulars. 15. Excessive inconvenience was caused in 1931 by the failure in 1921, to associate subsequent corrections made with the original circulars issued. The resulting position was that circulars were issued on the lines of those in 1921 and subsequent amendments were found necessary which had already been made in 1921 but of which no knowledge was obtained when the circular first issued in 1931. To remedy this difficulty, a collection (File No. 13-Misc.), was made this time of circulars issued and distributed according to subject instead of date, so that in issuing any circular on the basis of a 1931 circular corrections found necessary subsequently can be ascertained before the original circular is issued. Some of them are worth examination, and the provincial administrative reports will be found exceedingly useful. I advise the careful perusal of them as soon as duties are assumed. *File No. 13-Misc.*

Schedule. 16. Notes with regard to important points in the census schedule, which will have to be decided before it is published, and which is one of the first forms it is necessary to draft, are indicated below :

Community. 17. Columns 4 and 8:—I urge the substitution of a return of *community* instead of that of caste and religion. This in effect abolishes the return of caste. The returns of caste, if obtained, have no statistical value and the attempts of innumerable castes to use the census for purposes for which it was not intended are excessively troublesome. This change would save a vast deal of perfectly futile correspondence (*vide* paragraph 182 of the Report and the file of caste representations in 1931). As for religion, that is no longer entirely coterminous with the communal unit to which a person belongs. There are individuals who may be Muslim or Hindu by association but agnostic by belief and such cross division is likely to increase rather than decrease. A return of community in preference to religion will evade a number of difficulties and I have already given some arguments for it above. The distinction of Arya and Brahmo as separate subheads of Hindu may also be abandoned entirely; it serves no useful purpose and complicates sorting; they should be amalgamated for all purposes with the main head of Hindu, unless they return themselves as non-Hindu. *File No. 1-Enmn. File No. 5-Enmn.*

Sex. 18. I suggest substituting for the sex symbols used in 1931 an open triangle for male and a simple circle for female. These may be treated in one of two ways. Either they should be left blank for unmarried, have a tick put on them for married, and a cross for widowed [*vide* Madras Administrative Report, II, 13]; or be treated as in 1931, substituting a tick for a dot as being quicker, clearer and safer. The reason why I chose to keep the blank symbol for 'married' was that as the married greatly predominate fewer modifications were involved by this course, but I admit the strength of the considerations urged by the Census Superintendent for Madras in section 13 of Chapter II of his Administrative Report in a passage which might well be incorporated into the next census code, if slip-copying be anywhere retained. The experience of the Census Superintendent of Bihar and Orissa (*vide* the Bihar and Orissa Census Report, Chapter VI, 2, and his Administrative Report II, 10) was exceptional and I disagree emphatically with his view that the 1931 system is inferior to that of previous censuses. The change was suggested originally by Mr. Sedgwick in Bombay in the 1921 report and there is no question about the saving in time as well as in slips.

Age. 19. Column 7.—Age was returned in 1931 as age in years to nearest birthday. Previously age last birthday was asked for. The change was made at the instance of the 1921 Actuary, Mr. H. W. Meikle. The age returns were much improved by accepting his recommendations. The 1931, the Actuary, Mr. L. S. Vaidyanathan wishes to have a reversion to the previous return of "age last birthday". Frankly it appears to me absurd to ask for a return in this form in a country like India in which the vast majority have no idea when their birthday is. Only 8 persons in every 100 in 1931 could read and write in the vernacular. Those that know the date of their birth can hardly be as many as 8 per 1,000. The return really received is the approximate age in years. The 1931 actuary considers that the age received is really the age to the last birthday rather than that to the nearest birthday, a view which is open to dispute, though I entirely agree that it makes not the least difference to the returns whether age last, next or nearest birthday is asked for. In either case the method he would apply to obtain smoothed age groups is not the method selected by the 1921 actuary. He has dealt with it in the Annexure to Chapter IV of the 1931 Report. The 1921 actuary, however, has written expressing strong views in favour of the method he adopted himself. Probably the question should be decided in consultation with the actuary who is to examine and report on the returns. This is a point therefore which it would be as well to get decided at once. It is, however, unlikely that an immediate decision on such a point will be possible and on this as well as on general grounds I should recommend that the instructions on the schedule should take this form :—*Age—Here state age in years and months; if precise date of birth unknown, state approximate age in years only*. The result would suit whatever system of grouping is adopted. The reason why the examination was not made in 1931 by the Actuary to the Government of India was that he would not guarantee that the work would not take him so long that it could not be ready for publication with the report, or indeed for a considerable time thereafter. He also required to be given expensive clerical assistance from this office, an unsatisfactory arrangement in my opinion, as I should have had no control over the work done. In consequence the Government of India agreed to pay a sum of Rs. 5,000 down provided the report and life-tables were completed in six months time so that they could be bound with my report. I think it was probably no more costly in the end and a great deal more satisfactory. The correspondence with both actuaries as to the best method of grouping the age returns and the formula for the return will be found in File No. 28-Genl. Two of Mr. Meikle's letters are printed as an appendix to this report.

File No. 28-Genl.

Earner or Dependant.

Assam, 7. C. P., (b). U. P. I, 31.

20. Although this column was a great deal simpler than that for "occupation on which dependent" of previous decades, it seems to have given a good deal of trouble, and the Census Superintendent for one province not only insisted on interpreting "earner" in the sense of "worker" in 1921, which was not intended, but has repeated a recommendation of his definition for his successor at next census in case the same return is called for again. A boy of 10 years is not ordinarily an earner in the sense used by other provinces in 1931. The India code was I admit reprehensible in the matter of the instance taken, which slipped in from the 1921 code, but it should be easy to mend this next time.

Occupation.

Assam, 7. Bihar and Orissa, I, 27. Central Provinces and Berar, 42 (b). Madras, I, 4.

21. Columns 9, 10, 11 and 12 are concerned with occupation. In columns 9, 10 and 11, I recommend retaining the 1931 the form, but should add a proviso that domestic service should not be admitted as a return unless actual earnings in money or kind were received in recompense, and another proviso that where the principal occupation was agricultural a non-agricultural subsidiary occupation should be returned by preference, and vice versa. The term *means of livelihood* should probably be substituted for *occupation*, at any rate in vernacular forms. The definition of industry, if it is to be reserved for organized labour, is a matter of serious difficulty. The return was made but not compiled in 1931. On the whole I am inclined to recommend collecting the necessary statistics on a separate form (as in 1911 and in 1921) but *not simultaneously* with the population census, if that be synchronous.

Language.

22. I should retain both mother tongue and subsidiary language (columns 14 and 15). The latter return gives little trouble and is of great interest. The opinions of superintendents who have recommended its abandonment appear to me parochial. One change in instructions should be made. It should be permissible to return either Urdu or Hindi for the spoken language *in the schedule*; such a instruction will save innumerable protests. Both must still be classified as Hindustani for abstraction purposes since it is not possible to draw any definite line between the two *as spoken languages*. The return of script is a different matter.

23. In the column for literacy I would suggest altering the enquiry to read "script in which literate", and instruct the enumerator to ask for the script (other than English) in which the enumerated would normally write his private correspondence; if none, to enter 'illiterate'. These instructions would enable a correct return of all persons using the Urdu script, and obviate the complaint of many Muslims in 1931 that their national language did not appear in the census returns. Literacy.

24. My recommendation to omit infirmities from the census was not accepted as it was opposed by the D. G., I. M. S. Both the United Kingdom and the United States of America have long abandoned the attempt to record infirmities at the population census, and the figures obtained for India have little absolute value, though a relative value may perhaps be claimed from census to census. If they are retained I should be inclined to advocate a reversion in the case of deafmuteness to the old definition of deafmute from birth but to put it last on the list. It was claimed that the qualification from birth was improperly applied to the other infirmities, but it is clear that its omission has led to the entry of dotards as deafmute. The professor of Opthalmic Surgery in Calcutta Medical College has urged a standard definition of blindness as follows :— Infirmities. Assam, 17. (iii).

> A person who cannot count fingers close to the eye should be counted as blind, a person who cannot count fingers over a distance of one arm's length (3 ft.) from the eyes should be counted as partially blind.

I consider that any attempt to introduce this distinction should be strenuously resisted. It is bad enough to have to record the blind and the introduction of an attempt to record the partially blind will merely destroy what value our present figures have. As for the definition of blind there must be some at any rate who could more easily count fingers held at a slight distance than close to the eye, and Colonel Russell's criticism is that if a man can see any fingers at all he is not blind, whether he can count them or not. He deprecates the introduction of such a definition.

25. The codes have also to be drafted and I should very strongly recommend that the schedule, the enumeration code, and as far as possible the compilation code, should be drafted in time to allow drafts to be sent for criticism to provincial superintendents as soon as they are appointed. This might make it possible to print off a single English version which would serve for all provinces. Great inconvenience will be experienced if the Railway and Cantonment codes are issued later than the main code. There is no need for this provided the departments concerned are approached as soon as possible for their concurrence. If the codes are not issued with the rest it will be found that census charge circles and blocks have to be remade differently, very troublesome to Superintendents of Census Operations. In drawing up the Cantonment Code it has to be remembered that military units and officers are liable to be moved about at short notice without any regard at all for the convenience of enumeration. Consequently it is advisable to keep the methods followed in the census of the purely military population as simple as possible and to avoid the use of block lists, charge lists, etc., which have to be transferred from one unit to another if transfers occur during census operations. The Cantonment Code as framed in 1931 seems to have generally been regarded as a decided improvement on previous codes, though one province dissented from this view. Attention is drawn to the possibility of double enumeration of Railway passengers, an easy means of enhancing communal numbers if communal feeling were strong as it was in the Punjab in 1931. A reference should be made to the Punjab Administration Report for that census. Codes. Rajputana-Ajmer-Merwara, I. Central India Agency, 24. Rajputana-Ajmer-Merwara, I 4. Central Provinces, 54. Punjab, 18. Punjab (1921), 17.

In drawing up the codes the following points are worth attention with particular reference to the administrative reports quoted against each :—

Changes in the schedules.—Where communal feelings are likely to run high, involving attempts to insist by threats on persons returning themselves under other terms than they would use if left to themselves, it may be advisable to prohibit, without the authority of the charge superintendent, any alteration at the final enumeration of returns of community or religion made at the preliminary enumeration. Such orders were found necessary in the Punjab in 1931. File No. 25-Misc. (Confidl.) with particular reference to Punjab.

File No. 44-Enum.

Government Servants and the Census.—Chapter V, Section 12 of Part I of the 1931 Code. It is most inadvisable to agree to any Local Government's granting any general exemption for census work to any class of Government servant. The code needs amendment in that respect. [Madras, I, 3].

District Census Offices.—See Bihar and Orissa Administrative Report I, 10.

Charge Register Abstract.—See Imperial Census Code (1931) V, 9 and Bihar and Orissa Administrative Report I, 18(2).

Household Schedules.—Central Provinces and Berar 44, Bihar and Orissa I, 41; Madras I, 3.

Census Contingent Charges.—Assam, 17.

Slip copying accommodation and furniture.—Assam, 19.

Order of Sorting.—Assam, 32.

Other points in which the code might be amended are suggested in the Bihar and Orissa, Administrative Report I, 41, 43.

Baroda, 69. Bihar and Orissa, I, 13. Madras, I, 8.

Whether the voluntary enumerator system be retained or abolished, I am inclined to think that a system of small prizes for enumeration work would be of a value great out of all proportion to the cost involved, and would do much to stimulate the great amount of unpaid effort which will be needed to obtain a census of India under any system. The printed sanads are no longer valued as they used to be, as they have proved to bring no material advantage in the way of employment.

Census Conference.

26. When Census Superintendents have had a short time to examine the drafts, at any rate of the enumeration code, I would strongly recommend calling a census conference of all superintendents at Delhi. This was a 1931 innovation and proved very useful, but it would have been of very much greater value had it been called at a much earlier stage in the operations, giving superintendents time to see and criticize the draft codes. Incidentally it might have made it possible to frame a combined code, the English version of which would have suited the needs of all provinces, making it possible to print one English version of the code only instead of a code in English as well as in vernacular for each province. The saving in time and expense would probably more than counterbalance the cost of the conference in this respect alone.

Rajputana-Ajmer-Merwara, I, 1.

iii.—Abstraction.

Slip copying.

27. The method since 1901 has been to have the schedules copied out on to slips as described in Chapters I and II of the Census Code, Part II—Tabulation and Compilation. A sample slip is there depicted. The alterations to the sex signs described in Section 3 of the Code (Part II) should be a tick and a cross instead of a dot which is more difficult to make clearly and quickly. Instead of two circles a triangle and a circle would be better.

Baroda, 59—62. Bihar and Orissa, II, 2, 3. Central Provinces, 76, 86. Travancore, 56—59. United Provinces II, 3.

I should recommend that wherever possible the *billets individuels* system be introduced. It is fully described in the Baroda Administrative Report, and Mr. S. V. Mukerjea made a great success of his innovation in that State. It requires, however, better enumerators than are available in many parts of British India, and it also requires very careful training of enumerators, a matter indeed upon which the whole census depends, in any case. Wherever suitable enumerators are available this *billets individuels* system should be used in preference to schedules and slip-copying as it saves at least a month, perhaps even two or three, in time and a great deal in money. One Census Superintendent (B. and O.) was opposed to it, but both the Madras and C. P. Superintendents considered that it could be generally introduced in their provinces with success. If the synchronous census be abandoned, as I have already suggested, it would probably be possible to employ this system wherever there are local village officers of intelligence—*e.g.* throughout most of Madras, and thus effect a great economy. If the census were mechanized, a card, to be punched later, on the lines of the one illustrated at page 6, could conceivably be substituted for the *billet* but I should strongly recommend retaining the schedule in that case. In fact the schedule and a punched card is to be preferred to the *billet* on many grounds. The period occupied by slip copying varies considerably. Ajmer and Rajputana with a population of over 11 million had finished in 1931 by May 2nd; Madras, Bengal, and the United Provinces had finished by the middle of that month, Bihar and Orissa, and Burma by the end of it. Assam and the Central Provinces finished sometime in June but Bombay not till late in June and Hyderabad did not finish until sometime in July. The difference in timing started in slip-copying tends to become progressively increased as operations proceed and is an important factor in delaying the India compilation. If a *de jure* census be substituted for a *de facto* and the village official, patwaris, etc., who undertake the enumeration carefully trained, it should be possible, by the use of *billets individuels*, to eliminate this stage to a considerable extent next census and at subsequent censuses entirely. The total cost of slip-copying in 1931 was approximately Rs. 78,400 for the United Provinces, 16,300 for the Central Provinces, and Rs. 69,600 for Burma. If the census be mechanized the *billet* system will be unsuitable, and the schedule should be retained as suggested above, the enumerators entering code numbers where possible. Punching and coding will then take the place of slip-copying.

All superintendents should be warned in plenty of time that if combustible buildings are used for slip-copying and sorting proper precautions should be taken either to prevent fire or for the keeping of schedules not in use, and of all duplicates in some reasonably fireproof building. It is probably advisable to insure against fire to the extent of the possible cost of repeating the preliminary enumeration, if terms can be obtained which are not prohibitive. Assam, 19. Baroda, 16 (e).

28. Short of mechanization the present system of sorting the slips, which is fully described in the code, does not offer much room for improvement, but if the *billet individuel* is adopted instead of the slip it might be advisable when sorting by religion (or community) to wash each slip with a splash of water-colour, or of coloured ink according to the community of the individual represented in order to make the slips as readily identifiable by community as they are under the present system. A modification, however, will be needed in the case of any tables to be sorted by age. It would have been advisable in 1931, and it would be advisable in 1941, to have the usual sort made for the individual age returns of 100,000 of each sex; for the remainder, sorting into groups is much more economical. The question of the grouping to be adopted for age has been examined exhaustively by the actuary in the annexure to Chapter IV of the report. The question will have to be decided whether these groups should be the same as those adopted for 1931 or should be formed on the '2-6' method recommended by the 1931 actuary. The 1931 method is described in the actuary's report on the 1921 census published by the Government of India in 1926; in the special note, which will be found in the file of circulars (it was one of the first issued); and in Section 7 of Chapter IV of part II of the 1931 Code. It should, however, be pointed out that this paragraph needs one definite amendment. The calculations should not be made to convert "sorters' groups" to "compilers' groups" but should be delayed until the final compilation sheet is to be made up. This will very greatly reduce the number of claculations to be made. The sorters' ticket should therefore not contain the form shown on page 45 but should be designed on the 1921 sorters' ticket, and the form on page 45 should be used for the compilation form only. In deciding as to the method of grouping to be adopted it will be well to take into consideration Mr. Meikle's views as well as those of Mr. Vaidyanathan. The views of the latter will be found as indicated above. Mr. Meikle's views are embodied in the letters printed at the end of this report. It is worth considering whether the varying advantages of the two methods advocated may not depend on the nature of the decade experienced. It will be noticed from Mr. Vaidyanathan's analysis that the ternary-septenary grouping advocated by Mr. Meikle would have been the most suitable in 1891 when conditions during the past 10 years had been similar to those of the decade 1921-31, whereas the 2-6 method was best in the intervening decades when the years were unprosperous and the age constitution of the population was different. Perhaps the most important point for the census, however, is that the method of transforming the sorters' groups to the compilers' groups should be essentially simple, and provided the statistical results of the two methods do not show a very marked preference for one or the other, the choice should be determined by ease of transmutation. As Mr. Vaidyanathan's Table XXI does not show very cleary the method by which the original groups are transferred to quinquennial groups of 1·5, 5-10, etc., a table is here inserted (for comparison with that on page 45 of part II of the 1931 census code) which will give the results required by Mr. Vaidayanathan. In either case odd numbers remaining on division should be relegated to the lower age group, Sorting. File No. 13-Misc.

as no allowance is made for mortality in this arithmetical adjustment. Which method of grouping should be adopted is a matter for determination when the next code is framed.

Compilation form for Table of age.

Sorter's age group.		Number of Persons. Unmd.	M.	W.	Formula.		Compiler's age group.	Number of Persons. Unmd.	M	W.
0	A				A	=	0 ..			
1	B				B	=	1 ..			
2	C				C	=	2 ..			
3	D				D	=	3 ..			
4	E				E	=	4 ..			
5	F				F+G+3/5 H	=	5—9 ..			
6	G				2/5 H+3/5 I	=	10—14 ..			
7—11	H				2/5 I+3/5 J	=	15—19 ..			
12—16	I				2/5 J+3/5 K	=	20—24 ..			
17—21	J				2/5 K+3/5 L	=	25—29 ..			
22—26	K				2/5 L+3/5 M	=	30—34 ..			
27—31	L				2/5 M+3/5 N	=	35—39 ..			
32—36	M				2/5 N+3/5 O	=	40—44 ..			
37—41	N				2/5 O+3/5 P	=	45—49 ..			
42—46	O				2/5 P+3/5 Q	=	50—54 ..			
47—51	P				2/5 Q+3/5 R	=	55—59 ..			
52—56	Q				2/5 R+3/5 S	=	60—64 ..			
57—61	R				2/5 S+3/5 T	=	65—69 ..			
62—66	S				2/5 T+U	=	70 and over			
67—71	T									
72 and over	U									
Total ..							Total ..			

The question of the sort for age has to be carefully considered with reference to Civil Condition and to any other table (*e.g.*, Literacy) in which classification by age is adopted. A reference to paragraph 92 of the Report will indicate the disturbance caused in the figures of civil condition by the application of the actuary's method of age grouping, a disturbance which was unfortunately not foreseen when the method was adopted. In the correspondence with Mr. Meikle appended to this report a method of treating the age groups to get accurate figures for civil condition is suggested by him. In my opinion it would be enough to apply his method to the age groups from 4 to 23 years, the remaining groups being accurate enough for all sociological purposes even under the biased grouping used in 1931. Instead of Mr. Meikle's mathematical formula, however, it would be possible to obtain a sufficiently accurate result by sorting *ab initio* into the following groups :—0 or A, 1 or B, 2 or C, 3 or D, 4-6 or E, 7 and 8 or F, 9-11 or G, 12 and 13 or H, 14-16 or I, 17 and 18 or J, 19-21 or K, 22 and 23 or L, 24-26 or M, 27-33 or N and thereafter in alternate ternary and septenary groups as in the scheme on page 45 of part II of the 1931 census code. For purposes of age, the numbers in F, G and H and in J, K and L can be combined to form septenary groups equivalent to F and H respectively in the scheme referred to. For the purposes of civil condition on the other hand they would be combined as follows to form compilers groups :—

Age group—

3-4 $= \frac{1}{2}$ D $+$ 1/6 E

4-5 $=$ 1/3 E

5-10 $= \frac{1}{2}$ E $+$ F $+ \frac{1}{2}$ G

10-15 $= \frac{1}{2}$ G $+$ H $+ \frac{1}{2}$ I

15-20 $= \frac{1}{2}$ I $+$ J $+ \frac{1}{2}$ K

20-25 $= \frac{1}{2}$ K $+$ L $+ \frac{1}{2}$ M

25-30 $= \frac{1}{2}$ M $+ \frac{1}{2}$ N

and thereafter as in the scheme of 1931. This method gives very much better results in the case of civil condition than the rougher one followed in 1931, and it is probable that it is more accurate than direct sorting for civil condition into quinquennial groups. For the sake of comparison the method has been applied to the Gwalior figures given in paragraph 92 of the census report (Chapter VI) and the results arrived at are compared below with those obtained by the original method of sorting into quinquennial groups which are weighted by the preferential digit bias, and undoubtedly very inaccurate, and with those obtained by the 1931 method which are unduly weighted by the halving of the septenary groups, as there explained. In comparing these figures it should be understood that the old *pre*-1931 method has not been followed precisely as the original sort was not into groups of those aged 0-1, 1-2, etc., but into groups of those aged 0-6 months, 6 months to 18 months, 18 months to 2½ years, etc., and allowance had to be made for this—

Age group.	Method of grouping.	Total figures of age group.	Total number of males. married or widowed.	Ratio of married, etc., per 1,000.	Total number of females married or widowed.	Ratio of married, etc., per 1,000 of 1931 age group.
3—4	of 1931 ..	100,749	796	8	1,767	18
	of 1921 ..	98,617	785	8	1,519	15
	here suggested.	100,749	796	8	1,767	18
4—5	of 1931 ..	98,699	988	10	2,275	23
	of 1921 ..	100,577	930	9	2,050	21
	here suggested.	98,699	988	10	2,275	23
5—10	of 1931 ..	447,808	16,918	38	45,331	101
	of 1921 ..	468,568	9,748	22	27,297	61
	here suggested.	461,031	10,257	23	28,428	63
10—15	of 1931 ..	430,180	41,563	97	92,723	216
	of 1921 ..	390,623	41,004	95	100,872	234
	here suggested.	416,954	48,223	112	109,626	255

It is therefore recommended that if the 1931 method of grouping be retained at next census it should be dealt with as indicated above for the purpose of determining the numbers of married and widowed in each age group, the unmarried being determined by the subtraction of the married and widowed thus obtained from the total of the age group *computed by the 1931* method. Obviously it is necessary that the total age group should tally throughout, and it is *only in the case of civil condition* that the above method is more accurate than that of 1931. From this point of view any formula which would serve equally well for both age and civil condition is much to be preferred. For the sake of comparison I give the results of the same Gwalior figures as they would appear treated by the method of grouping suggested by Mr. Vaidyanathan :—

Age group.	Total figures.	Number of males married or widowed.	Ratio.	Number of females married or widowed.	Ratio.
3	102,798	603	6	1,258	12
4	94,436	967	10	1,780	19
5—9	458,961	10,500	23	29,384	64
10—14	430,448	47.041	109	103,155	240

A similar modification of this method could perhaps be used for civil condition on the following plan. For Mr. Vaidyanathan's age groups the following may be substituted :—

3=D, 4=E, 5=F, 6=G, 7+8=H, 9+10+11=I, 12+13=J, 14+15+16=K.

Then for the sort for civil condition we may take—

Age group—

3=D

4=E

5-9=F+G+H+1/3 I.

10-14=2/3 I+J+1/3 K

The result works out as follows :—

Age group.	Number of males married or widowed.	Ratio calculated on groups according to Mr. Vaidyanathan's figures.	Number of females married or widowed.	Ratio per 1,000 of Mr. Vaidyanathan's age group.
3	603	6	1,258	12
4	967	10	1,780	19
5—9	8,973	20	24,878	54
10—14	41,312	96	97,874	227

It is to be noted that the ratios have throughout been calculated on the total age group not on the age group of the sex concerned. This has been done to save trouble as the ratios are merely used as a standard of comparison. It is assumed that whatever system of grouping is adopted the age group will be determined purely from the point of view of age and will be kept constant for other tables as the total of the numbers at that age.

It will be seen that the variation between the figures for civil condition according to Mr. Vaidyanathan's method of grouping in its original form and in the proposed adjustment do not vary very greatly, and if it can be held that this variation is immaterial and that the figures in the original grouping are accurate enough to be taken as they are, for they are nearer than the modified figures are to figures obtained by Mr. Meikle's method, then this is a strong argument for the adoption or Mr. Vaidyanathan's grouping. On general grounds, however, I should prefer Mr. Meikle's method. The grouping may have to be carried out by unskilled and rather stupid persons. The division of each sorted age group into two halves leaves less room for confusion and error than when the division is into 2/5 and 3/5 which may too easily be interchanged and give rise to errors which will never be discovered. Perhaps the greatest disadvantage in adopting Mr. Vaidyanathan's method is that it means another break in continuity weakening the comparative values of successive censuses. Some change there had to be, for the Indian age groups were clearly absurd as they stood, but if changes are made without finality, continuity and comparative value will be lost and on that ground alone I should recommend adhering to the 1931 method of age grouping, while obtaining the numbers of married and widowed at each age by some such method as has been here suggested. An actuary's advice would be worth having, provided the method he proposes is not only simple but reasonably foolproof.

Compilation.

29. The compilation of the India Tables must wait on those of the provinces, and their irregular and dilatory submission often prevents the final completion of tables which wait the returns of a single unit some times for months. I recommend that next time the compilation of subsidiary tables should be taken up simultaneously with that of India Tables. It would be found greatly to facilitate the writing of the report, and it is convenient to start this early as the census commissioner has little but routine work while tabulation is proceeding. On this occasion I had to work out my own proportional figures with a mechanical calculator in order to form my conclusions and get on with the report, and they needed checking (and a good deal of correction) afterwards.

It is important that census superintendents should pay attention to the form taken by the India Tables. They did not all do this in 1931, and I had omitted to warn them to do so. The result was that I had great difficulty in separating some of the figures for provinces and states and in getting correct figures for the previous populations of cities, towns and cantonments. It is important that the census should provide self-governing urban units with the exact figure of the population with which each self-governing unit deals. It is also necessary for certain purposes to have inclusive figures of large urban areas which may contain more than one municipality. These two aspects have to be kept in mind in framing definitions of 'City' and 'Town.' Failure, however, to keep these two aspects of urban figures separate in some provinces made it very difficult to correlate the figures of self-governing units shown in Table IV to the figures of migration, literacy, occupation, etc., as tabulated for cities. Similarly some provinces failed to distinguish in all cases between the figures of British territory and those of states, a distinction which is required for all the India Tables. Again some difficulty was caused in states by the confusing of groups 159 and 160 of the occupation scheme. I would recommend the introduction of another group at that point and of calling 159 *Servants of the State* (*i.e.*, of the Imperial, British India or Provincial Government) while splitting up No. 160 into *Servants of Indian States* and *Servants of Foreign States.* All Indian States should then be instructed to return their own servants in the second of the three groups. If they require a separate count of their own servants they can subdivide it for state purposes. As it was in 1931, some returned them in 159 and others in 160 and the correct figures could not thereafter be obtained for the India Tables.

I would suggest that India Table IV should be reduced next census, though not of course the corresponding table in the provincial volumes. It would probably be enough in the case of India to tabulate individually the towns of classes I and II at most for that table, retaining the individual tabulation of class III in Table V. Several of the subsidiary tables in the report volume could also be omitted without any serious loss, and it is worth considering how far it is necessary (where they are not required to illustrate the text) to reproduce tables, *e.g.*, of vital statistics from other reports.

The actuary's report was perhaps unusually long at this census. It should not be necessary to print so long an actuarial report next time.

30. The following notes are recorded with reference to compilation of Imperial Tables as they may be found useful when drafting the code. **Notes on Tables.**

Table I.—The necessity of obtaining correct areas from the Survey Department at the earliest possible date has already been mentioned. It is to be noted that the number of towns has to correspond with the numbers given in Table IV, and cantonments and civil lines, etc., which are treated for that table, as separate towns on account of their possession of individual self-governing bodies must also be treated as separate units for this table. The areas of British administration in different states which appear in the appended statements should be verified through the Foreign and Political Department at the earliest opportunity.

Table II.—Great care has to be taken in the case of all units affected by transfers of areas since the previous census. When compiling one is liable to find that the adjusted populations of various units for previous decades when taken collectively do not add up to the corresponding unadjusted totals. Much trouble is given to the central compiling staff which could easily be avoided if provincial offices would take care that their figures were correct. The discrepancies in the totals are not always apparent till India total is struck. It would be well if definite instructions were given that the provincial figures should be verified before the preliminary totals were submitted to the central compiling office.

Table III.—This table should not be compiled till after the compilation of Table IV has been approved, any alteration in Table IV naturally affecting the compilation of Table III. Much trouble was caused in 1931 by provinces having ignored the instructions to keep municipalities and cantonments separate; having amalgamated them for Table III they had to be separated for Table IV, and then Table III had to be changed, as also Table V.

Table IV.—It would be well to compile this table before Tables I, III, or V are taken up. It should also be pointed out that much inconsistency has occurred in the past in the treatment of the totals of classes for the past decades. Obviously if the totals under classes are adjusted for past decades to fit the towns that appear below them, these totals can have no meaning whatever, since they represent no population total that ever existed or that now exists; consequently the totals of classes for past decades should be retained unaltered, so that they represent the numbers of persons living in the towns of that particular class at that particular time. Owing to the fact that some of the towns will have changed to another class either by increase or decrease since that time, the total will not correspond to the totals appearing below it in the same column; it will however have some meaning, which it will certainly not have if it is adjusted, and it would be better to omit the total altogether than to adjust it. Special instructions should perhaps be issued to Aden, whose urban and rural (if any) figures have given much trouble at the last two censuses, owing to the absence of clear distinctions between different urban and cantonment units particularly in regard to their decennial variation. The statement appended to Table IV should be scrutinized by the Army Department.

Table VI.—Much trouble was caused in the India compilation of this table by the fact that provinces had ignored the form in which the India table was to be compiled. They were all told, but they did not all obey the instructions. Consequently they were unable to give the necessary information for this table, which under the instructions of the Government of India was to be compiled in much more detail for all India than for the Provinces, since it was considered that the details, omitted in the abbreviated form prescribed for provincial reports, were necessary in the India Tables. If the 1931 form of the table be retained, it is recommended that after columns 2, 3 and 4, as they appear in 1931, corresponding columns should be inserted for Provinces, and another for states after columns 47—49. This will provide figures for intermigration between provinces and states and a check for the table the absence of which gave trouble in 1931.

In connection with this table it may also be pointed out that the provinces failed to supply one another with proper migration figures, consequently their figures of inter-provincial migration differ from and are less complete than those available for the India Tables.

Table IX.—Here again the provinces failed to keep in mind the requirements of the India Tables. Separate details for States and British districts were required for both parts of this table and also a detailed record of dual infirmities, making it possible for those with multiple infirmities to be distinguished from the numbers recorded with single infirmities. This also should have been sufficiently clear from the instructions which were not always regarded.

Table X.—Here again separate details are required for states and for agencies as distinct from British territory. Suggestions have already been made as to the classification of groups 159 and 160. Group 192 also gave considerable trouble because the provinces failed to pay attention to the instructions given. Possibly they did not always approve of those instructions, but that was no reason for ignoring them. The result was that it was not possible to get complete figures of inmates of jails distinguished according to whether they were suffering sentences of rigorous or simple imprisonment.

In printing this table in the India Tables in 1931 complete details were given by sex for all groups. It would be worth considering the reduction of the size of this table in part II only (Part I is not excessive) by giving complete details by sex for orders only and reducing the columns under groups to persons instead of showing males and females.

Table XI.—Here again some provinces made the inclusion of their figures in the India Tables impossible by not following instructions. The heading of sub-class 12 in the sorters' ticket for this table might be modified by the exclusion of the words 'Inmates of jails and asylums'.

Table XIII.—Trouble was given in this table by failure to follow instructions as to the treatment of those returned as illiterate for purposes of this table. For the sake of continuity it is probable that the percentage of literacy will again be calculated on population aged 5 and over, and though the total population may be shown in this table that part of it which is aged under 5 should appear as illiterate and the figures for literacy should not contain any persons whose age was under 5.

Separate details for Aryas and Brahmos should probably be omitted. It is doubtful if they serve any purpose, and I suggest that even if tabulation by religion is retained Hindus should be tabulated without sub-totals. Separate figures for Indian Christians on the other hand are frequently asked for, and are unavailable under the existing code unless special instructions are issued. This was overlooked in 1931 with the result that accurate figures for Indian Christians are absent. Provincial offices should be forcibly reminded (if tabulation by religion is retained) that separate details are required for India tables of the religions included by them under the head 'Others'. In some provinces religions which are important for India purposes may be almost entirely negligible, but when compiling India tables details of these (to them negligible items) are required, and several of them ignored this possibility.

Table XV.—Classification should be checked clearly before compiling and provinces might be warned not to make returns of people whose language is shown as "Swiss" or "Belgian"; both these were used in 1931 as synonyms for a Teutonic language, but they are not justified by the conventional linguistic nomenclature, and it is only the provinces that can make certain whether persons returned as speaking these languages are really speakers of German, French or Italian in the one case, or of Flemish or French in the other.

The treatment of Hindustani is a point that needs special consideration. The same applies to Punjabi and Western Punjabi or Lahnda. In 1931 speakers of Hindustani were classified for the India Table as speakers of Eastern, Mediate or Western Hindi according to the area from which the return came, the area being determined by the Linguistic Survey. The same system was applied as far as possible to Punjabi and Lahnda. In the one case all the returns, even those of Bihari, appear either as Hindi or Urdu and in the other case most of them appear as Punjabi and the other return of Jatki is in itself ambiguous.

Table XVI.—Here again care has to be taken that the provinces give full details by British territory and by States of minor religions and religions not returned, which they are inclined to amalgamate for their own purposes.

Table XVII.—This table will not appear if my recommendation to omit the return of caste, at any rate for compilation purposes, be accepted. In any case the returns cannot be regarded as accurate and they will become less accurate from census to census.

Table XVIII.—If this table which from certain points of view is of some importance be retained (as I am inclined to recommend that it should be retained for tribes only, omitting castes) it would probably be enough to give the variation from 1931 only. The previous figures in so far as they are obtainable have been recorded in 1931, but they are seriously defective, whereas the 1931 figure ought to make a correct starting point. In the provincial tables it will probably be possible and advantageous to go further back, but not for the Imperial Tables.

Table XIX.—Most provinces in 1931 omitted to keep the separate total for Armenians for purposes of the India Tables.

31. In the matter of accuracy from the point of view of supplying the necessary data for the India Tables the Burma Tables stood first in 1931 with Madras second. Among the provinces the Punjab Tables came last, and among the States Hyderabad and Jammu and Kashmir were rivals for that place. I consider that the cheapest method of compiling the India Tables, and by cheapest I mean quickest, as long as the present system is in vogue would be to have half a dozen extra men in the Assistant Grade who really knew what they were going to do and how to do it. To give them experience I should engage these men and depute them each to a different province when the provinces were at the sorting stage. As soon as the India compilation started in earnest they would be brought to headquarters and each one given an assistant who would be quite a cheap compiler of matriculation standard merely for purposes of a human addiator. The betwixt and between class, neither one thing nor the other, are too expensive for addiators and not good enough for real compilers, they need too much supervision and assistance. For the Head compiler, if one was still found necessary, or if not at any rate for one or two of the compiler assistants it would probably be advisable to have men with permanent posts to which they would ultimately revert. **Compilation suggestions.**

One more point is of great importance with regard to the India compilation, and that is that all provinces and states should give totals and sub-totals for all their tables. The Bombay tables were possibly the completest in this respect, and finding complete totals for the provinces, for British districts and for states all separable and readily available makes a great difference to the rate at which the India Tables can be compiled. The necessity of striking sub-totals from provincial tables for the purposes of the India tables, as had to be done with several of the provincial tables, *e.g.*, Bihar and Orissa, was most inconvenient and caused much delay. Similarly in the case of the states the India summary of Table VII was held up from June to September, because Jammu and Kashmir State could not supply details of religions included as 'Others', which should have been available from the first.

iv.—Finance.

32. Several points of the general financial position have already been alluded to, but one will bear repetition and that is that it cannot be stated too emphatically that enumeration should be a provincial charge. The question really arose in an acute form in 1931 for the first time. In 1921 census was not made a central charge until after the enumeration stage was over, and even then neither provincial governments, nor audit officers nor district officers at once appreciated in full the implications of the change ; the result was that all sorts of census expenditure which could have been debited to the central government was in point of **Enumeration a provincial charge.**

fact debited to provincial governments as usual. These charges included the travelling allowance of all Local Government officers and all the minor stationery used on census work in districts. In 1931 however the idea of certain debits being made to central funds was unfortunately familiar, and few failed to seize the golden opportunity, so that in addition to census travelling at the expense of the Central Government and the debit to the Central Government of various minor items of stamps and stationery on a scale which may have been insignificant locally but soon mounted up when the whole of India and Burma were concerned, the central expenditure was further affected by the inevitable slackening of control by officers whose own budgets were not concerned at all. It would be impossible to sidetrack the district officer and his staff for census purposes or to carry out a census without their co-operation, but although the services of the district census officers were given free by local governments the position was very different from that in which the district magistrate was directly responsible for district census expenditure to his own local government. Further, even where the district officer did his best to follow the rather belated instructions that all census touring was to be combined with other work and therefore not charged to the Central Government, audit officers discovered themselves most inconveniently assiduous in detecting census work combined with other activities and in insisting on debiting to the Central Government a share sometimes unfairly large of the touring expenses affected. In this connection reference should be made to the following census Administrative Reports for 1931—Assam, 17 (*i*), Bihar and Orissa, III 4, Central Provinces and Berar, 4, Madras, I, 2, and III, 3 and 4. The conclusion is inescapable that enumeration should be an entirely provincial charge. The same arguments do not apply to the abstraction stages where the control is concentrated in a few offices under the direct administration of the census superintendents, though they might apply in a very modified degree to slip-copying if carried out, as in the Punjab, at tahsil headquarters. If the census were mechanized then the best arrangement would probably be for the province to pay the costs of the census down to the completion of card-punching, when the punched cards would be sent to the central sorting office for the extraction of totals ; that is to say that the equivalent of the enumeration stage down to and including slip-copying would be a provincial charge, and on this score it might be better in any case to include the slip-copying stage with enumeration.

Cost.

33. A method of computing the cost of census operations on the present lines has been indicated above (paragraph 11). Whatever method be followed it would be useful as a guide to local governments in making their estimate for the first stage which has to be done before the census superintendents are appointed. Estimates for the later stages are made by the superintendents. A statement showing in as much detail as possible the cost of the 1931 census in British India is appended. Some attention is required to travelling allowance rules for Census Superintendents who have to do a great deal of touring at the enumeration stage. In this connection a scheme was prepared by Mr. Tennant who had some experience himself of the touring done by a gazetted officer during the enumeration stage of the census, and it would be as well to apply the same or a similar scheme next time, as the ordinary rules are by no means always the fairest or the most economical when much touring ought to be done by road which can (but should not) be done by rail.

Madras. III. 4.

The cost of the 1931 census works out at Rs. 48,000,000 as far as can be determined at the time of going to press, that is to say at Rs. 12 per 1,000 persons enumerated and tabulated. This is to be compared with Rs. 14 per 1,000, the cost of the 1921 census, when the two are reduced to the same basis as far as possible. Really however the cost of the 1931 census was considerably less than that of 1921 when all travelling allowances and much stationery at the enumeration stage were debited to provincial administrations and not to the Government of India at all. Also on that occasion the overhead charges for printing were not debited to census and their inclusion in costing since 1921 has made the debit for printing to the census grant more than double in 1931 what it was in 1921, though the real difference in cost cannot have been anything like so great. Had the debits on account of enumeration costs and printing been made on the same principles as in 1921, the census of 1931 would have shown a very pronounced reduction in the cost per mille of population censused. A detailed statement of expenditure and receipts is appended to this report. Reference may also be made to the introduction to the general report where the question of cost is briefly discussed. In estimating the cost the populations of the seven states which take their own census independently have been excluded from the calculations and also all population not actually enumerated in 1931.

v.—*Miscellaneous.*

34. It will be found very useful to have a map made out at the start showing the geographical census units and to have a number of copies printed in blue on drawing paper. If ordinary paper is used it is difficult to make any alteration in the ink drawing. Printing in blue makes it very simple to insert or omit any feature of the maps at will, as the blue matter will not show in reproduction. It will be found convenient to have this blue map printed by the Survey of India, but for the making of blocks, whether for printing maps in black or for diagrams and graphs, the Calcutta Chromotype Co., of 52-53 Bowbazar, Calcutta, will be found much quicker and cheaper. For elaborate coloured maps, such as the three coloured maps in the 1931 report, the Survey of India is better as they are able to use their own existing plates to form the basis of the map. **Maps.**

35. No superintendent should be allowed to waste money on addiator typewriters. Both at this census and at last census they have been tried in one province or another and have proved comparatively useless as the totals to be added are more horizontal than vertical. Calculating machines are a necessity and a Dalton addiator will be useful as well as a " Britannic " or " Muldivo " calculator, but it should not be combined with a typewriter. A cylindrical " Fuller's Calculating Slide Rule " is invaluable for working out ratios and proportions and for rapid division and saves a great deal of time and labour at the later stages of the census, while I consider that the Rs. 18 spent on a little Otis-King calculator, which enabled me to work out ratios roughly when examining the figures before the subsidiary tables were ready, saved Government considerably more than Rs. 1,800. Both these patterns are obtainable from the Mathematical Instrument Officer, and the ones used this time have been put away for next census : the Otis-King may need to have the figures renewed ; when in use it is enough to clean them from time to time with petrol. **Calculating machines.**

36. There are a number of minor errors in some of the lists and schemes issued in 1931. No 1931 list or scheme should be reissued without reference to the file by subjects and the correction slips issued, while in some cases, *e.g.*, language, mistakes have not been corrected and the scheme needs checking by the actual tables in part II. The same applies to the occupational list, and to some extent to the occupational key. The figures of area given in the 1931 Report and Tables are already out of date at the time of writing, and the latest authoritative figures of area should be obtained from the Survey of India for all provinces and states down to the figures of individual districts and states before the compilation stage of the census is reached and circulated at once, as subsequent alterations are exceedingly difficult to carry out, a change in the area of one province alone, when possible changes in contiguous areas are unknown, invalidating the India figures. **Erroneous lists.**

37. Considerable expense and trouble were saved in printing in 1931 by changes in the format of the tables. The omission of vertical rules saves the press much trouble and in consequence makes for speed as well as economy. Vertical rules are obviously unnecessary except where the totals are so high that the columns tend to become contiguous. In such cases vertical rules may be needed, but it is necessary to insert them from the start, as once the long horizontal leads are inserted vertical rules cannot be inserted without breaking up and resetting the page. For this reason they were not inserted in the 1931 occupation table, where it is obvious that rules separating India totals, British India and States would have made part I of the occupation table much easier to follow. **Printing.**

There were other minor points in which printing could have been made much easier had the difficulties been realized beforehand. Thus in the case of maps inset in the text it would have been a great advantage to have adhered to a single size for all inset maps. The use of a uniform base of 5 3/5 inches in length for all text maps would have given maps exactly fitting the width of the print and would have avoided the difficulty of setting narrow margins of type without any loss of appearance. Some of the maps inset in the text of the 1931 report are too small and some unnecessarily large. By using maps of the size suggested many of the difficulties of overruning in the press could be avoided. The same principle could advantageously be applied to many of the graphs and diagrams.

Another point arises in the matter of marginal captions. The use of these in 1931 made the matter too wide to go on a normal eight page machine, and so delayed printing in that way; besides making the type more difficult to set up. Shoulder notes -in which the marginal caption is given inside the text instead of in the margin- are said by the press to give less trouble on the whole than marginal captions, though I had avoided them because I thought they would be more troublesome. Easiest of all for the press to deal with would be bold type at the beginning of the paragraph—as in the Baroda report for instance, and it would probably be found worth while to adopt this method at another census.

In any case a preliminary consultation with the Manager of the press would be found of great value, and if blocks other than line blocks are to be used his assistance is essential, as he can advise on the screen to be used by the block-makers in reproducing. The block-maker normally prints on art paper, but for printing on paper of various textures different screens should be used and the block-maker instructed accordingly. Neglect of this precaution spoiled some of the 1931 blocks.

Records.

38. The census records have for the most part been sealed up and entrusted to the care of the Imperial Record Keeper in Delhi. There they are to remain in boxes until the next census commissioner assumes office. A few files to which references were likely to be needed have been made over to the Home Department and can be obtained from them. On previous occasions the census records have been unscrupulously looted during the intercensal period, which accounts for the incompleteness of printed census volumes of past decades. For this reason I have tried to put the 1931 records beyond the reach of interference. The file that contains the sorted series of circulars by subjects also contains a complete file index and the draft of a note on census administration drawn up by the superintendent of my office, which is worth perusal as supplementary to this report.

File No. 1S, IX.

A new use for Census Reports.

39. One of the census superintendents has suggested that the Provincial Census Report including the Administrative Report should be a prescribed subject for the departmental examinations for Indian Civil Service and Police probationers. The suggestion seems a sound one and might be brought to the notice of the Public Services Commission in case they can make similar use of the idea in connection with the India Report. At least it might increase sales. There has also been voiced from time to time a demand for an abridged edition of the census Report in octavo form, for which it is likely that there would be a ready sale if the price were moderate.

APPENDIX I.

Copy of a letter from the Census Superintendent, Central Provinces and Berar, to the Census Commissioner for India, No. 1600, dated the 17th September 1931:

I am sending for your information a copy of a paragraph in the rough draft of the first part of my Administrative Report. As the matter is one regarding which you may have received different opinions from other provinces, I thought it would be interesting at this stage to know what your own views are. I asked for a book of *Billets Individuels* from Baroda which I have now received and personally I see no reason why the system should not at the next Census be worked successfully in this province with the resultant saving of time and money. It appears to me that the only extra sorting necessitated is the separation of slips by religion and as I suggested to you at Bastar, it would be possible to identify the separate religions after the first sorting by drawing a distinguishing line over each kind in water colour paint.

The enumerators were all honorary workers and generally non-officials. What actually happened in the rural area was that in almost every case the patwaris themselves wrote up the preliminary record for all the blocks in their circles and the enumerators went round and checked it on the night of the census. This system produced records which were in many places almost perfect, except when there was some difficulty in understanding instructions, and such being the case I would strongly advise the adoption in Central Provinces at the next census of the system of *Billets Individuels* which entirely eliminates slip-copying and is explained in the chapter on that subject.

In towns where the Land Records Staff was not available for Census work results were incomparably inferior to those in rural areas, and I would therefore recommend that in 1941 paid supervisors should be appointed for a period of three months. They would be able to prepare a complete preliminary record, which would be checked by honorary enumerators on the night of the Census as is now generally done in rural areas. Charge Superintendents could be drawn as heretofore from Municipal officials or Government servants. If this system is adopted it should be possible to use *Billets Individuels* in towns also, thus saving a large sum on slip-copying which would more than balance the expenditure on paid supervisors.

APPENDIX II.

Extract from a letter from Mr. Meikle (late Actuary to the Govt. of India), to the Census Commissioner for India, dated the 15th December 1932.

With regard to the defect to which you refer when the system is applied to Civil Condition I would suggest a sub-division of each septenary group at those portions of the table where the incidence in the numbers from age to age varies at a rapid rate, such as in the 7-13 group where the married and the unmarried are being dealt with separately. Instead of combining the figures for seven ages in a single group it should be divided into three parts, *viz.*, 7 and 8, 9, 10 and 11 and 12 and 13. All the old ternary groups would of course, remain unaltered, as well as the septenary groups at the older ages. I presume there will possibly be two, or at the most three septenary groups which would require sub-division in the way here suggested. It will generally be found that in the septenary group 7-13 the largest shortage is at age 13, and the largest excess at age 12—the one being about equal to the other. The next largest shortage is at 11, then at 9. The second largest excess is at 10, thereby indicating the soundness of combining the numbers at 12 and 13 in one group, those at 9 and 11 with those at 10 for the middle group, and 7 combined with 8 for the remaining group. Similar results are seen in the higher septenary groups. This method of grouping gives more trustworthy results, or rather less misleading results, than if we relied more on the numbers in individual age groups. In order to arrive at the numbers in each quinary group it becomes necessary to divide the new ternary groups 9-11 into those under exact age 10 and those over that age. This can be done with considerable accuracy by the use of the following formula :—

If groups 7 and 8, *i.e.*, those over $6\frac{1}{2}$ and under $8\frac{1}{2}$ be represented by *a*
those over $11\frac{1}{2}$ and under $13\frac{1}{2}$ be represented by *b*
those over $8\frac{1}{2}$ and under 10 be represented by *c*
those over 10 and under $11\frac{1}{2}$ be represented by *d*

we know a, b and (c+d) and require to find c and d. Then $c = (c+d)\left\{\frac{\cdot 65a + \cdot 35b}{a+b} + \cdot 01\right\}$ d will of course be equal to the balance of the group (c+d) and should be calculated for the purpose of a check by the formula $d = (c+d)\left\{\frac{\cdot 35a + \cdot 65b}{a+b} - \cdot 01\right\}$. I am certain you will find this worthy of adoption for the next Census.

Extract from a letter from Mr. Meikle, to the Census Commissioner for India, dated the 21st March 1933.

Mr. Vaidyanathan tells me he is recommending the 4th-place method of quinary grouping of ages for adoption in future. I agree that *provided* the preliminary grouping *must* be quinary then the 4th place method gives a better balance of error than any other form of quinary grouping (see the last 6 lines on page 30 of my report)—also that from data grouped in that way it is possible—though not easy—to redistribute it into the ordinary form of quinary grouping with the quinquennial ages in the 1st place. This is shown in Table XV on page 33 of my report. That, however, is not the way to consider the problem. In my mind the problem is the determining of a form of preliminary grouping not necessarily of 5 ages in each group—which will enable non-experts to redistribute the data, with ease and reasonable accuracy into the ordinary form of quinary grouping and in a form suitable for dealing with some of the problems connected with Civil Condition, and also which will enable the expert, afterwards, to arrive at an accurate redistribution according to individual ages. I shall be very surprised if Mr. Vaidyanathan's report will prove that for either of these purposes there is any method so good as that suggested in my note of 17th October 1929, amended as stated in my recent letter to you and in two long letters to him. As septenary groups have been found to be inconveniently large let some or even all of them be replaced by two groups of 2 ages and one of 3. The groups would then be as follows :—

0
1
2
3
4, 5 and 6
7 and 8
9, 10 and 11 (nearest ages in every case).
12 and 13
14, 15 and 16 and so on in twos and threes

alternately right on to group 69, 70 and 71 inclusive. These ternary groups can afterwards be split up and regrouped in the way suggested in my last letter to you. I hope you wont mind my expressing to you my strongly held opinion on the matter.

Extract from a letter from Mr. Meikle, to the Census Commissioner for India, dated the 29th April 1933.

I have looked over the copy of my letter of 21st March to you and am satisfied of its soundness. Data grouped in twos and threes as therein suggested could, if required for any peculiar reason, be afterwards shown in quinary groups of the 4th place form merely by taking these smaller groups in pairs in such a way that quinquennial ages come in the 4th place—such as 27 and 28+29, 30 and 31 and so on for all other pairs—but for the purpose of getting the data in the final 1st place form no method will prove so easy to work and so accurate as the dividing of each of the ternary groups into two parts—such as over 28½ and under 30 as one portion and over 30 as the balance of that ternary group. Redistribution in the ordinary 1st place form can then be done as suggested by me.

APPENDIX III.

Staff entertained by the Census Commissioner in Delhi and Simla.

Serial No.	Name of post.	Duration.	Pay. Rs.	Remarks.
1	Statistical Assistant	16-10-29	325 }	Amalgamated on 1st May 1930.
2	Superintendent	1-5-30 to 7-6-33	400—475 }	
3	Budget Assistant and Cashier	10-8-31 to 7-6-33	175—185	
4	Stenographer and Camp Assistant	11-3-30 to 7-6-33	150—175	
5	1st Head Compiler	12-1-31 to 15-5-33	120—128	
6	2nd Head Compiler	15-9-31 to 7-6-33	100—108	

APPENDIX III—*contd.*

Staff entertained by the Census Commissioner in Delhi and Simla—contd.

Serial No.	Name of post.	Duration.	Pay. Rs.
7	Clerk	4-11-29 to 9-8-31	105—125
8	Clerk	11-4-30 to 21-9-32	60—83
9	Clerk	8-12-30 to 7-6-33	75—83
10	Clerk	26-2-31 to 31-10-32	75—79
11	Clerk	7-3-31 to 14-9-31	60—75
12	Compiler	27-10-31 to 25-3-33	75—79
13	Compiler	28-10-31 to 7-6-33	75—79
14	Compiler	9-10-31 to 31-10-32	55—75
15	Compiler	9-10-31 to 31-10-32	55—75
16	Compiler	9-10-31 to 31-10-32	55—75
17	Compiler	13-10-31 to 31-10-32	55—75
18	Compiler	16-9-31 to 19-1-32 and 14-3-32 to 7-6-33	50—75
19	Compiler	9-10-31 to 30-11-31 and 12-4-32 to 7-6-33	75
20	Compiler	8-7-32 to 31-10-32	75
21	Compiler	1-8-32 to 5-11-32	50
22	Compiler	27-7-31 to 7-6-33	50—54
23	Compiler	27-7-31 to 30-4-33	35—39
24	Compiler	1-2-33 to 15-4-33	75
25	Typist	25-9-31 to 31-5-33	50—75
26	Draftsman	7-11-31 to 31-7-32	50
27	Draftsman	29-1-32 to 1-5-33	75—79

APPENDIX III—*concld.*

Staff entertained by the Census Commissioner in Delhi and Simla—concld.

Serial No.	Name of post.	Duration.	Pay. Rs.
	Inferior Servants.		
1	Duftry	11-4-30 to 7-6-33	16—21
2	Jamadar	29-10-29 to 7-6-33	25—27
3	Peon	7-12-29 to 31-5-33	14
4	Peon	7-4-30 to 7-6-33	14
5	Peon	17-10-31 to 7-6-33	14
6	Peon	9-5-32 to 31-10-32	14

APPENDIX IV.

Statement marking the progress made by the various Provinces and States in the Compilation of Imperial and Provincial Tables in 1931-32.

APPEN

Statement marking the progress made by the various Provinces and States

Province, State or Agency.	I	II	III	IV	V	VI	VII	VIII	IX	X	XI
1. Ajmer-Merwara ..	20-5-31	20-5-31	20-5-31	30-5-31	8-6-31	22-9-31	21-6-31	17-8-31	30-5-31	14-9-31	17-8-31
2. Baroda State ..	22-4-31	22-4-31	22-4-31	22-4-31	22-4-31	10-8-31	22-7-31	3-9-31	12-8-31	16-9-31	9-10-31
3. Cochin State ..	3-8-31	3-8-31	3-8-31	3-8-31	3-8-31	3-8-31	18-8-31	19-10-31	26-8-31	24-10-31	24-10-31
4. North-West Frontier Province.	31-8-31	10-8-31	31-8-31	10-8-31	31-8-31	7-9-31	21-9-31	31-8-31	31-8-31	20-11-31	24-11-31
5. Andamans and Nicobars.	14-8-31	14-8-31	14-8-31	*	*	14-8-31	14-8-31	1-10-31	14-8-31	13-10-31	*
6. Rajputana Agency	20-5-31	20-5-31	20-5-31	30-5-31	8-6-31	3-8-31	17-7-31	18-9-31	30-5-31	5-10-31	3-8-31
7. Gwalior State ..	20-7-31	20-7-31	20-7-31	23-7-31	23-7-31	15-10-31	14-8-31	10-11-31	23-9-31	22-1-32	22-1-32
8. Mysore State ..	21-8-31	21-8-31	21-8-31	21-8-31	21-8-31	23-10-31	28-9-31	23-12-31	7-9-31	30-1-32	29-1-32
9. Travancore State	26-8-31	26-8-31	26-8-31	26-8-31	26-8-31	10-11-31	10-11-31	2-2-32	7-9-31	17-2-32	29-2-32
10. Sikkim State ..	22-1-32	22-1-32	14-12-31	*	*	4-1-32	30-1-32	22-2-32	10-12-31	26-3-32	4-3-32
11. Baluchistan ..	8-8-31	8-8-31	8-8-31	8-8-31	8-8-31	21-12-31	10-2-32	4-2-32	10-8-31	28-3-32	28-3-32
12. Bengal	22-1-32	22-1-32	14-12-31	16-3-32	26-1-32	4-1-32	30-1-32	22-2-32	3-9-31	7-3-32	4-3-32
13. Delhi	6-9-31	28-9-31	10-9-31	10-9-31	10-9-31	10-9-31	16-9-31	10-11-31	8-9-31	27-4-32	29-1-32
14. United Provinces of Agra and Oudh.	22-8-31	22-8-31	10-9-31	10-9-31	14-9-31	12-11-31	30-10-31	21-12-31	4-9-31	7-5-32	4-1-32
15. Punjab	2-10-31	2-10-31	2-10-31	2-10-31	2-10-31	3-11-31	10-11-31	23-2-32	16-9-31	30-5-32	9-5-32
16. Central Provinces and Berar.	31-8-31	31-8-31	31-8-31	16-11-31	6-11-31	19-12-31	23-1-32	11-3-32	22-12-31	1-6-32	29-4-32
17. Coorg	14-1-32	14-1-32	14-1-32	14-1-32	14-1-32	14-1-32	2-2-32	7-3-32	14-1-32	9-4-32	*
18. Madras	8-1-32	22-1-32	22-1-32	16-5-32	27-4-32	8-3-32	2-3-32	28-3-32	17-11-31	9-4-32	* *
19. Assam	14-9-31	31-8-31	14-9-31	7-9-31	7-9-31	15-2-32	12-9-31	24-11-31	24-11-31	29-4-32	2-5-32
20. Jammu and Kashmir State.	8-10-31	8-10-31	8-10-31	8-10-31	8-10-31	10-11-31	5-2-32	5-2-32	21-10-31	13-6-32	12-10-31
21. Central India Agency.	19-12-31	18-9-31	8-9-31	7-9-31	3-2-32	10-11-31	19-10-31	25-1-32	21-9-31	12-2-32	29-2-32
22. Bihar and Orissa ..	19-10-31	19-10-31	2-2-32	26-10-31	19-10-31	30-1-32	21-1-32	22-2-32	21-1-32	27-5-32	22-1-32
23. Hyderabad State ..	18-9-31	31-8-31	28-12-31	18-9-31	1-10-31	2-2-32	18-4-32	17-6-32	12-10-31	29-8-32	3-8-32
24. Western India States Agency.	24-3-32	14-4-32	30-1-32	14-3-32	24-3-32	14-1-32	27-4-32	18-5-32	29-12-31	6-7-32	13-9-32
25. Bombay ..	30-1-32	11-4-32	30-1-32	19-4-32	8-4-32	14-1-32	28-4-32	18-5-32	29-12-31	8-8-32	12-9-32
26. Burma	11-2-32	6-2-32	13-2-32	29-2-32	29-2-32	24-2-32	24-2-32	21-5-32	23-2-32	6-9-32	5-11-32

*Not Compiled.

The date of the receipt of the first table submitted to

The date of the receipt of the last table submitted to

DIX IV.

in the Compilation of Imperial and Provincial Tables in 1931-32.

XII	XIII	XIV	XV	XVI	XVII	XVIII	XIX	XX	Provincial Tables. I	II
8-6-31	14-6-31	17-8-31	15-7-31	15-6-31	17-8-31	24-8-31	16-6-31	21-6-31	27-6-31	17-8-31
29-6-31	31-7-31	28-8-31	14-8-31	22-4-31	4-9-31	20-8-31	30-7-31	*29-10-31*	22-4-31	16-9-31
26-8-31	3-8-31	14-10-31	3-8-31	14-7-31	12-10-31	12-10-31	22-8-31	26-8-31	3-8-31	*2-11-31*
31-8-31	12-9-31	31-8-31	3-12-31	22-8-31	22-9-31	*3-12-31*	31-8-31	31-8-31	31-8-31	10-9-31
*	31-8-31	31-8-31	31-8-31	27-7-31	31-8-31	*5-12-31*	31-8-31	14-8-31	*	*
8-6-31	20-7-31	17-8-31	25-7-31	30-6-31	*18-12-31*	3-11-31	25-7-31	21-6-31	26-6-31	21-11-31
15-10-31	26-8-31	10-11-31	15-10-31	*22-1-32*	4-11-31	4-11-31	17-8-31	15-8-31	23-7-31	14-10-31
27-11-31	8-10-31	26-11-31	30-10-31	3-8-31	26-11-31	23-12-31	8-10-31	2-1-32	4-1-32	22-12-31
7-9-31	2-1-32	2-2-32	2-1-32	17-7-31	2-2-32	2-2-32	26-8-31	1-10-31	2-10-31	10-2-32
*	2-2-32	11-3-32	26-3-32	30-1-32	*26-3-32*	18-3-32	14-12-31	25-1-32	*	*
15-8-31	25-1-32	7-3-32	10-2-32	11-8-31	15-2-32	22-2-32	17-8-31	17-8-31	17-8-31	10-2-32
27-8-31	2-2-32	11-3-32	6-2-32	30-1-32	26-3-32	18-3-32	14-12-31	25-1-32	*12-4-32*	26-3-32
28-9-31	16-9-31	12-11-31	12-2-32	9-9-31	15-10-31	15-10-31	8-9-31	16-9-31	*	*
22-8-31	12-12-31	9-1-32	15-10-31	14-7-31	10-11-31	21-12-31	12-10-31	2-11-31	24-8-31	6-2-32
28-9-31	13-11-31	12-11-31	11-2-32	9-9-31	19-2-32	19-5-32	9-9-31	3-11-31	8-4-32	24-3-32
10-11-31	23-1-32	29-2-32	8-4-32	13-1-32	10-3-32	1-6-32	3-9-31	9-1-32	5-12-31	17-3-32
*	2-2-32	7-3-32	19-3-32	14-1-32	7-3-32	*7-6-32*	14-1-32	*	2-2-32	2-2-32
20-10-31	2-3-32	13-4-32	1-6-32	8-1-32	11-4-32	25-5-32	8-1-32	*	20-5-32	*9-6-32*
28-12-31	28-12-31	24-11-31	21-5-32	31-8-31	6-5-32	13-6-32	23-9-31	13-6-32	13-6-32	*13-6-32*
13-10-31	25-1-32	26-1-32	6-5-32	25-1-32	25-1-32	9-1-32	10-11-31	21-3-32	21-3-32	28-3-32
*	29-10-31	25-1-32	26-11-31	6-8-31	25-1-32	3-2-32	7-9-31	15-12-31	4-5-32	*17-6-32*
14-12-31	10-3-32	5-3-32	29-1-32	26-10-31	22-2-32	*1-7-32*	23-1-32	26-1-32	2-2-32	21-3-32
31-8-31	18-4-32	29-6-32	27-5-32	6-8-31	14-5-32	28-9-31	23-9-31	4-3-32	8-10-31	29-7-32
7-12-31	14-5-32	8-5-32	29-12-31	29-12-31	20-4-32	6-6-32	29-12-31	4-4-32	10-10-32	*10-10-32*
7-12-31	25-5-32	4-3-32	29-12-31	18-8-31	20-4-32	6-6-32	29-12-31	24-3-32	21-6-3	*27-10-32*
19-1-32	21-5-32	21-5-32	16-7-32	23-2-32	26-7-32	10-8-32	26-2-32	*	*15-11-32*	1-8-32

the Census Commissioner for India is shown in heavy type.
the Census Commissioner for India is shown in heavy *italics*.

APPENDIX V.

Statement showing the final date of closing Provincial Census offices and date of publication of their main Report.

Office.	*Date of closing.*	*Month of publication of Report.*
Andaman and Nicobar Islands	1st April 1932	November 1932.
Assam	19th July 1932	September 1932.
Baluchistan	30th November 1932	Not yet published.
Bengal	28th February 1933	April 1933.
Bihar and Orissa	December 1932	January 1933.
Bombay	31st October 1932	Not yet published on 1st June 1933.
Burma	30th March 1933	May 1933.
Central India Agency	15th November 1932	May 1933.
Central Provinces and Berar	28th February 1933	February 1933.
Madras	30th June 1932	February 1933.
North-West Frontier Province	15th January 1933	Not yet published.
Punjab	31st March 1933	April 1933.
Rajputana and Ajmer-Merwara	31st August 1932	August 1932.
United Provinces	31st December 1932	March 1933.
Baroda State	4th August 1932	June 1932.
Cochin State	11th February 1933	March 1933.
Gwalior State	No intimation received	Not yet published on 1st June 1933.
Hyderabad State	Do.	Do.
Jammu and Kashmir State	27th January 1933	Do.
Mysore State	31st December 1932	December 1932.
Travancore State	12th April 1933	February 1933.

APPENDIX VI.

Statement showing the expenditure on Census Operations distributed under the heads prescribed by the Census Commissioner in India.

APPEN

Statement showing the expenditure on Census Operation distributed under

Name of sub-head, item, etc.	India. Total.	1929-30.	1930-31.	1931-32.	1932-33.	1933-34.	Total.	1929-30.
	Rs.	Rs.	Rs.	Rs.	Rs.	Rs.	Rs.	Rs.
Total	48,75,772	21,288	12,70,286	28,65,777	6,53,476	64,995	2,72,791	21,288
Total — Non-voted	7,52,806	16,345	2,61,407	2,69,662	1,91,092	14,800	1,35,128	16,345
Total — Voted	41,22,966	4,943	10,08,829	25,96,115	4,62,384	50,695	1,37,663	4,943
A.—Superintendence — Non-voted	7,45,091	16,345	2,59,688	2,63,721	1,91,092	14,800	1,35,128	16,345
A.—Superintendence — Voted	7,20,327	4,943	2,44,756	2,80,420	1,55,383	34,825	1,07,476	4,943
A-1.—Pay of officers — Non-voted	6,56,606	14,051	2,18,020	2,37,251	1,77,084	10,200	1,17,148	14,051
A-1.—Pay of officers — Voted	2,23,491	..	68,977	98,686	40,398	15,430	..	..
Pay of Officers — Non-voted	..	..	..	..	..	..	..	..
Pay of Officers — Voted	..	..	..	..	..	..	..	..
Special pay of officers on deputation — Non-voted	..	..	..	..	..	..	..	..
Special pay of officers on deputation — Voted	..	..	..	..	..	..	..	..
A-2.—Pay of Establishments—Voted	2,91,184	2,073	77,931	1,20,752	80,683	9,745	59,823	2,073
Pay of men deputed to Census duty	..	..	..	..	..	..	..	..
Special pay of men on deputation for Census	..	..	..	..	..	..	..	..
Pay of men without substantive appointments	..	..	..	..	..	..	..	..
A-3.—Allowances, Honoraria, etc. — Non-voted	72,089	2,024	37,724	19,204	9,237	3,900	15,710	2,024
A-3.—Allowances, Honoraria, etc. — Voted	68,717	783	35,662	17,655	9,867	4,750	17,941	783
Travelling and other Allowances	..	..	..	..	..	..	..	..
Officers	..	..	..	..	..	..	..	..
Establishments	..	..	..	..	..	..	..	..
A-4.—Contingencies—Voted	1,36,935	2,087	62,186	43,327	24,435	4,900	29,712	2,087
Office Rent	..	..	..	..	..	..	..	..
Purchase and repair of furniture	..	..	..	..	..	..	..	..
Stationery	..	..	..	..	..	..	..	..
Postage and telegram charges	..	..	..	..	..	..	..	..
Freight	..	..	..	..	..	..	..	..
Miscellaneous	..	..	..	..	..	..	..	..
Telephone charges	..	..	..	..	..	..	..	..
Rewards	..	..	..	..	..	..	..	..
Hot and cold weather charges	..	..	..	..	..	..	..	..
Purchase of books and maps	..	..	..	..	..	..	..	..
Liveries and warm clothing	..	..	..	..	..	..	..	..
Purchase and repair of tents	..	..	..	..	..	..	..	..
Camel gear	..	..	..	..	..	..	..	..
Other contingencies	..	..	..	..	..	..	..	..
A-5.—Grants-in-aid, contributions, etc.—Non-voted	16,396	270	3,889	7,266	4,771	200	2,270	270
B.—Enumeration — Non-voted	1,774	..	1,774	..	..	..	..	..
B.—Enumeration — Voted	4,78,545	..	[illegible]	2,26,268	2,877	..	..	..
B-1.—Pay of Establishments—Voted	38,790	..	32,930	5,860	..	..	..	..
District Office	..	..	..	..	..	..	..	..
Remuneration of Census Staff	..	..	..	..	..	..	..	..
B-2.—Allowances, Honoraria, etc. — Non-voted	1,774	..	1,774	..	..	..	..	..
B-2.—Allowances, Honoraria, etc. — Voted	3,31,696	..	1,24,153	2,04,856	2,687	..	..	..
Travelling allowance — Non-voted	..	..	..	..	..	..	..	..
Travelling allowance — Voted	..	..	..	..	..	..	..	..
Honoraria and other allowances	..	..	..	..	..	..	..	..
B-3.—Contingencies—Voted	1,08,059	..	92,317	15,552	190	..	..	..
Stationery	..	..	..	..	..	..	..	..
Postage and telegram charges	..	..	..	..	..	..	..	..
House numbering charges	..	..	..	..	..	..	..	..
Freight	..	..	..	..	..	..	..	..
Miscellaneous, including rewards to outsiders	..	..	..	..	..	..	..	..
C.—Abstraction and Compilation — Non-voted	5,941	..	..	5,941	..	..	..	..
C.—Abstraction and Compilation — Voted	21,50,114	..	87,218	19,84,204	74,423	4,270	8,800	..
C-1.—Pay of officers — Non-voted	5,633	..	..	5,633	..	..	..	..
C-1.—Pay of officers — Voted	94,388	..	335	92,848	1,205	..	..	..
C-2.—Pay of Establishments—Voted	14,94,877	..	5,406	14,38,906	48,695	1,870	1,500	..
Correspondence and accounts establishments	..	..	..	..	..	..	..	..
Pay of men deputed on Census duty	..	..	..	..	..	..	..	..
Special pay of men on deputation for Census	..	..	..	..	..	..	..	..
Pay of men without substantive appointments	..	..	..	..	..	..	..	..
Menial establishments	..	..	..	..	..	..	..	..
Working Staff including Superintendence	..	..	..	..	..	..	..	..
Officials	..	..	..	..	..	..	..	..
Non-officials	..	..	..	..	..	..	..	..
C-3.—Allowances, Honoraria, etc. — Non-voted	308	..	..	308	..	..	..	..
C-3.—Allowances, Honoraria, etc. — Voted	66,318	..	1,963	61,113	1,642	1,600	1,500	..
Travelling Allowance	..	..	..	..	..	..	..	..
Honoraria and other allowances	..	..	..	..	..	..	..	..
C-4.—Contingencies—Voted	4,94,531	..	79,514	3,91,337	22,880	800	800	..
Office Rent	..	..	..	..	..	..	..	..
Purchase and repair of furniture	..	..	..	..	..	..	..	..
Stationery and paper	..	..	..	..	..	..	..	..
Postage and telegram charges	..	..	..	..	..	..	..	..
Freight	..	..	..	..	..	..	..	..
Miscellaneous	..	..	..	..	..	..	..	..
Petty construction	..	..	..	..	..	..	..	..
Hot and cold weather charges	..	..	..	..	..	..	..	..
Liveries	..	..	..	..	..	..	..	..
Rewards	..	..	..	..	..	..	..	..
D.—Miscellaneous Staff—Voted	70,812	..	31,460	28,380	8,992	7,000	15,551	..
Officers	..	..	..	..	..	..	..	..
Establishments	..	..	..	..	..	..	..	..
Other allowances	..	..	..	..	..	..	..	..
E.—Printing and other stationery charges—Voted	7,11,368	..	3,95,995	81,863	2,28,910	4,600	10,836	..
Enumeration	..	..	..	..	..	..	..	..
Printing at Government Presses	..	..	..	..	..	..	..	..
Printing at Private Presses	..	..	..	..	..	..	..	..
Other charges	..	..	..	..	..	..	..	..
Abstraction and Compilation	..	..	..	..	..	..	..	..
Printing at Government Presses	..	..	..	..	..	..	..	..
Printing at Private Presses	..	..	..	..	..	..	..	..
Other charges	..	..	..	..	..	..	..	..
F.—*Deduct*—**Expenditure recovered from Provincial Governments.**	—8,200	..	..	—5,000	—3,200	..	..	..

DIX VI.

the heads prescribed by the Census Commisioner for India.

Census Commissioner's Office.				Andamans and Nicobars.				Assam.				Baluchistan.			
1930-31.	1931-32.	1932-33.	1933-34.*	Total.	1930-31.	1931-32.	1932-33.	Total.	1930-31.	1931-32	1932-33.	Total.	1930-31.	1931-32.	1932-33.
Rs.	Rs.	Rs.	Rs.	Rs.	Rs.	Rs.	Rs.	Rs.	Rs.	Rs.	Rs.	Rs.	Rs.	Rs.	Rs.
59,443	71,657	74,103	46,300	12,115	4,152	7,921	42	1,92,385	67,095	1,06,238	19,052	1,35,264	60,293	55,443	19,528
38,279	35,448	30,756	14,300	..	..	..	..	52,961	22,639	22,869	7,953	220	220	..	..
21,164	36,209	43,347	32,000	12,115	4,152	7,921	42	1,39,424	44,456	83,869	11,099	1,35,044	60,073	55,443	19,528
38,279	85,448	30,756	14,300	..	..	..	..	52,131	21,809	22,369	7,953	..	..	..	..
21,164	29,789	84,680	16,900	11,404	3,954	7,408	42	18,278	8,492	6,290	3,496	83,951	41,467	34,766	7,718
32,011	31,666	29,220	10,200	..	..	..	..	47,836	18,823	21,310	7,703	..	..	..	..
..	..	..	..	8,250	2,750	5,500	..	..	..	..	..	38,904	16,920	20,358	1,620
..	..	..	..	..	..	..	..	42,743	16,900	18,970	6,873	..	..	..	..
..	..	..	..	8,250	2,750	5,500	..	..	..	..	..	26,930	11,954	14,976	..
..	..	..	..	..	..	..	..	5,093	1,023	2,340	830	..	..	..	..
..	..	..	..	..	..	..	..	..	..	..	..	11,974	4,972	5,382	1,620
..	..	..	..	..	..	..	..	10,934	4,779	4,384	1,771	22,597	9,609	8,657	4,331
10,312	17,253	22,485	7,700	1,685	579	1,106	..	..	3,882	3,054	..	7,945	3,174	2,898	1,873
..	..	..	..	..	..	..	..	..	..	..	..	3,293	1,278	1,279	736
..	..	..	..	..	..	..	..	..	897	1,330	..	11,359	5,157	4,480	1,722
..	..	..	..	1,685	579	1,106	..	2,895	2,430	459	..	..	..	..	..
5,668	3,182	936	3,980	..	..	..	..	1,104	609	90	405	10,255	7,023	2,656	576
4,586	4,923	3,349	4,300	1,148	490	616	42	3,999	3,045	549	405	10,255	7,023	2,656	576
..	..	..	..	1,148	490	616	42	2,895	2,436	459	..	7,046	5,104	1,942	..
..	..	..	..	1,043	413	600	..	1,104	609	90	405	3,209	1,919	714	576
..	..	..	..	105	47	16	42	6,240	3,104	1,816	1,320	12,195	7,909	3,095	1,191
6,266	7,013	8,846	4,900	321	135	186	..	..	988	1,380	..	2,205	1,100	580	525
..	..	..	..	..	..	..	..	..	148	..	..	1,698	1,500	143	55
..	..	..	..	134	12	122	..	..	134	16	..	2,164	1,477	590	97
..	..	..	..	160	50	50	..	..	904	56	..	1,320	1,000	285	35
..	..	..	..	8	8	..	..	..	180	120	..	..	..	..	..
..	..	..	..	3	..	3	..	..	692	189	..	617	159	316	142
..	..	..	..	..	..	..	..	..	..	..	..	272	235	37	..
..	..	..	..	..	..	..	..	..	..	..	..	300	..	150	150
..	..	..	..	..	..	..	..	..	18	44	..	1,076	526	511	39
..	..	..	..	..	..	..	..	..	20	11	..	677	292	258	127
..	..	..	..	76	65	11	..	..	..	..	..	365	365	..	..
..	..	..	..	..	..	..	..	..	..	..	..	..	..	..	..
..	..	..	..	..	..	..	..	..	..	..	..	1,501	1,255	225	21
..	..	..	..	..	..	..	..	..	20	..	..	..	..	..	..
600	600	600	200	..	..	..	..	1,400	550	600	250	..	..	..	..
..	..	..	..	..	..	..	..	830	830	..	..	220	220	..	..
..	..	..	..	711	198	513	..	36,710	17,922	18,599	189	10,885	10,385	..	..
..	..	..	..	343	..	343	..	558	541	17	..	9,061	9,061	..	..
..	..	..	..	..	..	..	..	558	541	17	..	4,357	4,357	..	..
..	..	..	..	343	..	343	..	..	..	..	..	4,704	4,704	..	..
..	..	..	..	..	..	..	..	830	830	..	..	220	220	..	..
..	..	..	..	..	..	..	..	32,930	15,491	17,250	189	1,266	1,265	..	..
..	..	..	..	238	68	170	..	..	..	..	..	220	220	..	..
..	..	..	..	..	..	..	..	33,760	16,321	17,250	189	1,265	1,265	..	..
..	..	..	..	170	..	170	..	..	..	..	..	..	..	..	..
..	..	..	..	68	68	..	..	3,222	1,800	1,332	..	59	59	..	..
..	..	..	..	130	130	..	..	508	477	31	..	48	48	..	..
..	..	..	..	..	..	..	..	235	219	16	..	11	11	..	..
..	..	..	..	..	..	..	..	398	342	56	..	..	..	..	..
..	..	..	..	..	..	..	..	572	562	10	..	..	..	..	..
..	..	..	..	..	..	..	..	1,509	290	1,219	..	..	..	..	..
..	..	..	..	130	130	..	..	..	..	..	..	..	..	..	..
..	..	..	..	..	..	..	..	62,918	4,535	58,383	..	29,975	5,284	19,428	5,263
..	..	..	3,800	..	..	..	..	..	..	..	..	..	..	..	..
..	..	..	..	..	..	..	..	6,121	335	5,786	..	..	..	..	..
..	..	..	..	..	..	..	..	48,751	31	48,720	..	25,924	3,297	17,859	4,768
..	..	..	1,500	..	..	..	..	..	..	..	..	25,924	3,297	17,859	4,768
..	..	..	..	..	..	..	..	..	..	..	..	4,747	..	3,622	1,125
..	..	..	..	..	..	..	..	..	..	..	..	2,360	..	1,685	675
..	..	..	..	..	..	..	..	..	..	..	..	18,068	3,297	12,022	2,749
..	..	..	..	..	..	..	..	..	..	..	..	749	..	530	219
..	..	..	..	..	..	..	..	..	..	..	..	..	..	..	..
..	..	..	..	..	..	..	..	1,206	226	980	..	122	22	100	..
..	..	..	1,500	..	..	..	..	..	..	..	..	122	22	100	..
..	..	..	..	..	..	..	..	6,840	3,943	2,897	..	3,929	1,965	1,469	495
..	..	..	800	..	..	..	..	2,320	22	2,298	..	800	104	583	113
..	..	..	..	..	..	..	..	2,904	2,692	212	..	1,700	1,395	258	47
..	..	..	..	..	..	..	..	293	224	69	..	282	135	99	48
..	..	..	..	..	..	..	..	2	..	2	..	..	..	..	..
..	..	..	..	..	..	..	..	687	669	18	..	332	..	315	17
..	..	..	..	..	..	..	..	340	57	283	..	..	..	..	..
..	..	..	..	..	..	..	..	294	279	15	..	545	331	214	..
..	..	..	..	..	..	..	..	..	..	..	..	270	..	..	270
..	5,150	8,401	7,000	..	..	..	..	..	..	..	..	..	..	..	..
—	1,270	5,266	4,300	..	..	..	..	21,518	13,507	597	7,414	10,733	2,937	1,249	6,547
..	..	..	..	..	..	..	..	..	13,507	..	..	2,461	2,461	..	..
..	..	..	..	..	..	..	..	..	6,201	..	..	..	..	..	..
..	..	..	..	..	..	..	..	..	631	..	..	1,816	1,816	..	..
..	..	..	..	..	..	..	..	..	6,075	..	..	645	645	..	..
..	..	..	..	..	..	..	..	..	..	597	..	8,272	476	1,249	6,547
..	..	..	..	..	..	..	..	..	..	587	..	7,567	89	1,084	6,394
..	..	..	..	..	..	..	..	..	..	10	..	705	387	165	153
..	..	..	..	..	..	..	..	..	..	..	..	..	..	..	..

* Budget figures filled in.

APPENDIX

Statement showing the expenditure on Census Operation distributed under

Name of sub-head, item, etc.		Bengal. Total.	Bengal. 1930-31.	Bengal. 1931-32.	Bengal. 1932-33.	Bihar and Orissa. Total.	Bihar and Orissa. 1930-31.	Bihar and Orissa. 1931-32.	Bihar and Orissa. 1932-33.
		Rs.	Rs.	Rs.	Rs.	Rs.	Rs.	Rs.	Rs.
Total		5,44,399	1,58,125	3,22,511	63,763	4,70,572	1,13,455	3,19,204	37,913
Total	Non-voted	52,712	20,139	20,882	11,691	59,854	20,572	23,366	15,916
	Voted	4,91,687	1,37,986	3,01,629	52,072	4,10,718	92,883	2,95,838	21,997
A.—Superintendence	Non-voted	52,712	20,139	20,682	11,691	59,354	20,572	23,366	15,916
	Voted	44,859	8,050	24,678	12,131	36,719	12,746	19,389	4,584
A-1.—Pay of officers	Non-voted	46,503	16,800	18,605	11,098	53,530	17,180	21,270	15,080
	Voted	9,598	..	5,527	4,071	13,526	2,916	10,610	..
Pay of Officers	Non-voted	..	..	..	..	..	..	..	..
	Voted	..	..	..	..	..	..	..	..
Special pay of officers on deputation for Census.	Non-voted	..	..	..	..	..	..	..	..
	Voted	..	..	..	..	..	..	..	..
A-2.—Pay of Establishments—Voted		26,452	4,795	14,634	7023	13,600	3,749	6,158	3,693
Pay of men deputed to Census duty		..	..	..	..	..	..	..	..
Special pay of men on deputation for Census		..	..	..	..	..	..	..	..
Pay of men without substantive appointments		26,452	4,795	14,634	7,023	..	..	..	..
A-3.—Allowances, Honoraria, etc.	Non-voted	5,226	3,339	1,677	210	4,716	2,834	1,496	386
	Voted	1,266	458	602	206	1,526	1,179	184	163
Travelling and other Allowances		6,492	3,797	2,279	416	6,242	4,013	1,680	549
Officers		5,668	3,339	2,119	210	5,030	3,148	1,496	386
Establishments		824	458	160	206	1,212	865	184	163
A-4.—Contingencies—Voted		7,543	2,797	3,915	831	8,067	4,902	2,437	728
Office Rent		150	..	150	..	..	201	240	..
Purchase and repair of furniture		706	193	399	114	..	338	426	..
Stationery		1,217	569	641	7	..	735	71	..
Postage and telegram charges		1,296	626	620	50	..	615	417	..
Freight		434	57	320	57	..	1,688	243	..
Miscellaneous		1,266	291	777	198	..	..	..	..
Telephone charges		641	516	..	125	..	..	..	..
Rewards		..	..	..	..	..	..	..	..
Hot and cold weather charges		68	..	68	..	..	22	99	..
Purchase of books and maps		507	76	396	35	..	2	154	..
Liveries and warm clothing		181	58	113	10	..	..	16	..
Purchase and repair of tents		..	..	..	..	..	..	..	..
Camel gear		..	..	..	..	..	..	..	..
Other contingencies		1,077	411	431	235	..	1,301	771	..
A-5.—Grants-in-aid, contributions, etc.—Non-voted		983	..	600	383	1,608	558	600	450
B.—Enumeration	Non-voted	..	..	..	..	..	..	..	..
	Voted	71,582	65,815	5,370	377	24,037	21,657	2,380	..
B-1.—Pay of Establishments—Voted		1,466	1,466	..	..	190	190	..	..
District office		1,466	1,466	..	..	..	..	..	..
Remuneration of Census Staff		..	..	..	..	..	..	..	..
B-2.—Allowances, Honoraria, etc.	Non-voted	..	..	..	..	..	..	..	..
	Voted	34,312	30,109	3,826	377	20,508	18,336	2,172	..
Travelling allowance		34,312	30,109	3,826	377	..	..	..	..
Honoraria and other allowances		..	..	..	..	..	..	..	..
B-3.—Contingencies—Voted		35,784	34,240	1,544	..	3,339	3,131	208	..
Stationery		20,448	20,314	134	..	123	123	..	..
Postage and telegram charges		3,755	3,127	628	..	475	475	..	..
House numbering charges		..	..	..	..	114	114	..	..
Freight		2,221	2,129	92	..	1,253	1,179	74	..
Miscellaneous, including rewards to outsiders		9,360	8,670	600	..	1,374	1,240	134	..
C.—Abstraction and Compilation—Voted		2,87,985	19,856	2,67,540	589	2,79,106	3,401	2,72,502	3,203
C-1.—Pay of officers—Voted		21,780	..	21,260	520	20,784	..	20,461	323
C-2.—Pay of Establishments—Voted		2,31,183	211	2,30,961	11	2,42,495	..	2,39,889	2,606
Correspondence and accounts establishments		16,257	211	16,035	11	97,241	..	94,649	2,592
Pay of men deputed on Census duty		9,901	169	9,732	..	..	..	..	..
Special pay of men on deputation for Census		1,898	42	1,856	..	..	..	..	..
Pay of men without substantive appointments		1,499	..	1,499	..	..	..	..	..
Menial establishments		2,959	..	2,948	11	..	..	..	..
Working Staff including Superintendence—		2,14,926	..	2,14,926	..	..	..	..	..
Officials		276	..	276	..	..	..	..	..
Non-officials		2,14,650	..	2,14,650	..	..	..	..	..
Remuneration of sorters and slip copying charges		..	..	..	..	1,45,254	..	1,45,240	14
C-3.—Allowances, Honoraria, etc.—Voted		823	..	823	..	2,591	..	2,391	200
Travelling Allowance		823	..	823	..	..	..	..	..
Honoraria and other allowances		..	..	..	..	..	..	..	..
C-4.—Contingencies—Voted		34,149	19,645	14,496	8	13,236	3,401	9,761	74
Office Rent		1,671	..	1,671	..	2,309	..	2,309	..
Purchase and repair of furniture		6,207	1,879	4,328	..	296	..	296	..
Stationery and paper		19,368	15,729	3,639	..	708	..	708	..
Postage and telegram charges		258	15	243	..	378	..	378	..
Freight		2,594	850	1,744	..	2,645	1,588	1,057	..
Miscellaneous including telephone charges		2,837	882	1,947	8	6,523	1,813	4,636	74
Petty construction		960	290	670	..	60	..	60	..
Hot and cold weather charges		240	..	240	..	233	..	233	..
Liveries		14	..	14	..	84	..	84	..
Rewards		..	..	..	..	..	..	..	..
Pay of men on daily wages		..	..	..	..	..	..	..	..
D.—Miscellaneous Staff—Voted		24,561	22,245	2,316	..	..	..	..	..
Officers		5,914	4,193	1,721	..	..	..	..	..
Establishments		14,494	14,494	..	..	..	..	..	..
Other allowances		4,153	3,558	595	..	..	..	..	..
E.—Printing and other stationery charges—Voted		62,770	22,020	1,725	39,025	70,856	55,079	1,567	14,210
Enumeration		20,082	20,082	..	..	..	31,981	..	..
Printing at Government Presses		20,082	20,082	..	..	..	12,358	..	..
Printing at Private Presses		..	..	..	..	..	605	..	..
Other charges		..	..	..	..	..	19,018	..	..
Abstraction and Compilation		42,688	1,938	1,725	39,025	..	23,098	1,567	..
Printing at Government presses		37,791	1,938	1,544	34,309	..	10,762	1,493	..
Printing at Private Presses		..	..	..	..	..	..	74	..
Other charges		4,897	..	181	4,716	..	12,336	..	..

VI—*contd.*

the heads prescribed by the Census Commissioner for India—contd.

Bombay.				Burma.				Central India Agency.				Central Provinces and Berar.			
Total.	1930-31.	1931-32.	1932-33.	Total.	1930-31.	1931-32.	1932-33.*	Total.	1930-31.	1931-32.	1932-33.	Total.	1930-31.	1931-32.	1932-33.
Rs.	Rs.	Rs.	Rs.	Rs.	Rs.	Rs.	Rs.	Rs.	Rs.	Rs.	Rs.	Rs.	Rs.	Rs.	Rs.
5,65,588	1,48,646	3,24,418	92,524	3,85,740	83,228	2,20,299	82,213	1,24,161	47,041	48,355	28,765	2,80,575	69,316	1,66,396	44,863
10,172	..	..	10,172	83,112	25,007	26,604	31,501	59,844	20,724	20,823	18,297	57,684	20,075	21,849	15,760
5,55,416	1,48,646	3,24,418	82,352	3,02,628	58,221	1,93,695	50,712	64,317	26,817	27,582	10,468	2,22,891	49,241	1,44,547	29,103
10,172	..	..	10,172	83,112	25,007	26,604	31,501	59,844	20,724	20,823	18,297	57,684	20,075	21,849	15,760
69,038	30,157	29,080	9,851	51,525	11,678	21,084	18,318	27,748	11,769	10,019	5,960	30,968	16,321	7,912	6,735
9,700	..	..	9,700	67,594	21,329	21,829	24,436	54,427	17,200	19,355	17,872	51,340	16,618	19,462	15,260
41,204	16,905	19,892	4,407	14,527	1,861	7,041	5,625	..	..	..	..	6,458	6,458	..	..
..	..	..	..	..	..	..	..	46,077	15,000	15,365	15,712	..	..	..	..
..	..	..	..	..	..	..	..	..	..	..	..	..	..	..	..
..	..	..	..	..	..	..	..	8,350	2,200	3,990	2,160	..	..	..	..
..	..	..	..	..	..	..	..	..	..	..	..	..	..	..	..
14,219	4,803	5,382	4,034	20,783	3,824	8,654	8,305	19,600	6,359	8,274	4,967	14,209	4,111	4,836	5,262
6,716	2,991	1,800	1,925	9,355	1,765	3,655	3,935	5,749	2,636	1,644	1,469	..	..	..	..
..	..	..	..	..	..	..	..	3,072	867	1,182	1,023	..	..	..	..
7,503	1,812	3,582	2,109	11,428	2,059	4,999	4,370	10,779	2,856	5,448	2,475	..	..	..	..
222	..	..	222	13,768	3,128	4,175	6,465	3,842	3,524	318	..	4,724	2,937	1,787	..
7,645	5,454	1,841	350	4,085	1,164	1,569	1,352	2,405	1,610	195	600	3,091	2,490	442	159
7,867	5,454	1,841	572	17,853	4,292	5,744	7,817	6,247	5,134	513	600	..	..	..	..
5,953	4,198	1,495	260	16,761	3,525	5,575	7,661	3,842	3,524	318	..	..	..	..	..
1,914	1,256	346	312	1,092	767	169	156	2,405	1,610	195	600	..	..	..	..
5,970	2,995	1,915	1,060	12,130	4,829	3,770	3,531	5,743	3,800	1,550	393	7,210	3,262	2,634	1,314
2,002	646	806	550	4,063	..	1,995	2,068	..	..	..	..	..	..	..	..
779	678	56	45	402	402	..	..	732	550	182	..	..	..	..	..
217	9	208	..	688	467	125	96	1,326	1,018	272	36	..	..	..	..
1,860	1,160	550	150	1,358	958	400	..	1,395	988	407	..	..	..	..	..
496	288	90	118	64	46	4	14	225	140	50	35	..	..	..	..
445	162	107	176	2,599	2,050	223	326	531	379	106	46	..	..	..	..
1	1	..	..	619	169	225	225	300	..	200	100	..	..	..	..
..	..	..	..	..	..	..	..	..	..	..	..	..	..	..	..
5	..	5	..	..	..	..	..	593	251	208	134	..	..	..	..
87	13	53	21	469	293	38	138	389	222	125	42	..	..	..	..
68	38	30	..	411	185	186	40	252	252	..	..	..	..	..	..
10	..	10	..	..	..	..	..	..	..	..	..	..	..	..	..
..	..	..	..	..	..	..	..	..	..	..	..	..	..	..	..
..	..	..	..	1,367	169	574	624	..	..	..	..	..	..	..	..
250	..	..	250	1,750	550	600	600	1,575	..	1,150	425	1,620	520	600	500
..	..	..	..	..	..	..	..	..	..	..	..	..	..	..	..
1,05,991	57,229	48,366	396	21,919	19,229	2,678	12	255	5	250	..	6,213	5,235	978	..
11,954	8,044	3,910	..	2,260	2,260	..	..	..	..	..	..	..	..	..	..
..	..	..	..	2,260	2,260	..	..	..	..	..	..	..	..	..	..
11,954	8,044	3,910	..	..	..	..	..	..	..	..	..	..	..	..	..
..	..	..	..	..	..	..	..	..	..	..	..	..	..	..	..
55,916	17,981	37,728	207	13,836	11,489	2,335	12	250	..	250	..	4,620	3,954	666	..
55,916	17,981	37,728	207	13,836	11,489	2,335	12	..	..	..	..	..	..	..	..
..	..	..	..	..	..	..	..	..	..	..	..	..	..	..	..
38,121	31,204	6,728	189	5,823	5,480	343	..	5	5	..	..	1,593	1,281	312	..
1,361	1,361	..	..	50	50	..	..	5	5	..	..	..	..	..	..
2,610	2,366	244	..	2,468	2,308	160	..	..	..	..	..	..	..	..	..
2,863	2,301	562	..	..	..	..	..	..	..	..	..	..	..	..	..
2,016	1,546	470	..	662	662	..	..	..	..	..	..	..	..	..	..
29,271	23,630	5,452	189	2,643	2,460	183	..	..	..	..	..	..	..	..	..
2,58,158	5,796	2,40,058	12,304	1,93,335	8,035	1,66,413	18,887	22,209	5,455	14,578	2,181	1,17,982	2,092	1,13,570	2,320
11,861	..	11,499	362	..	..	..	..	..	..	..	..	8,860	..	8,860	..
81,748	20	70,942	10,786	16,726	214	16,512	..	13,804	179	11,776	1,849	93,742	..	91,622	2,120
81,748	20	70,942	10,786	16,726	214	16,512	..	10,879	179	10,190	510	..	..	..	..
7,081	..	5,461	1,620	14,010	136	13,874	..	} 1,744	..	1,744	{ ..	..	..	..	..
..	..	..	..	2,716	78	2,638	..				..	..	..	..	..
72,008	20	63,166	8,822	..	..	..	..	7,669	179	6,980	510	..	..	..	..
2,659	..	2,315	344	..	..	..	..	1,466	..	1,466	..	..	..	..	..
..	..	..	..	..	..	..	..	2,925	..	1,586	1,339	..	..	..	..
..	..	..	..	..	..	..	..	2,925	..	1,586	1,339	..	..	..	..
..	..	..	..	..	..	..	..	..	..	..	..	..	..	..	..
..	..	..	..	..	..	..	..	..	..	..	..	..	..	..	..
790	175	435	180	345	..	345	..	200	..	..	200	2,868	..	2,773	95
790	175	435	180	345	..	345	..	..	..	..	..	..	..	..	..
..	..	..	..	..	..	..	..	200	..	..	200	..	..	..	..
1,63,759	5,601	1,57,182	976	1,76,264	7,821	1,49,556	18,887	8,205	5,276	2,797	132	12,512	2,092	10,315	105
3,104	..	3,104	..	..	..	3,750	..	57	..	57	..	..	..	..	..
6,303	3,078	3,062	163	..	1,815	345	..	2,946	1,964	982	..	..	..	..	..
1,524	12	1,502	10	..	258	530	..	2,709	2,306	403	..	..	..	..	..
1,083	80	853	150	..	..	154	..	285	..	285	..	..	..	..	..
5,488	1,660	3,780	48	..	2	528	..	511	436	64	11	..	..	..	..
7,870	747	6,998	125	..	5,602	1,44,249	..	1,348	525	702	121	..	..	..	..
..	..	..	..	..	144	..	..	..	..	..	..	..	..	..	..
337	8	329	..	..	..	..	..	349	45	304	..	..	..	..	..
29	16	13	..	..	..	..	..	..	..	..	..	..	..	..	..
570	..	570	..	..	..	..	..	..	..	..	..	..	..	..	..
1,37,451	..	1,36,971	480	..	..	..	..	..	..	..	..	15,388	..	15,338	..
2,821	1,875	446	..	..	..	..	..	..	..	..	..	..	..	..	..
..	..	..	..	..	..	..	..	..	..	..	..	..	..	..	..
..	..	..	..	..	..	..	..	..	..	..	..	..	..	..	..
2,321	1,875	446	..	..	..	..	..	..	..	..	..	..	..	..	..
1,19,908	53,589	6,518	59,801	35,849	19,279	3,570	13,000	14,105	9,088	2,690	2,327	52,840	25,598	6,699	20,048
53,589	53,589	..	..	12,562	12,562	..	..	8,568	7,898	670	..	..	..	..	..
20,685	20,685	..	..	5,404	5,404	..	..	42	42	..	..	..	..	..	..
357	357	..	..	550	550	..	..	4,089	3,419	670	..	..	..	..	..
32,547	32,547	..	..	6,608	6,608	..	..	4,437	4,437	..	..	..	..	..	..
66,319	..	6,518	59,801	23,287	6,717	3,570	13,000	5,537	1,190	2,020	2,327	..	..	..	..
61,276	..	4,327	56,949	15,540	2,248	2,493	10,799	249	170	79	..	..	..	..	..
..	..	..	..	2,071	..	..	2,071	2,746	1,014	1,732	..	..	..	..	..
5,043	..	2,191	2,852	5,676	4,469	1,077	130	2,542	6	209	2,327	..	..	..	..
		..	..												

* Includes some of the charges to be incurred in 1933-34.

APPENDIX

Statement showing the expenditure on Census Operation distributed under

Name of sub-head, item, etc.	Coorg, Sikkim (and Bhutan) and Hyderabad. Total.	1930-31.	1931-32.	1932-33.	Madras. Total.	1930-31.	1931-32.	1932-33.
	Rs.	Rs.	Rs.	Rs.	Rs.	Rs.	Rs.	Rs.
Total	4,874	1,305	1,764	1,805	6,25,388	1,49,783	4,48,417	27,188
Total — Non-voted	..	..	..	..	56,258	26,159	24,660	5,484
Total — Voted	4,874	1,305	1,764	1,805	5,69,135	1,23,624	4,23,757	21,754
A.—Superintendence — Non-voted	..	..	..	..	56,258	26,159	24,660	5,434
A.—Superintendence — Voted	..	..	..	..	18,306	7,883	7,970	2,453
A-1.—Pay of officers — Non-voted	..	..	..	..	45,902	20,169	20,466	5,267
A-1.—Pay of officers — Voted	..	..	..	..	..	..	..	..
Pay of officers — Non-voted	..	..	..	..	..	16,969	16,956	..
Pay of officers — Voted	..	..	..	..	..	..	..	..
Special pay of officers on deputation for Census. — Non-voted	..	..	..	..	..	3,200	3,510	..
Special pay of officers on deputation for Census. — Voted	..	..	..	..	..	..	..	..
A-2.—Pay of Establishments—Voted	..	..	..	..	13,095	4,781	6,177	2,137
Pay of men deputed to Census duty	..	..	..	..	..	2,207	2,616	..
Special pay of men on deputation for Census	..	..	..	..	..	889	1,098	..
Pay of men without substantive appointments	..	..	..	..	..	1,685	2,463	..
A-3.—Allowances, Honoraria, etc. — Non-voted	..	..	..	..	8,868	5,990	2,878	..
A-3.—Allowances, Honoraria, etc. — Voted	..	..	..	..	511	295	216	..
Travelling and other Allowances	..	..	..	..	9,379	6,285	3,094	..
Officers	..	..	..	..	8,868	5,990	2,878	..
Establishments	..	..	..	..	511	295	216	..
A-4.—Contingencies—Voted	..	..	..	..	4,700	2,807	1,577	316
Office Rent	..	..	..	..	..	249	..	..
Purchase and repair of furniture	..	..	..	..	..	228	47	..
Stationery	..	..	..	..	..	521	21	..
Postage and telegram charges	..	..	..	..	..	950	651	..
Freight	..	..	..	..	..	167	233	..
Miscellaneous	..	..	..	..	..	343	335	..
Telephone charges	..	..	..	..	..	187	256	..
Rewards	..	..	..	..	..	..	..	..
Hot and cold weather charges	..	..	..	..	..	1	..	..
Purchase of books and maps	..	..	..	..	..	47	34	..
Liveries and warm clothing	..	..	..	..	..	..	..	..
Purchase and repair of tents	..	..	..	..	..	..	..	..
Camel gear	..	..	..	..	..	..	..	..
Other contingencies	..	..	..	..	..	114	..	..
A-5.—Grants-in-aid, contributions, etc.—Non-voted	..	..	..	..	1,483	..	1,316	167
B.—Enumeration — Non-voted	..	..	..	..	..	..	..	..
B.—Enumeration — Voted	..	..	..	..	1,51,208	15,077	1,34,223	1,908
B-1.—Pay of Establishments—Voted	..	..	..	..	5,537	4,446	1,091	..
District Office	..	..	..	..	4,395	3,458	937	..
Remuneration of Census staff	..	..	..	..	1,142	988	154	..
B-2.—Allowances, Honoraria, etc. — Non-voted	..	..	..	..	..	..	..	..
B-2.—Allowances, Honoraria, etc. — Voted	..	..	..	..	1,40,581	7,041	1,31,638	1,902
Travelling Allowance	..	..	..	..	..	7,041	1,31,638	..
Honoraria and other allowances	..	..	..	..	..	..	..	..
B-3.—Contingencies—Voted	..	..	..	..	5,085	3,590	1,494	1
Stationery	..	..	..	..	432	337	95	..
Postage and telegram charges	..	..	..	..	1,042	897	145	..
House numbering charges	..	..	..	..	1,924	1,065	859	..
Freight	..	..	..	..	230	172	58	..
Miscellaneous, including rewards to outsiders	..	..	..	..	1,457	1,119	337	1
C.—Abstraction and Compilation — Non-voted	..	..	..	..	..	..	..	..
C.—Abstraction and Compilation — Voted	..	..	..	..	2,82,382	21,798	2,56,146	4,438
C-1.—Pay of officers — Non-voted	..	..	..	..	..	..	..	..
C-1.—Pay of officers — Voted	..	..	..	..	3,026	..	3,026	..
C-2.—Pay of Establishments—Voted	..	..	..	..	2,43,366	612	2,38,652	4,102
Correspondence and accounts establishments	..	..	..	..	..	..	..	..
Pay of men deputed on Census duty	..	..	..	..	..	..	..	..
Special pay of men on deputation for Census	..	..	..	..	..	..	..	..
Pay of men without substantive appointments	..	..	..	..	..	..	..	..
Menial establishments	..	..	..	..	..	..	..	..
Working Staff including Superintendence	..	..	..	..	..	612	2,38,652	..
Officials	..	..	..	..	..	612	44,903	..
Non-officials	..	..	..	..	..	..	1,93,749	..
Remuneration of sorters and slip copying charges	..	..	..	..	..	..	..	..
C-3.—Allowances, Honoraria, etc. — Non-voted	..	..	..	..	..	..	..	..
C-3.—Allowances, Honoraria, etc. — Voted	..	..	..	..	3,997	1,443	2,369	185
Travelling Allowance	..	..	..	..	..	1,443	2,369	..
Honoraria and other allowances	..	..	..	..	..	..	..	..
C-4.—Contingencies—Voted	..	..	..	..	31,993	19,743	12,099	151
Office Rent	..	..	..	..	..	175	6,345	..
Purchase and repair of furniture	..	..	..	..	..	17,384	1,692	..
Stationery and paper	..	..	..	..	..	..	173	..
Postage and telegram charges	..	..	..	..	..	150	588	..
Freight	..	..	..	..	..	958	1,321	..
Miscellaneous	..	..	..	..	..	430	1,950	..
Petty construction	..	..	..	..	..	646	..	..
Hot and cold weather charges	..	..	..	..	..	..	50	..
Liveries	..	..	..	..	..	..	..	..
Rewards	..	..	..	..	..	..	..	..
D.—Miscellaneous Staff—Voted	3,474	1,305*	1,764†	405‡	6,715	6,035	494	186
Officers	..	..	..	..	..	..	..	..
Establishments	..	..	..	..	..	6,035	494	..
Other allowances	..	..	..	..	..	..	..	..
E.—Printing and other stationery charges—Voted	1,400	..	..	1,400§	1,10,529	72,831	24,924	12,774
Enumeration	..	..	..	..	..	56,917	6,181	..
Printing at Government Presses	..	..	..	..	..	17,868	5,656	..
Printing at Private Presses	..	..	..	..	..	13,907	..	..
Other charges	..	..	..	..	..	25,142	525	..
Abstraction and Compilation	..	..	..	..	..	15,914	18,743	..
Printing at Government presses	..	..	..	..	..	2,192	17,035	..
Printing at Private Presses	..	..	..	..	..	..	..	..
Other charges	..	..	..	..	..	13,722	1,708	..
F.—*Deduct*—Expenditure recovered from Provincial Governments.	..	..	..	..	..	--	--	..

* Rs. 746 for Hyderabad and balance for Coorg.

† Rs. 1,608 for Sikkim and balance for Coorg.

‡ Rs. 5 for Sikkim and balance for Coorg.

§ For Coorg.